TEXAS CIVIL PROCEDURE PRETRIAL

CASES AND MATERIALS

2019
EDITION

RICHARD E. FLINT
L. WAYNE SCOTT
PROFESSORS OF LAW
ST. MARY'S UNIVERSITY SCHOOL OF LAW

IMPRIMATUR PRESS

1325 GATEWAY TOWER
8111 LBJ FREEWAY
DALLAS, TEXAS 75251
TELEPHONE (214) 366-1155
FACSIMILE (214) 879-9939
800-811-6725
EMAIL: BOOKS@IMPRIMATURPRESS.COM
WWW.IMPRIMATURPRESS.COM

Printed in the United States of America

ISBN 978-1-60503-129-3

These materials are prepared for classroom use. It is not a substitute for specific legal research. The cases and laws are discussed generally and the author's comments should not be relied on for the basis of a legal opinion or course of action, without careful review of applicable authorities including those cases decided since the publication of this book.

TABLE OF CONTENTS

CHAPTER 1.
PRESERVATION OF ERROR AND THE HARMFUL ERROR RULE

1. Introduction 1
2. Why Require That Error Be Preserved 1
   In re The Prudential Insurance Co. of America 2
3. Fundamental Error 5
   Note 5
   McCauley v. Consolidated Underwriters 5
   USAA Texas Lloyds Co. v. Menchaca 6
   Pirtle v. Gregory 9
   Notes 10
   Texas Association of Business v. Texas Air Control Board, et al. 11
   Note 14
   Allstate Indemnity Company v. Forth 14
   Note 15
   Mapco, Inc. v. Carter 16
4. Methods of Preservation of Error 17
   Note 18
   Bay Area Healthcare Group, LTD. v. McShane 18
   Bushell v. Dean 20
   Notes 21
   Bridges v. Richardson 22
   Notes 23
   4M Linen & Uniform Supply Co. v. W.P. Ballard & Co. 25
   Notes 28
5. Failure to Properly Preserve Error Results in a Waiver 29
6. The Preserved Error must be Harmful 30
   Reliance Steel & Aluminum Co. v. Sevcik 30
   Notes 33
   McCraw v. Maris 34
   Notes 35
   Mentis v. Barnard 36
   Note 37

CHAPTER 2.
COURTS AND SUBJECT MATTER JURISDICTION

1. Jurisdiction and the Judicial Function 39
   Notes 39
   Clayton v. Hurt 39
   Notes 41
   Dubai Petroleum Company v. Kazi 42
   Note 45
   Morrow v. Corbin 45
   Notes 48
   Waldron v. Waldron 49
   Notes 51
   Jud v. City of San Antonio 51
   Notes 52
2. The Basic Court System in Texas 53
   Note 53
   Court Structure of Texas 54

3. Constitutional and Statutory Provisions Relating to Subject Matter Jurisdiction 55
Notes 57
Note 58
Amigo Helicopters, Inc. v. Jones 58
4. Nature of Suit as Basis for Subject Matter Jurisdiction 58
Ex parte Bryant 58
Note 59
Bailey v. Cherokee County Appraisal District 59
Note 60
Palmer v. Coble Wall Trust Co. 61
Notes 64
Carroll v. Carroll 65
Schlichting v. Lehman Brothers Bank FSB 66
Notes 67
5. Amount in Controversy as Basis for Jurisdiction 68
Flynt v. Garcia 68
Notes 69
Peek v. Equipment Serv. Co. of San Antonio 69
Note 71
Note 71
United Services Auto. Ass'n v. Brite 72
Note 74
6. Problems of Multiple Parties and Claims 74
Texas Employment Commission v. International Union of Electrical, Radio and Machine Workers, Local Union No. 782 74
7. Consequences of a Lack of Jurisdiction over the Subject Matter 75
Notes 75
Attorney General v. Sailer 76
8. Jurisdiction over Counterclaims 77
Andel v. Eastman Kodak Company 78
Smith v. Clary Corporation 78
Notes 79
9. Limits on Jurisdictional Power 80
University of Texas v. Morris 80
Donovan v. City of Dallas 80
Harris County v. Sykes 80

CHAPTER 3.
DISPOSITION WITHOUT TRIAL

1. Default Judgment 85
Paramount Pipe & Supply Co. v. Muhr 85
Holt Atherton Indus. v. Heine 86
Notes 87
2. Dismissal for Lack of Prosecution 90
Note 90
Villarreal v. San Antonio Truck & Equipment 91
In re Conner 94
Note 95
Walker v. Harrison 96
Notes 98
Smith v. Babcock & Wilcox Construction Company, Inc. 99
Alexander v. Lynda's Boutique 100
3. Nonsuit and Other Dismissals 100

Notes 101
Hyundai Motor Co. v. Alvarado 102
In re Bennett 103
4. Consent Judgment 106
Notes 106
Padilla v. LaFrance 107
Notes 111

CHAPTER 4.
FINALITY OF JUDGMENTS AND THE TRIAL COURT'S PLENARY POWER

1. Introduction 115
Notes 115
2. Interlocutory Appeals 115
Notes 115
Notes 118
Del Valle Indep. Sch. Dist. v. Lopez 118
In re Office of the Attorney General 120
Notes 121
De Ayala v. Mackie 121
Notes 124
3. Refinement of the Concept of Finality 125
North East Independent School District v. Aldridge 125
Notes 128
John v. Marshall Health Services, Inc. 130
Note 132
4. The Trial Court's Plenary Power 132
a. The Motion for New Trial 132
Deen v. Kirk 132
Note 134
Fruehauf Corp. v. Carrillo 134
In re Baylor Medical Center at Garland 134
Faulkner v. Culver 136
In re Lovito-Nelson 137
In re Brookshire Grocery Company 138
Notes 138
Jamar v. Patterson 138
Garza v. Garcia 139
Notes 139
b. Motions to Modify, Correct or Reform Judgments 140
L.M. Healthcare, Inc. v. Childs 140
Notes 142
Mackie v. McKenzie 142
Note 143
c. Nunc Pro Tunc Orders 144
Comet Aluminum Co. v. Dibrell 144
Note 146
Escobar v. Escobar 146
Note 147
d. Motions to Reinstate 147
Levit v. Adams 147
Note 148
e. Motions for Sanctions 148
Lane Bank Equipment Co. v. Smith Southern Equipment, Inc. 148

CHAPTER 5.
JUDGMENTS AND THE PRESUMPTIONS OF VALIDITY

1. Introduction 151
2. Direct Attacks on Judgments 151
   a. Equitable Motion for New Trial 151
      Note 151
      Craddock v. Sunshine Bus Lines 152
      Fidelity and Guaranty Insurance Company v. Drewery Construction Company, Inc. 154
      Notes 156
      State Employees Workers' Compensation v. Evans 157
      Carpenter v. Cimarron Hydrocarbons Corporation 160
      Dolgencorp of Texas, Inc. v. Lerma 161
      Notes 161
   b. Restricted Appeal to Court of Appeals in Civil Cases 165
      Note 165
      McEwen v. Harrison 165
      Note 167
      Texaco v. McEwen 168
      Notes 170
      Texaco, Inc. v. Central Power & Light Company 170
      Notes 172
   c. Bill of Review 173
      Notes 173
      Alexander v. Hagedorn 174
      Notes 179
      Hanks v. Rosser 180
      Note 186
      Baker v. Goldsmith 186
      Note 188
      Caldwell v. Barnes 188
      PNS Stores, Inc. v. Rivera 191
      Note 195
      Ross v. National Center for the Employment of the Disabled 196
      Notes 197
3. Collateral Attack on Judgments 201
   Crawford v. McDonald 201
   Note 203
   Templeton v. Ferguson 203
   Note 205
   Browning v. Prostok 206
   Stewart v. USA Custom Paint & Body Shop 209
   Notes 211
4. Full Faith and Credit of Foreign Judgments 214
   Note 214
   Mayhew v. Caprito 214
   Note 215

CHAPTER 6.
JURISDICTION OVER THE PERSON

1. Due Process Requirements of Personal Jurisdiction: Minimum Contacts 217
   Note 217
   Schlobohm v. Schapiro 217
   Spir Star AG v. Kimich 221
   Notes 225
   Moki Mac River Expeditions v. Drugg 227
   TV Azteca v. Ruiz 228
   Notes 234
2. The Notice Requirement of Due Process 236
   Peralta v. Heights Medical Ctr. 236
   Note 238
   Note 239
3. The Texas Long Arm Statute 239
   Notes 239
   McKanna v. Edgar 240
4. The Special Appearance under Texas Law 242
   a. Historical Background 242
      York v. Texas 242
      Note 243
   b. Special Appearance Hearing 244
      Kawasaki Steel Corporation v. Middleton 244
      Notes 244
   c. The Availability of Mandamus Relief—Interlocutory Appeal 246
      Note 246
5. Process and Service 246
   a. Actual Service upon a Resident Defendant 246
      In the Interest of K.M.L., a Child 246
      Notes 249
      Citation 250
      Note. 252
      Higginbotham v. General Life & Accident In. Co. 252
      Smith v. Commercial Equip. Leasing Co. 252
      Pleasant Homes v. Allied Bank of Dallas 253
      Note 254
      Primate Constr. v. Silver 254
      Note 255
      In the Interest of E.A., et al. 256
      Ashley v. Hawkins 258
   b. Substituted and Constructive Service of Resident Defendants 261
      State Farm Fire & Casualty Co. v. Costley 261
      Wilson v. Dunn 262
      Note 265
   c. Service upon Nonresidents 266
      Notes 266
      Whitney v. L & L Realty Corporation 268
      Campus Investments, Inc. v. Cullever 270
      Note 270
      Wood v. Brown 271
      In the Interest of E.R. 272
      Notes 276

CHAPTER 7.
VENUE: SELECTING AND MAINTAINING THE COUNTY OF SUIT

1. Introduction 277
Notes 277
Acevedo v. Commission for Lawyer Discipline 278
2. The General Venue Rule 278
Snyder v. Pitts 279
Notes 282
3. Exceptions to the General Venue Rule 283
a. Mandatory Venue 283
Notes 285
Acker v. Denton Publishing Company 286
Note 288
In re Applied Chemical Magnesias Corporation 289
Note 289
In re Texas Association of School Boards, Inc. 289
Notes 290
In re Missouri Pacific Railroad Company 291
Notes 295
b. Permissive Venue 297
Note 297
Trafalgar House Oil & Gas Inc. v. De Hinojosa 298
Notes 300
Gonzalez v. Reliant Energy, Inc. 302
4. Other Ways to Establish Venue 305
Notes 305
In re Team Rocket, L.P. 306
5. The Procedural Aspects of Venue 309
a. Requisites of the Motion to Transfer 309
b. Responses 309
c. Prima Facie Proof 309
d. The Time Table 310
6. The Venue Hearing 310
Note 310
WTFO, Inc. v. Braithwaite 311
Note 315
7. Review of Venue Decisions by Appellate Courts 316
Notes 316
In re Texas Dept. of Trans. 316
Notes 319
8. Problems Associated with an Impartial Trial 319
Notes 319
9. Problems Associated with Multiple Parties 321
Note 321
Note 322
American Home Products Corporation v. Clark 322
Ramirez v. Collier, Shannon, Scott, PLLC 326
10. The Convenience of the Parties—The "General Rule" 326
Garza v. Garcia 327
11. Forum Non Conveniens 329
Notes 329

CHAPTER 8.
PLEADINGS OF THE PARTIES TO A SUIT

1. Plaintiff's Pleadings 331
   Civil Case Information Sheet 331
   Notes 332
   a. Pleading a Cause of Action 334
      Edwards Feed Mill v. Johnson 334
      White v. Jackson 336
   b. Fair Notice Requirement of Petition 338
      Notes 338
      Stoner v. Thompson 340
      Notes 343
   c. Alternative Claims 344
      Jenkins v. Northwestern Pipe & Supply Co. 344
      Note 346
   d. Pleading of Damages 346
      Sherrod v. Bailey 346
      Notes 349
   e. Prayer 350
      Notes 350
   f. Truth in Pleadings 350
      Note 350
      Low v. Henry 351
      Note 355
2. Defendant's Pleadings 355
   Notes 355
   a. Plea in Abatement 356
      Wyatt v. Shaw Plumbing Co. 356
      Notes 358
   b. Special Exceptions 360
      Texas Dep't of Corrections v. Herring 360
      Notes 362
      McCamey v. Kinnear 362
      Note 364
   c. General Denial 365
      Moulton v. Alamo Ambulance Serv. 365
      Note 367
   d. Verified Denials 367
      Note 367
      The Ray Malooly Trust v. Juhl 367
   e. Affirmative Defenses 369
      Hassell Constr. Co., Inc. v. Stature Commercial Co., Inc. 369
      Phillips v. Phillips 371
      Notes 371
   f. Special Pleas 372
      Greathouse v. Charter Nat'l Bank 372
   g. Amendment of Pleadings 374
      Greenhalgh v. Service Lloyds Insurance Company 374
      Notes 376
      Chapin & Chapin v. Texas Sand & Gravel Co. 377
      State Bar of Texas v. Kilpatrick 378
      Sosa v. Central Power & Light 380
      Notes 381

h. Supplemental Pleadings 382
Note 382
3. Special Pleading Forms 382
a. Suit on a Sworn Account 382
Rizk v. Financial Guardian Ins. Agency 382
Note 384
b. Trespass to Try Title 384
Martin v. Amerman 384
Notes 385
Notes 386
c. Other Special Pleading Forms 386

CHAPTER 9. PARTIES AND ACTIONS

1. Capacity of Parties 387
Coastal Liquids Transportation, L.P. v. Harris County Appraisal District 387
Notes 387
2. Joinder of Parties 388
Note 388
Provident Tradesmens Bank & Trust Co. v. Patterson 388
Cooper v. Texas Gulf Indus. 389
Notes 391
Note 392
Ruthart v. First State Bank 393
Trueheart v. Braselton 394
Ford Motor Co. v. Garcia 394
Notes 399
3. Misjoinder of Claims 402
Flour Bluff Independent School District v. Bass 402
4. Joinder of Claims 403
Allison v. Arkansas Louisiana Gas Co. 403
Note 404
Akers v. Simpson 404
Notes 405
5. Interpleader 406
Clayton v. MONY Life Insurance Co. of America. 406
Notes 411
6. Intervention, Severance and Separate Trials 412
In re Union Carbide Corporation 412
Note 415
Notes 415
7. Class Actions 416
Ford Motor Company v. Sheldon 416
Notes 420

CHAPTER 10. DISCOVERY

1. Discovery Control Plans 423
Note 424
2. Scope of Discovery 424
Notes 424

Lunsford v. Morris 426
Notes 428
K Mart Corporation v. Sanderson 428
In re Ford Motor Company 430
Notes 430
Notes 430
3 Types of Discovery 431
a. Interrogatories 431
Notes 431
Braden v. Downey 434
Notes 435
b. Requests for Disclosure 435
In re C.D. Morse 437
c. Request for Admissions 437
Notes 437
Stelly v. Papania 438
Notes 439
d. Request for Production 440
Notes 440
Notes 443
In re Marion Shipman. 444
In re State Farms Lloyds 449
e. Oral Depositions 449
Notes 449
Crown Central Petroleum Corporation v. Garcia 452
In re Alcatel USA, Inc. f/k/a DSC Communications Inc. 452
Notes 456
f. Pre-Suit Discovery 457
Notes 457
In re John Doe a/k/a "Trooper" 457
Notes 458
4. Limitations on Discovery 458
a. Privileges and Exemptions 458
Scott v. McIlhany 458
Axelson v. McIlhany 460
Notes 463
National Union Fire Ins. Co. v. Valdez 464
Notes 467
National Tank Co. v. Brotherton 468
Notes 470
Notes 470
b. Asserting Exemptions and Privileges 471
Notes 471
In re Union Pacific Resources Company 472
Note 473
Humphreys v. Caldwell 474
Notes 474
Note 475
In re Christus Spohn Hospital Kleberg 475
5 Relief from Improper Discovery Orders 476
Walker v. Packer 476
Note 478
Paradigm Oil, Inc. v. Retamco Operating, Inc. 478
6. Failure to Comply with Discovery and Related Problems of Discovery Abuse and Sanctions 483

Alvarado v. Farah Mfg. Co. 483
Notes 486
Aluminum Co. of America v. Bullock 487
Note 487
Notes 487
Transamerican Natural Gas Corp. v. Powell 489
Notes 492
Cire v. Cummings 494
Notes 497
Occidental Chemical Corporation v. Banales 498
Note 500
7. Privacy of Discovery 500

TEXAS RULES OF CIVIL PROCEDURE 501

TEXAS RULES OF APPELLATE PROCEDURE 671

TABLE OF CASES 751

INTRODUCTION

THE DILEMMA OF INTERPRETING RULES OF CIVIL PROCEDURE: A PROPOSAL FOR ELASTIC FORMALISM

* * *

The Texas Rules of Civil Procedure are constructed in such a way as to grant guaranteed rights of procedure to all litigants, in the same sense that drivers on a highway are assured that other drivers (at least in the United States) will drive on the right side of the road.[1] In trial, however, it is the duty of a party to call attention to any deviation from the rules, through timely, contemporaneous[2] preservation of error.[3] Judges, while they do police trials, are not forced (placed at risk of reversal) to act, until a mistake or deviation from the rules has occurred during a trial, and is called to their attention.[4] Once error is preserved through some form of objection,[5] the complaining party is entitled to a new trial, if that party loses, appeals, and the error is found to be erroneous and harmful.[6]

---

1 *See* TEX. R. CIV. P. 1 ("The proper objective of rules of civil procedure is to obtain a just, fair, equitable and impartial adjudication of the rights of litigants under established principles of substantive law.").

2 *In re* Toyota Motor Sales, U.S.A., Inc., 407 S.W. 3d 746, 770 (Tex. 2013).

3 *See* Punch v. Gerlach, 263 S.W.3d 770, 771 (Tex. 1954) (The spirit of the rules is to charge the attorneys of the litigants with the responsibility of preserving the legal rights of their clients in the progress of litigation by timely action.").

4 *See generally* TEX. R. APP. P. 33.1 (outlining the rules of preservation). For a look at other sources that discuss preservation, see generally TEX. R. EVID. 103, 104; *In re* L.M.I, 119 S.W.3d 707 (2003) ("In an action to terminate parental rights, adhering to the preservation of error rules isn't a mere technical nicety; the interests at stake are too important to relax rules that serve a critical purpose. Appellate review of potentially reversible error, never presented to a trial court, would undermine the Legislature's dual intent to ensure finality in these cases and expedite their resolution."); Bushell v. Dean, 803 S.W. 2d 711 (Tex. 1991) (In order to preserve a complaint for appellate review, a party must present to the trial court a timely (contemporaneous) request, objection or motion, state the specific grounds therefore, and obtain a ruling.); John M. O'Quinn & L. Wayne Scott, *Exclusion of Evidence and Preservation of Error*, STATE BAR OF TEXAS GENERAL EVIDENCE: HOW TO PRESENT AND EXCLUDE EVIDENCE (1979); David F. Johnson, *Reservation of Error and Standards of Review Regarding the Admission or Exclusion of Expert Testimony in Texas*, 48 S. TEX. L. REV. 49 (2006); Sean M. Reagan, *Recurring Themes in Preserving Error in Civil Cases*, 22 APP. ADVOC. 392 (2010).

5 The objection may be to evidence, argument, conduct, judicial action or inaction, special appearance, motion to change venue, objection to charge, receipt of charge, post-verdict actions, and any other procedural or substantive mistake made by the trial court.

6 *See* Reliance Steel & Aluminum Co. v. Sevcik, 267 S.W.3d 867, 871 (Tex. 2008) (stating "[e]rroneous admission of evidence is harmless unless the error probably (though not necessarily) caused rendition of an improper judgment). The court continues, recognizing

> "the impossibility of prescribing a specific test" for harmless-error review, as the standard "is more a matter of judgment than precise measurement." A reviewing court must evaluate the whole case from voir dire to closing argument, considering the "state of the evidence, the strength and weakness of the case, and the verdict"

Id.; Gee v. Liberty Mut. Fire Ins. Co., 765 S.W.2d 394, 396 (Tex. 1989) ("[The Texas Supreme Court] will ordinarily not find reversible error for erroneous rulings on admissibility of evidence where the evidence in question is cumulative and not controlling on a material issue dispositive of the case"); 6 ROY W. MCDONALD & ELAINE A. GRAFTON CARLSON, TEX. CIV. PRAC. APP. PRAC. § 3:14 (2d ed.) (discussing the effect of error in

* * *

It is clear that the rules and the interpretation of the rules, as they have accumulated over time, have created a user friendly system that allows the correction of mistakes with relative ease, depending upon when the mistake is caught and the correction is sought. The earlier in the process the problem is found, the easier it is to correct. If one can picture a container holding a controversy, with the container wide at the bottom, but which narrows to the smallest opening possible at the top, one would see the nature of the Texas procedural system and how that system is designed to deal with procedural problems in contested litigation. It is easy to correct mistakes before judgment (when in the broad base of the container), harder on appeal in the intermediate court of appeal (as the container narrows), and difficult in the Texas Supreme Court (when the container is at its most narrow point).

III. THE TEXAS RULES OF CIVIL PROCEDURE ARE FRIENDLY WITH BUILT-IN ELASTICITY, WITHOUT REINTERPRETATION—TRIAL COURTS

Great flexibility is granted to trial courts in their attempts to apply rules. If a mistake is made,[7] and the error is promptly[8] and plainly[9] called to the court's attention, and a ruling from the trial court is obtained[10] or implied, it can be corrected by the trial judge until the judgment becomes final.[11] That is to say, the trial court has a period of plenary power[12] over the judgments, when corrections can be made after a judgment has been signed and entered. If not corrected, appeal is the general remedy for correction of the mistake, if error has been preserved.[13]

There exists a broad range of corrections a trial court can make post-judgment during the trial court's period of plenary power. For example, the court can grant a new trial, a judgment *non obstante veredicto*, a remittitur,

---

selecting the wrong court, one without jurisdiction, and the general remedy that comes along with it—dismissal of the case).

7 TEX. R. EVID. 103. (describing the procedure by which a party may claim and preserve an error in admitting or excluding evidence).

8 *See* Bushell v. Dean, 803 S.W. 2d 711, 712 (Tex. 1991) (requiring a timely objection in order to preserve error for appellate review).

9 *See* Campbell v. State, 85 S.W.3d 176, 185 (Tex. 2002) (finding an objection insufficient when it did not specify the statute which authorized the objection and when it did not specify the "things" prohibited under the unnamed statute); *McDaniel v. Yarbrough,* 898 S.W.2d 251, 252 (Tex. 1995) (requiring an objection to "state the specific grounds for the desired ruling if those grounds are not apparent from the context of the objection" because it will "[allow] the trial judge to make an informed ruling and the other party to remedy the defect"); Bridges v. Richardson, 354 S.W.2d 366, 368 (Tex. 1962) (recognizing an exception to the rule that a general objection does not preserve error: "a general objection that it is immaterial and irrelevant is sufficient to preserve right to review of error contained in admitting it").

10 *See In re* ZLT, 124 S.W.3d 163, 165 (Tex. 2003) (emphasizing the necessity of a trial court expressly or implicitly ruling on a request, objection, or motion in order to preserve error for appellate review).

11 *See Orion Enters., Inc. v. Pope,* 927 S.W.2d 654, 658 (Tex. App.—San Antonio 1996, orig. proceeding) (describing the trial court's power to reconsider its judgment and interlocutory orders "until thirty days after the date a final judgment is signed or, if a motion for new trial or its equivalent is filed, until thirty days after the motion is overruled by signed, written order or operation of law, whichever first occurs").

12 *Orion Enters., Inc. v. Pope,* 927 S.W.2d 654, 659 (Tex. App.—San Antonio 1996, orig. proceeding): ("Plenary power" is "that which is '[f]ull, entire, complete, absolute, perfect, unqualified.'") (quoting *Mesa Agro v. R.C. Dove & Sons,* 584 S.W.2d 506, 508 (Tex. Civ. App.—El Paso 1979, writ ref'd n.r.e.); *see also*, Deen v. Kirk, 508 S.W.2d 70, 72 (Tex. 1974) (recognizing, thirty days after the rendition of a judgment, a court will lack "jurisdictional power to hear and adjudicate").

13 TEX. R. APP. P. 33.1 (listing the requirements to show error has been preserved so that a complaint can be presented on appeal); *In re* L.M.I, 119 S.W.3d 707, 711 (Tex. 2003) (explaining the need for objecting with timeliness and specificity and obtaining a ruling because of the dangers of allowing an appeal based on unpreserved error).

or other similar relief.[14] Until recently, that power was broader. Trial courts could grant new trials "in the interest of justice."[15] Now, they may do so only, when there is an announced and detailed reason for such a new trial.[16] In other words, a statement by a trial court that grants a new trial "in the interest of justice" is an insufficient explanation for setting aside a jury verdict.[17] There must be an "articulable reason" given for the new trial.[18]

> A trial court does not abuse its discretion so long as its stated reason for granting a new trial (1) is a reason for which a new trial is legally appropriate (such as a well-defined legal standard or a defect that probably resulted in an improper verdict), and (2) is specific enough to indicate that the trial court did not simply parrot a pro forma template, but rather derived the articulated reasons from the particular facts and circumstances of the case at hand . . . .[19]

However, once jurisdiction is properly passed to the appellate courts, only those errors that have been properly preserved or are fundamental may then be considered.[20] To pass jurisdiction[21] once a final[22] judgment is entered, a notice of appeal must be filed within thirty or ninety days following the signing of the judgment.[23]

---

[14] *See* 5 ROY W. MCDONALD & ELAINE A. GRAFTON CARLSON, TEXAS CIVIL PRACTICE § 28:44 (2d. ed. 2015) (describing a remittitur as "frequently appropriate when the complaint is that the verdict is so excessive as to shock the conscience of the court," a remedy on which the refusal of a new trial may be conditioned, and results in a remittance "in an amount, set by the judge, that reduces the reward to a proper sum that comports with the evidence"); *id.* § 27:77 ("[U]pon motion and reasonable notice the court may render judgment *non obstante veredicto* if a directed verdict would have been proper, and . . . the court may, upon like motion and notice, disregard any jury finding on a question that has no support in the evidence").

[15] *See In re* United Scaffolding, Inc., 377 S.W.3d 685, 689 (Tex. 2012) (holding "an order based solely on 'the interest of justice' is insufficient" as is one that "could just as well be construed as relying solely on 'the interest of justice and fairness'").

[16] *See In re* United Scaffolding, Inc., 377 S.W.3d 685, 688-689 (Tex. 2012) (concluding there is no abuse of discretion when a trial court's reasons for granting a new trial are "specific enough to indicate that the trial court did not simply parrot a pro forma template, but rather derived the articulated reasons from the particular facts and circumstances of the case at hand").

[17] *See In re* Columbia Med. Ctr. of Las Colinas, 290 S.W.3d 204, 215 (Tex. 2009) (directing the trial court to state reasons why it refused to enter judgment, because "[b]road statements such as 'in the interest of justice' are not sufficiently specific"). *See generally* Robert W. Calvert, *In the Interest of Justice,* 4 ST. MARY'S L.J. 291 (1972).

[18] *See In re* United Scaffolding, Inc., 377 S.W.3d 685, 686 (Tex. 2012) ("[A] trial court's order granting a motion for a new trial must provide a reasonably specific explanation of the court's reasons for setting aside a jury verdict.").

[19] *Id.* at 688-89.

[20] *See* Bay Area Healthcare, Grp., Ltd. v. McShane, 239 S.W.3d 231 (Tex. 2007) ("Even if a trial court errs by improperly admitting evidence, reversal is warranted only if the error probably caused the rendition of an improper judgment" and the reviewing court will "review the entire record and require the complaining party to demonstrate that the judgment turns on the particular evidence admitted."); Bradley v. State *ex rel.* White, 990 S.W.2d 245, 247 (Tex. 1999) ("When both sides move for summary judgment and the trial court grants one motion and denies the other, the reviewing court should review both sides' summary judgment evidence and determine all questions presented."); Tex. Ass'n of Bus. v. Tex. Air Control Bd., 852 S.W.2d 440, 443 (Tex. 1993) (holding standing is an indispensable tool of a court in deciding a case and "is implicit in the concept of subject matter jurisdiction" even though standing was not raised by a party and that is normally fundamental error); Mapco Inc. v. Carter, 817 S.W.2d 686, 687 (Tex. 1991) ("[L]ack of jurisdiction is fundamental error and may be raised for the first time before [the Supreme Court of Texas]"); Pirtle v Gregory, 629 S.W.2d 919, 920 (Tex. 1982) ("Fundamental error survives today in those rare instances in which the record shows the court lacked jurisdiction or that the public interest is directly and adversely affected as that interest is declared in the statutes or the Constitution of Texas."); McCauley v. Consol. Underwriters, 304 S.W.2d 265, 266 (Tex. 1957) ("When

A. *Mistakes in the Trial Court*

1. Jurisdictional—Plenary Power, Service, Invoking and Terminating Trial Court Jurisdiction

In the trial courts, jurisdiction[24] is conferred by filing a pleading and effecting service upon the defendant.[25] Once jurisdiction is obtained, a trial court retains that jurisdiction until a final judgment is entered and, thereafter, for either thirty days after the judgment is signed or thirty days after the last post judgment remedy is determined[26]—and longer if a party does not receive notice of the entry of a judgment.[27] Once those time periods pass, jurisdiction over a case in the trial court ends, and a notice of appeal[28] is required to continue a direct ordinary appeal.[29] A short extension for the filing of the notice of appeal is possible under Texas Rules of Civil Procedure 5, with the noted limitation that a trial court "may not enlarge the period for taking any action under the rules relating to new trial except as stated in these rules."

"Judicial action taken after the trial court's plenary power has expired is void and a nullity."[30] Filing a jurisdictionally necessary document outside a mandated timetable that is one or more day(s) late is fatal to continued jurisdiction.[31]

---

the record affirmatively and conclusively shows that the court rendering the judgment was without jurisdiction of the subject matter, the error will also be regarded as fundamental.").

21 "After determining that the order may be taken up on appeal, the second and equally important issue is the timing of taking the steps to bring the order before the court of appeals." Tom Cowart, *The Appellate Clock*, 29 THE ADVOC. 110, 112 (Winter 2004). Cowart notes: "This issue is critical because the court of appeals cannot exercise jurisdiction over an order if its jurisdiction is not properly invoked. Thus, blowing a deadline in perfecting an appeal is the kiss of death for the attempt to obtain relief from an adverse order." *Id.*

22 Separate rules exist for limited interlocutory appeals, and possible mandamus actions.

23 TEX. R. CIV. P. 26.

24 Jurisdiction relates to the power to hear and decide lawsuits. Morrow v. Corbin, 62 S.W.2d 641, 644 (Tex. 1933).

25 State v. G.C. Olsen, 360 S.W.2d 398, 400 (Tex. 1960) (requiring jurisdiction to be "legally invoked; and when not legally invoked, the power to act is as absent as [if] it did not exist"), *overruled on other grounds*, Jackson v. State, 548 S.W.2d 685 (Tex. Crim. App. 1977); Waldron v. Waldron, 614 S.W.2d 648, 650 (Tex. Civ. App.—Amarillo, 1981, no writ) (demanding, in order to invoke the jurisdiction of a court, "that persons or property over which the court has potential jurisdiction be brought before the court by service of process").

26 *See* TEX. R. CIV. P. 329b (promulgating the thirty-day time frame within which a motion for new trial must be filed).

27 5 ROY MCDONALD & ELAINE A. CARLSON, TEXAS CIVIL PRACTICE § 28:2 (2d ed.).

28 *See* TEX. R. APP. P. 26 (noting a trial court's jurisdiction is terminated upon expiration of its plenary power).

29 *See* Elaine A. Carlson & Karlene S. Dunn, *Navigating Procedural Minefields: Nuances in Determining Finality of Judgments, Plenary Power, and Appealability*, 41 S. TEX. L. REV. 953, 1016 (2000) ("One party's filing invokes the appellate court's jurisdiction over all parties, but absent good cause, the court may not grant more favorable relief than the trial court in favor of a party who did not file a notice of appeal.").

30 Moore Landry LLP. v. Hirsch & Westheimer, PC, 126 S.W.3d 536, 543 (Tex. App.—Houston [1st Dist.] 2003, no pet.) (first citing *In re* Dickason, 987 S.W.2d 570, 571 (Tex. 1998); then citing *In re* T.G., 68 S.W.3d 171, 177 (Tex. App.—Houston [1st Dist.] 2002)); *see also* Jackson v. Van Winkle, 660 S.W.2d 807, 808 (Tex. 1983) ("The trial court loses plenary jurisdiction [thirty] days after judgment in the absence of a timely filed motion for new trial, so any action taken after the expiration of [thirty] days from judgment would be a nullity.").

31 *See* TEX. R. APP. P. 2, 25.1(b), 26.3 (promulgating the rules for perfecting and timely filing an appeal); *see also* Harris Cty. Toll Rd. Auth. v. Sw. Bell Tel., LP, 263 S.W.3d 48, 56 (Tex. App.—Houston [1st Dist.] 2006) ("The time for filing a notice of appeal is jurisdictional in nature, and absent a timely filed notice of appeal or extension request, we must dismiss an appeal for lack of jurisdiction), *aff'd*, 282 S.W.3d 59 (Tex. 2009); *In re*

Jurisdiction is a matter of power, but even here, there is a built-in flexibility in the trial courts of Texas. The elasticity of the Texas Rules of Civil Procedure, as construed by the courts, is illustrated through the ease by which default judgments are set aside, clerical mistakes are corrected, and a cushion is built in for missed deadlines and delayed mail.[32]

a. Example—setting aside default judgments

The clearest example of the friendly nature (the elasticity) of the Texas Procedural Rules is evident in the handling of default judgments. If a party fails to answer a citation, and a default judgment is taken, it is possible to set that judgment aside with ease, *if done in time*.[33] If the party does not act within time for a new trial in the trial court, within six months, it may seek a reversal by restricted appeal.[34] Failing that, one more difficult procedure remains: the bill of review.[35] That formalized procedure is allowed for four years.[36]

Dickason, 987 S.W.2d 570, 570 (Tex. 1998) (stating when a trial court's plenary power expires, any judgment from the trial court is void); Verburgt v. Dorner, 959 S.W.2d 615, 617 (Tex. 1997) (discussing timing requirements for filing notice of appeal); Levit v. Adams, 850 S.W.2d 469, 470 (Tex. 1993) (stating ninety-first-day notice under Rule 306a is one-day too late).

[32] *See* TEX. R. CIV. P. 5 ("[P]roperly addressed and stamped and is deposited in the mail on or before the last day for filing same, the same, if received by the clerk not more than ten days tardily, shall be filed by the clerk and be deemed filed in time.").

[33] *See* Craddock v. Sunshine Bus Lines Inc., 133 S.W.2d 124, 126 (Tex. Comm'n App. 1939) (analyzing the conditions upon which a default judgment may be properly set aside).

[34] TEX. R. APP. P. 30.

[35] *See* Caldwell v. Barnes, 975 S.W.2d 535, 537 (Tex. 1998) (defining a bill of review and listing the three factors that allow a judgment to be set aside by a bill of review); State v. 1985 Chevrolet Pickup Truck, VIN: 1GCEK14HLFS165672, 778 S.W.2d 463, 464 (Tex. 1989) (per curiam) ("[T]his court has enunciated in specific detail the steps necessary to be followed in a bill of review proceeding."); Transworld Fin. Servs. Corp. v. Briscoe, 722 S.W.2d 407, 408 (Tex. 1987) (discussing the narrow grounds upon which a bill of review can set a judgment aside); Baker v. Goldsmith, 582 S.W.2d 404, 406 (Tex. 1979) (stating "Texas courts have enunciated several requirements that must be satisfied" in filing a bill of review); Schwartz v. Jefferson, 520 S.W.2d 881, 889 (Tex. 1975) (explaining a bill of review is an original proceeding, separate and distinct from the underlying judgment).

[36] *See* TEX. CIV. PRAC. & REM. CODE ANN. § 16.051 (West 2011) (noting the four-year, residual statute of limitations); Caldwell v. Barnes, 975 S.W.2d 535, 538 (Tex. 1998) (providing the residual statute of limitations applies to bill of review actions).

b. Correction of clerical errors[37]

Again, elasticity is shown by the ease with which clerical errors,[38] as opposed to judicial errors,[39] in a judgment may be corrected at any time.[40] Then, if it becomes obvious on appeal that a party has made a clerical error—such as entering the wrong cause number—in an, otherwise, properly identified appeal document, correction will be allowed.[41] The rules relating to nunc pro tunc correction of judgments, in reality, extend the trial

[37] The failure to pay a filing fee is similar to a clerical error but is not separately discussed. The Supreme Court Supreme Court has dealt with this problem in a proper fashion. *See* Tate v. E.I. Dupont de Nemours & Co., 934 S.W.2d 83 (Tex. 1996). The filing of a post-judgment motion without paying the filing fee results in the extension of the trial court's plenary power, thus, also extending the appellate timetable if the filing fee is paid within the period of plenary power. The failure to pay the filing fee before the motion for new trial is overruled by operation of law may forfeit altogether the movant's opportunity to have the trial court consider the motion. However, the court failed to express an opinion on whether the failure to pay retroactively invalidated the conditional filing for purposes of the appellate timetable. That was laid to rest, and properly so, in *Garza v. Garcia*. Garza v. Garcia 137 S.W.3d 36 (Tex. 2004). There, Garcia timely filed a motion for new trial but never paid the fee. *Held*: A motion for new trial extends appellate timetables, even if the requisite filing fee is never paid. The court construes the Rules of Appellate Procedure liberally, so that decisions turn on substance, rather than procedural technicality. Nothing in those rules requires a fee to accompany a motion for new trial, or that such a fee be paid at all. Moreover, once a motion for new trial is conditionally filed, and timetables extended, all litigants benefit from knowing what timetables apply, even if they do not know whether the requisite fee was paid. The alternative would breed uncertainty, as the deadlines might automatically jump forward when the fee is quietly paid, or revert backwards if it is not. This is not to say filing fees are irrelevant. Absent emergency or other rare circumstances, a motion for new trial should not be considered, until the filing fee is paid. Here, Garcia's factual sufficiency complaint had to be presented to the trial judge, but because she never paid the $15 fee, the trial court was not required to review it. Thus, because no new trial fee was ever paid, the court of appeals correctly never addressed Garcia's factual sufficiency complaint, but correctly considered her venue complaint.

[38] *See* Andrews v. Koch, 702 S.W.2d 584, 585 (Tex. 1986) (emphasizing a nunc pro tunc judgment may only be entered to correct a clerical error not a judicial error).

[39] *See* Escobar v. Escobar, 711 S.W.2d 230, 231 (Tex. 1986) (reiterating, once a trial court's plenary power has expired, it may only modify a judgment to correct a clerical error); Wallace v. Rogers, 517 S.W.2d 301, 303 (Tex. Civ. App.—Dallas 1974, writ ref'd n.r.e.) (evaluating the differences between clerical and judicial errors).

[40] *See* Comet Aluminum Co. v. Dibrell, 450 S.W.2d 56, 58 (Tex. 1970) (outlining the timing during which clerical errors may be corrected).

[41] The Supreme Court has had no problem, in the last thirty-plus years, in correcting obvious attorney/party mistakes that do not reflect a lack of intent to act. Thus, in *City of San Antonio v. Rodriguez*, the appealing party placed the wrong cause number on the notice of appeal; all other information was correct. City of San Antonio v. Rodriguez, 828 S.W.2d 417 (pin) (Tex. 1992). While the court of appeals dismissed the appeal for want of jurisdiction, the Texas Supreme Court reinstated the appeal, saying:

> We have held that a court of appeals has jurisdiction over an appeal when the appellant files an instrument that is "a bona fide attempt to invoke appellate court jurisdiction." More recently, we reaffirmed the policy that "the decisions of the courts of appeals [should] turn on substance rather than procedural technicality." Here, there can be no doubt that the city's attempt to perfect an appeal was "bona fide" because, but for the erroneous cause number, the city's notice of appeal complied with the provisions of TEX. R. APP. P. 40(a) (2). We hold that the city's notation of the incorrect cause number on its notice of appeal does not defeat the jurisdiction of the court of appeals.

City of San Antonio v. Rodriguez, 828 S.W.2d 417, 418 (Tex. 1992) (alteration in original) (citations omitted) (first quoting Grand Prairie Indep. Sch. Dist. v. S. Parts Imports, Inc., 813 S.W.2d 499, 500 (Tex. 1991) (per curiam); and then quoting Crown Life Ins. v. Estate of Gonzales, 820 S.W.2d 121 (Tex. 1991) (per curiam)). This was akin to the correction of a clerical (as opposed to a judicial) error in a final judgment, which may be made even after plenary power has otherwise expired.

court's plenary power for an indefinite period, but only to correct the clerical errors.[42] Any nunc pro tunc corrections are subject to appellate review.[43] This nunc pro tunc power, however, does not reawaken the entire case for review—only the clerical mistake is subject to correction.[44]

JURISDICTIONAL POWER—INVOKING AND TERMINATING APPELLATE JURISDICTION

Once a timely notice of appeal is filed, jurisdiction passes to the appellate courts. Normally, appellate courts may only alter a trial court judgment, or remand, when harmful error is found to exist on appeal,[45] although in extremely rare circumstances, the Texas Rules of Appellate Procedure allow the reversal of errorless judgments where it is "in the interest of Justice."[46]

"When reversing the court of appeals' judgment, the Supreme Court may, in the interest of justice, remand the case to the trial court even if a rendition of judgment is otherwise appropriate."[47] One such exception exists, where remand is allowed in the interest of justice, because the law changes pending the appeal or, as a result of the appeal.[48]

When a plaintiff's judgment is reversed for legal insufficiency, the appellate court is required to render a take-nothing judgment.[49] However, even there, an exception has been created where both post-answer and no-answer default judgments have been reversed on appeal for legally insufficient evidence.[50]

The appellee will be required to perfect an appeal if the party seeks to alter the trial court's judgment.[51] In passing on the appeal, any procedural problems must be dealt with by the appellate courts before moving on to substance, if substantive matters are even reached. Normally, there is no difficulty with rule interpretation when a plain reading approach is used. However, if circumstances cause a perceived injustice, and the rules do not provide a means for correction, the courts must determine what to do. Several such situations and their solutions are dealt with here.

* * *

---

[42] *See* TEX. R. CIV. P. 329(b)(f) ("[T]he court may at any time correct a clerical error in the record of a judgment and render judgment nunc pro tunc under Rule 316, and may also sign an order declaring a previous judgment or order to be void because signed after the court's plenary power had expired.").

[43] *See* Escobar v. Escobar, 711 S.W.2d 230 (Tex. 1986) (conducting appellate review of nunc pro tunc order).

[44] *See* TEX. R. CIV. P. 329(b) (h).

[45] TEX. R. APP. P. 44.1; *see also Holt Atherton Indus., Inc. v. Heine,* 835 S.W.2d 80, 86 (Tex. 1992) ("As a general matter, when we sustain a no evidence point of error after a trial on the merits, we render judgment on that point."); *Mobil Oil Corp. v. Frederick,* 621 S.W.2d 595, 596 (Tex. 1981) ("[A]bsent circumstances of additional evidence to be developed or uncertainty of the decree, the appellate court has a duty to render the judgment which the trial court should have rendered."); TEX. R. APP. P. 43.3 (stating when an appellate court should render a trial court judgment); TEX. R. APP. P. 60.2 ("The Supreme Court may reverse the lower court's judgment in whole or in part and render the judgment that the lower court should have rendered.").

[46] Robert W. Calvert, *In the Interest of Justice*, 3 ST. MARY'S L.J. 291 (1972).

[47] TEX. R. APP. P. 60.3.

[48] *See* Westgate, Ltd. v. State, 843 S.W.2d 448, 455 (Tex. 1992), *quoted in* Kerr-McGee Corp. v. Helton, 133 S.W.3d 245, 258 (Tex. 2004); Bulanek v. West Tex. 66 Pipeline Co., 209 S.W.3d 98 (Tex. 2006).

[49] *See* Dolgencorp of Texas, Inc. v. Lerma, 288 S.W.3d 922, 929 (Tex. 2009) (providing the circumstances under which an appellate court is required to render a judgment).

[50] *See* Dolgencorp of Texas, Inc. v. Lerma, 288 S.W.3d 922, 929 (Tex. 2009) (noting the split between court of appeals as to the proper disposition of a case when there is insufficient evidence to support a post-answer default judgment).

[51] *See* TEX. R. APP. P. 43.3(b) (describing the circumstances under which a court of appeals must remand a case).

Chapter 1.
Preservation of Error and the Harmful Error Rule

1. *Introduction*

Before launching into a detailed presentation of the procedural intricacies of Texas Civil Procedure, one of its more fundamental aspects needs to be addressed. In the following pages of this book the student will be reading real decisions by real courts in Texas concerning Texas Civil Procedure. The majority of decisions in this book are from appellate courts in Texas. By in large the cases contained in this book discuss various alleged errors which occurred during the pretrial and trial process of the particular case. As a general rule a lawyer needs to bring the alleged error to the attention of the trial court for its consideration and decision in order for an appellate court to have the ability to consider the alleged error on appeal. The concept of preservation of error refers to those procedures which must be taken by a lawyer in a lower court to ensure that any alleged errors made by a lower court are available for review by an appellate court. *See* Rule 33 of the Texas Rules of Appellate Procedure.

Another fundamental aspect of Texas Civil Procedure that will be presented in this chapter concerns the manner in which an appellate court determines whether the error preserved and presented to it on appeal is of such a nature as to lead to a reversal of the case. As a general rule, even if error of law is determined to have occurred in the trial court level, appellate courts will not reverse the trial court unless the error which was committed "probably caused the rendition of a improper judgment or probably prevented the appellant from properly presenting the case" to the appellate court. This concept of reversible error has been given the popular name of the "harmful error rule". *See* Rules 44.1 and 61.1 of the Texas Rules of Appellate Procedure.

In the following pages the concepts of preservation of error and the "harmful error rule" will be briefly introduced. Throughout the remainder of the book the student needs to be very mindful of these basic concepts and of the various exceptions which can arise depending on the nature of the error or the type of proceeding which is presented to the court.

2. *Why Require That Error Be Preserved*

Most procedural rules are written to guide the parties and the courts in the conduct of litigation. When the rule is violated, an error occurs. The party aggrieved by that error has the alternative of insisting that the error be corrected, or of waiving the error. Parties regularly waive rules, and allow the rules to be ignored. When the party wishes to insist upon the observation of the rule, that party must preserve error at any time the other party or the court violate the rule. By complaining of the violation (preserving error),

a) the opposing party is given an opportunity to cure any error that may occur;
b) the trial court is given an opportunity to cure any error that may occur;
c) trial by ambush is prevented; and
d) appeal by ambush is prevented.

Following the trial of a case, a party seeking to alter a trial court's appealable order must perfect his appeal by filing a notice of appeal with the information required and in the manner dictated by Rule 25 of the Texas Rules of Appellate Procedure and within the time specified in Rule 26 of the Texas Rules of Appellate Procedure. Once the appeal has been perfected, and the record brought forward to the appellate court, the party seeking to alter the trial court's appealable order may through his brief request the court of appeals to review the alleged errors that had been properly preserved.

In addition, certain procedural errors committed by the trial court may be reviewed by an appellate court in an original mandamus proceeding pursuant to Rule 52 of the Texas Rules of Appellate Procedure. As will be shown in the following case, the basic requirements for an appellate court to exercise its original mandamus jurisdiction are an abuse of discretion by the trial court and no adequate remedy by appeal.

In re The PRUDENTIAL INSURANCE CO. OF AMERICA
148 S.W.3d 124
(Tex. 2004)

Gino John Rossini, John A. Mackintosh Jr., G. Luke Ashley and Camille Knight, Thompson & Knight, L.L.P., Dallas, for Relators.

Luke Madole, Russell F. Nelms, Dena Jean Denooyer, Carrington Coleman Sloman & Blumenthal, Dallas, for Respondents.

JUSTICE HECTH delivered the opinion of the Court, in which JUSTICE OWEN, JUSTICE SMITH, JUSTICE WAINWRIGHT, and JUSTICE BRISTER joined.

The parties to a commercial lease agreed to waive trial by jury in any future lawsuit involving the lease, but when the tenant and its guarantors later sued for rescission and damages, they nevertheless demanded a jury trial. The trial court denied the landlord's motion to quash the demand. In this original proceeding, the landlord petitions for mandamus relief directing the trial court to enforce the parties' contractual jury waiver. We conditionally grant relief.

I

Francesco Secchi, a native of Italy, and his wife Jane, a native of England, moved to Dallas in 1981, where they have lived ever since and have become naturalized citizens. The Secchis have been in the restaurant business since 1983, and they (or entities controlled by them) own and operate two Dallas restaurants, Ferrari's and Il Grano. In October 2000, a limited partnership the Secchis controlled, Italian Cowboy Partners, Ltd., leased space in a Dallas shopping center for another restaurant. The lease agreement was the product of six months' active negotiations with the landlord, The Prudential Insurance Co. of America, and its agent, Four Partners L.L.C. doing business as Prizm Partners (collectively, "Prudential"). The Secchis had negotiated at least two other leases over the years, and they and their lawyer successfully insisted on a number of changes in Prudential's proposals. Offers went back and forth, and the agreement went through seven drafts. Francesco, whose formal education extended only to about the eighth grade, did not read the lease but left that to Jane, whose educational background was similar but whose English was better. Jane went over the agreement with their attorney but focused on the economic terms. When the Secchis and Prudential finally reached an understanding, Francesco signed the lease as manager of the partnership's general partner, Secchi, L.L.C. Prudential insisted that the Secchis personally guarantee the lease, and that agreement was also negotiated and changed by the Secchis before they signed it.

The lease contains the following paragraph:

> Counterclaim and Jury Trial. In the event that the Landlord commences any summary proceeding or action for nonpayment of rent or other charges provided for in this Lease, Tenant shall not interpose any counterclaim of any nature or description in any such proceeding or action. Tenant and Landlord both waive a trial by jury of any or all issues arising in any action or proceeding between the parties hereto or their successors, under or connected with this Lease, or any of its provisions.

Prudential did not specifically point out this provision to the Secchis, and Jane testified that she never noticed it. She also testified that notwithstanding the clear meaning of the second sentence, she never intended to waive a jury trial in any future litigation. The guaranty agreement does not contain a similar waiver but does state that the Secchis agree to guarantee the tenant's "full and timely performance and observance of all the covenants, terms, conditions, provisions, and agreements" in the lease, and in the event of the tenant's default, to "faithfully perform and fulfill all of such terms, covenants, conditions, provisions, and agreements".

Some nine months after the lease was executed, the Secchis and their limited partnership (collectively, "ICP") sued Prudential in statutory county court, claiming in part that it was impossible to do business on the premises because of a persistent odor of sewage. Prudential counterclaimed for amounts allegedly due under the lease and guaranty. When the trial court notified the parties that a date for non-jury trial had been set, ICP filed a jury demand and paid the jury fee, as required by Rule 216 of the Texas Rules of Civil Procedure. The court then notified the parties that a date for jury trial had been set. Prudential moved to quash the jury demand, based on the waiver in the lease. ICP responded that contractual jury waivers in general, and the waiver in the lease in particular, are unenforceable. * * *

After a hearing, the court denied the motion in a brief order without explanation.

Prudential petitioned the court of appeals for mandamus relief, which that court denied with a short memorandum opinion, 2002 WL 1608233, explaining only that "the relators have not shown themselves entitled to the relief requested." Prudential then petitioned for relief from this Court, and we agreed to hear argument. * * *

* * *

Having concluded that the parties' contractual jury waiver is enforceable, we turn to whether Prudential is entitled to relief by mandamus. Prudential must meet two requirements. One is to show that the trial court clearly abused its discretion. We have concluded as a matter of law that Prudential was entitled to enforcement of the jury waiver. Since "[a] trial court has no 'discretion' in determining what the law is or applying the law to the facts", even when the law is unsettled, the trial court's refusal to enforce the jury waiver was a clear abuse of discretion. Thus, Prudential has met the first requirement.

The other requirement Prudential must meet is to show that it has no adequate remedy by appeal. The operative word, "adequate", has no comprehensive definition; it is simply a proxy for the careful balance of jurisprudential considerations that determine when appellate courts will use original mandamus proceedings to review the actions of lower courts. These considerations implicate both public and private interests. Mandamus review of incidental, interlocutory rulings by the trial courts unduly interferes with trial court proceedings, distracts appellate court attention to issues that are unimportant both to the ultimate disposition of the case at hand and to the uniform development of the law, and adds unproductively to the expense and delay of civil litigation. Mandamus review of significant rulings in exceptional cases may be essential to preserve important substantive and procedural rights from impairment or loss, allow the appellate courts to give needed and helpful direction to the law that would otherwise prove elusive in appeals from final judgments, and spare private parties and the public the time and money utterly wasted enduring eventual reversal of improperly conducted proceedings. An appellate remedy is "adequate" when any benefits to mandamus review are outweighed by the detriments. When the benefits outweigh the detriments, appellate courts must consider whether the appellate remedy is adequate.

This determination is not an abstract or formulaic one; it is practical and prudential. It resists categorization, as our own decisions demonstrate. Although this Court has tried to give more concrete direction for determining the availability of mandamus review, rigid rules are necessarily inconsistent with the flexibility that is the remedy's principal virtue. Thus, we wrote in *Walker v. Packer* that "an appellate remedy is not inadequate merely because it may involve more expense or delay than obtaining an extraordinary writ." While this is certainly true, the word "merely" carries heavy freight. In *In re E.I. duPont de Nemours & Co.*, we concluded that defending the claims of more than 8,000 plaintiffs in litigation that would last for years was not mere expense and delay, and that mandamus review of the denial of duPont's special appearance was justified, even though duPont could eventually appeal and did not appear to be in any danger of succumbing to the burden of the litigation. In *Travelers Indemnity Co. v. Mayfield*, we granted mandamus review of an order requiring a carrier to pay the plaintiff's attorney fees as incurred in a compensation case, even though the carrier could have appealed from the final judgment and won recovery for the amounts paid, because the order not only cost the carrier money but "radically skew[ed] the procedural dynamics of the case" by requiring the defendant to fund the plaintiff's prosecution of her claims. In *In re Masonite Corp.*, the trial court on its own motion and without any authority whatever, split two cases into sixteen and transferred venue of fourteen of them to other counties. We held that the defendants were not required to wait until appeal to complain:

> Walker does not require us to turn a blind eye to blatant injustice nor does it mandate that we be an accomplice to sixteen trials that will amount to little more than a fiction. Appeal may be adequate for a particular party, but it is no remedy at all for the irreversible waste of judicial and public resources that would be required here if mandamus does not issue.

These cases, among a great many others that could be cited, serve to illustrate that whether an appellate remedy is "adequate" so as to preclude mandamus review depends heavily on the circumstances presented and is better guided by general principles than by simple rules.

Nor is the consideration whether to grant mandamus review confined to private concerns. No one suggested in *Masonite* that any individual party would suffer more by waiting to complain on appeal of the venue order than would any other party complaining of any other venue order in any other case. Two factors drove our decision in *Masonite*: the complete lack of authority for the trial court's order, and the impact on the legal system. We simply could not justify putting the civil justice system itself to the trouble of grinding through proceedings that were certain to be "little more than a fiction." The trial court's ruling in Travelers was novel but might easily have become a repeated error. Either way, the error was clear enough, and correction simple enough, that mandamus review was appropriate.

Prudent mandamus relief is also preferable to legislative enlargement of interlocutory appeals. The unavailability of mandamus relief increases the pressure for expanded interlocutory appeals. For example, when this Court refused to review venue decisions by mandamus, the Legislature responded by authorizing mandamus review of all decisions involving mandatory venue provisions. When we held that the denial of a special appearance would ordinarily not warrant mandamus review, the Legislature responded by creating an interlocutory appeal from the denial of a special appearance. When questions arose concerning the availability of mandamus to review the sufficiency of expert reports required in medical malpractice cases, the Legislature responded by creating an interlocutory appeal from the denial of dismissals of such cases for insufficient expert reports. Interlocutory appeals lie as of right and must be decided on the merits, increasing the burden on the appellate system. "Mandamus," on the other hand, "is an extraordinary remedy, not issued as a matter of right, but at the discretion of the court. Although mandamus is not an equitable remedy, its issuance is largely controlled by equitable principles." As a selective procedure, mandamus can correct clear errors in exceptional cases and afford appropriate guidance to the law without the disruption and burden of interlocutory appeal. Appellate courts must be mindful, however, that the benefits of mandamus review are easily lost by overuse.

The issue before us in the present case—whether a pre-suit waiver of trial by jury is enforceable—fits well within the types of issues for which mandamus review is not only appropriate but necessary. It is an issue of law, one of first impression for us, but likely to recur (it has already arisen in another case in the court of appeals, also on petition for mandamus. It eludes answer by appeal. In no real sense can the trial court's denial of Prudential's contractual right to have the Secchis waive a jury ever be rectified on appeal. If Prudential were to obtain judgment on a favorable jury verdict, it could not appeal, and its contractual right would be lost forever. If Prudential suffered judgment on an unfavorable verdict, Prudential could not obtain reversal for the incorrect denial of its contractual right "unless the court of appeals concludes that the error complained of . . . probably caused the rendition of an improper judgment". Even if Prudential could somehow obtain reversal based on the denial of its contractual right, it would already have lost a part of it by having been subject to the procedure it agreed to waive.

* * *

Only if a contractual waiver of trial by jury is enforced in the trial court can its propriety effectively be reviewed on appeal. The denial of trial by jury is harmless error only if there are no material fact issues to submit to a jury. But the denial of trial by jury is also reviewable by mandamus. A sentence in our opinion in *General Motors Corp. v. Gayle* suggests that this is not true, but we granted mandamus in that case to correct the trial court's denial of a jury trial, and we cited without disapproval three courts of appeals that we said "ha[d] reviewed jury trial orders by mandamus." To afford relief for the denial of a jury trial both by mandamus and by appeal, and to deny relief by either means for the refusal to enforce a jury waiver, unacceptably contorts review of the issue. Mandamus relief in a situation like this, in Professor Charles Alan Wright's words, "provides a valuable ad hoc relief valve for the pressures that are imperfectly contained by the statutes permitting appeals from final judgments and interlocutory orders."

* * *

The dissent suggests that mandamus relief should not be used to enforce contractual rights, but we used it for precisely that purpose only recently in *In re Allstate County Mutual Insurance Co.* to enforce the parties' agreement to submit to an appraisal process for determining the value of a vehicle claimed to be a total loss. The dissent states that we took "the United States Supreme Court's pronouncement that appellate delays defeated the 'core purpose' of contracts to arbitrate" as a "mandate . . . to provide an extraordinary remedy." Perhaps so, but the Supreme Court's "pronouncement" was also a statement of fact: lawsuits followed by appeals defeat the core purpose of arbitration agreements. For exactly the same reason, trial to a jury followed by appeal, if one were even allowed, defeats the reasons for agreeing to waive a jury in the first place.

The dissent argues that "authorizing mandamus relief to enforce a contractual jury waiver while relegating a party to its appellate remedy when denied its constitutional right to a jury trial" creates a procedural anomaly. If the premise were true, an anomaly would exist; but the premise is not true. We have never held that the denial of a jury trial, which can certainly be reviewed by appeal, cannot also be reviewed by mandamus. As we have already noted, we have faced the issue only once, in *General Motors Corp. v. Gayle*, and while one sentence of that opinion states that mandamus is "generally not available" to review the denial of a jury trial, we nevertheless directed the trial court to abort or mistry the nonjury trial it had commenced and to set the case on its jury docket. We also cited three court of appeals cases that had "reviewed jury trials by mandamus." *General Motors* does not preclude review of the denial of a jury trial by mandamus.

Finally, the dissent argues that "[e]ven if parties may freely waive their right to trial by jury, there is no public policy reason for encouraging them to do so." Of course, enforcing an agreement is not the same as encouraging parties to make it. By enforcing contractual jury waivers, we no more encourage them than we encourage arbitration by enforcing arbitration agreements. Parties are free to agree to such remedies as they choose, and as we have noted, they may have good reasons for agreeing to waive a jury trial. What the dissent ignores is that there is a compelling public policy reason to enforce legal agreements freely made. The dissent does not find the jury trial waiver in this case illegal or contrary to public policy, yet it would deny all viable means of enforcement.

* * *

For these reasons, we direct respondent, the Honorable Sally Montgomery, to vacate her order of June 6, 2003, and the prior order of June 19, 2002, to grant Prudential's motion to quash the jury demand and payment of jury fee, and to return the case to the nonjury docket. We are confident she will promptly comply. Our writ will issue only if she does not.

CHIEF JUSTICE PHILLIPS, joined by JUSTICE O'NEILL, JUSTICE JEFFERSON, and JUSTICE SCHNEIDER, dissenting [omitted].

3. *Fundamental Error*

Fundamental or unassigned error is an exception to the general rule that error must be preserved during the lower court proceeding in order for an appellate court to consider any complaints about the specific error. The definition of fundamental error was fairly broad for a period of time. The current view of fundamental error, however was set in 1941, and is extremely restrictive.

Note

From time to time a significant primary holding from a case will be presented as a "Abbreviated Case". An "Abbreviated Case" is a short summary of a case that decides an important point that is printed in this book in outline form to reduce the length of the book. These notes are as important as "full" cases but add nothing significant other than the primary holding or holdings. The following short summary of the *McCauley* case is an example of an "Abbreviated Case".

MCCAULEY
v.
CONSOLIDATED UNDERWRITERS
157 Tex. 475, 304 S.W.2 265
(1957)

Facts: This is an appeal from the order of a district court setting aside a default judgment rendered at a previous term (after the trial court lost jurisdiction). The court of appeals affirmed.

Issues: Is this fundamental error? Yes. Fundamental error is an error which directly and adversely affects the interest of the public generally, as that interest is declared by the statutes or Constitution of Texas. A court's lack of jurisdiction is fundamental error.

Issues: Is there a difference between fundamental error in the Supreme Court and Court of Appeals? No. There used to be, but there is no longer any difference.

USAA TEXAS LLOYDS CO.
v.
MENCHACA
545 S.W.3d 479
(Tex. 2018)

Wallace B. Jefferson, Rachel A. Ekery, Alexander Dubose, Jefferson & Townsend LLP, Mary Margaret Roark, Thomas R. Phillips, Baker Botts LLP, Austin TX, Charles T. Frazier Jr., Alexander Dubose, Jefferson & Townsend LLP, Dallas TX, Bruce E. Ramage, Martin Disiere Jefferson & Wisdom LLP, Christopher W. Martin, Levon G. Hovnatanian, Paul Wayne Pickering, Robert T. Owen, Martin Disiere Jefferson & Wisdom LLP, Tanya Dugas, Raley & Bowick, LLP, Houston TX, for Petitioner USAA Texas Lloyds Company.

Jennifer Bruch Hogan, James C. Marrow, Richard P. Hogan Jr., Hogan & Hogan, Pennzoil Place, John Steven Mostyn, The Mostyn Law Firm, Houston TX, Gilberto Hinojosa, Law Offices of Gilberto, Hinojosa & Associates, P.C., Brownsville TX, Randal G. Cashiola, Cashiola & Bean, Beaumont TX, for Respondent Menchaca, Gail.

Michael A. Choyke, Thomas C. Wright, Lisa Wright, Wright, Close & Barger, LLP, Houston TX, for Amicus Curiae, Lexington Insurance Company.

Brendan K. McBride, The McBride Law Firm, Marc E. Gravely, Matthew R. Pearson, Gravely & Pearson, LLP, San Antonio TX, for Amicus Curiae, Brass Real Estate Funds, Texas Automobile Dealers Association, Texas Independent Automobile Dealers Association, Texas Organization of Rural & Community, Hospitals.

Russell S. Post, Beck Redden LLP, Houston TX, for Amicus Curiae, Cameron, a Schlumberger Company.

Dale Wainwright, Kendyl Taylor Hanks, Greenberg Traurig, LLP, Austin TX, Lindsay E. Hagans, Houston TX, for Amicus Curiae, Chamber of Commerce of the United States of America.

Catherine L. Hanna, Hanna & Plaut LLP, Austin TX 7870, for Amicus Curiae, Insurance Council of Texas.

Hugh Rice Kelly, Texans for Lawsuit Reform, Houston TX, for Amicus Curiae, Texans for Lawsuit Reform.

Marc S. Tabolsky, Penelope E. Nicholson, Schiffer Odom Hicks & Johnson PLLC, Houston TX, for Amicus Curiae, United Policyholders.

JUSTICE BOYD announced the Court's judgment and delivered the Court's opinion as to Parts I, II, and III.A, in which CHIEF JUSTICE HECHT, JUSTICE GREEN, JUSTICE GUZMAN, JUSTICE LEHRMANN, JUSTICE DEVINE, and JUSTICE BROWN joined, a plurality opinion as to Parts III.B and III.C, in which CHIEF JUSTICE HECHT, JUSTICE LEHRMANN, and JUSTICE DEVINE joined, and an opinion as to Parts III.D, III.E, III.F, and III.G, in which JUSTICE LEHRMANN and JUSTICE DEVINE joined.

After Hurricane Ike struck Galveston Island in September 2008, Gail Menchaca contacted her homeowner's insurance company, USAA Texas Lloyds, and reported that the storm had damaged her home. The adjuster USAA sent to investigate Menchaca's claim found only minimal damage. Based on the adjuster's findings, USAA determined that its policy covered some of the damage but declined to pay Menchaca any benefits because the total estimated repair costs did not exceed the policy's deductible. About five months later, at Menchaca's request, USAA sent another adjuster to re-inspect the property. This adjuster generally confirmed the first adjuster's findings, and USAA again refused to pay any policy benefits. Menchaca sued USAA for breach of the insurance policy and for unfair settlement practices in violation of the Texas Insurance Code.

* * *

* * * the jury in this case (1) failed to find in answer to Question 1 that USAA failed to comply with its obligations under the insurance policy; (2) found in answer to Question 2 that USAA violated the Insurance Code by failing to pay Menchaca's claim for policy benefits "without conducting a reasonable investigation with respect to" that claim; and (3) found in answer to Question 3 that USAA's statutory violation resulted in Menchaca incurring damages of $11,350, representing the amount of policy benefits USAA "should have paid" Menchaca.

* * *

* * * Here, the jury's answer to Question 3 (USAA "should have paid" $11,350 in policy benefits to Menchaca) necessarily addresses the same material fact as its answer to Question 1 (USAA "fail[ed] to comply with the terms of the insurance policy"), because both requested findings on whether USAA failed to pay benefits Menchaca was entitled to under the policy. The answers conflict because if USAA "should have paid"

Menchaca benefits under the policy and did not, then USAA necessarily failed to comply with the policy's terms.

* * *

When an irreconcilable conflict involves one jury answer that would require a judgment in favor of the plaintiff and another that would require a judgment in favor of the defendant, the conflict is fatal. *Little Rock Furniture Mfg. Co. v. Dunn*, 148 Tex. 197, 222 S.W.2d 985, 991 (1949). Here, both questions address the decisive issue—whether USAA failed to pay benefits Menchaca was entitled to under the policy. Without Questions 2 and 3, the jury's answer to Question 1 would require a judgment in USAA's favor. But without Question 1, the jury's answers to Questions 2 and 3 would require a judgment in Menchaca's favor. We thus conclude that the answers created a fatal conflict.

Our determination that the verdict contained a fatal conflict does not end the inquiry. Of course, a trial court should not enter judgment based on a verdict containing a fatal conflict until "the disputed question of fact . . . has been resolved." *Meyer*, 502 S.W.2d at 679. But we must decide whether we can consider a trial court's error in entering such a judgment when neither party has objected to the conflict.

Generally, as "a prerequisite to presenting a complaint for appellate review, the record must show that . . . the complaint was made to the trial court by a timely request, objection, or motion." TEX. R. APP. P. 33.1(a)(1)(A). This rule "conserves judicial resources by giving trial courts an opportunity to correct an error before an appeal proceeds," promotes "fairness among litigants" by prohibiting them from surprising their opponents on appeal, and furthers "the goal of accuracy in judicial decision-making" by allowing the parties to "develop and refine their arguments" and allowing the trial court to "analyze the questions at issue." *In re B.L.D.*, 113 S.W.3d 340, 350 (Tex. 2003). Under, this rule, we will not consider an error that was not properly raised in the trial court "unless a recognized exception exists." *Id.*

An exception to the preservation-of-error requirement applies when the alleged error is "fundamental." "Except for fundamental error, appellate courts are not authorized to consider issues not properly raised by the parties." *Mack Trucks, Inc. v. Tamez*, 206 S.W.3d 572, 577 (Tex. 2006). Thus, "we have used the term 'fundamental error' to describe situations in which an appellate court may review error that was neither raised in the trial court nor assigned on appeal." *B.L.D.*, 113 S.W.3d at 350. Beginning in the 1800s, we held that a trial court's entry of a judgment based on inconsistent or insufficient jury answers constitutes fundamental error because the error is "an error of law apparent on the face of the record," *Van Valkenberg v. Ruby*, 68 Tex. 139, 3 S.W. 746, 748 (1887), courts are not "permitted to speculate" about a jury's intentions, *Moore v. Moore*, 67 Tex. 293, 3 S.W. 284, 285-86 (1887), and the law deprives courts of "the power to render judgment, which is given by law and not by consent of the parties," *Radford v. Auto. Underwriters of Am.*, 299 S.W. 852, 853 (Tex. Comm'n App. 1927) (internal citations omitted).

In the decades that followed these decisions, the courts of appeals applied the fundamental-error doctrine in numerous cases, concluding that a jury verdict containing a fatal conflict constitutes fundamental error requiring a new trial even if no party complained of or preserved the error. In 1949, we at least appeared to confirm these holdings in *Little Rock Furniture*, noting that the "law seems to be established that such a conflict cannot be waived by the parties and that a judgment on a verdict containing such a conflict must be set aside." 222 S.W.2d at 991 (citing *Radford* 299 S.W. 852; *Interstate Tr.*, 88 S.W.2d at 1110; *Kilgore*, 204 S.W.2d at 1005; *Marshall*, 151 S.W.2d at 919). But we had no opportunity to apply the exception in *Little Rock Furniture* because we concluded that the verdict in that case did not "disclose a fatal conflict." *Id.*

Shortly before we decided *Little Rock Furniture*, however, we began to reconsider the fundamental-error doctrine in light of recent statutory revisions and our adoption of the Texas Rules of Civil Procedure. *See Ramsey v. Dunlop*, 146 Tex. 196, 205 S.W.2d 979, 982-83 (1947). The fundamental-error doctrine "in civil actions arose in Texas under old statutes that stated that cases on appeal could be reviewed 'on an error in law either assigned or apparent on the face of the record.' " *Pirtle*, 629 S.W.2d at 920 (citing 2 Gammel's Laws of Texas 1562 (1898); 3 Gammel's Laws of Texas 393 (1898)). But after the Legislature repealed those statutes and we adopted the Rules of Civil Procedure in 1941, no law remained that authorized appellate courts to consider unpreserved or unassigned errors. *Id.* We concluded in *Ramsey*, however, that despite the lack of any express legal authorization, it remained "both the province and the duty" of appellate courts to consider errors that are "truly fundamental," such as "an error which directly and adversely affects the interest of the public generally, as that interest is declared in the statutes or Constitution of this state." *Ramsey*, 205 S.W.2d at 983. We later concluded that fundamental error also exists when "the record affirmatively and conclusively shows that the court rendering the judgment was without jurisdiction of the subject matter." *McCauley v. Consol. Underwriters*, 157 Tex. 475, 304 S.W.2d 265, 266 (1957). Citing *Ramsey* and *McCauley*, we have since repeatedly explained that the fundamental-error doctrine applies only in those two "rare instances," in which "the record shows the court lacked jurisdiction or that the public interest is directly and adversely affected as that interest is declared in the statutes or the Constitution of Texas." *In re L.D.C.*, 400 S.W.3d 572, 574 (Tex. 2013) (quoting *In re C.O.S.*, 988 S.W.2d 760, 765 (Tex. 1999)). Although we have not hesitated to apply the doctrine when the error is jurisdictional or adversely affects the public's (as opposed to the current parties') interests, we have repeatedly refused to apply the fundamental-error doctrine to other types of errors and have instead consistently restricted appellate review to properly preserved errors. For this reason, we have characterized the fundamental-error doctrine as "a rarity," *Am. Gen. Fire & Cas. Co. v. Weinberg*, 639 S.W.2d 688, 689 (Tex. 1982), and "a discredited doctrine," *B.L.D.*, 113 S.W.3d at 350 (quoting *Cox*, 638 S.W.2d at 868).

Soon after our decisions in *Little Rock Furniture* and *Ramsey*, we warned that cases "discussing fundamental error decided before the adoption of the Rules of Civil Procedure in 1941 must be considered in the light of changes in the concept of fundamental error made by the adoption of the new rules." *Lewis v. Tex. Emp'rs' Ins. Ass'n*, 151 Tex. 95, 246 S.W.2d 599, 600 (1952). The result of those changes, we later explained, is that the scope of "truly fundamental" error is "much narrower" than it was before the 1941 amendments. *McCauley*, 304 S.W.2d at 266; *see also Estate of Pollack v. McMurrey*, 858 S.W.2d 388, 394 (Tex. 1993) (noting that we have since "taken a more restrictive view of fundamental error").

Before we clearly restricted the application of the fundamental-error doctrine to jurisdictional and public-interest errors in *McCauley*, courts of appeals continued to rely on *Little Rock Furniture* to hold that a fatal conflict in jury answers creates a fundamental error that appellate courts may review even if unassigned. But five years after *McCauley*, we rejected the statement in *Little Rock Furniture* and expressly held that, in light of the fundamental-error doctrine's restricted scope, the "entry of judgment by a trial court on conflicting findings does not constitute fundamental error." *St. Paul Fire & Marine Ins. Co. v. Murphree*, 163 Tex. 534, 357 S.W.2d 744, 749 (1962) (citing *Ramsey*, 205 S.W.2d at 979; *McCauley*, 304 S.W.2d at 265). We have since confirmed and reaffirmed that holding in several cases. With the exception of a few opinions that erroneously relied on *Little Rock Furniture* without citing or considering *Murphree*, the courts of appeals have repeatedly done the same.

We did not hold otherwise in our 1973 opinion in *Meyer*, 502 S.W.2d at 679. The trial court in *Meyer* entered judgment for the defendant based on the jury's verdict, but the court of appeals reversed and remanded the case "for further proceedings," concluding, "There being a fatal and irreconcilable conflict in the jury's answers, the verdict cannot stand, and the judgment based thereon must be set aside." *Meyer v. Union Mut. Life Ins. Co.*, 483 S.W.2d 7, 10 (Tex. Civ. App.—Dallas 1972), *aff'd*, 502 S.W.2d 676 (Tex. 1973). We agreed that the verdict contained a fatal conflict and affirmed, stating that such a verdict "cannot be regarded as an acceptable resolution of the disputed question of fact, and judgment should not be rendered until that fact issue has been resolved." *Meyer*, 502 S.W.2d at 679. Neither the court of appeals in *Meyer* nor this Court, however, addressed the question of whether error based on conflicting jury answers is fundamental or must be preserved, nor did they cite *Little Rock Furniture*, *Ramsey*, *McCauley*, *Murphree*, or any other authorities on that issue. In fact, neither the court of appeals nor this Court cited *any* authority for reversing the trial court's judgment in *Meyer*.

Until today, this Court has never cited, relied on, or discussed *Meyer* as authority on any issue. Only three courts of appeals have ever cited it, and none cited it as authority on the issue of whether error based on conflicting jury answers is fundamental or must be preserved. That is not to suggest that the Court wrongly decided *Meyer*; rather, it appears to simply confirm that the issue was not *at issue* in *Meyer*. Neither our opinion nor the court of appeals' opinion in *Meyer* ever mentioned or addressed whether any party objected to the conflicting answers or whether they should have. As best we can tell, the plaintiff in *Meyer* never complained that the defendant did not preserve the error, and the Court simply never addressed that issue. We cannot agree that *Meyer*—which never addressed the preservation requirement—somehow overruled or trumps *Murphree*, *Duke*, *Sunland Supply*, and the dozens of other opinions that directly addressed the issue. Consistent with these numerous applicable precedents, we conclude that the fatal conflict in the jury's verdict in this case does not constitute fundamental error, and as a result, we cannot consider that conflict unless the error was properly preserved. *Mack Trucks*, 206 S.W.3d at 577.

* * *

Having concluded that the trial court and court of appeals erred in disregarding the jury's answer to Question 1, we are left with findings that support the judgment in Menchaca's favor based on statutory violations but that also contain a fatal conflict. We could render judgment for Menchaca based on the jury's verdict because USAA failed to preserve that conflict. In the interest of justice, however, we could also "remand the case to the trial court even if a rendition of judgment is otherwise appropriate." TEX. R. APP. P. 60.3. Such a remand is particularly appropriate when it appears that one or more parties "proceeded under the wrong legal theory," *Boyles v. Kerr*, 855 S.W.2d 593, 603 (Tex. 1993), especially when "the applicable law has . . . evolved between the time of trial and the disposition of the appeal." *Nat. Gas Pipeline Co. of Am. v. Justiss*, 397 S.W.3d 150, 162 (Tex. 2012); *see Hamrick v. Ward*, 446 S.W.3d 377, 385 (Tex. 2014) (remanding in the interest of justice "in light of our clarification of the law"); *Moriel*, 879 S.W.2d at 26 (same, in light of our "substantial clarification"). In light of the parties' obvious and understandable confusion over our relevant precedent and the effect of that confusion on their arguments in this case, as well as our clarification of the requirements to preserve error based on conflicting jury answers, we conclude that a remand is necessary here in the interest of justice.

* * *

For the reasons explained, we reverse the court of appeals' judgment and remand the case to the trial court for a new trial in the interest of justice.

CHIEF JUSTICE HECHT filed a concurring opinion (omitted).

JUSTICE BLACKLOCK concurs in the judgment without opinion.

JUSTICE GREEN filed a dissenting opinion in which JUSTICE GUZMAN and JUSTICE BROWN joined as to Parts I, II, and IV, and a plurality opinion as to Part III, in which CHIEF JUSTICE HECHT, JUSTICE GUZMAN, and JUSTICE BROWN joined (omitted).

JUSTICE JOHNSON did not participate in the decision.

PIRTLE
v.
GREGORY
629 S.W.2d 919
(Tex. 1982)

Sudderth, Woodley & Dudley, Keith Woodley, Comanche, for petitioner.

Thompson & Cook, John R. Cook, Breckenridge, for respondents.

PER CURIAM.

Stanley Pirtle brought suit for specific performance and for removal of cloud on 512 acres of land. Pirtle sued Layne Gregory, Grady Gregory, and Kathy Coker because they had contracted in writing but failed to execute an oil and gas lease to Pirtle, as lessee. Layne and Grady Gregory later executed an oil and gas lease on the property to James P. Flanagan. Plaintiff Pirtle originally sued Flanagan as one of the defendants, but took a nonsuit as to him. The trial court rendered judgment for Pirtle commanding the Gregorys and Coker to execute the oil and gas lease, but the court of appeals reversed that judgment, believing that the absence of Flanagan from the suit constituted fundamental error. 623 S.W.2d 955 (Tex. App.).

"Fundamental error" in civil actions arose in Texas under old statutes that stated that cases on appeal could be reviewed "on an error in law either assigned or apparent on the face of the record." 2 GAMMEL, LAWS OF TEXAS 1562 (1898); 3 GAMMEL, LAWS OF TEXAS 393 (1898). The practice of appellate courts in considering unassigned errors was the source of much mischief, and when the Texas Supreme Court promulgated its Rules of Civil Procedure in 1941, old article 1837 was repealed. Since that time, there has been no rule or statute that authorizes appellate consideration of errors for which there was no trial predicate that complained of the error. *McCauley v. Consolidated Underwriters*, 157 Tex. 475, 304 S.W.2d 265, 266 (1957); *Ramsey v. Dunlop*, 146 Tex. 196, 205 S.W.2d 979, 984 (1947) (ALEXANDER, J., concurring). Fundamental error survives today in those rare instances in which the record shows the court lacked jurisdiction or that the public interest is directly and adversely affected as that interest is declared in the statutes or the Constitution of Texas. STATE BAR OF TEXAS, APPELLATE PROCEDURE IN TEXAS § 11.5 (2d ed. 1979).

The reason for the requirement that a litigant preserve a trial predicate for complaint on appeal is that one should not be permitted to waive, consent to, or neglect to complain about an error at trial and then surprise his opponent on appeal by stating his complaint for the first time.

Flanagan is said to be an indispensable party to this cause, because the defendants gave him an oil and gas lease and the validity of that lease has not been adjudicated. The defendants should not be heard to complain for the first time on appeal, however, because they did not complain at the trial level by exception, plea in abatement, motion to join other parties or otherwise.

We reaffirm the views we expressed in *Cooper v. Texas Gulf Industries, Inc.*, 513 S.W.2d 200 (Tex. 1974). We there stated: Under the provisions of our present Rule 39 it would be rare indeed if there were a person whose presence was so indispensable in the sense that his absence deprives the court of jurisdiction to adjudicate between the parties already joined. *Id.* at 204.

In a case such as this, parties who participate in the trial without complaint will not be heard to complain at the appellate stage when "there is reason not to throw away a judgment just because it did not theoretically settle the whole controversy." *Continental Insurance Co. of New York v. Cotten*, 427 F.2d 48, 51 (9th Cir. 1970) (*citing Provident Tradesmens Bank & Trust Co. v. Patterson*, 390 U.S. 102, 88 S.Ct. 733, 19 L.Ed.2d 936 (1967).

Pursuant to Texas Rules of Civil Procedure, Rule 483, we grant the writ of error and, without hearing oral argument, reverse the judgment of the court of appeals and remand this cause to that court for disposition of the other points not reached.

Notes

1. In *Ramsey v. Dunlop*,[1] CHIEF JUSTICE ALEXANDER, in his concurring opinion stated: "[I]n so far as the rights of the litigants are concerned they are not entitled to have the court consider any error not assigned by them. It is my opinion that the Court of Civil Appeals is authorized to reverse a judgment of the trial court upon an unassigned error only when it involves a matter of public interest and when the record affirmatively and conclusively shows that the appellee was not entitled to recover, where the record affirmatively shows that the court rendering the judgment was without jurisdiction over the subject matter."

2. Examples of fundamental error, that do not relate to jurisdictional defects, are difficult to find. *Bradley v. State of Texas ex rel White*,[2] however, is a recent case that reflects non-jurisdictional fundamental error. Under TEX. R. EVID. 605 "[T]he judge presiding at the trial may not testify in that trial as a witness. No objection need be made in order to preserve this point." In *Bradley*, city council members sitting as a court to remove the mayor of the city were held to be sitting as judges. The council members were, thus, bound by Rule 605, and violated the rule by testifying as witnesses in the removal proceeding. Under that section, a harm analysis is not necessary.

3. In *Waco Independent School District v. Gibson*, 22 S.W.3d 849 (Tex. 2000) the Court held that because subject matter jurisdiction is essential to the authority of a court to decide a case, it cannot be waived and may be raised for the first time on appeal. Thus, ripeness and standing, which are components of subject matter jurisdiction, cannot be waived.

4. *Burbage v. Burbage*, 447 S.W.3d 249, 258 (Tex. 2014): "Our procedural rules are technical, but not trivial. We construe such rules liberally so that the right to appeal is not lost unnecessarily. *Arkoma Basin Exploration Co. v. FMF Assocs. 1990-A, Ltd.*, 249 S.W.3d 380, 388 (Tex. 2008). But when an objection fails to explain the nature of the error, we cannot make assumptions. Preservation of error reflects important prudential considerations recognizing that the judicial process benefits greatly when trial courts have the opportunity to first consider and rule on error. *In re B.L.D.*, 113 S.W.3d at 350 (citing *In re C.O.S.*, 988 S.W.2d 760, 765 (Tex. 1999)). Affording courts this opportunity conserves judicial resources and promotes fairness by ensuring that a party does not neglect a complaint at trial and raise it for the first time on appeal. *Id.* (citing *Pirtle v. Gregory*, 629 S.W.2d 919, 920 (Tex. 1982) (per curiam)). Nor may we stray from these rules because Chad represented himself at trial. See *Mansfield State Bank v. Cohn*, 573 S.W.2d 181, 184-85 (Tex.1978)."

---

[1] 146 Tex. 196, 205 S.W.2d 979 (1947).

[2] 990 S.W.2d 245 (Tex. 1999).

TEXAS ASSOCIATION OF BUSINESS
v.
TEXAS AIR CONTROL BOARD, et al

852 S.W.2d 440
(Tex. 1993)

R. Kinnan Golemon, James W. Checkley, Jr., Albert R. Axe, Jr., Scott R. Kidd and Douglas W. Alexander, Austin, for appellant.

Douglas G. Caroom, Mary E. Kelly, Dan Morales, Nancy N. Lynch, William D. Dugat, III and Amy R. Johnson, Austin, for appellees.

CORNYN, JUSTICE.

The Texas Association of Business (TAB), on behalf of its members, brought this declaratory judgment action seeking a ruling that statutes empowering two state administrative agencies to levy civil penalties for violations of their regulations conflict with the open courts and jury trial provisions of the Texas Constitution. The administrative agencies denied TAB's claims, and along with two Intervenors, filed counterclaims seeking a declaration that the same statutes and regulations comport with those constitutional provisions.

* * *

TAB alleges that it is a Texas not-for-profit corporation, that its members do business throughout Texas, and that it is authorized to represent its members on any matter that may have an impact on their businesses.

TAB filed this suit under the Uniform Declaratory Judgments Act, TEX.CIV.PRAC. & REM.CODE §§ 37.001-37.011, alleging that some of its members had been subjected to civil penalties assessed by either the Air Control Board or the Water Commission. TAB further alleged that all of its other members that operate their businesses pursuant to the pertinent provisions of the Texas Clean Air Act, the Texas Water Code, or the Texas Solid Waste Disposal Act or any rules or orders issued pursuant to those provisions were put at "substantial risk (if not certainty)" of being assessed civil penalties by the Air Control Board or the Water Commission. Thus this suit does not challenge specific instances of the Air Control Board's or the Water Commission's exercise, or threatened exercise, of the civil penalty power. Instead, TAB's suit is a facial challenge to the constitutionality of this administrative enforcement scheme under the Texas Constitution.

* * *

Before we reach the merits of this case, we first consider the matter of the trial court's jurisdiction, as well as our own; specifically we determine whether TAB has standing to challenge the statutes and regulations in question. Because TAB's standing to bring this action is not readily apparent, and because our jurisdiction as well as that of the trial court depends on this issue, we requested supplemental briefing on standing at the oral argument of this case. In response, the parties insist that any question of standing has been waived in the trial court and cannot be raised by the court for the first time on appeal. We disagree.

Subject matter jurisdiction is essential to the authority of a court to decide a case. Standing is implicit in the concept of subject matter jurisdiction. The standing requirement stems from two limitations on subject matter jurisdiction: the separation of powers doctrine and, in Texas, the open courts provision. Subject matter jurisdiction is never presumed and cannot be waived.

One limit on courts' jurisdiction under both the state and federal constitutions is the separation of powers doctrine. *See* TEX.CONST. art. II, § 1; * * * Under this doctrine, governmental authority vested in one department of government cannot be exercised by another department unless expressly permitted by the constitution. Thus we have construed our separation of powers article to prohibit courts from issuing advisory opinions because such is the function of the executive rather than the judicial department. *Firemen's Ins. Co. v. Burch,* 442 S.W.2d 331, 333 (Tex. 1969); *Morrow v. Corbin,* 122 Tex. 553, 62 S.W.2d 641, 644 (Tex.1933). Accordingly, we have interpreted the Uniform Declaratory Judgments Act, TEX.CIV.PRAC. & REM.CODE §§ 37.001-.011, to be merely a procedural device for deciding cases already within a court's jurisdiction rather than a legislative enlargement of a court's power, permitting the rendition of advisory opinions. *Firemen's Ins. Co.,* 442 S.W.2d at 333; *United Serv. Life Ins. Co. v. Delaney,* 396 S.W.2d 855, 863 (Tex. 1965); *California Prods., Inc. v. Puretex Lemon Juice, Inc.,* 160 Tex. 586, 334 S.W.2d 780 (1960).

The distinctive feature of an advisory opinion is that it decides an abstract question of law without binding the parties. *Alabama State Fed'n of Labor v. McAdory,* 325 U.S. 450, 461, 65 S.Ct. 1384, 1389, 89 L.Ed. 1725 (1945); *Firemen's Ins. Co.,* 442 S.W.2d at 333; *Puretex Lemon Juice, Inc.,* 160 Tex. at 591, 334 S.W.2d at 783. An opinion issued in a case brought by a party without standing is advisory because rather than remedying an actual or imminent harm, the judgment addresses only a hypothetical injury. *See Allen v. Wright,* 468 U.S. 737, 751, 104 S.Ct. 3315, 3324, 82 L.Ed.2d 556 (1984). Texas courts, like federal courts, have no jurisdiction to render such opinions.

The separation of powers doctrine is not the only constitutional basis for standing. Under federal law, standing is also an aspect of the Article III limitation of the judicial power to "cases" and "controversies." *Sierra Club v. Morton,* 405 U.S. 727, 731, 92 S.Ct. 1361, 1364, 31 L.Ed.2d 636 (1972). To comport with Article III, a federal court may hear a case only when the litigant has been threatened with or has sustained an injury. *Valley Forge Christian College,* 454 U.S. at 471, 102 S.Ct. at 758. Under the Texas Constitution, standing is implicit in the open courts provision, which contemplates access to the courts only for those litigants suffering an injury. Specifically, the open courts provision provides:

> All courts shall be open, and every person for an **injury** done him, in his lands, goods, person or reputation, shall have remedy by due course of law.

TEX. CONST. art. I, § 13 (emphasis added). Because standing is a constitutional prerequisite to maintaining a suit under both federal and Texas law, we look to the more extensive jurisprudential experience of the federal courts on this subject for any guidance it may yield.

Under federal law, a lack of standing deprives a court of subject matter jurisdiction because standing is an element of such jurisdiction. * * * Other states have followed this analysis in construing their own constitutions. * * *

Subject matter jurisdiction is an issue that may be raised for the first time on appeal; it may not be waived by the parties. *Texas Employment Comm'n v. International Union of Elec., Radio and Mach. Workers, Local Union No. 782,* 163 Tex. 135, 352 S.W.2d 252, 253 (1961); RESTATEMENT (SECOND) OF JUDGMENTS § 11, comment c (1982). This court recently reiterated that axiom in *Gorman v. Life Insurance Co.,* 811 S.W.2d 542, 547 (Tex.), *cert. denied,* 502 U.S. 824, 112 S.Ct. 88, 116 L.Ed.2d 60 (1991). Because we conclude that standing is a component of subject matter jurisdiction, it cannot be waived and may be raised for the first time on appeal.

If we were to conclude that standing is unreviewable on appeal at least three undesirable consequences could result. First and foremost, appellate courts would be impotent to prevent lower courts from exceeding their constitutional and statutory limits of authority. Second, appellate courts could not arrest collusive suits. Third, by operation of the doctrines of res judicata and collateral estoppel, judgments rendered in suits addressing only hypothetical injuries could bar relitigation of issues by a litigant who eventually suffers an actual injury. We therefore hold that standing, as a component of subject matter jurisdiction, cannot be waived in this or any other case and may be raised for the first time on appeal by the parties or by the court.

* * *

Because standing is a component of subject matter jurisdiction, we consider TAB's standing under the same standard by which we review subject matter jurisdiction generally. That standard requires the pleader to allege facts that affirmatively demonstrate the court's jurisdiction to hear the cause. *Richardson v. First Nat'l Life Ins. Co.,* 419 S.W.2d 836, 839 (Tex. 1967). When reviewing a trial court order dismissing a cause for want of jurisdiction, Texas appellate courts "construe the pleadings in favor of the plaintiff and look to the pleader's intent." *Huston v. Federal Deposit Ins. Corp.,* 663 S.W.2d 126, 129 (Tex. App.—Eastland 1983, writ ref'd n.r.e. 1984); *see also* W. Wendell Hall, *Standards of Appellate Review in Civil Appeals,* 21 ST. MARY'S L.J. 865, 870 (1990).

Here, however, we are not reviewing a trial court order of dismissal for want of jurisdiction, we are considering standing for the first time on appeal. A review of only the pleadings to determine subject matter jurisdiction is sufficient in the trial court because a litigant has a right to amend to attempt to cure pleading defects if jurisdictional facts are not alleged. *See* TEX.R.CIV.P. 80. Failing that, the suit is dismissed. When an appellate court questions jurisdiction on appeal for the first time, however, there is no opportunity to cure the defect. Therefore, when a Texas appellate court reviews the standing of a party sua sponte, it must construe the petition in favor of the party, and if necessary, review the entire record to determine if any evidence supports standing.

TAB asserts standing on behalf of its members. The general test for standing in Texas requires that there "(a) shall be a real controversy between the parties, which (b) will be actually determined by the judicial declaration sought." *Board of Water Engineers v. City of San Antonio,* 155 Tex. 111, 114, 283 S.W.2d 722, 724 (1955). Texas, however, has no particular test for determining the standing of an organization, such as TAB. * * * While we agree with the statement of the general test for standing set out in *Board of Water Engineers,* we foresee difficulties in relying on it alone to determine the standing of an organization like TAB. For instance, when members of an organization have individual standing, but the organization was not established for the purpose of protecting the particular interest at issue, it is not necessarily in the members' best interest to allow such a disinterested organization to sue on their behalf. Furthermore, an organization should not be allowed to sue on behalf of its members when the claim asserted requires the participation of the members individually rather than as an association, such as when the members seek to recover money damages and the amount of damages varies with each member.

The United States Supreme Court has articulated a standard for associational standing that lends itself to our use. We adopt that test today. In *Hunt v. Washington State Apple Advertising Commission,* the Court held that an association has standing to sue on behalf of its members when "(a) its members would otherwise have standing to sue in their own right; (b) the interests it seeks to protect are germane to the organization's purpose; and (c) neither the claim asserted nor the relief requested requires the participation of individual members in the lawsuit." 432 U.S. 333, 343, 97 S.Ct. 2434, 2441, 53 L.Ed.2d 383 (1977); *see also New York State Club Ass'n v. City of New York,* 487 U.S. 1, 9, 108 S.Ct. 2225, 2231, 101 L.Ed.2d 1 (1988); *International Union, United Auto., Aerospace and Agric. Implement Workers of Am. v. Brock,* 477 U.S. 274, 282, 106 S.Ct. 2523, 2528, 91 L.Ed.2d 228 (1986). This standard incorporates the standing analysis we adopted in *Board of Water Engineers,* yet addresses the additional concerns we have noted.

We now apply the *Hunt* standard to the case before us. Reviewing the record in its entirety for evidence supporting subject matter jurisdiction, and resolving any doubt in TAB's favor, we conclude that TAB has standing to pursue the relief it seeks in this case.

The first prong of the *Hunt* test requires that TAB's pleadings and the rest of the record demonstrate that TAB's members have standing to sue in their own behalf. This requirement should not be interpreted to impose unreasonable obstacles to associational representation. In this regard the United States Supreme Court stated that "the purpose of the first part of the *Hunt* test is simply to weed out plaintiffs who try to bring cases, which could not otherwise be brought, by manufacturing allegations of standing that lack any real foundation." *New York State Club Ass'n,* 487 U.S. at 9, 108 S.Ct. at 2232. We are satisfied that TAB has not manufactured this lawsuit. A comparison of the association's membership roster with the list of businesses subjected to state penalties indicates individual TAB members have been assessed administrative penalties pursuant to the challenged enactments. Additionally, TAB has alleged that other of its members remain at substantial risk of penalty. A substantial risk of injury is sufficient under *Hunt. See e.g., Pennell v. City of San Jose,* 485 U.S. 1, 7 n. 3, 108 S.Ct. 849, 855 n. 3, 99 L.Ed.2d 1 (1988) (concluding that association of landlords had standing based on pleadings that individual members would likely be harmed by rent ordinance). Thus TAB satisfies the first prong of the *Hunt* test.

The second prong of *Hunt* requires that TAB's pleadings and the rest of the record demonstrate that the interests TAB seeks to protect are germane to the organization's purpose. TAB was chartered to "represent the interests of its members on issues which may impact upon its members' businesses." Considering a very similar question in *New York State Club Association,* the United States Supreme Court held that: "[T]he associational interests that the consortium seeks to protect are germane to its purpose: appellant's certificate of incorporation states that its purpose is 'to promote the common business interests of its [member clubs].' " 487 U.S. at 10 n. 4, 108 S.Ct. at 2232, n. 4 (bracketed language in original). Likewise, the interests TAB desires to protect are germane to the organization's purpose, and thus the second prong is met.

Under the third and final prong of the *Hunt* test, TAB's pleadings and the record must demonstrate that neither the claim asserted nor the relief requested require the participation of individual members in the lawsuit. The Supreme Court has interpreted this prong as follows:

> [W]hether an association has standing to invoke the court's remedial powers on behalf of its members depends in substantial measure on the nature of the relief sought. If in a proper case the association seeks a declaration, injunction, or some other form of prospective relief, it can reasonably be supposed

that the remedy, if granted, will inure to the benefit of those members of the association actually injured.

Hunt, 432 U.S. at 343, 97 S.Ct. at 2441 (quoting *Warth,* 422 U.S. at 515, 95 S.Ct. at 2213).

By seeking damages on behalf of its members, necessitating that each individual prove lost profits particular to its operations, the organization in *Warth* lacked standing to sue; rather, each individual member had to be a party to the suit. These facts are distinguishable from *Brock,* in which the union challenged an administrative interpretation of statutory provisions relating to unemployment compensation. 477 U.S. 274, 106 S.Ct. 2523. Recognizing that the suit raised "a pure question of law," and that "the individual circumstances" of any aggrieved member were not in issue, the Court held that the UAW had standing to challenge the government's actions. *Id.* at 287-88, 290, 106 S.Ct. at 2531-32, 2533; *see also Pennell,* 485 U.S. at 7 n. 3, 108 S.Ct. at 855 n. 3 (facial challenge to rent ordinance does not require participation of individual landlords). Here, TAB seeks only prospective relief, raises only issues of law, and need not prove the individual circumstances of its members to obtain that relief, thus meeting the third prong of *Hunt.*

Having found that TAB meets all three prongs of the *Hunt* test, we conclude that TAB has standing to pursue the relief it seeks in this case.

* * *

Concurring and dissenting opinions by DOGGETT, GAMMAGE and SPECTOR, JJ(omitted). HIGHTOWER, J., not sitting.

Note

Meyers v. JDC/Firethorne, Ltd., 548 S.W.3d 477 (Tex. 2018): Under Texas law, the standing inquiry begins with determining whether the plaintiff has *personally* been injured, that is, "he must plead facts demonstrating that he, himself (rather than a third party or the public at large), suffered the injury." The second element requires that the plaintiff's alleged injury be "fairly traceable" to the defendant's conduct because "a court [can] act only to redress injury that fairly can be traced to the challenged action of the defendant, and not injury that results from the independent action of some third party not before the court." This required showing of a causal connection between the plaintiff's injury and the defendant's conduct serves as a means of identifying the proper defendants. *See* To establish the third standing requirement—often referred to as "redressability"—a plaintiff must show that there is a substantial likelihood that the requested relief will remedy the alleged injury. ("The redressability prong deprives courts of jurisdiction over cases in which the likelihood of the requested relief redressing the plaintiff's injury is only speculative."). "If, for example, a plaintiff suing in a Texas court requests injunctive relief . . . but the injunction could not possibly remedy his situation, then he lacks standing to bring that claim."

ALLSTATE INDEMNITY COMPANY
v.
FORTH

204 S.W.3d 795
(Tex. 2006)

Roger Higgins, Thompson Coe Cousins and Irons, L.L.P., Dallas, Jeffrey P. Lennard, Sonnenschein Nath & Rosenthal LLP, Chicago, IL, for Petitioner.

G. Laird Morgan, Stephen Gardner, Law Office of Stephen Gardner, PC, John M. Phalen Jr., Daniel Sheehan & Associates, L.L.P., Dallas, for Respondent.

PER CURIAM.

In this breach of contract suit, we consider whether an insured has standing to sue her insurance company for settling her medical bills in what the insured considered to be an arbitrary and unreasonable manner. In reversing the trial court and remanding the case for trial, the court of appeals concluded that the insured had standing even though the insured had no out-of-pocket expenses, and her health care providers had not, and now could not, collect any additional sum from her. 151 S.W.3d 732, 738. Because there are no allegations that the insured suffered damages or that the manner in which the insurance company settled the insured's medical expenses caused her any injury, we conclude that the trial court was correct to dismiss her suit, and accordingly we reverse the court of appeals' judgment.

Pat Forth's daughter required medical treatment in 1997 as the result of an auto accident. The personal-injury-protection (PIP) of Forth's Allstate auto insurance policy, covered "reasonable medical expenses incurred for necessary medical services." Allstate settled Forth's medical bills for less than the actual amount billed. Forth sued Allstate for injunctive and declaratory relief, alleging that it arbitrarily reduced her bills without using an independent and fair evaluation to determine what amount of her medical expenses were reasonable. According to Forth, Allstate routinely discounts medical expenses by comparing those charges to a third-party contractor's computerized database. Allstate then offers about eighty-five percent of the medical expenses reflected in that database for the same treatment or procedure. Forth did not claim that Allstate's conduct had caused her any damage.

In the trial court, Allstate filed a motion to dismiss, arguing that Forth lacked standing because she had no claim for damages, and Allstate had not caused her any actual injury. The trial court granted Allstate's motion, and the court of appeals affirmed in part and reversed in part, holding that Forth lacked standing to seek prospective relief because Allstate no longer insured her, but that she could seek retrospective relief for any injury suffered while she was a policy holder. The court concluded that if a fair and independent evaluation of the medical bills revealed that Allstate paid less than the full amount of Forth's "reasonable expenses," then Forth could claim injury because the terms of the insurance contract required that reasonable expenses be paid.

The court of appeals relied on *Black v. American Bankers Insurance Co.*, 478 S.W.2d 434 (Tex. 1972) and *American Indemnity Co. v. Olesijuk*, 353 S.W.2d 71, 72 (Tex. Civ. App.—San Antonio 1961, writ dism'd w.o.j.) to support its view that the insured had standing to sue her insurance company despite its settlement of her medical claims to the apparent satisfaction of the medical providers. Both *Black* and *Olesijuk* held that the insurance companies' obligation to pay under the respective policies was triggered by the insured's incurrence of medical expenses and was not affected by the fact that the insured had not, in fact, had to pay those expenses. In both cases, a third party paid the medical expenses, but the respective courts concluded that such fact did not alter the obligation of the insurance company to pay under its policy. Unlike the insurance companies in Olesijuk and Black, Allstate did not question whether Forth had incurred medical expenses and did not refuse to pay the medical providers. Instead, Allstate paid the medical bills according to its own evaluation.

Under Texas law, to have standing a party must have suffered a threatened or actual injury. Forth does not claim that she has any unreimbursed, out-of-pocket medical expenses. She does not assert that these providers withheld medical treatment as a result of Allstate reducing their bills, or threatened to sue her for any deficiency, or harassed her in any other manner. Moreover, Forth has no exposure in the future because limitations has now run on the medical claims. From all appearances, her medical providers have accepted the amount Allstate paid them without complaint, thereby satisfying Allstate's obligation under the policy.

Because Forth does not claim that the manner in which Allstate settled her claim caused her any injury, we conclude that she does not have standing in this case. Accordingly, we reverse the court of appeals' judgment and, without hearing oral argument, render judgment dismissing Forth's claims against Allstate.

Note

In *Belt v. Oppenheimer, Blend, Harrison & Tate, Inc.*, 192 S.W.3d 780 (Tex. 2006), the Court held that there is no legal bar preventing an estate's personal representative from maintaining a legal malpractice claim on behalf of the estate against the decedent's estate planners for pure economic loss, because such claims are necessarily limited to recovery for property damage. In that case the joint, independent executors of an estate sued several attorneys and their law firm, for legal malpractice. The Court noted that even though an estate may suffer significant damages after a client's death, this does not preclude survival of an estate-planning malpractice claim.

MAPCO, INC.
v.
CARTER
817 S.W.2d 686
(Tex. 1991)

Roger Townsend, Lee A. Hunnell, Houston, Royse M. Parr, Tulsa, Okl., for Mapco.
Thomas Lee Bartlett, Tom F. Coleman, Houston, for Carter.

PER CURIAM.

We consider whether a judgment may be entered against a party not before the trial court. We conclude that it may not.

Clarence, James Ross, and Mrs. Clyde Carter (Carters), Mapco Underground Storage of Texas, Inc. (MUST) and Texasgulf, Inc. (Texasgulf) owned, in undivided interests, a 126.378-acre mineral estate (5/8's by the Carters, 2/8's by Texasgulf, and 1/8 by MUST). MUST owned the surface estate in its entirety. MUST created an underground cavern on a portion of the tract from a salt dome formation to store natural gas and other hydrocarbons. The Carters sued MUST for waste and sought a partition of the mineral estate. The waste claim was severed and is not a part of this appeal.

After a bench trial, the trial court found that the mineral estate was susceptible to a partition in kind. In accord with a request by MUST, the trial court awarded a 15.797-acre tract surrounding the cavern to Gordon Speer (Speer) (successor to MUST), a 31.582-acre tract to Landmark Trust (successor to Texasgulf), and a 78.999-acre tract to be divided equally among the Carters. In addition, the trial court entered a $450,000 owelty award against Mapco, Inc. (Mapco, Inc.) and imposed a lien against the property set aside to Speer, to be foreclosed in the event the owelty award was not paid. The court of appeals affirmed, holding, among other things, that a judgment against Mapco, Inc. was permissible. 808 S.W.2d 262. The parties do not contest the partition and we consider only the portion of the judgment pertaining to Mapco, Inc.

Mapco, Inc. argues that the owelty award entered against it was erroneous because it was not a party in the trial court. We agree.

In no case shall judgment be rendered against any defendant unless upon service, or acceptance or waiver of process, or upon an appearance. TEX. R. CIV. P. 124. *See, e.g., Patrick v. Patrick*, 728 S.W.2d 864, 868 (Tex. App.—Fort Worth 1987, writ ref'd n.r.e.). The Carters' pleadings identified only MUST as a party and indicated only that service could be made upon MUST's designated agent. Furthermore, each answer filed was only on behalf of MUST and there is no indication in the record that Mapco, Inc. waived service of process. *See* TEX. R. CIV. P. 120. The fact that MUST was generically referred to by the parties and the trial court as "Mapco, Inc." is not sufficient to place Mapco, Inc. before the court. *See also Fuqua v. Taylor*, 683 S.W.2d 735, 738 (Tex. App.—Dallas 1984, writ ref'd n.r.e.) ("Judgment may not be granted in favor of a party not named in the suit as a plaintiff or a defendant.").

The Carters argue that Mapco, Inc. and MUST waived this point because they did not raise it until their motion for rehearing in the court of appeals. Generally, a point not assigned as error in the court of appeals and raised for the first time in a motion for rehearing cannot be considered by this court. *See Watson v. Glens Falls Ins. Co.*, 505 S.W.2d 793, 797 (Tex. 1974). However, lack of jurisdiction is fundamental error and may be raised for the first time before this court. *Grounds v. Tolar Indep. School Dist.*, 707 S.W.2d 889, 893 (Tex. 1986). *See also Texas Alcoholic Beverage Comm'n v. Sfair*, 786 S.W.2d 26, 27 (Tex. App.—San Antonio 1990, writ denied).

* * *

Pursuant to Rule 170 of the Texas Rules of Appellate Procedure, a majority of the court grants the application for writ of error of Mapco, Inc. and MUST and, without hearing oral argument, reverses that portion of the judgment of the court of appeals concerning entry of judgment against Mapco, Inc., renders judgment that the Carters take nothing against Mapco, Inc. and remands this cause to the trial court solely to determine against whom the owelty award may properly be entered.

4. *Methods of Preservation of Error*

Error occurring during a lower court proceeding that is not fundamental requires some sort of affirmative action on the part of a complaining attorney to preserve error. As will be shown throughout this book the types of affirmative action necessary to preserve error for appellate review will vary depending on the nature of the alleged error as well as the time in the lower court proceeding in which the alleged error occurred.

One of the more frequent errors complained of on appeal relates to the admission or exclusion of evidence. Therefore, in the remaining portion of this Chapter the focus will be on steps which must be taken when alleged *improper evidence* is admitted during a trial or when purported proper evidence is excluded. An "objection" made to the introduction of evidence claimed to be inadmissible is the most frequent affirmative action which is taken to preserve the alleged error of admitting inadmissible evidence. An "offer of proof" [prior to September 1, 1997, this was also referred to an "informal bill of exception"; *see* Rule 52(b) of the former Texas Rules of Appellate Procedure] is the typical method to preserve error in the event that the trial court refuses to admit evidence. In the following pages a brief introduction to these two methods of preservation of error will be made. The proper procedures necessary to preserve other types of errors will be presented throughout the remainder of this book.

Texas Rules of Evidence 103. Rulings on Evidence.

(a) Effect of Erroneous Ruling. Error may not be predicated upon a ruling which admits or excludes evidence unless a substantial right of the party is affected, and

(1) Objection. In case the ruling is one admitting evidence, a timely objection or motion to strike appears of record, stating the specific ground of objection, if the specific ground was not apparent from the context. When the court hears objections to offered evidence out of the presence of the jury and rules that such evidence be admitted, such objections shall be deemed to apply to such evidence when it is admitted before the jury without the necessity of repeating those objections.

(2) Offer of proof. In case the ruling is one excluding evidence, the substance of the evidence was made known to the court by offer, or was apparent from the context within which questions were asked.

(b) Record of Offer and Ruling. The offering party shall, as soon as practicable, but before the court's charge is read to the jury, be allowed to make, in the absence of the jury, its offer of proof. The court may add any other or further statement which shows the character of the evidence, the form in which it was offered, the objection made, and the ruling thereon. The court may, or at the request of a party shall, direct the making of an offer in question and answer form.

(c) Hearing of Jury. In jury cases, proceedings shall be conducted, to the extent practicable, so as to prevent inadmissible evidence from being suggested to the jury by any means, such as making statements or offers of proof or asking questions in the hearing of the jury.

(d) Fundamental Error in Criminal Cases. In a criminal case, nothing in these rules precludes taking notice of fundamental errors affecting substantial rights although they were not brought to the attention of the court.

Texas Rules of Appellate Procedure 33.1. Preservation; How Shown.

(a) In General. As a prerequisite to presenting a complaint for appellate review, the record must show that:

(1) the complaint was made to the trial court by a timely request, objection, or motion that:

(A) stated the grounds for the ruling that the complaining party sought from the trial court with sufficient specificity to make the trial court aware of the complaint, unless the specific grounds were apparent from the context; and

(B) complied with the requirements of the Texas Rules of Civil or Criminal Evidence or the Texas Rules of Civil or Appellate Procedure; and

(2) the trial court:

(A) ruled on the request, objection, or motion, either expressly or implicitly; or

(B) refused to rule on the request, objection, or motion, and the complaining party objected to the refusal.

(b) Ruling by Operation of Law. In a civil case, the overruling by operation of law of a motion for new trial or a motion to modify the judgment preserves for appellate review a complaint properly made in the motion, unless taking evidence was necessary to properly present the complaint in the trial court.

(c) Formal Exception and Separate Order Not Required. Neither a formal exception to a trial court ruling or order nor a signed, separate order is required to preserve a complaint for appeal.

Note

1. *In the Interest of ZLT*, 124 S.W.3d 163 (Tex. 2003): Under Rule 33.1(a)(2) of the Rules of Appellate Procedure, in order to present a complaint for appellate review, the record must reflect that the trial court (A) ruled on the request, objection, or motion, either expressly or implicitly; or (B) refused to rule and the complaining party objected to the refusal. In this case, the trial court proceeded to trial without ruling expressly on Thompson's request for a bench warrant. Consistent with Rule 33.1(a)(2)' s language, an implicit ruling may be sufficient to present an issue for appellate review. By proceeding to trial, without issuing the bench warrant, it is clear that the trial court implicitly denied Thompson's request.

2. *Michiana Easy Livin' Country, Inc. v. Holten,* 168 S.W.3d 777, 783 (2005): It is true that a dozen years ago in *Piotrowski v. Minns* we stated: "[a] litigant who fails to request that the reporter record pretrial proceedings risks waiver of any complaint with respect to error occurring during those proceedings." But the appellant there conceded that the special appearance hearing was evidentiary. Moreover, since that time the rules have changed so that court reporters no longer attend court and make a record only "when requested" but now must do so "unless excused by agreement of the parties." The former rule implied a lack of diligence when the losing party requested no record; the current rule implies an agreement that no record was made because none was needed.

BAY AREA HEALTHCARE GROUP, LTD.
v.
MCSHANE
239 S.W.3d 231
(Tex. 2007)

R. Brent Cooper, Diana L. Faust, Stephen J. Rodolf, Leslie C. Weeks, Russell H. McMains, Rick Rogers, A. Scott Johnson, for Petitioners.

Mark R. Mueller, Max E. Freeman II, Vincent L. Marable III, Kathleen P. McCartan, for Respondents.

PER CURIAM.

In this medical malpractice case, Deborah Sue McShane and James Patrick McShane, individually and as next friends of their daughter, Maggie Yvonne McShane, sued Bay Area Healthcare Group, Ltd., Columbia Hospital Corporation of Bay Area, and South Texas Surgicare, Inc. (collectively, "Bay Area") to recover for injuries that Maggie allegedly sustained during her birth at a Bay Area Healthcare Group hospital. After a jury found in the hospital's favor, the trial court signed a take-nothing judgment. The court of appeals reversed, holding that the trial court abused its discretion in admitting evidence that two doctors involved in the incident were originally sued by the plaintiffs, but were nonsuited before trial. 174 S.W.3d 908, 912. Bay Area presents several issues on appeal: (1) whether the court of appeals misapplied the Texas Rules of Evidence regarding the admissibility of information in superseded pleadings; (2) whether the court of appeals incorrectly concluded that the error was harmful; and (3) whether the court of appeals misapplied Texas Rule of Appellate Procedure 44.1 We hold that the trial court did not abuse its discretion in admitting information from the superseded pleadings. Because that issue is dispositive, we do not reach Bay Area's remaining complaints.

* * *

In 1999, Deborah Sue McShane gave birth to Maggie Yvonne McShane. Maggie allegedly sustained injuries during the delivery that left her with brain damage and other physical complications. Deborah and James

McShane sued Bay Area and two doctors, Dr. Rothschild and Dr. Eubank, but nonsuited the doctors before trial. The McShanes filed a motion in limine to prevent Bay Area from introducing into evidence the superseded pleadings that listed Rothschild and Eubank as defendants. The trial court denied that motion. At trial, neither party attempted to introduce the superseded pleadings into evidence, but attorneys for both sides discussed Rothschild and Eubank's status during voir dire, and witnesses testified over objection that the McShanes had previously sued Rothschild and Eubank.

After a three-week trial, the jury returned a 10-2 verdict in Bay Area's favor, and the trial court signed a take-nothing judgment. A divided court of appeals reversed and remanded, concluding that the trial court abused its discretion by admitting evidence that the McShanes had, at one point, sued the two physicians. 174 S.W.3d at 912. The dissent would have held that the complained-of evidence was merely cumulative and the McShanes had not shown reversible error. *Id.* at 924 (Castillo, J., dissenting).

The first issue is whether statements from the superseded pleadings were admissible at trial. Evidentiary rulings are committed to the trial court's sound discretion. *Interstate Northborough P'ship v. State,* 66 S.W.3d 213, 220 (Tex. 2001); *City of Brownsville v. Alvarado,* 897 S.W.2d 750, 753 (Tex. 1995). Even if a trial court errs by improperly admitting evidence, reversal is warranted only if the error probably caused the rendition of an improper judgment. Tex. R. App. P. 61.1(a); *Nissan Motor Co. Ltd. v. Armstrong,* 145 S.W.3d 131, 144 (Tex. 2004); *Owens-Corning Fiberglas Corp. v. Malone,* 972 S.W.2d 35, 43 (Tex. 1998). We review the entire record and require the complaining party to demonstrate that the judgment turns on the particular evidence admitted. *Nissan Motor,* 145 S.W.3d at 144.

Statements from pleadings, depending on their content, could potentially be excluded as irrelevant or unfairly prejudicial. *See* Tex.R. Evid. 402, 403. The McShanes, however, cannot make this complaint here because their attorney was the first to allude to the doctors' party status by telling the jury panel that a doctor's conduct "could have been brought before this Court in this trial" but "both sides have not done that at this trial." *See McInnes v. Yamaha Motor Corp., U.S.A.,* 673 S.W.2d 185, 188 (Tex. 1984) (plaintiff's counsel opened door to plaintiff's alcohol consumption by discussing it during opening statements, thus preventing plaintiffs from complaining on appeal of similar evidence later introduced by the defendant); *see also* W. Jeremy Counseller & Charles D. Brown, Handbook of Texas Evidence § 401.03 (2005) ("A party can make otherwise irrelevant evidence relevant by injecting collateral issues into a lawsuit. This is called 'opening the door.' Once a party opens the door . . . the opposing party may offer rebuttal evidence on the collateral issue." (citations omitted)). Moreover, testimony is not inadmissible on the sole ground that it is "prejudicial" because in our adversarial system, much of a proponent's evidence is legitimately intended to wound the opponent. Here, however, we conclude that the information's probative value is not substantially outweighed by the danger of *unfair* prejudice.

The Rules of Evidence govern admissibility of evidence in court proceedings. Tex. R. Evid. 101(b). Bay Area introduced statements from superseded pleadings indicating that Bay Area sued Rothschild and Eubank. Normally, out-of-court statements are excluded as hearsay. *Id.* 801(d) (hearsay is a "statement, other than one made by the declarant while testifying at the trial or hearing, offered in evidence to prove the truth of the matter asserted"). But because the McShanes made the statements, they are considered admissions by a party-opponent and are not hearsay. *Id.* 801(e)(2) ("A statement is not hearsay if . . . [t]he statement is offered against a party and is . . . the party's own statement . . . ."). Rule 801(e)(2) is straightforward: subject to other Rules of Evidence that may limit admissibility, *any* statement by a party-opponent is admissible against that party. *Id.*

Thus, the court of appeals erred in concluding that statements from the pleadings would only be admissible if they contained "some statement relevant to a material issue in the case" that is "inconsistent with the position taken by the party against whom it is introduced." 174 S.W.3d at 920. Before the Rules of Evidence were promulgated, our cases required an inconsistency between the superseded pleading and the party's position at trial. *See Hartford Accident and Indem. Co. v. McCardell,* 369 S.W.2d 331, 337-39 (Tex. 1963); *Kirk. v. Head,* 137 Tex. 44, 152 S.W.2d 726, 729 (Tex. 1941). But the Rules of Evidence no longer require inconsistency when it comes to admissibility of superseded pleadings. *See* Tex.R. Evid. 801(e)(2) (statements made by a party and offered against that party are admissible). Cases that hold otherwise are distinguishable because they were decided before the Rules of Evidence became effective in 1983, or they rely on pre-1983 case law without discussing the Rules' effect. *See, e.g., Drake Ins. Co. v. King,* 606 S.W.2d 812, 817 (Tex. 1980); *McCardell,* 369 S.W.2d at 337-39; *Kirk,* 152 S.W.2d at 729; *Loy v. Harter,* 128 S.W.3d 397, 407 (Tex. App.—Texarkana 2004, pet. denied) (relying on *Kirk,* 152 S.W.2d at 729); *Huff v. Harrell,* 941 S.W.2d 230, 239 (Tex. App.—Corpus Christi 1996, writ denied) (same). We hold that there is no requirement that the statement be inconsistent with the party's position at trial, and the court of appeals erred in finding the superseded pleadings inadmissible on that basis.

* * *

For the reasons stated in this opinion, we grant the petition for review and without hearing argument, TEX. R. APP. P. 59. 1, we reverse the court of appeals' judgment and render judgment that the McShanes take nothing. *Id.* 60.2(c).

BUSHELL
v.
DEAN

803 S.W.2d 711
(Tex. 1991)

PER CURIAM.

Syndex's motion for rehearing is granted in part and overruled in part. This court's opinion and judgment of November 21, 1990, are withdrawn, and the following is substituted in their place.

Mary Dean brought this action against Bill Bushell and the Syndex Corporation, her former manager and employer, claiming assault, intentional infliction of emotional distress, and sexual harassment pursuant to TEX. REV. CIV. STAT. ANN. art. 5221k, § 5.01 (1985). Dean obtained a favorable jury determination on each cause and the trial court rendered judgment awarding Dean $195,600 in actual and punitive damages and $123,000 in attorney's fees. The court of appeals reversed that part of the judgment awarding damages and attorney's fees for the sexual harassment claim and remanded that part of the cause for new trial. 781 S.W.2d 652. Because the court of appeals based this part of its judgment on unpreserved error, we reverse the judgment of the court of appeals and remand the cause to that court for further proceedings.

By three points of error to the court of appeals, Syndex attacked the trial court's admission of testimony by one of Dean's experts, Dr. Lucia Gilbert. Syndex asserted that the testimony was irrelevant, TEX. R. CIV. EVID. 402; that the probative value of the testimony was substantially outweighed by unfair prejudice, TEX. R. CIV. EVID. 403; and that the testimony was inadmissible character evidence. TEX. R. CIV. EVID. 404. The court of appeals sustained all three points of error.

Syndex did not preserve its objection to Dr. Gilbert's testimony at trial. On direct examination, Dr. Gilbert indicated that he was going to give a "working definition" of sexual harassment, including "general things that are true about a person who harasses." Syndex's counsel objected, stating, I am objecting to the testimony of this expert witness as a whole to the extent that it goes to questions of profile of someone who harasses . . . . I think it is likely to create a great deal of prejudice and to confuse the jury and issues that they actually have to decide in this case, and that involves a mixture of law and fact. The trial judge responded, I [have] expressed a concern that at some point I did not think that the questions to the witness had crossed the point yet, but at some point it might cross the line into character evidence prohibitions, at which time if you believe that it does you will need to reurge your—any objection. Some time later, Dr. Gilbert testified about the "profile" of a sexual harasser, but Syndex did not make any further objection.

In order to preserve a complaint for appellate review, a party must present to the trial court a timely request, objection or motion, state the specific grounds therefor, and obtain a ruling. TEX. R. APP. P. 52(a). Therefore, Syndex's points of error relating to this testimony were not before the appellate court for review, and the court of appeals erred in holding that the testimony was inadmissible. *See Lemons v. EMW Mfg. Co.*, 747 S.W.2d 372 (Tex. 1988).

The court of appeals did not consider several of Syndex's points of error. These points include arguments which, if sustained, would require a modification of the trial court's judgment or a remand for new trial. Therefore, we remand the cause to the court of appeals for consideration of these points of error. *See McKelvy v. Barber*, 381 S.W.2d 59, 64 (Tex. 1964).

The applications for writ of error brought by Bill Bushell and Syndex Corporation are denied.

Pursuant to TEX. R. APP. P. 170, a majority of the court, without hearing oral argument, reverses the judgment of the court of appeals and remands the cause to that court for further consideration in accordance with this opinion.

Notes

"objection sufficient"

1. In *Campbell v. State of Texas*, 85 S.W.3d 176 (Tex. 2002) the court noted that an objection is sufficient to preserve error for appeal, if it allows the trial judge to make an informed ruling and the other party to remedy the defect, if he can. Campbell's statement, that an unidentified statute prohibited the trial court from compelling Campbell to engage in certain unidentified "things," was inadequate to inform the trial court of the precise objection. Thus, the objection was insufficient to preserve error for appellate review.

2. *Maritime Overseas Corporation v. Ellis.*[1] To preserve a complaint that scientific evidence is unreliable and thus, no evidence, a party must object to the evidence before trial, or when the evidence is offered.

Maritime did not object before trial, or when the evidence was offered, that the scientific evidence offered by Ellis's experts was scientifically unreliable. On appeal, Maritime argues that the federal standard articulated in *Daubert*[2] and the state standard articulated in *Robinson*[3] and *Havner*[4] are the proper standards for reviewing the sufficiency of Ellis's damages evidence. Maritime does not complain about the trial court's admissions of any of the scientific evidence from any of Ellis's five experts. Rather, Maritime's position is that, if the court of appeals applied a proper scientific methodology test to Ellis's experts' testimony, the testimony would be legally insufficient to show that the long-term conditions, which Ellis claims he suffers, were caused by delayed neurotoxicity. Thus, Maritime concludes, by way of its complaints about the court of appeals" factual sufficiency review, that there is *no evidence* of *some* of Ellis's actual damages.

Held: Affirmed. Maritime's argument is flawed. *To preserve a complaint that scientific evidence is unreliable and thus, no evidence, a party must object to the evidence before trial or when the evidence is offered.* In *Daubert,* the U. S. Supreme Court considered "the standard for admitting expert scientific testimony in a federal *trial*." *Daubert's* focus is on the trial court's discretion, when faced with an objection to scientific evidence, to admit or exclude such evidence before or during the trial. When the trial court concludes that the disputed scientific evidence is insufficient to go to the jury, the trial court may grant a summary judgment or a directed verdict. However, *Daubert* does not support the proposition that a reviewing court can in effect exclude expert testimony that was not objected to, based on its scientific reliability before trial, or when it was offered at trial, and then render judgment against the offering party.

Similarly, in *Robinson*, the special nature of scientific expert testimony was recognized. There, it was recognized that the trial court's role is as a "gatekeeper," and that "[t]he trial court is responsible for making the preliminary determination of whether the proffered testimony meets the standards for scientific reliability." Like *Daubert*, *Robinson's* focus is on a trial court's discretion in admitting or excluding scientific evidence after a party lodges an objection to the reliability of its opponent's scientific expert testimony before trial, or when the evidence is offered.

Under *Havner*, a party may complain on appeal that scientific evidence is unreliable, and thus, no evidence to support a judgment. *Havner* recognizes that a no evidence complaint may be sustained when the record shows one of the following: (a) a complete absence of a vital fact; (b) the reviewing court is barred by rules of law or evidence from giving weight to the only evidence offered to prove a vital fact; (c) the evidence offered to prove a vital fact is no more that a mere scintilla; or (d) the evidence establishes conclusively the opposite of the vital fact.

Without requiring a timely objection to the reliability of the scientific evidence, the offering party is not given an opportunity to cure any defect that may exist, and will be subject to trial and appeal by ambush. Reviewing courts may not exclude expert scientific evidence after trial to render a judgment against the offering party,

---

[1] 971 S.W.2d 402 (Tex. 1998).

[2] Daubert v. Merrell Dow Pharm., Inc., 509 U.S. 579 (1993).

[3] E.I. duPont de Nemours v. Robinson, 923 S.W.2d 549 (Tex. 1995).

[4] Merrell Dow Pharm., Inc. v. Havner, 953 S.W.2d 706 (Tex. 1997).

because that party relied on the fact that the evidence was admitted. To hold otherwise is unfair. To prevent trial or appeal by ambush, the complaining party must object to the reliability of scientific evidence before trial, or when the evidence is offered. When the reliability of scientific evidence is contested, attempts at persuasion before the jury and reiterated on appeal cannot amount to preservation of error for appeal. To allow otherwise would impermissibly permit a party to strip away the trial court's role as gate keeper in the first instance, when a party wishes to contest the reliability of scientific evidence. It is impossible for a trial court to exercise its gatekeeper function after the evidence has been admitted and the jury discharged. [Emphasis added.]

3. *In the Interest of ZLT*, 124 S.W.3d 163 (Tex. 2003). Under Rule 33.1(a)(2) of the Rules of Appellate Procedure, in order to present a complaint for appellate review, the record must reflect that the trial court (a) ruled on the request, objection, or motion, either expressly or implicitly; or (b) refused to rule and the complaining party objected to the refusal. In this case, the trial court proceeded to trial without ruling expressly on Thompson's request for a bench warrant. Consistent with Rule 33.1(a)(2)' s language, an implicit ruling may be sufficient to present an issue for appellate review. By proceeding to trial without issuing the bench warrant, it is clear that the trial court implicitly denied Thompson's request.

4. In *Low v. Henry*, 221 S.W.3d 609 (Tex. 2007) the court held that a trial court does not abuse its discretion in denying a party's request for a running objection, if the party fails to plainly identify the source of the objectionable testimony, the subject matter of the witness's testimony, and the ways the testimony will be brought before the court.

BRIDGES
v.
RICHARDSON

163 Tex. 292, 354 S.W.2d 366
(1962)

Woodgate, Richards & McElhaney, Dallas, for petitioners.
Strasburger, Price, Kelton, Miller & Martin, Dallas, for respondents.

PER CURIAM.

The opinion of the Court of Civil Appeals is reported in 349 S.W.2d 644.

We approve the judgment entered by the Court of Civil Appeals, but we are not satisfied that the opinion of the court "in all respects has correctly declared the law." Normally that conclusion would call for no other action on our part than the stamping of the application for writ of error, "Refused. No Reversible Error." *See* Rule 483, Texas Rules of Civil Procedure. But some of the general holdings of the Court of Civil Appeals, express and implied, which we regard as erroneous are so far-reaching that we deem it wise to disapprove them specifically lest they be regarded by lawyers, trial judges and judges of the Courts of Civil Appeals as having our tacit approval.

The holdings to which we refer and our views with respect thereto are:

1. That in order to complain successfully on appeal of the erroneous admission of evidence, a party must have filed a proper motion in limine to suppress the evidence or to instruct counsel not to offer it.

The purpose in filing a motion in limine to suppress evidence or to instruct opposing counsel not to offer it is to prevent the asking of prejudicial questions and the making of prejudicial statements in the presence of the jury with respect to matters which have no proper bearing on the issues in the case or on the rights of the parties to the suit. It is the prejudicial effect of the questions asked or statements made in connection with the offer of the evidence, not the prejudicial effect of the evidence itself, which a motion in limine is intended to reach. A proper objection made at the time evidence is offered is sufficient to preserve right of review of error committed in admitting it, and a motion in limine is not a necessary predicate for complaint on appeal that the admission of the evidence was error and that the error was prejudicial.

2. That in order to complain successfully on appeal of the erroneous admission of evidence, a party must have requested that the jury be retired until the judge had heard and ruled upon the admissibility of the evidence.

A request to retire the jury while evidence is being offered cannot be a necessary predicate to the right to complain on appeal of a trial court's error in admitting evidence over proper objection. The purpose in retiring a jury is to prevent prejudice through development of questionable evidence in the presence of the jury if the evidence is later excluded, or to permit the perfecting of a bill of exceptions after the evidence has been excluded.

3. That an objection that proffered evidence is "immaterial and irrelevant" is not sufficient to preserve right of review of error committed in admitting it.

The rule stated is a correct general rule but there is a limitation on or an exception to the rule: When the evidence is not relevant to any issue in the case and can have no material bearing thereon, a general objection that it is immaterial and irrelevant is sufficient to preserve right of review of error committed in admitting it. 1 MCCORMICK & RAY, TEXAS LAW OF EVIDENCE, 2d ed., § 25, p. 24; 1 WIGMORE, EVIDENCE, 3d ed. § 18, p. 336.

4. That a conclusion that the erroneous admission of evidence was not reasonably calculated to cause and probably did not cause an improper judgment leads to the further conclusion that "no error resulted in (from) the admission of the evidence."

If evidence is erroneously admitted, error exists; if its admission was not reasonably calculated to cause and probably did not cause an improper judgment, it is still error but is not reversible error. The question of whether a particular error is reversible error depends upon whether it was reasonably calculated to cause and probably did cause an improper judgment and presupposes the existence of error. *Aultman v. Dallas Ry. & Term. Co.*, 152 Tex. 509, 260 S.W.2d 596.

In pointing out the foregoing errors in the opinion of the Court of Civil Appeals we are not to be understood as approving all other holdings and statements in the opinion.

The application for Writ of Error is "Refused. No Reversible Error." Rule 483, Texas Rules of Civil Procedure.

Notes

1. *Hartford Accident and Indemnity Co. v. McCardell,* 369 S.W.2d 331, 335 (Tex. 1963): "The Court of Civil Appeals held that the trial court erred in not sustaining a portion of respondent's motion in limine which sought to suppress evidence of claims, settlements or payments arising out of three other injuries. We sustain petitioner's point of error complaining of this holding.

We held in *Bridges v. City of Richardson*, Tex., 354 S.W.2d 366 (1962), that a party need not file a motion in limine in order to preserve the right to appellate complaint about erroneous admission of evidence. Proper objection made at the time of the offer of the evidence is sufficient. We stated that the purpose of a motion in limine is to prevent the asking of prejudicial questions and the making of prejudicial statements in the presence of the jury. It seems that the converse of our holding in the Bridges case is that although the overruling of a motion in limine may be error, it is never reversible error.

If a motion in limine is overruled, a judgment will not be reversed unless the questions or evidence were in fact asked or offered. If they were in fact asked or offered, an objection made at that time is necessary to preserve the right to complain on appeal that such questions asked or such evidence tendered were so prejudicial that the mere asking or tendering should require a reversal. In neither case-(1) questions not asked or evidence not offered, or (2) questions asked or evidence offered-should the error of the trial court in overruling the motion in limine be regarded as harmful or reversible error."

2. *In re Toyoto Motor Sales, U.S.A., Inc.*, 407 S.W. 3d 746, 760 (Tex. 2013): The trial court initially granted the Kings' motion in limine to preclude Officer Coon's deposition testimony regarding King's seat belt usage at the time of the crash. But a protective limine order alone does not preserve error. *See Pool v. Ford Motor Co.,* 715 S.W.2d 629, 637 (Tex. 1986) (noting that "to preserve error as to an improper question asked in contravention of a sustained motion in limine, a timely objection is necessary"). Furthermore, where, as here, the party that requested the limine order *itself* introduces the evidence into the record, and then fails to immediately object, ask for a curative or limiting instruction or, alternatively, move for mistrial, the party waives any subsequent alleged error on the point. *See, e.g., Bay Area Healthcare Grp., Ltd. v. McShane,* 239 S.W.3d 231, 235 (Tex. 2007) ("Error is waived if the complaining party allows the evidence to be introduced without objection."); *State Bar of Tex. v. Evans,* 774 S.W.2d 656, 659 n. 6 (Tex. 1989) ("Failure to request the court to instruct

the jury to disregard the inadmissible testimony results in waiver of the alleged error where the instruction would have cured the error."); *see also* TEX.R.APP. P. 33.1(a) (detailing requirements for preservation of appellate complaints); TEX.R. EVID. 103(a) (describing effects of erroneous admission or exclusion of evidentiary rulings); John Henry Wigmore, WIGMORE'S CODE OF THE RULES OF EVIDENCE IN TRIALS AT LAW § 140 (3d ed. 1942) ("The objector waives an objection when he himself *subsequently introduces* evidence which is directed to prove or disprove the same matter and is liable to the same objection.")".

3. *In the Interest of R.V. Jr. and C.V.*, 977 S.W.2d 777, 780 (Tex. App.—Ft. Worth, 1998, no pet.): "A motion in limine merely precludes reference to certain issues without first obtaining a ruling on the admissibility of those issues outside the presence of the jury. *See Sims v. State*, 816 S.W.2d 502, 504 (Tex. App.—Houston [1st Dist.] 1991, writ denied). A trial court's ruling on a motion in limine does not preserve error. *See Chavis v. Director, State Worker's Compensation Div.*, 924 S.W.2d 439, 446 (Tex. App.—Beaumont 1996, no writ). Thus, on appeal, a party may not predicate his complaint on a motion in limine. *See id; Methodist Hospitals v. Corporate Communicators, Inc.*, 806 S.W.2d 879, 883 (Tex. App.—Dallas 1991, writ denied). In addition, the complaint on appeal must be the same as that presented in the trial court."

4. *Greenberg Traurig of N.Y., P.C. v. Moody*, 161 S.W.3d 56, 91 (Tex. App.—Houston [14th Dist.] 2004, no pet.): "A motion in limine is a procedural device that permits a party to identify, prior to trial, certain evidentiary rulings the trial court may be asked to make. *Weidner v. Sanchez*, 14 S.W.3d 353, 363 (Tex. App.—Houston [14th Dist.] 2000, no pet.). The purpose of the motion in limine is to prevent the other party from asking prejudicial questions or introducing prejudicial evidence in front of the jury without first asking the trial court's permission. *Hartford Acc. & Indem. Co. v. McCardell*, 369 S.W.2d 331, 335 (Tex. 1963); *Weidner*, 14 S.W.3d at 363. Because a trial court's ruling on a motion in limine preserves nothing for review, a party must object at trial when the testimony is offered to preserve error for appellate review. *Hartford Acc. & Indem. Co.*, 369 S.W.2d at 335. However, not all pretrial motions are motions in limine. *See Huckaby v. A.G. Perry & Son, Inc.*, 20 S.W.3d 194, 203 (Tex. App.—Texarkana 2000, pet. denied). There is a distinction between a motion in limine and a pretrial ruling on admissibility. *Id.*; *see also Norfolk S. Ry. Co. v. Bailey*, 92 S.W.3d 577, 583 (Tex. App.—Austin 2002, no pet.) (stating that "[a] ruling on a pretrial motion to exclude evidence . . . can be a ruling on the admission of evidence"). The trial court has the authority to make a pretrial ruling on the admissibility of evidence. *Huckaby*, 20 S.W.3d at 203; *Owens-Corning Fiberglas Corp. v. Malone*, 916 S.W.2d 551, 557 (Tex. App.—Houston [1st Dist.] 1996), aff'd, 972 S.W.2d 35 (1998)."

5. The *Bridges* case introduces another important concept of Texas Civil Procedure—the precedential value of orders by the Supreme Court. The refusal of a petition for review by the Texas Supreme Court indicates that the opinion of the court of appeals has the same precedential value as an opinion of the Supreme Court. Since June 24, 1927, such a notation [either writ refused or petition refused] has indicated that the opinion and judgment of the court of appeals are correction. [Prior to 1997, the method of appealing from a court of appeals to the Supreme Court of Texas was by application for writ of error, and hence a writ refused was the designation used to indicate that the opinion and judgment of a court of appeals was correct.] The denial of a petition for review carries no precedential value, and does not indicate approval of the opinion or judgment of the court of appeals. It only means that 4 justices did not agree that the appeal is important to the jurisprudence of the state. TEX. R. APP. P. 56.1.

From February 1, 1946, until December 31, 1987, the Supreme Court's most common notation when refusing to review a case was "writ refused, n.r.e." This designation indicated that the Supreme Court approved of the result (reverse and remand, reverse and render, affirm) of the court of appeals, but did not necessarily approve of the court's reasoning or language. *See* Frank Wilson, "*Hints on Precedent Evaluation*," 24 TEX. BAR J. 1037 (1961).

[Note that the Texas Courts of Civil Appeals became Courts of Appeal on September 1, 1981, and were, at that time, given jurisdiction to review criminal, as well as civil appeals.]

From September 1, 1941 to February 1, 1946, the notation "writ ref'd w.o.m.," was used to indicate approval of the Court of Civil Appeals judgment, but not the opinion.

From March 1, 1939 to September 1, 1941, the designation "Writ Dismissed, Judgment Correct," was used to indicate approval of the Court of Civil Appeals judgment, but not the opinion.

Prior to June 24, 1927, the designation "writ refused" meant only that the decision of a Court of Civil Appeals was correct in the result, even though the Supreme Court might not agree with the reasoning used to reach that result.

From February 1, 1946 until December 31, 1987, the designation "writ dismissed, w.o.j. (want of jurisdiction)" meant that the Supreme Court lacked jurisdiction to review the case or that the application on writ of error failed to properly present the error. The designation, petition dismissed for want of jurisdiction, currently in use, means the same thing.

Prior to February 1, 1946, the designation dismissed, w.o.j. could have one of several meanings. *See Bain Peanut Co. v. Pinson and Guyger*, 119 Tex. 572, 34 S.W.2d 1090, 1091 (1931).

6. In *Hartford Accident & Indem. Co. v. McCardell*,[1] the Court noted that "[i]f a motion in limine is overruled, a judgment will not be reversed unless the questions or evidence were in fact asked or offered. If they were in fact asked or offered, an objection made at that time is necessary to preserve the right to complain on appeal that such questions asked or such evidence tendered were so prejudicial that the mere asking or tendering should require a reversal. In either case—(1) questions not asked or evidence not offered, or (2) questions asked or evidence offered—should the error of the trial court in overruling the motion in limine be regarded as harmful or reversible error."

7. *In the Interest of M. N.*, 262 S.W.3d 799 (Tex. 2008): "This Court is obligated to promulgate rules of practice and procedure in civil cases. *See* TEX. CONST. art. V, § 31(b) ("The Supreme Court shall promulgate rules of civil procedure for all courts not inconsistent with the laws of the state as may be necessary for the efficient and uniform administration of justice in the various courts."); TEX. GOV'T CODE § 22.003(d) ("The supreme court from time to time shall promulgate suitable rules, forms, and regulations . . . ."); *id.* § 22.004(a) ("The supreme court has the full rulemaking power in the practice and procedure in civil actions, except that its rules may not abridge, enlarge, or modify the substantive rights of a litigant."); *see generally Stillman v. Hirsch,* 128 Tex. 359, 99 S.W.2d 270, 273-74 (1936). Rules promulgated by this Court repeal conflicting laws and parts of laws governing practice and procedure so long as the laws are non-substantive. *See* TEX. CONST. art. V, § 31(c); TEX. GOV'T CODE § 22.004(c) ("So that the supreme court has full rulemaking power in civil actions, a rule adopted by the supreme court repeals all conflicting laws and parts of laws governing practice and procedure in civil actions, but substantive law is not repealed."). The rules of civil procedure are intended to promote just, fair, and equitable resolution of issues."

4M LINEN & UNIFORM SUPPLY CO.
v.
W.P. BALLARD & CO.

793 S.W.2d 320
(Tex. App.—Houston [1st Dist.] 1990, writ denied)

Andrew J. Mytelka, John A. Buckley, Jr., Galveston, for appellant.
Robert E. Lapin, Galveston, for appellee.

O'CONNOR, JUSTICE.

This is an appeal from a suit on a sworn account. We grant appellant's motion for rehearing, withdraw our original opinion issued November 16, 1989, and substitute the following opinion.

W.P. Ballard & Co., Inc. (Ballard & Co.) filed suit on a sworn account against 4M Linen & Uniform Supply Co., Inc. (4M Linen). In response, 4M Linen filed a counterclaim alleging breach of implied warranty, breach of contract, and violation of the Deceptive Trade Practices Act (DTPA). Before trial, on stipulated facts, the court entered an instructed verdict for Ballard & Co. for $51,996.11 on its sworn account claim and on 4M Linen's counterclaim. After the evidence, the trial court submitted Ballard & Co.'s issue on attorney's fees, and 4M Linen's defensive issues on misrepresentations and breach of warranties. The jury answered all the issues in favor of Ballard & Co. The trial court disregarded the finding on attorney's fees, and signed a judgment awarding Ballard & Co. $51,996.11, plus interest. Both parties appealed. We modify and affirm the judgment.

---

[1] 369 S.W.2d 331 (Tex. 1963).

This suit arises out of a contract between Ballard & Co. and 4M Linen, under which Ballard & Co. supplied laundry products, produced and recommended by Diamond Shamrock, to 4M Linen. A sales representative for Ballard & Co. visited the 4M Linen plant each week to inventory 4M Linen's supplies. Based on that inventory, Ballard & Co. delivered chemicals. 4M Linen paid Ballard & Co. for the chemicals until July 1985. Beginning in June, 4M Linen started having problems with mildew. 4M Linen refused to pay Ballard & Co. for the supplies that it delivered from July 1985 through October 1985. The main issue at trial was whether Ballard & Co. had a duty to tell 4M Linen that Tex-Stat, one of the chemicals recommended by Diamond Shamrock and supplied by Ballard & Co., was not a mildewcide.

* * *

In its second point of error, 4M Linen contends the trial court erred in excluding part of the testimony of its expert witness, Chad Keith, which it preserved in an informal bill of exceptions. In our earlier opinion, we overruled the point because 4M Linen did not make an informal bill before the court submitted the charge to the jury. On rehearing, 4M Linen contends the trial court erred when it refused to permit it to make an informal bill of exceptions before the jury retired to consider the charge. We agree and reconsider our holding on appellant's second point of error.

When 4M Linen tried to question Keith about a statement in a letter Diamond Shamrock sent to 4M Linen, Ballard & Co. objected. After the court sustained the objection, 4M Linen deferred further questions of that witness on that subject until a later bill of exceptions. 4M Linen did not outline what it planned to prove through Keith's testimony.

At the charge conference, 4M Linen reminded the court that it wanted to make its bill of exceptions before the court submitted the charge to the jury. The court refused, but said it would permit 4M Linen to make a bill during the jury's deliberations. The court noted that if it decided it was error to exclude the evidence, it could grant 4M Linen a new trial.

After the jury retired to consider the charge, 4M Linen made its bill of exceptions by eliciting testimony from Keith before the court and opposing counsel, for the court reporter to include in the statement of facts. To begin the bill, 4M Linen asked that the two questions 4M Linen asked Keith during the trial be read to him from the court reporter's notes. In response to those questions, Keith testified that a product identified as a mildewcide should kill and prevent mildew, and that the letter did not supply a lot of information about the product. In response to questions that were not asked during the trial, Keith testified that a linen supply dealer in the Gulf Coast area would have reason to know that a linen company required a mildewcide, and that a linen supply company in this area would have run across the mildew problem many times.

There are two kinds of bills of exception: the informal bill and the formal bill. Compare TEX. R. APP. P. 52(b) to 52(c). An informal bill of exception preserves error if: (1) an offer of proof is made before the court, the court reporter, and the opposing counsel, outside the presence of the jury; (2) it is preserved as part of the statement of facts; (3) and it is made before the charge is read to the jury. TEX. R. APP. P. 52(b).

Rule 52(b) permits a party to make an informal bill of exception before the court reads the charge to the jury. *McKinney v. National Union Fire Ins. Co.*, 747 S.W.2d 907, 910 (Tex. App.—Fort Worth 1988), aff'd, 772 S.W.2d 72 (Tex. 1989). 4M Linen made its informal bill of exception after the charge was read to the jury.

Rule 52(b) states: When the court excludes evidence, the party offering same shall as soon as practicable, but before the court's charge is read to the jury, be allowed to make, in the absence of the jury, an offer of proof in the form of a concise statement. (Emphasis added.)

The rule is mandatory. The trial court must permit a party to make an informal bill before the jury is charged. *Dorn v. Cartwright*, 392 S.W.2d 181, 185-86 (Tex. Civ. App.—Dallas 1965, writ ref'd). Here, 4M Linen specifically reminded the court that it wanted to make an informal bill before the court read the charge to the jury. The court refused, and granted 4M Linen permission to make the bill after the charge was read.

Under rule 52, it was error to refuse 4M Linen permission to make an informal bill. Our task now is to determine whether the error was reasonably calculated to cause and probably did cause harm. TEX. R. APP. P. 81(b)(1); *see also Houston Lighting & Power Co. v. Russo Properties, Inc.*, 710 S.W.2d 711, 717 (Tex. App.—Houston [1st Dist.] 1986, no writ).

To appeal the trial court's exclusion of evidence, the complaining party must present the evidence that was excluded to the appellate court in a bill of exception. *Huckaby v. Henderson*, 635 S.W.2d 129, 131 (Tex. App.—

Houston [1st Dist.] 1981, writ ref'd n.r.e.). Because the appellate courts cannot evaluate excluded evidence unless it is preserved in a bill, it is reversible error for the trial court to refuse to permit a party to make a bill of exceptions. Here, however, although the trial court incorrectly prevented 4M Linen from making an informal bill before the charge was read to the jury, 4M Linen made a late informal bill, preserving that testimony.

On the late informal bill, Keith testified that a linen supply dealer in the Gulf Coast area would have reason to know that a linen company required a mildewcide, and that a linen supply company in this area would have run across the mildew problem many times. We hold this testimony was not relevant. There was no evidence in this case that Ballard & Co. had a duty to 4M Linen to do anything but supply the chemicals 4M Linen ordered. The laundry products were recommended to 4M Linen by Diamond Shamrock, not by Ballard & Co.

We overrule 4M Linen's second point of error.

* * *

We modify the judgment to reinstate the jury's award of attorney's fees for Ballard & Co., and, as modified, affirm the judgment.

ON SECOND MOTION FOR REHEARING

On appellant's first motion for rehearing, we held the trial court erred in refusing to allow 4M Linen to make an informal bill of exception, but we found the error was harmless. On second motion for rehearing, appellant claims the error was harmful. 4M Linen refers us to *In re Marriage of Goodwin*, 562 S.W.2d 532 (Tex. Civ. App.—Texarkana 1978, no writ); *Ledisco Fin. Serv., Inc. v. Viracola*, 533 S.W.2d 951 (Tex. Civ. App.—Texarkana 1976, no writ); and *Dorn v. Cartwright*, 392 S.W.2d 181 (Tex. Civ. App.—Dallas 1965, writ ref'd n.r.e.).

In all three cases cited by 4M Linen, the party who attempted to make a bill to preserve excluded testimony was prevented from preserving a record of the excluded testimony. *Dorn* directly supports our holding. In *Dorn*, the Dallas Court of Appeals held it was not reversible error to refuse a bill of exception when the information appellant attempted to offer was immaterial to the outcome of the suit. 392 S.W.2d at 186. We said the same thing in this case: the evidence offered in the late bill was not relevant to the issue of defendant's liability.

We do not think Ledisco assists 4M Linen's cause either. In *Ledisco*, the trial court refused to permit appellant to make a bill of exception to preserve cross-examination testimony of a witness. 533 S.W.2d at 958. On appeal, the court held the objections, the questions, and the statements of counsel were sufficient to apprise both courts of the nature of the evidence appellant expected to produce. 533 S.W.2d at 959. Here, as in *Ledisco*, we can look at the record and find the testimony the trial court excluded.

Neither should Goodwin offer 4M Linen any comfort. In *Goodwin*, the trial court announced it would render judgment without taking any evidence. 562 S.W.2d at 533. Before the judgment was signed, appellant filed a motion to make a bill of exception to preserve evidence. *Id.* Without ruling on the bill, the court rendered a judgment reciting that it heard evidence and the parties waived a record. *Id.* On appeal, the Texarkana Court of Appeals reversed because appellant did not have the opportunity to present evidence. That is not the case here. The record before us contains the testimony 4M Linen attempted to offer at trial.

4M Linen complains about the timing of the bill: it was not permitted to make a bill before the trial court charged the jury, as required in TEX. R. APP. P. 52(b). 4M Linen, however, was permitted to present the excluded evidence to the trial court after the charge was read to the jury. That evidence was brought forward for our consideration in the statement of facts.

After finding the trial court erred, we reviewed the evidence in the late bill and held the evidence was not relevant. 4M Linen now insists it has a right to a reversal and retrial because the trial court did not permit it to make a timely bill of exception.

If the purpose of the procedure for a bill of exception is to afford a party the opportunity to preserve excluded testimony for appellate review, the late informal bill did so. We find the late informal bill was the equivalent of a formal bill of exception, which can be filed as late as 60 days after the judgment is signed or, if a motion for new trial was filed, as here, 90 days after the judgment was signed.

We overrule 4M Linen's second motion for rehearing.

Notes

1. Rule 52(b) of the former Texas Rules of Appellate Procedure provided the procedural requirements for preservation of error by an informal bill of exception. The new Rules of Appellate Procedure eliminated mention of the informal bill of exception on grounds that it was unnecessary, as it was already provided for in Rule 103(a)(2) ["Offer of Proof"] of the Texas Rules of Civil Evidence. It is clear, therefore, that all of the procedures for the preservation of error by means of an informal bill of exception as outlined in the former case law have survived the enactment of the new appellate rules.

2. In *Raw Hide Oil & Gas v. Maxus Exploration*,[1] the Court stated succinctly: "To preserve error concerning the exclusion of evidence by offer of proof, the appellate record must show that (1) the substance of the evidence sought to be admitted was made known to the court, and (2) the court either ruled adversely to its admission or, after timely request, affirmatively refused to rule.[2] An objection to the trial court's refusal to rule is sufficient to preserve error for appellate complaint.[3] An offer of proof or objection to the refusal to rule on the offer must be made prior to the court's charge being read to the jury."[4]

3. a. *Presenting a formal bill of exception.* TEX. R. APP. P. 33.2 requires:

> "The objection to the court's ruling or action, and the ruling complained of, must be stated with sufficient specificity to make the trial court aware of the complaint." TEX. R. APP. P. 33.2(a).
>
> "If the evidence needed to explain the bill is in the record, the complainant may refer to it and attach a transcription of the record certified by the court reporter." TEX. R. APP. P. 33.2(b).

b. *The procedure for preserving error by use of a bill of exception.* The requirements are:

The bill be presented first to the trial court. TEX. R. APP. P. 33.2(c)(1).

If the parties agree to the bill, the judge must sign it. TEX. R. APP. P. 33.2(2).

If the parties do not agree to the bill, the judge must:

Sign the bill if the judge finds it to be correct. TEX. R. APP. P. 33.2(a).

Suggest correction to the complaining party if the judge believes they are necessary to make it accurately reflect the proceedings in the trial court. If the party agrees to the correction, then the judge signs and files the bill. TEX. R. APP. P. 33.2(b).

If the party will not make corrections suggested by the judge, then the judge returns the bill with the judge's refusal noted on it. The judge then prepares and files a bill that accurately reflects the proceedings in the court. TEX. R. APP. P. 33.2(c).

If the party is dissatisfied with the judge's bill, the party may file the bill rejected by the judge, supported by the affidavits of three people who observed the matter to which the bill of exceptions is addressed, who attest to the correctness of the bill. The opposing party may contest this 'by-standers' bill, and the appellate court will determine the truth of the exception. TEX. R. APP. P. 33.2(c)(3).

c. *Conflict with the record.* "If a formal bill *of* exceptions conflicts with the reporter's record, the bill controls." TEX. R. APP. P. 33.2(d).

d. *Time.* A formal bill of exceptions must be filed no later than 30 days after the filing party's notice of appeal is filed. TEX. R. APP. P. 33.2(e). Unlike the prior practice, the deadline does not vary depending on timely filing of a post verdict motion. The time for filing the formal bill may be extended if, "within 15 days after the deadline for filing the bill, the party files in the appellate court a motion complying with Rule 10.5(b)." TEX. R. APP. P. 33.2(e)(3).

---

[1] 766 S.W.2d 264, 274 (Tex. App—Amarillo 1988, writ denied).

[2] *See* Disposal Supply Co. v. Perryman Bros. Trash Service, Inc., 664 S.W.2d 756, 762 (Tex. App.—San Antonio 1983, writ ref'd n.r.e.); O'Shea v. Coronado Transmission Co., 656 S.W.2d 557, 564 (Tex. App.—Corpus Christi 1983, writ ref'd n.r.e.); TEX. R. CIV. EVID. 103(a)(2) & (b); TEX. R. APP. P. 52(a).

[3] TEX. R. APP. P. 52(a).

[4] TEX. R. APP. P. 52(a) & (b).

e. *Inclusion in the record:* "When filed, a formal bill of exceptions should be included in the appellate record."

4. *Mack Trucks, Inc. v. Tamez*, 206 S.W.3d 572, 577 (Tex. 2006): The purpose of a bill of exceptions is to allow a party to make a record for appellate review of matters that do not otherwise appear in the record, such as evidence that was excluded.

5. When it is impossible to preserve error by informal bill, and the trial court will not approve a formal bill of exception, the parties only recourse is to what has been called the "bystanders bill of exceptions." While, under the 1997 appellate rule changes, these may no longer be technically "bystanders bills," since the term "bystander" was eliminated from Rule 33.2, it is expected that the "old" terminology will continue to be used to describe this procedure.

6. A bill of exceptions that is not approved by either the trial judge or opposing counsel, and that is not a bystanders' bill, presents nothing for appellate review. *See Goodpasture v. Coastal Industrial Water Authority.*[5]

7. Under *old* TEX. R. APP. P. Rule 52(c), a bystanders bill of exceptions required the affidavits of "three respectable bystanders." The *new* TEX. R. APP. P. Rule 33.2 dispenses with the language "three respectable bystanders" and merely states "three people." Does this reflect a change in actual practice? Will the affidavits of attorneys still not suffice? Must the affiant still be one who has no concern in the outcome of the case?

8. In *Smith v. United Gas Pipe Line Co.*,[6] the Court held that bystander's bills are defective if supported only by affidavits of the attorneys participating in the case. The court in *Harris County Flood Control Dist. v. Cohen*,[7] held that the term "bystander" "relates to one who has no concern in the outcome of the case on trial."[8] Both *Smith v. United Gas Pipe Line Co.* and *Harris County Flood Control Dist. v. Cohen* dealt with TEX. R. APP. P. 52(c)(8)'s predecessor, TEX. R. CIV. P. 372(j). However, since the language of the two rules is virtually identical on the bystanders bill there is no reason to believe that these two cases are not still the law.

9. Before the 1997 amendments, formal bills of exception had to be filed 60 days after the judgment was signed if there was not post-judgment motion, and 90 days after the judgment was signed, if there was a post-verdict motion. Former TEX. R. APP. P. 52(c)(11). Under the current TEX. R. APP. P. 33.2(1), the formal bill of exception is to be filed 30 days after the filing party perfects appeal. TEX. R. APP. P. 33.2(e)(3) provides for extending that deadline, upon proper motion, filed within 15 days after the deadline. *See* Richard Orsinger, *The New Texas Rules of Appellate Procedure*, STATE BAR OF TEXAS INSTITUTE ON PRACTICING UNDER THE NEW TEXAS RULES OF APPELLATE PROCEDURE, 1997, at page B-9.

5. *Failure to Properly Preserve Error Results in a Waiver*

In order to preserve the right to complain on appeal about the admission of testimony one must have objected at the time the testimony was offered; the objection must have been specific enough to enable the trial court to understand the precise nature of the objection; and the party needed to have obtained a ruling on the objection. Thus, any complaint is waived if the objection is made after the admission of the testimony. Furthermore, the preceding section established that in order to preserve the right to complain on appeal about the exclusion of evidence one must have properly made an offer of proof. The failure to properly preserve error results in a waiver. Absent fundamental error, an appellate court is not authorized to reverse a trial court judgment in the absence of properly assigned error. *See Gulf Consolidated International Inc. v. Murphy.*[9]

---

5 90 S.W.2d 883 (Tex. App.—Houston [1st Dist] 1973, no writ).

6 149 Tex. 69, 228 S.W.2d 139 (1950).

7 282 S.W.2d 917 (Tex. Civ. App.—Galveston 1955, writ ref'd n.r.e.).

8 *Id.* at 919.

9 568 S.W.2d 565 (Tex. 1983).

6. *The Preserved Error must be Harmful*

Texas Rules of Appellate Procedure 44.1. Reversible Error in Civil Cases.

(a) Standard for Reversible Error. No judgment may be reversed on appeal on the ground that the trial court made an error of law unless the court of appeals concludes that the error complained of:

(1) probably caused the rendition of an improper judgment; or

(2) probably prevented the appellant from properly presenting the case to the court of appeals.

(b) Error Affecting Only Part of Case. If the error affects part of, but not all, the matter in controversy and that part is separable without unfairness to the parties, the judgment must be reversed and a new trial ordered only as to the part affected by the error. The court may not order a separate trial solely on unliquidated damages if liability is contested.

Texas Rules of Appellate Procedure 61.1. Standard for Reversible Error.

No judgment may be reversed on appeal on the ground that the trial court made an error of law unless the Supreme Court concludes that the error complained of:

(a) probably caused the rendition of an improper judgment; or

(b) probably prevented the petitioner from properly presenting the case to the appellate courts.

The reversible error rules under the former Texas Rules of Appellate procedure included language that error must be one that "was reasonably calculated to cause and probably did cause the rendition of an improper judgment in the case" in order to result in the reversal of the case. *See* Rules 81(b)(1) and 184(b) of the former Texas Rules of Appellate Procedure. The Supreme Court did not make any substantive changes in the new Rules of Appellate Procedure by dropping the phrase "reasonable calculated to cause" and leaving only "probably caused the rendition of an improper judgment."

RELIANCE STEEL & ALUMINUM CO.
v.
SEVCIK
267 S.W.3d 867
(Tex. 2008)

Chad Michael Forbes, Thomas C. Wright, Wright Brown & Close, LLP, Houston TX, Russell H. McMains, Law Offices of Russell H. McMains, Corpus Christi, TX, for Reliance Steel & Aluminum Co. and Samuel Alvarado.

David W. Holman, The Holman Law Firm, P.C., Houston TX, Macklin Keith Johnson, Hallettsville, TX, for Michael Sevcik and Cathy Loth.

JUSTICE BRISTER delivered the opinion of the Court.

Neither a plaintiff's poverty nor a defendant's wealth can help a jury decide whose negligence caused an accident. Even though punitive damages were not at issue in this collision case, the plaintiffs tendered evidence that the defendant's annual revenues were $1.9 billion. Because this evidence was inadmissible, and the record reflects that it probably caused an improper verdict, we reverse and remand for a new trial.

I. Background

Michael Sevcik and Cathy Loth were injured in a highway accident west of Houston when they were hit from behind by a tractor trailer owned by Reliance Steel & Aluminum Co. and driven by Sam Alvarado. Sevcik and Loth filed suit in Waller County, and at trial they offered the following testimony from the deposition of Reliance's corporate representative:

Q: How big a company is Reliance?

A: I believe last year's annual sales approximated $1.9 billion.

Q: About how many employees do they have? Do you know?

A: Just guessing, I think we're close to 3,000 I think, nationwide.

Q: And are the headquarters for Reliance in California? Is that what I-

A: Yes, sir. They're in Los Angeles, California.

Outside the presence of the jury, counsel for the defendants objected to the offer:

Defense counsel: Judge, on this and the next couple pages, [plaintiffs' counsel] is talking to the witness-this is the corporate rep for Reliance Steel & Aluminum. He is talking to him about how big a company it is, how many people do you employ, you're all over the country. And I think that is irrelevant and it is also inflammatory to the jury because that plants a seed in their mind that this is a huge company with huge dollars and they can afford a huge verdict.

The Court: [to plaintiff's counsel] You are not seeking punitives?

Plaintiffs' counsel: No, sir.

The Court: Therefore it becomes less relevant.

Plaintiffs' counsel: Right. The thing is, we are definitely entitled to show they are not a mom and pop operation, and we are going to talk-It says they are a California corporation. Then he says they are a division. I'm entitled to bring all of that in.

Defense counsel: I don't think it is relevant at all. We have the truck driver here, the man who drove the truck who was involved in the accident. Why do we need all this information about the company? That only plants the seed in their mind-

Plaintiffs' counsel: He is asking Mike Sevcik if he bought a new truck. I think everything

Defense counsel: This, I think, only tends to make the jurors start thinking about how much money is behind Mr. Alvarado, which isn't something they need to reach their verdict

Plaintiffs' counsel: Your Honor, some of what we get into in his deposition and then in the testimony of the driver is-part of it is how much-how many hours they have these people riding on the road, 15- and 16-hour days.

The Court: I'm going to overrule the objection

At the end of the four-day trial, the jury awarded the plaintiffs more than $3 million. The defendants appealed, challenging several of the damage awards and the admission of evidence of its $1.9 billion in revenues. After transfer for docket equalization, the court of appeals reduced one damage item by $6,000, affirmed the rest, and held admission of the gross sales evidence was harmless. The defendants then petitioned this Court for review.

II. Evidence of Wealth

Even when a party's wealth has no logical relevance to a case, the prejudicial effect of such evidence often creates strong temptations to use it. As we have stated before, "highlighting the relative wealth of a defendant has a very real potential for prejudicing the jury's determination of other disputed issues in a tort case." To avoid such situations, Texas courts "historically have been extremely cautious in admitting evidence of a party's wealth." Even when wealth can be used on the issue of punitive damages, we take the unusual step of bifurcating a trial so that it cannot be used for any other purpose.

* * * We hold the trial court abused its discretion in allowing admission of Reliance's gross annual sales.

III. Harmless Error?

Erroneous admission of evidence is harmless unless the error probably (though not necessarily) caused rendition of an improper judgment. We have recognized "the impossibility of prescribing a specific test" for harmless-error review, as the standard "is more a matter of judgment than precise measurement." A reviewing court must evaluate the whole case from voir dire to closing argument, considering the "state of the evidence, the strength and weakness of the case, and the verdict."

A. The Effect

The starting point for harmless-error review is the judgment. Obviously, a party that wins a favorable judgment has usually not suffered harm from any errors during trial. In this case, several parts of the verdict on which the judgment was based show that something beyond the relevant evidence was guiding the jury's deliberations.

During trial, plaintiffs' counsel introduced a chart showing that Loth's past medical expenses totaled $33,985.23, and he asked for precisely that amount in closing argument. Nevertheless the jury awarded $40,000. As the court of appeals held, there was no evidence for this amount as "the record is devoid of any testimony or affidavits" supporting it.

The same is true of the jury's verdict that Loth's future medical expenses were $250,000. Reliance concedes there was some evidence that she would incur $37,000 for future medications, and there was also some evidence she could incur as much as $90,000 for a six-month rehabilitation program in Houston. But there was no evidence she would incur anything more. To the contrary, her expert testified that "when we see a patient like Cathy, who is several years past their brain injury, all of the healing and recovery that is going to take place has taken place." While there was evidence that Loth would suffer permanent brain damage (for which the jury awarded $1.75 million in future impairment and mental anguish), there was no evidence that further medical treatment could do anything about it. The jury's finding on future medical expenses was simply twice as much as the evidence would support.

The jury's finding of $750,000 for future earning capacity was also surprisingly large given the evidence. Loth's tax returns leading up to the accident showed a total income of $7,562 for all five years combined; at that rate, the future award represented almost 500 years. Similarly, the jury's award for her earning capacity lost in the three years before trial was $15,000; at that rate the future award represented 150 years. It is of course true that Loth was entitled to damages for future earning capacity, not just future earnings. But the jury's findings still must be based on "such facts as are available" and "on something more than mere conjecture." We need not decide whether this particular award was erroneous; we conclude only that in combination with the other awards it shows that the jury's findings probably were the result of something other than the admissible evidence in the case.

The plaintiffs argue that the verdict was not inflated because the jury awarded them only half of what they requested in closing argument. But whether a jury awarded less than the plaintiffs requested is not the same question as whether they awarded the plaintiffs more than the evidence supported. The primary damage requests rejected by the jury related to future pain and mental anguish and future physical impairment, matters as to which the lack of specific proof available makes it very hard to say whether the jury's award was either "too low" or "too high." But in those parts of the verdict where such evidence was available, the jurors' findings generally exceeded it by a substantial amount.

B. The Evidence

In reviewing whether erroneous admission of evidence was harmful, we have also looked to the role the evidence played in the context of the trial. Thus, if erroneously admitted or excluded evidence was crucial to a key issue, the error was likely harmful. By contrast, admission or exclusion is likely harmless if the evidence was cumulative, or if the rest of the evidence was so one-sided that the error likely made no difference.

As already noted, a defendant's wealth has "a very real potential" for prejudice. The Legislature has deemed it so potentially prejudicial that it must be separated from the jury's deliberations regarding liability and actual damages. That concern is especially relevant here because the more impressive the wealth, the more likely it is to make an impression. Had Reliance's gross sales been $190,000 or perhaps even $1.9 million, the plaintiffs might be right that it would have been unlikely to turn jurors' heads. But sales of $1.9 billion are surely enough to catch any juror's attention. If evidence of gross sales is ever likely to be harmful, the evidence offered here surely must qualify.

Further, that evidence must be considered in the context of this case. Liability here was largely uncontested; as plaintiffs' counsel told the jury in his opening statement, "You're going to hear the driver tell you that it was his fault." Instead, he correctly noted that the key issue was damages: "The biggest issue, the biggest issue, in my opinion, that you're going to have at the end of the week or later in the week when you deliberate is going to involve how much should be paid." In that respect, most of the damages here were difficult to gauge, stemming as they did from soft-tissue injuries and impairments whose effects were hard to measure objectively. Given that the trial focused primarily on setting damage amounts as to which jurors have few clear guideposts, it is probable that proof of Reliance's huge revenues played a crucial role on the key issue at trial.

C. The Emphasis

In harmless-error review, we have also looked to efforts by counsel to emphasize the erroneous evidence. In this case, the court of appeals held that evidence of Reliance's wealth was harmless because it was mentioned only once. If that were the only rule, there would be little use for the rules of evidence as everyone could ignore them once with impunity.

Moreover, this argument conflicts with the plaintiffs' additional argument that evidence of Reliance's wealth was "buried in the larger context of testimony that concerned the size of the Reliance Steel operation, the number of employees, the number of divisions, and so forth." While plaintiffs' counsel mentioned the gross revenues figures only once, he mentioned Reliance's large size from voir dire to closing argument. * * *

D. The Effort

In harmless-error review, we have also considered whether admission of improper evidence was calculated or inadvertent. As this Court has stated before, a party's insistence on introducing inadmissible testimony "indicates how important he thought it was to his case." In the related area of improper evidence of insurance, Texas courts often look to whether the injection of insurance was inadvertent or not. When attorneys insist that prejudicial evidence be admitted, that can be some evidence that at least they thought it would have some likely effect.

Here, of course, admission was no accident. Proof of Reliance's income was not offered in the heat of the moment, but as a deposition excerpt prepared in advance and offered outside the presence of the jury, giving the plaintiffs time to overcome the defendants' objection and the trial court's reservations.

Intentionally leading the trial court into error does not always make the error harmful. But when issues like race, religion, gender, and wealth are injected into a case unnecessarily, there is the potential for damage not just to a litigant but to the civil justice system. Courts must provide equal justice to all, regardless of their circumstances, and efforts to suggest that jurors should do otherwise cannot be lightly disregarded.

* * *

We recognize that evidence of a party's wealth is sometimes admissible, and sometimes unavoidable; a large company may be so well known that jurors need no evidence about its ability to pay a judgment. But we also recognize "the potential that juries will use their verdicts to express biases against big businesses, particularly those without strong local presences." We reiterate today that gratuitous evidence about either party's financial circumstances is not what trials should be about.

Accordingly, we reverse the judgment of the court of appeals, and remand the case for a new trial.

Notes

1. *Texas Department of Transportation v. Able*, 35 S.W.3d 608 (Tex. 2000): The inclusion and exclusion of evidence is committed to the trial court's sound discretion. Even if the excluded evidence was admissible, and that the trial court erred in not admitting it, the complainant still must show that the error was harmful. To put it another way, a successful challenge to evidentiary rulings usually requires the complaining party to show that the judgment turns on the particular evidence excluded or admitted. In determining if the excluded evidence probably resulted in the rendition of an improper judgment, a court must review the entire record. Courts ordinarily will not reverse a judgment for erroneous rulings on admissibility of evidence when the evidence in question is cumulative and not controlling on a material issue dispositive to the case.

2. *Nissan Motor Company Ltd. v. Armstrong*, 145 S.W.3d 131(Tex. 2004): The erroneously admitted evidence probably made the judgment improper. The evidence of other incidents was far more than cumulative: it was emphasized at every opportunity; it was used to prove a defect when the actual evidence had been destroyed; and it was calculated to show Nissan was malicious rather than mistaken in suggesting the accident was Armstrong's fault. It also violated the long-standing rule in Texas that proof of unintended acceleration is not proof of a defect. Under that rule, proof of many instances of unintended acceleration cannot prove a defect ei-

ther; a lot of no evidence is still no evidence. For all these reasons, the evidence improperly admitted in this case probably resulted in an improper judgment.

3. In *Service Corp. International v. Guerra*, 348 S.W.3d 221 (Tex. 2011) the court stated: "An error in admitting evidence requires reversal if it probably caused the rendition of an improper judgment. TEX.R.APP. P. 61.1; *Nissan Motor Co. v. Armstrong,* 145 S.W.3d 131, 144 (Tex. 2004). In determining whether the error was harmful we evaluate the entire case from voir dire to closing argument, considering the evidence, strengths and weaknesses of the case, and the verdict. *Reliance Steel & Aluminum Co. v. Sevcik*, 267 S.W.3d 867,871 (Tex. 2008). We also consider whether counsel emphasized the erroneous evidence and whether the admission of the evidence was calculated or inadvertent. *Id.* at 874; *Nissan Motor Co.,* 145 S.W.3d at 144 ("[W]hether erroneous admission is harmful is more a matter of judgment than precise measurement.")."

4. *JLG Trucking, LLC v Garza*, 466 S.W.3d 157 (2015): We explained in *Sevcik* that "if erroneously admitted or excluded evidence was crucial to a key issue, the error was likely harmful." *Id.* at 873. "By contrast, admission or exclusion is likely harmless if the evidence was cumulative, or if the rest of the evidence was so one-sided that the error likely made no difference."

McCRAW
v.
MARIS

828 S.W.2d 756
(Tex. 1992)

Joe D. Gregory, Grapevine, Gary W. Sibley, Dallas, for petitioner.
David S. Stubblefield, Dallas, for respondent.

HIGHTOWER, JUSTICE.

The issue before this court is whether certain evidence was admissible in an action to determine whether the surviving spouse or the surviving children of Donna Ann Maris are entitled to the proceeds of her life insurance policy. After excluding certain evidence, the trial court determined that the surviving spouse was entitled to the life insurance proceeds. The court of appeals affirmed. ___ S.W.2d ___. We reverse the judgment of the court of appeals and remand the cause to the trial court for further proceedings on all issues.

Donna Ann Maris was an employee of the United States Department of Labor and had obtained life insurance under a Federal Employee's Group Life Insurance policy. Under federal statute, the life insurance proceeds are paid to the surviving spouse of the deceased employee unless the employee signed a written beneficiary designation form and filed it with the employing office. At her death in 1987, Donna Ann Maris was survived by her estranged husband, Jimmie L. Maris ("Maris"), and two children from a prior marriage, Tracy L. McCraw and Kristina N. McCraw ("McCraws"). The McCraws, the surviving children, filed suit for declaratory judgment asserting that they were entitled to the life insurance proceeds because Donna Ann Maris signed and filed the appropriate form with the employing office designating them as beneficiaries and the beneficiary designation form was subsequently lost. Maris, the surviving spouse, counterclaimed asserting that he was entitled to the life insurance proceeds. During trial, the court admitted testimony that two co-employees witnessed Donna Ann Maris' signature on some forms and that it was Donna Ann Maris' habit to complete handwritten duplicate forms prior to typing and filing the original form. However, the court excluded, among other things, a "duplicate beneficiary designation form" in the handwriting of Donna Ann Maris. The trial court determined that the surviving spouse was entitled to the life insurance proceeds. The court of appeals held that the trial court did not err in excluding the "duplicate beneficiary designation form."

* * *

Since we have determined that exclusion of the "duplicate beneficiary designation form" was erroneous, we must determine whether the exclusion constituted reversible error. For the exclusion of evidence to constitute reversible error, the complaining party must show (1) that the trial court committed error and (2) that the error was reasonably calculated to cause and probably did cause rendition of an improper judgment. *Gee v. Liberty Mut. Ins. Co.*, 765 S.W.2d 394, 396 (Tex. 1989); TEX. R. APP. P. 81(b)(1). Since we have determined that the trial court committed error when it excluded the "duplicate beneficiary designation form," we must determine whether the error was reasonably calculated to cause and probably did cause rendition of an improper judgment. This court has recognized "the impossibility of prescribing a specific test for determining whether any error . . . [including] the improper admission or exclusion of evidence . . . 'was reasonably calculated to cause and probably did cause the rendition of an improper judgment.' " *Lorusso v. Members Mut. Ins. Co.*, 603 S.W.2d 818, 821 (Tex. 1980). "Such a determination necessarily is a judgment call entrusted to the sound discretion and good senses of the reviewing court." *Id.* However, it is not necessary for the complaining party to prove that "but for" the exclusion of evidence, a different judgment would necessarily have resulted. The complaining party is only required to show that the exclusion of evidence probably resulted in the rendition of an improper judgment. *Howard v. Faberge, Inc.*, 679 S.W.2d 644, 648 (Tex. App.—Houston [1st Dist.] 1984, writ ref'd n.r.e.). *See King v. Skelly*, 452 S.W.2d 691, 696 (Tex. 1970). In making this determination, the court must review the entire record. *Gee v. Liberty Mut. Ins. Co.*, 765 S.W.2d at 396; *Lorusso v. Members Mut. Ins. Co.*, 603 S.W.2d at 821.

Under the McCraws' theory of the case, it is necessary that they prove (either directly or by circumstantial evidence) that Donna Ann Maris signed and filed the appropriate form with the employing office designating them as beneficiaries. Evidence of the duplicate beneficiary designation form in the handwriting of Donna Ann Maris combined with admitted evidence that it was Donna Ann Maris' habit to complete handwritten duplicate forms prior to typing and filing the original constitutes crucial circumstantial evidence concerning proof that Donna Ann Maris signed and filed the appropriate beneficiary designation form. Under these circumstances, the McCraws have demonstrated that exclusion of the "duplicate beneficiary designation form" was reasonably calculated to cause and probably did cause rendition of an improper judgment.

We reverse the judgment of the court of appeals and remand the cause to the trial court for further proceedings on all issues.

GONZALEZ, JUSTICE, dissenting [opinion omitted].

CORNYN, JUSTICE, dissenting.

* * *

Even if the majority is impelled to the conclusion that exclusion of this evidence was error, Petitioners have not met their burden to show any error was reasonably calculated to cause and probably did cause rendition of an improper judgment. TEX. R. APP. P. 81(b)(1). The excluded evidence of the duplicate beneficiary designation form is cumulative of other evidence admitted on this point and, thus, even erroneous exclusion is harmless error. *Rose v. O'Keefe*, 39 S.W.2d 877, 879 (Tex. Comm'n App. 1931, opinion adopted); *Thrailkill v. Montgomery Ward & Co.*, 670 S.W.2d 382, 387 (Tex. App.—Houston [1st Dist.] 1984, writ ref'd n.r.e.). Certainly, the inferences which petitioners seek to have drawn from the excluded evidence are cumulative of the inferences that they sought to have drawn from the evidence admitted and considered by the trial court. Moreover, how the majority can hold that in this non-jury trial—where the trier of fact actually heard all the evidence, both admitted and excluded, albeit on a bill of exception—that admission would have probably resulted in a different judgment is beyond me. I would affirm the judgment of the court of appeals.

Notes

1. As shown above a successful challenge to properly preserved evidentiary rulings usually requires the complaining party to show that the judgment turns on the particular evidence excluded or admitted. That determination is made by the appellate court by reviewing the entire record. *See City of Brownsville v. Alvarado.*[1]

2. Please note as you read the remainder of this book that often times the courts do not address the harmless error rule. Many times that failure is an oversight on the part of the court. However, in a few special instances, it is because a different standard—other than the harmless error rule—is being used to determine whether the error will lead to a reversal of the case being appealed. Please be alert to this possibility.

---

[1] 897 S.W.2d 750 (Tex. 1995).

MENTIS
v.
BARNARD
870 S.W.2d 14
(1994)

Gary W. Sibley and Robert T. Baskett, Dallas, for petitioner.

Charles M. Bradshaw, Dallas, for respondent.

JUSTICE DOGGETT delivered the opinion of the Court, in which CHIEF JUSTICE PHILLIPS, JUSTICE GONZALEZ, JUSTICE HIGHTOWER, JUSTICE HECHT, JUSTICE GAMMAGE, and JUSTICE ENOCH join.

We consider trial court exclusion of the testimony of an expert witness on the grounds that he had not been designated "as soon as practical" under Rule 166b(6)(b) of the Texas Rules of Civil Procedure.

While crossing a street, Thelma Mentis was struck and killed by an automobile driven by John Barnard. Although suit was filed shortly after her death, the attorney who tried the case was not retained until about three months before trial. In response to discovery, that attorney designated an accident reconstruction expert as a testifying witness thirty-two days before trial. After jury selection and opening statements had been completed, Barnard's attorney was successful in having barred any testimony from this expert because he had not been identified "as soon as practical." Based upon the remaining evidence it was permitted to consider, the jury found that the negligence of both Mentis and Barnard constituted a proximate cause of the accident, with 85 percent of the negligence attributable to the former, and 15 percent to the latter. The trial court entered a take-nothing judgment. The court of appeals affirmed. 853 S.W.2d 119. We reverse.

* * *

A trial court's exclusion of an expert who has not been properly designated can be overturned only upon a finding of abuse of discretion. *Morrow*, 714 S.W.2d at 298. Barnard's only objection was that "the designation of the [Mentis's] expert one month before trial, after a lawsuit ha [d] been filed almost two years, is not as soon as practical." Though later arguing that he lacked the expert's deposition, Barnard's counsel admitted that he had never sought it. A litigant who seeks to deny an opponent the right to use a witness has the burden of producing evidence to show that the designation was not "as soon as practical." *See Williams*, 734 S.W.2d at 193. Simply advising the court as to how long the case had been pending did not by itself establish that designation at an earlier date would have been practical. The trial court abused its discretion in granting Barnard's motion.

Our analysis is not complete, however, without determining whether the error constituted reversible error. TEX. R. APP. P. 81(b). An error in the exclusion of evidence requires reversal if it is both controlling on a material issue and not cumulative. *See Gee v. Liberty Mut. Fire Ins. Co.*, 765 S.W.2d 394, 396 (Tex. 1989). Here the excluded witness was an accident reconstruction expert who planned to address a central issue of the comparative negligence of the pedestrian and driver. The expert's noncumulative calculations and opinions, based on examination and measurement of the scene, that Barnard was driving between 6 and 20 miles above the 40 mile per hour speed limit on a dark, rainy morning were controlling, though not conclusive, as to whether excessive speed caused the death.

Given the harmful effect of the trial court's abuse of discretion in excluding expert testimony, we reverse the court of appeals and remand for a new trial.

CORNYN, JUSTICE, joined by SPECTOR, J., in Part I of this opinion, dissenting.

* * *

The court further errs when it concludes that exclusion of Murray's testimony was harmful error. After the trial court excluded Murray's testimony, Murray testified on bill of exception that Barnard's car was travelling between forty-five and sixty miles per hour at the time of the accident.

Three eyewitnesses testified to the speed of Barnard's vehicle before the accident, the main subject of contention at trial. Barnard testified that he was travelling about thirty-five miles per hour at the time of the collision; one disinterested witness, Carolyn Hubacek, testified that Barnard was travelling at a speed of twenty to twenty-five miles per hour. A second disinterested eyewitness, Joy Soby, testified that Barnard was travelling "approximately forty miles-an-hour" at the time his car hit Mentis.

Given this eyewitness testimony, Murray's testimony was probably cumulative. And the court offers no reason to assume that the testimony of what Learned Hand once referred to as a "hired champion" will carry the day with the jury. *See* Learned Hand, *Historical and Practical Considerations Regarding Expert Testimony*, 15 HARV. L. REV. 40, 53 (1901). Even if exclusion of Murray's testimony was error, however, the court's opinion does not show that such error probably caused the jury to reach an improper verdict when the jury assigned eighty-five percent of the fault for the accident to Mentis, and fifteen percent of the fault to Barnard. I would conclude that the trial court did not err by rendering judgment on the verdict. *See* TEX. R. APP. P. 81(b)(1).

For the foregoing reasons, I respectfully dissent.

Note

GTE Southwest v. Bruce.[1] In this action for intentional infliction of emotional distress, three GTE employees, Bruce, Davis, and Poelstra, sued GTE for intentional infliction of emotional distress premised on the constant humiliating and abusive behavior of their supervisor, Shields. The employees obtained opinion evidence from three different expert witnesses that Shields's conduct was extreme and outrageous. GTE objected to this testimony at trial, and complained of the trial court's admission of the testimony of two of the witnesses on appeal. The court of appeals held that the trial court's admission of expert testimony on the issue of whether Shields's conduct was extreme and outrageous was error. The Supreme Court affirmed, holding that the error was harmless.

> Last, GTE complains about the trial court's admission of expert testimony that Shields's conduct was extreme and outrageous. The employees obtained opinion evidence from three different expert witnesses that Shields's conduct was extreme and outrageous. GTE objected to this testimony at trial, and complained of the trial court's admission of the testimony of two of the witnesses on appeal.
>
> The court of appeals held that the trial court's admission of expert testimony on the issue of whether Shields's conduct was extreme and outrageous was error. 956 S.W.2d at 641. We agree. "[A]n expert may state an opinion on a mixed question of law and fact as long as the opinion is confined to the relevant issues and is based on proper legal concepts." *Birchfield v. Texarkana Mem'l Hosp.*, 747 S.W.2d 361, 365 (Tex. 1987). But to be admissible, expert testimony must generally involve "scientific, technical, or other specialized knowledge" as to which a witness could be qualified as an expert by "knowledge, skill, experience, training, or education," and it must assist the trier of fact. TEX. R. EVID. 702; *Warner v. Hurt*, 834 S.W.2d 404, 406 (Tex. App.—Houston [14th Dist.] 1992, no writ) ("Admissibility of the expert's opinion hinges on whether or not the expert has special knowledge concerning [the] matter on which his opinion is sought."). Except in highly unusual circumstances, expert testimony concerning extreme and outrageous conduct would not meet this standard. Where, as here, the issue involves only general knowledge and experience rather than expertise, it is within the province of the jury to decide, and admission of expert testimony on the issue is error.
>
> Nevertheless, the court of appeals correctly concluded that the error was harmless. The court applied our reasoning in *Louder v. De Leon*, 754 S.W.2d 148, 149 (Tex. 1988), that "[j]urors realize that they are the final triers to decide the issues. They may accept or reject an expert's view. Thus there is little danger in an expert's answer to an all-embracing question on a mixed question of law and fact."
>
> Texas Rule of Appellate Procedure 44.1(a)(1) mandates that no judgment may be reversed on appeal on the ground that the trial court made an error of law unless the error complained of probably caused the rendition of an improper judgment. TEX. R. APP. P. 44.1(a)(1). GTE argues that "it is inconceivable that expert opinion on the ultimate issue could be harmless." To demonstrate that it was harmed by the expert's testimony, GTE relies solely on the jury's answers to the charge, pointing out that the jury did not find malice, upon which there was no expert opinion, but did find intentional infliction of emotional distress, upon which there was expert testimony. This questionable logic is insufficient to demonstrate that admitting the testimony harmed GTE. *See Templeton v. Dreiss*, 961 S.W.2d

1 998 S.W.2d 605 (Tex. 1999).

645, 672 (Tex. App.—San Antonio 1998, pet. denied). Absent the expert testimony, there was an abundance of evidence from the employees and other witnesses establishing the continuing assaults and humiliation by Shields. At most, the expert testimony GTE finds objectionable was merely cumulative of evidence demonstrating that Shields's conduct amounts to intentional infliction of emotion distress. *See Southwestern Elec. Power Co. v. Burlington N. R.R.*, 966 S.W.2d 467, 474 (Tex. 1998). This non-expert testimony is sufficient to support the jury's verdict.

* * *

[JUSTICE OWEN concurred on grounds unrelated to this point.]

CHAPTER 2.
COURTS AND SUBJECT MATTER JURISDICTION

1. *Jurisdiction and the Judicial Function*

Notes

1. **TEXAS CONSTITUTION** Art. 5 provides in part:

> Sec. 1. The judicial power of this State shall be vested in one Supreme Court, in one Court of Criminal Appeals, in Courts of Appeals, in District Courts, in County Courts, in Commissioners Courts, in Courts of Justices of the Peace, and in such other courts as may be provided by law.
>
> The Legislature may establish such other courts as it may deem necessary and prescribe the jurisdiction and organization thereof, and may conform the jurisdiction of the district and other inferior courts thereto.

2. All courts in this state are of limited jurisdiction, in the sense that the jurisdiction of each is specifically defined as well be described below in Section 3; but, within the limits so defined, they are courts of general jurisdiction, as distinguished from tribunals of special jurisdiction. This is no less true of the justices' courts than of the district courts. *Koehler v. Earl*, 77 Tex. 188, 14 S.W. 28 (1890); *County of Angelina v. O'Quinn*, 429 S.W.2d 211, 214 (Tex. Civ. App.—Beaumont 1968, no writ). Some courts in Texas have been given special statutory jurisdiction over matters. *See, e.g.*, V.T.C.A., **Education Code** § 21.307 ("Either party may appeal the commissioner's decision to: (1) a district court in the county in which the district's central administrative offices are located; or (2) if agreed by all parties, a district court in Travis County); V.T.C.A., **Family Code** § 51.04(b). In each county, the county's juvenile board shall designate one or more district, criminal district, domestic relations, juvenile, or county courts or county courts at law as the juvenile court").

3. *Oncor Electric Delivery Co. LLC v. Chaparral Energy LLC, 546 S.W.3d 133 (Tex. 2018):* There is a presumption that district courts are constitutionally authorized to resolve legal disputes. To overcome that presumption, the Constitution or another law must grant exclusive jurisdiction to another court or an administrative agency. Unlike courts, an administrative agency is "a legislative creation with only those powers expressly conferred and necessary to accomplish its duties." Whether an agency has exclusive jurisdiction presents a question of statutory interpretation we review de novo.

CLAYTON
v.
HURT
88 Tex. 595, 32 S.W. 876
(1895)

L. E. Trezevant, for appellants.
Spencer & Kincaid, for appellees.

DENMAN, J.

[Facts abridged by editor. This was an action commenced in the justice court to expel a tenant from property. The owner gave the tenant only two days notice of the termination of the lease, when he was legally required to have given thirty days notice of termination. The justice court ordered the tenant off, despite the procedural irregularities. The county court affirmed. The tenant sued in district court to enjoin the enforcement of the justice court judgment alleging that such judgment was void, since the plaintiff did not plead that there had been thirty days notice.]

Where a court of general jurisdiction, in the exercise of its ordinary judicial functions, renders a judgment in a cause in which it has jurisdiction over the person of the defendant and the subject-matter of the controversy, such judgment is never void, no matter how erroneous it may appear, from the face of the record or otherwise, to be. An analysis and application of this rule to the facts stated will answer the questions certified. Whether a court is to be classed as one of general or one of special and limited jurisdiction depends, not upon the classification of courts of similar names in other jurisdictions, but upon the duties and powers devolved upon it, and the manner of their exercise, as prescribed by the organic law. The constitution of this state, in distributing the judicial power of the government among the various courts, and defining their relation to each other, after providing for the division of the county into precincts, and the election of a justice of the peace in each precinct, provides that "justices of the peace shall have jurisdiction . . . in civil matters of all cases where the amount in controversy is two hundred dollars or less, exclusive of interest, of which exclusive original jurisdiction is not given to the district or county courts; and such other jurisdiction, criminal and civil, as may be provided by law, under such regulations as may be prescribed by law. * * *" CONST. art. 5, § 19. In pursuance of the power therein conferred, the legislature has by law conferred upon such justices jurisdiction of forcible entry and detainer cases. The language of the constitution, that "the justices of the peace shall have jurisdiction," etc., confers upon them the general judicial powers of the government over the subjects therein specified, subject to the limitations therein prescribed; and such jurisdiction is as general and exclusive as is that of the various other courts mentioned in the constitution over the subjects committed to them. The fact that their judgments are subject to revision in the various forms prescribed by law does not tend to show that they are courts of limited or special jurisdiction; for such judgments can be revised or annulled only in the instances and in the manner prescribed by the constitution in fixing the jurisdiction of the other courts, and, until so revised or amended, are of as much binding force as the judgments of any other court. We therefore hold them to be courts of general jurisdiction, within the meaning of the rule above stated. *Williams v. Ball*, 52 Tex. 603; *Holmes v. Buckner*, 67 Tex. 107, 2 S.W. 452.

It is contended, however, that the justice court, in forcible entry and detainer proceedings, under our statute, is not "in the exercise of its ordinary judicial functions," but exercises only special and summary powers, and that, therefore, each step in the proceeding must appear to have been done in accordance with the statute regulating same, before the judgment can be held valid. In order to determine this question we must look to the statute conferring this jurisdiction upon the court, and regulating the manner of its exercise. The statute provides for the beginning of the proceedings by complaint; for the issuance and service of process upon the defendant, and return thereof by the officer serving same; for the summoning by the executive officer of a jury to try said cause; for the summoning and compelling the attendance of witnesses; for the postponement of the trial upon application of either party for good cause shown; for the impaneling and swearing of the jury "as in other cases;" for the docketing and trial of the cause "as in other cases;" for the rendition of a judgment by the justice upon and in accordance with the verdict of the jury; and, finally, for appeal by either party from such judgment to the county court. It is clear that during the trial the court is to be governed by the ordinary rules of law applicable in other cases. It is true that the statute expressly provides that "the only issue shall be as to the right of actual possession, and the merits of the title shall not be inquired into;" but this does not authorize the court, in the trial of such issue, to apply any other than the ordinary rules of law governing its proceedings. The question as to what evidence can properly be admitted upon such issue is often of difficult determination, and must be decided by the court trying the cause, governed by the rules of law. The decision of such questions, as well as various questions which may arise from the beginning to the end of the proceedings, including the motion for a new trial, calls into exercise the ordinary judicial functions of the court. We are therefore of the opinion that the contention above stated, that the court is not in the exercise of ordinary judicial functions, cannot be maintained. Therefore, if it be conceded that the ruling of the justice to the effect that the landlord was only required to give the notice for the length of time stated on the face of the complaint was erroneous in point of law, such error did not render the judgment void, under the rule above stated. *Railway Co. v. Dowe*, 70 Tex. 1, 6 S.W. 790.

No question is raised as to the jurisdiction of the justice over the person of the defendant, for he appears not only to have been served with process, but to have entered his appearance, and after the trial of the cause appealed to the county court, but it is contended that it appears from the face of the complaint that the justice had no jurisdiction of the subject-matter of the controversy. The ground upon which this contention is based is that the justice has no jurisdiction to entertain a suit of forcible detainer by a landlord against a tenant until the term has terminated, and that since it appears from the face of the complaint that it was a lease from month-to-month, the notice given on the 5th of December, only two days prior to the ending of the month, on the 7th of December, 1893, did not in law terminate the lease. We are not called upon to determine whether the justice erred, as a matter of law in holding such notice sufficient. The sole question for us to determine is, did the justice have jurisdiction of the suit? For if he had jurisdiction, as stated above, his judgment is not void, though it be conceded that his ruling as to the sufficiency of the notice was erroneous. The statute provides that "if any person shall willfully and without force hold over any lands, tenements or other real property after the termination of the time for which such lands, tenements or other real property were let to him, or to the person under whom he claims, after demand made in writing for the possession thereof by the person or persons entitled to such possession, such person shall be adjudged guilty of forcible detainer." The class of cases of which jurisdiction is conferred by this section of the statute is that where a landlord, or some one entitled to his rights, seeks to recover possession from his tenant or some one claiming under him, urging as cause of action that the lease under which the possession was obtained has been terminated. The jurisdiction of the court attaches when a case belonging to this class is stated on the face of the complaint. After the jurisdiction attaches, it then becomes the duty of the court, on exceptions raised to the complaint; of the jury, upon the evidence adduced in support thereof; and of the court, again, on motion for new trial,—to determine (1) whether the lease had in fact terminated; and (2) whether demand had been made in writing for the possession; and (3) whether the holding over thereafter was willful. The improper determination of either or all of these questions are merely errors occurring on the trial, which, under the rule above indicated, does not render the judgment void, although such errors appear on the face of the record. If one be sued in a justice court upon a contract to which he is not a party, or a married woman be sued upon a note which she had no power to contract, the judgment rendered thereon, though palpably erroneous, is not void. *Railway Co. v. Dowe*, 70 Tex. 1, 6 S.W. 790; *Trimble v. Miller*, 24 Tex. 215. These cases fall within the general rule stated in the beginning of this discussion. We are therefore of the opinion that the judgments of the justice and county courts referred to in the questions certified are not void.

Notes

1. *Dallas County v. Halsey*, 87 S.W.3d 552 (Tex. 2002). "When entitled to the protection of derived judicial immunity, an officer of the court receives the same immunity as a judge acting in his or her official judicial capacity—absolute immunity from liability for judicial acts performed within the scope of jurisdiction. *Stump v. Sparkman*, 435 U.S. 349, 356-57, 98 S.Ct. 1099, 55 L.Ed.2d 331 (1978) (stating that "[a] judge will not be deprived of immunity because the action he took was in error, was done maliciously, or was in excess of his authority; rather, he will be subject to liability only when he has acted in the 'clear absence of all jurisdiction.' " (*quoting Bradley v. Fisher*, 80 U.S. (13 Wall.) 335, 351, 20 L.Ed. 646 (1871)); *Turner v. Pruitt*, 161 Tex. 532, 342 S.W.2d 422, 423 (Tex.1961) (noting that in judicial proceedings in which the court has jurisdiction, a judge is immune for his or her actions). While protecting the individual judge, this policy likewise serves to protect the public "whose interest it is that the judges should be at liberty to exercise their functions with independence, and without fear of consequences." *Bradley v. Fisher*, 80 U.S. (13 Wall.) 335, 349 n. 16, 20 L.Ed. 646 (1871); *see Delcourt v. Silverman*, 919 S.W.2d 777, 781 (Tex. App.—Houston [14th Dist.] 1996, writ denied). The policy reasons for judicial immunity are also implicated when a judge delegates or appoints another person to perform services for the court or when a person otherwise serves as an officer of the court. *See Delcourt*, 919 S.W.2d at 782. In this circumstance, the immunity attaching to the judge follows the delegation, appointment, or court employment. *See Clements v. Barnes*, 834 S.W.2d 45, 46 (Tex.1992); *City of Houston v. West Capital Fin. Servs. Corp.*, 961 S.W.2d 687, 689 (Tex. App.—Houston [1st Dist.] 1998, pet. dism'd w.o.j.); *Byrd v. Woodruff*, 891 S.W.2d 689, 707 (Tex. App.—Dallas 1994, writ dism'd by agr.). The person acting in such a capacity also enjoys absolute immunity, known as derived judicial immunity. *See Clements*, 834 S.W.2d at 46; *Delcourt*, 919 S.W.2d at 782."

2. *Shepherd v. San Jacinto Junior College Dist.*, 363 S.W.2d 742 (Tex. 1962): "A state constitution, unlike the federal constitution, is in no sense a grant of power but operates solely as a limitation of power. 'All power which is not limited by the constitution inheres in the people, and an act of a state legislature is legal when the Constitution contains no prohibition against it.'

DUBAI PETROLEUM COMPANY
v.
KAZI
12 S.W.3d 71
(Tex. 2000)

Larry Funderburk, Michael A. Plotz, Michael K. Bell, Tracy J. Willi, Gregory G. Funderburk, JoAnn Storey, Houston, for Petitioners.
Jeffrey W. Mankoff, Dallas, for Respondents.

CHIEF JUSTICE PHILLIPS delivered the opinion of the Court, in which JUSTICE HECHT, JUSTICE OWEN, JUSTICE BAKER, JUSTICE ABBOTT, JUSTICE HANKINSON, JUSTICE O'NEILL and JUSTICE GONZALES joined.

We withdraw our January 6 opinion and substitute the following.

Section 71.031 of the Texas Civil Practice and Remedies Code permits suit for the personal injury or wrongful death of a citizen of a foreign country, if the decedent or injured party's country of citizenship has "equal treaty rights" with the United States. In this wrongful death case, we hold that the "equal treaty rights" requirement is not jurisdictional and that the plaintiffs have satisfied their initial burden to show that the decedent's country of citizenship offers "equal treaty rights" to United States citizens. Accordingly, we affirm the judgment of the court of appeals, which reversed the trial court's order dismissing the case for lack of subject-matter jurisdiction. 961 S.W.2d 313.

I

Alimuddin Sirajuddin Kazi, a citizen of India, was killed while working on an oil rig off the coast of the United Arab Emirates. Kazi's survivors, all citizens of India, brought this wrongful death suit in Harris County district court, basing their claim on Texas Civil Practice and Remedies Code section 71.031. When the Kazis filed this suit in 1993, section 71.031 provided:

(a) An action for damages for the death or personal injury of a citizen of this state, of the United States, or of a foreign country may be enforced in the courts of this state, although the wrongful act, neglect, or default causing the death or injury takes place in a foreign state or country, if:

(1) a law of the foreign state or country or of this state gives a right to maintain an action for damages for the death or injury;

(2) the action is begun in this state within the time provided by the laws of this state for beginning the action; and

(3) in the case of a citizen of a foreign country, the country has equal treaty rights with the United States on behalf of its citizens.

TEX. CIV. PRAC. & REM. CODE § 71.031(a) (1997).

Defendants, Dubai Petroleum Company, Inc., Conoco, Inc., Dresser Industries, Inc. d/b/a Dresser-Rand Co., Aeroquip Corporation, Solar Turbines Incorporated, and Energy Service International, LTD a/k/a ESI., Inc., responded that the trial court lacked subject-matter jurisdiction because India does not have "equal treaty rights" with the United States as section 71.031(a)(3) required. The court agreed and dismissed the case.

Unlike section 71.051(a), which applies only to plaintiffs who are not legal residents of this country, section 71.031's "equal treaty rights" requirement applies to all citizens of foreign countries, including legal residents of this country. *Compare* TEX. CIV. PRAC. & REM. CODE § 71.031(a)(4) (Supp. 2000), *with id.* § 71.051(a). The federal Constitution limits the states' ability to discriminate against foreign citizens who reside in this country. *See, e.g., Bernal v. Fainter*, 467 U.S. 216, 104 S.Ct. 2312, 81 L.Ed.2d 175 (1984); *Plyler v. Doe*, 457 U.S. 202, 102 S.Ct. 2382, 72 L.Ed.2d 786 (1982). As the decedent in this case was not a United States resident, we need not determine whether the "equal treaty rights" requirement can constitutionally be applied to resident aliens. Because section 71.031 frames the "equal treaty rights" requirement in terms of the injured party's citizenship, this opinion discusses the effect of that requirement on suits by or on behalf of foreign citizens. We caution, however, that one should not view our use of the word "citizen" as resolving the constitutionality of the "equal treaty rights" requirement as applied to resident aliens.

The court of appeals reversed, holding that the International Covenant on Civil and Political Rights, adopted by the U.N. General Assembly Dec. 16, 1966, 999 U.N.T.S. 171, reprinted in 6 I.L.M. 368 ("Covenant"), confers "equal treaty rights" between India and the United States. 961 S.W.2d at 318. The court of appeals sought guidance from a footnote in our opinion in *Dow Chemical Co. v. Alfaro*, 786 S.W.2d 674, 675 n. 2 (Tex. 1990), which requires the existence of treaty provisions "similar" to those in the Friendship, Commerce, and Navigation ("FCN") Treaty between Costa Rica and the United States to satisfy subsection (a)(3) of section 71.031. Determining that the Covenant's provisions were sufficiently "similar" to the rights extended in the FCN Treaty, which include (1) protection to persons and property, (2) free and open access to the courts, (3) the ability to employ counsel, and (4) the same rights and privileges as native citizens, the court of appeals held that Texas courts have subject-matter jurisdiction over the Kazis' wrongful death action. 961 S.W.2d at 318. For different reasons than the court of appeals gave, we affirm that judgment.

II

It is well-settled that "[a] judgment may properly be rendered against a party only if the court has authority to adjudicate the type of controversy involved in the action." RESTATEMENT (SECOND) OF JUDGMENTS § 11 (1982). For federal district courts or state trial courts of limited jurisdiction, the authority to adjudicate must be established at the outset of each case, as jurisdiction is never presumed. *See* 13 CHARLES A. WRIGHT, ARTHUR R. MILLER & EDWARD H. COPPER, FEDERAL PRACTICE & PROCEDURE § 3522, at 62 (1984). A Texas district court, however, is a court of general jurisdiction. Our Constitution provides that the jurisdiction of a district court "consists of exclusive, appellate, and original jurisdiction of all actions, proceedings, and remedies, except in cases where exclusive, appellate, or original jurisdiction may be conferred by this Constitution or other law on some other court, tribunal, or administrative body." TEX. CONST. art. V, § 8. By statute, district courts have "the jurisdiction provided by Article V, Section 8, of the Texas Constitution," TEX. GOV'T CODE § 24.007, and "may hear and determine any cause that is cognizable by courts of law or equity and may grant any relief that could be granted by either courts of law or equity." TEX. GOV'T CODE § 24.008.[1] For "courts of general jurisdiction, . . . the presumption is that they have subject matter jurisdiction unless a showing can be made to the contrary." 13 WRIGHT ET AL., *supra*, at § 3522, at 60; *see also* 16 CASAD ET AL., MOORE'S FEDERAL PRACTICE § 108.04[2], at 108-19 (3d ed.1999); *Dean v. State ex rel. Bailey*, 88 Tex. 290, 30 S.W. 1047, 1048 (1895) ("No other court having jurisdiction over the cause, the district court has the power to determine the right of the case, and to apply the remedy."); *Bowles v. Angelo*, 188 S.W.2d 691, 693 (Tex. Civ. App.—Galveston 1945, no writ) ("[I]f the jurisdiction necessary to relieve against a wrong is not to be found in the specific grants of jurisdiction to the justice or the county court, then it has either been specifically granted to the district court, or conferred upon that court in the grant to it of all residuary jurisdiction."); 2 BRADEN, ET AL., THE CONSTITUTION OF THE STATE OF TEXAS, AN ANNOTATED AND COMPARATIVE ANALYSIS 411 (1977). Thus, all claims are presumed to fall within the jurisdiction of the district court unless the Legislature or Congress has provided that they must be heard elsewhere.

However, this Court has held that this presumption does not apply to actions grounded in statute rather than the common law. For example, this Court held in *Mingus v. Wadley*, 115 Tex. 551, 285 S.W. 1084 (1926):

> The general rule is where the cause of action and remedy for its enforcement are derived not from the common law but from the statute, the statutory provisions are mandatory and exclusive, and must be complied with in all respects or the action is not maintainable. *Id.* at 1087.

---

[1] A third general jurisdictional statute, section 24.009, provides that "[i]f two or more persons originally and properly join in one suit, the suit for jurisdictional purposes is treated as if one party is suing for the aggregate amount of all their claims added together, excluding interests and costs." TEX. GOV'T CODE § 24.009. This section may be irrelevant to district courts, where there may no longer be a jurisdictional minimum, but it does apply to statutory county courts, where suits clearly must allege a certain minimum value for the court to exercise jurisdiction unless by law the jurisdiction of the statutory county court has been made equivalent to the district court in civil cases. TEX. GOV'T CODE § 25.0003(c)(1); *see also Smith v. Clary Corp.*, 917 S.W.2d 796, 797 (Tex. 1996) (holding that the statute applies to statutory county courts only "to allow multiple plaintiffs to aggregate their claims to achieve the minimum jurisdictional amount for a court, not to defeat jurisdiction"); *Peek v. Equipment Serv. Co.*, 779 S.W.2d 802, 803-04 n. 4 (Tex. 1989) (discussing without deciding whether a jurisdictional minimum still exists for Texas district courts).

Further, the Court stated: ". . . there is no presumption of jurisdiction where a court, although it is one of general jurisdiction, exercises special statutory powers in a special statutory manner or otherwise than according to the courts of the common law, since under such circumstances the court stands with reference to the special power exercised on the same footing with courts of limited and inferior jurisdiction." *Id.* at 1089 (*quoting* 15 CORPUS JURIS *Courts*, § 148(c), at 831-32). We have repeatedly reaffirmed this dichotomy between common-law and statutory actions. *See, e.g., Grounds v. Tolar Indep. Sch. Dist.*, 707 S.W.2d 889, 891 (Tex. 1986); *Texas Catastrophe Property Ins. Ass'n v. Council of Co- Owners of Saida II Towers Condominium Ass'n*, 706 S.W.2d 644, 646 (Tex. 1986); *Alpha Petroleum Co. v. Terrell*, 122 Tex. 257, 59 S.W.2d 364, 367-68 (1933); *see also Cunningham v. Robison*, 104 Tex. 227, 136 S.W. 441, 442 (1911). Likewise, the court of appeals below concluded that a claim must satisfy all the requisites of section 71.031 in order for the district court to assert subject-matter jurisdiction. 961 S.W.2d at 314. This approach is consistent with the language of other appellate decisions. *See Owens- Corning Fiberglas Corp. v. Baker*, 838 S.W.2d 838, 841 n. 2 (Tex. App.—Texarkana 1992, no writ); *Alfaro v. Dow Chem.*, 751 S.W.2d 208, 208-09 (Tex. App.—Houston [1st Dist.] 1988), *aff'd*, 786 S.W.2d 674 (Tex. 1990).

But while conceptualizing subject-matter jurisdiction in this way has an initial appeal, the resulting practical difficulties suggest underlying logical flaws. Because of the longstanding principle that subject-matter jurisdiction is a power that "exists by operation of law only, and cannot be conferred upon any court by consent or waiver," *Federal Underwriters Exch. v. Pugh*, 141 Tex. 539, 174 S.W.2d 598, 600 (1943), a judgment will never be considered final if the court lacked subject-matter jurisdiction. "The classification of a matter as one of [subject-matter] jurisdiction . . . opens the way to making judgments vulnerable to delayed attack for a variety of irregularities that perhaps better ought to be sealed in a judgment." RESTATEMENT (SECOND) OF JUDGMENTS § 12 cmt. b, at 118 (1982). When, as here, it is difficult to tell whether or not the parties have satisfied the requisites of a particular statute, it seems perverse to treat a judgment as perpetually void merely because the court or the parties made a good-faith mistake in interpreting the law. Thus, the rationale of *Mingus* has been criticized as "more suited to a eulogy for the common law than to a businesslike administration of justice." Dobbs, *Trial Court Error as an Excess of Jurisdiction*, 43 TEXAS L. REV. 854, 878 (1965). It wrongly assumes that a court exercising its common-law authority would never be "willing to introduce new procedures, new remedies, and new substantive rules," and that "something is functionally different about a non-common law proceeding, and that, therefore, courts are justified in regarding such proceedings in a harsher light." *Id.* at 878-79.

Although *Mingus* represented the dominant approach when it was decided, "the modern direction of policy is to reduce the vulnerability of final judgments to attack on the ground that the tribunal lacked subject matter jurisdiction." RESTATEMENT (SECOND) OF JUDGMENTS § 11 cmt. e, at 113 (1982). *See generally* Boskey & Braucher, *Jurisdiction and Collateral Attack*, 40 COLUM. L. REV. 1006 (1940); Note, *Filling the Void: Jurisdictional Power and Jurisdictional Attacks on Judgements*, 87 YALE L.J. 164 (1977). We therefore overrule *Mingus* to the extent that it characterized the plaintiff's failure to establish a statutory prerequisite as jurisdictional. The trial court in this case had jurisdiction because a claim for wrongful death was within its constitutional jurisdiction, not because the plaintiffs satisfied all the grounds listed in former section 71.031(a). Thus, while defendants in this Court and the Kazis in the court of appeals framed their argument in terms of whether the district court did or did not have subject- matter jurisdiction, we consider those arguments in the context of whether the Kazis established their right under the statute to go forward with this suit. "The right of a plaintiff to maintain a suit, while frequently treated as going to the question of jurisdiction, has been said to go in reality to the right of the plaintiff to relief rather than to the jurisdiction of the court to afford it." 21 C.J.S. *Courts* § 16, at 23 (1990).

III

Having made the preliminary determination that section 71.031 is not jurisdictional, we now discuss the meaning of "equal treaty rights" in order to determine whether plaintiffs met its requirements. We hold that "equal treaty rights" means that a country grants—based on a treaty—to United States citizens the same rights to sue in its courts for personal injury or death that it grants to its own citizens. This does not mean that the substantive law, remedies, or procedures in Texas and the foreign country have to coincide, or even be remotely similar. But it does require that the decedent's or injured party's country of citizenship allow United States citizens to pursue available remedies for personal injury or death in its courts to the same extent that it allows its own citizens to pursue those remedies.

* * *

Because the language of the Covenant provides for equal access to courts and equal treatment in civil proceedings, it satisfies the Kazis' initial burden of establishing "equal treaty rights." Under the procedure we authorize today, however, the defendants can still put this requirement at issue by producing evidence that, under Indian law, these rights do not exist. Accordingly, we express no opinion regarding whether the Kazis will ultimately meet their burden of proving this statutory condition. Because the plaintiffs have satisfied their initial burden of establishing that India provides "equal treaty rights" to United States citizens, however, we affirm the court of appeals' judgment reversing the trial court's order and remanding this case to that court.

JUSTICE ENOCH did not participate in the decision.

Note

Hubenak v. San Jacinto Gas Transmission Company, 141 S.W.3d 172 (Tex. 2004): Subject matter jurisdiction cannot be waived. If the "unable to agree" requirement, found in TEX. PROP. CODE § 21.012 (one of the requirements of a condemnation petition is to state that the parties were unable to agree on a value of the taking) were necessary to confer subject matter jurisdiction, then judgments in condemnation proceedings would be subject to collateral attack. In construing other mandatory statutory provisions, the modern direction of policy is to reduce the vulnerability of final judgments to attack on the ground that the tribunal lacked subject matter jurisdiction. Thus, the "unable to agree" requirements of § 21.012 are not jurisdictional, although they are mandatory.

MORROW
v.
CORBIN

122 Tex. 553, 62 S.W.2d 641
(1933)

B. R. Wall, of Grapevine, for plaintiff.
M. Hendricks Brown, of Fort Worth, for defendant.

[Facts abridged by the editor. Under a Texas statute, the district or county courts were authorized to certify any question raised by a party concerning the constitutionality of any law or any order, rule, or regulation of any officer, board, or other State commission directly to the Court of Civil Appeals before the trial on the merits. The statute also provided that the courts of civil appeals could further certify the question to the Supreme Court.]

CURETON, CHIEF JUSTICE.

* * *

It is obvious that the purpose of this act is to obtain before judgment in the trial court the advice of the Court of Civil Appeals and the Supreme Court as to "the constitutionality of any law or any order, rule or regulation of any officer, board, or other State Commission," which may be involved in any case pending but undetermined in a trial court. In other words, by the terms of this enactment in so far as involved in the case before us we are required to advise the district and county judges how to try their cases as to all constitutional questions, not to revise, reverse, affirm, or otherwise affect their decrees. Ordinarily, we believe the rendition of advisory opinions is to be regarded as the exercise of executive rather than judicial power. This seems to have been the conception of those who framed the Constitution, since by that instrument the Attorney General, a member of the Executive Department, is the only state officer expressly authorized to render such opinions. State Constitution, article 4, §§ 1, 22. At any rate, the rendition of advisory opinions has generally been held not to be the exercise of judicial power. 7 HARVARD LAW REVIEW, p. 153; *Matter of State Industrial Commission*, 224 N. Y. 13, 119 N. E. 1027; *Laughlin v. Portland*, 111 Me. 486, 90 A. 318, 51 L. R. A. (N. S.) 1143, Ann. Cas. 1916C, 734; Opinion of Justices, 126 Mass. 567; *Anway v. Grand Rapids R. Co*., 211 Mich. 592, 179 N. W. 350, 12 A. L. R. 26 (overruled in the later case, 68 A. L. R. 105, but not on the above question); 15 Corpus Juris, p. 785, ss 78, 79, and authorities cited in the notes; authorities post. We shall inquire, however, whether or not such power may be exercised by the appellate courts of this state, either as an express grant under the Constitution or as incidental to any granted power.

Section 1, article 5, of the Constitution states in what "magistracy" the judicial power shall be vested. It declares: "The judicial power of this State shall be vested in one Supreme Court, in Courts of Civil Appeals, in a Court of Criminal Appeals, in District Courts, in County Courts, in Commissioners Courts, in Courts of Justices of the Peace, and in such other courts as may be provided by law." The Constitution has thus erected a system of trial and appellate courts quite similar to that of the United States and those of the American states generally, all of which are an outgrowth of the judicial system of England, out of which the common law grew and attained its renown.

"Judicial power" is the power of a court to decide and pronounce a judgment and carry it into effect between persons and parties who bring a case before it for a decision. *Muskrat v. United States*, 219 U. S. 346, 31 S. Ct. 250, 55 L. Ed. 246; *Liberty Warehouse Co. v. Grannis*, 273 U. S. 70, 47 S. Ct. 282, 71 L. Ed. 541; 11 TEXAS JURISPRUDENCE, pp. 711, 712, § 9, and cases cited in the notes.

"Jurisdiction" of a particular court is that portion of the judicial power which it has been authorized to exercise by the Constitution or by valid statutes.

Since the Constitution has erected a system of both trial and appellate courts, it is obvious that it was never the purpose of the Organic Law to permit one tribunal to interfere with the lawful exercise by another of the judicial power allocated to it. It was the purpose of the framers of the Constitution to make each tribunal independent of all others in the exercise of the authority confided to it, except in so far as powers of revision or direction may be given in the Organic Law or valid statutes thereunder to appellate over trial tribunals. * * *

The Constitution is specific in confiding trial jurisdiction to the district and county courts, and other inferior courts. State Constitution, article 5, §§ 8, 16, 19. These provisions mean that those courts are to exercise that portion of the judicial power allocated to them unimpeded by the supervision of any other tribunal, except in so far as powers of revision may be confided to other tribunals. The jurisdiction of these trial or inferior courts, without any exception, embraces the "power to hear and determine the matter in controversy according to established rules of law, and to carry the sentence or judgment of the court into execution." * * *

One Court of Civil Appeals or district court will not be permitted to interfere with the previously attached jurisdiction of another court of co-ordinate power, nor can an appellate court interfere with the jurisdiction of a district court, except upon appeal in the usual way. *Cleveland v. Ward*, 116 Tex. 1, 285 S. W. 1063. Briefly stated, what we here intend to say is that the jurisdiction of trial courts, under the Constitution, once it attaches, embraces every element of judicial power allocated to those tribunals, and includes: (1) The power to hear the facts, (2) the power to decide the issues of fact made by the pleadings, (3) the power to decide the questions of law involved, (4) the power to enter a judgment on the facts found in accordance with the law as determined by the court, (5) and the power to execute the judgment or sentence. These duties this court will, by mandamus, require them to perform. Authorities *supra*. And further: That with the right of the trial court to exercise the powers thus confided to it, no appellate court can interfere, except in accordance with the authority given in the Constitution or valid statutes thereunder. *Cleveland v. Ward, supra*.

We are equally clear that the power thus confided to our trial courts must be exercised by them as a matter of nondelegable duty, that they can neither with nor without the consent of parties litigant delegate the decision of any question within their jurisdiction, once that jurisdiction has been lawfully invoked, to another agency or tribunal, and that any legislative act attempting to authorize such a delegation of authority is inconsistent with those provisions of the Constitution which confer jurisdiction on the trial tribunals. * * *

An analysis of the vital portions of this section shows that:

(a) The Supreme Court has "appellate jurisdiction only" (except where authorized to exercise original jurisdiction);

(b) This "appellate jurisdiction only" is limited in two particulars, viz.: (1) "To questions of law," (2) "Arising in cases of which the Courts of Civil Appeals have appellate jurisdiction."

The jurisdictional provisions of the Constitution relating to Courts of Civil Appeals are found in section 6 of article 5 of the Constitution. * * *

These provisions leave no room for doubt as to the types of jurisdiction which may be conferred upon Courts of Civil Appeals. They are (1) "original" and (2) "appellate." The italicized words in the quotations above definitely and conclusively settle this question.

We think the plain reading of the Constitution concludes the question that the Supreme Court and the Courts of Civil Appeals may exercise only these two classes of jurisdiction. *Yett v. Cook*, 115 Tex. 175, 180, 268 S. W. 715, 281 S. W. 843. Neither is given any advisory power by the organic law and since not given, under the rule expressio unius est exclusio alterius it is denied and can not be conferred by the Legislature.

Since advisory jurisdiction generally is not given under the Constitution and cannot be conferred by the Legislature, and since that authorized by the act before us is not original jurisdiction, it is obvious that if the enactment under which the certificate is before us is to stand the jurisdiction provided for must be found to be within the appellate powers of the Supreme Court and the Courts of Civil Appeals, either as an express grant or incidental to the exercise of the authority granted. The power to determine the constitutionality of a statute or order, etc., is certainly within the appellate power of the revisory courts, but this power can only be invoked in a case within their appellate jurisdiction (or in a case within their original jurisdiction), and in the manner and under conditions contemplated by the Constitution. The question then is when may the appellate jurisdiction of the Supreme Court and of the Courts of Civil Appeals be invoked. The rule in Texas, with exceptions to be hereafter noted, has always been that appellate jurisdiction may be invoked only after trial. * * *

Not only must there be a trial in the inferior court, but the trial must result in a final judgment disposing of all issues and parties before appellate jurisdiction may attach. These rules have been stated and adhered to by the courts without any special discussion of the Constitution, but from a consideration of the statutes then existing. However, a proper interpretation of the Constitution leads us to the same conclusion. The Constitution does not in so many words say that appeals lie only from final judgments, but it does erect a system of trial and appellate courts and gives the latter (aside from their original jurisdiction) only appellate power. The Constitution is to be interpreted in the light of the common law, which has been the rule of decision with us since 1840. The common law limits and determines the meaning of words and phrases used in the Constitution when the context or some other provision of the instrument or some previous enactment existing when the Organic Law was framed does not determine them. * * *

The fact that the statute before us authorizes certified questions to be presented to the appellate courts upon agreement of counsel, and that such an agreement was actually entered into in the instant case, cannot have the effect of conferring jurisdiction upon the appellate courts, nor of relieving the act of its constitutional infirmity. Jurisdiction over the subject-matter of litigation cannot be conferred by agreement. This type of jurisdiction exists by reason of the authority vested in the court by the Constitution, or by statutes not in conflict therewith.

* * *

So interpreting the jurisdictional provisions heretofore quoted by us, it is obvious that the appellate jurisdiction of the Courts of Civil Appeals and that of the Supreme Court (subject to exceptions next to be noted) cannot be invoked until after final judgment of the trial courts of the state. This interpretation of the Organic Law as to the appellate power is not only consistent with the construction given similar language of previous Constitutions, but in complete harmony with our view above expressed that the jurisdiction of our trial courts embraces not only the power and duty to hear causes, but the power and duty to pass upon the facts and law and enter final decrees in accordance therewith; and then to execute their judgments, without interference by any other tribunal, except and until the appellate power of a revisory court is invoked.

The exceptions as to the necessity for final judgments before appeal to which we have referred above are those where the statutes permit appeals from certain interlocutory orders of trial courts, namely, those granting or refusing temporary injunctions, appointing receivers, and determining pleas of privilege. Under these statutes appeals are predicated upon judgments, which though interlocutory in form as effectively deprive the litigant of his rights or his property for the time being as do final judgments or decrees.

The validity of these statutes is referable to the practice in common law chancery courts, to "stare decisis" and the amendment and consequent re-adoption of the jurisdictional section of the Constitution as to the Supreme Court as previously interpreted, and is not here involved. In the case before us neither an interlocutory nor final judgment has ever been rendered and the statute in so far as here involved does not require the entry of decrees before certification.

We know of no rule by which the constitutional basis for existing certification statutes may be extended to the act before us, which calls for advisory action only, and requires no judgment or decree upon which the appellate power of the revisory courts may act.

In view of the importance of the questions involved in the certificate of the district judge, we regret that the jurisdiction of the appellate courts has not been invoked in a constitutional way, so that we might have assisted in their solution at this time.

However, we are clear that we have no jurisdiction of the certificate, that the act under which the certified questions are before us is unconstitutional and void, and no other action may lawfully be taken by us than to dismiss the certificate, as provided by the rules of this court. The certificate of the Court of Civil Appeals is accordingly dismissed.

Notes

1. While advisory opinions are generally prohibited, advisory opinions are permitted by the Texas Supreme Court for federal circuit courts on certified questions. TEX. CONST., Art 5, sec 3-C(a), and TEX. R. APP. PROC. 58. While the constitutional amendment and rules give the Texas Supreme Court jurisdiction to answer the certified question, *Humana Hosp. Corp. v. American Med. Sys. Inc.*, 785 S.W.2d 144, 145 (Tex. 1990), the court will not apply the answer to the facts of the case—that is for the federal court. *Amberboy v. Societe de Banque Privee,* 831 S.W.2d 793, 798 (Tex. 1992). "Any response other than that necessary to answer the question authorized by the Constitution or the enabling rules would be dicta." *Rose v. Doctors Hosp.,* 801 S.W.2d 841, 844 (Tex. 1990).

2. *In the Interest of M. N.*, 262 S.W.3d 799 (Tex. 2008): Under Tex. Const. art. V, § 31(b), the Supreme Court is obligated to promulgate rules of practice and procedure in civil cases. Rules promulgated by the Supreme Court repeal conflicting laws, and parts of laws governing practice and procedure, so long as the laws are non-substantive. The rules of civil procedure are intended to promote just, fair, and equitable resolution of issues.

3. *Hagen v. Hagen,* 282 S.W.3d 899 (Tex. 2009): Doris and Raoul Hagens' 1976 divorce decree awarded a percentage of Raoul's military retirement pay to Doris to be paid if, as, and when he received it. After Raoul's subsequent retirement from the Army, he was determined by the Veterans' Administration (VA) to have a service-connected disability. He then elected to be paid VA disability benefit payments, which are not subject to federal income taxes, in place of part of his military retirement payments, which are subject to income taxes. Raoul's election reduced the amount of military retirement pay he received. When Doris began receiving her percentage of the reduced Army retirement pay Raoul received, she sought enforcement and clarification of the divorce decree. The trial court determined that the decree divided only the military retirement pay being received by Raoul, it did not divide his VA disability benefits, and Doris was entitled to only a percentage of the military retirement pay. The court of appeals reversed. The appeals court held that the trial court modified the 1976 decree instead of clarifying it, and the modification was barred by res judicata principles. ***Held:*** The judgment of the court of appeals is reversed and the judgment of the trial court is affirmed. The trial court correctly clarified the unambiguous original decree, and its action was not a modification barred by res judicata principles. The Hagens' 1976 divorce decree is unambiguous. It provides Doris is to receive a percentage of the Army Retirement Pay or Military Retirement Pay Raoul receives. It does not provide she is to receive payments calculated on any other basis, or that she is to receive part of his VA disability compensation. The trial court's order was a proper clarification of, and not an impermissible modification of, the decree.

4. TEX. R. APP. P. 30: Restricted Appeal to Court of Appeals in Civil Cases

> A party who did not participate—either in person or through counsel—in the hearing that resulted in the judgment complained of and who did not timely file a postjudgment motion or request for findings of fact and conclusions of law, or a notice of appeal within the time permitted by Rule 26.1(a), may file a notice of appeal within the time permitted by Rule 26.1(c). Restricted appeals replace writ of error appeals to the court of appeals. Statutes pertaining to writ of error appeals to the court of appeals apply equally to restricted appeals.

WALDRON
v.
WALDRON
614 S.W.2d 648
(Tex. Civ. App.—Amarillo 1981, no writ).

Arthur J. Lamb, Amarillo, for appellant.
Miner & Hill, Hal Miner, Amarillo, for appellee.

COUNTISS, JUSTICE.

This default judgment divorce case is before us on petition for writ of error[1] perfected in accordance with TEX. REV. CIV. STAT. ANN. art. 2249, et seq. (Vernon 1971) and TEX. R. CIV. P. 359-363. Petitioner Ronald Gordon Waldron (hereafter "Ronald") alleges and Respondent Donna Lee Waldron (hereafter "Donna") judicially admits reversible error. The questions before us are whether (1) a partial, or total, reversal is required and (2) that which is reversed should be rendered or remanded. We reverse the entire judgment and remand the case.

Donna filed suit for divorce in Potter County. She alleged her residence as Amarillo, Potter County, Texas, and Ronald's as Amarillo, Texas. Service of citation was obtained on Ronald in the state of Florida. The Florida sheriff's return on the citation did not comply with Rule 108 because the person serving the citation did not, among other things, state under oath that he was a disinterested person competent to make oath of that fact. Ronald did not make an appearance in the divorce case prior to entry of judgment. The parties have stipulated that no evidence was introduced at the trial to prove Ronald's residence. Donna obtained judgment granting the divorce and awarding her certain items of property, including "The sum of $13,235.00 to be paid to Petitioner (Donna) by Respondent (Ronald) from community funds and property in his possession." Thereafter, she instituted an action against Ronald to enforce property rights granted her under the decree. Ronald then initiated this writ of error proceeding in the divorce case.

Ronald urges two alternative points of error. Under his first point he requests a take-nothing rendition of the portion of the judgment awarding Donna $13,235.00 and affirmance of the remainder of the judgment. Alternatively, under his second point of error, Ronald requests a reversal and remand of the entire case because he was not served in accordance with Rule 108.

Donna admits reversible error because of the defective service. By motion filed prior to submission, and in her brief on the merits, she urges remand of the entire case for new trial.

The service of citation on Ronald was fatally defective because of the incomplete return. *Scucchi v. Woodruff*, 503 S.W.2d 356, 358-60 (Tex. Civ. App. Ft. Worth 1973, no writ). That much is conceded by the parties. However, in arguing his first point, Ronald does not rely on the defective service. Instead, he contends that Donna's failure to prove his residence combined with the fact of service on him in Florida means Donna did not prove facts sufficient to invoke Texas' long-arm jurisdiction over him. Absent such evidence, says Ronald, the trial court never acquired in personam jurisdiction of him. Thus, it could not award Donna the sum of $13,235.00 "from community funds and property in his possession" because that award is a money judgment to be paid from personal property in his possession outside Texas. Yet, because the court did have jurisdiction of the cause of action, Ronald argues, the remainder of the judgment should be affirmed.

In order to resolve the issue, an analysis of the nature of the trial court's jurisdictional power is necessary. The district court in which this case originated had the jurisdictional power to try all issues in the case. TEX. CONST. art. 5, § 8; TEX. REV. CIV. STAT. ANN. art. 1906 (Vernon 1964). That jurisdictional power, however, is dormant potential jurisdiction until it is awakened in the proper manner. "Jurisdiction of a court must be legally invoked; and when not legally invoked, the power to act is as absent as if it did not exist." *State v. Olsen*, 360 S.W.2d 398, 400 (Tex. 1962). In order to invoke the court's jurisdiction various procedural steps must be taken.

[1] Author's note: The procedure formerly known as the Petition for Writ of Error was revised in 1997, and is now referred to as a "restricted appeal." TEX. R. APP. P. 30. Many attorneys were confused because, before this, Texas had a procedure referred to as an "Application for Writ of Error," which was used to appeal from the court of appeals to the Supreme Court. That procedure is now referred to as a Petition for Discretionary Review. TEX. R. APP. P. 53.

See 1 R. McDONALD, TEXAS CIVIL PRACTICE, § 1.04 (rev. 1965). Pertinent to this case is the requirement that persons or property over which the court has potential jurisdiction be brought before the court by service of process that (1) is consistent with due process and (2) follows, with reasonable strictness, the procedure designed by the state for notification of the pending action. *Colson v. Thunderbird Bldg. Materials*, 589 S.W.2d 836, 839-40 (Tex. Civ. App. Amarillo 1979, writ ref'd n. r. e.); 1 R. McDONALD, *supra* § 1.04. Until the court's potential jurisdiction is activated, the court is not authorized to exercise its jurisdictional power.

The effect of an unauthorized exercise of jurisdictional power varies, depending on its demonstrability and the manner in which the judgment is attacked. If a court having potential jurisdiction renders a judgment when the potential jurisdiction has not been activated, and the defect is apparent from the face of the judgment, then the judgment is void and subject to either direct or collateral attack. *Fulton v. Finch*, 162 Tex. 351, 346 S.W.2d 823 (1961). If, as in this case, the court having potential jurisdiction renders a judgment regular on its face that contains recitations stating that potential jurisdiction has been activated, i.e., recitations of due service, then the judgment is voidable, not void, and may be set aside only by a direct attack. *Akers v. Simpson* 445 S.W.2d 957 (Tex. 1969). The latter result is because a court of potential jurisdiction has the power to determine whether its jurisdiction has been activated, and the recitations making that determination are immune from attack in a collateral proceeding. *McEwen v. Harrison*, 162 Tex. 125, 345 S.W.2d 706, 710 (1961). In a direct attack recitations of due service are not conclusive; the record must affirmatively show that the potential jurisdiction was properly activated. *See Whitney v. L & L Realty Corporation*, 500 S.W.2d 94, 95 (Tex. 1973).

The appeal before us is a direct attack on the judgment of the trial court. Despite recitations of due service in the judgment, it is apparent from the record that the potential jurisdiction of the trial court to render the default judgment was never activated, because the procedure designed by the state for notification of the pending action was not followed with reasonable strictness. *Scucchi v. Woodruff*, 503 S.W.2d at 358. Therefore, "the power to act is as absent as if it did not exist," *State v. Olsen*, 360 S.W.2d at 400, and we must declare the judgment void in its entirety.

We cannot, as Ronald requests under his first point, reverse and render part of the judgment and affirm the remainder. First, the record will not support his contention that the judgment awarding Donna $13,235.00 is an attempt by the trial court to exercise control over personal property located outside the state of Texas. The record does not reflect the location of the $13,235.00, which the judgment characterizes as community property. The fact that Ronald was served in Florida is no more than a scintilla of evidence that the $13,235.00 "in his possession" is in his possession outside the state of Texas.

Second, and of greater importance, we cannot ignore a patent jurisdictional defect and approve, in part, action taken by the trial court when it had no power to act. To do so would be to permit Ronald to activate the trial court's jurisdictional power in a manner not sanctioned by statute or rule.

It is also the failure to activate the trial court's jurisdictional power that distinguishes this case from, and makes inapplicable, the cases upon which Ronald relies. In *Fox v. Fox*, 559 S.W.2d 407 (Tex. Civ. App. Austin 1977, no writ), and *Risch v. Risch*, 395 S.W.2d 709 (Tex. Civ. App. Houston 1965, writ dism'd), *cert. denied*, 386 U.S. 10, 87 S.Ct. 881, 17 L.Ed.2d 703 (1967), the spouse who was the respondent in the trial court was apparently served in the manner required by the Rules, but proved an absence of minimum contacts with Texas. The courts held that the divorce, being in rem, could be affirmed but in personam relief against the respondent spouse was a nullity and that portion of the judgment in each case was reversed and rendered in the respondent spouse's favor. In those cases, however, the trial court's jurisdictional power was activated by service on the non-resident spouse that apparently was proper. Thereafter, the in personam jurisdiction over the respondent spouse was carved out because of the absence of minimum contacts. The in rem jurisdiction, however, remained viable. In our case, neither in rem nor in personam jurisdiction having been activated, there is no basis upon which we can affirm any part of the judgment. Notwithstanding a statement to the contrary in *Fox v. Fox*, 559 S.W.2d at 410, even the in rem aspect of a divorce cannot be ex parte.

Ronald's first point of error is overruled. His second point of error is sustained. The judgment of the trial court is reversed and the case is remanded for new trial.

Notes

1. In *Blum v. Savell*, 1994 WL 389039 (Tex. App.—Hous. (1st Dist.) 1994, no writ): Blum argues that Savell's foreclosure and his trustee's deed are invalid because the hearing in the bankruptcy court on the debtor's motion for authorization to incur secured debt was conducted without notice to debtor's creditors. There is conflicting evidence in the record regarding notice. Blum argues that the hearing was void because it violated her due process rights under the United States Constitution. Blum contends the bankruptcy order, which is void, is vulnerable to a collateral attack in any other court of proper jurisdiction. Blum cites *Waldron* to support her argument that the order is void *ab initio*, and may be collaterally attacked. Instead of supporting Blum's claim, the *Waldron* case exposes its weakness. In *Waldron*, the court held that:

> If . . . the court having potential jurisdiction renders a judgment regular on its face that contains recitations stating that potential jurisdiction has been activated, i.e., recitations of due service, then the judgment is voidable, not void, and may be set aside only by a direct attack.

The order authorizing debtor to incur secured debt contains similar recitations of service. The order was not void *ab initio*; it cannot be attacked as void for lack of due process in a collateral proceeding such as this.

2. In *Heth v. Heth*, 661 S.W.2d 303 (Tex App.—Fort Worth 1983, no writ): The primary question on appeal was whether the trial court lacked jurisdiction to enter the divorce decree due to the failure of proper service upon Mrs. Heth. James Heth contends that the trial court's decree was proper because the court had "in rem" jurisdiction over the marital status of the parties based on his domicile within the state. A divorce proceeding has been characterized as quasi in rem. This characterization does not dispense with the due process requirement of adequate notice to a non-resident spouse as noted by the *Waldron* court. Because Nancy Heth was a non-resident of Texas, TEX. R. CIV. P. 108 controlled as to the manner of service of citation upon her. Said rule authorizes service by the same methods as provided by Rule 106, one of which is to leave a copy of the citation and petition with anyone over the age of sixteen at the location specified in the movant's affidavit. *See* TEX. R. CIV. P. 106(b)(2). The rule, however, expressly requires that there be a motion for and order authorizing the use of such substituted service. TEX. R. CIV. P. 106(b). James Heth concedes that there was no such motion nor order authorizing the manner of service used in the instant case, but he argues that Nancy Heth had actual notice of the Texas divorce proceedings. We have been cited to no authority nor have we found any authority for the proposition that actual notice of pending proceedings is sufficient to activate the potential jurisdictional powers of a court. To the contrary, it has been held that where a defendant has not been served in the manner required by law, the court's jurisdiction is not invoked notwithstanding actual notice of the suit on the part of the defendant.

JUD
v.
CITY OF SAN ANTONIO
143 Tex. 303, 184 S.W.2d 821
(1945)

HICKMAN, COMMISSIONER.

This suit was instituted by George F. Jud against the City of San Antonio, the Board of Firemen, Policemen, and Fire Alarm Operator's Pension Fund Trustees of San Antonio, Texas, referred to hereinafter as the Pension Board, and against the Mayor and other individuals alleged to be members of the Pension Board. The plaintiff labeled his pleading a 'petition for declaratory judgment.' To this pleading the defendants filed an answer consisting of a plea to the jurisdiction, exceptions to plaintiff's petition, answer on the alleged facts, and a special answer. The Court set the case for a hearing on the plea to the jurisdiction only and after such hearing entered an order sustaining the plea and dismissing the case at plaintiff's cost. That order was affirmed by the Court of Civil Appeals, 182 S.W.2d 260. * * *

* * *

It is not presently material whether plaintiff alleged a cause of action against the members of the Board individually. It is sufficient for present purposes to note that he does undertake to connect them in some manner with the original fund collected from the City employees, claiming that it was a trust fund in which he had a vested interest, and that in denying his application the Board acted illegally, arbitrarily and maliciously. While he does seek to have the Court supervise the Pension Board and 'rescind their minutes to place the plaintiff on their pension rolls,' and substitute its discretion for that of the Board on the question of granting him a pension, still, as noted, that is not all the relief sought.

It is familiar law that jurisdiction is the power to hear and determine a controversy, which, of course, includes the power to decide whether or not a pleading filed in the court is sufficient to state a cause of action as against the exceptions filed thereto. *Morrow v. Corbin*, 122 Tex. 553, 62 S.W.2d 641; *Texas Employers' Ins. Ass'n v. Ezell, Tex.Com.App.*, 14 S.W.2d 1018; 11 TEX. JUR. p. 711 et seq., Sec. 9.

By Texas Rule of Civil Procedure, No. 90, it is provided that a general demurrer shall not be used. To dismiss a plaintiff's case upon sustaining a plea to the jurisdiction on the ground that his petition is insufficient to state a cause of action when he is praying for judgment for an amount within the jurisdiction of the Court, is even a more summary proceeding than to sustain a general demurrer. This is true for the reason that, upon sustaining a demurrer the Court does not dismiss the case until the plaintiff has been afforded an opportunity to amend, whereas, upon sustaining such plea the plaintiff is not afforded that opportunity.

It would seem that the defendants have proceeded upon the theory that they could establish want of jurisdiction in the Court by showing upon a hearing on the plea to the jurisdiction that certain fact allegations were untrue. They did not stand upon the proposition in the trial court that, as a matter of law on the face of the pleadings, the Court had no potential jurisdiction to hear the case. Their plea contemplated a hearing on the facts, and upon being granted that hearing they placed upon the witness stand one of the members of the Pension Board who testified, under the questioning of their attorney, to the facts in connection with the hearing on plaintiff's application for a pension. In substance and effect his testimony was that the Board did not act arbitrarily or maliciously, but that it accorded the plaintiff a fair hearing and based its order denying the application upon its conclusion that, under the facts plaintiff should not be granted a pension. They argue here that 'in view of the allegations of the petition, and the evidence introduced on the hearing on the plea to the jurisdiction' the Court had no jurisdiction to hear the case. The jurisdiction of a court is not to be determined on that basis. In passing on the plea to its jurisdiction the Court was not authorized to base its ruling upon the conclusion drawn from the evidence that the Board exercised a legitimate discretion in denying the pension and did not act arbitrarily and maliciously, as alleged. The question of whether or not the Board or the individual members thereof should be held liable for money paid into the pension fund is not a question to be determined in limine on a hearing of the plea to the jurisdiction.

* * *

It is ordered that the judgments of both courts below be reversed and the case remanded to the trial court with instructions to reinstate same on its docket. Opinion adopted by the Supreme Court.

Notes

1. *Bullock v. Briggs*, 623 S.W.2d 508 (Tex. 1981). "Appellants' proposition ignores the fundamental difference between subject matter and in personam jurisdiction. The former exists when the nature of the case falls within a general category of cases the court is empowered, under applicable statutory and constitutional provisions, to adjudicate. The latter exists when the statutory procedures for bringing a party within the court's control are followed, and those procedures comport with due process of law; or, it exists if a party appears voluntarily in the proceedings. * * * Whereas subject matter jurisdiction is a fundamental stricture on the power of the court, and appellants' argument would be valid in that respect, in personam jurisdiction may be waived, as it was here, by a voluntary participation in the trial of the suit. *Leroy v. Great Western United Corp.*, 443 U.S. 173, 99 S.Ct. 2710, 61 L.Ed.2d 464 (1979)."

2. *Texas Department of Parks and Wildlife v. Miranda*, 133 S.W.3d 217 (Tex. 2004): Sovereign immunity from suit defeats a trial court's subject matter jurisdiction and thus is properly asserted in a plea to the jurisdiction. The trial court must determine at its earliest opportunity whether it has the constitutional or statutory authority to decide the case before allowing the litigation to proceed.

3. In *Westbrook v. Penley*, 231 S.W.3d 389 (Tex. 2007) the Court discussed whether ecclesiastical matters fell within the jurisdiction of the courts of Texas. Westbrook, the pastor of a church and also a licensed professional counselor, directed his congregation to shun Penley, a former parishioner, for engaging in a "biblically

inappropriate" relationship, which the ecclesiastical disciplinary process outlined in the church's constitution required him to do. Claiming Westbrook had learned the disclosed information in a secular counseling session, Penley filed this suit against him for professional negligence. The trial court dismissed the case, because it was an ecclesiastical dispute, concerning church discipline, which the First and Fourteenth Amendments to the U. S. Constitution precluded the trial court from adjudicating. The court of appeals affirmed the trial court's dismissal of all claims against Westbrook except for professional negligence, which it held concerned Westbrook's role as Penley's secular professional counselor and did not invoke First Amendment concerns. 146 S.W.3d 220, 233. ***Held:*** Reversed and dismissed for want of jurisdiction. It is assumed for purposes of review that the counseling at issue was purely secular in nature. Even so, the Court cannot ignore Westbrook's role as Penley's pastor. In his dual capacity, Westbrook owed Penley conflicting duties; as Penley's counselor he owed her a duty of confidentiality, and as her pastor he owed Penley and the church an obligation to disclose her conduct. Parsing those roles for purposes of determining civil liability in this case, where health or safety are not at issue, would unconstitutionally entangle the court in matters of church governance and impinge on the core religious function of church discipline.

4. *American K-9 Detection Services LLC v Freeman*, 556 S.W.3d 246 (2018): To protect the separation of powers essential to the structure and function of American governments, the political question doctrine teaches that the Judicial Branch will abstain from matters committed by constitution and law to the Executive and Legislative Branches. The complex[,] subtle, and professional decisions as to the composition, training, equipping, and control of a military force are essentially professional military judgments, subject *always* to civilian control of the Legislative and Executive Branches." Among United States military troops stationed in war zones are dogs who protect soldiers and others by sniffing out enemy improvised explosive devices ("IEDs"). The claim in this case is that because of negligent training and handling by private military contractors, one such dog bit the plaintiff on a U.S. Army base in Afghanistan. The defense is that the incident was caused by the Army's use and prescribed manner of quartering the dog. We conclude that the dispute cannot be resolved without inquiry into military judgments that the political question doctrine precludes. We hold that the claim is nonjusticiable and, therefore, the district court correctly dismissed it.

2. *The Basic Court System in Texas*

Note

Jurisdiction can be understood as the power of the court to exercise its judicial function as authorized by the Constitution or statute. In order to be able to exercise power a court must have both actual subject matter jurisdiction over the case or controversy and actual personal jurisdiction over the named party defendant. The Texas Constitution establishes three different types of trial courts—the district court, the constitutional county court, and the justice court. The Constitution gives the legislature the power to establish the jurisdiction of these various courts. Furthermore the Constitution gives the legislature the power to create additional courts by legislative enactment. In response to this power the legislature has established legislative county courts (referred to as county courts at law), statutory probate courts, and municipal courts. The subject matter jurisdiction of all of these courts is determined by either the amount in controversy or the nature the of the suit itself. The Texas Government Code must be consulted in order to determine the exact parameters of a particular court's subject matter jurisdiction.

Of the courts established by the Constitution, the Texas Supreme Court, the Courts of Appeal and the Court of Criminal Appeals are primarily courts of appellate jurisdiction. The intermediate appellate courts in Texas—the courts of appeals—have jurisdiction over both criminal and civil matters. Appeal to these courts in civil cases is a matter of right [assuming the amount in controversy is in excess of $100]. The Texas Supreme Court is the highest court for appeals of civil matters; while the Court of Criminal Appeals is the highest court for criminal appeals. It needs to be noted that each of the appellate courts has limited original jurisdiction. The one which is most frequently used in civil cases is mandamus jurisdiction [the original jurisdiction of appellate courts is the subject of the last chapter of this book].

In the following pages the general constitutional provisions and the basic legislative enactments are included to give the student a basic understanding of the general Texas court jurisdictional scheme. The chart on the next page provides a general overview of the court structure in Texas.

Court Structure of Texas

September 1, 2013

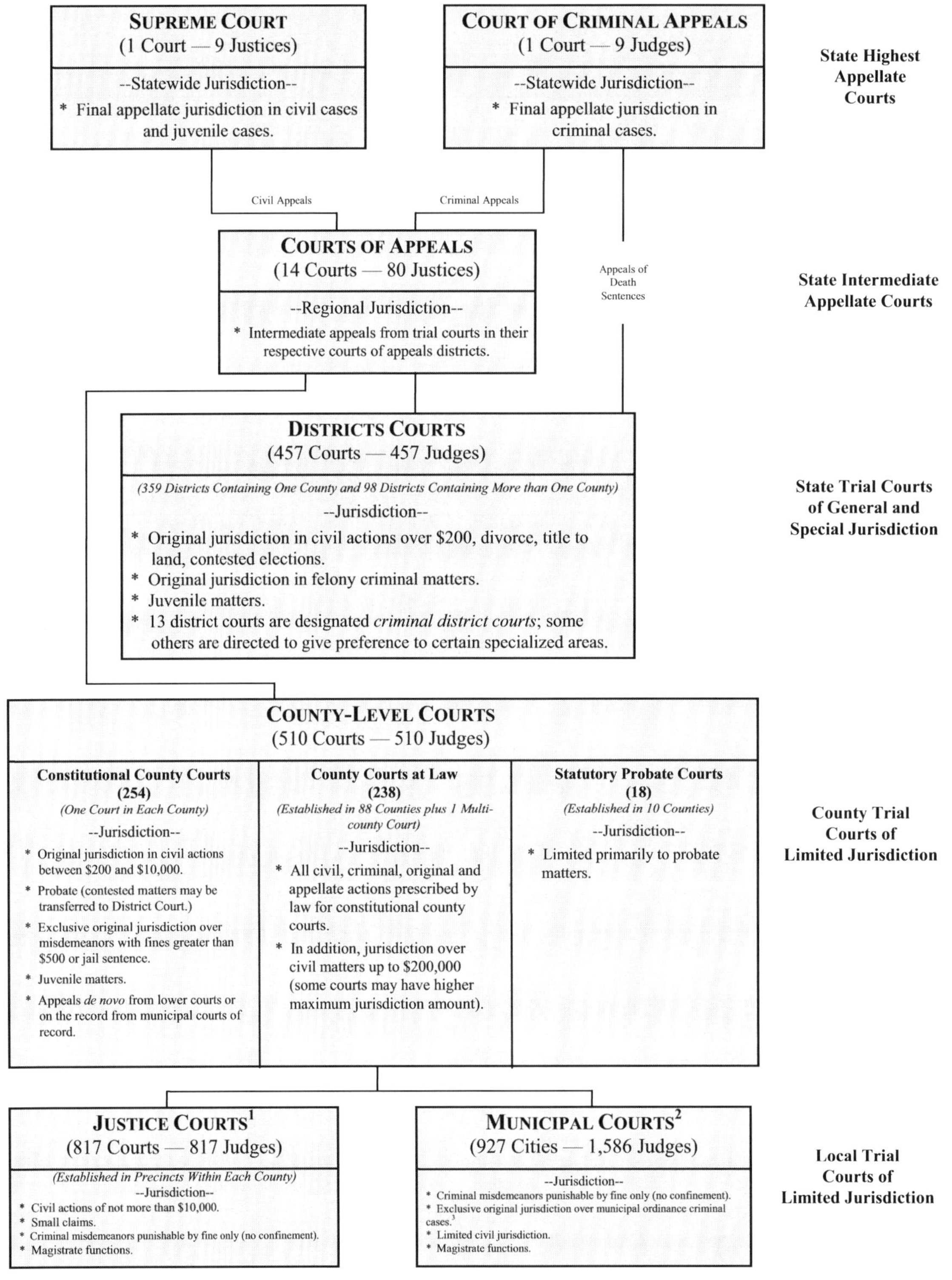

1. All justice courts and most municipal courts are not courts of record. Appeals from these courts are by trial de novo in the county-level courts, and in some instances in the district courts.
2. Some municipal courts are courts of record – appeals from those courts are taken on the record to the county-level courts. As of September 2013, 151 courts indicated that they were a court of record; a list is posted at http://www.courts.state.tx.us/oca/judinfo.asp
3. An offense that arises under a municipal ordinance is punishable by a fine not to exceed: (1) $2,000 for ordinances that govern fire safety, zoning, and public health or (2) $500 for all others.

3. *Constitutional and Statutory Provisions Relating to Subject Matter Jurisdiction*

TEX. CONST. Art. 5

Sec. 1. The judicial power of this State shall be vested in one Supreme Court, in one Court of Criminal Appeals, in Courts of Appeals, in District Courts, in County Courts, in Commissioners Courts, in Courts of Justices of the Peace, and in such other courts as may be provided by law.

The Legislature may establish such other courts as it may deem necessary and prescribe the jurisdiction and organization thereof, and may conform the jurisdiction of the district and other inferior courts thereto.

Sec. 8. District Court jurisdiction consists of exclusive, appellate, and original jurisdiction of all actions, proceedings, and remedies, except in cases where exclusive, appellate, or original jurisdiction may be conferred by this Constitution or other law on some other court, tribunal, or administrative body. District Court judges shall have the power to issue writs necessary to enforce their jurisdiction.

The District Court shall have appellate jurisdiction and general supervisory control over the County Commissioners Court, with such exceptions and under such regulations as may be prescribed by law.

Sec. 16. The County Court has jurisdiction as provided by law. The County Judge is the presiding officer of the County Court and has judicial functions as provided by law. County court judges shall have the power to issue writs necessary to enforce their jurisdiction . . . .

Sec. 19. Justice of the peace courts shall have original jurisdiction in criminal matters of misdemeanor cases punishable by fine only, exclusive jurisdiction in civil matters where the amount in controversy is two hundred dollars or less, and such other jurisdiction as may be provided by law. Justices of the peace shall be ex officio notaries public.

TEX. GOV'T CODE

§ 24.007 District Courts

(a) The district court has the jurisdiction provided by Article V, Section 8, of the Texas Constitution.

(b) A district court has original jurisdiction of a civil matter in which the amount in controversy is more than $500, exclusive of interest.

§ 25.0003 Statutory County Courts

(a) A statutory county court has jurisdiction over all causes and proceedings, civil and criminal, original and appellate, prescribed by law for county courts.

(b) A statutory county court does not have jurisdiction over causes and proceedings concerning roads, bridges, and public highways and the general administration of county business that is within the jurisdiction of the commissioners court of each county.

(c) In addition to other jurisdiction provided by law, a statutory county court exercising civil jurisdiction concurrent with the constitutional jurisdiction of the county court has concurrent jurisdiction with the district court in:

(1) civil cases in which the matter in controversy exceeds $500 but does not exceed $200,000, excluding interest, statutory or punitive damages and penalties, and attorney's fees and costs, as alleged on the face of the petition; and

(2) appeals of final rulings and decisions of the division of workers' compensation of the Texas Department of Insurance regarding workers' compensation claims, regardless of the amount in controversy.

(d) Except as provided by Subsection (e), a statutory county court has, concurrent with the county court, the probate jurisdiction provided by general law for county courts.

(e) In a county that has a statutory probate court, a statutory probate court is the only county court created by statute with probate jurisdiction.

(f) A statutory county court does not have the jurisdiction of a statutory probate court granted statutory probate courts by the Texas Probate Code.

§ 26.041 Constitutional County Courts

A county court has the jurisdiction conferred by this subchapter and other law.

§ 26.042. Constitutional County Courts; Civil Jurisdiction; Juvenile Jurisdiction

(a) A county court has concurrent jurisdiction with the justice courts in civil cases in which the matter in controversy exceeds $200 in value but does not exceed $10,000, exclusive of interest.

(b) A county court has juvenile jurisdiction as provided by Section 23.001.

(c) If under Subchapter E a county court has original concurrent jurisdiction with the justice courts in all civil matters in which the justice courts have jurisdiction, an appeal or writ of error may not be taken to the court of appeals from a final judgment of the county court in a civil case in which:

(1) the county court has appellate or original concurrent jurisdiction with the justice courts; and

(2) the judgment or amount in controversy does not exceed $250, exclusive of interest and costs.

(d) A county court has concurrent jurisdiction with the district court in civil cases in which the matter in controversy exceeds $500 but does not exceed $5,000, exclusive of interest.

(e) A county court has appellate jurisdiction in civil cases over which the justice courts have original jurisdiction in cases in which the judgment appealed from or the amount in controversy exceeds $250, exclusive of costs.

§ 27.031 Justice Courts

(a) In addition to the jurisdiction and powers provided by the constitution and other law, the justice court has original jurisdiction of:

(1) civil matters in which exclusive jurisdiction is not in the district or county court and in which the amount in controversy is not more than $10,000, exclusive of interest;

(2) cases of forcible entry and detainer;

(3) foreclosure of mortgages and enforcement of liens on personal property in cases in which the amount in controversy is otherwise within the justice court's jurisdiction; and

(4) cases arising under Chapter 707, Transportation Code, outside a municipality's territorial limits.

(b) A justice court does not have jurisdiction of:

(1) a suit in behalf of the state to recover a penalty, forfeiture, or escheat;

(2) a suit for divorce;

(3) a suit to recover damages for slander or defamation of character;

(4) a suit for trial of title to land; or

(5) a suit for the enforcement of a lien on land.

(c) A justice court has concurrent jurisdiction with a municipal court in cases that arise in the municipality's extraterritorial jurisdiction and that arise under an ordinance of the municipality applicable to the extraterritorial jurisdiction under Section 216.902, Local Government Code.

(d) A corporation need not be represented by an attorney in justice court.

Given the various constitutional and statutory provisions which confer general jurisdiction on other courts, it can be said that district courts generally have the following jurisdiction in civil cases: cases of divorce, suits for title to land or enforcement of liens on land, contested elections, suits for slander or defamation, suits in behalf of the State for escheat; and all civil cases where the amount in controversy is $200 or more. In those counties having statutory county courts at law, the district courts generally have exclusive jurisdiction in civil cases where the amount in controversy is $100,000 or more and concurrent jurisdiction with the statutory county courts where the amount in controversy exceeds $500 but is less than $100,000.

The legislature as created substantial confusion by creating a multitude of subject matter jurisdictions for the various statutory county courts. As of September 1, 1996, the legislature has created 172 statutory county courts and 19 statutory probate courts. Forty-five of the county courts at law have concurrent jurisdiction with the district court in appeals from decisions of the Texas Workers' Compensation Commission and civil cases when the matter in controversy does not exceed $100,000. One county court has concurrent jurisdiction with the district court in all matters. Four county courts at law have concurrent jurisdiction with district courts in all matters except felony official misconduct, contested elections, and family cases. Fifty three county courts at law have concurrent jurisdiction with district courts in specified family law matters, appeals from decisions of Texas Workers' Compensation Commission, and in civil cases when the matter in controversy does not exceed $100,000. Other statutory county courts have jurisdiction over all family law matters; still others have jurisdiction over suits involving title to land, eminent domain suits, and suits involving slander and defamation. One statutory probate court has concurrent jurisdiction with the district court in eminent domain cases and suits involving title to real or personal property. The list could go on. The point is that in order to determine the exact subject matter jurisdiction of the statutory county court at law or statutory probate court one needs to look at a specific section for the particular county in Chapter 25 of the Texas Government Code. The complexity of the system is shown in the case that follows.

Notes

1. *In re United Services Auto. Ass'n*, 307 S.W.3d 299 (Tex. 2010): The Court noted that Texas has some 3,241 trial courts within its 268,580 square miles. Jurisdiction is limited in many of the courts; it is general in others. Compare TEX. GOV'T CODE § 25.0021 (describing jurisdiction of statutory probate court), with *id.* § 24.007-.008 (outlining district court jurisdiction); *Thomas v. Long*, 207 S.W.3d 334, 340 (Tex. 2006) (noting that Texas district courts are courts of general jurisdiction). We have at least nine different types of trial courts, although that number does not even hint at the complexities of the constitutional provisions and statutes that delineate jurisdiction of those courts. *See* Office of Court Administration, 2008 Annual Report, Texas Judicial System, Subject-Matter Jurisdiction of the Courts passim (2008), available at http:// www.courts.state.tx.us/pubs/AR 2008/jud branch/2a-subject-matter-jurisdiction-of-courts.pdf; George D. Braden et al., *The Constitution of the State of Texas: An Annotated and Comparative Analysis* 367 (1977). Statutory county courts (of which county courts at law are one type) usually have jurisdictional limits of $100,000, *see* TEX. GOV'T CODE § 25.0003(c)(1), unless, of course, they do not, *see, e.g.*, TEX. GOV'T CODE §§ 25.0732(a) (El Paso County), 25.0862(a) (Galveston County), 25.0942(a) (Gregg County), 25.1322(a) (Kendall County), 25.1802(a) (Nueces County), 25.2142(a) (Smith County); *see also Sultan v. Mathew*, 178 S.W.3d 747, 756 (Tex. 2005) (HECHT, J., dissenting) (observing that "[m]onetary jurisdictional limits on statutory county courts are generally from $500 to $100,000, but they vary widely from county to county, and many such courts have no monetary limits"). Appellate rights can vary depending on which court a case is filed in, even among trial courts with concurrent jurisdiction, and even when the same judge in the same courtroom presides over two distinct courts. *See, e.g., Sultan*, 178 S.W.3d at 752 (holding that there was no right of appeal to courts of appeals from cases originating in small claims courts, but recognizing that justice court judgment would be appealable); *see also id.* at 754-55 (HECHT, J., dissenting) (noting that the same justice of the peace hears small claims cases and justice court cases).

The Court also noted the five-step process involved in determining the jurisdiction of any particular trial court:

> [R]ecourse must be had first to the Constitution, second to the general statutes establishing jurisdiction for that level of court, third to the specific statute authorizing the establishment of the particular court in question, fourth to statutes creating other courts in the same county (whose jurisdictional provisions may affect the court in question), and fifth to statutes dealing with specific subject matters (such as the Family Code, which requires, for example, that judges who are lawyers hear appeals from actions by non-lawyer judges in juvenile cases).

Office of Court Administration, Subject-Matter Jurisdiction of the Courts at 1.

In conclusion the Court stated that our court system has been described as "one of the most complex in the United States, if not the world." *Braden*, The Constitution of the State of Texas, at 367; *see also Continental Coffee Prods. Co. v. Cazarez*, 937 S.W.2d 444, 449 (Tex. 1996) (voicing "concern over the difficulties created for the bench, the bar, and the public by the patchwork organization of Texas' several trial courts"); *Sultan*, 178 S.W.3d at 753 (HECHT, J., dissenting) (noting that Texas courts' "jurisdictional scheme . . . has gone from elaborate . . . to Byzantine"); *Camacho v. Samaniego*, 831 S.W.2d 804, 807 n. 4, 811 (Tex. 1992) (stating that "confusion and inefficiency are endemic to a judicial structure with different courts of distinct but overlapping jurisdiction" and observing that "there are still more than fifty different jurisdictional schemes for the statutory county courts"); Texas Judicial Council, Assessing Judicial Workload in Texas' District Courts 2 (2001), available at http://www.courts.state.tx.us/tjc/TJC Reports/Final Report.pdf (observing that " 'the Texas trial court system, complex from its inception, has become ever more confusing as ad hoc responses are devised to meet the needs of an urban, industrialized society' " (quoting Citizens' Commission on the Texas Judicial System, Report and Recommendations-Into the Twenty-First Century 17 (1993).

2. *PR Investments and Specialty Retailers, Inc. v. Texas*, 251 S.W.3d 472 (Tex. 2008): In this condemnation proceeding, the trial court had jurisdiction to try the case de novo and was obliged to exercise that jurisdiction. A court possessed of jurisdiction generally must exercise it. Unless the dismissal was an appropriate sanction for improper conduct, the trial court should have exercised its jurisdiction to decide the case on the merits.

Note

There are additional "courts" in Texas. For example, Title IV-D of the Social Security Act requires states to "provide services relating to the establishment of paternity or the establishment, modification, or enforcement of child support obligations . . . ." 42 U.S.C. § 654(4). The Family Code designates the Attorney General as Texas' Title IV-D agency and sets forth its rights and responsibilities to collect child support. TEX. FAM. CODE §§ 231.001, .0011, .101. The Family Code allows presiding judges to appoint associate judges to handle Title IV-D matters. TEX. FAM. CODE § 201.101, .104.

AMIGO HELICOPTERS, INC.
v.
JONES
488 S.W. 2d 473
(Tex. 1972)

Facts: P filed suit , in a constitutional county court for $3,019.50, plus $1,207.80 in attorneys fees. At that time, the maximum amount in controversy for the constitutional county court was $1,000.

Issue: Does an action above the dollar jurisdiction of a court deprive that court of jurisdiction?

Held: Yes, the court could not take jurisdiction of this case.

There is a distinction between constitutional county courts and statutory county courts. An action for more than the dollar amount jurisdiction of the constitutional county court (then $1,000—now $5,000) was beyond the jurisdiction of the constitutional county court, and had to be brought in the legislative county court or the district court.

4. *Nature of Suit as Basis for Subject Matter Jurisdiction*

***Ex parte* BRYANT**
155 Tex. 219, 285 S.W.2d 719
(1956)

Issue: Did the Constitutional County Court have jurisdiction to issue an injunction enjoining the operation of a bawdy house (a house of prostitution)?

Held: No. There must be a fixed amount in controversy for a constitutional county court to have jurisdiction to issue an injunction. Thus, the constitutional county court does not have jurisdiction to enjoin the operation of a bawdy house. [The district court has residual jurisdiction, and, thus, has jurisdiction of such a case.]

Note

AIC Management v. Crews, 246 S.W.3d 640 (Tex. 2008): Generally, pursuant to TEX. GOV'T CODE § 25.0003(c)(1), the subject-matter jurisdiction of statutory county courts is limited to "cases in which the matter in controversy exceeds $500 but does not exceed $100,000." Without reference to amounts in controversy, TEX. PROP. CODE § 21.002 requires a county court at law before which an eminent-domain proceeding is pending to transfer the case to the district court upon determining that the controversy involves "an issue of title." Finally, section 25.1032 of the Government Code grants specific jurisdiction over "all civil matters and causes, original and appellate, prescribed by law for county courts" and exclusive jurisdiction "in Harris County of eminent domain proceedings, both statutory and inverse, regardless of the amount in controversy." Section 25.1032 also provides that such courts have jurisdiction to decide the issue of title to real or personal property. In Harris County, the county civil courts' jurisdiction to decide issues of title, arising out of condemnation proceedings, is in addition to their general concurrent jurisdiction described in section 25.0003(c) and is not dependent upon the amount in controversy.

BAILEY
v.
CHEROKEE COUNTY APPRAISAL DIST.

862 S.W.2d 581
(Tex. 1993)

William E. Bailey, Dallas, for petitioners.
F. Duane Force, Peter W. Low, Austin, Rodney B. Dowd, Longview, Tab Beall, Tyler, for respondents.

SPECTOR, JUSTICE.

Respondents' motions for rehearing are granted in part and overruled in part. The court's opinion and judgment of June 3, 1993 are withdrawn, and the following is substituted therefor.

This cause presents the question whether a suit to collect ad valorem taxes accruing on estate property during administration is a claim against the estate, properly filed in probate court, or a claim for which heirs are personally liable. The court of appeals held that the heirs are personally liable for the taxes and that a district court has concurrent jurisdiction with a statutory probate court over this matter. 817 S.W.2d 117 (1991). Because we hold that the present suit constitutes a claim against the estate which should have been filed in the probate court in which the administration was pending, we reverse the judgment of the court of appeals and dismiss the taxing authorities' claims without prejudice.

In 1973, W.E. Bailey died intestate in Cherokee County, Texas, survived by his wife, Petitioner Alibe Carter Bailey, and two adult sons, Petitioners William E. Bailey and Robert E. Bailey. At the time of his death, W.E. and Alibe Carter Bailey owned as community property land located in Cherokee County. Alibe Carter Bailey was appointed administrator of the estate in the intestate dependent administration.

Following commencement of the dependent administration, Respondents, Cherokee County, Cherokee County Appraisal District, and the City of Jacksonville, filed suit in the District Court of Cherokee County against the Baileys jointly and severally, seeking a personal judgment in the amount of $90,608.48 for tax years 1976-1986, and foreclosure of tax liens for delinquent property taxes, interest, and fees which had accrued subsequent to the decedent's death. The district court rendered a judgment ordering foreclosure of the tax liens, but denied the taxing authorities' prayers for personal judgment against the Baileys. The court of appeals reversed and remanded, holding that the taxing authorities were entitled to the personal judgment. 817 S.W.2d at 120. * * * [The Court first determined that ad valorem taxes accruing on estate property during administration were a claim against the estate].

Because the present action constitutes a claim against the estate filed after administration had begun in the county court at law sitting in probate, jurisdiction lies with the county court.

In those counties where there are statutory courts exercising probate jurisdiction, such courts share original jurisdiction over probate proceedings with the constitutional county court, to the exclusion of the district court.

TEX. PROB. CODE § 5(c). Accordingly, administration of the Bailey estate was properly initiated in the Cherokee County Court at Law.

The Probate Code further provides that "[a]ll courts exercising original probate jurisdiction shall have the power to hear all matters incident to an estate." TEX. PROB. CODE § 5(e). With regard to proceedings in statutory county courts, "matters incident to an estate" are defined to include "all claims by or against an estate" and "all actions for trial of title to land and for the enforcement of liens thereon incident to an estate." TEX. PROB. CODE § 5A(a). The instant suit constitutes a "claim against the estate" rather than a claim for which the putative heirs may be held personally liable. The suit is, moreover, an action "for the enforcement of liens" on land which is "incident to the estate." In sum, this suit pertains to matters incident to the estate and the county court at law is vested with jurisdiction over it. *See Blair v. State*, 640 S.W.2d 867, 869 (Tex. 1982) ("The scheme for administration of estates is that claims should be submitted to the probate court for classification and then paid through orders of the probate court.").

When sitting in probate, the county court at law is empowered to enforce creditors' claims against the estate. A creditor may petition the court to order payment of the claim; if funds on hand are insufficient, the court may order the sale of estate property. TEX. PROB. CODE § 326; *see also Rivera v. Morales*, 733 S.W.2d 677, 678 (Tex. App.—San Antonio 1987, writ ref'd n.r.e.) (an administrator has a duty to pay creditors pursuant to orders of the probate court). If the administrator refuses to make a court-ordered payment, the creditor may have execution issued against the property for the amount owed, plus interest and costs. TEX. PROB. CODE § 328(a). Alternatively, the court may cite the representative and sureties to show cause why they should not be held liable for the debt, as well as interest, costs and damages. TEX. PROB. CODE § 328(b).

Instead of submitting their claim to the county court, the taxing authorities filed suit in the district court. The record reflects that the Baileys filed a "Plea in Abatement and Motion for Dismissal of Cause" in the district court, urging that the taxing authorities' action be dismissed for want of jurisdiction. The district court in its final judgment denied the Baileys' motion to dismiss.

The taxing authorities argue that because the district court is empowered with original probate jurisdiction, it has jurisdiction to hear matters incident to the estate. We disagree. A court empowered with probate jurisdiction may only exercise its probate jurisdiction over matters incident to an estate when a probate proceeding related to such matters is already pending in that court. *See Interfirst Bank-Houston v. Quintana Petroleum*, 699 S.W.2d 864, 873 (Tex. App.—Houston [1st Dist.] 1985, writ ref'd n.r.e.). Thus, because the ongoing administration in the county court at law sitting in probate was the only probate proceeding pending, that court alone had jurisdiction over matters incident to the estate.

Furthermore, the court in which suit is first filed acquires dominant jurisdiction to the exclusion of coordinate courts. *Curtis v. Gibbs*, 511 S.W.2d 263, 267 (Tex. 1974). Because the administration was already pending in the county court when this suit was filed in the district court, the jurisdiction of the county court is dominant. *See Thomas v. Tollon*, 609 S.W.2d 859, 860 (Tex. App.—Houston [14th Dist.] 1981, writ ref'd n.r.e.) (where county court originally exercised jurisdiction over the estate of decedent it was the proper court to determine matters incident to the estate).

We hold that the estate bears the liability for ad valorem taxes accruing during administration and that therefore the Bailey heirs may not be held personally liable prior to distribution. The present suit to collect the taxes is a claim against the estate over which the probate court maintained exclusive jurisdiction once the administration commenced in that court. We reverse the judgment of the court of appeals and dismiss the taxing authorities' claims. Our disposition of this cause is without prejudice to any right of the taxing authorities to present claims incident to the estate in the county court at law sitting in probate. * * *

GONZALEZ, J., dissenting, joined by HIGHTOWER and ENOCH, JJ. [opinion omitted].

Note

In 1973 the legislature amended Section 5 of the Probate Code to limit probate court jurisdiction to matters "appertaining to" and "incident to" estates. The legislature was trying to limit probate court jurisdiction to matters in which <u>the controlling issue</u> was the settlement, partition, or distribution of an estate. In *Seay v. Hall*, 677 S.W.2d 19 (1984), the Court held that the probate court lacked jurisdiction to try a wrongful death or survival action, because it was not a matter incident to or appertaining to an estate, i.e., <u>the controlling issue</u> in the wrongful death action was not the settlement, partition or distribution of the estate. Furthermore, such action was not a claim against the estate because it was not for a specified sum owed. A claim is a debt of a liquidated nature due an estate. In 1985 and again in 1987 Section 5 of the Probate Code was amended to give the statutory probate courts concurrent jurisdiction with district courts in actions by or against a personal representative or in matters involving an inter vivos trust. Hence, the direct result in *Seay v. Hall* was reversed by the legislature, i.e., the statutory probate court has jurisdiction of a survival action or one for wrongful death *where a personal representative is joined.*

PALMER
v.
COBLE WALL TRUST CO.
851 S.W.2d 178
(Tex. 1992)

Thomas C. Hall, San Antonio, for petitioners.
Tony L. Schaffer, Barry A. McClenahan, San Antonio, for respondents.

GONZALEZ, JUSTICE.

This case addresses the scope of a statutory probate court's jurisdiction under § 5A(b) of the Texas Probate Code as it existed in 1985. William Palmer, the independent administrator of an estate, brought this suit in statutory probate court against Coble Wall Trust Company, Inc., the estate's former temporary administrator, and Elwood Cluck, president of Coble Wall. The suit alleged negligence, gross negligence, and violations of the DTPA, which included breach of fiduciary duty and misrepresentations of the estate plan's characteristics. Based on favorable jury findings for the plaintiff, the probate court rendered judgment for Palmer. The court of appeals reversed and rendered for Coble Wall and Cluck on the basis that the probate court lacked subject matter jurisdiction over the suit. 848 S.W.2d 696. Because the probate court did not exceed its subject matter jurisdiction, we reverse the judgment of the court of appeals and remand the cause to that court for consideration of the unaddressed points of error.

I.

In April 1985, the statutory probate court appointed Coble Wall as guardian of the estate of Booney M. Moore, an adjudicated incompetent. In November 1985, Cluck, an attorney and the sole stockholder and president of Coble Wall, applied for an order to authorize the establishment of an administrative plan for Moore's estate. The probate court issued an order approving the estate plan, and Moore's properties were then either sold or conveyed to her beneficiaries, pledged as collateral for bonds, or converted into various types of corporate shares. The probate court subsequently approved an order that Coble Wall be paid the greater of either $75,000 or 10% of the reduction in federal taxes achieved by the plan, plus 5% of the gross value of various property and stocks when sold.

Upon Moore's death in December 1985, Coble Wall was appointed temporary administrator of the estate with the power to complete the previously approved estate plan. Coble Wall continued as temporary administrator until March 1986, when the probate court removed it and appointed Palmer as independent administrator of Moore's estate.

In 1987, Palmer filed suit against Coble Wall and Cluck in the probate court alleging the aforementioned causes of action. Palmer also alleged that the estate plan had been ineffective, exorbitant, and needlessly complex, all of which forced the estate to pay useless and excessive fees. The jury found that Coble Wall and Cluck were guilty of negligence, gross negligence, breach of fiduciary duties, and breach of the DTPA; the jury also found that Coble Wall was the alter ego of Cluck. Based upon these findings, the probate court rendered judgment for Palmer and awarded damages of $1,757,600 against Coble Wall and $1,757,600 against Cluck.

II.

Texas Probate Code § 5A(b) sets forth the subject matter jurisdiction of statutory probate courts.[2] The court of appeals determined that the 1985 version of the Code applied to this cause of action. This version stated that:

> In proceedings in the statutory probate courts and district courts, the phrases "appertaining to estates" and "incident to an estate" in this Code include the probate of wills, the issuance of letters testamentary and of administration, and the determination of heirship, and also include, but are not limited to, all claims by or against an estate, all actions for trial of title to land and for the enforcement of liens thereon, all actions for trial of the right of property, all actions to construe wills, the interpretation and administration of testamentary trusts and the applying of constructive trusts, and generally all matters relating to the settlement, partition, and distribution of estates of wards and deceased persons. All statutory probate courts may, in the exercise of their jurisdiction, notwithstanding any other provisions of this Code, hear all suits, actions, and applications filed against or on behalf of any guardianship, heirship proceeding, or decedent's estate, including estates administered by an independent executor . . . . In situations where the jurisdiction of a statutory probate court is concurrent with that of a district court, any cause of action appertaining to estates or incident to an estate shall be brought in a statutory probate court rather than in the district court. In actions by or against a personal representative, the statutory probate courts have concurrent jurisdiction with the district courts. TEX. PROB. CODE § 5A(b) (1985).[3]

---

[2] Texas probate jurisdiction is, to say the least, somewhat complex. The Probate Code vests general probate jurisdiction in the constitutional county courts. TEX. PROB. CODE § 4 (1980). The Government Code, however, extends probate jurisdiction to the statutory county courts as follows: (d) Except as provided by Subsection (e), a statutory county court has, concurrent with the county court, the probate jurisdiction provided by general law for county courts. (e) In a county that has a statutory probate court, a statutory probate court is the only county court created by statute with probate jurisdiction. TEX. GOV'T CODE § 25.0003 (Supp.1992). Thus, a statutory county court has concurrent probate jurisdiction, unless there is also in that county a "statutory probate court." In the latter case, only the statutory probate court exercises probate jurisdiction concurrent with the constitutional county court. *See* TEX. GOV'T CODE § 25.0021 (1988). A "statutory probate court" is defined as: [A]ny statutory court . . . the jurisdiction of which is limited by statute to the general jurisdiction of a probate court, and such courts whose statutorily designated name contains the word "probate." County courts at law exercising probate jurisdiction are not statutory probate courts under this Code unless their statutorily designated name includes the word "probate." TEX. PROB. CODE § 3(ii) (1980). A statutory probate court is not considered to be a statutory county court, except in Brazoria County. TEX. GOV'T CODE § 21.009(2) (Supp.1992). However, there are statutory courts in two other counties designated as "Probate and County" courts which exercise both probate and county court at law jurisdiction. TEX. GOV'T CODE § 25.0171(a) (Supp.1992) (Bexar); § 25.0861(b) (Supp.1992) (Galveston). To further complicate matters, the district courts exercise some probate jurisdiction. The Probate Code provides that "[t]he district court shall have original control and jurisdiction over executors, administrators, guardians and wards under such regulations as may be prescribed by law." TEX. PROB. CODE § 5(a) (Supp.1992). In those counties where there is no statutory court exercising probate jurisdiction, most probate matters must be filed in the constitutional county court, *id.* § 5(b); however, the county judge may transfer contested matters to the district court, which may then hear them "as if originally filed in district court." *Id.* In this situation the county court retains jurisdiction over the uncontested portions of the case. *Id.* The county judge may also request the assignment of a statutory probate judge to hear contested matters. *Id.* In counties where there is a statutory court exercising probate jurisdiction, most probate matters must be filed and heard in the statutory court or the constitutional county court, rather than the district court, "unless otherwise provided by the legislature." *Id.* § 5(c). The county judge may transfer contested probate matters to one of the statutory courts, but not to the district court. *Id.* Examples of where the legislature has altered the general rule of Section 5 are Anderson County, where the statutory county court has concurrent jurisdiction with the district court over all probate matters, and Parker County, where the statutory county court has concurrent jurisdiction with the district court over contested probate matters. *See* TEX. GOV'T CODE §§ 25.0032, 25.1863 (1992). District courts and statutory probate courts have concurrent jurisdiction "in all actions by or against a person in the person's capacity as a personal representative, in all actions involving an inter vivos trust, in all actions involving a charitable trust, and in all actions involving a testamentary trust." TEX. PROB. CODE § 5(d) (1992).

[3] The 1987 amendment to the Texas Probate Code § 5A(b) modified the last sentence of that section to read: "In actions by or against a personal representative, or in matters involving an inter vivos trust, the statutory pro-

The court of appeals held that the probate court lacked subject matter jurisdiction over the suit, because it was not a suit "appertaining to" or "incident to" the estate. 848 S.W.2d at 701-02. In making this determination, the court relied heavily on our decision in *Seay v. Hall*, 677 S.W.2d 19 (Tex. 1984), in which this Court held that probate courts did not have jurisdiction over wrongful death and survival claims. In *Seay*, we stated that the "appertaining to an estate and incident to an estate" language was designed to limit probate court jurisdiction to matters in which the controlling issue was the settlement, partition, or distribution of an estate. *Id.* at 24. Thus, the court of appeals reasoned that the outcome of Palmer's claims failed to meet this test and was "not necessary to the resolution of the estate." 848 S.W.2d at 703. In 1985, the legislature responded to Seay by amending the Texas Probate Code to broaden statutory probate court jurisdiction. The 1985 amendment added the last sentence to § 5A which provided that "[i]n actions by or against a personal representative, the statutory probate courts have concurrent jurisdiction with the district court." TEX. PROB. CODE § 5A(b) (1985). We agree with the court of appeals' assessment in *Pearson v. K-Mart*, 755 S.W.2d 217, 219 (Tex. App.—Houston [1st Dist.] 1988 no writ) that "it is readily apparent that the purpose of [House Bill 479] was to overrule *Seay v. Hall*." Nevertheless, many courts of appeals have continued to apply the "controlling issue" test set out in Seay in their determination of whether a claim is "appertaining to" or "incident to" an estate. *See, e.g., Bruflat v. Rodeheaver*, 830 S.W.2d 821, 823 (Tex. App.—Houston [1st Dist.] 1992, no writ); *Carlisle v. Bennett*, 801 S.W.2d 589, 591 (Tex. App.—Corpus Christi 1990, no writ); *Crawford v. Williams*, 797 S.W.2d 184, 185 (Tex. App.—Corpus Christi 1990, no writ); *Qwest Microwave, Inc. v. Bedard*, 756 S.W.2d 426, 436 (Tex. App.—Dallas 1988, no writ). However, continued application of this test in the context of the 1985 amendment is inconsistent with that amendment's purpose. The controlling issue in wrongful death and survival actions is not the settlement, partition, and distribution of the estate. A wrongful death recovery is a means of providing the statutory beneficiaries a remedy for the loss of their loved one because of another's wrongful conduct; the estate does not benefit from this recovery. While a survival recovery may impact the assets of the estate to be distributed, this is obviously not the controlling issue. Therefore, to apply the "controlling issue" test in the context of the 1985 amendment would be to deny probate courts jurisdiction over wrongful death and survival actions, in direct contravention of the purpose of the amendment. The court of appeals, in denying the probate court jurisdiction over Palmer's claims, relied on *Qwest Microwave, Inc. v. Bedard, supra*. We agree with the holding in *Qwest* that the 1985 amendment to § 5A(b) "conferred jurisdiction upon the probate courts to hear claims that might not be fully liquidated but that nonetheless are brought by a personal representative in his capacity of personal representative administering an estate." 756 S.W.2d at 436-37. However, as previously discussed, we disagree with *Qwest* insofar as it states that by amending the statute in 1985, "the legislature did not intend to expand probate jurisdiction to matters other than those in which the controlling issue was the settlement, partition, or distribution of an estate." *Id.* at 436.

When the 1985 amendment is not implicated, the "controlling issue" test has useful application in determining whether a claim is "appertaining to" or "incident to" an estate. In 1989, the legislature again amended § 5A and gave probate courts jurisdiction over claims by or against personal representatives "whether or not the matter is appertaining to or incident to an estate." TEX. PROB. CODE § 5A(e).[4] This amendment dispensed with the need to make this inquiry in suits involving a personal representative. However, the need for an ascertainable meaning of "appertaining to or incident to" an estate still exists in certain circumstances. Therefore, we confirm our reasoning in Seay that a suit is "appertaining to or incident to" an estate when the controlling issue is the settlement, partition, or distribution of an estate insofar as it does not apply to suits by or against a personal representative.[5]

---

bate courts have concurrent jurisdiction with the district courts." *See* Act of June 17, 1987, 70th Leg., R.S. ch. 459, § 1, 1987 TEX. GEN. LAWS 2043, 2044.

[4] The 1989 amendment to § 5A reads as follows: A statutory probate court has concurrent jurisdiction with the district court in all actions: (1) by or against a person in the person's capacity as a personal representative; (2) involving an inter vivos trust; (3) involving a charitable trust; and (4) involving a testamentary trust. (d) A statutory probate court may exercise the pendent and ancillary jurisdiction necessary to promote judicial efficiency and economy. (e) Subsections and (d) apply whether or not the matter is appertaining to or incident to an estate.

[5] Because of the 1989 amendment, which separates the "appertaining to" or "incident to" an estate language from suits involving a personal representative, today's decision only impacts suits brought before September 1, 1989.

While it is true that the 1985 amendment was enacted in order to give probate courts jurisdiction over wrongful death and survival actions, the wording of this amendment and the legislative history behind its enactment contemplates a broader application. In fact, as noted in the House Research Organization report on the amendment, the original HB 479 stated specifically that statutory probate courts would have jurisdiction over survival and wrongful death actions, but it was changed to the more expansive wording of "in actions by or against a personal representative." It is evident that this suit falls within the plain meaning of the 1985 amendment.

The Texas Probate Code § 3(aa) defines "personal representative" as including "executor, independent executor, administrator, independent administrator, temporary administrator, guardian, and temporary guardian, together with their successors." TEX. PROB. CODE § 3(aa) (1980). As independent administrator of the estate, Palmer was Moore's personal representative. Further, as temporary administrator, Coble Wall acted as Moore's personal representative. Therefore, this suit filed by Palmer, the current independent administrator, against Coble Wall, the prior temporary administrator, was a suit filed by a personal representative against a personal representative. As such, under the 1985 Probate Code, the probate court had concurrent jurisdiction with the district court.

We reverse the judgment of the court of appeals and remand the cause to that court so that it can resolve the remaining unaddressed points of error.

CORNYN, J., dissenting [opinion omitted].

Notes

1. Before 1987, the Government Code specified that district courts had exclusive jurisdiction over divorces. The revised section, TEX. GOV'T CODE § 24.007, states that "[t]he district court has the jurisdiction provided by Article V, Section 8, of the Texas Constitution." In turn, article V, section 8 bridles the exclusive jurisdiction of district courts, when jurisdiction is conferred on another court. The Probate Code confers jurisdiction on statutory probate courts to hear matters appertaining to or incident to a guardianship estate. Thus, current Texas law does not impede a probate court from providing all necessary relief in a divorce action, when it properly transfers to itself a cause of action appertaining or incident to a guardianship estate.

2. *In Re Graham,* 971 S.W.2d 56 (Tex. 1988): A statutory probate court has authority under Probate Code section 608 to transfer to itself from district court a divorce proceeding when one party to the divorce is a ward of the probate court. Section 608 of the Probate Code authorizes a statutory probate court to transfer to itself a matter appertaining to or incident to a pending estate. A cause of action is appertaining or incident to an estate, if section 607 of the Probate Court explicitly defines it as such, or if the controlling issue in the suit is the settlement, partition, or distribution of an estate. Section 607 defines the term "appertaining to or incident to an estate" to include, among other things, "all actions for trial of the right of property incident to a guardianship estate, and generally all matters relating to the settlement, partition, and distribution of a guardianship estate." The divorce proceeding itself is appertaining to or incident to the guardianship estate.

CARROLL
v.
CARROLL
304 S.W.3d 366
(Tex. 2010)

Johnny Carroll, Whitney, pro se.

William Brent Shellhorse, Whitaker Chalk Swindle & Sawyer, L.L.P., Fort Worth, TX, Patrick Gordon Barkman, Cleburne, TX, for petitioner.

Bennett Brantley Aufill, Hillsboro, TX, S. Clinton Nix, Bradbury & Nix, Abilene, TX, for respondents.

PER CURIAM.

In this case, the 66th District Court of Hill County transferred a suit seeking the removal of a trustee and other relief to the county court at law. When the suit was filed, the Texas Property Code provided that district courts have original and exclusive jurisdiction over all proceedings concerning trusts, including proceedings to appoint or remove a trustee, determine the liability of a trustee, or require an accounting by a trustee. Act of May 26, 1997, 75th Leg., R.S., ch. 1375, § 5, 1997 Tex. Gen. Laws 5162, 5163 (amended 2005 and 2007) (current version at TEX. PROP. CODE § 115.001(a)). Because the Texas Property Code vests exclusive jurisdiction over the claims in this case in the district court, we hold that the county court at law had no jurisdiction to grant the relief sought and the judgment it rendered was void.

Letha and Ray Carroll were the parents of Johnny and Donald. Ray Carroll died in 1987, leaving an irrevocable testamentary trust called the Johnny Carroll Trust. Ray named Johnny as the trustee and Letha as the beneficiary of the trust. In November 2005, Donald and Letha sued Johnny, individually and as trustee, in the 66th District Court of Hill County. They alleged that Johnny failed to provide an accounting, engaged in self-dealing, wasted trust assets, and failed to file income tax returns. Donald and Letha requested that the court order an accounting, remove Johnny as trustee, and award damages for his alleged misconduct.

In February 2006, the case was transferred to the Hill County Court at Law. By partial summary judgment that court removed Johnny as trustee, ordered him to provide an accounting, and ordered the trust records to be turned over to Donald, the successor trustee. In a final default judgment signed October 3, 2006, the county court awarded Donald and Letha $1 million for breach of fiduciary duty, $2.8 million in exemplary damages, and $15,000 in attorney's fees. Johnny filed a motion for new trial on January 5, 2007, claiming he never received notice of the October 3 trial setting and did not receive notice of the default judgment until December 4. The county court never ruled on the motion and it was overruled by operation of law.

Johnny appealed, and Letha filed a brief in support requesting that the default judgment be set aside and the case remanded for a jury trial. The court of appeals treated the county court's failure to rule on the motion for new trial as an implied finding that Johnny received timely notice of the default judgment. 304 S.W.3d 414, 2008 WL 2404548. Thus, the court of appeals treated Johnny's motion for new trial as untimely and deemed his appeal a restricted appeal. *Id.* at 420. Finding no error apparent on the face of the record, the court denied Johnny's restricted appeal. *Id.* at 420. The court of appeals did, however, strike the $2.8 million exemplary damages award because Donald and Letha's pleadings failed to assert any claim that would support punitive damages. *Id.* at 417. Johnny filed this petition for review, to which only Letha responded, again in favor of Johnny's petition.

Johnny challenges the county court's jurisdiction over the case for the first time in this Court. Jurisdiction over the subject matter of an action may not be conferred or taken away by consent or waiver, and its absence may be raised at any time. *Tex. Ass'n of Bus. v. Tex. Air Control Bd.,* 852 S.W.2d 440, 445 (Tex. 1993). Accordingly, Johnny's failure to assert the jurisdictional defect below does not preclude our review.

When the suit was filed, section 115.001 of the Texas Property Code provided:

> a district court has original and exclusive jurisdiction over all proceedings concerning trusts, including proceedings to . . . appoint or remove a trustee; . . . determine the . . . liability of a trustee; [and] require an accounting by a trustee.

TEX. PROP. CODE § 115.001(a). The only exceptions to the district court's exclusive jurisdiction are limited and do not apply here.

Texas Government Code section 25.0003 governs the jurisdiction of county courts at law, also known as statutory county courts, and vests them with concurrent jurisdiction with the district courts in certain worker's compensation cases and in civil cases in which the matter in controversy exceeds $500, but does not exceed $100,000, as alleged on the face of the petition. TEX. GOV'T CODE § 25.0003(c). However, that section also explicitly states that statutory county courts do not have the jurisdiction granted to statutory probate courts by the Texas Probate Code. *Id.* § 25.0003(f). The jurisdiction of the Hill County Court at Law is specifically governed by Texas Government Code section 25.1112, which grants the court concurrent jurisdiction with the district court in felony cases and family law cases and proceedings. *Id.* § 25.1112(a). The district courts may only assign cases to the county courts at law that are within the county court at law's jurisdiction. *See id.* §§ 25.1112(g), (h). Neither section 25.1112 nor section 25.0003 provide a statutory county court with concurrent jurisdiction when another court is vested with exclusive jurisdiction. *See, e.g., AIC Mgmt. v. Crews,* 246 S.W.3d 640 (Tex. 2008) (holding that subject matter jurisdiction is determined by the more specific statute). *See also* TEX. GOV'T CODE § 25.0001(a). Nothing in the Texas Government Code confers jurisdiction upon the Hill County Court at Law over proceedings listed in Texas Property Code section 115.001. *See id.* §§ 25.0003, 25.1112.

In this case, Johnny and Letha sought removal of a trustee, an accounting by a trustee, and appointment of a successor trustee, together with money damages and attorney's fees. Removal of a trustee, an accounting by a trustee, and appointment of a successor trustee are all "proceedings concerning a trust" expressly governed by the statute and fall under the exclusive jurisdiction of the district court. TEX. PROP. CODE § 115.001(a). As such, transfer to the Hill County Court at Law was improper because it was apparent from the pleadings that the county court lacked jurisdiction over the claims. Because the Hill County Court at Law had no jurisdiction over the claims, its judgment was void. *See State ex rel. Latty v. Owens,* 907 S.W.2d 484, 485 (Tex. 1995). Because the county court's judgment was void, we do not reach Johnny's other arguments challenging the judgment.

Accordingly, without hearing argument, we grant the petition for review, reverse the court of appeals' judgment, vacate the county court's judgment, and remand the case to the county court with instructions to transfer the case back to the 66th District Court of Hill County for further proceedings. *See* TEX. R. APP. P. 59.1.

SCHLICHTING
v.
LEHMAN BROTHERS BANK FSB

346 S.W.3d 196
(Tex. App.—Dallas 2011, pet. filed)

Facts: Purchaser of property at non-judicial foreclosure sale brought forcible entry and detainer action, seeking writ of possession of property after mortgagor failed to vacate premises. The County Court at Law No. 4, Dallas County, Ken Tapscott, J., entered judgment of possession in purchaser's favor, and mortgagor appealed.

Appellant concedes that a justice court or county court at law is not deprived of jurisdiction in a forcible detainer action merely because of the existence of a title dispute. Indeed, in most cases the right to immediate possession can be determined separately from the right to title. The trial court is deprived of jurisdiction only if the determination of the right to immediate possession necessarily requires the resolution of the title dispute. This is not such a case.

Where a foreclosure pursuant to a deed of trust establishes a landlord and tenant-at-sufferance relationship between the parties, the trial court has an independent basis to determine the issue of immediate possession without resolving the issue of title to the property. In this case, as stated above, the foreclosure pursuant to the deed of trust created a landlord and tenant-at-sufferance relationship between appellant and Lehman Brothers. Thus, it was not necessary for the trial court to resolve the title dispute to determine the right of immediate possession.

Notes

1. In *Orange Laundry Co. v. Stark*, 179 S.W.2d 841 (Tex. Civ. App.—Amarillo 1944, no writ) the Bank had leased the property to the Defendants for one year (1937-1938), but the lease was not renewed. The Defendants, however, held over, and stayed in possession, paying rent to the Bank until July 6, 1942. On December 12, 1942, the Bank sold the property to Stark, notifying the Defendants of the sale. Stark, now the landlord, sued the Defendants, (the tenants) for forcible entry and detainer (FED) in justice court, alleging ownership of the land. The Defendants challenged Stark's title because the bank had held title to the land for more than five years in violation of a federal statute. Stark specially excepted to the Defendants' pleadings. The special exception was sustained. Stark, the landlord won, and it was held that the justice court had jurisdiction.

2. In *Rodriquez v. Sullivan*, 484 S.W.2d 592 (Tex. Civ. App.—El Paso 1972, no writ), Sandoval, sued in justice court for possession (FED), seeking to expel Rodriquez from the property. Sandoval sold the property to Rodriguez in 1961 on a contract for sale. Sandoval alleged that Rodriquez had become delinquent and sought to regain possession of the property. The justice court issued a writ of possession to Sandoval. The district court issued a temporary injunction to prevent the sheriff from executing on the writ of possession issued by the justice court. This was affirmed. A forcible entry and detainer proceeding is an action for possession and the question of right of possession is the only issue involved in the justice court. Justice courts have no jurisdiction for suits for title to land, and hence cannot try a forcible detainer action that involves trial of title to land. Here, the Defendant had the right to possession unless he lost equitable title to the property.

3. Are the two decisions consistent? Yes. In *Rodriguez* the issue was title and the district court had jurisdiction; in *Stark* the issue was possession and the justice court had jurisdiction. In *Stark,* the tenant did not claim title (ownership), but rather sought to show that the landlord was not the owner, and thus had no right to possession. In *Rodriguez* one or the other of the parties was entitled to ownership, and the ownership issue determined the possession issue.

4. A claimant may properly join in justice court a detainer action with a suit for unpaid rent, provided the amount requested does not exceed the jurisidictional limits of the justice court in which the suit is brought.

5. Although an appeal from a justice court judgment is tried de novo in the county or district court, TEX. R. CIV. P. 574b, the appellate jurisdiction of the county court is confirmed to the jurisdictional limits of the justice court. The county court has no jurisdiction over the appeal unless the justice court had jurisdiction over the case. *Tile v. Ramsey*, 905 S.W.2d 620, 622 (Tex.App.—Houston [14th Dist.] 1995, no writ); *Wattley v. Turner*, WL (Tex. App.—Dallas, 1998, ordered not published).

6. Texas Civil Practice & Remedies Code § 51.001:

(a) In a case tried in justice court in which the judgment or amount in controversy exceeds $20, exclusive of costs, or in which the appeal is expressly provided by law, a party to a final judgment may appeal to the county court.

(b) In a county in which the civil jurisdiction of the county court has been transferred to the district court, a party to a final judgment in a case covered by this section may appeal to the district court.

7. In *Coinmach Corp. v. Aspenwood Apt. Corp.*, 417 S.W.3d 909, 919 (Tex. 2013) the court stated:

> "The only issue in a forcible detainer action is the right to actual possession of the premises." *Marshall v. Hous. Auth. of the City of San Antonio,* 198 S.W.3d 782, 785 (Tex.2006). Such an action "is intended to be a speedy, simple, and inexpensive means to obtain immediate possession of property." *Id.* at 787. The judgment in a forcible detainer action is a final determination only "of the right to immediate possession;" it is not "a final determination of whether the eviction is wrongful" or whether the tenant's continued possession was a trespass. *Id.; see also House v. Reavis,* 89 Tex. 626, 35 S.W. 1063, 1067 (1896) (holding that FED action did not affect "merits of the title" and was "no bar to the recovery of the plaintiffs" in subsequent action for title and damages); *Johnson v. Highland Hills Drive Apartments,* 552 S.W.2d 493, 494 (Tex. Civ. App.—Dallas 1977, no writ) (holding that predecessor to section 24.008 "prevents a judgment of possession in a forcible entry and detainer action from barring a subsequent action for damages for wrongful eviction")."
>
> "We hold that chapter 24's procedural protections do not grant to tenants at sufferance any legal interests in or possessory rights to the property at issue; rather, the statute provides procedural protections

that apply once the tenant has lost, or allegedly lost, all legal interests and possessory rights. Although the landlord must comply with the statute's procedural requirements to evict the tenant at sufferance, eviction is allowed only if the tenant has no remaining legal or possessory interest, which makes the tenant a tenant at sufferance. The FED action and judgment do not bar a separate action for trespass or for wrongful eviction, and if it is determined in that action that the tenant lacked any legal interest or right of possession, the tenant at sufferance is a trespasser. Nothing in the statute indicates that the procedural protections grant legal or possessory rights to a tenant at sufferance. To the contrary, the statute states that the "person entitled to possession of the property" is not the tenant but the person seeking the eviction, that is, the one who "must comply with the [procedural] requirements." TEX. PROP. CODE § 24.002(b). And, even more directly, the statute expressly provides that a suit for eviction under the FED statute "does not bar a suit for trespass." *Id.* § 24.008. Thus, despite the so-called "grace periods" and chapter 24's other procedural protections, the tenant at sufferance remains a trespasser on the property."

5. *Amount in Controversy as Basis for Jurisdiction*

FLYNT
v.
GARCIA
587 S.W.2d 109
(Tex. 1979)

Fred Riepen, Houston, for petitioner.
Milton Schwartz, Houston, for respondent.

PER CURIAM.

This case involves the jurisdiction of a county court at law to entertain suit and render judgment after a trial amendment raised the amount in controversy over the maximum jurisdictional limit of $5,000.

We will recite only those facts necessary for our disposition of the case and will not repeat the full statement made by the court of civil appeals at 574 S.W.2d 587.

The record before us does not contain pleadings prior to the fourth amended original petition filed April 18, 1977. By that pleading, Sue Ann Flynt sought to recover $1,778.40 plus interest under a fully matured obligation, and $3,100 plus interest in monthly payments accrued through August, 1976, under another obligation not yet fully matured. The total sought at that time was $4,778.40 plus interest. By trial amendment, she increased her demand to $6,242.40 by including accrued payments on the second obligation through the end of trial.

The court of civil appeals has held that the county court at law retained jurisdiction to "entertain the suit," citing this Court's opinions in *Isbell v. Kenyon-Warner Dredging Co.*, 113 Tex. 528, 261 S.W. 762 (1924); and *Haginas v. Malbis Memorial Foundation*, 163 Tex. 274, 354 S.W.2d 368 (1962). However, the court further held that the trial court had no "jurisdiction to enter a judgment in excess of the jurisdictional amount."

We think the opinion of the court of civil appeals is in conflict with the general rule announced in *Isbell*, *supra* and *Haginas*, *supra* ; and, therefore pursuant to TEX. R. CIV. P. 483, we grant the application of Sue Ann Flynt, and without hearing oral argument, reverse the judgment of the court of civil appeals.

The general rule stated in the two prior opinions is that "where jurisdiction is once lawfully and properly acquired, no subsequent fact or event in the particular case serves to defeat that jurisdiction." We see no reason why that general rule should not apply to a case where the original suit is within the jurisdictional limits of the court and subsequent amendments seek only additional damages that are accruing because of the passage of time. This is especially so where there is no allegation of bad faith or fraud in invoking the jurisdiction of the court.

The rule applied here will serve the purposes of judicial economy. The opinion of the court of civil appeals would reverse the judgment and remand the cause for another trial in the county court at law while allowing only a partial recovery of the amount due. If another suit is required to recover the balance, three lawsuits will result from this single claim.

The judgment of the court of civil appeals is reversed and the judgment of the trial court is affirmed.

Notes

1. For jurisdictional purposes, the amount in controversy must be determined from the allegations of fact contained in the pleadings of the party seeking to invoke the court's jurisdiction, unless the adverse party alleges and proves that the allegations of his adversary with respect to the amount in controversy were falsely made for the fraudulent purpose of wrongfully conferring jurisdiction. *See, e.g., Dwyer v. Bassett*, 63 Tex. 274; *Clonts v. Johnson*, 116 Tex. 489, 294 S.W. 844.

2. It also appears to be well settled that the word 'interest,' as used in the Constitutional and statutes provisions above referred to, means interest *eo nomine* as distinguished from interest as an element of recoverable damages. *See, e.g., Smelser v. Baker*, 88 Tex. 26, 29 S.W. 377; *Watkins v. Junker*. Interest as interest or interest *eo nomine* is compensation allowed by law or fixed by the parties for the use of detention of money; interest as damages is compensation allowed by law as additional damages for lose use of the money due as damages during the lapse of time between the accrual of the claim and the date of judgement. *See, e.g., Cavnar v. Quality Control Parking*, 696 S.W.2d 549 (1985). Thus, in determining the amount in controversy interest as damages are included in the amount in controversy. In addition, exemplary damages and attorneys' fees are included in the amount in controversy.

3. In *Mr. W. Fireworks v. Mitchell*, 622 S.W.2d 576 (Tex. 1981) the Court applied the same general principles expressed in the *Flynt* case to a case in which additional attorney's fees accrued from the time of filing the suit until judgment.

4. In *Bybee v. Fireman's Fund Ins. Co.*, 331 S.W.2d 910 (Tex. 1960) the Court noted that when jurisdiction is dependent upon the amount in controversy, a mere unfounded claim to a penalty or attorney's fees will not serve to place the case within the exclusive jurisdiction of a particular court.

5. *Richardson v. First National Life Insurance Company*, 419 S.W.2d 836 (Tex. 1967). The residual power of Texas trial courts rests in the district courts. Thus, a suit for an accounting was properly brought in the district court.

PEEK
v.
EQUIPMENT SERV. CO. OF SAN ANTONIO

779 S.W.2d 802
(Tex. 1989)

PHILLIPS, CHIEF JUSTICE.

These cases present the question of whether a plaintiff seeking damages under the wrongful death and survival statutes invokes the jurisdiction of a district court by filing a petition which fails to allege either a specific amount of damages or that the damages sustained exceed the court's minimum jurisdictional limits. The district court held that its jurisdiction was not invoked by such a pleading. Because plaintiffs did not file a pleading properly alleging damages until after the applicable statute of limitations had run, the district court dismissed the suit. The court of appeals, in two unpublished opinions, affirmed. We reverse the judgments of the court of appeals and remand this consolidated cause to the trial court because the original pleading, although defective, was sufficient to invoke the court's jurisdiction and prevent the running of limitations.

This matter arose out of the murder of Clyde Peek on December 18, 1984. The plaintiffs were Clyde's widow, Lucie Allen Peek, acting in her individual capacity and as representative of Clyde's estate, and Clyde's four surviving children. They brought suit on November 18, 1986, under the wrongful death and survival statutes. TEX. CIV. PRAC. & REM. CODE ANN. §§ 71.001-.003, § 71.021 (Vernon 1986). The Peeks sued six defendants: Marvin Wiley DeBerry, Jr., who shot and killed Peek; Equipment Service Company, DeBerry's employer; Victor J. Weiss, M.D. and Burton O. Neeswig, M.D., two doctors who had treated DeBerry for mental illness; Suzanne Cude, DeBerry's estranged wife; and Oshman's Sporting Goods, Inc., the owner of the store in which DeBerry purchased the murder weapon. The Peeks plead for lost care, nurture, guidance, education, wages in the past and future, pain and suffering, mental anguish, grief, loss of companionship, and loss of enjoyment of life (hedonic damages), together with interest and costs. What they did not plead, however, was the amount of damages sought, either by properly alleging that damages exceeded the minimum jurisdictional limits of the court, *see* TEX. R. CIV. P. 47(b), or by alleging a sum certain.

The Peeks amended their petition on December 16, 1986, but made no changes in their defective allegations of damages. In a second amended pleading, filed January 14, 1987, the Peeks sought $3,750,000 actual damages and $5,000,000 exemplary damages against the defendants, jointly and severally. This pleading, however, came more than two years after Clyde's death. All defendants except Oshman's Sporting Goods, Inc. filed motions to dismiss, alleging that the Peeks had failed to invoke the jurisdiction of the district court prior to the running of the two-year statute of limitations. TEX. CIV. PRAC. & REM. CODE ANN. § 16.003(b) (Vernon 1986). The trial court granted these motions at various times, and severance orders were signed so that these judgments became final.

The Peeks timely appealed to the court of appeals, which affirmed the judgments of the trial court in two opinions. From both judgments of the court of appeals, the Peeks applied to this court for writ of error. After granting both writs, we consolidated the two causes for oral argument and decision.

The parties here have assumed the minimum monetary jurisdictional limit of the district court to be $500.00. Although recent constitutional and legislative changes call this assumption into question, we will also assume, for purposes of our decision, that the jurisdiction of the district court does not extend to controversies involving sums of less than $500.00.

In this case, all parties agree that the trial court's jurisdiction was invoked not later than the filing of the Peeks' second amended petition. The respondents, however, argue that the Peeks did not invoke jurisdiction by the first two pleadings, and hence did not obtain jurisdiction until after limitations had run. The Peeks, on the other hand, assert that their original petition did invoke the trial court's jurisdiction. Although the petition did not expressly allege that the amount sought was within the court's jurisdiction, neither did anything in the petition suggest that the court lacked jurisdiction. In fact, the Peeks argue that the nature of the loss sustained and the claims asserted made it absolutely apparent that plaintiffs sought damages far in excess of five hundred dollars.

The court of appeals held, however, that the Peeks' claims were time barred because the second amended petition, which alleged sufficient jurisdictional facts, was not filed prior to the expiration of limitations. In so holding, the court of appeals rejected the Peeks' theory that their second amended petition should relate back to the date of original filing. Instead, the court concluded that a petition which does not affirmatively state that the amount in controversy is above the minimum monetary jurisdiction of the district court is, in effect, no pleading.

In reaching this conclusion, the court relied heavily on our decision in *Richardson v. First National Life Insurance Co.*, 419 S.W.2d 836 (Tex. 1967). In that case, Richardson sued for breach of contract, alleging in his petition that he believed that "at least the amount of $314.37" was due to him, and also seeking an accounting and general relief. *Id.* at 837. The defendant attacked Richardson's pleading with special exceptions and, after Richardson failed to amend, the trial court dismissed his claim. The court of appeals and this court both affirmed. We held that because Richardson had specifically pleaded an amount under the minimum jurisdiction of the district court, he could not rely on his more general allegations to sustain jurisdiction. *Id.* at 839. Richardson, in effect, pleaded himself out of court.

In the instant case, however, the Peeks' original and first amended petitions did not affirmatively demonstrate an absence of jurisdiction. Under these circumstances, a liberal construction of the pleadings is appropriate. As we wrote in *Pecos & Northern Texas Railway Co. v. Rayzor*, 106 Tex. 544, 548, 172 S.W. 1103, 1105 (1915): "In any doubtful case all intendments of the plaintiff's pleading will be in favor of the jurisdiction." Unless it is clear from the pleadings that the court lacks jurisdiction of the amount in controversy, it should retain the case. *Dwyer v. Bassett & Bassett*, 63 Tex. 274, 276 (1885). As one court recently said: "[W]e must presume in favor of the jurisdiction unless lack of jurisdiction affirmatively appears on the face of the petition." *Smith v. Texas Improvement Co.*, 570 S.W.2d 90, 92 (Tex. Civ. App.—Dallas 1978, no writ).

The failure of a plaintiff to state a jurisdictional amount in controversy in its petition, without more, thus will not deprive the trial court of jurisdiction. *See* W. DORSANEO, 1 TEXAS LITIGATION GUIDE § 11.02(4)(a)

(1989); Newton, *Conflict of Laws*, 33 Sw.L.J. 425, 431-32 (1979). Even if the jurisdictional amount is never established by pleading, in fact, a plaintiff may recover if jurisdiction is proved at trial. DORSANEO, *supra*, § 2.01(4)(b); 2 R. MCDONALD, TEXAS CIVIL PRACTICE IN DISTRICT AND COUNTY COURTS § 6.09.1 (rev. 1982). This result is consistent with our holdings in cases when a plaintiff has failed to plead facts which state a cause of action. Unless the petition affirmatively demonstrates that no cause of action exists or that plaintiff's recovery is barred, we require the trial court to give the plaintiff an opportunity to amend before granting a motion to dismiss or a motion for summary judgment. *Texas Dept. of Corrections v. Herring*, 513 S.W.2d 6, 10 (Tex. 1974), *Killebrew v. Stockdale*, 51 Tex. 529, 532 (1879); *Southern Sur. Co. v. Sealy I.S.D.*, 10 S.W.2d 786, 789 (Tex. Civ. App.—Austin 1928, writ ref'd). And unless defendant objects, the plaintiff may proceed to trial, however defective its allegations. So it is here. In the absence of special exceptions or other motion, defendant waives the right to complain of such a defect if plaintiff establishes the trial court's jurisdiction before resting its case. *See Olivares v. Service Trust Co.*, 385 S.W.2d 687 (Tex. Civ. App.—Eastland 1964, no writ).

In summary, we hold that the omission of any allegation regarding the amount in controversy from plaintiff's petition did not deprive the court of jurisdiction, but was instead a defect in pleading subject to special exception and amendment. Although defective, the original petition filed in this cause was sufficient to invoke the jurisdiction of the district court. The court of appeals therefore erred in affirming the judgments of dismissal, as the Peeks amended their petition and cured the defect prior to the rendition of the judgments which dismissed their claims. Accordingly, the judgments of the court of appeals are reversed and the causes remanded to the trial court for further proceedings.

Note

Rule 47. Texas Rules of Civil Procedure: Claims for Relief

An original pleading which sets forth a claim for relief, whether an original petition, counterclaim, cross-claim, or third party claim, shall contain:

(a) a short statement of the cause of action sufficient to give fair notice of the claim involved;

(b) a statement that the damages sought are within the jurisdictional limits of the court;

(c) except in suits governed by the Family Code, a statement that the party seeks:

(1) only monetary relief of $100,000 or less, including damages of any kind, penalties, costs, expenses, pre-judgment interest, and attorney fees; or

(2) monetary relief of $100,000 or less and non-monetary relief; or

(3) monetary relief over $100,000 but not more than $200,000; or

(4) monetary relief over $200,000 but not more than $1,000,000; or

(5) monetary relief over $1,000,000; and

(d) a demand for judgment for all the other relief to which the party deems himself entitled.

Relief in the alternative or of several different types may be demanded; provided, further, that upon special exception the court shall require the pleader to amend so as to specify the maximum amount claimed. A party that fails to comply with (c) may not conduct discovery until the party's pleading is amended to comply.

Note

It will be helpful in understanding the following case to know that at the time of Mr. Brite's termination from USAA, his annual salary was almost $74,000, he was 52 years old, and intended to work until he was 65.

UNITED SERVICES AUTO. ASS'N
v.
BRITE
215 S.W.3d 400
(Tex. 2007)

Raquel G. Perez, Kathleen A. Devine, United Services Automobile Association, Judy K. Jetelina, Bracewell & Patterson, San Antonio, W. Carl Jordan, Vinson & Elkins LLP, Houston, J. Joe Harris, Southwest Airlines Co., Dallas, Lacey L. Gourley, Bracewell & Patterson, L.L.P., Pamela Stanton Baron, Austin, for Petitioner.

Jeffrey D. Small, Law Office of Jeff Small, Jeffrey Alan Goldberg, Cynthia A. Cano, San Antonio, Douglas Alexander, Alexander Dubose Jones & Townsend, LLP, Austin, for Respondent.

Kathryn S. Vaughn, Baker Botts LLP, Houston, for Amicus Curiae Texas Employment Law Council.

Jeffrey C. Londa, Ogletree Deakins Nash Smoak & Stewart, P.C., Houston, for Amicus Curiae Texas Association of Business.

JUSTICE MEDINA delivered the opinion of the Court.

County courts at law are courts of limited jurisdiction and many, including the county court at law in this case, lack jurisdiction over a "matter in controversy" that exceeds $100,000. *See* TEX. GOV'T CODE § 25.0003(C)(1); *see also id.* § 25.0172 (Bexar County Court at Law Provisions). The question here is whether the value of this case at filing (commonly referred to as the amount in controversy) exceeded the court's $100,000 jurisdictional limit. To answer that question, we must decide whether the amount in controversy includes the total amount of the damages the plaintiff seeks to recover, or whether it excludes damages that are uncertain in duration or amount. Because we hold that the "matter in controversy" includes all of the damages the plaintiff seeks to recover at the time suit is filed, we conclude that the case's value here at the time of filing exceeded $100,000 and that the county court at law therefore lacked jurisdiction over this matter. Accordingly, we reverse the judgment of the court of appeals and dismiss the case for want of jurisdiction.

James Steven Brite was employed by United Services Automobile Association (USAA) from 1977 to 2001. In 2001, USAA undertook a reduction in force and terminated Brite's employment. Brite subsequently filed an age-discrimination lawsuit against USAA, alleging that he was selected for a layoff because of his age.

Brite filed his suit in the Bexar County Court at Law No. 7, which has jurisdiction concurrent with that of the district court in "civil cases in which the matter in controversy exceeds $500 but does not exceed $100,000, excluding interest, statutory or punitive damages and penalties, and attorney's fees and costs, as alleged on the face of the petition . . . ." TEX. GOV'T CODE § 25.0003(C)(1). In his original petition, Brite pleaded that his damages exceeded the statutory minimum of $500, but he did not plead that his damages were below the $100,000 maximum limits. Although he did not specify amounts, his pleadings did seek the recovery of back pay, front pay, punitive damages, and attorney's fees. Brite's pleading did not use the terms "back pay" and "front pay" but rather described his damages as "compensation due Plaintiff that accrued at the time of filing this Petition" (back pay) and "the present value of unaccrued wage payments" (front pay).

Subsequently, Brite amended his petition to state that he sought damages of $1.6 million. He did not specify how much of that amount consisted of punitive damages or attorney's fees, but in a later discovery response, Brite admitted that "his lost wages and benefits in the future, until age 65, total approximately $1,000,000.00."

USAA filed a plea to the jurisdiction, asserting that the county court at law lacked jurisdiction because Brite sought damages greater than $100,000. The trial court denied the plea, and, after a jury trial, the court ultimately awarded Brite $188,406 for back pay, $350,000 for front pay, $300,000 in punitive damages, $129,387 in attorney's fees, and prejudgment interest. The court of appeals, with one justice dissenting, affirmed the trial court's judgment. 161 S.W.3d 566.

USAA argues here that the court of appeals erred in affirming the trial court's judgment because the amount in controversy at the time Brite filed suit exceeded $100,000, thus depriving the county court at law of jurisdiction over the matter. We agree.

Texas Rule of Civil Procedure 47(b) requires that an original pleading "contain . . . the statement that damages sought are within the jurisdictional limits of the court." Moreover, we have said that "[t]he general rule is that the allegations of the plaintiff's petition must state facts which affirmatively show the jurisdiction of the court in which the action is brought." *Richardson v. First Nat'l Life Ins. Co.*, 419 S.W.2d 836, 839 (Tex. 1967). Brite's petition did not comply with these authorities because it failed to assert that the matter in controversy was within the monetary limitations of the county court at law's jurisdiction. His petition was therefore defective. He could have remedied this defect, however, by proving jurisdiction in the trial court, as his original petition did not "affirmatively demonstrate an absence of jurisdiction." *See Peek v. Equip. Serv. Co.*, 779 S.W.2d 802, 804 (Tex. 1989) ("Even if the jurisdictional amount is never established by pleading, in fact, a plaintiff may recover if jurisdiction is proved at trial.").

Brite asserts that he established jurisdiction by proof at trial that, at the time he filed his petition, his back-pay damages totaled less than $100,000. USAA, on the other hand, argues that Brite's request for front-pay damages must also be included in calculating the amount in controversy. Because Brite's alleged front-pay damages alone exceeded $100,000 at the time he filed suit, including these damages would mean that the county court at law did not have jurisdiction over the case. TEX. GOV'T CODE § 25.0003(C)(1).

We have previously held that the amount in controversy is determined by the amount the plaintiff seeks to recover. *Tune v. Tex. Dep't of Pub. Safety*, 23 S.W.3d 358, 361 (Tex. 2000) ("It has long been the law that the phrase 'amount in controversy,' in the jurisdictional context, means 'the sum of money or the value of the thing originally sued for . . . .' " *quoting Gulf, C. & S.F. Ry. Co. v. Cunnigan*, 95 Tex. 439, 67 S.W. 888, 890 (1902) (emphasis in original)). Brite argues, however, that we should abandon this rule in favor of another that takes into consideration the probability that plaintiff will succeed. Thus, he submits that the amount in controversy should not be calculated by the damages originally sued for, but instead by the amount of damages that, more likely than not, the plaintiff would recover. Under his proposed rule, Brite asserts that front pay should not be included in the amount in controversy because it was unlikely that he would recover those damages at the time he filed suit. Although Brite sued for front pay, asserting that he would "[i]n all reasonable probability" sustain those damages, he now submits that he was unlikely to prevail on this claim because the front-pay remedy is disfavored by the courts.

The court of appeals accepted this argument, holding that because of the "speculative nature of the front-pay damages," the trial court did not err in excluding those damages from its calculation of the amount in controversy. 161 S.W.3d at 573 n. 1. A dissenting justice disagreed, noting that "[f]or purposes of determining the 'amount in controversy,' the question is not what a plaintiff will recover or is likely to recover; it is what the plaintiff seeks to recover." *Id.* at 586 (DUNCAN, J. dissenting). We agree with the dissenting justice.

The jurisdictional statute for county courts at law values the matter in controversy on the amount of damages "alleged" by the plaintiff, not on the amount the plaintiff is likely to recover. As previously stated, it grants county courts at law jurisdiction over "civil cases in which the matter in controversy exceeds $500 but does not exceed $100,000, excluding interest, statutory or punitive damages and penalties, and attorney's fees and costs, as alleged on the face of the petition . . . ." TEX. GOV'T CODE § 25.0003(C)(1). And although the statute excludes several items when determining the amount in controversy, front pay is not among them. *See Mid-Century Ins. Co. of Tex. v. Kidd*, 997 S.W.2d 265, 273-74 (Tex. 1999) (doctrine of expressio unius est exclusio alterius—the inclusion of a specific limitation excludes all others—a statutory interpretation tool of some use under these circumstances). Moreover, the statute is not ambiguous, and courts are required to interpret unambiguous language according to its plain meaning. *McIntyre v. Ramirez*, 109 S.W.3d 741, 745 (Tex. 2003). Because the statute bases jurisdiction on the damages "alleged on the face of the petition" and makes no exclusion based on the plaintiff's likelihood of recovery, it does not allow front-pay damages to be excluded from the amount in controversy. We therefore hold that front-pay damages must be included when determining the amount in controversy.

The amount in controversy in this case exceeded $100,000 at the time Brite filed suit, and thus the county court at law lacked jurisdiction over this matter. Accordingly, we reverse the court of appeals' judgment and, without reference to the merits, dismiss the case for want of jurisdiction.

JUSTICE GREEN did not participate in the decision.

Note

See Texas Rules of Civil Procedure 91A. **Dismissal of Baseless Causes of Action**.

6. *Problems of Multiple Parties and Claims*

Section 24.009 of the Texas Government Code provides in part:

If two or more persons originally and properly joined in one suit, the suit for jurisdictional purposes is treated as if one party is suing for the aggregate amount of all their claims added together, excluding interest and costs.

TEXAS EMPLOYMENT COMMISSION
v.
INTERNATIONAL UNION OF ELECTRICAL, RADIO AND MACHINE WORKERS, LOCAL UNION NO. 782

165 Tex. 135, 352 S.W.2d 252
(Tex. 1961)

Will Wilson, Atty. Gen., C. K. Richards, Sam Lane, Asst. Attys. Gen., for Texas Employment Commission.
Ramey, Brelsford, Hull & Flock, Tyler, Wm. J. Barron, New York City, L. Mason Harter, De Witt, N. Y., and Jack W. Flock, Tyler, of counsel, for General Electric Company.
Sam Houston Clinton, Jr., Austin, for respondents.

STEAKLEY, JUSTICE.

This case as it reaches us with the Texas Employment Commission and General Electric Company as petitioners involves the right of eighty-eight respondents to unemployment compensation benefits for the week of August 4, 1957, during which the plant of General Electric Company at Tyler was shut down. The facts common to all of the respondents require a construction of certain provisions of their collective bargaining contract in the light of the applicable provisions of the Texas Unemployment Compensation Act. The claims of the respondents were denied by the Commission in one proceeding and suit was brought by all the respondents in the District Court of Smith County to review the adverse decision. The district court sustained the Commission. The Court of Civil Appeals reversed the district court and entered judgment 'directing the Texas Employment Commission to grant the claims of the eighty-eight claimants. * * *

Preliminarily, petitioners urge two jurisdictional pleas. The first is that the district court was without jurisdiction in the fact that the claim of each respondent was approximately $25.00 although aggregating, of course, more than $500.00. This plea to the jurisdiction was not raised in the trial court but was urged in the Court of Civil Appeals, and is urged here, as fundamental error. Lack of jurisdiction in the district court would be fundamental error and a plea to such effect is subject to review although first presented on appeal. We hold, however, that the plea is without merit.

There was proper joinder of the claimants under Rule 40, Texas Rules of Civil Procedure. *Hindman v. Texas Lime Co.*, 157 Tex. 592, 305 S.W.2d 947, 954. The rights jointly asserted by the several claimants arose out of the same transactions and occurrences within the purview and purposes of the Rule. The determining questions of law and of fact are common to all.

Article 1906a, Vernon's Ann.Civ.St., provides: 'Where two or more persons originally and properly join in one suit, the suit for jurisdictional purposes shall be treated as if one party were suing for the aggregate amount of all their claims added together, exclusive of interest and cost; provided that this statute shall not prevent jurisdiction from attaching on any other ground. Provided further, that the passage of this Act shall not affect any pending litigation.' Acts 1945, 49th Leg., p. 543, ch. 329, § 1.

Article V, Section 8 of the Constitution, Vernon's Ann. St., provides that 'The District Court shall have * * * such other jurisdiction, original and appellate, as may be provided by law.' *See Oilmen's Reciprocal Ass'n v. Franklin*, 116 Tex. 59, 286 S.W. 195, 197.

Respondents were originally and properly joined and the statute makes the aggregate amount controlling for jurisdictional purposes. Article 1906a was enacted for the express purpose of curing what the Legislature described as a 'jurisdictional defect' in *Long v. City of Wichita Falls*, 142 Tex. 202, 176 S.W.2d 936; the 'defect' was the holding in Long that the claims of several plaintiffs cannot be added together to achieve a jurisdictional amount. *Southwestern Drug Co. v. Webster*, Tex. Civ. App., 246 S.W.2d 241 (no writ hist.) and *Kasishke v. Ekern*, Tex. Civ. App., 278 S.W.2d 274 (ref., n.r.e.), cited by petitioners, are not in point because of their reliance on Long and under their facts. In the case before us there is proper joinder of claims aggregating more than $500.00 giving the district court jurisdiction under the express provisions of Article 1906a.

* * *

7. *Consequences of a Lack of Jurisdiction over the Subject Matter*

Notes

1. A Texas court which does not have subject matter jurisdiction must dismiss the proceeding before it. Thus, if the trial court proceeds to judgment and the case is appealed the appellate court can make no order other than reversing the judgment of the court below and dismissing the cause. *See City of Garland v. Louton*, 691 S.W.2d 603 (Tex. 1985).

2. Texas Civil Practice & Remedies Code § 16.064 provides:

> (a) The period between the date of filing an action in a trial court and the date of a second filing of the same action in a different court suspends the running of the applicable statute of limitations for the period if:
>
> (1) because of lack of jurisdiction in the trial court where the action was first filed, the action is dismissed or the judgment is set aside or annulled in a direct proceeding; and
>
> (2) not later than the 60th day after the date the dismissal or other disposition becomes final, the action is commenced in a court of proper jurisdiction.
>
> (b) This section does not apply if the adverse party has shown in abatement that the first filing was made with intentional disregard of proper jurisdiction.

3. *In re United Services Auto. Ass'n*, 307 S.W.3d 299 (Tex. 2010): TEX. CIV. PRAC. & REM. CODE § 16.064 tolls limitations for those cases filed in a trial court that lacks jurisdiction, provided the case is refiled in a proper court within sixty days of dismissal. The tolling provision does not apply, however, to those cases in which the first filing was made with "intentional disregard of proper jurisdiction." When, as here, the plaintiff intentionally disregarded the jurisdictional limits applicable to county courts at law in Bexar County, in a way that cannot be cured by ordinary appellate review, mandamus relief will be granted.

Once an adverse party has moved for relief under the "intentional disregard" provision, the nonmovant must show that he did not intentionally disregard proper jurisdiction when filing the case. As it is the nonmovant who has this information, he should bear the burden of producing it. Section 16.064's intent standard is similar to that required for setting aside a default judgment, and a mistake of law may be a sufficient excuse. Moreover, section 16.064 was drafted precisely because "capable lawyers" often make "good faith" mistakes about the jurisdiction of Texas courts. But while the tolling statute protects plaintiffs who mistakenly file suit in a forum that lacks jurisdiction, it does not apply to a strategic decision to seek relief from such a court—which is what happened here. Because Brite unquestionably sought damages in excess of the county court at law's jurisdiction, it matters not that he subjectively anticipated a verdict within the jurisdictional limits. For that reason, limitations was not tolled. His second suit, filed long after the expiration of the two-year statute, is therefore barred.

4. *Texas Department of Transportation, Petitioner v. Ramirez,* 74 S.W.3d 864 (Tex. 2002): In considering jurisdictional pleas, an appellate court reviews the pleadings and any evidence relevant to the jurisdictional issue, construing the pleadings liberally in the plaintiff's favor. To sue the State for a tort, the pleadings must state a claim under the Tort Claims Act. Mere reference to the Act is not enough. A plaintiff has a right to

amend its pleadings to attempt to cure pleading defects, if he has not alleged enough jurisdictional facts. However, if the pleadings show a state of facts under which it is impossible to amend the pleadings to invoke jurisdiction, the trial court should dismiss the plaintiff's suit.

5. *FKM Partnership, Ltd v. Board of Regents of University of Houston System*, 255 S.W.3d 619 (2008): The trial court is allowed to conduct a hearing on a plea to the jurisdiction or motion to dismiss for lack of jurisdiction in a manner similar to how it hears a summary judgment motion, and may consider affidavits and other summary judgment-type evidence. If the evidence presents a fact question on the jurisdictional issue, the motion should be denied.

ATTORNEY GENERAL
v.
SAILER

871 S.W.2d 257
(Tex. App.—Houston [14th Dist.] 1994, writ denied)

Rhonda Amkraut Pressley, Tod L. Adamson, Austin, for appellant.
Bruce A. Baughman, Baytown, for appellee.

SEARS, JUSTICE.

The Attorney General appeals an order dismissing a motion to modify child support with prejudice. The Attorney General claims that the trial court lacked subject matter jurisdiction and could not dismiss the case with prejudice. We agree, reform the order to delete the words "with prejudice," and affirm the order as reformed.

Joyce Barrett and David Sailer were divorced in Iowa on November 4, 1982. Ms. Barrett was awarded custody of the couples' two minor children, and Mr. Sailer was ordered to pay $140.00 a month per child in child support. Subsequently, all the parties moved to Texas.

On January 14, 1991, Ms. Barrett instituted an action in the 308th District Court in Harris County, Texas, to enforce the Iowa decree and obtain past due child support. The Texas court granted judgment to Ms. Barrett for $15,640.00 in past due child support, found Mr. Sailer in contempt for failure to pay his child support, and sentenced him to three years in jail and a $500.00 fine. The court suspended the commitment order, on the condition that Mr. Sailer comply with a schedule to pay off the amount in arrears and stay current with his support obligations.

Ms. Barrett then applied to the Attorney General for child support services. On August 5, 1991, the 308th district court signed an order assigning Ms. Barrett's right to child support to the Attorney General. The Attorney General filed a motion to modify support in the 308th District Court. That motion was dismissed on jurisdictional grounds. On May 13, 1992, the Attorney General filed a second, identical motion in the 308th court to modify support. The motion again erroneously identified the "order to be modified" as an order signed on "November 4, 1982, by order of this Court." The motion identified by date the order signed by an Iowa court, but told the Texas court that it was an order the Texas court had entered. As a result, on August 12, 1992, Appellee again objected to the court's jurisdiction and filed a motion to dismiss the motion to modify support. He argued "there is no support order in the State of Texas to be modified." On September 15, 1992, the trial court dismissed the motion to modify support "with prejudice." In a hearing on a motion for new trial and in their briefs before this court, both parties agree that the trial court lacked subject matter jurisdiction to hear the motion to modify.

If a trial court learns that it lacks jurisdiction to hear a cause, it becomes the duty of the court to dismiss the cause. *General Tel. Co. of the Southwest v. City of Point Comfort*, 553 S.W.2d 808, 811 (Tex. Civ. App.—Corpus Christi 1977, no writ), and *Southwestern Bell Tel. Co. v. City of Kountze*, 543 S.W.2d 871, 873 (Tex. Civ. App.—Beaumont, no writ). In rendering the judgment of dismissal, the trial court must refrain from rendering a judgment on the merits of the suit. *State v. Schless*, 815 S.W.2d 373, 376 (Tex. App.—Austin 1991, original proceeding [leave denied]), and *Berger v. Berger*, 497 S.W.2d 453, 454 (Tex. Civ. App.—El Paso 1973, no writ). "It is well established that a dismissal with prejudice functions as a final determination on the merits." *Mossler v. Shields*, 818 S.W.2d 752, 754 (Tex. 1991). Therefore, a dismissal for want of jurisdiction with prejudice is error. *Stephanou v. Texas Medical Liab. Ins. Underwriting Ass'n*, 792 S.W.2d 498, 500 (Tex. App.—Houston [1st Dist.] 1990, writ denied).

We recognize that Appellee relies on two cases which indicate that, even if a trial court lacks jurisdiction, a dismissal with prejudice is proper if the appellant has shown that he is not entitled to recovery. This proposition, found in *Zimmerman v. Texaco, Inc.*, 409 S.W.2d 607, 614 (Tex. Civ. App.—El Paso 1966), writ ref'd, n.r.e., 413 S.W.2d 387 (Tex. 1967) and *Liland v. Dallas County Appraisal Dist.*, 731 S.W.2d 109 (Tex. App.—Dallas 1987, no writ) has never been cited nor followed by any other Texas court. Further, *Zimmerman* and *Liland* are both distinguishable as administrative cases, which turn on the issue of exhaustion of administrative remedies. Finally, this is not a case which "cannot be tried for jurisdictional reasons" and for which the plaintiff "is not entitled to recovery." The Attorney General may simply refile and allege the proper order to be modified, and then the 308th district court may consider the merits of the claim. *See, In re S.A.V.*, 837 S.W.2d 80 (Tex. 1992).

We order that the words "with prejudice" be deleted from the trial court's order, and reform the order to be a dismissal without prejudice. The judgment of the trial court is affirmed as reformed.

8. *Jurisdiction over Counterclaims*

Rule 97. Texas Rules of Civil Procedure: Counterclaim and Cross-Claim

(a) Compulsory Counterclaims. A pleading shall state as a counterclaim any claim within the jurisdiction of the court, not the subject of a pending action, which at the time of filing the pleading the pleader has against any opposing party, if it arises out of the transaction or occurrence that is the subject matter of the opposing party's claim and does not require for its adjudication the presence of third parties of whom the court cannot acquire jurisdiction; provided, however, that a judgment based upon a settlement or compromise of a claim of one party to the transaction or occurrence prior to a disposition on the merits shall not operate as a bar to the continuation or assertion of the claims of any other party to the transaction or occurrence unless the latter has consented in writing that said judgment shall operate as a bar.

(b) Permissive Counterclaims. A pleading may state as a counterclaim any claim against an opposing party whether or not arising out of the transaction or occurrence that is the subject matter of the opposing party's claim.

(c) Counterclaim Exceeding Opposing Claim. A counterclaim may or may not diminish or defeat the recovery sought by the opposing party. It may claim relief exceeding in amount or different in kind from that sought in the pleading of the opposing party, so long as the subject matter is within the jurisdiction of the court.

(d) Counterclaim Maturing or Acquired After Pleading. A claim which either matured or was acquired by the pleader after filing his pleading may be presented as a counterclaim by amended pleading.

(e) Cross-Claim Against Co-Party. A pleading may state as a cross-claim any claim by one party against a co-party arising out of the transaction or occurrence that is the subject matter either of the original action or of a counterclaim therein. Such cross-claim may include a claim that the party against whom it is asserted is or may be liable to the cross-claimant for all or part of a claim asserted in the action again the cross-claimant.

(f) Additional Parties. Persons other than those made parties to the original action may be made parties to a third party action, counterclaim or cross-claim in accordance with the provisions of Rules 38, 39 and 40.

(g) Tort shall not be the subject of set-off or counterclaim against a contractual demand nor a contractual demand against tort unless it arises out of or is incident to or is connected with same.

(h) Separate Trials; Separate Judgments. If the court orders separate trials as provided in Rule 174, judgment on a counterclaim or cross-claim may be rendered when the court has jurisdiction so to do, even if the claims of the opposing party have been dismissed or otherwise disposed of.

ANDEL
v.
EASTMAN KODAK COMPANY
400 S.W.2d 584
(Tex. Civ. App.—Houston 1966, no writ)

Facts: Ps sued D for negligence (causing the auto accident). D counterclaimed for an amount below the jurisdictional limit of the court. When Ps' motion for continuance was denied, they took a nonsuit.

Issue: Does a trial court retain jurisdiction of a counterclaim, below its jurisdictional amount, when the Ps' claim within its jurisdictional amount is nonsuited?

Held: Yes. Where a court by the plaintiff's pleading obtains jurisdiction over the case, a defendant may assert against the plaintiff a counter-claim in an amount that is below the minimum jurisdiction of the court where the case is filed. Once the court has obtained jurisdiction over the controversy between the parties by the filing of a counter-claim, dismissal of plaintiff's case does not deprive the court of jurisdiction of the counter-claim.

SMITH
v.
CLARY CORPORATION
917 S.W.2d 796
(Tex. 1996)

Anne Gardner and John J. Drake, Fort Worth, for petitioners.

Sloan B. Blair, Fort Worth, Carey Frank Walker and David Lewallen, Arlington, Kevin Norton, Fort Worth, for respondent.

PER CURIAM.

* * *

This issue in this case is whether counterclaims of multiple defendants should be aggregated to determine whether the amount in controversy in a county court at law exceeds that court's maximum statutory jurisdictional limit and divests it of jurisdiction. The court of appeals held that a statute required aggregation. We hold that the legislature enacted TEX. GOV'T CODE section 24.009, the aggregating statute, to allow multiple plaintiffs to aggregate their claims to achieve the minimum jurisdictional amount for a court, not to defeat jurisdiction for multiple defendants each of whose counterclaims is within the jurisdictional limit. Accordingly, the statute does not apply to require that multiple counterclaims be aggregated to determine the amount in controversy for statutory county court jurisdiction. Without hearing argument, the Court reverses the judgment of the court of appeals and remands the cause to that court for further proceedings. *See* TEX. R. APP. P. 170.

Daniel Smith and Michael Smith formed Fairfield Distributors and contracted with Clary Corporation to sell Clary's pallet products. Clary sued the Smiths, individually, and d/b/a Fairfield Distributors in Tarrant County Court at Law Number Three for $19,821.85 balance on an open account. The Smiths and Fairfield counterclaimed against Clary alleging deceptive trade practices, negligent misrepresentation, and tortious interference with business relations.

In their original counterclaims, the Smiths and Fairfield generally alleged damages in excess of the minimum jurisdiction of the Tarrant County Court at Law. Later, the three parties amended their counterclaims to allege damages of $100,000 each, for an aggregate of $300,000. A jury awarded Clary $14,155.57 on its open account claim. However, the jury found for the Smiths and Fairfield on their counterclaims. After deducting the $14,155.57 plus attorney's fees, the court rendered a net judgment for the Smiths and Fairfield for $264,271.61, including pre-judgment interest, statutory penalties, treble damages, attorney's fees and costs. Clary appealed this judgment arguing that the aggregate amount of the counterclaims exceeded the jurisdictional limit of the county court's authority. The court of appeals reversed the judgment and remanded the cause. 886 S.W.2d 570.

County courts at law generally have statutorily prescribed jurisdiction in civil cases where the amount in controversy exceeds $500 but does not exceed $100,000, excluding mandatory damages and penalties, attorney's fees, interest, and costs. TEX. GOV'T CODE ANN. § 25.0003(c) (Vernon Supp. 1995). A counterclaim, whether permissive or compulsory, must be within the court's jurisdiction. 2 ROY W. MCDONALD, TEXAS CIVIL PRACTICE § 9.76 (rev. 1992); *see also Wyatt v. Shaw Plumbing Co.*, 760 S.W.2d 245, 247 (Tex. 1988) (counterclaim is compulsory if "it is within the jurisdiction of the court."). A counterclaim is not within the court's jurisdiction when the amount in controversy exceeds the maximum jurisdictional limit of the court. *Kitchen Designs, Inc. v. Wood*, 584 S.W.2d 305, 307 (Tex. Civ. App.—Texarkana 1979, writ ref'd n.r.e.); 2 ROY W. MCDONALD, TEXAS CIVIL PRACTICE § 9.77 (rev. 1992); 16 TEX. JUR. 3D *Courts* §70 (1981). Daniel Smith, Michael Smith, and Fairfield individually pleaded $100,000 in damages. Each claim is within the jurisdictional purview of Tarrant County Court at Law Number Three. However, the court of appeals held that the counterclaim amounts should be aggregated under section 24.009 of the Government Code which provides, in relevant part:

> If two or more persons originally and properly join in one suit, the suit for jurisdictional purposes is treated as if one party is suing for the aggregate amount of all their claims added together, excluding interest and costs. This section does not prevent jurisdiction

TEX. GOV'T CODE ANN. § 24.009 (Vernon 1988). The court of appeals concluded that this statute applies to county courts at law through section 25.2222(m) of the Government Code. *See* TEX. GOV'T CODE ANN. § 25.2222(m) (Vernon Supp.1996). We initially assume, without deciding, that the aggregating statute applies to county courts at law. However, we disagree with the court of appeals' conclusion that the aggregating statute applies to the counterclaims the multiple defendants presented in this case. The courts have never applied the aggregating statute to counterclaims of multiple defendants who are properly joined. The legislature enacted the aggregating statute in 1945 to statutorily overrule this Court's holding in *Long v. City of Wichita Falls*, 142 Tex. 202, 176 S.W.2d 936, 940 (1944). *Long* involved two plaintiffs' claims against the same defendant, properly subject to joinder under Rule 40, one of which was below the minimum jurisdictional amount of the trial court. We held the trial court lacked jurisdiction over the smaller claim. The legislature sought to overturn what we quoted as the majority rule prevailing in 1944: "Where several claimants have separate and distinct demands against a defendant or defendants, and join in a single suit to enforce them, they cannot be added together to make up the required jurisdictional amount but each separate claim furnishes the jurisdictional test." *Long*, 176 S.W.2d at 940. Thus, Clary Corporation's reliance on *Long* is misplaced because neither *Long* nor any case cited in *Long* considered aggregation of counterclaims of separate defendants to defeat jurisdiction.

* * *

The courts have not and should not apply aggregation to divest a court of jurisdiction on counterclaims asserted by multiple defendants, whose joinder normally is not voluntary, and who have not chose the forum. *See* TEX. R. CIV. P. 38, 39. Moreover, co-defendants have no control over the number of defendants joined or the amounts of their counterclaims. Permitting aggregation of counterclaims to defeat jurisdiction under such circumstances would encourage races to the courthouse and forum shopping by parties to set arbitrary limits on anticipated claims by adversaries. We reverse the judgment of the court of appeals and remand the cause to that court for further proceedings.

Notes

1. A court must not only have jurisdiction over the amount in controversy, but it must also have subject matter jurisdiction over a counterclaim. *See Camacho v. Samaniego*, 831 S.W.2d 804, 806-807 (Tex.1992).

2. *Moritz v. Byerly*, 185 S.W.2d 589 Tex. Civ. App. 589 (Tex. Civ. App.—Austin 1945, writ refused): ". . . [A] court (here the district court) has jurisdiction of a counterclaim which is in amount below its minimum jurisdiction, the counterclaim not arising out of the same transaction as plaintiff's claim, but being of the general character warranting set off; and being pleaded only by way of set-off, without prayer for affirmative relief.

3. A permissive or compulsory counterclaim may be for an amount within or below the court's minimum jurisdiction, but it cannot be for an amount above the court's maximum jurisdiction. *See* TEX. R. CIV. P. 97(a); *Kitchen Designs, Inc. v. Wood*, 584 S.W.2d 305, 307 (Tex. Civ. App.—Texarkana 1979, writ ref'd n.r.e.).

4. An order that severs a compulsory counterclaim from the main suit is an abuse of discretion. *Goins v. League Bank & Trust*, 857 S.W.2d 628, 630 (Tex. App.—Houston [1st Dist.] 1993, no writ) (citing *Guaranty Fed. Sav. Bank v. Horseshoe Operating Co.* 793 S.W.2d 652, 658 (Tex. 1990)).

5. When the counterclaim is for an amount in excess of the jurisdictional limits of the court, the trial court should dismiss the counterclaim. *Kitchen Designs, Inc. v. Wood*, 584 S.W.2d 305 (Tex. Civ. App.—Texarkana 1979, writ ref'd n.r.e.); 2 MCDONALD'S TEXAS CIVIL PRACTICE, § 7.51.2, p. 293 (1970); 15 TEX. JUR. 2D *Courts*, § 81, p. 520 (1960).

9. *Limits on Jurisdictional Power*

UNIVERSITY OF TEXAS
v.
MORRIS
162 Tex. 60, 344 S.W.2d 426
(1961)

A district court having jurisdiction of the parties and the subject matter may enjoin a party from prosecuting a cause of action in another court when such relief is necessary to prevent a multiplicity of suits, avoid vexatious litigation, or prohibit the use of the judicial processes for purposes of harassment. [This is limited on intra-state litigation by the holding in ***Donovan v. City of Dallas,*** *infra.*]

DONOVAN
v.
CITY OF DALLAS
377 U. S. 408, 84 S.Ct. 1579, 12 L. Ed. 2d 409
(1964)

A state court cannot enjoin a person from prosecuting an action in personam in a district or appellate court of the United States which has jurisdiction both of the parties and of the subject matter.

Congress has authorized federal courts to restrain state-court proceedings in some special circumstances.

However, in cases of in rem or quasi in rem proceedings the state or federal court having custody of the property has exclusive jurisdiction to proceed.

HARRIS COUNTY
v.
SYKES
136 S.W.3d 635
(Tex. 2004)

Kevin D. Jewell, Chamberlain Hrdlicka White Williams & Martin, Casey Todd Wallace and Michael A Stafford, Harris County Atty., Michael R. Hull, Harris County Attorney's Office, Houston, for Petitioner.
Okon J. Usoro, Okon J. Usoro, P.C., Houston, for Respondent.

CHIEF JUSTICE PHILLIPS delivered the opinion of the Court, in which JUSTICE HECHT, JUSTICE OWEN, JUSTICE JEFFERSON, JUSTICE SMITH, and JUSTICE WAINWRIGHT joined.

This case raises two issues. First, we address whether an order granting a governmental unit's plea to the jurisdiction should be with or without prejudice when the claimant has failed to state a claim that is cognizable under the Texas Tort Claims Act. Regardless of the answer, we must then decide whether such a dismissal is a judgment for the purposes of section 101.106 of the Texas Tort Claims Act, that would bar a plaintiff from proceeding against governmental agents for claims arising from the same subject matter. *See* TEX. CIV. PRAC. &

REM.CODE § 101.106. The court of appeals held that a dismissal pursuant to a plea to the jurisdiction is a dismissal without prejudice, and as such, not a judgment under the Texas Tort Claims Act. 89 S.W.3d 661, 670. We hold that such a dismissal is with prejudice because it fully and finally adjudicates whether the claims that were asserted, or that could have been asserted, come within the Texas Tort Claims Act's waiver of sovereign immunity. We further hold that such a dismissal is a judgment under section 101.106 of the Texas Tort Claims Act. Accordingly, we modify the judgment of the court of appeals to render judgment dismissing the plaintiff's claims with prejudice and render judgment that the plaintiff take nothing.

I

George Sykes and his wife, Faye, brought this suit for injuries Mr. Sykes allegedly sustained in the Harris County jail. While incarcerated there, Mr. Sykes was assigned to a bed next to an inmate who was infected with tuberculosis. The Sykeses claimed that the county was negligent in failing to quarantine the infected inmate and in failing to warn Mr. Sykes of the inmate's infection. Several months after filing suit, Faye Sykes filed a suggestion informing the trial court of her husband's death. At the same time, she filed a motion, on which the trial court apparently never ruled, requesting that Trenard Battle, Mr. Sykes's minor son, be added as a plaintiff and that the estate of George Sykes be substituted in the place of her late husband.

Asserting governmental immunity from suit, Harris County filed a plea to the jurisdiction arguing that the Legislature has not waived immunity from suits like the Sykes's. Sykes responded that immunity was waived by the Texas Tort Claims Act because her husband's injuries arose out of the condition or use of property. TEX. CIV. PRAC. & REM.CODE § 101.021. Specifically, Sykes argued that the words "housed," "room," and "sleeping space" in their pleadings all connote use of the tangible personal or real property that caused Mr. Sykes's injury and eventual death.

By amended petition, Sykes added Carl Borchers, the major of the Harris County jail, as a defendant both individually and in his official capacity. The trial court subsequently granted Harris County's plea to the jurisdiction and dismissed Sykes's claims against Harris County with prejudice. Borchers then moved for summary judgment, urging that the trial court's dismissal of Harris County entitled him to derivative immunity under section 101.106 of the Texas Tort Claims Act. *See id.* § 101.106; *Thomas v. Oldham*, 895 S.W.2d 352, 357 (Tex. 1995). The trial court granted Borchers's motion and signed an order that Sykes take nothing.

Sykes appealed, arguing that the trial court erred in granting the plea to the jurisdiction and dismissing her claims against Harris County because the Texas Tort Claims Act waives immunity when a condition or use of tangible personal property causes injury. *See* TEX. CIV. PRAC. & REM.CODE § 101.021. Sykes also argued that the trial court further erred in granting Borchers's motion for summary judgment because Harris County's dismissal was not a judgment for purposes of section 101.106. *See id.* § 101.106. The court of appeals affirmed the trial court's dismissal of Harris County, holding that Sykes's amended petition did not affirmatively plead facts sufficient to confer jurisdiction on the trial court. 89 S.W.3d at 667. But the court decided that, in granting the plea to the jurisdiction, the trial court could only dismiss the suit without prejudice, which did not qualify as a judgment under section 101.106 of the Texas Tort Claims Act. 89 S.W.3d at 668. Accordingly, the court of appeals reversed Carl Borchers's summary judgment and remanded the case to the trial court. We granted Carl Borchers and Harris County's petition for review.

II

Sovereign immunity from suit defeats a trial court's subject matter jurisdiction unless the state expressly consents to suit. *Tex. Dep't of Transp. v. Jones*, 8 S.W.3d 636, 638 (Tex. 1999). Governmental immunity operates like sovereign immunity to afford similar protection to subdivisions of the State, including counties, cities, and school districts. *See Wichita Falls State Hosp. v. Taylor*, 106 S.W.3d 692, 694 n. 3 (Tex. 2003) (recognizing that sovereign immunity and governmental immunity are distinct concepts although courts often use the terms interchangeably). The Texas Tort Claims Act provides a limited waiver of governmental immunity if certain conditions are met. *See* TEX. CIV. PRAC. & REM.CODE §§ 101.021, 101.025.

A plea to the jurisdiction is a dilatory plea that seeks dismissal of a case for lack of subject matter jurisdiction. *Bland Indep. Sch. Dist. v. Blue*, 34 S.W.3d 547, 554 (Tex. 2000). Because governmental immunity from suit defeats a trial court's jurisdiction, it may be raised by such a plea. *Tex. Dep't of Parks & Wildlife v. Miranda*, 133 S.W.3d 217, 225-26 (Tex. 2004); *Jones*, 8 S.W.3d at 639. Whether a court has subject matter jurisdiction is a legal question. *State ex rel. State Dep't of Highways & Pub. Transp. v. Gonzalez*, 82 S.W.3d 322, 327 (Tex. 2002); *Mayhew v. Town of Sunnyvale*, 964 S.W.2d 922, 928 (Tex. 1998). If the trial court denies the governmental entity's claim of no jurisdiction, whether it has been asserted by a plea to the jurisdiction, a motion for summary judgment, or otherwise, the Legislature has provided that an interlocutory appeal may be brought. *See* TEX. CIV. PRAC. & REM.CODE § 51.014; *San Antonio State Hosp. v. Cowan*, 128 S.W.3d 244, 245 n. 3 (Tex. 2004). However, if the court grants the plea to the jurisdiction, as the trial court did in this case, the plaintiff may take an appeal once that judgment becomes final. See *Cash Am. Int'l Inc. v. Bennett*, 35 S.W.3d 12, 15 (Tex. 2000).

A trial court must grant a plea to the jurisdiction, after providing an appropriate opportunity to amend, when the pleadings do not state a cause of action upon which the trial court has jurisdiction. See *Bybee v. Fireman's Fund Ins. Co.*, 160 Tex. 429, 331 S.W.2d 910, 917 (1960) (citing *Lone Star Fin. Corp. v. Davis*, 77 S.W.2d 711, 715 (Tex. App.—Eastland 1934, no writ)). This was such a case. After Harris County filed its plea to the jurisdiction, Sykes amended her petition to state with greater particularity the theory that Harris County waived governmental immunity by placing Mr. Sykes in the same room with, and assigning him a bed near, an inmate infected with tuberculosis. The trial court dismissed Sykes's claims, and the court of appeals agreed that "any effect that the room's walls and Sykes's bed had on Sykes's alleged exposure to tuberculosis is too attenuated to constitute a waiver of immunity under the [Texas Tort Claims Act]." 89 S.W.3d at 667 (citing *Dallas County Mental Health & Mental Retardation v. Bossley*, 968 S.W.2d 339, 343 (Tex. 1998)).

The court of appeals disagreed with the trial court, however, on whether such a dismissal should be with or without prejudice. In general, a dismissal with prejudice is improper when the plaintiff is capable of remedying the jurisdictional defect. See *Dahl v. State*, 92 S.W.3d 856, 862 (Tex. App.—Houston [14th Dist.] 2002, no pet.); *Thomas v. Skinner*, 54 S.W.3d 845, 847 (Tex. App.—Corpus Christi 2001, pet. denied); *Bell v. State Dep't of Highways & Pub. Transp.*, 945 S.W.2d 292, 295 (Tex. App.—Houston [14th Dist.] 1997, writ denied). The court of appeals in this case relied on Bell to hold that Sykes's claims should have been dismissed without prejudice. In so doing, the court ruled contrary to a line of decisions stating that dismissal with prejudice is appropriate when a trial court lacks subject matter jurisdiction because of the sovereign immunity bar. . . . We granted Borchers and Harris County's petition to resolve this conflict.

If a plaintiff has been provided a reasonable opportunity to amend after a governmental entity files its plea to the jurisdiction, and the plaintiff's amended pleading still does not allege facts that would constitute a waiver of immunity, then the trial court should dismiss the plaintiff's action. Such a dismissal is with prejudice because a plaintiff should not be permitted to relitigate jurisdiction once that issue has been finally determined. Before dismissing this case, the trial court allowed Sykes to file an amended petition, after which the court made a final adjudication that the Legislature has not waived governmental immunity under the Texas Tort Claims Act with respect to any claim that Sykes brought against Harris County.

Therefore, Sykes is foreclosed from relitigating whether the Texas Tort Claims Act waives immunity in this case. Accordingly, the court below erred in reversing the dismissal with prejudice, and we modify the court of appeals' judgment to dismiss Sykes's claims against Harris County with prejudice.

III

Next, we address the court of appeals' holding reversing the summary judgment granted by the trial court in favor of Carl Borchers. The Texas Tort Claims Act states: "A judgment in an action or a settlement of a claim under this chapter bars any action involving the same subject matter by the claimant against the employee of the governmental unit whose act or omission gave rise to the claim." TEX. CIV. PRAC. & REM.CODE § 101.106. The purpose of section 101.106 is to protect employees of a governmental unit from liability when a judgment or settlement has been obtained from the government employer pursuant to a claim under Chapter 101 of the Texas Tort Claims Act. *Thomas v. Oldham*, 895 S.W.2d 352, 357 (Tex. 1995). Section 101.106 applies not only when there has been a judgment against a governmental entity prior to the suit against the employee, but also when the settlement or judgment against the governmental entity occurs at any time before or during the pendency of the action against the employee. *Id.* at 355. The bar applies regardless of whether the judgment is favorable or adverse to the governmental unit. *Dallas County Mental Health & Mental Retardation v. Bossley*, 968 S.W.2d 339, 343 (Tex. 1998).

This Court has never addressed whether a dismissal on a plea to the jurisdiction is a judgment for purposes of section 101.106 of the Texas Tort Claims Act. Several courts of appeals, however, have considered this issue. In *Brown v. Prairie View A & M Univ.*, the Fourteenth Court of Appeals held that dismissing Prairie View A & M pursuant to a plea to the jurisdiction was not a judgment that triggered the bar of the Texas Tort Claims

Act. 630 S.W.2d 405, 408 (Tex. App.—Houston [14th Dist.] 1982, writ ref'd n.r.e.). Since *Brown*, however, that court, as well as two other courts of appeals, have held that a dismissal pursuant to a plea to the jurisdiction is a judgment for purposes of section 101.106 of the Texas Tort Claims Act. . . .

Sykes argues that a granted plea to the jurisdiction does not qualify as a judgment because it does not dispose of the claims' merits. As we have already held, however, a dismissal constitutes a final determination on the merits of the matter actually decided. *See Ritchey v. Vasquez*, 986 S.W.2d 611, 612 (Tex. 1999) (per curiam); *Mossler v. Shields*, 818 S.W.2d 752, 754 (Tex. 1991) (per curiam). In this case, there is a final adjudication that the Legislature has not waived Harris County's immunity on the facts of this case. Since the trial court properly dismissed Sykes's claims against Harris County with prejudice, Carl Borchers is entitled to derivative immunity under section 101.106 of the Texas Tort Claims Act.

The court of appeals erred in holding that the claims against Harris County should be dismissed without prejudice and that such a dismissal is not a judgment under section 101.106 of the Texas Tort Claims Act. Accordingly, we modify the judgment of the court of appeals and render judgment that the plaintiff's suit is dismissed with prejudice. We also reverse the portion of the court of appeals' judgment reversing Carl Borchers's summary judgment and render judgment that the plaintiff take nothing.

JUSTICE BRISTER, joined by JUSTICE O'NEILL, concurring (omitted).

JUSTICE SCHNEIDER did not participate in the decision.

CHAPTER 3.
DISPOSITION WITHOUT TRIAL

1. *Default Judgment*

Rule 99a. Texas Rules of Civil Procedure: Issuance of Citation:

The citation shall direct the defendant to file a written answer to the plaintiff's petition on or before 10:00 a.m. on the Monday next after the expiration of twenty days after the date of service thereof. The requirement of subsections 10 and 12 of this section shall be in the form set forth in section c of this rule.

Rule 107(h). Texas Rules of Civil Procedure:

No default judgment shall be granted in any cause until proof of service as provided by this rule or by Rules 108 or 108a, or as ordered by the court in the event citation is executed by an alternative method under Rule 106, shall have been on file with the clerk of the court ten days, exclusive of the day of filing and the day of judgment.

Read Rules 241 and 243 Texas Rules of Civil Procedure

PARAMOUNT PIPE & SUPPLY CO.
v.
MUHR
749 S.W.2d 491
(Tex. 1988)

Marc O. Knisely and Robert C. Alden, McGinnis, Lochridge & Kilgore, Austin, Don Johnson, Johnson, Jones & Autry, Coleman, Travis Hartgraves, Abilene, for petitioner.

W.K. Rutledge and Evans S. Rutledge, Rutledge & Rutledge, Abilene, for respondent.

KILGARLIN, JUSTICE.

These causes concern the validity of two default judgments. Paramount Pipe & Supply Co., Inc. and Winters Flexline Service Company are oil and gas field equipment suppliers. In separate lawsuits (consolidated for argument in our court), Paramount Pipe and Winters Flexline sued Western International Petroleum Corporation and Ulrich Muhr, seeking payment for materials and services furnished in connection with the drilling and operation of oil and gas wells. Paramount Pipe and Winters Flexline also sought foreclosure of mechanics' and materialmen's liens.

Neither Western International nor Ulrich Muhr filed an answer. The trial court rendered default judgments in both cases ($16,825.21 plus interest, and $4,000 attorney's fees for Paramount Pipe; $21,688.98 plus interest, and $7,000 attorney's fees for Winters Flexline). Ulrich Muhr appealed by writ of error. Western International did not seek relief from the default judgments. The court of appeals reversed and remanded for new trial Paramount Pipe's claims against Muhr * * * 737 S.W.2d 385. In a separate unpublished opinion, the court of appeals similarly reversed and remanded Winters Flexline's claims. We reverse the judgments of the court of appeals and affirm the judgments of the trial court.

* * *

Next, Ulrich Muhr argues there is no evidence to support the finding that he was indebted to either Paramount Pipe or Winters Flexline. Muhr submits that nothing in the record evidences any sale or delivery of materials or services to him. As to default judgments, however, the non-answering party has "admitted" the facts properly pleaded and the justice of the opponent's claim. *Stoner*, 578 S.W.2d at 682. Also, and as noted above, a petition providing fair notice of the claims asserted, absent other deficiencies, will support a default judgment. The original petitions in question alleged agency and documented the indebtedness of Western International. We overrule this no evidence contention.

Muhr further argues there was no evidence to support the amount of damages awarded to Paramount Pipe. It is true that when damages are unliquidated or not proved by an instrument in writing, the court must conduct a hearing as to damages before a final default judgment may be granted. TEX. R. CIV. P. 243. The record reflects testimony by an officer from Paramount Pipe as to the reasonableness of the charges and the amount of the unpaid accounts. His testimony was consistent with the damages pleaded and the invoices attached to the petition. We further reject as meritless Muhr's apparent claim that, as to one of the leases, a fifty-seven cent discrepancy between the amount alleged in the petition and the amount shown by the attached invoices is fatal to Paramount Pipe's claim.

Muhr likewise alleges error in the trial court's award of attorney's fees to Paramount Pipe and Winters Flexline. Muhr relies on TEX. CIV. PRAC. & REM. CODE § 38.002 (Vernon 1986). He urges that neither Paramount Pipe nor Winters Flexline alleged proper presentation of their claims to Muhr nor his failure to tender the just amount owed before the expiration of the thirtieth day after such presentation. However, both petitions specifically alleged that: Plaintiff has provided Defendant Ulrich Muhr with notice, by certified mailings, of the Liens claimed by Plaintiff on the [aforementioned leases], and Defendant Ulrich Muhr has failed and refused to pay the sums lawfully due and owing to Plaintiff. Both petitions also specifically prayed for recovery of attorney's fees. Certainly the omission to allege that Muhr failed to tender payment within thirty days would have been subject to attack by special exception. We conclude, however, that the petitions gave Muhr fair notice that Paramount Pipe and Winters Flexline were seeking recovery of attorney's fees. We hold there was no error in the judgments awarding attorney's fees against Muhr.

Lastly, Muhr urges that the trial court erred in ruling that Paramount Pipe and Winters Flexline's mechanic's and materialman's liens are valid. We reject these contentions. The affidavits and exhibits before us satisfy the requirements of TEX. PROP. CODE ANN. § 56.022 (Vernon 1986). In addition, both the petitions allege that the plaintiffs "performed services and provided materials to mineral leasehold properties" and that "defendant, Ulrich Muhr, knew or reasonably should have known of the business activities of defendant Western . . . in connection with mineral development of the Moon and Creswell leases . . . ." We find no error.

We reverse the judgments of the court of appeals and affirm the judgments of the trial court.

HOLT ATHERTON INDUS.
v.
HEINE
835 S.W.2d 80
(Tex. 1992)

G. Wade Caldwell, Michael Golightly, Rebecca Simmons, San Antonio, for petitioner.
David C. Griffin, Cynthia T. Sheppard, John Griffin, Victoria, for respondents.

COOK, JUSTICE.

This case presents two questions: 1) whether the trial court abused its discretion in denying the motion of defendant Holt Atherton Industries, Inc. to set aside default judgment and for new trial; and 2) whether there is any evidence to support recovery of lost profits. We hold that the trial court did not abuse its discretion in denying the motion for new trial and that the evidence is legally insufficient to support recovery of lost profits. Therefore, we affirm in part and reverse in part the judgment of the court of appeals. 797 S.W.2d 250.

In January 1987, Roy and Kitty Heine took their bulldozer to Holt Machinery Company for repairs under an alleged oral warranty. Holt Machinery did not recognize the oral warranty. The bulldozer remained in the possession of Holt Machinery but it was not being repaired because Holt Machinery did not recognize the warranty and the Heines did not agree to pay for repairs. In August of 1987, Holt Machinery merged into Holt Atherton Industries, Inc. Holt Atherton then merged into B.D. Holt Company. In September of 1987, the Heines agreed to pay for the repairs to their bulldozer. In March 1988, the Heines brought this action against B.D. Holt, B.D. Holt Co., and Holt Co. of Texas alleging violations of the Deceptive Trade Practices Act (TEX. BUS. & COM. CODE §§ 17.41-17.63), breach of express and implied warranties, breach of contract, negligence, and tortious interference with business relations. In July 1988, the Heines' Second Amended Original Petition added Holt Atherton as a defendant and was properly served on Holt Atherton's registered agent, Stevenson Atherton. In August 1988, the trial court rendered default judgment against Holt Atherton due to its failure to appear and answer. The Heines severed their cause of action against Holt Atherton to obtain a final judgment. Subsequently, the trial court stayed the actions against the other defendants pending the outcome of this appeal. Holt Atherton moved to set aside the default judgment and for new trial. The trial court denied Holt Atherton's motion, and the court of appeals affirmed. 797 S.W.2d 250.

* * *

Once a default judgment is taken on an unliquidated claim, all allegations of fact set forth in the petition are deemed admitted, except the amount of damages. *Morgan v. Compugraphic Corp.*, 675 S.W.2d 729, 731 (Tex. 1984). A court rendering a default judgment must hear evidence of unliquidated damages. TEX. R. CIV. P. 243; *see Morgan*, 675 S.W.2d at 731. The trial court, in this case, held a hearing and determined that the Heines suffered damages in the amount of $159,665 including $120,000 for lost profits.

Holt Atherton argues that there is no evidence supporting the trial court's award of damages for lost profits. "In a nonjury trial, where no findings of fact or conclusions of law are filed or requested, it will be implied that the trial court made all the necessary findings to support its judgment." *Burnett v. Motyka*, 610 S.W.2d 735, 736 (Tex. 1980) (*citing Goodyear Tire and Rubber Co. v. Jefferson Construction Co.*, 565 S.W.2d 916 (Tex. 1978); *Lassiter v. Bliss*, 559 S.W.2d 353 (Tex. 1978)). When, as in this case, a statement of facts is brought forward, these implied findings may be challenged by factual or legal sufficiency points. *Roberson v. Robinson*, 768 S.W.2d 280, 281 (Tex. 1989); *Burnett*, 610 S.W.2d at 736. In determining a legal sufficiency question, a court must consider only the evidence and inferences that tend to support the finding, and disregard all evidence and inferences to the contrary. *Best v. Ryan Auto Group, Inc.*, 786 S.W.2d 670, 671 (Tex. 1990); *King v. Bauer*, 688 S.W.2d 845, 846 (Tex. 1985). If there is more than a scintilla of evidence to support the finding, the no evidence challenge fails. *Stafford v. Stafford*, 726 S.W.2d 14, 16 (Tex. 1987); *Kindred v. Con/Chem, Inc.*, 650 S.W.2d 61, 63 (Tex. 1983). * * * [After reviewing the evidence the court determined that it was] legally insufficient to provide a reasonable basis for determining the Heines' lost profits.

III.

We affirm the court of appeals' holding that the trial court did not abuse its discretion in denying Holt Atherton's motion for new trial and reverse the court of appeals' holding that the evidence supporting an award of lost profits was legally sufficient. As a general matter, when we sustain a no evidence point of error after a trial on the merits, we render judgment on that point. TEX. R. APP. P. 81(c); *Mobil Oil Corp. v. Frederick*, 621 S.W.2d 595, 596 (Tex. 1981); *National Life and Accident Ins. Co. v. Blagg*, 438 S.W.2d 905, 909 (Tex. 1969); *Garza v. Alviar*, 395 S.W.2d 821, 823 (Tex. 1965). Texas courts view an appeal from a default judgment somewhat differently than an appeal from a trial on the merits. In part, this is because an adjudication on the merits is preferred in Texas. *See, e.g., In re T.B.S.*, 601 S.W.2d 539, 543 (Tex. Civ. App.—Tyler 1980, no writ).

After a default judgment is granted, the trial court must hear evidence of unliquidated damages. TEX. R. CIV. P. 243. However, as a practical matter, in an uncontested hearing, evidence of unliquidated damages is often not fully developed. This is particularly true when the trial judge expresses a willingness to enter judgment on the evidence that has been presented. Therefore, when an appellate court sustains a no evidence point after an uncontested hearing on unliquidated damages following a no-answer default judgment, the appropriate disposition is a remand for a new trial on the issue of unliquidated damages.

We remand the cause to the trial court for a new trial on the issue of lost profits.

DOGGETT, J., concurring and dissenting, joined by JUSTICE MAUZY [opinion omitted].

Notes

1. There are four types of default judgments:

1) The "true default" occurs when the D fails to appear on "answer day" (or the day on which default is entered). Then the P must prove unliquidated damages and, at least in a personal injury case, a causal nexus between the event sued upon and the P's injuries.

2) A nihil dicit judgment exists where the D has appeared but has had a plea or motion not dealing with the merits of the case overruled leaving D with no answer.

3) A post-answer default occurs where there is a failure to appear (or an impossibility of appearance). Here there is no admission of liability & the P must prove both liability & damages.

4) A post-appearance default. Once a defendant has made an appearance in a cause, he is entitled to notice of the trial setting as a matter of due process under the Fourteenth Amendment to the federal constitution, as set forth in *Peralta v. Heights Medical Center, Inc*., 485 U.S. 80, 108 S.Ct. 896, 99 L.Ed.2d 75 (1988). *LBL Oil Co. v. International Power Services, Inc*.,777 S.W.2d 390, 391 (Tex. 1989.

2. *Sedona Pacific. Housing Partnership v. Ventura*, 408 S.W.3d 507, 511 (Tex. App.—El Paso, 2013, no pet,).

"There are several types of default judgments. They generally fit into pre- or post-answer default judgments, but other variations exist which do not fit neatly into either category. *Paradigm Oil, Inc. v. Retamco Operating, Inc*., 372 S.W.3d 177, 184 (Tex. 2012).

"A traditional no-answer default judgment can be taken when the defendant is properly served with citation but fails to answer or appear. TEX. R. CIV. P. 239. A defendant who has not answered or otherwise appeared in the case is not entitled to notice of a default judgment proceeding. *Wilson v. Wilson*, 132 S.W.3d 533, 536 (Tex. App.—Houston [1st Dist.] 2004, pet. denied). A judgment nihil dicit is usually "limited to situations in which either (1) the defendant has made a plea, usually dilatory in nature, but the pleading has not placed the merits of the plaintiff's case in issue before it is overruled, or (2) the defendant has placed the merits of the case in issue by filing an answer, but has withdrawn that answer." *Paradigm Oil*, 372 S.W.3d at 184 n. 8, quoting 7 William V. Dorsaneo III, TEXAS LITIGATION GUIDE § 100.01[3] at 100-11 (2011).

"A no-answer default and a judgment nihil dicit are so similar that the same rules apply to each with respect to the effect and validity of the judgment. *Stoner*, 578 S.W.2d at 682. In both instances, the non-answering party has "admitted" the facts properly pled and the justice of the opponent's claim, although a judgment nihil dicit carries an even stronger confession than the no-answer default judgment. *Id*.

"A post-answer default occurs when the defendant has filed an answer but fails to appear for trial. It differs from the no-answer default and the judgment nihil dicit in that it does not constitute an abandonment of the defendant's answer and it is not an implied confession of any issues joined by the defendant's answer. *Stoner*, 578 S.W.2d at 682. Consequently, judgment cannot be entered on the pleadings, and the plaintiff is required to offer evidence and prove his case as in a judgment upon a trial. *Id*.

"The Supreme Court had also recognized a fourth category of default judgment: a post-appearance default judgment. *LBL Oil Co. v. International Power Services, Inc*., 777 S.W.2d 390 (Tex. 1989). This type of default judgment occurs when the defendant makes a general appearance but fails to answer or appear for trial. Once a defendant has made an appearance, he is entitled to notice of the trial setting as a matter of due process under the Fourteenth Amendment. *Peralta v. Heights Medical Center, Inc*., 485 U.S. 80, 108 S.Ct. 896, 99 L.Ed.2d 75 (1988); *LBL Oil*, 777 S.W.2d at 390-91; *In re Brilliant*, 86 S.W.3d 680, 693 (Tex. App.—El Paso 2002, orig. proceeding). A party enters a general appearance when he (1) invokes the judgment of the court on any question other than the court's jurisdiction, (2) recognizes by his acts that an action is properly pending, or (3) seeks affirmative action from the court. *Exito Electronics Co., Ltd. v. Trejo*, 142 S.W.3d 302, 304 (Tex. 2004); *Dawson-Austin v. Austin*, 968 S.W.2d 319, 322 (Tex. 1998)."

3. *Morgan v. Compugraphic Corporation,* 675 S.W.2d 729 (Tex. 1984). In this case, the plaintiff sued the defendant for negligence and products liability alleging injuries (ultimately to her circulatory, digestive and nervous systems) resulting from her exposure to chemical fumes emitting from a typesetting machine installed in her office. Compugraphic did not appear and answer and a default judgment was entered upon proof of damages. The Supreme Court held that in addition to proving the amount of unliquidated damages, the plaintiff taking the default judgment was required, at a hearing held in accordance with TEX. R. CIV. P. 243, to prove a causal nexus between the event sued upon and the plaintiff's injuries [which is not admitted by default).

The Court continued by noting that, in a personal injury case the plaintiff must establish two causal nexuses in order to recover: (a) a causal nexus between the defendant's conduct and the event sued upon [which is admitted by default] and (b) a causal nexus between the event sued upon and the plaintiff's injuries [which is not admitted by default]. It is the causal nexus between the conduct of the defendant and the event sued upon that is admitted by default. Proving that the event sued upon caused the plaintiff's alleged injuries is part and parcel of proving the amount of damages to which the plaintiff is entitled. *The causal nexus between the event sued upon and the plaintiff's injuries must be shown by competent evidence.*

4. In order to take a default judgment, the return of citation must be on file with the clerk for at least ten (10) days. TEX. R. CIV. P. 107: "No default judgment shall be granted in any cause until the citation . . . shall have been on file with the clerk of the court ten days, exclusive of the day of filing and the day of judgment."

5. Rule 239a of the TEX. R. CIV. P. provides that the individual who obtains a default judgment shall file with the clerk of the court a default judgment certificate containing the last known mailing address of the party against whom the default judgment was rendered, and the clerk of the court shall mail to such party at the address contained in the certificate notice of the rendition of such judgment. However, the rule notes that "[f]ailure to comply with the provisions of this rule shall not affect the finality of the judgment".

6. In *Dolgencorp of Texas, Inc. v. Lerma*, 288 S.W.3d 922, 929-30 (Tex. 2009) the Court discussed the appropriate appellate remedy when reversing a post-answer default judgment as follows:

> Generally, if an appellate court holds there is legally insufficient evidence to support a judgment after a trial on the merits, the proper disposition is to reverse and render judgment. *Holt Atherton Indus., Inc. v. Heine,* 835 S.W.2d 80, 86 (Tex. 1992); *Mobil Oil Corp. v. Frederick,* 621 S.W.2d 595, 596 (Tex. 1981); *see* TEX.R.CIV. P. 43.3, 60.2. But in *Holt Atherton,* we held that when a plaintiff fails to present legally sufficient evidence at an uncontested hearing on unliquidated damages following a *no-answer* default judgment, the proper disposition is to remand for a new trial on the issue of damages. 835 S.W.2d at 86. We reasoned that the plaintiff should be afforded a second opportunity to present evidence in support of its claims because "as a practical matter, in an uncontested hearing, evidence of unliquidated damages is often not fully developed." *Id.*
>
> Courts of appeals have reached differing results as to the proper disposition of a case when there is legally insufficient evidence to support a *post-answer* default judgment. *Compare Renteria v. Trevino,* 79 S.W.3d 240, 243 (Tex. App.—Houston [14th Dist.] 2002, no pet.) (rendering judgment without discussion), *and Wallace v. Ramon,* 82 S.W.3d 501, 506 (Tex. App.—San Antonio 2002, no pet.) (same), *and Sutton v. Hisaw & Assocs. Gen. Contractors, Inc.,* 65 S.W.3d 281, 286 (Tex. App.—Dallas 2001, pet. denied) (same), *with In re Estate of Wilson,* 252 S.W.3d 708, 715 & n. 8 (Tex. App.—Texarkana 2008, no pet.) (noting authorities allowing a case reversed on no evidence grounds to be remanded when the facts have not been fully developed, such as in a post-answer default judgment), *and Armstrong v. Benavides,* 180 S.W.3d 359, 364 (Tex. App.—Dallas 2005, no pet.) (remanding under *Holt Atherton* because facts had not been fully developed), *and Raines v. Gomez,* 143 S.W.3d 867, 869 (Tex. App.—Texarkana 2004, no pet.) (remanding without discussion), *and Thorp v. Adair & Myers,* 809 S.W.2d 306, 308-09 (Tex. App.—Houston [14th Dist.] 1991, no writ) (remanding for further factual development in the interest of justice).
>
> No-answer and post-answer default judgments differ in the issues a plaintiff is required to prove. In cases of no-answer default, such as *Holt Atherton,* a defaulting defendant admits all facts properly pled in the plaintiff's petition except for the amount of unliquidated damages. *Holt Atherton,* 835 S.W.2d at 83. Thus, the plaintiff is only required to prove its claim for unliquidated damages. *Id.; see* TEX.R. CIV. P. 243. But if the defendant files an answer, as in this case, a trial court may not render judgment on the pleadings and the plaintiff is required to offer evidence and prove all aspects of its claim. *Bradley Motors, Inc. v. Mackey,* 878 S.W.2d 140, 141 (Tex. 1994); *Stoner,* 578 S.W.2d at 682. We, however, see no reason why this difference should result in judgment being rendered rather than remanded in cases of post-answer default.
>
> In both types of default judgment, a plaintiff must present evidence, but the uncontested proceedings are often abbreviated and perfunctory. In the absence of opposing counsel, an uncontested trial, like an uncontested damages hearing, is less likely to result in a fully-developed factual record. *See Holt Atherton,* 835 S.W.2d at 86; *see also U.S. Fire Ins. Co. v. Carter,* 473 S.W.2d 2, 3 (Tex. 1971) (noting an appellate court may remand when the case has not been fully developed). That is reflected in this case. Although Lerma had the burden to prove all elements of its claim, the trial court opined "[t]his will be only an issue of damages, not negligence, [so] prove it up the way you want to prove it up."
>
> We conclude that the better rule is the one expressed in *Holt Atherton* and by the courts of appeals that have remanded for a new trial after a post-answer default judgment rather than rendering judgment.

2. *Dismissal for Lack of Prosecution*

Read Rule 165a Texas Rules of Civil Procedure

Note

1. The appellate standard of review of a dismissal for want of prosecution is whether the trial court committed a clear abuse of discretion. *Bevil v. Johnson*, 157 Tex. 621, 307 S.W.2d 85, 87 (1957). To determine if there is an abuse of discretion, the appellate court must look to see if the trial court acted without reference to any guiding rules and principles. *Morrow v. H.E.B., Inc.*, 714 S.W.2d 297 (Tex. 1986). On the issue of dismissal for want of prosecution, the sole test is whether the case was prosecuted to judgment with reasonable diligence and the court has the inherent power to dismiss if the plaintiff fails to do this. *See generally, Bard v. Frank B. Hall & Co.*, 767 S.W.2d 839 (Tex. App.—San Antonio 1989, writ denied); *Stromberg Carlson Leasing Corp. v. Central Welding Supply Co.*, 750 S.W.2d 862, 864 (Tex. App.—Houston [14th Dist.] 1988, no writ). In addition, TEX. R. CIV. P. 165a expressly authorizes trial courts to dismiss a case which was not prosecuted diligently. However, the trial court's right to dismiss a suit for failure to prosecute it with due diligence is not an unbridled discretion, but a judicial discretion subject to review.

2. The Texas Rules of Judicial Administration provide as follows:

Rule 6. Time Standards for the Disposition of Cases.

Rule 6.1 District and Statutory County Courts.

District and statutory county court judges of the county in which cases are filed should, so far as reasonably possible, ensure that all cases are brought to trial or final disposition in conformity with the following time standards:

(a) Criminal Cases. As provided by Article 32A.02, Code of Criminal Procedure.

(b) Civil Cases Other Than Family Law.

(1) Civil Jury Cases. Within 18 months from appearance date.

(2) Civil Nonjury Cases. Within 12 months from appearance date.

(c) Family Law Cases.

(1) Contested Family Law Cases. Within 6 months from appearance date or within 6 months from the expiration of the waiting period provided by the Family Code where such is required, whichever is later.

(2) Uncontested Family Law Cases. Within 3 months from appearance date or within 3 months from the expiration of the waiting period provided by the Family Code where such is required, whichever is later.

(d) Juvenile Cases. In addition to the requirements of Title 3, Texas Family Code:

(1) Detention Hearings. On the next business day following admission to any detention facility.

(2) Adjudicatory or Transfer (Waiver) Hearings.

(a) Concerning a juvenile in a detention facility: Not later than 10 days following admission to such a facility, except for good cause shown of record.

(b) Concerning a juvenile not in a detention facility: Not later than 30 days following the filing of the petition, except for good cause shown of record.

(3) Disposition Hearing. Not later than 15 days following the adjudicatory hearing. The court may grant additional time in exceptional cases that require more complex evaluation.

(4) Nothing herein shall prevent a judge from recessing a juvenile hearing at any stage of the proceeding where the parties are agreeable or when in the opinion of the judge presiding in the case the best interests of the child and of society shall be served.

(e) Complex Cases. It is recognized that in especially complex cases or special circumstances it may not be possible to adhere to these standards.

Rule 6.2 Appeals in Certain Cases Involving the Parent-Child Relationship.

In an appeal of a suit for termination of the parent-child relationship or a suit affecting the parent-child relationship filed by a governmental entity for managing conservatorship, appellate courts should, so far as reasonably possible, ensure that the appeal is brought to final disposition in conformity with the following time standards:

(a) Courts of Appeals. Within 180 days of the date the notice of appeal is filed.
(b) Supreme Court. Within 180 days of the date the petition for review is filed.

VILLARREAL
v.
SAN ANTONIO TRUCK & EQUIPMENT

994 S.W.2d 628
(Tex. 1999)

Luis R. Vera, Jr., Les Mendelsohn, San Antonio, for Petitioner.
Peter Y. Henry, San Antonio, for Respondents.

CHIEF JUSTICE PHILLIPS delivered the opinion of the Court, in which JUSTICE HECHT, JUSTICE OWEN, JUSTICE ABBOTT, JUSTICE HANKINSON, JUSTICE O'NEILL, and JUSTICE GONZALES, joined.

The issue presented is whether the standard notice of dismissal used by the district courts of Bexar County, which warns that a case will be dismissed "if no announcement is made" at the dismissal hearing, adequately apprises parties of the trial court's intent to dismiss for want of prosecution in the exercise of its inherent power. Because we hold that it does not, we reverse the judgment of the court of appeals, 974 S.W.2d 275, and remand this cause to the trial court for further proceedings.

On June 21, 1994, Martin Villarreal sued San Antonio Truck and Equipment, Inc., and Robert Gonzales ("Defendants") in Bexar County district court for failure to maintain a safe work environment. The parties engaged in discovery during the summer of 1994, but no further action was taken until the trial court, on its own motion, notified Villarreal on August 30, 1996, that the case was set on the October 1996 dismissal docket. The notice of setting stated:

> BY DIRECTION OF THE PRESIDING JUDGE OF SAID COURT[,] NOTICE IS HEREBY GIVEN YOU THAT THE ABOVE CAUSE(S), UPON ORDER OF THE COURT[,] IS SET FOR DISMISSAL ON THE 22ND DAY OF OCTOBER, 1996 . . . . YOU ARE REQUESTED TO BE PRESENT AND MAKE YOUR ANNOUNCEMENT. IF NO ANNOUNCEMENT IS MADE, THIS CAUSE WILL BE DISMISSED FOR WANT OF PROSECUTION. ALL ORDERS THAT WILL REMOVE A CASE FROM THE DISMISSAL DOCKET MUST BE SUBMITTED TO THE DISMISSAL DEPARTMENT ON OR BEFORE THE DATE WHEN THE DOCKET IS CALLED. YOU ARE REMINDED THAT THIS IS NOT A DOCKET FOR THE RE-SETTING OF CASES, BUT FOR THEIR DISMISSAL.

On October 21, 1996, Villarreal filed a motion to set the case on the jury docket. On October 22, 1996, he filed a motion to retain the case, asserting that he was ready to proceed to trial. That same day, the trial court held the dismissal hearing. Although the record on appeal does not contain a reporter's record of the hearing, Defendants conceded in their brief to this Court that "[t]he plaintiff and his attorney did appear at the docket [call]." At oral argument, Defendants further acknowledged that "[the plaintiff] did announce that he was ready." Because the sole issue on appeal is the adequacy of the Bexar County notice of dismissal, these statements provide a sufficient factual basis to resolve the case.

Villareal contends that the dismissal was improper because he complied with the notice's conditions of (1) presence at the dismissal docket hearing, and (2) announcement of readiness for trial. The notice, he says, limited the trial court's discretion to dismiss to those instances where "no announcement is made." Thus, Villareal argues, the trial court abused its discretion by dismissing the case for want of prosecution on the ground that "[i]t appear[ed] to the Court that there is good and sufficient reason for dismissal of these cases for want of prosecution . . . ."

Defendants maintain that the trial court committed no abuse because the Bexar County dismissal docket notice "did not mislead Villarreal. It clearly stated that the case was being set for dismissal and did not state that all Villarreal had to do as he argues, is to show up and announce ready." Defendants argue that the notice provided adequate warning that Villarreal was required to show good cause why his case should not be dismissed at the docket call hearing. The court of appeals affirmed, with one justice dissenting. 974 S.W.2d 275.

The trial court's authority to dismiss for want of prosecution stems from two sources: (1) Rule 165a of the Texas Rules of Civil Procedure, and (2) the court's inherent power. *See Veterans' Land Bd. v. Williams*, 543

S.W.2d 89, 90 (Tex. 1976); *Bevil v. Johnson*, 157 Tex. 621, 307 S.W.2d 85, 87 (1957). A trial court may dismiss under Rule 165a on "failure of any party seeking affirmative relief to appear for any hearing or trial of which the party had notice," TEX. R. CIV. P. 165a(1), or when a case is "not disposed of within the time standards promulgated by the Supreme Court . . . ." TEX. R. CIV. P. 165a(2).[3] In addition, the common law vests the trial court with the inherent power to dismiss independently of the rules of procedure when a plaintiff fails to prosecute his or her case with due diligence. *See Rizk v. Mayad*, 603 S.W.2d 773, 776 (Tex. 1980); *Williams*, 543 S.W.2d at 90.

However, a party must be provided with notice and an opportunity to be heard before a court may dismiss a case for want of prosecution under either Rule 165a or its inherent authority. *See* TEX. R. CIV. P. 165 a(1) ("Notice of the court's intention to dismiss and the date and place of the dismissal hearing shall be sent by the clerk to each attorney of record . . . ."); *General Elec. Co. v. Falcon Ridge Apartments, Joint Venture*, 811 S.W.2d 942, 943 (Tex. 1991); *Gutierrez v. Lone Star Nat'l Bank*, 960 S.W.2d 211, 214 (Tex. App.—Corpus Christi 1997, pet. denied) (requiring notice for dismissals under Rule 165a); *see also State v. Rotello*, 671 S.W.2d 507, 508-09 (Tex. 1984); *Callahan v. Staples*, 139 Tex. 8, 161 S.W.2d 489, 491 (1942) (requiring notice for dismissals under the court's inherent power). The failure to provide adequate notice of the trial court's intent to dismiss for want of prosecution requires reversal. *See Donnell v. Spring Sports, Inc.*, 920 S.W.2d 378, 386 (Tex. App.—Houston [1st Dist.] 1996, writ denied); *Davis v. Laredo Diesel, Inc.*, 611 S.W.2d 943, 946-47 (Tex. Civ. App.—Waco 1981, writ ref'd n.r.e.).

The notice of setting sent to Villarreal warned of dismissal for the failure to make an announcement at the dismissal hearing. Thus, the notice apprised Villarreal of a possible Rule 165a(1) dismissal for failure to make an appearance. Because it is undisputed that Villarreal did appear, the trial court could not have dismissed this case for want of prosecution under Rule 165a(1). Nonetheless, Defendants contend that the dismissal was warranted under the trial court's inherent power to dismiss[4] and argue that the notice of setting warned of the trial court's intent to invoke this power.

The court of appeals agreed:

> The notice in the instant case expressly stated that the case was set on the dismissal docket upon the court's own motion. The placement of a case on the dismissal docket on a court's own motion is nothing but an exercise of the trial court's inherent authority to control its docket. Therefore, it cannot be said that Villarreal was not alerted that the trial court was invoking its inherent power to dismiss for lack of diligent prosecution when the court, on its own motion, placed his case on the dismissal docket.

974 S.W.2d at 278(citations omitted). We disagree.

The Fourth Court of Appeals has considered the adequacy of the Bexar County dismissal notice twice before, reaching conflicting results. In the more recent case of *Goff v. Branch*, 821 S.W.2d 732 (Tex. App.—San Antonio 1991, writ denied), the court found that the Bexar County notice "merely gave the appellants notice that the dismissal setting was pursuant to the provisions of Rule 165a(1)." *Id.* at 734. The court rejected an argument that, although a Rule 165a(1) dismissal was not warranted, the dismissal and failure to reinstate the case were justified under the court's inherent power to dismiss for failure to diligently prosecute. The court reasoned:

> [W]e can find no authority for a court to invoke for the first time, without prior notice, its inherent power to dismiss for want of prosecution in a reinstatement hearing clearly involving only the review of a dismissal order under TEX. R. CIV. P. 165a(1). This is especially true when notice received by the party whose cause has been dismissed was pursuant only to Rule 165a(1). If a trial court had authority to invoke its inherent powers to dismiss for want of prosecution at any time, with or without proper notice, cases could be summarily dismissed at random in the privacy of the court's chambers. Such a situation would be unjust and untenable. *Id.* at 736.

---

[3] Rule 6 of the Rules of Judicial Administration provides that civil jury cases must be disposed of within 18 months from the appearance date. *See* TEX. R. JUD. ADMIN. 6.

[4] Although the Defendants make brief reference to the ability to dismiss a case pursuant to Rule 165a(2), warranting dismissal for failure to adhere to the Supreme Court time standards, they do not urge that Villarreal violated this standard. Thus, we do not consider the possibility of dismissal under Rule 165a(2), except to state that adequate notice of the court's intent to dismiss on this ground is also required.

Earlier, in *Ozuna v. Southwest Bio-Clinical Laboratories*, 766 S.W.2d 900 (Tex. App.—San Antonio 1989, writ denied), the court reached the opposite result. It concluded that the Bexar County notice was adequate to provide for dismissal "on two separate and independent grounds: (1) failure to appear at the dismissal hearing, and (2) failure to litigate the case with due diligence." *Id.* at 901. Because the record was unclear on whether the parties had in fact appeared at the dismissal hearing, the court affirmed the dismissal on the sole ground of the trial court's inherent power to dismiss for failure to diligently prosecute. *See id.* In deciding this case, the court of appeals relied upon Ozuna, determining that Goff was not binding authority because "we are not presented with the issue of whether reinstatement was required under Rule 165a(3), rather we are asked to determine whether the trial court properly concluded that Villarreal's case had not been prosecuted with due diligence." 974 S.W.2d at 278. This statement mischaracterizes the issue on appeal. Before deciding whether the trial court properly concluded that Villarreal failed to exercise diligent prosecution, the court must first determine whether the trial court gave adequate notice of its intent to invoke its inherent authority to dismiss on such ground. Thus, although this case does not involve a reinstatement hearing, as does Goff's rationale regarding the adequacy of the Bexar County dismissal notice is persuasive here.

We reject Defendants' contention that "[t]he dismissal notice clearly indicated that the plaintiff's case would be dismissed unless the plaintiff could show good cause why it should not be dismissed for want of prosecution." A plain reading of the Bexar County standard dismissal notice informs parties only of a possible Rule 165a(1) dismissal. *See Goff*, 821 S.W.2d at 734. In response to that notice, the plaintiff appeared and announced ready for trial at the dismissal docket call. Because Villarreal complied with all the requirements of the notice, the trial court abused its discretion by invoking its inherent authority to dismiss for failure to prosecute diligently. *Cf. Shook v. Gilmore & Tate Mfg. Co.*, 951 S.W.2d 294, 297 (Tex. App.—Waco 1997, pet. denied) (declining to decide appeal on plaintiff's failure to prosecute case diligently when the trial court failed to give notice that "the diligence of prosecution would be a factor in the judge's deciding whether to reinstate the case").

Defendants contend that the notice's language, "if no announcement is made, this cause will be dismissed for want of prosecution," was not intended to be literally interpreted. They urge that a literal interpretation would permit even an announcement of "not ready for trial" to save the case from dismissal. However, language "will not be so construed or interpreted as to lead to absurd conclusions . . . if the provision is subject to another, more reasonable interpretation." *C & H Nationwide, Inc. v. Thompson*, 903 S.W.2d 315, 322 n. 5 (Tex. 1994). Because a reasonable litigant would understand that only an announcement of ready for trial would justify removal from the dismissal docket, we reject Defendants' alternative construction.

Defendants also argue that Villarreal should be charged with notice of the court's inherent authority to dismiss for lack of diligent prosecution through Local Rule 3.26 of the Bexar County District Courts Local Rules, which provides:

> Pursuant to Rule 165a, T.R.C.P., cases that have not been disposed of within the Supreme Court's time standards shall be scheduled for hearing to show cause why they should not be dismissed for want of prosecution. The local administrative judge shall periodically assign judges to preside over the dismissal docket.

BEXAR COUNTY (TEX.) DIST. CT. LOC. R. 3.26. Defendants rely on our decision in *Rotello*, where we held that the plaintiffs were "charged with notice of the trial court's intention to dismiss this cause at the . . . dismissal docket by their attorney's knowledge of the [Brazos County district courts'] local rule." *Rotello*, 671 S.W.2d at 508. This case is distinguishable from *Rotello*. The Brazos County local rule explicitly states that " '[t]his rule shall constitute notice of [the dismissal] hearings,' " *id.* (*quoting* BRAZOS COUNTY (TEX.) DIST. CT. LOC. R. 11.1), while the Bexar County local rule omits such language. Furthermore, the Bexar County notice flatly contradicts the local rule by suggesting that an announcement will cure the lack of prosecution and by failing to warn that good cause must be shown to avoid dismissal. We therefore conclude that *Rotello* is not controlling in this case.

Finally, Defendants contend that the last sentence of the dismissal docket notice, which reminds litigants that "this is not a docket for the re-setting of cases, but for their dismissal," serves as adequate notice that the court will dismiss the case for want of prosecution unless good cause is shown at the docket call. We do not read the sentence in this way. Nothing in this language notifies a party that good cause must be shown to avoid dismissal, nor does it otherwise cure the misleading effect of the earlier language.

To the extent that *Ozuna* can be read to hold that the Bexar County notice of dismissal apprises parties of the court's intent to dismiss on a ground other than the failure to appear under Rule 165a(1), or that *Knight v. Trent*, 739 S.W.2d 116 (Tex. App.—San Antonio 1987, no writ), *Gaebler v. Harris*, 625 S.W.2d 5 (Tex. App.—San Antonio 1981, writ ref'd n.r.e.), and *Laird v. Jobes*, 580 S.W.2d 413 (Tex. Civ. App.—San Antonio 1979, no writ), imply that a party may be charged with such notice, we disapprove of the language of those cases. We, therefore, reverse the judgment of the court of appeals and remand this cause to the trial court for further proceedings consistent with this opinion.

JUSTICE ENOCH filed a dissenting opinion, in which JUSTICE BAKER joined.

JUSTICE ENOCH, joined by JUSTICE BAKER, dissenting.

I share the sentiment that, I think, motivates the Court to reach its result—frustration at the Bexar County District Clerk's apparent refusal to change a badly worded dismissal notice, even after the court of appeals has expended significant judicial resources in several reported decisions to answer parties' questions about the notice's wording. *See Goff v. Branch*, 821 S.W.2d 732 (Tex. App.—San Antonio 1991, writ denied); *Ozuna v. Southwest Bio-Clinical Laboratories*, 766 S.W.2d 900 (Tex. App.—San Antonio 1989, writ denied). But frustration should not decide cases. The issue here is whether the notice is sufficient to warn litigants that the trial court might, under its inherent power, dismiss a case for want of prosecution. While the notice is not a model of clarity or good writing, it is sufficient. I dissent.

* * *

In re CONNER

458 S.W.3d 532
(Tex. 2015)

J. S. Freels Jr., J. S. Freels, Jr., P.C., 114 S. Crockett St., Sherman, TX, for Real Party in Interest.

Bryan Kyle Briscoe, The Peavler Group, P.C., 3400 Carlisle Street, Suite 430, Daron L. Janis, Kirsten M. Castaneda, Locke Lord LLP, 2200 Ross Avenue, Suite 2200, Donna C. Peavler, The Peavler Group, P.C., 3400 Carlisle Street, Suite 430, Dallas, Mike A. Hatchell, Locke Lord LLP, 600 Congress Avenue, Suite 2200, Austin, TX, for Relator.

PER CURIAM

A plaintiff has a duty to "prosecut[e] the suit to a conclusion with reasonable diligence," failing which a trial court may dismiss for want of prosecution. *Callahan v. Staples*, 139 Tex. 8, 161 S.W.2d 489, 491 (1942). The issue here is whether a trial court abuses its discretion by refusing to grant a motion to dismiss for want of prosecution in the face of unmitigated and unexplained delay. We hold that it does.

In December 2002, Donald and Crystal Peel were traveling in their van along a highway when they were struck by a truck driven by Michael Conner and owned by his employer, IESI Solid Waste Services. One day short of two years later, the Peels sued Conner and IESI (collectively "Conner") for damages. Conner timely answered and requested discovery, but the Peels did not respond. In June 2007, two months before a trial setting, Conner moved for summary judgment. The Peels responded. The trial setting was cancelled, and the motion was never heard.

By September 2011, the Peels had taken no other action to advance the case, and Connor moved to dismiss for want of prosecution. The Peels responded that the delay was due to their counsel's health issues, including a stroke requiring hospitalization and, later, bypass surgery. The Peels did not indicate when counsel's health issues had occurred. The trial court refused to dismiss the case.

In October 2013, when the Peels had still done nothing to pursue their claims, Conner again moved to dismiss for want of prosecution. At the hearing on the motion, the Peels offered no other excuse for their delay than they had before. Conner cited court records showing that the Peels' counsel had appeared in many different matters in the prior two years. The trial court again refused to dismiss, directed the Peels to respond to Connor's discovery requests served more than eight years earlier, and set the case for trial.

Conner petitioned the court of appeals for mandamus directing the trial court to dismiss the case. The court of appeals denied relief, and Connor then petitioned this Court.

Trial courts are generally granted considerable discretion when it comes to managing their dockets. Such discretion, however, is not absolute. It has long been the case that "a delay of an unreasonable duration . . . , if not sufficiently explained, will raise a conclusive presumption of abandonment of the plaintiff's suit." *Callahan*, 161 S.W.2d at 491. This presumption justifies the dismissal of a suit under either a court's inherent authority or Rule 165a of the Texas Rules of Civil Procedure. *Villarreal v. San Antonio Truck & Equip.*, 994 S.W.2d 628, 630 (Tex. 1999) (recognizing both common law source of power and rule based source of power); *see, e.g., Veterans' Land Bd. v. Williams*, 543 S.W.2d 89, 90 (Tex. 1976) (finding seven-and-one-half year delay as failing to satisfy the demands of reasonable diligence); *Denton Cnty. v. Brammer*, 361 S.W.2d 198, 201 (Tex. 1962) (same for five-year delay); *Bevil v. Johnson*, 157 Tex. 621, 307 S.W.2d 85, 88 (1957) (same for eight-year delay).

Under Rule 165a, there are two grounds for dismissal for want of prosecution. One is when a "party seeking affirmative relief [fails] to appear for any hearing or trial of which the party had notice." TEX. R. CIV. P 165a(1). In such cases, "[a] court shall dismiss . . . unless there is good cause for the case to be maintained on the docket." *Id.* The other is when a case is "not disposed of within [the] time standards promulgated by the Supreme Court." TEX. R. CIV. P. 165a(2). And while Rule 165a(2) does not refer to Rule 165a(1)'s procedural requirements, including notice and a hearing, neither does it suggest a basis for deviating from those procedures.

The Peels' failure to provide good cause for their nearly decade-long delay mandates dismissal under Rule 165a(2). Our Rules of Judicial Administration require district and statutory county courts to ensure, "so far as reasonably possible," that civil cases in which a jury has been demanded, other than those arising under the Family Code, are brought to trial or final disposition within eighteen months of the appearance date. TEX. R. JUD. ADMIN. 6.1(b)(1). The Peels' suit well exceeded this time frame. Absent any reasonable explanation for the delay, the trial court clearly abused its discretion by disregarding the conclusive presumption of abandonment. *See Walker v. Packer*, 827 S.W.2d 833, 840 (Tex. 1992) ("[A] clear failure by the trial court to analyze or apply the law correctly will constitute an abuse of discretion, and may result in appellate reversal by extraordinary writ."); *see also Downer v. Aquamarine Operators, Inc.*, 701 S.W.2d 238, 241-42 (Tex. 1985).

Mandamus will issue to correct such an abuse of discretion when there is no adequate remedy by appeal. *In re Prudential Ins. Co. of Am.*, 148 S.W.3d 124, 136 (Tex. 2004). A trial court's erroneous refusal to dismiss a case for want of prosecution cannot effectively be challenged on appeal. A defendant should not be required to incur the delay and expense of appeal to complain of delay in the trial court. To deny relief by mandamus permits the very delay dismissal is intended to prevent. In addition, the danger that a trial will be hampered by stale evidence and lost or clouded memories is particularly distinct after the delay in this case. *See So. Pac. Transp. Co. v. Stoot*, 530 S.W.2d 930, 931 (Tex. 1975) ("[P]ossibilities for error multiply rapidly as time elapses between the original fact and its judicial determination.").

Accordingly, we conditionally grant the petition for writ of mandamus, and without hearing oral argument, direct the trial court to vacate its order denying Conner's motion to dismiss filed October 24, 2013, and to dismiss this suit for want of prosecution. TEX. R. APP. P. 52.8(c). We are confident the trial court will promptly comply, and our writ will issue only if it does not.

Note

Please note that Rule 165a of the Texas Rules of Civil Procedure has been changed since the case of *Walker v. Harrison*. However, the case is still valid law for the points discussed therein.

WALKER
v.
HARRISON
597 S.W.2d 913
(Tex. 1980)

DeLange, Hudspeth, Pitman & Katz, Eugene J. Pitman, Houston, for relator.
Hirsch, Westheimer, Block & Wilk, Joe Holzer, Houston, for respondents.

SPEARS, JUSTICE.

Relator Walker petitions this court in an original proceeding for a writ of mandamus to compel District Judge Harrison to vacate his order reinstating a case previously dismissed for want of prosecution. We conditionally grant the writ of mandamus.

The question presented is whether Judge Harrison reinstated the case in accordance with rule 165a before the trial court lost jurisdiction to do so. The pertinent part of rule 165a provides:

> Within thirty days after the signing of the order of dismissal, the court shall reinstate the case upon finding, after hearing, that the failure of the party or his attorney was not intentional or the result of conscious indifference but was due to an accident or mistake. Where after a hearing the court finds that neither the party nor his attorney received a mailed notice, or acquired actual notice in any manner, of either the court's intention to dismiss or the order of dismissal prior to the expiration of twenty days after the signing of such order, the court may reinstate the case at any time within thirty days after the party or his attorney first received either a mailed notice or actual notice, but in no event later than six months after the date of signing the order of dismissal.

Relator Walker was the plaintiff in the trial court in a suit styled *Walker v. Oak Ridge Townhouse Apartments, Ltd., et al.* One of the defendants, Houston National Bank, a respondent here, filed a counterclaim seeking to recover on several promissory notes. The court clerk, sometime prior to April 2, 1979, mailed a notice of intent to dismiss to the parties. The postcard notice stated that the case would be dismissed for want of prosecution on April 2, 1979 unless affirmative action was taken to retain it on the docket. No action was taken, and on April 12, the trial judge signed an order dismissing the case.

Counsel for the bank received actual notice of the dismissal on April 16 and on April 24 filed a motion to reinstate the counterclaim. A hearing on the motion was held on April 30. An entry on the docket sheet of the court dated April 30 reads: "Motion to reinstate denied, pleadings to be amended then granted." Nothing further appears to have occurred until the trial judge rendered a signed order of reinstatement bearing the date of October 15.

The written order of reinstatement recites that it "came on to be heard" on April 30. As originally typed, the order read "Entered this 30th day of April 1979," but the day and month have been marked through and "15" and "October" inserted, apparently in the handwriting of Judge Harrison whose name is signed at the end of the order. There is also a May 2 file mark on the order.

The bank acknowledged in its motion to reinstate that its attorney received actual notice on April 16, within 20 days from the signing of the order of dismissal. Under rule 165a, the trial court had only 30 days from the signing of the order of dismissal to reinstate the case. The 30-day period expired on Saturday, May 12; therefore, the last day on which the trial court could have reinstated the case was Monday, May 14. *See* rule 4.

This court has repeatedly held that the time limits provided in rule 165a are mandatory and jurisdictional and that orders of reinstatement entered after their expiration are void. *Harris County v. Miller*, 576 S.W.2d 808, 809 (Tex. 1979); *Danforth Memorial Hosp. v. Harris*, 573 S.W.2d 762, 763 (Tex. 1978); *N-S-W Corp. v. Snell*, 561 S.W.2d 798, 798 (Tex. 1977). When the party seeking reinstatement of the case has actual knowledge of the dismissal within 20 days of the order of dismissal, an attempt to reinstate the case more than 30 days after the order has been signed is void because the court is without jurisdiction. In *N-S-W Corp. v. Snell, supra*, at 799 we held that a docket entry showing that reinstatement occurred within 30 days was ineffective to contradict or impeach the written order of reinstatement signed after 30 days had expired; thus, the order was void.

Respondent bank argues that the trial court did act within the 30-day limit by orally granting the motion on April 30 and entering its action on the docket sheet. This contention is supported, it is argued, by the clerk's file stamp indicating that the written order was filed on May 2. The bank, *citing Comet Aluminum Co. v. Dibrell*, 450 S.W.2d 56, 58 (Tex. 1970) *and Knox v. Long*, 152 Tex. 291, 257 S.W.2d 289, 292 (1953), contends that an order or judgment is rendered when the decision is officially announced either orally in open court or by memorandum filed with the clerk. The bank points out that under rule 306a oral judgments or orders are valid. *See Dunn v. Dunn*, 439 S.W.2d 830, 832-33 (Tex. 1969).

There is, however, no statement of facts to support the bank's assertion that the trial court orally granted the motion for reinstatement. In fact, the docket entry indicates that the motion was denied. Moreover, the clerk's file mark on an order is not instructive. Orders of the court are not required to be filed by the clerk; they are signed by the judge and entered on the minutes of the court by the clerk. Neither the date of filing nor the date of entering a judgment is indicative of the date of signing. *See Heard v. Heard*, 305 S.W.2d 231, 234 (Tex. Civ. App. Galveston 1957, writ ref'd).

While it is true that orders and judgments may be orally pronounced in open court, a different rule applies when there is a time limit placed on the court's jurisdiction to act on a matter. When there is a time limit within which the court has jurisdiction to act, the order must be in writing, specific, and signed by the trial judge. *See Reese v. Piperi*, 534 S.W.2d 329, 331 (Tex. 1976). In the recent case of *McCormack v. Guillot*, 597 S.W.2d 345 (Tex. 1980) we noted the general rule: During the time in which a court may vacate, set aside, modify or amend its previous order, such action must, to be effective, be by written order that is express and specific. Thus, a written order signed by the trial judge was required within the 30-day time limit imposed by rule 165a; otherwise the trial court was without jurisdiction to reinstate the case. Since the written order was dated October 15, outside the 30-day limit, the attempted order of reinstatement was void.

There is one final matter to consider. At the end of the order of October 15 it is stated: "Entered this 15th day of October 1979." Although the use of the word "entered" is not helpful in determining when the order was actually signed by the judge, the record establishes that this is the date the trial judge signed the order, and there is nothing to indicate otherwise. Moreover, relator Walker's verified petition in this court asserts that October 15 was the date of signing. In the absence of a verified denial of that fact, it is admitted as true. *Burgemeister v. Anderson*, 113 Tex. 495, 259 S.W. 1078 (1924).

Relying on *Dean v. Warren*, 464 S.W.2d 672 (Tex. Civ. App. Tyler 1971, no writ), respondent bank contends that because no date of signing is recited in the judgment, the date of rendition of the order should be deemed to be the date of the hearing. *Dean* and the authorities cited therein involve the question whether steps for appeal were timely taken by an appellant under rule 306a. Under rule 306a, "the date of rendition of a judgment or order shall be deemed to be the date upon which the written draft thereof was signed by the trial judge as stated therein." (emphasis added). When there is a recital of the date of signing on the face of the judgment, that date controls. *Polis v. Alford*, 267 S.W.2d 918, 919 (Tex. Civ. App. San Antonio 1954, no writ); *Cox v. Payne*, 231 S.W.2d 957, 958 (Tex. Civ. App. Amarillo 1950, no writ). When the judgment does not recite the date it was signed, it has been held that the critical time limits for determining steps for appeal are calculated from the date of rendition of the judgment as shown on the face of the judgment. *Heard v. Heard*, 305 S.W.2d 231, 235 (Tex. Civ. App. Galveston 1957, writ ref'd); *Magic Valley Produce Co. v. Baldridge*, 393 S.W.2d 418, 420 (Tex. Civ. App. Corpus Christi 1965, no writ); *Headley Indep. School Dist. v. Doneghy*, 358 S.W.2d 724, 726 (Tex. Civ. App. Amarillo 1962, no writ). These cases are not controlling here, however. They involve a determination of when a judgment is rendered for the purpose of calculating the time from which the various steps of appeal must be taken under rule 306a. In the case before us, an entirely different question is presented has the trial court acted within the time limit imposed by rule 165a before the court lost jurisdiction?

Finally, we are constrained to point out that the use of the word "entered" indicates that both trial counsel, who approved the order as to form, and the trial judge, who signed the order, ignored the clear mandate of this court in *Burrell v. Cornelius*, 570 S.W.2d 382, 384 (Tex. 1978) that all orders and judgments reflect the date of signing, not that of entering. "'Entered' is synonymous with neither 'Signed' nor 'Rendered.'" *Id.* Entry is done by the clerk in the minutes of the court and occurs after the judge has signed the order or judgment.

We assume that Judge Harrison will vacate his October 15 order of reinstatement voluntarily, and a writ of mandamus will issue only if he refuses to do so.

Notes

1. As shown in *Villarreal* proper notice must be given of the court's intention to dismiss a case. Furthermore, if the court determines at the hearing to keep the case on the docket, the court must render a pretrial order assigning a trial date for the case, and setting deadlines for joining new parties, discovery, and other pretrial matters. After this, the case may only be continued for valid and compelling reasons determined by court order.

2. *If case is dismissed, notice must be given.* Notice of the signing of an order of dismissal for want of prosecution must be given as provided in TEX. R. CIV. P. 306a. However, if a party receives timely notice of the court's intention to dismiss for want of prosecution, the fact that the party does not also receive notice of the actual dismissal within 20 days after the dismissal order is signed cannot serve as a basis for extending the 30-day limit on the trial court's jurisdiction to reinstate the case. *Harris County v. Miller,* 576 S.W.2d 808 (Tex. 1979). Further, the failure of the record to reflect that the notices were sent is not error on the face of the record for purposes of an appeal by writ of error. *General Electric Co. v. Falcon Ridge Apartments*, 811 S.W.2d 942 (Tex. 1991).

3. *Reinstatement.* If a motion for reinstatement has been timely filed by any party, the trial court has plenary power to reinstate the case until 30 days after all such timely filed motions are overruled, or within the period allowed by Rule 306a. The motion to reinstate has to be decided by signed order within 75 days after the judgment is signed, or as otherwise allowed by Rule 306a, or the motion will be deemed overruled by operation of law.

4. *Motion to Reinstate.* The motion to reinstate must be (1) verified, (2) set forth grounds for reinstatement, and (3) be filed with the court within 30 days of the dismissal (4) with a copy served on each party. As shown in *Walker* failure to comply with the time requirements deprives the trial court of jurisdiction to set aside the dismissal.

5. *Order.* A court order for reinstatement of a case must be in writing. An oral pronouncement and docket entry may not be used in lieu of a written order to reinstate the case. *Emerald Oaks Hotel/Conference Center, Inc. v. Zardenetta* 776 S.W.2d 577 (Tex. 1989).

6. *Refiling.* The order of dismissal does not decide the merits of the case. Thus, subject to any limitation defense that may exist, the dismissed litigant may refile the dismissed action.

7. *Pending Venue Motions.* When the suit is dismissed for want of prosecution while the motion to transfer venue is pending, it is not effective to fix venue in the county named in the motion to transfer venue. *Ruiz v. Conoco, Inc.*, 868 S.W.2d 752 (Tex. 1993).

8. *In Re Lovito-Nelson*, 278 S.W.3d 773 (Tex. 2009): An order granting a new trial, or modifying, correcting or reforming a judgment, must be written and signed. A trial judge's oral pronouncement, granting a motion for new trial, together with a docket entry, indicating that such motion was granted, and a scheduling order setting various pretrial deadlines, and a final trial date and time, cannot substitute for a written order required by TEX. R. CIV. P. 329b.

9. *Ginn v. Forrester*, 282 S.W. 430 (Tex. 2009): The Forresters filed suit against the defendants (collectively Ginn) on 1/29/2004, for damages arising out of a traffic accident. On 5/18/ 2005, the trial court notified all parties that, unless either a judgment or scheduling order was signed or a verified motion to retain was filed by 6/27, the case would be dismissed for want of prosecution. On 6/27, Forrester filed a verified motion to retain the case, which the trial court granted after inserting the words "for 60 days" at the end of the paragraph ordering retention. The trial court subsequently granted Forrester's motion to substitute counsel, but the record reflects no further activity until 12/2 when the trial court dismissed the case for want of prosecution. Six months later, Forrester filed a notice of restricted appeal. The clerk's supplemental record contains a notation that the clerk's office was unable to locate documents indicating notice was sent or a hearing was held on the trial court's dismissal for want of prosecution. Construing the notation as affirmative evidence that the trial court failed to provide notice, a divided court of appeals concluded the requirements for a restricted appeal were met. ***Held:*** Reversed and judgment rendered dismissing the case. A restricted appeal requires error that is apparent on the face of the record; error that is merely inferred will not suffice. Because the clerk has no affirmative duty to record the giving of notice, however, a statement that the record reflects none cannot establish error on the face of the record.

SMITH
v.
BABCOCK & WILCOX CONSTRUCTION COMPANY, INC.

913 S.W.2d 467
(Tex. 1995)

Charles T. Frazier, Jr., Dallas, Charles B. Lord, Austin, for Petitioners.
David S. Lill, Austin, Iris J. Jones, Austin, James N. Rader, Austin, for Respondents.

PER CURIAM.

We decide in this case whether the trial court abused its discretion in refusing to reinstate a case dismissed for want of prosecution when plaintiffs' attorney failed to appear for trial. The court of appeals affirmed the dismissal. 915 S.W.2d 22. We reverse.

James Smith was injured on a construction jobsite while employed by a subcontractor and received compensation benefits from Lumbermen's Mutual Casualty Co. Smith and his wife then filed this suit for damages in Travis County against the general contractor, Babcock & Wilcox Construction Co., and the project owner, the City of Austin (together, Babcock). Lumbermen's intervened to assert its subrogation rights. After the Smiths' attorney obtained a date for trial, he requested a trial setting for an unrelated case in Freestone County which had been filed after this case and involved a more recent incident. Trial of the case in Freestone County was set on the same date as trial of the Smiths' case.

The Smiths' attorney did not notify the parties or the court in this case of the conflicting setting until twelve days before trial, in an unverified motion for continuance. The motion misstated that the Freestone County case was older and preferentially set. The trial court heard argument by telephone and denied the continuance. No record was made of this conference call. Following the call the Smiths' attorney stated in a letter to the trial court that he understood from what the court had said during the call that it would reconsider his motion for continuance on the date of trial if the Freestone County case actually went to trial at the same time. The other parties did not share this understanding. The Smiths' attorney never requested a continuance in the Freestone County case and never mentioned the conflict to that trial court.

Neither the Smiths nor their attorney appeared on the trial date. Apparently anticipating this occurrence, Babcock's attorney came to court with a prepared motion to dismiss the case with prejudice for want of prosecution, together with exhibits and an order. Lumbermen's counsel appeared, advised the court that the Smiths' attorney was in trial in Freestone County, and re-urged the continuance. The court denied the continuance and granted Babcock's motion to dismiss. The court later denied the Smiths' and Lumbermen's motions to reinstate the case. The court of appeals affirmed. 915 S.W.2d 22.

When a case is dismissed for want of prosecution, "[t]he court shall reinstate the case upon finding after a hearing that the failure of the party or his attorney [to appear] was not intentional or the result of conscious indifference but was due to an accident or mistake or that the failure has been otherwise reasonably explained." TEX. R. CIV. P. 165a(3). The operative standard is essentially the same as that for setting aside a default judgment. *See Craddock v. Sunshine Bus Lines*, 134 Tex. 388, 133 S.W.2d 124 (1939). A failure to appear is not intentional or due to conscious indifference within the meaning of the rule merely because it is deliberate; it must also be without adequate justification. Proof of such justification—accident, mistake or other reasonable explanation—negates the intent or conscious indifference for which reinstatement can be denied. *Bank One, Texas, N.A. v. Moody*, 830 S.W.2d 81, 84 (Tex. 1992). Also, conscious indifference means more than mere negligence. *Ivy v. Carrell*, 407 S.W.2d 212, 213 (Tex. 1966).

The Smiths' attorney reasonably explained his failure to appear for trial. He was actually in trial in another county and believed, based upon his credible explanation, that the court would grant a continuance for that reason. Even if the Smiths' attorney was not as conscientious as he should have been, his actions did not amount to conscious indifference. Also, while the Smiths' attorney was wrong to state in his motion for continuance that the Freestone County suit was older and preferentially set when it was neither, that misconduct would be ground for sanctions, not dismissal or denial of reinstatement.

Babcock argues that the Smiths' attorney was obliged to attempt to postpone the Freestone County trial, *citing Smock v. Fischel*, 146 Tex. 397, 207 S.W.2d 891, 892 (1948). In that case we held that a trial court did not abuse its discretion in proceeding to trial when defendant's counsel was in trial in another county because, among other things, he had made no effort to resolve the conflicting settings and had failed to contact the judge on the day of trial to tell him of his whereabouts. By contrast, the Smiths' attorney tried to resolve the conflict by moving for continuance in this case, and mistakenly understood that a continuance would be granted. His explanation was reasonable.

The denial of the Smiths' and Lumbermen's motions for reinstatement was an abuse of discretion. Accordingly, a majority of the Court grants the Smiths' application for writ of error and, without hearing oral argument, reverses the judgment of the court of appeals and remands this case to the trial court with instructions to reinstate the case. TEX. R. APP. P. 170.

ALEXANDER
v.
LYNDA'S BOUTIQUE
134 S.W.3d 845
(Tex. 2004)

TEX. R. CIV. P. 165a(1) does not require that a separate hearing to adjudicate dismissal be held, before a trial court may dismiss a case, for want of prosecution for failure to appear at a pre-trial hearing, when notice of that pre-trial hearing stated that failure to appear may result in dismissal.

A trial court may dismiss a case for want of prosecution, for failure to appear at a pre-trial hearing, when notice of that pre-trial hearing stated that failure to appear may result in dismissal.

3. *Nonsuit and Other Dismissals*

Rule 91a. Texas Rules of Civil Procedure: Dismissal of Baseless Causes of Action

91a.1. Motion and Grounds. Except in a case brought under the Family Code or a case governed by Chapter 14 of the Texas Civil Practice and Remedies Code, a party may move to dismiss a cause of action on the grounds that it has no basis in law or fact. A cause of action has no basis in law if the allegations, taken as true, together with inferences reasonably drawn from them, do not entitle the claimant to the relief sought. A cause of action has no basis in fact if no reasonable person could believe the facts pleaded.

91a.2. Contents of Motion. A motion to dismiss must state that it is made pursuant to this rule, must identify each cause of action to which it is addressed, and must state specifically the reasons the cause of action has no basis in law, no basis in fact, or both.

91a.3. Time for Motion and Ruling. A motion to dismiss must be:

(a) filed within 60 days after the first pleading containing the challenged cause of action is served on the movant;

(b) filed at least 21 days before the motion is heard; and

(c) granted or denied within 45 days after the motion is filed.

91a.4. Time for Response. Any response to the motion must be filed no later than 7 days before the date of the hearing.

91a.5. Effect of Nonsuit or Amendment; Withdrawal of Motion.

(a) The court may not rule on a motion to dismiss if, at least 3 days before the date of the hearing, the respondent files a nonsuit of the challenged cause of action, or the movant files a withdrawal of the motion.

(b) If the respondent amends the challenged cause of action at least 3 days before the date of the hearing, the movant may, before the date of the hearing, file a withdrawal of the motion or an amended motion directed to the amended cause of action.

(c) Except by agreement of the parties, the court must rule on a motion unless it has been withdrawn or the cause of action has been nonsuited in accordance with (a) or (b). In ruling on the motion, the court must not consider a nonsuit or amendment not filed as permitted by paragraphs (a) or (b).

(d) An amended motion filed in accordance with (b) restarts the time periods in this rule.

91a.6. Hearing; No Evidence Considered. Each party is entitled to at least 14 days' notice of the hearing on the motion to dismiss. The court may, but is not required to, conduct an oral hearing on the motion. Except as required by 91a.7, the court may not consider evidence in ruling on the motion and must decide the motion based solely on the pleading of the cause of action, together with any pleading exhibits permitted by Rule 59.

91a.7. Award of Costs and Attorney Fees Required. Except in an action by or against a governmental entity or a public official acting in his or her official capacity or under color of law, the court must award the prevailing party on the motion all costs and reasonable and necessary attorney fees incurred with respect to the challenged cause of action in the trial court. The court must consider evidence regarding costs and fees in determining the award.

91a.8. Effect on Venue and Personal Jurisdiction. This rule is not an exception to the pleading requirements of Rules 86 and 120a, but a party does not, by filing a motion to dismiss pursuant to this rule or obtaining a ruling on it, waive a special appearance or a motion to transfer venue. By filing a motion to dismiss, a party submits to the court's jurisdiction only in proceedings on the motion and is bound by the court's ruling, including an award of attorney fees and costs against the party.

91a.9. Dismissal Procedure Cumulative. This rule is in addition to, and does not supersede or affect, other procedures that authorize dismissal.

Notes

1. A dismissal without prejudice means the claimant has the right to sue again on the same cause of action and prevents "the decree of dismissal from operating as a bar to a subsequent suit." BLACK'S LAW DICTIONARY 469 (6th ed. 1990). If a suit is dismissed without prejudice, res judicata has not occurred. *See, e.g., Bell v. Moores*, 832 S.W.2d 749, 755 (Tex. App.—Houston [14th Dist.] 1992, writ denied). If dismissal is with prejudice, res judicata applies and bars the right to bring an action on the same cause. *Id.*

2. A nonsuit is a voluntary discontinuance of a pending action against a party. A nonsuit affects all claims against the nonsuited party. If the litigant wishes to discontinue as to a claim, but retain others, the litigant abandons the claim, by formally stating the fact of abandonment of record by pleadings or otherwise, before, and not after, trial of the cause and entry of judgment. Any such dismissal that terminates the case will authorize the clerk to tax court costs against the dismissing party unless otherwise ordered by the court.

3. A nonsuit may be taken at anytime before the plaintiff has introduced all evidence other than rebuttal evidence. Notice of the dismissal or nonsuit must be served in accordance with Rule 21a, TEX. R. CIV. P. on any party who has answered or has been served with process. A court order is not required. A plaintiff's right to take a nonsuit is unqualified and absolute as long as the defendant has not made a claim for affirmative relief. *BHP Petroleum Co. Inc. v. Millard*, 800 S.W.2d 838 (Tex. 1990). However, if an adverse party has made a claim for affirmative relief, the dismissal shall not prejudice the right of an adverse party to be heard on a pending claim for affirmative relief.

4. The trial court retains jurisdiction, at least for 30 days, to reinstate the cause of action previously dismissed by voluntary nonsuit. *McClendon v. State Farm Ins Co.*, 796 S.W.2d 229, 232 (Tex. App.—El Paso 1990, writ denied); *Chester v. Texas Employers Ins. Ass'n*, 265 S.W.2d 648, 649 (Tex. Civ. App.—Texarkana 1954, writ ref'd n.r.e).

5. *Villafani v. Trejo*, 251 S.W.3d 466 (Tex. 2008): Under TEX. R. CIV. P. 162 parties have an absolute right to nonsuit their own claims for relief at any time during the litigation until they have introduced all evidence other than rebuttal evidence at trial. One effect of a nonsuit is that it can vitiate certain interlocutory orders, rendering them moot and unappealable. However, the plaintiff's nonsuit does not control the non-moving party's independent claims for affirmative relief. A party makes a claim for affirmative relief by alleging grounds on which he could recover benefits, compensation or relief and does more than resist a plaintiff's right to recover. Thus, a nonsuit under Rule 162 also has no effect on any motion for sanctions, attorney's fees or other costs, pending at the time of dismissal. Additionally, a party's right to nonsuit cannot be used to disturb a

court's judgment on the merits of a claim, such as a partial summary judgment against the nonsuiting party. Rule 162 protects a party's pending claim for affirmative relief from the general rule that a party is required to get a ruling (or a refusal to rule) from a trial court to preserve a right to appeal.

Whether a particular sanction is considered a claim for affirmative relief that survives a nonsuit for later enforcement or appeal depends on the purpose of the sanction. A party makes a claim for affirmative relief by alleging grounds on which he could recover benefits, compensation or relief, and does more than resist a plaintiff's right to recover. If, for example, a trial court imposes a discovery sanction, excluding witnesses, to insure a party is afforded a fair trial, a nonsuit obviates the reason for the sanction—to protect the integrity of the proceeding—and thus the sanction does not survive the nonsuit. Monetary sanctions, on the other hand, may serve compensatory and punitive purposes, beyond the specific proceeding and, therefore, survive a nonsuit and can be the subject of an appeal. A claim for attorney's fees is not an affirmative claim where it is based solely on the defense against the other party's claims, but is an affirmative claim where it is based on an independent ground or as a sanction.

6. *In re Greater Houston Orthopaedic Specialists, Inc.*, 295 S.W.3d 232 (Tex. 2009): The plaintiff (Greater Houston Orthopaedic Specialists) took a nonsuit, but misnamed itself ("Orthopaedic Specialists, L.L.P.) in the motion for nonsuit. Thereafter, the defendants filed a counterclaim. ***Held:*** Despite the misnomer, GHOS filed a valid notice of nonsuit before the defendants, Griswold and Zavaletta, filed counterclaims. Therefore, the trial court abused its discretion in setting the case for trial. Since nonsuit preceded the counterclaim, the trial court abused its discretion in refusing to dismiss the case. Granting a nonsuit is a ministerial act, and a plaintiff's right to a nonsuit exists from the moment a written motion is filed, or an oral motion is made in open court, unless the defendant has, prior to that time, sought affirmative relief.

HYUNDAI MOTOR CO.
v.
ALVARADO

892 S.W.2d 853
(Tex. 1995)

PER CURIAM.

The issue in this case is whether a partial summary judgment survives a nonsuit. We hold that when a defendant obtains a partial summary judgment on certain of the plaintiffs' causes of action and the plaintiff thereafter moves for a nonsuit as to the whole case, that nonsuit results in a dismissal with prejudice as to the issues decided in the partial summary judgment.

In 1989, Mario and Fidel Alvarado were injured in a car accident involving a 1988 Hyundai Excel. They sued Hyundai Motor Company and others in Webb County, alleging several theories, including failure to equip the front seats with seat belts, failure to instruct, and failure to warn of increased danger. Hyundai filed a motion for partial summary judgment asserting that all claims but the failure to instruct claims were preempted by federal law, specifically, 15 U.S.C. § 1392(d) and 49 C.F.R. § 571.208. The trial court granted the motion. On January 30, 1991, the plaintiffs filed a motion to nonsuit in the trial court and then filed a separate petition in Duval County, bringing the same claims against Hyundai, including those on which Hyundai had obtained the partial summary judgment. After the original trial court signed an order of nonsuit, Hyundai filed a motion to modify the nonsuit order to provide that the Alvarados could not refile those claims against which the partial summary judgment had been granted. The trial court granted the motion and entered an order stating that the claims adjudicated by the summary judgment were dismissed with prejudice. On appeal, the court of appeals reversed, holding that the right to nonsuit continues until the plaintiffs have put on all their evidence. Since the plaintiffs had not put on any evidence, the court of appeals reasoned that a summary judgment could not withstand the plaintiffs' right of nonsuit.

In Texas, our general rule is that plaintiffs have the right to take a nonsuit at any time until they introduce all evidence other than rebuttal evidence. *Aetna Casualty & Surety Co. v. Specia*, 849 S.W.2d 805, 806 (Tex. 1993); TEX. R. CIV. P. 162. Such a nonsuit may have the effect of vitiating earlier interlocutory orders. *See Ault v. Mulanax*, 724 S.W.2d 824, 828 (Tex. App.—Texarkana 1986, orig. proceeding). A decision on the merits, such as a summary judgment, however, is not vitiated. *See Mainland Savings Ass'n v. Wilson*, 545 S.W.2d 491, 493 (Tex. Civ. App.—Houston [1st Dist.] 1976, no writ). This includes partial summary judgments.

In summary judgment practice, a plaintiff need not produce any evidence. TEX. R. CIV. P. 166a (a)-(b). If Rule 162 provided the only cut-off point after which a plaintiff could no longer take a nonsuit, the plaintiff could in effect avoid any summary judgment by merely requesting a nonsuit after the case was adjudicated by the summary judgment. To give any force to the partial summary judgment provisions, those judgments must withstand a nonsuit. *See Wood v. Moers*, 289 S.W. 1017, 1018 (Tex. Civ. App.—Galveston 1926, no writ) ("[W]ere the rule otherwise, there would rarely, if ever, be such a result in a trial as a judgment upon an instructed verdict for the defendant, because in such cases, the plaintiff would probably resort to a nonsuit rather than suffer the consequences of an instructed verdict against him."). A partial summary judgment is a decision on the merits unless set aside by the trial court. *See Krenek v. Texstar N.A., Inc.*, 787 S.W.2d 566, 569 (Tex. App.—Corpus Christi 1990, writ denied). It becomes final upon the disposition of the other issues of the case. *Chase Manhattan Bank, N.A. v. Lindsay*, 787 S.W.2d 51, 53 (Tex. 1990). Once a judge announces a decision that adjudicates a claim, that claim is no longer subject to the plaintiff's right to nonsuit. *See Wood*, 289 S.W. at 1018. A nonsuit sought after such a judicial pronouncement results in a dismissal with prejudice as to the issues pronounced in favor of the defendant. Thus, we reverse the judgment of the court of appeals concerning the finality of the nonsuit. The dismissal is with prejudice as to the issues disposed of by the summary judgment.

Because the court of appeals held that the entire cause of action should have been dismissed without prejudice, it did not consider the Alvarados' claim that the trial court erred in finding their particular claims preempted by federal law. We remand this case to the court of appeals for disposition of the preemption issue.

Pursuant to Rule 170 of the Texas Rules of Appellate Procedure, a majority of the court grants the application for writ of error of Hyundai Motor Company and, without hearing oral argument, reverses the court of appeals' judgment with respect to the partial summary judgment and remands to the court of appeals for the disposition of issues not addressed.

In re BENNETT
960 S.W.2d 35
(Tex. 1997)

Carlos Villarreal, Corpus Christi, for Relator.
Eric Brown, Austin, Linda C. Breck, Corpus Christi, for Respondent.

PER CURIAM.

In this mandamus proceeding we hold that neither the filing of a nonsuit nor the subsequent removal of a case to federal court deprived the state court of jurisdiction to consider, sua sponte, whether sanctions should be imposed on attorneys for pre-removal conduct when the sanctions are unrelated to the merits of the removed case. We further hold that the trial court did not abuse its discretion in imposing sanctions under the facts of this case. Accordingly, we conditionally issue a writ of mandamus directing the court of appeals to vacate the writ of mandamus in which it ordered the trial court to vacate sanctions, 925 S.W.2d 338.

I

This case arises out of a deliberate circumvention of the random assignment of cases in a county in which eight district courts preside. The attorneys who were sanctioned by the Honorable Max Bennett of the 319th District Court of Nueces County for their conduct are Robert C. Hilliard and Andrew Schirrmeister, III. They represent approximately seven hundred Peruvian plaintiffs who claim to have been injured by toxic gases and chemicals released by the Southern Peru Copper Corporation.

On August 30, 1995, plaintiffs' counsel filed the first of seventeen lawsuits in Nueces County. The first suit was brought on behalf of three claimants. In accordance with the local rules of Nueces County, the case was randomly assigned to Judge Bennett's court.[5] Plaintiffs' counsel then filed sixteen more lawsuits, each having no

---

[5] Rule 3 of the Local Rules of the District Courts of Nueces County (Dec. 6, 1988) and the Substitute Order on Assigning Criminal and Civil Cases in the District Courts of Nueces County (Nov. 19, 1992) both provide that the district clerk of Nueces County shall randomly assign cases to the district courts of the county. The

more than five plaintiffs. The petitions were filed one after the other, only minutes apart, late in the afternoon of August 30 and on the morning of August 31, 1995. Each suit named different plaintiffs, all citizens of Peru, but the same defendants were sued in every case, and each petition contained identical factual allegations and legal claims. Each case was randomly assigned to one of the eight district courts in the county, but plaintiffs' counsel instructed the clerk of the court not to prepare citation for service in any of the first sixteen cases that had been filed.

None of the first sixteen suits was assigned to the 105th District Court. But the seventeenth was. Two hours after that assignment, plaintiffs' counsel filed an amended petition in the 105th District Court adding approximately seven hundred plaintiffs, though none of the claimants in the other sixteen suits were ever joined. Once counsel for plaintiffs had finally succeeded in lodging a case in the 105th District Court, they instructed the clerk of the court to issue citation for service on the defendants. Service was never requested in any of the sixteen other suits.

On September 5, 1995, five days after securing the 105th District Court as the forum of choice, plaintiffs' counsel filed notices of nonsuit in all sixteen previously filed suits pursuant to TEX. R. CIV. P. 162. Judge Bennett apparently was skeptical of this turn of events. He did not sign an order of nonsuit in the case pending in his court, but instead, on October 2, 1995, signed a "Sua Sponte Order Abating Dismissal and Setting Hearing on Transfer, Consolidation and Sanctions." The order required plaintiffs' counsel to appear on November 10, 1995 to show cause why the other sixteen lawsuits should not be transferred and consolidated into the case before Judge Bennett and why plaintiffs' counsel should not be sanctioned for intentionally violating local rules implementing random assignment of cases in Nueces County or the Texas Rules of Civil Procedure, including Rules 1, 2, 3a, 41, and 174.

Prior to the hearing on sanctions before Judge Bennett, the defendants removed all seventeen cases to federal court, including the case pending before Judge Bennett. Shortly after removal, plaintiffs' counsel filed with the federal district court a "Notice of Prior Filing of Nonsuit, and, in the Alternative, Notice of Dismissal pursuant to FRCP 41(a)(1)."

Judge Bennett nevertheless went forward with a hearing on the matter of sanctions on November 10, as scheduled. At that hearing, counsel for the plaintiffs were themselves represented by counsel and were given the opportunity to call witnesses. Plaintiffs' counsel asserted that they acted in good faith and intended to diligently prosecute the case remaining in the 105th District Court. Hilliard admitted, however, that the filing process he used was designed to get his clients' claims before a particular judge. At the close of the hearing, Judge Bennett announced from the bench that he intended to enter an order requiring plaintiffs' counsel each to pay $10,000 as a sanction.

Meanwhile, on November 16, 1995, before Judge Bennett had reduced his rulings to a written order, the federal district court consolidated all seventeen cases that had been removed. That same day, the federal district court dismissed, but did not remand, all the cases that had been nonsuited, including the one removed from Judge Bennett's court, leaving pending only the case removed from the 105th District Court. (The federal district court eventually entered final judgment in the case removed from the 105th District Court on January 22, 1996, dismissing the case under the doctrines of comity of nations and forum non conveniens. The United States Court of Appeals for the Fifth Judicial Circuit has affirmed that judgment. *Torres v. Southern Peru Copper Corp.*, 113 F.3d 540 (5th Cir.1997).)

In January 1996, Judge Bennett proceeded to memorialize his rulings from the sanctions hearing in formal written orders. Among the express findings included in those orders, Judge Bennett found that counsel had knowingly and intentionally violated the Local Rules of Practice of the District Courts of Nueces County that provide for the random assignment of cases and had violated the Texas Rules of Civil Procedure, in particular Rules 13 and 1. Judge Bennett never signed an order dismissing the case pursuant to the notice of nonsuit.

Plaintiffs' counsel filed a motion for leave to file a petition for writ of mandamus in the court of appeals challenging Judge Bennett's sanctions. The court of appeals conditionally issued a writ of mandamus directing Judge Bennett to vacate that order and to sign an order dismissing the case pursuant to the notice of nonsuit.

105th District Court, however, is to receive one half the share of civil case assignments received by other district courts.

Judge Bennett has now instituted this mandamus proceeding and requests that this Court issue a writ directing the court of appeals to vacate its writ of mandamus. We first consider the extent of Judge Bennett's authority to sanction counsel after the notice of nonsuit was filed.

II

The court of appeals held that because no affirmative relief had been requested by any defendant, the filing of a nonsuit deprived the trial court of jurisdiction to take any action other than the ministerial act of signing an order dismissing the case. 925 S.W.2d at 341. That holding gives an inordinate amount of weight to a notice of nonsuit and strips a trial court of authority to sanction the conduct of counsel when appropriate.

Generally, plaintiffs have the right under TEX. R. CIV. P. 162 to take a nonsuit at any time until they have introduced all evidence other than rebuttal evidence. *See Hyundai Motor Co. v. Alvarado*, 892 S.W.2d 853, 854 (Tex. 1995); *Aetna Cas. & Sur. Co. v. Specia*, 849 S.W.2d 805, 806 (Tex. 1993). Such a nonsuit may have the effect of vitiating earlier interlocutory orders and of precluding further action by the trial court, with some notable exceptions. *See Hyundai*, 892 S.W.2d at 854-55 (holding that once a trial court announces a decision on a motion for partial summary judgment, that claim is no longer subject to the plaintiff's right to nonsuit); *Greenberg v. Brookshire*, 640 S.W.2d 870, 872 (Tex. 1982) (stating that the rule recognizing a plaintiff's right to nonsuit should not be confused with the rule recognizing the power of a court to grant injunctive relief to prevent a multiplicity of groundless suits).

However, the signing of an order dismissing a case, not the filing of a notice of nonsuit, is the starting point for determining when a trial court's plenary power expires. Appellate timetables do not run from the date a nonsuit is filed, but rather from the date the trial court signs an order of dismissal. *See Farmer v. Ben E. Keith Co.*, 907 S.W.2d 495, 496 (Tex. 1995) ("The appellate timetable does not commence to run other than by a signed, written order, even when the signing of such an order is purely ministerial."); *see also Shadowbrook Apartments v. Abu-Ahmad*, 783 S.W.2d 210, 211 (Tex. 1990); TEX. R. CIV. P. 329b(d).

While we have recognized that generally, a trial court has no discretion to refuse to sign an order of dismissal once notice of a nonsuit has been filed, this broad principle necessarily has exceptions. Rule 162 expressly states that a dismissal under the rule "shall have no effect on any motion for sanctions, attorney's fees or other costs pending at the time of dismissal." TEX. R. CIV. P. 162. Further, a trial court is free to "impose sanctions while it retain[s] plenary jurisdiction" even when a motion for sanctions is filed after the notice of nonsuit is filed. *Scott & White Mem'l Hosp. v. Schexnider*, 940 S.W.2d 594, 596 (Tex. 1996). It is only after plenary jurisdiction has expired that a trial court may not sanction counsel for pre-judgment conduct. *Id.* at 596 & n. 2; *see also BHP Petroleum Co. v. Millard*, 800 S.W.2d 838, 840 (Tex. 1990) (right to nonsuit is absolute unless there is a pending claim for affirmative relief or a motion for sanctions).

The removal to federal court placed this case in an unusual procedural posture. On the date of removal, Judge Bennett had not signed an order of dismissal, but he would have been well within his authority to defer signing such an order pending the disposition of the sanctions issues. A trial court has the discretion to allow a reasonable amount of time for holding a hearing on sanctions and, once the question of sanctions has been resolved, to then sign an order of dismissal. The court of appeals erred when it held otherwise. Judge Bennett would have had plenary power when he signed the order imposing sanctions but for the removal.

The opinion of the court of appeals is devoid of any mention of removal and erroneously focused only on Judge Bennett's plenary power in the context of a nonsuit. The court of appeals should have considered what authority Judge Bennett had to enter an order sanctioning counsel for pre-removal conduct after the case had been removed and after the federal court had dismissed the case at the request of plaintiffs. We turn to that issue.

III

* * *

From our review of federal precedent and in light of the practical ramifications, we conclude that state courts retain jurisdiction after removal of a case to federal court to sanction lawyers for pre-removal conduct so long as the sanction does not operate upon the merits of the underlying action. Accordingly, the court of appeals erred in concluding that Judge Bennett did not have jurisdiction to consider the imposition of sanctions in this case. The final issue is whether the imposition of sanctions was appropriate under the facts of this case.

IV

Counsel for the plaintiffs contend that the trial court abused its discretion by sanctioning them. The court of appeals agreed, writing in dicta that even if Judge Bennett had plenary jurisdiction, he had no authority to impose sanctions sua sponte. 925 S.W.2d at 341-42. We disagree.

Courts possess inherent power to discipline an attorney's behavior. *See Lawrence v. Kohl*, 853 S.W.2d 697, 700 (Tex. App.—Houston [1st Dist.] 1993, no writ) (holding that trial courts have the power to sanction parties for bad faith abuse of the judicial process not covered by rule or statute); *Kutch v. Del Mar College*, 831 S.W.2d 506, 509-10 (Tex. App.—Corpus Christi 1992, no writ) (same); *see also Public Util. Comm'n v. Cofer*, 754 S.W.2d 121, 124 (Tex. 1988) (recognizing the inherent power of courts to ensure an adversarial proceeding); *Eichelberger v. Eichelberger*, 582 S.W.2d 395, 398- 99 (Tex. 1979) (recognizing that a court has inherent power "which it may call upon to aid in the exercise of its jurisdiction, in the administration of justice, and in the preservation of its independence and integrity"). A court has the inherent power to impose sanctions on its own motion in an appropriate case.[6]

Plaintiffs' counsel admitted that the filing scheme was designed to ensure adjudication by a particular judge. The practice of filing multiple cases without intent to prosecute most of them, in search of a court perceived to be sympathetic, subverts random assignment procedures that are in place in many multi-court counties and is an abuse of the judicial process. This type of conduct, if tolerated, breeds disrespect for and threatens the integrity of our judicial system.

The power to sanction is of course limited by the due process clause of the United States Constitution, as urged by plaintiffs' counsel. The lawyers sanctioned in this case cannot deny that they were fully aware of the purposes of the random assignment system. They intentionally attempted to circumvent those purposes. Counsel were given notice of the court's intention to consider sanctions and were given an opportunity to respond. Due process was not violated in this case. The court of appeals abused its discretion in directing Judge Bennett to vacate the order sanctioning counsel in this case.

* * *

Accordingly, the Court grants Relators' motion for leave to file, and, without hearing oral argument, conditionally grants the writ of mandamus. TEX. R. APP. P. 59.1. The writ will issue only if the court of appeals fails to vacate its writ of mandamus.

4. *Consent Judgment*

Notes

1. *Kennedy v. Hyde*, 682 S.W. 2d 525 (Tex. 1984): Consent to an agreed judgment must exist at the time the judgement is entered.

2. *Middleton v. Murff*, 689 S.W.2d 212 (Tex. 1985) (per curiam): While consent must exist at the time a consent judgment is entered, the entry of a consent judgment after consent has been withdrawn is a procedural error which must be attacked directly.

3. *Shamrock Psychiatric Clinic, P.A. v. Tex. Dep't of Health and Human Services*, 540 S.W.3d 553 (Tex. 2018): A trial court has a ministerial duty to enforce a valid Rule 11 agreement. Litigants' Rule 11 agreements are contracts relating to litigation, and thus we construe them under the same rules as a contract. We do not give a Rule 11 agreement greater effect than the parties intended. If a contract can be given a certain or definite legal meaning or interpretation, it is not ambiguous, and we construe it as a matter of law. To be effective, a Rule 11 agreement must consist of "a written memorandum which is complete within itself in every material detail, and

[6] For suits commenced on or after September 1, 1995, the Texas Civil Practice and Remedies Code authorizes a trial court to impose sanctions on its own initiative for certain conduct if the show cause order is issued before a voluntary dismissal or settlement of claims. *See* TEX. CIV. PRAC. & REM.CODE §§ 10.002(b), 10.004(e) and historical notes [Act of May 4, 1995, 74th Leg., R.S., ch. 137, § 2, 1995 Tex. Gen. Laws 977, 978]. We need not decide whether the conduct in this case is covered by these statutes.

which contains all of the essential elements of the agreement. We have held that a series of letters between the parties is sufficient to constitute a Rule 11 agreement. Here, the alleged agreement, made via email and memorialized in the Inspector General's status report, was in writing, signed, and filed with the court, as required by Rule 11.

PADILLA
v.
LaFRANCE

907 S.W.2d 454
(Tex. 1995)

James B. Lewis, Ronald P. Schramm, Glover Anderson Chandler & Uzick, Houston, for petitioner.

John Stevenson, Jr., Stevenson Albright & Ammons, Dennis R. Mundy, D. Craig Olivier, Jeffrey W. Hitt, Olivier & Steidley, Houston, for respondents.

PHILLIPS, CHIEF JUSTICE, delivered the opinion of the Court, joined by GONZALEZ, HIGHTOWER, HECHT, CORNYN, SPECTOR, and OWEN, JUSTICES.

The primary issue presented is whether a series of letters between the parties' representatives constituted a written settlement agreement enforceable under Texas Rule of Civil Procedure 11, even though plaintiffs withdrew their consent to the settlement before the letters were filed with the court and before judgment was rendered on the agreement. The court of appeals held that any agreement was unenforceable under Rule 11 because plaintiffs revoked consent before the letters were filed with the court. 875 S.W.2d 730. Because we hold that the letters constituted an enforceable Rule 11 agreement, we reverse the judgment of the court of appeals and remand to the trial court with instructions to enforce the parties' settlement agreement.

I

One member of the LaFrance family was killed and two others were seriously injured when their vehicle collided with that driven by Enrique Padilla. After the LaFrances sued Padilla, his insurer, State Farm Mutual Automobile Insurance Company, assumed defense of the claims. The parties subsequently engaged in settlement negotiations and, as discussed below, vigorously dispute whether an enforceable settlement agreement was consummated. On April 10, 1991, Jeffrey Steidley, the LaFrances' attorney, mailed a settlement demand to Brian Chandler, Padilla's attorney, providing in pertinent part as follows:

> Dear Mr. Chandler:
>
> You are quite familiar with the facts and circumstances surrounding the above referenced matter. At this time we make demand for policy limits of $40,000.00 for full and final settlement of this case against the insured that you represent. Payment of this sum should be made on or before Tuesday, April 23, 1991 at 5:00 p.m., by delivery of checks in the appropriate amount to the offices of the undersigned made payable in the following amounts and to the following payees:
>
> One check in the amount of $20,000.00 to Madeleine LaFrance As Next Friend of Michelle LaFrance and Olivier & Steidley.
>
> One check in the amount of $20,000.00 made payable to Ernest J. LaFrance, Marlene Luther, Marilyn Koenig, Madeleine LaFrance and Olivier & Steidley, their attorneys of record.
>
> * * *
>
> Please be advised that although I will be more than happy to discuss this case with you or any of your representatives, no oral discussion that we may have will serve to alter the time limits expressed in the correspondence. I look forward to receipt of the checks on or before date specified, failing which this offer to settle will be withdrawn and my clients will proceed to perfect their rights under Texas law, the substance of which I know you are well aware.

Chandler forwarded this letter to Phil Bradshaw, the State Farm adjuster handling the claim, who telephoned Steidley's office on April 15 and spoke with Sherea Carry. Bradshaw informed Carry of an outstanding $1,600 medical lien for treatment to Michelle LaFrance that needed to be cleared up in connection with the settlement.

Carry responded that she would have Steidley call Bradshaw to discuss the lien. When Bradshaw did not hear back from Steidley, he called Steidley's office on April 18 and again on the morning of April 23 to discuss the lien. Each time he was able to speak only with Carry, who informed Bradshaw that the lien had not yet been resolved.

When Bradshaw still had not heard from Steidley by the afternoon of April 23, the settlement deadline, he faxed this handwritten letter to Steidley:

> Dear Mr. Steidley,
>
> This will confirm our settlement agreement of 4/18/91, whereby State Farm agreed to meet the policy limit demands set out in your letter of 4/10/91. The only thing holding up resolution of this is the hospital lien re: Michelle. I await word from you regarding the lien so I know to whom to make drafts payable.

It is unclear from the record what Bradshaw was referring to by the "agreement of 4/18/91." Steidley responded before 5:00 p.m. the same day, by fax and regular mail, with this letter:

> Dear Mr. Bradshaw:
>
> This letter will confirm that the above referenced matter has been settled for all applicable policy limits, which have been represented to us to be $40,000.00. Please forward settlement checks in the above referenced matter. This office will agreed [sic] to take care of the lien filed by Medical Center Hospital out of the settlement funds forwarded by your office. Your attention to this matter is greatly appreciated.

Bradshaw did not see Steidley's response until he arrived at his office the next morning, April 24. Approximately one week later, Chandler tendered two settlement checks for $20,000 each to Steidley, along with a formal settlement agreement. Steidley, however, refused to accept the checks or sign the agreement, contending that Padilla had not timely accepted the April 10 settlement offer.

Padilla subsequently filed Steidley's April 23 letter with the court, describing it as "an acceptance of a settlement." Padilla then filed a counterclaim in the pending suit, seeking enforcement of the alleged settlement agreement, and both sides moved for summary judgment on the counterclaim. Padilla argued that the letters between the parties' representatives constituted a written settlement agreement. Although acknowledging that the court could not render a consent judgment incorporating the terms of the settlement, as the LaFrances had revoked consent, he nonetheless contended that the court could enforce the settlement by summary judgment. The LaFrances countered that the parties did not have an enforceable agreement under Texas Rule of Civil Procedure 11, which requires agreements regarding pending suits to "be in writing, signed and filed with the papers as part of the record . . . ." The LaFrances further argued that, even if an otherwise valid Rule 11 agreement existed, it could not be enforced since the LaFrances had revoked consent prior to any judgment being rendered on the agreement. The LaFrances also moved to sever the counterclaim.

After a hearing on May 1, 1992, the court orally ruled that an enforceable settlement agreement did not exist, granting the LaFrances' motion for summary judgment and denying Padilla's. The court also granted the motion for severance, noting on the docket that a final judgment would be granted to the LaFrances on the counterclaim. The court, however, did not sign a written judgment or order of severance at that time.

On June 11, 1992, Padilla filed a "Motion for Reconsideration on his Motion for Summary Judgment," raising the same arguments contained in his original motion for summary judgment and adding one additional argument.[1] Although this motion was apparently set for oral hearing on June 22, there is no indication in the record or the briefs that any hearing occurred. On June 19, Padilla filed another motion, styled simply as a "Motion for Summary Judgment," setting forth essentially the same arguments contained in the motion for reconsideration.

---

[1] The new argument was based on section 154.071(a) of the Texas Civil Practice and Remedies Code, which provides:

> If the parties reach a settlement and execute a written agreement disposing of the dispute, the agreement is enforceable in the same manner as any other written contract.
>
> This section is contained in Title 7 of the Civil Practice and Remedies Code, regarding referral of cases to alternative dispute resolution.

No oral hearing was held on this subsequent motion for summary judgment, and neither it nor the motion for reconsideration was submitted for a ruling on Harris County's submission docket. See Local Rule 3.3.2 of the Harris County District Courts. On October 19, 1992, the court signed an order granting the LaFrances' motion for summary judgment and denying Padilla's. This order referred only to the cross motions for summary judgment argued on May 1, mentioning neither Padilla's motion for reconsideration nor his later successive motion for summary judgment. On November 20, 1992, the court signed an order severing Padilla's counterclaim and assigning it a new cause number, thus finalizing the earlier summary judgment.

Padilla appealed from this severed cause. The LaFrances moved the court of appeals to dismiss the appeal, contending that the transcript, which Padilla filed 82 days after the judgment became final on November 20, 1992, was untimely. Under Texas Rule of Appellate Procedure 54(a), the transcript must be filed within sixty days after judgment, or within 120 days if a timely motion for new trial or motion to modify the judgment has been filed. The court of appeals originally dismissed the appeal, but reinstated it on rehearing. The court concluded that Padilla's motion for rehearing of the trial court's oral summary judgment ruling was the equivalent of a motion for new trial, extending the appellate deadlines under Rule 54(a). 875 S.W.2d at 732.

As to the merits, the court of appeals concluded that the parties did not have an enforceable settlement agreement under Texas Rule of Civil Procedure 11. The court held that, under Rule 11, consent to the settlement agreement must exist at the time it is filed with the court. 875 S.W.2d at 734. Although not expressly deciding whether Steidley's April 23 letter constituted a signed writing sufficient under Rule 11, the court noted that the LaFrances had revoked any consent prior to that letter being filed with the court. *Id.* The court accordingly affirmed the trial court's summary judgment in favor of the LaFrances.

II

* * *

III

Texas Rule of Civil Procedure 11 provides as follows:

> Unless otherwise provided in these rules, no agreement between attorneys or parties touching any suit pending will be enforced unless it be in writing, signed and filed with the papers as part of the record, or unless it be made in open court and entered of record.

This rule has existed since 1840 and has contained the filing requirement since 1877. *See Kennedy v. Hyde*, 682 S.W.2d 525, 526 (Tex.1984) (tracing the history of Rule 11). The rationale for the rule is straightforward:

> Agreements of counsel, respecting the disposition of causes, which are merely verbal, are very liable to be misconstrued or forgotten, and to beget misunderstandings and controversies; and hence there is great propriety in the rule which requires that all agreements of counsel respecting their causes shall be in writing, and if not, the court will not enforce them. They will then speak for themselves, and the court can judge of their import, and proceed to act upon them with safety.

The rule is a salutary one, and ought to be adhered to whenever counsel disagree as to what has transpired between them. *Birdwell v. Cox*, 18 Tex. 535, 537 (1857). A settlement agreement must comply with Rule 11 to be enforceable. *Kennedy*, 682 S.W.2d at 528.[2]

issues

The LaFrances argue that 1) the writings in this case do not evidence a binding agreement, 2) even if there was an agreement, it did not comply with Rule 11 because the LaFrances withdrew their consent before the writings were filed with the court, and 3) any agreement was further unenforceable because the LaFrances withdrew their consent before judgment was rendered on the agreement. We consider each of these arguments in turn.

A

Rule 11 requires settlement agreements to "be in writing." Although we have never articulated what is necessary to satisfy this "in writing" requirement, we may analogize to the statute of frauds, which requires certain contracts to be in writing. *See* TEX. BUS. & COM. CODE § 26.01. To satisfy the statute of frauds, "there must be a written memorandum which is complete within itself in every material detail, and which contains all of the essential elements of the agreement, so that the contract can be ascertained from the writings without resorting to

[2] Because the primary purpose of Rule 11 is to require the parties to reduce their agreements to writing, the Court in Kennedy refused to enforce an oral settlement agreement.

oral testimony." *Cohen v. McCutchin*, 565 S.W.2d 230, 232 (Tex. 1978). The written memorandum, however, need not be contained in one document. *See Adams v. Abbott*, 151 Tex. 601, 254 S.W.2d 78, 80 (1952).

These principles apply equally to Rule 11 agreements. Applying them here, we hold that the series of letters between Steidley, Bradshaw and Chandler are sufficient to constitute an agreement in writing satisfying Rule 11. Steidley's initial letter to Chandler offered to settle the case for the $40,000 policy limits, making clear that the offer could only be accepted by payment of the money by a specific deadline. It is undisputed that Padilla did not tender the $40,000 within that deadline. Where an offer prescribes the time and manner of acceptance, those terms must ordinarily be complied with to create a contract. *See Town of Lindsay v. Cooke County Elec. Cooperative Ass'n*, 502 S.W.2d 117, 118 (Tex.1973), *cert. denied*, 416 U.S. 970, 94 S.Ct. 1993, 40 L.Ed.2d 559 (1974). However, a different method of acceptance may be effectual where the "original offeror thereafter manifests his assent to the other party." *Id.* That was the case here. The later writings reflect that Steidley agreed to a modification of the terms of acceptance set out in the original letter. Bradshaw's letter—faxed to Steidley on the afternoon of April 23—agreed to pay the $40,000 policy limits, specifically confirming a "settlement agreement" between the parties. That letter, however, noted uncertainty as to one detail, payment of the hospital lien, and requested guidance from Steidley. Steidley responded that same day with a letter indicating that plaintiffs would pay the hospital lien out of the settlement funds, specifically stating that "[t]his letter will confirm that the above referenced matter has been settled for all applicable policy limits . . . ." (emphasis added). Steidley used this language, indicating a consummated settlement, notwithstanding that no checks had not yet been forwarded by Padilla. Steidley, therefore, assented to Padilla's alteration of the mode of acceptance set out in Steidley's original offer. Rather than requiring actual payment by a particular deadline, Steidley accepted Padilla's agreement to pay the policy limits as acceptance of his earlier offer. Moreover, the letters reflect all material terms of the agreement; i.e., Padilla agreed to pay $40,000 in settlement of all claims, and the LaFrances agreed to pay the hospital lien out of those proceeds. We accordingly hold that the parties entered into a binding settlement agreement, evidenced by a writing sufficient to satisfy Rule 11.

B

Rule 11 requires settlement agreements to be filed "with the papers as part of the record." Padilla did not file any of the settlement letters until after the LaFrances had refused to accept the settlement checks tendered by Padilla. The court of appeals accordingly held that the agreement did not comply with Rule 11 because it was not filed until after the LaFrances had revoked their consent.

Although Rule 11 requires the writing to be filed in the court record, it does not say when it must be filed. The purpose of the rule—to avoid disputes over the terms of oral settlement agreements—is not furthered by requiring the writing to be filed before consent is withdrawn. As noted by the dissent below, "[t]o require the parties to immediately rush to the courthouse with a signed document in order to quickly comply with the requirements of Rule 11 before the other party reneges on his agreement goes against the grain of the policy in Texas jurisprudence which favors the settlement of lawsuits." 875 S.W.2d at 735. The purpose of the filing requirement, in the language of *Birdwell v. Cox*, is to put the agreement before the court so that "the court can judge of [its] import, and proceed to act upon [it] with safety." 18 Tex. at 537. This purpose is satisfied so long as the agreement is filed before it is sought to be enforced. Padilla met that requirement here by filing each of the settlement letters with his motion for summary judgment on the counterclaim.

C

Finally, the LaFrances argue that the settlement is unenforceable because they withdrew consent before judgment was rendered on the agreement. The LaFrances rely on *Kennedy v. Hyde*, where we held that "notwithstanding a valid Rule 11 agreement, consent must exist at the time an agreed judgment is rendered." 682 S.W.2d at 528. *See also Burnaman v. Heaton*, 150 Tex. 333, 240 S.W.2d 288, 291 (1951).

The LaFrances, however, confuse the requirements for an agreed judgment with those for an enforceable settlement agreement. Although a court cannot render a valid agreed judgment absent consent at the time it is rendered, this does not preclude the court, after proper notice and hearing, from enforcing a settlement agreement complying with Rule 11 even though one side no longer consents to the settlement. The judgment in the latter case is not an agreed judgment, but rather is a judgment enforcing a binding contract. In *Burnaman*, for example, the plaintiff wanted to repudiate a settlement that her attorney had agreed to on the record in open court, claiming that she had not authorized such settlement. Although aware of the plaintiff's objection, the court subsequently rendered a consent judgment incorporating the terms of the settlement. We held that the consent judgment was improper since contemporaneous consent was lacking. "It is not sufficient to support the judgment that a party's consent thereto may at one time have been given; consent must exist at the very moment the court undertakes to make the agreement the judgment of the court." 240 S.W.2d at 291. In reversing the agreed judgment, however, we noted as follows:

> Since the judgment of the trial court is reversed, we cannot pass on the effect of the agreement made by the attorneys or the notation of that agreement on the docket. We can only say that the announcement of the agreement in open court and its notation on the docket cannot give it the force of a judgment. It follows that the reversal of the judgment should be without prejudice to the right of defendants to plead the agreement in bar of plaintiff's suit and without prejudice also to plaintiff's right to avoid the agreement by pleading that her attorney was without authority to make it. These are issues to be settled by the jury or the court in a trial of the case.

240 S.W.2d at 292. Similarly in *Quintero v. Jim Walter Homes, Inc.*, 654 S.W.2d 442 (Tex.1983), we held that the trial court erred by rendering an agreed judgment of dismissal based on a release signed by plaintiff because plaintiff did not consent to the judgment at the time it was rendered. We noted, however, that "our reversal of the judgment of dismissal is without prejudice to the rights of the Jim Walter Homes in its attempt to plead and prove an enforceable settlement agreement under the release." 654 S.W.2d at 444. . . .

An action to enforce a settlement agreement, where consent is withdrawn, must be based on proper pleading and proof. *See Quintero*, 654 S.W.2d at 444; *Browning*, 620 S.W.2d at 615. In this case, for example, Padilla filed a counterclaim seeking enforcement of the parties' agreement, and both sides moved for summary judgment on that claim. As previously discussed, the summary judgment evidence established an enforceable settlement agreement as a matter of law. The trial court therefore should have granted Padilla's motion for summary judgment and enforced the agreement.

For the foregoing reasons, we reverse the judgment of the court of appeals and remand this cause to the trial court for further proceedings consistent with this opinion.

ENOCH, JUSTICE, joined by GAMMAGE, JUSTICE, dissenting (Opinion omitted).

Notes

1. *See* L. Wayne Scott, *The Law of Mediation in Texas*, 37 ST. MARY'S LAW J. 325, 365 (2006).

2. A serious split of authority existed concerning the effect of Section 154.071, TEX. CIV. PRAC. & REM. CODE, which provides, in part: "(a) If the parties reach a settlement and execute a written agreement disposing of the dispute, the agreement is enforceable in the same manner as any other written contract." In *Matter of the Marriage of Ames*, 860 S.W.2d 590, 591 (Tex. App.—Amarillo 1993, no writ), the court held that settlement agreements reached through court-ordered mediation may not be unilaterally repudiated. Two other courts, however, have refused to support the entry of agreed judgments based on repudiated mediated settlement agreements (repudiated before the agreed judgment could be entered). *Cary v. Cary,* 894 S.W.2d 111, 112 (Tex. App.—Houston [1st Dist.] 1995, no writ) and *Clopton v. Mountain Peak Water Supply Corp.*, 911 S.W.2d 525 (Tex. App.—Waco, 1995, no writ). Both the *Cary* and the *Clopton* courts agree that the mediated agreement is still enforceable as a contract. As stated in *Clopton*, 911 S.W.2d, 527:

> "We do not determine whether Clopton may repudiate the settlement agreement. Clopton's withdrawing his consent to entry of a judgment does not necessarily make the settlement agreement unenforceable. A party can enforce the agreement even though the other party has withdrawn consent to the judgment. However, the party seeking to enforce the agreement must provide proper pleading and proof to support enforcing the settlement agreement under contract law. * * *"

Any doubt about the *Ames* questions, that might arguably have remained after *Padilla,* seems to have been settled by the Texas Supreme Court in *Mantas v. Fifth Court of Appeals,* 925 S.W.2d 656 (Tex. 1996). Stated simply, although *Ames* is not cited, *Ames* is effectively overruled.

3. *Leal v Cortez,* 569 S.W.2d 536 (Tex. Civ. App.—Corpus Christi 1978, no writ). The court has no power to alter the agreement or supply additional terms; it only had the power to put the agreement as made by the parties themselves into judgment form.

4. The language in TEX. R. CIV. P. 11 was amended in 1987 to add the language: "Unless otherwise provided in these rules" to the beginning of the rule. The effect is to allow discovery agreements, and other informal arrangement allowed elsewhere in the rules.

5. A special provision for enforcement of mediated settlement agreements in certain family law cases is found in TEX. FAM. Code section § 6.602:

(a) On the written agreement of the parties or on the court's own motion, the court may refer a suit for dissolution of a marriage to mediation.

(b) A mediated settlement agreement is binding on the parties if the agreement:

(1) provides, in a prominently displayed statement that is in boldfaced type or capital letters or underlined, that the agreement is not subject to revocation;

(2) is signed by each party to the agreement; and

(3) is signed by the party's attorney, if any, who is present at the time the agreement is signed.

(c) If a mediated settlement agreement meets the requirements of this section, a party is entitled to judgment on the mediated settlement agreement notwithstanding Rule 11, Texas Rules of Civil Procedure, or another rule of law.

(d) A party may at any time prior to the final mediation order file a written objection to the referral of a suit for dissolution of a marriage to mediation on the basis of family violence having been committed against the objecting party by the other party. After an objection is filed, the suit may not be referred to mediation unless, on the request of the other party, a hearing is held and the court finds that a preponderance of the evidence does not support the objection. If the suit is referred to mediation, the court shall order appropriate measures be taken to ensure the physical and emotional safety of the party who filed the objection. The order shall provide that the parties not be required to have face-to-face contact and that the parties be placed in separate rooms during mediation.

6. In *In re Lee*, 411 S.W.3d 445 (Tex. 2013) the court held that a mediated settlement agreement, under Fam. Code § 153.0071(e), had to be enforced by the trial court, without an inquiry into the child's best interest.

7. *Milner v. Milner*, 361 S.W.3d 615 (Tex. 2012): Unlike other settlement agreements in family law, the trial court is not required to determine if the property division is "just and right" before approving an mediated settlement agreement. And once signed, an mediated settlement agreement cannot be revoked like other settlement agreements. As a general rule, a party may revoke its consent to a settlement agreement before the court renders judgment on the agreement. An agreed judgment may not be rendered thereafter, although the revoking party may be liable for breaching the settlement agreement. Mediated settlement agreements that comply with Texas Family Code § 6.602 are an exception to this general rule.

8. *Cayan v. Cayan*, 38 S.W.3d 161, 166 (Tex. App.—Houston [14th Dist.] 2000, *pet. denied*): Under this provision, an agreement that complies with section 6.602 may be enforced by the family court without a determination that the agreement is "just or right," as generally required by section 7.006.

> ". . ., [T]he language of section 6.602 reflects that when the Legislature enacted that section, it definitely and deliberately created a procedural shortcut for enforcement of mediated settlement agreements in divorce cases. Equally apparent is that section 6.602 does not conflict with, but is an exception to, section 7.006. We are similarly persuaded that section 6.602 is also an exception to sections 7.001 and 7.006 in allowing a judgment to be entered on a section 6.602 agreement without a determination by the trial court that the terms of the agreement are just and right. Importantly, however, section 6.602 cannot be imposed on parties against their wishes. Rather, they remain free to enter mediated settlement agreements that do not fall within section 6.602 and, in fact, must take affirmative steps to qualify for section 6.602 treatment.

9. *Boyd v. Boyd*, 67 S.W. 3d 398 (Tex. App.—Fort Worth 2002, no pet.): "Ordinarily, settlement agreements arising from mediation are not binding where one party withdraws consent to the agreement, unless the other party successfully sues to enforce the settlement agreement as a contract that complies with rule 11 of the Texas Rules of Civil Procedure. *See* TEX. CIV. PRAC. & REM.CODE Ann. § 154.071(a) (Vernon 1997) (providing that settlement agreements arising from mediation are enforceable in the same manner as any other written contract); *Padilla v. LaFrance*, 907 S.W.2d 454, 461- 62 (Tex. 1995) (holding that, once consent to settlement

agreement is withdrawn, agreement can only be enforced as a binding contract that complies with rule 11, as established by proper pleading and proof); *Alcantar v. Okl. Nat'l Bank*, 47 S.W.3d 815, 819 (Tex. App.—Fort Worth 2001, no pet.)."

"Unilateral withdrawal of consent does not, however, negate the enforceability of a mediated settlement agreement in a divorce proceeding, and a separate suit for enforcement of a contract is not necessary. *Alvarez v. Reiser*, 958 S.W.2d 232, 234 (Tex. App.—Eastland 1997, writ denied). Rather, section 6.602 creates a procedural short cut for the enforcement of mediated settlement agreements in divorce cases. *Cayan v. Cayan*, 38 S.W.3d 161, 166 (Tex. App.—Houston [14th Dist.] 2000, pet. denied). Thus, a mediated settlement agreement that meets the requirements of section 6.602(b) is binding, and a party is entitled to judgment on the agreement notwithstanding rule 11 or another rule of law. TEX. FAM.CODE Ann. § 6.602(c); *see also id.* § 153.0071(e); *Alvarez*, 958 S.W.2d at 234."

"In his first issue, Randall contends that the "notwithstanding rule 11 or another rule of law" language in the statute means that a mediated settlement agreement that complies with section 6.602(b) is not subject to [trial court] review and that a trial court's failure to enforce the agreement is reversible error. We decline to construe section 6.602(c) in such a restrictive manner.

In construing a statute, our objective is to determine and give effect to the legislature's intent. *Nat'l Liab. & Fire Ins. Co. v. Allen*, 15 S.W.3d 525, 527 (Tex. 2000). When terms are not defined in a statute, we apply their ordinary meaning. TEX. GOV'T CODE Ann. §§ 311.011, 312.002(a) (Vernon 1998); *Nat'l Liab. & Fire Ins. Co.*, 15 S.W.3d at 527. We also presume that the legislature intended a just and reasonable result in enacting a statute. TEX. GOV'T CODE ANN. § 311.021(3). A court will not construe a statute in a manner that will lead to a foolish or absurd result when another alternative is available. *Del Indus., Inc. v. Tex. Workers' Comp. Ins. Fund*, 973 S.W.2d 743, 747-48 (Tex. App.—Austin 1998), aff'd, 35 S.W.3d 591 (Tex. 2000).

"Construing the phrase "notwithstanding rule 11 or another rule of law" to mean that a mediated settlement agreement that complies with section 6.602(b) must be enforced no matter what the circumstances could require enforcement of an agreement that was illegal or that was procured by fraud, duress, coercion, or other dishonest means. We do not believe that the legislature intended such an absurd result in enacting section 6.602. Rather, we construe this phrase to mean that the requirements of rule 11 and the common law that ordinarily apply to the enforcement of settlement agreements do not apply to mediated settlement agreements in divorce proceedings, if the agreements meet the three requirements listed in section 6.602(b). *See Cayan*, 38 S.W.3d at 166 (stating that section 6.602 was enacted to create a procedural short cut for the enforcement of mediated settlement agreements in divorce cases).

"We hold that the phrase "notwithstanding rule 11 or another rule of law" does not require a trial court to enforce a mediated settlement agreement simply because it complies with section 6.602(b), irrespective of what the agreement provides for or how it was procured. *See In re Kasschau*, 11 S.W.3d 305, 311 (Tex. App.—Houston [14th Dist.] 1999, orig. proceeding) (op. on reh'g) (holding that trial court did not err by refusing to enforce mediated settlement agreement that contained an illegal provision); *see also Cayan*, 38 S.W.3d at 166 n. 8. We overrule the portion of Randall's point first in which he contends that a mediated settlement agreement that complies with section 6.602(b) is not subject to review."

10. In *Knapp Medical Center v. De La Garza*, --- S.W.3d ----, 51 Tex. Sup. Ct. J. 105, 2007 WL 3230144 (Tex) Dr. De La Garza, M.D., sued Knapp Medical Center. During that trial, De La Garza's attorney offered to settle the case, for the hospital's insurance policy limits of $1,000,000. When this settlement demand was made, De La Garza's attorney understood that the hospital would contribute an additional $200,000 to the settlement. After making the policy-limits demand, he learned that the hospital did not plan to contribute to the settlement, but that the insurer had agreed to settle for the $1,000,000 policy limits. The hospital's attorney acknowledged, that the insurer had agreed to settle the case for policy limits. He further acknowledged, that an additional contribution from the hospital had been discussed, but that no agreement had been reached, and that the hospital would not contribute anything further to the settlement. Despite the disagreement about what had been promised, De La Garza agreed, on the record, to settle the underlying claims for $1,000,000, while purporting to reserve his right to collect an additional $200,000 from the hospital, in another lawsuit. The court accepted the agreement, and discharged the jury. De La Garza, thereafter, signed a Release, acknowledging the settlement funds as complete satisfaction of the claims asserted in the underlying litigation. De La Garza then sued the hospital for the disputed $200,000, alleging fraud, and breach of an oral agreement that pre-dated the September 15 hearing, at which the settlement terms were dictated into the record, and accepted by the court. The trial court

rendered judgment for De La Garza's damages and attorney's fees. The court of appeals concluded, that the parol testimony of one of the attorneys was sufficient, to support the existence and breach of the settlement agreement, and affirmed the trial court's judgment. ***Held:*** Reversed and rendered. Texas Rule of Civil Procedure 11 bars enforcement of a disputed oral settlement agreement. Rule 11 requires that agreements between attorneys or parties, touching any pending suit, be in writing, signed, and filed of record, or be made in open court, and entered of record, as a condition to enforcement. The failure to comply with TEX. R. CIV. P. 11 bars the present claims.

11. In *McCalla v. Baker's Campground, Inc.*, --- S.W.3d ----, 2013 WL 4493899, 56 Tex. Sup. Ct. J. 965, (Tex. August 23, 2013) the court held that a settlement agreement that contained all necessary terms was enforceable even though some terms contemplated an additional future contract.

CHAPTER 4.
FINALITY OF JUDGMENTS AND THE TRIAL COURT'S PLENARY POWER

1. *Introduction*

Notes

1. Section 51.012 of the Texas Civil Practice and Remedies Code states:

> In a civil case in which the judgment or amount in controversy exceeds $250, exclusive of interest and costs, a person may take an appeal or writ of error to the court of appeals from a final judgment of the district or county court.

2. Texas law and public policy dictate that certain limitations be imposed upon the supervisory role of appellate courts upon decisions made by lower courts. This policy is expressed in terms of limiting appellate review to some minimum amount in controversy and, more importantly, limiting appeals to "final judgments". The Texas courts have steadfastly adhered to the principle, with certain statutory exceptions, that an appeal may be prosecuted only from a final judgment. Thus, if an order is merely interlocutory it is not appealable, unless specifically made so by statute. A final judgment is one that determines the rights of all the parties and disposes of all the issues so that no further action by the trial court is necessary in order to settle and determine the entire controversy. *See Wagner v. Warhasch*, 156 Tex. 334, 295 S.W.2d 890 (1956). An interlocutory order leaves something further to be determined and adjudicated in disposing of the rights of the parties. *See Kinney v. Tri-State Telephone Co.*, 222 S.W. 227 (Tex. Comm'n App. 1920, judgm't approved).

2. *Interlocutory Appeals*

Notes

1. Section 51.014 of the Texas Civil Practice and Remedies Code states:

(a) A person may appeal from an interlocutory order of a district court, county court at law, or county court that:

(1) appoints a receiver or trustee;

(2) overrules a motion to vacate an order that appoints a receiver or trustee;

(3) certifies or refuses to certify a class in a suit brought under Rule 42 of the Texas Rules of Civil Procedure;

(4) grants or refuses a temporary injunction or grants or overrules a motion to dissolve a temporary injunction as provided by Chapter 65;

(5) denies a motion for summary judgment that is based on an assertion of immunity by an individual who is an officer or employee of the state or a political subdivision of the state;

(6) denies a motion for summary judgment that is based in whole or in part upon a claim against or defense by a member of the electronic or print media, acting in such capacity, or a person whose communication appears in or is published by the electronic or print media, arising under the free speech or free press clause of the First Amendment to the United States Constitution, or Article I, Section 8, of the Texas Constitution, or Chapter 73;

(7) grants or denies the special appearance of a defendant under Rule 120a, Texas Rules of Civil Procedure, except in a suit brought under the Family Code;

(8) grants or denies a plea to the jurisdiction by a governmental unit as that term is defined in Section 101.001;

(9) denies all or part of the relief sought by a motion under Section 74. 351(b), except that an appeal may not be taken from an order granting an extension under Section 74.351;

(10) grants relief sought by a motion under Section 74.351(l); or

(11) denies a motion to dismiss filed under Section 90.007.

(b) An interlocutory appeal under Subsection (a), other than an appeal under Subsection (a)(4), stays the commencement of a trial in the trial court pending resolution of the appeal. An interlocutory appeal under Subsection (a)(3), (5), or (8) also stays all other proceedings in the trial court pending resolution of that appeal.

(c) A denial of a motion for summary judgment, special appearance, or plea to the jurisdiction described by Subsection (a)(5), (7), or (8) is not subject to the automatic stay under Subsection (b) unless the motion, special appearance, or plea to the jurisdiction is filed and requested for submission or hearing before the trial court not later than the later of:

(1) a date set by the trial court in a scheduling order entered under the Texas Rules of Civil Procedure; or

(2) the 180th day after the date the defendant files:

(A) the original answer;

(B) the first other responsive pleading to the plaintiff's petition; or

(C) if the plaintiff files an amended pleading that alleges a new cause of action against the defendant and the defendant is able to raise a defense to the new cause of action under Subsection (a)(5), (7), or (8), the responsive pleading that raises that defense.

(d) On a party's motion or on its own initiative, a trial court in a civil action may, by written order, permit an appeal from an order that is not otherwise appealable if:

(1) the order to be appealed involves a controlling question of law as to which there is a substantial ground for difference of opinion; and

(2) an immediate appeal from the order may materially advance the ultimate termination of the litigation .

(d-1) Subsection (d) does not apply to an action brought under the Family Code.

(e) An appeal under Subsection (d) does not stay proceedings in the trial court unless:

(1) the parties agree to a stay; or

(2) the trial or appellate court orders a stay of the proceedings pending appeal.

(f) An appellate court may accept an appeal permitted by Subsection (d) if the appealing party, not later than the 15th day after the date the trial court signs the order to be appealed, files in the court of appeals having appellate jurisdiction over the action an application for interlocutory appeal explaining why an appeal is warranted under Subsection (d). If the court of appeals accepts the appeal, the appeal is governed by the procedures in the Texas Rules of Appellate Procedure for pursuing an accelerated appeal. The date the court of appeals enters the order accepting the appeal starts the time applicable to filing the notice of appeal.

2. Section 74.351 of the Texas Civil Practice and Remedies Code states as follows:

(a) In a health care liability claim, a claimant shall, not later than the 120th day after the date the claim was filed, serve on each party or the party's attorney one or more expert reports, with a curriculum vitae of each expert listed in the report for each physician or health care provider against whom a liability claim is asserted. The date for serving the report may be extended by written agreement of the affected parties. Each defendant physician or health care provider whose conduct is implicated in a report must file and serve any objection to the sufficiency of the report not later than the 21st day after the date it was served, failing which all objections are waived.

(b) If, as to a defendant physician or health care provider, an expert report has not been served within the period specified by Subsection (a), the court, on the motion of the affected physician or health care provider, shall, subject to Subsection (c), enter an order that:

(1) awards to the affected physician or health care provider reasonable attorney's fees and costs of court incurred by the physician or health care provider; and

(2) dismisses the claim with respect to the physician or health care provider, with prejudice to the refiling of the claim.

(c) If an expert report has not been served within the period specified by Subsection (a) because elements of the report are found deficient, the court may grant one 30-day extension to the claimant in order to cure the deficiency. If the claimant does not receive notice of the court's ruling granting the extension until after the 120-day deadline has passed, then the 30-day extension shall run from the date the plaintiff first received the notice.

[Subsections (d)-(h) reserved]

(i) Notwithstanding any other provision of this section, a claimant may satisfy any requirement of this section for serving an expert report by serving reports of separate experts regarding different physicians or health care providers or regarding different issues arising from the conduct of a physician or health care provider, such as issues of liability and causation. Nothing in this section shall be construed to mean that a single expert must address all liability and causation issues with respect to all physicians or health care providers or with respect to both liability and causation issues for a physician or health care provider.

(j) Nothing in this section shall be construed to require the serving of an expert report regarding any issue other than an issue relating to liability or causation.

(k) Subject to Subsection (t), an expert report served under this section:

(1) is not admissible in evidence by any party;

(2) shall not be used in a deposition, trial, or other proceeding; and

(3) shall not be referred to by any party during the course of the action for any purpose.

(l) A court shall grant a motion challenging the adequacy of an expert report only if it appears to the court, after hearing, that the report does not represent an objective good faith effort to comply with the definition of an expert report in Subsection (r)(6).

[Subsections (m)-(q) reserved]

(r) In this section:

(1) "Affected parties" means the claimant and the physician or health care provider who are directly affected by an act or agreement required or permitted by this section and does not include other parties to an action who are not directly affected by that particular act or agreement.

(2) "Claim" means a health care liability claim.

[(3) reserved]

(4) "Defendant" means a physician or health care provider against whom a health care liability claim is asserted. The term includes a third-party defendant, cross-defendant, or counterdefendant.

(5) "Expert" means:

(A) with respect to a person giving opinion testimony regarding whether a physician departed from accepted standards of medical care, an expert qualified to testify under the requirements of Section 74.401;

(B) with respect to a person giving opinion testimony regarding whether a health care provider departed from accepted standards of health care, an expert qualified to testify under the requirements of Section 74.402;

(C) with respect to a person giving opinion testimony about the causal relationship between the injury, harm, or damages claimed and the alleged departure from the applicable standard of care in any health care liability claim, a physician who is otherwise qualified to render opinions on such causal relationship under the Texas Rules of Evidence;

(D) with respect to a person giving opinion testimony about the causal relationship between the injury, harm, or damages claimed and the alleged departure from the applicable standard of care for a dentist, a dentist or physician who is otherwise qualified to render opinions on such causal relationship under the Texas Rules of Evidence; or

(E) with respect to a person giving opinion testimony about the causal relationship between the injury, harm, or damages claimed and the alleged departure from the applicable standard of care for a podiatrist, a podiatrist or physician who is otherwise qualified to render opinions on such causal relationship under the Texas Rules of Evidence.

(6) "Expert report" means a written report by an expert that provides a fair summary of the expert's opinions as of the date of the report regarding applicable standards of care, the manner in which the care rendered by the physician or health care provider failed to meet the standards, and the causal relationship between that failure and the injury, harm, or damages claimed.

(s) Until a claimant has served the expert report and curriculum vitae as required by Subsection (a), all discovery in a health care liability claim is stayed except for the acquisition by the claimant of information, including medical or hospital records or other documents or tangible things, related to the patient's health care through:

(1) written discovery as defined in Rule 192.7, Texas Rules of Civil Procedure;

(2) depositions on written questions under Rule 200, Texas Rules of Civil Procedure; and

(3) discovery from nonparties under Rule 205, Texas Rules of Civil Procedure.

(t) If an expert report is used by the claimant in the course of the action for any purpose other than to meet the service requirement of Subsection (a), the restrictions imposed by Subsection (k) on use of the expert report by any party are waived.

(u) Notwithstanding any other provision of this section, after a claim is filed all claimants, collectively, may take not more than two depositions before the expert report is served as required by Subsection (a).

3. *See* Section 90.007 of the Texas Civil Practice and Remedies Code concerning the dismissal of certain actions and claims involving asbestos and silica.

4. *See* Section 27.003 of the Texas Civil Practice and Remedies Code concerning the dismissal of actions and claims involving the exercise of certain Constitutional rights.

Notes

1. *In re The City of Georgetown,* 531 S.W.3d 328 (Tex. 2001) represents a special circumstance in which the writ of mandamus comes into play. As a general proposition, when rights may be enforced by suit in a trial court, review of determinations by that court are through an appeal to a court of appeals and then petition for review in the Supreme Court after entry of a final judgment. This is so even if the relief sought in the trial court is a writ of mandamus. Where these ordinary remedies are complete and adequate, the extraordinary original jurisdiction of the Supreme Court or of the Court of Civil Appeals cannot be successfully invoked. Where, however, the trial court enters a writ of mandamus which grants partial relief, and is interlocutory, the order is not appealable to the court of appeals, and an application for writ of mandamus to the Supreme Court is the appropriate procedural vehicle to seek relief.

2. A temporary restraining order is not, as such, subject to an interlocutory appeal. A writ of mandamus must be used when the time for restraining order is improperly extended. *In Re: Texas Natural Resource Conservation Commission*, 85 S.W.3d 201 (Tex. 2002). (A district court may not extend a temporary restraining order by forty-two days without the restrained party's consent). TEX. R. CIV. P. 680 governs an extension of a temporary restraining order, whether issued with or without notice, and permits but one extension for no longer than fourteen days, unless the restrained party agrees to a longer extension. Mandamus is available to remedy a temporary restraining order that violates Rule 680's time limitations.

DEL VALLE INDEP. SCH. DIST.
v.
LOPEZ

845 S.W.2d 808
(Tex. 1992)

John T. Fleming, Austin, for petitioners.
Judith Bagley, Austin, Judith Sanders-Castro, Jose Garza, San Antonio, James C. Harrington, and Maria-Elena Cigarrora, Austin, for respondents.

DOGGETT, JUSTICE.

In this proceeding, we determine that the dismissal of an interlocutory appeal for want of jurisdiction was erroneous.

Through a class action filed in December 1989, Enrique Lopez, Felix Rosales, and Maurice Walker sought a declaration that the at-large system of electing board members for the Del Valle Independent School District violated the Texas Constitution by diluting minority voting strength, an injunction against further use of this system, and implementation of a constitutionally-permissible election plan. The District thereafter revised its system to provide for the selection of five members from single-member districts and two at-large. The Plaintiffs amended their petition to challenge this new plan and urged that all seven positions be selected from single member districts.

After severing the claims against the 5-2 plan from those against the at-large plan, the trial court entered an "Order Adopting and Implementing Interim Election Plan", which required the holding of an election on May 2, 1992 with six members selected from single-member districts and one at-large. All parties objected to this order, and the District appealed.

While review was pending, the election was held under the court-mandated plan. Shortly thereafter, the court of appeals dismissed the appeal for want of jurisdiction based on its finding that the trial court's order was not a temporary injunction permitting review. 845 S.W.2d 916.

This Court has jurisdiction to determine whether the court of appeals had jurisdiction over the appeal. *See Long v. Humble Oil & Ref. Co.*, 380 S.W.2d 554, 555 (Tex. 1964). Though appellate review is generally limited to final judgments, a court of appeals may consider an interlocutory order that grants a temporary injunction. *See* TEX. CIV. PRAC. & REM. CODE §§ 51.012, 51.014(4). Thus, whether jurisdiction was conferred on the court of appeals depends on whether the trial court's order can properly be characterized as a temporary injunction.

Although recognizing that the trial court provided mandatory, temporary relief by implementing an interim election plan pending the final resolution of the case, the court of appeals nevertheless held that the order did not grant "injunctive" relief. The only articulated basis for distinguishing the order from an injunction was the trial court's failure to issue a writ of injunction in accordance with TEX. CIV. PRAC. & REM. CODE § 65.022. We reject the notion that such matters of form control the nature of the order itself—it is the character and function of an order that determine its classification. *See Brines v. McIlhaney*, 596 S.W.2d 519, 524 (Tex. 1980); *Conway v. Irick*, 429 S.W.2d 648, 649 (Tex. Civ. App.—Fort Worth 1968, writ ref'd); *see also Gensco, Inc. v. Thomas*, 609 S.W.2d 650, 651 (Tex. Civ. App.—San Antonio 1980, no writ) ("The true character of an injunction is to be determined by its characteristics and functions."). In *Brines*, we concluded that: A temporary restraining order is one entered as part of a motion for a temporary injunction, by which a party is restrained pending the hearing of the motion. A temporary injunction is one which operates until dissolved by an interlocutory order or until the final hearing. 596 S.W.2d at 523 (citations omitted). An order such as that at issue here, which directs the conduct of a party but does not contemplate imminent disposition of a request for a temporary or permanent injunction, cannot be categorized as a non-appealable temporary restraining order. *See* TEX. R. CIV. P. 680.[1] To reject the order's status as a temporary injunction based on a deficiency in form is to deny review of any defects that may render the order void. Because the order constitutes a temporary injunction, and not a temporary restraining order, the District was entitled to seek review in the court of appeals pursuant to TEX. CIV. PRAC & REM. CODE § 51.014(4).

We make this determination despite the claim that this appeal has been rendered moot by both the completion of the election ordered by the trial court and the Justice Department's denial of preclearance under the Voting Rights Act. *See Clark v. Roemer*, _____ U.S. _____, 111 S.Ct. 2096, 114 L.Ed.2d 691 (1991). While, as the trial court anticipated when it ordered the parties to obtain preclearance review, the action by the Justice Department will undoubtedly impact the ultimate resolution of this case, we believe that the arguments regarding the effect of that ruling are best presented to the courts below. At this time, the order has not been dissolved or superseded by final judgment, and by its terms, it has a continuing effect on the Del Valle Independent School District. Under these circumstances, we are unwilling to consider the appeal of this order moot.

Accordingly, we reverse the judgment of the court of appeals and remand this cause to it for consideration of the merits of the District's appeal.

---

1 *See also* Plant Process Equip., Inc. v. Harris, 579 S.W.2d 53, 54 (Tex. Civ. App.—Houston [14th Dist.] 1979, no writ) ("The controlling factor is . . . whether the relief granted does more than preserve the status quo during the ten day span of a temporary restraining order."); Global Natural Resources v. Bear, Stearns & Co., 642 S.W.2d 852, 854 (Tex. App.—Dallas 1982, no writ) ("[T]he temporary restraining order [is] tantamount to a temporary injunction because the effect of it on the parties went beyond protecting the status quo for a ten-day period.").

In re OFFICE OF THE ATTORNEY GENERAL

257 S.W.3d 695
(Tex. 2008)

Kristofer S. Monson, Assistant Solicitor General, Greg W. Abbott, Jeffrey L. Rose, Attorney General of Texas, Kent C. Sullivan, First Assistant Attorney General, David S. Morales, Clarence Andrew Weber, Rafael Edward Cruz, Brantley David Starr, James C. Ho, Office of the Attorney General of Texas, Austin TX, for Relator.

Bob O'Donnell, Attorney at Law, Garland TX, for Real Party in Interest.

PER CURIAM.

In this case, the district court issued a temporary restraining order against the Office of the Attorney General and later signed two orders purporting to extend the original order. Because we conclude the orders are procedurally void, we conditionally grant the Attorney General's petition for writ of mandamus.

These proceedings concern several orders from the 301st District Court directing that child-support payments be remitted by the Attorney General to Guardian Ad Litem ("GAL"), a private company that collects and disburses child-support payments for its clients in exchange for a fee. After the Fifth Circuit held that federal law prohibited the Attorney General from remitting child-support payments to GAL absent parental authorization, *see O'Donnell v. Abbott*, 481 F.3d 280, 282 (5th Cir.2007), the Attorney General sought a writ of mandamus in the court of appeals seeking to modify approximately 560 child-support orders from Dallas and Collin Counties that ordered payment to GAL. On February 25, 2008, the 301st District Court-which had issued sixteen of the challenged orders-entered an ex parte temporary restraining order directing the Attorney General to continue to make payments in accordance with the child-support orders issued by that court and set a hearing for February 29th. On February 26th, the court of appeals stayed the hearing, but on February 28th that court denied mandamus relief and lifted the stay. On February 29th, the day set for the hearing, the Attorney General filed two petitions for writs of mandamus in this Court-one challenging the temporary restraining order issued by the 301st District Court in this case and another seeking modification of all 560 Dallas- and Collin-County child-support orders (Cause No. 08-0166). He also filed a motion requesting an emergency stay of the temporary restraining order and the scheduled hearing. While that motion was pending, the district court issued two amended orders, the first extending the prior temporary restraining order for a period of fourteen days and setting a hearing on March 12, 2008, and the second extending the order indefinitely as a temporary injunction. On February 29th, this Court stayed the original temporary restraining order pending resolution of this petition and the Attorney General's mandamus petition in the related case.

In the related case, the Attorney General sought a writ of mandamus ordering modification of the approximately 560 child-support orders in Dallas and Collin Counties, which require the Attorney General to remit payments to GAL. We denied that petition for mandamus on April 4th, and appeals regarding some of those orders are still pending in the lower courts. The present petition addresses only the temporary orders issued by the 301st District Court. The Attorney General contends the temporary orders require violations of federal law by ordering payment of child-support to GAL, *see O'Donnell v. Abbott*, 393 F.Supp.2d 508, 515-17 (W.D. Tex. 2005), aff'd 481 F.3d at 282, thus jeopardizing Texas's receipt of federal funding, and are procedurally void for failure to comply with the Texas Rules of Civil Procedure. Because we agree that the orders are void for failure to comply with mandatory procedural requirements, we conditionally grant the writ.

Texas Rules of Civil Procedure 680 and 684 require a trial court issuing a temporary restraining order to: (1) state why the order was granted without notice if it is granted ex parte, TEX.R. CIV. P. 680; (2) state the reasons for the issuance of the order by defining the injury and describing why it is irreparable, *id.*; (3) state the date the order expires and set a hearing on a temporary injunction, *id.*; and (4) set a bond, TEX.R. CIV. P. 684. Orders that fail to fulfill these requirements are void. *InterFirst Bank San Felipe, N.A. v. Paz Constr. Co.*, 715 S.W.2d 640, 641 (Tex. 1986); *Lancaster v. Lancaster*, 155 Tex. 528, 291 S.W.2d 303, 308 (1956).

The temporary restraining order and amended orders issued by the trial court violate these rules. The original and first amended orders were granted ex parte but fail to explain why they were granted without notice, *see* TEX.R. CIV. P. 680; they do not define the injury they were designed to prevent or explain why such injury would be irreparable, *see id.*; and they were issued without meeting the bond requirement, *see* TEX.R. CIV. P.

684. The second amended order purports to carry forth the original temporary restraining order as a temporary injunction, but the trial court issued it without a hearing; thus, it is not properly considered a temporary injunction but, rather, a continuation of the temporary restraining order. *See* TEX.R. CIV. P. 680; *Del Valle Indep. Sch. Dist. v. Lopez*, 845 S.W.2d 808, 809 (Tex. 1992). This second amended order, although it does set a bond, again fails to explain the reason for granting the order without notice or to define the injury to be suffered. *See* TEX.R. CIV. P. 680, 684.

Because temporary restraining orders are not appealable, the Attorney General has no remedy by appeal. *In re Tex. Natural Res. Conservation Comm'n,* 85 S.W.3d 201, 205 (Tex. 2002); *In re Newton*, 146 S.W.3d 648, 652-53 (Tex. 2004). Furthermore, the Attorney General has presented evidence that Texas could lose federal funding if he is forced to comply with the orders pending the outcome of proceedings to amend the underlying child-support orders. *See* 42 U.S.C. § 602 (2000). Given the unavailability of appeal and the gravity of interests at issue in this case, we accordingly-without hearing oral argument, pursuant to Texas Rule of Appellate Procedure 52.8(c)-conditionally grant relief and direct the court to withdraw all three of its temporary orders. We are confident that the trial court will comply, and the writ will issue only if the trial court fails to do so.

Notes

1. *In re: Texas Natural Resource Conservation Commission*, 85 S.W.3d 201 (Tex. 2002): In an original mandamus proceeding the court held that a district court may not extend a temporary restraining order by forty-two days without the restrained party's consent. The court noted that TEX. R. CIV. P. 680 governs an extension of a temporary restraining order, whether issued with or without notice, and permits but one extension for no longer than fourteen days, unless the restrained party agrees to a longer extension. Finally the court held that a mandamus is available to remedy a temporary restraining order that violates Rule 680's time limitations.

2. *In re Norman F. Newton*, 146 S.W.3d 648 (Tex. 2004). ART PAC, a political-action committee, had solicited and expended funds on elections for at least 4 years. Based solely upon pleadings, and without hearing evidence, the trial court, found that this activity violated the Texas Election Code, and entered a temporary restraining order (TRO) enjoining ART PAC, from continuing to solicit and expend funds, to the detriment of the plaintiffs' election campaigns. The trial court set the hearing on the TRO 14 days after its issuance, on November 3, the day after the election. *Held*: Writ of mandamus will issue. While the continuation of illegal conduct cannot be justified as preservation of the status quo, neither should conduct be adjudicated illegal, based merely on pleadings and a brief, non-evidentiary TRO hearing, when substantial rights are involved, and the issues are far from clear. The position of the parties just prior to the issuance of the TRO is the last peaceable uncontested status between these parties that must be preserved. The determination whether the status quo was a violation of the law, is the central question of the suit, and should be determined with a full trial on the merits.

DE AYALA
v.
MACKIE

193 S.W.3d 575
(Tex. 2006)

W. Wendell Hall, Rosemarie Kanusky, Lara Michelle Johnson, Fulbright & Jaworski L.L.P., San Antonio, Carlos Zaffirini, Zaffirini & Castillo, Laredo, for Petitioner.

Homero G. Martinez, Homero G. Martinez, PLLC, Laredo, Shannon H. Ratliff, Ratliff Law Firm, P.L.L.C., Austin, Randall A. Pulman, Alcide Federico Longoria, Pulman, Bresnahan & Pullen, L.L.P., San Antonio, Bruce John Werstak, III, Sames & Werstak, L.L.P., Laredo, for Respondent.

Kenneth A. Valls, Wilson Trevino Freed Valls & Trevino, LLP, Laredo, for Amicus Curiae.

Michael W. Perrin, Adam P. Schiffer, Christian Garza, King & Spalding, LLP, Houston, Julio A. Garcia, Laredo, Jason Murray Davis, Law Office of Jason Davis, P.C., San Antonio, for Others.

CHIEF JUSTICE JEFFERSON delivered the opinion of the Court.

We deny the motion for rehearing. We withdraw our opinion of April 21, 2006 and substitute the following in its place.

Maria Cristina Brittingham-Sada de Ayala ("Ayala"), defendant below, alleged that the trial court lacked subject matter jurisdiction over this ancillary probate proceeding involving the estate of her father, a Mexican testator whose will was probated in Mexico. The trial court denied Ayala's motion to dismiss, and she pursued an interlocutory appeal. The court of appeals concluded it had jurisdiction over the appeal, and the parties now agree. Because we disagree, we reverse the court of appeals' judgment and dismiss the appeal.

I
Factual Background

Juan Roberto Brittingham McLean ("Brittingham"), a Mexican resident, died testate in Mexico on January 14, 1998. His will was admitted to probate in a Mexican court, and two executors, Raul Hernandez Garcia and Harold Turk, were named. Brittingham's wife, Ana Maria de la Fuente de Brittingham, sued his estate in that proceeding and asked that court to set aside their property agreement. The Mexican probate court denied her request, and an appeal is pending in Mexico. The Mexican probate proceeding remains open.

Subsequently, in August 2000, Ms. Brittingham filed an application to have Brittingham's will admitted to probate in Texas, as she alleged that he owned personal property (described as bank deposits, portfolio investments, and claims against third parties) in Webb County. Later that month, the trial court issued ancillary letters testamentary to Ms. Brittingham, naming her the independent executor of Brittingham's estate (the "Estate"). On behalf of the Estate, Ms. Brittingham sued Brittingham's daughters and grandchildren (who, pursuant to Brittingham's will, were the beneficiaries of ninety-five percent of his residuary estate), accusing them of pillaging the Estate's assets. Brittingham's only son, John R. Brittingham Aguirre ("Aguirre"), intervened, alleging an interest as a creditor of the Estate.

Ayala moved to dismiss the ancillary probate proceeding for lack of subject matter jurisdiction or, alternatively, to have Ms. Brittingham removed as executor. The trial court denied the motion, and Ayala appealed.

The Estate and Aguirre moved to dismiss the appeal for lack of appellate jurisdiction. *Citing Crowson v. Wakeham*, they argued that, because numerous pleadings and issues remained pending in the trial court, the trial court's order was an unappealable interlocutory order. *See Crowson*, 897 S.W.2d 779 (Tex. 1995). The court of appeals disagreed and concluded that it had jurisdiction. 131 S.W.3d 3, 7. Relying on *Crowson*, the court noted that the probate court order addressed all the relief requested by Ayala's motion, resolved the question of subject matter jurisdiction, and confirmed both the admission of the will to probate and the appointment of Ms. Brittingham as executor. *Id.* Thus, the court held that the probate court's order "complete[d] the initial phase of the probate proceeding and [was] final for purposes of appeal." *Id.* The court then held that the trial court had subject matter jurisdiction over the ancillary probate proceeding, but that Ms. Brittingham should be removed as executor due to a conflict of interest. *Id.* at 8-9.

After the court of appeals issued its opinion, Ms. Brittingham resigned as representative of the ancillary estate and withdrew from the litigation. Subsequently, Roberto Tijerina, the Mexican estate's successor independent executor, applied to be named Ms. Brittingham's successor in the Texas case. On April 14, 2004, the trial court denied Tijerina's application and appointed Kevin Michael Mackie as the Estate's successor administrator. Mackie has entered an appearance on behalf of the Estate in this matter.

II

Appellate Jurisdiction

We first consider whether the court of appeals had jurisdiction over Ayala's appeal, even though respondents apparently no longer contest that jurisdiction. *See Univ. of Tex. Med. Branch v. Barrett*, 159 S.W.3d 631, 633 n. 8 (Tex. 2005). Generally, appeals may be taken only from final judgments. *Lehmann v. Har-Con Corp.*, 39 S.W.3d 191, 195 (Tex. 2001). Probate proceedings are an exception to the "one final judgment" rule; in such cases, "multiple judgments final for purposes of appeal can be rendered on certain discrete issues." *Id.* at 192. The need to review "controlling, intermediate decisions before an error can harm later phases of the proceeding" has been held to justify this rule. *Logan v. McDaniel*, 21 S.W.3d 683, 688 (Tex. App.—Austin 2000, pet. denied). Not every interlocutory order in a probate case is appealable, however, and determining whether an otherwise interlocutory probate order is final enough to qualify for appeal, has proved difficult.

In the past, courts relied on the "substantial right" test to decide whether an ostensibly interlocutory probate order had sufficient attributes of finality to confer appellate jurisdiction. *See, e.g., Huston v. F.D.I.C.*, 800 S.W.2d 845, 848 (Tex. 1990); *Estate of Wright*, 676 S.W.2d 161, 163 (Tex. App.—Corpus Christi 1984, writ ref'd n.r.e.). Under that standard, once the probate court adjudicated a "substantial right," the order was appealable. That phrase soon became a fruitful source of litigation as appellate courts struggled to delineate its parameters. Eleven years ago, we attempted to clarify appellate jurisdiction in this complex area. *See Crowson v. Wakeham*, 897 S.W.2d 779, 783 (Tex. 1995) (acknowledging that "our language heretofore has been somewhat ambiguous"). We noted that, while adjudication of a "substantial right" was one factor to be considered, equally important was our earlier precedent requiring that the order dispose of all issues in the phase of the proceeding for which it was brought. *Id.* at 782-83. To sidestep "potential confusion" about the appropriate test for jurisdiction, we adopted this test:

> If there is an express statute, such as the one for the complete heirship judgment, declaring the phase of the probate proceedings to be final and appealable, that statute controls. Otherwise, if there is a proceeding of which the order in question may logically be considered a part, but one or more pleadings also part of that proceeding raise issues or parties not disposed of, then the probate order is interlocutory.

Id. at 783. Recognizing the inherent difficulties in applying any test to determine appealability, we urged parties to seek severance orders to eliminate ambiguities about whether the order was intended to be final and appealable. *Id.* at 783 (explaining that "[l]itigants can and should seek a severance order either with the judgment disposing of one party or group or parties, or seek severance as quickly as practicable after the judgment").

The parties in this case did not seek a severance before appealing the order. They could hardly be faulted, however, as an order denying a motion to dismiss an entire proceeding for want of subject matter jurisdiction is more like a prelude than a finale. It certainly does not dispose of a claim that, if asserted independently, would be the proper subject of a lawsuit. *See Guar. Federal Sav. Bank v. Horseshoe Operating Co.*, 793 S.W.2d 652, 658 (Tex.1990); *see also Crowson*, 897 S.W.2d at 783 (urging severance of a claim only "if it meets the severance criteria"); *see, e.g., Forlano v. Joyner*, 906 S.W.2d 118, 120 (Tex. App.—Houston [1st Dist.] 1995, no writ) ("The [venue] transfer order, on the other hand, does not resolve a 'claim' at all, and is thus not severable."); *H.E. Butt Grocery Co. v. Currier*, 885 S.W.2d 175, 177 (Tex. App.—Corpus Christi 1994, no writ) (holding that an order granting a motion to compel discovery could not be severed because it "does not address a 'claim' that may be severed under the rules").

Moreover, under *Crowson*, the trial court's order was interlocutory because it did not dispose of all parties or issues in a particular phase of the proceedings. Because an order denying a plea to the jurisdiction and refusing to remove an executor does not end a phase of the proceedings, but sets the stage for the resolution of all proceedings, the order is interlocutory. *See, e.g., Fischer v. Williams*, 160 Tex. 342, 331 S.W.2d 210, 213-14 (1960) ("Since the order overruling respondents' motion to dismiss [in a probate proceeding] failed to finally dispose of the controverted issue [whether will contestants had shown an interest in the case], it, therefore, amounts to no more than an interlocutory order, inconclusive in its nature, made in the progress of the trial, and, therefore, not appealable."); *In re O'Bryant*, No. 04-04-00359-CV, 2004 WL 2616323, at *1, 2004 Tex. App. LEXIS 7147, at *2-*3 (Tex. App.—San Antonio Aug.11, 2004, no pet.) (dismissing appeal for lack of jurisdiction, as order denying plea to the jurisdiction in probate case was interlocutory); *Mobil Oil Corp. v. Shores*, 128 S.W.3d 718, 721 (Tex. App.—Fort Worth 2004, no pet.) (court of appeals lacked jurisdiction to review probate court's denial of plea to the jurisdiction).

The court of appeals did not reach Ayala's other alleged basis for appellate jurisdiction: that the trial court's failure to remove Ms. Brittingham as executor was immediately appealable as an order that "overrules a motion to vacate an order that appoints a receiver or trustee." TEX. CIV. PRAC. & REM. CODE § 51.014(a)(2). Accordingly, we must decide whether the Legislature intended by that language to give appellate courts jurisdiction over all orders refusing to remove estate executors. To support her contention, Ayala relies on our statement in *Bailey v. Cherokee County Appraisal District*, that "the administrator is designated the trustee of the estate property." *Bailey*, 862 S.W.2d 581, 584 (Tex. 1993).

The Legislature enacted the statute permitting interlocutory appeal of orders overruling motions to vacate orders appointing receivers or trustees in 1917, and the provision remains substantially unchanged today. *See* Act of March 30, 1917, 35th Leg., R.S., ch. 168, § 1, 1917 TEX. GEN. LAWS 379, 379 (now codified at TEX. CIV. PRAC. & REM. CODE § 51.014(a)(2)). At no time during the statute's almost ninety-year history have we held that it applies to a motion to remove an estate's executor. Our statement in *Bailey*—that an administrator is designated trustee of estate property—referred to the administrator's obligation, as holder of legal title to the estate's property, to pay ad valorem taxes accruing during administration. *Bailey*, 862 S.W.2d at 583, 586. It did not equate an executor to a trustee for all purposes, and there is no evidence that the Legislature intended to permit immediate appeals of orders refusing to remove estate executors. Accordingly, we conclude that section 51.014(a)(2) does not permit Ayala to pursue an interlocutory appeal of the trial court's order.[2]

IV
Conclusion

Because the court of appeals was without jurisdiction, we reverse the court of appeals' judgment and dismiss the appeal. TEX. R. APP. P. 60.2(c).

JUSTICE O'NEILL and JUSTICE GREEN did not participate in the decision.

Notes

1. Section 51.014 TEX. CIV. PRAC. & REM. CODE grants jurisdiction to the courts of appeal to review the enumerated interlocutory orders. As stated in *Del Valle Indep. Sch. Dist. v. Lopez,* the Supreme Court of Texas has jurisdiction to determine whether the court of appeals had jurisdiction over the appeal.

2. Section 22.001 of the Texas Government Code provides:

(a) The supreme court has appellate jurisdiction, except in criminal law matters, of an appealable order or judgment of the trial courts if the court determines that the appeal presents a question of law that is important to the jurisprudence of the state. The supreme court's jurisdiction does not include cases in which the jurisdiction of the court of appeals is made final by statute.

(b) A case over which the court has jurisdiction under Subsection (a) may be carried to the supreme court by petition for review.

(c) Except as provided by this subsection or other law, an appeal may be taken to the supreme court only if the appeal was first brought to the court of appeals. An appeal may be taken directly to the supreme court from an order of a trial court granting or denying an interlocutory or permanent injunction on the ground of the constitutionality of a statute of this state.

(d) The supreme court has the power, on affidavit or otherwise, as the court may determine, to ascertain the matters of fact that are necessary to the proper exercise of its jurisdiction.

(e) Repealed by Acts 2017, 85th Leg., ch. 150 (H.B. 1761), § 4(1).

3. *Coastal Corp. v. Garza,* 979 S.W.2d 318 (Tex. 1998). For the Supreme Court to have jurisdiction on the ground of conflict, it must appear that the rulings in the two cases are so far upon the same state of facts that the decision of one case is necessarily conclusive of the decision in the other. The conflict must be on the very question of law actually involved, and determined, in respect of an issue in both cases. The test is whether one would operate to overrule the other, in case they were both rendered by the same court.

4. *Butnaru v. Ford Motor Company*, 44 Tex. Sup. Ct. J. 808 (2001 WL 618149)(Tex. 2001). A temporary injunction's purpose is to preserve the status quo of the litigation's subject matter pending a trial on the merits. *Walling v. Metcalfe*, 863 S.W.2d 56, 57 (Tex. 1993); *Electronic Data Sys. Corp. v. Powell*, 508 S.W.2d 137, 139 (Tex. Civ. App.—Dallas 1974, no writ). A temporary injunction is an extraordinary remedy and does not issue as a matter of right. *Walling*, 863 S.W.2d at 57. To obtain a temporary injunction, the applicant must plead and prove three specific elements: (1) a cause of action against the defendant; (2) a probable right to the relief sought; and (3) a probable, imminent, and irreparable injury in the interim. *Walling*, 863 S.W.2d at 57; *Sun Oil*

---

[2] We note that, since *Crowson*, the Legislature has given litigants seeking immediate appellate review another option. If the parties and the trial court agree, the parties may seek a permissive interlocutory appeal under certain circumstances. *See* TEX. CIV. PRAC. & REM. CODE § 51.014(d) (authorizing trial courts to order an interlocutory appeal if (1) the parties agree that the order involves a controlling question of law as to which there is a substantial ground for difference of opinion; (2) an immediate appeal from the order may materially advance the ultimate termination of the litigation; and (3) the parties agree to the order); *Liberty Mut. Ins. Co. v. Griesing*, 150 S.W.3d 640, 643 n.3 (Tex. App.—Austin 2004, pet. filed). That avenue is unavailable to the parties in this case, however, as this suit was filed August 3, 2000, and the statute applies only to suits filed on or after the statute's September 1, 2001 effective date. *See* Act of May 17, 2001, 77th Leg., R.S., ch. 1389, § 3, 2001 TEX. GEN. LAWS 3575, 3575.

Co. v. Whitaker, 424 S.W.2d 216, 218 (Tex. 1968); *Fasken v. Darby*, 901 S.W.2d 591, 592 (Tex. App.—El Paso 1995, no writ); *Henderson v. KRTS, Inc.*, 822 S.W.2d 769, 773 (Tex. App.—Houston [1st Dist.] 1992, no writ). An injury is irreparable if the injured party cannot be adequately compensated in damages or if the damages cannot be measured by any certain pecuniary standard. *Canteen Corp. v. Republic of Tex. Props., Inc.*, 773 S.W.2d 398, 401 (Tex. App.—Dallas 1989, no writ); *Minexa Ariz., Inc. v. Staubach*, 667 S.W.2d 563, 567 (Tex. App.—Dallas 1984, no writ).

Whether to grant or deny a temporary injunction is within the trial court's sound discretion. *Walling*, 863 S.W.2d at 58; *State v. Walker*, 679 S.W.2d 484, 485 (Tex. 1984). A reviewing court should reverse an order granting injunctive relief only if the trial court abused that discretion. *Walling*, 863 S.W.2d at 58. The appellate court must not substitute its judgment for that of the trial court and determine that the trial court abused its discretion by granting injunctive relief unless the trial court's action was so arbitrary that it exceeded the bounds of reasonable discretion. *Davis v. Huey*, 571 S.W.2d 859, 861-62 (Tex. 1978); *Rugen v. Interactive Bus. Sys., Inc.*, 864 S.W.2d 548, 551 (Tex. App.—Dallas 1993, no writ). Moreover, the appellate court should draw all legitimate inferences from the evidence in a manner most favorable to the trial court's judgment. *Rugen*, 864 S.W.2d at 551.

3. *Refinement of the Concept of Finality*

NORTH EAST INDEPENDENT SCHOOL DISTRICT
v.
ALDRIDGE
400 S.W.2d 893
(Tex. 1966)

Foster, Lewis, Langley, Gardner & Hawn, Willis T. Taylor, San Antonio, with above firm, for petitioner.
Frank Y. Hill, Jr., San Antonio, for respondent.

CALVERT, CHIEF JUSTICE.

Guy Aldridge appealed from a trial court judgment awarding a recovery from him by North East Independent School District of damages in the sum of $30,000.00. The Court of Civil Appeals dismissed the appeal upon a holding that the trial court's judgment was not a final judgment. 392 S.W.2d 607. We reverse the judgment of the Court of Civil Appeals and order the appeal reinstated.

School District's suit was based upon an alleged breach of a written contract between it and Aldridge. By the terms of the contract Aldridge agreed to sell and School District agreed to buy a tract of 20.963 acres of land at a price of $3,500.00 per acre, and Aldridge obligated himself to construct a sewer line along a section of the southern boundary and streets along the northern and western boundaries of the tract. The petition alleged that School District had fully performed its obligations, but that Aldridge had failed to construct the sewer line and the streets. Aldridge's amended answer included a plea in abatement, a general denial, a plea that the contract was in reality made by School District with King-O-Hills Development Company for which he acted only as agent in executing the contract, and, with permission of the court, a cross-action against King-O-Hills Development Company to recover any sum which he might be adjudged liable to pay to School District. At a later date he filed a supplemental answer in which he pleaded that School District was estopped to assert its claim against him. King-O-Hills was duly cited and filed its answer to the cross-action. The record indicates that on June 5, 1964, the case was set for trial on the jury calender for the month of October, 1964.

School District moved for summary judgment on its claim against Aldridge for the damages sued for, or, alternatively, on the issue of Aldridge's personal liability for damages for breach of the contract. Aldridge filed an answer to the motion in which he asserted that there was an issue of fact concerning his personal liability inasmuch as School District knew that in executing the contract he was acting only as agent for King-O-Hills Company, and also an issue of fact concerning the amount of the damages. On July 8, 1964, the trial court granted School District's motion on its alternative prayer and rendered judgment that Aldridge was personally liable for damages for breach of the contract. The judgment also directed that 'this cause proceed to trial upon the sole remaining issue of the amount of damages to which the plaintiff is entitled.'

On October 5, 1964, the attorneys for School District and the attorney for Aldridge entered into a written stipulation that the damages suffered by School District as a result of the failure to construct the sewer line and streets amounted to $30,000.00. Thereupon, the court rendered judgment that North East School District recover of and from Guy Aldridge the sum of $30,000.00 with interest and costs. The judgment was approved as to form by the attorneys for both parties. There is no mention in the judgment of the third-party defendant, King-O,-Hills Company, and no disposition is made therein of the crossaction by Aldridge against such defendant. It was because of the failure of the judgment to dispose of the cross-action that the Court of Civil Appeals held that it was not a final judgment. It is that holding which we are called upon to review.

The finality of judgments for appealability has been a recurring and nagging problem throughout the judicial history of this State. We have steadfastly adhered through the years to the rule, with certain exceptions not applicable here, that an appeal may be prosecuted only from a final judgment and that to be final a judgment must dispose of all issues and parties in a case. *Gulf C. & S. F. Ry. Co. v. Fort Worth & N. O. Ry. Co.*, 68 Tex. 98, 2 S.W. 199, 3 S.W. 564 (1886); *Davis v. McCray Refrigerator Sales Corp.*, 136 Tex. 296, 150 S.W.2d 377 (1941). The rule is deceiving in its apparent simplicity and vexing in its application. In *Linn v. Arambould*, 55 Tex. 611 (1881), this Court reviewed many of the earlier decisions and announced rules for determining finality which no doubt were thought adequate to settle all future questions in the area. If so, the thought died aborning. In one of the rules announced, the Court said that to be final 'the judgment must in substance show intrinsically, and not inferentially, that the matter in the record had been determined in favor of one of the litigants, or the rights of the parties in litigation had been adjudicated.' 55 Tex. 619. That rule has long since passed into limbo. It was too simple. By its application most judgments easily became black or white-final or interlocutory; but all too often judgments which were obviously intended to be final were being held interlocutory because of careless draftsmanship. The rule had to be changed to accommodate oversight or carelessness.

In 1896 this Court decided *Rackley v. Fowlkes*, 89 Tex. 613, 36 S.W.77. No question of finality of a judgment was involved; only a question of res judicata. In a prior suit the plaintiff sought to recover title to land and rents from the land. The trial court's judgment awarded recovery of title to the land but did not mention the issue of rents. The plaintiff then filed a second suit for rents. This Court held that the defendant's plea of res judicata should have been sustained in the absence of a showing by the plaintiff that in his first suit he withdrew his court for rents or the court refused to decide it. The holding was bottomed upon a rule stated by the Court, as follows (36 S.W.78):

> 'The proposition seems to be sound in principle and well supported by authority that where the pleadings and judgment in evidence show that the pleadings upon which the trial was had put in issue plaintiff's right to recover upon two causes of action, and the judgment awards him a recovery upon one, but is silent as to the other, such judgment is prima facie an adjudication that he was not entitled to recover upon such other cause.'

The Court arrived at the rule by indulging 'the presumption that the (trial) court performed the duty devolved upon it upon the submission of the cause by disposing of every issue presented by the pleadings so as to render its judgment final and conclusive of the litigation * * *.' Taking no notice of the rule announced in *Linn v. Arambould*, or of the distinction between rules governing finality of judgments and those relating to res judicata, the Court in *Davies v. Thomson*, 92 Tex. 391, 49 S.W. 215 (1899), applied the rule quoted from *Rackley v. Fowlkes* in holding that a judgment which awarded plaintiffs relief they sought in one particular would 'be construed' to deny relief they sought in another particular. *Davies v. Thomson* has been followed by our latest decisions on the subject. *See Gamble v. Banneyer*, 137 Tex. 7, 151 S.W.2d 586 (1941); *Vance v. Wilson*, Tex.Sup., 382 S.W.2d 107 (1964).

The decision in *Davies v. Thomson* obviously did not necessarily settle the issue of finality of a judgment which granted relief to a plaintiff but failed to dispose expressly of a cross-action or counterclaim by the defendant against the plaintiff. The Courts of Civil Appeals were badly divided in their rulings on the finality of judgments of that character. The issue was settled by this Court in favor of finality in *Trammell v. Rosen*, 106 Tex. 132, 157 S.W. 1161 (1913). The Court dealt a final blow in that case to the rule announced in *Linn v. Arambould* by indicating, in effect, that it was a dictum. For the first time the Court spoke of the disposition of issues by implication and by necessary implication; but it did so only in referring to holdings of various Courts of Civil Appeals. It should be noted that the Court did not hold that the defendants' cross-action in *Trammell v. Rosen* was disposed of by necessary implication, or even by implication. Instead, the Court stated that the 'principle' which controlled *Rackley v. Fowlkes* and *Davies v. Thomson* was 'applicable in great measure to this case.' 157 S.W. 1163. That 'principle' was, of course, that a presumption would be indulged that the court's judgment disposed 'of every issue presented by the pleadings so as to render its judgment final and conclusive of the litigation;' and, in the absence of a showing that a claim for relief had been withdrawn or that the court refused to decide it, that the judgment would be 'construed' to deny all relief not expressly granted. The Court need not have gone quite so far in *Trammell v. Rosen.* Instead of holding that the judgment would be construed as denying all relief sought in the pleadings and not expressly granted, the Court needed to hold only that the judgment would be construed as disposing of all issues made by the pleadings in the case. Whether the judgment was construed as denying all relief not expressly granted or as dismissing all claims for relief not expressly granted was immaterial to the holding of finality. The distinction becomes important when the subsequent opinion of the *Commission of Appeals in Burton Lingo Co. v. First Baptist Church of Abilene*, Tex.Com.App., 222 S.W.203 (1920), is considered.

In *Burton Lingo Co. v. First Baptist Church of Abilene*, Burton Lingo Co. sued a number of defendants, including a contractor and the sureties on his bond, on an account for materials furnished the contractor. A joint answer was filed on behalf of the contractor and the sureties. Bankruptcy was pleaded as a defense on behalf of the contractor, and the sureties pleaded their suretyship, and by cross-action sought a recovery over against the contractor. At the conclusion of the evidence the trial court instructed a verdict against the plaintiff on its claim against the contractor, and in favor of the plaintiff against the sureties. No instruction was given with respect to the sureties' cross-action. The trial court's judgment decreed that the plaintiff recover the amount of its account from the sureties, but it neither disposed of nor mentioned the sureties' cross-action against the contractor. The sureties appealed. The Court of Civil Appeals held that the judgment was not a final judgment and dismissed the appeal. 198 S.W. 1013. The Commission of Appeals called attention to the fact that a joint answer had been filed on behalf of the contractor and the sureties and observed that the record did not show that the sureties had objected to the failure of the trial court to instruct a verdict in their favor on their cross-action, or that they had complained of the failure of the trial court to award them a recovery on their cross-action at the time the judgment was rendered, in their motion for new trial, or in their appeal to the Court of Civil Appeals. Under these circumstances, said the court, 'It is not unreasonable to presume in favor of the finality of the judgment that the sureties elected to waive and abandon their cross-action, or that a dismissal or discontinuance was had with reference thereto.' 222 S.W.204. Here, as in *Trammell v. Rosen*, the Court was presuming that the trial court made disposition of the cross-action in a particular manner, when all that was necessary to a holding of finality was a presumption that the claim had been disposed of, as in *Rackley v. Fowlkes* and *Davies v. Thomson*.

Notice should be taken of the holding in *Davis v. McCray Refrigerator Sales Corp.*, 136 Tex. 296, 150 S.W.2d 377 (1941). In that case the defendant filed a plea in abatement and a cross-action against the plaintiff. The trial court entered a judgment sustaining the plea in abatement and dismissing the suit. No disposition was made of the cross-action. The plaintiff appealed. This Court held that the judgment dismissing the plaintiff's suit did not by necessary implication dispose of the defendant's cross-action against the plaintiff and was not final. The rationale of the decision is found in the Court's statement that had the trial court intended to retain the cross-action for further consideration, it would have entered the very judgment which it did enter. The effect of the holding is to engraft an exception upon the general rule formulated by the decisions preceding *Davis*. The exception may be stated thusly: It will not be presumed that a judgment dismissing a plaintiff's suit on nonsuit, plea to the jurisdiction, plea in abatement, for want of prosecution, etc., also disposed of the issues in an independent cross-action.

There are a great number of decisions by Courts of Civil Appeals and by the Commissions of Appeals dealing with finality of judgments in various fact situations. It would serve no good purpose to review them here. Analysis of the decisions we have discussed is sufficient to lead us to the statement of a rule for determining, in most instances, whether judgments in which parties and issues made by the pleadings are, not disposed of in express language are, nevertheless, final for appeal purposes. When a judgment, not intrinsically interlocutory in character, is rendered and entered in a case regularly set for a conventional trial on the merits, no order for a separate trial of issues having been entered pursuant to Rule 174, Texas Rules of Civil Procedure, it will be presumed for appeal purposes that the Court intended to, and did, dispose of all parties legally before it and of all issues made by the pleadings between such parties. A claim duly severed under Rule 41 is a 'case' within the meaning of the foregoing rule. The rule will be subject to the exception created by *Davis v. McCray Refrigerator Sales Corporation*; but it will apply to separate claims of the plaintiff, cross-actions and counterclaims by defendants against the plaintiff, cross-actions by defendants against other defendants and cross-actions by defendants against third-party defendants. Of course, the problem can be eliminated entirely by a careful drafting of judgments to conform to the pleadings or by inclusion in judgments of a simple statement that all relief not expressly granted is denied.

* * *

The proper judgment to be rendered by this Court is one reversing the judgment of the Court of Civil Appeals and ordering the cause reinstated on the docket of that court for consideration of the appeal on its merits. *See Bay v. Mecom*, Tex.Sup., 393 S.W.2d 819 (1965); *Trammell v. Rosen*, 106 Tex. 132, 157 S.W. 1161 (1913). It is so ordered.

Notes

1. *Farm Bureau County Mutual Insurance Co. v. Rogers,* 455 S.W.3d 161 (Tex. 2015): ". . . a Mother Hubbard clause—by which we mean the statement, 'all relief not granted is denied', or essentially those word . . ."

2. *M. O. Dental Lab v. Rape*, 139 S.W.3d 671 (Tex. 2004): The trial court entered summary judgment, as to all named parties, but did not dispose of Smith, a named defendant, who had never been served with citation, and who had never appeared. *Held*: The trial court's order, granting summary judgment, was final for purposes of this appeal, because Smith was never served, and the record contains no pleadings or motions filed by Smith. In these circumstances, the case stands as if there had been discontinuance, as to the unserved party, and the judgment is to be regarded as final, for the purposes of appeal.

3. *Vaughn v. Drennon*, 324 S.W.3d 560 (Tex. 2010): The trial court's judgment issued after a conventional trial on the merits was final for purpose of appeal. The Drennon's grandchildren were joined as parties due to their shared interest in the subject property, but no claims against the grandchildren were addressed at trial nor were any jury questions submitted on the grandchildren. The grandchildren were not mentioned in the trial court's judgment, and this raised finality concerns in the court of appeals. Under the Aldridge presumption, any judgment following a conventional trial on the merits creates a presumption that the judgment is final for purpose of appeal. A judgment following a conventional trial on the merits need not dispose of every party and claim for the Aldridge presumption of finality to apply.

4. *In re Vaishangi, Inc.*, 442 S.W.3d 256 (Tex. 2014): Writ of mandamus will issue to set aside the trial court's order enforcing a Rule 11 agreement. The trial court did not have jurisdiction to enforce a Rule 11 agreement when the defendant filed a motion to enforce almost one year after the case had been dismissed. The Rule 11 agreement was not an agreed judgment. Because the trial court's plenary power expired thirty days after the dismissal order, the court lacked power to enforce the agreement.

Read Rule 329b(a)-(g) of the Texas Rules of Civil Procedure and refer to the following diagram.

RULE 329b-TRIAL COURT'S PLENARY POWER

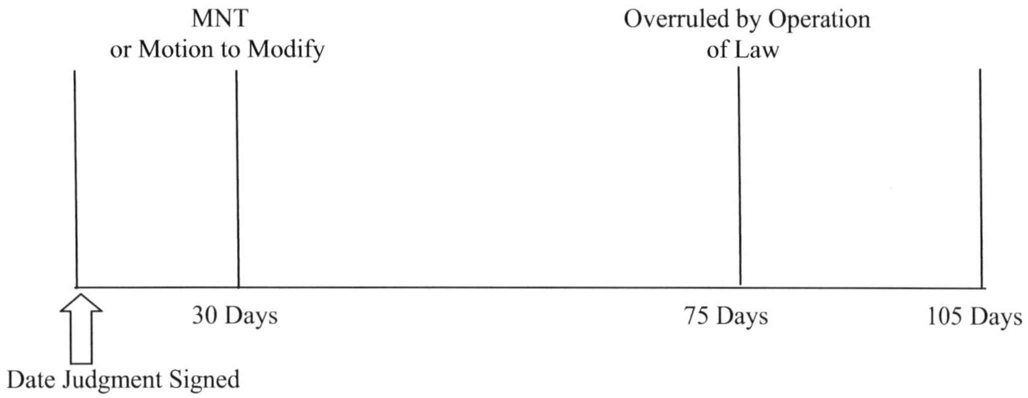

Read Rule 306a and refer to the following diagram.

RULE 306a(4)

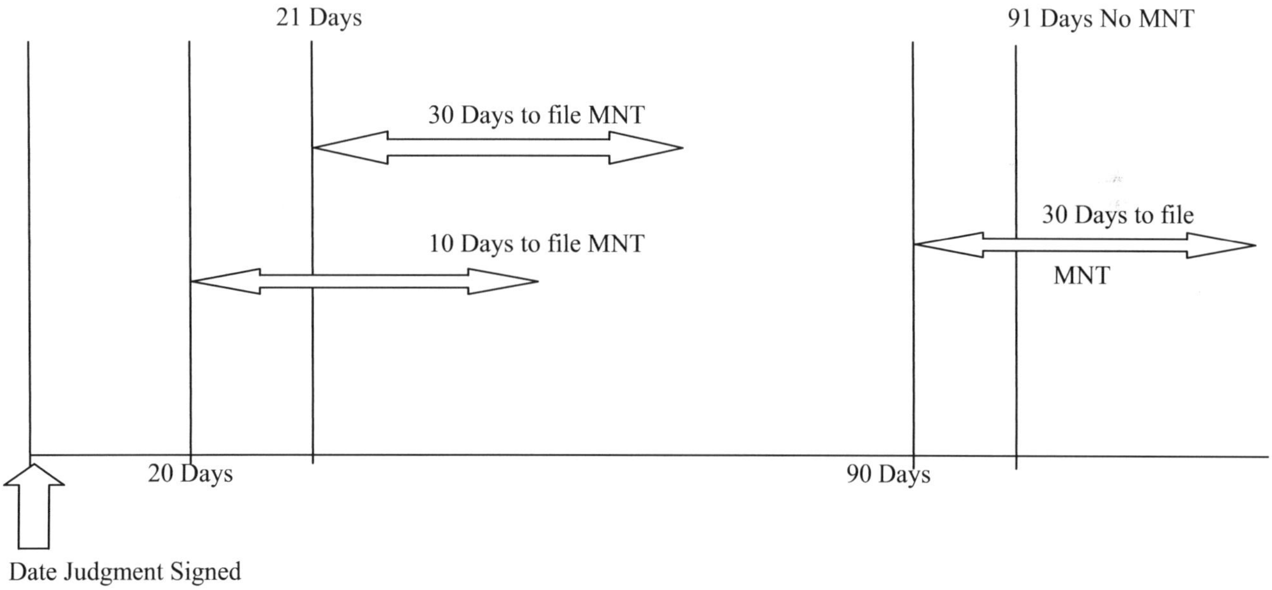

JOHN
v.
MARSHALL HEALTH SERVICES, INC.
58 S.W.3d 738
(Tex. 2001)

Derek Shane Hollingsworth, Harris County Dist. Atty. Office, Houston, Weston C. Loegering, Davis LeClair Loegering & Daniel, David J. Schenck, Gregory M. Bair, Hughes & Luce, Dallas, Kenneth L. Ross, Ross Hudgens & Associates, Longview, for Petitioner.

Otis W. Carroll, Deborah J. Race, Ireland Carroll & Kelley, Tyler, for Respondents.

PER CURIAM.

There are two questions here. First: is a judgment rendered after the close of trial final and appealable if it does not expressly dispose of the plaintiff's claims against defendants with whom the plaintiff was negotiating settlement? Second: must a motion to extend post-judgment deadlines under Rule 306a(5) of the Texas Rules of Civil Procedure be filed within thirty days of the date the movant learned that judgment had been signed? The court of appeals answered both in the affirmative and dismissed the appeal for want of jurisdiction. We agree that the trial court's judgment was final and appealable, but not that the appeal was untimely perfected. Accordingly, we reverse the judgment of the court of appeals and remand the case to that court for consideration of the merits.

Plaintiff Christopher Leigh John sued six defendants: Trinity Mother Frances Health System, Tom Cammack, and Trincare Inc. ("the Trinity defendants"); Harrison County Hospital Association, Inc. and Marshall Health Services ("the Marshall defendants"); and Dianna Taylor. John alleged fraud, breach of contract, and tortious interference. The trial court granted partial summary judgment for the Marshall defendants on John's breach-of-contract claims. Shortly before trial, John reached a preliminary settlement with the three Trinity defendants, but no final agreement was made and the Trinity defendants were not dismissed from the case. The other three defendants moved for a continuance because of uncertainty about the effect of the settlement on the trial. The trial court denied the motion, and the case proceeded to trial on John's claims against Taylor and the Marshall defendants. John nonsuited Taylor during the trial, and only his claims against the Marshall defendants were submitted to the jury. After the jury failed to reach a verdict, the trial court at first declared a mistrial, then withdrew that ruling and granted the Marshall defendants' earlier motion for a directed verdict. The Marshall defendants drafted and submitted a judgment, which the trial court signed on September 8. Entitled "Final Judgment", it recited the nonsuit of Taylor and ordered that John take nothing against the Marshall defendants. The judgment awarded costs against John and contained a "Mother Hubbard" clause, that "[a]ll other relief not expressly granted in this judgment is denied." The judgment did not mention the three settling Trinity defendants, and the record does not reflect whether their settlement was finalized.

The judgment was not filed by the clerk until September 13. John did not receive the defendants' proposed draft until several days later, and never received written notice from the clerk that a final judgment had been signed.[3] John first learned of the judgment in a telephone conversation with the clerk on September 30. The clerk stated that the judgment had been signed September 13. John filed a motion for new trial on October 13, more than thirty days after the judgment was signed when such motions must ordinarily be filed. Post-judgment deadlines may be extended under Rule 306a, but John did not file the requisite motion under Rule 306a(5) until December 10. After a hearing, the trial court agreed that John first learned of the judgment on September 30, but that the Rule 306a(5) motion was filed too late, and therefore the time for filing a motion for new trial was not extended. On December 13, John filed a notice of appeal which was timely only if post-judgment deadlines ran from September 30 instead of September 8.

On appeal, John argued that the judgment was not final because it did not dispose of the claims against the Trinity defendants. The court of appeals held that because the judgment followed a conventional trial on the merits and contained a "Mother Hubbard" clause, it was presumed final, citing this Court's opinions in *North*

[3] Rule 306a(3) provides in part: "When the final judgment or other appealable order is signed, the clerk of the court shall immediately give notice to the parties or their attorneys of record by first-class mail advising that the judgment or order was signed."

East Independent School District v. Aldridge and *Mafrige v. Ross*. The court of appeals further held that John's Rule 306a(5) motion should have been filed within thirty days of the date he first learned of the judgment and because it was not, neither the motion for new trial nor the notice of appeal were timely filed. Accordingly, the court of appeals dismissed John's appeal for want of jurisdiction.

We first consider whether the judgment was final. Recently in *Lehmann v. Har-Con Corp.*, we observed that "[t]he presumption that a judgment rendered after a conventional trial on the merits is final and appealable has proved fairly workable for nearly a century . . . ." John here argues that this presumption should not be rigidly applied to make judgments final contrary to litigants' reasonable expectations. We do not disagree with this argument in general, especially given today's frequency of separate trials of parties and claims in a single case, and bifurcated trials required in certain instances. However, we believe the presumption is entirely appropriate in a case like this. John did not move for separate trials; he went to trial against the only defendants against whom he still wished to prosecute his claims. The trial court and all of the parties were aware of the pending settlement, and there is nothing to indicate that the trial court did not intend the judgment to finally dispose of the entire case. John did not move for dismissal of his claims against the Trinity defendants or for an agreed judgment. Whether the judgment was final should not depend on one party's testimony that he did or did not finalize a settlement with parties from whom he sought no relief at trial. The *Aldridge* presumption fits just such circumstances.

We next consider the Rule 306a issue. Rule 306a(1) provides that the periods within which parties may file various post-judgment motions and trial courts may exercise their plenary jurisdiction all run from the date the judgment is signed. Rule 306a(3) requires clerks to notify parties or their attorneys immediately when a judgment is signed. Rule 306a(4) provides the following exception to Rule 306a(1):

> If within twenty days after the judgment or other appealable order is signed, a party adversely affected by it or his attorney has neither received the notice required by paragraph (3) of this rule nor acquired actual knowledge of the order, then with respect to that party all the periods mentioned in paragraph (1) shall begin on the date that such party or his attorney received such notice or acquired actual knowledge of the signing, whichever occurred first, but in no event shall such periods begin more than ninety days after the original judgment or other appealable order was signed.

Rule 306a(5) prescribes the procedure for claiming this exception:

> In order to establish the application of paragraph (4) of this rule, the party adversely affected is required to prove in the trial court, on sworn motion and notice, the date on which the party or his attorney first either received a notice of the judgment or acquired actual knowledge of the signing and that this date was more than twenty days after the judgment was signed.

The rules do not set a deadline for filing a motion under Rule 306a(5).

Nevertheless, the court of appeals in this case held that such a motion must be filed within thirty days of the date a party or his attorney first either receives the clerk's notice of a judgment or acquires actual knowledge that the judgment was signed. Three other courts have reached the same conclusion, but two courts have concluded that Rule 306a(5) does not prohibit a motion from being filed at any time within the trial court's plenary jurisdiction measured from the date determined under Rule 306a(4). The latter courts are plainly correct: Rule 306a simply imposes no deadline, and none can be added by decision, other than the deadline of the expiration of the trial court's jurisdiction. We disapprove the cases that have reached a contrary result.

Because the trial court here found that John did not have notice of the judgment until September 30, more than twenty days after it was signed, time periods based on the signing of the judgment ran instead from that date. Thus, under Rule 329b(a) the plaintiff had thirty days to file a motion for new trial, and he did so. Because the trial court did not rule on the motion, it was overruled by operation of law on the seventy-fifth day after September 30, which was December 14. The trial court's plenary jurisdiction did not expire until thirty days later, on January 13, 2000. The plaintiff's notice of appeal was due ninety days from September 30, which was December 29, and was therefore timely when filed on December 13.

We thus conclude that the court of appeals erred by dismissing the appeal for want of jurisdiction. Accordingly, the Court grants John's petition for review, and without hearing oral argument, reverses the judgment of the court of appeals and remands the case to that court for consideration of the parties' other arguments.

Note

Edwards Aquifer Authority v. Chemical Lime, Ltd., 291 S.W.3d 392 (Tex. 2009): A deadline is not something one can substantially comply with. A miss is as good as a mile. The notion that a filing deadline can be complied with by filing sometime after the deadline falls due is, to say the least, a surprising notion, and it is a notion without limiting principle. If 1-day late filings are acceptable, 10-day late filings might be equally acceptable, and so on in a cascade of exceptions that would engulf the rule erected by the filing deadline; yet regardless of where the cutoff line is set, some individuals will always fall just on the other side of it. Filing deadlines, like statutes of limitations, necessarily operate harshly and arbitrarily with respect to individuals who fall just on the other side of them, but if the concept of a filing deadline is to have any content, the deadline must be enforced. Any less rigid standard would risk encouraging a lax attitude toward filing dates. A filing deadline cannot be complied with, substantially or otherwise, by filing late—even by one day.

4. *The Trial Court's Plenary Power*

a. *The Motion for New Trial*

Read Rule 329b(a)-(f) Texas Rules of Civil Procedure.

DEEN
v.
KIRK

508 S.W.2d 70
(Tex. 1974)

C. Coit Mock and W. J. Fleniken, Jr., Fort Worth, for relator.
Clyde Fillmore, Wichita Falls, for respondents.

WALKER, JUSTICE.

This is an original mandamus proceeding. It was instituted by Betty L. Deen, relator, against F. Edgar Deen, Jr., and the Honorable Stanley C. Kirk, Judge of the 78th Judicial District of Wichita County, to require the latter to expunge an order purporting to set aside a divorce judgment previously rendered by him. We agree with relator that the judgment in question had become final and that Judge Kirk had no power to set it aside as he attempted to do. In accordance with our usual procedure in cases of this nature, the writ of mandamus will be granted conditionally.

On June 22, 1973, F. Edgar Deen, Jr., hereinafter referred to as respondent, instituted suit for divorce against relator in Cause No. 94,536-B in the 78th District Court of Wichita County. At the same time he filed a waiver of citation previously executed by relator. The jurat on the waiver is dated June 21, 1973. On August 22, 1973, without further notice, citation or waiver, Judge Kirk rendered judgment granting respondent a divorce and approving an undescribed property settlement agreement. Relator first learned of these proceedings on October 27, 1973.

On November 30, 1973, relator filed suit for divorce against respondent in the Domestic Relations Court No. 4 of Tarrant County. Temporary injunctions were issued in that suit, and both parties were ordered to file written inventories. Apparently no further action has been taken in that case, which is still pending in the trial court. It has no bearing on our disposition of this mandamus proceeding.

On December 3, 1973, relator filed in Cause No. 95,544-B in the 78th District Court of Wichita County a petition in the nature of a bill of review, praying that the judgment in Cause No. 94,536-B be set aside. On December 13, 1973, Judge Kirk on his own motion entered an order in Cause No. 94,536-B setting aside the judgment previously rendered in that case. A few days later relator was served with citation in the original divorce case. Respondent then filed in Cause No. 95,544-B a motion to dismiss, alleging that since the judgment in Cause No. 94,536-B had been set aside, the bill of review proceeding was moot. On January 3, 1974, the motion was granted and the bill of review proceeding was dismissed. The original divorce case was also set for trial on the merits.

It is our understanding that relator appealed the judgment of dismissal in Cause No. 95,544-B to the Court of Civil Appeals. So far as we know, she did not attempt to carry the original divorce judgment in Cause No. 94,536-B to the Court of Civil Appeals by writ of error. In the present proceeding she seeks a writ of mandamus to require Judge Kirk to set aside the order of December 13, 1973, whereby he attempted to give her the relief she sought by her petition for a bill of review.

Under the provisions of Rule 119, Texas Rules of Civil Procedure, a defendant may waive the issuance and service of citation by filing among the papers of the cause a verified written memorandum 'signed by him, or by his duly authorized agent or attorney, after suit is brought.' Article 2224, Vernon's Ann. Civ. St., prohibits the waiver of process by an instrument executed prior to institution of suit. It is clear then that the waiver executed by relator prior to institution of the divorce suit in Wichita County did not subject her to the jurisdiction of the court. *McAnelly v. Ward*, 72 Tex. 342, 12 S.W. 206.

Respondents say that since the lack of jurisdiction over relator was apparent from the record, the judgment rendered on August 22, 1973, was void and could properly be set aside by Judge Kirk at any time. * * *

The present case is governed by the following provisions of Rule 329b, T.R.C.P.: 5. Judgments shall become final after the expiration of thirty (30) days after the date of rendition of judgment or order overruling an original or amended motion for new trial. After the expiration of thirty (30) days from the date the judgment is rendered or motion for new trial overruled, the judgment cannot be set aside except by bill of review for sufficient cause, filed within the time allowed by law . . . .

The history of these provisions was reviewed in *McEwen v. Harrison*, 162 Tex. 125, 345 S.W.2d 706, ...

The opinion in *McEwen* recognizes that a bill of review might not be an appropriate method for attacking in the trial court, more than thirty days after the rendition of judgment or order overruling motion for new trial, a judgment in a case which the court was without jurisdictional power to hear and adjudicate. The words 'jurisdictional power' as used in that opinion mean jurisdiction over the subject matter, the power to hear and determine cases of the general class to which the particular one belongs. We were not speaking of jurisdiction over the parties. The examples given were the rendition by a county court of judgment for divorce or for title to land. In each instance the court would have been utterly without power to render an effective judgment on the merits of the controversy.

The quoted provisions of Rule 329b were construed in *McEwen* as follows: Accordingly, we construe the emphasized provision of Rule 329b—to mean that when the time for filing a motion for new trial has expired and relief may not be obtained by appeal, a proceeding in the nature of a bill of review is the exclusive method of vacating a default judgment rendered in a case in which the court had jurisdictional power to render it. Into this category will fall those cases in which a default judgment is asserted to be void for want of service, or of valid service, of process. This is in harmony with our holding in *Brown v. Clippenger*, 113 Tex. 364, 256 S.W. 254. With this construction of the Rule, we may assume, without deciding, that Texaco is correct when it says that the default judgment against it is a void judgment and that its motion to vacate is a direct attack on the judgment. We are yet compelled to hold that the order vacating the default judgment is unauthorized and void because the district court had jurisdictional power to determine the validity of service (Indeed, it was its duty to do so) and to render the judgment, and Texaco's motion to vacate it does not qualify as a bill of review. (Emphasis supplied)

Paraphrasing the italicized portion of the opinion just quoted, the 78th District Court of Wichita County had jurisdictional power to determine the validity and effectiveness of the waiver and to render a judgment for divorce. Relator's petition for a bill of review was never heard but was dismissed. In these circumstances and under the provisions of Rule 329b, the order of December 13, 1973, purporting to set aside the divorce judgment previously rendered in Cause No. 94,536-B is void and should itself be set aside. We are not to be understood as saying that a bill of review was the only effective remedy available to relator when she learned of the divorce judgment. *See* Art. 2255, V.A.C.S.; *Whitney v. L & L Realty Corp.*, Tex., 500 S.W.2d 94; *Flynt v. City of Kingsville*, 125 Tex. 510, 82 S.W.2d 934. It was, however, the only remedy then available to her in the trial court.

We assume that Judge Kirk will set aside his order of December 13, 1973, promptly after our judgment in this proceeding becomes final. In the event he fails to do so, a writ of mandamus will issue.

Note

In *Orion Enters., Inc. v. Pope,* 927 S.W.2d 654, 659 (Tex. App.—San Antonio 1996, orig. proceeding) the court stated:

> "A trial court has plenary power over, and therefore the jurisdiction and authority to reconsider, not only its judgment but also its interlocutory orders until thirty days after the date a final judgment is signed or, if a motion for new trial or its equivalent is filed, until thirty days after the motion is overruled by signed, written order or operation of law, whichever first occurs. *Fruehauf Corp. v. Carrillo,* 848 S.W.2d 83, 84 (Tex. 1993); *Bollard v. Berchelmann,* 921 S.W.2d 861, 863-64 (Tex. App.—San Antonio 1996, orig. proceeding); *see* TEX.R. CIV. P. 329(b). "Plenary power" is "that which is '[f]ull, entire, complete, absolute, perfect, unqualified.' " *Mesa Agro v. R.C. Dove & Sons,* 584 S.W.2d 506, 508 (Tex. Civ. App.—El Paso 1979, writ ref'd n.r.e.) (quoting BLACK'S LAW DICTIONARY 1313 (4th ed. rev. 1968))."

FRUEHAUF CORP.
v.
CARRILLO
848 S.W.2d 83
(Tex. 1993)

Facts: This is a negligence action arising out of an auto collision. A take-nothing judgment against the Ps was signed on 9/21/90. Ps filed motions for new trial, which the trial court granted on 12/4/90, the 74th day after the date of judgment. On 12/5/90, the 75th day after judgment, the trial court set aside its order granting the motions for new trial & overruled the motions.

Issue: Does a trial court have the power to vacate the grant of a motion for new trial during the period of the trial court's plenary power? Yes.

Held: A trial court has the authority to vacate an order for a new trial during the 75 day period. A trial court has plenary power over its judgment until it becomes final. The trial court also retains continuing control over interlocutory orders and has the power to set those orders aside any time before a final judgment is entered.

In re BAYLOR MEDICAL CENTER AT GARLAND
280 S.W.3d 227
(Tex. 2008)

R. Brent Cooper, Michelle E. Robberson, John A. Scully, Cooper & Scully, P.C., Derek S. Davis, Founders Square, Dallas TX, for Relator.

William M. Hayner Jr., William M. Hayner, William M. Hayner & Associates, Gil L. Daley II, Law Office of Gil L. Daley, II, P.C., Dallas TX, for Real Party in Interest.

JUSTICE BRISTER delivered the opinion of the Court, in which CHIEF JUSTICE JEFFERSON, JUSTICE HECHT, JUSTICE O'NEILL, JUSTICE WAINWRIGHT, JUSTICE GREEN, JUSTICE MEDINA and JUSTICE WILLETT joined.

Mandamus will not issue against a new judge for what a former one did. In this medical malpractice case, the jury found for the defendant hospital, but the trial judge granted a new trial, allegedly based on juror affidavits prohibited by the rules. As a new judge now presides over the trial court, Rule 7.2 requires abatement of this original proceeding to allow the successor to reconsider the order.

But another rule prevents a trial judge from "ungranting" (i.e., vacating) a new trial order more than 75 days after it is signed. As that deadline has passed, we can hardly ask the new judge to reconsider this order if he has no power to do so. The hospital urges us to reconsider this deadline, pointing out that it contradicts the general rules of plenary power and is unsupported by the current rules of civil and appellate procedure, stemming instead from a provision that has long since been repealed.

We agree. As with any other order, a trial court should be able to reconsider a new trial order as long as a case is still pending. Accordingly, we abate this proceeding for the current judge to reconsider the order.

I. Background

Tammy and Steve Williams brought a medical malpractice lawsuit against Baylor Medical Center at Garland. The case was tried to a jury, which found in Baylor's favor. On May 6, 2005, Judge Joe Cox signed a final take-nothing judgment, but 82 days later granted a new trial after further hearings. Baylor unsuccessfully sought mandamus relief in the court of appeals, and then sought [mandamus] relief in this Court.

In the meantime Judge Nancy Thomas succeeded Judge Cox, . . .

* * *

Two months later, Judge Thomas vacated the new trial order and reinstated judgment on the jury verdict. As required by our order, Baylor notified us of the development and moved to dismiss its petition as moot. But the same day we did so, the Williamses asked Judge Thomas to reconsider, which she did and once again reinstated Judge Cox's new trial order.

Baylor petitioned this Court for relief. While the case was pending, Judge Jim Jordan was elected to take Judge Thomas's place.

* * *

Nowhere but Texas can one find a single appellate opinion discussing when a court can "ungrant" a motion. Texas has more than 20, almost all dealing with our unique rule that an order granting a new trial cannot be "ungranted" more than 75 days after it is signed.

This ungrammatical rule stems from *Fulton v. Finch*, a 1961 opinion in which we held that an order granting a new trial could not be set aside after the deadline for ruling on new trial motions. That was because rule 329b at the time provided that all motions for new trial "must be determined" within 45 days:

> All motions and amended motions for new trial must be determined within not exceeding forty-five (45) days after the original or amended motion is filed, unless by written agreement of the parties in the case, the decision of the motion is postponed to a later date.

Because reinstating the original judgment was "tantamount to overruling [the] motion for new trial," we held the 45-day deadline imposed an absolute limit on when an order of new trial could be " un determined" and the original judgment reinstated

> Rule 329b was amended effective January 1, 1981 to eliminate this "must be determined" provision. Now, the rule terminates the trial court's plenary power 30 days after all timely motions for new trial are overruled, but there is no provision limiting its plenary power if such motions are granted. Under the current rules, if no judgment is signed, no plenary-power clock is ticking.

But some 33 years after *Fulton* this Court issued *Porter v. Vick*, a five-paragraph per curiam opinion that read *Fulton* to render void any attempt to vacate a new-trial order after plenary power would have expired had the original judgment not been set aside. But *Fulton* did not even mention plenary power; it turned on a rule, since repealed, requiring new trial orders to be decided within 45 days. The *Porter* opinion neither recognizes nor addresses the 1981 changes to rule 329b.

Instead, *Porter* imposed a deadline based on a purely hypothetical event: the expiration of plenary power assuming that a vacated judgment had instead become final. Plenary power of course expires only after final judgments, not vacated judgments. So *Porter's* deadline is highly unusual; it is hard to think of any other case in which a deadline runs from a vacated order.

Moreover, rather than enforcing the rules of plenary power, the deadline in *Porter v. Vick* is inconsistent with them. When a new trial is granted, the case stands on the trial court's docket "the same as though no trial had been had." Accordingly, the trial court should then have the power to set aside a new trial order "any time before a final judgment is entered."

It is possible (though not mentioned in the opinion) that *Porter v. Vick* sought to prevent a situation where reinstatement of a previous judgment would prevent a party from having time to file an appeal. As parties have 90 days to appeal when a motion for new trial is filed, retroactively reinstating an original judgment more than 90 days after it was signed arguably might prevent any appeal at all. But we recently clarified that "a trial judge who modifies a judgment and then withdraws the modification has modified the judgment twice rather than never." Rule 329b(h) provides that if a judgment is modified " in any respect " the appellate timetables are restarted. Surely a judgment that is set aside by a new trial order has been modified in some respect, even if it is later reinstated. Thus, if a new trial is granted and later withdrawn, the appellate deadlines run from the later order granting reinstatement rather than the earlier order.

It is true that if trial judges constantly reconsider prior orders, time and money can be wasted waiting for closure. But a rule preventing trial judges from ever reconsidering a prior order would be wasteful too. New trial orders are rare, and the long list of cases in footnote 8 shows that trial judges often think better of them. Perhaps a rule should be adopted placing a deadline on reinstating a judgment, even though no rule currently sets a deadline on signing a judgment in the first place. But a deadline that appears only in case law sets a trap for judges and litigants like the one they fell into here.

"A trial court's plenary jurisdiction gives it not only the authority but the responsibility to review any pretrial order upon proper motion." This principle is violated by the rule of *Porter v. Vick*, as succinctly noted by one Texas justice:

> [A]fter a motion for new trial has been granted, how can a trial court have ongoing plenary power to re-try the case, etc., but lack plenary power to vacate the decision to grant the motion for new trial?; (2) once a trial court determines that a motion for new trial has been improvidently granted and that a proper adjudication was, in fact, reached, why must the time and other resources of the parties and judicial system nevertheless be wasted to relitigate it?; and (3) why have such anomalies been allowed to persist?

Federal courts and commentators agree: "There is no sound reason why the court may not reconsider its ruling [granting] a new trial" at any time.

Accordingly, we overrule *Porter v. Vick*, and abate this case for Judge Jordan to reconsider whether to enter judgment on the jury verdict or to grant a new trial.

JUSTICE JOHNSON filed a dissenting opinion (opinion omitted).

FAULKNER
v.
CULVER

851 S.W.2d 187
(Tex. 1993)

David A. Livingston, Dion C. Raymos, Houston, for relator.
Valorie W. Davenport, Houston, for respondent.

PER CURIAM.

In this original proceeding, Relator Dale Faulkner, M.D. (Faulkner) seeks a writ of mandamus directing the trial judge to vacate an order entered November 8, 1990 vacating summary judgment for Faulkner. Pursuant to Rule 170 of the Texas Rules of Appellate Procedure, a majority of this court conditionally grants the application for writ of mandamus.

In February 1988, Betty and Dan Krock (Krock) sued Dale Faulkner, M.D. (Faulkner) for medical malpractice. On December 15, 1989, Judge Charles Dickerson granted a take-nothing summary judgment. On January 15, 1990, Krock filed a motion for rehearing of the summary judgment and, in the alternative, motion for new trial. Judge Dickerson orally vacated the summary judgment at a hearing on March 1, 1990 and made a entry on the docket sheet to this effect. While Krock's attorney apparently tried to ascertain whether Judge Dickerson signed a written order to this effect, both a clerk in the Fort Bend County District Clerk's office and Judge Dickerson's secretary indicated that the order vacating the summary judgment had been signed but the case file was in the Judge's chambers and could not be retrieved. Judge Dickerson did not vacate the summary judgment by written order until November 8, 1990.

In December 1990, Judge Dickerson resigned and was replaced by Thomas Culver. Faulkner moved to vacate Judge Dickerson's November 8, 1990, order vacating the summary judgment. On April 1, 1992, Judge Culver ruled that Judge Dickerson's order was effective and the case would proceed to trial.

Faulkner argues that Judge Dickerson did not have plenary power when he signed the November 8, 1990 order vacating the summary judgment. We agree.

If a party moves for a new trial or to modify, correct, or reform a judgment, the trial judge has plenary power for thirty days after the motion for new trial is overruled. TEX. R. CIV. P. 329b. A motion for new trial or motion to modify, correct, or reform the judgment is overruled by operation of law seventy-five days after the judgment was signed. TEX. R. CIV. P. 329b(c). An order granting a new trial or modifying, correcting, or reforming a judgment must be written and signed. TEX. R. CIV. P. 329b(c); *McCormack v. Guillot*, 597 S.W.2d 345, 346 (Tex. 1980). A trial judge's oral pronouncement granting a motion for new trial or motion to modify, reform, or correct a judgment and a docket entry indicating that such motion was granted cannot substitute for a written order required by Rule 329b. *Clark & Co. v. Giles*, 639 S.W.2d 449, 450 (Tex. 1982).

Judge Dickerson's oral pronouncement and docket entry vacating the summary judgment could not be substituted for a written order required by Rule 329b. *See Clark & Co. v. Giles*, 639 S.W.2d at 450. Since no written order was signed by Judge Dickerson within the required time, Krock's alternative motions were overruled by operation of law on February 28, 1990. The judgment became final 30 days later and the trial judge lost jurisdiction over the case. Therefore, the order of November 8, 1990, purporting to vacate the summary judgment is a nullity.

Pursuant to Rule 170 of the Texas Rules of Appellate Procedure, a majority of this court, without hearing oral argument, conditionally grants Faulkner's petition for writ of mandamus. The mandamus will only issue if the trial judge refuses to act in accordance with this opinion.

In re LOVITO-NELSON
278 S.W.3d 773
(Tex. 2009)

"We have been clear that Rule 329b(c) requires a written order to grant a new trial. In *Faulkner v. Culver,* 851 S.W.2d 187, 188 (Tex. 1993) (per curiam), we held that a trial court's "oral pronouncement and docket entry . . . could not be substituted for a written order required by Rule 329b." We added that under Rule 329b(c), "[a]n order granting a new trial or modifying, correcting, or reforming a judgment must be written and signed." We reached the same holding in *Clark & Co. v. Giles,* 639 S.W.2d 449, 450 (Tex. 1982) (per curiam). More recently, we "decline[d to] overrule our precedent (and ignore Texas Rule of Civil Procedure 329b) requiring written orders granting new trials." *Horizon/CMS Healthcare Corp., Inc. v. Fischer,* 111 S.W.3d 67, 68 (Tex. 2003) (per curiam). Although we have never had occasion to apply the rule to scheduling orders, the courts of appeals have, and have mostly held that such orders do not grant new trials." * * * "

"It is important that the requirement of a written order granting a motion for new trial be a bright-line rule. Otherwise, one might argue that all sorts of conduct should be given the same effect—a trial setting or other setting, a status conference, a hearing on a discovery motion, a request for discovery—the list is endless. The uncertainty would carry over to appellate deadlines and possibly give rise to mandamus proceedings, like this one. The requirement is not difficult to meet, and the movant who fails to satisfy it is not left without possibility of relief. He may still attempt to prosecute an appeal, a restricted appeal, or a bill of review. But a motion for new trial is not granted without a signed, written order explicitly granting the motion."

In re BROOKSHIRE GROCERY COMPANY

250 S.W.3d 66
(Tex. 2008)

This is an original mandamus action. A motion for new trial filed within thirty days of judgment, but after a prior motion for new trial has been overruled, is not "timely" for purposes of extending plenary power under TEX. R. CIV P. 329b(e). Leave of court has no effect on the timeliness of a motion for new trial filed after a preceding motion has been overruled. This holding does not preclude a party whose motion for new trial has been overruled from continuing to seek a new trial while the trial court is still empowered to act.

Pursuant to TEX. R. CIV. P. 329b(e), the trial court retains plenary power for thirty days after overruling a motion for new trial; thus, the losing party may ask the trial court to reconsider its order denying a new trial—or the court may grant a new trial on its own initiative—so long as the court issues an order granting new trial within its period of plenary power. Additionally, under Rule 329b, a trial court's plenary power to grant a new trial expires thirty days after it overrules a motion for new trial, only provided no other type of 329b motion (such as a motion to modify, correct, or reform the judgment) is "timely filed." Thus, a party whose motion for new trial is overruled within thirty days of judgment may still file a motion to modify, correct, or reform the judgment—provided it is filed within thirty days of judgment—and thereby extend the trial court's plenary power.

Mandamus relief is appropriate when a trial court issues an order after its plenary power has expired.

Notes

1. *Moritz v. Preiss,* 121 S.W.3d 715, 719 (Tex. 2003): An untimely amended motion for new trial does not preserve issues for appellate review.

2. In *Brighton v. Koss*, --- S.W.3d ----, 2013 WL 4493580 (Tex.), 56 Tex. Sup. Ct. J. 953 (August 23, 2013) the court stated that "[g]enerally, a postjudgment motion is subsumed by a subsequent judgment that grants all of the relief requested in the motion. *Wilkins v. Methodist Health Care Sys.,* 160 S.W.3d 559, 563-64 (Tex.2005). When subsumed by the subsequent judgment, the motion does not extend the appellate deadlines after the subsequent judgment. *Id.* at 562. But when a subsequent judgment does not grant all requested relief, the motion remains as a viable complaint about the subsequent judgment and extends the appellate deadlines after that judgment. *Id.*"

JAMAR
v.
PATTERSON

868 S.W.2d 318
(Tex. 1993)

Martin L. Peterson, Stephenville, for petitioner.
Russell Scott Briggs, Houston, for respondent.

PER CURIAM.

This case presents the issue of what constitutes "filing" a motion for new trial for purposes of calculating the appellate timetable. After a jury trial the trial judge signed a judgment for Gayle Patterson, individually and as next friend of Brandi Istre (Patterson), against Hewell Jamar. The judgment is dated October 16, 1992. On November 12, 1992, counsel for Jamar tendered his motion to the district clerk, who did not "accept" the motion for filing because Jamar had not paid the requisite $15.00 statutory filing fee. Despite its other deficiencies, the clerk file-stamped the motion on November 30, 1992, when the $15.00 filing fee was received.

Jamar then filed an appeal bond which was timely if his motion for new trial were timely filed to extend the appellate deadline, but untimely if he were limited to thirty days after judgment. *See* TEX. R. APP. P. 41(a). The court of appeals, in a two-paragraph unpublished opinion, stated that Jamar's motion was "filed" on November 30, 1992, when it was file-stamped, and dismissed his appeal. The court of appeals did not state either that the file-stamp was controlling or that payment of the filing fee was a requirement for filing, but presumably it impliedly made one or the other of those holdings.

In a long line of cases, this court has held that a document is "filed" when it is tendered to the clerk, or otherwise put under the custody or control of the clerk. *Mr. Penguin Tuxedo Rental & Sales, Inc. v. NCR Corp.*, 787 S.W.2d 371, 372 (Tex. 1990); *Biffle v. Morton Rubber Indus., Inc.*, 785 S.W.2d 143 (Tex. 1990); *Standard Fire Ins. Co. v. LaCoke*, 585 S.W.2d 678, 681 (Tex. 1979). We therefore assume the court of appeals did not mean the file stamp was controlling. That means the court held that payment of the filing fee controlled when the document was "filed" for appellate timetable purposes.

TEX. R. CIV. P. 329b(a) provides that "[a] motion for new trial, if filed, shall be filed prior to or within thirty days after the judgment or other order complained of is signed." The rule does not define "filed." It is our policy to construe rules reasonably but liberally, when possible, so that the right to appeal is not lost by creating a requirement not absolutely necessary from the literal words of the rule. *See McRoberts v. Ryals*, 863 S.W.2d 450, 455 (Tex. 1993); *Pool v. Ford Motor Co.*, 715 S.W.2d 629, 632-33 (Tex. 1986). Consistent with that rule and our prior holdings that the date of filing is when the document is first tendered to the clerk, we hold that Jamar's motion for new trial was conditionally filed on November 12, 1992, when he tendered it to the clerk. That date controls for appellate purposes. The filing was completed, as the trial court clerk implicitly recognized, when Jamar paid the filing fee.

Without hearing argument, a majority of the court grants the application for writ of error, holds that the date of original tender of the motion for new trial governs for appellate time calculation purposes, reverses the judgment of the court of appeals and remands the cause to that court for further proceedings consistent with this opinion. TEX. R. APP. P. 170.

GARZA
v.
GARCIA

137 S.W.3d 36
(Tex. 2004)

Garcia timely filed a motion for new trial, but never paid the fee. ***Held:*** A motion for new trial extends appellate timetables, even if the requisite filing fee is never paid. The Court construes the Rules of Appellate Procedure liberally, so that decisions turn on substance, rather than procedural technicality. Nothing in those rules requires a fee to accompany a motion for new trial, or that such a fee be paid at all. Moreover, once a motion for new trial is conditionally filed, and timetables extended, all litigants benefit from knowing what timetables apply, even if they do not know whether the requisite fee was paid. The alternative would breed uncertainty, as the deadlines might automatically jump forward when the fee is quietly paid, or revert backwards if it is not. This is not to say filing fees are irrelevant. Absent emergency or other rare circumstances, a motion for new trial should not be considered, until the filing fee is paid. Here, Garcia's factual sufficiency complaint had to be presented to the trial judge, but because she never paid the $15 fee, the trial court was not required to review it. Thus, because no new trial fee was ever paid, the court of appeals correctly never addressed Garcia's factual sufficiency complaint, but correctly considered her venue complaint.

Notes

1. In *Tate v. E.I. DuPont de Nemours & Co.*, 934 S.W.2d 83 (Tex. 1996) the Court held that "a motion for new trial timely presented to the district clerk without the required filing fee extends the appellate timetable, where the movant pays the filing fee after the motion is overruled by operation of law but before the trial court loses plenary jurisdiction." However, the Court refused to express an opinion as to whether the appellate timetable would be extended if the fee were not paid within the period of time of the trial court's plenary jurisdiction.

2. *Board of Trustees of Bastrop Independent School District v. Toungate*, 958 S.W.2d 365 (Tex. 1997). Under TEX. R. CIV. P. 306(a), it is the signing of the modified judgment that determines whether the trial court acted within its plenary power. The modified judgment was rendered when signed on 1/10/95. Notification of the parties and filing of the judgment are not required for rendition of the judgment. Under TEX. R. CIV. P

306(a)(4), the school district's right to appeal was still protected, even though the parties did not receive timely notice of the judgment. The appellate timetable did not start to run until the school district was notified of the judgment on 2/10/95. The trial court should have submitted the modified judgment to the clerk immediately upon signing it, to avoid the burden of the notification hearing.

3. *In re Columbia Medical Center of Las Colinas*, 290 S.W.3d 204 (Tex. 2009): Mandamus relief is conditionally granted, directing the trial court to more specifically set out the reasons for which it set aside the jury verdict, and granted a new trial. The trial court has not stated its specific grounds for refusing to enter judgment on the jury verdict, and granting a new trial. Thus, the Court declines to consider whether mandamus relief is available, as to the trial court's action in disregarding the jury verdict. The Court denies, without prejudice, Columbia's request for a writ of mandamus directing the trial court to enter judgment on the verdict. Trial courts have significant discretion in granting new trials. However, such discretion should not, and does not, permit a trial judge to substitute his or her own views for that of the jury, without a valid basis. A trial court's actions in refusing to disclose the reasons it set aside, or disregarded, a jury verdict is no less arbitrary to the parties and public than if an appellate court did so. The trial court's action, in failing to give its reasons for disregarding the jury verdict, as to Columbia, was arbitrary and an abuse of discretion. Once a jury has rendered its verdict, the trial court may not disregard that verdict, grant a new trial, and explain its action only as being "in the interests of justice and fairness." Just as appellate courts that set aside jury verdicts are required to detail reasons for doing so, trial courts must give more explanation than "in the interest of justice" for setting aside a jury verdict.

b. *Motions to Modify, Correct or Reform Judgments*

Read Rule 329b(g)-(h) Texas Rules of Civil Procedure.

L.M. HEALTHCARE, INC.
v.
CHILDS
929 S.W.2d 442
(Tex. 1996)

Thomas W. McQuage, Galveston, for Petitioner.
Daniel B. Childs, Jacksonville, for Respondent.

PER CURIAM.

We grant Respondent's motion for rehearing. We withdraw our opinion and judgment of April 12, 1996 and substitute the following.

L.M. Healthcare, Inc., d/b/a Longmeadow Care Center filed suit as an alleged creditor against the estate of Dorothy "Dot" H. Childs. On January 28, 1994, the trial court held that Longmeadow could not recover from Childs because it did not present a properly authenticated claim under the Texas Probate Code.

Longmeadow filed a motion for new trial on February 7, 1994, and the trial court set a hearing for March 3, 1994. At the hearing, the trial court signed both the January 28, 1994 judgment and an order denying the motion for new trial.

On April 4, 1994, Longmeadow filed a motion to modify judgment. Longmeadow asked the trial court to alter its judgment to reflect that it was without prejudice to Longmeadow's refiling its suit. The trial court held a hearing on the motion on May 11, 1994. On May 17, 1994, the trial court rendered an order modifying judgment as requested in Longmeadow's motion. The trial court also added the following finding to its judgment:

> The Court further finds that on May 11, 1994 a properly authenticated claim was filed with the Court and personally served on [Childs] in open court and that the thirty (30) day time to respond by the guardian would expire on June 13, 1994.

Childs brought two points of error before the court of appeals complaining that the trial court did not have plenary power to modify its judgment and one point complaining about the trial court's additional finding. The court of appeals sustained all three points. 908 S.W.2d 593. Before this Court, Longmeadow challenges only the court of appeals decision that the trial court did not have plenary power to modify its judgment.

Childs claimed that the trial court signed a modified judgment after its plenary jurisdiction expired. The court of appeals concluded that a motion to modify judgment filed within the time the Texas Rules of Civil Procedure permits, but after the trial court overruled a motion for new trial, cannot extend the trial court's plenary jurisdiction. 908 S.W.2d 593. Thus, the court of appeals held the trial court lacked the plenary power to modify the judgment. We disagree.

A party shall file a motion to modify judgment within the time prescribed for a motion for new trial. *See* TEX. R. CIV. P. 329b(g). A party must file a motion for new trial no later than the thirtieth day after the judgment was signed. *See* TEX. R. CIV. P. 329b(b). The court of appeals acknowledged that Longmeadow timely filed its motion to modify on Monday, April 4, 1994. *See* TEX. R. CIV. P. 4. That the trial court overruled Longmeadow's motion for new trial does not shorten the trial court's plenary power to resolve a motion to modify judgment. According to the rules:

> A motion to modify, correct, or reform a judgment . . . , if filed, shall be filed and determined within the time prescribed by this rule for a motion for new trial and shall extend the trial court's plenary power . . . in the same manner as a motion for new trial.

TEX. R. CIV. P. 329b(g).

> The overruling of a [motion to modify] shall not preclude the filing of a motion for new trial, nor shall the overruling of a motion for new trial preclude the filing of a motion to modify, correct, or reform.

TEX. R. CIV. P. 329b(g).

> If a motion for new trial is timely filed by any party, the trial court, regardless of whether an appeal has been perfected, has plenary power to grant a new trial or to vacate, modify, correct, or reform the judgment until thirty days after all such motions are overruled, either by written and signed order or by operation of law, whichever occurs first.

TEX. R. CIV .P. 329b(e).

> These rules do not reduce the seventy-five day plenary power period in which a trial court can determine a motion to modify judgment. *See* TEX. R. CIV. P. 329b(c). These rules do provide that a timely filed motion to modify judgment extends the trial court's plenary power, separate and apart from a motion for new trial.

The court of appeals held that the trial court's plenary power can be extended only once. Otherwise, a party could create indefinite delay through the carefully timed filing of subsequent motions to modify. However, an indefinite delay is not possible under the rules.

Only timely filed motions extend the trial court's plenary jurisdiction. *See* TEX. R. CIV. P. 329b(e),(g). A party must file a motion to modify judgment and motion for new trial within thirty days from the date the trial court signed the judgment. *See* TEX. R. CIV. P. 329b(b),(g). The trial court's plenary jurisdiction cannot extend beyond 105 days after the trial court signs the judgment. *See* TEX. R. CIV. P. 329b(c) (seventy-five days) and TEX. R. CIV. P. 329b(e) (30 days); *See also* TEX. R. CIV. P. 5 (trial court may not enlarge the period for taking any action under the rules relating to new trials except as stated in the rules).

Accordingly, we hold that the trial court possessed plenary power to modify the judgment in this case. Under Texas Rule of Appellate Procedure 170, without hearing oral argument, we reverse the court of appeals' judgment in part. We render judgment reinstating the trial court's judgment as modified that Longmeadow's claim was not properly authenticated and that it take nothing against Childs, individually or as guardian of Dorothy H. Childs, but that the judgment does not act as res judicata or preclude a properly authenticated claim from being filed. However, we affirm the court of appeals holding that the portion of trial court's modified order finding that Longmeadow had made a properly authenticated claim was premature because the claim had not been presented to and rejected by the guardian.

Notes

1. *Board of Trustees of Bastrop I.S.D. v. Toungate*, 958 S.W.2d 365 (1997): "The initial judgment, which was the take-nothing judgment against Toungate, was rendered on November 29, 1994. Toungate filed a timely motion to modify or reform the judgment, and the trial court signed the modified judgment in favor of Toungate on January 10, 1995, well within its plenary power. *See* TEX.R. CIV. P. 329b. Upon signing the modified judgment, the trial court then had plenary power to set aside or to further modify or reform that judgment within 30 days, absent another motion extending the time periods. *See* TEX.R. CIV. P. 329b(h), 329b(d)."

2. *In the Interest of J.Z.P. et al., Minor Children,* 484 S.W.3d 924 (Tex. 2016): Fifty-seven days after trial court entered an order modifying divorce decree, following substituted service, W filed a motion "to reopen and vacate an order" alleging that she had discovered service. The trial court denied the motion. The court of appeals dismissed W's appeal for want of jurisdiction, finding that W's motion did not extend the trial court's plenary jurisdiction and post-judgment deadlines to run from the date she received notice of the trial court's order, because it was not captioned a motion under R 306a.

Held: Reversed and remanded. Under R 71, "[w]hen a party has mistakenly designated any plea or pleading, the court, if justice so requires, shall treat the plea or pleading as if it had been properly designated." Courts should acknowledge the substance of the relief sought despite the formal styling of the pleading.

MACKIE
v.
McKENZIE

890 S.W.2d 807
(Tex. 1995)

Bennett J. Roberts, III, Houston, for petitioners.
Charles T. Frazier, Jr., Andrea M. Kuntzman, Dallas, for respondents.

PER CURIAM.

Stephanie S. Mackie, Charles W. Settle, Jr. and Katherine S. Nelson appeal from a dismissal for want of jurisdiction ordered by the court of appeals, 872 S.W.2d 11. We reverse that judgment and remand to that court for consideration of the merits of the appeal.

Mackie sued William A. McKenzie, Jay M. Wallace and McKenzie and Baer, alleging negligence and deceptive trade practices arising out of McKenzie's legal representation of Mackie. On January 8, 1993, the trial court signed an order granting an interlocutory summary judgment in favor of McKenzie. The summary judgment order did not discuss or dispose of a counterclaim filed by McKenzie. McKenzie moved to sever the counterclaim, but after the trial court overruled the severance motion, McKenzie determined that he no longer wished to pursue the counterclaims and filed a motion for nonsuit.

An order nonsuiting McKenzie's counterclaim was signed on June 1, 1993. At the request of Mackie's counsel, the trial court, on June 25, 1993, signed a "Final Judgment" that stated: On the 25th of June, 1993, this Court, having granted Defendants' Motion for Summary Judgment on or about January 8, 1993 and subsequently dismissing Defendants' counterclaim without prejudice on or about June 1, 1993, finds that said Summary Judgment is final. IT IS THEREFORE ORDERED, ADJUDGED AND DECREED that the Summary Judgment granted in favor of Defendants on January 8, 1993 is hereby made final. All relief not expressly granted herein is DENIED.

Mackie filed an appeal that was dismissed for want of jurisdiction. The court of appeals held that the appellate timetable began to run when the order of nonsuit was signed—not when the final judgment was signed—and therefore, Mackie's cost bond was not timely filed. Mackie here argues that the issuance of the final judgment was a correction or modification of an earlier judgment, and the commencement of the appellate timetable was delayed until the date of the final judgment.

In *Anderson v. Casebolt*, 493 S.W.2d 509, 510 (Tex. 1973), this Court held that a new judgment filed after a final judgment and serving "no purpose other than to enlarge the time for appeal" is without effect. *Anderson* involved two judgments that were "identical except for the date of entry" and the court issued the latter order because the "counsel for plaintiff did not discover such entry until too late to file a motion for new trial . . . ." *Id.*

At the time *Anderson* was decided, the Texas Rules of Civil Procedure did not contain a provision specifying the effect of a modified judgment on the commencement of the appellate timetable. After *Anderson* was decided, this Court added subsection (h) to TEX. R. CIV. P. 329b, which provides: If a judgment is modified, corrected or reformed in any respect, the time for appeal shall run from the time the modified, corrected or reformed judgment is signed . . . . After this amendment, we decided *Check v. Mitchell*, 758 S.W.2d 755 (Tex. 1988). In *Check* the new judgment varied from the original judgment "in that, among other things, the docket number was changed to the new number assigned in the severance order, it reflected that a severance had been ordered and language was added to the effect that all writs and processes might issue and that all relief not expressly granted was denied." *Id.* at 756. In *Check* we held that "any change, whether or not material or substantial, made in a judgment while the trial court retains plenary power, operates to delay the commencement of the appellate timetable until the date the modified, corrected or reformed judgment is signed." After *Check*, *Anderson* is limited to cases in which the face of the record reveals that the trial court entered the new order for the sole purpose of extending the appellate timetable.

In this case, the latter order stated that the interlocutory summary judgment and nonsuit order were final and added "Mother Hubbard" language. The trial judge issued the latter order while he still had plenary power over the case and there is no indication that the trial judge issued the order solely for the purpose of extending the appellate timetable.

Under these circumstances, the court of appeals erred when it failed to measure the appellate timetable from the date of the latter order. Accordingly, without hearing oral argument, a majority of this Court reverses the judgment of the court of appeals and remands to that court for further proceedings consistent with this decision.

Note

Naaman v. Grider, 126 S.W.3d 73 (Tex. 2003): Four weeks after the trial court rendered a final judgment, it issued an order granting the defendant's motion for judgment but did not issue a new judgment. The Supreme Court held that the time for the plaintiff to perfect appeal ran from the date of final judgment and not from the date of the court's order granting the defendant's motion for judgment. An order that merely grants a motion for judgment is in no sense a judgment itself. It adjudicates nothing. The only judgment in this case was signed four weeks earlier.

c. *Nunc Pro Tunc Orders*

Read Rules 306a(6), 316, and 329b(h) of the Texas Rules of Civil Procedure and refer to the following diagram.

Rule 316, Rule 306a(6), Rule 329b(h)

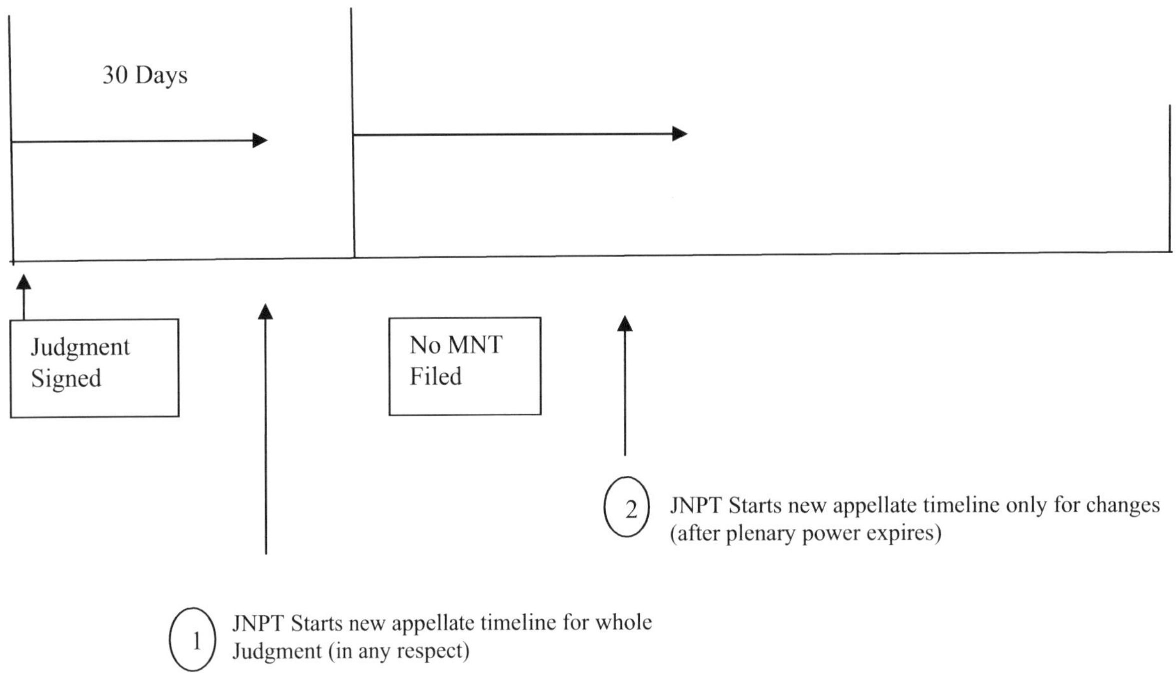

COMET ALUMINUM CO.
v.
DIBRELL
450 S.W.2d 56
(Tex. 1970)

John H. Holloway, Houston, for relator.
Carr, Osorio, Palmer, Dickson, Long & Coleman, William Dickson, Houston, for respondents.

CALVERT, CHIEF JUSTICE.

In this original proceeding in this court, relator, Comet Aluminum Company, Inc., seeks a writ of mandamus directing Honorable Joe B. Dibrell, District Judge, one of the respondents, to set aside a nunc pro tunc judgment and a judgment ordering a new trial rendered and entered in Cause No. 689,616, styled *Comet Aluminum Company, Inc. v. San Levine, Individually and d/b/a Tele-Sales*, on the docket of the 125th Judicial District Court of Harris County. The writ is ordered conditionally issued.

The chronological sequence of events in the suit by Comet against Levine which led to the filing of this proceeding is as follows: 1-9-67: Comet filed its First Amended Original Petition by which it sought a recovery of $4,354.98, alleged to be due on a debt for money lent, 'together with interest thereon at the maximum legal rate from September 12, 1964,' and 'attorney's fees in the sum of $1,000.00.' 8-21-68: The case was tried by Judge Dibrell, and at the conclusion of the trial, he announced: 'Gentlemen, . . . I am going to have to award judgment to the plaintiff in the amount of $4,354.98. . . . And since no attorneys fees were proved up, or no actual demand, I am not allowing any attorney's fees.' Thereupon, he made the following notation in the docket: '. . . Judgment announced in favor of plaintiff against defendant for amount of $4,354.98—Notice of appeal.' 8-23-68: Judge Dibrell signed a written draft of judgment, approved as to form and substance by the attorneys for both parties, awarding a recovery of $4,354.98, and continuing,'. . . with interest thereon at the rate of six percent (6%) per annum from September 12, 1964; and for all costs in this behalf expended, for all of which let execution issue. All recovery not specifically awarded herein is expressly denied. . . .' Above the signature of the judge was this legend: 'RENDERED, SIGNED and ENTERED this the 23 day of August, 1968.' Notice of appeal by Levine was contained in the draft of judgment, but the appeal was not perfected. 12-5-68: Levine filed a 'Motion for Entry of Judgment Nunc Pro Tunc' by which he sought the entry of a judgment correcting the draft of judgment of 8-23-68 by eliminating therefrom the award of pre-judgment interest from September 12, 1964. 1-16-69: Judge Dibrell refused and denied the motion for judgment nunc pro tunc 'for want of merit,' and Levine gave notice of appeal. 3-3-69: Judge Dibrell, on his own motion, rendered and entered a nunc pro tunc judgment which, after reciting that judgment for pre-judgment interest had not been rendered on 8-21-68 and that inclusion of such interest in the 8-23-68 draft of judgment was, therefore, a clerical error, awarded Comet judgment for only the principal sum of $4,354.98. The judgment also contained a recitation that '(a)ll recovery not specifically awarded herein is expressly denied.' On some date not shown in the record, Comet filed a motion to set aside this judgment. 3-6-69: Levine filed a one-paragraph motion for new trial. 3-17-69: Hearing was had on Comet's motion to set aside the nunc pro tunc judgment of 3-3-69 and on Levine's motion for new trial. 3-28-69: Judgment was rendered and entered refusing and denying Comet's motion to set aside the nunc pro tunc judgment, but such judgment was 'modified' to strike the recitation, '(a)ll recovery not specifically awarded herein is expressly denied.' A separate judgment was then rendered granting Levine's motion for new trial.

The position of Comet in this court is that the 3-3-69 nunc pro tunc judgment was void, and that the subsequent judgment setting aside that judgment and granting Levine a new trial is likewise void. Levine defends the validity of the 3-3-69 judgment on the ground that the court's 'pronouncement' on 8-21-68 of judgment for Comet for the sum of $4,354.98 constituted the 'rendition' of judgment in the case, and that any other adjudicative provisions in the 8-23-68 written draft of judgment were nothing more than clerical errors in the 'entry' of judgment which errors the trial judge was authorized to correct by a judgment nunc pro tunc. Having thus concluded that the 3-3-69 nunc pro tunc judgment was valid, Levine then turns to the provisions of Rule 306a, Texas Rules of Civil Procedure, as authority for the judgment granting his motion for a new trial. We will first examine the validity of the nunc pro tunc judgment; if it is void, the judgment granting a new trial falls automatically. *Finlay v. Jones*, 435 S.W.2d 136 (Tex. Sup. 1968).

The law is now well settled in this state that clerical errors in the 'entry' of a judgment, previously rendered, may be corrected after the end of the court's term by a nunc pro tunc judgment, but that judicial errors in the 'rendition' of a judgment may not be so corrected. *Finlay v. Jones*, 435 S.W.2d 136 (Tex. Sup. 1968); *Knox v. Long*, 152 Tex. 291, 257 S.W.2d 289 (1953); *Love v. State Bank & Trust Co. of San Antonio*, 126 Tex. 591, 90 S.W.2d 819 (1936); *Coleman v. Zapp*, 105 Tex. 491, 151 S.W. 1040 (1912); Rule 316, Texas Rules of Civil Procedure. Judicial errors committed in the rendition of judgment must be corrected by appeal, writ of error or bill of review. *Finlay v. Jones, supra*. The crucial inquiry in this proceeding is, therefore, whether the trial court 'rendered' judgment for Comet for pre-judgment interest by its 8-23-68 written draft of judgment, or whether, to the contrary, the award of pre-judgment interest by such draft was, as the court subsequently found, a mere clerical error in the entry of judgment.

Before applying the law to the facts of this case, it will be well to summarize the material and relevant facts once again. By its first amended petition, Comet expressly sought three items of recovery, to wit: (1) a debt of $4,354.98; (2) pre-judgment interest 'at the maximum legal rate from September 12, 1964'; and (3) 'attorney's fees in the sum of $1,000.00.' At the conclusion of the evidence on the trial of the case, the trial judge pronounced judgment in open court on the first and third issues tendered by the pleadings, but did not pronounce judgment on the second issue of pre-judgment interest. The docket entry indicated that judgment had been rendered only on the first issue. Conversely, the court's written draft of judgment, executed on 8-23-68, disposed of all three issues. It (1) awarded Comet a recovery of the principal amount of the debt in the sum of $4,354.98; (2) awarded a recovery of pre-judgment interest at the rate of 6% from September 12, 1964; and (3) denied a recovery of attorney's fees by denying a recovery of all relief not specifically awarded. Thus, while it may correctly and properly be said that the written instrument signed by the judge on 8-23-68 was but a written memorandum of a judgment previously rendered on the first and third issues, it contained the first words spoken by the judge, either orally or in writing, with respect to the second issue.

In *Coleman v. Zapp*. 105 Tex. 491, 151 S.W. 1040, at 1041 (1912), we stated that a judgment's 'rendition is the judicial act by which the court settles and declares the decision of the law upon the matters at issue.' And in *Knox v. Long*, 152 Tex. 291, 257 S.W.2d 289, at 292 (1953), we quoted FREEMAN ON JUDGMENTS as stating that a judgment is "rendered' when the decision is officially announced either orally in open court or by memorandum filed with the clerk.' We then quoted with approval from *Appeal of Bulkeley*, 76 Conn. 454, 57 A. 112, 113, as follows:

> 'A judgment is in fact rendered whenever the trial judge officially announces his decision in open court, or out of court signifies to the clerk, in his official capacity and for his official guidance—whether orally or by written memorandum—the sentence of the law pronounced by him in any cause.'

Pre-judgment interest is always recoverable as damages 'when the principal damages are fixed by conditions existing at the time the injury is inflicted.' *Texas Company v. State*, 154 Tex. 494, 281 S.W.2d 83, at 89 and 92-93 (1955). Such damages having been expressly sought by Comet, the trial court had a duty to decide the issue and to render judgment with respect thereto. This duty was not discharged or terminated by the oral rendition of judgment on the other two issues on 8-21-68; and it is immaterial that a denial of recovery of pre-judgment interest would have been implied in the absence of an actual decision of the issue. *See Vance v. Wilson*, 382 S.W.2d 107 (Tex. Sup. 1964).

We hold that the provision in the 8-23-68 written draft of judgment awarding Comet a recovery of pre-judgment interest was a 'rendition' of judgment as to that item, and, if error, was judicial and not clerical error, the trial court's finding to the contrary notwithstanding. Therefore, the nunc pro tunc judgment of 3-3-69 purporting to eliminate the item as clerical error was void; and subsequent judgment of 3-28-69 granting Levine a new trial is likewise void.

Levine insists that a writ of mandamus should not issue to require Judge Dibrell to set aside the two judgments because Comet had a remedy by appeal from the nunc pro tunc judgment. We cannot accept this premise. The record discloses that the trial judge had granted Levine a new trial before Comet could possibly have obtained relief from the nunc pro tunc judgment by appeal, and there is no right of appeal from a trial court judgment granting a new trial.

We assume that Judge Dibrell will set aside the nunc pro tunc judgment of 3-3-69 and his judgment of 3-28-69 granting Levine a new trial. Writ of mandamus will issue to require that action if he should refuse.

Note

Clerical errors are those which do not result from judicial reasoning or determination. *Nolan v. Bettis,* 562 S.W.2d 520, 522 (Tex. Civ. App.—Austin 1978, no writ). Stated another way, a clerical error is one that is not the result of judicial reasoning, evidence or determination. *Anderes v. Koch,* 702 S.W.2d 584, 585 (Tex. 1986). A judicial error is one made by the court in rendering judgment, as opposed to a failure to accurately recite the judgment rendered. *Wallace v. Rogers,* 517 S.W.2d 301 (Tex. Civ. App.—Dallas 1974, writ ref'd n.r.e.).

ESCOBAR
v.
ESCOBAR
711 S.W.2d 230
(Tex. 1986)

Facts: In a suit over title to 200 tracts of land, the trial court, in a 1978 docket entry, stated that "tracts 34 & 38" awarded as per the Trimble Map." (The Trimble map showed 265.42 acres for tract 38 & 70 acres for tract 34). In the 1982 final judgment, tract 34 was listed at 72.954 acres, and tract 38 was listed at 315.2 acres. Ramon claims tract 34; Rodolfo Escobar claims tract 38. Ramon Escobar filed a motion for judgment nunc pro tunc to correct the judgment. The district court signed a motion for judgment nunc pro tunc, and removed tract 38 from the 1982 judgment, and found that tract 38 had been previously awarded at 265.42 acres. The court of appeals concluded that the trial court could not correct an incorrect rendering by judgment nunc pro tunc.

Issue: Was this a clerical or judicial error? The trial court found as a matter of fact that this was a clerical error, by finding, as a matter of fact, that the trial court did render judgment in 1979 on the Trimble map. Docket entries are some evidence of rendered judgment and its contents. If that finding is supported by sufficient evidence, it stands.

Issue. Who determines whether it is a clerical or judicial error? The decision of whether an error in a judgment is judicial or clerical is a question of law. However, whether the court pronounced judgment orally, and the terms of the pronouncement are questions of fact. The judicial or clerical question becomes a question of law only after the trial court factually determines whether it previously rendered judgment, and the judgment's contents.

A judicial error is an error which occurs in the rendering, as oppose to the entering, of a judgment. The court can only correct the entry of a final written judgment that incorrectly states the judgment actually rendered.

Note

In re Elizondo, 544 S.W.3d 824 (Tex. 2018): Our conclusion that the original order was final also decides the issue whether the amended order was void as an attempt to correct judicial error. A trial court may correct clerical errors in a judgment even after its plenary power has expired. *See* TEX. R. CIV. P. 329b(d), (f). But it must correct judicial errors within thirty days of judgment or not at all. *See Escobar v. Escobar*, 711 S.W.2d 230, 231 (Tex. 1986) ("After the trial court loses its jurisdiction over a judgment, it can correct only *clerical* errors in the judgment by judgment nunc pro tunc." (emphasis added)).

The trial court's inclusion of the finality phrase in the original order constituted judicial error. It is settled that "only errors made in entering a judgment are clerical; an error in rendition is judicial." *Daredia*, 317 S.W.3d at 249 (citing *Escobar*, 711 S.W.2d at 231). Here, as in *Daredia*, the trial court signed an order that one of the parties submitted. *See Daredia*, 317 S.W.3d at 249. As such, the finality phrase was part of the judgment that the trial court rendered. *See id.* ("[P]rovisions alleged to have been inserted by mistake of the attorney nevertheless become a part of the court's judgment and therefore are judicial errors when thus rendered in writing by the court." (quoting *Dikeman v. Snell*, 490 S.W.2d 183, 185-86 (Tex.1973))). Since the amended order sought to correct judicial error after the trial court's plenary power had expired, the amended order was void.

d. *Motions to Reinstate*

Read Rule 165a(3) and 306a of the Texas Rules of Civil Procedure.

LEVIT
v.
ADAMS
850 S.W.2d 469
(Tex. 1993)

Issue: Does notice of dismissal after the 90th day trigger R 306a and restart the time-table? No!

Held: Under Rule 306a (4) the party gets an extra 30 days, if the party does not have notice of the judgment within 20 days. However, notice must be obtained by the 90th day from the date the judgment was entered, in order to gain the extra 30 days. Thus, learning of the order of dismissal on the 91st day did not extend the time.

The actual knowledge acquired by P on the 91st day after dismissal did not suffice under Rule 306a(4) to restart the trial court's jurisdiction to entertain a motion to reinstate. Notice received after the 90th day is not covered by the Rule.

This is an appeal from a dismissal for want of prosecution. After a dismissal for want of prosecution, a party may file a motion to reinstate within 30 days after the order of dismissal is signed or within the period provided by TEX.R. CIV. P. 306a. In this case, the court of appeals concluded that when P learned of the dismissal for want of prosecution on the 91st day, Rule 306a(4) gave him until the 120th day to file a reinstatement motion. 841 S.W.2d 483. **Held:** Reversed and remanded to the trial court. The actual knowledge acquired by P on the

91st day after dismissal did not suffice under Rule 306a(4) to restart the trial court's jurisdiction to entertain a motion to reinstate. Notice received after the 90th day is not covered by the Rule.

Note

When a trial court erroneously reinstates a case after the expiration of the court's plenary jurisdiction, mandamus will issue. *See Emerald Oaks Hotel v. Zardenetta*, 776 S.W.2d 577 (Tex. 1989).

e. *Motions for Sanctions*

LANE BANK EQUIPMENT CO.
v.
SMITH SOUTHERN EQUIPMENT, INC.

10 S.W.3d 308
(Tex. 2000)

Walter J. Kronzer, III, Charles R. Kaufmann, Houston, for Petitioner.
John M. Mings, Houston, for Respondent.

CHIEF JUSTICE PHILLIPS delivered the opinion of the Court, in which JUSTICE BAKER, JUSTICE ABBOTT, JUSTICE HANKINSON, JUSTICE O'NEILL and JUSTICE GONZALES joined.

In this case, we decide whether a timely filed postjudgment motion seeking to add an award of sanctions to an existing judgment extends the thirty-day period in which a trial court may exercise plenary power over its judgment. The court of appeals held that such a motion qualified as a motion to modify, correct, or reform a judgment under Texas Rule of Civil Procedure 329b(g), thus extending the trial court's plenary power to change its judgment beyond the initial thirty-day period. 981 S.W.2d 302. Because we agree, we affirm the court of appeals' judgment.

Lane Bank Equipment Company and Smith Southern Equipment, Inc., each design, install, and supply equipment to banks. In 1995, Lane sued Smith for unfair competition. Smith answered and subsequently sought to recoup its attorney's fees as a sanction, asserting that Lane's suit was frivolous. On the eve of trial, Lane nonsuited. The trial court granted the nonsuit without prejudice to Smith's claim for attorney's fees should Lane elect to refile suit.

Two weeks after the dismissal, Lane refiled, adding claims of tortious interference with contract and misappropriation of trade secrets to the former unfair competition complaint. After another year of litigation, the trial court granted Smith's motion for summary judgment. The trial court's order, signed on June 5, 1997, stated that "Defendant Smith Southern Equipment, Inc.'s Motion for Summary Judgment is granted." Three weeks later, Smith moved for sanctions and for rendition of a new final judgment in the case. Smith alleged that Lane's claims were baseless and filed solely for purposes of harassment. *See* TEX. CIV. PRAC. & REM. CODE § 10.001(1), (3); TEX. R. CIV. P. 13. The trial court agreed; and on July 11, 1997, it signed an order stating that Lane's petition and discovery responses were "in bad faith and for the improper purposes of harassing and imposing needless costs upon Smith Southern." As a sanction for this conduct, the trial court awarded Smith more than $46,000 for attorney's fees and expenses reasonably incurred in defending the litigation, together with additional sums for appellate attorney's fees in the event Lane pursued an unsuccessful appeal. *See* TEX. CIV. PRAC. & REM. CODE § 10.002(c). The trial court also signed a new judgment on that date, referring to the previous order granting summary judgment in Smith's favor and awarding the attorney's fees and expenses found to be reasonable and necessary in the sanctions order. Lane appealed, and the court of appeals affirmed the summary judgment and sanctions. 981 S.W.2d 302.

In this Court, Lane abandons its attack on the summary judgment and focuses solely on whether the trial court had jurisdiction to render its July 11th order awarding sanctions. Lane contends that the original summary judgment signed on June 5, 1997, became final after thirty days so that the trial court's plenary power expired on July 5, 1997. Thus, Lane concludes the trial court had no authority to order sanctions on July 11, 1997.

A trial court retains jurisdiction over a case for a minimum of thirty days after signing a final judgment. TEX. R. CIV. P. 329b(d). During this time, the trial court has plenary power to change its judgment. *Check v. Mitchell*, 758 S.W.2d 755, 756 (Tex. 1988). The period of plenary power may be extended, however, by timely filing an appropriate postjudgment motion. Thus, the filing of a motion for new trial, TEX.R.CIV. P. 329b(e), or a motion to modify, correct or reform the judgment, TEX. R. CIV. P. 329b(g), within the initial thirty-day period extends the trial court's jurisdiction over its judgment up to an additional seventy-five days, depending on when or whether the court acts on the motions. *Philbrook v. Berry*, 683 S.W.2d 378, 379 (Tex. 1985); TEX. R. CIV. P. 329b(c). In this case, the court of appeals concluded that Smith's postjudgment motion for sanctions extended the trial court's plenary jurisdiction over the June 5th judgment as a motion to modify, correct or reform the judgment under Rule 329b(g). 981 S.W.2d at 303.

* * *

While we agree that a judgment does not have to resolve pending sanctions issues to be final, that principle does not control this case. Even if a sanctions order is not required to be included in a final judgment, it may be included there. And a motion made after judgment to incorporate a sanction as a part of the final judgment does propose a change to that judgment. Such a motion is, on its face, a motion to modify, correct or reform the existing judgment within the meaning of Rule 329b(g).

A number of courts of appeals, beginning with *Brazos Electric Cooperative, Inc. v. Callejo*, 734 S.W.2d 126, 128 (Tex. App.—Dallas 1987, no writ), have said that a Rule 329b(g) motion must seek to substantively change the existing judgment to qualify as a motion to modify under subpart (g). In this case, Smith's postjudgment motion for sanctions sought to change the court's June 5th judgment by adding an award of attorney's fees as a sanction for frivolous litigation. *See* TEX. CIV. PRAC. & REM. CODE § 10.002(c). The motion accordingly proposed a substantive modification to the former judgment.

Although Smith's motion here satisfies the substantive requirement of *Callejo* and its progeny, Smith argues that its motion did not have to seek a substantive change to extend the trial court's plenary jurisdiction under our decision in *Check v. Mitchell*, 758 S.W.2d 755, 756 (Tex. 1988). *Check*, however, was not concerned with a Rule 329b(g) motion. Instead, *Check* applied subpart (h) of this rule which provides that "[i]f a judgment is modified, corrected or reformed in any respect, the time for appeal shall run from the time the modified, corrected, or reformed judgment is signed . . . ." TEX. R. CIV. P. 329b(h). In interpreting subpart (h), we held that "any change, whether or not material or substantial, made in a judgment while the trial court retains plenary power" restarts the appellate timetable. *Check*, 758 S.W.2d at 756. Applying *Check* here, Smith submits that because subparts (g) and (h) share the same triggering language, that of modification, correction or reformation of a judgment, they should be interpreted in the same way. Thus, if a change in the judgment, "whether or not material or substantial," triggers rule 329(h), then any timely postjudgment motion requesting such a change should also trigger Rule 329b(g). We do not agree that subparts (g) and (h) share a common trigger.

Rule 329b(h) provides that "[i]f a judgment is modified, corrected or reformed in any respect " the appellate timetable runs from the date of the new judgment. TEX. R. CIV. P. 329b(h)(emphasis added). Thus, in *Check*, we concluded that the appellate timetable should restart whenever a court changes its judgment whether or not the change is "material or substantial." *Check*, 758 S.W.2d at 756. Subpart (g), on the other hand, is not concerned with a court changing its judgment but rather with a party's request that some change be made. Rather than the expansive "in any respect" of subpart (h), subpart (g) begins, "[a] motion to modify, correct, or reform a judgment (as distinguished from motion to correct the record of a judgment under Rule 316)" extends the trial court's plenary jurisdiction and the appellate deadlines as would a motion for new trial. Subpart (g)'s omission of the "in any respect" language found in subpart (h) and its pointed distinction between motions to modify and motions seeking purely clerical corrections indicate that the respective provisions have different triggers. Thus, any change to a judgment made by the trial court while it retains plenary jurisdiction will restart the appellate timetable under Rule 329b(h), *Check*, 758 S.W.2d at 756, but only a motion seeking a substantive change will extend the appellate deadlines and the court's plenary power under Rule 329b(g). *See Cavalier Corp. v. Store Enter., Inc.*, 742 S.W.2d 785, 786 (Tex. App.—Dallas 1987, writ denied). JUSTICE HECHT'S concurring opinion questions the wisdom of requiring that a Rule 329b(g) motion actually seek a substantive change. He argues that such a requirement creates a trap for the unwary appellate practitioner—a trap that is not warranted by the rule's language or its history. But his historical view demonstrates, and he concedes, that there is almost no history pertaining to subpart (g) in the minutes of the Rules Advisory Committee. He therefore must impute the Committee's concerns about subpart (h) to subpart (g), suggesting that the Committee impliedly intended for a party's rights under subpart (g) to mirror the trial court's power under subpart (h). We disagree. The history upon which Justice Hecht relies and the language adopted by this Court indicate that a party's right to move for a modification and the court's power to change its judgment are not coextensive.

A motion to modify, correct or reform a judgment was always intended to embody something other than a motion for judgment nunc pro tunc.[7] That distinction continues in the express language of Rule 329b(g) today. Even Justice Hecht ultimately concludes that a motion seeking a purely clerical change cannot qualify under Rule 329b(g). 10 S.W.3d at 313 (HECHT, J. concurring). But any change made by the court under subpart (h) prior to losing jurisdiction, even a clerical change, will restart the appellate timetable. Accordingly, JUSTICE HECHT must concede that the modifications that trigger subpart (h) are not identical to those that trigger subpart (g). Because we are in agreement on this point, JUSTICE HECHT manufactures a dispute by imagining that the Court intends for the application of Rule 329b(g) to depend upon the relative degree of substance contained in the motion. In fact, we intend no such thing. A timely filed postjudgment motion to incorporate sanctions into a new final judgment qualifies under Rule 329b(g) without regard to the relative value of the sanction imposed or even whether the sanction has any express monetary value. In contrast, a timely filed postjudgment motion that merely seeks to correct clerical errors, such as punctuation, grammar or misspellings, will not qualify under Rule 329b(g).

We accordingly hold that a timely filed postjudgment motion that seeks a substantive change in an existing judgment qualifies as a motion to modify under Rule 329b(g), thus extending the trial court's plenary jurisdiction and the appellate timetable. *See Gomez v. Texas Dep't of Crim. Justice*, 896 S.W.2d 176, 176-77 (Tex. 1995) (*citing Miller Brewing Co. v. Villarreal*, 822 S.W.2d 177, 179 (Tex. App.—San Antonio 1991), *rev'd on other grounds*, 829 S.W.2d 770 (Tex. 1992)) (timely postjudgment motion seeking substantive change extends appellate timetable). The court of appeals' judgment is correct, and it is therefore affirmed.

JUSTICE HECHT filed a concurring opinion [opinion omitted].

JUSTICE ENOCH filed a concurring opinion, in which JUSTICE OWEN joined [opinion omitted].

[7] As CHIEF JUSTICE GUITTARD explained, the "kind of a motion, which is filed to correct a judgment within the period of the courts plenary power, is to be distinguished from a motion to correct the record of a judgment nunc pro tunc under rules 316 and 317." 10 S.W.3d at 318 (HECHT, J. concurring)(quoting from Minutes of the May 5, 1979 meeting of the Advisory Committee for the Supreme Court of Texas, at 174 (on file with the Supreme Court of Texas)).

CHAPTER 5.
JUDGMENTS AND THE PRESUMPTION OF VALIDITY

1. *Introduction*

This chapter is really in two parts. The first deals with default judgments and the direct methods available to set those judgments, or any other judgments aside. The second deals with the finality (which could almost be the sanctity) of final judgments. This second parts is reviewed in the second book in this series (Texas Civil Procedure: Trial and Appeal), which deals with the attack on judgments that are no longer subject to a direct attack: res judicata.

This chapter focuses on another important concept which extends throughout the law of Texas Civil Procedure—the presumptive validity of judgments rendered by Texas courts. A judgment entered by a court may contain many errors, but unless and until that judgment is set aside it carries a presumption of validity. As shown in the last chapter, error in a trial court's judgment even if properly preserved and presented to an appellate court may not lead to a reversal of a case unless that error is harmful. This Chapter focuses on the Texas concept of the void judgment. In general under Texas law a judgment which is considered void is one that is entered by a court which did not have personal jurisdiction over of the defendant, or did not have subject matter jurisdiction, or which did not have the jurisdictional power to enter the judgment entered. However, even in the case of a void judgment, some affirmative action in a court on the part of the judgment defendant is necessary in order to set aside or avoid the effects of that judgment. Texas courts have developed different procedural approaches to assist individuals to either set aside a void judgment or to avoid the effects of the judgment.

Although void judgments can arise in a variety of circumstances, most of the reported cases involve default judgments—that is a case where the defendant failed to make either an appearance or show up for trial. In many default judgments, there is not anyone present to complain prior to the entry of judgment that the court lacks jurisdiction to enter the judgment. The difficulty in setting aside or avoiding the effects of such judgments varies depending on the procedural method selected. Each procedural method has its own requirements which must be established in order to set aside or avoid the effects of a default judgment. Just as important, however, is the fact that each method has a specific time frame in which it must be brought in order to even be considered by a court.

A knowledge of the procedural devises used in attacking existing judgments other than the ordinary appeal is fundamental to a thorough understanding of the jurisdiction power of Texas courts and will continually appear throughout this book. The purpose of this chapter is to introduce the basic parameters of direct and collateral attacks on judgments. The student needs to be mindful of these basic parameters as they will come up constantly throughout the remainder of this book.

2. *Direct Attacks on Judgments*

a. *Equitable Motion for New Trial*

Read Rule 329b(a) and (d) Texas Rules of Civil Procedure.

Note

A motion for new trial is a procedural devise for presenting alleged error to a trial court following the entry of a judgment. Prior to 1978, a specific complaint concerning an alleged error contained in a motion for new trial was a prerequisite in order to have an appellate court consider the particular error. Of course, even under the old rule, most errors had to be properly preserved prior to the filing of the motion for new trial. Since 1978, it is no longer necessary in most cases to file a motion for new trial as a prerequisite for presenting an alleged error to an appellate court assuming that the error had been properly preserved pursuant to Rule 33 of the Texas Rules of Appellate Procedure. Rule 329(b) fully explains the procedures involved in a motion for new trial. That rule will be studied in detail later in this book. However, at this time, an investigation of the equitable motion for new trial will be made. It may be filed by a defendant within thirty days following the signing of a default judgment against him. It is referred to as an equitable motion for new trial because the courts used their equitable powers to assist the absent defendant in setting aside the default judgment. However, in order to be successful, the defendant must meet the requirements for an equitable motion for new trial as developed by the case law.

CRADDOCK
v.
SUNSHINE BUS LINES

134 Tex. 388, 133 S.W.2d 124
(Tex. 1939)

Wynne & Wynne, of Wills Point, for plaintiff in error.

Thompson, Knight, Baker, Harris & Wright, Pinkney Grissom, and Rhodes S. Baker, all of Dallas, and A. A. Dawson, of Canton, for defendant in error.

HICKMAN, COMMISSIONER.

Judgment by default for $15,400 was rendered in favor of plaintiff in error Irl Craddock, hereinafter called plaintiff, against defendant in error Sunshine Bus Lines, Inc., hereinafter called defendant, for damages for personal injuries sustained by plaintiff and his wife and also injuries to their automobile, all resulting from a collision between the automobile in which they were riding and a bus belonging to defendant. On the day following the rendition of the default judgment a motion to set same aside and grant a new trial was filed by defendant, which motion was later amended and the amended motion overruled. On appeal the Court of Civil Appeals at Fort Worth reversed the trial court's judgment and remanded the cause with instructions to that court to vacate the default judgment and set the case down for trial on its merits in its regular order. 112 S.W.2d 248.

The suit was filed in the trial court on August 25, 1936, and at the same time two citations were issued, one to Van Zandt county and the other to Kaufman county, both citations being returnable on September 7th. The Van Zandt county citation was served on the agent of defendant in that county on the day it was issued and the Kaufman county citation was served the following day by leaving a copy thereof at the business office of defendant in that county. Defendant carried indemnity insurance with the Travelers Insurance Company, and, by the terms of the policy, the Insurance Company was obligated to defend law suits of the nature of the instant one.

In its motion for a new trial defendant alleged that after the citations were served in the manner above indicated they were sent to John H. Awtry & Company, general agents of the Insurance Company; that Awtry & Company transmitted them with a letter to the Insurance Company on August 28th; that the envelope containing the letter and citations was opened by a lady employee in the claims department and by her passed on to a Mr. Morrison, who was in charge of that department, along with other mail received on that day; that Morrison checked the letter in such manner as to indicate that it related to urgent business and was to be returned to his desk with the files on the case either that afternoon or the next day; that due to a recent hail and wind storm in Dallas, which produced 400 claims against the company, the claims department was running behind with its work, and in order to meet the situation thus created the important mail was separated from that which was not so important and the former received first attention; that in some unexplained manner, the letter transmitting the citation became mixed with the general, or less important mail after being checked by Morrison, and was not discovered until September 10, the day upon which the default judgment was rendered in Van Zandt county; that upon its discovery, Morrison immediately took the citation to the attorneys of the Insurance Company, who proceeded with dispatch to ascertain the status of the matter, and on the following day filed a motion for a new trial; and that the attorneys representing plaintiff were advised of the foregoing facts and were also advised that the defendant was willing to try the case on its merits on the day the motion was filed or on any subsequent day. Facts were alleged which, if true, constitute a meritorious defense to the cause of action. Facts were also alleged which, if true, would establish that the judgment for $15,400 is grossly excessive.

Upon a hearing of the motion evidence was offered in support of all the material allegations therein contained. It was made further to appear upon the hearing that, if the judgment by default had been set aside on September 11, and a new trial granted, the plaintiff could have obtained a trial as soon as he could have done had an answer been filed before appearance day. It was also made to appear at the hearing that one of defendant's attorneys, on the date the motion was filed, offered, on behalf of his client, to pay the plaintiff all of the expenses incurred in obtaining the default judgment. In short, it was shown, at least prima facie, that, had the default judgment been set aside and the case tried in its regular order, the plaintiff would have been in no worse position than he would have been had an answer been filed prior to the rendition of the default judgment.

An investigation of the question presented for decision by the above facts leads naturally for a beginning point to the case of *Dowell v. Winters*, 20 Tex. 793. In that case the defendant employed an attorney to answer for him, and the only excuse for his failure to do so was his mistake as to the law. The court, speaking through Justice Wheeler, recognized that the excuse was "certainly very slight;" but held that, since some excuse was proffered, the trial court should have set aside the default and granted a new trial. The opinion pointed out that it was not the intention of the attorney to suffer judgment to go by default. There was, of course, a showing made upon the hearing of the motion for a new trial of a meritorious defense, and it was also made to appear that the trial would not have been delayed, nor would the plaintiff otherwise have been injured, by the granting of the motion. Our court at that early date recognized the importance of setting up a guiding principle to rule in the decision of this important question of practice, as is manifest from this language taken from its opinion: "But the practice in our own Courts ought to be referable to some general principle, to produce uniformity . . . ." The Court then announced that principle in this language:

> "But where the trial has not been delayed, and there is an affidavit of merits, we think the default should be set aside and the answer received, upon some showing by way of excuse for the failure to plead in time. . . ."

Some excuse, but not necessarily a good excuse, was the test there prescribed. When the opinion in that case is analyzed, it seems clear that the absence of an intentional failure to answer rather than a real excuse for not answering was the controlling fact.

In the case of *Houston & T. C. Ry. Co. v. Burke*, 55 Tex. 323, 40 Am.Rep. 808, the facts with reference to the excuse for failure to answer in time were strikingly similar to those in the instant case. The agent of the Railway Company who was served with citation should have forwarded same to Houston, but by mistake forwarded it to the general freight agent at another place. The freight agent was absent from his office and the citation remained on his desk until after default was taken. The trial court overruled a motion to set aside the default judgment and, in reversing the trial court's judgment, the Supreme Court, speaking through Justice Gould, used this language:

> ". . . We think the facts stated so far excused the failure to answer, that, if there was also a showing of a valid and meritorious defense, the court should have allowed the defendant an opportunity to make that defense available. The case made out is one of mistake and accident appealing strongly for relief from the judgment, if it be made to appear that the defendant would otherwise be deprived of a valid and meritorious defense. . . ."

There are many other cases by the courts of this state of the same general import as the two above singled out, of which the following may be cited: *Janes v. Laugham*, 33 Tex. 604; *Sedberry v. Jones*, 42 Tex. 10, 11; *Cowan v. Williams*, 49 Tex. 380; *Springer v. Gillespie*, Tex. Civ. App., 56 S.W. 369; *Clewis v. Snell*, Tex. Civ. App., 59 S.W. 910; *Mistrot Bros. & Co. v. Wilson*, 41 Tex. Civ. App. 160, 91 S.W. 870; *Pecos & N. T. Ry. v. Pearce*, Tex. Civ. App. 117 S.W. 911; *International Travelers Ass'n v. Peterson*, Tex. Civ. App., 183 S.W. 1196; *Miller v. First State Bank*, Tex. Civ. App., 184 S.W. 614; *Jackson v. Pure Oil Operating Co.*, Tex. Civ. App., 217 S.W. 959; *Walker v. Harris*, Tex. Civ. App., 227 S.W. 360; *First National Bank v. Southwest National Bank*, Tex. Civ. App., 273 S.W. 951; *Borger v. Mineral Wells Clay Products Co.*, Tex. Civ. App., 80 S.W.2d 333.

Applying the rule announced in the *Dowell-Winters* case and followed in the other cited cases to the facts of the case before us, the certain conclusion is reached that the trial court should have granted the motion of the defendant to set aside the default judgment and reinstate the case on its docket. The failure to answer was on account of a mistake and was not intentional. The press of business resulting from the storm certainly constituted some excuse for the oversight; and the showing that there existed a meritorious defense, and that the plaintiff would not have suffered any injury by the granting of the motion, makes a strong appeal for relief from the judgment.

An inspection of the many decisions by our several courts on the question here involved reveals that the purpose of the court in the *Dowell-Winters* case in announcing the principle to which the practice should be referable, namely, to produce uniformity, has not been fully realized. Some lack of uniformity still exists. This is probably due, in part at least, to the fact that the question is controlled by principles of equity and it accordingly has been announced many times that its decision is directed to the sound discretion of the trial court. Naturally appellate courts will differ on the delicate question of whether trial courts have abused their discretion. While trial courts have some measure of discretion in the matter, as, in truth, they have in all cases governed by equitable principles, it is not an unbridled discretion to decide cases as they might deem proper, without reference to any guiding rule or principle. Trial judges desire and are entitled to have a principle or rule to guide them, and we, therefore, reannounce, in slightly changed language the rule established by the above authorities, as follows: A default judgment should be set aside and a new trial ordered in any case in which the failure of the defendant to answer before judgment was not intentional, or the result of conscious indifference on his part, but was due to a mistake or an accident; provided the motion for a new trial sets up a meritorious defense and is filed at a time when the granting thereof will occasion no delay or otherwise work an injury to the plaintiff. This is a just rule. It prevents an injustice to the defendant without working an injustice on the plaintiff. Such a rule has the sanction of equity.

The judgment of the Court of Civil Appeals is affirmed.

Opinion adopted by the Supreme Court.

FIDELITY AND GUARANTY INSURANCE COMPANY
v.
DREWERY CONSTRUCTION COMPANY, INC.

186 S.W.3d 571
(Tex. 2006)

Douglas J. McCarver, Nacogdoches, for Respondent.

Gregory M. Weinstein, Shawn Malcolm McCaskill, Dennis M. Weinstein, Godwin Gruber, LLP, Julia F. Pendery, Daon M. Ward, Godwin Pappas Langley Ronquillo, LLP, Dallas, for Petitioner.

PER CURIAM.

In this suit on a surety bond, Drewery Construction Company, Inc., a subcontractor, obtained a default judgment for $158,131.05 plus interest and attorney's fees against Fidelity and Guaranty Insurance Company, surety for the general contractor, JenCra, Inc. Fidelity filed a motion for new trial explaining that the service papers had been lost. The trial court denied the motion, and the court of appeals affirmed. 188 S.W.3d 672, 2005 WL 468323. Fidelity asserts three grounds for reversal, the last of which is well-taken. Accordingly, we reverse.

First, Fidelity complains of a minor omission in the citation. Rule 99 requires (among other things) that citation be directed to the defendant and show the names of parties. TEX. R. CIV. P. 99(b)(7)-(8). Citation here was correctly addressed to "Fidelity and Guaranty Ins. Co." but the style of the case listed only "JenCra, Inc. & Fidelity and" due to space constraints, omitting the remainder of Fidelity's title. The parties cite and rely on cases concerning restricted appeals (or before 1997, writs of error). But this appeal is from a motion for new trial. A brief review of the differences in these procedures shows why cases concerning one do not necessarily apply to the other.

A restricted appeal is filed directly in an appellate court. *See* TEX. R. APP. P. 30. As in any other appeal, the appellate court does not take testimony or receive evidence. Instead, the review is limited to errors apparent on the face of the record. *See Alexander v. Lynda's Boutique*, 134 S.W.3d 845, 848 (Tex. 2004). In such appeals, "[t]here are no presumptions in favor of valid issuance, service, and return of citation." *Primate Const., Inc. v. Silver*, 884 S.W.2d 151, 152 (Tex. 1994) (citations omitted). Circumstances require this last rule, because presumptions can neither be confirmed nor rebutted by evidence in an appellate court. Thus, for example, if the citation says an amended petition was attached (which named the defaulted party) and the return says the original petition was served (which did not), an appellate court cannot tell from the record which is true. *Id.* Similarly, if the petition says the registered agent for service is "Henry Bunting, Jr." but the citation and return reflect service on "Henry Bunting," an appellate court cannot tell whether those persons are different or the same. *See Uvalde Country Club v. Martin Linen Supply Co., Inc.*, 690 S.W.2d 884, 885 (Tex. 1985).

By contrast, when a default judgment is attacked by motion for new trial or bill of review in the trial court, the record is not so limited. In those proceedings, the parties may introduce affidavits, depositions, testimony, and exhibits to explain what happened. *See Gold v. Gold*, 145 S.W.3d 212, 214 (Tex. 2004) (per curiam). That being the case, these procedures focus on what has always been and always should be the critical question in any default judgment: "Why did the defendant not appear?"

If the answer to this critical question is "Because I didn't get the suit papers," the default generally must be set aside. *See Peralta v. Heights Med. Ctr., Inc.*, 485 U.S. 80, 84, 108 S.Ct. 896, 99 L.Ed.2d 75 (1988) ("Failure to give notice violates the most rudimentary demands of due process of law."); *Caldwell v. Barnes*, 154 S.W.3d 93, 96-97 (Tex. 2004). Exceptions to this rule exist when nonreceipt is uncorroborated, *see Primate Constr.*, 884 S.W.2d at 152, or was a bill-of-review claimant's own fault, *see Campus Invs., Inc. v. Cullever*, 144 S.W.3d 464, 466 (Tex. 2004).

But if the answer to the critical question is "I got the suit papers but then . . .," the default judgment should be set aside only if the defendant proves the three familiar *Craddock* elements. *See Craddock v. Sunshine Bus Lines*, 134 Tex. 388, 133 S.W.2d 124, 126 (1939) (requiring new trial if defendant shows (1) default was neither intentional nor conscious indifference, (2) meritorious defense, and (3) new trial would cause neither delay nor undue prejudice).

In this case, undisputed evidence presented on the motion for new trial showed that Fidelity's registered agent received the suit papers. Thus, the only relevance of the partial omission of Fidelity's name is its possible role in the *Craddock* analysis. While errors in suit papers might mislead a defendant into failing to answer, Fidelity makes no such assertion here. Because Fidelity's failure to answer had nothing to do with this omission, it provides no ground for setting aside the default judgment by motion for new trial.

Second, Fidelity argues that the default should be set aside because it was served with Drewery's original petition, which was later amended before the default judgment. But the only difference in the two petitions was an amendment to allow long-arm service on JenCra by serving the Secretary of State. *See generally* TEX. CIV. PRAC. & REM. CODE, Chapter 17. Service of an amended petition on a party that has not appeared is necessary only when a plaintiff "seeks a more onerous judgment than prayed for in the original pleading." *Weaver v. Hartford Accident & Indem. Co.*, 570 S.W.2d 367, 370 (Tex. 1978). That was not the case here.

Fidelity's last argument finds better traction. Of the three *Craddock* elements needed to set aside a default, Drewery argues, and the court of appeals held, that Fidelity failed to establish only the first—whether the default was the result of accident or mistake. Fidelity attached four affidavits to its motion for new trial that establish the following facts. Fidelity's registered agent for service, Corporation Service Company (CSC), received Drewery's petition and citation. Though in the ordinary course of business CSC would forward an electronic scan of the documents to a Fidelity affiliate, computer records show this never occurred. As a backup, in the ordinary course of business CSC would forward the service documents themselves to the same affiliate, where they were compared with the electronic copy and then discarded after 90 days. As 90 days had passed before Fidelity learned of the default, all the records received during that time had been discarded. Thus, neither CSC nor Fidelity could verify whether Drewery's suit papers were actually forwarded by CSC to Fidelity. CSC averred that an employee of Fidelity's affiliate "acknowledged receipt of the Petition," but the Fidelity agent who should have received them averred that she never did.

The court of appeals refused relief on the ground that Fidelity's affidavits did not explain what happened to the service documents:

> [T]here is no affidavit from a person who actually handled the citation explaining how the citation was lost or where in the chain of communication a breakdown occurred that led to Fidelity's failure to answer the citation. In this case, none of the affidavits Fidelity submitted explain what happened to the citation. Each affidavit stated that Fidelity's failure to answer was not intentional. However, a trial court cannot vacate a default judgment based only upon general allegations or conclusions.

188 S.W.3d at 679, 2005 WL 468323, at *5-6 (citations omitted).

We disagree that Fidelity's four affidavits were general or conclusory. To the contrary, they detail the procedures for handling service papers in general and what is known about Drewery's papers in particular. In the case of the electronic records, they explain precisely where the breakdown occurred—at data entry by CSC.

We also disagree that to establish that papers were lost there must be an affidavit from the person who lost them describing how it occurred. People often do not know where or how they lost something—that is precisely why it remains "lost." This Court has often set aside default judgments when papers were misplaced, though no one knew precisely how. *See Old Republic Ins. Co. v. Scott*, 873 S.W.2d 381, 382 (Tex. 1994) (reversing default when investigator averred that she believed suit papers were inadvertently included among files transferred to another adjustment company); *Estate of Pollack v. McMurrey*, 858 S.W.2d 388, 391 (Tex. 1993) (reversing default when unidentified person signed for papers and never delivered them to executrix); *Hanks v. Rosser*, 378 S.W.2d 31, 32, 36 (Tex. 1964) (reversing default when druggist testified he placed suit papers "on his prescription counter," that he "just lost them" and "never did find them").

We agree that a conclusory statement that documents were "lost" must generally be supported by some explanation from the person most likely to have seen them, or of the efforts made to find them. But the *Craddock* standard is one of intentional or conscious indifference—that the defendant knew it was sued but did not care. An excuse need not be a good one to suffice. *See Craddock*, 133 S.W.2d at 125.

The affidavits here show neither intent nor indifference. Instead, they detail Fidelity's efforts to establish a system that would avoid precisely what happened. As Drewery did not controvert this proof, the trial court was not at liberty to disregard it. *See Dir., State Employees Workers' Comp. Div. v. Evans*, 889 S.W.2d 266, 269 (Tex. 1994).

Accordingly, without hearing oral argument, we reverse the court of appeals' judgment and remand the case to the trial court for further proceedings consistent with this opinion. TEX. R. APP. P. 59.1.

Notes

1. *Levine v. Shackelford, Melton & McKinley, L.L.P.*, 248 S.W.3d 646 (Tex. 2008): Three law firms sued the Levine for legal fees. Levine's attorney knew of the 11/29/2004 deadline for answer in the suit. He agreed to file a general denial by that date, but he did not do so. He again failed to meet an extended deadline. Although he eventually emailed a draft denial to the parties, he never attempted to confirm that an answer was filed, despite repeated discussions, emails, and contact with the opposing party, warning him that if he did not file an answer, the law firms would take a default judgment. A default judgment was entered on 12/15/2004. The attorney did not even know until 12/23/2004, when his client informed him of the default judgment, that the clerk had not received the answer. The court of appeals affirmed the trial court's refusal to set aside the default judgment. In applying the *Craddock v. Sunshine Bus Lines, Inc.*, 133 S.W.2d 124, 126 (Tex. 1939), test to this case, the court of appeals stated that the evidence "showed a pattern of conduct that disregarded deadlines, promises, procedures, and simple steps that a person of reasonable sensibilities would have taken to ensure that the answer was properly and timely filed." Held: Affirmed. Though the court of appeals articulated the "conscious indifference" requirement of the *Craddock* test incorrectly, it properly applied the test. The *Craddock* standard is one of intentional or conscious indifference—that the defendant knew it was sued, but did not care. Still, the facts of this case show conscious indifference that was more than mere negligence.

2. *In the Interest of E.A.* , 287 S.W.3d 1 (2009): If a defendant is properly served with process, in order to have a default judgment set aside, she must prove the three elements set out in *Craddock v. Sunshine Bus Lines, Inc.*, 133 S.W.2d 124, 126 (Tex. 1939). But if the defendant never received the suit papers, she is generally entitled to a new trial without any further showing.

3. *Sutherland v. Spencer*, 376 S.W.3d 752 (Tex. 2012): Spencer sued Southern Customs under the DTPA for damages he allegedly sustained as a result of Southern Customs's failure to properly restore his 1965 Corvette. After Southern Customs failed to file an answer timely, Spencer obtained a default judgment. Southern Customs timely moved for a new trial under *Craddock v. Sunshine Bus Lines, Inc.*, 133 S.W.2d 124, 126 (Tex. 1939). The trial court denied the motion; and the court of appeals affirmed. ***Held*:** Contrary to the court of appeals' conclusion, Southern Custom's stated reason for failing to answer timely—"that the citation was left in a stack of papers on a desk and forgotten about because of limited time spent at the office due to weather conditions over a nearly three-week period during the Christmas holiday season"—if true, satisfies *Craddock*'s first requirement that the defendant establish that "the failure of the defendant to answer before judgment was not intentional, or the result of conscious indifference on his part, but was due to a mistake or an accident."

4. *Milestone Operating Inc. v. ExxonMobil Corp.*, --- S.W.3d ----, 56 Tex. Sup. Ct. J. 70, 2012 WL 5285085 (Tex.2012): The issue is whether Milestone established that it's no answer-default judgment in ExxonMobil's contract-breach action was unintentional and not the result of conscious indifference. Milestone moved for a new trial after the default judgment, arguing that service was defective service and that its failure to

answer satisfied the *Craddock v. Sunshine Bus Lines* elements to set aside the judgment. The trial court denied the motion and the court of appeals affirmed in part, holding that Milestone's argument on the first *Craddock* element—unintentional or without conscious indifference—failed. The Supreme Court HOLDS that Milestone's failure to answer was neither intentional nor indifferent. A defendant satisfies its burden under this first element when its factual assertions, if true, negate intentional or consciously indifferent conduct and the plaintiff does not controvert these factual assertions. Milestone contended that its registered agent, a director, did not recall being served with ExxonMobil's petition, even after reviewing his office notes and speaking to the people with whom he works about that day's events. He testified that Milestone had been sued at least four times before ExxonMobil's suit, he was served in each of those suits and his routine was to turn over the suit papers to Milestone's legal counsel. Yet he testified that he did not remember being served or turning over any suit papers to Milestone's legal counsel in this case. Although the process server's fiancée's testified she saw Milestone's agent take the papers, ExxonMobil did not controvert his testimony that he did not recall being served.

STATE EMPLOYEES WORKERS' COMPENSATION
v.
EVANS

889 S.W.2d 266
(Tex. 1994)

Barbara L. Stroud, Austin, for petitioner.
Tom L. Ragland, Waco, for respondent.

GONZALEZ, JUSTICE.

The dispositive issue presented in this workers' compensation case is whether the trial court abused its discretion in refusing to set aside a default judgment and grant a motion for new trial. Specifically at issue is whether a movant is required to introduce evidence at the hearing on its motion for new trial in order to satisfy the test in *Craddock v. Sunshine Bus Lines, Inc.*, 134 Tex. 388, 133 S.W.2d 124 (1939), when the movant has attached affidavits in support of its motion. The trial court, without the State being present, proceeded to trial and found the worker totally and permanently incapacitated and awarded her lump-sum benefits of $92,218.80. The trial court overruled the State's motion for new trial, and the court of appeals affirmed. 835 S.W.2d 230. We reverse the judgment of the court of appeals and remand for trial.

Paulette Evans filed a workers' compensation action against the State for injuries allegedly sustained during her employment at the Mexia State School. The trial was originally set for March 26, 1990, but Ms. Evans moved for a continuance. The trial was reset for March 25, 1991, with an alternate setting of May 28, 1991. On February 28, 1991, the assistant attorney general handling the case, Lance Sharp, requested that the trial date be changed to April 22, 1991. Counsel for Ms. Evans agreed, and a letter was sent to the clerk resetting the case for April 22.

Mr. Sharp subsequently resigned from the attorney general's office effective April 19, 1991. Barbara Stroud, who assumed responsibility for Mr. Sharp's case load, was informed that this case was set for trial on May 28, 1991. Ms. Stroud asserts that she was unaware that the State and Ms. Evans had agreed to an April 22, 1991 trial date due to Mr. Sharp's failure to record the trial date on his calendar or to note the trial date in the case file. The State did not make an appearance at the trial, and a post-answer default judgment was taken against the State.

After Ms. Stroud received a copy of the judgment, the State timely filed a Motion to Set Aside Default Judgment and Motion for New Trial. The State contended in its motion that it was entitled to a new trial because Ms. Evans failed to comply with the statutory ten-day notice requirement applicable to default judgments against the State and because the State met the three-part *Craddock* test. The trial court denied the State's motion. The court of appeals affirmed, 835 S.W.2d at 232, holding that the court could not consider the State's affidavits attached to its motion for new trial since they were not introduced at the hearing. We reverse the judgment of the court of appeals because the trial court abused its discretion in refusing to grant a new trial.

MOTION FOR NEW TRIAL

The court of appeals held that the trial court "did not abuse its discretion in denying the motion for new trial because the State did not meet its burden on any of the *Craddock* tests when it failed to offer any evidence." 835 S.W.2d at 232. The court of appeals erred in relying on *Carey Crutcher, Inc. v. Mid-Coast Diesel Services, Inc.*, 725 S.W.2d 500, 502 (Tex. App.—Corpus Christi 1987, no writ), which held that the failure to offer into evidence affidavits attached to a motion for new trial precludes the affidavits from being considered for purposes of the meritorious defense element of the *Craddock* test. *Carey Crutcher*, the cornerstone of the court of appeals' analysis, is clearly wrong. The holding in *Carey Crutcher* conflicts with the procedure for motions for new trial set out in *Strackbein v. Prewitt*, 671 S.W.2d 37, 38-39 (Tex. 1984), and *Ivy v. Carrell*, 407 S.W.2d 212, 215 (Tex. 1966). Affidavits attached to the motion for new trial do not have to be offered into evidence in order to be considered by the trial court for the meritorious defense element or any other element of the *Craddock* test. *See Strackbein*, 671 S.W.2d at 38-39. It is sufficient that the affidavits are attached to the motion for new trial and are part of the record.

Craddock Test

Craddock provides that a default judgment should be set aside and a new trial ordered in any case in which: [1] the failure of the defendant to answer before judgment was not intentional, or the result of conscious indifference on his part, but was due to a mistake or an accident; [2] provided the motion for a new trial sets up a meritorious defense and [3] is filed at a time when the granting thereof will occasion no delay or otherwise work an injury to the plaintiff. 133 S.W.2d at 126; accord, *Old Republic Ins. Co. v. Scott*, 873 S.W.2d 381 (Tex. 1994); *Estate of Pollack v. McMurrey*, 858 S.W.2d 388, 390 (Tex. 1993). The prerequisites for setting aside a no-answer default judgment have been applied to post-answer default judgments. *See, e.g., Cliff v. Huggins*, 724 S.W.2d 778, 779 (Tex. 1987); *Grissom v. Watson*, 704 S.W.2d 325, 326 (Tex. 1986). A motion for new trial is addressed to the trial court's discretion and the court's ruling will not be disturbed on appeal in the absence of a showing of an abuse of discretion. *Cliff*, 724 S.W.2d at 778-79. However, a trial court abuses its discretion by not granting a new trial when all three elements of the *Craddock* test are met. *Bank One, Texas, N.A. v. Moody*, 830 S.W.2d 81, 85 (Tex. 1992).

Consciously Indifferent or Intentional Conduct

In *Strackbein*, we held that when the factual allegations in a movant's affidavits are not controverted, the question of conscious indifference must be determined in the same manner as a claim of meritorious defense. 671 S.W.2d at 38. As with a claim of meritorious defense, it is sufficient if the motion and affidavits set forth facts which, if true, would negate intentional or consciously indifferent conduct. *Id.* at 38-39. The trial court is required to test the motion for new trial and the accompanying affidavits against the requirements of *Craddock*. *Id.* at 39; *Cliff*, 724 S.W.2d at 780. If the motion and affidavits meet those requirements, a new trial should be granted. *Strackbein*, 671 S.W.2d at 39; *See Cliff*, 724 S.W.2d at 778.

In *Strackbein*, since there was no record of the hearing and the nonmovant did not file controverting affidavits, the movant's evidence was uncontroverted and supported the requirements of *Craddock*. The court of appeals could only look to the evidence before it (the motion and supporting affidavits) to determine if the trial court abused its discretion in denying a new trial. *Strackbein* does not require a movant to introduce its supporting affidavits as evidence in order for them to be considered by the trial court. In the case at hand, although there were affidavits filed by the nonmovant and a record of the hearing was preserved, nothing presented was sufficient to controvert the factual assertions in the State's motion for new trial and attached affidavits.

"In determining whether the failure to appear was due to intentional disregard or conscious indifference we must look to the knowledge and acts of the defendant." *Strackbein*, 671 S.W.2d at 39. If the factual assertions in the defendant's affidavit are not controverted by the plaintiff, the defendant satisfies his burden if his affidavit sets forth facts that, if true, negate intentional or consciously indifferent conduct by the defendant. *Id.* at 38-39. In determining if the defendant's factual assertions are controverted, the court looks to all the evidence in the record. The evidence in this record consists of the State's motion and affidavits, including those of Defendant's Counsel, Barbara Stroud and Lance D. Sharp, Ms. Evans' response to the motion and affidavits, and Ms. Evans' evidence (oral testimony and exhibits) introduced at the hearing.

The State's motion and the affidavits of Ms. Stroud and Mr. Sharp state facts that negate the possibility that the State's failure to appear was intentional or the result of conscious indifference. Ms. Stroud's predecessor simply misdated the trial date on his calendar and conveyed the wrong information to Ms. Stroud when she replaced him. Ms. Stroud believed the case was set for a later date, thus, her failure to appear was not intentional, but was due to an accident or mistake. Ms. Stroud's affidavit states that she did not become aware of the actual trial setting until after the default judgment. Ms. Stroud then checked with Mr. Sharp's former secretary, Connie Hughes, who showed her Mr. Sharp's reading files which included the letter from Mr. Sharp to Ms. Evans setting the trial date for April 22, 1991. The State's motion and supporting affidavits clearly satisfy the requirements of *Craddock*, if uncontroverted.

Ms. Evans' response to the motion for new trial alleges that the State failed to negate that three employees of the State Employees Workers' Compensation Division and the secretary to the attorney for the defendant had knowledge of the trial setting. In addition, Ms. Evans' response states that in Ms. Stroud's affidavit Ms. Stroud states that she "reviewed the files maintained by Mr. Sharp [former attorney for the defendant] 'and found a February 28, 1991 letter from Sharp' that 'stated that trial was scheduled for April 22, 1991.' " Ms. Evans further alleged that the State "failed to establish that its failure to appear at the trial on the merits, at its request, was not intentional and was not the result of conscious indifference." Ms. Evans' supporting affidavit by Tom Ragland, her attorney, does not controvert any facts related to conscious indifference or delay.

At the hearing, the State presented its arguments to the judge and the affidavits submitted with the motion for new trial were brought to the attention of the trial court. Ms. Evans' attorney, Mr. Ragland, presented oral testimony and exhibits establishing the trial date setting and the letters sent to Mr. Sharp and other State employees regarding the case.

Although Ms. Evans argues that employees of the State, including Mr. Sharp and Ms. Stroud's secretary, knew about the trial setting, Ms. Evans does not specifically controvert the statement of Ms. Stroud's belief that the case was set for a later date. *See Bank One, N.A.*, 830 S.W.2d at 85 (holding that the nonmovant did not controvert the statement of the movant's belief and thus, the first element of the *Craddock* test was satisfied). In the absence of controverting evidence that the State's failure to appear was due to its intentional act or conscious indifference, the State's affidavits should, for the purpose of establishing lack of conscious indifference, be taken as true.[1] *Estate of Pollack*, 858 S.W.2d at 391.

Meritorious Defense

Setting up a meritorious defense is determined on the facts alleged in the movant's motion and supporting affidavits, regardless of whether those facts are controverted. *See e.g., Ivy*, 407 S.W.2d at 214; *see also Strackbein*, 671 S.W.2d at 38-39. It is sufficient that the movant's motion and affidavits set forth facts which in law constitute a meritorious defense. *Id.; Estate of Pollack*, 858 S.W.2d at 392.

---

1 [For the purposes of this book, only selected footnotes which appear in the various court's opinions will be used. Instead of using the specific court's numbering system all footnotes will be numbered consecutively in each Chapter.] For examples of cases in which intentional disregard or conscious indifference was not found and a new trial was granted, *see Strackbein*, 671 S.W.2d at 39 (secretary was told to mail documents, but did not because she thought the defendant had mailed them); *Craddock*, 133 S.W.2d at 125 (insurance company inadvertently placed defendant's citation with mail not requiring immediate attention); State Farm Life Ins. Co. v. Mosharaf, 794 S.W.2d 578 (Tex. App.—Houston [1st Dist.] 1990, writ denied) (insurance company made a filing mistake and the file never made it to the right person); Southland Paint Co. v. Thousand Oaks Racket Club, 724 S.W.2d 809 (Tex. App.—San Antonio 1986, writ ref'd n.r.e.) (answer was filed late due to staff shortage at defendant's insurance broker's office); Evans v. Woodward, 669 S.W.2d 154 (Tex. App.—Dallas 1984, no writ) (failure to file answer was due to confusion in attorney's office rather than indifference on defendant's part); Drake v. McGalin, 626 S.W.2d 786 (Tex. Civ. App.—Beaumont 1981, no writ) (answer prepared by secretary was presumably lost by volunteer exchange student who was assisting defendant's attorney as an office boy); Dallas Heating Co., Inc. v. Pardee, 561 S.W.2d 16 (Tex. Civ. App.—Dallas 1977, writ ref'd n.r.e.) (suit papers were inadvertently misplaced in defendant's office); Leonard v. Leonard, 512 S.W.2d 771 (Tex. Civ. App.—Corpus Christi 1974, writ dism'd w.o.j.) (attorney misplaced file); Continental Airlines Inc. v. Carter, 499 S.W.2d 673 (Tex. Civ. App.—El Paso 1973, no writ) (inadvertence by secretary in failing to note on calendar date answer was due); Republic Bankers Life Ins. Co. v. Dixon, 469 S.W.2d 646 (Tex. Civ. App.—Tyler 1971, no writ) (attorney forgot to prepare answer when his secretary placed the file with his general files rather than his active files); *and* Reynolds v. Looney, 389 S.W.2d 100 (Tex. Civ. App.—Eastland 1965, writ ref'd n.r.e.) (the citation was mislaid in insurance company's office).

The State alleges that Ms. Evans was injured in an automobile accident following her alleged job-related injury and that this accident, and not the job-related injury, was the cause of her damages. The facts, if true, would establish a sole cause defense. The State also alleges the defense of a credit or offset.

Delay or Injury

The third requirement of *Craddock* is that the motion for new trial be filed at a time when the granting thereof will occasion no delay or otherwise work an injury to the plaintiff. *Craddock*, 133 S.W.2d at 126. Once a defendant has alleged that granting a new trial will not injure the plaintiff, the burden of going forward with proof of injury shifts to the plaintiff. *Cliff*, 724 S.W.2d at 779; *Angelo v. Champion Restaurant Equip. Co.*, 713 S.W.2d 96, 98 (Tex. 1986). An equitable principle is involved and the court should deal with the facts on a case by case basis in order to do equity. *Id.* The goal to be achieved is to not unduly delay or injure the plaintiff by granting the motion. *Id.*

In its motion for new trial, in supporting affidavits, and at the hearing, the State offered to go to trial immediately and to reimburse Ms. Evans for the expenses incurred in obtaining the default judgment.[2] Ms. Evans' attorney testified that granting the motion for new trial would provide a financial hardship to Ms. Evans because the State has not paid her weekly benefits, or her medical bills, nor offered to provide her medical care. Mr. Ragland further testified that he had upcoming trials that might conflict with a new trial setting. The purpose of this element of the *Craddock* test, however, is to protect a plaintiff against the sort of undue delay or injury that would disadvantage her in presenting the merits of her case at a new trial, such as a loss of witnesses or other valuable evidence. *Id.* Thus, Ms. Evans' allegations fail to show an injury that would negate the State's showing of no undue delay or injury.

In summary, the State's motion for new trial and uncontroverted attached affidavits satisfy the *Craddock* test. Thus, the trial court's denial of the State's motion for new trial was an abuse of discretion. Accordingly, we reverse the judgment of the court of appeals and remand for trial.

CARPENTER
v.
CIMARRON HYDROCARBONS CORPORATION

98 S.W.3d 682
(Tex. 2002)

Issue: Is it reversible error for a trial court to deny a motion to file a late response?

Issue stated another way: Does Craddock apply to aid a party, who fails to timely respond to a motion for summary judgment, when another remedy, such a motion for continuance, is available under the Rules?

Held: Not if another remedy was available to the complaining party. *Craddock v. Sunshine Bus Lines*, 133 S.W.2d 124 (Tex. 1939) does not apply to a motion for new trial filed after summary judgment is granted on a motion to which the nonmovant failed to timely respond when the respondent had notice of the hearing and an opportunity to employ the means our civil procedural rules make available to alter the deadlines TEX. R. CIV. P. 166a imposes. When the rules provide the defaulting party a remedy, Craddock does not apply. Here, the rules provided the plaintiff an opportunity to obtain leave to file a late response to the summary-judgment motion.

Issue: When should a trial court grant a motion for leave to file a late response to a motion for summary judgment?

A motion for leave to file a late summary-judgment response should be granted when the nonmovant establishes good cause by showing that the failure to timely respond (1) was not intentional or the result of conscious indifference, but the result of an accident or mistake, and (2) that allowing the late response will occasion no

---

[2] The willingness of a party to go to trial immediately and pay the expenses of the default judgment are important factors for the court to look to in determining whether it should grant a new trial. They are not dispositive of whether the motion should be granted. *See Cliff*, 724 S.W.2d at 779 (holding that an offer to reimburse plaintiff for costs is not a precondition, but an important factor for trial court to look at in determining whether it should grant a new trial); *Angelo*, 713 S.W.2d at 98 (noting that courts look more favorably upon defendants ready, willing and able to go to trial almost immediately).

undue delay or otherwise injure the party seeking summary judgment. Because the plaintiff here did not establish good cause, the trial court did not abuse its discretion in denying plaintiff's motion. Nor did the trial court err in denying plaintiff's motion for new trial on this basis.

DOLGENCORP OF TEXAS, INC.
v.
LERMA
288 S.W.3d 922
(Tex. 2009)

Facts: This appeal arises from a post-answer default judgment, entered against Dolgencorp of Texas, Inc., d/b/a Dollar General Store ("Dollar General"), when its counsel failed to appear for trial, because he was in a preferential trial setting in another county. Dollar General filed a motion for new trial, asserting that Harrison's failure to appear was not intentional, nor the result of conscious indifference, and the default judgment should be set aside. Dollar General established it was entitled to a new trial pursuant to the factors set out in *Craddock v. Sunshine Bus Lines, Inc*., 133 S.W.2d 124, 126 (Tex. 1939). Harrison was actually in trial in Harris County when he failed to appear in Cameron County for the Dollar General suit. At the motion for new trial hearing, Harrison testified, that when he realized he had a conflicting preferential trial setting, he sent his associate, Sachitano, to announce the conflict at docket call for the Dollar General suit. In addition, while he was in trial in Harris County, he asked the Harris County judge and trial coordinator to call and notify the Cameron County trial court that he was still in trial. He also instructed his associate and secretary to call and apprise the Cameron County court of his status. The court coordinator for the Cameron County trial court submitted an affidavit confirming the fact that she received calls from the Harris County judge and trial coordinator, as well as Sachitano and his secretary, each of whom confirmed that Harrison would be in trial in Harris County, beyond his scheduled trial date for the Dollar General suit. Dollar General provided affidavits from Sachitano, his secretary, and the Harris County coordinator verifying the communications. After conducting an evidentiary hearing, the trial court denied the motion. The court of appeals affirmed. 241 S.W.3d 584. **Held**: Reversed and remanded for a new trial. The attorney's failure to appear was not intentional or due to conscious indifference, because he was actually in trial in another county, and believed, based upon his credible explanation, that the court would grant a continuance for that reason. He did not know that trial was scheduled for Feb. 26, when the trial court started without him. The attorney attempted to resolve the conflict before trial, apprised the court of his whereabouts the day of trial, and provided a credible explanation for why he believed the court would delay trial.

Issue: When A post-judgment default judgment is reversed, should it be remanded, even though the Plaintiff's evidence was insufficient?

Held: Yes. Generally, if an appellate court holds that there is legally insufficient evidence to support a judgment, after a trial on the merits, the proper disposition is to reverse and render judgment. But, in *Holt Atherton Indus., Inc. v. Heine,* 835 S.W.2d 80, 86 (Tex. 1992); it was determined that when a plaintiff fails to present legally sufficient evidence at an uncontested hearing on unliquidated damages, following a no-answer default judgment, the proper disposition is to remand for a new trial on the issue of damages. It was reasoned that the plaintiff should be afforded a second opportunity to present evidence in support of its claims, because, as a practical matter, in an uncontested hearing, evidence of unliquidated damages is often not fully developed. *Held*: The rule expressed *in Holt Atherton,* should apply to post-answer default judgments, as well as no answer defaults. Thus, when the default is reversed on appeal, the case should be remanded for a new trial, after a post-answer default judgment, rather than rendering judgment.

Judges and lawyers should extend common and professional courtesies to other judges and lawyers.

Notes

1. During the period 1918-1945 the Commission of Appeals assisted the Supreme Court with its workload. Cases were assigned to the Commission by the Supreme Court. The Commission would hear a case, enter a judgment, and issue a written opinion. If the Supreme Court adopted the opinion of the Commission, the opinion had the full authority of a Texas Supreme Court decision. Approval by the Texas Supreme Court of the holding of a Commission decision, signified that the Court approved the judgment and adopted each specific holding of

the Commission, but did not necessarily approve the reasoning of the Commission. If the Supreme Court merely adopted the judgment of the Commission, the Supreme Court neither approved specific holdings, nor reasonings, but found no compelling reason to reverse the Commission's decision. The opinion in every case decided by the Commission of Appeals after 1934 was adopted by the Texas Supreme Court.

2. It is an abuse of discretion for a trial court to overrule an uncontested timely filed motion for new trial, supported by affidavit proof containing factual evident that, if true, satisfies the *Craddock* requirements.[1]

3. A mistake of law is sufficient to satisfy the first prong of the *Craddock* test.[2]

4. a. *Time to Act.*

1) *Original Motion.* The motion must ". . . be filed prior to or within thirty days after the judgment or other order complained of is signed."[3] TEX. R. CIV. P. 5 expressly prohibits that trial court from enlarging the period for taking a new trial.[4] However, the trial court can, within its discretion, consider late filed motions, filed during its period of plenary power.[5]

Citation By Publication. TEX. R. CIV. P. 329 sets up a special two-year period for new trials following service of citation by publication. The procedure to be followed in such a situation is discussed in W. DORSANEO, 6 TEXAS LITIGATION GUIDE § 140.01[7] (1989).

2) *Amended Motions.* Before this decade of procedural change, a party could file only one amended motion for new trial. Now, one or more amendments to the motion may be filed, but the filing must be within the same thirty day period of time following the signing of the judgment and must be before the motion for new trial is overruled.[6] The filing of the amendment does not gain extra time.[7] However, an amended motion filed after the thirty day period can be considered by the trial court, if it is filed during the period when the court has plenary power.[8] The late filed amended motion does not preserve error for appeal, and is meaningless unless acted upon by the trial court.[9]

3) *Late Notice.* Under TEX. R. CIV. P. 306a (4) and (5), a party who does not receive notice, or gain actual knowledge, of the signing of a judgment, has up to ninety additional days to perfect the appeal. The party must:

a) not have received notice or actual knowledge within twenty days after the judgment is signed;

b) receive notice or acquire actual knowledge within ninety days after the judgment was signed;

c) prove in the trial court, on sworn motion and notice, the date on which the party first acquired notice or actual knowledge of the signing <u>and</u> that this date was more than twenty days after the judgment was signed.

When this is done, all the periods mentioned in TEX. R. CIV. P. 306a(1) begin on the date of notice or actual knowledge of the signing, ". . . but in no event shall such periods begin more than ninety days after the original judgment or other appealable order was signed."[10] Motions for new trial are expressly mentioned in TEX. R. CIV. P. 306a(1) as one of the periods which can be extended.

---

1 Old Republic v. Scott, 873 S.W.2d 381, 873 S.W.2d 381 (Tex. 1994).

2 Bank One, Texas v. Moody, 830 S.W.2d 81 (Tex. 1992).

3 Jackson v. Van Winkle, 660 S.W.2d 807, 808 (Tex. 1983); TEX. R. CIV. P. 329b(a).

4 Smith v. Caney Creek Estates Club, Inc., 631 S.W.2d 233, 234 (Tex. App.—Corpus Christi 1982, no writ).

5 Independent Life Ins. Co. of Am. v. Work, 124 Tex. 281, 77 S.W.2d 1036, 1040 (1934). *But see* Equinox Enter. Inc. v. Associated Media Inc., 730 S.W.2d 872 (Tex. App.—Dallas 1987, no writ).

6 Lind v. Gresham, 672 S.W.2d 20 (Tex. App.—Houston [14th Dist.] 1984, no writ).

7 TEX. R. CIV. P. 329b(a)(b).

8 Baker v. Wal-Mart Stores, Inc., 727 S.W.2d 53 (Tex. App.—Beaumont 1987, no writ).

9 Jackson v. Van Winkle, 660 S.W.2d 807 (Tex. 1983).

10 TEX. R. CIV. P. 306a (4).

Stated simply, motions for new trial filed within thirty days after the defaulting defendant receives notice or actual knowledge of a default judgment are timely,[11] if not more than ninety days has passed since the original judgment was signed.[12]

4) *Court Action.*[13]

a) *General Power.* The court has until seventy-five days after the judgment is signed in which to act on the original or amended motions. Stated another way, the motion is overruled seventy-five days after the judgment is signed, unless it is determined by written order signed before the seventy-fifth day.[14] This is true whether there was a hearing on the motion for new trial or not.[15] Withdrawal of the motion for new trial by the movant terminates the trial court's power to act more than 30 days after the judgment is signed.[16]

b) *Plenary Power.* The trial court has plenary power over its judgment for thirty days after the judgment is signed, and if a motion for new trial is filed, until thirty days after the motion for new trial is overruled by operation of law or by written order.[17]

b. *Required Use.* A motion for new trial is required in a number of circumstances, but in particular, is required ". . . on a complaint on which evidence must be heard such as . . . [the] failure to set aside a judgment by default; . . . ." TEX. R. CIV. P. 324(b)(1).

c. *Procedural Requirements.*

1) *Leave of Court.* Leave of court is not required for the filing of the original or the amended motion.[18]

2) *Written.* The motion must be in writing and signed by the party or attorney.[19]

3) *Points.* The motion must detail the points (not grounds—the Rule was amended in 1981) relied on; it is insufficient to incorporate previous objections from other motions (such as motions for judgment n.o.v., etc.).[20]

4) *The Craddock Requirements.* A default judgment should be set aside and a motion for new trial should be granted where:

(a) The failure of the defendant to answer before judgment was not intentional, or the result of conscious indifference on the part of the defendant;

(b) but was due to a mistake or an accident;

---

[11] Equinox Enterprises, Inc. v. Associated Media Inc., 730 S.W.2d 872, 874 (Tex. App.—Dallas 1987, no writ).

[12] *But see* Looney v Gibraltar Sav. Ass'n, 695 S.W.2d 336 (Tex. App.—Amarillo 1985, no writ).

[13] It should be remembered that a trial court can grant a motion for new trial for a period of 30 days after the judgment is signed, even if no motion for new trial is filed. This power exists without the necessity for a motion, or it can be exercised for reasons not stated in a filed motion. 4 R. MCDONALD, TEXAS CIVIL PRACTICE § 18.03 (F. Elliott rev. 1984); *Spikes v. Smith*, 386 S.W.2d 346 (Tex. Civ. App.—Corpus Christi 1965, mandamus overruled); TEX. R. CIV. P. 320. The Court's discretion is practically unlimited. *Sandoval v. Rattikin*, 395 S.W.2d 889, 892 (Tex. Civ. App.—Corpus Christi 1965, writ ref'd n.r.e.), *cert. denied*, 385 U.S. 901 (1966), *rehearing denied*, 385 U.S. 964 (1966).

[14] Clark & Co. v. Giles, 639 S.W.2d 449 (Tex. 1982).

[15] Jackson v. Van Winkle, 660 S.W.2d 807, 808 (Tex. 1983).

[16] Rogers v. Clinton, 33 Tex. Sup. Ct. J. 554 (June 16, 1990).

[17] Philbrook v. Berry, 683 S.W.2d 378 (Tex. 1985); Mathes v. Kelton, 569 S.W.2d 876 (Tex. 1978) (the motion is voluntarily withdrawn by the movant); Transamerican Leasing Co. v. Three Bears, Inc., 567 S.W.2d 799 (Tex. 1978); TEX. R. CIV. P. 329b(d) & (e); Rogers v. Clinton, 33 Tex. Sup. Ct. J. 554 (June 16, 1990).

[18] TEX. R. CIV. P. 329b.

[19] TEX. R. CIV. P. 320.

[20] Wagner v. Foster, 161 Tex. 333, 341 S.W.2d 887 (1960); TEX. R. CIV. P. 321.

(c) provided the motion for a new trial sets up a meritorious defense and

(d) is filed at a time when the granting thereof will occasion no delay or otherwise work an injury to the plaintiff.

(1) *Conscious Indifference/Mistake or Accident.* The courts have been liberal in interpreting this element.[21] Only a "slight excuse" is necessary to justify setting aside the default judgment.[22]

Set Up. Where no controverting affidavits are filed, the conscious indifference question must be determined in the same manner as a claim of meritorious defense; i.e., it is enough to set up the lack of conscious indifference in the pleading and affidavit. Then, the motion should be granted if the movant's motion and affidavits set forth facts which, if true, would negate intentional or consciously indifferent conduct.[23]

(2) *Meritorious Defense. Craddock* does not require *proof* of a meritorious defense, only that it be *set up* by a motion alleging facts which would constitute a defense to the cause, and supported by affidavit or other evidence proving, prima facie, that the defendant has such meritorious defense. Once the meritorious defense is set up, it is improper to try the issue.[24]

Exceptions. In the context of a bill of review proceeding, the United States Supreme Court held *in Peralta v. Heights Medical Center, Inc.*,[25] that where the defendant had no notice of the suit, the requirement of proof of a meritorious defense offended due process. This holding has been extended to motions for new trial and the meritorious defense element will be dispensed with where the defendant is not given proper notice.[26]

(3) *Grant Will Not Delay/Reimbursement.* As pointed out in *Angelo v. Champion Restaurant Equip. Co.*,[27] courts of appeal look more favorably on those defendants, seeking motions for new trial, who are ready to go to trial almost immediately, and some courts of appeal require that the defendant offer to reimburse the plaintiff for costs involved in obtaining the default. The Supreme Court, in *Angelo*, however, held that the failure to offer reimbursement should not, in every instance, preclude the granting of a new trial. The goal is not to injure the plaintiff or unduly delay him by granting the motion.

(4) *Applicability of* Craddock. *Craddock* applies to post-answer defaults.[28] Included are defaults resulting from sanctions of striking the pleadings.[29]

d. *Post Answer Default.*

Post answer default judgments, where the defendant has answered, but fails to appear at trial, require that the plaintiff offer evidence and prove the case.[30] In this context, there is no admission of liability.[31]

---

[21] Harlen v. Pfeffer, 693 S.W.2d 543 (Tex. App.—San Antonio 1985, no writ) (mistake shown by both parties was each thought other contacted attorney to answer suit when neither had.)

[22] Butler v. Dal Tex Mach. & Tool Co., Inc., 627 S.W.2d 258 (Tex. App.—Fort Worth 1982, no writ); Beard v. McKinney 456 S.W.2d 451, 453 (Tex. Civ. App.—Houston [1st Dist.] 1970, no writ).

[23] Strackbein v. Prewitt, 671 S.W.2d 37 (Tex. 1984).

[24] Ivy v. Carrell, 407 S.W.2d 212, 214 (Tex. 1966).

[25] 485 U.S. 80, 108 S. Ct. 896, 99 L.Ed.2d 75 (1988).

[26] Lopez v. Lopez, 757 S.W.2d 721, 723 (Tex. 1988).

[27] 713 S.W.2d 96, 98 (Tex. 1986),

[28] *See* Cliff v. Huggins, 724 S.W.2d 778, 779 (Tex. 1987) *and* Grissom v. Watson, 704 S.W.2d 325, 326 (Tex. 1986).

[29] Equinox Enter., Inc. v. Associated Media Inc., 730 S.W.2d 872, 874 (Tex. App.—Dallas 1987, no writ).

[30] Frymire Eng'g Co., Inc. v. Grantham, 524 S.W.2d 680, 681 (Tex. 1975).

[31] Stoner v Thompson, 578 S.W.2d 679, 682 (Tex. 1979); W. DORSANEO, TEXAS LITIGATION GUIDE, § 100.07 (1990).

b. *Restricted Appeal to Court of Appeals in Civil Cases*

Read Rule 30 Texas Rules of Appellate Procedure.

Note

The procedure now known as a restricted appeal was formerly known as an appeal by writ of error from a trial court to a court of appeals. *See* Rule 45 of the former Texas Rules of Appellate Procedure. Although some of the procedures for perfecting an appeal by one who did not participate in a hearing that resulted in the judgment complained of have been modified under the new rule, there is no indication that the new rule concerning restricted appeals was intended to change the substantive law which had developed concerning the old writ of error. That law had been fairly well developed and defined as shown by the following cases. The new Rule, however, has been clarified to explicitly limit the application of the restricted appeal to an individual who did not participate in the hearing that resulted in the judgment complained of and who did not timely file a postjudgment motion or request for findings of facts and conclusion of law.

McEWEN
v.
HARRISON

162 Tex. 125, 345 S.W.2d 706
(1961)

Woodgate, Richards & McElhaney, Dallas, Robert A. Fanning, Dallas, for relator.

Thompson, Knight, Wright & Simmons, Dallas, David S. Kidder, Dallas, with firm, for respondent.

CALVERT, CHIEF JUSTICE.

In this direct proceeding in this court relator seeks a writ of mandamus against Honorable A. M. Harrison, Judge of the District Court of the 6th Judicial District and, alternatively, against Honorable W. L. Thornton, Judge of the District Court of the 44th Judicial District. Texaco, Inc., is also made a respondent. The writ is sought to compel the setting aside of an order entered by Judge Harrison while sitting for Judge Thornton.

The facts giving rise to the proceeding are as follows: On September 20, 1960 relator, seeking a recovery of damages for personal injuries, filed suit in the District Court of the 44th Judicial District against Texaco, Inc., Warren A. Roach, d/b/a Bob Roach Service Station, and L. F. Corrigan. It was alleged in relator's petition that service of citation could be had on Texaco by serving one of its agents at 3900 Singleton Blvd. in Dallas. Citation was duly issued and the sheriff's return thereon recites that it was executed as to Warren A. Roach d/b/a Bob Roach Texaco Service Station by delivering a copy of the citation and of the petition to Warren A. Roach and as to Texaco, Inc. by delivering copies to "Warren A. Roach."

Texaco failed to appear or answer, and on October 19, 1960 Judge Thornton, after hearing evidence as to the extent of relator's injuries, rendered a default judgment against Texaco. The judgment is regular on its face and recites that "though duly served with process" Texaco, Inc. failed to appear or answer but wholly made default. On November 22, 1960 relator non-suited the other two defendants and the default judgment against Texaco thereupon became final. No motion for new trial was filed by Texaco within the time prescribed by the Texas Rules of Civil Procedure.

On January 14, 1961, long after the judgment had become final, Texaco filed a motion to vacate the judgment on the ground that it was void because citation had not been served on any person designated by law as its agent for service. Judge Harrison, sitting for Judge Thornton, heard and granted the motion and entered an order vacating the judgment. Relator asserts that the order is expressly prohibited by Rule 329-b and is therefore a void order.

The parties agree that the motion to vacate which was granted by Judge Harrison may not be treated as a motion for new trial. It was not filed within the time prescribed by Rule 329-b of the Texas Rules of Civil Procedure for the filing of motions for new trial. They also agree that it may not be treated as a bill of review. It does not contain the allegations required to qualify it as such.

Rule 329-b, which governs time for filing and time for action on motions for new trial, contains the following provision: 'Judgments . . . shall become final after the expiration of thirty (30) days after the date of rendition of judgment or order overruling an original or amended motion for new trial. After the expiration of thirty (30) days from the date the judgment is rendered or motion for new trial overruled, the judgment cannot be set aside except by bill of review for sufficient cause, filed within the time allowed by law.'

Our question is whether the emphasized provision of the Rule provides the exclusive method by which the default judgment can be set aside. Respondent Texaco asserts it does not because the record reflects affirmatively that the default judgment is void for want of legal service of citation, and that a void judgment may be set aside in any recognized legal proceeding in the nature of a direct attack. It contends that a motion to vacate is a direct attack. * * *

The emphasized provision of Rule 329-b has had but little attention during its existence, even in cases tried in courts to which it was applicable. In cases involving the right to set aside a default judgment litigants and courts have been prone to ignore or overlook the provision, whether of statute or of Rule, and to decide them under common law rules. * * *

In none of the cases mentioned (and in none we have discovered), did the court undertake to point out the full extent of the applicability of the quoted provision or to mark out its limitations. It may be stated categorically that in adopting the emphasized provision of Rule 329-b it was not, and could not have been, the intention of this Court, nor could it have been the intention of the Legislature in enacting the statute, to limit the legal remedy of nonappealing victims of all default judgments to a bill of review. A bill of review filed in the proper court and against proper parties is one authorized method of making a direct attack on a judgment, *Hamblen v. Knight*, 60 Tex. 36; *Dunklin v. Land*, Tex. Civ. App., 297 S.W.2d 360, 362; 25 TEX. JUR. 586, Judgments, § 186, but to hold that it is the only method of doing so would, in some instances, lead to absurd results. That would be true in cases in which the court was without jurisdictional power to hear the case and render a judgment. By way of example, but not of limitation: If a suit for divorce or a suit for title to land should be filed in a county court and the court should render a judgment against a defaulting defendant, it would be absurd to hold that the defendant, although filing no timely motion for new trial and perfecting no appeal, could have the judgment vacated only by bill of review. In a bill of review proceeding the plaintiff must allege and prove that he was not negligent in suffering the default judgment to be rendered against him and that he has a meritorious defense to the suit. Our decisions require that the two issues be tried together so that the court may render a new final judgment. *Texas Employers' Ins. Ass'n v. Arnold*, 126 Tex. 466, 88 S.W.2d 473, 474; *Humphrey v. Harrell*, Tex. Com. App., 29 S.W.2d 963, 964. But after a trial of the bill of review in the cases used as examples, the county court would still have no jurisdictional power to render a judgment on the merits.

On the other hand, it would be equally absurd to hold that in spite of the provision of Rule 329-b all remedies in the nature of direct attacks available at any time in the history of our jurisprudence for review of void judgments are still available for review of all void judgments; that as to judgments deemed void in law, for whatever reason, the limiting express language of the Rule is wholly meaningless. We should give effect to the provision of the Rule when it may be done without denying relief from an unwarranted judgment to a diligent litigant. Accordingly, we construe the emphasized provision of Rule 329-b to mean that when the time for filing a motion for new trial has expired and relief may not be obtained by appeal, a proceeding in the nature of a bill of review is the exclusive method of vacating a default judgment rendered in a case in which the court had jurisdictional power to render it. Into this category will fall those cases in which a default judgment is asserted to be void for want of service, or of valid service, of process. This is in harmony with our holding in *Brown v. Clippenger*, 113 Tex. 364, 256 S.W. 254. With this construction of the Rule, we may assume, without deciding, that Texaco is correct when it says that the default judgment against it is a void judgment and that its motion to vacate is a direct attack on the judgment. We are yet compelled to hold that the order vacating the default judgment is unauthorized and void because the district court had jurisdictional power to determine the validity of the service (Indeed, it was its duty to do so) and to render the judgment, and Texaco's motion to vacate it does not qualify as a bill of review.

Our construction of the emphasized provision of the Rule will expedite the final disposition of litigation. To that extent it will aid in the administration of justice. It can lead to no grave injustice. If a defendant in a suit negligently suffers a default judgment to be rendered against him by a court having the jurisdictional power to render it, or negligently permits it to become final, he should not be heard to say that the judgment is void. And if he has no meritorious defense to the suit, the setting aside of the judgment would be a vain act and a trespass on the time of the court. If, on the other hand, a defendant has not been negligent in suffering a default judgment to be rendered against him by a court which had jurisdictional power to render it, or in permitting it to become final, and if he has a meritorious defense to the suit, he may still have the suit tried on its merits with the right to require the plaintiff to prove his case and the corresponding right to establish his defense. *Texas Employers' Ins. Ass'n v. Arnold*, 126 Tex. 466, 88 S.W.2d 473, 474; *Wear v. McCallum*, 119 Tex. 473, 33 S.W.2d 723, 724.

Our construction of the Rule will give a diligent defendant with a meritorious defense every opportunity to protect himself against an unwarranted default judgment. If he is not served with citation and learns of the judgment within 30 days after its rendition, he may file a motion for new trial, which the court is at liberty to grant, and if his motion is overruled he may obtain relief by appeal. If he does not learn of the judgment within 30 days after its rendition but does learn of it within six months, and the invalidity of the judgment is disclosed by the papers on file in the case, he may obtain relief by prosecuting writ of error to a Court of Civil Appeals. Article 2255, *V.A.T.S.; Flynt v. City of Kingsville*, 125 Tex. 510, 82 S.W.2d 934.

If the judgment is one which the court had jurisdictional power to render but it is invalid, he may obtain relief by bill of review as provided in Rule 329-b whether the invalidity is or is not disclosed by the papers on file in the case. Only if a court had no jurisdictional power to render the judgment should a negligent defendant or one with no meritorious defense to the suit be able to relieve himself of the burdens and consequences of a default judgment.

We are not unmindful of the recent cases of *Consolidated Underwriters v. McCauley*, Tex.Civ.App., 320 S.W.2d 60, writ refused, n. r. e. (on prior appeal, Tex.Civ.App., 301 S.W.2d 181, reversed, 157 Tex. 475, 304 S.W.2d 265), and *Freeman v. Freeman*, Tex.Sup., 327 S.W.2d 428, in which we upheld orders on motions, in substantially the same form as the motion before us, to vacate void judgments. In McCauley, the default judgment was rendered after the case had been removed to and while it was pending in a United States District Court. The state district court therefore had no jurisdictional power to render the default judgment because no case in which it could be rendered was pending before it. In Freeman, exclusiveness of remedy by bill of review as provided in Rule 329-b was not presented or decided.

We hold that appeal by writ of error or a bill of review to set aside the judgment are the exclusive methods by which Texaco may have the default judgment vacated or set aside. It follows that the order entered by Judge Harrison is void. We assume that Hon. W.L. Thornton or Honorable A.M. Harrison will set aside the order vacating the default judgment and will reinstate that judgment. Writ of mandamus will issue only if they decline to do so.

Our judgment here is without prejudice to the right of Texaco, Inc. to file an appeal by writ of error or to file a bill of review to set aside the default judgment against it.

WALKER, J., not sitting.

Note

Mandamus is not an appropriate means of reviewing a final default judgment rendered while the trial court had jurisdiction to do so. Instead, after the time for regular appeal has run, such a judgment may be attacked only by restricted appeal or equitable bill of review.[1]

[1] *In re Barber*, 982 S.W.2d 364 (Tex. 1998) (Opinion by CHIEF JUSTICE PHILLIPS, dissenting opinion by JUSTICE BAKER, joined by JUSTICE SPECTOR).

TEXACO
v.
McEWEN

356 S.W.2d 809
(Tex. Civ. App.—Dallas 1962, writ ref'd n.r.e.)

Fanning, Billings, Harper, Pierce & Gilley
Woodgate, Richards & McElhaney, Dallas, for respondent.

WILLIAMS, JUSTICE.

This case reaches this Court by petition for Writ of Error filed by Texaco, Inc., against Faye McEwen, a feme sole, seeking to set aside a default judgment against petitioner. Arts. 2249, 2249a and 2255, Vernon's Ann. Civ. St.

On September 20, 1960 Faye McEwen, sued three defendants, Warren A. Roach, d/b/a Bob Roach Texaco Service Station; Texaco, Inc.; and L. F. Corrigan. In her petition in the District Court she alleged that on February 19, 1960 she was caused to fall and injure herself while crossing a driveway of the Bob Roach Texaco Service Station in Dallas, Texas. She alleged that each of the named defendants were negligent and sought recovery, jointly and severally in the amount of $56,486.73. Her petition alleged that "plaintiff is a resident of Dallas County, Texas; defendant, Warren A. Roach can be served for process at the Bob Roach Texaco Service Station, 4700 block Lemmon Ave., Texaco, Inc. is a corporation licensed to do business in this State and can be served for process, through one of its agents, 3900 Singleton Blvd., Dallas, Texas; L. F. Corrigan can be served for process at the Corrigan Tower Building, Dallas, Texas." The petition did not allege any legal relationship between the three named defendants.

Citation, with return thereon, was filed on September 23rd, 1960, the essential part of said return being as follows: "Came to hand on the 20th day of Sept. 1960 at 11:39 o'clock A.M. Executed at Dallas, Texas, within the County of Dallas at _____ o'clock _ M on the day of ___ 19 __, by delivering to the within named Warren A. Roach, d/b/a Bob Roach Texaco Service Station, Texaco, Inc. by delivering to Warren A. Roach on September 20, A.D. 1960 at 2:10 o'clock P.M., and L. F. Corrigan on September 22, A.D. 1960 at 2:25 o'clock P.M., defendants, each, in person, a true copy of this citation together with the accompanying copy of this petition, having first indorsed on same the date of delivery."

The return was signed by M. M. Gossett, Deputy for Roby Love, Constable, Precinct No. 1, Dallas County, Texas. Thereafter answers were filed by Warren A. Roach, d/b/a Bob Roach Texaco Service Station and by L. F. Corrigan. On October 19, 1960 default judgment was entered against Texaco, Inc. in the sum of $30,000, plus cost, said judgment reciting that Texaco, Inc. 'though duly served with process had failed to appear and therefore made default.' In the judgment of October 19, 1960, no disposition was made of the other two defendants. However, on November 22, 1960 Faye McEwen voluntarily non-suited Warren A. Roach, d/b/a Bob Roach Texaco Service Station and L. F. Corrigan. In January 1961 execution was issued and levy was attempted against Texaco, Inc. It was alleged that this was the first notice that Texaco, Inc. had that suit had been filed against it and that default judgment had been taken. Thereafter a motion to vacate said default judgment was filed in the 44th District Court of Dallas County, Texas. The trial court granted the motion and the default judgment was set aside by order dated January 20th, 1961.

Original application for Writ of Mandamus was then made by Faye McEwen in the Supreme Court of Texas in Cause styled: *McEwen v. Harrison et al.* The Supreme Court in its opinion, 345 S.W.2d 706, granted the Writ of Mandamus and ordered the trial court to vacate the order setting aside the default judgment. The Supreme Court, speaking through Chief Justice Calvert, pointed out that the only question passed upon was whether or not the trial court had the power to set aside a default judgment after the expiration of more than 30 days from its entry even when the record upon which default judgment was based reflected that the court did not have jurisdiction of the person of the defendant at the time it was entered. The Court said: "We hold that appeal by writ of error or a bill of review of set aside the judgment are the exclusive methods by which Texaco may have the default judgment vacated or set aside. * * * Our judgment here is without prejudice to the rights of Texaco, Inc. to file an appeal by writ of error or to file a bill of review to set aside the default judgment against it."

Pursuant to instructions of the Supreme Court an order was entered on May 4, 1961, by the District Court setting aside its prior order vacating the default judgment. Prior thereto, on April 28, 1961, petition for Writ of Error was perfected to this Court.

Petitioner directly attacks the default judgment rendered against it in three points of error, (1) because jurisdiction of the person of petitioner has not been obtained; (2) because the record shows that service of citation and petition were not had upon petitioner; and (3) because the record did not affirmatively reflect that service of citation and petition was had upon petitioner in accordance with the applicable statutes. * * *

We now turn to the consideration of petitioner's points of error. Since petitioner's mode of review is by way of Writ of Error, which constitutes a direct attack upon the default judgment against it, the decisive question presented is whether there is error apparent on the face of the record which would vitiate the trial court's order. *Milam County v. Robertson*, 47 Tex. 222; *Cruger v. McCracken*, 87 Tex. 584, 30 S.W. 537; *Crawford v. McDonald*, 88 Tex. 626, 33 S.W. 325; *American Standard Life Ins. Co. v. Denwitty*, Tex. Civ. App., 256 S.W.2d 864; Art. 2249a, V.A.C.S.; 3 TEX. JUR. 2D Sec. 17, p. 287. The record here consists of more than the recitations contained in the default judgment concerning service. The question, then, is: What does the "face of the record" reveal? In her petition respondent named three parties defendant (1) L. F. Corrigan; (2) Warren A. Roach, d/b/a Bob Roach Texaco Service Station, 4700 Block Lemmon Ave.; and Texaco, Inc., a corporation licensed to do business in the State of Texas and who can "be served for process, through one of its agents, 3900 Singleton Blvd., Dallas, Texas." Insofar as Texaco, Inc., is concerned no definite officer or agent is named upon whom service may be had. Warren A. Roach is not alleged to have been an agent of Texaco, Inc. for any purpose, whether for service of process or otherwise. Roach and Texaco, Inc. are co-defendants and nothing else. While she sued three defendants, respondent's attorney in a letter to the District Clerk, stated significantly: "Enclosed herewith are the original and two copies of our pleadings in the above entitled cause. Please file the original, issue citation, and forward same to Constable Roby Love's office in order that service might be obtained upon the defendant. Please place your file mark on the extra copy and return same to this office." (Emphasis ours).

The cost bill prepared by the District Clerk indicates only the original and "two copies" of the citation were prepared. The citation request from the respondent's attorney gave no instructions concerning upon whom service might be had against Texaco, Inc. Since only two copies of the citation were issued by the Clerk it becomes apparent that the Deputy Constable delivered one copy of the citation to L. F. Corrigan and another copy to Warren A. Roach. According to the Constable's return on the citation he served Texaco, Inc. by delivering to "Warren A. Roach" on September 20, A.D. 1960, at 2:10 o'clock P.M. The default judgment recites that Texaco, Inc. was "duly served with process." There is no controversy but that Texaco, Inc. did not appear or participate in the trial court proceedings either in person, by agent or attorney.

Art. 2031, V.A.C.S. (1948) provided for service: "in any suit against a foreign corporation" on the president, vice-president, secretary, treasurer, general manager or any local or traveling agent or traveling salesman. Art. 2031a, V.A.C.S. (1948) applies to a foreign corporation which shall transact or do any business within this State, and requires such foreign corporation to designate a resident agent for service, and authorize service on the Secretary of State in the event such resident agent cannot be found. Considerable difficulty and confusion resulted from the provision of the statute authorizing service on "local or traveling agent or traveling salesman," as evidenced by the adjudicated cases. In 1955, the Legislature enacted what is known as the Business Corporation Act, Art. 8.10, V.A.T.S. thereof providing for service of process on foreign corporations. It is there provided that the president and all vice-presidents of the foreign corporation authorized to transact business in this State and the registered agent so appointed by the foreign corporation shall be agents of such corporations upon whom any process, notice, or demand required are permitted by law to be served upon the corporation may be served. It is further provided that when a foreign corporation shall fail to appoint or maintain a registered agent that service may be had upon the Secretary of State. These statutes provide for the only method of obtaining service or process upon a foreign corporation authorized to do business in this State. There is no alternative method for obtaining jurisdiction of the person of such a corporation in the courts of this State unless such corporation voluntarily appears or waives service or process. 14 TEX. JUR. 2D § 484, p. 588.

It has long been the established law of this State that it is imperative and essential that the record affirmatively shows a strict compliance with the provided mode of service. * * *

It is evident that the "face of the record" in this case does not affirmatively reveal that Texaco, Inc., a corporation authorized to do business in this State, was served with process in the plain and specific manner provided by either the old or new statute. The petition itself does not designate Warren A. Roach as agent or officer of the corporation. The instructions to the serving officer does not designate Roach as the proper person for service upon the corporation. The return of the serving officer merely indicates that he served Texaco, Inc. by serving someone named Roach. This obviously, is not sufficient to comply with the law relating to service and the default judgment based thereon cannot stand. Petitioner's points are therefore sustained, and respondent's cross-points are overruled.

The default judgment against petitioner is ordered vacated and set aside and the cause remanded to the trial court for trial on the merits.

Reversed and remanded.

Notes

1. In *DSC Finance Corp. v. Moffitt,*[1] the Court noted that in determining whether the error complained of is apparent on the face of the record, the court may consider all of the papers on file in the appeal including the statement of facts.

2. Review by writ of error affords an appellant the same scope of review as an ordinary appeal; that is, a review of the entire case. The only restriction on the scope of writ of error review is that the error must appear on the face of the record. The face of the record, for purposes of writ of error review, consists of all the papers on file in the appeal, including the statement of facts. It necessarily follows that review of the entire case includes review of legal and factual insufficiency claims.[2]

3. In any direct attack upon a judgment rendered by a court with jurisdictional power, the record must always show a strict compliance with the provided mode of service.

4. In *Stubbs v. Stubbs,*[3] the court held: (1) signing the waiver of citation and the filing of an agreement incident to divorce was not participation in the actual trial, and (2) the trial court's decision could be reversed because a statement of facts was not made at the divorce hearing.

5. In *Wachovia Bank of Delaware, N.A. v. Gilliam*, 215 S.W.3d 848 (Tex. 2007) the Court noted that in a restricted appeal from a default judgment, based on substituted service, the face of the record must show that service was forwarded to a statutorily required address. No presumptions are made in favor of valid service in a restricted appeal from a default judgment. Thus, for a default judgment to survive a restricted appeal, the face of the record must reflect that service was forwarded to the address required by statute.

TEXACO, INC.
v.
CENTRAL POWER & LIGHT COMPANY
925 S.W.2d 586
(Tex. 1996)

Facts: This is an appeal by writ of error. Espinoza, the employee of an independent contractor, IEC, hired by Texaco to fix a transformer, was burned when he brushed against an electrical line, provided by CP&L. Espinoza sued Texaco and CP&L. CP&L cross-claimed against Texaco for indemnity. After the jury was selected and trial had begun, Texaco settled with Espinoza for $350,000, with an agreement from Espinoza to indemnify Texaco against any claim by the workers' compensation carrier. The settlement was announced outside the presence of the jury, and the Texaco's lawyer was told by the judge that he could go. Texaco did not participate further in the trial. On the last day of trial, CP&L filed a motion to take judicial notice of a tariff on file with the PUC, which CP&L claimed established Texaco's duty to indemnify it. It served the motion on Texaco's lawyers. The trial court did take judicial notice of the tariff. The jury allocated 20% of the negligence to CP&L, 50% to Texaco, and 30% to Espinoza. It found the Espinozas' damages to be $1,129,033. The trial court entered judgment for Espinoza, and found that, under the indemnity provisions of the tariff, Texaco owes CP&L

[1] 815 S.W.2d 551 (Tex. 1991),

[2] Norman Communications v. Texas Eastman Co., 955 S.W.2d 269 (Tex. 1997).

[3] 685 S.W.2d 643 (Tex. 1985).

complete indemnity for all amounts. Texaco sought to appeal by writ of error. The court of appeals disputed Texaco's need to appeal by writ of error, because Texaco had notice of CP&L's theory of indemnity from service of the motion to take judicial notice and receipt of the judgment. The court of appeals dismissed the appeal, concluding that Texaco's participation in the trial was such that it was barred from an appeal by writ of error. 897 S.W.2d 854. **Held**: Reversed and remanded to the court of appeals for consideration of Texaco's point of error.

Issue: Does participation in the primary matters leading up to the trial, including an announcement of ready, constitute an appearance at trial, which would preclude the use of the restricted appeal?

Issue stated another way: Is the announcement of ready participation at trial?

Held: No. Because Texaco did not participate in the trial that led to judgment against it, it may appeal by writ of error. TEX. R. APP. P. 45 (now 30) extends the right to appeal by writ of error (now restricted appeal) to a party to the suit, who did not participate in the actual trial, within six months of the judgment.

Issue: At what point does one participate in the actual trial, precluding an appeal by writ of error?

Held: The actual trial of a case is the hearing in open court, leading up to the rendition of judgment, on the questions of law, if the case is disposed of on the questions of law, or on the questions of fact, if the final judgment is rendered on the facts. The question is whether the appellant has participated in the decision-making event that results in judgment adjudicating the appellant's rights. Here, the jury trial, establishing liability against CP&L, resulting in judgment against Texaco, is the relevant decision-making event. While, Texaco's announcement of ready was a general appearance, it does not follow that Texaco, thereby, participated at trial. Mere appearance is not participation. Further, Texaco's decision not to participate in the trial does not preclude appeal by writ of error. There is no equitable component to appeal by writ of error. Writ of error is but another mode of appeal. As in an ordinary appeal, a writ of error appellant is not required to show diligence, or lack of negligence, before its complaints will be heard. It is the fact of nonparticipation, not the reason for it, that determines the right to appeal by writ of error.

Issue: Does participation in a summary judgment proceeding constitute participation that would preclude the use of a restricted appeal?

Held: It depends. TEX. R. APP.P. 45 extends the right to appeal by writ of error to a party to the suit, who did not participate in the actual trial, within six months of the judgment. A party who has taken part in all steps of a summary judgment proceeding, except the hearing on the motion, has participated in the "actual trial" that determined the parties rights.

Issue: What is purpose of the restricted appeal (writ of error)?

Held: The policy behind the nonparticipation requirement, for an appeal by writ of error, is to deny appeal by writ of error, to those who should reasonably resort to the quicker method of appeal. Those who participate in the trial leading up to the rendition of judgment are familiar with the record, and are, therefore, in position to prepare for appeal on short notice; whereas, those who do not so participate in the actual trial, and are therefore, unfamiliar with the record, may need additional time in which to familiarize themselves with the record. The distinction based on familiarity with the record means that, in a jury trial, an appellant who does not participate in the hearing of evidence that leads to an unfavorable judgment, is not disqualified from writ of error. In this case, CP&L's liability to the Espinozas, and the amount of damages, which CP&L seeks to pass on to Texaco, were established through the evidentiary stage of trail. Texaco is in no better position to prepare those issues for appeal than if it had never announced ready for trial, never appeared to inform the court of settlement, or never received notice of CP&L's theory of judgment.

Notes

1. In *Withem v. Underwood,*[1] a malicious prosecution case, the trial court struck the defendant's answer and entered a partial summary judgment on liability. The defendant failed to appear at the separate hearing on damages. The defendant was subsequently allowed to appeal by writ of error, since he did not participate in the decision-making event that resulted in judgment adjudicating the appellant's rights. *Participation means taking part in a hearing in open court, leading up to the rendition of judgment, on the questions of law, if the case is disposed of on the questions of law, or on the questions of fact, if the final judgment is rendered on the facts.*

2. As a result of the *Texaco* case and the efforts of the appellate attorneys for Texaco, Rule 30 of the Texas Rules of Appellate Procedure was amended. *Under TEX. R. APP. P. 30, to obtain a restricted appeal:*

(a) the notice of appeal must be brought within six months of the date of judgment;
(b) by a party to the suit;
(c) who did not participate in the trial; and
(d) error must be apparent from the face of the record.

Thereafter, the procedure is as in any other appeal. One major change occurred with the 1997 amendments, that should be noted. It can be treated as a fifth element.

(e) Unlike the writ of error procedure, the petitioner must not have filed a timely post-judgment motion or request for findings of fact and conclusions of law.

3. *Insufficient Participation—Writ of Error (Restricted Appeal) Allowed.*

(a) Waiver of Citation and Agreement Incident to Divorce.
(b) Answer. Filing an answer is not participation.
(c) Appearance. Likewise, an appearance through a plea to the jurisdiction is insufficient to constitute participation.
(d) Physical Presence. Physical presence in the courtroom is not enough if the party has not answered and is not participating in the trial. Thus, a party who's attorney was present to file a nonsuit, was not allowed to appeal by writ of error, even though the attorney remained in the courtroom for the hearing.
(e) Motions for New Trial and Other Post-Judgment Motions. Before 1997, the filing of a motion for new trial was not enough to preclude appeal by writ of error. By rule amendment, however, the filing of a post-judgment motion precludes the use of a restricted appeal. TEX. R. APP. PROC. 30.

4. In the following instance, the participation of the parties was found to be sufficient to preclude an appeal by writ of error (restricted appeal):

(a) Summary Judgments. Appearance at a summary judgment hearing may, or may not be sufficient participation.
(b) Discovery Sanctions Hearing. A party's appearance at a discovery sanction hearing, that resulted in the striking of that party's pleading, was participation at the hearing where the party's rights were determined.
(c) Confession of Judgment. A Confession of judgment by an attorney of record constitutes participation.

5. *Usability—Restrictions on Use.*

(a) Form of Ordinary Appeal. The restricted appeal is a form of ordinary appeal.
(b) No Evidentiary Hearing/Error on Face of Record. There is no evidentiary hearing, and the error must appear on the face of the record. The record includes the transcript, statement of facts, and all papers in the case.
(c) Need for Statement of Facts. In the absence of a statement of facts presented by the appellant, the evidence is presumed to support the judgment, unless the appellant is improperly deprived of the statement of facts.
(d) Filing Is Appearance. Finally, it must be remembered that one attacking a default judgment by writ of error makes an appearance by so doing, if one has not be previously made.

---

[1] 922 S.W.2d 956 (Tex. 1997).

6. *Practical Considerations*. The restricted appeal may only work in a limited range of cases where there is fundamental error, a failure to serve the defendant, or to give notice of a hearing, where the evidence or pleadings are insufficient to support the judgment, and in any other context where error appears without the necessity for objection.

7. *Dakota Pike-Grant v. Grant*, ___ S.W.3d ___, 2014 WL 4933010 (Tex. 2014): The issue is whether the appeals court erred by dismissing a restricted appeal from a divorce decree that contained two conflicting recitals, one noting that Pike-Grant attended the hearing to modify, the other that she did not. The first recital indicates the hearing occurred in November 2011, and that she was present. But the other recital indicates the hearing occurred in September 2011, and she was not present, which would not foreclose her restricted appeal under Rule of Appellate Procedure 30. The Supreme Court HOLDS no record evidence shows the hearing occurred in November 2011 and at least eight references, including portions of the trial court's docket sheet and the reporter's record, conclusively confirm the hearing occurred in September 2011 without Pike-Grant's participation.

c. *Bill of Review*

Notes

Valdez v. Hollenbeck, 465 S.W.3d 217 (Tex. 2015): "A bill of review is brought as a direct attack on a judgment that is no longer appealable or subject to a motion for new trial." *Frost Nat'l Bank*, 315 S.W.3d at 504. Because it is a direct attack, a bill of review must be filed in the court that rendered the original judgment, and only that court may exercise jurisdiction over the bill. *Id.* Courts have long recognized bills of review rooted in general principles of equity or as prescribed by the Legislature, but courts do not readily grant them "[b]ecause it is fundamentally important in the administration of justice that some finality be accorded to judgments." *Alexander v. Hagedorn*, 148 Tex. 565, 226 S.W.2d 996, 998 (1950); *see Crouch v. McGaw*, 134 Tex. 633, 138 S.W.2d 94, 96 (1940) (noting that a bill of review requires "something more than injustice").

Equitable bills of review are not a novel legal concept and can be traced as far back as seventeenth century England. *See Finality of Equity Decrees in the Light of Subsequent Events*, 59 HARV. L. REV. 957, 958 (1946) ("In equity a decree may be re-examined by a bill of review, a procedure going back at least as far as Lord Bacon's Ordinances in 1619."). To obtain an equitable bill of review, a petitioner must generally plead and prove (1) a meritorious claim or defense to the judgment, (2) which the petitioner was prevented from making by official mistake or by the opposing party's fraud, accident, or wrongful act, (3) unmixed with any fault or negligence on the petitioner's own part. *King Ranch, Inc. v. Chapman*, 118 S.W.3d 742, 751-52 (Tex. 2003); *Alexander*, 226 S.W.2d at 998; *see also* Patrick J. Dyer, *A Practical Guide to the Equitable Bill of Review*, 70 TEX. B.J. 20, 22 (2007). Unless otherwise specified by statute, equitable bills of review carry a four-year statute of limitations. *Caldwell v. Barnes*, 975 S.W.2d 535, 538 (Tex. 1998) (citing TEX. CIV. PRAC. & REM. CODE § 16.051).

Statutory bills of review are more scarce, existing predominantly in the probate and guardianship contexts. *See, e.g.*, TEX. ESTATES CODE §§ 55.251, 202.203, 1056.101; *cf.* TEX. CODE CRIM. PROC. art. 22.17. At all times relevant to this proceeding, section 31 of the Texas Probate Code allowed for a statutory bill of review in connection with probate proceedings, providing:

> Any person interested may, by a bill of review filed in the court in which the probate proceedings were had, have any decision, order, or judgment rendered by the court, or by the judge thereof, revised and corrected on showing error therein; but no process or action under such decision, order or judgment shall be stayed except by writ of injunction, and no bill of review shall be filed after two years have elapsed from the date of such decision, order, or judgment.

Former TEX. PROB. CODE § 31 (current version at TEX. ESTATES CODE § 55.251). In contrast to equitable bills of review, section 31 has been interpreted to require a showing of "substantial error" in a prior decision, order, or judgment. *See, e.g., Nadolney v. Taub*, 116 S.W.3d 273, 278 (Tex. App.—Houston [14th Dist.] 2003, pet. denied) ("The purpose of a section 31 bill of review is to revise and correct errors, not merely to set aside decisions, orders, or judgments rendered by the probate court."); *McDonald v. Carroll*, 783 S.W.2d 286, 288 (Tex. App.—Dallas 1989, writ denied); *cf. Norton v. Cheney*, 138 Tex. 622, 161 S.W.2d 73, 74 (1942) (holding that standard for obtaining equitable bill of review did not apply to statutory bill of review in guardianship proceeding, citing *Jones v. Parker*, 67 Tex. 76, 3 S.W. 222, 224 (1886)). Fidelity and Valdez contend the Legislature intended section 31 to displace equitable bills of review in probate proceedings, but to the extent it does not, they argue the statute plainly establishes the outer temporal limits for attacking a probate judgment. *Cf. Gramercy Ins. Co. v. State,* 834 S.W.2d 379, 381 (Tex. App.—San Antonio 1992, no pet.) (holding that the Legislature intended to abrogate equitable-bill-of-review requirements when it enacted the special statutory bill of review in Tex. Code Crim. Proc. art. 22.17)."

ALEXANDER v. HAGEDORN

148 Tex. 565, 226 S.W.2d 996
(1950)

William Yelderman, Austin, for petitioners.
Richards & Richards, Lockhart, Hart, Brown & Sparks, Austin, J. H. Hart, Austin, for respondent.

BREWSTER, JUSTICE.

This is a proceeding by bill of review brought by William Hagedorn, respondent, against W.C. Alexander et ux., petitioners, to set aside a judgment rendered in their favor against respondent at a former term of court. A trial court judgment for Hagedorn was affirmed by the Court of Civil Appeals. 220 S.W.2d 196.

In the original suit, the Alexanders alleged that while they were riding on a public highway at night in their automobile and while they were meeting another automobile, a mule stepped from behind the latter vehicle and immediately in front of their own; that to avoid striking the mule, Mrs. Alexander was compelled to steer their automobile into a ditch, which action overturned the car causing damage to it and severe injuries to her; that Hagedorn was the owner of the mule and had permitted it to run at large and unattended upon the highway in violation of a local stock law.

Hagedorn was not born "in this country" and at the time of the trial of his bill of review was 75 years old, but he had lived in Gonzales, Hays and Caldwell Counties for 52 years. He cannot read or write the English language. So, when the citation was served on him in the damage suit, he requested the deputy sheriff to explain its meaning. The officer explained that it meant that the Alexanders were suing Hagedorn for damages. He told Hagedorn what they alleged in support of their demands and that the citation required Hagedorn to appear in district court at Lockhart on September 1, 1947, to answer the suit.

According to the trial judge's findings of fact, Hagedorn went to the district courtroom on September 1 but found nobody there, whereupon he went to the district clerk's office and told the clerk he was there to answer the Alexanders' suit. The clerk told Hagedorn that the district judge was not in Lockhart and that no court would be held that week. Asked by the clerk whether he had an attorney, Hagedorn replied that he did not. He then gave the clerk his address, requesting the clerk to notify him when to return to defend the suit. Hagedorn "understood that the Clerk would notify him when he should return to Lockhart for the purpose of defending" the suit but "did not understand that he was required to employ an attorney or to do anything more than he had done in response to the process served on him." Then Hagedorn went home; he employed no attorney; and, receiving no word from the clerk "or from any other person" relative to the suit, he did nothing further about it until after April 1, 1948, when he learned that garnishment had been run against his bank account following a judgment rendered against him on December 8, 1947, three months and one week after he had his conversation with the clerk. Then he did employ attorneys and filed this action.

The trial court found that Hagedorn "had a complete and absolute defense" to the Alexanders' suit in that he did not own the mule and was not responsible for it being on the highway when the Alexanders' car was forced off the road; that the court would not have entered judgment for the Alexanders on December 8, 1947, if he "had not understood from the testimony given and the statements made to the Court at that time that defendant William Hagedorn admitted that the mule which was on the highway and which was alleged to have caused the accident . . . was his mule and was a mule for the custody of which he was responsible;" that when Hagedorn came to the courtroom on September 1, 1947, he came to inform the court that he did not own, and was not responsible for, the mule at the time of the accident; and that the mule belonged to, and was under the control of, Hagedorn's son, Robert, at the time of the accident, which fact was known to the Alexanders when they filed suit "and at all times thereafter."

Petitioners complain that the Court of Civil Appeals erred in holding that these facts showed that Hagedorn had suffered the judgment to be rendered against him "through fraud, accident or acts of the opposing party, wholly unmixed with any fault or negligence of his own."

Although the bill of review is an equitable proceeding, before a litigant can successfully invoke it to set aside a final judgment he must allege and prove: (1) a meritorious defense to the cause of action alleged to support the judgment, (2) which he was prevented from making by the fraud, accident or wrongful act of the opposite party, (3) unmixed with any fault or negligence of his own. *Garcia et al. v. Ramos et al.*, Tex. Civ. App., 208 S.W.2d 111, er. ref. Because it is fundamentally important in the administration of justice that some finality be accorded to judgments, these essentials have been uniformly recognized by our courts; therefore, bills of review seeking relief from judgments "are always watched by courts of equity with extreme jealousy, and the grounds on which interference will be allowed are narrow and restricted;" and the rules are not to be relaxed merely because it may appear in some particular case that an injustice has been done. *Harding v. W. L. Pearson & Co. et al.*, Tex. Com. App., 48 S.W.2d 964. As said by the Supreme Court of California, "Endless litigation, in which nothing was ever finally determined, would be worse than occasional miscarriages of justice." *Pico v. Cohn et al.*, 91 Cal. 129, 25 P. 970, 971, 27 P. 537, 13 L.R.A. 336, 25 Am. St. Rep. 159.

Although negligence is a question of fact for the trial court, it is a question of law whether, when the facts are so established, they amount to any evidence to sustain that issue. *Crawford v. Houston & T. C. Ry. Co.*, 89 Tex. 89, 33 S.W. 534; *San Antonio Brewing Ass'n v. Wolfshohl*, Tex. Civ. App., 155 S.W. 644, er. ref.; *Houston E. & W. T. R. Co. v. Boone*, 105 Tex. 188, 146 S.W. 533. So the question is whether respondent's conversation with the clerk and his understanding of its import, as found by the trial court, tend to show diligence on respondent's part in defending the suit.

"Reliance upon the statements or promises of third persons even though they may occupy some official position or seem to be in a position to have better information than the party himself, does not ordinarily entitle to relief for failing to make a defense." FREEMAN, LAW OF JUDGMENTS (5th Ed.), Vol. 3, Sec. 1245, p. 2592.

Under any other rule it would be very difficult if not impossible for a trial court to function in the field of default judgments. For it would mean that before the court could enter a valid judgment against a non-answering defendant, he would have to call in the clerk, the sheriff and perhaps all other courthouse officials and their deputies to ascertain whether any of them had made any extra-official agreement to notify the defendant when his case would be on call, even though the judge, as is true in this case, may have no intimation whatever from any source that any such agreement has been made. Obviously, such a situation would be intolerable. * * *

The true rule is stated in 31 AM. JUR., Sec. 745, p. 286. "The failure of a clerk of court to inform a party or his attorney as to the status of a cause is ordinarily regarded as insufficient ground for the opening or vacating of a judgment resulting therefrom. This rule has even been applied where the clerk failed to answer letters inquiring about the status of the case, and where he failed to keep his promise to keep the party informed. On the other hand, relief has been granted where a judgment was rendered against a party in consequence of some mistake or fault of a clerk of the court, where there was no negligence on the part of the litigant, or where the negligence was excusable. This rule has been applied where a party has in good faith endeavored to ascertain from the clerk of the court the condition of the cause upon the court's calendar, and is honestly misled by information received. Thus, it has been decided to be proper to open a default against a defendant, where his attorney was informed by the clerk that no business would be transacted by the court until after a certain date, and relying upon this statement he did not appear until such date, when he found that his pending demurrer had been overruled."

This statement recognizes the difference between promises or statements made by the clerk within the scope of his official duties and those made outside of it. For example, it is not the clerk's official duty to undertake to keep a party informed as to the status of his case or when it will be reached on the docket. It is his official duty to know when sessions of the court will be held, what class of business will or will not be disposed of at a given time and what his office records show with respect to pending litigation, therefore when he gives an inquiring litigant the wrong information within that field the litigant is not at fault. * * *

When respondent requested the district clerk to notify him when he should return to court to defend the suit he was requesting the clerk to undertake something that the latter was in no sense required to do in his official capacity. So, as to that, the clerk became respondent's agent, and negligence of the clerk must be charged to respondent; it became his own negligence.

* * *

Again, Hagedorn cannot prevail because he has not shown that he was prevented from making his defense to the Alexanders' suit by their fraud or wrongful act.

Fraud in its relation to attacks on final judgments is either extrinsic or intrinsic. Only extrinsic fraud will entitle a complainant to relief because it is a wrongful act committed "by the other party to the suit which has prevented the losing party either from knowing about his rights or defenses, or from having a fair opportunity of presenting them upon the trial. Such, for instance, as where he has been misled by his adversary by fraud or deception, did not know of the suit, or was betrayed by his attorney. In other words, fraud which denied him the opportunity to fully litigate upon the trial all the rights or defenses he was entitled to assert. "Intrinsic fraud" in the procurement of a judgment is not ground, however, for vacating such judgment in an independent suit brought for that purpose. And within that term is included such matters as fraudulent instruments, perjured testimony, or any matter which was actually presented to and considered by the trial court in rendering the judgment assailed." *State v. Wright*, Tex. Civ. App., 56 S.W.2d 950, 952, which was cited with approval and substantially quoted by this court in *Crouch et al. v. McGaw*, 134 Tex. 633, 138 S.W.2d 94.

The Supreme Court of the United States gives these illustrations of extrinsic fraud: "Where the unsuccessful party has been prevented from exhibiting fully his case, by fraud or deception practiced on him by his opponent, as by keeping him away from court, a false promise of a compromise; or where the defendant never had knowledge of the suit, being kept in ignorance by the acts of the plaintiff" and then says: "The court will not set aside a judgment because it was founded on a fraudulent instrument, or perjured evidence, or for any matter which was actually presented and considered in the judgment assailed." (Italics ours.) *United States v. Throckmorton*, 98 U.S. 61, 25 L.Ed. 93.

* * *

This wealth of authority compels the conclusion that the wrongful act of petitioners in stating to the trial court in the default judgment proceedings that respondent admitted ownership of the mule was intrinsic fraud. The fundamental issues which petitioners had to establish in order to prevail in the original suit were: (1) that respondent owned a mule, (2) which he permitted to run at large in violation of law, (3) thereby proximately causing the damages sued for. When respondent defaulted, all of them were to be taken as proved and admitted and the right of petitioners as well as the liability of respondent was foreclosed, except as to the amount of damages. *Southern S. S. Co. v. Schumacher Co.*, Tex. Civ. App., 154 S.W.2d 283, er. ref. want merit; *Johnson v. Brown*, Tex. Civ. App., 218 S.W.2d 317, er. ref. n. r. e. Nevertheless respondent's ownership of the mule remained an essential element of the cause of action alleged by petitioners. The cautious trial judge recognized this when, although the law says the issue was to be taken as confessed, he required assurance that respondent owned the mule. That he was satisfied by an unsworn statement by petitioners and did not require their testimony under oath does not alter the fact that it related to a basic phase of the case; it still had to do with the merits between the parties. We fail to see how any statement made by petitioners that respondent had admitted ownership of the mule, made to the trial judge for the purpose of getting a default judgment, could be extrinsic fraud if made without the sanction of an oath, but intrinsic fraud if made under that sanction.

At one point in his findings the trial court states that if he had not 'understood from the testimony given and statements made to the court at that time' that respondent admitted ownership of the mule he would have postponed the case. Under that version of what happened, we cannot hold that the 'testimony given' was intrinsic fraud but that the 'statements made' were extrinsic fraud, when the testimony was given and the statements made at the same place and time, for the same purpose and on the same issue.

Having wholly failed to establish two of the three essential elements of a cause of action for bill of review, respondent is not entitled to recover.

Accordingly, both judgments below are reversed and judgment is rendered for petitioners.

HART, J., not sitting.

SMEDLEY, JUSTICE (dissenting).

I find it impossible to agree to the opinion of the majority and the judgment reversing and rendering the judgments of the Court of Civil Appeals and the District Court, because that opinion and the resulting judgment treat the applicable equitable rules as inflexible rules, ignoring the fact that the rules of equity are in a measure flexible and adaptable to particular exigencies. In doing so the Court is permitting one party in this case to suffer gross wrong at the hands of the other party, and is denying to this Court, although it is a court of equity and this is an equitable proceeding, authority to apply the established rules to the peculiar facts of this case in such way as to prevent gross injustice. I do not suggest that the rules be changed or disregarded, but only that they should be reasonably and fairly adapted and fitted to the facts of the case. If this cannot be done, what is a court of equity for?

The majority admits and must admit that respondent Hagedorn had and has a meritorious defense to the original suit. The trial court found from abundant evidence that respondent Hagedorn "had a complete and absolute defense." He did not own the mule that caused the accident and he did not permit it to run at large. According to the opinion of the majority respondent is required to pay to petitioners more than $3,000 as damages for which he was in no way responsible.

The opinion of the majority, in denying to respondent relief from the default judgment rendered against him, holds first that the fraudulent or wrongful act on the part of petitioner Alexander was intrinsic rather than extrinsic fraud and, second, that respondent was not sufficiently diligent in defending against the original suit.

As to the first of these holdings, the material facts found by the trial court are as follows: When he was served with citation in the original suit respondent Hagedorn, being uneducated and not able to read or write, requested the deputy sheriff to explain to him what the citation meant, and was told that petitioners were suing him for damages, alleging that he was the owner of the mule which was struck by them on the highway, with resulting injuries to them, and that the citation required him to be in the courthouse in Lockhart, Texas, on September 1, 1947, and at that time to appear in the District Court.

Respondent went to the district courtroom in the courthouse at Lockhart on September 1, 1947, for the purpose of informing the court that he did not own the mule and was not responsible for the mule's being on the highway. Finding no one in the courtroom, he went to the office of the district clerk and told him that he had come to the courthouse in obedience to the notice served on him to appear in the District Court on September 1, 1947, to answer in the suit which petitioners had filed against him. The clerk told him that the district judge was not in Lockhart and that no district court would be held there during that week. When asked by the clerk whether he had an attorney, respondent hold him he did not, and he gave the clerk his address, requesting the clerk to notify him when he should return for the purpose of defending the suit. The clerk took respondent's address, and respondent understood that the clerk would notify him when to return. Respondent did not understand that he was required to employ an attorney or to do anything more than he had done in response to the process that had been served on him. He did not employ an attorney and returned home. He received no word from the district clerk or from any other person concerning the suit, and did not know that any action had been taken in the suit until he learned early in April 1948, that petitioners, on December 8, 1947, had taken a judgment against him in that suit for $3,126.84.

On December 8, 1947, petitioners and their attorney appeared in the District Court of Caldwell County and requested the Court to render default judgment in their favor against respondent, and at that time it was stated to the Court either by petitioners or their attorney that respondent Hagedorn admitted that the mule which was on the highway was his mule and was under his control. These statements were made, although petitioner Alexander, even before the suit was instituted, knew that the mule was the property of Robert Hagedorn (not respondent William Hagedorn) and that Robert Hagedorn had admitted that he owned it and that the mule had escaped from his premises at the time it was on the highway. The judge who rendered the judgment in the original suit and who tried this case states in his findings of fact that if these statements had not been made to him by petitioner Alexander or his attorney he would have postponed the hearing in the original suit "until defendant William Hagedorn should be notified of the fact that the suit would be tried at a certain time."

Thus the wrongful act of petitioner was a false statement made to the district judge for the purpose of inducing him to hold the hearing in the absence of respondent Hagedorn. It did induce the district judge to proceed, and but for that statement no hearing would have been held and no judgment would have been rendered. It is very clear that petitioner's statement was extrinsic rather than intrinsic fraud. By it respondent Hagedorn was deprived of the opportunity which the trial judge undoubtedly would have given him to appear and show that he had a complete defense. Respondent not having answered, there was no occasion for the introduction of evidence bearing upon liability. The trial judge could have heard evidence merely as to damages without inquiry as to ownership of the mule, but being careful and conscientious he hesitated to hold the hearing in respondent's absence and without giving him opportunity to be present, and he would not have proceeded if the representation that respondent admitted ownership of the mule had not been made either by petitioners or by petitioners' attorney. The wrongful act, the statement made before the hearing began, was extrinsic in that it was the inducement for the court to proceed in respondent's absence and was not evidence offered to prove a fact in issue.

The opinion of the majority seizes upon a statement made at one place in the trial judge's findings that he would not have rendered the judgment in the original suit "if the court had not understood from the testimony given and statements made to the court at that time" that the defendant admitted ownership of the mule. And the opinion argues therefrom that the wrongful act of petitioner must be considered intrinsic fraud rather than extrinsic fraud because it was false testimony given at the hearing on the issue of ownership. This is an unnecessary straining in support of an inequitable and unjust judgment. If the phrase quoted from the findings means that after the trial judge decided to hold the hearing the petitioner, when testifying to the amount of damages, repeated in his testimony the false statement that he had made before the hearing was begun to induce the judge to proceed with the hearing, the fact remains, clearly shown by the findings, that before the hearing was begun petitioner Alexander or his attorney made the false statement that respondent had admitted ownership of the mule and that only because that statement was made did the trial judge proceed to hold the hearing and render judgment against respondent in his absence. The distinction between extrinsic fraud and intrinsic fraud in bill of review cases is very clearly drawn in the decisions. *Crouch v. Panama Refining Co.*, 134 Tex. 633, 138 S.W.2d 94; *Mohammed v. McDonald*, Tex. Civ. App., 214 S.W.2d 896; *State v. Wright*, Tex. Civ. App., 56 S.W.2d 950; *United States v. Throckmorton*, 98 U.S. 61, 25 L.Ed. 93. Relief is granted when, as here, a party by the wrongful or fraudulent act of the other party has been prevented from presenting his case or defense to the court. It is not granted on account of perjured testimony on the trial. It is of no consequence in this case whether there was or was not perjured testimony at the hearing. The point is that the false statement made before the hearing, and that only, induced the court to proceed to hold the hearing and to render judgment in respondent's absence. There is no sound reason for the action of the majority in holding that the statement made before the hearing was intrinsic fraud, and not extrinsic fraud, merely because there may have been, or was, intrinsic fraud in the making of a like statement in the testimony at the hearing.

The opinion of the majority denies relief to respondent on the further ground that he was not diligent in appearing to make defense to the original suit. The facts as to what he did after he was served with citation have been stated above. The further facts, as shown by the trial court's findings and supported by evidence, are: Respondent is seventy-five years old. He was not born "in this country." He cannot read or write the English language. His testimony shows that he is uneducated and not well informed. When he appeared at the courthouse on September 1, 1947, in answer to the citation and found that the district judge was not in Lockhart and that no court would be held during that week, he gave his address to the district clerk and requested the clerk to notify him when he should return for the purpose of defending the suit. He understood from his conversation with the clerk that the clerk would notify him when to return. He did not understand that he was required to employ an attorney or to do anything more than he had done in response to the process that had been served on him.

If this were an action at law, as for example a suit for damages caused by negligence, the conduct of the parties with respect to negligence would be measured by the conduct of the ordinary, reasonable man. And the majority have made the mistake of applying that measure to respondent's conduct and of holding as a matter of law that respondent was negligent, notwithstanding the trial court's finding that he was not. But this proceeding is a suit in equity. It is permitted to prevent manifest injustice. * * *

* * *

In view of the principles mentioned and the authorities cited above, I am firmly convinced that the Court, in deciding the question whether respondent was negligent, should take into consideration all of the facts, including respondent's handicaps, his age, his want of information and of education, and his inexperience with courts and litigation. * * *

Respondent was diligent to the extent of his capacity, understanding and information. Following the deputy sheriff's explanation to him that the citation meant petitioners had sued him for damages, claiming that he was the owner of the mule which caused the accident, and that he was required to appear in the district courtroom on September 1, 1947, he went to the courthouse and the district courtroom on the morning of that day for the purpose of obeying the citation and making known to the court that he was not the owner of the mule. Finding no one in the courtroom, he sought out the clerk of the court and explained to him the reason why he had come to the courthouse. When told by the clerk that the judge was absent and there would be no court held that week, he gave the clerk his address and requested him to notify him when he should return for the purpose of defending the suit, and the clerk caused him to understand that he would be notified. He was not notified and the record indicates that the clerk did not make known to the district judge that respondent had come to the courthouse in answer to the citation and did not make an entry showing that respondent had appeared. It is clear from this record that had the clerk made such an entry or called to the attention of the district judge the fact that respondent had thus appeared to answer the citation, the judgment would not have been rendered against respondent in his absence.

The trial court found that "William Hagedorn did not understand that he was required to employ an attorney or to do anything more than he had done in response to the process served on him." Under these circumstances, and in view of respondent's meager information and his inexperience, he could not be expected to anticipate that the case would be heard without notice to him and a judgment rendered against him for damages in a very substantial amount for which he was in no way liable. Under the record in this case a court of equity should not be required by too strict an application of a common law measure of negligence to enter a decree which, to use the language of the trial judge, would be "inequitable and unjust" and would "result in a miscarriage of justice."

* * *

The careful and able trial judge and the Court of Civil Appeals rendered correct judgments in this case. The settled rules do not require the rendition of the harsh and inequitable judgment that this Court is rendering. There would be no departure from the rules and the working of gross injustice would be avoided if only the rules were applied fairly and reasonably to the facts of this case. The judgments of the District Court and the Court of Civil Appeals should be affirmed.

TAYLOR, J., joins in this dissent.

Notes

1. Only extrinsic fraud will support a bill of review's requirement of fraud by the opposing party. Extrinsic fraud is fraud that denies a party the opportunity to fully litigate upon the trial all the rights or defenses he was entitled to assert. Proof of one's own attorney's negligence is not extrinsic fraud.[1] Furthermore, proof of a litigant's own attorney's fraudulent and wrongful acts is not sufficient to establish extrinsic fraud.[2]

2. The requirement of showing extrinsic fraud or wrongful conduct by the opposing party is not necessary in all cases. The Court has held that if a litigant has been misled from filing a motion for new trial by misinformation of an officer of the court, acting within his official duties, the litigant will be excused from the necessity of proving extrinsic fraud.[3] Proof of fraud is also excused in the case where the clerk of the court fails to give a defaulting party notice of the final judgment as required by Rule 306a of the Texas Rules of Civil Procedure.[4]

3. *King Ranch, Inc. v. Chapman*, 118 S.W.3d 742 (Tex. 2003): Various heirs of the Chapmans, seek title to an undivided one-half interest in 15,449.4 acres of property (the Rincon), much of it contained within the storied King Ranch in South Texas. The Chapman heirs allege that, in the late 1800s, their forebears' lawyer conspired with Captain Richard King to deprive the Chapman heirs of rightful title to the property. Seeking to avoid an 1883 agreed judgment, they have filed a bill of review and a trespass to try title action. The Supreme Court held that the claims of the Chapman's are rejected. Allegations of fraud or negligence on the part of a party's attorney are insufficient to support a bill of review. Thus, a bill of review petitioner, who alleges that the wrongful act of his or her attorney caused an adverse judgment, is not excused from the necessity of pleading and prov-

[1] Gracey v. West, 422 S.W.2d 913 (Tex. 1968).

[2] Transworld Financial Services Corporation v. Briscoe, 722 S.W.2d 407 (Tex. 1987).

[3] Hanks v. Rosser, 378 S.W.2d 31 (1964).

[4] Petro-Chemical Transp., Inc. v. Carroll, 514 S.W.2d 240, 245 (Tex. 1974).

ing his or her opponent's extrinsic fraud. The grounds upon which a bill of review can be obtained are narrow, because the procedure conflicts with the fundamental policy that judgments must become final at some point. A bill of review requires something more than injustice.

Fraud, in relation to attacks on final judgments, is either extrinsic or intrinsic. Only extrinsic fraud will support a bill of review. Extrinsic fraud is fraud that denied a party the opportunity to fully litigate at trial, all the rights or defenses that could have been asserted. Intrinsic fraud, by contrast, relates to the merits of the issues that were presented, and presumably were or should have been, settled in the former action. Within that term are included such matters as fraudulent instruments, perjured testimony, or any matter which was actually presented to and considered by the trial court in rendering the judgment assailed. Such fraud will not support a bill of review because each party must guard against adverse findings on issues directly presented. Issues underlying the judgment attacked by a bill of review are intrinsic, and thus have no probative value on the fraud necessary to a bill of review. The fact that Robert Kleberg may have simultaneously represented King and Chapman in unrelated cases was neither unethical nor fraudulent. Simultaneous representation in unrelated matters is not evidence of a fraudulent conspiracy between one party's attorney, and their opponent, who is represented by the same lawyer in another matter. Such dual representation is permissible under today's ethical rules and was not prohibited in the 1880s. The rule prohibiting an attorney, once retained by a client from acting for the opposing party, applies only in the case of conflicting interest.

In a November 3, 1880 letter from Powers, of the Powers & Wells law firm, in which he advised Richard King to compromise Cause No. 1279, because "I don't see how you are to get over Mrs. Chapman's title to the Santa Gertrudis interest." The Supreme Court further held that the decision to settle cannot support an inference that King committed extrinsic fraud. The fact of settlement establishes only that both sides wanted to compromise. By going to trial, the Chapman estate could have lost all. Settlement—particularly a settlement like this one, that awarded the Chapman estate $5,811.75 (over three times what King and Chapman agreed to pay for Lewis's one-half interest in the Rincon thirty years earlier) and title to 240 acres of property—may have been the most prudent course. At the time of the consent judgment, both William and Helen Chapman were dead, and the heirs were litigating via long distance.

HANKS
v.
ROSSER

378 S.W.2d 31
(Tex. 1963)

Stephenson, Stephenson & Thompson, Jim I. Graves, with above firm, Orange, A. A. DeLee, Port Arthur, for petitioner.

Fred A. Carver, Beaumont, for respondent.

GREENHILL, JUSTICE.

Joseph Rosser brought suit against Jerry Hanks for services which he alleged he had rendered to Hanks and for which Hanks had agreed to pay him. Hanks was served with process on April 24, 1961. Appearance day was May 16, 1961. Hanks failed to file an answer by May 16, 1961; and on May 25, 1961, Rosser took a default judgment. Hanks is seeking equitable relief from that default judgment. The district court set aside the default judgment, and entered judgment in Hanks' Favor on a cross-action. The Court of Civil Appeals modified the lower court judgment, by reinstating the default judgment but affirming that portion of the judgment allowing Hanks recovery on his cross-action. 369 S.W.2d 643.

Hanks was a full-time independent druggist. He had a relief druggist only once or twice a week. On the same day that Hanks was served with process, he called an attorney, Thomas, and told him of the lawsuit. Thomas advised Hanks to bring the papers to his office and that he would advise him what to do after reading them. Hanks did not go to Thomas' office, and Thomas never saw the papers. Hanks misplaced the citation. He said they were placed on his prescription counter with his prescriptions and that he just lost them. He never did find them. He thought he had more time in which to answer. As a result, he did not file an answer in time.

Sometime between the day of service of citation and appearances day, Rosser's attorney conversed about the suit with Thomas, the attorney with whom Hanks had talked. On May 24, 1961, after appearance day, Rosser's attorney again saw Thomas and told him that appearance day had passed without an answer having been filed by Hanks, and that a default judgment was going to be taken. Thomas explained that he did not represent Hanks, but would inform Hanks of the matter. Thomas called Hanks that same afternoon, and told him that he had better file an answer to avoid having a default judgment taken against him. Thomas declined to represent Hanks, and recommended another attorney, A. A. DeLee, whose office was in Port Arthur. Hanks telephoned DeLee and made an appointment for the next morning, May 25, 1961. In their meeting in Port Arthur on the morning of May 25, Hanks explained the situation. DeLee immediately telephoned the district clerk's office in Beaumont and was informed by the clerk that while the suit was ripe for action, no judgment had yet been taken; that nothing had been done except the filing of the petition.

DeLee prepared an answer, which Hanks signed about 4:15 that afternoon. DeLee again called the district clerk, and was informed that still no judgment had been taken. It was too late to drive from Port Arthur to Beaumont and file the answer before the clerk's office would close for the day; so the answer was not filed until 9:18 the next morning. Again, at the time he filed the answer DeLee asked if a judgment had been taken in the case, and "the person (asked) went back and picked up a file and said, 'No'." He also testified that at this time he "was advised by the clerk there that nothing had been done. (So) I filed the answer." DeLee did not personally examine the file, the docket sheet, or the minutes of the district clerk. In fact, the judge's civil docket sheet showed that a default judgment had been taken May 25, 1961, and the judgment had been entered on the court minutes that same day.

DeLee sent a copy of the answer to Rosser's attorney, who stipulated that he received his copy May 26, 1961, the day it was filed. Rosser's counsel did not inform DeLee that judgment had been taken. Neither party took any further action until about July 18, 1961, when Rosser had an execution to the default judgment issued by the district court. The execution was delivered to the sheriff for proper levy and sale of Hank's property, all of his interest in the drug store and its contents. This was the first that Hanks or his attorney heard of the May 25, 1961, default judgment.

Hanks' counsel promptly sought equitable relief. He brought to the district court a plea for equitable relief based on contentions that he was not negligent in failing to file timely answer to Rosser's petition; that he did not file motion for new trial only because he relied on false information given to him by the district clerk, that he had a meritorious defense to the lawsuit, and that the granting of this equitable relief would be in keeping with justice and would cause no undue delay or prejudice to Rosser. The district court agreed with his position and, setting aside the default judgment, granted him a trial on the merits.

In the trial on the merits, Hanks' defense was sustained so that Rosser recovered nothing, and Hanks recovered on his cross action $1,000 plus interest. The Court of Civil Appeals found that the facts "would perhaps be sufficient to establish that appellee (Hanks) had not failed to use due diligence in availing himself of all adequate remedies at law to prevent the judgment from becoming final. That is to say, that in reliance upon such information, he was justified in not having timely filed motion for new trial prior to his petition for Bill of Review." 369 S.W.2d at 643. That court further stated that it recognized that "the record unquestionably reflects that a grave injustice will result to appellee (Hanks)." Nevertheless, the court, with one justice dissenting, held that it had no alternative but to reinstate the default judgment. 369 S.W.2d at 646.

Relief by bill of review is made available in this state by Rule 329b(5) of the Texas Rules of Civil Procedure. The rule does not prescribe the standards by which the actions of a defaulting party must be measured except to say that the bill must be "for sufficient cause" and be "filed within the time allowed by law." This bill, beyond question, was filed within the time allowed by law. The question is whether "sufficient cause" existed.

(1) Since the rule does not attempt to specify what "sufficient cause" is, the courts have done so in particular cases. A bill of review proceeding is an equitable one designed to prevent manifest injustice. But while manifest injustice to the defaulting party is a material consideration, another is the necessity for there being finality to judgments. The litigating parties are entitled to know when the contest is at an end; and others, including title examiners and purchasers and sellers of land and interests in land have a need for knowledge as to whether or not litigation involving title to land has been finally concluded.

The general rules on the granting of a bill of review are set out in *Alexander v. Hagedorn*, 148 Tex. 565, 226 S.W.2d 996 (1950). This Court there said that before a litigant can successfully set aside a final judgment, he must allege and prove, within the time allowed, (1) a meritorious defense to the cause of action alleged to support the judgment, (2) which was prevented from making by fraud, accident or wrongful act of the opposite party, (3) unmixed with any fault or negligence on his own part.

The litigant in *Hagedorn* attempted to rely upon the alleged promise of the clerk of the court to inform him as to when to return to court to defend that suit. The clerk failed to inform Hagedorn, and a default judgment was rendered against him. After an extensive review of the authorities within and without this state, the Court held that this act (or failure to act) on the part of the clerk was not part of his official duties, and that Hagedorn was not entitled to a bill of review under those circumstances.

This Court in *Hagedorn*, however, went to some length to distinguish cases where parties or their counsel had relied upon official acts of officers of the Court. After quoting from AMERICAN JURISPRUDENCE, this Court stated:

> It is his (the clerk's) official duty to know when sessions of the court will be held, what class of business will or will not be disposed of at given time and what his office records show with respect to pending litigation; therefore when he gives an inquiring litigant the wrong information within that field the litigant is not at fault.
>
> (Emphasis added.)

In *Hagedorn*, there was no fault of the opposite party, his counsel, or of an officer of the court in the performance of his official duties.

The trial court here found that Hanks was not negligent in failing to file an answer because of his having misplaced the citation, and that the default judgment was not caused by his negligence. It will be here assumed that, viewing the matter under bill of review standards, there is no evidence to support these findings, and that Hanks was negligent as a matter of law. This negligence, however, was in failing to file an answer in time, not in his failure to timely file a motion for new trial.

(2) Under the law, Hanks had two rights or remedies: (1) to file an answer to prevent a default judgment, and (2) to file a motion for new trial within ten days after the judgment was taken. Rule 329b (1), TEX. R CIV. P.

Since there was a reliance on the erroneous official information given by the clerk, it was unnecessary for Hanks to show, as was required under other circumstances in Hagedorn, that he was prevented from filing his motion for new trial because of some accident, fraud, or wrongful act of the opposing party.

Here, because of the incorrect information given by the clerk, within his official duties as set out in Hagedorn, Hanks was misled, and filed an answer instead of a motion for new trial. The Court of Civil Appeals, nevertheless, reversed this cause because it found that Hanks, by bill of review standards as contrasted with those required in an ordinary motion for new trial, was negligent in failing to file an answer. *Compare Craddock v. Sunshine Bus Lines*, 134 Tex. 388, 133 S.W.2d 124 (1939) *to Johnson v. Templeton*, 60 Tex. 238 (1883). As we view the case, this was not of controlling importance. Assuming that to be true, Hanks was nevertheless entitled to file a motion for new trial.

The controlling facts under these circumstances are: (1) whether the failure to file the answer was either intentional or the result of conscious indifference. *Craddock v. Sunshine Bus Lines*, *supra*; (2) whether Hanks was misinformed by the clerk within the time for filing the motion for new trial, and (3) was thus prevented from filing, or misled into not filing, his motion in time; (4) whether Hanks had a meritorious defense; and (5) whether the plaintiff Rosser would not be caused to suffer injury by the granting of the bill of review.

(3) Accordingly, we hold, within the spirit of the *Hagedorn* opinion, and assuming that the failure to file an answer is not intentional or the result of conscious indifference, that if a litigant is misled or prevented from filing a motion for new trial by misinformation of an officer of the court, acting within his official duties, and this misinformation is given to the party or his counsel within the ten-day period for filing the motion for new trial so as to bring about the failure to file a motion for new trial in time, the trial court, upon finding that the party has a meritorious defense and that no injury will result to the opposite party, may grant the bill of review.

We shall look again at the evidence to determine, if we can, whether, under these standards, the facts support the judgment of the Court of Civil Appeals; and if not, what judgment this Court should enter.

The bill of review was tried before the court. It was the judgment of the court that the bill of review should be in all things granted. Rosser requested the court to make findings of fact and conclusions of law on the bill of review action. The fact findings which were made are substantially the same as the facts set out herein. The court accepted the testimony of A. A. DeLee as to the inquiries of the clerk and the answers received by him. The court further found that Rosser's attorney received a copy of Hanks' answer the same day it was filed; that he knew that Hanks' attorney was attempting to protect Hanks' rights; but Rosser's attorney stated to the court that he owed no duty to anyone to advise that a default judgment had been taken. The court further found that upon learning that execution had been served, Hanks' counsel acted immediately and as expeditiously as possible to file the bill of review.

The trial court, in addition to his findings on want of negligence on Hanks' part in filing the answer, concluded that Hanks had a good defense to the asserted cause of action; that he had a meritorious defense to the suit, and that upon the trial, the result would be different from that rendered upon the default; and that it would be against the conscience to allow the judgment obtained by Rosser against Hanks to stand.

In the trial upon the merits, it was stipulated that the Statement of Facts in the bill of review hearing would be introduced and the evidence there adduced would be used for all purposes. In addition to that evidence, reviewed above, Hanks gave testimony, as to the arrangement between himself and Rosser whereby Rosser was to do some work for Hanks; that Rosser had not only been paid all that he was due, but had taken money from the venture without authority and had not repaid it. Hanks further testified that Rosser had asked Hanks to lend him $1,000 to pay off some of Rosser's creditors; that Hanks had done so, and had not been repaid. This is the basis of Hanks' cross-action.

The defendant Rosser, though represented by counsel, offered no evidence either on the bill of review or upon the trial upon the merits, except that he joined with counsel for Hanks in tendering the attorney Thomas as a witness. Thomas' testimony is undisputed. As to the cross-action, Rosser's counsel stated, ". . . we will confess that he (Hanks) has a counter claim. Let the Court's ruling stand on the basis that he had a successful counter claim for $1,000. All that I ask in this suit is final determination on the merits on the Bill of Review.'

Looking then at the five controlling elements set out above as to the bill of review, we find that the trial court specifically concluded that Hanks had a meritorious defense. The fact findings of the trial court are to the effect that Hanks was misinformed by the clerk within the time for filing a motion for new trial and was thus misled into not filing his motion in time. We construe the opinion of the Court of Civil Appeals to hold in context that there was sufficient evidence to support these findings. In fact, the evidence in this regard is undisputed.

The court found that Hanks was not negligent in failing to file his answer in time, and that the failure to answer was due to accident or mistake. By necessary implication, this means that the trial court was of the opinion that Hanks did not intentionally fail to answer, and that his failure to answer was not caused by conscious indifference.

The remaining element is that Rosser would not be caused to suffer injury by the granting of the motion. He was shown to be in the television repair business under the name of Rosser Electronics. The clear implication is that he was still in the immediate vicinity and could have been in attendance upon the court without substantial inconvenience. There was evidence that Hanks did not owe Rosser the money. Under these circumstances Hanks made out a prima facie case of proving the negative: no injury to Rosser. The burden of going forward shifted to Rosser. There was no evidence that Rosser would have been damaged in any respect by the granting of the bill of review, and no effort was made to introduce any such evidence.

The only point of error which Rosser brought to the Court of Civil Appeals was that the trial court erred in setting aside the default judgment against Hanks and entering judgment for the defendant Hanks. Rosser does not argue or even suggest in his brief in that court or his reply to the application for writ of error in this Court that any injury to himself was, or would have been, occasioned by the granting of the bill of review. His argument in both courts was as to the negligence of Hanks in failing to file the original answer.

All of the necessary elements set out above, therefore, were fulfilled. Accordingly, we hold that the Court of Civil Appeals erred in reversing the judgment of the trial court in the suit by Rosser against Hanks. Rosser had no other points in the Court of Civil Appeals which could be looked to for the purpose of supporting its judgment, and he has none here.

* * *

Accordingly, the judgment of the Court of Civil Appeals, in so far as it reversed the trial court's judgment in the suit of Rosser against Hanks is concerned, is reversed and that of the trial court is affirmed. On the cross-action by Hanks against Rosser, the action of the Court of Civil Appeals (in affirming the trial court) is affirmed.

GRIFFIN, JUSTICE (dissenting).

The law with regard to bills of review as it has existed since the beginning of Texas jurisprudence has been changed by the majority opinion herein.

A bill of review is an equitable proceeding and is so recognized by the majority. Heretofore there has been a clearly recognized distinction between a bill of review and a motion for new trial. . . . As late as 1961, in the case of *Fulton v. Finch*, 162 Tex. 351, 346 S.W.2d 823, in a unanimous opinion, this Court held that after the time prescribed in Rule 329-b, Texas Rules of Civil Procedure, that a judgment should become final, any action of the trial judge was absolutely void, and that a writ of mandamus would be issued, ordering the trial judge to expunge the order.

Also, in 1961, this Court had before it the case of *McEwen v. Harrison*, 162 Tex. 125, 345 S.W.2d 706, which involved the question whether the trial court, after the expiration of thirty days from the date of judgment and with no motion for new trial being filed, had the power to set aside a default judgment rendered against a party not served with process, and, therefore, the trial court had no jurisdiction over such non-served party. In a unanimous opinion, this Court said:

> 'Accordingly, we construe the emphasized provision of Rule 329-b to mean that when the time for filing a motion for new trial has expired and relief may not be obtained by appeal, a proceeding in the nature of a bill of review is the exclusive method of vacating a default judgment rendered in a case in which the court had jurisdictional power to render it. Into this category will fall those cases in which a default judgment is asserted to be void for want of service, or of valid service, of process.'

Further this Court said:

> 'Our construction of the Rule will give a diligent defendant with a meritorious defense every opportunity to protect himself against an unwarranted default judgment.'

In the case at bar, it is undisputed that the defendant in the main suit, Mr. Hanks, was duly and legally served by a legal and proper citation commanding him 'to appear by filing a written answer to the plaintiff's petition, at or before 10:00 o'clock A.M. of the Monday next after the expiration of 20 days after the date of service thereof . . . .' The record shows that was not the first citation served on Hanks, but that there had been at least two other and different suits filed against him and process served on him prior to the service of this citation.

The provision of 'to appear by filing a written answer to the plaintiff's petition' was inserted after this Court's decision in the *Hagedorn* case (226 S.W.2d 996) and for the very purpose of preventing those served seeking to justify their not filing a written answer within the time prescribed by law.

In the present case no answer was filed by appearance day plus approximately one week thereafter, and there is no claim made by petitioner Hanks that he was prevented from filing an answer at any time, either before or after appearance day by any action or conduct of plaintiff or his attorney, nor by any conduct, information or action of the clerk's office until May 25th-which was the ninth day after appearance day.

Further, there is no showing that the information that no judgment had been taken, given by the clerk's office in answer to the first telephone call made by Hanks' attorney around 11:00 A.M. was not true and correct. The hour of the taking of the default judgment is not in this record. Even though informed by the clerk that time was ripe for a judgment the morning of May 25th, and even though the name and residence of the plaintiff's attorney was at that time known, as well as the name of the judge presiding over the court where the action was pending, no effort was made to have the court clerk enter the name of defendant's attorney on the judge's trial docket, or to contact plaintiff's attorney or the trial judge and inform both or either of them that an answer for defendant Hanks was being filed. Any one of the three last above mentioned actions would have prevented the taking of a default judgment, or would have informed defendant that a default judgment had been taken that day.

The law prior to the decision in this case, required in bill of review cases, three very clear, simple, easily understood and universally and unanimously recognized things to exist, viz: (1) a meritorious defense to the cause of action alleged to support the judgment-and for this case we can assume such a defense was pleaded by Hanks, (2) which he was prevented from making by the fraud, accident or wrongful act of the apposite party-and here there is no contention, allegation by pleading or proof of this requisite and necessary element; (3) unmixed with any fault or negligence of his own. Here the majority has set aside this third test and has changed it to read 'that the failure to answer (was) not intentional or the result of conscious indifference.'

In connection with the last above test, the majority holds as a matter of law that under all the circumstances of this case, Mr. Hanks misplacing his citation and paying no attention to it was not conscious indifference or intentional failure to answer by appearance day. There is no finding by the trial court to this effect. The findings of the trial court are that Mr. Hanks was not negligent in permitting the default judgment to be taken against him; that Jerry Hanks used due diligence to prevent the judgment being had against him after he learned that the accident or mistake had occurred. It is interesting to note that Mr. Hanks in his testimony swore that he thought he had plenty of time to file an answer-not that when he misplaced the citation, he forgot about the suit. All the findings of the trial court were to the effect that Mr. Hanks was without fault and not negligent, because of losing the citation. Such conduct as misplacing the citation, or forgetting about it, has been held to be negligence prior to this holding. *Woods v. Gamboa* (Tex.Civ.App., 1950, writ refused, n. r. e.), 229 S.W.2d 1021; *Banks v. Crawford* (Tex.Civ.App., 1959, writ refused, n. r. e.), 330 S.W.2d 243.

The three requisites to be pleaded and proved as set out in the *Hagedorn* case were not original with the court in that case. These three requisites were first mentioned in the jurisprudence of this State in the case of *Goss v. McClaren*, 17 Tex. 107 (1856). . . .

The above are a few of the myriad of authorities, but I do not want to unduly lengthen this opinion. There has also been a well-recognized distinction between the pleadings and proof necessary to secure a retrial on a motion for new trial and on a bill of review. Many of the cases cited immediately above set out the distinction. A clear statement of this difference, and the reason therefor, is found in the case of *Smith v. Ferrell* (Comm. of App., 1932), 44 S.W.2d 962 (1 & 2) & (7), opinion expressly approved by the Supreme Court.

> 'It has been well said that in ordinary cases the trial judge has a certain amount of discretion in granting new trials during the term. However, no such discretion can be exercised after the expiration of the term. The judgment then becomes a vested right which can only be divested by a direct proceeding filed for that purpose, and, when such a proceeding is resorted to, the person presenting the bill must bring himself strictly within the rules of law providing for relief in such cases. It is not enough that he plead and prove that he had a meritorious defense in the first instance, but he must go further and show that he was then free from negligence.'

The case of *State v. Newman* (Tex.Civ.App., 1951, writ refused), 237 S.W.2d 417, expressly refused to recognize as a test in a bill of review case that the failure to file an answer before judgment taken could be excused by showing such failure was not intentional nor the result of conscious indifference. The trial court found that the failure of the defendant to file an answer before default was not intentional nor the result of conscious indifference on his part, but was due to a mistake or an accident which prevented him from making his defense, etc., etc.

The court said:

> 'No intimation is made that Mr. Newman was prevented from making his defense by the fraud, accident or wrongful act of plaintiff; or that there was not any fault or negligence of the defendant, and under all of the circumstances and facts in this case it is apparent that the failure of the defendant to file an answer was occasioned by the negligence or lack of diligence by the defendant and/or his attorneys, and he cannot be relieved of the effect of the judgment.'

That part of the *Hagedorn* case quoted by the majority opinion holds only that the reliance on the clerk's statements as to the contents of his official records, is an excuse for the defendant's negligence in not filing a motion for new trial, nor for failure to file an answer by appearance day plus eight days. *Hagedorn* does not hold that misinformation given by the clerk can be imputed to the plaintiff herein so as to satisfy the second well-recognized requirement, that defendant was prevented from making his defense by the fraud, accident or wrongful act of plaintiff herein. As we have said before, it is affirmatively shown that plaintiff was guilty of no such conduct, but on the contrary the record shows that plaintiff's attorney on the eighth day after appearance day sent word to defendant Hanks that no answer had been filed and a default judgment would be taken. In spite of this information received by plaintiff on May 24th, no answer was filed until May 26th.

Although the majority relies solely on *Hagedorn* as authority for its holding that misinformation from the court clerk-unmixed with any fault of the opposite party-will entitle a negligent defendant to set aside a default judgment after term time, it overlooks the following holding in *Hagedorn*: 'Again, *Hagedorn* cannot prevail because he has not shown that he was prevented from making his defense to the Alexanders' suit by their fraud or wrongful act.' This quote is just as much a declaration of the law as that part quoted in the majority opinion.

A bill of review is an equitable proceeding and one of the fundamental maxims of equity is that 'equity rewards the diligent, not one who has slept on his rights.' In this case the majority has deprived an innocent plaintiff of a judgment of a court of record entered not on appearance day but on the ninth day thereafter and before an answer was filed. This judgment became a final judgment thirty days after its entry. Our rules and our decisions deny to a trial judge the right or jurisdiction to grant a new trial therein, but the majority opinion herein applies new trial rules to a bill of review, and affirms the trial court's action granting a new trial and hearing the case.

I cannot bring myself to disregard the well-established precedents as set out in such a multitude of well reasoned opinions by this Court and by the Courts of Civil Appeals for more than one hundred years. The experience of this State has been that these rules are best in order that justice may prevail. As said by this Court in *Wear v. McCallum* (1930), 119 Tex. 473, 33 S.W.2d 723, 725:

> 'A judgment by default in a trial court must be respected and upheld when there was no fraud or mistake in its procurement, and where fair and ample opportunity was afforded the defendant to controvert and contest on their merits the allegations of the plaintiff.'

I would affirm the judgment of the Court of Civil Appeals because it follows what was, at the time it was rendered, the well-established and never- questioned law of all the cases decided by all the courts of this State.

Note

Mabon Ltd.v. Afri-Carib Enterprises, Inc. 369 S.W.3d 809 (Tex. 2012): A defendant seeking a bill of review is not required to prove its diligence in monitoring the status of its underlying case, when that bill-of-review plaintiff was represented by counsel, who had been suspended from practice for non-payment of dues and state occupation tax, and non-compliance with CLE requirements, but proves that, through no fault of its own, it did not receive notice of the trial setting that led to a default judgment. A defendant that proves (1) it had no notice of the trial setting or the default judgment within an adequate time to pursue alternative legal remedies, and (2) the lack of notice was not because of its own fault or negligence, the first two traditional bill-of-review requirements—that a defendant show proof of a meritorious defense to the underlying cause of action, which it was prevented from making by fraud, accident, or wrongful act of the opposing party or by official mistake—are rendered unnecessary, and the final traditional requirement—lack of negligence—is conclusively established. The Due Process Clause of the Fourteenth Amendment requires that once a defendant makes an appearance, that defendant is entitled to notice of the trial setting. While the third bill-of-review element, lack of fault or negligence, requires a party to show that it diligently pursued all adequate legal remedies, a party is not required to show that it diligently monitored the case status, especially after a party hires an attorney to represent it.

BAKER
v.
GOLDSMITH

582 S.W.2d 404
(Tex. 1979)

Facts: The Bakers sued the Goldsmiths, and others, alleging that they had conspired to sell them a gift shop, that they had made fraudulent representations, etc. Edward Goldsmith sent a letter by certified mail to the district judge, substantially denying the material allegations in the Bakers' petition. The letter was received on 12/11/73. On 1/4/74, the Bakers' severed the other defendants, and took a default against Edward and Juliette Goldsmith. On 3/10/74, the Goldsmiths file this bill of review, asserting that the letter to the judge constituted an answer, and that the answer had been lost at the courthouse.

The trial court found as a matter of fact that the letter was received and forwarded to the judge of the court, and that it disappeared through no fault of the Goldsmiths. The trial court concluded that the letter was an answer, and the Goldsmiths' had not received notice of the default within 30 days of its rendition. The trial court, however, found that the Goldsmith's had failed to establish their meritorious defense by a preponderance of the evidence. The court of appeals reversed and remanded. Held: Affirmed.

Issue: What is a bill of review?

A bill of review is an independent equitable action brought by a party to a former action seeking to set aside a judgment, which is no longer appealable or subject to motion for new trial. After 30 days from the date of judgment or overruling of a motion for new trial, the judgment cannot be set aside except by bill of review for sufficient cause, filed within the time allowed by law.

Issue: What is sufficient cause for a bill of review?

To be successful on a bill of review, the complainant must allege and prove:

(1) a meritorious defense to the cause of action alleged to support the judgment,
(2) which the movant was prevented from making by the fraud, accident or wrongful act of the opposite party,
(3) unmixed with any fault or negligence on the part of the movant.

Issue: What if the defendant relies upon erroneous official information given by an official court functionary?

To the extent there is reliance on the erroneous official information given by an official court functionary preventing the filing of a motion for new trial, the bill of review plaintiff is excused from showing the wrongful conduct, fraud or accident of the opposite party.

Where an officer of the court gives wrong information which prevents the filing of a motion for new trial, the complainant in a bill of review is excused from showing that the judgment was rendered as a result of the wrongful conduct of the opposite party. It is also acceptable for the complainant to allege and prove that he was prevented from presenting his contentions in the former action by a mistake or error of the court or a functionary thereof in the discharge of official duties. The circumstances of this case obviate the necessity of pleading and providing accident, fraud, or wrongful act of the Bakers.

Issue: What is the trial procedure for a bill of review?

(1) The bill of review petitioner must file a petition, alleging factually, and with particularity, that the prior judgment was rendered as the result of fraud, accident or wrongful act of the opposite party, or official mistake unmixed with the negligence of the bill of review petitioner.

(2) The bill of review petitioner must further allege, with particularity, sworn facts sufficient to constitute a defense, and as a pretrial matter, present prima facie proof to support the contention. (This is to make sure the court will not waste valuable judicial resources).

Issue: What is a meritorious defense?

Held: A meritorious defense is not one that would probably be different on retrial. Rather, a prima facie meritorious defense is made out when it is determined that the complainant's defense is not barred as a matter of law that the bill of preview petitioner will be entitled to judgment on retrial if no evidence to the contrary is offered. This is a question of law for the court.

Issue: What is prima facie proof of a meritorious defense?

Held: Prima facie proof may be comprised of documents, answers to interrogatories, admission, and affidavits on file along with such other evidence that the trial court may receive in its discretion.

Issue: May the bill of review defendant respond to the prima facie proof?

Held: Yes, the defendant may respond with proof showing that the defense is barred as a matter of law, but factual questions arising out of factual disputes are resolved in favor of the complainant of the purposes of this pretrial, legal determination.

Issue: What happens if the court determines that a meritorious defense has not been made out?

Held: The proceeding is terminated, and the trial court shall dismiss the bill of review case.

Issue: What happens if the meritorious defense has been shown?

Held: The court will then conduct a trial on the hearing. The trial, within the discretion of the court, may be done in one hearing, or in separate hearings. Either way, only one final judgment may be rendered in a bill of review proceeding either granting or denying the requested relief.

Issue: Who has the burden of persuasion?

Held: The complainant must open and assume the burden of proving that the judgment was rendered as the result of the fraud, accident or wrongful act of the opposite party or official mistake, unmixed with any negligence of his own. The bill of review defendant must assume the burden of proving the original cause of action.

Note

Amer v. Rozicki, 2011 WL 904404 (Tex. App.—Dallas 2011): "Since the *Baker* hearing [in this bill or review proceeding] conducted in the underlying case involved only a question of law, we conclude Amer was not entitled to findings of fact and conclusions of law. Accordingly, Amer's request for findings and conclusions did not operate to extend the normal thirty-day deadline to file a notice of appeal. * * *"

CALDWELL
v.
BARNES
154 S.W.3d 93
(Tex. 2004)

Gus E. Pappas, Todd S. Gaines, for Petitioner.
Thomas O. Matlock Jr., Kelly K. McKinnis, McAllen, for Respondent.

PER CURIAM.

This case arises from a bill of review proceeding that challenged a default judgment for lack of service. After holding a pretrial hearing and taking evidence on the question of whether a bill of review plaintiff had been served with process in the underlying lawsuit, the trial court issued a finding of fact that the plaintiff had been served and rendered judgment against him. The court of appeals affirmed. The issue before this Court is whether the plaintiff was entitled to submit the question of service to a jury at trial, or whether the trial court properly resolved the matter in a pretrial hearing. Because we conclude (1) that the plaintiff was entitled to submit the question of service to a jury at trial and the trial court erred by resolving the matter in a pretrial hearing, and (2) the plaintiff preserved his right to a jury trial, we reverse the court of appeals' judgment and remand the case to the trial court for further proceedings.

Robert F. Barnes sued Harold Caldwell, a Colorado resident, in Texas in 1989, alleging various causes of action stemming from a contract dispute. Barnes arranged for Caldwell to be personally served with process in Colorado through a private process server, DeWayne Perdew. The return of service filed with the trial court reflects that Perdew hand-delivered process to Caldwell in Jefferson County, Colorado on July 30, 1989. Caldwell contends that he was never served with process, and as a result, did not file an answer. When Caldwell did not answer, Barnes obtained a $15,500,000 default judgment against him.

In 1993, Caldwell filed a petition for a bill of review in the trial court, claiming he was never served with process. In support of his claim, Caldwell submitted (1) an affidavit stating that he had never been served; (2) a second affidavit from Perdew in which Perdew contradicted his earlier affidavit by stating that he had not, in fact, ever served Caldwell; (3) an affidavit from Perdew's ex-girlfriend, Lucy Lackey, corroborating Perdew's retraction by stating that Perdew could not have served Caldwell on July 30, 1989, because on that date he was attending a George Strait concert with her in Cheyenne, Wyoming; (4) the affidavits of four litigants in unrelated lawsuits, whom Perdew claimed to have served on July 30, 1989, but who similarly denied service; and (5) the affidavit of a landlord stating that no one resided at an apartment where Perdew claimed to have served a tenant with process on that same date.

Both parties moved for summary judgment. Caldwell asserted that the above-mentioned affidavits established that he was never served with process, and therefore the default judgment against him should be set aside.

Barnes, however, asserted that Caldwell's bill of review should be denied because Caldwell had failed to exhaust his legal remedies in Colorado and because a bill of review was barred by laches since Caldwell had failed to diligently exercise his right to challenge notice when he was informed of the default judgment against him. The trial court granted summary judgment in favor of Barnes, and the court of appeals affirmed. 941 S.W.2d 182, 190.

On review, this Court reversed the court of appeals' judgment and remanded the case to the trial court. This Court held that Barnes was not entitled to summary judgment because Caldwell was not required to exhaust his legal remedies in Colorado as a prerequisite to relief in Texas, and because a bill of review was not barred by laches since it was brought within the statutory limitations period. 975 S.W.2d 535, 538-39. This Court further held that "because the original return of service conflict[ed] with Caldwell's, Perdew's, and the others' subsequent affidavits," a genuine issue of fact existed as to whether Caldwell had been served in the underlying proceeding. *Id.* at 537.

In June 2000, on remand from this Court, the trial court conducted a pretrial hearing on the question of Caldwell's service. At the hearing, Caldwell offered evidence suggesting that he was never served with process, including the above-mentioned affidavits, Caldwell's own testimony that he was not served with process on July 30, 1989, or at any other time, and Lackey's testimony that on July 30, 1989, Perdew was with her in Wyoming and therefore did not serve process on Caldwell. During cross-examination, however, Caldwell admitted that in the past he had purposely allowed approximately a dozen default judgments to be taken against him, even after being properly served with process, because defaulting was often less costly than defending the underlying suits. In addition, during Lackey's cross-examination, she admitted that she could not remember who prepared her affidavit or where it was signed. She also testified that she could not produce receipts and concert ticket stubs supporting her trip with Perdew to Wyoming, because in 1991, she had relinquished them to Caldwell's agents after they arranged to meet with her at the Taco Bell where she worked in Colorado. Caldwell, however, never introduced any receipts or ticket stubs into evidence to support Lackey's claims.

After the pretrial hearing, the trial court made the following factual findings: (1) the credibility and interest of the witnesses present at the hearing was in issue; (2) Caldwell had a practice of being served with process and not answering, thus allowing default judgments to be entered against him; (3) Perdew gave at least two completely contradictory statements under oath regarding service; (4) Lackey's credibility had been called into question; and (5) Caldwell had been served. Based on these findings, the trial court declined to proceed to trial and denied Caldwell's bill of review. The court of appeals affirmed the trial court's judgment. --- S.W.3d ----, 2003 WL 359453. Caldwell petitioned this Court for review. We must decide whether (1) Caldwell was entitled to submit the question of service of process to a jury at trial, and if the trial court therefore erred by resolving the matter in a pretrial hearing, and (2) whether the error was harmful because Caldwell preserved his right to a jury trial on the issue.

We begin by considering what a bill of review plaintiff must prove when claiming lack of service of process. A bill of review is an equitable proceeding brought by a party seeking to set aside a prior judgment that is no longer subject to challenge by a motion for new trial or appeal. *Baker v. Goldsmith*, 582 S.W.2d 404, 406 (Tex. 1979). Bill of review plaintiffs must ordinarily plead and prove (1) a meritorious defense to the underlying cause of action, (2) which the plaintiffs were prevented from making by the fraud, accident or wrongful act of the opposing party or official mistake, (3) unmixed with any fault or negligence on their own part. *Id.* at 406-08; 975 S.W.2d at 537.

Bill of review plaintiffs claiming non-service, however, are relieved of two elements ordinarily required to be proved in a bill of review proceeding. 975 S.W.2d at 537; *see Tex. Indus., Inc. v. Sanchez*, 525 S.W.2d 870, 871 (Tex. 1975). First, if a plaintiff was not served, constitutional due process relieves the plaintiff from the need to show a meritorious defense. *Peralta v. Heights Med. Ctr., Inc.*, 485 U.S. 80, 86- 87, 108 S.Ct. 896, 99 L.Ed.2d 75 (1988) (holding that the meritorious defense requirement in a bill of review proceeding violates due process where the bill of review plaintiff has no notice of the proceeding in which the default judgment was rendered); 975 S.W.2d at 537. Second, the plaintiff is relieved from showing that fraud, accident, wrongful act or official mistake prevented the plaintiff from presenting such a defense. 975 S.W.2d at 537; *Sanchez*, 525 S.W.2d at 871.

Bill of review plaintiffs alleging they were not served, however, must still prove the third and final element required in a bill of review proceeding that the judgment was rendered unmixed with any fault or negligence of their own. In *Caldwell*, we said this third and final element is conclusively established if the plaintiff can prove that he or she was never served with process. 975 S.W.2d at 537. An individual who is not served with process cannot be at fault or negligent in allowing a default judgment to be rendered. Proof of non-service, then, will conclusively establish the third and only element that bill of review plaintiffs are required to prove when they are asserting lack of service of process as their only defense.[4]

We next consider whether Caldwell was entitled to submit the question of service of process to a jury at trial or whether the trial court could properly resolve the question in a pretrial proceeding. In *Goldsmith*, we outlined the procedure to be utilized in a bill of review proceeding. 582 S.W.2d at 408-09; *see also State v.1985 Chevrolet Pickup Truck*, 778 S.W.2d 463, 464-65 (Tex. 1989). We held in *Goldsmith* that a bill of review plaintiff is required, as a pretrial matter, to present prima facie proof of a meritorious defense to the underlying cause of action. 582 S.W.2d at 408-09; *see also Beck v. Beck*, 771 S.W.2d 141, 142 (Tex. 1989). This requirement, as we have stated, is dispensed with when the plaintiff is claiming lack of service of process. We further held that once prima facie proof of a meritorious defense has been established, the court should conduct a trial in which the plaintiff must negate his or her fault or negligence. *Goldsmith*, 582 S.W.2d at 409. Because proof of non-service conclusively negates a plaintiff's fault or negligence, then, the question of service is properly resolved at trial and not by the trial court in a pretrial proceeding if the material facts are disputed.

In sum, when a plaintiff seeks a bill of review based solely on a claim of non-service, the bill of review procedure outlined in *Goldsmith* must be slightly modified. *See id.* at 408-09. When a plaintiff claims lack of service, the trial court should: (1) dispense with any pretrial inquiry into a meritorious defense, (2) hold a trial, at which the bill of review plaintiff assumes the burden of proving that the plaintiff was not served with process, thereby conclusively establishing a lack of fault or negligence in allowing a default judgment to be rendered, and (3) conditioned upon an affirmative finding that the plaintiff was not served, allow the parties to revert to their original status as plaintiff and defendant with the burden on the original plaintiff to prove his or her case.

Finally, we consider whether the denial of a jury trial on the issue of service of process was harmful error. Because the trial court considered conflicting evidence, made findings of fact based on the evidence, and ultimately determined that Caldwell was served with process, Barnes argues that it was harmless error for the trial court not to present the question of service to the jury. Specifically, Barnes relies on the court of appeals' holding that "in a non-jury case, the trial court's findings of fact have the same force and dignity as does a jury verdict on special issues." --- S.W.3d ----, 2003 WL 359453. We do not agree with Barnes, however, that this was a "non-jury" case.

The record indicates that Caldwell never assented to a non-jury determination on the issue of service. Caldwell's attorney specifically asserted to the trial court that service of process was a "question of fact" and that Caldwell was entitled to a trial on the issue. Similarly, Barnes's attorney argued that service of process presented a fact question for the jury to decide. Further, the record reflects that the jury fee had been paid and the case had been placed on the jury trial docket. When a party timely demands a jury and pays the fee, the trial court may not remove the case from the jury docket over the objection of the opposing party. *See* TEX.R. CIV. P. 216, 220; *Mercedes-Benz Credit Corp. v. Rhyne*, 925 S.W.2d 664, 667 (Tex. 1996). The wrongful denial of a jury trial is harmful when the case contains a question of material fact. *Rhyne*, 925 S.W.2d at 666. The question of whether Caldwell was served with process is a question of material fact, and therefore the denial of a jury trial was harmful error.

Caldwell must be given a jury trial because he preserved his right to have a jury decide whether he was served with process. At trial, he must establish by a preponderance of the evidence that he was never served. Pursuant to Rule 59.1 of the Texas Rules of Appellate Procedure, we grant Caldwell's petition for review, and without hearing oral argument, we reverse the court of appeals' judgment and remand the case to the trial court for further proceedings consistent with this opinion. *See* TEX.R.APP. P. 59.1.

---

[4] *Cf.* Campus Invs., Inc. v. Cullever, 144 S.W.3d 464, 466 (Tex. 2004) (holding that when bill of review plaintiffs are properly served with process, they must show they were not at fault or negligent in allowing a default judgment to be rendered); Gold v. Gold, 145 S.W.3d 212, 214 (Tex. 2004) (failure to seek reinstatement, new trial, or appeal, if available, normally would be negligence).

PNS STORES, INC.
v.
RIVERA
379 S.W.3d 267
(Tex. 2012)

Peter D. Kennedy, Graves Dougherty Hearon & Moody PC, Austin, TX, for Amicus Curiae CSC—Lawyers Incorporating Service Company.

David A. Oliver, Jr., Paul Brown Kerlin, Tiffany Sue Bingham, Vorys, Sater, Seymour and Pease LLP, Houston, TX, for Petitioner PNS Stores, Inc.

Bernard Wm. Fischman, Attorney at Law, Richard Tinsman, Daniel J.T. Sciano, Tinsman & Sciano, Inc., San Antonio, TX, Kimberly S. Keller, Keller Stolarczyk PLLC, Boerne, TX, for Respondent Rivera, Anna E.

JUSTICE GUZMAN delivered the opinion of the Court.

In this appeal from a summary judgment dismissal of a direct and collateral attack, the petitioner, PNS Stores, Inc., contends the underlying judgment is void and subject to collateral attack at any time. In this regard, PNS argues that the trial court rendering the default judgment never acquired personal jurisdiction over it because the service of process was defective. Alternatively, PNS argues that its adversary's extrinsic fraud prevented it from learning about the underlying default judgment and that limitations was thereby tolled, making its direct attack through a bill of review timely.

The court of appeals affirmed the summary judgment, concluding that the underlying default judgment was not void and that there was no evidence of extrinsic fraud that would toll limitations. 335 S.W.3d 265, 277. We agree with the court below that the alleged defects in service of process were not sufficient to render the default judgment void, but we hold that summary judgment was improperly granted because there is some evidence of extrinsic fraud. Accordingly, we reverse the court of appeals' judgment and remand the case to the trial court for further proceedings.

I. Factual and Procedural Background

On December 29, 1998, Rachael Rivera filed suit against PNS Stores, Inc. in state court for injuries she allegedly sustained when she slipped and fell at a MacFrugal's Bargain Closeouts Store, owned by PNS. PNS removed the case to federal court, and after discovery, the federal district court granted PNS's motion for summary judgment and dismissed the case "without prejudice on January 7, 2000." No appeal was taken.

Three months later, Rivera, through her attorney Oscar Tamez, sued again in state court for the same slip and fall claims, serving PNS through its registered agent for service of process, Prentice Hall Corporation. PNS failed to answer, and Rivera obtained a no-answer default judgment for $1,480,677.74 plus post-judgment interest. Rivera then waited six years to abstract the judgment and about nine years to attempt execution. By then, the judgment had more than doubled to $3,513,070.55. The writ of execution was served at the PNS corporate headquarters in Columbus, Ohio and at its place of business in San Antonio on February 10, 2009.

Thirteen days later, PNS filed a bill of review seeking to set aside the default judgment and quash the writ. After limited discovery, both Rivera and PNS moved for summary judgment. Rivera moved for summary judgment based on the four-year statute of limitations applicable to a bill of review. In its summary judgment motion, PNS argued that the default judgment was barred by res judicata and void due to errors in service of process. Alternatively, PNS argued that if the judgment was merely voidable, its bill of review was nonetheless timely filed because its adversary's extrinsic fraud tolled limitations.

The trial court granted Rivera's motion for summary judgment and denied PNS's. PNS appealed. The court of appeals affirmed the summary judgment, concluding that: (1) PNS's attack was a direct attack; (2) PNS's only possible means of direct attack was by bill of review that would be barred by limitations unless there was evidence of extrinsic fraud sufficient to toll the bill's four-year limitations period; and (3) there was no evidence of extrinsic fraud. 335 S.W.3d 265, 275-77.

II. Analysis

PNS argues the court of appeals erred in affirming Rivera's summary judgment because (1) defects in service rendered the default judgment void, and therefore assailable at any time, and (2) even if the judgment was merely voidable, the summary judgment was nevertheless erroneous because fact issues remained regarding the existence of extrinsic fraud sufficient to toll the bill of review's limitations period. Although we disagree that the alleged defects in service render the default judgment void, we agree there is some evidence of extrinsic fraud sufficient to raise a fact issue about whether PNS's bill of review is barred by limitations.

A. Void and Voidable Judgments

Because there is some inconsistency in our state's jurisprudence concerning important distinctions between void and voidable judgments and direct and collateral attacks, we begin our analysis with a discussion of clarifying principles. It is well settled that a litigant may attack a void judgment directly or collaterally, but a voidable judgment may only be attacked directly. *Hagen v. Hagen,* 282 S.W.3d 899, 902 (Tex. 2009) (holding that a divorce decree must be "void, not voidable, for a collateral attack to be permitted"); *Ramsey v. Ramsey,* 19 S.W.3d 548, 552 (Tex. App.—Austin 2000, no pet.). A direct attack—such as an appeal, a motion for new trial, or a bill of review—attempts to correct, amend, modify or vacate a judgment and must be brought within a definite time period after the judgment's rendition. A void judgment, on the other hand, can be collaterally attacked at any time. *In re E.R.,* —— S.W.3d ——, —— (Tex. 2012). A collateral attack seeks to avoid the binding effect of a judgment in order to obtain specific relief that the judgment currently impedes. *Browning v. Prostok,* 165 S.W.3d 336, 346 (Tex. 2005). After the time to bring a direct attack has expired, a litigant may only attack a judgment collaterally.

The distinction between void and voidable judgments is critical when the time for a direct attack has expired. Before then, the distinction is less significant because—whether the judgment is void or voidable—the result is the same: the judgment is vacated. We have described a judgment as void when "the court rendering judgment had no jurisdiction of the parties or property, no jurisdiction of the subject matter, no jurisdiction to enter the particular judgment, or no capacity to act." *Travelers Ins. Co. v. Joachim,* 315 S.W.3d 860, 863 (Tex. 2010) (quoting *Browning,* 165 S.W.3d at 346). Some confusion persists, however, over collateral attacks premised on the absence of personal jurisdiction over a party. *See, e.g., Skadden v. Alfonso,* 217 S.W.3d 611, 619-20 (Tex. App.—Houston [14th Dist.] 2006) (noting "dicta" from this Court that courts may allow collateral attack if defendant is not served with process, but concluding that because *McEwen v. Harrison,* 162 Tex. 125, 345 S.W.2d 706 (1961), had not been overruled or disapproved, the court was bound to follow it), *rev'd on other grounds,* 251 S.W.3d 52 (Tex. 2008) (per curiam).

This confusion can be traced to our decision in *McEwen. McEwen* purported to distinguish the absence of personal jurisdiction from a lack of subject matter jurisdiction, observing that a default judgment rendered by a court without subject matter jurisdiction would be void whereas a judgment rendered by a court lacking personal jurisdiction over the parties might only be voidable. 345 S.W.3d at 710 (suggesting that the bill of review was the exclusive method to vacate a default judgment allegedly void for "want of service, or of valid service, of process"); *see also Deen v. Kirk,* 508 S.W.2d 70, 72 (Tex. 1974) (noting that *McEwen* was concerned about "jurisdiction over the subject matter . . . not . . . jurisdiction over the parties"). To the extent that *McEwen* may be read to foreclose a collateral attack on a judgment based on the failure to serve a party with notice, it has been overruled by *Peralta v. Heights Medical Center, Inc.,* 485 U.S. 80, 108 S.Ct. 896, 99 L.Ed.2d 75 (1988). *E.R.,* —— S.W.3d at ——.

In *Peralta,* the United States Supreme Court held that "a judgment entered without notice or service is constitutionally infirm," and some form of attack must be available when defects in personal jurisdiction violate due process. 485 U.S. at 84, 108 S.Ct. 896. The Court stated, " '[a]n elementary and fundamental requirement of due process in any proceeding which is to be accorded finality is notice reasonably calculated, under the circumstances, to apprise interested parties of the pendency of the action . . . .' " *Id.* (quoting *Mullane v. Cent. Hanover Bank & Trust Co.,* 339 U.S. 306, 314, 70 S.Ct. 652, 94 L.Ed. 865 (1950)). Thus, the "[f]ailure to give notice violates 'the most rudimentary demands of due process of law.' " *Id.* (quoting *Armstrong v. Manzo,* 380 U.S. 545, 550, 85 S.Ct. 1187, 14 L.Ed.2d 62 (1965)). In light of *Peralta,* we hold that a judgment may also be challenged through a collateral attack when a failure to establish personal jurisdiction violates due process.

Turning to the case at hand, PNS argues that defects in service prevented the trial court from acquiring personal jurisdiction over it and asserts that the citation: (1) fails to list the exact time service was performed; (2) fails to state that PNS was served through its registered agent; (3) states that Prentice Hall was served "VIA USPS" as well as "in person;" (4) does not state that service was by certified mail; (5) does not recite that Prentice Hall was served by registered or certified mail; and (6) lacks any proof that it was on file for ten days preceding the default judgment. *See generally* TEX.R. CIV. P. 106, 107. PNS concludes that the default judgment is void and therefore must be set aside because of these defects. Rivera counters that the alleged defects do not create a jurisdictional problem but that, in any event, the Court may not look beyond the jurisdictional recitals on the face of the judgment to determine whether the trial court lacked jurisdiction.

Although we do not agree that we must confine our review to the face of the judgment, we nevertheless conclude that these asserted defects in service do not render the default judgment void. When attacked collaterally, a judgment is presumed valid. *Stewart v. USA Custom Paint & Body Shop, Inc.,* 870 S.W.2d 18, 20 (Tex. 1994). But that presumption disappears when the record establishes a jurisdictional defect. *Alfonso,* 251 S.W.3d at 55 (holding that "[t]he presumption supporting judgments does not apply when the record affirmatively reveals a jurisdictional defect"). Accordingly, although we presume Rivera's default judgment is valid, we may look beyond its face to determine whether the record affirmatively demonstrates that the trial court lacked jurisdiction.

The record affirmatively demonstrates a jurisdictional defect sufficient to void a judgment when it either: (1) establishes that the trial court lacked subject matter jurisdiction over the suit; or (2) exposes such personal jurisdictional deficiencies as to violate due process. Here, PNS filed its attack outside the bill of review's four-year statute of limitations period and its complaints amount to no more than allegations of improper service. We must therefore determine whether PNS's complaints rise to the level of a due process violation that would render the default judgment void and subject to collateral attack. The defects PNS identifies are technical in nature. After *Peralta,* Texas courts of appeals have correctly distinguished between technical defects in service and a complete failure or lack of service, concluding that only the latter violates due process. *Compare Wagner v. D'Lorm,* 315 S.W.3d 188, 194 (Tex. App.—Austin 2010, no pet.) (construing an attack as collateral where a complete lack of service was alleged), *with Layton v. Nationsbanc Mortg. Corp.,* 141 S.W.3d 760, 763 (Tex. App.—Corpus Christi 2004, no pet.) (holding that improper service alone does not render a judgment void). This distinction strikes a reasonable balance between the need for finality of judgments and the requirement that the power underlying judicial authority must be based on a litigant's fair opportunity to be heard.

PNS nevertheless argues that a default judgment must be vacated when the prevailing party fails to strictly comply with statutory notice provisions. *See, e.g., Wilson v. Dunn,* 800 S.W.2d 833, 836 (Tex. 1990). But the cases on which it relies simply reiterate the strict compliance requirement in the context of a direct attack on a default judgment. *See, e.g., Primate Constr. Inc. v. Silver,* 884 S.W.2d 151, 152 (Tex. 1994) (per curiam) (noting that strict compliance is necessary to withstand a direct attack). Extending these stringent standards to collateral attacks involving mere technical defects in service would pose a serious threat to the finality of judgments. *See King Ranch, Inc. v. Chapman,* 118 S.W.3d 742, 751 (Tex. 2003). "While no system is infallible, '[e]ndless litigation, in which nothing was ever finally determined, would be worse than the occasional miscarriages of justice.' " *Browning,* 165 S.W.3d at 348 (alteration in original) (quoting *Alexander v. Hagedorn,* 148 Tex. 565, 226 S.W.2d 996, 998 (1950)). Exercising personal jurisdiction under these circumstances does not violate due process.

Moreover, although the service is technically defective, the record shows that Rivera requested service of process on PNS's registered agent for service, and its agent's (Prentice Hall's) computer records reveal that it received the service and accompanying documents and forwarded them to PNS. Although PNS claims it did not receive notice of the suit until February 10, 2010, some nine years after the default was taken, service effected on a registered agent within the scope of its agency is imputed to the litigant. *See Preston Farm & Ranch Supply, Inc. v. Bio-Zyme Enters.,* 625 S.W.2d 295, 300 (Tex. 1981) (holding that notice to an agent, in the scope of his agency, is notice to the principal). And further, its agent's records reflect that PNS acknowledged receipt.

In sum, a judgment is void if the defects in service are so substantial that the defendant was not afforded due process. None of the defects at issue here deprived PNS of a meaningful opportunity to appear and answer Rivera's claims. When a defective citation is served, but the citation puts the defendant on notice of asserted claims in a pending suit, and the technical defects are not of the sort that deprive a litigant of the opportunity to be heard, we reject them as grounds sufficient to support a collateral attack. Because the trial court had jurisdiction over the subject matter of Rivera's claims and the technical defects in service at best render the default judgment voidable, not void, PNS may not collaterally attack the judgment.

B. Extrinsic Fraud

Having rejected PNS's collateral attack on the judgment, PNS must rely on its bill of review to attack the default judgment directly. A direct attack can be in the form of a motion for new trial, appeal, or bill of review. *Frost Nat'l Bank v. Fernandez,* 315 S.W.3d 494, 504 (Tex. 2010). A bill of review is an equitable proceeding to set aside a prior judgment that is no longer subject to challenge by a motion for new trial or direct appeal. *Id.* It must, however, be brought within four years of the rendition of the judgment. *Caldwell v. Barnes,* 975 S.W.2d 535, 537 (Tex. 1998) (citing TEX. CIV. PRAC. & REM.CODE § 16.051). Here, PNS did not file its bill of review until approximately nine years after the default was rendered. If PNS can prove extrinsic fraud, however, the bill of review's four-year limitations period may be tolled. In affirming the summary judgment, the court of appeals concluded that there was no evidence of extrinsic fraud. We disagree.

A direct attack on "a judgment on the basis of extrinsic fraud is allowed because such fraud distorts the judicial process to such an extent that confidence in the ability to discover the fraudulent conduct through the regular adversarial process is undermined." *Browning,* 165 S.W.3d at 348. Extrinsic fraud is fraud that denies a litigant the opportunity to fully litigate at trial all the rights or defenses that could have been asserted. *King Ranch,* 118 S.W.3d at 752. It occurs when a litigant has been misled by his adversary by fraud or deception, or was denied knowledge of the suit. *Alexander,* 226 S.W.2d at 1001. PNS argues that Tamez's failure to comply with Texas Rule of Civil Procedure 239a, his violations of the Texas Lawyer's Creed, and his extensive history of unethical conduct, including his disbarment, are indicative of extrinsic fraud.

We first address PNS's argument that Tamez misled the trial court by providing the clerk with PNS's registered agent's address as the last known address for PNS. Texas Rule of Civil Procedure 239a requires in relevant part:

> At or immediately prior to the time . . . [a] final default judgment is rendered, the party taking the same or his attorney shall certify to the clerk in writing the last known mailing address of the party against whom the judgment is taken . . . . Immediately upon the signing of the judgment, the clerk shall mail written notice thereof to the party against whom the judgment was rendered at the address shown in the certificate . . . .

TEX.R. CIV. P. 239a. PNS argues that Tamez knew: (1) PNS's contact information including the address of its corporate headquarters and its local store in San Antonio; (2) the name and address of the local attorneys who had defended PNS in the previous case involving the same claim; and (3) that PNS would certainly defend any refiled claim. This knowledge, according to PNS, is some evidence that Tamez purposefully provided the clerk with Prentice Hall's address instead of PNS's last known address to prevent PNS from discovering the default. This is especially so, PNS argues, in light of PNS's failure to appear after the previous service through Prentice Hall. Rule 239a is intended to ensure that the party in default receives personal notice.

Rivera responds that Tamez's violation of Rule 239a is not evidence of extrinsic fraud and points us to two cases. In *Layton,* Layton provided the clerk with the address she had been given by defendant Nationsbanc as the place to receive her payments. 141 S.W.3d at 764. The court of appeals stated that Nationsbanc had failed to demonstrate why that address would be fraudulent for the purpose of receiving notices of judgment. *Id.* In *Alderson v. Alderson,* the defendant failed to provide any evidence to show that the plaintiff engaged in a purposeful act of deception, because although the motion for summary judgment was mailed to the wrong address, there was no evidence that this was due to anything other than mistake or accident. 352 S.W.3d 875, 878 (Tex. App.—Dallas 2001, pet. denied).

We conclude that under the specific circumstances presented in this case, Tamez's failure to provide the clerk with PNS's last known address, which he knew, is some evidence of extrinsic fraud. In contrast to *Layton* and *Alderson,* Tamez knew PNS's mailing address, had corresponded with PNS and its counsel at this last known address only months earlier and instead chose to provide the clerk with the address of PNS's registered agent, Prentice Hall.

Next, PNS argues that Tamez's violations of the Texas Lawyer's Creed is evidence of extrinsic fraud. The Texas Lawyer's Creed, promulgated by this Court and the Court of Criminal Appeals, was intended to encourage lawyers to be mindful that abusive tactics—ranging from hostility to obstructionism—do not serve the justice we pursue. The Texas Lawyer's Creed—A Mandate for Professionalism, *reprinted in* TEXAS RULES OF COURT 865, 865 (West 2012). The Lawyer's Creed serves as an important reminder that the conduct of lawyers "should be characterized at all times by honesty, candor, and fairness." *Id.* The Lawyer's Creed states that an attorney "will not take advantage, by causing any default or dismissal to be rendered, when [he] know[s] the identity of an opposing counsel, without first inquiring about that counsel's intention to proceed." *Id.* at 867.

PNS argues that Tamez, in blatant violation of the Texas Lawyer's Creed, purposefully took a default judgment against PNS without contacting PNS's known attorneys and that he did so only three months after the federal court granted summary judgment in the first suit with full knowledge that PNS would defend the second lawsuit as vigorously as it had the first. The Lawyer's Creed, however, is aspirational. It does not create new duties and obligations enforceable by the courts beyond those existing as a result of (1) the courts' inherent powers and (2) the rules already in existence. *Id.* at 865. The failure to notify opposing counsel of an intent to take a default judgment does not trigger the courts' inherent powers. *See Cont'l Carbon Co. v. Sea-Land Serv., Inc.,* 27 S.W.3d 184, 189 (Tex. App.—Dallas 2000, pet. denied). A lawyer's failure to adhere to the Texas Lawyer's Creed may be evidence of a lack of professionalism or character, but Tamez's failure to adhere to the spirit and letter of this aspirational standard in this case is not itself evidence of extrinsic fraud.

Finally, PNS argues that Tamez's history of unethical conduct, including grievances filed against him, his subsequent disbarment, and his refusal to give deposition testimony, is evidence of extrinsic fraud. But "[e]vidence of other wrongs or acts is not admissible to prove character in order to show 'action in conformity therewith.' " *Serv. Corp. Int'l v. Guerra,* 348 S.W.3d 221, 235 (Tex. 2011) (quoting TEX.R. EVID. 404(a)). Such evidence may be admissible to show intent, however, if "the prior acts are 'so connected with the transaction at issue that they may all be parts of a system, scheme or plan.' " *Id.* (quoting *Oakwood Mobile Homes, Inc. v. Cabler,* 73 S.W.3d 363, 375 (Tex. App.—El Paso 2002, pet. denied)). Unless some connection can be drawn between PNS's failure to assert its rights in this case and Tamez's grievances and disbarment, they will not suffice as evidence of extrinsic fraud. *See King Ranch,* 118 S.W.3d at 752. Because PNS offers no connection here, these prior acts are not evidence of extrinsic fraud.

In sum, although Tamez's failure to abide by the Texas Lawyer's Creed and his unethical conduct are not evidence of extrinsic fraud, under the specific facts of this case, his failure to comply with Texas Rule of Civil Procedure 239a is sufficient to raise a genuine issue of material fact regarding extrinsic fraud and its effect on limitations.

III. Conclusion

The alleged technical defects in service render the judgment voidable, not void. Therefore, PNS cannot collaterally attack the judgment. But because there is some evidence of extrinsic fraud, a material fact issue remains regarding Rivera's limitations defense. Accordingly, we reverse the judgment of the court of appeals and remand the case to the trial court for further proceedings.

Note

Evidence of extrinsic fraud does not toll the bill of review's limitations period indefinitely. *See Defee v. Defee,* 966 S.W.2d 719, 722 (Tex. App.—San Antonio 1998, no pet.); *Maddux v. Brownen,* 759 S.W.2d 183, 185 (Tex. App.—Waco 1988, writ denied). A bill of review's four-year limitations period begins to run when the litigant knew or should have known about the default judgment.

ROSS
v.
NATIONAL CENTER FOR THE EMPLOYMENT OF THE DISABLED

197 S.W.3d 795
(Tex. 2006)

John P. Mobbs, Attorney At Law, El Paso, for Petitioner.
Ken Slavin, Kemp Smith, LLP, El Paso, for Respondent.

PER CURIAM.

In one of several suits between these parties, a trial court entered a $10 million default judgment against a party who was never served. When the trial court denied a bill of review to set aside that default, the court of appeals affirmed, pointing to evidence that the unserved party failed to file a motion for a new trial in the original default, and resisted postjudgment enforcement of it. 176 S.W.3d 642, 646-49. But the trial court had no jurisdiction either to enter judgment or to enforce it against a party who had neither been properly served nor appeared. Accordingly, we reverse.

In 1998, Tamarack Capital, LLC and Tamarack Insurance, LLC ("Tamarack") sued Access Healthsource, Inc. in Arizona state court for breach of a stock merger agreement. Access removed the case to federal court, and added a counterclaim against Tamarack and misrepresentation crossclaims against Richard Ross (the owner of the Tamarack entities) and others. After a bench trial, the federal court in Arizona entered judgment against Access for about $1 million, and the 9th Circuit affirmed. *See* 91 F.App'x. 551 (9th Cir. 2004).

Meanwhile, ten Access shareholders sued Ross and two others on fraud claims in El Paso County Court No. 7. It is undisputed that service was defective in many respects and that Ross never received citation. *See* 176 S.W.3d at 645. Nevertheless, the El Paso court granted a default judgment against him for $5 million actual and $5 million exemplary damages.

The shareholders assigned this default judgment to Access, which thereafter assigned it to an entity named National Center for the Employment of the Disabled. The latter attempted to domesticate the default judgment in Arizona. Ross successfully persuaded the Arizona court to set it aside for lack of service.

Ross also filed a bill of review in El Paso to set aside the default. The trial court dismissed his bill of review by summary judgment, but the Eighth Court of Appeals reversed, finding a fact issue whether Ross had pursued his legal remedies with diligence. *See* 2003 WL 22870629 at *4. At a bench trial on remand, the trial court found against Ross and again denied his bill of review. This time the court of appeals affirmed, on two grounds.

The court of appeals held Ross had not shown diligence in pursuing his legal remedies. Traditionally, a bill of review requires proof of three elements: (1) a meritorious defense, (2) that was not asserted due to fraud, accident, or wrongful act of an opponent or official mistake, (3) unmixed with any fault or negligence by the movant *See Baker v. Goldsmith*, 582 S.W.2d 404, 407 (Tex. 1979); *Sedgwick v. Kirby Lumber Co.*, 130 Tex. 163, 107 S.W.2d 358, 359 (1937). But in *Caldwell v. Barnes,* we held that a defendant who is not served with process is entitled to a bill of review without a further showing, because the Constitution discharges the first element, and lack of service establishes the second and third. *See* 154 S.W.3d 93, 96-97 (Tex. 2004).

The court of appeals found Ross at fault because, though he learned of the February 29, 2000 default judgment by regular mail on April 12, 2000, he did not file an out-of-time motion for new trial in that case. *See* TEX. R. CIV. P. 306a. In the first place, if a postjudgment postcard giving notice of default triggers a duty to enter an appearance, service of process would become obsolete. A defendant who responded to such a postcard would make a general appearance, rendering service unnecessary; a defendant who ignored it would be barred from attacking it later and simply have to pay the default judgment. Proper service is not a technicality so easily discarded.

More important, "[a] party who becomes aware of the proceedings without proper service of process has no duty to participate in them." *Caldwell*, 154 S.W.3d at 97 n. 1; *accord, Wilson v. Dunn*, 800 S.W.2d 833, 837 (Tex. 1990) ("[M]ere knowledge of a pending suit does not place any duty on a defendant to act."); *Harrell v. Mexico Cattle Co.*, 73 Tex. 612, 11 S.W. 863, 865 (1889) ("A defendant . . . is not bound to take action until he has been duly served with process."). While diligence is required from properly served parties or those who have appeared, *see Gold v. Gold,* 145 S.W.3d 212, 214 (Tex. 2004), those not properly served have no duty to act, diligently or otherwise. *See Caldwell*, 154 S.W.3d at 97 ("An individual who is not served with process cannot be at fault or negligent in allowing a default judgment to be rendered."). Ross filed his bill of review well within the applicable four-year limitations period, *see Caldwell v. Barnes*, 975 S.W.2d 535, 538-39 (Tex. 1998), and proved that he had never been properly served. We hold the court of appeals erred in requiring Ross to act diligently in a case in which he was never served.

The court of appeals also affirmed on the basis that Ross did not have clean hands. The court first cited Ross's failure to appear at the trial of his bill of review after receiving a subpoena. 176 S.W.3d at 649. But there is nothing in the record indicating the district court considered or tried lesser sanctions before denying his bill of review. While the range of sanctions available for nonappearance is quite broad, it generally does not include dismissing a party's case as an initial step. *See TransAmerican Natural Gas Corp. v. Powell*, 811 S.W.2d 913, 919 (Tex. 1991).

The court of appeals also faulted Ross for failing to cooperate with postjudgment efforts to collect the earlier default judgment-in the case in which he was never properly served. As already noted, a party has no duty to participate in proceedings absent proper service of process. *See Caldwell,* 154 S.W.3d at 97; *Wilson*, 800 S.W.2d at 836-37. Moreover, "death penalty" sanctions are inappropriate unless a party's conduct "justifies a presumption that its claims or defenses lack merit," *Cire v. Cummings*, 134 S.W.3d 835, 840 (Tex. 2004); refusing to appear in court without proper citation does not justify such a presumption. Finally, a bill of review is a separate proceeding from the underlying suit, *see Caldwell*, 154 S.W.3d at 98 (ordering separate jury trial for bill of review issues); the court of appeals did not explain why the trial court could sanction Ross in this proceeding for misconduct in another. We hold the court of appeals erred in finding that a party never served can challenge a default judgment only if he first complies with it.

Accordingly, without hearing oral argument, we reverse the court of appeals, render judgment for Ross setting aside the default judgment, and remand for trial on the merits of the underlying allegations. *See* TEX. R. APP. P. 59.1.

Notes

1. *The Bill of Review.*

"A bill of review is an equitable proceeding by a party to a former action who seeks to set aside a judgment that is no longer appealable or subject to a motion for new trial."[1]

a. *Time to Act.*

i. *After the End of the Trial Court's Plenary Power.*

TEX. R. CIV. P. 329b(f) provides that:

> "On expiration of the time within which the trial court has plenary power, a judgment cannot be set aside by the trial court except by bill of review for sufficient cause, filed within the time allowed by law; . . ."

This, of course, does not affect the ability of the appellate courts, in an ordinary appeal or appeal by writ of error, to set aside the judgment of the trial court. But the trial court cannot further change the judgment for judicial error without the filing of the bill of review.[2]

An exception exists when the court rendering the judgment had no jurisdictional power to do so.[3]

---

[1] Ortega v. First Republic Bank Fort Worth, 33 Tex. Sup. Ct. J. 285 (March 3, 1990); Transworld Fin. Serv. Corp. v. Briscoe, 722 S.W.2d 407 (Tex. 1987).

[2] McEwen v. Harrison, 162 Tex. 125, 345 S.W.2d 706 (1961); Deen v Kirk, 508 S.W.2d 70, 71 (Tex. 1974); State of Texas v. 1985 Chevrolet Pickup Truck, 778 S.W.2d 463, 464 (Tex. 1989).

[3] Middleton v. Murff, 689 S.W.2d 212, 213 (Tex. 1985); Hicks v. First National Bank in Dalhart, 778 S.W.2d 98, 101 (Tex. App.—Amarillo 1989, no writ).

ii. *Limitations*. Commence Within Four Years. The residual four year statute of limitations, TEX. CIV. PRAC. & REM. CODE ANN. § 16.051 (Vernon 1986), applies,[4] but caution should be used since the defense of laches has been raised successfully.[5]

Note: Were Texas to adopt §§ 72 & 73, RESTATEMENT OF JUDGMENTS (1980), § 74 would require that the movant use reasonable diligence in discovering the GROUND for relief and that efforts to set aside the judgment be made with diligence after the discovery of the ground to set aside the judgment. Assuming the RESTATEMENT to be applicable, the Texas Supreme Court has indicated that a party would be precluded from seeking relief if they waive over four years to seek the relief.[6]

The only exception to the four-year limitation is when the petitioner proves extrinsic fraud. *Defee v. Defee,* 966 S.W.2d 719, 722 (Tex. App.—San Antonio 1998, no pet.); *Law v. Law,* 792 S.W.2d 150, 153 (Tex. App.—Houston [1st Dist.] 1990, writ denied).

b. *Procedural Requirements.*

i. *The Elements Be Plead and Proven.* In *Alexander v. Hagedorn,*[7] the Supreme Court stated that to be successful in a bill of review the complaining party must allege and prove:

(1) a meritorious defense to the cause of action alleged to support the judgment,
(2) which he was prevented from making by the fraud, accident or wrongful act of the opposite party,
(3) unmixed with any fault or negligence of his own.

Legal Insufficiency of Bill. "Where the movant's allegations are legally insufficient to support a bill of review, a writ of prohibition will issue."[8]

a) *Meritorious Defense.* A meritorious defense is shown when the ". . . result reached in the prior case would have been different had the defensive matter been presented."[9] The Court concluded in *Baker v.* Goldsmith:[10]

> ". . . a prima facie meritorious defense is made out when it is determined that the complainant's defense is not barred as a matter of law and that he will be entitled to judgment on retrial if no evidence to the contrary is offered. This is a question of law for the court."

Note: The Texas Supreme Court implies that a prior judicial decision, based on erroneous law might be a valid meritorious defense.[11]

(1) *Burden of Proof.* The movant need not prove the meritorious defense by a preponderance of the evidence. Rather, a prima facie meritorious defense must be made out in order to go to trial.[12]

(2) *Excused When Defendant Not Served.* Where a defendant is not served the meritorious defense requirement violates the fourteenth amendment's due process clause and need not be shown as a condition to the granting of a bill of review.[13]

---

4 Levy v. Roper, 113 Tex. 356, 256 S.W. 251, 253 (1923).

5 Calloway v. Elliot, 440 S.W.2d 99, 103 (Tex. Civ. App.—Tyler 1969, writ dism'd w.o.j.).

6 Ortega v. First Republic Bank Fort Worth, 33 Tex. Sup. Ct. J. 285, 287 (March 3, 1990).

7 148 Tex. 565, 226 S.W.2d 996, 998 (1950).

8 Trice v. City of Pasadena, 767 S.W.2d 700, 702 (Tex. 1989).

9 Crosby v. Di Palma, 141 S.W. 321 (Tex. Civ. App.—El Paso 1911, writ ref'd) cited in Baker v. Goldsmith, 582 S.W.2d 404, 408, 409 (Tex. 1979).

10 582 S.W.2d 404, 408, 409 (Tex. 1979).

11 Ortega v. First Republic Bank Fort Worth, 33 Tex. Sup. Ct. J. 285 (March 3, 1990).

12 Baker v. Goldsmith, 502 S.W.2d, 404, 408 (Tex. 1979).

13 Peralta v. Heights Medical Center, Inc., 485 U.S. 80, 108 S. Ct. 896, 99 L.Ed.2d 75 (1988).

b) *Fraud.*

(1) *Extrinsic Fraud Required.* Only extrinsic fraud will support a bill of review.[14] This is fraud which comes from somewhere other than the witness stand. Thus, perjury is intrinsic fraud which will not support a bill of review.[15] The distinction is not always easy. *See Montgomery v. Kennedy*[16] where it was held that a fiduciary's concealment of material facts, used to induce an agreed or uncontested judgment, which prevented a party from presenting at trial his legal rights, constitutes extrinsic fraud.

(2) *Proof of Fraud Excused—Official Mistake.* Where a party relies on erroneous official information given by a court clerk and is thereby prevented from filing a motion for new trial, the party is excused from showing, on bill of review, the wrongful conduct, fraud or accident of the opposite party.[17] The same result obtains when a court clerk misplaces a letter that would have constituted an answer,[18] and when the clerk of the trial court fails to give a defaulting party notice of the final judgment as required by TEX. R. CIV. P. 306a.[19] Indeed, where there is a lack of diligence in determining the whereabouts of a defendant cited by publication, the judgment is voidable and should be set aside by bill of review.[20]

Attorney Negligence Insufficient. One's own attorney is not an "officer of the court" who's negligence will justify a bill of review.[21]

c) *Due Diligence.* The movant must show that the fraud, accident or wrongful act of the opposite party was unmixed with the fault or negligence of the movant. In short, the movant must show the absence of negligence and the exercise of due diligence in protecting its rights in the original action.[22]

ii. *The Procedure.* The procedure to be followed in bill of review proceedings is not set forth in the rules, but is controlled by case law. The most significant case on the procedure itself is *Baker v. Goldsmith*[23] which should be read in its entirety.

a) *Petition.* A bill of review is commenced by the filing of a petition in the court that rendered the judgment in question.

b) *Docketing.* The action is separate from the original suit and should receive a different cause number.

c) *Parties.* All parties who would be affected by setting aside the original judgment must be made parties.

d) *Prima Facie Case.* The petition must set forth facts presenting prima facie proof of a meritorious defense. The petition must be supported by affidavits, discovery, or documents supporting the prima facie case. If the prima facie case is shown, the case proceeds to trial; if not, the case is dismissed.

e) *Hearing.* The court, after concluding that there is prima facie evidence of a meritorious defense may hear the case in one hearing or in separate hearings leading to one judgment.

---

14 Alexander v. Hagedorn, 148 Tex. 565, 226 S.W.2d 996, 1001 (1950).

15 Tice v. City of Pasadena, 767 S.W.2d 700, 702 (Tex. 1989); Crouch v. McGaw, 134 Tex. 633, 138 S.W.2d 94 (1940).

16 669 S.W.2d 309 (Tex. 1984).

17 Gracey v. West, 422 S.W.2d 913, 915 (Tex. 1968); Hanks v. Rosser, 378 S.W.2d 31, 34 (Tex. 1964).

18 Baker v. Goldsmith, 582 S.W.2d 404, 407 (Tex. 1979).

19 Petro-Chemical Transp., Inc. v. Carroll, 514 S.W.2d 240, 245 (Tex. 1974).

20 Anderson v. Collum, 514 S.W.2d 230, 231 (Tex. 1974); Commercial Credit Corp. v. Smith, 143 Tex. 612, 187 S.W.2d 363, 366 (1945).

21 Transworld Fin. Services Corp. v. Briscoe, 722 S.W.2d 407 (Tex. 1987).

22 Crispin v. Crispin, 529 S.W.2d 310 (Tex. Civ. App.—Austin 1975, no writ); Texas Mach. & Equip. Co. v. Gordon Knox Oil & Explo. Co., 442 S.W.2d 315, 317-318 (Tex. 1969); Alexander v. Hagedorn, 148 Tex. 565, 226 S.W.2d 996, 998 (1950).

23 582 S.W.2d 404 (Tex. 1979).

f) *Burdens of Proof.* The movant opens, with the burden of showing that the judgment was the result of fraud, accident or wrongful act of the opposite party, or official mistake, unmixed with any negligence of his own. The opposite party must then prove the original cause of action.

g) *The Charge.* The first issue inquires whether the prior judgment is rendered as a result of fraud, accident or wrongful act of the opposite party or official mistake unmixed with negligence on the complainant's part. Conditioned on an affirmative answer to that issue, the next question, or series of questions, is whether the bill of review defendant has proven the elements of the original cause of action.

c. *Availability—Conditions to Use.* The party bringing the bill of review must have standing as a party to the original lawsuit, or as one who had a then-existing interest or right prejudiced by the judgment in that suit.

d. *Usability—Restrictions on Use.*

1. *No Supersedeas.* The bill of review does not suspend the first judgment and there is no provision for the use of a supersedeas bond in connection with this procedure.[24]

2. *Cost.* The bill of review is a new lawsuit, requiring new evidence, another trial, and the probability of another appeal.

3. *Onerous Burden.* The onerous burden of proving fraud, accident, or wrongful act of the opposite party or official mistake unmixed with any negligence of the movant, makes the bill of review the last of the direct attacks to be chosen.

e. *Practical Considerations.* The bill of review will be used only when the time for an ordinary appeal (and motion for new trial) has passed, in addition, an evidentiary hearing is required. Bluntly, this is a procedural remedy of desperation, but a most necessary and useful one in the rare case of great wrong.

2. *Caldwell v. Barnes.*[25]

a. It is not necessary to exhaust legal remedies in another state before seeking to set utilize a bill of review in Texas.

b. The residual four-year statute of limitations applies to bills of review.[26] The bill of review filed within the four year limitation period will not be barred by laches, *unless allowing the action would work a grave injustice (usually in cases where the principles of estoppel would apply).*

3. *Peralta v. Heights Medical Center, Inc.*, 485 U.S. 80, 108 S.Ct. 896 (1988). The "meritorious defense requirement for a bill of review violates the due process clause in the limited situation in which the bill is based upon absence of service.

4. *Lopez v. Lopez*, 757 S.W.2d 721 (Tex. 1988) (per curiam). *Peralta* applies to motions for new trials. I.e., the defendant who is not served does not have to set up a meritorious defense in order to obtain a new trial.

5. *French v. Brown* (noted in footnote 7 of note 1 *supra*) was distinguished in *Gold v. Gold*, 145 S.W.3d 212 (Tex. 2004). In *Gold* the Court held on the facts of that case that a restricted appeal was not a prerequisite to a bill of review. There are three prerequisites for a bill of review: (1) a meritorious defense, (2) that was not made due to fraud, accident, or wrongful act by an opponent or official mistake by a clerk, and (3) unmixed with any fault or negligence of the party filing the bill. Failure to file a restricted appeal could only be relevant to the last, and then only if it constituted fault or negligence. It did not in this case. If a motion to reinstate, motion for new trial, or direct appeal is available, it is hard to imagine any case in which failure to pursue one of them would not be negligence. But the same cannot be said about choosing to appeal by bill of review rather than a restricted appeal, for several reasons. First, a bill of review allows trial courts to rectify their own errors, eliminating the need for lengthy appellate review. Second, all facts may be considered, not just those appearing on the face of the record. Third, discovery is available to find out what all the facts are. It is true the Court has sometimes stated that relief by bill of review is available only if a party has exercised due diligence in pursuing all adequate legal remedies and not if legal remedies were available but ignored. But a party is not "ignoring" its

[24] Kantor v. Herald Publishing Co., Inc., 632 S.W.2d 656 (Tex. App.—Tyler 1982, no writ).

[25] 975 S.W.2d 535 (Tex. 1998).

[26] TEX. CIV. PRAC. & REM. CODE § 16.051.

remedies when it chooses one appellate avenue rather than another. If closely read, the Supreme Court decision could be viewed as holding across the board that the use of restricted appeal is not a prerequisite for a bill of review. However, if an evidentiary hearing is needed, the restricted appeal is not an adequate remedy, which need not be pursued. An evidentiary hearing was required in *Gold*, hence the restricted appeal (even though it was not filed) would not have been adequate.

6. In *Kiefer v. Touris*, 197 S.W.3d 300 (Tex. 2006) the court held that a summary judgment, in a bill of review proceeding, that sets aside a parentage adjudication, but does not make a new parentage adjudication, is not an appealable judgment. A bill of review that sets aside a prior judgment, but does not dispose of all the issues of the case on the merits, is interlocutory in nature and not a final judgment appealable to the court of appeals or the Supreme Court.

3. *Collateral Attack on Judgments*

CRAWFORD
v.
McDONALD
88 Tex. 626, 33 S.W. 325
(1895)

Brown & Bliss and H.G. Robertson, for plaintiffs in error.
Decker & Harris, for defendant in error.

DENMAN, J.

[Facts abridged by editor. This case was a trespass to try title action which turns on whether an earlier sale of the property ordered by a probate court was proper. Only if the order of the probate court was void and subject to collateral attack was the sale improper.]

The first ground upon which plaintiffs in error claim such sale to be void is that it was made at Denison, instead of at Sherman, the county seat of Grayson county, where the courthouse was then situated, in violation of the statute requiring same to be made at the door of the courthouse of the county. Where a domestic judgment is sought to be impeached in order to determine the rules of law governing the particular proceeding, it becomes necessary to consider (1) whether such judgment was rendered by a court of general jurisdiction over the subject-matter of the suit or proceeding in which same was rendered; (2) whether the attack is being made by parties thereto or their privies, or by strangers; (3) whether the attack is direct or collateral; (4) whether the evidence adduced to support the attack is apparent on the face of the record of the proceedings in which such suit was rendered, and, if not, whether evidence aliunde is competent; and (5) whether the ground of the complaint is one which, if true, goes to the power of the court to render the judgment, or is a mere matter of procedure. We will confine ourselves to the determination, in their order, of such of said questions and the discussion of such principles of law applicable thereto as may be necessary to the decision of the case before us, without attempting to discuss the many interesting questions which may be suggested.

Previous decisions, which meet with our entire approval, have settled beyond controversy the proposition that our probate courts are courts of general jurisdiction in matters pertaining to estates of decedents. *Murchison v. White*, 54 Tex. 83. The proceedings in probate to sell the property in controversy herein being quasi in rem, the devisees (plaintiffs in error) were parties thereto. *Murchison v. White*, 54 Tex. 83. A direct attack on a judgment is an attempt to amend, correct, reform, vacate, or enjoin the execution of same in a proceeding instituted for that purpose, such as a motion for a rehearing, an appeal, some form of writ of error, a bill of review, an injunction to restrain its execution, etc. A collateral attack on a judgment is an attempt to avoid its binding force in a proceeding not instituted for one of the purposes aforesaid as where, in an action of debt on a judgment, defendant attempts to deny the fact of indebtedness, or where, in a suit to try the title to property, a judgment is offered as a link in the chain of title, and the adverse party attempts to avoid its effect, etc. Tested by these principles, it is clear that the attack on the judgment of the probate court confirming the sale in the case before us is collateral. It does not appear from the face of the record of the court in the probate proceedings where the sale was made. The undisputed verbal testimony in the case, however, shows that after said order of sale was made,

Acheson, the trustee in said trust deed, acting under the power contained therein, sold the land in controversy, together with the other land described in said trust deed, at public venue, within the hours prescribed by law, on the first Tuesday in December, 1874, in the city of Denison, about 10 miles distant from Sherman, the county seat of Grayson county, at which sale said executor was present, taking part as executor, it being announced by the trustee, in crying off the property, that he, as trustee, would convey to the purchasers at such sale the title of the surviving partner, L.W. Shepard, and that the executor would convey the title of the estate of C.W. Nelson.

The question, then, is, can this judgment of confirmation of sale, rendered by a domestic court of general jurisdiction of estates of decedents, in a matter to which its jurisdiction had attached by the granting of an application for an order of sale in a pending administration, be attacked by evidence of matters dehors the record? The proper determination of this question on sound legal principles is of the greatest importance, since, on the one hand, great injustice may sometimes result to persons against whom judgments are asserted, by a rule precluding inquiry, even in a collateral attack, into matters dehors the record affecting the validity of such judgments; while, on the other hand, if such evidence be allowed, no title held under a judgment of any court, however regular its proceedings appear, would be of much value, as such collateral attack can be made after any lapse of time, it not being an action or suit within the meaning of any statute of limitations, but merely a means of rebutting and destroying the effect of the judgment as evidence; and the attack, if successful, establishes the nullity of the judgment from its inception, under which no one, however innocent, can acquire many of the rights which the courts, under settled rules of law, will protect where the judgment is attacked directly. The general rule is well established that a judgment rendered by a court even of general jurisdiction is void if it had, at the time of the rendition of the judgment, no jurisdiction of the person of the defendant or the subject-matter of the litigation. This principle is self-evident, because until the court acquires jurisdiction it has no power to proceed to investigate and determine private rights. Logically, it can make no difference as to the validity of the judgment whether the lack of jurisdiction of the person or the subject-matter appears from the face of the record or is made to appear by evidence aliunde; for if, for instance, no service was had upon the defendant, he not appearing in the case, the court, having no jurisdiction whatever over his person, is absolutely without power to bind him by an adjudication that he had been in fact duly served; and, logically, this want of power is the same whether the lack of jurisdiction appears on the face of the record or not. There is, however, another rule of law, equally well settled upon principles of public policy, which precludes inquiry by evidence aliunde the record in a collateral attack upon a judgment of a domestic court of general jurisdiction, regular on its face, into any fact which the court rendering such judgment must have passed upon in proceeding to its rendition. Therefore it is well settled that, where a personal judgment has been rendered against a defendant by a domestic court of general jurisdiction, and under the same his property has been seized and sold, he will not, in a contest over the title to the property, be allowed to show by evidence dehors the record that the judgment was rendered without any service whatever upon him. Logically, the judgment is, in fact, void, but on grounds of public policy the courts, in order to protect the property rights, apply the rule aforesaid, which precludes inquiry into facts dehors the record for the purpose of showing the invalidity of the judgment; and therefore, for all practical purposes, in such collateral attack, the judgment is held valid. This rule is analogous to, and probably as important as, the rule forbidding the introduction of verbal testimony to vary or contradict the terms of a written contract, except in a proceeding instituted for the purpose of correcting, reforming, or annulling the same. These principles have long been acted upon by this court as applicable to judgments of the district, probate, and justice courts, and have become settled rules of property in this state. *Murchison v. White*, 54 Tex. 78; *Williams v. Ball*, 52 Tex. 603; *Brown v. Christie*, 27 Tex. 73; *Heck v. Martin*, 75 Tex. 469, 13 S.W. 51; *Fowler v. Simpson*, 79 Tex. 611, 15 S.W. 682; *Martin v. Burns*, 80 Tex. 677, 16 S.W. 1072; *Hardy v. Beaty*, 84 Tex. 562, 19 S.W. 778. Whether an exception has been ingrafted upon this rule by the decision of the supreme court of the United States in *Pennoyer v. Neff*, 95 U.S. 565, and, if so, what is the effect thereof, is foreign to this discussion. *Martin v. Burns*, 80 Tex. 676, 16 S.W. 1072; *Hardy v. Beaty*, 84 Tex. 564, 19 S.W. 778. Since the rule of public policy above referred to precludes inquiry into even a jurisdictional fact when it does not appear from the face of the record, it must follow for stronger reasons that the judgment in this case affirming the sale cannot be attacked collaterally by evidence dehors the record to the effect that the sale was not in fact made at the place required by law. The court, in confirming the sale, will be conclusively presumed in this collateral attack to have investigated and determined correctly that the sale was made at the proper place, and no evidence aliunde to the contrary will be permitted to impeach the correctness of the judgment. The only relief, if any, permitted by the rules of law against an improper determination of such question by the court in rendering such judgment of confirmation is to be found in a direct attack upon the judgment where the court has full power to adjust the equities of the parties litigant. We are therefore of the opinion that this judgment cannot be attacked by the evidence dehors the record of the probate court that the sale was not made at the courthouse door of Grayson county. *Brown v. Christie*, 27 Tex. 73.

Since we have disposed of the first objection raised by plaintiffs in error on the ground above stated, we deem it unnecessary to determine whether, if it had appeared on the face of the record that the sale was made at Denison, such fact would have rendered the judgment of confirmation and sale thereunder void.

* * *

The judgment will be affirmed.

BROWN, J., did not sit in this case.

Note

In a direct attack, the challenger alleging that he was not served with citation is not limited to the face of the record or bound by jurisdictional recitations in the challenged judgment. *Min v. Avila*, 991 S.W.2d 495, 499-500 (Tex.App.-Houston [1st Dist.] 1999, no pet.).

TEMPLETON
v.
FERGUSON

89 Tex. 47, 33 S.W. 329
(1895)

Rector, Thomson & Rector, for plaintiffs in error.
Thomas M. Joseph, for defendants in error.

[Facts abridged by editor. James B. Murphy, a soldier under Fannin was killed at Goliad during the war for independence in 1836. In 1837, one application was made in Harrisburg county of the Republic of Texas for administration of the estate of Murphy and two other deceased soldiers on behalf of an individual who alleged to have purchased the claims of the deceased from their legal representatives. Administrators for the estate of Murphy were appointed. Shortly thereafter a land certificate for 640 acres was issued by the Republic of Texas to Murphy for his service during the war. The administrators were authorized to sell the land. The administrators subsequently sold the land to Snydor and filed with the court a report of sale and final accounting of the estate. In 1840, the probate judge approved the final accounting. There was no direct evidence during the subsequent trial that the administrators ever executed a conveyance of the 640 acres to Snydor. The land in question was surveyed in Harris county; patented to Murphy; and Snydor paid taxes on the property. The deed records of Harris county showed that in 1849 that Syndor conveyed the land to Ware.]

DENMAN, J.

* * *

This is an ordinary action of trespass to try title, brought by plaintiffs in error, heirs of James B. Murphy, against defendants in error, heirs of said Ware, who pleaded not guilty. The case was tried before the court below, who rendered a judgment for plaintiffs in error for the land. Thereupon defendants in error appealed to the court of civil appeals, which court reversed the judgment of the court below, and rendered judgment for defendants in error, and plaintiffs in error thereupon brought the case by writ of error to this court. If the administration sale passed the title to said certificate to John S. Snydor, the judgment of the court of civil appeals must be affirmed.

The first assignment is to the effect that the court erred in not holding that the probate court of Harrisburg county had no jurisdiction of the estate of Murphy, and that the entire administration proceedings were for that reason void, in that Murphy was not at the time of his death an inhabitant or resident of said county, did not die therein, and did not, at the time administration was granted, nor at any time prior thereto, have any property therein. Jurisdiction is the power of a court to hear and determine a cause and enforce its decree. The exact legal signification of the word varies with the circumstances under which it is used, and a failure to observe this fact often produces confusion, and leads to the statement of inaccurate legal propositions. The question of the validity of judicial proceedings for want of jurisdiction arises in two classes of cases. Thus there are classes of cases over which a court has not, under the very law of its creation, any possible power; e.g. an administration upon the estate of a living person, administration upon the estate of a deceased soldier when prohibited by statute, an administration in bankruptcy upon the estate of a person deceased before the institution of the proceedings, a suit for divorce in a foreign country in which neither of the parties is domiciled, or a suit to recover against a nonresident, upon service by publication, a purely personal judgment. In such cases the entire proceedings are coram non judice. The law raises no presumptions in their support, and the facts bringing any particular case within one of such classes may be established by evidence dehors the record, either in a direct or collateral attack, for the purpose of destroying the apparent binding force of such proceedings. This is upon the principle that the court, being as a matter of law without power to investigate or determine any question connected with such matters, cannot, by a clear usurpation of power, preclude inquiry into the facts establishing such usurpation, and the consequent nullity of its proceedings. In such cases the court is without jurisdiction of the subject-matter, the status of the parties, or the person of the defendant, as the case may be; and other courts have no difficulty or hesitation in ignoring its proceedings or decrees. Again, there are classes of cases over which the law has conferred upon the court general judicial power, but its right to exercise such power in a particular case is challenged, and the nullity of its proceedings urged, not upon the ground that the case does not belong to one of such classes, but upon the ground that no such state of facts existed, or that no such preliminary steps had been taken as authorized the court to exercise its powers in the given case; e.g. where the power of a probate court to grant an administration of an estate or to make an order of sale in a pending administration is called in question, and the validity of its proceedings denied on the ground that no necessity therefor existed, or where the validity of a personal judgment against a resident is questioned upon the ground that the court had not, by service of process or otherwise, acquired jurisdiction over the person of the defendant. Much difficulty has been encountered by the courts, in passing upon this class of cases, in their efforts to shield the citizen from the unwarranted and oppressive exercise of judicial power without unduly prejudicing the property interest of the country, largely dependent upon the validity of judicial proceedings. The validity of the proceedings for want of jurisdiction may be raised in this class of cases, as in the other, in either a direct or collateral attack. On account, however, of the legal presumptions indulged in favor of the validity of the proceedings in this class, which we have seen do not obtain in the other, the time and circumstances under which the attack can be made, the character of evidence by which it must be supported, especially when the attack is collateral, the power of the court to impose terms as a condition of relief against the record supported by such presumptions, and the ultimate rights of the parties in case the attack is successful, are in many instances entirely different in the two classes. What is a direct and what a collateral attack, and the reason why, in a collateral attack on a judgment of the class under consideration, evidence of matters dehors the record will not be received, having been discussed in the case of *Crawford v. McDonald*, 33 S.W. 325 (recently decided by this court), and cases therein cited, need not be here restated. It may be well to state, however, that the opinion in that case had no reference whatever to the first class of causes above noticed.

Plaintiffs in error contend that under a proper construction of the act of 1836, under which this administration was granted, the probate court of Harrisburg county had no power to grant administration upon an estate unless the decedent was an inhabitant or resident of such county at the time of his death, and that, therefore, said court, under the evidence in this case, had no jurisdiction over the estate of Murphy, and its proceedings were wholly void under the rules of law applicable to the first class of cases above discussed. This question was decided adversely to this contention in *Pleasants v. Dunkin*, 47 Tex. 343, and followed in *Brockenborough v. Melton*, 55 Tex. 504, and may be considered settled law. It is true that the subsequent legislation referred to in the opinion in the first case as persuasive of the construction adopted had not been enacted when the administration herein was granted. Such legislation, however, did not enlarge, but restricted, the jurisdiction of the probate court under said act of 1836 as to a certain class of nonresident soldiers, thereby indicating that in the opinion of the law-making power such courts were not restricted in their jurisdiction by said act, as contended by plaintiffs in error. The court simply adopted the legislative construction, and we see no reason to question its correctness. We are of the opinion that the assignment is not well taken; that the court had jurisdiction over the class of cases to which Murphy's estate belonged, and that this case belongs to the second class of cases above discussed. It will be so considered in passing upon the remaining assignments.

* * *

The next assignment is to the effect that the court erred in not holding the administration void because the application was made for administration on three estates in one petition and granted in one order. This was a mere error in procedure, which cannot affect the validity of the proceedings in this collateral attack. It is well settled that where a court of general jurisdiction, in the exercise of its ordinary judicial functions, renders a judgment in a cause of which it has jurisdiction, such judgment is never void, no matter how erroneous it may appear from the face of the record or otherwise to be. *Clayton v. Hurt* (recently decided by this court) 32 S.W. 876, and cases cited.

The next two assignments are as follows: "The court erred in not holding said administration void, because the record shows that there were no debts due from said estate," and "The court erred in not holding the sale void, because the record shows that it was not ordered or made to satisfy debts against the estate of Murphy." These assignments raise the question indicated in the discussion of the second class of cases mentioned under the first assignment, to the effect that, though the court may have had power to grant administration in the class of cases to which Murphy's estate belonged, and may have had power to grant orders of sales of property, yet "no such state of facts existed as authorized the court to exercise its powers" in this case, either to grant administration or order the sale. They will therefore be considered together. We pass without comment the question as to whether the existence of debts was necessary to authorize the grant of administration. Assuming that it was necessary to the validity of the order granting administration, as well as the order authorizing the sale, the question presents itself, does the record negative the existence of debts when read in view of the presumptions indulged by the law in support of the validity of such orders? Under repeated adjudications in this state, by these assignments a collateral attack is made upon judgments of a domestic court of general jurisdiction of estates of decedents by parties to the proceedings in which such judgments were rendered. *Crawford v. McDonald, supra.* In such cases it may be considered the settled rule that if the record of the cause in which such judgments were rendered does not negative the existence of the facts authorizing the court to make the particular order, the law conclusively presumes that such facts are established by the evidence before the court when such orders or judgments were rendered, and evidence of matters dehors the record to the contrary will not be received. As said by Justice Stayton in his able opinion on this subject in *Martin v. Robinson*, 67 Tex. 375, 3 S.W. 550: "Such a court must determine whether the facts exist which make it lawful for administration to be granted in the county in which the court sits; and if, in this respect, having power to make the inquiry, it comes to an erroneous conclusion, its decree founded on such conclusion is voidable, but not void." *Crawford v. McDonald, supra.* The petition for administration is silent as to the existence of debts, and the application for the order of sale has been lost, and its contents not shown. In such cases it must be presumed that the court found the existence of debts. The fact that the final account did not show any debts antedating the administration does not rebut the presumption in favor of the judgment of the court, for such debts may have existed and never have been presented or allowed. There is no fraud shown in this case. The administration purports to have been had at the instance of the legal assignee of the heirs. No question is made as to the truth of the recitals in the petition for administration, and therefore we are not called upon the decide the question as to whether any presumptions will be indulged in support of decrees rendered in a fraudulent administration.

* * *

The judgment of the court of civil appeals is affirmed.

Note

York v. State, 373 S.W.3d 32 (Tex. 2012): York sued for a declaration that a final judgment awarding his property to the State was rendered in violation of the Bankruptcy Code's automatic stay and is therefore void. ***Held*:** Agreeing with most of the circuit courts (but not the Fifth Circuit), the Court holds that a judgment rendered in violation of the Bankruptcy Code's automatic stay is void and therefore subject to collateral attack in state court; consequently, Texas's rule barring the use of extrinsic evidence in a collateral attack does not apply. The Court noted that as a general rule extrinsic evidence is not admissible in a collateral attack, it noted that the *Templeton* case had made an exception to this general rule in those situation where the court has not under its very law of creation any possible power. The Court noted that it had not been asked to reconsider the rule here, nor need we attempt to define exceptions with greater certainty. This case fits comfortably under *Templeton*'s exclusion from the rule.

BROWNING
v.
PROSTOK
165 S.W.3d 336
(Tex. 2005)

JUSTICE WAINWRIGHT delivered the opinion of the Court.

This dispute arises out of highly contentious bankruptcy proceedings. During the bankruptcy proceedings, a committee representing bond and trade unsecured creditors vigorously disputed the valuation of the debtor as presented by the debtor's management. The committee sought to replace the debtor's management with a bankruptcy trustee, based in part on allegations of intentional undervaluation of the debtor. In addition, the committee objected to the debtor's plan of reorganization, again raising allegations of intentional undervaluation. Over two years after the bankruptcy court entered its order confirming the reorganization plan proposed by the debtor, a class of bondholders brought this suit. The class of bondholders alleges that the officers and directors breached their fiduciary duties by intentionally undervaluing the debtor during the bankruptcy proceedings. The trial court granted summary judgment against the class and entered a take-nothing judgment. We consider whether the class claims, based on conduct occurring during bankruptcy proceedings, can be maintained in state court years after the bankruptcy court's final order confirming the debtor's reorganization plan. We conclude that the claims cannot.

* * *

Prostok, individually and on behalf of all other Junior Bondholders, filed the current case in state court in October 1995 against the former officers and directors of National Gypsum (Officers and Directors) and their financial advisor, Donaldson, Lufkin & Jenrette Securities Corporation (DLJ). Prostok amended his petition to add one of the Senior Bondholders, TCW. Prostok sued for breach of fiduciary duties, fraud and constructive fraud, and civil conspiracy against all the defendants. Prostok also brought claims against DLJ and the Officers and Directors for gross negligence, and alternative claims against TCW and DLJ for participating, aiding, assisting, and/or inducing breach of fiduciary duties.

Prostok alleges that during the course of the bankruptcy proceedings, the Senior Bondholders, the Officers and Directors, and their financial advisors intentionally undervalued National Gypsum by concealing a plan to dramatically reduce the company's operating expenses. Specifically, Prostok alleges that the Officers and Directors represented that National Gypsum was worth $300 to $375 million, based on management's "best estimate and intention of how the company would operate once out of bankruptcy," though the Officers and Directors were fully aware of the cost-savings plan later announced in October 1993. Prostok alleges that this cost-savings plan resulted in an increase in the market value of New NGC's outstanding stock from $350 million to almost $1 billion. According to Prostok, had the Officers and Directors disclosed the plan to cut expenses to the bankruptcy court, the value assigned to National Gypsum would have been higher, and the distribution to the Junior Bondholders would have been greater. Prostok claims that as a result of the cost-savings plan, the value in stock acquired by Senior Bondholders by reorganization far exceeded its initial value, resulting in a windfall for Senior Bondholders. Prostok alleges that in exchange for their participation in concealing the cost-savings plan, the Officers and Directors maintained their positions in New NGC and received lucrative incentive deals.

* * *

On February 1, 1999, the Officers and Directors, DLJ, New NGC, and TCW (except The TCW Group, Inc.) joined in a motion for summary judgment asserting that Texas law did not recognize Prostok's claims. TCW (except The TCW Group, Inc.) filed a separate supplemental motion for summary judgment against Prostok, asserting statute of limitations, res judicata, collateral estoppel, and lack of a fiduciary duty.

On March 1, 1999, the trial court specifically denied TCW's motion for summary judgment on limitations grounds but granted summary judgment in favor of the Officers and Directors, TCW, and New NGC without specifying grounds. On April 21, 1999, the trial court signed a final judgment . . . .

Prostok appealed the trial court's final take-nothing judgment. . . . The court of appeals held that none of the theories asserted by the Officers and Directors could support summary judgment. The court of appeals reversed the summary judgment granted in favor of the Officers and Directors against Prostok.

TCW cross-appealed the trial court's denial of its motion for summary judgment on statute of limitations grounds. The court of appeals held that TCW's motion for summary judgment on statute of limitations grounds was meritorious. Thus, the court of appeals effectively affirmed the trial court's judgment in favor of TCW on different grounds than the trial court articulated in its judgment. . . .

The Officers and Directors petitioned this Court for review, arguing that the court of appeals erred in reversing summary judgment. Specifically, they argue that summary judgment was proper because: 1) Prostok's claims are an impermissible collateral attack on the bankruptcy court's final judgment; . . .

* * *

Section 1144 of the United States Bankruptcy Code provides that upon proper request made within 180 days of the entry of the confirmation order and after notice and a hearing, the bankruptcy court may revoke the order if and only if the order was procured by fraud. 11 U.S.C. 1144. Section 1144 provides the exclusive means for revoking a confirmation order. *Dale C. Eckert Corp. v. Orange Tree Assocs.* (*In re Orange Tree Assocs.*), 961 F.2d 1445, 1447 n. 6 (9th Cir.1992) (*quoting In re Longardner & Assocs.*, 855 F.2d 455, 460 (7th Cir.1988)); *In re Newport Harbor Assocs.*, 589 F.2d 20, 23-24 (1st Cir.1978). Any attempt to revoke a confirmation order after expiration of the 180-day limitations period is barred even if the alleged fraud is not discovered until then. *In re Orange Tree Assocs.*, 961 F.2d at 1447; *see also Farley v. Coffee Cupboard, Inc.* (*In re Coffee Cupboard, Inc.*), 119 B.R. 14, 19 (E.D.N.Y.1990) ("The 180 day time limit in Section 1144 has been strictly enforced by the courts . . . even to the extent of enforcing it in those cases where the alleged fraud of the debtor is not discovered until after the limitations period.") (citations omitted).

* * *

An attempt to revoke a confirmation order in a separate proceeding is a collateral attack on the order. *See id.* (holding that creditors' complaint was "not an attempt to revoke or otherwise collaterally attack the confirmation order that is subject to the limitations period of Section 1144"). An action which, in effect, attempts to revoke a confirmation order is also a collateral attack. *See Miller*, 462 F.2d at 360 ("[I]t is a collateral attack if it must in some fashion overrule a previous judgment."). Thus, if Prostok's claims constitute an impermissible collateral attack on the confirmation order, Section 1144 of the Bankruptcy Code provides his exclusive remedy. We now turn to whether Prostok's claims constitute an impermissible collateral attack.

Collateral attacks on final judgments are generally disallowed because it is the policy of the law to give finality to the judgments of the courts. *Tice v. City of Pasadena*, 767 S.W.2d 700, 703 (Tex. 1989) (*quoting Crouch v. McGaw*, 134 Tex. 633, 138 S.W.2d 94, 96 (1940)).

> [T]he mischief of retrying every case in which the judgment or decree rendered on false testimony, given by perjured witnesses, or on contracts or documents whose genuineness or validity was in issue, and which are afterwards ascertained to be forged or fraudulent, would be greater, by reason of the endless nature of the strife, than any compensation arising from doing justice in individual cases.

United States v. Throckmorton, 98 U.S. 61, 68-69, 25 L.Ed. 93 (1878). This policy of finality is especially important in a Chapter 11 bankruptcy, where the proceedings are intended to rehabilitate a business. A confirmation plan affects the rights of, and restructures the relationships between, the debtor and its creditors. *In re Newport Harbor Assocs.*, 589 F.2d at 22. If the rehabilitative purpose of Chapter 11 is to be realized, Chapter 11 proceedings must be "concluded with reasonable expedition and finality so as to allow certainty for future business planning." *Id.; see also Kaufman v. Pub. Serv. Co.* (*In re Pub. Serv. Co.*), 43 F.3d 763, 768 (1st Cir.1995) ("[T]he willingness of future claimants and creditors to compromise in chapter 11 proceedings depends on giving the reorganization court's approval a due measure of finality."); *Christopher v. Am. Universal Ins. Group* (*In re Christopher*), 148 B.R. 832, 837 (Bankr. N.D. Tex. 1992) ("A strong policy favors enforcement of the plan of reorganization because too many rights of too many interests have relied on the finality of the confirmation order."). A collateral attack runs counter to this strong policy of finality because a collateral attack attempts to bypass the appellate process in challenging the integrity of a judgment.

A collateral attack is an attempt to avoid the binding force of a judgment in a proceeding not instituted for the purpose of correcting, modifying, or vacating the judgment, but in order to obtain some specific relief which the judgment currently stands as a bar against. *Crawford v. McDonald*, 88 Tex. 626, 33 S.W. 325, 327 (1895); *see also Biaza v. Simon*, 879 S.W.2d 349, 353 (Tex. App.—Houston [14th Dist.] 1994, writ denied) (*citing Crawford*, 33 S.W. at 327). Only a void judgment may be collaterally attacked. *Browning v. Placke*, 698 S.W.2d 362, 363 (Tex. 1985). A judgment is void only when it is apparent that the court rendering judgment "had no jurisdiction of the parties or property, no jurisdiction of the subject matter, no jurisdiction to enter the particular judgment, or no capacity to act." *Id.* (*citing Austin Indep. Sch. Dist. v. Sierra Club*, 495 S.W.2d 878, 881 (Tex. 1973)). A confirmation order issued by a bankruptcy court has the effect of a judgment rendered by a district court. *Miller*, 462 F.2d at 360; *In re Emmer Bros.*, 52 B.R. at 390. Prostok does not argue that the bankruptcy order was void; therefore, any collateral attack is improper.

* * *

The court of appeals held that Prostok's claims do not collaterally attack the confirmation order because they are based on conduct extrinsic to the confirmation order. 112 S.W.3d 876, 905. This Court has held that when a party does not seek to set aside a prior judgment, but instead brings suit based on extrinsic fraud, the action is not a collateral attack. *State v. Durham*, 860 S.W.2d 63, 67 (Tex. 1993) (recognizing, in a suit brought by the state for fraud in obtaining court approval for an oil and gas lease, that the State had not sought to set aside the judgment but had "alleged fraud extrinsic to the judgment, and invoke[d] the equity powers of the court to impose a constructive trust"); *cf. Spera v. Fleming, Hovenkamp & Grayson, P.C.*, 25 S.W.3d 863, 871 (Tex. App.—Houston [14th Dist.] 2000, no pet.) (holding that extrinsic conduct that formed the basis of claims for attorney malpractice and breach of fiduciary duty were not a collateral attack on trial court's order apportioning attorneys' fees). In contrast, the underlying issues resolved by a judgment are considered intrinsic. *See King Ranch, Inc. v. Chapman*, 118 S.W.3d 742, 752 (Tex. 2003) ("Issues underlying the judgment attacked by a bill of review are intrinsic and thus have no probative value on the fraud necessary to [support] a bill of review."). An attack on a final judgment, otherwise constituting a collateral attack, cannot be maintained on grounds that the judgment was obtained through fraudulent conduct intrinsic to the judgment. *See Neill v. Neill*, 386 S.W.2d 642, 647 (Tex. Civ. App.—Austin 1965, writ dism'd) ("Neither a collateral nor a direct attack upon a prior judgment can be based upon intrinsic fraud.").

Extrinsic fraud is fraud that denies a losing party the opportunity to fully litigate at trial all the rights or defenses that could have been asserted. *Montgomery v. Kennedy*, 669 S.W.2d 309, 312 (Tex. 1984) (*citing Alexander v. Hagedorn*, 148 Tex. 565, 226 S.W.2d 996, 1001 (1950)). It generally includes wrongful conduct occurring outside of the adversarial proceedings. *See Hagedorn*, 226 S.W.2d at 1002 (*citing Phillips Petroleum Co. v. Jenkins*, 91 F.2d 183, 187 (8th Cir. 1937)). The fraud must be collateral to the matter tried and not something which was actually or potentially in issue. *Montgomery*, 669 S.W.2d at 312. For example, a fiduciary's concealment of material facts to induce an agreed or uncontested judgment, which prevents a party from presenting his legal rights at trial, is extrinsic fraud. *Id.* at 313.

Intrinsic fraud, by contrast, "relates to the merits of the issues [that] were presented and presumably were or should have been settled in the former action." *Tice*, 767 S.W.2d at 702. Intrinsic fraud includes fraudulent instruments, perjured testimony, or any matter which was actually presented to and considered by the trial court in rendering judgment. *Id.*; *see also Montgomery*, 669 S.W.2d at 313 ("It is particularly well-established that the alleged perjury of a witness on a contested issue, which the opposing party had the opportunity to refute, is intrinsic fraud."). Allegations that a plaintiff conspired to suborn perjury is an allegation of intrinsic fraud. *Tice*, 767 S.W.2d at 702. In addition, when the fraudulent acts themselves are in issue, or could have been in issue, in the prior proceeding, the fraud is intrinsic. *Montgomery*, 669 S.W.2d at 313 (*citing Mills v. Baird*, 147 S.W.2d 312, 316 (Tex. Civ. App.—Austin 1941, writ ref'd)). This Court has noted that while concealment of a material fact by a fiduciary charged with the duty of full disclosure generally is extrinsic fraud, where "the alleged specific fraudulent acts were known and in issue in the prior suit, the fraud is intrinsic." *Id.* at 313-14. Similarly, the First Circuit affirmed a bankruptcy court's injunction barring a civil action for fraud occurring in Chapter 11 proceedings "[b]ecause the alleged inaccuracies could have been, and in part were, litigated in the bankruptcy court." *In re Pub. Serv. Co.*, 43 F.3d at 768.

The distinction between extrinsic and intrinsic fraud as grounds for attacking a judgment represents a balance of competing concerns. On one hand, the sound policy of promoting finality in judgments arises from a general level of confidence that the adversarial process leading to judgment is reasonably effective to ascertain the merits of the controversy. *See* Restatement (Second) of Judgments § 70 cmt. a (1982). While no system is infallible, "[e]ndless litigation, in which nothing was ever finally determined, would be worse than occasional miscarriages of justice." *Hagedorn*, 226 S.W.2d at 998 (*quoting Pico v. Cohn*, 91 Cal. 129, 25 P. 970, 971 (1891)). On the other hand, to fully insulate judgments from attack would give great protections to the most devious parties. *See* Restatement (Second) of Judgments § 70 cmt. a (1982) ("[I]f judgments were wholly immune it would give powerful incentive to use . . . fraudulent tactics in obtaining a judgment."). As such, an attack upon a judgment based on intrinsic fraud is not allowed because the fraudulent conduct may be properly exposed and rectified within the context of the underlying adversarial process itself. In contrast, a collateral attack on a judgment on the basis of extrinsic fraud is allowed because such fraud distorts the judicial process to such an extent that confidence in the ability to discover the fraudulent conduct through the regular adversarial process is undermined. . . .

* * *

In this case, Prostok complains that the Officers and Directors intentionally misled the bankruptcy court regarding the proper valuation of National Gypsum. The controlling question is "whether the alleged fraud prevented the party from knowing about and presenting [their] legal rights at trial." *Montgomery*, 669 S.W.2d at 314. The alleged fraudulent conduct, the misrepresentation of the value of National Gypsum, is a material issue that was presented and considered by the bankruptcy court over two years before Prostok filed this suit. The conduct was considered by the bankruptcy court in rendering judgment—specifically, when the trial court denied the BT Committee's motion to appoint a trustee and again in overruling the BT Committee's objection to the confirmation of National Gypsum's proposed reorganization plan. The fraud Prostok now alleges did not prevent the Junior Bondholders from presenting their legal rights in the bankruptcy proceedings. In fact, the BT Committee raised and litigated at the bankruptcy court the fraud Prostok now alleges. Fraud is intrinsic when the fraudulent conduct was in issue in the prior proceedings, even when the acts are committed by a fiduciary. *Id.* at 313-14. Because the fraud Prostok alleges was litigated in the bankruptcy proceedings, the alleged fraudulent conduct is intrinsic to the confirmation order. Therefore, Prostok's allegations based on intrinsic fraud constitute an impermissible collateral attack on the bankruptcy's confirmation order.

* * *

. . . Accordingly, we reverse the judgment of the court of appeals in part and affirm in part, and render judgment that Prostok take nothing.

JUSTICE O'NEILL did not participate in the decision.

STEWART
v.
USA CUSTOM PAINT & BODY SHOP

870 S.W.2d 18
(Tex. 1994)

Brett W. Arnold, Houston, for petitioner.
L. David Sosebee, Richmond and Kenneth L. Smith, Houston, for respondent.

HIGHTOWER, JUSTICE.

At issue is the validity of the judgment underlying a writ of garnishment. This case requires that we decide whether a captionless sheet purporting to dismiss an undesignated case and a later attached computer printout listing a number of cases meet the requisites of a valid judgment, dismissing one of the cases included on the printout. The trial court concluded that the case had not been dismissed and the court of appeals reversed. 856 S.W.2d 227. For the reasons explained herein, we reverse the judgment of the court of appeals and remand this cause to the trial court for further proceedings consistent with this opinion.

In 1985, Brad Stewart (Stewart) sued USA Custom Paint & Body Shop, Inc. (USA Custom) for damages allegedly arising from a car repair. In response to the trial court's notice, Stewart timely filed a motion to retain to prevent dismissal of his suit for want of prosecution. On October 20, 1987, the trial court signed a captionless sheet, noting the dismissal of a case for want of prosecution. Subsequently, Stewart's case was included on a computer printout listing a number of cases dismissed for want of prosecution. The printout has a run date of October 24, 1987, four days after the trial court signed the captionless sheet. At some point, the computer list and the captionless sheet were stapled together and placed in Stewart's file. Although it is unclear how any error in including Stewart's case on the dismissal list came to light, in April and May 1990 correction reports noted that the dismissal was erroneous and the case was reactivated. The trial court rendered a nihil dicit judgment against USA Custom in March 1991.

In November 1991, Stewart initiated this proceeding by filing for a writ of garnishment against Lockwood National Bank, claiming that it had possession of USA Custom's funds. Stewart based his request for garnishment on the nihil dicit judgment against USA Custom. USA Custom intervened and filed a motion to dissolve the writ of garnishment, asserting that the nihil dicit judgment was void because it was signed after the trial court's jurisdiction had expired. USA Custom argued that the trial court had lost jurisdiction because it already had rendered judgment by dismissing the suit for want of prosecution. USA Custom further argued that, because the suit was never reinstated and because there was no evidence of a clerical error in rendering judgment, the judgment became final. After a hearing, the trial court rendered judgment, allowing garnishment from any accounts held at Lockwood National Bank in the name of USA Custom, overruling the motion to dissolve in relation to those accounts, but granting the motion to dissolve with respect to any other accounts. Finding that there had been a dismissal for want of prosecution so that the trial court lacked jurisdiction when it entered the nihil dicit judgment against USA Custom, the court of appeals reversed the trial court's judgment and rendered judgment for Lockwood National Bank, quashing the writ of garnishment.

Because this is a collateral attack, USA Custom must show that the nihil dicit judgment is void. *Kelly v. Gibbs*, 84 Tex. 143, 19 S.W. 563, 563 (1892) (stating that a garnishment proceeding may be defeated by a showing that the judgment relied on by the plaintiff does not, in fact, exist, or that it is void); *Tom Benson Chevrolet Co. v. Beall*, 567 S.W.2d 857, 859 (Tex. Civ. App.—San Antonio 1978, writ ref'd n.r.e.) (noting that, in a writ of garnishment proceeding, the attack on the underlying judgment must show that it is nonexistent or void); *see Fleming v. Seeligson*, 57 Tex. 524, 531 (1882) (stating that the only issue in a collateral attack is whether the underlying judgment is void); *Owen Elec. Supply, Inc. v. Brite Day Constr., Inc.*, 821 S.W.2d 283, 287 (Tex. App.—Houston [1st Dist.] 1991, writ denied) (holding that a garnishment proceeding could not proceed because the underlying judgment was null and void). In a collateral attack, the judgment under attack is presumed valid. *White v. White*, 142 Tex. 499, 179 S.W.2d 503, 506 (1944); *Bouldin v. Miller*, 87 Tex. 359, 28 S.W. 940, 941 (1894).

Stewart contends that the captionless sheet, although it was titled as an order of dismissal, was not sufficiently definite and certain on its face to effect a dismissal and that the later attachment of the computer printout did not cure any defect in the order. We agree.

A properly executed order of dismissal is a judgment. *Texas State Bd. of Examiners in Optometry v. Lane*, 337 S.W.2d 801, 803-04 (Tex. Civ. App.—Fort Worth 1960, writ ref'd). However, an order of dismissal must meet the requisites of a valid judgment. A judgment must be sufficiently definite and certain to define and protect the rights of all litigants, or it should provide a definite means of ascertaining such rights, to the end that ministerial officers can carry the judgment into execution without ascertainment of facts not therein stated. *Steed v. State*, 143 Tex. 82, 183 S.W.2d 458, 460 (1944) (quoting 25 TEX. JUR. § 84 & (Supp. 1939)); *see also Hinde v. Hinde*, 701 S.W.2d 637, 639 (Tex. 1985) (per curiam); *Taylor v. Hicks*, 691 S.W.2d 839, 840 (Tex. App.—Fort Worth 1985, no writ) (per curiam); *Roberts v. Brittain*, 659 S.W.2d 750, 751 (Tex. App.—Tyler 1983, no writ); *American Casualty & Life Ins. Co. v. Boyd*, 394 S.W.2d 685, 688 (Tex. Civ. App.—Tyler 1965, no writ) (concluding that an order unintelligible on its face is a nullity with no legal force and effect); *Hatton v. Burgess*, 167 S.W.2d 260, 262-63 (Tex. Civ. App.—Beaumont 1943, writ ref'd w.o.m.) (finding a judgment void for want of certainty).

The captionless sheet is labeled as an order, but it identifies no parties or docket numbers. The computer printout, which was not incorporated by reference into the captionless sheet and which listed over a dozen other cases, was not generated until several days after the trial court signed the captionless "order." It is impossible to discern from the face of the captionless sheet whose rights are affected by the attempted dismissal, and a ministerial officer could not have carried the "order" into execution without ascertaining additional facts. Consequently, we hold that the self-described "order" did not constitute a judgment and, accordingly, that Stewart's case was not dismissed.

For the reasons explained herein, we reverse the judgment of the court of appeals and remand this cause to the trial court for further proceedings consistent with this opinion.

Notes

1. The law is settled in Texas that in a collateral attack brought by a Texas resident the recitations in the judgment prevail over the rest of the record. Therefore, even if other parts of the record show a lack of personal jurisdiction, if the judgment recites the contrary [for example if the judgment recites: "the defendant although duly cited failed to appear"], the collateral attack fails.[1]

2. Unless a judgment of a court of general jurisdiction is void, it is not subject to collateral attack in another court of equal jurisdiction.[2] And a judgment is void only when it is shown that the court had no jurisdiction of the parties or property, no jurisdiction of the subject matter, no jurisdiction to enter the particular judgment, or no capacity to act as a court.[3] All errors other than jurisdictional deficiencies render the judgment merely voidable, and such errors must be corrected on direct attack. When time for direct attack by appeal has elapsed, a bill of review in the court rendering the initial judgment is the exclusive remedy to attack the judgment.[4]

3. As shown above, it is the firmly established rule in Texas that a *resident* defendant who is not served and who does not appear may not as a matter of public policy, attack the verity of a judgment in a collateral proceeding; the jurisdictional recitals import absolute verity.[5] In *Hicks v. Sias*[6] the Court held that a *nonresident* of Texas was entitled to go beyond the fact of the record in a collateral attack. The Court noted that in the case of a citizen of Texas, the courts of Texas have potential jurisdiction, and thus on grounds of public policy, a collateral attack should not inquire into facts dehors of the record in order to establish its invalidity. However, the court noted "the 'public policy' of Texas can not support judgments by its courts against nonresidents for the simple reason that the courts of Texas have no potential jurisdiction over of citizen of another state."

4. *Summary of the law concerning collateral attacks.*

The primary authority on this subject is Gus M. Hodges. Anyone with a problem in this area must turn to his article entitled *Collateral Attacks on Judgments*, 41 TEX. L. REV. 163 (1962). Hodges' work is used freely herein, and is cited as Hodges. His introduction to the subject is the best that can be found:

> The significance of the problem to be considered is suggested by the fact that the judgment of a court completely without jurisdiction of the person, the subject matter, or the judgment entered may nevertheless be completely binding on a person and his property. This result will be reached because of overweighing policies in favor of maintaining the reliability of records and setting a limit of finality to judgments. Hodges, 41 TEX. L. REV. 163 (1962).

Note: While this statement appears to be true today, it must be mentioned that the concepts of due process have greatly expanded since the writing of Hodges' article and most of the cases on collateral attack. The due process concepts must always be considered in evaluating any collateral attack problem.

a. *Time to Act.* There is no timetable and no statute of limitations for a collateral attack.[7]

b. *No Need for Meritorious Defense.* Further, the collateral attack does not require the pleading or proof of a meritorious defense.[8] However, it would be an unusual case where an attorney would consciously choose to mount a collateral attack when a direct attack is available. This is so, if for no other reason, because the collateral attack, if valid, will always be available, while the direct attack passes beyond reach with the passage of time.

---

1 *See* Pure Oil Co. v. Reese, 124 Tex. 476, 78 S.W. 2d 932 (Tex. Comm'n App. 1935, opinion adopted).

2 *See, e.g.,* Austin Indep. Sch. Dist. v. Sierra Club, 495 S.W.2d 878, 881 (Tex. 1973).

3 *Id.*

4 *See. e.g.,* Middleton v. Murff, 689 S.W.2d 212 (Tex. 1985).

5 *See also* Akers v. Simpson, 445 S.W.2d 957 (Tex. 1969).

6 102 S.W.2d 460 (Tex. Civ. App. 1937, writ ref'd).

7 Carlton v. Hoff, 292 S.W. 642, 644 (Tex. Civ. App.—Eastland 1927, no writ).

8 Galveston, Harrisburg & San Antonio Ry. Co. v. Ware, 74 Tex. 47, 11 S.W. 918 (1889).

c. *Procedural Requirements*. There is no set procedure for a collateral attack. Any proceeding which would avoid the effect of a prior judgment is a collateral attack. It is also any direct attack which, though made in the form of a direct attack, is unavailable as such because of some limitation or qualification of the direct attack chosen. Hodges, 41 TEX. L. REV., 164 (1962).

d. *Availability—Conditions to Use*. Assuming that the judgment in question is one rendered by a court of general jurisdiction, and that the attack is made by a party (or one in privity with a party), the general grounds for a collateral attack are that the trial court: 1) had no jurisdiction of the person of a party, or of the property of that party; 2) had no jurisdiction of the subject matter; 3) had no jurisdiction to enter the particular judgment; 4) and/or had no capacity to act as a court.[9]

e. *Usability—Restrictions on Use*.

i. *The Power to Decide Includes the Power to Decide Wrongly*. The true problem with collateral attacks is that they may not be used to overturn prior judicial error, as opposed to jurisdictional errors. In this context, a judicial error is one made by a court, directly or by implication, in deciding a case. This may include errors in determining whether the defendant has been properly served, whether the plaintiff's petition states a cause of action, or whether sufficient evidence was offered to support the judgment entered. Unless the error is fundamental, it must have been corrected by direct attack, or it cannot be corrected by collateral attack. "Errors are corrected by appeal, and a judgment that has become final may be attacked only by way of bill of review."[10] This is so because the power to decide includes the power to decide wrongly. Once a judicial decision has been made, the only remedy for a party aggrieved by the ruling is a direct attack. The exception to this statement occurs when the error is jurisdictional or fundamental.

ii. *The Concept of Fundamental Error*. The concept of "void" judgments and fundamental error are closely related. The current law of collateral attack has evolved in much the same way as fundamental error. The latter concept has changed radically since the 1941 repeal of old art. 1837, TEX. REV. CIV. STAT. ANN.[11]

> "Fundamental error survives today in those rare instances in which the record shows the court lacked jurisdiction or that the public interest is directly and adversely affected as that interest is declared in the statutes or the Constitution of Texas." *Pirtle v. Gregory*, 629 S.W.2d 919, 920 (Tex. 1982).

f. *Examples*. The law of collateral attack has evolved since the decision in *McEwen v. Harrison*.[12] There McEwen had obtained a default judgment against Texaco. Long after the time for filing a motion for new trial had passed, Texaco filed a motion to vacate the judgment on the ground that it was void because citation had not been served on any person served on any person designated by law as its agent for service. Judge Harrison granted the motion and ordered the judgment vacated. The Supreme Court found that order to be void and decreed that it be set aside. Tracing the history of TEX. R. CIV. P. 329b, the Court construed it:

> . . . to mean that when the time for filing a motion for new trial has expired and relief may not be obtained by appeal, a proceeding in the nature of a bill of review is the exclusive method of vacating a default judgment rendered in a case in which the court had jurisdictional power to render it. Into this category will fall those cases in which a default judgment is asserted to be void for want of service, or of valid service of process . . . . With this construction of the Rule, we may assume, without deciding, that Texaco is correct when it says that the default judgment is a void judgment and that its motion to vacate is a direct attack on the judgment. We are yet compelled to hold that the order vacating the default judgment is unauthorized and void because the district court had jurisdictional power to determine the validity of the service (Indeed, it was its duty to do so) and to render the judgment, and Texaco's motion to vacate it does not qualify as a bill of review. *McEwen v. Harrison*, 162 Tex. 125, 345 S.W.2d 706, 710-711 (1961).

---

[9] Cook v. Cameron, 733 S.W.2d 137, 140 (Tex. 1987); Browning v. Placke, 698 S.W.2d 362, 363 (Tex. 1985); Austin Indep. School Dist. v. Sierra Club, 495 S.W.2d 878, 881 (Tex. 1973).

[10] Mann v. Gonzalez, 595 S.W.2d 102 (Tex. 1979).

[11] McCauley v. Consolidated Underwriters, 157 Tex. 475, 304 S.W.2d 265 (1957); Ramsey v. Dunlop, 146 Tex. 196, 205 S.W.2d 979, 984 (1947).

[12] 162 Tex. 125, 345 S.W.2d 706 (1961).

In *Dean v. Kirk*,[13] the wife signed a waiver of citation before the husband filed the petition for divorce. The petition and waiver were filed at the same time, and the trial court granted the divorce. More than thirty days after the divorce decree became final the trial judge purported to set the decree aside as void. It was argued in the Texas Supreme Court that the lack of jurisdiction over the wife was apparent from the record or the "judgment roll" (the papers on file in the case). The Supreme Court rejected the argument and held that Judge Kirk was without power to set aside the judgment after thirty days had passed. Citing to *McEwen v. Harrison*[14] which, in turn, relied upon *Brown v. Clippenger*,[15] the Court held that *the judgment of a court with subject matter jurisdiction could only be directly attacked, even if there was a want of service, or of valid service, of process.*[16]

In *El Paso Pipe and Supply Co. v. Mountain State Leasing, Inc.*,[17] as in *Mann v Gonzales*,[18] the trial court had dismissed an action for want of prosecution, and had erroneously ordered that the dismissal be with prejudice. No direct attack was made on that judgment. The plaintiff filed a new suit alleging the identical cause of action that had been dismissed with prejudice. Since this new suit was clearly a collateral attack on the first judgment, the trial court entered a summary judgment for the defendant. The court of appeals reversed.[19] The Supreme Court reversed the court of appeals reiterating that TEX. R. CIV. P. 329b provides the exclusive remedy to attack a judgment which has become final. The Court held that the defendant's only remedy was by appeal or bill of review.

In *Middleton v. Murff*[20] the Supreme Court ended any question about the matter. The Court expressly disapproved of the language in prior opinions that "[i]f a judgment rendered by a trial court is void it may be set aside by that court at any time." They held that TEX. R. CIV. P. 329b provided the exclusive remedy for a trial court to correct an improper judgment.[21] They did reiterate the limited exception recognized in *McEwen* and *Deen*:

> . . . where the court rendering the judgment had no 'jurisdictional power' to do so. We have defined 'jurisdictional power' in this sense to mean 'jurisdiction over the subject matter, the power to hear and determine cases of the general class to which the particular one belongs.' *Deen v. Kirk*, 508 S.W.2d 70, 72 (Tex. 1974).

This exception, then, is the permissible range for collateral attack in Texas.

g. *No Evidence Outside the Record.* Domestic Judgments. At least in the case of domestic judgments regular on their face, in collateral proceedings, no evidence outside the record will be considered in determining the collateral attack.[22]

h. *Face of Judgment.* There is a well settled principle of public policy:

> ". . . which precludes inquiry by evidence aliunde the record in a collateral attack upon a judgment of a domestic court of general jurisdiction, regular on its face, into any fact which the court rendering such

---

13 508 S.W.2d 70 (Tex. 1974).

14 162 Tex. 125, 345 S.W.2d 706 (1961).

15 113 Tex. 364, 256 S.W. 254 (1923).

16 Akers v. Simpson, 445 S.W.2d 957 (Tex. 1969) is in accord.

17 617 S.W.2d 189 (Tex. 1981).

18 595 S.W.2d 102 (Tex. 1979).

19 Mountain States Leasing, Inc. v. El Paso Pipe & Supply Co., 612 S.W.2d 633 (Tex. App.—El Paso 1981).

20 689 S.W.2d 212, 213 (Tex. 1985).

21 The trial court can correct the judgment by the grant of a new trial or by a bill of review. The appellate courts can correct the judgment by an ordinary appeal, an appeal by writ of error, or appeal by writ of error from a bill of review judgment. Otherwise there is no procedural device available to set aside a judgment in Texas.

22 Huffstutlar v. Koons, 789 S.W.2d 707 (Tex. App.—Dallas 1990, no writ); Davis v. Boone, 786 S.W.2d 85 (Tex. App.—San Antonio 1990, no writ); Fender v. Moss, 696 S.W.2d 410 (Tex. App.—Dallas 1985, writ ref'd n.r.e); Crawford v. McDonald, 88 Tex. 626, 33 S.W. 325 (1895). *See* Akers v. Simpson, 445 S.W.2d 959 (Tex. 1969); Graham v. Graham, 733 S.W.2d 374 (Tex. App.—Amarillo, 1987, writ ref'd n.r.e.). *But cf.* Ex parte Cardwell, 416 S.W.2d 382 (Tex. 1967) (allowing extrinsic evidence on service in a habeas corpus proceeding, since such review is quasi-criminal.).

judgment must have passed upon in proceeding to its rendition. Therefore. . . where a personal judgment has been rendered against a defendant by a domestic court of general jurisdiction, and recitals in a domestic judgment, regular on its face, against a resident defendant, will control and may not be contradicted by the judgment roll or record. They import absolute verity." *Templeton v. Ferguson*, 89 Tex. 47, 33 S.W. 325, 328 (1895).

Recitations in the judgment control the rest of the record on collateral attack, so that even though other parts of the record show a lack of jurisdiction, if the judgment recites the contrary, the collateral attack fails.[23]

Accord Lewright v. Manning,[24] The limitation of extrinsic evidence to vary judgment recitals does not apply against nonresidents who are not otherwise subject to potential jurisdiction.[25]

i. *Defending Against the Collateral Attack.* Plead res judicata and collateral estoppel.[26] Appeal if the judgment is adverse. The writ of prohibition is usually not available.[27]

j. *Practical Considerations.* Collateral attacks are used when nothing else can be done.

4. ***Full Faith and Credit of Foreign Judgments***

Note

In *Durfee v. Duke*[1] the Supreme Court held that under Article IV, Section 1 of the United States Constitution a court in one state, when asked to give effect to the judgment of a court in another state, may constitutionally inquire into the foreign court's jurisdiction to render that judgment. However, the Court noted that the scope of such an inquiry is extremely limited. As a general rule a judgment is entitled to full faith and credit—even as to questions of jurisdiction [subject matter or jurisdiction over the person]—when the second court's inquiry discloses that those questions have been fully and fairly litigated and finally decided in the court which rendered the original judgment.

MAYHEW
v.
CAPRITO
794 S.W.2d 1
(Tex. 1990)

George Barron, Orange, Jim Boyle, Austin, for petitioners.
Pannal Alan Sanders, Orange, for respondents.

PER CURIAM

The question presented is what effect the Texas courts should give to a Louisiana judgment.

This is a will contest. Contestants seek to litigate in Texas issues of the decedent's domicile and validity of the will, even though those issues were litigated by the parties in the courts of Louisiana. The trial court granted the will proponents' motion for summary judgment, finding that the deceased was domiciled in Louisiana at

[23] Huffstutlar v. Koons, 789 S.W.2d 707 (Tex. App.—Dallas 1990, no writ), *citing* Pure Oil Co. v. Reese, 124 Tex 476, 481, 78 S.W.2d 932, 934-35 (Tex. Comm'n App. 1935, opinion adopted).

[24] 392 S.W.2d 466 (Tex. Civ. App.—Corpus Christi 1965, no writ).

[25] Hicks v. Sias, 102 S.W.2d 460 (Tex. Civ. App.—Beaumont 1937, writ ref'd).

[26] Joiner v. Vasquez, 632 S.W.2d 755 (Tex. App.—Dallas 1981), 104 S. Ct. 422.

[27] Holloway v. Fifth Court of Appeals, 767 S.W.2d 680 (Tex. 1989); Milam County Oil Mill Co. v. Bass, 106 Tex. 260, 163 S.W. 577 (1914); Mid Plains Reeves, Inc. v. Baskin, ____ S.W.2d ____ (Tex. App.—El Paso 08-90-0203-CV, June 27, 1990).

[1] 375 U.S. 106, 84 S.Ct. 242 (1963).

death and that the Louisiana will was valid. In an unpublished opinion, the court of appeals reversed and remanded, holding that the will proponents were not entitled to the summary judgment because it was not established whether the decedent was domiciled in Texas or Louisiana at the time of his death. We reverse the judgment of the court of appeals and affirm the judgment of the trial court.

The decedent, Salvador Caprito, lived in Fort Worth, Texas from 1955 until 1977. In 1977, Caprito was adjudged mentally incompetent and guardianship proceedings were instituted in Tarrant County, Texas. Guardianship proceedings were transferred to Orange County, Texas, in 1978. In 1981, Caprito was placed in a nursing home in Pineville, Louisiana. At the time of his death in March 1982, in Louisiana, guardianship proceedings were still pending in Texas.

There are two wills at issue—the 1982 will (the Louisiana will) and the 1977 will (the Texas will). The decedent's children (will proponents) initially probated the Louisiana will in Louisiana, alleging that the deceased was domiciled in Louisiana at the time of his death. The decedent's niece and nephew (will contestants) initially probated the Texas will in Orange County, Texas, claiming that the Texas court had jurisdiction because of the guardianship proceedings previously filed with the Texas court. The contestants challenged the Louisiana will in Louisiana and their objections were overruled by the Louisiana court, which determined that the decedent was a Louisiana domiciliary. This ruling was affirmed on appeal.

The will proponents moved for summary judgment in this Texas proceeding on the grounds that: (1) the issue of domicile was fully litigated in the Louisiana suit; and (2) none of the grounds for contesting the 1982 will provided for in section 100 of the Texas Probate Code are present in this case. The issue before this court is whether the court of appeals must recognize the judgment of the Louisiana Supreme Court that Caprito was a Louisiana domiciliary when he died.

The United States Constitution requires that "[f]ull Faith and Credit shall be given in each State to the . . . judicial Proceedings of every other State." U.S. Const. art. IV, § 1. The United States Supreme Court has stated that "the judgment of a state court should have the same credit, validity, and effect, in every other court of the United States, which it had in the state where it was pronounced." *Underwriters Nat'l Assurance Co. v. North Carolina Life and Accident and Health Ins. Guar. Ass'n*, 455 U.S. 691, 704, 102 S.Ct. 1357, 1365, 71 L.Ed.2d 558 (1982). In *Durfee v. Duke*, 375 U.S. 106, 84 S.Ct. 242, 11 L.Ed.2d 186 (1963), the Supreme Court limited the scope of a jurisdictional review by a court of a sister state, holding that "a judgment is entitled to full faith and credit—even as to questions of jurisdiction—when the second court's inquiry discloses that those questions have been fully and fairly litigated and finally decided in the court which rendered the original judgment." *Id.* at 111, 84 S.Ct. at 245. The Supreme Court stated: We see no reason why a court, in the absence of an allegation of fraud . . . should examine again the question whether the court making the earlier determination on an actual contest over jurisdiction between the parties, did have jurisdiction of the subject matter of the litigation . . . a collateral attack upon the decision as to jurisdiction . . . merely retries the issue previously determined.

There is no reason to expect that a second decision will be more satisfactory than the first. *Id.* at 113-14, 84 S.Ct. at 246 (*quoting Stoll v. Gottlieb*, 305 U.S. 165, 172, 59 S.Ct. 134, 137, 83 L.Ed. 104 (1938)). We have jurisdiction to correct a decision of the court of appeals which is contrary to a decision of the United States Supreme Court. *Eichelberger v. Eichelberger*, 582 S.W.2d 395, 400 (Tex. 1979).

Because the court of appeals' decision directly conflicts with the United States Supreme Court's holding in *Durfee v. Duke*, 375 U.S. 106, 84 S.Ct. 242, 11 L.Ed.2d 186 (1963), a majority of the court grants the application for writ of error and, without hearing oral argument, reverses the judgment of the court of appeals and affirms the judgment of the trial court. *See* Tex. R. App. P. 133(b).

Note

A Texas Court must give full faith and credit to a foreign judgment when the question of jurisdiction and the validity of the judgment have been fully and fairly litigated and finally decided in a court of a sister state. This is so even if the judgment is based on a cognovit clause (allowing the confession of judgment upon default in the performance of a contract) which is prohibited by law in Texas under Sec 30.001, Tex. Civ. P. & Rem. Code. *See Roark v. Sweigart*, 848 S.W.2d 387 (Tex. App.—Amarillo 1993, no writ)

CHAPTER 6.
JURISDICTION OVER THE PERSON

1. *Due Process Requirements of Personal Jurisdiction: Minimum Contacts*

Note

Section 17.042 of the Texas Civil Practices and Remedies Code specifies the acts which constitute doing business in the state as follows:

> In addition to other acts that may constitute doing business, a nonresident does business in this state if the nonresident:
>
> (1) contracts by mail or otherwise with a Texas resident and either party is to perform the contract in whole or in part in this state;
>
> (2) commits a tort in whole or in part in this state; or
>
> (3) recruits Texas residents, directly or through an intermediary located in this state, for employment inside or outside this state.

This statute is the essence of the principal Texas long-arm statute in that if sets forth the permissible scope of Texas jurisdiction over nonresidents served beyond the borders of the state of Texas, consistent with limits prescribed by the Fourteenth Amendment to the United States Constitution, through the doing business concept. Satisfaction of the doing business standard as spelled out in this section is a necessary prerequisite in order to utilize the principal Texas long-arm jurisdiction. It enables a state court to assert personal jurisdiction over a nonresident doing business in Texas to the federal constitutional limits.

Read Rule 120a Texas Rules of Civil Procedure.

SCHLOBOHM
v.
SCHAPIRO
784 S.W.2d 355
(Tex. 1990)

James H. Baumgartner, David Reese, Dallas, for petitioners.
Howard V. Tygrett, Dallas, for respondents.

COOK, JUSTICE.

This case presents us with a Pennsylvania defendant and the question whether a Texas court has the power to adjudicate a Texan's claims against him. The courts below found that the defendant's contacts with Texas were too minimal to allow the exercise of in personam jurisdiction. Because we hold that his contacts with Texas were continuing and systematic enough to permit the imposition of jurisdiction, we reverse the judgment of the court of appeals.

The Pennsylvania defendant is Rolf Schapiro ("Schapiro"). His son, Douglas, lives in Dallas. In July 1984, Schapiro invested $10,000 in a corporation named Hangers, Inc., which was formed by Douglas and his wife to establish a dry cleaning business in Dallas. Schapiro received stock in Hangers and became its sole director. Douglas became president. Although Schapiro did not participate in the incorporation, he conducted Hangers' first meeting in Dallas. Corporate records were kept by his attorney in Pittsburgh.

Hangers leased space for some of its outlets, and Schapiro guaranteed some of the leases. In late 1984, Charles and Joneen Schlobohm leased a building to Hangers. A sixty month lease was negotiated and signed by Douglas, as president. Schapiro did not participate in the negotiations, and he did not guarantee the lease.

In November, Schapiro loaned Hangers $30,000 of his personal funds to buy equipment to expand the business. He later visited Dallas and obtained financing for the rest of the plant, signing a promissory note in his individual capacity for $136,702.10. Schapiro owned the equipment and leased it to Hangers.

Schapiro's involvement in Hangers' plant expansion was not an unusual event in the history of his entanglement with Hangers. He frequently provided funds during start-up, expansion, and throughout Hangers' decline. Hangers' payroll and other expenses were continually covered by Schapiro's deposits. These sums, which were characterized as loans, totaled an estimated $474,000. Schapiro claimed that Douglas signed promissory notes for the loans, but the notes are not in the record.

The growing financial commitment induced Schapiro to adopt various measures to protect his investment. He first demanded that all shares in the corporation be transferred to him. The transfer was made by Douglas and another shareholder in late 1984 or early 1985, making Schapiro both sole shareholder and sole director of Hangers. In the summer of 1985, as a result of continuous but unsatisfactory communications about the status of the business, Schapiro sent his personal accountant to Dallas to ensure the use of proper accounting procedures. In October 1985 and January 1986, Schapiro went to Dallas himself to investigate Hangers. The visits did nothing to allay his anxiety about the condition of the business, and he resigned as director of Hangers later that month. After another visit to Dallas by Schapiro's accountant to assess Hangers, Schapiro discontinued his relationship with Hangers.

In August 1986, Hangers stopped paying rent on the building leased from the Schlobohms. The Schlobohms sued Hangers, Douglas, and Schapiro for non-payment of rent from August until the end of the lease term in 1989. Schapiro made a special appearance pursuant to TEX. R. CIV. P. 120a. The trial court sustained Schapiro's challenge to jurisdiction and dismissed the cause. The court of appeals affirmed. 759 S.W.2d 470.

I. THE TEXAS LONG-ARM STATUTE

A Texas court may exercise jurisdiction over a nonresident if two conditions are met. First, the Texas long-arm statute must authorize the exercise of jurisdiction. Second, the exercise of jurisdiction must be consistent with federal and state constitutional guarantees of due process. *See* TEX. CIV. PRAC. & REM. CODE ANN. § 17.041-§ 17.069 (Vernon 1986).

Our long-arm statute authorizes the exercise of jurisdiction over those who do business in Texas. *Id.* at § 17.042. The statute lists particular acts that constitute "doing business." The statute provides, however, that "other acts" of the nonresident may place him within the "doing business" requirement. *Id.; see generally Zac Smith & Co. v. Otis Elevator Co.*, 734 S.W.2d 662 (Tex. 1987), *cert. denied* 484 U.S. 1063, 108 S.Ct. 1022, 98 L.Ed.2d 986 (1988). Although Schapiro's acts in Texas do not fit into any of the particularly described acts listed under Section 17.042 of the long-arm statute, his acts do concern a business enterprise. Jurisdiction, therefore, is authorized by the "other acts" language of Section 17.042.

We must now determine whether the exercise of jurisdiction under the long-arm statute is consistent with due process. This court has decided that the broad language of the long-arm statute's doing business requirement allows the statute to reach as far as the federal constitution permits. *See U-Anchor Advertising, Inc. v. Burt*, 553 S.W.2d 760, 762 (Tex. 1977), *cert. denied*, 434 U.S. 1063, 98 S.Ct. 1235, 55 L.Ed.2d 763 (1978). Our inquiry, therefore, focuses on the decisions of this court and of the United States Supreme Court outlining the constitutional test for in personam jurisdiction.

II. THE FEDERAL TEST

Under the federal constitutional test of due process, a plaintiff must overcome two hurdles to justify the exercise of jurisdiction over a nonresident defendant. The plaintiff must initially show that the defendant has established minimum contacts with the forum state. *International Shoe Co. v. Washington*, 326 U.S. 310, 316, 66 S.Ct. 154, 158, 90 L.Ed. 95 (1945). He must then show that the assertion of jurisdiction comports with fair play and substantial justice. *Id.*

The United States Supreme Court has extensively developed the first prong of the test, the minimum contacts analysis. We now know that an essential goal of the test is to protect the defendant. *World-Wide Volkswagen Corp. v. Woodson*, 444 U.S. 286, 292, 100 S.Ct. 559, 564, 62 L.Ed.2d 490 (1980). This goal requires that we focus upon his intentional activities and expectations in deciding whether it is proper to call him before the courts of the forum. He must do something purposeful to avail himself of the privilege of conducting activities in the forum, thus invoking the benefit and protection of its laws. *Hanson v. Denckla*, 357 U.S. 235, 253, 78 S.Ct. 1228, 1239, 2 L.Ed.2d 1283 (1958). Those activities, whether they consist of direct acts within the forum or conduct outside the forum, must justify a conclusion that the defendant should reasonably anticipate being called into court there. *World-Wide Volkswagen*, 444 U.S. at 297, 100 S.Ct. at 567.

The Court has refined the minimum contacts analysis by identifying recurring fact patterns and outlining guidelines for application of the due process test to these patterns. Where the activities of a defendant in a forum are isolated or disjointed, for example, jurisdiction is proper if the cause of action arises from a particular activity. In these cases, jurisdiction is said to be specific. *Helicopteros Nacionales de Colombia v. Hall*, 466 U.S. 408, 414 n. 8, 104 S.Ct. 1868, 1872 n. 8, 80 L.Ed.2d 404 (1984). The minimum contacts analysis is somewhat narrow, focusing on the relationship among defendant, forum, and litigation. *Id.*, (*citing Shaffer v. Heitner*, 433 U.S. 186, 204, 97 S.Ct. 2569, 2579, 53 L.Ed.2d 683 (1977)). On the other hand, where the defendant's activities in the forum are continuing and systematic, jurisdiction may be proper without a relationship between defendant's particular act and the cause of action. In these cases, jurisdiction is often said to be general. *Helicopteros*, 466 U.S. at 414, n. 9, 104 S.Ct. at 1872, n. 9. The minimum contacts inquiry is broader and more demanding when general jurisdiction is alleged, requiring a showing of substantial activities in the forum state.

Under the second prong of the test of due process, plaintiffs must show that the exercise of in personam jurisdiction comports with fair play and substantial justice. *International Shoe*, 326 U.S. at 316, 66 S.Ct. at 158. Because the minimum contacts analysis now encompasses so many considerations of fairness, it has become less likely that the exercise of jurisdiction will fail a fair play analysis. Courts must consider the fair play analysis, however, because the case law makes it clear that this analysis is separate and distinct from the minimum contacts issue. *See Asahi Metal Indus. Co. v. Superior Court*, 480 U.S. 102, 113, 107 S.Ct. 1026, 1033, 94 L.Ed.2d 92 (1987); *Burger King Corp. v. Rudzewicz*, 471 U.S. 462, 476-77, 105 S.Ct. 2174, 2184-85, 85 L.Ed.2d 528 (1985).

III. THE TEXAS TEST

In an effort to ensure compliance with the federal constitutional standard, Texas has designed its own formula for specific jurisdiction: (1) The nonresident defendant or foreign corporation must purposefully do some act or consummate some transaction in the forum state; (2) The cause of action must arise from, or be connected with, such act or transaction; and (3) The assumption of jurisdiction by the forum state must not offend traditional notions of fair play and substantial justice, consideration being given to the quality, nature, and extent of the activity in the forum state, the relative convenience of the parties, the benefits and protection of the laws of the forum state afforded the respective parties, and the basic equities of the situation. *O'Brien v. Lanpar Co.*, 399 S.W.2d 340, 342 (Tex. 1966).

The Texas formula tracks elements of the jurisdictional test that have evolved in United States Supreme Court decisions. The first part of the Texas formula reflects the key component of the minimum contacts analysis, the requirement that a defendant purposefully avail himself of the benefits of the forum and reasonably expect to be called to court there. The third part reflects the fair play and substantial justice prong of the jurisdictional test and specifies the factors that this state considers important in the fair play analysis.

In its second part, the Texas formula reflects the concept of specific jurisdiction. The formula does not, however, include the concept of general jurisdiction. For this reason, the formula is incomplete and could give litigants the false idea that jurisdiction may be premised only on an act or transaction of the defendant that gives rise to a cause of action. We believe that the Texas formula should be as complete an outline of the constitutional standard as possible. Accordingly, we modify the second part of the formula to state that jurisdiction may also arise from the continuing and systematic contacts of the defendant with Texas, even if the cause of action does not arise from a specific contact. The requirement should now read: (2) The cause of action must arise from, or be connected with, such act or transaction. Even if the cause of action does not arise from a specific contact, jurisdiction may be exercised if the defendant's contacts with Texas are continuing and systematic. In adopting this modification, we do not change the law. We simply clarify what federal and state cases have acknowledged for many years, that is, that jurisdiction is possible whether either single or numerous contacts between forum and defendant exist. *See Helicopteros*, 466 U.S. at 414-15, 104 S.Ct. at 1872-73; *Zac Smith*, 734 S.W.2d at 663.

IV. APPLICATION

In considering how far our courts may constitutionally reach in the instant case, we reject mechanical application of any test, including the Texas formula. We believe, however, that the Texas formula provides us with a useful jurisdictional checklist, one which helps ensure that we have considered all aspects of the necessary analysis.

Our first inquiry centers on the second part of the formula, the question whether jurisdiction in this case is premised on continuing and systematic activity or on a cause of action that arises from isolated and sporadic activity. The Schlobohms rely on the number and continuity of Schapiro's actions to support their proposition that an activity in which Schapiro did not directly participate, that is, the negotiation and signing of their lease, subjects him to jurisdiction. Their claim of jurisdiction is, therefore, based on continuing and systematic activity. Schapiro agrees that the assertion of jurisdiction in this case must be based on such activity. Schapiro further agrees that he did maintain a number of contacts with Texas. Despite this concession, however, he insists that his "primary" contacts amount to nothing more than his negotiation for the equipment loan and his status as sole stockholder of Hangers.

Schapiro's condensation of activities into two "primary" contacts suggests an unfamiliar approach to the minimum contacts inquiry. The inquiry does not authorize defendants to review their relationship with the forum and excise the contacts they regard as most pertinent to the jurisdictional issue. It demands instead that all contacts be carefully investigated, compiled, sorted, and analyzed for proof of a pattern of continuing and systematic activity. By adopting this approach, we conclude that Schapiro's "primary" contacts are but two of many activities in his continuing relationship with this state.

Our second inquiry concentrates on the first part of the Texas formula, purposeful availment. The issue is whether Schapiro's Texas-related activities, irrespective of their volume, justify our conclusion that Schapiro purposefully directed his activities into this forum. By framing this issue in the common-sense language of *World-Wide Volkswagen*, we clarify it: should Schapiro have reasonably anticipated the call to a Texas court? *World-Wide Volkswagen*, 444 U.S. at 297, 100 S.Ct. at 567.

Schapiro became actively involved in a Texas business and voluntarily continued his commitment for almost two years. He was investor, stockholder, director, advisor, lender, and guarantor for Hangers. He visited the state and maintained regular communications with some of its citizens. When we consider the degree of his involvement, we regard it difficult to believe that anyone in Schapiro's position could have been surprised by the call to litigation in Texas. It is clear that he purposefully availed himself of the benefits of this forum. We hold that Schapiro's minimum contacts with Texas were continuing and systematic enough to subject him to the jurisdiction of a Texas court.

Having determined that Schapiro had minimum contacts with Texas, we must now proceed to the final inquiry, which is expressed in the third part of the Texas formula. The question is whether, despite the existence of minimum contacts, there is any reason why our assertion of jurisdiction in this case would offend traditional notions of fair play and substantial justice. In considering the factors suggested in the Texas formula, we note that the quality, nature and extent of Schapiro's activity in Texas justify a conclusion that he should expect to be called to our courts. Nothing in the record indicates that litigation in a Texas court would be excessively burdensome or inconvenient to him. Finally, litigation in Texas will provide both parties with the benefits and protection of our laws. We hold that the exercise of jurisdiction over Schapiro by a Texas court does not offend traditional notions of fair play and substantial justice.

We reverse the judgment of the court of appeals. We remand the cause to the trial court for trial on the merits.

HECHT, J., not sitting.

SPIR STAR AG
v.
KIMICH
310 S.W.3d 868
(Tex. 2010)

Sarah B. Duncan, Elissa Gail Underwood, Mike A. Hatchell, Locke Lord Bissell & Liddell, LLP, Austin, TX, Rick Lee Oldenettel, Oldenettel & Associates, P.C., Houston, TX, for Petitioner.

Scott Rothenberg, Law Offices of Scott Rothenberg, Keith M. Fletcher, Simmons & Fletcher, Houston, TX, for Respondent.

CHIEF JUSTICE JEFFERSON delivered the opinion of the Court.

A foreign manufacturer sold its products in Texas through a Texas distributor. We must decide whether the use of that distributorship insulates the manufacturer from the reach of a Texas court when one of the products injures a Texas citizen. We hold that a manufacturer is subject to specific personal jurisdiction in Texas when it intentionally targets Texas as the marketplace for its products, and that using a distributor-intermediary for that purpose provides no haven from the jurisdiction of a Texas court. Because, in this case, personal jurisdiction comports with traditional notions of fair play and substantial justice, we affirm the court of appeals' judgment.

I. Factual and Procedural Background

Spir Star AG ("AG"), a German corporation headquartered in Rimbach, Germany, manufactures high-pressure hoses and fittings for sale throughout the world. AG is owned by three German citizens: Werner Büchner, Gerhard Strobach, and Walter de Graaf. In 1995, AG decided that Houston would be the optimal location for a distributorship because the Texas coastal region's numerous refineries were well suited for AG's energy-related products. AG's executives traveled to Houston, leased office space, and established a Texas distributorship, Spir Star Inc., now Spir Star Limited ("Limited"). AG's directors gave Limited permission to use the trademarked "Spir Star" name free of charge. Although it sells products other than AG's, Limited is AG's exclusive distributor in Texas and North America.

AG manufactures hoses that are used primarily in the energy industry. Each month, Limited purchases a maritime container full of AG's products, which are then shipped to the port of Houston. Limited assembles the hoses using AG-provided training and tools and sells them to customers in Texas and elsewhere. Title to the hoses passes to Limited in Europe. The Texas distributorship accounts for thirty-five percent of AG's annual sales, although Limited and AG do not share profits or finances with each other.

De Graaf, AG's president, is also the president of Limited. He splits his time between Houston and Germany, and regularly conducts AG's business in Texas. De Graaf and AG's other two officers own seventy-five percent of Limited; twenty-five percent is owned by Limited employees.

In 2003, an AG high-pressure hose ruptured and seriously injured Louis Kimich. AG had sold the hose to Limited, which in turn sold it to Kimich's employer. Kimich sued his employer and the premises owner, and later added claims against AG and Limited.

AG filed a special appearance, which the trial court and the court of appeals denied. 311 S.W.3d 1. We granted AG's petition for review, 51 Tex. Sup.Ct. J. 1403, 1416 (Sept. 26, 2008), and now affirm.

II. Applicable Law

To render a binding judgment, a court must have both subject matter jurisdiction over the controversy and personal jurisdiction over the parties. *CSR Ltd. v. Link*, 925 S.W.2d 591, 594 (Tex. 1996). Whether a court has personal jurisdiction over a defendant is determined as a matter of law, which appellate courts review de novo. *BMC Software Belg., N.V. v. Marchand*, 83 S.W.3d 789, 794 (Tex. 2002). When, as here, a trial court does not issue findings of fact or conclusions of law to support its special-appearance determination, we presume that all factual disputes were resolved in favor of the trial court's ruling. *Id.*

Texas courts have personal jurisdiction over a nonresident defendant when (1) the Texas long-arm statute provides for it, and (2) the exercise of jurisdiction is consistent with federal and state due process guarantees. *Am. Type Culture Collection, Inc. v. Coleman*, 83 S.W.3d 801, 806 (Tex. 2002). Our long-arm statute reaches

" 'as far as the federal constitutional requirements for due process will allow.' " *Id.* (*quoting Guardian Royal Exch. Assur., Ltd. v. English China Clays, P.L.C.*, 815 S.W.2d 223, 226 (Tex.1991)). Consequently, the statute's requirements are satisfied if exercising jurisdiction comports with federal due process limitations. *Id.*

If a defendant has never invoked the protections that a forum offers its residents, or has no purposeful contact with it, the forum court's jurisdiction is confined. Personal jurisdiction over nonresident defendants is constitutional only when: (1) the defendant has established minimum contacts with the forum state, and (2) the exercise of jurisdiction comports with traditional notions of fair play and substantial justice. * * *

Although this "fair play" and "substantial justice" test is well known to appellate courts, the expression is imprecise. It gains meaning, however, when viewed in light of the "minimum contacts" a defendant has with the forum. *Int'l Shoe*, 326 U.S. at 316, 66 S.Ct. 154. Significant contacts suggest that the defendant has taken advantage of forum-related benefits, while minor ones imply that the forum itself was beside the point. When a nonresident defendant has purposefully availed itself of the privilege of conducting business in a foreign jurisdiction, it is both fair and just to subject that defendant to the authority of that forum's courts. *Burger King Corp. v. Rudzewicz*, 471 U.S. 462, 475, 105 S.Ct. 2174, 85 L.Ed.2d 528 (1984).

A defendant's contacts with a forum can give rise to either specific or general jurisdiction. *CSR*, 925 S.W.2d at 595. General jurisdiction exists when a defendant's contacts are continuous and systematic, even if the cause of action did not arise from activities performed in the forum state. *Id.* Here, the court of appeals concluded that AG's continuous and systematic contacts with Texas established general jurisdiction. 311 S.W.3d at 5. We do not reach that issue, however, because we conclude instead that the trial court had specific jurisdiction over AG.

III. AG satisfies the "additional conduct" standard required for specific jurisdiction.

A court has specific jurisdiction over a defendant if its alleged liability arises from or is related to an activity conducted within the forum. *CSR*, 925 S.W.2d at 595. Unlike general jurisdiction, which requires a "more demanding minimum contacts analysis," *id.* at 595, specific jurisdiction "may be asserted when the defendant's forum contacts are isolated or sporadic, but the plaintiff's cause of action arises out of those contacts with the state." 4 Charles Alan Wright & Arthur R. Miller, FEDERAL PRACTICE & PROCEDURE § 1067.5 (3d ed. 2002). In such cases, "we focus on the 'relationship among the defendant, the forum[,] and the litigation.' " *Moki Mac*, 221 S.W.3d at 575-76 (*quoting Guardian Royal*, 815 S.W.2d at 228). Specific jurisdiction is appropriate when (1) the defendant's contacts with the forum state are purposeful, and (2) the cause of action arises from or relates to the defendant's contacts. *See Retamco*, 278 S.W.3d at 338.

The "touchstone of jurisdictional due process [is] 'purposeful availment.' " *Michiana Easy Livin' Country, Inc. v. Holten*, 168 S.W.3d 777, 784 (Tex. 2005). Purposeful availment requires a defendant to seek some "benefit, advantage, or profit by 'availing' itself of the jurisdiction." *Id.* at 785. Thus, sellers who reach beyond one state and create continuing relationships with residents of another state are subject to the specific jurisdiction of the latter in suits arising from those activities. *Moki Mac*, 221 S.W.3d at 575.

Notably, however, a seller's awareness " 'that the stream of commerce may or will sweep the product into the forum State does not convert the mere act of placing the product into the stream into an act purposefully directed toward the forum State.' " *CSR*, 925 S.W.2d at 595 (*quoting Asahi Metal Indus. Co., Ltd. v. Superior Court of Cal.*, 480 U.S. 102, 112, 107 S.Ct. 1026, 94 L.Ed.2d 92 (1987) (plurality opinion)). Instead, our precedent generally follows Justice O'Connor's plurality opinion in *Asahi,* which requires some "additional conduct"—beyond merely placing the product in the stream of commerce—that indicates "an intent or purpose to serve the market in the forum State." *Asahi*, 480 U.S. at 112, 107 S.Ct. 1026; *Moki Mac*, 221 S.W.3d at 577; *Michiana*, 168 S.W.3d at 786. Examples of this additional conduct include: (1) "designing the product for the market in the forum State," (2) "advertising in the forum State," (3) "establishing channels for providing regular advice to customers in the forum State," and (4) "marketing the product through a distributor who has agreed to serve as the sales agent in the forum State." *Asahi*, 480 U.S. at 112, 107 S.Ct. 1026; *see also Moki Mac*, 221 S.W.3d at 577; *Michiana*, 168 S.W.3d at 786; *Kawasaki Steel Corp. v. Middleton*, 699 S.W.2d 199, 201 (Tex.1985). In this case, Kimich argues that AG's substantial sales plus utilization of Limited as its distributor meets this standard.

* * *

When an out-of-state manufacturer like AG specifically targets Texas as a market for its products, that manufacturer is subject to a product liability suit in Texas based on a product sold here, even if the sales are conducted through a Texas distributor or affiliate. *See Asahi*, 480 U.S. at 112, 107 S.Ct. 1026 ("Additional conduct of the defendant may indicate an intent or purpose to serve the market in the forum State, for example, . . . marketing the product through a distributor who has agreed to serve as the sales agent in the forum State."). In such cases, it is not the actions of the Texas intermediary that count, but the actions of the foreign manufacturer who markets and distributes the product to profit from the Texas economy. As the United States Supreme Court stated in *World-Wide Volkswagen Corp. v. Woodson*, purposeful availment of local markets may be either direct (through one's own offices and employees) or indirect (through affiliates or independent distributors) * * *

There are several limitations inherent in this rule. First, it is limited to the specific jurisdiction context, because stream-of-commerce analysis "is relevant only to the exercise of specific jurisdiction; it provides no basis for exercising general jurisdiction over a nonresident defendant." * * * If sales alone created general jurisdiction, a foreign manufacturer like AG could be sued in Texas for labor practices occurring in Germany even though they had nothing to do with Texas.

Second, specific jurisdiction is limited to claims that "arise out of or relate to" a nonresident's forum contacts. *Burger King*, 471 U.S. at 472, 105 S.Ct. 2174; *Retamco*, 278 S.W.3d at 338. In such cases, there must be a "substantial connection" between the defendant's contacts and the operative facts of the litigation. *See Moki Mac*, 221 S.W.3d at 585. So when a nonresident's only contacts with Texas involve indirect sales through a distributor or subsidiary, specific jurisdiction is limited to claims arising out of those sales. * * *

Third, not every product claim against a foreign manufacturer is included; there must be a substantial connection. That similar products were sold in Texas would not create a substantial connection as to products that were not. Similarly, a nonresident that buys a Texas distributor might have no substantial connection with sales that occurred before that purchase. *See Commonwealth Gen. Corp. v. York*, 177 S.W.3d 923, 924 (Tex. 2005).

Finally, the manufacturer must have intended to serve the Texas market. *CSR*, 925 S.W.2d at 596. While use of a Texas distributor may satisfy this requirement, there may be situations in which it does not. A Texas distributorship may increase the manufacturer's bottom line because it is more efficient or has greater access to economies of scale, and not because it is intended to serve Texas consumers. *Cf. Asahi*, 480 U.S. at 112, 107 S.Ct. 1026 ("Additional conduct" may include "marketing the product through a distributor who has agreed to serve as the sales agent in the forum State." (emphasis added)).

Many transactions can be structured to avoid any benefit from or availment of Texas law—but not all. A nonresident manufacturer does not avoid Texas law merely by forming a Texas affiliate or utilizing a Texas distributor to sell its products in Texas markets. Just as manufacturers cannot escape liability for defective products by selling them through a subsidiary or distributor, neither can they avoid jurisdiction related to such claims by the same means.

The question is whether AG has purposefully directed acts towards Texas or purposefully availed itself of the benefits and protections of Texas law. We conclude that it has.

A. AG marketed its products exclusively through Limited, a Texas distributor.

AG argues that its individual owners-rather than AG itself-established Limited. Even if that were true, by "marketing [its] product through a distributor who has agreed to serve as the sales agent in the forum state," AG has met *Asahi's* "additional conduct standard." *Asahi*, 480 U.S. at 112, 107 S.Ct. 1026.

AG also contends that, because it receives none of Limited's profits and relinquishes title to the hoses before they reach Texas, AG does not benefit from Limited's Texas connections. But AG reaps substantial economic gain through its sales to Limited, its largest distributor by far, responsible for over one-third of AG's annual sales. *See Moki Mac*, 221 S.W.3d at 578 (finding purposeful availment because of foreign corporation's "additional conduct through which it aimed to get extensive business in or from this state"). Indeed, specific jurisdiction over foreign manufacturers is often premised on sales by independent distributors. * * *

Thus, it is not persuasive that title to the hoses passed in Europe, rather than in Texas. * * *

B. AG intended to serve the Texas market, and Kimich's claim arose from AG's purposeful direction of acts towards Texas.

Not only did AG market its products through a distributor in the forum state, AG directly targeted the Texas market. In CSR, we held that there was no specific jurisdiction over CSR, a foreign asbestos supplier whose product wound up in Texas: CSR's knowledge that its buyer, a pipe manufacturer, had a plant in Texas was not determinative because that manufacturer also had plants in at least four other states, and CSR's awareness that the stream of commerce may sweep the product into Texas " '[did] not convert the mere act of placing the product into the stream into an act purposefully directed toward the forum State.' " *CSR*, 925 S.W.2d at 595 (*quoting Asahi*, 480 U.S. at 112, 107 S.Ct. 1026). Instead, we held that "there must be some indication that CSR intended to serve the Texas market." *Id.* at 595.

This is consistent with federal authority holding that no specific jurisdiction exists over a manufacturer whose product just happens to end up in the forum state. For example, the Seventh Circuit Court of Appeals recently held that a Danish jack manufacturer was not subject to specific jurisdiction in Indiana, because there was no evidence that the manufacturer had "an awareness or expectation that some of its products would be purchased in Indiana" * * *

Contrast those cases with the situation here. AG's board of directors created Limited because AG wanted to take advantage of "the biggest economy in the world." Strobach testified that "the whole board . . . decided that [Houston would be the best place for a distributor] because we knew that—we thought that would be the greatest need, because of the immediate vicinity of all the refineries." Strobach traveled to Houston because "we wanted to establish an office in Houston." The Board's selection of a Houston office preceded by a few days the arrival of Walter De Graaf, president of both AG and Limited and an employee of each, who signed the documents that created Limited. De Graaf spends half the year working in Houston and is paid by both AG and Limited while there; his contract with AG authorizes him to act on its behalf no matter where he is.

After deciding to establish Limited, AG authorized Limited to use the "Spir Star" name, and Limited became AG's exclusive distributor in Texas and throughout North America. According to one of AG's directors, Limited has been "very successful indeed," and it is AG's largest customer by far. AG has sold millions of dollars worth of hoses to Limited; each month, AG sells Limited a maritime container full of reels of hose, which are shipped to the port of Houston. AG supplies Limited with crimping and assembly tools and written assembly standards, and AG personnel train Limited's employees in hose assembly.

AG's website, authored by one of its employees, states that:

> In order to cover the world-wide market and provide quick service to our customers, office [sic] were opened in the following countries: SPIR STAR France, S.A.R.L. 1991 in Haguenau/France, SPIR STAR Inc. [Limited] 1995 in Housten [sic]/Texas (U.S.A.) and SPIR STAR Asia Pty. Ltd. 1999 in Singapore.

Limited's website, which is written from AG's perspective, states that "the decision was made that the company should expand its activities outside of Europe" and that "we ventured across the Atlantic and founded SPIR STAR, Ltd. in Houston, Texas." The same website touts Limited as "the main link for our growing market share in North and South America." Under the heading "Spir Star Companies," four entities are listed: AG, Limited, Spir Star France, and Spir Star Asia, PTE Ltd. De Graaf, AG's president, testified that he reviewed the content of both websites prior to their publication. The trial court could have believed, as Kimich argues, that AG, acting through its directors and officers, created Limited or that the website statements were admissions by AG. Or the trial court simply could have determined that AG "marketed [its] product through a distributor who has agreed to serve as the sales agent in the forum State." *Asahi*, 480 U.S. at 112, 107 S.Ct. 1026. If the foregoing evidence does not indicate "an intent or purpose to serve the market in [Texas]," it is difficult to imagine what would. *Cf. id.* (finding no specific jurisdiction in California because "respondents have not demonstrated any action by Asahi to purposefully avail itself of the California market").

Finally, Kimich's claim arose from AG's Texas contacts. * * *

IV. Exercising jurisdiction over AG comports with traditional notions of fair play and substantial justice.

Because AG's Texas contacts support specific jurisdiction, we must now determine whether jurisdiction is consistent with traditional notions of fair play and substantial justice. *Retamco*, 278 S.W.3d at 341. "Only in rare cases, however, will the exercise of jurisdiction not comport with fair play and substantial justice when the nonresident defendant has purposefully established minimum contacts with the forum state." *Guardian Royal*, 815 S.W.2d at 231 (*citing Burger King*, 471 U.S. at 477, 105 S.Ct. 2174). To evaluate this component, we must consider AG's contacts in light of: (1) "the burden on the defendant"; (2) "the interests of the forum state in adjudicating the dispute"; (3) "the plaintiff's interest in obtaining convenient and effective relief"; (4) the interstate or international judicial system's interest in obtaining the most efficient resolution of controversies; and (5) the shared interest of the several nations or states in furthering fundamental substantive social policies. *Id.* at

231. To defeat jurisdiction, AG must present " 'a compelling case that the presence of some consideration would render jurisdiction unreasonable' "—something AG has not done. *See id.* (*quoting Burger King*, 471 U.S. at 477, 105 S.Ct. 2174).

Requiring AG to defend Kimich's claim in Texas would not pose an undue burden for the company. The fact that AG is headquartered in Germany cannot, by itself, defeat jurisdiction. *See id.* at 231 ("Nor is distance alone ordinarily sufficient to defeat jurisdiction: 'modern transportation and communication have made it much less burdensome for a party sued to defend himself in a State where he engages in economic activity.' " (*quoting McGee v. Int'l Life Ins. Co.*, 355 U.S. 220, 223, 78 S.Ct. 199, 2 L.Ed.2d 223 (1957))). Houston is familiar territory for AG's leadership: its president spends six months of the year there (and can carry on AG's business while there), two of AG's directors traveled to Houston to establish Limited, and one of them returned-at AG's expense—to celebrate Limited's fifth anniversary. *Cf. id.* at 232-33, 78 S.Ct. 199 (finding jurisdiction unreasonable because, among other things, the English defendant was unaffiliated with any American companies). Three of AG's directors collectively own seventy-five percent of Limited, which will be litigating in Houston.

Moreover, Texas has a significant interest in exercising jurisdiction over controversies arising from injuries a Texas resident sustains from products that are purposefully brought into the state and purchased by Texas companies. *Cf. Asahi*, 480 U.S. at 114, 107 S.Ct. 1026 ("Because the plaintiff is not a California resident, California's legitimate interests in the dispute have considerably diminished."); *Guardian*, 815 S.W.2d at 233 ("[S]ince Guardian Royal and U.S. Fire are neither Texas consumers nor insureds, Texas' interest in adjudicating the dispute . . . is considerably diminished."). Not only would Kimich face an undue burden were he forced to litigate his product liability claim against AG in Germany, but because the claims against Limited will be heard in Texas, it would be more efficient to adjudicate the entire case in the same place. *See Retamco*, 278 S.W.3d at 341 ("[The plaintiff] has an interest in resolving this controversy in Texas because that is where the litigation began."). We recognize "the unique and onerous burden placed on a party called to defend a suit in a foreign legal system." *CSR*, 925 S.W.2d at 595 (*citing Asahi*, 480 U.S. at 114, 107 S.Ct. 1026). In this case, that burden is minimal and is outweighed by Kimich's and Texas's interests in adjudicating the dispute here. *See Asahi*, 480 U.S. at 114, 107 S.Ct. 1026. Asserting personal jurisdiction over AG comports with traditional notions of fair play and substantial justice.

V. Conclusion

Under the appropriate standard of review, our task ends when, as here, some evidence supports the trial court's denial of AG's special appearance. *BMC*, 83 S.W.3d at 794-95. AG did not merely set its products afloat in a stream of commerce that happened to carry them to Texas. AG "marketed [its] product through a distributor who has agreed to serve as [its] sales agent in [Texas]," *Asahi*, 480 U.S. at 112, 107 S.Ct. 1026, and AG undoubtedly "intended to serve the Texas market," *CSR*, 925 S.W.2d at 595. Further, AG's potential liability arises out of its contacts with Texas, and exercising personal jurisdiction over AG does not offend traditional notions of fair play and substantial justice. The court of appeals and the trial court correctly concluded that Texas courts have personal jurisdiction over this claim against AG. We affirm the court of appeals' judgment. TEX. R. APP. P. 60.2(a).

Notes

1. *Michiana Easy Livin' Country, Inc. v. Holten*, 168 S.W.3d 777 (Tex. 2005): Holten decided to buy a $64,000 Coachmen recreational vehicle, sight unseen. Eschewing every RV dealer in Texas, he sought a lower price from Michiana Easy Livin' Country, Inc., an outlet store that only did business in Indiana. Holten called Michiana in Indiana, sent payment to Indiana, paid for delivery from Indiana, and agreed to resolve every dispute in Indiana. But when a dispute actually arose, he filed suit in Texas. The trial court and court of appeals denied Michiana's special appearance. Held: Reversed, and judgment is rendered, dismissing the claims against Michiana for want of jurisdiction. Michiana's only contact with Texas was Holten's decision to place his order from there. Michiana did not have minimum contacts with Texas. Michiana did not place large numbers of RVs in a "stream of commerce" flowing to Texas; stream-of-commerce jurisdiction requires a stream, not a dribble. Nor is there any evidence of any "additional conduct"—Michiana did not design, advertise, or distribute RVs in Texas.

Allegations, that a tort was committed in Texas, satisfy the Texas Long-Arm Statute, but not necessarily the U.S. Constitution; the broad language of the former extends only as far as the latter will permit. Although it has been argued that foreseeability of causing injury in another State should be sufficient to establish such contacts there, when policy considerations so require, the U. S. Supreme Court has consistently held that this kind of foreseeability is not a sufficient benchmark for exercising personal jurisdiction. Jurisdiction cannot be based solely upon the effects or consequences of an alleged conspiracy in the forum state. Instead, it is the defendant's conduct, and connection with the forum, that are critical. The Texas Supreme Court disapproves of those opinions holding that (1) specific jurisdiction is necessarily established by allegations, or evidence that a nonresident committed a tort in a telephone call from a Texas number, or that (2) specific jurisdiction turns on whether a defendant's contacts were tortious, rather than the contacts themselves.

The touchstone of jurisdictional due process has been "purposeful availment." It is essential, in each case involving a non-resident defendant, that there be some act, by which the defendant purposefully avails itself of the privilege of conducting activities within the forum State, thus invoking the benefits and protections of its laws. Three aspects of this requirement are relevant here:

> First, it is only the defendant's contacts with the forum that count. Purposeful availment ensures that a defendant will not be haled into a jurisdiction, solely as a result of the unilateral activity of another party or a third person.
>
> Second, the acts relied on must be "purposeful" rather than fortuitous. Sellers who reach out beyond one state and create continuing relationships and obligations with citizens of another state are subject to the jurisdiction of the latter, in suits based upon their activities. By contrast, a defendant will not be haled into a jurisdiction, solely based on contacts that are random, isolated, or fortuitous.
>
> Third, a defendant must seek some benefit, advantage, or profit by "availing" itself of the jurisdiction. Jurisdiction is premised on notions of implied consent—that by invoking the benefits and protections of a forum's laws, a nonresident consents to suit there. By contrast, a nonresident may purposefully avoid a particular jurisdiction by structuring its transactions, so as neither to profit from the forum's laws nor be subject to its jurisdiction.

2. *Moncrief Oil Intern., Inc. v. OAO Gazprom*, --- S.W.3d ----, 2013 WL 4608672 (Tex.), 56 Tex. Sup. Ct. J. 1023 (August 30, 2013): The court held that there were sufficient contacts with the state of Texas to exercise personal jurisdiction over a non-resident defendant on a trade secret misappropriation claim; however, there were not sufficient contacts with the state of Texas for the court to exercise personal jurisdiction over that same nonresident on a tortious interference claim.

3. *Retamco Operating, Inc. v. Republic Drilling Co***.**, 278 S.W.3d 333 (Tex. 2009)**:** Retamco Operating, Inc. (ROI), a Texas corporation, sued Paradigm Oil, Inc. (Paradigm), another Texas corporation, in a Texas district court, over unpaid royalties, related to oil and gas interests in several Texas counties. After a finding of discovery abuse, sanctions were assessed against Paradigm, and the trial court entered a $16 million default judgment against Paradigm. Following this interlocutory judgment, ROI amended its petition to include a claim against Republic Drilling Company (Republic), a California corporation, for violation of the Uniform Fraudulent Transfer Act, TEX. BUS. & COM. CODE § 24.001–.013. ROI claimed that during the pendency of the litigation, Paradigm assigned to Republic a 72% interest in Paradigm's oil and gas wells and leases in Fayette County and a 72% interest in an option to acquire an interest in a lease in Dimmit and Webb Counties. ROI alleged that these transfers were fraudulent, and that they led to Paradigm's insolvency, rendering it unable to satisfy ROI's claims. In response to the amended petition, Republic filed a special appearance, arguing that it does not have minimum contacts with Texas, and that, even if it did, ROI's cause of action did not arise from, or relate to, those contacts. The trial court denied Republic's special appearance, making no findings of fact or conclusions of law. The court of appeals reversed, holding that Republic is not subject to personal jurisdiction in Texas. ***Held:*** Reversed and remanded. By its actions Republic subjected itself to the jurisdiction of Texas courts. Republic's contacts with Texas were purposeful, not random, fortuitous, or attenuated. The purchase of real property in Texas does not establish a single contact, but, rather, the purchase and ownership of real property could involve many contacts over a long period of time, which would carry with it certain continuing obligations. Should Republic ever wish to enforce rights under its interest in Texas oil and gas leases and wells, it is this state where those rights can be enforced, not California. Republic's contacts with Texas were also not the result of the unilateral actions of a third party. Republic was a willing participant in a transaction with an affiliated Texas company to purchase Texas real property. Lastly, Republic has sought a benefit, advantage or profit. The assignment gave Republic valuable assets in Texas, including the right to enforce warranties and covenants related to the real property.

Three issues are considered in determining whether a defendant purposefully availed itself of the privilege of conducting activities in Texas: First, only the defendant's contacts with the forum are relevant, not the unilateral activity of another party or a third person. Second, the contacts relied upon must be purposeful rather than random, fortuitous, or attenuated. Thus, sellers who reach out beyond one state and create continuing relationships and obligations with citizens of another state are subject to the jurisdiction of the latter in suits based on their activities. Finally, the defendant must seek some benefit, advantage or profit by availing itself of the jurisdiction. Additionally, the minimum-contacts analysis is focused on the quality and nature of the defendant's contacts, rather than their number. Here, these considerations lead to the conclusion that Republic purposefully availed itself of the privilege of conducting activities in Texas. Purposeful availment alone will not support an exercise of specific jurisdiction, unless the defendant's liability arises from, or relates to, the forum contacts. The courts look for a substantial connection between the defendant's forum contacts and the operative facts of the litigation.

MOKI MAC RIVER EXPEDITIONS
v.
DRUGG
221 S.W.3d 569
(Tex. 2007)

Specific Personal Jurisdiction. Liability Must Arise From, Or Relate To, The Forum Contacts.

P-Betsy Drugg alleges she was induced to send Andy on a rafting trip in Arizona by Moki Mac's direct solicitation, which included statements made in Moki Mac's brochures, and in the release it sent to the Druggs. Andy was killed while on the trip. The trial court denied the special appearance of Moki Mac, Utah-based river-rafting outfitter. The court of appeals affirmed. Held: Reversed and remanded to the court of appeals to consider Ps' general jurisdiction claim. Claims arising out of personal injury that occurs outside the forum do not arise from or relate to a defendant's forum advertising. The plaintiff's death on a Grand Canyon hiking trail did not arise from or relate to its in-state commercial activities so as to establish specific jurisdiction over it in Texas. Purposeful availment alone will not support an exercise of specific jurisdiction. Specific-jurisdiction analysis has two co-equal components. For specific-jurisdiction purposes, purposeful availment has no jurisdictional relevance, unless the defendant's liability arises from or relates to the forum contacts. For a nonresident defendant's forum contacts to support an exercise of specific jurisdiction, there must be a "substantial connection" between those contacts and the operative facts of the litigation. The operative facts of the Druggs' suit concern principally the guides' conduct of the hiking expedition and whether they exercised reasonable care in supervising Andy. The events on the trail and the guides' supervision of the hike will be the focus of the trial. In sum, the alleged misrepresentation is not the subject matter of the case nor is it related to the operative facts of the negligence action.

In establishing a test for determining this issue, the Court examines, and rejects, the "but-for relatedness" test as too broad and conceptually unlimited in scope, the "substantive-relevance/proximate-cause" test as posing too narrow an inquiry, and the "sliding-scale" analysis as conflating the fundamental distinction between general and specific jurisdiction that is firmly embedded in Texas jurisprudence. Rather, the Court adopts a middle ground, more flexible than substantive relevance but more structured than but-for relatedness, in assessing the strength of the necessary connection between the defendant, the forum, and the litigation.

TV AZTECA
v.
RUIZ

490 S.W.3d 29
(Tex. 2016)

JUSTICE BOYD delivered the opinion of the Court.

This is an interlocutory appeal from the denial of Petitioners' special appearances. Petitioners are Mexican citizens who broadcast television programs on over-the-air signals that originate in Mexico but travel into parts of Texas. Respondents are Texas residents who allege Petitioners defamed them in some of those programs. We hold that the allegations and evidence that Petitioners harmed Texas residents in Texas, Petitioners' broadcasts were viewable in Texas, and Petitioners knew Texans could watch the programs in Texas are insufficient to establish that Petitioners purposefully availed themselves of the benefits of conducting activities in Texas. However, that evidence, taken together with evidence that Petitioners exploited the Texas market to capitalize on the broadcasts that traveled into Texas, does establish purposeful availment and provides a constitutional basis for exercising jurisdiction over Petitioners in this case. Because Respondents' claims arise from and relate to those broadcasts, and the exercise of jurisdiction comports with traditional notions of fair play and substantial justice, we affirm the court of appeals' judgment.

I. Background

Mexican recording artist Gloria de Los Angeles Trevino Ruiz, popularly known as Gloria Trevi (and sometimes referred to as "Mexico's Madonna"), now lives in Texas. Near the height of Trevino's fame in the late 1990s, she was accused of luring underage girls into sexual relationships with her manager. Authorities arrested Trevino and her manager in Brazil on charges of sexual assault and kidnapping. Trevino spent nearly five years in prisons in Brazil and Mexico, but a Mexican judge ultimately found her not guilty and dismissed all charges in 2004.

After her acquittal, Trevino moved to McAllen, Texas, and later married Armando Gomez, a Mexican attorney who had defended her in the criminal proceedings. In the late 2000s, as the ten-year anniversary of the scandal approached, various Mexican media outlets ran stories discussing the events and Trevino's activities following her acquittal. In 2009, Trevino, acting individually and on behalf of her minor son, and Gomez (collectively, Trevino) filed this lawsuit in Hidalgo County, alleging that several media defendants defamed them in their broadcasts. Trevino asserts that she and others viewed the defamatory programs on their televisions in Texas.

The relevant defendants are two Mexican television broadcasting companies, TV Azteca, S.A.B. de C.V., and Publimax, S.A.B. de C.V., and a Mexican citizen, Patricia Chapoy, a news anchor and producer for TV Azteca. Trevino alleges that TV Azteca, Publimax, and Chapoy (collectively, Petitioners) defamed her on several occasions, primarily in stories on a television program called Ventaneando, a Spanish-language entertainment news program that TV Azteca produced, Chapoy hosted, and Publimax aired on television stations affiliated with TV Azteca. Petitioners filed special appearances challenging the trial court's jurisdiction over them. The trial court denied the special appearances, and this interlocutory appeal followed. The court of appeals affirmed the trial court's denial of the special appearances, —— S.W.3d ——, 2014 WL 346031, and we granted review to consider, as a matter of first impression in this Court, whether a television broadcast that originates outside Texas but travels into the state can support personal jurisdiction over the broadcaster in Texas.

II. Jurisdictional Requirements

We begin by summarizing the well-established limits on a trial court's jurisdiction. A court has power to decide a case only if it has "both subject matter jurisdiction over the controversy and personal jurisdiction over the parties." *Spir Star AG v. Kimich*, 310 S.W.3d 868, 871 (Tex. 2010). Subject matter jurisdiction involves a court's "power to hear a particular type of suit," while personal jurisdiction "concerns the court's power to bind a particular person or party." *CSR Ltd. v. Link*, 925 S.W.2d 591, 594 (Tex. 1996). Petitioners argue that Texas courts lack personal jurisdiction over them.

Courts have personal jurisdiction over a nonresident defendant when the state's long-arm statute permits such jurisdiction and the exercise of jurisdiction is consistent with federal and state due-process guarantees.

Moncrief Oil Int'l Inc. v. OAO Gazprom, 414 S.W.3d 142, 149 (Tex. 2013). The Texas long-arm statute broadly allows courts to exercise personal jurisdiction over a nonresident who "commits a tort in whole or in part in this state." TEX. CIV. PRAC. & REM. CODE § 17.042(2). Because this statute reaches "as far as the federal constitutional requirements for due process will allow," Texas courts may exercise jurisdiction over a nonresident so long as doing so "comports with federal due process limitations." *Spir Star*, 310 S.W.3d at 872 (quoting *Am. Type Culture Collection, Inc. v. Coleman*, 83 S.W.3d 801, 806 (Tex. 2002)).

Consistent with federal due process protections, a state court can exercise jurisdiction over a nonresident defendant only if (1) the defendant has established "minimum contacts" with the state and (2) the exercise of jurisdiction comports with "traditional notions of fair play and substantial justice." *Int'l Shoe Co. v. Washington*, 326 U.S. 310, 316, 66 S.Ct. 154, 90 L.Ed. 95 (1945); *see Moncrief Oil*, 414 S.W.3d at 150. We will address both requirements in turn, in light of the allegations and evidence in this case.

III. Minimum Contacts

The minimum-contacts requirement protects due-process rights by permitting a state to exercise jurisdiction over a nonresident defendant only when the defendant "could reasonably anticipate being haled into court there." *Moncrief Oil*, 414 S.W.3d at 152. Minimum contacts may create either general or specific personal jurisdiction. *Id.* at 150. A court has general jurisdiction over a nonresident defendant whose "affiliations with the State are so 'continuous and systematic' as to render [it] essentially at home in the forum State." *Daimler v. Bauman*, — U.S. —, 134 S.Ct. 746, 754, 187 L.Ed.2d 624 (2014) (quoting *Goodyear Dunlop Tires Operations, S.A. v. Brown*, 564 U.S. 915, 919, 131 S.Ct. 2846, 180 L.Ed.2d 796 (2011)). This test requires "substantial activities within the forum" and presents "a more demanding minimum contacts analysis than for specific jurisdiction." *BMC Software*, 83 S.W.3d at 797. When a court has general jurisdiction over a nonresident, it may exercise jurisdiction "even if the cause of action did not arise from activities performed in the forum state." *Spir Star*, 310 S.W.3d at 872.

By contrast, courts may exercise specific jurisdiction when the defendant's forum contacts are "isolated or sporadic," as opposed to "continuous and systematic," but only if the plaintiff's cause of action arises from or relates to those contacts. *Id.* at 872-73 (quoting 4 Charles Alan Wright & Arthur R. Miller, FEDERAL PRACTICE AND PROCEDURE § 1067.5 (3d ed. 2002)); see also *Moncrief Oil*, 414 S.W.3d at 150 ("[S]pecific jurisdiction exists when the cause of action arises from or is related to purposeful activities in the state."). For specific jurisdiction, we must analyze the defendant's contacts "on a claim-by-claim basis" to determine whether each claim arises out of or is related to the defendant's minimum contacts. *Moncrief Oil*, 414 S.W.3d at 150.

Trevino alleged that the trial court has both general and specific personal jurisdiction over Petitioners. The trial court denied Petitioners' special appearances without specifying which type of jurisdiction it found. Affirming the trial court's decision, the court of appeals found that the trial court has specific jurisdiction, and it did not reach the general-jurisdiction issue. — S.W.3d at —, 2014 WL 346031, at *26. We therefore also address specific jurisdiction. Because we conclude the evidence establishes that Petitioners purposefully availed themselves of the benefits of conducting activities in Texas and that Trevino's claims arise from or relate to those purposeful contacts, we do not reach the general-jurisdiction issue.

A. Purposeful Availment

To establish minimum contacts for both general and specific jurisdiction, the defendant must have "purposefully avail[ed] itself of the privilege of conducting activities within the forum state, thus invoking the benefits and protections of its laws." *Moncrief Oil*, 414 S.W.3d at 150 (quoting *Retamco Operating, Inc. v. Republic Drilling Co.*, 278 S.W.3d 333, 338 (Tex. 2009)). Due process requires purposeful availment because personal jurisdiction "is premised on notions of implied consent—that by invoking the benefits and protections of a forum's laws, a nonresident consents to suit there." *Michiana Easy Livin' Country, Inc. v. Holten*, 168 S.W.3d 777, 785 (Tex. 2005). Three principles guide our analysis of whether a nonresident has purposefully availed itself of the privilege of conducting activities in Texas:

> First, only the defendant's contacts with the forum are relevant, not the unilateral activity of another party or a third person. Second, the contacts relied upon must be purposeful rather than random, fortuitous, or attenuated. Finally, the defendant must seek some benefit, advantage or profit by availing itself of the jurisdiction. *Moncrief Oil*, 414 S.W.3d at 151 (quoting *Retamco*, 278 S.W.3d at 338-39).

To constitute purposeful availment, the defendant's contacts must be "purposefully directed" to the state, *Guardian Royal Exch. Assurance, Ltd. v. English China Clays, P.L.C.*, 815 S.W.2d 223, 228 (Tex. 1991), and must result from the defendant's own "efforts to avail itself of the forum." *Moki Mac River Expeditions v. Drugg*, 221 S.W.3d 569, 576 (Tex. 2007). "[A] defendant will not be haled into a jurisdiction solely based on contacts that are 'random, isolated, or fortuitous," *Michiana*, 168 S.W.3d at 785 (quoting *Keeton v. Hustler Magazine, Inc.*, 465 U.S. 770, 774, 104 S.Ct. 1473, 79 L.Ed.2d 790 (1984)), or on the "unilateral activity of another party or a third person." *Guardian Royal*, 815 S.W.2d at 226 (quoting *Burger King Corp. v. Rudzewicz*, 471 U.S. 462, 475, 105 S.Ct. 2174, 85 L.Ed.2d 528 (1985)). Through its purposeful forum contacts, the defendant must have sought "some benefit, advantage, or profit by 'availing' itself of the jurisdiction." *Michiana*, 168 S.W.3d at 785. In conducting this analysis, we assess "the quality and nature of the contacts, not the quantity." *Moncrief Oil*, 414 S.W.3d at 151.

TV Azteca is a Mexican national broadcasting company that provides programs to affiliated network-television stations. Publimax operates two such stations in Monterrey, Mexico, which are licensed by the Mexican government. Publimax pays TV Azteca for the exclusive right to broadcast TV Azteca programs in northeastern Mexico. Chapoy produces and hosts one of those programs, Ventaneando. Both TV Azteca and Publimax are Mexican corporations, are not registered in Texas or any of the United States, and do not have any offices, employees, agents, or representatives in Texas. Chapoy is a Mexican citizen and resident, has never been a Texas citizen or resident, does not have an office or agent for service of process in Texas, and has never been a party to a lawsuit in Texas other than this suit. Nevertheless, Trevino contends that Texas courts have specific personal jurisdiction over all three Petitioners because they purposefully availed themselves of the benefits of conducting activities in Texas when they defamed her in broadcasts that aired in Texas. As this is our first opportunity to address specific jurisdiction in the context of defamation claims arising from media broadcasts, we begin by reviewing four key precedents that are crucial to our analysis. We then apply those precedents to the allegations and evidence to determine whether Petitioners purposefully availed themselves of the benefits of doing business in Texas.

1. Guiding precedents

Numerous other courts, including the United States Supreme Court, have addressed specific personal jurisdiction in cases involving claims based on alleged defamatory or false statements and in cases involving claims arising out of media broadcasts. * * *

The Supreme Court recently confirmed our understanding of *Calder* and *Keeton* [two earlier Supreme Court cases] in *Walden v. Fiore*, —— U.S. ——, 134 S.Ct. 1115, 188 L.Ed.2d 12 (2014). The defendant in *Walden*, a Georgia police officer assigned to a federal drug-interdiction team, confiscated money from the plaintiffs at the Atlanta airport. *Id.* at 1119. The plaintiffs were Nevada residents catching a connecting flight in Atlanta on their way from Puerto Rico. *Id.* They sued the Georgia defendant in Nevada, alleging he violated their Fourth Amendment rights by seizing and attempting to forfeit their money, in part by signing a false affidavit. *Id.* at 1119-20. The Ninth Circuit concluded that Nevada courts had specific jurisdiction over the Georgia defendant because the defendant had " 'expressly aimed' his submission of the allegedly false affidavit at Nevada by submitting the affidavit with knowledge that it would affect persons with a 'significant connection' to Nevada." *Id.* at 1120. The Supreme Court reversed, holding that "the mere fact that [the defendant's] conduct affected plaintiffs with connections to the forum State does not suffice to authorize jurisdiction." Id. at 1126.

The Court reaffirmed that the specific-jurisdiction inquiry "focuses 'on the relationship among the defendant, the forum, and the litigation.' " *Id.* at 1121 (quoting *Keeton*, 465 U.S. at 775, 104 S.Ct. 1473). Thus, "the relationship must arise out of contacts that the 'defendant himself ' creates with the forum State," *id.* at 1122 (quoting *Burger King*, 471 U.S. at 475, 105 S.Ct. 2174), and the "analysis looks to the defendant's contacts with the forum State itself, not the defendant's contacts with persons who reside there," *id.* (citing *Int'l Shoe Co. v. Washington*, 326 U.S. 310, 319, 66 S.Ct. 154, 90 L.Ed. 95 (1945)). The Court explained that *Calder* focused on the "various contacts the defendants had created with California (and not just with the plaintiff)." *Id.* at 1123. The defendants' contacts were sufficient in *Calder* because they had relied on "California sources" for information, they had written "the story about the plaintiff's activities in California," and they had caused the "brunt of the injury" in California "by writing an allegedly libelous article that was widely circulated in the State." *Id.* (quoting *Calder*, 465 U.S. at 788-89, 104 S.Ct. 1482). "In sum, California [wa]s the focal point both of the story and of the harm suffered." *Id.* (quoting *Calder*, 465 U.S. at 789, 104 S.Ct. 1482). Under *Calder*, "mere injury to a forum resident is not a sufficient connection to the forum." Instead, "an injury is jurisdictionally relevant only insofar as it shows that the defendant has formed a contact with the forum State," and "[t]he proper question is not where the plaintiff experienced a particular injury or effect but whether the defendant's conduct connects him to the forum in a meaningful way." *Id.* at 1125.

2. Petitioners' Contacts

With these precedents and principles in mind, we now consider Trevino's allegations and the evidence regarding Petitioners' contacts with Texas to determine whether they support the trial court's finding that Petitioners purposefully availed themselves of the benefits of conducting activities in the state. * * *

Trevino contends that evidence of Petitioners' additional conduct demonstrates that they intended to serve the Texas market with their broadcasts. Relying on *Calder*, Petitioners argue that the evidence does not establish that they intentionally targeted Texas because the subject matter of the allegedly defamatory broadcasts had no relation to Texas and Petitioners did not rely on Texas sources to prepare those broadcasts. * * *

(1) Subject-and-sources test

The Supreme Court found that the defendants in Calder were "not charged with mere untargeted negligence," but instead had "expressly aimed" their actions at California, because their article "concerned the California activities of a California resident" and "was drawn from California sources." 465 U.S. at 788-89, 104 S.Ct. 1482. Petitioners rely on three Fifth Circuit cases to argue that, under *Calder*, an allegedly defamatory broadcast targets the forum state only if the subject matter of the article involves events in the state and the broadcaster prepared the article by relying on sources in the state. First, in *Revell v. Lidov*, the Fifth Circuit held that "the sources relied upon and activities described in an allegedly defamatory publication should in some way connect with the forum if *Calder* is to be invoked." 317 F.3d 467, 474 (5th Cir.2002). Then, in *Fielding v. Hubert Burda Media, Inc.*, the court relied on *Revell* for the proposition that "[t]his Court has held that, to exercise specific jurisdiction in a libel action, the 'aim' of the plaintiff under the *Calder* test must be demonstrated by showing that (1) the subject matter of and (2) the sources relied upon for the article were in the forum state." 415 F.3d 419, 426 (5th Cir.2005) (citing *Revell*, 317 F.3d at 474 & n. 48). Finally, in *Clemens v. McNamee*, the court again stated, "We read *Calder* as requiring the plaintiff seeking to assert specific personal jurisdiction over a defendant in a defamation case to show '(1) the subject matter of and (2) the sources relied upon for the article were in the forum state.' " 615 F.3d 374, 380 (5th Cir.2010) (quoting *Fielding*, 415 F.3d at 426).

We agree with Petitioners that the subject-and-sources test is consistent with *Calder's* approach to determining whether a defamation defendant "expressly aimed" its communication to a forum state. We also agree that the evidence in this case does not support specific jurisdiction under this test. The subject matter of the allegedly defamatory broadcasts is completely unrelated to Texas. Trevino alleges that Petitioners defamed her by making statements that are almost exclusively about events that occurred outside of and completely unrelated to Texas. * * *

We agree with Petitioners that these broadcasts did not "concern[ ] the [Texas] activities of a [Texas] resident," *Calder*, 465 U.S. at 788, 104 S.Ct. 1482, or describe activities having a connection with Texas, *Revell*, 317 F.3d at 474, as the subject-and-sources test requires. * * * Thus, the evidence does not support a finding of purposeful availment under the *Calder* subject-and-sources test sufficient to make Texas "the focal point" of the broadcasts at issue. See *Calder*, 465 U.S. at 789, 104 S.Ct. 1482.

(2) Intentional efforts to serve the Texas market

Citing the Fifth Circuit's decision in *Clemens*, Trevino asserts that the subject-and-sources test is only one method of proving that a defamation defendant targeted the forum state, and it need not be met when evidence otherwise establishes that the defendant's statement was "aimed at or directed to" the state. See *Clemens*, 615 F.3d at 380. Petitioners disagree, arguing that "whether the forum state is the focal point of the story is a crucial criterion in determining whether the story is directed at the forum state." We agree with Trevino.

* * *

As we have explained, the mere facts that Petitioners' signal reaches into Texas and that Petitioners know it does do not establish that Petitioners purposefully sought to serve the Texas market through their broadcasts. Petitioners cite to evidence to show that is, in fact, not their intent. TV Azteca's contract with Publimax, for example, limits Publimax's right to broadcast TV Azteca's programs like Ventaneando only to three Mexican states: Nuevo Leon, Coahuila, and Tamaulipas. Chapoy testified that her programs reported stories deemed appealing to Mexican viewers and that her intended viewership included "primarily Mexican citizens and residents, and not viewers located in the State of Texas." In short, Petitioners' evidence tends to establish that the signals "involuntarily strayed" into Texas as a result of "signal 'spill-over,' " which occurs naturally from the broadcasts in Mexico.

Trevino submitted evidence, however, that Petitioners made substantial and successful efforts to benefit from the fact that the signals travel into Texas, as well as additional efforts to promote their broadcasts and expand their Texas audience. This evidence generally falls into three categories of activities. First, Trevino points to evidence that Petitioners actually physically "entered into" Texas to produce and promote their broadcasts. Between 2005 and 2009, for example, when Petitioners were producing and airing the allegedly defamatory stories about Trevino, TV Azteca had a business office and production studio in South Texas. In 2006-2007, Publimax sent or hired an employee to work in Texas on a project to expand Publimax's broadcasts through cable distribution. Chapoy, meanwhile, traveled to Laredo to promote her books about the Ventaneando program (THE BEST OF VENTANEANDO AND THE FILES OF VENTANEANDO) and to Dallas to host a live broadcast of Ventaneando. While this evidence might not be sufficient on its own, we agree that it is relevant and supports Trevino's allegation that Petitioners purposefully availed themselves of the benefits of conducting activities in Texas.

Second, Trevino points to evidence that Petitioners derived substantial revenue and other benefits by selling advertising time to Texas businesses. As we previously noted, Publimax's website included a map of its viewing market that at least arguably promoted that the stations (which Publimax operates and TV Azteca owns) had over 1.5 million viewers in South Texas. Trevino points to evidence that Petitioners took advantage of this Texas audience as a means to increase their advertising revenue in Texas. * * *

But the evidence here relates as much to Petitioners' own efforts to target Texas with their broadcasts as it does to AIC's [ed. TV Azteca's wholly owned subsidiary and not a party to the suit] and the other contractors' efforts. To be sure, courts may lack specific jurisdiction over a nonresident defendant who made no independent efforts to purposefully avail itself of Texas and merely contracted with a third party who did. See, e.g., *Zinc Nacional*, 308 S.W.3d at 396 (holding that a Mexican company "using a third-party trucking service to transport its goods through Texas to an out-of-state customer" did not purposefully avail itself of Texas). But a defendant who "intentionally targets Texas as the marketplace for its products" is subject to specific jurisdiction, and "using a distributor-intermediary for that purpose provides no haven from the jurisdiction of a Texas court." *Spir Star*, 310 S.W.3d at 871. We conclude that this evidence would support a finding that Petitioners made substantial and successful efforts to distribute their programs in Texas, not just that they contracted with other companies that happened to have contacts with Texas.

We acknowledge Petitioners' evidence that their broadcasts originated in Mexico and were directed primarily at northeastern Mexico and their argument that no evidence suggests that they took steps to direct the signals into Texas or that they reasonably could have stopped that from happening. But whether Petitioners intentionally directed the signals into Texas or not, we must look for evidence that each of the Petitioners took specific and substantial actions to take advantage of the fact that the signals reach into Texas and to financially benefit from that fact. We conclude such evidence exists.

* * *

The evidence that Petitioners physically "entered into" Texas to produce and promote their broadcasts, derived substantial revenue and other benefits by selling advertising to Texas businesses, and made substantial efforts to distribute their programs and increase their popularity in Texas supports the trial court's finding that Petitioners "continuously and deliberately exploited the [Texas] market." *Keeton*, 465 U.S. at 781, 104 S.Ct. 1473. We thus conclude that the evidence supports the trial court's finding that through their broadcasts, Petitioners purposefully availed themselves of the benefits of conducting activities in Texas, such that they "could reasonably anticipate being haled into court there." *Moncrief Oil*, 414 S.W.3d at 152.

B. "Arising from or related to"

Because we are addressing the issue of specific—as opposed to general—jurisdiction, we must also determine whether Trevino's claim "arises from or is related to [Petitioners'] purposeful activities in the state." *Id.* at 150. "For specific-jurisdiction purposes, purposeful availment has no jurisdictional relevance unless the defendant's liability arises from or relates to the forum contacts." *Moki Mac*, 221 S.W.3d at 579. A claim arises from or relates to a defendant's forum contacts if there is a "substantial connection between those contacts and the operative facts of the litigation." *Id.* at 585; see *Spir Star*, 310 S.W.3d at 874 (stating same); *Walden*, 134 S.Ct. at 1121 ("For a State to exercise jurisdiction consistent with due process, the defendant's suit-related conduct must create a substantial connection with the forum State.").

This "substantial connection" standard does not require proof that the plaintiff would have no claim "but for" the contacts, or that the contacts were a "proximate cause" of the liability. *Moki Mac*, 221 S.W.3d at 584 ("[T]he but-for relatedness test is too broad and conceptually unlimited in scope, the substantive-relevance/proximate-cause test poses too narrow an inquiry. . . ."). Instead, we consider what the claim is "principally concerned with," *Moncrief Oil*, 414 S.W.3d at 157, whether the contacts will be "the focus of the trial" and "consume most if not all of the litigation's attention," and whether the contacts are "related to the operative facts" of the claim, *Moki Mac*, 221 S.W.3d at 585.

Petitioners contend that, even if the evidence we have described establishes that they purposefully availed themselves of the benefits of doing business in Texas, Trevino's claims are not substantially connected to those Texas contacts. The map showing their Texas viewership, for example, "contains no alleged defamation," and the advertising contracts and revenues from Texas are not "in any way attributable to the subject broadcasts." They thus compare this case to the circumstances we addressed in *Moki Mac*, in which Texas plaintiffs, the Druggs, sought specific jurisdiction over an Arizona outfitter company based in part on the company's advertising of its programs in Texas. 221 S.W.3d at 585-86. The Druggs sued the Arizona outfitter, Moki Mac, after their son, Andy, fell off a cliff and died while on a hiking trip Moki Mac led in Arizona, asserting wrongful-death claims for negligence and claims for intentional and negligent misrepresentation. *Id.* at 573. We held that Moki Mac's Texas advertisements were not substantially connected to the Druggs' claims, because "claims arising out of personal injury that occurs outside the forum do not arise from or relate to a defendant's forum advertising." *Id.* at 586. We concluded that "the injuries for which the Druggs seek recovery [were] based on Andy's death on the hiking trail in Arizona, and the relationship between the operative facts of the litigation and Moki Mac's promotional activities in Texas [were] simply too attenuated to satisfy specific jurisdiction's due-process concerns." *Id.* at 588. Petitioners here argue that, as in *Moki Mac*, Trevino's defamation claims do not arise from or relate to Petitioners' map, advertising contracts, studio, promotional tour, and other Texas contacts.

Petitioners overlook a key distinction between *Moki Mac* and this case. In *Moki Mac*, the evidence of the defendant's Texas contacts was insufficient to support specific jurisdiction in Texas because the "operative facts" of the suit occurred in Arizona. *Id.* at 585. In other words, Moki Mac's "actionable conduct," from which the claim arose, occurred in Arizona, and its "additional conduct" of advertising in Texas did not transform its actionable conduct in Arizona into a contact with Texas. * * *

But the fact that the actionable conduct occurred in Texas is only one stage of the analysis, and it is not enough. For jurisdiction to exist, the actionable conduct within Texas must be conduct through which Petitioners purposefully had contact with Texas and sought some "benefit, advantage, or profit by 'availing' itself of the jurisdiction." *Michiana*, 168 S.W.3d at 785. Thus, unlike in *Moki Mac*, the question here is not whether Trevino's claims arise from Petitioners' additional conduct in Texas (the promotional map, advertising contracts, the promotional tour, etc.), but whether that additional conduct establishes that Petitioners purposefully availed themselves of Texas through their actionable conduct in Texas (the broadcasts). The relevance of the additional conduct, in other words, is not to establish that those contacts constitute Petitioners' minimum contacts with Texas, but to establish that the actionable conduct in Texas itself constitutes minimum contacts.

* * *

* * * The evidence of "additional conduct" here (the advertising, promotional tour, map, etc.) establishes that Petitioners purposefully availed themselves of Texas in connection with their actionable conduct (the allegedly defamatory broadcasts), which occurred and caused harm in Texas. And since Trevino's claims arise directly out of those broadcasts, we hold that the evidence supports the trial court's conclusion that Petitioners have minimum contacts sufficient to support specific jurisdiction in Texas.

IV. Fair Play and Substantial Justice

Even when a nonresident has established minimum contacts with a state, due process permits the state to assert jurisdiction over the nonresident only if doing so comports with "traditional notions of fair play and substantial justice." *Int'l Shoe*, 326 U.S. at 316, 66 S.Ct. 154; *Moncrief Oil*, 414 S.W.3d at 154. Typically, "[w]hen a nonresident defendant has purposefully availed itself of the privilege of conducting business in a foreign jurisdiction, it is both fair and just to subject that defendant to the authority of that forum's courts." *Spir Star*, 310 S.W.3d at 872. Thus, "[i]f a nonresident has minimum contacts with the forum, rarely will the exercise of jurisdiction over the nonresident not comport with traditional notions of fair play and substantial justice." *Moncrief Oil*, 414 S.W.3d at 154-55.

Nevertheless, we consider several factors to evaluate the fairness and justness of exercising jurisdiction over a nonresident defendant: (1) the burden on the defendant; (2) the interests of the forum in adjudicating the dispute; (3) the plaintiff's interest in obtaining convenient and effective relief; (4) the international judicial system's interest in obtaining the most efficient resolution of controversies; and (5) the shared interest of the several nations in furthering fundamental substantive social policies. *Id.* at 155. When the defendant is a citizen of a foreign country, and not just another state, we consider more specifically (6) "the unique burdens placed upon the defendant who must defend itself in a foreign legal system;" (7) the state's regulatory interests; and (8) "the procedural and substantive policies of other nations whose interests are affected as well as the federal government's interest in its foreign relations policies." *Guardian Royal*, 815 S.W.2d at 229. "To defeat jurisdiction, [the defendant] must present 'a compelling case that the presence of some consideration would render jurisdiction unreasonable' " *Spir Star*, 310 S.W.3d at 878-89 (quoting *Guardian Royal*, 815 S.W.2d at 231).

* * *

We hold that Texas courts have jurisdiction over Petitioners not because their broadcast signals "strayed" and "crossed national boundaries," but because some evidence establishes that Petitioners intentionally targeted Texas with those broadcasts and thereby purposefully availed themselves of the benefits of Texas laws. Requiring nonresidents to comply with the laws of the jurisdictions in which they choose to do business is not unreasonable, burdensome, or unique.

V. Conclusion

Trevino submitted evidence in this case that Petitioners intentionally targeted Texas through their broadcasts that aired in Texas, and Trevino's claims arise from and relate to those broadcasts. Because the evidence supports the trial court's conclusion that Petitioners have minimum contacts with Texas and the exercise of specific personal jurisdiction over Petitioners will not offend traditional notions of fair play and substantial justice, we affirm the court of appeals' judgment and remand this case to the trial court.

Notes

1. *Kelly v. General Interior Construction, Inc.*, 301 S.W3d 653 (Tex. 2010): To establish personal jurisdiction in Texas courts over nonresident defendants, plaintiffs must plead a connection between the defendants' alleged wrongdoing and the forum state. Asserting statutory and common law claims, General Interior Construction, Inc. (GIC), a Texas corporation, sued Daniel Kelly and Laura Hofstatter (collectively, the Officers), both Arizona residents. Absent from GIC's pleadings, however, is any allegation that Kelly and Hofstatter committed any acts giving rise to these claims in Texas. Because the Officers filed a special appearance proving that they do not live in Texas, they successfully negated all alleged bases for personal jurisdiction in Texas courts.

Texas special-appearance jurisprudence dictates that the plaintiff and the defendant bear shifting burdens of proof in a challenge to personal jurisdiction. The plaintiff bears the initial burden to plead sufficient allegations to bring the nonresident defendant within the reach of Texas's long-arm statute. Once the plaintiff has pleaded sufficient jurisdictional allegations, the defendant filing a special appearance bears the burden to negate all bases of personal jurisdiction alleged by the plaintiff. Because the plaintiff defines the scope and nature of the lawsuit, the defendant's corresponding burden to negate jurisdiction is tied to the allegations in the plaintiff's pleading. If the plaintiff fails to plead facts bringing the defendant within reach of the long-arm statute (i.e., for a tort claim, that the defendant committed tortious acts in Texas), the defendant need only prove that it does not live in Texas to negate jurisdiction. When the pleading is wholly devoid of jurisdictional facts, the plaintiff should amend the pleading to include the necessary factual allegations, thereby allowing jurisdiction to be decided based on evidence rather than allegations. The defendant can negate jurisdiction on either a factual or legal basis. Factually, the defendant can present evidence that it has no contacts with Texas, effectively disproving the plaintiff's allegations. The plaintiff can then respond with its own evidence that affirms its allegations, and it risks dismissal of its lawsuit if it cannot present the trial court with evidence establishing personal jurisdiction. Legally, the defendant can show that even if the plaintiffs alleged facts are true, the evidence is legally insufficient to establish jurisdiction; the defendant's contacts with Texas fall short of purposeful availment; for specific jurisdiction, that the claims do not arise from the contacts; or that traditional notions of fair play and substantial justice are offended by the exercise of jurisdiction.

But the mere existence of a cause of action does not automatically satisfy jurisdictional due process concerns. A state is powerless to create jurisdiction over a nonresident by establishing a remedy for a private wrong and a mechanism to seek that relief. Instead, jurisdictional analysis always centers on the defendant's actions and choices to enter the forum state and conduct business. The concept of minimum contacts is rooted in the notion that a defendant may reasonably be haled into the forum state's courts when it purposefully, not randomly or fortuitously, engages in activities there. Thus, merely pleading that Kelly and Hofstatter (defendants) violated the Texas Trust Fund Act is not enough; GIC (plaintiff) must also plead and, when challenged by the defendants, present evidence that the Officers' relevant acts (i.e., those connected to GIC's claims) occurred, at least in part, in Texas. There must also be allegations and evidence that a part of the claim originated from the defendant's conduct in Texas. Allegations that the corporate officers (defendant's) fraud was purposefully directed toward Texas is insufficient.

2. In *IRA Resources, Inc. v. Griego*, 221 S.W.2d 592 (Tex. 2007) the Court noted that while a foreign choice-of-law provision does not prevent Texas courts from also exercising personal jurisdiction, a choice-of-law provision cannot be ignored when weighing purposeful availment. Though the IRA agreement here does not require that disputes be litigated in California, this choice-of-law provision, when combined with the fact that Griego initiated contact with IRA Resources, which rendered all of its services within California, demonstrates that IRA Resources never anticipated Texas jurisdiction.

3. In *PHC-Minden, L.P v. Kimberly-Clark Corporation*, 235 S.W.3d 163 (Tex. 2007) the Court addressed some additional issue concerning general jurisdiction. The Court noted that TEX. CIV. PRAC. & REM. CODE § 17.042 permits Texas courts to exercise jurisdiction over a nonresident defendant that "does business" in Texas, and the statute identifies some activities that constitute "doing business." The list, however, is not exclusive. Section 17.042's language extends Texas courts' personal jurisdiction as far as the federal constitutional requirements of due process will permit. Personal jurisdiction over nonresident defendants is constitutional when: (1) the defendant has established minimum contacts with the forum state, and (2) the exercise of jurisdiction comports with traditional notions of fair play and substantial justice. The terms "specific" and "general" are used to describe the differing types of personal jurisdiction. Specific jurisdiction arises out of, or relates to, the defendant's contacts with the forum. General jurisdiction is personal jurisdiction over a defendant in a suit not arising out of or related to the defendant's contacts with the forum. Purchases and related trips, standing alone, are not a sufficient basis for a State's assertion of general jurisdiction. A general jurisdiction inquiry, therefore, is very different from a specific jurisdiction inquiry, and involves a more demanding minimum contacts analysis. General jurisdiction has been described as "dispute-blind," an exercise of the court's jurisdiction, made without regard to the nature of the claim presented. The appropriate time period for assessing contacts, for purposes of general jurisdiction, ends at the time suit is filed. A mere one-time snapshot of the defendant's in-state activities may not be sufficient, and contacts should be assessed over a reasonable number of years, up to the date suit is filed. This includes contacts at the time the cause of action arose. A general jurisdiction inquiry can be tedious, as it demands that all contacts be carefully investigated, compiled, sorted, and analyzed for proof of a pattern of continuing and systematic activity.

4. *Zinc Nacional, S. A. v. Bouche Trucking, Inc.*, 308 S.W.3d 395 (Tex. 2010): A non-resident defendant does not have minimum contacts with Texas, for purposes of establishing specific jurisdiction, by using a third-party trucking service to transport its goods through Texas to an out-of-state customer. The mere fact that goods have traveled into a state, without more, does not establish the minimum contacts necessary to subject a manufacturer to personal jurisdiction within that state. The fact that a seller knows his goods will end up in the forum state does not support jurisdiction when the seller made no attempt to market its goods there. The exercise of jurisdiction over a merchant requires that the merchant actually direct sales *to* the forum state, not *through* it. Accordingly, a merchant's decision to ship its goods with a third-party shipper that will travel through Texas to a recipient outside of Texas does not, by itself, constitute purposeful availment. Here, there is no evidence that Zinc has attempted to serve the market in Texas. It has no offices, employees, agents, or representatives in Texas, nor does it advertise or market its paper products here. As such, Zinc lacks the minimum contacts with Texas necessary to establish specific jurisdiction. Although Zinc does have three or four customers for its other products in Texas, and does receive some raw materials from Texas, these facts are unrelated to the accident in this case and are thus irrelevant to the question of specific jurisdiction. However, they may have some bearing on the existence of general jurisdiction, an issue the court of appeals did not consider.

5. *Choice Auto Brokers, Inc. v. Dawaon*, 274 S.W.3d 172, 177-78 (Tex. App.—Houston [1st Dist.] 2008, no pet.) "Internet usage is divided into three categories, using a sliding scale, for the purposes of establishing

personal jurisdiction. *Reiff v. Roy,* 115 S.W.3d 700, 705 (Tex. App.—Dallas 2003, pet. denied). "At one end of the scale are websites clearly used for transacting business over the Internet, such as entering into contracts and knowing and repeated transmission of files of information, which may be sufficient to establish minimum contacts with a state." *Id.* "On the other end of the spectrum are 'passive' websites that are used only for advertising over the Internet and are not sufficient to establish minimum contacts even though they are accessible to residents of a particular state." *Id.* at 705-06. "In the middle are 'interactive' websites that allow the 'exchange' of information between a potential customer and a host computer." *Id.* at 706. "Jurisdiction in cases involving interactive websites is determined by the degree of interaction. *Id.*"

6. *Old Republic Nat'l Title Ins. Co. v. Bell,* 549 S.W.3d 550 (Tex. 2018): The issue is whether a Texas court has personal jurisdiction over Goldsmith a Louisiana resident who got proceeds from a house sale by Bell in Texas in an alleged fraudulent transfer. Old Republic sued Bell a Texas resident and Goldsmith to recoup money that it paid the home buyer to satisfy a lien against the house sold by Bell. To establish specific jurisdiction in Texas Old Republic noted 81 money transfers from Goldsmith to Bell, the Goldsmith's liens against three of Bell's vehicles, years of telephone calls between Goldsmith and Bell, and Bell's transfer to Goldsmith of the house sale proceeds by cashier's check. The trial court granted Goldsmith's special appearance contesting personal jurisdiction in Texas and the court of appeals affirmed. The Texas Supreme Court affirmed holding that Goldsmith's contacts with Texas were insufficient to establish either general or specific jurisdiction over Goldsmith. The test for establishing purposeful availment has three factors: (1) only the defendant's contacts with the forum are relevant, not the unilateral activity of another party or a third person; (2) the contacts relied upon must be purposeful rather than random, fortuitous, or attenuated; and (3) the defendant must seek some benefit, advantage, or profit by availing itself of the jurisdiction. The "effects test" is not an alternative to our traditional "minimum contacts" analysis, and it does not displace the factors we look to in determining whether a defendant purposefully availed itself of the state. The court held even if a tort was committed and even if Goldsmith knew her actions would cause an injury in Texas, her contacts did not rise to the level of purposeful availment simply because the alleged harm occurred in Texas.

2. *The Notice Requirement of Due Process*

PERALTA
v.
HEIGHTS MEDICAL CTR.
485 U.S. 80, 108 S.Ct. 896
(1988)

JUSTICE WHITE delivered the opinion of the Court.

Heights Medical Center, Inc. (hereafter appellee), sued appellant Peralta in February 1982 to recover some $5,600 allegedly due under appellant's guarantee of a hospital debt incurred by one of his employees. Citation issued, the return showing personal, but untimely, service. Appellant did not appear or answer, and on July 20, 1982, default judgment was entered for the amount claimed, plus attorney's fees and costs.

In June 1984, appellant began a bill of review proceeding in the Texas courts to set aside the default judgment and obtain other relief. In the second amended petition, it was alleged that the return of service itself showed a defective service[1] and that appellant in fact had not been personally served at all. The judgment was therefore void under Texas law. It was also alleged that the judgment was abstracted and recorded in the county real property records, thereby creating a cloud on appellant's title, that a writ of attachment was issued, and that, unbeknownst to him, his real property was sold to satisfy the judgment and for much less than its true value. Ap-

[1] The petition alleged that the record contained a return of service of process, showing that service was effected more than 90 days after its issuance, contrary to Texas Rule of Civil Procedure 101 (repealed effective Jan. 1, 1988). Record 41. The parties agree that under Texas law at the time of this suit, the citation lost its official status after 90 days. Texas courts have held that service after the 90th day is a nullity, depriving the court of personal jurisdiction over the defendant. Lewis v. Lewis, 667 S.W.2d 910, 911 (Tex. App. 1984); Kem v. Krueger, 626 S.W.2d 143, 144 (Tex. App. 1981); Lemothe v. Cimbalista, 236 S.W.2d 681, 682 (Tex. Civ. App. 1951).

pellant prayed that the default judgment be vacated, the abstract of judgment be expunged from the county real property records, the constable's sale be voided, and that judgment for damages be entered against the Medical Center and Mr. and Mrs. Paul Seng-Ngan Chen, the purchasers at the constable's sale and appellees here.

Appellee filed a motion for summary judgment asserting that in a bill of review proceeding such as appellant filed, it must be shown that petitioner had a meritorious defense to the action in which judgment had been entered, that petitioner was prevented from proving his defense by the fraud, accident, or wrongful act of the opposing party, and that there had been no fault or negligence on petitioner's part. Although it was assumed for the purposes of summary judgment that there had been defective service and that this lapse excused proof of the second and third requirement for obtaining a bill of review, it was assertedly necessary, nevertheless, to show a meritorious defense, which appellant had conceded he did not have. In response to the motion, appellant repeated the allegations in his petition and filed an affidavit denying that he had ever been personally served or had ever been notified of the entry of default judgment [as required by rule 239a author] or of the sale of his property. Appellee's motion for summary judgment was granted. Record 54.

Appellant's motion for rehearing for the first time asserted federal constitutional claims under the Fourteenth Amendment. Appellee answered that under Texas law there were three avenues by which to attack a judgment on the grounds that it was void for want of service: an appeal within 30 days of the judgment; by writ of error within 6 months; and by bill of review. It being too late to seek either of the first two courses, appellee urged that the bill of review was the only route then open to appellant, and that route was not available to him—even assuming he did not receive notice of the action filed against him—since he had no meritorious defense. Appellee denied that the meritorious-defense requirement threatened any federal constitutional rights. Rehearing was denied.

On appeal to the Texas Court of Appeals, appellant repeated his claims that in the absence of valid service of process and notice of the judgment, showing a meritorious defense was not necessary under Texas law and requiring it violated the Fourteenth Amendment. Appellee argued that despite the allegation of no service and no notice of judgment, the meritorious-defense requirement prevented relief and that even though the bill of review was the only avenue of relief, the State could constitutionally insist on the showing of a meritorious defense. The Court of Appeals affirmed, reciting the three elements essential for granting a bill of review and holding that a meritorious defense must be shown whether there had been proper service and notice or not. 715 S.W.2d 721 (1986). The court rejected the due process challenge because it viewed the meritorious-defense requirement as "not onerous." *Id.*, at 722. Rehearing was denied, as was the application for a writ of error filed with the Texas Supreme Court, that court noting, "No Reversible Error." App. to Juris. Statement 2a.

Because the holding below appeared problematic in light of our precedents, we noted probable jurisdiction. 481 U.S. 1067, 107 S.Ct. 2458, 95 L.Ed.2d 868 (1987). The case was briefed and argued, and we now reverse.

In opposition to summary judgment, appellant denied that he had been personally served and that he had notice of the judgment. The case proceeded through the Texas courts on that basis, and it is not denied by appellee that under our cases, a judgment entered without notice or service is constitutionally infirm. "An elementary and fundamental requirement of due process in any proceeding which is to be accorded finality is notice reasonably calculated, under the circumstances, to apprise interested parties of the pendency of the action and afford them the opportunity to present their objections." *Mullane v. Central Hanover Bank & Trust Co.*, 339 U.S. 306, 314, 70 S.Ct. 652, 657, 94 L.Ed. 865 (1950). Failure to give notice violates "the most rudimentary demands of due process of law." *Armstrong v. Manzo*, 380 U.S. 545, 550, 85 S.Ct. 1187, 1190, 14 L.Ed.2d 62 (1965). *See also World-Wide Volkswagen Corp. v. Woodson*, 444 U.S. 286, 291, 100 S.Ct. 559, 564, 62 L.Ed.2d 490 (1980); *Mathews v. Eldridge*, 424 U.S. 319, 333, 96 S.Ct. 893, 902, 47 L.Ed.2d 18 (1976); *Zenith Radio Corp. v. Hazeltine Research, Inc.*, 395 U.S. 100, 110, 89 S.Ct. 1562, 1569, 23 L.Ed.2d 129 (1969); *Pennoyer v. Neff*, 95 U.S. (5 Otto) 714, 733, 24 L.Ed. 565 (1878).

The Texas courts nevertheless held, as appellee urged them to do, that to have the judgment set aside, appellant was required to show that he had a meritorious defense, apparently on the ground that without a defense, the same judgment would again be entered on retrial and hence appellant had suffered no harm from the judgment entered without notice. But this reasoning is untenable. As appellant asserts, had he had notice of the suit, he might have impleaded the employee whose debt had been guaranteed, worked out a settlement, or paid the debt. He would also have preferred to sell his property himself in order to raise funds rather than to suffer it sold at a constable's auction.

Nor is there any doubt that the entry of the judgment itself had serious consequences. It is not denied that the judgment was entered on the county records, became a lien on appellant's property, and was the basis for issuance of a writ of execution under which appellant's property was promptly sold without notice. Even if no execution sale had yet occurred, the lien encumbered the property and impaired appellant's ability to mortgage or alienate it; and state procedures for creating and enforcing such liens are subject to the strictures of due process. *See Mitchell v. W.T. Grant Co.*, 416 U.S. 600, 604, 94 S.Ct. 1895, 1898, 40 L.Ed.2d 406 (1974); *Hodge v. Muscatine County*, 196 U.S. 276, 281, 25 S.Ct. 237, 239, 49 L.Ed. 477 (1905). Here, we assume that the judgment against him and the ensuing consequences occurred without notice to appellant, notice at a meaningful time and in a meaningful manner that would have given him an opportunity to be heard. *Armstrong v. Manzo, supra*, 380 U.S., at 552, 85 S.Ct., at 1191.

In this Court, appellee insists that appellant has other remedies to escape the consequences of an invalid judgment and should be left to pursue those avenues. This argument, which is made for the first time in this litigation and which appellant disputes, is apparently offered as an alternative ground for affirming the judgment below. We are not required, however, to entertain such submissions, particularly when there is no indication that they were raised below, and we are especially disinclined to become involved in resolving disputes about Texas law that should have been presented to the state courts. We shall deal with the case as it came here and affirm or reverse based on the ground relied on below.

Appellee's position below was that appellant either had a remedy by bill of review or not at all, and that that remedy was unavailable since no meritorious defense had been shown. It appears to us that the Texas courts decided the case on this basis. There was no mention of other remedies, no suggestion that appellant had sought the wrong remedy; and it seems obvious that had a meritorious defense been shown, and the allegations on service and notice found to be true, the offending judgment would have been vacated. The Texas court held that the default judgment must stand absent a showing of a meritorious defense to the action in which judgment was entered without proper notice to appellant, a judgment that had substantial adverse consequences to appellant. By reason of the Due Process Clause of the Fourteenth Amendment, that holding is plainly infirm.

Where a person has been deprived of property in a manner contrary to the most basic tenets of due process, "it is no answer to say that in his particular case due process of law would have led to the same result because he had no adequate defense upon the merits." *Coe v. Armour Fertilizer Works*, 237 U.S. 413, 424, 35 S.Ct. 625, 629, 59 L.Ed. 1027 (1915). As we observed in *Armstrong v. Manzo*, 380 U.S., at 552, 85 S.Ct., at 1191, only "wip[ing] the slate clean . . . would have restored the petitioner to the position he would have occupied had due process of law been accorded to him in the first place." The Due Process Clause demands no less in this case.

The judgment below is

Reversed.

Note

In re Discount Rental, Inc., 216 S.W.3d 831 (Tex. 2007) involved a restricted appeal in which the court of appeals reversed a default judgment against relator Discount Rental, Inc., because service was improper. Discount Rental did not supersede the judgment, so while the appeal was pending, the plaintiffs obtained a writ of execution on Discount Rental's property. The constable seized Discount Rental's property, and at a hearing on the Carters' motion to sell the property, the parties reached agreement on how the property should be sold. The trial court signed an order reflecting the parties' agreement, but the court of appeals reversed the default judgment before the sale occurred. Discount Rental moved for the return of its property under section 34.021 of the Texas Civil Practice and Remedies Code, which states: "A person is entitled to recover his property that has been seized through execution of a writ issued by a court if the judgment on which execution is issued is reversed or set aside and the property has not been sold at execution." The trial court denied the motion, and directed that the sale take place. ***Held:*** Writ of mandamus will issue. The trial court is directed to vacate its orders for sale, and directed to return the property to Discount Rental. Even assuming that Discount Rental could waive these statutory rights, Discount Rental's agreement was premised on the trial court's authority to force a sale of its property. Because the default judgment was taken without proper service, it was void, and "any attempt, by process based upon the void judgment to reach Discount Rental's property is devoid of lawful authority." Mandamus will lie to correct the error.

Note

In *Lopez v. Lopez*, 757 S.W.2d 721 (Tex. 1988) the court held that *Peralta* applies to motions for new trials. Therefore a defendant who is not served does not have to set up a meritorious defense in order to obtain a new trial.

3. *The Texas Long Arm Statute*

Notes

1. As noted above Section 17.042 of the Texas Civil Practice and Remedies Code establishes the substantive right of a Texas resident to seek a remedy from a nonresident with the limits of federal due process. The remaining sections of the principal Texas long arm statute are procedural in nature as they prescribe the methods of service of process that must be followed in order to obtain redress from a nonresident. Section 17.043 provides for actual service upon the nonresident as follows:

> In an action arising from a nonresident's business in this state, process may be served on the person in charge, at the time of service, of any business in which the nonresident is engaged in this state if the nonresident is not required by statute to designate or maintain a resident agent for service of process.

2. Section 5.255 of the Texas Business Organization Code: Agent for Service of Process, Notice, or Demand as Matter of Law provides:

> For the purpose of service of process, notice, or demand:
>
> (1) the president and each vice president of a domestic or foreign corporation is an agent of that corporation;
>
> (2) each general partner of a domestic or foreign limited partnership and each partner of a domestic or foreign general partnership is an agent of that partnership;
>
> (3) each manager of a manager-managed domestic or foreign limited liability company and each member of a member-managed domestic or foreign limited liability company is an agent of that limited liability company;
>
> (4) each person who is a governing person of a domestic or foreign entity, other than an entity listed in Subdivisions (1)-(3), is an agent of that entity; and
>
> (5) each member of a committee of a nonprofit corporation authorized to perform the chief executive function of the corporation is an agent of that corporation.

3. Section 17.044 of the Texas Civil Practices and Remedies Code provides for substituted service on the Secretary of State in certain circumstances as specified below:

> (a) The secretary of state is an agent for service of process or complaint on a nonresident who:
>
> > (1) is required by statute to designate or maintain a resident agent or engages in business in this state, but has not designated or maintained a resident agent for service of process;
> >
> > (2) has one or more resident agents for service of process, but two unsuccessful attempts have been made on different business days to serve each agent; or
> >
> > (3) is not required to designate an agent for service in this state, but becomes a nonresident after a cause of action arises in this state but before the cause is matured by suit in a court of competent jurisdiction.
>
> (b) The secretary of state is an agent for service of process on a nonresident who engages in business in this state, but does not maintain a regular place of business in this state or a designated agent for service of process, in any proceeding that arises out of the business done in this state and to which the nonresident is a party.
>
> (c) After the death of a nonresident for whom the secretary of state is an agent for service of process under this section, the secretary of state is an agent for service of process on a nonresident administrator, ex-

ecutor, or personal representative of the nonresident. If an administrator, executor, or personal representative for the estate of the deceased nonresident is not appointed, the secretary of state is an agent for service of process on an heir, as determined by the law of the foreign jurisdiction, of the deceased nonresident.

(d) If a nonresident for whom the secretary of state is an agent for service of process under this section is judged incompetent by a court of competent jurisdiction, the secretary of state is an agent for service of process on a guardian or personal representative of the nonresident.

4. Under Section 17.045 of the Texas Civil Practice and Remedies Code, process is mailed immediately by registered or certified mail return receipt requested from the Secretary of State's office. There are other Texas "long-arm" statutes, such as sec 17.061-067 of the Texas Civil Practice and Remedies Code, permitting service on the Chair of State Highway & Public Transportation Commission, for civil actions arising from operation of motor vehicles in Texas. Sections 1.14 and 1.142 of the Texas Insurance Code permit service on the Insurance Commissioner when foreign insurance companies engage in violations of the Code.

5. *Mechanics of serving a non resident by serving the Secretary of State.* Citation is prepared by the proper court clerk or by the attorney. The petition and citation must be served on the Secretary by the clerk or by the Plaintiff or his representative or by a sheriff or constable in accordance with section 17.025 of the Texas Civil Practice and Remedies Code. The Secretary of State sends the papers to the Defendant at the address provided by the person requesting the process.

Read Rule 123 Texas Rules of Civil Procedure.

McKANNA v. EDGAR

388 S.W.2d 927
(Tex. 1965)

Dan Moody, Jr., and John E. Clark, Austin, for petitioner.
Tom Higgins, Austin, for respondent.

GREENHILL, JUSTICE.

Some time before this proceeding was instituted, Eileen Ann McKanna, a resident of California, executed and delivered a note to Joe Edgar, Jr., of Austin, Texas. The note was payable in Austin. McKanna did not pay the note when due, and Edgar brought suit. Edgar had a problem in obtaining personal service of process because McKanna lived in California. There is a Texas statute which provides for substituted service upon corporation and individuals doing business in Texas, Article 2031b. Edgar served, or attempted to serve, McKanna by serving the Secretary of State of the State of Texas under that statute. The Secretary of State in turn forwarded the citation to McKanna. McKanna did not appear in the Texas Court in person or by attorney. Article 2249a. Based on that service, Edgar obtained a judgment by default against McKanna on the note. McKanna thereafter instituted this action, within the time allowed, by way of writ of error to the Court of Civil Appeals to set aside the default judgment based on the substituted service. Articles 2249 and 2255. The Court of Civil Appeals refused to set aside the judgment. 380 S.W.2d 889 (1964).

McKanna, the nonresident defendant, contends that the judgment should be set aside for lack of jurisdiction over her person because (1) the substituted service of citation upon her was not made in accordance with the provisions of Article 2031b in that the record fails to show the existence of the conditions which, under the statute, are a prerequisite to service on her by serving the Secretary of State; and (2) Article 2031b is unconstitutional if it confers jurisdiction under the facts and circumstances of this case.

We reverse both judgments below on the basis of McKanna's first contention. It is therefore unnecessary to consider the constitutional question. For an analysis of Article 2031b, *see generally* Thode, *In Personam Jurisdiction; Article 2031b, the Texas "Long Arm" Jurisdiction Statute; and the Appearance to Challenge Jurisdiction in Texas and Elsewhere*, 42 TEX. L. REV. 279, 303-10 (1964); *Wilson, in Personam Jurisdiction over Non-*

residents: An Invitation and a Proposal, 9 BAYLOR L. REV. 363 (1957); Counts, *More on Rule 120a*, 28 TEX. B.J. 95, 96 (Feb. 1965).

Since McKanna's mode of review by way of writ of error in the Court of Civil Appeals constitutes a direct attack on the default judgment, the question to be decided is whether there is a lack of jurisdiction apparent on the face of the record which would vitiate the trial court's judgment. *Flynt v. City of Kingsville*, 125 Tex. 510, 82 S.W.2d 934 (1935); *Texaco Inc. v. McEwen*, 356 S.W.2d 809 (Tex. Civ. App. 1962, wr. ref., n. r. e.); *Doak v. Biggs*, 235 S.W. 957 (Tex. Civ. App. 1921, no writ).

Section 3 of Article 2031b, here to be construed, reads in part as follows: "Any . . . non-resident natural person that engages in business in this State . . . and does not maintain a place of regular business in this State or a designated agent upon whom service may be made . . . , the act or acts of engaging in such business . . . shall be deemed equivalent to an appointment . . . of the Secretary of State of Texas as agent upon whom service of process may be made . . . ."

Section 4 of that Article provides that a nonresident "shall be deemed doing business in this State by entering into contract by mail or otherwise with a resident of Texas to be performed in whole or in part by either party in this State . . . ." The parties agree that McKanna was doing business in Texas; so that problem is not before us.

Edgar alleged in his petition the Eileen Ann McKanna resided in Orange County, California, and that she executed and delivered to Edgar her note "payable to the order of plaintiff at 1210 Perry-Brooks Building, Austin, Texas . . . ." These allegations comply with the requirements of Section 3 of Article 2031b that McKanna be a nonresident and, as stipulated, be doing business in this State. But there are no allegations that McKanna "does not maintain a place of regular business in this State or a designated agent upon whom service may be made." The nonexistence of those two conditions is shown to be a necessary prerequisite to the applicability of Section 3 because of the language used in Section 2. Section 2 provides: "When any . . . non-resident natural person . . . shall engage in business in this State . . . service may be made by serving a copy of the process with the person who . . . is in charge of any business in which the defendant or defendants are engaged . . . ."

If the defendant had a regular place of business or a designated agent in Texas, we doubt that it could be successfully contended that service of process could be made on the Secretary of State. We hold under the clear language of Article 2031b that "the intent is to permit resort to Section 3 only if Section 2 is not available." Counts, *More on Rule 120a*, 28 TEX. B.J. 95, 137 (Feb. 1965). This holding is in accord with the established law of this State that it is imperative and essential that the record affirmatively show a strict compliance with the provided mode of service. *Roberts v. Stockslager*, 4 Tex. 307 (1849); *Texaco Inc. v. McEwen*, 356 S.W.2d 809 (Tex. Civ. App. 1962, wr. ref., n. r. e.); *Parker v. Scobee*, 36 S.W.2d 303 (Tex. Civ. App. 1931, no writ).

The Court of Civil Appeals, in its opinion, leaned heavily on its conclusion that "a legitimate inference might be drawn from the petition that appellee did not maintain a place of regular business in Texas or a designated agent for service," *citing Kelley v. First Nat'l Bank*, 270 S.W.2d 644, 646-647 (Tex. Civ. App. 1954, no writ). That case is distinguishable because the question before the court was whether the petition stated a cause of action which would support a default judgment. The court construed the pleadings in favor of the pleader in order to determine whether there was a cause of action alleged. This rule does not apply with respect to jurisdictional facts. While ordinarily presumptions are made in support of a judgment (including presumptions of due service of citation when the judgment so recites), no such presumptions are made in a direct attack upon a default judgment. *See Flynt v. City of Kingsville*, 125 Tex. 510, 82 S.W.2d 934 (1935). We think the same rule would apply to inferences of jurisdictional facts in a direct attack. *Cf. Walker v. Koger*, 99 S.W.2d 1034 (Tex. Civ. App. 1936, wr. dism.); *National Cereal Co. v. Earnest*, 87 S.W. 734 (Tex. Civ. App. 1905, no writ). As noted above, jurisdiction in this type of case must affirmatively appear on the face of the record. The provisions of Article 2031b are clear, and plaintiff has the burden of making sufficient allegations to bring the defendant within its provisions. *Cf. Sgitcovich v. Sgitcovich*, 150 Tex. 398, 241 S.W.2d 142 (1951); *Steele v. Caldwell*, 158 S.W.2d 867 (Tex. Civ. App. 1942, no writ); *Parker v. Scobee*, 36 S.W.2d 303 (Tex. Civ. App. 1931, no writ). We find nothing in the record that compels the inference that McKanna had neither a place of regular business nor a designated agent in this State.

The Court of Civil Appeals relied on *Employer's Reinsurance Corp. v. Brock*, 74 S.W.2d 435 (Tex. Civ. App. 1934, wr. dism.), for the proposition that a citation return showing service on a defendant by serving his agent is sufficient, without proof of such agency, to warrant a default judgment. The question in that case was whether the judgment was invalid because "no proof was offered respecting the agency of the said John R. Young . . . ." (Emphasis supplied.) The plaintiff alleged that Young was in charge of defendant's office and was a duly authorized attorney for service of legal process. The court held that in view of the sheriff's amended return which recited that service was had on the defendant through its "local agent John R. Young," it was unnecessary for the plaintiff to introduce proof of his agency. The case at bar is distinguishable in that the question here is whether the plaintiff made sufficient allegations to confer jurisdiction under Article 2031b. A return showing service on the Secretary of State cannot supply the missing jurisdictional facts upon which such service must depend.

McKanna, having now appeared to attack the judgment, is presumed to have entered her appearance to the term of the court at which the mandate shall be filed. Rule 123, Texas Rules of Civil Procedure. The judgments of the courts below are reversed, and the cause remanded to the District Court for a trial on the merits.

4. *The Special Appearance under Texas Law*

a. *Historical Background*

Read Rules 120a and 121 Texas Rules of Civil Procedure.

YORK
v.
TEXAS
137 U.S. 15, 11 S.Ct. 9
(1890)

Rufus H. Thayer, for plaintiff in error.
J. S. Hogg, Atty. Gen. Tex., for the State.

BREWER, J.

On the 14th day of November, 1888, a personal judgment was rendered in the district court of Travis county, Tex., against the plaintiff in error, which judgment was subsequently affirmed by the supreme court of the state. 11 S. W. Rep. 869. Error is now alleged in this: that the district court had no jurisdiction of the person of the defendant. The record discloses that on October 20, 1885, the defendant leased from the state certain school lands, at a stipulated rental. The lease provided that in all suits thereunder the venue should be laid in Travis county, Tex. The state filed its petition on February 15, 1888, alleging nonpayment of the rent due in 1886 and 1887. The defendant being a non-resident, a citizen of St. Louis, Mo., a notice in accordance with the provisions of the statute was served upon him personally in that city. No question is made but that the service was in strict conformity with the letter of the statute. On March 9, 1888, the defendant appeared by his counsel, and filed a special plea, challenging the jurisdiction of the court, on the ground that he was a non-resident and had not been served personally with process within the limits of the state. This plea was overruled. Thereafter, and on the 5th day of October, 1888, the defendant appeared by his attorneys in open court, demanded a jury, paid the jury fee, and had the cause transferred to the jury docket. On the 6th day of October he again filed a plea to the jurisdiction, on the same ground, which was also overruled. On the 14th day of November, when the cause was reached and called for trial, he again appeared by his attorneys, waived his right of trial by a jury and his demand of a jury, and declined to further answer to the cause, relying solely upon his plea to the jurisdiction. The court thereupon proceeded to render judgment against him, which, as heretofore stated, was affirmed by the supreme court.

It was conceded by the district and the supreme courts that the service upon the defendant in St. Louis was a nullity, and gave the district court no jurisdiction; but it was held that, under the peculiar statutes of the state of Texas, the appearance for the purpose of pleading to the jurisdiction was a voluntary appearance, which brought the defendant into court. Plaintiff in error questions this construction of the Texas statutes; but, inasmuch as the supreme court, the highest court of the state, has so construed them, such construction must be accepted here as correct, and the only question we can consider is as to the power of the state in respect thereto. It must be conceded that such statutes contravene the established rule elsewhere, a rule which also obtained in Texas at an earlier day, to-wit, that an appearance which, as expressed, is solely to challenge the jurisdiction is not a general appearance in the cause, and does not waive the illegality of the service, or submit the party to the jurisdiction of the court. *Harkness v. Hyde*, 98 U. S. 476; *Raquet v. Nixon*, Dall. Dig. 386; *Dewitt v. Monroe*, 20 Tex. 289; *Hagood v. Dial*, 43 Tex. 626; *Robinson v. Schmidt*, 48 Tex. 19. The difference between the present rule in Texas and elsewhere is simply this: Elsewhere the defendant may obtain the judgment of the court upon the sufficiency of the service without submitting himself to its jurisdiction; in Texas, by its statute, if he asks the court to determine any question, even that of service, he submits himself wholly to its jurisdiction. Elsewhere he gets an opinion of the court before deciding on his own action; in Texas he takes all the risk himself. If the service be in fact insufficient, all subsequent proceedings, including the formal entry of judgment, are void; if sufficient, they are valid. And the question is whether, under the constitution of the United States, the defendant has an inviolable right to have this question of the sufficiency of the service decided in the first instance and alone. The fourteenth amendment is relied upon as invalidating such legislation. That forbids a state to 'deprive any person of life, liberty, or property without due process of law.' And the proposition is that the denial of a right to be heard before judgment simply as to the sufficiency of the service operates to deprive the defendant of liberty or property. But the mere entry of a judgment for money, which is void for want of proper service, touches neither. It is only when process is issued thereon, or the judgment is sought to be enforced, that liberty or property is in present danger. If at that time of immediate attack protection is afforded, the substantial guaranty of the amendment is preserved, and there is no just cause of complaint. The state has full power over remedies and procedure in its own courts, and can make any order it pleases in respect thereto, provided that substance of right is secured without unreasonable burden to parties and litigants *Antoni v. Greenhow*, 107 U. S. 769, 2 Sup. Ct. Rep. 91. It certainly is more convenient that a defendant be permitted to object to the service, and raise the question of jurisdiction, in the first instance, in the court in which suit is pending. But mere convenience is not substance of right. If the defendant had taken no notice of this suit, and judgment had been formally entered upon such insufficient service, and under process thereon his property, real or personal, had been seized or threatened with seizure, he could by original action have enjoined the process, and protected the possession of his property. If the judgment had been pleaded as defensive to any action brought by him, he would have been free to deny its validity. There is nothing in the opinion of the supreme court or in any of the statutes of the state of which we have been advised gainsaying this right. Can it be held, therefore, that legislation simply forbidding the defendant to come into court, and challenge the validity of service upon him in a personal action, without surrendering himself to the jurisdiction of the court, but which does not attempt to restrain him from fully protecting his person, his property, and his rights against any attempt to enforce a judgment rendered without due service of process, and therefore void, deprives him of liberty or property, within the prohibition of the fourteenth amendment? We think not. The judgment is affirmed.

BRADLEY and GRAY, JJ., dissent.

Note

In 1962, the Texas Supreme Court, at the urging of Professor Wayne Thode, passed TEX. R. CIV. P. 120a, and again established a special appearance procedure in Texas. *See* E Wayne Thode, *In Personam Jurisdiction; Article 2031B, The Texas "Long Arm" Jurisdiction Statute; and the Appearance To Challenge Jurisdiction in Texas and Elsewhere*, 42 TEX. L. REV. 279, 332 (1964).

b. *Special Appearance Hearing*

KAWASAKI STEEL CORPORATION
v.
MIDDLETON
699 S.W.2d 199
(Tex. 1985)

The only issue that can be reached by a special appearance is the defendant's amenability to process. The words "not amenable to process" in R 120a mean that the special appearance is available solely to establish that the Texas court cannot, validly obtain jurisdiction over the person or property of the defendant.

All else must be raised by a motion to quash. Defective jurisdictional allegations in the petition, defective service of process, and defects in the citation must be challenged by a motion to quash, not a special appearance. All that is gained by filing a motion to quash is additional time to file and answer. *See* Rule 122, Texas Rules of Civil Procedure.

The non-resident defendant asserting a special appearance has the burden of proof to negate all bases of personal jurisdiction.

Notes

1. A specially appearing defendant may not go to trial on the merits before a court rules on his special appearance. To do so would be a general appearance in the lawsuit, and a defendant would be deemed to have waive his right to complain of a lack of personal jurisdiction. Furthermore, a defendant waives his special appearance by not timely requesting a hearing on his special appearance. *See Bruneio v. Bruneio*, 890 S.W.2d 150 (Tex. App.—Corpus Christi 1994, no writ). However, the rules specifically permit discovery to be conducted on the issue of jurisdiction without resulting in a waiver of the special appearance.

2. *GFTA Trendanalysen B.G.A. Herrdum GMBH & Company v. Varme,* 991 S.W.2d 785 (1999). A special appearance is not waived by including, in the same document, a challenge to the method of servicing citation, at least where the complaintant challenged jurisdiction and did not seek the trial court's decision on any other matter. "[In Kawaskaki], we did not hold that a party waives a due process challenge for want of minimum contacts by challenging the method of service in the special appearance. To the contrary, although the defendant in Kawasaki had challenged the method of service in its special appearance, we did not suggest that the defendant had thereby waived its contest to jurisdiction based on minimum contacts. *See id.* at 200. Instead, we carefully reviewed the record of the defendant's contacts with the forum before holding the defendant was amenable to suit. *Id.* at 201, 203. More recently, we considered whether an unsworn special appearance constituted waiver and a general appearance. *See Dawson-Austin v. Austin*, 968 S.W.2d 319 (Tex. 1998). We held that it did not, because the defendant neither acknowledged the trial court's jurisdiction in any way nor sought court action other than a dismissal for lack of jurisdiction. *Id.* at 322-23. Likewise, in the present case GFTA challenged jurisdiction and did not seek the trial court's decision on any other matter. The court of appeals erred when it held that GFTA consented to suit. Accordingly, without hearing oral argument, we reverse the judgment of the court of appeals and remand to that court to consider issues not reached by that court. TEX. R. APP. P. 59.1."

3. *Exito Electronics Company, Ltd. v. Trejo*, 142 S.W.3d 302 (Tex. 2004): A party enters a general appearance when it (1) invokes the judgment of the court on any question other than the court's jurisdiction, (2) recognizes by its acts that an action is properly pending, or (3) seeks affirmative action from the court. A Rule 11 Agreement, which extends a defendant's time to file an initial responsive pleading, and which is filed in the trial court before the defendant files a special appearance, even if the agreement is not expressly made subject to the special appearance, does not violate Rule 120a's "due-order-of-pleading" requirement and thus does not constitute a general appearance. A trial court's resolution of discovery matters related to the special appearance does not amount to a general appearance by the party contesting personal jurisdiction. An unverified special appearance does not concede jurisdiction. Also, there was more in the record for the trial court's consideration at the time of the special appearance hearing than the verification and affidavit, including the pleadings and

the deposition of Exito's corporate representative. If Exito did not provide sufficient evidence in support of its jurisdictional challenge, the trial court should have denied the motion, which it did. That does not, however, absolve the court of appeals from reviewing the merits of Exito's appeal of that ruling. Any defect in proof goes to the merits; it is simply not a waiver issue. The court of appeals, therefore, erred in holding that a defective verification and affidavit resulted in a waiver of Exito's special appearance.

4. *Dawson-Austin v. Austin,* 968 S.W.2d 319 (Tex. 1998). A party enters a general appearance whenever it invokes the judgment of the court on any question other than the court's jurisdiction; if a defendant's act recognizes that an action is properly pending or seeks affirmative action from the court, that is a general appearance. Or stated negatively, although an act of defendant may have some relation to the cause, it does not constitute a general appearance, if it in no way recognizes that the cause is properly pending, or that the court has jurisdiction, and no affirmative action is sought from the court. Thus, the Court held that a motion for continuance of the hearing on a special appearance did not constitute a general appearance.

5. *BMC Software Belgium, N.V. v. Marchand*, 83 S.W.3d 789, 794 (Tex. 2002) in discussing the standard of review in a special appearance stated: "The plaintiff bears the initial burden of pleading sufficient allegations to bring a nonresident defendant within the provisions of the long- arm statute. *See McKanna v. Edgar*, 388 S.W.2d 927, 930 (Tex. 1965). A defendant challenging a Texas court's personal jurisdiction over it must negate all jurisdictional bases. *Kawasaki Steel Corp. v. Middleton*, 699 S.W.2d 199, 203 (Tex. 1985). This Court has never clearly articulated the standard for reviewing a trial court's order denying a special appearance. The Fourth Court of Appeals has held that, because personal jurisdiction involves both legal and factual questions, appellate courts should review the trial court's decision for an abuse of discretion. *See, e.g., Klenk v. Bustamante*, 993 S.W.2d 677, 681 (Tex. App.—San Antonio 1998, no pet.). However, other courts of appeals review the trial court's factual findings for legal and factual sufficiency and review the trial court's legal conclusions de novo. *See, e.g., E.L.M. LeBlanc v. Kyle*, 28 S.W.3d 99, 101 (Tex. App.—Texarkana 2000, pet. denied); *In re Estate of Judd*, 8 S.W.3d 436, 440-41 (Tex. App.—El Paso 1999, no pet.); *C-Loc Retention Sys., Inc. v. Hendrix*, 993 S.W.2d 473, 476 (Tex. App.—Houston [14th Dist.] 1999, no pet.); *Cadle v. Graubart*, 990 S.W.2d 469, 471 (Tex. App.—Beaumont 1999, no pet.); *Ball v. Bigham*, 990 S.W.2d 343, 347 (Tex. App.—Amarillo 1999, no pet.); *Garner v. Furmanite Australia Pty, Ltd.*, 966 S.W.2d 798, 802 (Tex. App.—Houston [1st Dist.] 1998, pet. denied); *Al-Turki v. Taher*, 958 S.W.2d 258, 260-61 (Tex. App.—Eastland 1997, pet. denied)."

"We agree with the latter view and disapprove of those cases applying an abuse of discretion standard only. Whether a court has personal jurisdiction over a defendant is a question of law. *See Hotel Partners v. Craig*, 993 S.W.2d 116, 120 (Tex. App.—Dallas 1994, writ denied) (stating that this Court's decision in *Guardian Royal Exch. Assurance, Ltd. v. English China Clays, P.L.C.*, 815 S.W.2d 223, 226 (Tex. 1991), suggests that personal jurisdiction is a legal question). However, the trial court frequently must resolve questions of fact before deciding the jurisdiction question. *See E.L.M. LeBlanc*, 28 S.W.3d at 101; *C-Loc Retention Sys.*, 993 S.W.2d at 476. If a trial court enters an order denying a special appearance, and the trial court issues findings of fact and conclusions of law, the appellant may challenge the fact findings on legal and factual sufficiency grounds. *See Hotel Partners v. KPMG Peat Marwick*, 847 S.W.2d 630, 632 (Tex. App.—Dallas 1993, writ denied). Our courts of appeals may review the fact findings for both legal and factual sufficiency. *Ortiz v. Jones*, 917 S.W.2d 770, 772 (Tex. 1996). This Court's review of the trial court's fact findings is limited to legal sufficiency. *Ortiz*, 917 S.W.2d at 772."

"Appellate courts review a trial court's conclusions of law as a legal question. *Hitzelberger v. Samedan Oil Corp.*, 948 S.W.2d 497, 503 (Tex. App.—Waco 1997, pet. denied). The appellant may not challenge a trial court's conclusions of law for factual insufficiency; however, the reviewing court may review the trial court's legal conclusions drawn from the facts to determine their correctness. *Templeton v. Dreiss*, 961 S.W.2d 645, 656 n. 8 (Tex. App.—San Antonio 1998, pet. denied); *Dallas County v. Sweitzer*, 881 S.W.2d 757, 763 (Tex. App.—Dallas 1994, writ denied). If the reviewing court determines a conclusion of law is erroneous, but the trial court rendered the proper judgment, the erroneous conclusion of law does not require reversal. *Scholz v. Heath*, 642 S.W.2d 554, 559 (Tex. App.—Waco 1982, no writ)."

c. *The Availability of Mandamus Relief—Interlocutory Appeal*

Note

There was a considerable battle over the availability of mandamus relief when a special appearance was denied. *Canadian Helicopters, Ltd. v. Wittig*, 876 S.W.2d 304 (Tex. 1994); *National Industrial Sand Association v. Gibson*, 897 S.W.2d 769 (Tex. 1995); and *CSR v. Link*, 925 S.W.2d 591 (Tex. 1996). While interesting, these cases became immaterial when, in 1997, the Texas Legislature enacted TEX. CIV. PRAC. & REM. CODE Ann section 51.0147(7), authorizing interlocutory appeals from the granting or denial of a special appearance. As noted in *BMC Software Belgium, N.V. v. Marchand*, 83 S.W.3d 789, 793 (Tex. 2002), a court of appeals judgment in an interlocutory appeal is conclusive and an appeal to this Court is not allowed. *See* TEX. GOV'T CODE § 22.225(b). However, if there is a dissent in the court of appeals, the Supreme Court may exercise jurisdiction over the case. *See* TEX. GOV'T CODE § 22.225(c).

5. *Process and Service*

Read Rules 99-107, & 123 & 124 Texas Rules of Civil Procedure.

a. *Actual Service upon a Resident Defendant*

In the Interest of K.M.L., a Child.
443 S.W.3d 101
(Tex. 2014)

Teressa Anderson, Huntsville, TX, pro se for Other interested party Teressa Anderson.

Melissa Hannah, Attorney at Law, Lufkin, TX, Attorney ad Litem for Other interested party Attorney ad Litem.

Kathleen E. Matheu, Attorney at Law, Coldspring, TX, for Petitioner 1, Melissa Levalley.

Diane Macfarlane, Law Office of Diane Macfarlane, Longview, TX, Michael L. Davis, Attorney at Law, Coldspring, TX, for Petitioner 2, John Andrew James.

Kerry C. Hagan, Attorney at Law, Oakhurst, TX, for Petitioner 3, Angali Tarneja.

Eric Tek Tai, Luisa P. Marrero, Michael Shulman, Susan Marie Wolfe, Austin, TX, for Respondent, Texas Department of Family and Protective Services.

JUSTICE GREEN delivered the opinion of the Court, in which CHIEF JUSTICE HECHT, JUSTICE WILLETT, JUSTICE GUZMAN, and JUSTICE BROWN joined, and in which JUSTICE JOHNSON and JUSTICE BOYD joined except as to Parts II.B, II.D, and IV, and in which JUSTICE LEHRMANN and JUSTICE DEVINE joined except as to Parts III and IV.

In this parental termination case, we consider whether the trial court properly terminated the parental rights of an intellectually disabled and mentally ill mother who executed a voluntary affidavit of relinquishment and the parental rights of an indigent father who was not appointed trial counsel nor provided notice of the trial. Following a jury trial, the trial court signed a judgment terminating both the mother's and the father's parental rights to their minor child, and appointed the Texas Department of Family and Protective Services (DFPS) as the child's sole managing conservator. The court of appeals affirmed both terminations . 442 S.W.3d 396, 399, 2012 WL 1951111 (Tex. App.—Beaumont 2012, pet. granted) (mem. op.). Because there is legally insufficient evidence that the mother knowingly and intelligently executed the affidavit of voluntary relinquishment, and because the father did not receive notice of trial and did not waive notice, we reverse the judgment of the court of appeals and hold that termination of both parents' rights was improper.

I. Factual and Procedural Background

Just days after her eighteenth birthday, high-school student Melissa gave birth to a daughter, K.M.L., in Tennessee. The baby's father, John, seventeen at the time, lived in Texas. During the pregnancy, Melissa, her two younger brothers, and her mother, Angali, moved from Texas to Tennessee. Melissa suffers from bipolar disorder and has intellectual disabilities, and she and her mother have had a tumultuous relationship. Angali and Melissa decided that Melissa should move back to Texas to live with her uncle to finish high school, leaving K.M.L. with Angali. Over the next two years, Melissa graduated high school, visiting her daughter occasionally, and shuffled from one friend's house to the next. Angali served as K.M.L.'s primary caretaker, a position Melissa never questioned. John knew about K.M.L., but never made any attempts to see her or support her during this period.

* * *

On August 6, 2009, left alone with her teenaged uncles, two-year-old K.M.L. fell off the stairs. As a result of the six-foot fall, she suffered injuries to her teeth and jaw, though none life-threatening. The very next day, DFPS removed K.M.L. from the home, placed her in foster care, and filed a petition to terminate Melissa's parental rights.

More than two months after suit was filed, DFPS served John by publication, without appointing an attorney ad litem. Over the next six months, John received no notice of the proceedings, nor did he have any involvement with K.M.L. After Angali contacted John and put him in touch with her attorney, John filed pro se pleadings on May 3, 2010, acknowledging paternity, requesting that his rights not be terminated, and providing his sister's address and phone number, where he was currently residing, along with his mother's contact information. Despite filing a response in opposition, John was not provided notice of any hearings in the case, nor is there evidence that he received notice of the trial. John continued to make little effort to see his daughter, even after opposing the termination.

* * *

On January 18, 2011, the first day of trial, the State served John with a subpoena to attend the trial, and John arrived by police escort. For the first hours of the trial, John sat in the hall outside the courtroom and missed pre-trial motions, jury selection, and part of DFPS's opening statement. Angali's attorney alerted the trial court to the fact that John was in the hallway halfway through DFPS's opening statement, and John came into the courtroom. The trial judge told John—after John gave a short opening statement—that he possibly could have been entitled to appointed counsel, but that it was "a little late for that now.

* * *

Following a four-day trial, the jury found that termination of Melissa and John's parental rights was in K.M.L.'s best interest. . . . The trial court ordered the termination of both Melissa and John's parental rights and appointed DFPS as K.M.L.'s sole managing conservator. [The court of appeals affirmed the trial court's judgment of termination] . . . .

John . . .petitioned this Court for review. His petition raises three issues: (1) whether he waived his right to notice of the termination hearings by appearing at trial after being subpoenaed; . . . Because we find the first issue determinative, we do not reach the other two issues.

John argues that he did not receive notice of the termination hearings and did not waive notice by appearing at the trial. Family Code section 263.301(a) provides, "[n]otice of a permanency hearing shall be given as provided by Rule 21a, Texas Rules of Civil Procedure, to all persons entitled to notice of the hearing." Rule 21a provides that citation may be served by delivering a copy to the party to be served, or the party's duly authorized agent or attorney of record, as the case may be, either in person or by agent or by courier receipted delivery or by certified or registered mail, to the party's last known address, or by telephonic document transfer to the recipient's current telecopier number, or by such other manner as the court in its discretion may direct.[7]

After John filed a general appearance and answer in opposition on May 3, 2010, acknowledging his paternity of K.M.L. and providing both his address and telephone number, he became entitled to ten days' notice of any permanency hearing under section 263.301. *See* TEX. FAM. CODE § 263.301(a), (b)(3). It is undisputed that John did not receive notice of the four permanency hearings held after his May 3, 2010, answer but before the trial on January 18, 2011. In fact, at two of the hearings—the May and October 2010 hearings—the trial court issued orders finding that John did not receive proper notice. At the two other hearings, in June and August,

7 TEX. R. CIV. P. 21a.

DFPS employees testified that John was served only by publication, a manner of citation not authorized by Rule 21a. *See* TEX. R. CIV. P. 21a.

John's lack of notice of the permanency hearings has significance in two ways. First, one of the grounds under which John's parental rights were terminated is section 161.001(1)(O)—failure to comply with the provisions of a court order specifically establishing the actions necessary for the parent to obtain the return of the child who has been in DFPS custody for at least nine months as a result of an abuse or neglect removal. *See* TEX. FAM. CODE § 161.001(1)(O). The court of appeals did not address his lack of notice of the permanency hearings because it affirmed termination on constructive abandonment grounds, an independent basis from the jury's findings relating to the permanency hearings. *See* 443 S.W.3d at 107. But second and more importantly, John's failure to receive notice of the permanency hearings has implications as it relates to his lack of counsel and his due process rights. While we note our concern about DFPS's admitted and repeated failure to notify a parent about proceedings in a termination suit, we need not resolve the case on these grounds because the record indicates that DFPS may have erred in failing to provide John notice of trial.

Rule 245 of the Texas Rules of Civil Procedure provides that a trial court "may set contested cases on written request of any party, or on the court's own motion, with reasonable notice of not less than forty-five days to the parties of a first setting for trial, or by agreement of the parties." TEX. R. CIV. P. 245. If a timely answer has been filed in a contested case or the defendant has otherwise made an appearance, due process rights are violated when a judgment is subsequently entered without the party having received notice of the setting of the case, *Peralta v. Heights Med. Ctr.,* 485 U.S. 80, 86-87, 108 S.Ct. 896, 99 L.Ed.2d 75 (1988), even when that party previously waived notice of citation. *See Delgado v. Hernandez,* 951 S.W.2d 97, 99 (Tex. App.—Corpus Christi 1997, no writ); *Gonzalez v. State,* 832 S.W.2d 706, 706-07 (Tex. App.—Corpus Christi 1992, no writ). A trial court's failure to comply with the notice requirements in a contested case deprives a party of his constitutional right to be present at the hearing and to voice his objections in an appropriate manner, resulting in a violation of fundamental due process. *Armstrong v. Manzo,* 380 U.S. 545, 550, 85 S.Ct. 1187, 14 L.Ed.2d 62 (1965).

The record does not show that John was served with actual notice of the trial setting. In his original answer, John provided his sister's address, where he resided at the time of trial. No return receipt of citation was included in the clerk's record, although the appellate rules do not require such documents to be automatically included in the clerk's record absent specific request, and DFPS did not request it, even though it knew that notice was being challenged. *See* TEX. R. APP. P. 34.5(a), (b)(2). Additionally, in this regard, the question of whether John had constructive notice of trial is, at most, inconclusive. John testified that he knew about the termination suit and had previously met with Angali's attorney. However, John appeared at trial under subpoena and, according to his testimony, was driven by a district attorney or possibly a police officer. When asked if he was given notice of the trial, John responded, "I have never gotten anything," and that he "didn't get anything in the mail." Failure to give a parent notice of pending proceedings "violates the most rudimentary demands of due process of law." *Peralta,* 485 U.S. at 84, 108 S.Ct. 896 (quoting *Armstrong,* 380 U.S. at 549, 85 S.Ct. 1187) (internal quotations omitted). Given the constitutional implications of parental rights termination cases, *see In re E.R.,* 385 S.W.3d at 554, and John's statements on the record that he did not receive notice of trial, and absent any evidence to the contrary, we must conclude that John did not receive notice of trial. *See Gonzalez,* 832 S.W.2d at 707.

DFPS next argues that John waived notice by appearing at trial and not moving for a continuance. The due process right to notice prior to judgment is subject to waiver. *D.H. Overmyer Co. Inc., of Ohio v. Frick Co.,* 405 U.S. 174, 185, 92 S.Ct. 775, 31 L.Ed.2d 124 (1972). But such waiver must be voluntary, knowing, and intelligently waived. *See id.* at 185-86, 92 S.Ct. 775. It is true that John attended and participated in all four days of trial and did not request a continuance based on his lack of notice. However, John was told by the trial judge on the first day of trial that it was too late for him to be appointed an attorney and that nobody would be looking out for him anymore. Further, John appeared at trial under subpoena and testified that, "I have a lot of stuff going through my head right now, and it's very difficult to sit up here, and be this nervous, and try not to burst into tears over y'all not letting me see my little girl." The due process requirement of notice must be provided "at a meaningful time and in a meaningful manner." *Mathews v. Eldridge,* 424 U.S. 319, 333, 96 S.Ct. 893, 47 L.Ed.2d 18 (1976) (quoting *Armstrong,* 380 U.S. at 552, 85 S.Ct. 1187). And, while we "certainly agree that pro se litigants are not exempt from the rules of procedure," when a determination "turns on an actor's state of mind . . . , application may require a different result when the actor is not a lawyer." *See Wheeler v. Green,* 157 S.W.3d 439, 444 (Tex. 2005) (per curiam). Based on the record before us, we cannot conclude that John voluntarily, knowingly, and intelligently waived his due process right to notice of trial by sitting, under subpoena, through trial without any help from counsel and failing to formally move for continuance. John raised this complaint in a motion for new trial, and the trial court erred by not granting that motion. "Only that would have wiped the slate clean. Only that would have restored [John] to the position he would have occupied had due process of law been accorded to him in the first place." *Armstrong,* 380 U.S. at 552, 85 S.Ct. 1187.

We hold that John was entitled to notice of the permanency hearings and the trial and that he did not waive that right to notice by appearing at trial, as the record does not show that he appeared voluntarily such as to waive his constitutional due process right to notice. This lack of notice renders any judgment unenforceable and void. Accordingly, we reverse the judgment of the court of appeals as it relates to John and remand the case to the trial court for a new trial.

Notes

1. *Texas v. v. Bristol Hotel Asset Company*, 65 S.W.3d 638 (Tex. 2001) (JUSTICE BAKER, dissenting): "In an ordinary judicial proceeding, an officer's return of service that meets all procedural requirements is valid on its face and carries a presumption of the truth of the facts stated on the return and a presumption of its regularity. *See Sauve v. State*, 638 S.W.2d 608, 610 (Tex. App.—Dallas 1982, writ ref'd.). The return of service is *prima facie* evidence of service because our procedural rules ensure that independent, uninterested, and legally authorized persons serve process and verify the return. *See* TEX. R. CIV. P. 103, 107. Therefore, in an ordinary judicial proceeding, unless the party contesting service presents a preponderance of evidence to the contrary—for example the party's testimony along with corroborating facts or circumstances—the officer's return of service is sufficient proof that the citation and petition were properly served. *See Ward v. Nava*, 488 S.W.2d 736, 738 (Tex. 1972); *Sauve*, 638 S.W.2d at 610."

2. In *Proulx v. Wells*, 235 S.W.3d 213 (Tex. 2007) the Court noted that a suit for personal injuries must be brought within two years from the time the cause of action accrues. But a timely-filed suit will not interrupt the running of limitations, unless the plaintiff exercises due diligence in the issuance and service of citation. If service is diligently effected after limitations has expired, the date of service will relate back to the date of filing. Generally, the question of the plaintiff's diligence in effecting service is one of fact, and is determined by examining the time it took to secure citation, service, or both, and the type of effort, or lack of effort, the plaintiff expended in procuring service. The Court also addressed the burden of proof involving the diligence issue in a summary judgment proceeding as follows: Once a defendant has affirmatively pled the limitations defense, and shown that service was effected after limitations expired, the burden shifts to the plaintiff to explain the delay. In some instances, the plaintiff's explanation may be legally improper to raise the diligence issue, and the defendant will bear no burden at all. In others, the plaintiff's explanation of its service efforts may demonstrate a lack of due diligence, as a matter of law, as when one or more lapses between service efforts are unexplained or patently unreasonable. But, if the plaintiff's explanation for the delay raises a material fact issue, concerning the diligence of service efforts, the burden shifts back to the defendant to conclusively show why, as a matter of law, the explanation is insufficient. In assessing diligence, the relevant inquiry is whether the plaintiff acted as an ordinarily prudent person would have acted under the same or similar circumstances, and was diligent up until the time the defendant was served.

CITATION FOR PERSONAL SERVICE - Judicial District Court - Jim Wells County

Accurate Printing Co., Inc. - Alice, Texas

THE STATE OF TEXAS ORIGINAL

TO: CURTIS H. AUSTIN, JR.
1300 Jefferson Drive
Alice, Texas 78332

Defendant , Greetings:

YOU HAVE BEEN SUED. You may employ an attorney. If you or your attorney do not file a written answer with the clerk who issued this citation by 10:00 a.m. on the Monday next following the expiration of twenty days after you were served this citation and petition a default judgment may be taken against you.

Said Plaintiff's Original Petition was filed in said court, on the 18th day of May A.D. 19 94 in this cause, numbered 94-05-32647 on the docket in the 79th Judicial District Court of Jim Wells County, Alice, Texas, and styled,

Plaintiff.

ETHYLE M. AUSTIN FAMILY PROPERTIES, LTD.

VS.

CURTIS H. AUSTIN, JR.

Defendant ,

The nature of Plaintiff's Demand is fully shown by a true and correct copy of Plaintiff's Original Petition accompanying this citation, and made a part hereof.

Issued and given under my hand and the seal of said Court at Alice, Texas, this the 18th day of May, A.D. 19 94

Attest: OLGA VILLARREAL, Clerk, District Court, Jim Wells County, Texas
P. O. Drawer 2219
Alice, Texas 78332

By Eloisa Sepulveda Deputy.

ATTORNEY FOR PLAINTIFF:
LUCINDA GARCIA
P.O. BOX 331
Alice, Texas 78333

(SEAL) DISTRICT COURT JIM WELLS COUNTY, TEXAS

Rule 106: "the citation shall be served by the officer delivering to each defendant, in person, a true copy of the citation with the date of delivery endorsed thereon and with a copy of the petition attached thereto."

SHERIFF'S RETURN

Came to hand on 19th day of May, 1994, at 9:45 o'clock A M., and executed in Jim Wells County, by delivering to each of the within named defendants, in person, a true copy of this Citation, having first endorsed thereon the date of delivery, together with the accompanying true and correct copy of the Plaintiff's Petition, at the following times and places, to-wit:

NAME	DATE Month	Day	Year	TIME Hour	Min.	M.	Place, and Course and Distance From Court House	Mileage
Curtis H. Austin, Jr.	05	19	94	11	16	A	1300 Jefferson	

POSTED

And not executed as to the defendant ________

the diligence used in finding said defendant ______ being: ________

and the cause of failure to execute this process is: ________

and the information received as to the whereabouts of the said defendant ______ being ________

I actually and necessarily traveled ________ miles in the service of this Writ in addition to any other mileage I may have traveled in the service of other process in the same case during the same trip.

FEES—Serving ______ cop ____ $ ______

Mileage ______ miles $ ______

Total ______ $40.00

OSCAR LOPEZ Sheriff

SHERIFF, JIM WELLS COUNTY County, Texas

By [signature], Deputy

File No. 94-05-32647

ETHYLE M. AUSTIN FAMILY PROPERTIES, LTD.

vs.

CURTIS H. AUSTIN, JR.

Citation for Personal Service

IN DISTRICT COURT
79th JUDICIAL DISTRICT
of Jim Wells County, Texas

Issued

This 18th day of May A. D. 1994

OLGA VILLAREAL, Clerk District Court

By [signature] Deputy

Do not mark below
(For Clerk's File Mark)

FILED AT ___ O'CLOCK ___ M
OLGA VILLARREAL
MAY 24 1994
CLERK DIST COURT JIM WELLS CO. TEXAS

Note

Rule 106(a) of the Texas Rules of Civil Procedure states:

(a) Unless the citation or an order of the court otherwise directs, the citation shall be served by any person authorized by Rule 103 by

(1) delivering to the defendant, in person, a true copy of the citation with the date of delivery endorsed thereon with a copy of the petition attached thereto, or

(2) mailing to the defendant by registered or certified mail, return receipt requested, a true copy of the citation with a copy of the petition attached thereto.

HIGGINBOTHAM
v.
GENERAL LIFE & ACCIDENT IN. CO.

796 S.W.2d 695
(Tex. 1990)

Facts: This is a suit for the failure of General Life and National (GFN) and National Benefit Life Insurance Company (NBLI) to pay medical expenses under insurance policies they had issued. Service was had upon GFN and NBLI, according to the return, "on the 18th day of March 1986 at 12:01 o'clock p.m.." [The statute permitted that service could be accomplished by leaving a copy of the citation at the home office during business hours.] A default was entered. The defendants filed a motion for new trial alleging that Joyce Brown [the employee who was at the home office and received the citation] was not an officer or registered agent and that service was improper. They did not raise an objection to the failure to the citation to recite that 12:01 p.m. was during business hours. The *trial court conducted an evidentiary hearing* and denied the motion for new trial. On appeal they seek reversal because service was not shown to have been made during business hours.

Issue: Can a defective return of citation be amended to reflect the truth of service? Yes. Will the failure to recite a statutory requirement for service invalidate the citation? No, at least not when the attack is a direct one by motion for new trial, and there is an opportunity to determine the true facts of service. TEX.R.CIV.P. 118 allows the amendment of the return to reflect the service that actually was had. The trial, by overruling the motion for new trial, impliedly took judicial knowledge that 12:01 p.m. was during business hours.

This does not conflict with the prior default judgment cases in which it is stated that strict compliance with service requirements will be required on a direct attack. That statement applies, particularly in writ of error cases attacking default judgments, when there is no record showing strict compliance with a valid method of service. Thus, when a default judgment is attacked directly, "failure to affirmatively show strict compliance with the Rules of Civil Procedure [concerning service requirements] renders the attempted service of process invalid and of no effect," but where the record [on its face, or developed at an evidentiary hearing] affirmatively shows strict compliance, Rule 118 allows the amendment of the citation return to reflect the strict compliance.

SMITH
v.
COMMERCIAL EQUIP. LEASING CO.

678 S.W.2d 917
(Tex. 1984)

Werner A. Gohmert, Alice, for petitioner.
Chilton Maverick, San Antonio, for respondent.

PER CURIAM.

This is an appeal from a default judgment rendered in favor of Commercial Equipment Leasing Company on February 7, 1983. Smith, the defendant, brought a suit in the nature of a bill of review to set aside the default judgment. The trial court denied this relief on July 5, 1983. Smith appealed the bill of review and appealed the original default judgment by petition for writ of error. The San Antonio court of appeals consolidated these appeals, denied the petition for writ of error, and affirmed the trial court's denial of the bill of review in an unpublished opinion. Pursuant to TEX. R. CIV. P. 483, we grant Smith's application for writ of error and, without hearing oral argument, reverse the judgment of the court of appeals.

Citation was served on Smith by the district clerk by certified mail, return receipt requested. The return receipt was signed by Smith, and it is undisputed that he received the process. The citation contains the following sentence: This citation may be served by the sheriff or constable of any county in the State of Texas in which the party to be served is found, and he shall deliver to the above named party, in person, a true copy of this citation with the date of delivery endorsed thereon. No other method of service is mentioned in the citation.

Rule 106(a) states that "[u]nless the citation or an order of the court otherwise directs, the citation shall be served by any officer authorized by Rule 103 by (1) delivering to the defendant, in person, a true copy of the citation . . . or (2) mailing to the defendant by . . . certified mail . . . return receipt requested, a true copy of the citation . . ." (emphasis added). The question thus presented is whether the quoted sentence from the citation foreclosed any other method of service by directing the proper manner.

The settled rule in this state is that the manner of service must strictly comply with the rules. *McKanna v. Edgar*, 388 S.W.2d 927 (Tex. 1965). The language of this citation has a potential to mislead a defendant to believe that delivery of the citation in person is required, and will subsequently occur. In order to uphold this citation and service, the sentence in the citation would have to be viewed as merely naming one permissive method, but not necessarily directing that manner. Because of the conspicuous omission in the citation of any other allowable method of service, such a construction is strained, and the clause is, at best, ambiguous. Due to the strong policy considerations behind the strict scrutiny of personal service, we hold that the manner of service conflicted with the terms of the citation, and therefore with Rule 106(a).

We conclude that the court of appeals' decision conflicts with Rule 106(a), and pursuant to TEX. R. CIV. P. 483 we reverse the court of appeals' denial of the petition for writ of error without hearing oral argument, and hold the default judgment of February 7, 1983 void. We therefore find it unnecessary to consider the bill of review. We remand the cause for trial, and in accordance with TEX. R. CIV. P. 123, the defendant shall be presumed to have entered his appearance, thus making further service of citation unnecessary.

PLEASANT HOMES
v.
ALLIED BANK OF DALLAS

776 S.W.2d 153
(Tex. 1989)

Joe N. Boudreaux, Gary Johnson, Dallas, for petitioners.
John A. Gilliam, Louis J. Weber, Jr., Charles A. Gall, Dallas, for respondent.

PER CURIAM.

The application for writ of error of petitioners, Pleasant Homes, Inc. and Ray J. Stockman, is denied, as the default judgment was properly reversed on other grounds. In so doing, however, the majority of the court disapproves of the court of appeals' conclusion that a default judgment against a bank could not stand because the record on appeal did not affirmatively show that the individual at the bank, who was served with process in accordance with Texas Revised Civil Statutes article 342-915 (1989), was in fact the bank's vice-president, cashier, or agent for service. 757 S.W.2d 460, 462-63.

A return showing delivery of process to a vice-president or president, as authorized by applicable statute, is prima facie evidence that the person served is in fact the officer as designated. It is not necessary for either the petition or citation to designate the officer to be served by name if the face of the record affirmatively shows the person's authority. *See Dentex Shoe Corp. v. F.E. Schmitz Co.*, 745 S.W.2d 503 (Tex. App.—Fort Worth 1988, writ denied); *NRTRX Corp. v. Story*, 582 S.W.2d 225 (Tex. Civ. App.—Fort Worth 1979, writ ref'd n.r.e.). A defendant who contends that the person served was not in fact a proper officer for service has the burden to present evidence to the trial court of improper service by motion for new trial or motion to set aside default judgment. Here, the defendant made no such showing. The statement in the return of service identifying Beverly

Waters as a "V.P." indicates that she was a vice-president of the bank. This return would have been sufficient to sustain a default judgment.

HECHT, J., not sitting.

Note

TEX. BUS. ORG. § 5. 255. Agent for Service of Process, Notice, or Demand as Matter of Law

For the purpose of service of process, notice, or demand:

(1) the president and each vice president of a domestic or foreign corporation is an agent of that corporation;

(2) each general partner of a domestic or foreign limited partnership and each partner of a domestic or foreign general partnership is an agent of that partnership;

(3) each manager of a manager-managed domestic or foreign limited liability company and each member of a member-managed domestic or foreign limited liability company is an agent of that limited liability company;

(4) each person who is a governing person of a domestic or foreign entity, other than an entity listed in Subdivisions (1)-(3), is an agent of that entity; and

(5) each member of a committee of a nonprofit corporation authorized to perform the chief executive function of the corporation is an agent of that corporation.

PRIMATE CONSTR.
v.
SILVER
884 S.W.2d 151
(Tex. 1994)

Rayborn C. Johnson, Jr., The Woodlands, William K. Conkin, Houston, for petitioner.
Jeffrey P. Norman, Houston, for respondents.

PER CURIAM.

On appeal by writ of error from default judgment, we consider whether Defendant Primate Construction Co., Inc. has shown error on the face of the record because the sheriff's pre-printed return of service states that Primate Construction was served with a version of the plaintiff's petition in which it was not named as a defendant. Pursuant to Rule 170 of the Texas Rules of Appellate Procedure, a majority of the court grants Petitioner's application for writ of error and, without hearing oral argument, reverses the judgment of the court of appeals and remands the cause to the trial court.

Jim Silver, Suzanne Silver and Silver Inspection Services, Inc. originally filed suit against Gary Wayne Martin, the driver of the car with which they collided and an employee of Primate Construction, Inc. Primate Construction was first named as a defendant in Plaintiffs' Second Amended Petition. The citation in the record indicates that the citation was attached to a true and correct copy of Plaintiffs' Second Amended Petition; however, the pre-printed return of service form, signed by the sheriff, indicates that Primate Construction was served with a true and correct copy of the Plaintiffs' Original Petition. When Primate Construction failed to answer, the plaintiffs took a default judgment, from which Primate Construction appealed by writ of error to the court of appeals.

In order to be entitled to reversal by writ of error, a party who did not participate at trial has six months in which to show error on the face of the record. *Brown v. McLennan County Children's Protective Services*, 627 S.W.2d 390, 392 (Tex. 1982). Because the sheriff's return shows that the defendant was served with a version of the plaintiffs' petition in which Primate Construction was not named as a defendant, the court of appeals erred in finding no error on the face of the record.

For well over a century, this court has required that strict compliance with the rules for service of citation affirmatively appear on the record in order for a default judgment to withstand direct attack. *Wilson v. Dunn*,

800 S.W.2d 833, 836 (Tex. 1990); *Uvalde Country Club v. Martin Linen Supply Co.*, 690 S.W.2d 884, 886 (Tex. 1985); *McKanna v. Edgar*, 388 S.W.2d 927, 929 (Tex. 1965); *Flynt v. Kingsville*, 125 Tex. 510, 82 S.W.2d 934 (1935); *Sloan v. Batte*, 46 Tex. 215, 216 (1876); *Roberts v. Stockslager*, 4 Tex. 307 (1849). There are no presumptions in favor of valid issuance, service, and return of citation in the face of a writ of error attack on a default judgment. *Uvalde*, 690 S.W.2d at 836; *McKanna*, 388 S.W.2d at 929; *Flynt*, 82 S.W.2d at 934. Here, the plaintiffs argue that there is no error because the blanks filled in on the citation show the correct petition was attached, while the only evidence to the contrary is a form on which the sheriff made no affirmative alteration. This argument ignores the weight given to the recitations in the sheriff's return as proof of service.

The return of service is not a trivial, formulaic document. It has long been considered prima facie evidence of the facts recited therein. *Pleasant Homes v. Allied Bank of Dallas*, 776 S.W.2d 153, 154 (Tex. 1989); *Gatlin v. Dibrell*, 74 Tex. 36, 11 S.W. 908, 909 (1889) ("The return of the officer imports absolute verity, and was sufficient to authorize the rendition of judgment upon default . . . ."). *See also Gerland's Food Fair, Inc. v. Hare*, 611 S.W.2d 113, 116 (Tex. Civ. App.—Houston [1st Dist.] 1980, writ ref'd n.r.e.); *Pierce-Fordyce Oil Ass'n v. Staley*, 190 S.W. 814, 815 (Tex. Civ. App.—Amarillo 1916, no writ). The recitations in the return of service carry so much weight that they cannot be rebutted by the uncorroborated proof of the moving party. *Ward v. Nava*, 488 S.W.2d 736, 738 (Tex. 1972); *Sanders v. Harder*, 227 S.W.2d 206, 209 (Tex. 1950); *Gatlin*, 11 S.W. at 909; *Pierce-Fordyce*, 190 S.W. at 815. The weight given to the return is no less when the recitations impeach the judgment than when they support it.

The officer's return does not cease to be prima facie evidence of the facts of service simply because the facts are recited in a form rather than filled in by the officer. It is the responsibility of the one requesting service, not the process server, to see that service is properly accomplished. TEX. R. CIV. P. 99(a). This responsibility extends to seeing that service is properly reflected in the record. The Rules of Civil Procedure allow for liberal amendment of the return of service to show the true facts of service. TEX. R. CIV. P. 118. If the facts as recited in the sheriff's return, pre-printed or otherwise, are incorrect and do not show proper service, the one requesting service must amend the return prior to judgment. Under the current state of the record, the only proof that Primate Construction was served with anything at all is a return which recites service of a pleading in which it had not been sued.

Proper service not being affirmatively shown, there is error on the face of the record, and the court of appeals erred in holding otherwise. Pursuant to Rule 170 of the Texas Rules of Appellate Procedure, a majority of the court grants the application for writ of error of Primate Construction Co., Inc. and, without hearing oral argument, reverses the judgment of the court of appeals and remands the cause to the trial court.

Note

In designating the person or entity to be served, the specific statute controlling the entity to be served should be consulted. Here are some examples:

> *Corporations*. Under the TEX. BUS. CORP. ACT, arts 2.11, 8.10, in an action against a corporation, the president and all vice presidents and the registered agent of the corporation are agents of the corporation upon whom any process required or permitted by law to be served upon the corporation may be served. It is not enough to leave the citation with an employee of the company, such as a bookkeeper.
>
> *Counties*. When suing a county, serve the county judge. TEX. CIV. PRAC. & REM. CODE § 17.024(a).
>
> Unincorporated Cities, Towns or Villages. When suing an unincorporated city, town, or village, serve the mayor, clerk, secretary, or treasurer. TEX. CIV. PRAC. & REM. CODE § 17.024(b).
>
> *School Districts*. When suing a school district, serve the president of the school board or on the superintendent. TEX. CIV. PRAC. & REM. CODE § 17.024(c).

IN THE INTEREST OF E.A., et al.
287 S.W.3d 1
(Tex. 2009)

Bethany Schendel Lucking, Legal Aid of North West Texas, Wichita Falls, TX, for Petitioner.
Stephen Bjordammen, Milissa Christina Barrick, Wichita Falls, TX, for Respondent.

CHIEF JUSTICE JEFFERSON delivered the opinion of the Court, joined by JUSTICE HECHT, JUSTICE O'NEILL, JUSTICE MEDINA, JUSTICE GREEN, and JUSTICE JOHNSON.

In *Weaver v. Hartford Accident and Indemnity Co.,* 570 S.W.2d 367, 370 (Tex. 1978), we held that "a new citation is necessary for a party who has not appeared when the plaintiff, by amended petition, seeks a more onerous judgment than prayed for in the original pleading." In 1990, however, Texas Rule of Civil Procedure 21a was amended to provide for a variety of methods of service, including certified or registered mail, for all pleadings and court papers except the original petition. We must decide whether, in light of Rule 21a, service of new citation is required for a default judgment based on a more onerous amended petition, or whether service under Rule 21a will suffice. We conclude that service under Rule 21a is sufficient. Accordingly, we reverse the court of appeals' judgment and remand to the trial court for further proceedings consistent with this opinion.

Emilio and Norma Avitia were married and had two children, E.A. and D.A. The Avitias later divorced, and the final decree appointed them joint managing conservators of the children. Norma was given the exclusive right to designate the children's primary residence, and Emilio was granted visitation. Five months later, Emilio filed this petition to modify the parent-child relationship, seeking the exclusive right to designate the children's primary residence. If a suit seeking such a modification is filed within one year of the prior order, the petitioner must attach an affidavit that contains, along with supporting facts, one of several allegations. TEX. FAM.CODE § 156.102(a), (b). Emilio's petition had no such affidavit attached. Norma was served with citation but did not file an answer or otherwise appear.

Approximately three months later, Emilio filed an amended petition alleging that Norma had a pattern or history of drug use and requesting that he be appointed sole managing conservator and given a credit on his child support arrearage for a period during which he had intermittent physical custody of the children. Emilio attached a supporting affidavit making an appropriate allegation under Family Code section 156.102(b). Although the amended petition did not contain a certificate of service, Emilio alleges he sent Norma the amended petition via certified mail. The amended petition, transmittal letter, return receipt, and court order modifying the parent-child relationship all included the same street address in Wichita Falls but reflected three different zip codes. The post office attempted delivery of the amended petition three times before it was returned to Emilio's counsel as unclaimed.

The trial court rendered a default judgment granting Emilio the exclusive right to designate the children's primary residence. The court ordered no visitation for Norma and required her to pay child support to Emilio. Norma moved to set aside the default judgment and for new trial, arguing that default judgment was improper because Norma was not served with the amended petition. The trial court denied both motions. The court of appeals affirmed, 287 S.W.3d 38, holding that Texas Rule of Civil Procedure 21a eliminated the requirement of an additional citation for service of an amended petition seeking a more onerous judgment on a nonanswering party. The court of appeals further held that Norma had constructive notice of the amended petition, and that this satisfied due process. Because we conclude that a new citation is not required for service of a more onerous amended petition on a nonanswering party, but that Norma was not properly served with the amended petition and did not have constructive notice of it, we reverse the court of appeals' judgment and remand to the trial court for further proceedings.

If a defendant is properly served with process, in order to have a default judgment set aside, she must prove the three elements set out in *Craddock v. Sunshine Bus Lines, Inc.,* 134 Tex. 388, 133 S.W.2d 124, 126 (1939). But if the defendant never received the suit papers, she is generally entitled to a new trial without any further showing. *Fidelity and Guar. Ins. Co. v. Drewery Constr. Co.,* 186 S.W.3d 571, 574 (Tex. 2006) (per curiam) (citing *Peralta v. Heights Med. Ctr., Inc.,* 485 U.S. 80, 84, 108 S.Ct. 896, 99 L.Ed.2d 75 (1988)). Here there is no dispute that Norma was properly served with Emilio's original petition. The parties dispute only whether Norma was properly served with the amended petition.

The parties agree that a nonanswering party is entitled to some form of notice of a more onerous amended petition, but they dispute the manner in which such a petition must be served. Norma argues that service of new citation is required, while Emilio contends that service under Texas Rule of Civil Procedure Rule 21a is sufficient. In *Weaver v. Hartford Accident and Indemnity Co.,* 570 S.W.2d 367, 370 (Tex. 1978), we held that "new citation is necessary for a party who has not appeared when the plaintiff, by amended petition, seeks a more onerous judgment than prayed for in the original pleading." However, in 1990, we amended Rule 21a to provide that several methods of delivery, including certified or registered mail, are appropriate for "[e]very notice required by these rules, and every pleading, plea, motion, or other form of request required to be served under Rule 21, other than the citation to be served upon the filing of a cause of action and except as otherwise expressly provided in these rules." TEX. R. CIV. P. 21a. The court of appeals held that Rule 21a "eliminated the requirement of an additional citation" set out in *Weaver.* 287 S.W.3d at 41.

We have never addressed this issue directly. Although we recently cited *Weaver* in *Fidelity and Guaranty Insurance Co. v. Drewery Construction Co.,* 186 S.W.3d 571, 574 (Tex. 2006) (per curiam), we did not reach the issue of whether the type of service required has changed in light of Rule 21a because we concluded that the amended petition in *Fidelity* was not more onerous than the original petition. *Id.*

* * *

Rule 21a applies to all pleadings required to be served under Rule 21 other than the original petition and except as provided in the rules. Nothing in the rules requires a plaintiff to serve a nonanswering defendant with new citation for a more onerous amended petition. While a nonanswering defendant must be served with a more onerous amended petition in order for a default judgment to stand, we agree with the court of appeals that Rule 21a service satisfies that requirement. This interpretation "eliminates the uncertainty and confusion that is found in the cases regarding what constitutes a 'more onerous judgment' or a new 'cause of action.' " *In re R.D.C.,* 912 S.W.2d at 856 (noting that Rule 21a now governs over "ambiguous rules that have evolved as to when a new citation must be served") (citing 2 ROY W. MCDONALD, TEXAS CIVIL PRACTICE §§ 10:15-16 (1992)). To the extent *Weaver* conflicts with Rule 21a, the rule prevails.

We must then determine, however, whether Emilio served the amended petition in compliance with Rule 21a. Under that rule, court papers served by certified mail must be sent "by certified or registered mail, to the party's last known address." TEX.R. CIV. P. 21a. Service by mail is "complete upon deposit of the paper, enclosed in a postpaid, properly addressed wrapper, in a post office or official depository . . . ." *Id.*

Even assuming that the amended petition was properly addressed, a point that Norma disputes, any presumption of service arising from Emilio's mailing of the amended petition was negated by the amended petition's return as unclaimed. 287 S.W.3d at 41. The presumption of service under Rule 21a "is not 'evidence' and it vanishes when opposing evidence is introduced that [a document] was not received." *Cliff v. Huggins,* 724 S.W.2d 778, 780 (Tex. 1987).

Rule 21a further provides that the party or attorney of record shall certify compliance with the rule "in writing over signature and on the filed instrument." TEX.R. CIV. P. 21a. A certificate of service is prima facie evidence of the fact of service, but nothing in the rule "preclude[s] any party from offering proof that the notice or instrument was not received, or, if service by mail, that it was not received within three days . . . ." *Id.* Because the amended petition does not include a certificate of service, Emilio has not made a prima facie case of the fact of service on this basis.

Nonetheless, the court of appeals concluded that Norma received constructive notice of the amended petition and that this satisfied due process. 287 S.W.3d at 42. The court of appeals relied on the post office's repeated attempts to deliver the petition, one of the children's testimony that Norma knew about the lawsuit, and Emilio's attorney's statement that she sent Norma a copy of the amended petition via regular mail and it was not returned. *Id.* The court of appeals also noted that despite the fact that the later modification order, like the amended petition, was returned unclaimed, Norma timely moved to set the order aside. *Id.* The court of appeals held that even when a party does not receive actual notice, if the serving party has complied with Rule 21a, constructive notice may be established " 'if the serving party presents evidence that the intended recipient engaged in instances of selective acceptance or refusal of certified mail relating to the case or that the intended recipient refused all deliveries of certified mail.' " *Id.* (quoting *Etheredge v. Hidden Valley Airpark Ass'n, Inc.,* 169 S.W.3d 378, 381-82 (Tex. App.—Fort Worth 2005, pet. denied)).

We have never decided whether constructive notice of a more onerous amended petition satisfies due process. Assuming, without deciding, that it does, the record in this case is insufficient to establish constructive notice. Emilio presented no evidence that Norma avoided or refused delivery of the amended petition, nor that she received the certified mail notices. The mere fact that the certified mail was returned unclaimed is not sufficient to show avoidance or refusal where, as here, the relevant documents reflect three different zip codes for Norma's address, and the pertinent pleading lacks a certificate of service. The child's testimony regarding Norma's knowledge of the lawsuit was vague and did not address Norma's knowledge of the amended petition. Moreover, that Norma learned of the modification order does not mean she received notice of the amended petition. Emilio's attorney asserted that she sent Norma a copy of the amended petition via regular mail and that copy was not returned. However, standing alone, this is insufficient to establish that Norma had constructive notice of the amended petition.

In order for a default judgment to stand, a nonanswering party must be served with a more onerous amended petition under Rule 21a. Service of new citation is no longer required. There is no evidence, however, that Norma was served with the amended petition under Rule 21a or that she had constructive notice of the amended petition. Accordingly, without hearing oral argument, we reverse the court of appeals' judgment and remand to the trial court for further proceedings consistent with this opinion. TEX.R.APP. P. 59.1.

JUSTICE BRISTER filed a concurring opinion, in which JUSTICE WAINRIGHT and Justice WILLETT joined (omitted).

ASHLEY
v.
HAWKINS

293 S.W.3d 175
(Tex. 2009)

Kimberley M. Spurlock, Carrie Holman Westbrook, Clara Ines Medina, The Spurlock, Law Firm, Humble, TX, R. Brent Cooper, Diana L. Faust, Cooper & Scully, P.C., Dallas, TX, for Petitioner.

James B. Manley, James B. Manley, P.C., Cleveland, TX, for Respondent.

Rance L. Craft, James C. Ho, David S. Morales, Office of Atty. Gen., Clarence Andrew Weber, First Asst. Atty. Gen., Greg W. Abbott, Atty. Gen., Austin, TX, for Amicus Curiae.

JUSTICE GREEN delivered the opinion of the Court.

In this case, we consider whether section 16.063 of the Texas Civil Practice and Remedies Code tolls the limitations period when a defendant leaves Texas following a motor vehicle collision, but is otherwise amenable to out-of-state service. We hold, consistent with our recent decision in *Kerlin v. Sauceda,* 263 S.W.3d 920 (Tex. 2008), that section 16.063 does not apply in these circumstances, and we also overrule our decision in *Vaughn v. Deitz,* 430 S.W.2d 487 (Tex. 1968). We, therefore, reverse the court of appeals' judgment and reinstate the trial court's grant of summary judgment.

On May 31, 2003, Gail Ashley and Doris Hawkins were involved in a motor vehicle collision in Montgomery County, Texas. After the wreck, sometime in 2004, Ashley moved to California, leaving behind no forwarding address. On April 1, 2005, approximately sixty days prior to the expiration of the two-year limitations period, Hawkins sued Ashley, alleging personal injuries and damages related to the wreck. Although Hawkins made attempts to serve Ashley, she was not actually served until May 10, 2006, by a Sacramento County sheriff, almost one year after the limitations period expired. Ashley sought summary judgment on a statute-of-limitations affirmative defense, arguing that Hawkins failed to exercise diligence in serving her. *See* TEX. CIV. PRAC. & REM.CODE § 16.003(a) (setting a two-year limitations period for personal injury actions). In response, Hawkins argued that she exercised diligence in attempting to serve Ashley, and that, regardless, Ashley's absence from the state tolled the limitations period under section 16.063 of the Texas Civil Practice and Remedies Code. The trial court granted Ashley's motion, but the court of appeals reversed, holding that section 16.063 tolled the limitations period while Ashley was outside Texas. 293 S.W.3d 209. We reverse.

Ashley argues that the court of appeals erred in applying section 16.063 because (1) the statute is unconstitutional under the Commerce Clause, as it burdens Ashley's right to interstate travel; and (2) alternatively, even if constitutional, the statute should apply only in very narrow circumstances, as it is inconsistent with Texas's out-of-state service provisions. Section 16.063 provides:

> Temporary Absence From State. The absence from this state of a person against whom a cause of action may be maintained suspends the running of the applicable statute of limitations for the period of the person's absence.

TEX. CIV. PRAC. & REM.CODE § 16.063. We recently held in *Kerlin v. Sauceda,* that: "[I]f a nonresident is amenable to service of process under the longarm statute and has contacts with the state sufficient to afford personal jurisdiction . . . then we can discern no reason why a nonresident's 'presence' in this state would not be established for purposes of the tolling statute." 263 S.W.3d at 927. Under the general longarm statute, a nonresident party is amenable to service through the Secretary of State, if he or she "engages in business in this state" and the proceeding at issue "arises out of the business done in this state and to which the nonresident is a party." TEX. CIV. PRAC. & REM.CODE § 17.044(b). A nonresident defendant engages in business in this state, "if, among other acts . . . the nonresident *commits a tort in whole or in part in this state." Kerlin,* 263 S.W.3d at 927 (citing TEX. CIV. PRAC. & REM.CODE § 17.042) (emphasis added). Thus, according to *Kerlin,* if a party engages in business in this state, then the party's presence is established, and the tolling statute does not apply. *Id.* In her petition, Hawkins alleged that Ashley committed a tort in Montgomery County, Texas. Therefore, Ashley was present in Texas and amenable to service under the longarm statute.

Unlike in *Kerlin,* however, we are now squarely presented with the issue of whether we should overrule our decision in *Vaughn v. Deitz,* 430 S.W.2d 487 (Tex. 1968). In *Deitz,* we held that the tolling statute, which preceded section 16.063 of the Civil Practice and Remedies Code, applied to an out-of-state defendant, despite the existence of former article 2039a (now codified as TEX. CIV. PRAC. & REM.CODE § 17.062), which provided for out-of-state service through the Chairman of the State Highway Commission. 430 S.W.2d at 490. In *Kerlin,* we recognized that *Deitz* did not address the effect of the general longarm statute, only the impact of amenability to service through the Chairman of the State Highway Commission (now the Chairman of the Texas Transportation Commission). 263 S.W.3d at 927; *see also* TEX. CIV. PRAC. & REM.CODE § 17.062. The general longarm statute not only provides for substituted service, but also establishes a nonresident's presence in the state for purposes of personal jurisdiction. *Kerlin,* 263 S.W.3d at 927. Former article 2039a, the statute addressed in *Deitz,* and current section 17.062, provide only for substitute service, but do not define a defendant's "presence." *Id.*

Kerlin did not involve an automobile accident, so substituted service through the Texas Transportation Commission was not possible. Here, although Hawkins did not choose to pursue these options, Ashley was amenable to service under both section 17.062 (service on the Chairman of the Transportation Commission) and section 17.044 (service on the Secretary of State) of the Civil Practice and Remedies Code. Thus, we are presented with a conflict: *Deitz* says a defendant is not "present" in Texas for purposes of the tolling statute, even if amenable to service through the Chairman of the Highway (Transportation) Commission, whereas *Kerlin* says a defendant is "present" if amenable to service under the general longarm statute. *Compare Kerlin,* 263 S.W.3d at 927, *with Deitz,* 430 S.W.2d at 490. These differing standards are unworkable and inefficient, and will only serve to create confusion when litigants attempt to determine if the tolling statute applies to their cases. *Cf. Sw. Bell Tel. Co., L.P. v. Mitchell,* 276 S.W.3d 443, 447 (Tex. 2008). ("We adhere to our precedents for reasons of efficiency, fairness, and legitimacy . . . ." (internal quotations omitted)). Therefore, we overrule *Deitz* and hold, as we did in *Kerlin,* that a defendant is "present" in Texas, for purposes of the tolling statute, if he or she is amenable to service under the general longarm statute, as long as the defendant has "contacts with the state sufficient to afford personal jurisdiction." *Kerlin,* 263 S.W.3d at 927. In most cases, the general longarm statute will establish this "presence," as its "broad doing-business language 'allows the statute to reach as far as the federal constitutional requirements of due process will allow.' " *Retamco Operating, Inc. v. Republic Drilling Co.,* 278 S.W.3d 333, 337 (Tex. 2009) (quoting *Moki Mac River Expeditions v. Drugg,* 221 S.W.3d 569, 575 (Tex. 2007)).

Because we hold that section 16.063 does not toll the limitations period, Hawkins was required to file suit and serve Ashley by May 31, 2005. She failed to serve Ashley by this date, so we must consider whether Hawkins exercised due diligence in pursuing service after the limitations period expired.

If a party files its petition within the limitations period, service outside the limitations period may still be valid if the plaintiff exercises diligence in procuring service on the defendant. *Gant v. DeLeon,* 786 S.W.2d 259, 260 (Tex. 1990) (per curiam) (citing *Zale Corp. v. Rosenbaum,* 520 S.W.2d 889, 890 (Tex. 1975) (per curiam)). When a defendant has affirmatively pleaded the defense of limitations, and shown that service was not timely, the burden shifts to the plaintiff to prove diligence. *Proulx v. Wells,* 235 S.W.3d 213, 216 (Tex. 2007) (per curiam) (citing *Murray v. San Jacinto Agency, Inc.,* 800 S.W.2d 826, 830 (Tex. 1990)). Diligence is determined by asking "whether the plaintiff acted as an ordinarily prudent person would have acted under the same or similar circumstances and was diligent up until the time the defendant was served." *Id.* at 216. Although a fact question, a plaintiff's explanation may demonstrate a lack of diligence as a matter of law, "when one or more lapses between service efforts are unexplained or patently unreasonable." *Id.* Thus, Hawkins has the burden to "present evidence regarding the efforts that were made to serve the defendant, and to explain every lapse in effort or period of delay." *Id.*

Hawkins alleges the collision occurred on May 31, 2003, setting May 31, 2005, as the date the two-year limitations period expired. TEX. CIV. PRAC. & REM.CODE § 16.003(a) (setting a two-year limitations period for personal injury actions). In her motion for summary judgment, Ashley pointed out that she was not served until May 10, 2006, almost a year after the limitations period expired. Therefore, the burden shifted to Hawkins to explain how she was diligent in attempting to serve Ashley. *See Proulx,* 235 S.W.3d at 216. The record reflects that Hawkins filed suit on April 1, 2005, and the clerk first mailed service to Ashley in Conroe, Texas, at an address found on Ashley's Texas drivers license and on the accident report. This citation was returned unclaimed. Then, on June 7, 2005, Hawkins requested, and the clerk mailed, service to an address in Sacramento, California. This was returned on July 27, 2005. No other service was attempted until March 17, 2006, at which time Hawkins provided the clerk with a new address in Rio Linda, California. Almost two months later, a Sacramento County sheriff personally served Ashley at that address. However, a period of almost eight months lapsed between July 27, 2005 and March 17, 2006. During this time, the record reflects that the trial court twice set the case for dismissal based on a want of prosecution, dismissing it on January 17, 2006, only to reinstate it following a motion by Hawkins. In her response to the motion for summary judgment, Hawkins asserted that she made a diligent effort to serve Ashley, citing the two attempts at service in April and June of 2005, and also explaining:

> Counsel for [Hawkins] and his assistants have spent approximately twenty (20) hours searching for [Ashley's] whereabouts. Many search engines, including Zabasearch, Google, DCS Information Systems (a reliable intelligence source for business), People Search, Intelius, and other sources have been utilized. Counsel for [Hawkins] personally went to the last known address of [Ashley] and canvassed the apartment project where she once resided. Although [Ashley] moved to California many months before she was finally served, she never changed her address on her driver's license.
>
> [Ashley] was finally located at a different address in Rio Linda, California and served with citation.

Hawkins also attached an affidavit from her counsel, stating that he was a licensed private investigator for over fifteen years, that he is "acquainted with the resources utilized by private investigators in skip tracing," and that he utilized those resources in attempting to locate Ashley. In addition to the methods listed in the motion, the affidavit listed other websites and public records he searched. She also contended that the Montgomery County Voter Registration Database listed Ashley's address in Conroe, Texas.

We agree with the trial court and hold that, as a matter of law, Hawkins' responses do not create a fact issue as to diligence, as this eight-month gap in time is left unexplained. *See, e.g., Gant,* 786 S.W.2d at 260. Hawkins stated that she spent approximately twenty hours searching for Ashley, although she does not specify when this time was spent. Either these twenty hours were expended early on, in which case, the diligence of the search later ceased; or, these hours were spread over eight months, in which case the search was never diligent. Either way, Hawkins failed to meet her burden.

* * *

Notably, the record does not indicate that Hawkins attempted any form of service other than service by mail or delivery. If Hawkins was unable to locate Ashley, or if Hawkins thought Ashley was evading service, other methods of service were available. In particular, no substitute service such as service by publication was attempted. *See* TEX.R. CIV. P. 109 (providing for service by publication when defendant's residence is unknown, the defendant is transient, or the defendant is absent or is a nonresident of the state); *see also Parmer v. DeJulian,* No. 12-07-00479-CV, 2008 WL 4225994, (Tex. App.—Tyler Sept.17, 2008, no pet.) (mem. op., not designated for publication) (finding lack of diligence as a matter of law where plaintiff relied on its own efforts only to locate defendant over a one-year period, rather than resorting to other methods such as hiring a private investigator or process server, or performing citation by publication); *Hodge v. Smith,* 856 S.W.2d 212, 215-17 (Tex.

App.—Houston [1st Dist.] 1993, writ denied) (finding diligence was not lacking as a matter of law where plaintiff requested service by publication, four months after suit was filed and after other attempts to locate the defendant). Hawkins recognized its availability by stating, in her October 11, 2005, motion to retain the case on the court's docket, that she "utilized various investigative resources to no avail" and that she "would like additional time to locate [Ashley] before resorting to service by publication [,] which is expensive." But from the time of that motion, an additional five months lapsed before service was attempted and seven months lapsed until service was achieved. Although service by publication should not be a first resort, when a plaintiff is continuously unable to locate a defendant, its availability should not be overlooked. *See Wood v. Brown,* 819 S.W.2d 799, 800 (Tex. 1991) (per curiam) (noting that service by publication is to be used only if the requirements of Rule 109 of the Texas Rules of Civil Procedure are met); *see also Carter v. MacFadyen,* 93 S.W.3d 307, 314-15 (Tex. App.—Houston [14th Dist.] 2002, pet. denied) ("A flurry of ineffective activity does not constitute due diligence if easily available and more effective alternatives are ignored.").

For these reasons, we reverse the court of appeals' judgment and reinstate the trial court's grant of summary judgment in favor of Ashley.

b. *Substituted and Constructive Service of Resident Defendants*

Read Rules 106-119 Texas Rules of Civil Procedure.

STATE FARM FIRE & CASUALTY CO.
v.
COSTLEY
868 S.W.2d 298
(Tex. 1993)

Kenneth S. Carroll, Dallas, William W. Kilgarlin, Austin, for petitioner.
Ed Walton, Jeffrey W. Shell, Amarillo, for respondents.

PER CURIAM.

Cathy Costley sued Robert Costley, her father-in-law, for personalty lost in a fire which occurred on Robert's property. Robert filed a third party action against his son Andy Costley, Cathy's husband, alleging that Andy's negligence caused the fire. Andy contacted State Farm, his homeowner's policy carrier, and made a demand that it defend him in the third party action. Apparently, Andy failed to cooperate with State Farm in defending his suit, and State Farm subsequently filed suit to rescind the policy.

State Farm made ten failed attempts to achieve personal service on Andy Costley before requesting substituted service under Rule 106(b) of the Texas Rules of Civil Procedure. State Farm filed an affidavit stating the location of Costley's usual place of abode and the specific facts describing the unsuccessful attempts at personal service. State Farm's affidavit complied with Rule 106(b), and the trial court authorized substituted service by mailing a copy of the petition and citation by certified mail, return receipt requested, with an additional copy sent by first-class mail, postage prepaid to Costley's mailing address. State Farm filed a return of service stating that Costley had been served in the manner authorized by the court. Costley failed to answer and a default judgment was entered by the trial court. The court of appeals reversed the default judgment concluding that service by first-class mail did not satisfy the Rule 106(b) requirement that substituted service "be reasonably effective to give defendant notice" because the service by U.S. mail did not show when Costley actually received notice. 844 S.W.2d 939, at 941-942.

Substituted service exists to allow plaintiffs to effect service where proof of actual notice under Rule 106(a) is impractical. *See Wilson v. Dunn*, 800 S.W.2d 833, 836 (Tex. 1992). Under Rule 106(b) a court may authorize substituted service only after a plaintiff has unsuccessfully tried to effect personal service or service by certified mail, return receipt requested, as required by Rule 106(a). TEX. R. CIV. P. 106(b). A plaintiff may resort to substituted service only upon the failure of these methods which provide proof of actual notice. Thus, to require proof of actual notice upon substituted service would frustrate Rule 106(b)'s purpose of providing alternate methods for plaintiffs in the position of State Farm. In fact, the rule itself contemplates other procedures which will not necessarily furnish evidence of actual notice. The rule allows service by leaving a copy of the citation and petition with someone over the age of sixteen at the defendant's place of abode as stated in the affidavit. TEX. R. CIV. P. 106(b)(1). This method of substituted service provides no evidence in the record of when defendant received actual notice, but rather only provides proof of when plaintiff actually left the copies with someone in compliance with the rule. Service by mail achieves a similar result because it allows a plaintiff to properly post a return of service which demonstrates that the plaintiff has precisely followed the court's order of service by means reasonably calculated to provide actual notice.

Upon receipt of an affidavit satisfying Rule 106(b) the trial court may authorize substituted service which, shown from the affidavit or other evidence, is reasonably calculated to provide notice. In the present case, the court of appeals found that "[n]either the affidavit nor any other evidence in the record demonstrates a method of service that will be reasonably effective to give Mr. Costley notice of the suit." 844 S.W.2d at 941. We disagree. State Farm presented the trial court with a copy of Costley's insurance policy, authenticated by an affidavit of the claim's superintendent, which contained Costley's mailing address; a copy of a letter sent by State Farm, to that same address, informing Costley of the attorney State Farm had retained for his defense; and a copy of a letter sent to State Farm from Costley's attorney which contained specific references to the letter sent to Costley by State Farm. This was sufficient evidence to establish that notice sent to this address would be reasonably effective to give Costley notice of the suit. Under these circumstances, the trial court properly authorized service by first-class mail, postage prepaid.

State Farm's return of service strictly complied with the rules of civil procedure as well. Rule 107 requires an adequate return of service before a court may grant a default judgment. Rule 107 provides, "[w]here citation is executed by an alternative method as authorized by Rule 106, proof of service shall be made in the manner ordered by the court." State Farm's return of service states the date of service by both certified and first-class mail, in accordance with the court order, and is thereby in strict compliance with the rules of civil procedure.

Pursuant to Rule 170 of the Texas Rules of Appellate Procedure, a majority of the Court grants State Farm's application for writ of error and, without hearing oral argument, reverses the judgment of the court of appeals and remands the case to that court for consideration of Andy Costley's unaddressed points of error.

WILSON
v.
DUNN

800 S.W.2d 833
(Tex. 1991)

Don Prager, Fort Worth, on appeal only, for petitioner.
Robert D. Frye, Fort Worth, for respondent.

HECHT, JUSTICE.

The district court in this case authorized substitute service of suit papers upon defendant without an affidavit or other evidence justifying such service as required by Rule 106(b) of the Texas Rules of Civil Procedure. Defendant nevertheless received citation and plaintiff's petition, but did not answer, and the trial court rendered default judgment against him. The court of appeals reversed the default judgment because of the defect in service and remanded the case to the trial court for further proceedings. 752 S.W.2d 15. We affirm.

I

Jesse Wilson sued Michael Dunn for damages resulting from Dunn's negligent operation of a motor vehicle. Wilson alleged that Dunn could be served with citation at his apartment, where, in fact, Dunn was then residing and has resided at all times material to this case. Repeated, sustained efforts to serve Dunn there, however, both in person and by mail, proved unsuccessful.

After several months, Wilson's attorney filed a motion for substitute service under Rule 106(b). Rule 106(b) states: Upon motion supported by affidavit stating the location of the defendant's usual place of business or usual place of abode or other place where the defendant can probably be found and stating specifically the facts showing that service has been attempted under either (a)(1) or (a)(2) at the location named in such affidavit but has not been successful, the court may authorize service (1) by leaving a true copy of the citation, with a copy of the petition attached, with anyone over sixteen years of age at the location specified in such affidavit, or (2) in any other manner that the affidavit or other evidence before the court shows will be reasonably effective to give the defendant notice of the suit. (Emphasis added.) Contrary to the explicit requirement of the rule, Wilson's motion was not verified or supported by affidavit or other evidence. Nonetheless, the judge of the 236th District Court to which the case was assigned granted the motion and ordered that citation be served upon Dunn either by attaching it to the door of his apartment or by delivering it to the apartment manager at Dunn's address. However, the judge instructed the clerk to attach a note to the docket sheet stating that no default judgment was to be taken. The return of citation authorized by the district court stated that it had been served by a deputy constable "by delivering to the within named Michael Donell [sic] Dunn by delivering to his agent for service, Carol Berlinger, apartment manager" a copy of the citation and plaintiff's original petition. Dunn actually received the papers, as he later acknowledged in a sworn statement given to Wilson's attorney:

> I received some suit papers from [Wilson's attorney]. These papers were placed in my apartment by the apartment manager where I live after the Constable served the papers on her. Within five days from the date that I received the suit papers, I hand delivered them to my insurance agent . . . .

Within a few weeks an adjuster for Dunn's insurer telephoned Wilson's attorney to discuss the case. Following up their conversation, the adjuster wrote Wilson's attorney requesting him to agree that, pending efforts to obtain Dunn's cooperation and to settle Wilson's claim, Dunn would not be required to file an answer in the case and no default judgment would be taken without ten days' notice. Wilson's attorney wrote at the bottom of the letter, "I agree to the above," signed it, and returned it to the adjuster. Shortly thereafter the adjuster retained an attorney to monitor the case. The attorney telephoned the clerk of the court on at least two occasions and was told that at the court's instruction a note had been attached to the file that no default judgment could be taken in the case. The attorney did not contact Dunn but the adjuster finally did, and obtained a statement from him. About the same time, however, the insurer transferred the case to another adjuster, and Wilson's attorney was not informed that Dunn had been contacted.

Concerned that the second anniversary of the accident was approaching, Wilson's attorney wrote Dunn a letter dated February 19, 1987, urging him to cooperate with his insurer and warning him of the possible consequences of failing to do so. Specifically, the letter stated, "we are going to ask the Court for the Default Judgment against you during the second week of March, 1987." Wilson's attorney sent a copy of the letter to the adjuster and the attorney retained by the adjuster. In response to the letter, the sometimes elusive Dunn contacted Wilson's attorney and arranged to meet with him. Dunn gave Wilson's attorney a sworn statement in which he indicated that he had not failed to communicate with his insurer.

Convinced that the adjuster had not been fully candid with him, Wilson's attorney went to the 236th District Court on February 27, 1987, to obtain a default judgment. Finding that the judge of that court was not available, Wilson's attorney requested the file from the clerk so that he could take it to another judge for hearing on his request for a default judgment. The clerk was reluctant to give Wilson's attorney the file because the judge had told her that default judgment was not to be taken in the case. She pointed out to Wilson's attorney the note the judge had instructed her to attach to the file, but he insisted on taking it, and she finally relented. On the way to a hearing before the judge of the 67th District Court, Wilson's attorney removed the note from the file and threw it away.

Wilson's original petition requested $144 damages for past medical expenses, and unspecified amounts for future medical expenses, lost wages, loss of earning capacity, and past and future physical pain and mental anguish. After hearing, the judge of the 67th District Court rendered default judgment for Wilson for $475,000. Later the same day Wilson's attorney told the judge who granted the default judgment that he had removed the prior judge's note from the file because Dunn had actual knowledge of the suit and default was therefore appropriate. The judge who granted the default judgment strongly reproved Wilson's attorney but did not set aside the judgment.

Neither Dunn nor his insurer learned of the default judgment until after it was signed. Dunn filed a motion for new trial, which was also presented to the judge of the 67th District Court. The motion did not complain of the defect in service. After hearing evidence, the trial court denied the motion. The trial court concluded that substitute service was appropriate, and that Dunn had received actual notice of the suit. The trial court also concluded that Dunn's failure to file an appearance was due to the conscious indifference of his insurer.

On appeal, Dunn argued that service was defective and could not support the default judgment. Dunn also argued that the trial court's conclusion that he was not entitled to a new trial was against the great weight of the evidence and manifestly unjust. The appeals court agreed with Dunn's defective service argument and did not address his other arguments. Thus, the only issue presented to us is the sufficiency of service.

II

For well over a century the rule has been firmly established in this state that a default judgment cannot withstand direct attack by a defendant who complains that he was not served in strict compliance with applicable requirements. *See, e.g., Uvalde Country Club v. Martin Linen Supply Co.*, 690 S.W.2d 884, 886 (Tex. 1985) (per curiam); *McKanna v. Edgar*, 388 S.W.2d 927, 929 (Tex. 1965); *Sloan v. Batte*, 46 Tex. 215, 216 (1876); *see also* R. MCDONALD, TEXAS CIVIL PRACTICE IN DISTRICT AND COUNTY COURTS § 17.23.2, at 134-144 (F. Elliott rev. 1984). This Court only recently reasserted: There are no presumptions in favor of valid issuance, service, and return of citation in the face of a [direct] attack on a default judgment . . . . Moreover, failure to affirmatively show strict compliance with the Rules of Civil Procedure renders the attempted service of process invalid and of no effect. *Uvalde*, 690 S.W.2d at 885. *See Higginbotham v. General Life & Acc. Ins. Co.*, 796 S.W.2d 695, 697 (Tex. 1990).

In this case, Dunn was not strictly served in compliance with Rule 106(b) because substitute service was not properly authorized absent the affidavit explicitly required by the rule. The express requirement of an affidavit in support of a motion for substitute service was added effective in 1981. 599-600 S.W.2d xxxviii-xxxix (Tex. Cases 1980). It appears, however, that prior to that change in the text of the rule the courts uniformly held that substitute service could be authorized only upon probative evidence of the impracticality of personal service. *See Stylemark Constr., Inc. v. Spies*, 612 S.W.2d 654, 656-657 (Tex. Civ. App.—Houston [14th Dist.] 1981, no writ); *Harrison v. Dallas Court Reporting College*, 589 S.W.2d 813, 815-816 (Tex. Civ. App.—Dallas 1979, no writ); *Kirkegaard v. First City Nat'l Bank*, 486 S.W.2d 893, 894-895 (Tex. Civ. App.—Beaumont 1972, no writ); *Franks v. Montandon*, 465 S.W.2d 800, 801 (Tex. Civ. App.—Austin 1971, no writ); *Spencer v. Texas Factors, Inc.*, 366 S.W.2d 699, 700 (Tex. Civ. App.—Dallas 1963, writ ref'd n.r.e.); *cf. Sgitcovich v. Sgitcovich*, 241 S.W.2d 142, 144, 148 (Tex. 1951) (trial court authorized substitute service on unverified motion but heard evidence of sufficiency of that service before rendering default judgment). Since the 1981 change in Rule 106(b) the courts have consistently held that substitute service may not properly issue on a motion supported by an affidavit that is conclusory or otherwise insufficient. *See Medford v. Salter*, 747 S.W.2d 519, 520 (Tex. App.—Corpus Christi 1988, no writ); *Garrels v. Wales Transp., Inc.*, 706 S.W.2d 757, 758-759 (Tex. App.—Dallas 1986, no writ); *Beach, Bait & Tackle, Inc. v. Holt*, 693 S.W.2d 684, 685-686 (Tex. App.—Houston [14th Dist.] 1985, no writ); *Mackie Constr. Co. v. Carpet Services, Inc.*, 645 S.W.2d 594, 596 (Tex. App.—Eastland 1982, no writ). We agree and hold that substitute service is not authorized under Rule 106(b) without an affidavit which meets the requirements of the rule demonstrating the necessity for other than personal service.

Wilson acknowledges that service on Dunn was defective because of the failure to comply with Rule 106(b), but argues that the default judgment rendered against Dunn should nevertheless stand because Dunn actually received the suit papers and actually knew of the pendency of the suit. We disagree. Actual notice to a defendant, without proper service, is not sufficient to convey upon the court jurisdiction to render default judgment against him. *See Harrell v. Mexico Cattle Co.*, 73 Tex. 612, 11 S.W. 863, 865 (1889). Rather, jurisdiction is dependent upon citation issued and served in a manner provided for by law. *Id.*; *Panhandle Constr. Co. v. Casey*, 66 S.W.2d 705, 707 (Tex. Civ. App.—Amarillo 1933, writ ref'd); *see C.W. Bollinger Ins. Co. v. Fish*, 699 S.W.2d 645, 655 (Tex. App.—Austin 1985, no writ). Absent service, waiver, or citation, mere knowledge of a pending suit does not place any duty on a defendant to act. *See Harrell*, 11 S.W. at 865; *Panhandle Constr. Co.*, 66 S.W.2d at 707. Consequently, Dunn's knowledge that Wilson had sued him and his actual receipt of suit papers is not sufficient to invoke the district court's jurisdiction to render default judgment against him.

Wilson relies heavily upon section 3 of the RESTATEMENT (SECOND) OF JUDGMENTS (1982), which states: "When actual notice of an action has been given, irregularity in the content of the notice or the manner in which it was given does not render the notice inadequate." Wilson fails to note, however, that this rule does not apply to default judgments. As comment d to section 3 explains: The objection to the regularity of notice also often arises in the context of an application for relief from a default judgment. Here again there is a rational basis for treating an irregularity in notice-giving as significant even though actual notice has been conferred. To do so is to apply a rule of parity among the parties concerning formal defects in procedure. A default judgment is awarded not because the court is entirely satisfied that the claim has substantive merit . . . but because the party in default was derelict in complying with the rules of procedure governing how he may make his defense. An applicant for relief from such dereliction must show that he acted with due diligence after having become aware of the default and that he has a good case on the merits. . .. Assuming he makes such a showing, the only ground supporting the judgment is that the defendant has failed to respond to the action in conformity with applicable procedure for doing so. If the defendant can then show that the person commencing the action was guilty of comparable nonconformity with procedural rules, under a principle of equality the derelictions offset each other and the merits of the controversy may be brought forward for consideration. This authority contradicts, rather than supports, Wilson's position.

Wilson also contends that Dunn is foreclosed from complaining that service was defective because he has admitted receipt of the suit papers. We agree that Dunn could have waived his complaint of defective service by conceding the issue, but he has not done so. Dunn has admitted receipt, not service. Indeed, the issue presented is whether actual receipt can cure defective service in this context. The two cases upon which Wilson relies demonstrate this distinction. *In both First Nat'l Bank v. Peterson*, 709 S.W.2d 276, 280 (Tex. App.—Houston [14th Dist.] 1986, writ ref'd n.r.e.), and *Hurst v. A.R.A. Manufacturing Co.*, 555 S.W.2d 141, 142 (Tex. Civ. App.—Fort Worth 1977, writ ref'd n.r.e.), the defendant admitted not simply that process was received, but that it was "duly served." The distinction between actual receipt and proper service is precisely what gives rise to the issue we address here. We hold that a default judgment is improper against a defendant who has not been served in strict compliance with law, even if he has actual knowledge of the lawsuit. *See Higginbotham v. General Life & Acc. Ins. Co.*, 796 S.W.2d 695, 697 (Tex. 1990).

Finally, Wilson argues that Dunn has failed to preserve any complaint of defective service by not raising the issue in his motion for new trial. Rule 324 imposes no such requirement for preservation of such error. TEX. R. CIV. P. 324; *see Bronze & Beautiful, Inc. v. Mahone*, 750 S.W.2d 28, 29 (Tex. App.—Texarkana 1988, no writ); *American Universal Ins. Co. v. D.B. & B., Inc.*, 725 S.W.2d 764, 765 (Tex. App.—Corpus Christi 1987, writ ref'd n.r.e.). We hold that Dunn's complaint was preserved for appeal.

III

Accordingly, we conclude that the default judgment against Dunn was improper. We therefore affirm the judgment of the court of appeals reversing the judgment of the district court and remanding the case to that court for further proceedings.

Note

The Rules of Civil Procedure specifically authorize service of citation by publication in a number of situations. It is not a favored method of service for the simple reason that it is highly unlikely that a defendant will receive actual notice of the suit. The due process problems have been clearly identified. *See Mullane v. Central Hanover Bank & Trust Co.*, 339 U.S. 306, 70 S.Ct. 652 (1950). Texas courts do, however, apparently permit personal judgments to be rendered against resident defendants following service by publication if the requirements of the rules have been strictly complied with. *See generally Sgitcovich v. Sgitcovich*, 150 Tex. 398, 241 S.W.2d 142 (1959). In *Sgitcovich* the Court was faced with a problem concerning the due process requirements of substituted service upon a recalcitrant defendant. However, by way of *dicta* the Court *quoting* AMERICAN JURISPRUDENCE noted:

> However, a state has more control over the form of service upon its own residents than upon nonresidents, and when a resident defendant cannot be found and served personally within the forum, it is competent for the legislature to authorize the recovery of a personal judgment on the basis of substituted service made by leaving a copy of the process at his residence, by constructive service by publication, or by personal service outside the jurisdiction.

c. *Service upon Nonresidents*

Read Rule 108 of the Texas Rules of Civil Procedure

Notes

1. In *Paramount Pipe & Supply Co. v. Muhr*, 749 S.W.2d 491 (Tex. 1988) the court held that service under Rule 108 does not confer jurisdiction over non-resident defendants; however, the Court noted that the rule is a valid procedural alternative to service under the long-arm statute. The Court stated:

> First, Muhr complains of improper service of citation. Muhr admits he was served with citation in Arizona pursuant to TEX. R. CIV. P. 108. However, according to Muhr, service under Rule 108 was insufficient to subject him to personal jurisdiction in the district court below. We agree that service under Rule 108 does not, by itself, confer jurisdiction over non-resident defendants. However, Rule 108 is a valid procedural alternative to service under the long-arm statute. TEX. CIV. PRAC. & REM. CODE §§ 17.041-17.045 (Vernon 1986). We further reject Muhr's contention that Rule 108 impermissibly abridges substantive rights. *See* Carlson, *General Jurisdiction and the Exercise of In Personam Jurisdiction Under the Texas Long-Arm Statute*, 28 S. TEX. L. REV. 307, 328-30 (1986). So long as the allegations confronting Muhr were sufficient to satisfy due process requirements, the trial court had jurisdiction to render judgment by default against him. The only question, then, is whether the jurisdictional allegations in the petitions were sufficient, under the Constitution of the United States, to require Muhr to answer. TEX. R. CIV. P. 108.
>
> The petitions in both cases alleged that the defendants, including Muhr, engaged in business in Texas and further that the causes of action arose from and were connected with "purposeful acts committed by Defendant Western International Petroleum Corporation, acting for itself and as agent for Defendant Ulrich Muhr." The petitions went on to allege, in substance, that Western International made and breached contracts in Texas as Muhr's agent and on his behalf. These allegations against Western International (which, by default, admittedly was acting for Muhr) are sufficient to satisfy the rule stated in *Siskind v. Villa Foundation for Education, Inc.*, 642 S.W.2d 434 (Tex. 1982), and we perceive no due process violation. We conclude that the trial court did have in personam jurisdiction and constitutionally rendered judgments by default on the allegations made against Muhr.

2. A Texas court has authority to exercise personal jurisdiction over a nonresident when the nonresident was voluntarily within the state and was personally served with a properly issued citation while within the state, whether or not the cause of action was related to the activities while within the state. *See Flores v. Melo-Palacios*, 921 S.W.2d 399 (Tex. App.—Corpus Christi 1996, writ denied) [*relying upon Burnham v. Superior Court of Calif., County of Marin*, 110 S.Ct. 2105 (1990)].

3. Although substituted service will support a personal judgment against a nonresident, it is apparently clear in Texas that constructive service, such as by publication, will not confer jurisdiction on a court to enter a personal judgment against a nonresident. *See, e.g., Ex parte Limoges*, 526 S.W.2d 707 (Tex. Civ. App.—Austin 1975, no writ). Substituted service will, however, support an *in rem* judgment which declares only the status of a person or thing. *See, e.g., In re S.A.V. & K.E.V.*, 837 S.W.2d 80 (Tex. 1992) (noting that personal jurisdiction is necessary in order for a court to enter a valid personal judgment for child support, but that since custody determinations are status adjudications no personal jurisdiction is necessary over the parents).

4. Section 17.043 of the Texas Civil Practice and Remedies Code provides as follows:

Service on Persons In Charge Of Business.

If the cause of action arises out of a nonresident's business in this state, process may be served on the person in charge, at the time of service, of any business in which the nonresident is engaged in this state if the nonresident is not required by statute to designate or maintain a resident agent for service of process.

5. As noted above, Section 17.044 of the Texas Civil Practices and Remedies Code appoints the Secretary of State as the agent to receive service of citation for certain nonresidents. Section 17.045 of the Texas Civil Practices and Remedies Code requires that certain notice be given to nonresidents of the state after service upon the Secretary of State as follows:

(a) If the secretary of state is served with duplicate copies of process for a nonresident, he shall require a statement of the name and address of the nonresident's home or home office and shall immediately mail a copy of the process to the nonresident.

(b) If the secretary of state is served with process under Section 17.044(a)(3), he shall immediately mail a copy of the process to the nonresident (if an individual), to the person in charge of the nonresident's business, or to a corporate officer (if the nonresident is a corporation).

(c) If the person in charge of a nonresident's business is served with process under Section 17.043, a copy of the process and notice of the service must be immediately mailed to the nonresident or the nonresident's principal place of business.

(d) The process or notice must be sent by registered mail or by certified mail, return receipt requested.

(e) If the secretary of state is served with duplicate copies of process as an agent for a person who is a nonresident administrator, executor, heir, guardian, or personal representative of a nonresident, the secretary shall require a statement of the person's name and address and shall immediately mail a copy of the process to the person.

6. In *Capital Brick v. Fleming Mfg. Co.*, 722 S.W.2d 399 (Tex. 1986), the Court addressed some of the problems associated with service upon the Secretary of State. The Court held that actual personal service under the Texas Long Arm Statute was not required to be made on the Secretary of State. In *Capital Brick* a constable delivered a copy of the citation and a copy of the Plaintiff's Original Petition to the clerk having charge of the corporation division of the Secretary of State's office. The clerk stamped the constable's return and signed it. A certificate was prepared by the Secretary of State showing receipt of process, the date received, the address to which it was forwarded by certified mail, the date forwarded, and the date the return receipt was received in the office of the Secretary of State. This certificate was filed with the trial court on February 7, 1984. The defendant complained that service was not personally served on the Secretary of State as it argued was required by the long arm statute. The Court held that proof of service under the long-arm statute is satisfied by a certificate from the Secretary of State. The Court noted that the mode of service on the Secretary of State did not affect the defendant's due process rights. The court then stated that absent fraud or mistake, the Secretary of State's certificate was conclusive evidence that the Secretary of State, as agent of Fleming, had received service of process for Fleming and had forwarded the service as required by the statute.

7. In *Royal Surplus Lines Ins. Co. v. Samaria Baptist Church*, 840 S.W.2d 382 (Tex. 1992) the Secretary of State had forward the citation and attached copy of the petition to the wrong address. The Secretary's certificate reflected that citation was sent to "1201 Bassie." The address of Samaria's registered agent was listed in the Secretary's public records as "1201 Bessie." The envelope and receipt card from the Secretary which had been return as undeliverable had "Bassie" marked out and "Bessie" written in. The Court held that typographical error in the forwarding address typed by the Secretary is grounds to set aside a default judgment based on substituted service.

8. As the Secretary of State is deemed to be the agent of the nonresident, the time for filing an answer begins to run from the date of service on the Secretary of State, not the date upon which the defendant receives a copy of the petition and citation from the Secretary of State. *See Bonewitz v. Bonewitz*, 726 S.W.2d 227 Tex. App.—Austin 1987, writ dismissed).

9. *Fidelety Funding, Inc. v. Pollution Research and Control Corp.*, 1999 WL 20955 (N.D.Tex. 1999): Plaintiff argues that Defendant's time to remove should start to run from the time the Secretary of State was served. In response, Defendant asserts that the removal period commences once Defendant receives "actual" notice. Under Texas state procedural law, service is complete when the Secretary of State is served, not when a defendant receives notice. *Bonewitz v. Bonewitz*, 726 S.W.2d 227, 230 (Tex.App—Austin 1987, writ re'fd n.r.e.) (service under the long-arm statute). Once the Secretary of State forwards process to a defendant, the defendant is considered served even if the process is returned to the Secretary of State. *BLS Limousine Serv., Inc. v. Buslease, Inc.*, 680 S.W.2d 543, 546 (Tex.App.—Dallas 1984, writ ref'd n.r.e.) (process returned with the notation "refused"). Under federal law, however, the majority of courts have found that service on the Secretary of State is insufficient to commence the time period for removal under 28 U.S.C. § 1446. Rather, the time for removal is commenced when a defendant receives a copy of the pleading. *Id.* However, one federal court has recently held that the removal period begins from when the Secretary of State is served with process, not when

the defendant actually receives notice. *Bodden v. Union Oil Co. of Cal. & Life Ins. Co. of North America*, No. CIV. A. 97-3372, 1998 WL 88048 (E.D.La. February 20, 1998). In reaching this conclusion, the *Bodden* court determined that the policies recognized in the Fifth Circuit case, *Reece v. Wal-Mart Stores, Inc*., 98 F.3d 839 (5thCir.1996), "uniformity and expediency" are best recognized by an interpretation of the removal statute that permits the commencement of the thirty-day period on the date of formal service on the Secretary of State. *Id.*

10. *Hubicki v. Festina*, 226 S.W.3d 405 (Tex. 2007) involved a restricted appeal from a default judgment. Plaintiff-Festina made a single attempt to serve Defendant-Hubicki under TEX. R. CIV. P. 106(a) before moving for alternative service, under Rule 106(b). There is no evidence that Hubicki was actually receiving mail at the address Festina provided. Furthermore, the process server's affidavit in support of Festina's motion for alternative service stated that Hubicki was "currently in Mexico" and "can usually be found at Casa Tranquilidad . . . when he is in Mexico." But Festina did not attempt to serve Hubicki until almost a month later. And Festina's petition alleges that Hubicki had a "residence address" in Dallas. The trial court authorized substituted service by first class mail and by certified mail, return receipt requested, on Frank Hubicki, at a post-office box associated with a house he owns in Mexico. Hubicki did not answer, and the court rendered a default judgment against him for actual and punitive damages. ***Held:*** Reversed and remanded. As a matter of law, Festina failed to establish that alternative service at the Casa Tranquilidad address was reasonably calculated to provide Hubicki with notice of the proceedings, in time to answer and defend. Service under Rule 108a, used for foreign service, "must be reasonably calculated, under all of the circumstances, to give actual notice of the proceedings to the defendant in time to answer and defend."

WHITNEY
v.
L & L REALTY CORPORATION

500 S.W.2d 94
(Tex. 1973)

Andress, Woodgate & Lodewick, William Andress, Jr., Dallas, for petitioners.
Johnson, Bromberg, Leeds & Riggs, Richard L. Jackson and Robert H. Bliss, Dallas, for respondent.

GREENHILL, CHIEF JUSTICE.

These suits by a landlord to collect rent from former tenants raise a question concerning the proof needed to support a default judgment where service of process was upon the Secretary of State. The solution turns upon the construction, and the requirements as to service, of Article 2031b, the Texas long-arm statute. The immediate question is whether, as a matter of jurisdiction, the long-arm statute involved requires not only service upon the Secretary of State but also requires a showing in the record that he forwarded the service to the defendant. We hold that it does.

Plaintiff, L & L Realty Corporation, leased apartment in Dallas to defendants Whitney and Parnass for one year terms. During the term, defendants moved out of the state, abandoned their apartments, and ceased rental payments. Plaintiff took default judgments against them after serving process on Secretary of State of Texas, as authorized by Article 2031b. Nothing in the record indicates whether or not the Secretary of State forwarded a copy of the process to either defendant.

The defendants challenged the default judgments by a petition for writ of error in the Dallas Court of Civil Appeals. They contended that, under the statute, in the absence of proof that the Secretary of State forwarded the citations, the district court lacked personal jurisdiction. The Court of Civil Appeals overruled the contention and affirmed the default judgments. *Whitney*, 496 S.W.2d 120; *Parnass*, 482 S.W.2d 944. We reverse.

A petition for writ of error in the Court of Civil Appeals is a direct attack on the trial court's judgment. Consequently a recitation of due service in the judgment is not conclusive as it is in a collateral proceeding. In such a writ of error proceeding, the record must affirmatively show that the court had jurisdiction of the defendant's person. *Flynt v. City of Kingsville*, 125 Tex. 510, 82 S.W.2d 934 (1935).

A record showing of jurisdiction necessary to support a default judgment upon substituted service, such as we have here, must meet two major requirements: (1) The pleadings must allege facts which, if true, would make the defendant responsible to answer,—or in the language of Rule 120a, contain allegations making the defendant 'amenable to process' by the use of the long-arm statute; and (2) there must be proof in the record that the defendant was, in fact, served in the manner required by statute.

We have no problem here as to the responsibility to answer, or 'amenability to process.' The allegations are sufficient, under Section 6 of Art. 2031b, to require the defendants to answer if they have in fact been served in accordance with the requirements of that statute. *McKanna v. Edgar*, 388 S.W.2d 927 (Tex. 1965). The fact of service, however, must be shown by proof appearing in the record. *Flynt v. City of Kingsville*, 125 Tex. 510, 82 S.W.2d 934 (1935); *Roberts v. Stockslager*, 4 Tex. 307 (1849); *De Proy v. Progakis*, 269 S.W. 78 (Tex. Com. App. 1925, holding approved).

In the present case, the record includes a citation and return showing service on the Secretary of State, the official designated by statute as eligible to receive it. Thus the question is squarely presented whether this is sufficient to confer jurisdiction, or whether, under the statute, the record must show compliance with the additional statutory requirement that the Secretary forward a copy of the process to defendant.

Under the facts alleged by plaintiff here, defendants were amenable to service by virtue of Section 6 of Article 2031b. That section reads in part that such corporation or natural person 'may be served with citation by serving a copy of the process upon the Secretary of State . . . , who shall be conclusively presumed to be the true and lawful attorney to receive service of process; Provided that the Secretary of State shall forward a copy of such service to the person in charge of such business or an officer of such company, Or to such natural person by certified or registered mail, return receipt requested.'

We regard the statute as being ambiguous. It could be construed to mean that service is complete when the Secretary of State is served, whether the forwards the service or not; but that as the agent of the defendant, he ought to forward the service to the defendant. Or it could mean that the legislature intended to require that in order for the Secretary of State to be conclusively presumed to be the attorney for the defendant in another state, he Must forward the service; i.e., the Secretary of State is to be deemed the defendant's agent If, or Provided, he forwards the service as required by the statute.

We regard the latter as being the intent of the statute. It achieves a result most consistent with justice and due process to both parties. *Roberts v. Stockslager*, 4 Tex. 307 (1849).

Under this construction, a showing in the record that the Secretary of State forwarded a copy of the process is essential to establish the jurisdiction of the court over the defendants' persons. This was not shown, and hence no jurisdiction was acquired over the defendants.

The requirement of proof of forwarding of process which we construe the statute to impose will not cause any significant hardship to plaintiffs seeking judgments against non-residents. A certificate from the office of the Secretary of State, which the plaintiff could obtain for a trivial fee, would suffice. A contrary result would entail a much more serious hardship for defendants. If the Secretary fails to forward the process, the defendant will probably not learn of the suit until long after the time for filing a motion for new trial. If we held that proof of forwarding was not required to sustain a judgment on writ of error review, the defendant would then be relegated to his remedy by bill of review. This remedy would be less satisfactory than a trial at which he would have an opportunity to present his defenses because, in a bill of review proceeding, our cases say that the defendant would face the initial burden of proving at least that he had a good defense and that he was free from fault in failing to appear. *Hanks v. Rosser*, 378 S.W.2d 31 (Tex. 1964); *Alexander v. Hagedorn*, 148 Tex. 565, 226 S.W.2d 996 (1950).

Furthermore, requiring proof of forwarding is consistent with our decisions which have insisted on compliance with statutes conferring personal jurisdiction. To support a default judgment, our decisions require particularity in pleading amenability to service, *McKanna v. Edgar*, 388 S.W.2d 927 (Tex. 1965), and in showing the fact of service, *Roberts v. Stockslager*, 4 Tex. 307 (1849). These decisions reflect a strong policy that defendants ought not to be cast in personal judgment without notice. *See Roberts v. Stockslager*, 4 Tex. at 309. As Justice Oliver Wendell Holmes said, speaking of statutes authorizing service by publication, '. . . great caution should be used not to let fiction deny the fair play that can be secured only by a pretty close adhesion to fact.' *McDonald v. Mabee*, 243 U.S. 90, 91, 37 S.Ct. 343, 61 L.Ed. 608 (1917).

Our decision requires that the default judgments be set aside on the ground that the record fails to show that the district court acquired personal jurisdiction of the defendants. Accordingly, the judgments below are reversed, and the causes are remanded to the district court.

CAMPUS INVESTMENTS, INC.
v.
CULLEVER
144 S.W.3d 464
(Tex. 2004)

The evidence at the trial of this bill of review showed that a certificate of service from the Secretary of State was on file ten days before the underlying default judgment was granted, but citation and return were not. The First Court of Appeals held this was sufficient. ***Held:*** Affirmed. When substituted service on a statutory agent is allowed, the designee is not an agent for *serving* but for *receiving* process on the defendant's behalf. A certificate like the one here from the Secretary of State *conclusively* establishes that process was served. As the purpose of Rule 107 is to establish whether there has been proper citation and service, the Secretary's certificate fulfills that purpose.

Note

Kerlin v. Sauceda, 263 S.W.3d 920 (Tex. 2008): In 1829, the State of Tamaulipas, Mexico, recognized the claims of Padre Nicolas Balli and his nephew, Juan Jose Balli, to Padre Island. Since then, the island's ownership has been the subject of numerous legal disputes, including the present one. In this case, more than 275 descendants of Juan Jose Balli sued Gilbert Kerlin, individually and as trustee, as well as his wholly owned companies, Windward Oil & Gas Corp. and PI Corp., asserting that Kerlin had defrauded them of oil and gas royalties and other interests in Padre Island. Kerlin plead limitations. The trial court rendered judgment in the Balli' favor for unpaid royalties, mineral lease rentals, and prejudgment interest, and attorneys fees. The trial court imposed a constructive trust on an undivided 37.5% mineral interest, but denied the Ballis' request for an equitable accounting. The court of appeals affirmed except for the trial court's ruling denying an accounting, which it reversed and remanded to the trial court for further proceedings. 164 S.W.3d at 903. Held: Reversed and rendered. The Ballis' claims were not subject to statutory tolling and, accordingly, are time-barred. Section 16.063 of the Texas Civil Practice and Remedies Code provides that "[t]he absence from this state of a person against whom a cause of action may be maintained suspends the running of the applicable statute of limitations for the period of the person's absence." TEX. CIV. PRAC. & REM. CODE § 16.063. Thus, unless Kerlin was somehow present in the state for more than four years (and the jury found that he was not physically present for either a two or four year period) since the *Havre v. Dunn* settlement, limitations has not run on the Ballis' claims against him. The jury found that Kerlin was receiving royalty payments that rightfully belonged to the Ballis from January 1, 1966, until February 8, 1991, and that he continued to deceive the Ballis about the *Havre v. Dunn* settlement from its execution until the same date. Thus, whether or not Kerlin was constructively present in Texas, because he was subject to service of process via the secretary of state, he was present by doing business in this state as the statute defines that term. Because Kerlin was doing business here, and was thus not absent from Texas, the tolling statute does not apply, and limitations bars the Ballis' claims. Because the Ballis' claims are time barred, Kerlin's other arguments need not be addressed.

The general long-arm statute, TEX. CIV. PRAC. & REM. CODE § 17.044(b), provides that "the secretary of state is an agent for service of process on a nonresident who engages in business in this state . . . in any proceeding that arises out of the business done in this state . . . ." In addition to providing for substituted service, the general long-arm statute specifically addresses a nonresident defendant's presence within the state's territorial limits for purposes of personal jurisdiction; specifically, the statute provides that a nonresident does business "in this state" if, among other acts, the nonresident contracts with a Texas resident and either party is to perform in whole or in part here, or the nonresident commits a tort in whole or in part in this state. But if a nonresident's contacts with the state are sufficient to afford personal jurisdiction under the general long-arm statute then there is no reason why a nonresident's "presence" in this state would not be established for purposes of the tolling statute.

WOOD
v.
BROWN
819 S.W.2d 799
(Tex. 1991)

Clifton M. Freeman, Dallas, for petitioner.
Harry P. Stuth, Jr., Dallas, for respondent.

PER CURIAM.

This case presents the question whether respondent Thomas Brown met the prerequisites for securing proper citation by publication under Rule 109 of the Texas Rules of Civil Procedure.

Brown filed suit against Calvin Wood for personal injury claims arising out of an automobile accident. Brown attempted to personally serve Wood with citation but was unable to locate Wood in Oklahoma at his last known address. Brown then made service by publication. After Wood failed to answer Brown's complaint, the trial court rendered default judgment in favor of Brown. In an unpublished opinion, the court of appeals affirmed the default judgment against Wood.

In order to properly make service by publication a party must comply with Rule 109. Rule 109 provides in part: When a party to a suit, his agent or attorney, shall make oath that the residence of any party defendant is unknown to affiant, and to such party when the affidavit is made by his agent or attorney, or that such defendant is a transient person, and that after due diligence such party and the affiant have been unable to locate the whereabouts of such defendant, or that such defendant is absent from or is a nonresident of the State, and that the party applying for the citation has attempted to obtain personal service of nonresident notice as provided for in Rule 108, but has been unable to do so, the clerk shall issue citation for such defendant for service by publication. TEX. R. CIV. P. 109.

The court of appeals determined that the affidavit sworn by Brown's attorney complied with the rule, and the court upheld the default judgment against Wood. The record indicates, however, that the affidavit does not meet the requirements of Rule 109. In his affidavit, Brown's counsel stated that the Oklahoma sheriff who attempted to make service of citation on Wood informed counsel that Wood had moved from his last known address in Oklahoma and that neighbors thought that Wood had moved to Florida. The affidavit, however, does not state that Wood's residence was unknown to Brown's attorney, that Wood was a transient person, that Wood was absent from Texas or that Wood did not reside in Texas. Therefore, the affidavit sworn by Brown's attorney did not meet any of the requirements for service by publication under Rule 109.

A default judgment cannot withstand direct attack by a defendant who complains that he was not served in strict compliance with applicable requirements. *See Wilson v. Dunn*, 800 S.W.2d 833, 836 (Tex. 1990); *Uvalde Country Club v. Martin Linen Supply Co.*, 690 S.W.2d 884, 885 (Tex. 1985) (per curiam).

Accordingly, we grant the application for writ of error pursuant to Rule 170 of the Texas Rules of Appellate Procedure, and without oral argument, a majority of this court reverses the judgment of the court of appeals and remands the cause to the trial court for a trial on the merits.

In the Interest of E.R.
268 S.W.3d 552
(Tex. 2012)

Jeremy C. Martin, Malouf & Nockels LLP, Georganna L. Simpson, Georganna L. Simpson, P.C., Dallas, TX, for E.R.

Craig M. Watkins, Dallas County District Attorney, Michael R. Casillas, Kimberly Joy Duncan, Dallas County District Attorney's Office, Michael Chad Kotwal, Henry Wade Juvenile Justice Center, Dallas, TX, for State of Texas.

Jonathan F. Mitchell, Solicitor General, Office of the Attorney General, Arthur Cleveland D'Andrea, Assistant Solicitor General, for Amicus Curiae Solicitor General of Texas.

CHIEF JUSTICE JEFFERSON delivered the opinion of the Court.

When the State seeks to sever permanently the relationship between a parent and a child, it must first observe fundamentally fair procedures. The most basic of these is notice. If the State cannot deliver notice in person, it may try other means that will likely reach the parent. We consider today whether serving the parent in a newspaper advertisement, "a poor and sometimes a hopeless substitute for actual service," is constitutionally acceptable when the State knew the mother's identity, was in regular contact with her, and had at least one in-person meeting with her after it sued to terminate the legal rights to her children. We conclude that the substituted service was poor, hopeless, and unjustifiable under these circumstances.

But that does not end our inquiry. A parental rights termination proceeding encumbers a value "far more precious than any property right" and is consequently governed by special rules. We are faced not with the ordinary dispute about how to allocate money in a contract or tort action. We must decide how to reconcile a parent's desire to raise her child with the State's responsibility to promote the child's best interest. The Legislature and our courts have labored to ensure that proceedings to terminate a parent's legal relationship to her child are handled efficiently. To promote permanency in child rearing at the earliest stage possible, the Legislature has enacted a strict six-month deadline to challenge a termination judgment following citation by publication. For reasons we explain below, that strict time limit cannot foreclose a challenge when the parent has no constitutionally adequate notice of the proceeding. On the other hand, because a parent must remain vigilant with respect to her child's welfare, and because courts must always consider the child's best interest, a parent who learns about a judgment terminating the bonds to her child must act diligently to restore that right.

We reverse the court of appeals' judgment affirming the termination of parental rights. We remand the case to the trial court to determine whether the mother unreasonably failed to act after knowing that a final judgment had taken away her children, and if so, whether granting relief would impair another person's substantial interest in reliance on that judgment.

Several months after removing L.R.'s four children from her home and becoming their temporary managing conservator, the Department of Family Protective Services petitioned the trial court to terminate L.R.'s parental rights. After an unsuccessful attempt at personal service, the Department decided to serve L.R. by publication. Felicia Chidozie, the caseworker, prepared an affidavit summarizing her attempts to locate L.R. Although she had L.R.'s phone number, Chidozie said that L.R. told her that she was in the process of moving and did not have a permanent address. Chidozie ran a background check through IMPACT, which confirmed the address Chidozie already possessed. Chidozie also checked a website, www.anywho.com, and found no listing. Chidozie's call to the Texas Vine System was fruitless, and the Salvation Army refused on confidentiality grounds to answer her query. Chidozie faxed TXU Electric, Missing Person's Clearinghouse, Voter Registration, and Adult Probation, but received no responses in the two days between sending the faxes and filing her affidavit stating that L.R. could not be located. Finally, Chidozie called the "motor vehicle Tax Roles" but was told that it could locate information only from property or motor vehicle numbers. Based on this affidavit, the trial court authorized service by publication.

The Department published the citation, and the trial court conducted a final hearing. L.R. did not appear. The hearing transcript spans twelve double-spaced pages. Two witnesses testified: Chidozie and Erica Finley, the children's guardian and "aunt." Chidozie testified that she searched diligently for L.R. and signed an affidavit chronicling her efforts. She stated that L.R. had visited the children at the Department's offices a month before the termination hearing. Chidozie said that L.R. gave her a phone number but would not provide an address.

Chidozie contacted L.R. at that phone number and gave her information about court hearings. Chidozie testified that L.R. attended the hearings, but was tardy each time. Chidozie said L.R. had knowingly placed or knowingly allowed the children to remain in conditions or surroundings that endangered their physical or emotional well-being. According to Chidozie, the children were physically abused, and L.R. tested positive for methamphetamine when she gave birth to her youngest child. Chidozie testified that the children were doing well in Finley's home and that termination would be in their best interest. She stated that the Department's plan was to be named the permanent managing conservator and for the children to be adopted.

Finley testified that the children had been living with her for approximately six months, that they were happy, and that she planned to adopt them. Joe Rosenfield, the children's guardian ad litem, stated that Finley wanted the children, and they were doing well under her care. He opined that termination would be in the children's best interest.

Brenda Hull Thompson, who appeared as "publication attorney," stated that L.R. was served by publication and that publication was "ripe" on October 15, 2007. Thompson apparently never met with L.R. and learned for the first time at the hearing that L.R. had personally visited the children at the Department's offices. Thompson made no other statements about L.R., nor did she opine that termination would be in the children's best interest. The trial court terminated L.R.'s parental rights as well as those of the putative fathers, and it appointed the Department permanent managing conservator.

L.R. moved for a new trial within two years of the judgment. *See* TEX.R. CIV. P. 329(a) (authorizing trial court to grant motion for new trial filed within two years of judgment, if judgment rendered on service by publication and defendant did not appear in person or by attorney of her own selection). She complained that service by publication was obtained by fraud and was invalid because, among other things, she had been in regular, personal contact with Chidozie and visited the children at the Department offices during the time the Department was attempting to serve her. L.R. denied ever telling Chidozie that she did not have an address at which she could be served; instead, she asserted that she told Chidozie she did not have an address separate from her mother's, which Chidozie already had. L.R. also challenged Chidozie's affidavit.

The Department argued that L.R.'s motion was untimely because it was filed beyond Rule 329's two-year deadline. Chidozie disputed L.R.'s characterization of their conversation about her address, but Chidozie admitted that she met with L.R. in the Department's offices for a prescheduled meeting in August 2007. The Department did not cite the Family Code's six-month deadline for attacking termination decrees. The trial court denied the motion, and L.R. appealed.

In her appellate brief, L.R. included a footnote citing Family Code section 161.211 but argued that the matter was an affirmative defense that the Department waived by failing to raise it in the trial court, citing *In re Bullock,* 146 S.W.3d 783, 790-91 (Tex. App.—Beaumont 2004, no pet.). The Department's brief cited the same case and agreed that "[t]he six-month limitation in section 161.211 is an affirmative defense, which is waived if not presented to the trial court . . . . If the State's argument regarding the timeliness of the motion was not sufficient to invoke the six-month limitation in section 161.211, appellant's November 16, 2009 motion for new trial was timely under rule 329(a) . . . ."

Three months after briefing had been completed, the Department filed an amended brief, now arguing that section 161.211 absolutely barred challenges made more than six months after the order was signed, and that the court of appeals should not reach the merits because L.R.'s motion was untimely.

A divided court of appeals agreed. 335 S.W.3d 816. The court held that section 161.211's six-month deadline was dispositive: "The mandatory language of family code section 161.211 leaves no room for a construction other than a requirement that any collateral or direct attack on the termination of parental rights, including a motion for new trial, be filed no more than six months after the termination order is signed." *Id.* at 820. Because L.R.'s challenge was not filed within that period, it was barred. The court of appeals held that L.R. had not raised a constitutional challenge and thus had not preserved or presented the issue for review. *Id.* at 823.

The dissent concluded that the six-month deadline applied only to people who were *validly* served by publication. *Id.* at 827 (MURPHY, J., dissenting). Because service on L.R. was invalid, the deadline was inapplicable * * *

The dissent determined that L.R. was never validly served by publication because the Department had L.R.'s working phone number and a contact address, the caseworker met with L.R. during the time service by publication was being pursued, the Department knew the whereabouts of at least one relative, and Chidozie's affidavit was inconsistent with her live testimony. *Id.* at 832.

* * *

Citation by publication is a form of substituted service that, through a small notice published in the classified section of a local newspaper, is meant to apprise a defendant that her rights are at stake. Courts have accepted this method for more than a century. *See, e.g., Pennoyer v. Neff,* 95 U.S. 714, 727, 24 L.Ed. 565 (1877); *Harris v. Daugherty,* 74 Tex. 1, 11 S.W. 921, 922 (1889). Sixty years ago, however, the Supreme Court squarely addressed the practice's due process implications. *See Mullane v. Cent. Hanover Bank & Trust Co.,* 339 U.S. 306, 70 S.Ct. 652, 94 L.Ed. 865 (1950). *Mullane* remains the seminal case involving notice by publication, and it explains how to evaluate the adequacy of notice. *See* 4A CHARLES ALAN WRIGHT & ARTHUR R. MILLER, FEDERAL PRACTICE AND PROCEDURE § 1074, at 368 (3d ed.2002) (noting that *Mullane* "is recognized as the keystone of the modern philosophy regarding the due process aspects of a notice requirement and the importance of the case should not be underestimated"). We measure the constitutionality of notice using *Mullane*'s analytical framework, rather than *Mathews v. Eldridge*'s balancing test. *Dusenbery v. United States,* 534 U.S. 161, 167-68, 122 S.Ct. 694, 151 L.Ed.2d 597 (2002).

Mullane involved a common trust fund, a mechanism for pooling small trusts to simplify their administration. *Mullane,* 339 U.S. at 307-08, 70 S.Ct. 652. Under New York law, once such a fund had been established, its beneficiaries could be served by publication for four successive weeks. *Id.* at 309-10, 70 S.Ct. 652. Central Hanover established a common trust fund and petitioned the court for settlement of its first account as common trustee. *Id.* at 309, 70 S.Ct. 652. Central Hanover provided publication notice to beneficiaries. *Id.* A court-appointed attorney retained to represent the beneficiaries complained that notice by publication was constitutionally inadequate. *Id.* at 311, 70 S.Ct. 652.

The Supreme Court agreed. The Court observed that "[m]any controversies have raged about the cryptic and abstract words of the Due Process Clause but there can be no doubt that at a minimum they require that deprivation of life, liberty or property by adjudication be preceded by notice and opportunity for hearing appropriate to the nature of the case." *Id.* at 313, 70 S.Ct. 652. The Court noted that personal service was the classic form of notice "always adequate in any type of proceeding." *Id.* at 313-14, 70 S.Ct. 652. But personal service is not always necessary, and "[a] construction of the Due Process Clause which would place impossible or impractical obstacles in the way could not be justified." *Id.* But "when notice is a person's due, process which is a mere gesture is not due process." *Id.* at 315, 70 S.Ct. 652. * * *

For missing or unknown persons, service by this "indirect and even . . . probably futile" means did not raise due process concerns. *Id.* at 317, 70 S.Ct. 652. But as to a known beneficiary with a known address, the Court concluded, notice by publication was constitutionally defective because it was not "reasonably calculated, under all the circumstances, to apprise interested parties of the pendency of the action and afford them an opportunity to present their objections." *Id.* at 314, 319, 70 S.Ct. 652.

The Court revisited *Mullane* thirty-three years later in *Mennonite Board of Missions v. Adams,* 462 U.S. 791, 103 S.Ct. 2706, 77 L.Ed.2d 180 (1983). There, a landowner signed a mortgage in favor of the Mennonite Board of Missions. *Mennonite,* 462 U.S. at 792, 103 S.Ct. 2706. After the landowner failed to pay property taxes, the county began proceedings to sell the property. *Id.* at 794, 103 S.Ct. 2706. Indiana law required that notice be posted at the county courthouse and published for three consecutive weeks. *Id.* at 793, 103 S.Ct. 2706. Afterwards, the county could sell the property to the highest bidder. *Id.* After the auction, a two-year redemption period commenced during which those with an interest in the property could pay the delinquency. *Id.* Failing that, the purchaser acquired the deed. *Id.* at 794, 103 S.Ct. 2706.

The county published notice and auctioned the property. *Id.* Adams, as the high bidder, sued to quiet title to the property. *Id.* at 794-95, 103 S.Ct. 2706. Mennonite did not learn of the tax sale until after the redemption period had expired. *Id.* at 794, 103 S.Ct. 2706. Mennonite argued that publication notice of the tax sale was constitutionally inadequate. *Id.* at 795, 103 S.Ct. 2706. The Indiana courts rejected this argument, but the Supreme Court held that "unless the mortgagee is not reasonably identifiable, constructive notice [by publication] alone does not satisfy the mandate of *Mullane.*" *Id.* at 798, 103 S.Ct. 2706. The Court observed that Mennonite's identity was known, and it assumed that Mennonite's address could have been ascertained by reasonably diligent efforts. *Id.* at 798 n. 4, 103 S.Ct. 2706. The Court held that "[n]otice by mail or other means as certain to ensure actual notice is a minimum constitutional precondition to a proceeding which will adversely affect the liberty or property interests of *any* party, whether unlettered or well versed in commercial practice, if its name and address are reasonably ascertainable." *Id.* at 800, 103 S.Ct. 2706. The Court reversed the Indiana Court of Appeals' judgment and held that publication notice failed to provide Mennonite with due process.

* * *

From these decisions, we can distill a common principle: when a defendant's identity is known, service by publication is generally inadequate. *See, e.g.,* 1 RESTATEMENT (SECOND) OF JUDGMENTS § 2, reporter's note cmt. a (1982) ("Some courts still do not seem to have appreciated the thrust of *Mullane* .... The critical distinction is between notice to known claimants and notice to persons unknown. Notice by publication meets the requirement of adequate notice as to the latter but not as to the former.").

* * *

Mullane's due process requirements displace state statutes that restrict the time for challenging a judgment. * * *

Most state courts that have considered the issue have reached a similar conclusion: due process prevails over a state law time limit, even one imposed on challenges to termination of parental rights or adoptions.

With these principles in mind, we examine whether citation by publication was proper in this case. Parental rights are "far more precious than any property right," and when the State initiates a termination proceeding, "it seeks not merely to infringe that fundamental liberty interest, but to end it." *Santosky v. Kramer,* 455 U.S. 745, 758-59, 102 S.Ct. 1388, 71 L.Ed.2d 599 (1982). We carefully scrutinize termination proceedings, and we strictly construe involuntary termination statutes in the parent's favor. *Holick v. Smith,* 685 S.W.2d 18, 20 (Tex. 1985); *cf. United States v. Kiriaze,* 172 F.2d 1000, 1002 (5th Cir. 1949) ("When, then, the United States, as here, seeks not by actual notice to the citizen but by substituted service by publication to deprive him of this priceless right [of citizenship], it must strictly comply with the statute authorizing such service.").

Personal jurisdiction, a vital component of a valid judgment, is dependent "upon citation issued and served in a manner provided for by law." *Wilson v. Dunn,* 800 S.W.2d 833, 836 (Tex.1990). If service is invalid, it is "of no effect" and cannot establish the trial court's jurisdiction over a party. *Uvalde Country Club v. Martin Linen Supply Co.,* 690 S.W.2d 884, 885 (Tex. 1985) (per curiam). When judgment is rendered on service of process by publication, a party has two years to move for a new trial, which the trial court may grant for "good cause." TEX.R. CIV. P. 329(a). But if service was invalid, a party is entitled to a new trial without showing good cause.

The Family Code permits service by publication for individuals who cannot be served personally or through the mail, or if a person's name is unknown. TEX. FAM.CODE § 102.010(a). Citation by publication is served "as in other civil cases," *id.,* and the trial court must "inquire into the sufficiency of the diligence exercised in attempting to ascertain the residence or whereabouts of the defendant . . . before granting any judgment on such service." TEX.R. CIV. P. 109; *see also* TEX. FAM.CODE § 161.107(b) ("If a parent of the child has not been personally served in a suit in which the Department of Family and Protective Services seeks termination, the department must make a diligent effort to locate that parent."). A lack of diligence makes service by publication ineffective. *Anderson v. Collum,* 514 S.W.2d 230, 231 (Tex. 1974).

We have said that "[i]f personal service can be effected by the exercise of reasonable diligence, substituted service is not to be resorted to." *Sgitcovich v. Sgitcovich,* 150 Tex. 398, 241 S.W.2d 142, 147 (1951) (quoting 42 AM. JUR. § 65, p. 54). Yet we have never explained what a diligent search involves. * * *

A diligent search must include inquiries that someone who really wants to find the defendant would make, and diligence is measured not by the quantity of the search but by its quality. Even disregarding the factual dispute about what L.R. told Chidozie about her address, the uncontroverted evidence here establishes a lack of diligence. Chidozie neglected "obvious inquiries" a prudent investigator would have made. *In the Interest of S.P.,* 672 N.W.2d at 848. She did not contact L.R.'s mother, nor she did attempt service by mail in an effort to obtain a forwarding address. She did not pursue other forms of substituted service that would have been more likely to reach L.R., such as leaving a copy with L.R.'s mother. *See* TEX.R. CIV. P. 106(b)(1); *see also McDonald v. Mabee,* 243 U.S. 90, 92, 37 S.Ct. 343, 61 L.Ed. 608 (1917) ("To dispense with personal service the substitute that is most likely to reach the defendant is the least that ought to be required if substantial justice is to be done."). Even if L.R.'s address was not "reasonably ascertainable," an address was unnecessary for personal service on L.R. because she visited the Department's offices during the relevant time period. When a known parent has not left the jurisdiction, when she has attended at least two court hearings and has come to the Department offices for a prescheduled, hour-long meeting with her children during the very period service was being attempted, and when the Department can reach her by telephone and can communicate with her family members, service by publication cannot provide the kind of process she is due. Sending a few faxes, checking websites, and making three phone calls—none of which were to L.R. or her family members—is not the type of diligent inquiry required before the Department may dispense with actual service in a case like this. *Mullane* authorized service by publication when "it is not reasonably possible or practicable to give more adequate warning." *Mullane,* 339 U.S. at 317, 70 S.Ct. 652. Here, it was both possible and practicable to more adequately warn L.R. of the impending termination of her parental rights, and notice by publication was therefore constitutionally inadequate. *Jones v. Flowers,* 547 U.S. 220, 237, 126 S.Ct. 1708, 164 L.Ed.2d 415 (2006).

We must next decide the effect of the failure to provide adequate notice. Family Code section 161.211 provides that "the validity of an order terminating the parental rights of a person who is served by citation by publication is not subject to collateral or direct attack after the sixth month after the date the order was signed." TEX. FAM.CODE § 161.211(b). L.R. contends—as did the dissent below—that this bar applies only to parents for whom service by publication is valid. Failing that, L.R. argues that the statute is unconstitutional as applied to her.

Whether we conclude that the statute applies only if service was valid or that the statute is unconstitutional as applied to L.R., the reasoning and result are the same in this case. A complete failure of service deprives a litigant of due process and a trial court of personal jurisdiction; the resulting judgment is void and may be challenged at any time. * * * Accordingly, the statute cannot place a temporal limit on a challenge to a void judgment filed by a defendant who did not receive the type of notice to which she was constitutionally entitled. Despite the Legislature's intent to expedite termination proceedings, it cannot do so at the expense of a parent's constitutional right to notice. *Cf. In the Interest of M.N.,* 262 S.W.3d 799, 803 (Tex. 2008) (noting that Family Code did not indicate legislative intent to unfairly or unreasonably preclude parents from appealing final orders).

* * *

The Department's allegations against L.R. are serious, and if proven, may justify terminating her parental rights. But that determination cannot be made before she is given notice and the opportunity to be heard. Service by publication deprived L.R. of due process. She is entitled to a new trial unless she unreasonably delayed in seeking relief after learning of the judgment against her, and granting relief would impair another party's substantial reliance on the judgment. We reverse the court of appeals' judgment and remand to the trial court for further proceedings consistent with this opinion. TEX.R.APP. P. 60.2(d).

Notes

1. Any default judgment based upon service by publication is subject to being set aside by motion for new trial filed within two years of the signing of the default judgment.

2. Service by publication is available in rem actions. It is also available in personam actions against residents, but not on a non-resident.

CHAPTER 7.
VENUE: SELECTING AND MAINTAINING THE COUNTY OF SUIT

1. *Introduction*

Read Rules 86-89 Texas Rules of Civil Procedure

Notes

1. In the last two chapters the questions of the jurisdiction or power of the court to act with respect to the subject matter of the suit and the parties before it have been investigated. In this chapter the focus will turn from the power of the court to act, to a discussion of the location or situs from which that power can be exercised. In Texas the concept of venue refers the specific county in which the particular court is located. In Texas, the legislature has enacted various statutory provisions which establish the county in which a suit can be properly brought depending upon the type of lawsuit and the type of defendant. The Texas Supreme Court has also promulgated rules which govern venue proceedings.

2. Unlike subject matter jurisdiction, proper venue can be waived by a defendant by failing to timely object.[1] Furthermore, venue can be conferred by written agreement of the parties.[2]

3. Although venue places restrictions upon which of the 254 Texas counties a plaintiff may file a suit, it should be noted at the beginning of the Chapter that the present venue scheme in Texas vests the situs of the lawsuit in the hands of a well-informed plaintiff. A individual plaintiff by filing his lawsuit containing properly plead venue facts in a county of proper venue can defeat almost all attempts by a defendant to move the suit to another county [assuming that the defendant can get a fair and impartial trial in the county of suit or the county of suit is inconvenient for the parties]. In the following pages it will be shown that venue can be proper under the general rule, or certain mandatory provisions, or other permissive provisions. It should be noted at this point that many other statutes [other than the specific venue statute contained in Chapter 15 of the Texas Civil Practices and Remedies Code] provide that venue may be either mandatory or permissive in various types of statutory causes of action. Examples of some of these other venue statutes will be provided in this Chapter.

4. Students should be apprised that significant changes were made in the venue statutes first in 1984 and then again in 1995.

5. TEX. CONST. Art 5, Sec. 7. The State shall be divided into judicial districts, with each district having one or more Judges as may be provided by law or by this Constitution. Each district judge shall be elected by the qualified voters at a General Election and shall be a citizen of the United States and of this State, who is licensed to practice law in this State and has been a practicing lawyer or a Judge of a Court in this State, or both combined, for four (4) years next preceding his election, who has resided in the district in which he was elected for two (2) years next preceding his election, and who shall reside in his district during his term of office and hold his office for the period of four (4) years, and who shall receive for his services an annual salary to be fixed by the Legislature. The Court shall conduct its proceedings at the county seat of the county in which the case is pending, except as otherwise provided by law. He shall hold the regular terms of his Court at the County Seat of each County in his district in such manner as may be prescribed by law. The Legislature shall have power by General or Special Laws to make such provisions concerning the terms or sessions of each Court as it may deem necessary.

The Legislature shall also provide for the holding of District Court when the Judge thereof is absent, or is from any cause disabled or disqualified from presiding.

---

[1] *See* Rule 86.1 of the Texas Rules of Civil Procedure.

[2] *See* Farris v. Ray, 895 S.W.2d 351 (Tex. 1995).

ACEVEDO
v.
COMMISSION FOR LAWYER DISCIPLINE
131 S.W.3d 99
(Tex. App.—San Antonio 2004, pet. denied)

Facts: Attorney disciplinary action filed in Bexar County. Dallas judge appointed to hear the case. She granted a partial motion for summary judgment after a hearing conducted by telephone conference. She was in Dallas at the time. Acevedo did not respond to the motion, but did participate in the telephone hearing. Acevedo was later disbarred.

Issue: Is venue waivable? Yes. Venue is a matter of procedure.

Issue: Was the failure of the judge to hold the hearing in Bexar County reversible error under Art. V, Sec. 7, Tex. Const.?

Held: No. Fact that judge was in chambers in different county during hearing on this disciplinary proceeding, as opposed to an ordinary case, did not deprive her of jurisdiction. Because original jurisdiction over a disciplinary petition is vested in the Texas Supreme court, the county in which the disciplinary proceeding is actually conducted is a matter not of jurisdiction but of venue.

Issue: Must ordinary suits be tried in the county where they were case is pending? Yes. This is a matter of jurisdiction.

Under article V, section 7 of the Texas Constitution, a district court "shall conduct its proceedings at the county seat of the county in which the case is pending, except as otherwise provided by law." TEX. CONST. ART. V, § 7. This "county seat" requirement has been held to be jurisdictional, so that "[i]f a district court [sits] outside its jurisdictional geographic area, its proceedings [are] fundamentally defective and any order based on those proceedings [is] void." Conversely, if the judgment is not based upon "extra-territorial proceedings, the judgment is not void due to the out-of-county . . . proceedings." In cases filed after September 1, 1999, the restriction imposed by the "county seat" requirement contained in article V, section 7 is somewhat liberalized by section 74.094(e) of the Texas Government Code, which provides that "[a] judge who has jurisdiction over a suit pending in one county may, unless objected to by any party, conduct any of the judicial proceedings except the trial on the merits in a different county."

Because original jurisdiction over a disciplinary petition is vested in the Texas Supreme Court, the county in which the disciplinary proceeding is actually conducted is a matter not of jurisdiction but of venue.

2. *The General Venue Rule*

The General Rule of venue in Texas is contained in the following two statutory provisions of the Texas Civil Practice & Remedies Code.

§ 15.001. Definitions.

In this chapter:

(a) "Principal office" means a principal office of the corporation, unincorporated association, or partnership in this state in which the decision makers for the organization within this state conduct the daily affairs of the organization. The mere presence of an agency or representative does not establish a principal office.

(b) "Proper venue" means:

(1) the venue required by the mandatory provisions of Subchapter B [Civil Practice & Remedies Code § 15.011 et seq. specifying the mandatory venue provisions] or another statute prescribing mandatory venue; or

(2) if Subdivision (1) does not apply, the venue provided by this subchapter or Subchapter C. [Civil Practice & Remedies Code § 15.031 et seq. specifying permissive venue]

§ 15.002. Venue: General Rule

(a) Except as otherwise provided by this subchapter or Subchapter B or C, all lawsuits shall be brought:

(1) in the county in which all or a substantial part of the events or omissions giving rise to the claim occurred;

(2) in the county of defendant's residence at the time the cause of action accrued if defendant is a natural person;

(3) in the county of the defendant's principal office in this state, if the defendant is not a natural person; or

(4) if Subdivisions (1), (2), and (3) do not apply, in the county in which the plaintiff resided at the time of the accrual of the cause of action.

(b) For the convenience of the parties and witnesses and in the interest of justice, a court may transfer an action from a county of proper venue under this subchapter or Subchapter C to any other county of proper venue on motion of a defendant filed and served concurrently with or before the filing of the answer, where the court finds:

(1) maintenance of the action in the county of suit would work an injustice to the movant considering the movant's economic and personal hardship;

(2) the balance of interests of all the parties predominates in favor of the action being brought in the other county; and

(3) the transfer of the action would not work an injustice to any other party.

(c) A court's ruling or decision to grant or deny a transfer under Subsection (b) is not grounds for appeal or mandamus and is not reversible error.

SNYDER
v.
PITTS

150 Tex. 407, 241 S.W.2d 136
(1951)

King Fike, Dalhart, Storey, Storey & Donaghey, Vernon, John D. Aikin, Mel R. Aikin and James W. Witherspoon, Hereford, J. H. Hart, Austin, for petitioners.
F. H. Richards, Dalhart, for respondent Earl Johnson.

WILSON, JUSTICE.

The question here is whether a defendant has established a second residence apart from his domicile within the meaning of the first sentence of art. 1995, R.C.S., Vernon's Ann. Civ. St. art. 1995. It arises in a suit involving a contract with a defense of accord and satisfaction. Both the trial court and the Court of Civil Appeals (with dissent) held that a second residence had been established and overruled the plea of privilege.[1] The defendants in the trial court (relators here) contend there is "no evidence" to support the trial court's judgment. See the opinion of the Court of Civil Appeals as reported in *Snyder v. Johnson*, 237 S.W.2d 741, for a detailed statement of the facts. The parties will be referred to as in the trial court.

Briefly, defendant Cecil Snyder was domiciled at Vernon in Wilbarger County where he had a permanent home with homestead exemption from taxes in which his wife lived and where he voted, paid his taxes, did his banking, and registered his automobile. He and a partner (his co-defendant), whose residence is not in issue here constructed approximately twenty-five houses and other buildings as a business in Dallam, Sherman and Hartley Counties, Texas, and in Oklahoma and Kansas. While supervising this construction for a period of fifteen

[1] Under Rule 86 of the Texas Rules of Civil Procedure the pleading of the Defendant to seek to change venue to another county from the one in which the lawsuit was originally filed is now referred to as a Motion to Transfer Venue.

months from a business headquarters in Dalhart, Dallam County, defendant Snyder had a room at a hotel part of the time and in a private residence part of the time. He spent most of his time in Dalhart during the weekend, according to his brief, "commuted" to Vernon on the weekends, holidays, and when "his work did not require his presence in Dallam County." On one occasion his wife visited him for a day or two in Dalhart.

* * *

The first sentence of art. 1995 provides that an inhabitant of this state shall be sued in the "county in which he has his domicile." By a series of early decisions it was established that the word domicile as used in the first sentence of the present art. 1995 did not mean domicile but rather meant residence.

* * *

Thus our problem narrows to that of determining whether there is any evidence in the case at bar which will support the trial court's judgment establishing a second residence in a different county from an established domicile.

Since a residence is a lesser-included element within the technical definition of domicile, *Evans v. American Pub. Co.*, 118 Tex. 433, 13 S.W.2d 358, we should start with the technical definition of domicile and eliminate as a test for a second residence those things which can be done only at a domicile. *In Taylor v. Wilson, supra*, where the defendant was admittedly domiciled in New York, the Supreme Court said: ". . . Decisions of this court holding that the terms 'domicile' and 'inhabitant' used in the first clause mean, respectively, the same things as 'residence' and 'resident,' have relieved the question before us of much of the difficulty which otherwise would attend it. *Brown v. Boulden*, 18 Tex. 434; *Pearson v. West*, 97 Tex. (238) 243, 77 S.W. 944. The certificate states that the defendant had a residence in Jefferson county, Tex., and, as citizenship and legal domicile within the state are not, according to the decisions referred to, essential to the privilege given by the first provision of the statute, he clearly falls within it, and is entitled to that privilege." (99 Tex. 651, 93 S.W. 110.)

The elements of the legal concept of domicile are:

1. An actual residence—
2. The intent to make it the permanent home.

The word home seems to mean a "true fixed and permanent home and principal establishment, and to which, whenever he is absent, he has the intention of returning." *Ex Parte Blumer*, 27 Tex. 734; *Switzerland Gen. Ins. Co. v. Gulf Ins. Co.*, Tex. Civ. App., 213 S.W.2d 161.

From the fact that there can be but one domicile and several residences, we arrive at the conclusion that the element of "intent to make it a permanent home" is not necessary to the establishment of a second residence away from the domicile.

The dissent of one member of the Court of Civil Appeals in the case at bar cites a line of Civil Appeals cases making the presence of the wife a test to determine whether or not a second residence has been established in so far as a married man is concerned. *Devereaux v. Rowe*, Tex. Civ. App. 1927, 293 S.W.2d 207. These cases are based upon an election statute, art. 2958, R.C.S., which states that the residence of a married man is the place where his wife resides. Since this statute defines the place a married man can vote and since a person cannot vote in but one county, this statute can have no application to our problem because obviously under art. 2958 a married man can have but one residence for voting purposes,—actually his domicile. *Wright v. Marquis*, Tex. Civ. App., 255 S.W. 637; *Major v. Loy*, Tex. Civ. App., 155 S.W.2d 617. There is no need to discuss the complications involved in this definition except to state generally that, in so far as this line of cases uses art. 2958 for a definition of residence, it amounts to a return to the legal concept of domicial and is, therefore, when used in construing art. 1995, no authority on this question because contrary in principle to *Brown v. Boulden*. *In Agey v. Red Star Supply Co.*, Tex. Civ. App. 1938, 113 S.W.2d 212, 213 (relied on by defendant in the case at bar to establish a conflict), although not citing art. 2958 or *Devereaux v. Rowe, supra*, the court makes the flat statement that the "residence" of a married man, unless permanently separated from his wife, is where his wife resides. This is not necessarily true if it be construed as establishing this point as a matter of law. It is in conflict with the decision of the Supreme Court in *Taylor v. Wilson, supra*, and is for that reason an incorrect statement of law. The same Court of Civil Appeals which wrote the opinion in the *Devereaux* case had previously written on this subject in *Benavides v. Gussett*, 8 Tex. Civ. App. 198, 28 S.W. 113, where its discussion is clearly contrary to *Brown v. Boulden*. Its opinion in *Pearson v. West*, Tex. Civ. App., 75 S.W. 334, was based upon *Benavides v. Gussett* and was reversed by the Supreme Court, 97 Tex. 238, 77 S.W. 944. What is said here about art. 2958 is said only to illustrate the mistake in *Devereaux v. Rowe* and related cases and is not a construction of art. 2958 as that statute is not in issue here.

Leaving aside any consideration of art. 2958, the presence of the wife living in a second place of abode is certainly evidence of the establishment of a second residence apart from a domicile, *Pearson v. West, supra*; *Caprito v. Weaver*, Tex. Civ. App. 1933, 63 S.W.2d 1043; *Wrenn v. Brooks*, Tex. Civ. App., 1924, 257 S.W. 299; *Kelly v. Egan*, Tex. Civ. App. 1911, 143 S.W. 1183; *Funk v. Walker*, Tex. Civ. App. 1922, 241 S.W. 720; but the failure of the wife to live in a second place of abode does not as a matter of law prevent it from becoming a second residence. *Taylor v. Wilson, supra; International & G. N. R. Co. v. Elder*, 1907, 44 Tex. Civ. App. 605, 99 S.W. 856; *Latham v. Continental Supply Co.*, Tex. Civ. App. 1921, 230 S.W. 230. Conversely, neither does the presence of the wife in the second place of abode for a considerable period of time establish a second residence as a matter of law. *Bolton v. Alley*, Tex. Civ. App. 1929, 25 S.W.2d 638; *Dixon v. McDonald*, Tex. Civ. App., 1939, 130 S.W.2d 884. Thus we find that the presence or absence of the wife in a second place of abode away from a domicile is not conclusive and does not determine the question of a second residence as a matter of law one way or the other, but is simply evidence to be considered. *Littlefield v. Clayton Bros.*, Tex. Civ. App. 1917, 194 S.W. 194.

A second residence away from a domicile within the meaning of the first sentence of art. 1995 must include the following elements:

1. A fixed place of abode within the possession of the defendant
2. Occupied or intended to be occupied consistently over a substantial period of time
3. Which is permanent rather than temporary.

Here defendant Snyder rented a room at a hotel for a period and then moved to a room rented in a private home. A rented room may be a residence under art. 1995. *Wilson v. Bridgeman, supra; International & G. N. Ry. Co. v. Elder, supra; Gilmer v. Graham*, Tex. Civ. App. 1930, 26 S.W.2d 687; *Kerr v. Davenport*, Tex. Civ. App. 1950, 233 S.W.2d 197. For a place of abode to become a residence under the first sentence of art. 1995 the defendant must have some right of possession and not be a mere visitor. The payment of rent satisfies this requirement. *Burns v. Napier*, Tex. Civ. App. 1929, 19 S.W.2d 578. Hence we hold there is some evidence upon the first element of residence to support the trial court.

Defendant Snyder spent about five days a week in Dalhart for about two years. In *Pearson v. West, supra*, the defendant spent about 6 months of each year in each residence. In *Caprito v. Weaver, supra*, a fact issue on residence was raised by a defendant spending all of 6 or 7 weeks together with his family in a second place of abode. In *Wilson v. Bridgeman, supra*, the defendant established a second residence in part of one year. In *Bolton v. Alley, supra*, a fact issue on residence was raised by defendant spending 1/4 of his time and his wife spending 2/3 of her time for a period of 2 years. In *Wrenn v. Brooks, supra*, the defendant established a residence by spending "most" of 18 months in a county. In *International & G. N. Ry. v. Elder, supra*, a residence was established by spending all of one year. In *Kelly v. Egan, supra*, defendant established a residence by spending all of 6 months. In *Taylor v. Wilson, supra*, the defendant established a residence in 14 months. In *Littlefield v. Clayton Bros., supra*, defendant established a second residence by spending from one to three days at a time every ten days or two weeks. In *Gilmer v. Graham, supra*, defendant established a second residence by staying from "ten to twenty days at the time." (26 S.W.2d 690.) In *Funk v. Walker, supra*, defendant established a residence by being present about one to five days twice a month over a period of one year and three months. In *Kerr v. Davenport, supra*, defendant established a residence in Bexar County by being present about one third of the time over a period of three years. By citing these cases, we do not necessarily approve each holding. We cite them to demonstrate the weight of authority on this point.

We conclude that there is some evidence to support the trial court's judgment upon the second element of residence, and that we cannot hold as a matter of law that 5 days a week with some interruptions over a fifteen-month period is not enough to establish a second residence.

The third element involves the question of whether the place of abode is permanent or temporary. In *Dixon v. McDonald, supra*, the court held that the proprietor of a traveling skating rink which had been operating in Beaumont for about two months had not established a residence under art. 1995 although he rented an apartment and had his family with him. The court held that defendant's stay in Beaumont was temporary and that "When he moved to a new location there was no fixed purpose on his part to return" (130 S.W.2d 885.) to Beaumont. The case of *Harrison v. Ward*, Tex. Civ. App. 1923, 277 S.W. 445, held that the stay of a cotton buyer in Corpus

Christi who bought cotton during the season (July through November) was temporary, hence no residence established.

In the case at bar the defendant Snyder had been regularly and consistently commuting between his room in Dalhart and his home in Vernon for a period of fifteen months at the time the plea of privilege was filed and for two years at the time it was tried. The question of whether a stay is temporary or permanent is a question of intent to be proved by declarations and acts. *O'Connor v. Cook*, Tex. Civ. App. 1894, 26 S.W. 1113; *Gulf Coast & S. F. R. Co. v. Rogers*, 1903, 37 Tex. Civ. App. 99, 82 S.W. 822. Here the defendant Snyder made excursions out from Dalhart and returned. It was headquarters for his business. Under the facts here there is no dispute that defendant Snyder had not abandoned his plan for living part time in Dalhart. *Faires v. Young, supra; Cross v. Johns*, Tex. Civ. App. 1922, 238 S.W. 354; *Seale v. Garvey*, Tex. Civ. App. 1923, 247 S.W. 672; *Eppenauer v. Schrup*, Tex. Civ. App. 1938, 121 S.W.2d 473.

Defendant Snyder occupied consistently and with continuity a fixed place of abode in Dalhart in such a manner that the trial court could find that he had ceased to be a visitor and that the proof supplied this element of the definition of a resident. Therefore we conclude that the trial court had some evidence upon which to base a finding that defendant's second residence in Dalhart was permanent and not temporary.

* * *

Having determined that there is some evidence to support the trial court's finding that the defendant Snyder has established a residence in Dallam County under the first sentence of art. 1995, we do not pass upon other questions brought forward.

* * *

Notes

1. *§ 15.006. Venue Determined by Facts Existing at the Time of Accrual.* A court shall determine the venue of a suit based on the facts existing at the time the cause of action that is the basis of the suit accrued.

2. *Smith v. Farmer.*[1] A person whose home is built on the county line between two counties is a resident of both counties and may be sued in either.

3. *Mijares v. Paze.*[2] In this paternity action brought in Lubbock County, the defendant, a university student, who lived in university housing, was found to be a resident of Lubbock for venue purposes, even though he claimed El Paso as the county of his domicile. The court of appeals held:

> Furthermore, the defendant could be a resident of Lubbock County for venue purposes even if his domicile were elsewhere. Although a person may have only one domicile, he may establish more than one residence for venue purposes. Even a rented room may qualify and the intent to make a permanent home is not necessary to the establishment of a second residence away from the domicile. *Snyder v. Pitts*, 150 Tex. 407, 241 S.W.2d 136 (1951). In *Snyder*, the Supreme Court announced a three element test to determine whether a second residence away from a domicile has been established. The proof must show that (1) the defendant possesses a fixed place of abode, (2) occupied or intended to be occupied consistently over a substantial period of time, (3) which is permanent rather than temporary.
>
> The court in *Ward v. Lavy*, 314 S.W.2d 381 (Tex. Civ. App.—Eastland 1958, no writ) applied the *Snyder* test to facts similar to those before us. It held that a student at Hardin-Simmons University located in Taylor County had established residence in Taylor County for venue purposes by virtue of his enrollment in that university with the intention of remaining one or two years together with his rental of an apartment there.

---

[1] 226 S.W. 485 (Tex. Civ. App.—Austin Dec 15, 1920).

[2] 534 S.W.2d 435, 436-437 (Tex. Civ. App.—Amarillo 1976, no writ).

3. *Exceptions to the General Venue Rule*

a. *Mandatory Venue*

The general rule is subject to various mandatory exceptions. The mandatory venue exceptions provide that an action "shall be brought" in a particular county. Mandatory venue exceptions trump the general rule, as well as the permissive exceptions discussed below. Therefore, if a plaintiff relies upon a permissive exception or the general rule, a defendant should be able [assuming that he complies with the rules of Texas Civil Procedure and does not waive the mandatory venue exception] to transfer a case to a county of mandatory venue. However, if a mandatory venue provision applies to the case, a well-informed plaintiff can prevent a defendant from transferring the case to another county by filing suit in the county of mandatory venue. The mandatory venue exceptions found in Subchapter B of Chapter 15 of the Texas Civil Practice and Remedies Code are:

§ 15.011. Land

Actions for recovery of real property or an estate or interest in real property, for partition of real property, to remove encumbrances from the title to real property, for recovery of damages to real property, or to quiet title to real property shall be brought in the county in which all or a part of the property is located.

§ 15.0115. Landlord—Tenant

(a) Except as provided by another statute prescribing mandatory venue, a suit between a landlord and a tenant arising under a lease shall be brought in the county in which all or a part of the real property is located.

(b) In this section, "lease" means any written or oral agreement between a landlord and a tenant that establishes or modifies the terms, conditions, or other provisions relating to the use and occupancy of the real property that is the subject of the agreement.

§ 15.012. Injunction Against Suit.

Actions to stay proceedings in a suit shall be brought in the county in which the suit is pending.

§ 15.013. Injunction Against Execution of Judgment.

Actions to restrain execution of a judgment based on invalidity of the judgment or of the writ shall be brought in the county in which the judgment was rendered.

§ 15.014. Head of State Department.

An action for mandamus against the head of a department of the state government shall be brought in Travis County.

§ 15.015. Counties.

An action against a county shall be brought in that county.

§ 15.016. Other Mandatory Venue.

An action governed by any other statute prescribing mandatory venue shall be brought in the county required by that statute.

§ 15.017. Libel, Slander, or Invasion of Privacy.

A suit for damages for libel, slander, or invasion of privacy shall be brought and can only be maintained in the county in which the plaintiff resided at the time of the accrual of the cause of action, or in the county in which the defendant resided at the time of filing suit, or in the county of the residence of defendants, or any of them, or the domicile of any corporate defendant, at the election of the plaintiff.

§ 15.018. Federal Employers' Liability Act.

(a) This section only applies to suits brought under the federal Employers' Liability Act (45 U.S.C. Section 51 et seq.).

(b) All suits brought under the federal Employers' Liability Act shall be brought:

(1) in the county in which all or a substantial part of the events or omissions giving rise to the claim occurred;

(2) in the county where the defendant's principal office in this state is located; or

(3) in the county where the plaintiff resided at the time the cause of action accrued.

§ 15.0181. Jones Act

(a) In this section:

(1) "Coastal county" means:

(A) a county in a coastal area, as defined by Section 33.004, Natural Resources Code; or

(B) a county having a United States Customs port through which waterborne freight is transported.

(2) "Coastal erosion" means the loss of land, marshes, wetlands, beaches, or other coastal features because of the actions of wind, waves, tides, storm surges, subsidence, or other forces.

(3) "Erosion response project" means an action intended to address or mitigate coastal erosion, including beach nourishment, sediment management, beneficial use of dredged material, creation or enhancement of a dune, wetland, or marsh, and construction of a breakwater, bulkhead, groin, jetty, or other structure.

(4) "Gulf Coast state" means Louisiana, Mississippi, Alabama, or Florida.

(5) "Inland waters" means the navigable waters shoreward of the navigational demarcation lines dividing the high seas from harbors, rivers, the Gulf Intracoastal Waterway, and other inland waters of Texas, Louisiana, Mississippi, Alabama, Arkansas, Tennessee, Missouri, Illinois, Kentucky, or Indiana or of Florida along the Gulf of Mexico shoreline of Florida from the Florida-Alabama border down to and including the shoreline of Key West, Florida. The term does not include the Great Lakes.

(b) This section applies only to suits brought under the Jones Act (46 U.S.C. Section 30104).

(c) Except as provided by this section, a suit brought under the Jones Act shall be brought:

(1) in the county where the defendant's principal office in this state is located;

(2) in the county in which all or a substantial part of the events or omissions giving rise to the claim occurred; or

(3) in the county where the plaintiff resided at the time the cause of action accrued.

(d) If all or a substantial part of the events or omissions giving rise to the claim occurred on the inland waters of this state, ashore in this state, or during the course of an erosion response project in this state, the suit shall be brought:

(1) in the county in which all or a substantial part of the events giving rise to the claim occurred; or

(2) in the county where the defendant's principal office in this state is located.

(e) If all or a substantial part of the events or omissions giving rise to the claim occurred on inland waters outside this state, ashore in a Gulf Coast state, or during the course of an erosion response project in a Gulf Coast state, the suit shall be brought:

(1) in the county where the defendant's principal office in this state is located if the defendant's principal office in this state is located in a coastal county;

(2) in Harris County unless the plaintiff resided in Galveston County at the time the cause of action accrued;

(3) in Galveston County unless the plaintiff resided in Harris County at the time the cause of action accrued; or

(4) if the defendant does not have a principal office in this state located in a coastal county, in the county where the plaintiff resided at the time the cause of action accrued.

§ 15.019. Inmate Litigation

(a) Except as provided by Section 15.014, an action that accrued while the plaintiff was housed in a facility operated by or under contract with the Texas Department of Criminal Justice shall be brought in the county in which the facility is located.

(b) An action brought by two or more plaintiffs that accrued while the plaintiffs were housed in a facility operated by or under contract with the Texas Department of Criminal Justice shall be brought in a county in which a facility that housed one of the plaintiffs is located.

(c) This section does not apply to an action brought under the Family Code.

§ 15.020. Major Transactions: Specification of Venue by Agreement

(a) In this section, "major transaction" means a transaction evidenced by a written agreement under which a person pays or receives, or is obligated to pay or entitled to receive, consideration with an aggregate stated value equal to or greater than $1 million. The term does not include a transaction entered into primarily for personal, family, or household purposes, or to settle a personal injury or wrongful death claim, without regard to the aggregate value.

(b) An action arising from a major transaction shall be brought in a county if the party against whom the action is brought has agreed in writing that a suit arising from the transaction may be brought in that county.

(c) Notwithstanding any other provision of this title, an action arising from a major transaction may not be brought in a county if:

(1) the party bringing the action has agreed in writing that an action arising from the transaction may not be brought in that county, and the action may be brought in another county of this state or in another jurisdiction; or

(2) the party bringing the action has agreed in writing that an action arising from the transaction must be brought in another county of this state or in another jurisdiction, and the action may be brought in that other county, under this section or otherwise, or in that other jurisdiction.

(d) This section does not apply to an action if:

(1) the agreement described by this section was unconscionable at the time that it was made;

(2) the agreement regarding venue is voidable under Section 35.52, Business & Commerce Code; or

(3) venue is established under a statute of this state other than this title.

(e) This section does not affect venue and jurisdiction in an action arising from a transaction that is not a major transaction.

Notes

1. Mandatory venue provisions control over the general venue provisions and over the permissive venue provisions. The phrase "mandatory venue" is misleading. It should really read "insistable venue," since it waivable.

2. Under the pre-1983 art. 1995, the mandatory and permissive venue provisions were mixed together. Twenty-three sub-divisions provided that suit "may" be brought in designated counties. These were the permissive provisions. The remainder, providing that suits "must" or "shall" be brought in designated counties, were mandatory. Now, there are six express mandatory provisions, and a seventh catch-all provision.

The mandatory venue provisions are of paramount importance in multiple party cases, for if one of the claims is governed by a mandatory venue provision, and "the claims or causes of action arise from the same transaction, occurrence, or series of transactions or occurrences," then the suit must "be brought in the county required by the mandatory venue provision." TEX. CIV. PRAC. & REM. CODE § 15.004. Stated another way, any of the joined defendants can insist upon the transfer of the case to the county of mandatory venue, if it arises out of the same transaction, and if the plaintiff fails to bring suit there originally.

3. Contractual provisions establishing venue in a stated county are generally against public policy, and are considered to be void and unenforceable. *See Leonard v. Paxson*, 654 S.W.2d 440 (Tex. 1983); *Fidelity Union Life Ins. Co. v. Evans*, 477 S.W.2d 535 (Tex. 1972).

4. Once a lawsuit has been filed the parties have the authority to consent to a transfer of venue to another county. Such action would be a waiver of the right of either party to complain on appeal concerning venue. *See In re Omni Hotels Management Corp.*, 159 S.W.3d 627 (Tex. 2005).

ACKER
v.
DENTON PUBLISHING COMPANY

937 S.W.2d 111
(Tex. App—Fort Worth 1996, no writ)

Gary L. Acker, Flower Mound, for appellant.
J. Shelby Sharpe, Fort Worth, for appellees.

HOLMAN, JUSTICE.

Gary Lewis Acker, pro se, appeals the summary judgment of a district court in Denton County that he take nothing on claims by which he sought $9.6 million in damages for alleged injury from newspaper articles written about him. Acker asserted causes of action for defamation, invasion of privacy, and deceptive trade practices. One defendant, Denton Publishing Company, publishes three newspapers, the Lewisville News, the Denton Record-Chronicle, and the Grapevine Sun. Other defendants were Fred W. Patterson, an officer of the publishing company, Fred W. Patterson, Jr., general manager of the publishing company, Tom Bateman, a vice president, Roy Appleton, a director, Cynthia Baker and James Florez, staff writers, and Dawn Cobb, managing editor of the Lewisville News. Finding no reversible error, we affirm.

Although there are seven points of error, we will not address them in numerical order. Instead, we will consider them in the chronological order in which the issues arose.

We begin with the complaint of the third point, that venue was erroneously transferred from Tarrant County to Denton County. This suit originated on August 7, 1995 in the 96th Judicial District Court, Tarrant County, where the defendants answered subject to their motion to transfer venue to Denton County. Mr. Acker is a resident of Denton County.

In the motion to transfer, the defendants asserted that venue in Denton County was mandated by TEX. CIV. PRAC. & REM. CODE ANN. s 15.017 (Vernon 1986). The motion recited that Denton Publishing Company is a corporation domiciled in Denton County, where its registered office and registered agent are located. The motion stated that all the defendant individuals except Tom Bateman reside in Denton County, where causes of action asserted by Mr. Acker allegedly arose. Although Tom Bateman works in Denton County, the motion concedes that he resides in Tarrant County where Mr. Acker filed suit. The portion of Section 15.017 that applies to the facts of this case is: A suit for damages for libel, slander, or invasion of privacy shall be brought and can only be maintained in the county in which the plaintiff resided at the time of the accrual of the cause of action . . . or in the county of the residence of defendants, or any of them, . . . at the election of the plaintiff. TEX. CIV. PRAC. & REM. CODE ANN. § 15.017 (Vernon 1986). Section 15.017 is a "mandatory" venue provision. *See* TEX. R. CIV. P. 87.2(a).

The defendants supported their motion with affidavits of Fred W. Patterson, Jr. and Tom Bateman, and because they sought to transfer venue to Denton County, the defendants had the burden to prove venue facts showing that venue was maintainable in Denton. *Id.* Venue facts for defendants to prove under Section 15.017 were: (1) that the causes of action alleged include libel, slander, or invasions of privacy; (2) that Mr. Acker resided in Denton County at the time the alleged causes accrued; (3) that all defendants reside in Denton, not Tarrant; and (4) that Tom Bateman, a resident of Tarrant, is not a proper defendant in this suit.

On the other hand, Mr. Acker had the burden to prove venue facts showing that venue was maintainable in Tarrant. TEX. R. CIV. P. 87.2(a). To meet his burden of proof and maintain the venue of this suit in the 96th District Court in Tarrant County under Section 15.017, Mr. Acker had to prove only two venue facts: (1) the causes of action alleged include libel, slander, or invasion of privacy; and (2) a defendant resides in Tarrant County.

Here, the 96th District Court in Tarrant County was required to resolve the defendants' venue challenge from the plaintiff's pleadings, the defendants' pleadings, and the affidavits filed by two of the defendants. TEX. CIV. PRAC. & REM. CODE ANN. § 15.064(a) (Vernon 1986); TEX. R. CIV. P. 87.3(b). From the pleadings, that court could reasonably conclude that two of Mr. Acker's causes of action were libel and invasion of privacy.

From the defendants' motion to transfer, that court could reasonably conclude that the motion was grounded upon the mandatory provision of Section 15.017.

Other than his pleadings, Mr. Acker did not offer the 96th District Court any proof that would support venue in Tarrant County. He did not file any affidavit, and his reply to the defendants' affidavits and motion to transfer venue consisted of bare conclusions that the motion was "premature and inappropriate" and that venue in Tarrant County could be established once discovery was completed. When a defendant pleads a venue fact and the plaintiff fails to specifically deny it, the trial court is required to consider that venue fact true. TEX. R. CIV. P. 87.3.(a).

Nevertheless, the first venue fact that Mr. Acker had to prove—that some of his causes of action were within the scope of Section 15.017—was established by the allegations of his pleadings that were on file in the 96th District Court. Mr. Acker was relieved of the burden of proving his second venue fact, but only because it was judicially admitted, both by the defendants' motion to transfer (conceding that defendant Tom Bateman resides in Tarrant County) and Tom Bateman's own affidavit verifying that he resides in Tarrant. Thus, Mr. Acker's pleadings proved one of the venue facts necessary to maintain venue in Tarrant County, and the defendants proved the second venue fact for him.

From the 96th District Court's order transferring venue, it appears that the transfer was made because the venue facts alleged in the defendants' motion to transfer were supported with the Patterson and Bateman affidavits as prima facie proof that the defendants were entitled to the transfer, and because Mr. Acker failed to controvert with sworn proof of his own. If venue is not proper in the county where suit is filed, a trial court must transfer the case to a county where venue is proper. TEX. CIV. PRAC. & REM. CODE ANN. § 15.063(1) (Vernon 1986). But if a plaintiff files suit in a county of proper venue, it is reversible error to transfer venue under section 15.063(1) even if the county of transfer would have been proper if originally chosen by the plaintiff. *Wilson v. Texas Parks & Wildlife Dept.*, 886 S.W.2d 259, 261 (Tex. 1994). In *Wilson*, the supreme court applies a principle of appellate review of venue challenges that it established a year earlier in *Ruiz v. Conoco, Inc.*, 868 S.W.2d 752, 757 (Tex. 1993). *See Wilson*, 886 S.W.2d at 261. Although the factual issues addressed in the two cases were not the same, *Wilson* and *Ruiz* make clear that in order for us to determine whether there was reversible error in this case, we are obligated to conduct an independent review of the entire record. TEX. CIV. PRAC. & REM. CODE ANN. § 15.064(b) (Vernon 1986); *Wilson*, 886 S.W.2d at 261; *Ruiz*, 868 S.W.2d at 756-57. In *Ruiz*, the Supreme Court commented on some very practical reasons for such a review: [A]n appellate court is obliged to conduct an independent review of the entire record to determine whether venue was proper in the ultimate county of suit . . . . If there is probative evidence to support the trial court's determination, even if the preponderance of the evidence is to the contrary, we believe the appellate court should defer to the trial court. A remand to reconsider the [venue] issue, which is the relief ordinarily afforded or factual insufficiency of the evidence, would only increase the expense and delay of litigation in order to resolve an issue which, though important, is unrelated to the merits. Moreover, it exacerbates the difficulties already present in the rule if the appellate court decides, based on all the evidence, that the case should be remanded for a redetermination of venue, based on prima facie proof. (Would a second trial be required?) [Section 15.064] does not mandate factual sufficiency review, and we believe it is neither necessary nor wise. Therefore, if there is any probative evidence in the entire record . . . that venue was proper in the county where judgment was rendered, the appellate court must uphold the trial court's determination . . . . Only if there is no probative evidence that venue was proper either in the county of suit or in the county to which transfer was sought should the appellate court remand the case to the trial court to conduct further proceedings on the issue of venue . . . . *Id.*, 868 S.W.2d at 758.

For trial judges, the parties' pleadings on file at the venue hearing are conclusive on the issues of the existence of a cause of action. *See* TEX. R. CIV. P. 87.3(a). This means that for venue purposes, a trial court is forced to take pleadings at face value and may find venue proper in the county of suit as long as the cause of action alleged and the residence of a named defendant will permit venue in that county. We have already quoted the *Ruiz* rationale for requiring appellate courts to review the entire record when improper venue is a complaint on appeal. *Wilson*, however, expands that rationale by explaining another significant and practical purpose served by having an appellate court review the entire record: the review satisfies the need to balance a plaintiff's right to select the county of proper venue against a defendant's right to protection from being forced to trial in a county that only later is understood to have been a county of improper venue. *Wilson*, 886 S.W.2d at 262.

A full review after final judgment may reveal that the prima facie venue proof considered by the trial court was simply misleading or wrong. *Ruiz*, 868 S.W.2d at 757. An appellate court's review of the full record once the case has ended in final judgment enables a defendant to have a just recourse from improper venue that a plaintiff wrongly gained by false or inaccurate pleadings that the trial court had to accept at face value in the venue process. *See Wilson*, 886 S.W.2d at 262.

For years, libel plaintiffs at venue hearings were required to offer prima facie proof of the existence of a cause of action against the defendant. *See General Motors Acceptance Corp. v. Howard*, 487 S.W.2d 708, 710 (Tex. 1972); *A.H. Belo Corp. v. Blanton*, 133 Tex. 391, 129 S.W.2d 619, 621-22 (Tex. 1939); *Betancourt v. Whittle*, 659 S.W.2d 895, 897 (Tex. App.—San Antonio 1983, no writ). It is no longer necessary to prove at a venue hearing that a cause of action exists. TEX. R. CIV. P. 87.3.(a). From the evidence in this case, the trial court was aware that all of the litigants except Tom Bateman reside or are domiciled in Denton County and Mr. Acker's claims had their origin in Denton County, not Tarrant County.

Facially, Mr. Acker's basis for claiming venue in Tarrant County was that he had joined Tom Bateman, a Tarrant County resident, as a defendant. The record, however, does not substantiate any claim by Mr. Acker against Tom Bateman for acts done by him in his individual capacity. Although Mr. Acker's petition names Mr. Bateman as one of the defendants, it does not allege that Bateman personally committed any wrongs. Tom Bateman's affidavit in support of the motion to transfer venue from Tarrant County was not controverted by Mr. Acker and is competent evidence that Mr. Bateman did not personally perform, assist, or supervise the alleged libel. Mr. Bateman's only relation to the matters alleged by Mr. Acker is that Mr. Bateman is a corporate officer of the publishing company.

After bathing Mr. Acker's Tarrant County venue claim in the light of the entire record, we must conclude that Mr. Bateman was not a proper defendant in the suit. *See ACF Indus., Inc. v. Carter*, 903 S.W.2d 423, 424 (Tex. App.—Texarkana 1995, writ dism'd by agr.). The record as a whole reveals no genuine issue of material fact that would support a cause of action by Mr. Acker against Mr. Bateman individually. Because our review of the entire record shows that the prima facie venue proof in the Tarrant County court was misleading, we conclude that Tarrant County was not a county of proper venue, and the 96th District Court's order to transfer venue to the proper county, Denton, was not reversible error. The third point of error is overruled.

* * *

Having found no reversible error, we affirm the judgment of the trial court.

Note

In the case of *In re* Fisher, 433 S.W.3d 523 (Tex. 2014) the court stated:

> "Next, Richey alternatively argues that if section 15.017 does not apply, venue is proper in Wise County under the general venue statute because a substantial part of the events giving rise to his claim occurred there. *See* TEX. CIV. PRAC. & REM.CODE § 15.002(a)(1) (providing that a lawsuit shall be brought in various enumerated places including "in the county in which all or a substantial part of the events or omissions giving rise to the claim occurred"). He cites *Acker v. Denton Publishing,* 937 S.W.2d 111, 115 (Tex. App.—Fort Worth 1996, no writ) for the proposition that if a plaintiff's choice of venue is proper, it is reversible error for a trial court to transfer venue even if the county of transfer would also have been proper if chosen by the plaintiff. But *Acker* did not address whether a case should be transferred when a mandatory venue provision for a different county was applicable. And we long ago explained that "[i]f the plaintiff's chosen venue rests on a *permissive* venue statute and the defendant files a meritorious motion to transfer based on a *mandatory* venue provision, the trial court must grant the motion." *Wichita Cnty. v. Hart,* 917 S.W.2d 779, 781 (Tex. 1996) (emphasis added). The permissive venue statute does not control over the mandatory venue provision applicable in this case."

In re APPLIED CHEMICAL MAGNESIAS CORPORATION

206 S.W.3d 114
(Tex. 2006)

Venue. A Declaratory Judgment Action To Determine The Rights Of The Parties To A Contract To Acquire Leases Is An Action Involving Real Estate.

This is an original mandamus proceeding. Held: A declaratory judgment suit to determine the rights of the parties to a contract, to acquire surface and mineral leases, is an action involving an interest in real property, thus making it subject to the mandatory venue provision of section 15.011 of the Texas Civil Practice and Remedies Code. Special distinctions are not made for real property suits, simply because they are couched in terms of a declaratory judgment action.

The improper transfer of venue can never be harmless error. TEX. CIV. PRAC. & REM. CODE Sec. 15.064(b): "On appeal from the trial on the merits, if venue was improper it shall in no event be harmless error and shall be reversible errors. In determining whether venue was or was not proper, the appellate court shall consider the entire record, including the trial on the merits."

Note

In the case of *In re* Lopez, 372 S.W.3d 174, 176-177 (Tex. 2012) the court stated:

> "Mandamus relief is the proper remedy to enforce a mandatory venue provision when the trial court has denied a motion to transfer venue. *In re Cont'l Airlines, Inc.,* 988 S.W.2d 733, 735 (Tex. 1998) (orig. proceeding); TEX. CIV. PRAC. & REM. CODE § 15.0642. Ordinarily, mandamus relief is proper when the trial court has abused its discretion and a party has no appellate remedy. *In re Prudential Ins. Co. of Am.,* 148 S.W.3d 124, 135-36 (Tex. 2004) (orig.proceeding). However, where a party seeks to enforce a mandatory venue provision a party is only required to show that the trial court clearly abused its discretion by failing to transfer the case and is not required to prove that it lacks an adequate appellate remedy. *In re Applied Chem. Magnesias Corp.,* 206 S.W.3d 114, 117 (Tex. 2006) (orig. proceeding); *In re Mo. Pac.,* 998 S.W.2d at 216; *In re Cont'l Airlines,* 988 S.W.2d at 735.
>
> Section 171.096(c) is a mandatory venue provision, as it says that a party "must" file the initial application in the county where the arbitration hearing was held. TEX. CIV. PRAC. & REM. CODE § 171.096(c); *see Helena Chem. Co. v. Wilkins,* 47 S.W.3d 486, 493 (Tex. 2001) (recognizing the word "must" as "mandatory, creating a duty or obligation"). Since section 171.096(c) is a mandatory venue provision, the Lopezes are not required to prove that they have no adequate appellate remedy in order to obtain mandamus relief. *See In re Applied Chem. Magnesias,* 206 S.W.3d at 117; *In re Mo. Pac.,* 998 S.W.2d at 216; *In re Cont'l Airlines,* 988 S.W.2d at 735."

In re TEXAS ASSOCIATION OF SCHOOL BOARDS, INC.

169 S.W.3d 653
(Tex. 2005)

"In this mandamus proceeding, the Texas Association of School Boards, Inc. and the Texas Association of School Boards Risk Management Fund seek to have a suit against them transferred from Duval County to Travis County based on a contractual choice of venue provision in a risk coverage agreement that is similar to an insurance contract. They assert that the agreement is a "major transaction" within the meaning of section 15.020 of the Civil Practice and Remedies Code. Section 15.020 is a mandatory venue provision. If there is a written agreement that suit arising from a "major transaction" may be brought in a particular county, suit must be brought in that county. A "major transaction" is "a transaction evidenced by a written agreement under which a person pays or receives, or is obligated to pay or entitled to receive, consideration with an aggregate stated value equal to or greater than $1 million." The relators agreed to provide more than $17 million in risk coverage at a cost of $41,973 per year. The trial court declined to enforce the parties' venue agreement without stating its reasons, and the court of appeals denied mandamus relief. We likewise deny mandamus relief. The mandatory venue provision in section 15.020 is inapplicable because the coverage agreement is not a "major transaction."

"If a trial court erroneously denies enforcement of a mandatory venue provision, mandamus relief is available without the necessity of showing an inadequate appellate remedy. Because trial courts have no discretion in determining the legal principles controlling their rulings or in applying the law to the facts, our focus in this case is whether the trial court failed to correctly apply section 15.020."

"The principal dispute in this case is what constitutes the "aggregate stated value" of the "consideration" "which a person pays or receives, or is obligated to pay or entitled to receive" under the parties' agreement."

"What is clear is that the consideration for an agreement like the one between the Fund and BISD is an exchange of promises. The Fund promised to pay any claims that were covered, up to the coverage limits, if, as, and when they occurred during the specified term. BISD promised to pay $41,973 for this coverage. The "aggregate stated value" of BISD's promise to pay is thus easily determinable."

"The dispute, however, is over the "aggregate stated value" of the Fund's promise. The Fund contends that this should be measured by the coverage limits. We disagree. The consideration the Fund furnished was its agreement to bear the risk that covered losses might occur. The value assigned in the coverage agreement to the risk the Fund assumed is the $41,973 annual contribution from BISD. Thus, the consideration to be valued is the undertaking of the risk that insured losses might occur."

"BISD agreed to pay what is in essence a premium of $41,973. That is the value the parties assigned to the risks the Fund assumed. The aggregate stated value of the consideration for the coverage agreement is the amount of the contribution specified in the agreement for assumption of the risk of loss from the enumerated perils, not the coverage limits."

Notes

1. *In re Fisher*, 433 S.W.3d 523 (Tex. 2014): The major transaction provision applies to all parts of the transaction. A specific agreement is not required. The provision is applicable to a note accompanying a partnership agreement.

2. One of the major changes in the overhaul of the venue statute in 1984 was the removal of the right of an interlocutory appeal from a venue determination. Texas law permits appeals from only a final judgment (one that disposes of all parties and cause of action) except in very limited circumstances [the concept of finality of judgments is the subject of Chapter 15 of this book]. As a venue decision does not even address the merits of the case it is clearly interlocutory, and thus not the subject to appeal unless a statutory exception applies. The statutory exception contained in the venue statute was eliminated in 1984. Of course, after the trial of the case, a losing party could assert an improper venue determination on appeal of the case. The amendments to the venue statute in 1995 reinstated the availability of an interlocutory appeal of a venue determination under very limited circumstances. *See* § 15.003 of the Texas Civil Practice and Remedies Code.

3. Prior to 1995, case law permitted the use of mandamus to review certain improper venue decisions prior to the entry of a final judgment. However, that same case law established that most venue determinations were not reviewable by mandamus. In *Polaris Inv. Management Corp. v. Abscal*[1] the Court stated:

> Venue is a creature of legislative grace, and because a change of venue was unknown to the common law, the power to make venue changes is purely statutory. Accordingly, appellate review of trial court venue rulings is generally limited to a determination of whether the trial court ruling was faithful to the relevant venue statute.

However, if a trial court had a mandatory duty to transfer the case, an appellate court would issue mandamus to force the transfer. *See, e.g., Proffer v. Yates*,[2] Furthermore, if a trial court issued a void order on venue, an ap-

---

[1] 892 S.W.2d 860 (Tex. 1995).

[2] 734 S.W.2d 671, 673 (Tex. 1987) (venue under § 11.06 of the Family Code, which was mandatory, could be enforced by mandamus).

pellate court would issue mandamus to correct the order.[3] Finally, if a trial court violated a mandatory notice procedure, an appellate court would issue mandamus to force the trial court to follow the rules.[4] The reason for the limited availability of mandamus was simple—even if the court had abused its discretion in making the venue determination, there was generally an adequate remedy by appeal following the trial of the case. The amendments to the venue statute in 1995 added a provision permitting mandamus as a statutory remedy to enforce a mandatory venue provision [this statutory mandamus procedure is in addition to the very limited use of mandamus that had been permitted by the case law].

4. § 15.0642 of the Texas Civil Practice and Remedies Code provides as follows:

§ 15.0642. Mandamus

A party may apply for a writ of mandamus with an appellate court to enforce the mandatory venue provisions of this chapter. An application for the writ of mandamus must be filed before the later of:

(1) the 90th day before the date the trial starts; or
(2) the 10th day after the date the party receives notice of the trial setting.

In re MISSOURI PACIFIC RAILROAD COMPANY

998 S.W.2d 212
(Tex. 1999)

JUSTICE GONZALES delivered the opinion for a unanimous court.

These consolidated mandamus proceedings concern the mandatory venue statute for suits brought under the Federal Employers' Liability Act (FELA). [TEX. CIV. PRAC. & REM. CODE § 15.018] In each case the key issue is whether the plaintiff in the underlying lawsuit sued the corporate defendant in a county where it maintains "a principal office," as defined in the venue statutes. We conclude that the plaintiffs in all of the suits failed to prove that the corporate defendant has a principal office in the county of suit, so we direct the trial courts in Jefferson County and Tarrant County to transfer the cases to a proper county.

I

These mandamus proceedings arise out of three FELA lawsuits filed in Jefferson County, and three filed in Tarrant County. Section 15.018(b) of the venue statutes gives three choices: (b) All suits brought under [FELA] shall be brought:

(1) in the county in which all or a substantial part of the events or omissions giving rise to the claim occurred;
(2) in the county where the defendant's principal office in this state is located; or
(3) in the county where the plaintiff resided at the time the cause of action accrued.

Subparts (b)(1) and (b)(3) do not apply here because none of the plaintiffs reside in the county of suit and none claim the cause of action arose there. All the plaintiffs in the Jefferson County cases claim damages for an injury occurring outside of Texas. . . . Each plaintiff in the Tarrant County suits against Union Pacific Railroad alleged he suffered an injury in his home state outside Texas. . . . The venue challenges proceeded much the same in all the cases. The plaintiff alleged that the railroad maintained a principal office in the county of suit. The railroad denied that it had a principal office in the county of suit or that venue was proper there, and moved to transfer venue to Harris County where the railroad had principal offices in Texas. In each case the trial court denied the motion and retained venue, resulting in these mandamus proceedings.

II

Section 15.0642 of the Texas Civil Practice and Remedies Code directs appellate courts to enforce the mandatory venue statutes by mandamus:

---

[3] *See, e.g.,* Dorchester Master Ltd. Partnership v. Anthony, 734 S.W.2d 151, 152 (Tex. App.—Houston [1st Dist.] 1987) (orig. proceeding) (trial court had no authority to consider second venue motion).

[4] *See, e.g.,* Henderson v. O'Neill, 797 S.W.2d 905, 905 (Tex. 1990) (trial court did not give party the required 45 days notice of the venue hearing).

A party may apply for a writ of mandamus with an appellate court to enforce the mandatory venue provisions of this chapter. An application for the writ of mandamus must be filed before the later of: (1) the 90th day before the date the trial starts; or (2) the 10th day after the date the party receives notice of the trial setting. Section 15.0642 does not detail the scope of mandamus review of mandatory venue decisions. Traditionally, mandamus will not issue (1) unless the trial court has committed a clear abuse of discretion, (2) for which appeal is not an adequate remedy. We determined in a prior case that the usual mandamus standard of review, abuse of discretion, applies to a section 15.0642 mandamus. But we have not considered whether a party challenging a mandatory venue decision also must show that appeal is an inadequate remedy. The railroads argue that it is presumed that there is no adequate remedy for a failure to enforce a mandatory venue statute, *citing KJ Eastwood Investments., Inc. v. Enlow.*[1] In that case, the court of appeals reasoned that it would undermine the purpose of section 15.0642 if a relator were forced to show inadequate remedy by appeal. We agree. We have repeatedly denied mandamus to review the merits of a venue decision because we considered it an incidental trial ruling correctable by appeal.

Before 1983, venue rulings were immediately correctable by interlocutory appeal under the former plea of privilege practice. In 1983, the Legislature replaced interlocutory venue appeals with the rule that in an ordinary post-trial appeal, improper venue is not subject to harmless error analysis, virtually guaranteeing reversal. We have held that an appeal is inadequate to remedy an erroneous venue decision in only one instance—mandatory transfer in a suit involving the parent-child relationship. In *Proffer v. Yates*,[2] we reasoned that the need to expeditiously resolve custody and support issues makes ordinary appeal inadequate. Outside of suits involving the parent-child relationship, our Court has steadfastly declined to review by mandamus whether venue was proper in the county of suit under the venue statues. We reiterated in early 1995 that "Texas law is quite clear that venue determinations are not reviewable by mandamus." But a few months later, the Legislature enacted section 15.0642 authorizing parties to seek mandamus "to enforce the mandatory venue provisions," along with a timetable for seeking mandamus. The Legislature left in place the "presumed harm" rule for challenging venue in an appeal after trial. Thus, section 15.0642 poses a conundrum: venue decisions are not reviewable by mandamus because they are correctable by appeal, but section 15.0642 authorizes mandamus review of mandatory venue decisions. Either the availability of mandamus relief under the statute is largely illusory, or we must dispense with the requirement of showing inadequate appellate remedy in mandatory venue cases. Our goal in construing a statute is to carry out the Legislature's intent. The language of section 15.0642 seems to contemplate a review of the merits of the trial court's decision on mandatory venue. Yet if we still insist on a particularized showing of inadequate remedy by appeal, then a court could rarely, if ever, "enforce the mandatory venue provisions" by mandamus. *Proffer* is the exception that illustrates the near-impossibility of showing that appeal is inadequate to remedy an erroneous venue decision. We do not lightly presume that the Legislature may have done a useless act. Rather, we presume the Legislature intended "a result feasible of execution." to effectuate the Legislature's intent, we conclude that adequacy of an appellate remedy is not a requisite of a mandatory venue mandamus under section 15.0642.

III

Thus, the focus of a mandamus proceeding under section 15.0642 is whether the trial court abused its discretion. The trial court has no discretion in determining the legal principles controlling its ruling or in applying the law to the facts. A trial court does not have the discretion to make an erroneous legal conclusion even in an unsettled area of law. Therefore, we review in these cases whether the trial courts failed to analyze or apply the law correctly when they refused to transfer the cases to the defendants' chosen venue. The parties' pleading and proof limits a trial court's discretion to determine venue. A plaintiff's choice of venue stands unless challenged by proper motion to transfer venue. Once challenged, the plaintiff has the burden to present prima facie proof by affidavit or other appropriate evidence that venue is maintainable in the county of suit. The plaintiff's prima facie proof is not subject to rebuttal, cross-examination, impeachment, or disproof. However, if the plaintiff fails to discharge the burden, the right to choose a proper venue passes to the defendant, who must then prove that venue is proper in the defendant's chosen county. The controlling issue here is what the plaintiffs had to plead and prove to establish venue in "the county where the defendant's principal office in this state is located" under the FELA venue statute.

1 923 S.W.2d 255 (Tex. App.—Fort Worth 1996, orig. proceeding).

2 734 S.W.2d 671, 673 (Tex. 1987).

The railroads contend that a foreign corporation only has one principal office under the mandatory venue statutes for FELA actions. If the FELA venue statute is read in isolation, the provision for suit "in the county where the defendant's principal office in this state is located" would indicate a company's Texas headquarters. However, that view is complicated by the general definition of "principal office" in section 15.001:

In this chapter:

(a) "Principal office" means a principal office of the corporation . . . in this state in which the decision makers for the organization within this state conduct the daily affairs of the organization. The mere presence of an agency or representative does not establish a principal office.

The plaintiffs respond that the phrase "a principal office" indicates that there can be more than one principal office. Further, the plaintiffs argue, the "daily affairs" of these defendants consist of operating trains, so that a principal office is wherever a railroad official makes decisions about operating trains.

We agree with the plaintiffs that a corporation can have more than one principal office. We are bound by the statutory definition of "principal office" as "a" principal office. Thus, when we apply the general definition of "principal office" to the FELA venue statute, we must assume a defendant company could have more than one principal office. But we reject the plaintiffs' argument that the statute clearly defines a principal office as any place where a company official makes decisions about the company's business. Such a broad definition would include agencies and representatives, which the statute expressly rejects. Agencies and representatives, as we defined them under the former venue statutes, are officials who possess broad power and discretion to act for the corporation.

Thus, "decision makers" who "conduct the daily affairs" are officials of a different order than agents or representatives. Moreover, even though "a principal office" suggests there can be more than one office, the term "principal" indicates some sort of primacy. It is unlikely that an office clearly subordinate to and controlled by another Texas office could be "a principal office." Finally, in context, "the daily affairs" of a company cannot mean relatively common, low-level managerial decisions.

Beyond these preliminary observations, the statute is not entirely clear in all its particulars. The language of the statute could support more than one reasonable interpretation and therefore is ambiguous. Because it is ambiguous, we may turn to extratextual sources such as the statute's legislative history.

IV

Sections 15.001 and 15.018 codify parts of Senate Bill 32, enacted by the 74th Legislature. The railroads contend that Senate Bill 32's legislative history supports its interpretation of the venue statutes. The plaintiffs argue to the contrary, that the bill's history supports their own interpretation. Both the House and Senate proposed changes to the venue statutes for corporations during the 74th regular session of the Legislature, House Bill 6 and Senate Bill 32. As the plaintiffs readily concede, and legislative history bears out, a major purpose of the 1995 amendments was to reduce or limit forum shopping. As initially proposed, Senate Bill 32 did not define "principal office." The Senate Committee on Economic Development added the definition of "a" principal office, but also provided that courts would determine a single county as the principal office in this state for any corporate defendant. The definition of "a principal office" remained in Senate Bill 32, but the provision for a single principal office was not included in the version the Senate adopted on April 19, 1995. The House substituted House Bill 6 with Senate Bill 32 and amended section 15.001(a) to provide that the mere presence of an agency or representative does not establish a principal office. The House passed Senate Bill 32 as amended on May 4, 1995, and the Senate concurred four days later. The railroads argue that the bill's history shows the Legislature intended to adopt the "nerve center" test to determine where a corporation has its principal office. This is the test federal courts use to decide a company's "principal place of business" for diversity jurisdictional purposes. When he introduced the bill in a meeting of the Senate Economic Development Committee, the sponsor of the bill, Senator John T. Montford, mentioned the test when he described the definition of "a principal office": [A] definition of the term principal office has been added, [to] bring focus to one location that adopts the nerve center test, used by the federal courts, to determine what constitutes a principal office, instead of having a variety of possible constructions of where a principal office could be. The railroads read too much into Senator Montford's statement. The federal court that originated the term "nerve center test" stated the test thusly: [A company's] principal place of business is the nerve center from which it radiates out to its constituent parts and from which its officers direct, control and coordinate all activities without regard to locale, in the furtherance of the corporate objective.

The nerve-center test focuses on where the activities of the corporation are controlled or directed. However, it is but one of several tests federal courts use to determine a corporation's principal place of business. Another is the "place of operations" or "corporate activity" test, which is where the bulk of the corporation's physical operations are located. The Fifth Circuit uses either or both tests depending on the facts of the case. However, as the court of appeals for the Seventh Circuit notes, federal courts all agree that regardless of the test, a corporation has only one principal place of business for diversity purposes. We agree with the plaintiffs that Senator Montford's reference in the committee meeting to the "nerve center test" signifies only a general approach, that a court should look at how a company is run rather than corporate activity or operations.

* * *

We find nothing in the legislative history to dissuade us from our initial observations about the meaning of section 15.001. Rather, the legislative history supports our conclusion that: (1) a company may have more than one principal office, (2) the "decision makers" who conduct the "daily affairs" of the company are officials who run the company day to day, (3) a mere agent or representative is not a "decision maker" nor is a principal office one where only decisions typical of an agency or representative are made, and (4) a principal office is not an office clearly subordinate to and controlled by another Texas office.

The debates on the floor of the House and the Senate confirm that the Legislature did not intend to limit venue to only one county where the company maintains a corporate office if the facts do not warrant it. A company may control or direct its daily affairs in Texas through decision makers of substantially equal responsibility and authority in different offices in the state. In that case each office may be a principal office of the company. Necessarily, courts must look at the corporation's structure to determine a company's principal office or offices. The titles of the company officials in a particular office are not as informative as a description of their responsibility and authority, relative to other company officials within the state. We recognize that our interpretation does not provide a precise test. But we believe the Legislature intended a flexible test to allow for the myriad forms that corporate structures can take.

V

Turning to the facts of the Jefferson County cases, Burleigh and the Spillers contend that they were not required to prove a prima facie case because the defendants failed to specifically deny that the railroad had "decision makers and other management personnel," in Jefferson County as required by Texas Rule of Procedure 87(3)(a). However, the railroads denied that they had a principal office in Jefferson County and enumerated the officers in Harris County versus those in Jefferson County. Thus the plaintiffs were required to present prima facie evidence that venue was proper in Jefferson County.

The plaintiffs' evidence focused largely on the extent of operations and equipment in Jefferson County, Texas. The evidence showed that the railroad's corporate headquarters were in Omaha, Nebraska, and many of the executive and administrative decisions were made there. The evidence did little to define the role of any of the decision makers in Jefferson County relative to the rest of the company in Texas. A party cannot prove a prima facie case that a county has a principal office without evidence of the corporate structure and the authority of the officers in the county of suit as compared with the remainder of the state. The only company officials in Jefferson County the plaintiffs' evidence identified were a manager of train operations, a manager of yard operations, and a "maintenance and way" foreman. There was testimony that the railroads' corporate headquarters delegated some policy-making to the local level. However, there is little evidence of the kinds of decisions the Jefferson County officials could make. More importantly, there is no evidence of how the Jefferson County officials' authority compared to others statewide, so that the court could make a meaningful determination whether Jefferson County is in any sense a "principal office."

VI

The Tarrant County plaintiffs put on more extensive evidence of Union Pacific's organization structure in Texas. Union Pacific is divided into four regions. The southern region includes most of Texas and parts of Louisiana. The southern region is further divided into six divisions. In answer to interrogatories, the railroad identified the "decision makers" who office in Harris County as a general solicitor, a vice president for transportation, a general manager, two general supervisors, a chief engineer, and two division superintendents. All but the division superintendents are considered executive officers of the company. The former general solicitor stated in a deposition that "the real policy decisions and real serious operational decisions are made by persons at the level of superintendent or above." The only official the plaintiffs claim is a "decision maker" in Tarrant County is a division superintendent for the Fort Worth service unit. He testified in his deposition that his duties included coordinating the movement of trains, staffing the crews within the area, and ensuring rules compliance and discipline. The division superintendent also said that the southern region is based in Houston, and his boss is the general manager in Harris County. This evidence is sufficient to characterize a division superintendent as a decision maker under the statute. However, it fails to establish prima facie that the Tarrant County office is a principal office when compared to the responsibility and authority exercised by company officials elsewhere in Texas. The evidence shows that the division superintendent in Tarrant County is not an executive officer and has the least authority of any of the decision makers) with any real discretion or authority. In contrast, there are six executive officers in Harris County. The two highest ranking officers in Texas, general solicitors, conduct the affairs of the railroad from offices in Harris County. They oversee legal affairs such as FELA litigation in Texas for the railroads. The general manager of transportation is responsible for the transportation plan for the southern region of the Company, which includes Texas and Louisiana. The general manager supervises the assistant general manager and the general superintendent. The general supervisor also supervises six division superintendents, two in Houston, three in other Texas offices, and one in Louisiana. The general superintendent performs the logistics for deciding train starts and yard starts. Finally, the chief engineer directs the activities of local maintenance-of-way and signal service units throughout the region.

VII

The plaintiffs failed to establish Jefferson County or Tarrant County as principal offices of the railroads. The burden shifted to the defendants to prove that Harris County is a proper venue. The venue facts bear out that Harris County is "a" principal office of the railroads, and therefore a proper venue under the mandatory FELA statute. The trial courts abused their discretion by not sustaining the motions to transfer. Accordingly, we conditionally issue writs of mandamus directing the trial courts to sustain the railroads' motions to transfer the cases to Harris County. The writs will not issue unless the trial courts fail to act in accordance with this opinion.

Notes

When Mandatory Venue Provisions Conflict.

1. *The Ventura v. Hunter Barrett & Co.*[1]

To establish venue under § 15.011, the plaintiff is required to show (1) that the nature of suit concerns land and (2) that the land is located in the county of suit (or the count to which transfer is sought).

Where land is involved and an injunction is sought, the test to determine which controls is well established. Whenever it can properly be said from the pleadings that the issuance of the injunction is ancillary to a judgment awarding recovery of land or quieting title thereto, section 15.011 controls. But, where the petition discloses that the primary relief sought is injunctive, then § 65.023 controls.

2. *Maranatha Temple, Inc. v. Enterprise Prods. Co.*[2]

The nature of the suit is determined from the facts alleged in the plaintiff's petitions, the rights asserted, and the relief sought.

3. *Stiba v. Bowers.*[3]

For venue purposes, a cause of action consists of the factual propositions, which establish plaintiff's primary right, and defendant's act or omission which violated such right. But it is only essential factual propositions that matter, and not mere evidentiary ones.

To establish venue under § 15.011 a plaintiff must prove two venue facts:

1) the location of the land, and
2) the nature of the plaintiff's claim. This is determined from the facts alleged in the plaintiff's petition, the rights asserted, and the relief sought.

---

[1] 552 S.W.2d 918 (Tex. App.—Corpus Christi 1977).

[2] 833 S.W.2d 736 (Tex. App.—Houston [1st Dist.] 1992, writ denied).

[3] 756 S.W.2d 835 (Tex. App.—Corpus Christi 1988, no writ).

4. In applying a mandatory venue provision, the *ultimate or dominant* purpose of the suit controls whether the mandatory venue provision applies. If the action only incidentally or secondarily, and not directly, involves title, then § 15.011 does not apply. Because this venue provision is mandatory, it is construed strictly. Where the action is cast as one for the recovery of land or to quiet title, and the parties rights are the sole issue, the mandatory venue rule for suits affecting an interest in land applies, regardless of the fact that the rights must be determined with reference to a will or lease.

5. The improper transfer of venue can never be harmless error. "On appeal from the trial on the merits, if venue was improper it shall in no event be harmless error and shall be reversible errors. In determining whether venue was or was not proper, the appellate court shall consider the entire record, including the trial on the merits." *See* TEX. CIV. PRAC. & REM. CODE Sec. 15.064(b).

6. *Wichita County, Texas v. Hart.*[4] Mandatory venue provisions control over permissive. Thus, under TEX. CIV. PRAC. & REM. CODE § 15.015, "[a]n action against a county *shall be brought* in that county." Under TEX. GOV'T CODE § 554.007, "a public employee *may sue* under this chapter in a district court of the county in which the employee resides or in a district court of Travis County." A trial court's erroneous denial of a motion to transfer venue requires reversal of the judgment and remand for a new trial. The Whistleblower Act's venue provision is not jurisdictional.

7. *In Re Continental Airlines, Inc.*[5] These are original mandamus proceedings. The City of Fort Worth filed suit in Tarrant County district court for a judgment declaring rights under compacts and agreements with the City of Dallas, concerning Dallas-Fort Worth International Airport, and the use of Love Field Airport. The suit was against the City of Dallas, the DFW Airport Board, Legend Airlines, and others. American Airlines intervened, seeking the same declaratory relief as Fort Worth. Continental Airlines filed a declaratory judgment action against Dallas and Fort Worth in Federal Court, asking that the Court declare that it had a right, under federal law, to commence flying from Love Field to Cleveland. Fort Worth and American amended their state court petitions to include a prayer for a judgment declaring that flights from Love Field to Cleveland would violate the 1968 contracts between the cites of Fort Worth and Dallas to establish a regional airport, and to limit interstate flights out of local airports such as Love Field Airport in Dallas. The DFW Board also filed a cross-claim against Continental for a declaratory judgment. Continental answered, and sought a change of venue to Harris County. On 6/19/98, Fort Worth and the DFW board requested a temporary restraining order and temporary injunction to keep Continental from commencing service. Each of the defendants moved to transfer venue, arguing that Fort Worth's causes of action, properly considered, are injunction suits that must be brought in a defendant's domicile county. The trial court denied the motions to transfer venue. At a later date, the district court granted the requested temporary injunctive relief. The court of appeals denied all mandamus relief. *Held:* Writ of mandamus is denied. The relators' motions fail to make out a case of mandatory venue. *Actions for declaratory judgments are governed by general venue rules for civil actions. However, injunction suits against a resident shall be tried in a district or county court in the county in which the party is domiciled. The statute placing venue in the county of the defendant's domicile is mandatory. The injunction venue statute applies only to suits in which the relief sought is purely or primarily injunctive.* The venue statues give plaintiffs some degree of choice over where to file their suits. The legislative plan allows a plaintiff to control venue to a certain extent, by deciding what relief to seek. *The legislature has expressly provided a special venue of injunction suits in cases where the plaintiff alleges that he/she has no adequate remedy at law, and hence is entitled to, and requests, injunctive relief. Here, Fort Worth's pleadings do not ask for, and would not support, a permanent injunction.* Conversely, the pleadings state a justiciable controversy that maybe fully resolved by declaratory judgment. The Supreme Court cannot reform Fort Worth's requests for relief to reflect the defendants' suspicions.

8. *Conflict between the Rules and the Statute.*

§ 15.066. Conflict with Rules of Civil Procedure

Subject to Section 22.004, Government Code, to the extent that this chapter conflicts with the Texas Rules of Civil Procedure, this chapter controls."

[Current through end of 1997 Reg. Sess.]

---

[4] 917 S.W.2d 779 (Tex. 1996).

[5] 988 S.W.2d 733 (Tex. 1998)

§ 22.004. Rules of Civil Procedure

(a) The Supreme Court has the full rulemaking power in the practice and procedure in civil actions, except that its rules may not abridge, enlarge, or modify the substantive rights of a litigant.

(b) The Supreme Court from time to time may promulgate a specific rule or rules of civil procedure, or an amendment or amendments to a specific rule or rules, to be effective at the time the Supreme Court deems expedient in the interest of a proper administration of justice. The rules and amendments to rules remain in effect unless and until disapproved by the legislature. The clerk of the supreme court shall file with the secretary of state the rules or amendments to rules promulgated by the supreme court under this subsection and shall mail a copy of those rules or amendments to rules to each registered member of the State Bar of Texas not later than the 60th day before the date on which they become effective.

(c) So that the Supreme Court has full rulemaking power in civil actions, a rule adopted by the Supreme Court repeals all conflicting laws and parts of laws governing practice and procedure in civil actions, but substantive law is not repealed. At the time the Supreme Court files a rule, the court shall file with the secretary of state a list of each article or section of general law or each part of an article or section of general law that in the court's judgment is repealed. The list has the same weight and effect as a decision of the court.

(d) The rules of practice and procedure in civil actions shall be published in the official reports of the Supreme Court. The Supreme Court may adopt the method it deems expedient for the printing and distribution of the rules.

(e) This section does not affect the repeal of statutes repealed by Chapter 25, page 201, General Laws, Acts of the 46th Legislature, Regular Session, 1939, on September 1, 1941.

b. *Permissive Venue*

Note

Subchapter C of Chapter 15 of the Texas Civil Practice and Remedies Code provides for various permissive exceptions to the general rule. A plaintiff can file his lawsuit in a county covered by one of these exceptions. A defendant can also rely upon one such exception to transfer a case to another county in the event that the county in which the case was originally filed is not a county of proper venue. The permissive exceptions are:

§ 15.031. Executor; Administrator; Guardian.

If the suit is against an executor, administrator, or guardian, as such, to establish a money demand against the estate which he represents, the suit may be brought in the county in which the estate is administered, or if the suit is against an executor, administrator, or guardian growing out of a negligent act or omission of the person whose estate the executor, administrator, or guardian represents, the suit may be brought in the county in which the negligent act or omission of the person whose estate the executor, administrator, or guardian represents occurred.

§ 15.032. Insurance

Suit against fire, marine, or inland insurance companies may also be commenced in any county in which the insured property was situated. A suit on a policy may be brought against any life insurance company, or accident insurance company, or life and accident, or health and accident, or life, health, and accident insurance company in the county in which the company's principal office in this state is located or in the county in which the loss has occurred or in which the policyholder or beneficiary instituting the suit resided at the time the cause of action accrued.

§ 15.033. Breach of Warranty by Manufacturer

A suit for breach of warranty by a manufacturer of consumer goods may be brought in any county in which all or a substantial part of the events or omissions giving rise to the claim occurred, in the county in which the manufacturer has its principal office in this state, or in the county in which the plaintiff resided at the time the cause of action accrued.

§ 15.035. Contract in Writing.

(a) Except as provided by Subsection (b), if a person has contracted in writing to perform an obligation in a particular county, expressly naming the county or a definite place in that county by that writing, suit on or by reason of the obligation may be brought against him either in that county or in the county in which the defendant has his domicile.

(b) In an action founded on a contractual obligation of the defendant to pay money arising out of or based on a consumer transaction for goods, services, loans, or extensions of credit intended primarily for personal, family, household, or agricultural use, suit by a creditor on or by reason of the obligation may be brought against the defendant either in the county in which the defendant in fact signed the contract or in the county in which the defendant resides when the action is commenced. No term or statement contained in an obligation described in this section shall constitute a waiver of these provisions.

§ 15.036. Corporations and Associations [Repealed]

§ 15.037. Foreign Corporations [Repealed]

§ 15.038. Other Permissive Venue.

An action governed by any other statute prescribing permissive venue may be brought in the county allowed by that statute.

§ 15.039. Transient Person.

A transient person may be sued in any county in which he may be found.

TRAFALGAR HOUSE OIL & GAS INC.
v.
De HINOJOSA
773 S.W.2d 797
(Tex. App.—San Antonio 1989)

Arnold G. Gonzalez, Wood, Boykin, Wolter & Keys, Corpus Christi, for appellants.
Terry A. Canales, Terry A. Canales, P.C., Premont, Timothy Patton, Pasqual & Pozza, San Antonio, for appellee.

BIERY, JUSTICE.

Appellants, Trafalgar House Oil & Gas, Inc., Hamill Energy Company and Linda D. Schibi, Trustee, appeal from a $20,600.00 judgment in favor of Trinidad C. De Hinojosa, appellee. The judgment followed a non-jury trial. Hinojosa's claims against Esenjay Petroleum Corporation, a bankrupt defendant, were severed from her claims against the other defendants prior to trial. Defendant Joseph P. Mueller did not appeal the judgment against him. Plaintiff, Trinidad C. De Hinojosa, sued defendants for breach of contract of an oil and gas lease. Plaintiff contended that defendants breached the "notice of assignment" provision and, therefore, plaintiff was entitled to recover liquidated damages of $1,000.00 for each breach as provided in the contract. By two points of error, defendants/appellants contend that the trial court erred in denying their motion to transfer venue and that the liquidated damage provision of the contract is an unenforceable penalty. We affirm the judgment of the trial court.

In point of error number one, appellants contend that venue was mandatory in Jim Hogg County or Duval County because the case involves an action to recover an interest in real property. TEX. CIV. PRAC. & REM. CODE ANN. § 15.011 (Vernon 1986).[1] In the alternative, appellants contend that venue was proper in Nueces County under the permissive venue provision requiring suits to be brought in the county of residence of the principal place of business of a corporation. *See* TEX. CIV. PRAC. & REM. CODE ANN. § 15.036 (Vernon Supp. 1989).

The ultimate or dominant purpose of the suit determines whether the case falls under the mandatory venue provision applicable to certain actions involving real property. *Scarth v. First Bank & Trust Co.*, 711 S.W.2d 140, 142 (Tex. App.—Amarillo 1986, no writ). Because of its mandatory nature, the venue provision applicable to suits concerning land is strictly construed by Texas courts and will not be applied unless the suit falls clearly within one of the categories set out by the statute. *Id.*

When construing the statutory predecessor to TEX. CIV. PRAC. & REM. CODE ANN. § 15.011, which was identical to the current venue law, this court recognized: "It is not enough that the suit merely involves land; it must be a suit for the recovery of land or damages thereto, or to quiet the title to land, or to prevent or stay waste on land." *Canales v. Estate of Canales*, 683 S.W.2d 77, 81 (Tex. App.—San Antonio 1984, no writ). Plaintiff's suit is not an action to recover land or quiet title; rather, it is a breach of contract action to recover liquidated damages for defendants' breaches of the notice requirements of the lease.

Appellants also claim that proper venue of the suit was Nueces County, the residence of defendants/appellants, under a permissive venue provision. If, however, the suit was properly filed in Jim Wells County pursuant to a different permissive venue provision, then the trial court correctly overruled the motions to transfer. *See* 1 R. MCDONALD, TEXAS CIVIL PRACTICE § 4.05 (1981). Venue was proper in Jim Wells County under the permissive venue provision, TEX. CIV. PRAC. & REM. CODE ANN. § 15.035(a), which states:

> [I]f a person has contracted in writing to perform an obligation in a particular county, expressly naming the county or a definite place in that county by that writing, suit on or by reason of the obligation may be brought against him either in that county or in the county in which the defendant has his domicile.

In paragraph five of the lease, the lessee and his assignees contracted in writing that:

> All payments due to LESSOR [Hinojosa] may be made by the check of LESSEE [defendants] mailed or delivered to the LESSOR at Post Office Box 14, Premont, Texas 78375, or THE FIRST STATE BANK in the City of Premont, Jim Wells County, Texas, on or before the due date of payment.

In paragraph nine of the lease, the lessee and any assignees agreed to pay Hinojosa $1,000.00 as liquidated damages if they failed to notify Hinojosa of an assignment within thirty days after that assignment. In paragraph thirty-one of the lease, the parties agreed that "all notices required" by the lease had to be delivered by the Lessee and assignees personally or by certified/registered mail to Trinidad C. De Hinojosa at P.O. Box 14, Premont, Texas 78375. Venue was therefore proper in Jim Wells County. *See Graham Homes, Inc. v. Bowyer Real Estate*, 619 S.W.2d 25, 26 (Tex. Civ. App.—Fort Worth 1981, no writ) (venue proper in county where brokers fee was payable by terms of contract); *Yanta v. Davenport*, 323 S.W.2d 636, 637 (Tex. Civ. App.—San Antonio 1959, writ dism'd) (provision for payment to order of plaintiff "at the Frost National Bank, of San Antonio, Texas" established venue); *Texas Gas Prods. Corp. v. Rowan*, 317 S.W.2d 815, 816 (Tex. Civ. App.—Fort Worth 1958, writ dism'd) (place of performance for venue purposes was fixed by parties when provision inserted for delivery of payment in specified county). Point of error number one is overruled.

* * *

The judgment of the trial court is affirmed.

---

1 Unless otherwise stated, all references to the Texas Civil Practice and Remedies Code are to Vernon 1986.

Notes

1. *Contract Actions. WTFO, Inc. v. Braithwaite*[1] is set forth *infra*, but the holding concerning permissive venue of contract actions belongs here. Refer to the full text of this case which appears later.

(This is an action by an assignee of promissory notes secured by deeds of trust against the borrower to collect deficiencies remaining after nonjudicial foreclosure sales.)

* * *

Appellant argues that it offered prima facie evidence that venue was proper in Harris County pursuant to section 15.035(a) of the Texas Civil Practice and Remedies Code. *See* TEX. CIV. PRAC. & REM. CODE ANN. § 15.035(a) (Vernon 1986) (permissive venue provision). Appellant claims that the notes provided for payment at the holder's address in Dallas County or "at such other county that holder may designate in writing." Appellant argues that to comply with this language it gave formal written notice in a letter to appellee that the place of payment was changed to Harris County. Appellant claims that this letter is valid venue proof that it comported with the terms of the contract under section 15.035(a).

Prima facie proof is made when the venue facts are properly pleaded and an affidavit and any duly proved attachments to the affidavit fully and specifically setting forth the facts supporting such pleading are filed. TEX. R. CIV. P. 87(3)(a); *Kansas City S. Ry. Co. v. Carter*, 778 S.W.2d 911, 914-15 (Tex. App.—Texarkana 1989, writ denied). Affidavits shall be made on personal knowledge, shall set forth specific facts as would be admissible in evidence, and shall show affirmatively that the affiant is competent to testify. TEX. R. CIV. P. 87(3)(a).

Appellant's sole prima facie proof that venue was proper in Harris County consisted of the letter sent to appellee two days before suit was filed. *Appellant's* letter is not an affidavit pursuant to rule 87(3)(a). *See* TEX. R. CIV. P. 87(3)(a). Accordingly, we conclude that appellant failed to make prima facie proof of the venue facts necessary to maintain venue in Harris County.

Assuming, arguendo, that appellant affirmatively proved its venue facts, its argument that the letter expressly designated the county of proper venue pursuant to section 15.035 is without merit. Section 15.035(a) provides for two locations where venue may be proper in a suit on a written contract to perform an obligation in a particular county: (1) where the contract expressly names the county or a definite place in that county or (2) in the county where the defendant is domiciled. TEX. CIV. PRAC. & REM. CODE ANN. § 15.035(a) (Vernon 1986). Although appellant relies on the first location for maintaining venue in Harris County, this exception applies only in a case where the defendant agreed at the time he executed the instrument to perform his obligation in a particular place other than his place of residence. *Hibbler v. Walker*, 598 S.W.2d 19, 20 (Tex. Civ. App.—Texarkana 1980, no writ) (*citing* section 5 of article 1995, the former venue statute); *see also Texas Workers' Compensation Assigned Risk Pool v. Perry-Packard Co.*, 643 S.W.2d 202, 203 (Tex. App.—Austin 1982, no writ). The place of performance for payment of a contract must be named specifically at the time the instrument was executed to avoid the loss of venue under section 15.035(a). *Hibbler*, 598 S.W.2d at 20. The ability to redesignate in writing the place of performance at some time in the future by appellant or any holder of the indebtedness makes the place of payment uncertain.

Otherwise, leaving open a contract's term of place of performance at the time of execution of the contract allows the appellant, as the holder, at some future time to determine venue at its own will and pleasure. *Id.*; *Yell v. Prock*, 238 S.W.2d 238, 239 (Tex. Civ. App.—Fort Worth 1951, writ dism'd). Accordingly, we conclude that such a unilateral designation by appellant does not establish prima facie proof that venue was proper in Harris County under section 15.035(a).

2. *Corporations.* Generally, under the current statute, venue of an action against a corporation is in the county of the defendant's principal office in this state. Venue in cases involving corporations was once a matter of permissive venue, expressly included within the permissive venue section of the venue statute. *See Ruiz v.*

[1] 899 S.W.2d 709, 715, 716 (Tex. App.—Dallas 1995, no writ).

Conoco.[2] For more on venue concerning the current venue provisions relating to corporations refer back to *In Re Missouri Pacific Railroad.*[3]

Even though the use of agents and representatives to determine the venue over a corporation ended in 1995, many cases remained on appeal. The sharply divided decision in *Ford Motor Company v. Miles*[4] demonstrates the deep divisions over the questions raised by the old statute.

3. *Accrual—Where the cause of action accrued.* Under the pre-1983 art. 1995 (9a), venue in cases involving negligent acts was in the county where the cause of action "occurred". This language was interpreted to mean that the place where damages was not part of the negligent occurrence, for venue purposes.[5] In the 1983 re-write of the venue statute, there was no special venue "exception" for negligence cases. Rather, it was assumed that negligence cases would be controlled by the "accrued" provision. This reasoning flowed from the decision in *Lubbock Manufacturing Co. v.* Sames,[6] a case against a non-resident manufacturer under Art. 1995 (23), in which the plaintiff sought to impose strict liability. There it was held that damages were an essential part of a cause of action for strict liability, under 402A of the RESTATEMENT (SECOND) OF TORTS. A strict liability cause of action, therefore, "arose" in the county where damages were sustained. The 1995 revision of the venue statute abandoned the use of the "accrued" language, and returned to the "occurred" language.

4. *"Occurred" Restricts Venue.* If it was clear that the 1983 legislation was intended to extend permissible venue into counties where the plaintiff's suffered damages, it is now equally clear that the legislature in 1995 intends to withdraw that extension. The replacement of the word "accrued" with "occurred" is significant. JUSTICE MEADE GRIFFIN, writing for the Supreme Court of Texas, in 1963, in *Leonard v. Abbott*[7] interpreted the language in Art. 1995 (9a), allowing suit in the "county where the act or omission of negligence occurred." He concluded that:

> "This is plain and unambiguous language. An act can only occur where the act actually takes place. 'Occur' does not include the results of the occurrence, but only the taking place, happening, or coming to pass. . . . The Legislature knew how to use appropriate language to confer venue where the cause of action or a part thereof arose, had it desired to do so. See subdivisions 23 and 27 of Article 1995." [The latter reference is to the "arose" language relied upon in *Sames*, which formed the basis for the "accrued" language of the 1983 legislation. These two subdivisions, as recodified, have been repealed.]

See Richards v. United States,[8] cited in *Leonard,* where the United States Supreme Court construed similar language in the Federal Tort Claims Act. They said: "We believe that it would be difficult to conceive of any more precise language Congress could have used to command application of the law of the place where the negligence occurred than the words it did employed in the Tort Claims Act" [would be liable to the claimant in accordance with the law of the place where the act or omission occurred]. *See also Chirbogha v. State Farm Mut. Auto. Ins.*, 96 S.W.3d (Tex. App.—Austin 2003, no pet.) (§ 15.002(a)(1) is substantially similar to 28 U.S.C. § 1391 (a)(2), (b)(2), and can be interpreted in the same way.

2 868 S.W.2d 752 (Tex. 1993).

3 42 Tex. Sup. Ct. J. 1018, ___ S.W.2d ___ (Tex. 1999), *supra.*

4 967 S.W.2d 377 (Tex. 1998).

5 Leonard v. Abbott, 366 S.W.2d 925 (Tex. 1963).

6 553 S.W.2d 234 (Tex. 1980).

7 366 S.W.2d 925, at 927 (Tex. 1963).

8 369 U.S. 1, 82 S.Ct. 585, 7 L.Ed. 492 (1962).

GONZALEZ
v.
RELIANT ENERGY, INC.
159 S.W.3d 615
(Tex. 2005)

Pamela Stanton Baron, Austin, Anthony F. Constant, Miguel Jose Chapa, Constant & Vela, Corpus Christi, Thomas C. Wright, Wright Brown & Close, LLP, Houston, for petitioner.

Macey Reasoner Stokes, David Michael Rodi, John Anaipakos, Stephen G. Tipps, Susanna Dokupil, Baker & Botts, L.L.P., Houston, for respondent.

Ben Taylor, Fulbright & Jaworski L.L.P., Dallas, for Zachry Construction Corporation and H.B. Zachry Company

JUSTICE OWEN delivered the opinion of the Court.

Two interlocutory appeals in the same underlying case present the issue of whether section 15.007 of the Texas Civil Practice and Remedies Code places venue limitations on a statutory probate court's discretionary authority, pursuant to section 5B of the Texas Probate Code, to transfer to itself a wrongful death, personal injury, or property damage case in which a personal representative of an estate pending in that court is a party. The court of appeals held that under section 15.007, a statutory probate court cannot effectuate such a transfer unless venue in the county in which the probate court is located would be proper under section 15.002 of the Civil Practice and Remedies Code. We affirm.

I

Guadalupe Gonzalez, Jr., lived with his wife Jannete and their children in Hidalgo County. Guadalupe Gonzalez was killed in an accident while working at a Reliant Energy power plant in Fort Bend County, near Houston. Jannete Gonzalez initiated an estate administration proceeding in statutory probate court in Hidalgo County and was appointed dependent administrator of her husband's estate. While the administration of the estate was pending, Gonzalez filed a wrongful death and survival action against Reliant in the Hidalgo County statutory probate court. Reliant moved to transfer venue of the wrongful death and survival case to a district court in Harris County, where its principal place of business is located. The probate court denied the motion.

Meanwhile, Gonzalez filed an identical wrongful death and survival action in a Harris County district court and ten days later filed a motion in the Hidalgo County probate court asking that court to transfer the Harris County suit to Hidalgo County and consolidate the two actions, citing former section 5B of the Texas Probate Code. The version of section 5B that was in effect prior to the 2003 amendments applies to this suit, and it provided:

> A judge of a statutory probate court, on the motion of a party to the action or on the motion of a person interested in an estate, may transfer to his court from a district, county, or statutory court a cause of action appertaining to or incident to an estate pending in the statutory probate court or a cause of action in which a personal representative of an estate pending in the statutory probate court is a party and may consolidate the transferred cause of action with the other proceedings in the statutory probate court relating to that estate.

Back in Harris County, Reliant answered in the Harris County suit and applied for an anti-suit injunction, requesting that Gonzalez be enjoined from pursuing the wrongful death and survival action in Hidalgo County. Reliant argued that section 15.007 of the Civil Practice and Remedies Code rendered venue of that suit improper in Hidalgo County and that the Harris County court had dominant jurisdiction over Gonzalez's wrongful death and survival claims even though they were first filed and remained pending in Hidalgo County. Section 15.007 provides:

> Notwithstanding Sections 15.004, 15.005, and 15.031, to the extent that venue under this chapter for a suit by or against an executor, administrator, or guardian as such, for personal injury, death, or property damage conflicts with venue provisions under the Texas Probate Code, this chapter controls.

Gonzalez countered by filing an amended motion to transfer in Hidalgo County, informing the probate court of the impending anti-suit injunction hearing in Harris County. The Hidalgo County probate court then advanced its hearing on the motion to transfer to itself the Harris County suit so that its hearing would occur before the Harris County anti-suit injunction hearing. Reliant responded by moving for and obtaining a temporary restraining order in the Harris County court requiring Gonzalez to contact the Hidalgo County court and reschedule the hearing on the motion to transfer for a date after the anti-suit injunction hearing.

In accordance with the Harris County district court's temporary restraining order, Gonzalez filed a request in the Hidalgo County probate court to reschedule the transfer hearing. The probate court denied that request, as well as Reliant's motion for a continuance, proceeded with its hearing, and granted Gonzalez's motion to transfer her suit out of the Harris County district court and into the Hidalgo County probate court. The Hidalgo County probate court also denied Reliant's motion to abate.

Subsequently, the hearing on Reliant's application for an anti-suit injunction went forward in the Harris County district court, and that court refused to grant injunctive relief. Reliant then initiated proceedings in two courts of appeals. It sought a writ of mandamus from the Thirteenth District Court of Appeals directing the Hidalgo County court to vacate its transfer order, and that request for relief was denied. Reliant also perfected an interlocutory appeal in the First District Court of Appeals from the Harris County district court's denial of temporary injunctive relief. One business day before the Hidalgo County wrongful death and survival case was set for trial, a divided court of appeals sitting en banc, held that the Harris County district court had abused its discretion in denying Reliant's request for an anti-suit injunction. The court of appeals remanded the case to the Harris County district court with instructions to enter a temporary injunction. In accordance with the court of appeals' directive, the Harris County district court enjoined Gonzalez "from engaging in proceedings with respect to the wrongful death suit" pending in the Hidalgo County probate court. Gonzalez filed a motion for rehearing of the court of appeals' decision and a separate interlocutory appeal of the district court's injunction.

The court of appeals, again sitting en banc and again divided, considered Gonzalez's motion for rehearing and her interlocutory appeal at the same time, though it denied her motion to consolidate. The court of appeals denied Gonzalez's motion for rehearing of its decision in Reliant's appeal from the denial of injunctive relief, withdrew that opinion, and dismissed the first (Reliant's) appeal. In the same opinion, the court of appeals affirmed the trial court's order granting Reliant's application for an anti-suit injunction, which had been issued in compliance with the court of appeals' directive in the first interlocutory appeal. The court of appeals concluded that section 5A of the Probate Code gives the Hidalgo County statutory probate court concurrent jurisdiction with the Harris County district court over the wrongful death and survival suit at hand, but held that section 5A does not "dispense with the requirement that proper venue must lie for a statutory probate court to exercise its concurrent jurisdiction." Similarly, the court of appeals held that section 5B of the Probate Code, which gives a statutory probate court discretionary authority to transfer to itself a cause of action in which a personal representative of an estate pending in that court is a party, does not dispense with the requirement that venue of the wrongful death and survival action must be proper in the probate court. The court rejected Gonzalez's argument that the Hidalgo County probate court had dominant jurisdiction over the case, holding "it is axiomatic that a court cannot have 'dominant jurisdiction' if it does not have proper venue."

Finally, the court of appeals concluded that venue was improper in Hidalgo County due to section 15.007 of the Civil Practice and Remedies Code, which states that "to the extent venue under this chapter for a suit by or against an executor, administrator, or guardian as such, for personal injury, death, or property damage conflicts with venue provisions under the Texas Probate Code, this chapter controls."

Gonzalez filed two petitions for review in this Court. We have jurisdiction over these interlocutory appeals because there were dissents in the court of appeals and because the court of appeals' opinion expressly declined to follow and conflicts with the holding in *In re Houston Northwest Partners, Ltd.* We granted Gonzalez's petitions and the petition in Houston Northwest Partners and consolidated the cases for oral argument. The Houston Northwest Partners controversy has since settled.

We note that we also have had pending before us in a separate proceeding Reliant's petition for a writ of mandamus directing the Hidalgo County probate court to withdraw its transfer order. We conditionally grant that request for mandamus relief today in a separate opinion.

II

It is undisputed that Gonzalez's estate administration proceeding was properly brought in the Hidalgo County statutory probate court. That court has jurisdiction over the proceeding pursuant to section 5 of the Texas

Probate Code, and venue is proper under section 6 of the Probate Code, which governs venue for the probate of wills and administration of estates.

It is also undisputed that the Hidalgo County statutory probate court has jurisdiction over Gonzalez's wrongful death and survival action. Former section 5A(c)(1), which governs this suit, provided that "[a] statutory probate court has concurrent jurisdiction with the district court in all actions: (1) by or against a person in the person's capacity as a personal representative." This Court held in *Palmer v. Coble Wall Trust Co.* that this provision, added in 1985 and then contained in section 5A(b), gave probate courts jurisdiction over wrongful death and survival actions. However, this provision does not confer venue. Venue in wrongful death and survival actions is governed by section 15.002 of the Civil Practice and Remedies Code, . . .

The accident that caused the death of Gonzalez's husband occurred in Fort Bend County, and Reliant's principal place of business is in Harris County. Accordingly, venue in Hidalgo County was not proper unless some provision of the Probate Code overrides section 15.002 with respect to wrongful death and survival actions. Gonzalez contends that even if she could not have filed and maintained her wrongful death and survival claims in Hidalgo County over Reliant's objection that venue was improper, the 1999 version of section 5B of the Probate Code, which governs this case, gave the probate court unfettered authority to transfer wrongful death and personal injury claims to itself. Accordingly, Gonzalez contends that the Hidalgo County probate court had the power to transfer her Harris County suit to Hidalgo County even though venue in Hidalgo County would otherwise be improper. Neither the wording nor the history of section 5B of the Probate Code or section 15.007 of the Civil Practice and Remedies Code supports this position.

* * *

Thus the question is whether section 5B of the Probate Code authorized the Hidalgo County statutory probate court's transfer of the wrongful death case to itself from the Harris County district court despite section 15.007 and the fact that venue of the suit is not otherwise proper in Hidalgo County. We hold that section 15.007 of the Civil Practice and Remedies Code prohibits such a transfer when there is a timely objection.

Section 15.007 clearly curbs a party's ability to initially bring a lawsuit involving personal injury, death, or property damage in a statutory probate court when venue of the suit is not proper under Chapter 15 in the county in which the probate court is located, even if the probate court has jurisdiction to hear the suit. Section 15.007 also limits the probate court's discretion to transfer those kinds of cases to itself if venue is improper under Chapter 15.

Gonzalez's main argument—that section 5B is not a venue provision and that section 15.007 is therefore inapplicable because it governs only when there is a conflict between Chapter 15 and the venue provisions of the Probate Code—is unpersuasive. Section 5B permits a transfer. The transfer of a case pertains to venue, not jurisdiction. While section 5A grants concurrent jurisdiction in probate and district courts, section 15.007 makes clear that the transfer authority granted in section 5B is limited by the venue constraints set forth in Chapter 15 for wrongful death, personal injury, and property damage claims. Hidalgo County is not a county of proper venue for the wrongful death suit under section 15.002, as it is not a "county in which all or a substantial part of the events or omissions giving rise to the claim occurred" or the "county of the defendant's principal office in this state." The venue provisions in Chapter 15 govern regardless of whether the issue is the propriety of bringing the suit in the Hidalgo County probate court in the first instance or the probate court's authority to transfer the case. The fact that suit was first brought in another county does not make venue any more proper in Hidalgo County.

The Legislature chose between competing policy considerations in enacting section 5B of the Probate Code and section 15.007 of the Civil Practice and Remedies Code. On the one hand, the Legislature has "persistent[ly] expan[ded]" the statutory probate courts' jurisdiction over the years. On the other hand, the venue statutes were revised in 1995—the same year section 15.007 was added—in an effort to reduce forum shopping.

Because Hidalgo County was not a county of proper venue for the wrongful death suit, the Hidalgo County statutory probate court erred in granting Gonzalez's section 5B motion to transfer. In doing so, the probate court "actively interfered with the jurisdiction" of the Harris County court.

III

With regard to the parties' arguments as to which court had "dominant jurisdiction" over the wrongful death suit, we agree with the court of appeals that unless venue would be proper in both Harris and Hidalgo counties, the concept of "dominant jurisdiction" is inapplicable to this case. The court in which suit is first filed generally acquires dominant jurisdiction to the exclusion of other courts if venue is proper in the county in which suit was first filed. "As long as the forum is a proper one, it is the plaintiff's privilege to choose the forum." Hidalgo County, however, was not a proper forum for Gonzalez's wrongful death suit, and the Hidalgo County statutory probate court therefore could not have acquired dominant jurisdiction over the suit even though it was first filed there.

* * *

For the foregoing reasons, we affirm the court of appeals' judgment.

4. *Other Ways to Establish Venue*

Notes

1. *Venue by Consent.* An agreement satisfying the requirements of TEX. R. CIV. P. 11, and consenting to the transfer of venue, constitutes a waiver of venue and precludes the challenge of venue on appeal.[1]

2. *Failure to Object.* There is nothing to indicate that there is any change in the requirement that the motion to transfer venue must be filed "prior to or concurrently with any other plea, pleading or motion except a special appearance motion provided by Rule 120a."[2] The failure to timely file, in due order, the motion to transfer venue waives any complaint about the venue selected by the plaintiff.

3. *Other statutes creating venue. In re Lopez*, 372 S.W.3d 174 (Tex. 2012): Regency Nursing Center Partners of Yoakum, Ltd. and the Lopezes entered into an agreement for the admission of San Juana Lopez to Yoakum's nursing home. The agreement contained an arbitration clause that specified that arbitration was to take place in Victoria County. After Mrs. Lopez died while in Yoakum's care, the Lopezes filed a demand for arbitration of their wrongful death and survival claims to the American Arbitration Association. Although the Lopezes' demand indicated that the location of the arbitration should be Victoria County, the parties subsequently agreed by email to a specific arbitrator located in Travis County. However, the arbitration agreement was never explicitly modified. The arbitration took place in Travis County, with a ruling in the Lopezes' favor. Yoakum filed an application in Victoria County to vacate the award. In response, since the arbitration had already been conducted in Travis County, the Lopezes asked the court to transfer venue to Travis County pursuant to Texas Civil Practices & Remedies Code section 171.096(c), which provides that "[i]f a hearing before the arbitrators has been held, a party must file the initial application [to vacate the arbitration award] with the clerk of the court of the county in which the hearing was held." Yoakum responded that venue was proper in Victoria County pursuant to section 171.096(b), which provides that "[i]f the agreement to arbitrate provides that the hearing before the arbitrators is to be held in a county in this state, a party must file the initial application [to vacate the arbitration award] with the clerk of the court of that county." The trial court denied the Lopezes request to transfer venue. The court of appeals denied the Lopezes' request for a writ of mandamus. ***Held*:** By using the past tense in section 171.096(c)—"has been held"—the Legislature indicated that this provision applies when the arbitration has already occurred; conversely, by using the future tense in section 171.096(b)—"is to be held"—the Legislature indicated that this provision applies when the arbitration has not yet occurred. Since the arbitration had already occurred, the trial court abused its discretion in applying subsection (b) rather than subsection (c). Because the Lopezes seek to enforce a mandatory venue provision, as indicated by subsection (c)'s use of "must," they are required to show only a clear abuse of discretion; they are not required to show they lack an adequate appellate remedy to be entitled to relief by mandamus.

4. *Perryman v. Spartan Texas Six Capital Partners Ltd.*, 546 S.W.3d 110 (Tex. 2018): Here, Spartan sued EOG for breach of contract and for an accounting in Harris County, EOG's principal place of business, under the general venue statute. EOG did not complain that venue was improper, although when it added the Perrymans as third-party defendants, it noted that Montague County was the mandatory and proper venue for its claims against the Perrymans. Although the Perrymans did indeed move to transfer venue, EOG never contested venue on its

---

[1] Farris v. Ray, 895 S.W.2d 351 (Tex. 1995).

[2] TEX. R. CIV. P. 81(1).

own motion and nothing in the record indicates that it filed anything in support of the Perrymans' motion. If the Perrymans were the original defendants to the main action, our statutes would have required the trial court to transfer venue on the Perrymans' motion. However, the Perrymans were joined as third-party defendants. And the venue statutes also state: "Venue of the main action shall establish venue of a counterclaim, cross claim, or third-party claim properly joined under the Texas Rules of Civil Procedure or any applicable statute." TEX. CIV. PRAC. & REM. CODE § 15.062(a). The Perrymans were properly joined by EOG, which then filed a proper third-party claim against them. Thus, the supreme court stated that section 15.062(a) appears to apply.

In re TEAM ROCKET, L.P.
256 S.W.3d 257
(Tex. 2008)

Robert C. McCreary, Law Offices of Lou McCreary, Austin, Cynthia T. Sheppard, Cuero, Mahon B. Garry Jr., Wright & Greenhill, Austin, TX, for Relator.

Gary L. Evans, George Andrew Coats, Coats & Evans, The Woodlands, TX, for Real Party In Interest.

JUSTICE GREEN delivered the opinion of the Court.

In this case, we decide whether a plaintiff who was denied his initial venue of choice can nonsuit his case in the transferee county and refile in a third county. We hold that a plaintiff cannot avoid a venue ruling in such a way. Because the trial court in the third county refused to enforce the prior order setting venue in the transferee county, we conditionally grant the writ of mandamus.

I

Thomas Creekmore died when the airplane he was flying crashed in Fort Bend County. His family brought negligence, strict liability, survival, and wrongful death claims in Harris County against Team Rocket, L.P., MLF Airframes, Inc., and Mark L. Frederick (collectively, Team Rocket), related to Team Rocket's manufacture and sale of the plane kit that Creekmore had purchased. Team Rocket moved to transfer venue, arguing that venue was improper in Harris County because they did not deliver the kit parts to Creekmore's residence there. The Harris County trial court agreed and transferred the case to Williamson County, Team Rocket's principal place of business and the residence of its representative. After the transfer, the Creekmores voluntarily nonsuited the case and immediately refiled the same claims against the same defendants in Fort Bend County. Team Rocket moved to transfer venue to Williamson County based on the Harris County trial court's prior venue order and the doctrine of collateral estoppel. The Fort Bend County trial court denied the motion. Team Rocket then sought mandamus relief in the court of appeals, which denied the petition. 256 S.W.3d 314, 2006 WL 1071213 (Tex. App.—Houston [14th Dist.] 2006).

II

We grant the extraordinary relief of mandamus only when the trial court has clearly abused its discretion and the relator lacks an adequate appellate remedy. *In re Prudential Ins. Co. of Am.*, 148 S.W.3d 124, 135-40 (Tex. 2004) (*citing Walker v. Packer*, 827 S.W.2d 833, 840 (Tex. 1992)). In this case, Team Rocket argues that they are entitled to mandamus relief because collateral estoppel bars reconsideration of the Harris County trial court's final venue ruling, and because the Fort Bend County trial court's refusal to transfer the case back to Williamson County violated Texas Rule of Civil Procedure 87(5). Team Rocket also argues that, rather than requiring the parties to proceed to trial following an erroneous venue ruling, exceptional circumstances exist to justify granting mandamus relief. The Creekmores contend that they had an absolute right to nonsuit their case and refile in Fort Bend County.

A

A plaintiff may nonsuit his case at any time prior to the close of the plaintiff's pre-rebuttal evidence. TEX. R. CIV. P. 162. "Subject to certain conditions, a plaintiff who takes a nonsuit is not precluded from filing a subsequent suit seeking the same relief." *Aetna Cas. & Sur. Co. v. Specia*, 849 S.W.2d 805, 806 (Tex. 1993). The issue in this case is whether that general rule allows a plaintiff to use the procedural vehicle of nonsuiting a case to avoid unfavorable venue rulings.

The plaintiff gets the first choice of venue by filing suit. *In re Masonite Corp.*, 997 S.W.2d 194, 197 (Tex. 1999). The defendant, however, may challenge that venue selection, and a court must "transfer an action to another county of proper venue if . . . the county in which the action is pending is not a proper county." TEX. CIV. PRAC. & REM. CODE § 15.063(1); *see* TEX.R. CIV. P. 87 (procedures for filing motions to transfer venue). In this case, the Creekmores initially filed suit in Harris County, their county of residence. Team Rocket challenged venue, asserting that the defendants did not reside there and that a substantial portion of the events giving rise to the cause of action did not occur there. *See* TEX. CIV. PRAC. & REM. CODE § 15.002(a)(1)-(2). The Harris County trial court determined that Harris County was not a proper venue, but that venue was proper in Williamson County.

Team Rocket argues that only one venue determination may be made in a proceeding and that Texas Rule of Civil Procedure 87 specifically prohibits changes in venue after the initial venue ruling. We agree. Once a trial court has ruled on proper venue, that decision cannot be the subject of interlocutory appeal. *Id.* § 15.064(a) ("No interlocutory appeal shall lie from the determination."); TEX.R. CIV. P. 87(6) ("There shall be no interlocutory appeals from such determination."). Moreover, Rule 87 states that "if an action has been transferred to a proper county in response to a motion to transfer, then no further motions to transfer shall be considered." TEX.R. CIV. P. 87(5). Although a trial court's ruling transferring venue is interlocutory for the parties, and thus not subject to immediate appeal, the order is final for the transferring court as long as it is not altered within the court's thirty-day plenary jurisdiction. *See In re Sw. Bell Tel. Co.*, 35 S.W.3d 602, 605 (Tex. 2000) (per curiam). Once a ruling is made on the merits, as in a summary judgment, that decision becomes final as to that issue and cannot be vitiated by nonsuiting and refiling the case. *See Hyundai Motor Co. v. Alvarado*, 892 S.W.2d 853, 855 (Tex. 1995) (per curiam) ("A nonsuit sought after [a partial summary judgment] results in a dismissal with prejudice as to the issues pronounced in favor of the defendant."). This concept is rooted in the long-standing and fundamental judicial doctrines of res judicata and collateral estoppel, which "promote judicial efficiency, protect parties from multiple lawsuits, and prevent inconsistent judgments by precluding the relitigation" of matters that have already been decided or could have been litigated in a prior suit. *Sysco Food Servs., Inc. v. Trapnell*, 890 S.W.2d 796, 801 (Tex. 1994); *accord Citizens Ins. Co. of Am. v. Daccach*, 217 S.W.3d 430, 449 (Tex. 2007). Just as a decision on the merits cannot be circumvented by nonsuiting and refiling the case, a final determination fixing venue in a particular county must likewise be protected from relitigation. *Cf. Wichita Falls & S. R.R. Co. v. McDonald*, 141 Tex. 555, 174 S.W.2d 951, 952-53 (1943) ("[A] ruling on a plea of privilege is treated as final in so far as it disposes of the issue as to the venue of the case . . . . [A]n interlocutory order of court overruling a plea of privilege shall become final in so far as the venue question is concerned, within the same time and under the same circumstances that a judgment on the merits of the case would become final.").

Reading Section 15.064 of the Texas Civil Practice and Remedies Code and Rule 87 together, we conclude that once a venue determination has been made, that determination is conclusive as to those parties and claims. Because venue is then fixed in any suit involving the same parties and claims, it cannot be overcome by a nonsuit and subsequent refiling in another county. *Cf. H.H. Watson Co. v. Cobb Grain Co.*, 292 S.W. 174, 177 (Tex. Comm'n App.1927, judgm't adopted) (holding that a plaintiff's nonsuit following the trial court's hearing on a plea of privilege "unalterably fixed the venue of any suit involving any subsequent controversy between the parties, relating to the subject-matter of the original suit in the county where the defendants reside," and that "[t]he venue of such subsequent suit, if any, has become res adjudicata."). Once the Harris County trial court transferred the cause to the proper venue of Williamson County, venue was fixed permanently in Williamson County for these causes of action between these parties. That venue was also proper in Fort Bend County does not change the result. The Fort Bend County trial court therefore abused its discretion by refusing to enforce the prior venue order issued by the Harris County trial court.

To interpret the provisions otherwise would allow forum shopping, a practice we have repeatedly prohibited. *See, e.g., In re Autonation, Inc.*, 228 S.W.3d 663, 667-68 (Tex. 2007). If a plaintiff has an absolute right to nonsuit and refile, as the Creekmores contend, nothing could stop him from filing in each of Texas's 254 counties until he finds a favorable venue. And, under the Creekmores' interpretation, defendants would be left with no remedy and would have to endure a trial in the wrong venue, while a plaintiff could avoid any number of venue rulings simply by nonsuiting and refiling his case. We do not believe that the Legislature intended such a situation. Indeed, the plea of privilege practice that existed before amendment of the predecessor to Section 15.064 prevented that outcome. *See H.H. Watson Co.*, 292 S.W. at 177; *Ruiz v. Conoco, Inc.*, 868 S.W.2d 752, 756-57 (Tex. 1993). When a plea of privilege was sustained and a cause then transferred, a plaintiff's nonsuit became res judicata as to venue if the plaintiff asserted the same cause of action against the defendant in a subsequent suit. *See GeoChem Tech Corp. v. Verseckes*, 962 S.W.2d 541, 543 (Tex. 1998) (recognizing that, under the previous plea of privilege practice, when a plaintiff took a nonsuit while a proper plea of privilege was pending, the dismissal was deemed an admission that venue was improper in the original county, and venue became fixed in the county to which transfer was sought); *Ruiz*, 868 S.W.2d at 756-57 (explaining that although referred to as "res judicata," the rule was really based on the dismissal being "deemed an admission of the merit of the plea"). Though we no longer have a plea of privilege under our statutes or rules, the rationale of "protect[ing] defendants from the harassment and expense of several contests on the issue of venue" remains. *First Nat'l Bank in Dallas v. Hannay*, 123 Tex. 203, 67 S.W.2d 215, 215 (1933) (per curiam).

The only remedy afforded by the Legislature when a party loses a venue hearing is to proceed with trial in the transferee county and appeal any judgment from that court on the basis of alleged error in the venue ruling. TEX. CIV. PRAC. & REM. CODE § 15.064(b) ("On appeal from the trial on the merits, if venue was improper it shall in no event be harmless error and shall be reversible error."). The Creekmores chose not to avail themselves of that prescribed remedy and instead attempted to circumvent the venue ruling by nonsuiting and refiling. As we said in *Masonite*, "the plaintiffs had the first choice, but not the second, of a proper venue." 997 S.W.2d at 198 (emphasis added).

* * *

B

The adequacy of an appellate remedy must be determined by balancing the benefits of mandamus review against the detriments. *Prudential Ins. Co. of Am.*, 148 S.W.3d 124, 136 (Tex. 2004). In evaluating benefits and detriments, we consider whether mandamus will preserve important substantive and procedural rights from impairment or loss. *Id.* Our venue statutes create a balance: a plaintiff has the first choice of venue when he files suit, and a defendant is restricted to one motion to transfer that venue. *See Masonite*, 997 S.W.2d at 197-98; TEX. R. CIV. P. 87(5). By defying the Harris County trial court's venue ruling by nonsuiting and refiling elsewhere, the Creekmores disrupted that balance in their favor and thereby impaired Team Rocket's procedural rights.

In addition to impairment of rights, we consider whether mandamus will "allow the appellate courts to give needed and helpful direction to the law that would otherwise prove elusive in appeals from final judgments." *Prudential*, 148 S.W.3d at 136. This petition involves a legal issue-the construction of Texas venue statutes and related rules in the context of voluntary nonsuit-that is likely to recur, as demonstrated by the court of appeals' decisions that have already addressed it. *See Fincher*, 141 S.W.3d 255; *Shell Oil*, 128 S.W.3d 694; *Hendrick Med. Ctr.*, 690 S.W.2d 42.

Finally, we consider whether mandamus will spare litigants and the public "the time and money utterly wasted enduring eventual reversal of improperly conducted proceedings." *Prudential*, 148 S.W.3d at 136. Although we generally do not grant a petition for mandamus for venue determinations absent extraordinary circumstances, we have granted mandamus relief when the trial court issued an improper order transferring venue that "wrongfully burdened fourteen other courts in fourteen other counties, hundreds of potential jurors in those counties, and thousands of taxpayer dollars in those counties." *Masonite*, 997 S.W.2d at 199. When, as in this case, a trial court improperly applied the venue statute and issued a ruling that permits a plaintiff to abuse the legal system by refiling his case in county after county, which would inevitably result in considerable expense to taxpayers and defendants, requiring defendants to proceed to trial in the wrong county is not an adequate remedy. *See Prudential*, 148 S.W.3d at 137. "[A]n appellate remedy is not inadequate merely because it may involve more expense or delay than obtaining an extraordinary writ," *Walker*, 827 S.W.2d at 842, but extraordinary relief can be warranted when a trial court subjects taxpayers, defendants, and all of the state's district courts to meaningless proceedings and trials. *See Prudential*, 148 S.W.3d at 137.

We have granted mandamus relief in the context of Rule 87 venue rulings where, as here, the trial court made no effort to follow the rule. *See Henderson v. O'Neill*, 797 S.W.2d 905, 905 (Tex. 1990) (per curiam); *cf. Bridgestone/Firestone, Inc. v. Thirteenth Court of Appeals*, 929 S.W.2d 440, 442 (Tex. 1996) (per curiam) (explaining that, in that Rule 87 venue case, no extraordinary circumstances existed to justify mandamus relief). In this case, the Creekmores defied the Harris County trial court's venue order by attempting to have another court revisit the question of venue, which had already been decided. To say that the Fort Bend County trial court, which violated statutory venue procedure and Rule 87(5), committed reversible error while declining to correct the injustice would compromise the integrity of the venue statute and result in an irreversible waste of resources. We hold that Team Rocket has no adequate appellate remedy.

III

For the reasons described above, we conditionally grant the writ of mandamus directing the Fort Bend County trial court to vacate its venue order and transfer the Creekmores' case to Williamson County. If the court fails to do so, the writ will issue.

JUSTICE WAINWRIGHT, concurring, joined by CHIEF JUSTICE JEFFERSON and JUSTICE O'NEILL (opinion omitted).

5. *The Procedural Aspects of Venue*

a. *Requisites of the Motion to Transfer*

i. *Verification?*

The motion to transfer and any amendments to the motion must state that the action should be transferred and the reasons (legal or factual) for the transfer. Unlike the old practice the motion to transfer does not have to be verified. TEX. R. CIV. P 86(3).

ii. *Required Statements*

TEX. R. CIV. P 86(3) provides:

The motion, and any amendments to it, shall state that the action should be transferred to another specified county of proper venue because:

(a) The county where the action is pending is not a proper county; or

(b) Mandatory venue of the action in another county is prescribed by one or more specific statutory provisions which shall be clearly designated or indicated.

iii. *Specific Denial of Venue Facts*

TEX. R. CIV. P 87(3)(2) provides that:

All venue facts, when properly pleaded, shall be taken as true *unless specifically denied by the adverse party. See Whitworth v. Kuhn.*[1]

b. *Responses*

TEX. R. CIV. P 86(4) states that:

Except as provided in paragraph 3(a) of TEX. R. CIV. P 87, a response to the motion to transfer is not required. Verification of a response is not required.

One should not be misled by this Rule, for if a venue fact is specifically denied, ". . . the party *pleading* the venue fact *must* make prima facie proof of that venue fact." TEX. R. CIV. P 87(3)(2). Thus, while the old controverting affidavit is gone, some form of prima facie proof must be made to avoid a transfer.

c. *Prima Facie Proof*

TEX. R. CIV. P 87(3)(a) provides that: "prima facie proof is made when the venue facts are properly pleaded and an affidavit, and any duly proved attachments to the affidavit, are filed fully and specifically setting forth the facts supporting such pleading."

---

[1] 734 S.W.2d 108, 111 (Tex. App.—Austin 1987, no writ) (party did not specifically deny the asserted allegations).

i. *The Affidavit.*

The affidavit must be based upon *personal knowledge*. The facts set forth in the affidavit must be *admissible*, and the affiant must be shown affirmatively to be competent to testify. TEX. R. CIV. P 87(3)(a).

Warning. The failure to affirmatively show the competence of the affiant on the admissibility of the evidence contained in an affidavit could be fatal. Note, however, that amendments are allowed. Rule 86(3). If neither party makes prima facie proof, the trial court may direct the parties to make further proof. TEX. R. CIV. P 87(3)(d).

ii. *The Attachments (Discovery)*

TEX. R. CIV. P 88 provides:

> Discovery shall not be abated or otherwise affected by pendency of a motion to transfer venue . . . . Depositions, responses to requests for admission, answers to interrogatories and other discovery products on file containing information relevant to a determination of proper venue may be considered by the court in making the venue determination *when* they are *attached* to, or incorporated by reference in, an affidavit of a party, a witness or an attorney who has knowledge of such discovery.

No specific provision is made for exhibits other than those generated by discovery, unless it is the provision in Rule 87(3)(a). ". . . and any duly proved attachments to the affidavit . . . ." To rely on this provision to incorporate matters not covered by discovery, one should be sure to establish the evidentiary predicate for the exhibit in the affidavit of a competent affiant by stating admissible facts. Any evidentiary predicate should be satisfied within the affidavit.

d. *The Time Table*

i. *Hearing*

TEX. R. CIV. P. 87 (1) provides that "The movant has the duty to request a setting on the motion to transfer. Except on leave of court each party is entitled to at least 45 days notice of a hearing on the motion to transfer. A trial court abuses its discretion by ruling on the motion to transfer without giving the opponent sufficient notice.

ii. *Response*

Any response or opposing affidavits are to be filed at least 30 days prior to the hearing.

iii. *Reply*

A *reply* by the Movant is not required, but if one is desired it is to be filed not later than 7 days prior to the hearing date, except on leave of court. TEX. R. CIV. P 87(1).

6. *The Venue Hearing*

Note

§ 15.064(a) of the Texas Civil Practice and Remedies Code provides:

In all venue hearings, no factual proof concerning the merits of the case shall be required to establish venue. The court shall determine venue questions from the pleadings and affidavits. No interlocutory appeal shall lie from the determination.

[Note, however, that § 15.003 of the Texas Civil Practices and Remedies Code permits limited interlocutory appeals.]

WTFO, INC.
v.
BRAITHWAITE

899 S.W.2d 709
(Tex. App.—Dallas 1995, no writ)

Jeffrey A. Lehmann, Lehmann & Associates, Houston, for appellant.

Ernest E. Figari, Jr., Thomas A. Graves, Michael G. Brown, Figari & Davenport, L.L.P., Dallas, for appellee.

LAGARDE, JUSTICE.

Appellant WTFO, Inc. appeals a summary judgment granted in favor of appellee Garlan Braithwaite in its suit to collect the deficiencies remaining after nonjudicial foreclosure sales of two pieces of real property resulting from the default on two promissory notes. In two points of error, appellant contends that the trial court erred in transferring venue and in granting summary judgment. We overrule the points and affirm the trial court's judgment.

FACTUAL AND PROCEDURAL BACKGROUND

In May 1987, appellee, along with Judy Poort and Robert Mayr, executed two promissory notes, each for approximately $96,500. The notes were payable to Forestwood National Bank (Forestwood), as holder, in Dallas County or "at such other place as holder may designate in writing." Each note was secured by a deed of trust covering different real property. An Assignment of Rents and Leases was also executed.

On July 5, 1990, the FDIC, acting as conservator and receiver for Forestwood, sent two demand letters to appellee at a "Hurst Address" to formally notify him of the maturity and default on each note. One of the letters was returned, "Attempted, Not Known." On July 24, 1990, the FDIC sent appellee another letter notifying him that it now had his current address at the "Brookridge Address." Enclosed in that letter were the July 5 demand letters.

On January 3, 1991, the FDIC sent appellee a letter indicating that the real estate securing one of his loans had been sold at public auction on January 1, 1991, for $63,600 and that appellee owed the deficiency on the loan. On July 17, 1991, the FDIC sent him another letter stating that the real estate securing both loans had been foreclosed upon and that he owed the remaining balances of $41,011.47 and $46,940.42. Both pieces of property were later sold by the FDIC to third parties.

On April 21, 1993, appellant notified appellee that it had been assigned the promissory notes and that it sought the deficiencies. Two days later, appellant filed suit in Harris County against appellee and Poort seeking the deficiencies.

Appellee filed an answer, a motion to transfer venue, and counterclaims against appellant. Appellee requested a venue hearing; the parties were notified that the hearing was set for August 2, 1993. Appellant requested thirty days to respond and forty-five days' notice of the hearing as required by the Texas Rules of Civil Procedure. TEX. R. CIV. P. 87. The trial court rescheduled the hearing for August 26, 1993. Appellant timely filed a response. On August 23, 1993, appellant received a call that the hearing had been moved to August 24, 1993. Appellant neither objected nor requested a continuance. After a hearing the next day, the trial court severed the action as to appellee and granted his motion to transfer venue to Dallas County.

In January 1994, appellee filed a motion for summary judgment based on three grounds: (1) the failure to provide written notice of the foreclosure sales pursuant to the Deeds of Trust and section 51.002 of the Texas Property Code; (2) lack of evidence to establish the fair market value of the foreclosed property; and (3) appellee's release from personal liability. On March 4, 1994, appellant filed its response to appellee's motion, incorporating by reference the affidavit of Jerald W. Rosen (Rosen affidavit) and numerous exhibits. The Rosen affidavit and the exhibits, however, were not filed until March 7, 1994.

On March 11, 1994, the trial court granted summary judgment. Later that day, appellee nonsuited his counterclaims against appellant, making the summary judgment final.

TRANSFER OF VENUE

In its first point of error, appellant contends that the Harris County trial court reversibly erred in sustaining appellee's motion transferring venue to Dallas County. Appellant argues that (1) it did not receive forty-five days' notice of the hearing, (2) venue was proper in Harris County under a permissive venue statute, and (3) a general appearance by one co-defendant makes venue proper as to all defendants. * * *

Burden of Proof

When a motion to transfer venue is filed, the initial burden of proof that venue is maintainable in the county of suit is on the plaintiff. TEX. R. CIV. P. 87(2)(a). If the defendant specifically denies the venue facts, the plaintiff must support his pleadings by prima facie proof of the venue facts. TEX. R. CIV. P. 87(3)(a). If the plaintiff meets that burden, the trial court must maintain the lawsuit in the county in which it was filed unless a mandatory provision applies. TEX. R. CIV. P. 87(3)(c). If the plaintiff fails in his burden, the defendant has the burden of showing that venue is maintainable in the county in which the transfer is sought under either a general, permissive, or mandatory venue rule. *See* TEX. CIV. PRAC. & REM. CODE ANN. §§ 15.001-.040 (Vernon 1986); TEX. R. CIV. P. 87(2)(a). If the defendant succeeds in that showing, the cause will be transferred to the appropriate county. TEX. R. CIV. P. 87(2)(a).

Standard of Review

As an appellate court, we are obligated to conduct an independent review of the entire record to determine whether venue is proper in the ultimate county of suit. *See* TEX. CIV. PRAC. & REM. CODE ANN. § 15.064(b) (Vernon 1986); *Wilson v. Texas Parks & Wildlife Dept.*, 886 S.W.2d 259, 261 (Tex. 1994); *Ruiz v. Conoco, Inc.*, 868 S.W.2d 752, 757-58 (Tex. 1993). We view evidence adduced after the issue of venue was decided by the trial court to determine if this evidence "destroys the prima facie proof on which the trial court relied." *Ruiz*, 868 S.W.2d at 757. If, within the entire record, there is probative evidence to support the trial court's determination, we defer to the trial court's ruling. *Wilson*, 886 S.W.2d at 262; *Ruiz*, 868 S.W.2d at 758. If there is no supporting evidence, the judgment must be reversed and the cause remanded to the trial court. *Ruiz*, 868 S.W.2d at 758. The purpose of reviewing the entire record is to strike a balance between preserving the plaintiff's right to select and maintain suit in a county of proper venue and protecting the defendant against "fraud or inaccuracy at the pleading stage." *Wilson*, 886 S.W.2d at 262.

Notice of Hearing

Appellant claims that the trial court failed to give the forty-five days' notice required by rule 87(1) of the Texas Rules of Civil Procedure. *See* TEX. R. CIV. P. 87(1). When the venue hearing was originally scheduled for August 2, 1993, appellant requested the trial court to give it forty-five days' notice. The trial court complied, moving the date to August 26, 1993. Appellant now argues that the court's later moving the date of the hearing two days earlier to August 24 erroneously deprived it of the full forty-five days' notice.

The trial court's order states that appellant lodged the same objections as it filed in its responsive pleadings. These pleadings contained no specific lack of notice objection. The trial court also stated that it was transferring venue over appellant's objection. Because appellant provided no statement of facts from the venue hearing, we are unable to determine appellant's specific objection. *See* TEX. R. APP. P. 53(a); *Flores v. Arrieta*, 790 S.W.2d 75, 76 (Tex. App.—San Antonio 1990, writ denied) (appellant must bring forth sufficient record to demonstrate error). A review of the record before us shows that appellant specifically objected to the lack of notice in its motion to vacate, which was filed over two months after the trial court signed the transfer order. Appellant's failure to timely and specifically object to the lack of notice or request a motion for continuance waives error. TEX. R. APP. P. 52(a); *Gonzalez v. Nielson*, 770 S.W.2d 99, 101 (Tex. App.—Corpus Christi 1989, writ denied). Accordingly, we conclude that there is no evidence in the record that appellant objected or requested a motion for continuance, either after it received notice that the hearing was scheduled for an earlier date or during the hearing. Error is not preserved.

Section 15.035(a)

Appellant argues that it offered prima facie evidence that venue was proper in Harris County pursuant to section 15.035(a) of the Texas Civil Practice and Remedies Code. *See* TEX. CIV. PRAC. & REM. CODE ANN. § 15.035(a) (Vernon 1986) (permissive venue provision). Appellant claims that the notes provided for payment at the holder's address in Dallas County or "at such other county that holder may designate in writing." Appellant argues that to comply with this language it gave formal written notice in a letter to appellee that the place of payment was changed to Harris County. Appellant claims that this letter is valid venue proof that it comported with the terms of the contract under section 15.035(a).

Prima facie proof is made when the venue facts are properly pleaded and an affidavit and any duly proved attachments to the affidavit fully and specifically setting forth the facts supporting such pleading are filed. TEX. R. CIV. P. 87(3)(a); *Kansas City S. Ry. Co. v. Carter*, 778 S.W.2d 911, 914-15 (Tex. App.—Texarkana 1989, writ denied). Affidavits shall be made on personal knowledge, shall set forth specific facts as would be admissible in evidence, and shall show affirmatively that the affiant is competent to testify. TEX. R. CIV. P. 87(3)(a).

Appellant's sole prima facie proof that venue was proper in Harris County consisted of the letter sent to appellee two days before suit was filed. Appellant's letter is not an affidavit pursuant to rule 87(3)(a). *See* TEX. R. CIV. P. 87(3)(a). Accordingly, we conclude that appellant failed to make prima facie proof of the venue facts necessary to maintain venue in Harris County.

Assuming, arguendo, that appellant affirmatively proved its venue facts, its argument that the letter expressly designated the county of proper venue pursuant to section 15.035 is without merit. Section 15.035(a) provides for two locations where venue may be proper in a suit on a written contract to perform an obligation in a particular county: (1) where the contract expressly names the county or a definite place in that county or (2) in the county where the defendant is domiciled. TEX. CIV. PRAC. & REM. CODE ANN. § 15.035(a) (Vernon 1986). Although appellant relies on the first location for maintaining venue in Harris County, this exception applies only in a case where the defendant agreed at the time he executed the instrument to perform his obligation in a particular place other than his place of residence. *Hibbler v. Walker*, 598 S.W.2d 19, 20 (Tex. Civ. App.—Texarkana 1980, no writ) (citing section 5 of article 1995, the former venue statute); *see also Texas Workers' Compensation Assigned Risk Pool v. Perry-Packard Co.*, 643 S.W.2d 202, 203 (Tex. App.—Austin 1982, no writ). The place of performance for payment of a contract must be named specifically at the time the instrument was executed to avoid the loss of venue under section 15.035(a). *Hibbler*, 598 S.W.2d at 20. The ability to redesignate in writing the place of performance at some time in the future by appellant or any holder of the indebtedness makes the place of payment uncertain. *Id.* Otherwise, leaving open a contract's term of place of performance at the time of execution of the contract allows the appellant, as the holder, at some future time to determine venue at its own will and pleasure. *Id.; Yell v. Prock*, 238 S.W.2d 238, 239 (Tex. Civ. App.—Fort Worth 1951, writ dism'd). Accordingly, we conclude that such a unilateral designation by appellant does not establish prima facie proof that venue was proper in Harris County under section 15.035(a).

Section 15.061

Appellant also contends that venue was proper under section 15.061 of the Texas Civil Practice Remedies and Code, which provides that where the court has venue of an action against any one defendant, the court has venue as to all defendants. *See* TEX. CIV. PRAC. & REM. CODE ANN. § 15.061 (Vernon 1986) (multiple defendants). Appellant argues that because co-defendant Poort filed an answer in Harris County without filing a motion to transfer venue, she waived her right to challenge venue; therefore, venue was proper in Harris County as to Poort and, thus, to appellee. We disagree.

The matter of venue is a personal privilege which may be waived by any party to a lawsuit. *Grozier v. L-B Sprinkler & Plumbing Repair*, 744 S.W.2d 306, 308 (Tex. App.—Fort Worth 1988, writ denied). Because venue may be proper in numerous counties, the plaintiff is given the first choice in the filing of a lawsuit. *Wilson*, 886 S.W.2d at 260. If a plaintiff files suit in an improper county, he waives his first choice of venue and the defendant may have the suit transferred to another county, as long as venue is proper in that county. *Maranatha Temple, Inc. v. Enterprise Prods. Co.*, 833 S.W.2d 736, 741 (Tex. App.—Houston [1st Dist.] 1992, writ denied); *Tieuel v. Southern Pac. Transp. Co.*, 654 S.W.2d 771, 775 (Tex. App.—Houston [14th Dist.] 1983, no writ). A defendant may also waive venue by failing to object by written motion prior to or concurrently with his first responsive pleading, except by special appearance. TEX. CIV. PRAC. & REM. CODE ANN. § 15.063 (Vernon 1986); TEX. R. CIV. P. 86; *see also Grozier*, 744 S.W.2d at 310 (listing numerous ways for a defendant to waive venue).

Under the current version of section 15.061, we have found no Texas case addressing the effect of one defendant's waiver of venue upon another defendant's right to challenge venue. Appellee argues, and we agree, that this Court should look for guidance in caselaw interpreting the prior venue statute.

Prior to September 1, 1983, the state's venue statute, article 1995, consisted of one general rule and thirty-four exceptions. Dan R. Price, *New Texas Venue Statute: Legislative Seminar*, 15 ST. MARY'S L.J. 855, 857-58 (1984). One exception, subdivision 29a, allowed a plaintiff to join all defendants who were necessary parties in a single lawsuit if venue could be maintained against any one of those defendants. *See* Act of June 7, 1927, 40th Leg., 1st C.S., ch. 72, § 2, 1927 TEX. GEN. LAWS 197, 197. Subdivision 29a was always considered with another exception in article 1995 because 29a dealt only with suits against nonresident defendants. *See Gray*, 125 S.W.2d at 286; *Schulz v. Schulz*, 478 S.W.2d 239, 243-44 (Tex. Civ. App.—Dallas 1972, no writ). In other words, the plaintiff was required to prove facts showing proper venue against one defendant before subdivision 29a's joinder provision would be applicable against the other defendants. *Gray*, 125 S.W.2d at 286. The fact that one defendant waived venue did not confer venue in the original county of suit under subdivision 29a when another defendant protested it. *See Stanford v. Dairy Queen Prods.*, 623 S.W.2d 797, 804 (Tex. Civ. App.—Austin 1981, writ ref'd n.r.e.); *Kott v. Faircloth*, 350 S.W.2d 668, 669 (Tex. Civ. App.—Beaumont 1961, no writ).

The passage of the 1983 Act was the first attempt to improve and clarify the venue rules. The newest version of the joinder rule is section 15.061 of the Texas Civil Practice and Remedies Code. Section 15.061 provides:

> When two or more parties are joined as defendants in the same action or two or more claims or causes of action are properly joined in one action and the court has venue of an action or claim against any one defendant, the court also has venue of all claims or actions against all defendants unless one or more claims or causes of action is governed by one of the provisions of Subchapter B requiring transfer of the claim or cause of action, on proper objection, to the mandatory county.

TEX. CIV. PRAC. & REM. CODE ANN. § 15.061 (Vernon 1986). Appellant urges this Court to construe section 15.061 as allowing a plaintiff who has established venue over one defendant by waiver to maintain venue over all defendants under section 15.061.

Basic rules of statutory construction provide guidance in determining the meaning of section 15.061. *Volunteer Council of Denton State Sch., Inc. v. Berry*, 795 S.W.2d 230, 239-40 (Tex. App.—Dallas 1990, writ denied). The dominant and fundamental aim of statutory construction is to give effect to the legislative intent. *Id.* at 240. Legislative intent must be ascertained from the entire act and not from isolated portions. *Calvert v. Texas Pipe Line Co.*, 517 S.W.2d 777, 781 (Tex. 1974). When a statute is amended, the entire statute must be construed to be harmonious, all sections mutually acting upon each other. *Berry*, 795 S.W.2d at 240. When the venue statute is read in its entirety, it becomes clear that the joinder rule is predicated on the mandatory and permissive provisions of prior subchapters. *See* TEX. CIV. PRAC. & REM. CODE ANN. § 15.001 (Vernon 1986) (Unless subchapters A, B, or C apply, venue is where a cause of action accrues or where a defendant resides.); *Burlington N. R.R. Co. v. Harvey*, 717 S.W.2d 371, 376 (Tex. App.—Houston [14th Dist.] 1986, writ ref'd n.r.e.). The joinder rule is not an independent basis for establishing the propriety of venue. *See* TEX. CIV. PRAC. & REM. CODE ANN. § 15.001 (Vernon 1986).

Furthermore, when the legislature amends a rule, the courts presume that the lawmakers knew of the decisions construing the former versions. *Berry*, 795 S.W.2d at 239-40. We presume the legislature knew about the caselaw preventing a plaintiff from establishing venue as to one defendant without proving that another venue provision was applicable. *See Berry*, 795 S.W.2d at 240. Courts are responsible for giving a true and fair interpretation of the statutes as written, which means an interpretation that is not forced or strained but one that the ordinary meaning of the words of the statute will fairly sanction and clearly sustain. *Railroad Comm'n v. Miller*, 434 S.W.2d 670, 672 (Tex. 1968); *Schulz*, 478 S.W.2d at 242. If such a significant oversight was made, it is for the legislature to acknowledge and set right by amendment. Accordingly, we hold that the waiver of venue by one defendant does not prevent another defendant from appropriately challenging venue by filing a motion to transfer.

Based on the facts of this case, appellant has failed to plead and prove that a permissive or mandatory venue provision other than section 15.061 is applicable to Poort. Accordingly, we conclude that appellant failed to prove that venue was proper in Harris County as to appellee.

Nevertheless, appellee has the burden to show that venue was maintainable in the county to which transfer was sought. TEX. R. CIV. P. 87(2)(a); *Kimmell v. Leoffler*, 791 S.W.2d 648, 653 (Tex. App.—San Antonio 1990, writ denied). Appellee sustained this burden by properly pleading venue facts supporting venue in Dallas County, and by filing an affidavit specifically stating that both defendants are residents of Dallas County. *See* TEX. CIV. PRAC. & REM. CODE ANN. § 15.035(a) (Vernon 1986) (Venue is proper in county where defendant is domiciled.); TEX. R. CIV. P. 87(3)(a). Accordingly, after reviewing the entire record, we conclude that the Harris

County court properly determined that venue should be transferred to Dallas County. *See* TEX. R. CIV. P. 87(3)(b).

* * *

Because the uncontroverted summary judgment evidence establishes as a matter of law that appellant's predecessor failed to give appellee notice of the foreclosure sales, we hold that the trial court properly granted summary judgment for appellee. Appellant's second point of error is overruled. The trial court's judgment is affirmed.

Note

While evidence may not be heard on the motion to transfer venue, there is to be a venue hearing if a motion to transfer is filed. The hearing resembles the hearing held on a motion for summary judgment.

A. *The Burden of Establishing Venue*

1. *The Party Seeking To Maintain Venue*

A party (usually the plaintiff or cross-plaintiff), who seeks to *maintain venue* of an action in the county where the suit is filed, has the burden ". . . to make proof . . . that venue is maintainable in the county of suit." TEX. R. CIV. P. 87(2).

2. *The Party Seeking To Transfer Venue*

A party (usually the defendant or cross-defendant), who seeks to *transfer venue* of the action to another specified court, has the burden ". . . to make proof . . . that venue is maintainable in the county to which transfer is sought." TEX. R. CIV. P. 87(2).

3. *Plead and Possibly Provide Prima Facie Proof of a Cause of Action*

The claimant does have to plead a cause of action, but does not have to prove the cause of action, *unless* the claimant's *allegations are specifically denied.* Then ". . . the pleader is required to support his pleadings, that the cause of action, or a part thereof, accrued in the county of suit by prima facie proof." TEX. R. CIV. P. 87 (2)(b).

4. *The Allegations Are Not Admissions But What Of The Proof?*

A defendant seeking a transfer to a county where the cause of action, or a part thereof, accrued may allege that ". . . if the cause of action exists, then the cause of action or a part thereof accrued in the specific county to which transfer is sought, and *such allegation* shall not constitute an admission that a cause of action in fact exists." A defendant seeking such a transfer does have to make prima facie proof that the cause of action, or part thereof, accrued in the county to which transfer is sought. TEX. R. CIV. P. 87(2)(b).

B. *Who Wins?*

If the *plaintiff* establishes by pleading and prima facie proof (i.e., all venue facts were plead and any specifically denied venue facts were established by affidavit), that venue is proper in the county of suit (either because a defendant resides in the county of suit, a mandatory venue provision applies, or a permissive venue provision applies), the plaintiff wins[1] *unless*:

1. An impartial trial cannot be had in the county of suit as provided in Rules 257-259, or

2. The defendant establishes the applicability of a mandatory venue provision (by making prima facie proof). Presumably, the old law concerning the priority between two or more mandatory venue provisions will

---

1 Humphrey v. May, ___ S.W.2d ___ (Tex. App.—Austin 1991, no writ at this time) (No. 3-89-102-CV) "Because the Mays [Plaintiffs] properly pleaded the relevant venue facts and filed affidavits specifically setting forth the facts supporting their petition, they succeeded in presenting prima facie evidence that venue was proper in Travis County. *See* E.D.S. Energy Dev. Serv., Inc. v. Bandera Trucking Co., 601 S. W. 2d 215 (Tex. Civ. App. 1980, no writ). Accordingly, the trial court was *required* by Rule 87 (3) (c), Texas Rules of Civil Procedure, to deny Humphrey's [Defendant's] motion. Rule 87 does not provide for the trial court to weight the credibility of the affiants."

apply to the new statute. Thus, ". . . their priorities will turn upon their construction in light of their statutory histories." 1 MCDONALD § 4.05

C. *No Jury*. [TEX. R. CIV. P. 87(4)]

Unlike the old practice, juries are not available on the question of venue.

D. *No Rehearing*. [TEX. R. CIV. P. 87(5)]

1. One hearing settles the question of venue as between the parties to the action (subject to appellate review).

2. A party joined after the venue hearing *is bound* by the result of that hearing, *unless* the motion to transfer filed by the new party:

a. is based on the ground that an impartial trial cannot by had under Rules 257-259, or

b. asserts a ground of mandatory venue that was not available to the other parties.

The party joined after the venue hearing who is precluded from being heard in the trial court may nevertheless have the question of venue review "*provided* the party has *timely filed a motion* to transfer."

7. *Review of Venue Decisions by Appellate Courts*

Notes

1. § 15.063 of the Texas Civil Practices and Remedies Code provides:

The court, on motion filed and served concurrently with or before the filing of the answer, shall transfer an action to another county of proper venue if:
(1) the county in which the action is pending is not a proper county as provided by this chapter;
(2) an impartial trial cannot be had in the county in which the action is pending; or
(3) written consent of the parties to transfer to any other county is filed at any time.

2. § 15.064(b) of the Texas Civil Practice and Remedies Code provides:

On appeal from the trial on the merits, if venue was improper it shall in no event be harmless error and shall be reversible error. In determining whether venue was or was not proper, the appellate court shall consider the entire record, including the trial on the merits.

In re TEXAS DEPT. OF TRANS.
218 S.W.3d 74
(Tex. 2007)

Greg Abbott, Atty. Gen., Barry Ross McBee, Edward D. Burbach, Rafael Edward Cruz, Rance L. Craft, Susan Desmarais Bonnen, Ronald E. Garner, Office of Atty Gen., Austin, William Henry, San Marcos, Kent C. Sullivan, First Asst. Atty. Gen., Randy Howry, Sean E. Breen, Scott Forrest Deshazo, Herman Howry & Breen, LLP, Austin, L. Chris Heinemeyer, Krenek & Heinemeyer, P.C., San Antonio, Scott Maynard Freshour, Andrew F. MacRae, Hull Hendricks & MacRea, LLP, Matthew B. Cano, Allensworth & Porter, L.L.P., Rex Jason Zgarba, Austin, for Real Party In Interest.

Charles S. Frigerio, Hector X. Saenz, Law Offices of Charles S. Frigerio, San Antonio, Wade Caven Crosnoe, Jeff D. Otto, Amy Elizabeth Stephenson, Thompson, Coe, Cousins & Irons, LLP, Austin, for Relator/Other.

PER CURIAM.

The Texas Department of Transportation (TxDOT) and Gillespie County each seek writ of mandamus directing the probate court of Travis County to transfer venue of a personal injury suit to Gillespie County. They assert that as to each of them, separately, venue is mandatory in Gillespie County. We conditionally grant relief.

On the evening of January 16, 2004 Courtney Foreman was a passenger in a car approaching a bridge over the Pedernales River in Gillespie County. As it neared the bridge the car slid off the roadway, through a gap between the guardrail and the adjacent embankment and into the river. Courtney drowned.

Courtney's parents, Barbara and Steven Foreman, sued TxDOT, the County, the Allen Keller Company, James Robbins (the car's driver) and others in Travis County probate court. Their claims against TxDOT and the County were brought pursuant to the Texas Tort Claims Act, TEX. CIV. PRAC. & REM.CODE §§ 101.001-.109. (TTCA). The Foremans classify their claims as falling into four categories: negligence, gross negligence, premises defect and special defect or injury-by-traffic-control-device. Venue is alleged to be proper in Travis County as to TxDOT pursuant to section 101.102(a) of the TTCA because part of the cause of action arose in Travis County, and as to Gillespie County under section 15.005 of the Civil Practice and Remedies Code because venue is proper in Travis County as to TxDOT. The basis for the claim that part of the cause of action arose in Travis County is that TxDOT, its bridge division, and other defendants maintained offices in Travis County and entered into and performed, at least in part, their contract and job duties in Travis County. It is alleged that the negligent performance of those duties in Travis County resulted in the defective roadway and approach to the bridge where the accident occurred.

TxDOT and the County filed motions to transfer venue to Gillespie County where the accident occurred. TxDOT asserted that the only claims which can be "properly pled" against it are claims for which sovereign immunity is waived by the TTCA, which in this instance are premises defect and special defect claims. TxDOT urges that because any actions taken and decisions made by its employees antecedent to the accident are not part of such causes of action, there is no "properly pled cause of action," part of which took place in Travis County and on which to sustain venue in Travis County. Gillespie County concurred in TxDOT's position and also asserted that regardless of whether all or some of the cause of action took place in Travis County, section 15.015 of the Civil Practice and Remedies Code made venue in Gillespie County mandatory for claims against the county. The motions were denied. The court of appeals denied mandamus relief. TxDOT and the County now seek mandamus relief from this Court.

Generally, chapter 15 of the Texas Civil Practice and Remedies Code governs venue of actions. Section 15.016 provides that if an action is governed by a separate mandatory venue provision, then the action shall be brought in the county required by the separate venue provision. Section 101.102(a) is such a mandatory provision. It requires claims made pursuant to the TTCA to be brought in the county in which all or a part of the cause of action arose. Chapter 15 also authorizes parties to seek mandamus relief to enforce its mandatory venue provisions. TEX. CIV. PRAC. & REM.CODE § 15.0642. In seeking mandamus under section 15.0642, a party need not prove the lack of an adequate appellate remedy, but need only show that the trial court abused its discretion by failing to transfer the case. *See In re Mo. Pac. R.R. Co.,* 998 S.W.2d 212, 216 (Tex. 1999).

The Foremans do not disagree with TxDOT's assertion that for venue to be proper in Travis County, one of the Foremans' claims under the TTCA must have arisen at least in part in Travis County. Citing *Wilson v. Texas Parks & Wildlife Department,* 886 S.W.2d 259 (Tex. 1994), they claim that negligent decisions and actions by TxDOT employees and agents in Travis County resulted in the condition of the premises at the accident site in Gillespie County and are part of a premise defect or special defect cause of action.

In *Wilson,* a fishing party waded across a riverbed which was, at least in part, in Pedernales Falls State Park in Blanco County. Later in the evening the water level in the riverbed began rising as a result of heavy rainfall upstream which resulted in an unusually large amount of water entering the river over a short period of time. Two members of the fishing party drowned as they tried to wade back through the rising water. Suit was filed in Travis County alleging, in part, that the Texas Parks and Wildlife Department owned the park and was negligent in training park personnel and in designing, implementing, maintaining, and operating an early warning system to alert park users of floods.

Pursuant to the Department's motion to transfer venue the suit was transferred to Blanco County where it was tried to a jury. In response to a general negligence submission the jury found the department negligent, but failed to find that its negligence was a proximate cause of the deaths. As the case was presented to this Court, it differed in two aspects from the matter now before us. First, the claims were to the effect that negligent actions and omissions by park personnel such as failing to warn of the impending high water in the riverbed and failing to activate existing systems designed to warn of anticipated rising water levels occurred contemporaneously with the occurrence and were proximate causes of the drownings. *See Wilson v. Tex. Parks & Wildlife Dep't,* 853 S.W.2d 825, 827-28 (Tex. App.—Austin), *rev'd,* 886 S.W.2d 259 (Tex. 1994). Second, the parties disagreed on whether the decedents were even on park premises. Premises liability questions were not submitted. Nevertheless, the charge asked the jury to find whether the decedents were fishing on park premises. The jury found that they were not. *Id.* at 828.

In this Court, the plaintiffs urged that Travis County was a county of proper venue and that transfer of the case to Blanco County was reversible error even though Blanco County was also a county of proper venue. We agreed. *Wilson,* 886 S.W.2d at 261. In doing so, we noted that decisions and actions taken in Travis County by employees of the Department constituted probative evidence that acts giving rise to the plaintiff's cause of action occurred in Travis County. We held that venue was proper in Travis County under section 101.102 of the Texas Civil Practice and Remedies Code. *Id.* at 262. Because of the posture of the case as presented, we did not address the question of whether suit had been properly brought as a negligence cause of action as opposed to a premises defect cause of action. In this case such question is directly presented because both TxDOT and Gillespie County urge that this is a premises defect claim, no contemporaneous negligent activities in Travis County have been alleged, Travis County is not a proper county of suit and Gillespie County is. Because we did not address the question in *Wilson,* we do not consider *Wilson* controlling.

We have distinguished between causes of action based on negligent activities and those based on premise defects. *See State v. Shumake,* 199 S.W.3d 279, 284 (Tex. 2006); *Timberwalk Apartments, Partners, Inc. v. Cain,* 972 S.W.2d 749, 753 (Tex. 1998); *Keetch v. Kroger Co.,* 845 S.W.2d 262, 264 (Tex. 1992). A negligent activity claim arises from activity contemporaneous with the occurrence, whereas a premises defect claim is based on the property itself being unsafe. *Shumake,* 199 S.W.3d at 284; *Keetch,* 845 S.W.2d at 264.

In *Keetch* a customer slipped on a slick spot on the floor of a grocery store. The slick spot was alleged to have been left by employees who had been spraying plants some time before Keetch slipped and fell. The employees were not spraying at the time of the incident. The trial court submitted only a premises defect theory of liability to the jury. The jury failed to find for Keetch. On appeal Keetch urged that the negligent spraying activity exposed the store's customers to unreasonable risk of a fall, and that the trial court erred by refusing to submit a negligent activity theory of liability to the jury as well as the premises defect theory. We held that the trial court's refusal to submit a negligent activity theory was not error. In doing so, we noted that

> There was no ongoing activity when Keetch was injured. Keetch may have been injured by a condition created by the spraying but she was not injured by the activity of spraying. At some point, almost every artificial condition can be said to have been created by an activity.

Keetch, 845 S.W.2d at 264.

So it is in this case. The Foremans allege that TxDOT failed to use ordinary care in designing, inspecting, maintaining, and employing others to inspect and maintain the bridge and surrounding roadway. But, they do not allege that such activities were actively ongoing at the time of the accident. Taking the Foremans' allegations as true for purposes of determining the venue issue, such negligent activities would be causes of the conditions at the scene of the accident, but not contemporaneous activities proximately causing the accident. *See id.* Accordingly, the Foremans properly pled only a cause of action for premises or special defect as to the roadway and bridge. They did not properly plead a contemporaneous-activity negligence cause of action which would include, as part of the cause of action, allegedly negligent actions or omissions which took place in Travis County. Thus, the Foremans failed to "properly plead" a negligence cause of action for which Travis County would be proper venue. Having failed to properly plead a negligence cause of action, they have also failed to properly plead a gross negligence cause of action for which Travis County would be proper venue. *See La.-Pac. Corp. v. Andrade,* 19 S.W.3d 245, 246 (Tex. 1999) ("[w]hat separates ordinary negligence from gross negligence is the defendant's state of mind.").

* * *

In sum, the Foremans properly pled premise and special defect causes of action, but neither of these claims arose, in any part, in Travis County. Allegations and evidence of TxDOT's employees' knowledge, decisions, or failure to make decisions in Travis County as to the condition of the roadway and bridge in Gillespie County do not allege or constitute *prima facie* evidence that part of the cause of action arose in Travis County.

Without hearing oral argument we conditionally grant mandamus relief and direct the probate court to transfer venue of the underlying case as to TxDOT and Gillespie County to Gillespie County. TEX.R.APP. P. 52.8(c). The writ will issue only if the probate court fails to comply.

Notes

1. *Tenneco, Inc. v. Salyer.*[1] If a claimant has adequately pleaded and made prima facie proof that venue is proper then the cause shall not be transferred. If the parties fail to make prima facie proof that the county of suit or specific county to which transfer is sought is a county of proper venue, then the court may direct the parties to make further proof. Rule 87 does not authorize transfer to a third county. Rule 89 provides that if a motion to transfer venue is sustained, the cause shall not be dismissed, but the court shall transfer the case to the proper court.

Neither the venue statue nor the amended rules allow a plaintiff to file a motion to transfer venue if he/she has improvidently bought suit in an improper county. I.e., a plaintiff cannot correct an improper choice of suit by motion to transfer.

2. *GeoChem Tech Corporation v. Verseckes.*[2] The plaintiff has "first choice" of venue. However, the statutes do not say that the plaintiff may choose venue only once. They simply say that if the county chosen is not proper, the case must be transferred, if a sufficient motion is filed and ruled upon. Thus, GeoChem did not lose the right, under the facts of this case, to choose between two counties in which mandatory venue is proper by filing its first suit in a county in which venue was improper. Because venue in Van Zandt County was proper under TEX. CIV. PRAC. & REM. CODE § 65.023, the trial court erred in transferring the case to Stephens County, after GeoChem took a nonsuit in the first suit.

8. *Problems Associated with an Impartial Trial*

Read Rules 257 & 258 Texas Rules of Civil Procedure.

Notes

1. A change of venue is proper because of prejudice in the county when Rule 257 is satisfied. The Rule requires affidavits of three credible person, who are residents of the county of suit.

There are three causes for transfer, plus a fourth general provision:

a. That there exists in the county where the suit is pending so great a prejudice against him that he cannot obtain a fair and impartial trial.

b. That there is a combination against him instigated by influential persons, by reason of which he cannot expect a fair and impartial trial.

c. That an impartial trial cannot be hand in the county where the action is pending.

d. For other sufficient cause to be determined by the court.

2. *Portwood v. Buckalew.*[1] This was an action on an oil and gas lease between the heirs of W.H. and Dottie Portwood, with a cross-action between some of the heirs of the Portwoods. The cross-action was by Buckalew, the surviving wife of Billy Sunday Portwood, and the mother , guardian and attorney if fact for Harley, Linda, and Billy, Jr. She sued the brothers and sisters of her late husband. Suit was in Baylor county, which has only 5,000 citizens. The trial court transferred venue from Baylor County to Wichita County, apparently on the motion of Buckalew. The court of appeals upheld the transfer of venue.

> "Rule 257, Texas Rules of Civil Procedure, authorizes the trial judge to order a change of venue where the evidence shows (a) that there exists in the county of suit so great a prejudice that the applicant cannot obtain a fair and impartial trial; (b) that there is a combination against the applicant instigated by influential persons by reason of which he cannot expect a fair and impartial trial; and (c) for other sufficient cause to be determined by the court.

---

1 739 S.W.2d 448 (Tex. App.—Corpus Christi 1987, no writ).

2 962 S.W.2d 541 (Tex. 1998).

1 521 S.W.2d 904, 920-922 (Tex. Civ. App.—Tyler 1975).

"The trial court is vested with wide discretion in passing on an application for change of venue. 59 TEX. JUR. 2D *Venue*, § 129. In the absence of an abuse of discretion an order denying or changing venue will not be disturbed on appeal. *Bennett v. Jackson*, 172 S.W.2d 395 (Tex. Civ. App.—Waco 1943, writ ref'd., w.o.m.).

"The evidence shows that Baylor County, the county in which the main suit was originally filed by Sam Portwood and his sister, Jessie Lee Hargrave, is a sparsely populated county with approximately 5,000 residents. At the time of the hearing on the application to change venue, appellants, Dannie Fancher and Harry Portwood, were residents of Baylor County and were engaged in various business activities in the county. Mrs. Fancher was well known because of her substantial gifts to the churches in the county and to the City of Seymour. The testimony shows that the Portwood family had a reputation for family litigation and a previous suit between appellee and Mrs. Fancher had resulted in a 'hung jury.' There is testimony showing that Mrs. Fancher transferred some of her funds out of a local bank after officials of the bank testified against her cause at the hearing for change of venue. The record reveals that the lawsuit had been pending approximately eight years before the hearing for change of venue. Tom Craddock testified that the existence of the lawsuit was common knowledge all over the county, and that there had never been a case in the county that had caused such widespread differences of opinion. Bob Farr testified that a great number of people identified with one faction of the family or another. A. F. Wirz, the only witness called by appellants, testified that he had heard very little discussion of the case and he was of the opinion that the parties could receive a fair and impartial trial in the county.

"Insofar as the appellee is concerned, we think the foregoing evidence is sufficient to support a change of venue under Subdivision (b) and (c) of Rule 257, Texas Rules of Civil Procedure. The evidence shows that a great number of the people had already identified themselves on one side of the family or another. Circumstantially, at least, there is some evidence that appellants had used their influence to 521 S.W.2d 904, 920-922 (Tex. Civ. App.—Tyler 1975): induce other persons in the county to side against appellee. The trial court heard the evidence and saw the witnesses and thereafter determined that a change of venue was required. Under the record before us, we do not believe we would be justified in finding an abuse of discretion.

"The trial has wide discretion in passing on a motion under Rule 257, and absent an abuse of discretion, the ruling will not be disturbed on appeal. Here there was sufficient evidence to satisfy TEX. R. CIV. PROC. 257. There was some evidence that Ps had used their influence to induce other persons in the county side against Appellee."

3. *Acker v. Denton Publishing Company.*[2] "In the fourth point of error, Mr. Acker complains about the 362nd District Court's denial of his motion to transfer venue from the 362nd District Court to either Dallas or Travis Counties. That motion appears to be grounded on Mr. Acker's concern that the case would not be tried fairly in Denton because the defendant publishing company owns and operates the only daily newspaper in the county. The inability to obtain a fair and impartial trial of a civil case may be grounds for a change of venue. TEX. R. CIV. P. 257. A motion on those grounds must be supported by competent affidavits of the party seeking the transfer and three credible residents of the county where the suit is pending. *Id.* Mr. Acker did not furnish the required number of affidavits, and because he did not comply with Rule 257, we find no error in the denial of his motion to transfer venue from Denton County. We overrule point of error number four."

4. In *Brainard v. State*, 968 S.W.2d 403 (Tex. App.—Amarillo 1998), *reversed in part and affirmed in part*, 12 S.W.3d 6 (2000), the Court of Appeals indicated that it was appropriate to hold an evidentiary hearing on the issue of prejudice. The Texas Supreme Court reviewed the case. However, they did not reach the question of venue. "Due to our disposition of this case, we also need not address the Landowners' conditional challenge to the trial court's change of venue from Roberts County to Hutchinson County."

[2] 937 S.W.2d 111 (Tex. App.—Fort Worth 1996, no writ).

9. *Problems Associated with Multiple Parties*

Note

§ 15.003. Multiple Plaintiffs and Intervening Plaintiffs

(a) In a suit in which there is more than one plaintiff, whether the plaintiffs are included by joinder, by intervention, because the lawsuit was begun by more than one plaintiff, or otherwise, each plaintiff must, independently of every other plaintiff, establish proper venue. If a plaintiff cannot independently establish proper venue, that plaintiff's part of the suit, including all of that plaintiff's claims and causes of action, must be transferred to a county of proper venue or dismissed, as is appropriate, unless that plaintiff, independently of every other plaintiff, establishes that:

(1) joinder of that plaintiff or intervention in the suit by that plaintiff is proper under the Texas Rules of Civil Procedure;

(2) maintaining venue as to that plaintiff in the county of suit does not unfairly prejudice another party to the suit;

(3) there is an essential need to have that plaintiff's claim tried in the county in which the suit is pending; and

(4) the county in which the suit is pending is a fair and convenient venue for that plaintiff and all persons against whom the suit is brought.

(b) An interlocutory appeal may be taken of a trial court's determination under Subsection (a) that:

(1) a plaintiff did or did not independently establish proper venue; or

(2) a plaintiff that did not independently establish proper venue did or did not establish the items prescribed by Subsections (a)(1)-(4).

(c) An interlocutory appeal permitted by Subsection (b) must be taken to the court of appeals district in which the trial court is located under the procedures established for interlocutory appeals. The appeal may be taken by a party that is affected by the trial court's determination under Subsection (a). The court of appeals shall:

(1) determine whether the trial court's order is proper based on an independent determination from the record and not under either an abuse of discretion or substantial evidence standard; and

(2) render judgment not later than the 120th day after the date the appeal is perfected.

(d) An interlocutory appeal under Subsection (b) has the effect of staying the commencement of trial in the trial court pending resolution of the appeal.

§ 15.005. Multiple Defendants

In a suit in which the plaintiff has established proper venue against a defendant, the court also has venue of all the defendants in all claims or actions arising out of the same transaction, occurrence, or series of transactions or occurrences.

§ 15.062. Counterclaims, Cross Claims, and Third-Party Claims

(a) Venue of the main action shall establish venue of a counterclaim, cross claim, or third-party claim properly joined under the Texas Rules of Civil Procedure or any applicable statute.

(b) If an original defendant properly joins a third-party defendant, venue shall be proper for a claim arising out of the same transaction, occurrence, or series of transactions or occurrences by the plaintiff against the third-party defendant if the claim arises out of the subject matter of the plaintiff's claim against the original defendant.

§ 15.0641. Venue Rights of Multiple Defendants

In a suit in which two or more defendants are joined, any action or omission by one defendant in relation to venue, including a waiver of venue by one defendant, does not operate to impair or diminish the right of any other defendant to properly challenge venue.

Note

Polaris Investment Management Corporation v. Abascal.[1] Under the 1983 venue statute, venue could be maintained in any county where venue was proper as to a properly joined defendant. The decision in *Polaris* gained great notoriety, and was one of the cases that lead directly to the 1995 amendments to the venue statute. It is primarily of historical interest, and much of the law discussed in the case has changed.

AMERICAN HOME PRODUCTS CORPORATION
v.
CLARK
38 S.W.3d 92
(Tex. 2000)

David C. Duggins, Marnie Ann McCormick, Burgain G. Hayes, Kenneth J. Ferguson, Clark, Thomas & Winters, Patrick L. DeLaune, Austin, Grant Liser, Brown Herman Dean Wiseman Liser & Hart, Fort Worth, Leslie A. Benitez, Susan Elizabeth Burnett, Clark Thomas & Winters, Austin, Brian P. Leitch, Denver, CO, for petitioners.

Michael Y. Saunders, Helm Pletcher Bowen & Saunders, Sharon S. McCally, Daryl L. Moore, Moore & McCally, J. Donald Bowen, Helm Pletcher Bowen & Saunders, Dan M. Boulware, MacLean & Boulware, J. Scott Nabors, Helm Pletcher Bowen & Saunders, Houston, for respondents.

JUSTICE BAKER delivers the opinion of the Court in which CHIEF JUSTICE PHILLIPS, JUSTICE ENOCH, JUSTICE ABBOTT, JUSTICE HANKINSON, JUSTICE O'NEILL, and JUSTICE GONZALES join.

This case requires us to interpret the interrelation between sections 15.002, 15.003, and 15.064 of the Texas Civil Practice and Remedies Code. American Home Products Corporation and its division, Wyeth-Ayerst Laboratories (American Home), challenged the propriety of venue in Johnson County, Texas, of the nonresident plaintiffs under sections 15.002 and 15.003 of the Code. The trial court held that each plaintiff had established venue against all defendants under sections 15.002(a)(2) and 15.005 of the Code. American Home filed an interlocutory appeal from the trial court's order. The court of appeals dismissed American Home's appeal for want of jurisdiction. 999 S.W.2d 908. The primary issue in this case is whether section 15.003(c) grants a court of appeals interlocutory appellate jurisdiction over all venue decisions that relate to intervention or joinder. We hold that the court of appeals correctly held it does not. Accordingly, we affirm its judgment.

I. JURISDICTION

A. THE CODE PROVISIONS

Under the Legislature's general venue scheme, except as otherwise provided, all lawsuits shall be brought in the county of the defendant's residence at the time the cause of action accrued if the defendant is a natural person. TEX. CIV. PRAC. & REM. CODE § 15 .002(a)(2). When a plaintiff has established proper venue against a defendant, the court also has venue of all the defendants in all claims or actions arising out of the same transaction, occurrence, or series of transactions or occurrences. TEX. CIV. PRAC. & REM. CODE § 15.005. In a suit in which more than one plaintiff is joined, each plaintiff must independently establish proper venue. TEX. CIV. PRAC. & REM. CODE § 15.003(a). The Legislature has provided that no interlocutory appeal shall lie from a trial court's determination of a venue question. TEX. CIV. PRAC. & REM. CODE § 15.064(a). But the Legislature has provided the right of limited interlocutory appeal in an intervention or joinder situation:

[1] 892 S.W.2d 860, 861 (Tex. 1995).

> Any person seeking intervention or joinder, who is unable to independently establish proper venue, or a party opposing intervention or joinder of such a person may contest the decision of the trial court allowing or denying intervention or joinder by taking an interlocutory appeal to the court of appeals' district in which the trial court is located under the procedures established for interlocutory appeals.

TEX. CIV. PRAC. & REM. CODE § 15.003(c).

B. PROCEDURAL HISTORY

Here, eleven plaintiffs sued ten defendants in Johnson County, Texas, claiming injuries resulting from taking diet drugs commonly known as Fen-Phen. Nine plaintiffs live outside Texas, one lives in Gregg County, Texas, and only one lives in Johnson County, the county of suit. American Home does not challenge venue as it relates to the Johnson County resident. American Home filed a Motion to Transfer Venue, Objection to Attempted Joinder, and a Motion to Strike or Sever the Plaintiffs. It challenged the propriety of venue of the non-resident plaintiffs in Johnson County under both sections 15.002 and 15.003 of the Code. The plaintiffs responded to these motions by filing affidavits of each plaintiff, an affidavit of one of their attorneys, and affidavits of their experts. The trial court conducted a nonevidentiary hearing and denied all American Home's motions without specifying the grounds for its decision.

American Home filed an interlocutory appeal of the trial court's order. American Home asserted that the plaintiffs could not establish venue under section 15.002(a) and that they had failed to establish joinder under section 15.003(a). The plaintiffs contended that they had established venue under section 15.002(a) because each had individually sued the Johnson County physician who had treated the Johnson County plaintiff.

The court of appeals observed that the trial court's order did not specify on what ground the trial court had denied American Home's Motion to Transfer. Thus, the court could not determine whether it had jurisdiction of American Home's appeal. Accordingly, it abated the appeal and requested the trial court to enter an order specifying the basis for its ruling. 3 S.W.3d 57.

The trial court signed a revised order, which held that (1) the plaintiffs each established venue against the Johnson County physician under section 15.002(a)(2), and (2) because the plaintiffs established venue against the physician, venue was proper against all other defendants under section 15.005. Subsequently, the court of appeals, with one judge dissenting, held that because the trial court's denial of American Home's motions was under section 15.002, it had no interlocutory-appeal jurisdiction. 999 S.W.2d 908.

Here, American Home raises [the issue of] . . . whether, under section 15 .003(c), a court of appeals has interlocutory appellate jurisdiction over all venue decisions that relate to intervention or joinder.

C. ANALYSIS

American Home recognizes that the law requires a party to wait until a final judgment is entered in a case to appeal an erroneous venue ruling. *See* TEX. CIV. PRAC. & REM. CODE § 15.064(a); *Wilson v. Texas Parks & Wildlife Dep't*, 886 S.W.2d 259, 262 (Tex.1994). However, American Home asserts that this rule does not apply in multi-plaintiff trials because the Legislature has provided an avenue for speedy pretrial appellate review in section 15.003.

American Home recognizes that a court of appeals may only exercise interlocutory jurisdiction under section 15.003 if the joining party is unable to establish proper venue independently under section 15.002. But American Home also notes that section 15.003 requires a court of appeals to decide the joinder issue based upon an independent determination from the record. Therefore, it contends that when a plaintiff argues venue under both sections 15.002 and 15.003, the court of appeals must independently determine whether the plaintiff can establish venue under section 15.002 to determine whether it has jurisdiction under section 15.003.

American Home further contends that a court of appeals must be able to review a trial court's decision to permit a multi-plaintiff case to proceed in the face of a venue or joinder challenge, regardless of the expressed basis for the trial court's decision, if section 15.003 is to retain any meaning. Thus, American Home argues, to determine its own jurisdiction under section 15.003(c), a court of appeals must decide whether a party is a person unable to independently establish proper venue.

On the other hand, the plaintiffs argue that the Legislature has expressly mandated that venue determinations are not subject to interlocutory appeal. *See* TEX. CIV. PRAC. & REM. CODE § 15.064(a). They argue that while section 15.003's plain language grants an interlocutory appeal to those opposing the joinder of persons who are unable to independently establish proper venue, that section does not grant an interlocutory appeal to those opposing the joinder of persons who are able to independently establish proper venue. Plaintiffs assert that, here, because the trial court determined that the plaintiffs independently established proper venue under sections 15.002 and 15.005, the trial court never reached the joinder issue under 15.003(a). Thus, the plaintiffs contend that interlocutory appellate jurisdiction does not exist under 15.003(c) to review the trial court's venue determination.

When we construe a statute, our objective is to determine and give effect to the Legislature's intent. TEX. GOV'T CODE § 312.005; *Liberty Mut. Ins. Co. v. Garrison Contractors, Inc.*, 966 S.W.2d 482, 484 (Tex. 1998). We endeavor to discover what the Legislature intended from the actual language that the Legislature used. *Mitchell Energy Corp. v. Ashworth*, 943 S.W.2d 436, 438 (Tex. 1997). We look first to the plain and common meaning of the statute's words. *Fitzgerald v. Advanced Spine Fixation Sys., Inc.*, 996 S.W.2d 864, 865 (Tex. 1999).

Section 15.003 is not a venue statute; it is a joinder statute. The statute allows an interlocutory appeal for one specific purpose: to contest the trial court's decision allowing or denying intervention or joinder. *See* TEX. CIV. PRAC. & REM. CODE § 15.003(c); *Surgitek, Inc. v. Adams*, 955 S.W.2d 884, 887 (Tex. App.—Corpus Christi 1997, pet. dism'd by agr.). Section 15.003(c) does not provide for an interlocutory appeal from the trial court's determination that a person seeking intervention or joinder has independently established proper venue. *See* TEX. CIV. PRAC. & REM. CODE § 15.003(c); *Bristol-Myers Squibb Co. v. Goldston*, 983 S.W.2d 369, 374 (Tex. App.—Fort Worth 1998, pet. dism'd by agr.); *Adams*, 955 S.W.2d at 887.

When the trial court's order necessarily determines an intervention or joinder issue under section 15.003(a), section 15.003(c) plainly allows for either party to contest that decision by taking an interlocutory appeal. *See* TEX. CIV. PRAC & REM. CODE § 15.003(c); *Surgitek v. Abel*, 997 S.W.2d 598, 601 (Tex. 1999). Conversely, if the trial court determines that venue is proper under section 15.002, the inquiry is over. This is because section 15.003(a) takes as its starting point a "person who is unable to establish proper venue." *Surgitek v. Abel*, 997 S.W.2d at 602. Thus, if the trial court, even erroneously, decides that venue is proper under section 15.002, an interlocutory appeal under section 15.003(c) is unavailable. *See* TEX. CIV. PRAC. & REM. CODE § 15.064(a); *Adams*, 955 S.W.2d at 887. Neither the court of appeals nor this Court can review the propriety of the trial court's venue decision.

American Home's argument that a court of appeals has interlocutory-appeal jurisdiction over all venue decisions that relate to intervention or joinder is without merit. Such an interpretation would make any trial court venue decision under § 15.002 in a multi-plaintiff case reviewable by interlocutory appeal, which is contrary to the plain language of the statute. *See* TEX. CIV. PRAC. & REM. CODE § 15.064 ("No interlocutory appeal shall lie from the [venue] determination."). The language the Legislature used clearly indicates its intent to limit interlocutory appellate review of a trial court's decision to whether certain plaintiffs may intervene or join in the suit. *See* TEX. CIV. PRAC. & REM. CODE § 15.003(c) ("Any person seeking intervention or joinder, who is unable to independently establish proper venue, or a party opposing intervention or joinder of such a person may contest the decision of the trial court allowing or denying intervention or joinder by taking an interlocutory appeal.") (emphasis added). Section 15.003(c) does not permit an interlocutory appeal under the circumstances that exist here. Accordingly, we conclude that the court of appeals correctly dismissed American Home's appeal for want of jurisdiction.

* * *

We . . . conclude that the court of appeals correctly dismissed American Home's appeal for want of jurisdiction. Accordingly, we affirm the court of appeals' judgment.

JUSTICE ENOCH, joined by CHIEF JUSTICE PHILLIPS, concurring [omitted].

JUSTICE OWEN, joined by JUSTICE HECHT, dissenting.

Section 15.003 was a cornerstone of the Legislature's tort reform efforts in the 1995 legislative session. It was designed to preclude the joinder of multiple parties in a forum in which venue over their claims does not lie. More to the point in this case, it was intended to give appellate courts the power to bring a quick end to instances of blatant forum shopping. There should be no mistake about legislative intent. The Court disregards that intent. I therefore dissent.

I

The Court today sanctions a sham and a fraud on the legal system. The trial court did not have even a colorable basis for finding that each plaintiff in this multi-plaintiff suit established venue "independently of any other plaintiff." TEX. CIV. PRAC. & REM. CODE § 15.003(a). Yet, the Court renders itself impotent to deal with the matter by adopting an untenable interpretation of section 15.003.

Eleven plaintiffs have joined in a single suit they filed in Johnson County, Texas. They have alleged that they were injured from taking drugs commonly called Fen Phen. Seven of the plaintiffs are residents of Utah, and one is a resident of North Carolina. None of these out-of-state plaintiffs received prescriptions for or took Fen-Phen in Texas. The remaining two plaintiffs are Texas residents, but only one of them, Glenda Gallup, is a resident of Johnson County. The other Texas resident had no contact with Johnson County or residents of Johnson County other than to file her suit there. There are nine defendants, but only one of them, Dr. Arthur L. Raines, is a resident of Johnson County. He treated Gallup, but none of the other plaintiffs has had any contact or dealings with Raines, and the plaintiffs do not contend otherwise.

In their petition, the plaintiffs asserted venue under sections 15.002(a)(1) and 15.003 of the Texas Civil Practice and Remedies Code. Several of the defendants, including American Home Products, joined in a motion to transfer venue that also contained objections to venue and joinder. The trial court denied that motion and overruled the objections without stating the grounds for its decision. American Home Products brought an interlocutory appeal.

* * *

It is true that section 15.003 requires a trial court to determine whether a plaintiff can independently establish venue in order to decide whether the plaintiff can join in a suit. Because section 15.003(c) authorizes an interlocutory appeal from a trial court's decision allowing or denying joinder, it necessarily authorizes an interlocutory appeal of the venue determination underlying this decision. *Masonite Corp.*, 951 S.W.2d at 817 (citation omitted).

Instead of determining, as directed by section 15.003, whether the plaintiffs in this case were unable to meet the requirements of section 15.003, the Court says that its hands have been tied by the Legislature. Even though the Legislature for the first time in our jurisprudence has expressly granted a right to an interlocutory appeal of joinder issues in section 15.003, the Court says there is nothing it can do to remedy improper joinder until after rendition of a final judgment. That may well be after a full trial on the merits. I am at a loss to understand why the Court denies power to appellate courts that the Legislature clearly wanted them to have.

In granting the right to an interlocutory appeal in section 15.003(c), the Legislature recognized the harm that can occur from forum shopping and the need for prompt relief. This case is a prime example. If the plaintiffs were to obtain a final judgment in their favor in Johnson County, they would face certain reversal on appeal because venue as to ten of the eleven plaintiffs is improper, and reversal is mandatory. TEX. CIV. PRAC. & REM. CODE § 15.064(b) (if venue is improper it "shall be reversible error"); *Ford Motor Co. v. Miles*, 967 S.W.2d 377, 382 (Tex.1998). Yet the plaintiffs obviously believe that the tactical advantages they will gain from maintaining venue in Johnson County outweigh that consideration.

III

Venue lies in Johnson County only with respect to Gallup's claims. No plaintiff other than Gallup is a resident of Johnson County. The only defendant who resides in Johnson County is Gaines. No plaintiff other than Gallup makes a claim against Gaines. There is no basis under sections 15.002 and 15.005 for maintaining venue as to the remaining plaintiffs' claims. Accordingly, those plaintiffs did not "independently of any other plaintiff, establish proper venue." TEX. CIV. PRAC. & REM. CODE § 15.003(a).

Nor do subsections (1) through (4) of section 15.003(a) rescue the plaintiffs. Our decision in *Surgitek, Bristol-Myers Corp. v. Abel*, 997 S.W.2d 598 (Tex.1999), dispenses with the plaintiffs' argument that they have an essential need to maintain venue in Johnson County. They contend only that they need to "pool resources for common experts and issues and to reach trial expeditiously." We held in *Surgitek* that the need to pool resources will not carry the day. 997 S.W.2d at 604. Nor will proof that a plaintiff can obtain an earlier trial date in the county of suit suffice. *See id.* We said in Surgitek that "essential need" as used in section 15.003 means that it is "indispensably necessary" to try claims in a particular county. *Id.* Speed of trial does not meet the "very high" burden that section 15.003 sets forth. *See id.*

* * *

Because the Court seriously undermines the Legislature's efforts to reform the legal system, I dissent. I would reverse the judgment of the court of appeals and remand this case to the trial court with instructions to grant the motion to transfer.

RAMIREZ
v.
COLLIER, SHANNON, SCOTT, PLLC
123 S.W.3d 43
(Tex. App.—Houston [1st Dist.] 2003, pet. denied)

In the 2003 session, the Texas Legislature clarified its intent as to the broad scope of interlocutory appeal under subsection 15.003, legislatively superseding the holding in *American Home Products* that interlocutory appeal does not lie from a ruling by the trial court that venue is proper as to an intervening plaintiff. Section 15.003 now reads, in relevant part, as follows:

(b) An interlocutory appeal may be taken of a trial court's determination under Subsection (a) that:
(1) a plaintiff did or did not independently establish proper venue; or
(2) a plaintiff that did not independently establish proper venue did or did not establish the items prescribed by Subsection (a)(1)-(4).

TEX. CIV. PRAC. & REM. CODE § 15.003.

While this appeal is brought under the prior version of the statute, there can be no doubt as to the Legislature's intent that interlocutory appeal lie from every determination by a trial court in a multiple-party case that a person seeking intervention or joinder as a plaintiff under section 15.003 "did or did not independently establish proper venue," as well as its intent that interlocutory appeal lie from the trial court's determination that "a plaintiff that did not independently establish venue did or did not establish" the four factors in subsection 15.003(a) that permit intervention or joinder in lieu of independently establishing proper venue. *See* TEX. CIV. PRAC. & REM. CODE § 15.003.

We hold that we have jurisdiction to consider Wiegel's interlocutory appeal both of the trial court's determination under section 15.003(b)(1) that he was unable to establish proper venue and of its determination under section 15.003(b)(2) that he failed to establish the four factors set out in 15.003(a) that permit intervention or joinder of a plaintiff unable to independently establish proper venue

10. *The Convenience of the Parties—The "General Rule"*

The 1995 revision of the venue law contains two intra-state *forum non conveniens* provisions. The first is in Section 15.002(b), the general venue rule. The second is found in Section 15.003, concerning multiple plaintiffs.

Under Section 15.002 (b), even when the plaintiff has filed suit in a county of proper venue, the trial court may, upon timely motion of the defendant, transfer venue "to any other county of proper venue on motion of a defendant." To do this the court must find:

"(1) maintenance of the action in the county of suit would work an injustice to the movant considering the movant's economic and personal hardship;

"(2) the balance of interests of all the parties predominates in favor of the action being brought in the other county; and

"(3) the transfer of the action would not work an injustice to any other party."

Judge's Ruling On Convenience Not Reviewable. The trial court's decision to transfer or not to transfer because of the issue of convenience of the parties and witnesses, and in the interest of justice, under Section 15.002 (b) "is not grounds for appeal or mandamus and is not reversible error." TEX. CIV. PRAC. & REM CODE § 15.002 (c).

GARZA
v.
GARCIA
137 S.W.3d 36
(Tex. 2004)

JUSTICE BRISTER delivered the opinion of the Court, in which JUSTICE HECHT, JUSTICE OWEN, JUSTICE O'NEILL, JUSTICE SCHNEIDER and JUSTICE SMITH joined.

The Legislature amended the venue statutes in 1995 to allow a trial court to transfer venue "[f]or the convenience of the parties and witnesses and in the interest of justice." At the same time, the Legislature mandated that a trial court's order granting or denying such a transfer for convenience is "not grounds for appeal or mandamus and is not reversible error."

In this case, a defendant filed a motion asserting both improper venue and inconvenience, which the trial court granted without specifying the grounds. Generally, we must affirm such general orders if any ground in the accompanying motion is meritorious. Because the motion here asserted convenience as one ground, and the statute precludes reversal of any ruling made on convenience grounds, we hold the court of appeals erred in considering and reversing the trial court's venue order.

* * *

The record reflects that petitioner Ines Gonzalez Garcia (a resident of Hidalgo County) brought suit against J & R Valley Oilfield Services, Inc. (a business in Hidalgo County) and Ramiro Garza (a resident of either Hidalgo or Starr County) concerning an auto accident occurring in Hidalgo County. Of sixteen potential lay and expert witnesses designated by the parties, fourteen were residents of Hidalgo County, and two of Mexico. None resided in Starr County. Nevertheless, suit was brought in Starr County, based on evidence that Garza lived there.

J & R's motion to transfer venue (which Garza joined) argued that Starr County was not a county of proper venue, and added "[a]lternatively, your Defendant would show that venue should be transferred to Hidalgo County for the convenience of the parties." The trial court's order stated that "after considering the motion, the pleadings, the affidavits, the responses as well as arguments of counsel and after a hearing, the Court grants Defendants' Motion to Transfer Venue."

At the trial in Hidalgo County, the jury awarded Garcia $120,000. Unsatisfied, she appealed seeking automatic reversal and a new trial based on the venue transfer.

The court of appeals reversed, refusing to presume a venue order was granted on convenience grounds unless the order specifically said so. In addition to reversing the traditional presumption applicable to all other orders, this rule would sometimes do just what the Legislature prohibited. Because the transfer order here includes no reasons, we cannot be certain on which of the two grounds it was granted; one ground was convenience, and the evidence showed most of the witnesses and all of the events took place in Hidalgo County. As the Starr County judge certainly might have intended to grant it on convenience grounds, we cannot ignore the Legislature's ban on reviewing such orders by adopting a new presumption so we can review them anyway.

The court of appeals refused to imply a finding on convenience grounds because the statutory prohibition on appellate review precluded reviewing the record for evidence that might support such an implied finding. But the statute precludes review not just of the evidence, but of the order itself. As a result, it is irrelevant whether a transfer for convenience is supported by any record evidence. Hypothetically, a trial judge could state there was no evidence for a convenience transfer, but grant it nonetheless, and (except for perhaps reporting it to the Judicial Conduct Commission) there is very little we could do about it.

We acknowledge the court of appeals' concern that the usual presumption in favor of nonspecific orders will make many venue orders "immune from review." But in transfer orders based on convenience, that appears to have been precisely the Legislature's intent. And even under the court of appeals' bright-line test, trial judges who are so inclined may make any venue order immune from review simply by adding "granted on convenience grounds."

Nor do we believe the potential for error or injustice here justifies making an exception to the general rule that trial judges and lawyers need not detail specific findings in every order. When a defendant files a motion based on both convenience and another venue ground, a trial judge may grant the motion on the former ground and we cannot review it. Or the judge may deny both, in which case we may review only the latter. The court of appeals was concerned a trial judge might intend to deny a motion based on convenience while granting (erroneously) the motion on an alternative ground. But most venue provisions are based on notions of convenience. As the county where the parties reside or the events occurred will often be the most convenient, we decline to change our usual presumption rules to presume the opposite.

Our dissenting colleagues conclude the trial court could not possibly have granted this transfer on convenience grounds, but do so only after looking beyond the motion and order to the supporting evidence and the attorneys' arguments—exactly the kind of appellate review the statute precludes. They would remand to Hidalgo County, where the case could be transferred again (using the magic words "for convenience" this time), tried again in Starr County, and appealed again. This is exactly the kind of piecemeal review and relitigation our usual presumption is intended to avoid.

Our dissenting colleagues argue our strict construction presumes the Legislature was either naive or cynical, but they appear willing to presume most trial judges who sign a venue order without specifying the grounds are ignorant of what they are signing or playing keep-away with appellate courts. They assert we have "swallowed" the defendants' arguments based on the literal words of this statute; but in a government of separate and limited powers, it is not our role to spit out those parts of a statute we find unpalatable. Nor can we make an exception "just this once" (as our colleagues suggest) because our venue rules are peculiar and of "critical importance;" undoubtedly, some might say the same about our rules for voir dire, the jury shuffle, or "the Rule." If we begin adding our own requirements to statutes, it becomes only a matter of personal preference as to where we should stop.

Finally, we do not believe the movant's convenience motion must be more specific than the one here, at least when it is part of a motion asserting other venue grounds and there is no special exception. For example, under the general venue rule in section 15.002(a), the movant must plead venue facts (and support them with affidavits if necessary) that show no individual defendant resides in the forum county, no defendant business has its principal Texas office there, and a substantial part of the events did not occur there. While a movant has every reason to add more facts in an effort to prevail, if those reasons alone are enough to convince the trial judge that the case would be more conveniently tried elsewhere, it would be mere formalism to reverse because they were not stated under two different headings.

While appellate justices may chafe at restrictions on appellate review, the Texas Constitution generally allows the Legislature to expand or limit such review as it sees fit. Nor is the restriction here unreasonable under these circumstances. Debates in the Legislature indicate the transfer for convenience statute was intended "to make sure that venue is not a game any longer" by giving trial judges some power to ensure cases were tried where they sensibly belonged, but without adding reversible error or additional delays. This case was tried four years ago, and has been on appeal ever since. The Legislature might reasonably have concluded that discretionary transfers would make litigation more convenient only if they did not have to be re-fought on appeal. Accordingly, we hold the court of appeals erred by reversing the venue order here.

Because the court of appeals should have affirmed the trial court's transfer order on convenience grounds, we reverse the court of appeals' judgment. Because Garcia failed to preserve her remaining factual sufficiency point (by failing to ever pay the filing fee), we render judgment reinstating the trial court's judgment.

JUSTICE WAINWRIGHT filed a dissenting opinion [omitted]
JUSTICE JEFFERSON did not participate in the decision.

CHIEF JUSTICE PHILLIPS, joined by JUSTICE WAINWRIGHT as to Parts I and II, dissenting.

The Court holds today that when a motion to transfer venue on several grounds includes a phrase in a sentence alleging that such transfer will be for the convenience of the parties, and the trial court grants the motion without any indication that it considered or even knew a transfer on convenience grounds was alleged, the transfer is immune from review by any appellate court. Although this result can be supported by a literal reading of the venue statute, I believe it exalts form over substance to undermine the essential purpose of the Legislature's venue scheme. Therefore, I respectfully dissent.

* * *

11. *Forum Non Conveniens*

Notes

1. In addition to the intrastate concept of a convenient forum, just discussed, there is also the "doctrine of forum non conveniens," which applies to actions that arise out of a jurisdiction, which become the subject of litigation within the jurisdiction. The doctrine of forum non conveniens is not, per se, a venue concept. However, it concerns the "place of trial," and should be mentioned.

2. *Baker v. Bell Helicopter Textron, Inc.*[1]

* * *

> "The doctrine of forum non conveniens is an equitable doctrine exercised by courts to resist imposition of an inconvenient jurisdiction on a litigant, even if jurisdiction is proper. *See, e.g., In re Smith Barney*, 975 S.W.2d 593, 596 (Tex. 1998) (orig. proceeding); *Direct Color Services, Inc. v. Eastman Kodak Co.*, 929 S.W.2d 558, 562 (Tex. App.—Tyler 1996, writ denied); *Sarieddine v. Moussa*, 820 S.W.2d 837, 839 (Tex. App.—Dallas 1991, writ denied). Although the Texas Supreme Court has neither enthusiastically embraced the doctrine of forum non conveniens, nor fully defined its application, it has acknowledged the existence of the doctrine as announced by the United States Supreme Court in *Gulf Oil Corp. v. Gilbert*, 330 U.S. 501, 67 S.Ct. 839, 91 L.Ed. 1055 (1947). *See Flaiz v. Moore*, 359 S.W.2d 872, 874 (Tex. 1962); *see also Direct Color Servs., Inc.*, 929 S.W.2d at 562. Texas recognizes the doctrine as a procedural rule that does not determine jurisdiction, but only determines that the jurisdiction that exists should not be exercised where another forum, also having jurisdiction, is better able to act. *See Direct Color Servs., Inc.*, 929 S.W.2d at 562; *McNutt v. Teledyne Indus.*, 985 S.W.2d 272 (Tex. App.—Fort Worth, 1999, petition for review filed May 13, 1999):*Inc.*, 693 S.W.2d 666, 668 (Tex. App.—Dallas 1985, writ dism'd).

* * *

> "The Texas Civil Practices and Remedies Code governs forum non conveniens in Texas." . . .

3. The present *forum non conveniens* statute can be found in TEX. CIV. PRAC. & REM CODE § 71.051.

4. *In re Fisher*, 433 S.W.3d 523 (Tex. 2014): Forum selection clauses establishing venue are presumptively valid and mandamus will issue to enforce such forum selection clauses.

[1] 985 S.W.2d 272 (Tex. App.—Fort Worth, 1999, petition for review filed May 13, 1999).

CHAPTER 8.
PLEADINGS OF THE PARTIES TO A SUIT

1. *Plaintiff's pleadings*

Read Rules 43-45 Texas Rules of Civil Procedure.

CIVIL CASE INFORMATION SHEET

CAUSE NUMBER *(FOR CLERK USE ONLY)*: ______________________ COURT *(FOR CLERK USE ONLY)*: ________________

STYLED ____

(e.g., John Smith v. All American Insurance Co; In re Mary Ann Jones; In the Matter of the Estate of George Jackson)

A civil case information sheet must be completed and submitted when an original petition or application is filed to initiate a new civil, family law, probate, or mental health case or when a post-judgment petition for modification or motion for enforcement is filed in a family law case. The information should be the best available at the time of filing.

1. Contact information for person completing case information sheet:

Name: ____________ Email: ____________

Address: ____________ Telephone: ____________

City/State/Zip: ____________ Fax: ____________

Signature: ____________ State Bar No: ____________

Names of parties in case:

Plaintiff(s)/Petitioner(s): ____________

Defendant(s)/Respondent(s): ____________

[Attach additional page as necessary to list all parties]

Person or entity completing sheet is:

☐Attorney for Plaintiff/Petitioner
☐*Pro Se* Plaintiff/Petitioner
☐Title IV-D Agency
☐Other: ____________

Additional Parties in Child Support Case:

Custodial Parent: ____________

Non-Custodial Parent: ____________

Presumed Father: ____________

2. Indicate case type, or identify the most important issue in the case *(select only 1)*:

Civil

Contract

Debt/Contract
☐Consumer/DTPA
☐Debt/Contract
☐Fraud/Misrepresentation
☐Other Debt/Contract: ____________

Foreclosure
☐Home Equity—Expedited
☐Other Foreclosure
☐Franchise
☐Insurance
☐Landlord/Tenant
☐Non-Competition
☐Partnership
☐Other Contract: ____________

Injury or Damage

☐Assault/Battery
☐Construction
☐Defamation
Malpractice
☐Accounting
☐Legal
☐Medical
☐Other Professional Liability: ____________
☐Motor Vehicle Accident
☐Premises
Product Liability
☐Asbestos/Silica
☐Other Product Liability List Product: ____________
☐Other Injury or Damage: ____________

Real Property

☐Eminent Domain/ Condemnation
☐Partition
☐Quiet Title
☐Trespass to Try Title
☐Other Property: ____________

Related to Criminal Matters

☐Expunction
☐Judgment Nisi
☐Non-Disclosure
☐Seizure/Forfeiture
☐Writ of Habeas Corpus—Pre-indictment
☐Other: ____________

Employment

☐Discrimination
☐Retaliation
☐Termination
☐Workers' Compensation
☐Other Employment: ____________

Other Civil

☐Administrative Appeal
☐Antitrust/Unfair Competition
☐Code Violations
☐Foreign Judgment
☐Intellectual Property
☐Lawyer Discipline
☐Perpetuate Testimony
☐Securities/Stock
☐Tortious Interference
☐Other: ____________

Family Law

Marriage Relationship

☐Annulment
☐Declare Marriage Void
Divorce
☐With Children
☐No Children

Post-judgment Actions (non-Title IV-D)

☐Enforcement
☐Modification—Custody
☐Modification—Other

Title IV-D

☐Enforcement/Modification
☐Paternity
☐Reciprocals (UIFSA)
☐Support Order

Other Family Law

☐Enforce Foreign Judgment
☐Habeas Corpus
☐Name Change
☐Protective Order
☐Removal of Disabilities of Minority
☐Other: ____________

Parent-Child Relationship

☐Adoption/Adoption with Termination
☐Child Protection
☐Child Support
☐Custody or Visitation
☐Gestational Parenting
☐Grandparent Access
☐Parentage/Paternity
☐Termination of Parental Rights
☐Other Parent-Child: ____________

Tax

☐Tax Appraisal
☐Tax Delinquency
☐Other Tax

Probate & Mental Health

Probate/Wills/Intestate Administration
☐Dependent Administration
☐Independent Administration
☐Other Estate Proceedings
☐Guardianship—Adult
☐Guardianship—Minor
☐Mental Health
☐Other: ____________

3. Indicate procedure or remedy, if applicable *(may select more than 1)*:

☐Appeal from Municipal or Justice Court
☐Arbitration-related
☐Attachment
☐Bill of Review
☐Certiorari
☐Class Action
☐Declaratory Judgment
☐Garnishment
☐Interpleader
☐License
☐Mandamus
☐Post-judgment
☐Prejudgment Remedy
☐Protective Order
☐Receiver
☐Sequestration
☐Temporary Restraining Order/Injunction
☐Turnover

4. Indicate damages sought *(do not select if it is a family law case)*:

☐Less than $100,000, including damages of any kind, penalties, costs, expenses, pre-judgment interest, and attorney fees
☐Less than $100,000 and non-monetary relief
☐Over $100, 000 but not more than $200,000
☐Over $200,000 but not more than $1,000,000
☐Over $1,000,000

Notes

Rule 4. Texas Rules of Civil Procedure: Computation of Time

In computing any period of time prescribed or allowed by these rules, by order of court, or by any applicable statute, the day of the act, event, or default after which the designated period of time begins to run is not to be included. The last day of the period so computed is to be included, unless it is a Saturday, Sunday, or legal holiday, in which event the period runs until the end of the next day which is not a Saturday, Sunday, or legal holiday. Saturdays, Sundays, and legal holidays shall not be counted for any purpose in any time period of five days or less in these rules, except that Saturdays, Sundays, and legal holidays shall be counted for purpose of the three-day periods in Rules 21 and 21a, extending other periods by three days when service is made by mail.

Rule 21. Texas Rules of Civil Procedure: Filing and Serving Pleadings and Motions

(a) *Filing and Service Required.* Every pleading, plea, motion, or application to the court for an order, whether in the form of a motion, plea, or other form of request, unless presented during a hearing or trial, must be filed with the clerk of the court in writing, must state the grounds therefor, must set forth the relief or order sought, and at the same time a true copy must be served on all other parties, and shall must be noted on the docket.

(b) *Service of Notice of Hearing.* An application to the court for an order and notice of any hearing thereon, not presented during a hearing or trial, must be served upon all other parties not less than three days before the time specified for the hearing, unless otherwise provided by these rules or shortened by the court.

(c) *Multiple Parties.* If there is more than one other party represented by different attorneys, one copy of each pleading must be served on each attorney in charge.

(d) *Certificate of Service.* The party or attorney of record, must certify to the court compliance with this rule in writing over signature on the filed pleading, plea, motion, or application.

(e) *Additional Copies.* After one copy is served on a party, that party may obtain another copy of the same pleading upon tendering reasonable payment for copying and delivering.

(f) *Electronic Filing.*

(1) Requirement. Except in juvenile cases under Title 3 of the Family Code, attorneys must electronically file documents in courts where electronic filing has been mandated. Attorneys practicing in courts where electronic filing is available but not mandated and unrepresented parties may electronically file documents, but it is not required.

(2) Email Address. The email address of an attorney or unrepresented party who electronically files a document must be included on the document.

(3) Mechanism. Electronic filing must be done through the electronic filing manager established by the Office of Court Administration and an electronic filing service provider certified by the Office of Court Administration.

(4) Exceptions.

(A) Wills are not required to be filed electronically.

(B) The following documents must not be filed electronically:

(i) documents filed under seal or presented to the court in camera; and

(ii) documents to which access is otherwise restricted by law or court order.

(C) For good cause, a court may permit a party to file other documents in paper form in a particular case.

(5) Timely Filing. Unless a document must be filed by a certain time of day, a document is considered timely filed if it is electronically filed at any time before midnight (in the court's time zone) on the filing deadline. An electronically filed document is deemed filed when transmitted to the filing party's electronic filing service provider, except:

(A) if a document is transmitted on a Saturday, Sunday, or legal holiday, it is deemed filed on the next day that is not a Saturday, Sunday, or legal holiday; and

(B) if a document requires a motion and an order allowing its filing, the document is deemed filed on the date that the motion is granted.

(6) Technical Failure. If a document is untimely due to a technical failure or a system outage, the filing party may seek appropriate relief from the court. If the missed deadline is one imposed by these rules, the filing party must be given a reasonable extension of time to complete the filing.

(7) Electronic Signatures. A document that is electronically served, filed, or issued by a court or clerk is considered signed if the document includes:

(A) a "/s/" and name typed in the space where the signature would otherwise appear, unless the document is notarized or sworn; or

(B) an electronic image or scanned image of the signature.

(8) Format. An electronically filed document must:

(A) be in text-searchable portable document format (PDF);

(B) be directly converted to PDF rather than scanned, if possible;

(C) not be locked; and

(D) otherwise comply with the Technology Standards set by the Judicial Committee on Information Technology and approved by the Supreme Court.

(9) Paper Copies. Unless required by local rule, a party need not file a paper copy of an electronically filed document.

(10) Electronic Notices From the Court. The clerk may send notices, orders, or other communications about the case to the party electronically. A court seal may be electronic.

(11) Non-Conforming Documents. The clerk may not refuse to file a document that fails to conform with this rule. But the clerk may identify the error to be corrected and state a deadline for the party to resubmit the document in a conforming format.

(12) Original Wills. When a party electronically files an application to probate a document as an original will, the original will must be filed with the clerk within three business days after the application is filed.

(13) Official Record. The clerk may designate an electronically filed document or a scanned paper document as the official court record. The clerk is not required to keep both paper and electronic versions of the same document unless otherwise required by local rule. But the clerk must retain an original will filed for probate in a numbered file folder.

Comment to 2013 Change: Rule 21 is revised to incorporate rules for electronic filing, in accordance with the Supreme Court's order—Misc. Docket No. 12-9206, amended by Misc. Docket Nos. 13-9092 and 13-9164—mandating electronic filing in civil cases beginning on January 1, 2014. The mandate will be implemented according to the schedule in the order and will be completed by July 1, 2016. The revisions reflect the fact that the mandate will only apply to a subset of Texas courts until that date.

Rule 21a. Texas Rules of Civil Procedure: Methods of Service

(a) *Methods of Service.* Every notice required by these rules, and every pleading, plea, motion, or other form of request required to be served under Rule 21, other than the citation to be served upon the filing of a cause of action and except as otherwise expressly provided in these rules, may be served by delivering a copy to the party to be served, or the party's duly authorized agent or attorney of record in the manner specified below:

(1) Documents Filed Electronically. A document filed electronically under Rule 21 must be served electronically through the electronic filing manager if the email address of the party or attorney to be served is on file with the electronic filing manager. If the email address of the party or attorney to be served is not on file with the electronic filing manager, the document may be served on that party or attorney under subparagraph (2).

(2) Documents Not Filed Electronically. A document not filed electronically may be served in person, by commercial delivery service, by fax, by email, or by such other manner as the court in its discretion may direct.

(b) *When Complete.*

(1) Service by mail or commercial delivery service shall be complete upon deposit of the document, postpaid and properly addressed, in the mail or with a commercial delivery service.

(2) Service by fax is complete on receipt. Service completed after 5:00 p.m. local time of the recipient shall be deemed served on the following day.

(3) Electronic service is complete on transmission of the document to the serving party's electronic filing service provider. The electronic filing manager will send confirmation of service to the serving party.

(c) *Time for Action After Service.* Whenever a party has the right or is required to do some act within a prescribed period after the service of a notice or other paper upon him and the notice or paper is served upon him by mail, three days shall be added to the prescribed period.

(d) *Who May Serve.* Notice may be served by a party to the suit, an attorney of record, a sheriff or constable, or by any other person competent to testify.

(e) *Proof of Service.* The party or attorney of record shall certify to the court compliance with this rule in writing over signature and on the filed instrument. A certificate by a party or an attorney of record, or the return of the officer, or the affidavit of any other person showing service of a notice shall be prima facie evidence of the fact of service. Nothing herein shall preclude any party from offering proof that the document was not received, or, if service was by mail, that the document was not received within three days from the date that it was deposited in the mail and upon so finding, the court may extend the time for taking the action required of such party or grant such other relief as it deems just.

(f) *Procedures Cumulative.* These provisions are cumulative of all other methods of service prescribed by these rules.

Comment to 2013 Change: Rule 21a is revised to incorporate rules for electronic service in accordance with the Supreme Court's order—Misc. Docket No. 12-9206, amended by Misc. Docket Nos. 13-9092 and 13-9164—mandating electronic filing in civil cases beginning on January 1, 2014.

Rule 78a. Texas Rules of Civil Procedure: Case Information Sheet

(a) *Requirement.* A civil case information sheet, in the form promulgated by the Supreme Court of Texas, must accompany the filing of:

(1) an original petition or application; and

(2) a post-judgment petition for modification or motion for enforcement in a case arising under the Family Code.

(b) *Signature.* The civil case information sheet must be signed by the attorney for the party filing the pleading or by the party.

(c) *Enforcement.* The court and clerk must take appropriate measures to enforce this rule. But the clerk may not reject a pleading because the pleading is not accompanied by a civil case information sheet.

(d) *Limitation on Use.* The civil case information sheet is for data collection for statistical and administrative purposes and does not affect any substantive right.

(e) *Applicability.* The civil case information sheet is not required in cases filed in justice courts or small-claims courts, or in cases arising under Title 3 of the Family Code.

a. Pleading a Cause of Action

EDWARDS FEED MILL
v.
JOHNSON
158 Tex. 313, 311 S.W.2d 232
(1958)

Wolff & Wolff, San Antonio, for petitioner.
Stahl & Sohn, H. Kyle Seale, San Antonio, for respondent.

GREENHILL, JUSTICE.

The controlling question in this case relates to the asserted voidness of a default judgment rendered against respondent, William Warren Johnson, by the District Court of Bexar County, Texas, on February 27, 1953, in Cause No. F-54,353. The District Court and the Court of Civil Appeals (by a divided court) have held that the judgment was void. We are not in agreement with such holding, and accordingly the judgments of the courts below will be reversed and the cause remanded to the district court.

The undisputed facts are fully set out in the majority opinion of the Court of Civil Appeals. 302 S.W.2d 151. We shall confine our statement to the essentials which bear directly upon the question of validity of the default judgment.

On April 1, 1949, petitioner, Edwards Feed Mill, Inc., as plaintiff brought suit against William Warren Johnson (respondent here) and his son, Woodson W. Johnson. They were sued as partners for feed sold and delivered to them. Neither the fact of partnership, the sale of the feed, or the receipt of the goods was or is denied. The suit was based upon two counts, a promissory note and a verified account. We are concerned here only with the action on the promissory note. William Warren Johnson, although duly served with citation, filed no answer. Woodson W. Johnson filed an answer but the suit as to him was subsequently dismissed and a final judgment upon both the promissory note and the sworn account was rendered against the defaulting defendant, William Warren Johnson, on February 27, 1953. No appeal was attempted. More than two years later, on May 16, 1955, William Warren Johnson filed a suit (Cause No. F-93,721) attacking that portion of the judgment based upon the promissory note upon the ground that it was void. The trial court sustained this position and rendered a summary judgment which left the judgment in Cause No. F-54,353 in full force and effect as to the sworn account but annulled the portion thereof based upon the promissory note.

In affirming this judgment, the majority of the Court of Civil Appeals recognized that: "Default judgments which are subject to be set aside for lack of pleadings or on faulty pleading, fall into two classes, first, those which are merely lacking in allegations of fact sufficient to fully state a cause of action (known as the general demurrer class), and can only be attacked by direct appeal or writ of error, and, second, those which, from the facts alleged, affirmatively show that plaintiff has no cause of action upon the facts stated." It concluded that the "petition in said Cause No. F-54,353, from the allegations therein contained, wholly negatived the existence of a cause of action against William Warren Johnson on said note."

In *Smith v. Pegram*, 80 S.W.2d 354, 356, the Amarillo Court of Civil Appeals quoted with approval *Ritch v. Jarvis*, Tex. Civ. App., 64 S.W.2d 831, setting out the following rule: "A judgment not based upon any pleadings is void. *Hart v. Hunter*, 52 Tex. Civ. App. 75, 114 S.W. 882. But there is difference between no pleadings, or a petition which from the facts alleged shows affirmatively that plaintiff has no cause of action upon the facts stated, and a petition which is merely lacking in allegations of fact sufficiently to fully state the cause of action. In the latter case, it may be subject to a general demurrer and would be reversed upon appeal from an adverse ruling of the trial court. Yet the same petition may be sufficient to prevent a judgment by default from being void; for, if it states the nature of the cause of action determined by the judgment and is of a class over which the court has potential jurisdiction, it invokes the active jurisdiction of the court, and its sufficiency in regard to the fullness of facts is a matter for determination by the trial judge entering the judgment. An error committed by the trial court in its deliberation upon the sufficiency of the petition in this respect would not in legal effect be different from an error committed in rendering the judgment upon insufficient facts proven, and would not render the judgment void. FREEMAN ON JUDGMENTS (5th Ed.) vol. 1, § 365, p. 765. However, if the pleadings do not invoke the jurisdiction of the court upon the subject matter determined by the judgment, it is void. *Sandoval v. Rosser*, Tex. Civ. App., 26 S.W. 930; *Morgan v. Davis*, Tex. Civ. App., 292 S.W. 610."

A writ of error was refused by this court without reservation in *Smith v. Pegram*.

We are of the opinion that the allegations in the petition filed by the Edwards Feed Mill do not show affirmatively that the plaintiff had no cause of action against William Warren Johnson on the facts stated. The petition asserted that defendants Woodson W. Johnson and William Warren Johnson "were on the dates of the transaction alleged below partners in the dairy business and were buying animal feed from plaintiffs. On the 29th day of September, 1948, defendant, Woodson W. Johnson, executed and delivered to plaintiff his promissory note bearing date of such day and year and thereby promised to pay it, or its order, thirty (30) days after date, the sum of Four Thousand Dollars ($4,000.00) . . . . Though repeated demands have been made by plaintiff upon defendants to pay such note, interest and attorney's fees, the defendants have failed and refused and still fail and refuse to pay the same, or any part thereof, to plaintiff's damage" in the sum of $3,500 and interest. (Italics ours).

The count upon the promissory note is followed by one based upon a sworn account.

The prayer is for judgment "against defendants, Woodson W. Johnson and Warren W. (William Warren) Johnson jointly and severally in the amount of Thirty-five Hundred Dollars ($3,500.00)" and interest, followed by a further prayer for the recovery of $3,292.67, being the amount alleged to be due upon the open account.

The note set forth in the petition is signed, 'W. W. Johnson,' but it is undisputed that the note was executed by the son, Woodson W. Johnson and that the Warren W. Johnson referred to in the petition and the judgment and served with citation is the same person as petitioner, William Warren Johnson.

Rule 45, Texas Rules of Civil Procedure, only requires that a petition consist of a statement in plain and concise language of the plaintiff's cause of action and provides that the fact "that an allegation be evidentiary or be of legal conclusion shall not be ground for objection when fair notice to the opponent is given by the allegations as a whole." In order to support a default judgment it is not necessary that a plaintiff set out in his pleadings the evidence upon which he relies to establish his asserted cause of action. As above pointed out, it is not requisite that a petition be technically sufficient to state a cause of action in order to sustain a default. We think a fair interpretation of the petition before us is that the plaintiff was thereby asserting that Woodson W. Johnson and William Warren Johnson were partners in the dairy business; that they were buying feed for their livestock from plaintiffs; that in the course of their business operations they delivered to plaintiff a promissory note signed by one of the partners, Woodson W. Johnson, which they had not paid. In other words, the petition was a declaration upon a partnership obligation. *First State Bank of Riesel v. Dyer*, 151 Tex. 650, 254 S.W.2d 92; 68 C.J.S. PARTNERSHIP §§ 147 and 161(c), pp. 581 and 606; 40 AM. JUR. 288, Partnership § 152. This being true, it cannot be said that the allegations of the petition affirmatively show that the plaintiff Edwards Feed Mill, Inc., had no cause of action against William Warren Johnson. MCCORMICK & RAY, TEXAS LAW OF EVIDENCE, (2d Ed.) § 398.

For the reasons stated, the judgments of the Courts below are reversed and the cause remanded to the trial court for further proceedings not inconsistent with this opinion.

Reversed and remanded.

WHITE
v.
JACKSON

358 S.W.2d 174
(Tex. Civ. App.—Waco 1962, writ ref'd n.r.e.)

Shields, Jones & Whittington and James W. Cantwell, Dallas, for appellant.
Sanders, Nolen & Stevenson, H. J. Dollinger, Jr., Dallas, for appellee.

TIREY, JUSTICE.

This is an appeal by writ of error from a default judgment.

In May 1961, Willie Jackson filed his original petition in the District Court of Dallas County against Henry White, a resident of Dallas County, and caused citation to be issued and served on White, but he failed to answer. We quote the pertinent parts of the petition:

> On or about the 7th day of June 1959, plaintiff sustained severe and extensive injuries and damages as a direct and proximate result of the negligence of defendant, all to the actual damage of plaintiff in an amount greatly in excess of One Thousand Dollars ($1000.00) and within the jurisdiction of the District Court.
>
> Wherefore, premises considered, plaintiff prays that defendant be cited to appear and answer herein, and that upon final trial, plaintiff have judgment against defendant for all damages proved, costs of court, interest at the rate of 6% per annum from the date of the judgment until same is paid, and for such other and further relief as to which plaintiff may be justly entitled, whether at law or in equity.

On June 12, 1961, judgment was rendered against defendant in favor of plaintiff, and in the judgment we find this recital:

> the matters of fact and things in controversy being submitted to the court in their due and regular order, and it appearing to the court upon good and sufficient evidence that plaintiff is entitled to recover of and from Henry White, defendant, the sum of $20,510.

And decreed accordingly. Thereafter on August 30, 1961, White filed his petition for writ of error and executed a supersedeas bond, and this cause was removed to the Dallas Court of Civil Appeals for review, and is here on transfer. It appears that no court reporter was present and there is no statement of facts, and it also appears that more than 30 days had expired since the rendition and entry of a default judgment, and no motion for new trial was filed. *See* Rule 329-b, T.R.C.P.

The judgment is assailed on 5 Points. They are substantially to the effect that the Trial Court erred in entering judgment: (1 and 2) Based upon appellee's petition for the reason that the petition is not sufficient to support a default judgment, because it failed to allege any facts or circumstances from which it could be found that appellant breached any duty whatsoever which he might have owed appellee in connection with whatever act or omission of the appellant is claimed as negligence; and failed to allege any act or omission whatsoever of appellant which could constitute negligence; (3 and 4) That the Court erred in entering judgment for any amount of money for the reason that appellee's petition failed to allege any injury, fact or act from which any damages could have resulted to appellee; and that the Court erred in entering judgment in the sum of $20,510.00 in favor of appellee for the reason that his petition could in no event support a judgment substantially in excess of $1,000.00; (5) That the judgment of $20,510.00 is erroneous, because such petition did not give appellant notice as to the nature of appellee's claim and the relief sought as required by the Fourteenth Amendment of the Constitution of the United States, and as also required by Article 1, Sec. 19 of the Constitution of the State of Texas, Vernon's Ann. St.

Going back to Points 1 and 2, we think that each of them must be sustained for reasons which we shall briefly mention. The Rule in Texas is that the petition must adequately allege a cause of action before it can support a default judgment. *See* 25 TEX. JUR., *Judgments*, Sec. 36. In *Griswold v. Carlson*, 151 Tex. 246, 249 S.W.2d 58, our Supreme Court made this statement:

> The rules authorize the taking of a judgment by default. In order to support such a judgment, it is essential that the petition show a good cause of action upon which a default judgment can be entered, and the parties seeking such judgment must comply with the requirements of the rules regarding same.'

The Court points out that Rule 90 of T.R.C.P., expressly excepts default judgments from its operation. Rules 45 and 47 T.R.C.P., are pertinent here. * * * The effect of Rules 45 and 47 . . . is apparent when they are considered in the light of Rule 90, T.R.C.P. It is likewise apparent from Rules 45 and 47 that the pleadings must give a party fair notice of the claim involved, and it is clear from Rule 90 aforesaid that a party seeking reversal of a default judgment because of defects, omissions or faults in pleadings, either in form or substance, does not waive the insufficiency of the pleading merely because of the default. *See* Vol. 4, MCDONALD, TEX. CIV. PRAC., Sec. 1723, p. 1372. *Edwards Feed Mill v. Johnson*, Tex. Civ. App., 302 S.W.2d 151, reversed by Supreme Court on other grounds not pertinent here, 311 S.W.2d 232. It is clear under the foregoing authority that our Supreme Court intended to retain the rule relating to a general demurrer as a test of the sufficiency of pleadings to support a judgment by default. In fact, under the express language of Rule 90, T.R.C.P., the same test is still valid. * * * It is clear to us that the petition of appellee could not withstand the test of a general demurrer. The Rule is that in order to be sufficient to support a default judgment, a plaintiff's petition must at least set forth sufficient of the facts and circumstances which constitute his cause of action as to fairly notify his adversary of the basis of his claim and of the relief which he is seeking.

Going back to appellee's petition, we find that it fails to allege any act or omission on the part of appellant which constituted negligence; we find no allegation of fact indicating that appellant owed appellee any duty whatsoever in connection with whatever might be the basis of appellee's claim against him. No facts are alleged in the petition. The only word contained in appellee's petition which might be considered any clue as to the nature of appellee's claim is the word 'negligence.' But, there can be no negligence unless a duty is present, and here none is alleged. The term 'negligence' is not used to characterize any specific act or omission made by appellant, and there is no way of ascertaining from the pleading that appellant may or might have owed appellee a duty of any kind whatsoever. So the word 'negligence', standing alone, provides the only starting point for determination of whether or not appellee's petition was sufficient to support a default judgment. It follows that in resolving Points 1 and 2, resort can be had only to the general rules pertaining to negligence actions. 30-B, TEX. JUR., *Negligence*, Sec. 4, states substantially that the essentials of actionable negligence are the elements of (1) duty, (2) breach and (3) injury. Certainly the element of duty of the defendant to plaintiff is not shown in the petition. * * *

> A mere general allegation of the existence of such duty without a statement of facts from which the duty arises is insufficient as being merely a statement of a legal conclusion.

See 30-B, TEX. JUR., *Negligence*, Sec. 125. When the foregoing rules are applied to the petition in this cause it shows that such petition is fatally defective. As above stated, no duty was alleged owing by the appellant to appellee, nor were any facts or circumstances alleged from which a duty could even be remotely implied or inferred. As to the relationship of the parties, it is not even shown by the pleading that they directly, or by any agency, were within miles of each other at the time in question. * * * It seems to us that appellee alleged no more than a legal conclusion to the effect that appellant was liable to him as a result of negligence; that appellee's pleading is and was fatally defective; that in effect it contained nothing more than the unsupported statement that appellant is liable to appellee because of some unknown act or omission of negligence resulting in some unknown injury or damage to appellee; such allegations are obviously a conclusion on the part of appellee and do not furnish any information whatsoever from which such conclusion could be drawn. The allegation of negligence is a mere conclusion of the pleader, and such allegation is not admitted by either a general demurrer or by default, and such allegation in the petition could in no event support a judgment by default under Rules 45, 47 and 90, T.R.C.P. *See also Cragin v. Lovell*, 109 U.S. 194, 197, 27 L.Ed. 903. Needless to say that appellee's pleading was wholly insufficient to permit appellant to identify anything or to estimate the scope of the dispute, which is well illustrated by a judgment for $20,510.00 against him, based upon a petition alleging damages only 'in excess of $1,000.00'. We think for the reasons stated that Points 1 and 2 must be sustained, and this will require that the cause be reversed and remanded.

Appellant's 3rd Point is substantially that the Court erred in entering judgment for any amount of money, for the reason that the petition failed to allege any injury, fact or act from which any damages could have resulted to appellee. We think it is obvious that this point must be sustained. For the rules prescribing the detail with which the damages must be alleged, *see* Vol. 2, MCDONALD, TEXAS CIV. PRAC., Sec. 6.17, at p. 576. Going back to the appellee's petition in this cause, the defendant was not advised of the alleged damages and injuries to appellee, either to his person or to his property. We think that a pleading which wholly failed to state whether or not the alleged injuries or damages were personal or whether the damage was to property, is fatally defective and will certainly not support a judgment by default for any amount. The petition, as we have stated before, does not allege any act, circumstance or injury from which damages normally flow or can be remotely implied. Certainly none can be supplied by the court. It is the general rule of pleadings that fair notice is a guide for determining whether or not a petition contains sufficient allegations on which to base an award of damages in any amount. *See* Rules 45 and 47 T.R.C.P. *See also* 17 Tex. Jur. 2d, *Damages*, Sec. 192. The petition here does not allege any facts from which the court can supply any measure of damages whatsoever, and we think such failure requires the judgment to be reversed and remanded. *See Caswell v. J. S. McCall & Sons*, Tex. Civ. App., 163 S.W. 1001, n.w.h. We have carefully considered Points 4 and 5, and we think each should be sustained. Since we are of the view that the cause must be reversed and remanded, it will unduly extend this opinion to make further comment on Points 4 and 5, and for that reason we do not do so. Accordingly, this cause is reversed and remanded.

MCDONALD, C. J., and WILSON, J., concur in the result.

b. *Fair Notice Requirement of Petition*

Read Rule 90 Texas Rules of Civil Procedure.

Notes

Rule 45. Texas Rules of Civil Procedure: Definition and System

Pleadings in the district and county court shall

(a) be by petition and answer;

(b) consist of a statement in plain and concise language of the plaintiff's cause of action or the defendant's grounds of defense. That an allegation be evidentiary or be of legal conclusion shall not be grounds for an objection when fair notice to the opponent is given by the allegations as a whole; and

(c) contain any other matter which may be required by any law or rule authorizing or regulating any particular action or defense. Pleadings that are not filed electronically must be in writing, on paper measuring approximately 8 ½ inches by 11 inches, and signed by the party or his attorney. The use of recycled paper is strongly encouraged. All pleadings shall be construed so as to do substantial justice.

Rule 47. Texas Rules of Civil Procedure: Claims for Relief

An original pleading which sets forth a claim for relief, whether an original petition, counterclaim, cross-claim, or third party claim, shall contain:

(a) a short statement of the cause of action sufficient to give fair notice of the claim involved;
(b) a statement that the damages sought are within the jurisdictional limits of the court;
(c) except in suits governed by the Family Code, a statement that the party seeks:

(1) only monetary relief of $100,000 or less, including damages of any kind, penalties, costs, expenses, pre-judgment interest, and attorney fees; or

(2) monetary relief of $100,000 or less and non-monetary relief; or

(3) monetary relief over $100,000 but not more than $200,000; or

(4) monetary relief over $200,000 but not more than $1,000,000; or

(5) monetary relief over $1,000,000; and

(d) a demand for judgment for all the other relief to which the party deems himself entitled.

Relief in the alternative or of several different types may be demanded; provided, further, that upon special exception the court shall require the pleader to amend so as to specify the maximum amount claimed. A party that fails to comply with (c) may not conduct discovery until the party's pleading is amended to comply.

Rule 57. Texas Rules of Civil Procedure: Signing of Pleadings

Every pleading of a party represented by an attorney shall be signed by at least one attorney of record in his individual name, with his State Bar of Texas identification number, address, telephone number, email address, and if available, fax number. A party not represented by an attorney shall sign his pleadings, state his address, telephone number, email address, and, if available, fax number.

Rule 169. Texas Rules of Civil Procedure: Expedited Actions

(a) *Application.*

(1) The expedited actions process in this rule applies to a suit in which all claimants, other than counter-claimants, affirmatively plead that they seek only monetary relief aggregating $100,000 or less, including damages of any kind, penalties, costs, expenses, pre-judgment interest, and attorney fees.

(2) The expedited actions process does not apply to a suit in which a party has filed a claim governed by the Family Code, the Property Code, the Tax Code, or Chapter 74 of the Civil Practice & Remedies Code.

(b) *Recovery.* In no event may a party who prosecutes a suit under this rule recover a judgment in excess of $100,000, excluding post-judgment interest.

(c) *Removal from Process.*

(1) A court must remove a suit from the expedited actions process:

(A) on motion and a showing of good cause by any party; or

(B) if any claimant, other than a counter-claimant, files a pleading or an amended or supplemental pleading that seeks any relief other than the monetary relief allowed by (a)(1).

(2) A pleading, amended pleading, or supplemental pleading that removes a suit from the expedited actions process may not be filed without leave of court unless it is filed before the earlier of 30 days after the discovery period is closed or 30 days before the date set for trial. Leave to amend may be granted only if good cause for filing the pleading outweighs any prejudice to an opposing party.

(3) If a suit is removed from the expedited actions process, the court must reopen discovery under Rule 190.2(c).

(d) *Expedited Actions Process.*

(1) Discovery. Discovery is governed by Rule 190.2.

(2) Trial Setting; Continuances. On any party's request, the court must set the case for a trial date that is within 90 days after the discovery period in Rule 190.2(b)(1) ends. The court may continue the case twice, not to exceed a total of 60 days.

(3) Time Limits for Trial. Each side is allowed no more than eight hours to complete jury selection, opening statements, presentation of evidence, examination and cross-examination of witnesses, and closing arguments. On motion and a showing of good cause by any party, the court may extend the time limit to no more than twelve hours per side.

(A) The term "side" has the same definition set out in Rule 233.

(B) Time spent on objections, bench conferences, bills of exception, and challenges for cause to a juror under Rule 228 are not included in the time limit.

(4) Alternative Dispute Resolution.

(A) Unless the parties have agreed not to engage in alternative dispute resolution, the court may refer the case to an alternative dispute resolution procedure once, and the procedure must:

(i) not exceed a half-day in duration, excluding scheduling time;

(ii) not exceed a total cost of twice the amount of applicable civil filing fees; and

(iii) be completed no later than 60 days before the initial trial setting.

(B) The court must consider objections to the referral unless prohibited by statute.

(C) The parties may agree to engage in alternative dispute resolution other than that provided for in (A).

(5) Expert Testimony. Unless requested by the party sponsoring the expert, a party may only challenge the admissibility of expert testimony as an objection to summary judgment evidence under Rule 166a or during the trial on the merits. This paragraph does not apply to a motion to strike for late designation.

Comments to 2013 change:

1. Rule 169 is a new rule implementing section 22.004(h) of the Texas Government Code, which was added in 2011 and calls for rules to promote the prompt, efficient, and cost effective resolution of civil actions when the amount in controversy does not exceed $100,000.

2. The expedited actions process created by Rule 169 is mandatory; any suit that falls within the definition of 169(a)(1) is subject to the provisions of the rule.

3. In determining whether there is good cause to remove the case from the process or extend the time limit for trial, the court should consider factors such as whether the damages sought by multiple claimants against the same defendant exceed in the aggregate the relief allowed under 169(a)(1), whether a defendant has filed a compulsory counterclaim in good faith that seeks relief other than that allowed under 169(a)(1), the number of parties and witnesses, the complexity of the legal and factual issues, and whether an interpreter is necessary.

4. Rule 169(b) specifies that a party who prosecutes a suit under this rule cannot recover a judgment in excess of $100,000. Thus, the rule in *Greenhalgh v. Service Lloyds Ins. Co.*, 787 S.W.2d 938 (Tex. 1990), does not apply if a jury awards damages in excess of $100,000 to the party. The limitation of 169(b) does not apply to a counter-claimant that seeks relief other than that allowed under 169(a)(1).

5. The discovery limitations for expedited actions are set out in Rule 190.2, which is also amended to implement section 22.004(h) of the Texas Government Code.

STONER
v.
THOMPSON

578 S.W.2d 679
(Tex. 1979)

Horkin & Horkin, Patrick J. Horkin, Jr., Corpus Christi, for petitioner.

Andrews, Kurth, Campbell & Jones, Hall E. Timanus, Houston, Fulbright & Jaworski, Simeon Lake, Houston, for respondents.

SPEARS, JUSTICE.

Petitioner, Roger Stoner, appeals from a judgment against him granting injunctive relief, declaratory relief and money damages to Texas Media, Inc. and Arnold and Audrey Malkan, intervenors and respondents herein. The judgment was entered on their interventions and counterclaim after Stoner, the original plaintiff, had taken a nonsuit and refused to participate in the trial on the merits. Stoner contends there were no pleadings to support the judgment given. The Court of Civil Appeals has disagreed and affirmed the trial court. 570 S.W.2d 511. We affirm except as to money damages awarded Texas Media, Inc.

The factual background and chronology of events is fully set out in the opinion of the Court of Civil Appeals. We will only recite here such facts as are necessary to decide the sufficiency of pleadings question.

Stoner filed the original suit in Harris County District Court on September 2, 1976, against Joe Glenn Thompson, seeking an injunction and specific performance.

The Malkans intervened on September 13, asking that injunctive relief sought by Stoner be denied and on September 29 filed a counterclaim for money damages, charging that Stoner interfered with their contractual relations. On November 10, the Malkans filed a supplemental petition in intervention asking for injunctive relief against Stoner. Texas Media intervened on October 8, asking for a declaratory judgment as to its rights and liabilities, and on November 29, filed an application seeking a restraining order, temporary injunction and permanent injunction against Stoner. Stoner filed answers to these pleadings.

On February 17, 1977, Stoner moved to nonsuit without prejudice his causes of action on file. The order of the trial court granting the motion provided that "nothing herein shall be prejudicial to any of the pleadings or rights asserted by the other parties (seeking relief) herein."

On June 13, the trial court granted a motion for preferential setting filed by the Malkans and set the case for trial on July 11. Stoner's motion and supplemental motion to set aside this order were denied after a hearing on July 8. On the morning of trial, July 11, Stoner's attorney, Mr. Horkin, appeared and urged a "special appearance," citing Rule 120a. Stoner was not present. After the trial court overruled the "special appearance," counsel for Stoner announced to the court that he represented Stoner solely for the purpose of making a special appearance and was not authorized to proceed further on his client's behalf. The Statement of Facts reflects the following:

"MR. HORKIN: Thank you, Your Honor. We decline to proceed further, Your Honor.

"THE COURT: That is your privilege to make that election. The Court says that you are here, and you say that you are leaving, so good day.

"MR. HORKIN: Thank you. "(Reporter's Note: Mr. Horkin retiring from the courtroom.)"

After a brief recess, the Malkans were granted leave to file a trial amendment asking for declaratory judgment relief under Art. 2524-1, and trial without a jury began. Evidence was then presented to the trial court by the Malkans and Texas Media with the resulting judgment in their favor.

The judgment of the trial court granted all of the relief sought by the interventions and counterclaims of Texas Media and the Malkans, and in addition, granted the following relief not asked for in pleadings at the time Mr. Horkin left the courtroom: (1) that Texas Media, Inc. recover $50,000.00 from Stoner, and (2) declaratory judgment relief for the Malkans, declaring their contract to purchase the stock in Texas Media binding and legally enforceable. Stoner complains, Inter alia, of both of these awards by the trial court as without pleadings to support them. All relief granted by the judgment of the trial court was supported by the evidence adduced.

The broad question presented is to what extent can a trial court grant relief to the petitioning parties on their pleadings where the opposing party, who has answered, fails to appear for trial or, as here, quits the trial.

The judgment in this case was neither a no-answer default judgment, nor a judgment Nihil dicit. * * *

While there is a difference between a no-answer default judgment and a judgment Nihil dicit, the general rule is that the two are so similar that the same rules apply to each with respect to the effect and validity of the judgment. *Storey v. Nichols*, 22 Tex. 87 (1858); *see* 49 C.J.S. JUDGMENTS § 187 at 325 (1947); Pohl and Kirlin, *Judgments By Default A Survey of Texas Law*, 31 SW.L.J. 465 (1977). In both instances, it is said that the non-answering party has "admitted" the facts properly pled and the justice of the opponent's claim, although a judgment Nihil dicit carries an even stronger confession than the default judgment. *Storey v. Nichols, supra*; *Texas Quarries v. Pierce*, 244 S.W.2d 571 (Tex. Civ. App. 1951, no writ). In one respect, both the no-answer default judgment and the judgment Nihil dicit differ from a post-answer default judgment where an answer is on file but defendant fails to appear at the trial. A post-answer "default" constitutes neither an abandonment of defendant's answer nor an implied confession of any issues thus joined by the defendant's answer. Judgment cannot be entered on the pleadings, but the plaintiff in such a case must offer evidence and prove his case as in a judgment upon a trial. *Frymire Engineering Company, Inc. v. Grantham, supra.*

A judgment must be based upon pleadings, and as this Court has stated, "(A) plaintiff may not sustain a favorable judgment on an unpleaded cause of action, in the absence of trial by consent . . . ." *Oil Field Haulers Association, Inc. v. Railroad Commission*, 381 S.W.2d 183, 191 (Tex. 1964). In determining whether a cause of action was pled, plaintiff's pleadings must be adequate for the court to be able, from an examination of the plaintiff's pleadings alone, to ascertain with reasonable certainty and without resorting to information aliunde the elements of plaintiff's cause of action and the relief sought with sufficient information upon which to base a judgment. *C & H Transportation Company v. Wright*, 396 S.W.2d 443 (Tex. Civ. App. 1965, writ ref'd n. r. e.). Mere formalities, minor defects and technical insufficiencies will not invalidate a default judgment where the petition states a cause of action and gives "fair notice" to the opposing party of the relief sought. *Edwards Feed Mill v. Johnson*, 158 Tex. 313, 311 S.W.2d 232 (1958).

The principle that a plaintiff will not be permitted to obtain relief on a cause of action which is not contained in pleadings of which the defendant can be said to have "fair notice" has been consistently applied by Texas courts to all three types of "default" judgments: (1) a default judgment as defined by Rule 239, where no answer has been filed, *Edwards Feed Mill v. Johnson, supra; Weatherford v. Van Alstyne*, 22 Tex. 22 (1858); (2) a judgment nihil dicit, where no answer placing the merits of the case in issue is on file, *Goodlett v. Stamps*, 29 Tex. 121 (1867); *Storey v. Nichols, supra; O'Quinn v. Tate*, 187 S.W.2d 241 (Tex. Civ. App. 1945, writ ref'd); *Spivey v. Saner-Ragley Lumber Co.*, 284 S.W. 210 (Tex. Comm'n App. 1926, judgmt. adopted); and (3) a post-answer "default" judgment where a defendant has answered but fails to appear for trial, *Mullen v. Roberts*, 423 S.W.2d 576, 579 (Tex. 1968); *City of Fort Worth v. Gause*, 129 Tex. 25, 101 S.W.2d 221 (Tex. Comm'n App. 1937, opinion adopted). The controlling principle has been correctly summarized: "The rules expressly countenance more general allegations than formerly were permitted, and the default judgment will stand if the plaintiff has alleged a claim upon which the substantive law will give relief, and has done so with sufficient particularity to give fair notice to the defendant of the basis of his complaint, even though he has stated some element or elements in the form of legal conclusions which will need to be revised if attacked by special exceptions." 4 MCDONALD, TEXAS CIVIL PRACTICE § 17.23.3 at 120 (1971). * * *

In the instant case, Stoner, at the time his attorney quit the courtroom, had answers on file to the pleadings of both Texas Media and the Malkans. Texas Media had pled for (1) a declaratory judgment, fixing and declaring its rights with regard to the Malkans, Stoner, and changing its own corporate structure, and (2) injunctive relief to force Stoner to turn over physical possession and control of the radio station KZFM and its books and records to Texas Media. Stoner assails the action of the trial court in granting Texas Media a $50,000.00 judgment for damages as being without support in the pleadings. There is no mention in the pleadings of Texas Media that it sustained money damages and there was no prayer therefor. Under these circumstances, it cannot be said that a party such as Stoner had "fair notice" that the trial court might award money damages against him in favor of Texas Media upon a trial. Nor will the inclusion in the prayer of the phrase "and for such other and further relief to which plaintiff (or cross-plaintiff, intervenor, etc.) may show himself entitled" enlarge a pleading to the extent that it embraces an entirely different cause of action for which fair notice does not exist.

Stoner next complains by point of error that the declaratory relief given the Malkans was not alleged or prayed for in their pleadings. The Malkans, when Stoner's attorney left the trial, had pleadings that (1) prayed that the court deny Stoner's requested injunction to enjoin another defendant, Thompson, from consummating the sale of his stock in Texas Media to the Malkans, the Malkans alleging that they had a valid, binding contract with Thompson for such sale; (2) sought damages of Stoner for $100,000.00 for tortious interference with their contract with Thompson; and (3) sought injunctive relief against Stoner to prohibit him from interfering with their asserted rights to inspect the business, its premises, books and records, under their contract.

The Malkans argue that their trial amendment asking for declaratory relief and filed shortly after Stoner's attorney quit the trial was properly allowed and thus supplied the necessary basis in the pleadings for the declaratory relief in the judgment. If the trial amendment had asserted a new or different cause of action of which Stoner did not have fair notice, it would not support a judgment based upon that new or different cause of action. In this case, however, we hold that apart from the trial amendment, Stoner had fair notice of this declaratory relief by the pleadings of the Malkans on file in the case. The Malkans had made the same contention in all three of their prior pleadings that they made in their trial amendment, i.e., that they had a valid contract with Thompson to buy the majority stock interest in Texas Media. Stoner was charged with notice of all pleadings that had been filed and served on him or his attorney prior to their withdrawal. A determination of the question of the validity of the Malkans' contract to buy the stock had to be made before the trial court could have granted the Malkans relief under any of their prior pleadings. Stoner cannot now say that he did not have fair notice that such declaration of validity or invalidity was going to be made upon a trial. *Edwards Feed Mill v. Johnson, supra; Chokas v. Donald*, 439 S.W.2d 870 (Tex. Civ. App. 1969, no writ).

Texas Media and the Malkans both argue that when Stoner quit the trial, he waived all his rights to complain about their pleadings. They contend that under Rule 90, providing that pleading defects are waived when not brought to the attention of the trial court before judgment, and Rule 67, providing that issues not raised by the pleadings can be tried by implied consent, Stoner has waived any and all defects in the pleadings. They cite *Willeford v. Walker*, 499 S.W.2d 190 (Tex. Civ. App. 1973, no writ); however, that case has no application here. There the party complaining was present during the trial and did participate. He was under those circumstances found to have waived his complaint about the pleadings and tried the unpled issue by implied consent. *See also J. D. Abrams, Inc. v. Sebastian*, 570 S.W.2d 81, 84 (Tex. Civ. App. 1978, writ ref'd n. r. e.).

The specific terms of Rule 90 exempt its application to default judgments, and this Court has so held. *Griswold v. Carlson*, 151 Tex. 246, 249 S.W.2d 58 (1952). In view of our holding that in measuring the sufficiency of pleadings to support a judgment a post-answer default is treated the same as a no-answer default judgment and a judgment Nihil dicit, it follows that Rule 90 does not apply to a post-answer default judgment. A default judgment admits facts which are properly alleged. *Fitz v. Toungate*, 419 S.W.2d 708 (Tex. Civ. App. 1967, writ ref'd n. r. e.); 4 MCDONALD, TEXAS CIVIL PRACTICE 119 § 17.23.3 (1971). While a petition which serves as the basis for a default judgment may be objectionable under Rule 90, the default judgment will be held erroneous only if (1) the petition (or other pleading of the non-defaulting party that seeks affirmative relief) does not attempt to state a cause of action that is within the jurisdiction of the court, or (2) the petition (or pleading for affirmative relief) does not give fair notice to the defendant of the claim asserted, or (3) the petition affirmatively discloses the invalidity of such claim. Likewise, an absent party will not be considered to have tried an unpled cause of action by implied consent under Rule 67 where fair notice of that cause of action is not in the pleadings. *Edwards Feed Mill v. Johnson, supra; Weatherford v. Van Alstyne, supra; City of Fort Worth v. Gause, supra; Spivey v. Saner-Ragley Lumber Co., supra; C & H Transportation Company v. Wright, supra.*

The judgment of the Court of Civil Appeals is reformed to eliminate the award of $50,000.00 damages to Texas Media, Rule 501; the remainder of the judgment is affirmed.

Notes

1. *In the Interest of E.A. , et al,* 287 S.W.3d 1 (2009): In *Weaver v. Hartford Accident and Indemnity Co.*, 570 S.W.2d 367, 370 (Tex. 1978), the Court held that "a new citation is necessary for a party who has not appeared when the plaintiff, by amended petition, seeks a more onerous judgment than prayed for in the original pleading." In 1990, however, Texas Rule of Civil Procedure 21a was amended to provide for a variety of methods of service, including certified or registered mail, for all pleadings and court papers, except the original petition. In light of Rule 21a, service of new citation is not required for a default judgment, based on a more onerous amended petition. Service under Rule 21a will suffice. Here, there is no evidence, however, that Defendant-Norma was served with the amended petition under Rule 21a, or that she had constructive notice of the amended petition. Accordingly, without hearing oral argument, the court of appeals' judgment is reversed and remanded to the trial court for further proceedings consistent with this opinion.

2. *Horizon/CMS Healthcare Corp. v. Auld*, 34 S.W.3d 887 (Tex. 2000): "Texas follows a "fair notice" standard for pleading, which looks to whether the opposing party can ascertain from the pleading the nature and basic issues of the controversy and what testimony will be relevant. See *Broom v. Brookshire Bros., Inc.*, 923 S.W.2d 57, 60 (Tex. App.—Tyler 1995, writ denied). Horizon's first amended answer pleaded sufficient facts to give adequate and fair notice to Auld and the trial court of Horizon's intent to invoke the punitive-damages cap found in the Texas Civil Practice and Remedies Code, even though the pleading referred to an incorrect version of the statute. See, e.g., *CKB & Assocs., Inc. v. Moore McCormack Petroleum, Inc.*, 809 S.W.2d 577, 586 (Tex. App.—Dallas 1991, writ denied) ("A pleading that gives adequate notice will not fail merely because the draftsman named it improperly."). "A petition is sufficient if it gives fair and adequate notice of the facts upon which the pleader bases his claim. The purpose of this rule is to give the opposing party information sufficient to enable him to prepare a defense." *Roark v. Allen*, 633 S.W.2d 804, 810 (Tex. 1982). Horizon satisfied this standard. Being that there was, and is, only one punitive-damages cap provision in Chapter 41, it is hard to imagine that Auld was unaware of exactly what Horizon was claiming."

3. *Bos v. Smith*, 555 S.W.3d 293 (Tex. 2018): Pleadings must give fair notice of the nature and basic issues, so the opposing party can prepare a defense. When, as here, no special exception is made, we liberally construe the pleadings in the pleader's favor. Even so, a liberal construction "does not require a court to read into a petition what is plainly not there." When a pleader provides both general and specific allegations, the specific controls, and the pleader cannot rely on the general allegations to expand the scope of the claim.

c. *Alternative Claims*

JENKINS
v.
NORTHWESTERN PIPE & SUPPLY CO.
299 S.W. 857
(Tex. Comm'n. App. 1927, holding approved)

Kenley, Dawson & Holliday, of Wichita Falls, for plaintiff in error.

Carrigan, Britain, Morgan & King, W. E. Wilson, and E. R. Surles, all of Wichita Falls, for defendant in error.

SHORT, P. J.

This suit grows out of a transaction wherein the plaintiff in error sold to the defendants in error a quantity of casing located in an abandoned well, the casing intended to be bought weighing 20 pounds to the lineal foot, for a consideration of $200 actually paid upon the delivery of the bill of sale. When the defendants in error began to extract the casing from the well, they discovered for the first time that the casing only weighed 13 pounds to the lineal foot. Whereupon the defendants in error tendered the casing back to the plaintiff in error and demanded the return of the $200. This tender having been declined, this suit was brought in the county court at law of Wichita county, Tex., and upon the trial to a jury, wherein special issues were presented and answered, a verdict for the defendants in error for $360 was rendered, the defendants in error having sued for $385, of which $200 represented the original purchase price and $185 represented the lost profits. The plaintiff in error having appealed to the Court of Civil Appeals at Amarillo, the judgment of the trial court was affirmed. Whereupon writ of error was granted by the Supreme Court.

The jury answered that the defendants in error, at the time they paid the $200 for the casing, did not rely upon their own knowledge or investigation as to the kind of casing they were purchasing, but did rely upon the provision in the bill of sale as to the weight of casing. In answer to special issue No. 3, the jury answered that, immediately after learning the casing was not a 20-pound casing the defendants in error proceeded with the pulling of the same, with the intention to accept it as in compliance with the contract. The testimony in the case is sufficient to support each of these findings.

There is also testimony in the case which would justify a finding by the trial court that the casing actually sold was worthless, and it is upon the assumption that the trial judge did so find this fact that the Court of Civil Appeals based its conclusion that the judgment of the trial court should be affirmed, since it is a familiar principle of the law that, where a case is tried on special issues and neither party tenders an issue and a judgment is rendered, the trial judge is presumed to have found any material fact in issue supported by testimony in harmony with the judgment rendered.

The defendants in error in their pleading, after alleging the contract of sale between the parties and their performance of their part of the terms and the discovery that the casing was not 20-pound casing, but was 13-pound casing, then alleged that immediately on such discovery they notified the plaintiff in error of said fact and refused to accept the casing and tendered it back and have at all times been ready and willing to deliver it to the plaintiff in error. They then alleged that the reasonable market value of the 20-pound casing in the condition and of the age of that supposed to be in the well was $510 and the reasonable cost and expense of pulling the casing would not have exceeded $125. They then alleged that they purchased the casing for the purpose of resale and that, if it had been 20-pound casing, they would have sold it at a profit of $185. They therefore alleged that they were entitled to recover the purchase price of $200 and the profit of $185, aggregating $385.

The plaintiff in error answered by general and special exceptions, general denial, and, among other things, specially answered that the defendants in error had elected to affirm the contract and accept the casing after discovering the casing to be of the weight of 13 pounds, and it has been seen that the jury found that the defendants in error had so elected to affirm the contract. There is no allegation in the petition that the casing actually sold was entirely worthless, nor is there any allegation in the petition that the property received and accepted was worth less than the value of the property mentioned in the contract. Since the court rendered a judgment for

$360, and since it appears that the defendants in error only paid $200 for the property, and since they alleged the profits were $185, upon which latter claim the testimony is not very clear, we must assume that this $360 was made up of the $200 purchase money and $160 found by the court to be the profits lost by the defendants in error. We must also assume, in view of the finding of the jury in answer to issue No. 3, that the judgment was based upon a finding that the defendants in error had suffered this amount of money in damages growing out of the admitted fact that the casing actually sold was different from that actually contracted for.

We are inclined to the opinion that the petition of the defendants in error evidences the fact that this is a suit for rescission. The jury found that the defendants in error were not entitled to a rescission, since they accepted the casing after discovery of its true condition with intention to accept it as in compliance with the terms of the contract. The petition is not sufficient to state a cause of action for damages after expunging from it those allegations upon which the defendants in error sought to base a recovery as upon rescission. The defendants in error might have so framed their petition as that, upon failure of the jury and the court to give them relief by treating the contract as having been rescinded and allowing a recovery of the money paid with interest, they would be able to recover their damages flowing from the failure of the plaintiff in error to comply with his contract. To have done this successfully would have required a pleading in the alternative. This was not done.

In Nass v. Chadwick, 70 Tex. 157, 7 S. W. 828, CHIEF JUSTICE WILLIE, speaking for the Supreme Court of this state on this subject, says:

> "It is well settled by frequent decisions of this court that, where the vendor reserves an express lien to secure the purchase money of the land, the contract is executory; and in default of payment of the purchase money the vendor may either affirm the contract, sue for the money, and foreclose his lien, or he may rescind the contract, and recover the land itself. *Tom v. Wollhoefer*, 61 Tex. 277; *Coddington v. Wells*, 59 Tex. 50; *Ransom v. Brown*, 63 Tex. 188. But it has never been held that he could affirm the contract in part and rescind as to the remainder. The contract is an entirety and as such must either be affirmed or rescinded."

The defendants in error cannot repudiate the contract of sale by asking rescission and at the same time affirm it by seeking damages for the breach of an alleged warranty therein. They must either rescind as a whole or treat the contract as binding and rely upon the warranty as a basis for damages. *Kesler v. Robson*, 16 Tex. 119; *Brantley v. Thomas*, 22 Tex. 271, 73 Am. Dec. 264; *Blythe v. Speake*, 23 Tex. 429; *Scalf v. Tompkins*, 61 Tex. 476.

The supposed finding of fact by the trial judge in support of the judgment rendered that the casing actually delivered was worthless, supported as it is by some testimony in the record, cannot be considered for the reason that there is no pleading upon which to base such a finding. Moreover, even if there was pleading upon which to base such finding and we should be in error that the petition evidences a suit for rescission, yet the judgment cannot be sustained for the reason that the jury, in answer to special issue No. 3, found that the defendants in error, after learning that the casing was not 20-pound casing, proceeded with the pulling of it, with the intention to accept it as in compliance with the contract. This finding of fact by the jury had the legal effect of denying to the defendants in error any recovery upon any theory of the case, whether of rescission or for damages.

The questions we have discussed were raised in due time and in a proper way by the plaintiff in error by appropriate assignments, and, these assignments having been brought forward in the application for the writ of error, they are therefore sustained.

We recommend that the judgment of the Court of Civil Appeals affirming that of the trial court, as well as the judgment of the trial court, be reversed and that the case be remanded for further proceedings not inconsistent with this opinion.

CURETON, C. J.

Judgments of the Court of Civil Appeals and trial court are both reversed, and cause remanded, as recommended by the Commission of Appeals.

We approve the holding of the Commission of Appeals on the questions discussed in its opinion.

Note

In Texas jurisprudence, the Texas Supreme Court first analyzed the appropriateness of a settlement offset under the One Satisfaction Rule in *Bradshaw v. Baylor University,* 126 Tex. 99, 84 S.W.2d 703, 705 (Tex. Com. App. 1935) (limiting an injured party to a single satisfaction for one injury, whether or not there was more than one wrongdoer who contributed to the injury). In *Bradshaw,* a plaintiff riding a Baylor University bus was injured when the bus collided with a train. He settled with the railroad company, and the court refused to let the suit against Baylor University continue because the prior settlement satisfied the amount found to be the plaintiff's total injury. *See id.*

The Court modified the manner in which the One Satisfaction Rule applied in product liability suits in 1984 with *Duncan v. Cessna Aircraft Co. See* 665 S.W.2d 414, 429, 434 (Tex. 1984) (outlining the common law contribution scheme based on comparative causation as applied to products cases involving strict liability, breach of warranty, and mixed theories of strict liability and negligence tried after July 13, 1983). The One Satisfaction Rule, as first discussed in *Bradshaw,* was endorsed again in *Stewart Title Guaranty Co. v. Sterling. See* 822 S.W.2d 1, 5 (Tex. 1991) (applying the *Bradshaw* One Satisfaction Rule to cases not covered by a comparative causation scheme). Since then, the rule has been widely applied.

d. *Pleading of Damages*

Read Rule 56 Texas Rules of Civil Procedure.

SHERROD
v.
BAILEY
580 S.W.2d 24
(Tex. App.—Houston [1st. Dist.] 1979, writ ref'd n.r.e.)

William W. Byrd, Houston, for appellant.
Robert H. Hull, Houston, for appellee.

PEDEN, JUSTICE.

This is an appeal by Jack L. Sherrod Et al. (Developers) from a judgment in favor of Victor R. Bailey Et al. (Residents) based primarily on fraudulent misrepresentations and breach of contract. The jury found in response to special issues that 1) Sherrod promised Residents he would build roads that conformed to Harris County standards, 2) he failed to do so, 3) he made the promises with intent that the roads would not be so built, 4) he made the promises to induce Residents to buy lots, and 5) that the Residents reasonably relied on the promises to their detriment. The jury assessed actual damages (Issue 6) and punitive damages (Issue 7). The trial court granted the Developers' motion to disregard the jury's finding of punitive damages but entered judgment for the Residents in accordance with the jury's answers to the first six special issues.

On appeal the Developers assert insufficiency of the plaintiffs' pleadings, improper measure of damages, violation of the parol evidence rule, erroneous admission of expert testimony, and no evidence that Sherrod made a verbal promise. Residents maintain by cross-points that there is evidence to support an award of punitive damages and that the trial court erred in disregarding the jury's award of them. We reverse and remand.

From 1971 until 1975, Sherrod sold residential lots in two subdivisions, Spring-Stuebner Estates and Spring-Stuebner Estates Section II. Residents are all owners of lots in these two unrecorded subdivisions located in north Harris County.

The Residents assert that Sherrod orally promised that the roads in the subdivision would be brought up to Harris County standards so that the county would maintain them; Sherrod denies ever having made such a promise. The Residents have been attempting to maintain the roads themselves, and photographs in evidence demonstrate that the roads contain deep ruts and potholes.

Developers' points of error 1, 2, 3, 4, and 6 assert insufficiency of the Residents' pleadings. In their first two points, the Developers say the trial court erred in rendering judgment for the plaintiffs because they did not specifically plead any facts or otherwise file pleadings to support the submission of Issue 6 asking what losses, if any, were sustained by the Residents on the current value of their lots and improvements with roads as they now exist as compared with what the value would be if the roads were built to Harris County standards. In their fourth point, the Developers complain that the trial court erred in overruling their objections to the court's charge based on the lack of pleadings to support the submission of Issue No. 6. That issue, together with its instruction, was submitted as follows: "What sum of money, if any, if paid now in cash, do you find from a preponderance of the evidence would fairly and reasonably compensate the plaintiffs listed below for their damages, if any, which you find from a preponderance of the evidence proximately resulted from the occurrences inquired about herein? You may consider the following element of damage, if any, and none other: Loss in market value, if any, of each particular lot and improvements situated thereon with roads as they now exist in said subdivision as compared to what the value would be if roads were to Harris County Standards. Answer in dollars and cents, if any."

The purpose of pleadings is to put one's opponent on notice as to the parameters of the forthcoming battle.

Defects in the opponent's pleadings are not waived if challenged by special exception, objection to evidence, motion to strike testimony, motion for instructed verdict, or objection to the charge. When specific complaint has been made and an adverse ruling obtained from the court, there will be no implied consent to the trial of issues outside the pleadings. 2 MCDONALD TEXAS CIVIL PRACTICE 49, Pleading: General § 5.18 (1970).

The relevant portions of the Residents' petition were:

Count III

(Stating a Cause of Action for Breach of Contract)

At the time Plaintiffs purchased their property in Spring-Stuebner Estates and Spring-Stuebner Estates Section II, Defendants made oral representation to Plaintiffs that the roads and streets in Spring-Stuebner Estates and Spring-Stuebner Estates Section II subdivisions would be brought up to Harris County standards so that the roads would be maintained by Harris County. The Defendants have not brought the roads in the subdivision up to Harris County standards at any time since selling of lots in the subdivisions began in 1971. Defendants have breached this agreement, which breach has caused Plaintiffs' loss. Plaintiffs pray for specific performance of the agreement to bring the roads in the subdivision up to county standards and have them maintained; or, in the alternative, Plaintiffs plead for the cost of bringing the roads up to county standards and have the county take them over. The cost of paving the roads and reworking the ditches to provide adequate drainage would be approximately One Hundred Seventy-Five Thousand Dollars ($175,000.00), of lowering the three Tenneco pipelines would be at least Two Hundred Fifty Thousand Dollars ($250,000.00), and of lowering the Amoco pipeline would be approximately Twenty Thousand Dollars ($20,000.00), for which Plaintiffs here pray judgment.

Count IV

(Stating a Cause of Action for Fraud under Texas Business and Commerce Code, Sec. 27.01)

XII.

Plaintiffs allege that Defendants willfully represented to Plaintiffs that the roads in the subdivision would be brought up to county standards and that maintenance would be assumed by Harris County. This material promise to bring the roads up to county standards was made by the Defendants with the intention of not fulfilling it and for the purpose of inducing the Plaintiffs to enter into the purchase contract with the Defendants herein. Plaintiffs relied upon these representations in entering into their contracts to purchase their several parcels of property. The difference in the value of the property as represented and the value of the property as sold exceeds Seventy-Five Thousand Dollars ($75,000.00), for which Plaintiffs herein pray. Additionally, Plaintiffs further ask this Honorable Court that punitive damages be awarded to Plaintiffs for Defendants' willful and fraudulent acts in the amount at least twice the actual damages found herein, but in no event less than One Hundred Fifty Thousand Dollars. ($150,000.00).

Count VI

(Stating a Cause of Action for Mandatory Injunctions Incorporating All Allegations from Paragraphs I through XIII).

XIV.

Plaintiffs plead in the alternative in equity that this Court issue a mandatory injunction against Defendants to force Defendants to cause the roads in Spring-Stuebner Estates and Spring-Stuebner Estates Section II to be brought up to Harris County standards as defined in Exhibit "F" attached hereto.

XVI.

In the alternative to all of the above, and without waiver thereof, if the agreements to provide a restricted subdivision were not sufficiently definite, then Defendants are estopped to deny this insufficiency because Plaintiffs herein have relied on these promises heretofore set out to their great detriment and loss. Plaintiffs would be entitled to recover the amounts herein sought.

WHEREFORE, premises considered, Plaintiffs pray that Plaintiffs be awarded damages as aforesaid or other remedies as aforesaid, all costs of court, and all such other and further relief, both in law and in equity, to which they may be justly entitled.

We sustain the appellants' first, second and fourth points of error. As to the roads in question, the Residents had asked in a prior petition for common law damages, but the Defendants were entitled to conclude from the deletion of that aspect of the claim, that it was being abandoned. As we have seen, their trial petition explicitly sought 1) specific performance of the oral representations, or 2) the cost of bringing the roads up to county standards, 3) the difference in the value of their properties As represented and As sold, 4) punitive damages, 5) a mandatory injunction to force defendants to bring the roads up to Harris County standards, and 6) general relief. (emphasis added)

When items of special damage are claimed, they shall be specifically stated." Rule 56, Texas Rules of Civil Procedure. Special damages are those that proximately result from the defendant's wrongful conduct but are of such an unusual nature that they would normally vary with the circumstances of the individual case in which they occur. General damages are those that are so usual an accompaniment of the kind of breach or wrongdoing alleged in the complaint that the mere allegation of the wrong gives sufficient notice. 2 MCDONALD, TEXAS CIVIL PRACTICE 124, § 6.17.1 (1970).

We cannot say that a necessary result of a fraudulent misrepresentation as to quality of roads in an undeveloped subdivision will be purchasers' losses in value of their properties as improved at the time of trial as compared to what they would be if the roads were as represented. This was an item of special damages, and facts raising them should have been specially pleaded.

Stated another way, it was held in a negligence case that if a plaintiff makes a general allegation of damages it will suffice as a basis for proof of those damages which naturally and necessarily result therefrom, for the law implies such damages. But if plaintiffs choose to particularize the injuries arising from a harm, all that they intended to prove must be alleged. *Weingartens, Inc. v. Price*, 461 S.W.2d 260 (Tex. Civ. App. 1970, writ ref. n.r.e.).

We have noted that in our case the jury was instructed to consider the loss in market value of each lot And its improvements with the roads in their present condition as compared to what their value would be if the roads met the county standards. (emphasis added)

Did the defendants have fair notice of the proof to be offered? This measure of damages, based on the market value of the improved lots at the time of trial, was not raised by the pleadings. The plaintiffs did not allege that improvements had been built on their lots, nor did they ask for damages to any improvements. By their only allegations concerning their damages based on the values of their properties, they asked for "the difference in value of the property as represented and . . . as sold." (Count IV, Paragraph XII, above). This pleaded measure of damages was, as they indicated in the heading of Count IV, the one provided by Section 27.01 of the Texas Business & Commerce Code, and it put the defendants on notice that damages were to be assessed based on values existing when they sold the respective tracts. The defendants were entitled to conclude that damages to the improvements were not being sought. The defendants raised this point in their objections to the trial court's charge.

We do not suggest that the plaintiffs may not recover, under proper pleadings, damages in addition to those provided in Section 27.01 of the Code. Section 27.01 replaced Article 4004, V.T.C.S. Neither Article 4004 nor Section 27.01 superseded the common law rule and neither provides an exclusive remedy for the recovery of damages in an action based on fraud in a real estate transaction. *Maddox v. Worsham*, 415 S.W.2d 222 (Tex. Civ.

App. 1967, writ ref. n. r. e.) *citing El Paso Development Co. v. Ravel*, 339 S.W.2d 360 (Tex. Civ. App. 1960, writ ref. n. r. e.). It should be noted that in both those cases the plaintiffs clearly alleged that the fraud was not discovered until after they had taken possession of the properties and had spent money in developing and utilizing them. It was held in both cases that the plaintiffs might recover "such additional damages as are directly traceable to the wrongful act complained of and which result therefrom."

It is well settled that a prayer for general relief will support any relief raised by the evidence and consistent with the allegations in the petition. We hold that the relief granted was not consistent with the plaintiffs' allegations.

The appellants' eleventh point complains that the plaintiffs' testimony about Sherrod's promises about the roads violated the parol evidence rule. We overrule this point. The parol evidence rule does not preclude enforcement of prior contemporaneous agreements which are not inconsistent with and do not vary or contradict the express or implied terms or obligations thereof. *Hubacek v. Ennis State Bank*, 159 Tex. 166, 317 S.W.2d 30, 32 (1958).

Our disposition of these points of error makes it unnecessary for us to decide the appellants' other points.

The appellees complain by cross-points of the trial court's having disregarded the jury's award of exemplary damages.

Having held that the plaintiffs were not entitled to recover actual damages under the pleadings and proof offered, we cannot hold that they could recover exemplary damages.

Reversed and remanded.

Notes

1. In *Henry S. Miller Co. v. Bynum*, 836 S.W.2d 160 (Tex. 1992) CHIEF JUSTICE PHILLIPS in a concurring opinion discussed the difference between general and special damages in the context of a deceptive trade practice case.

> At common law, actual damages can be either "direct" or "consequential." *See generally, Nobility Homes of Texas, Inc. v. Shivers*, 557 S.W.2d 77, 78 n. 1 (Tex. 1977); DAN B. DOBBS, THE LAW OF REMEDIES § 9.2 (1973). "Direct damages," also known as "general damages," compensate for the loss, damage or injury that is conclusively presumed to have been foreseen or contemplated by the party as a consequence of his breach of contract or wrongful act. *Id.* For misrepresentation, there are two recognized measures of direct damages. The "out of pocket" measure, which operates on a restitutionary theory, measures the difference between the value of that which was parted with and the value of that which was received. The "benefit of the bargain" measure, which utilizes an expectancy theory, evaluates the difference between the value as represented and the value actually received. * * * The DTPA allows the injured consumer to recover either the "out of pocket" measure or the "benefit of the bargain" measure of damages, whichever is greater. *W.O. Bankston Nissan*, 754 S.W.2d at 128.
>
> On the other hand, "consequential damages," also known as "special damages," are those damages which result naturally, but not necessarily, from the acts complained of. *Dan B. Dobbs, The Law of Remedies* § 9.2 (1973). Under the common law, they are not recoverable unless the defendant had notice that the plaintiff would suffer such damages. *Mead v. Johnson Group, Inc.*, 615 S.W.2d 685, 687 (Tex. 1981) (*citing Hadley v. Baxendale*, 9 Exch. 341, 354 (1854)). Even though the notice or foreseeability requirement may not be necessary under the DTPA, . . . , if the damages are too remote, too uncertain, or purely conjectural and speculative, they cannot be recovered. *See White v. Southwestern Bell Telephone Co., Inc.*, 651 S.W.2d 260 (Tex. 1983). A consumer may recover consequential damages under the DTPA for a variety of injuries, including, but not limited to, lost profits, *White*, 651 S.W.2d 260, loss of credit, *see, e.g., Roberts v. U.S. Homes Corp.*, 694 S.W.2d 129 (Tex. App.—San Antonio 1985, no writ), loss for improvements made, *see Village Mobile Homes, Inc. v. Porter*, 716 S.W.2d 543 (Tex. App.—Austin 1986, writ ref'd n.r.e.), interest on indebtedness, *Kold-Serve Corp. v. Ward*, 736 S.W.2d 750 (Tex. App.—Corpus Christi 1987), *writ dism'd, Ward v. Kold-Serve Corp.*, 748 S.W.2d 227 (Tex. 1980), and related and reasonably necessary expenses. *Kish*, 692 S.W.2d at 466. In order to be recoverable, however, consequential damages must be specifically pled. TEX. R. CIV. P. 56. *See*

generally, Weingartens, Inc. v. Price, 461 S.W.2d 260, 263 (Tex. Civ. App.—Houston [14th Dist.] 1970, writ ref'd n.r.e.).

2. An example of special damages that must be plead can be found in *Interstate Northborough Partnership v. State of Texas*, 66 S.W. 3d 213 (Tex. 2001): The community-damages rule in a condemnation case does not bar recovery of increased-proximity damages. Rather, the nature of the injury and whether it affects the remainder in some special, unique way determines whether damages are community or special. Under the facts in this condemnation case, damages due to increased proximity to the roadway are resulting from a commercial property's increased proximity to a roadway, with attendant loss of curb appeal, green space, and "buffer" zone, are special rather than community damages, and thus compensable. Here, the difference in injury to the property is not one of degree, it is one of kind.

e. *Prayer*

Notes

1. In *Arrington v. McDaniel*, 119 Tex. 148, 14 S.W.2d 1009 (Tex. 1929) "the prayer, for 'other and further relief to which they may be entitled at law or in equity,' cannot enlarge the recovery to embrace a cause of action not within the pleadings." Furthermore, the court will not grant relief inconsistent with or entirely different from that asked in the special prayer.

2. In *Benavides v. Isles Constr. Co.*, 726 S.W.2d 23 (Tex. 1987) the Court noted that:

> [w]e recognize that as a general rule plaintiffs are required to plead for prejudgment interest sought at common law as an element of damages, whereas statutory or contractual interest may be predicated on a prayer for general relief. *Republic National Bank v. Northwest National Bank*, 578 S.W.2d 109, 116-17 (Tex. 1978); *Black Lake Pipe Line Co. v. Union Construction Co.*, 538 S.W.2d 80, 96 (Tex. 1976). In *Republic National Bank*, we stated: Where prejudgment interest is sought at common law as an element of damages, the plaintiff must plead for it [editor: this pleading can be in the prayer itself: "Plaintiff prays that after notice and hearing that he recover of and from the Defendant for the damages as hereinabove set out, for interest and costs, and for such other relief both general and special, at law and equity, to which it may show itself justly entitled."]. Such is not the case where prejudgment interest is sought on the basis of a written contract fitting the description of article 5069-1.03. An award of this statutory interest, or interest eo nomine as it is known, may be supported by a prayer for general relief. 578 S.W.2d at 117 [editor: "other relief both general and special, at law and equity, to which it may show itself justly entitled"].

f. *Truth in Pleadings*

Note

Texas Civil Practice and Remedies Code § 10.001. Signing of Pleadings and Motions.

The signing of a pleading or motion as required by the Texas Rules of Civil Procedure constitutes a certificate by the signatory that to the signatory's best knowledge, information, and belief, formed after reasonable inquiry:

(1) the pleading or motion is not being presented for any improper purpose, including to harass or to cause unnecessary delay or needless increase in the cost of litigation;

(2) each claim, defense, or other legal contention in the pleading or motion is warranted by existing law or by a nonfrivolous argument for the extension, modification, or reversal of existing law or the establishment of new law;

(3) each allegation or other factual contention in the pleading or motion has evidentiary support or, for a specifically identified allegation or factual contention, is likely to have evidentiary support after a reasonable opportunity for further investigation or discovery; and

(4) each denial in the pleading or motion of a factual contention is warranted on the evidence or, for a specifically identified denial, is reasonably based on a lack of information or belief.

(a) A court that determines that a person has signed a pleading or motion in violation of Section 10.001 may impose a sanction on the person, a party represented by the person, or both.

(b) The sanction must be limited to what is sufficient to deter repetition of the conduct or comparable conduct by others similarly situated.

(c) A sanction may include any of the following:

(1) a directive to the violator to perform, or refrain from performing, an act;

(2) an order to pay a penalty into court; and

(3) an order to pay to the other party the amount of the reasonable expenses incurred by the other party because of the filing of the pleading or motion, including reasonable attorney's fees.

(d) The court may not award monetary sanctions against a represented party for a violation of Section 10.001(2).

(e) The court may not award monetary sanctions on its own initiative unless the court issues its order to show cause before a voluntary dismissal or settlement of the claims made by or against the party or the party's attorney who is to be sanctioned.

(f) The filing of a general denial under Rule 92, Texas Rules of Civil Procedure, shall not be deemed a violation of this chapter.

LOW
v.
HENRY
221 S.W.3d 609
(Tex. 2007)

Carlos Villarreal, Brian Charles Miller, Robert J. Seerden and J. Kevin Oncken, for Petitioners.
Paul D. Andrews, Keith Matthew Gould and Paul D. Andrews, for Respondents.
John C. Marshall, III, Marshall & McCracken, Melanie Sky Breedlove, Lanette Lurleen Lutich, Cooper & Scully, P.C., Houston, Michael L. Hurst, Hermes Sargent & Bates, Michael Berry, Thompson & Knight, John A. Scully, Cooper & Scully, P.C., Dallas, Jennifer P. Henry, Thompson & Knight, Fort Worth, for Other.
Donald P. Wilcox, Susan G. Taylor, Austin, for Amicus Curiae.

JUSTICE WAINWRIGHT delivered the opinion of the Court.

Texas follows a "fair notice" standard for pleading, in which courts assess the sufficiency of pleadings by determining whether an opposing party can ascertain from the pleading the nature, basic issues, and the type of evidence that might be relevant to the controversy. *See Tex. Dep't of Parks & Wildlife v. Miranda,* 133 S.W.3d 217, 230 (Tex. 2004); *Horizon/CMS Healthcare Corp. v. Auld,* 34 S.W.3d 887, 896-97 (Tex. 2000); *Boyles v. Kerr,* 855 S.W.2d 593, 601 (Tex. 1993); *see also* TEX.R. CIV. P. 47(a). However, the actual facts and evidence of a specific case limit this relatively liberal standard. Chapter 10 of the Texas Civil Practice and Remedies Code requires a pleading's signatory to certify that he or she conducted a reasonable inquiry into the allegations and concluded that each allegation or other factual contention in the pleading has or is likely to have evidentiary support. Because the attorney who filed the petition in this case obtained and directed the review of evidence that disproved some of the allegations pled against some of the defendants, the trial court correctly found that the attorney violated Chapter 10. However, we hold that the trial court abused its discretion in not providing a sufficient basis to support the imposition of a $50,000 penalty. We reverse the court of appeals' judgment and remand the case to the trial court for proceedings consistent with this opinion.

On November 20, 1999, Henry White was admitted to Columbia North Bay Hospital after suffering a stroke. Dr. Stephen Smith treated White in the emergency room for less than one hour. Dr. Robert Low cared for him for four days before White was transferred to another hospital. White was comatose at the time of the transfer. He died in December 1999.

On January 31, 2002, Joyce White (both individually and as representative of her husband Henry White's estate) sued the alleged manufacturers, designers, and distributors of the drug known as Propulsid, Coastal Bend Hospital, Inc. d/b/a Columbia North Bay Hospital, eight physicians and nurse Donna McMahon for damages flowing from Henry White's death. Although most of the claims involved the drug Propulsid, some alleged that the physicians and hospital were negligent in Henry White's medical treatment.

Attorney Thomas J. Henry represented Joyce White when he filed the petition. His office received copies of Henry White's medical records months before he filed the petition. Henry filed a motion to withdraw as counsel on the same day he filed the petition. Henry continued to represent Joyce White until the trial court granted the motion to withdraw on May 6, 2002.

On May 28, 2002, Dr. Smith filed a motion for sanctions against Joyce White and Henry for alleged violations of Texas Rule of Civil Procedure 13 and chapters 9 and 10 of the Texas Civil Practice and Remedies Code. Dr. Low filed the same motion. Both physicians argued that none of the medical records from the hospital at which the physicians treated White contained any reference to either doctor having prescribed or provided Propulsid to White. On June 10, Joyce White nonsuited the case. The physicians' motions for sanctions remained pending.

The trial court held a hearing on the physicians' motions on July 30, 2002. Henry did not attend or testify but appeared through counsel. On July 31, 2002, the trial court granted the motions and ordered Henry to pay $25,000 in sanctions on each motion, for a total of $50,000. On August 2, 2002, the trial court entered a revised judgment that incorporated findings of fact and conclusions of law. On August 26, 2002, Henry filed a motion for new trial and a motion to vacate, modify, correct, or reform the sanctions order. On September 23, 2002, Henry filed a supplemental motion. On October 15, 2002, the trial court held a hearing on Henry's motions. After hearing more testimony, including Henry's, the trial court ultimately denied admission of all additional evidence and denied Henry's motion to modify the judgment. Henry filed a motion to reconsider, challenging the adequacy of the trial court's findings of fact and conclusions of law for the first time. The trial court denied this motion and rejected as untimely all arguments not contained in the original motion for new trial and motion to vacate, modify, correct or reform the judgment as untimely. Henry appealed.

An en banc court of appeals reversed, holding that because the allegations against the physicians were made in the alternative, sanctions under chapter 10 of the Texas Civil Practice and Remedies Code were inappropriate. 132 S.W.3d 180, 187. The court also held that the physicians' motions did not support sanctions under Chapter 10 for unrelated prior litigation and that the trial court's order failed to meet the specificity requirements of Chapter 10. *Id.* at 187-88. The dissenting justices argued that the trial court did not abuse its discretion and that Henry waived his other complaints. *Id.* at 190-91. The physicians petitioned this Court for review.

We review the imposition of sanctions here under the same standard we review sanctions under Rule 13-abuse of discretion. *See Am. Flood Research, Inc. v. Jones,* 192 S.W.3d 581, 583 (Tex. 2006); *Cire v. Cummings,* 134 S.W.3d 835, 838 (Tex. 2004). An appellate court may reverse the trial court's ruling only if the trial court acted without reference to any guiding rules and principles, such that its ruling was arbitrary or unreasonable. *Cire,* 134 S.W.3d at 838-39. To determine if the sanctions were appropriate or just, the appellate court must ensure there is a direct nexus between the improper conduct and the sanction imposed. *Spohn Hosp. v. Mayer,* 104 S.W.3d 878, 882 (Tex. 2003) (citing *TransAmerican Natural Gas Corp. v. Powell,* 811 S.W.2d 913, 917 (Tex. 1991)). Generally, courts presume that pleadings and other papers are filed in good faith. *GTE Commc'ns Sys. Corp. v. Tanner,* 856 S.W.2d 725, 730 (Tex. 1993). The party seeking sanctions bears the burden of overcoming this presumption of good faith. *Id.* at 731.

Chapters 9 and 10 of the Texas Civil Practice and Remedies Code and rule 13 of the Texas Rules of Civil Procedure allow a trial court to sanction an attorney or a party for filing motions or pleadings that lack a reasonable basis in fact or law. Chapter 9 of the Texas Civil Practice and Remedies Code only applies in proceedings in which neither Rule 13 nor Chapter 10 applies. TEX. CIV. PRAC. & REM.CODE § 9.012(h). Rule 13 authorizes the imposition of the sanctions listed in Rule 215.2(b), which only provides for a monetary penalty based on expenses, court costs, or attorney's fees. Because the trial court ordered Henry to pay $50,000 in penalties not based on expenses, court costs, or attorney's fees, and because the trial court's written order specifically orders the penalty pursuant to chapter 10 of the Texas Civil Practice and Remedies Code, we review the trial court's order in light of chapter 10. Chapter 10 provides that:

> The signing of a pleading or motion as required by the Texas Rules of Civil Procedure constitutes a certificate by the signatory that to the signatory's best knowledge, information, and belief, formed after reasonable inquiry:
>
> (1) the pleading or motion is not being presented for any improper purpose, including to harass or to cause unnecessary delay or needless increase in the cost of litigation;
> (2) each claim, defense, or other legal contention in the pleading or motion is warranted by existing law or by a nonfrivolous argument for the extension, modification, or reversal of existing law or the establishment of new law;
> (3) each allegation or other factual contention in the pleading or motion has evidentiary support or, for a specifically identified allegation or factual contention, is likely to have evidentiary support after a reasonable opportunity for further investigation or discovery; and
> (4) each denial in the pleading or motion of a factual contention is warranted on the evidence or, for a specifically identified denial, is reasonably based on a lack of information or belief.

TEX. CIV. PRAC. & REM.CODE § 10.001. Under Section 10.001, the signer of a pleading or motion certifies that *each* claim, *each* allegation, and *each* denial is based on the signatory's best knowledge, information, and belief, formed after reasonable inquiry. The statute dictates that each claim and each allegation be individually evaluated for support. *Id.* The fact that an allegation or claim is alleged against several defendants-so-called "group pleadings"—does not relieve the party from meeting the express requirements of Chapter 10. Each claim against each defendant must satisfy Chapter 10.

Likewise, alternative pleading under Texas Rule of Civil Procedure 48 does not excuse noncompliance with Chapter 10. Pleading in the alternative allows multiple allegations, which may even conflict, to be alleged against a defendant, but there still must be a reasonable basis for each alternative allegation. Pleading in the alternative does not permit alleging a claim with no reasonable basis in fact or law "in the alternative" of a claim that does have support. That is simply not permitted by Texas law. *See* TEX. CIV. PRAC. & REM.CODE § 10.001. Each allegation and factual contention in a pleading or motion must have, or be likely to have, evidentiary support after a reasonable investigation. *Id.*

* * *

The physicians argue that by filing the pleading in this case, Henry certified that to the best of his knowledge, information, and belief, the factual contentions in the pleading had or were likely to have evidentiary support. A reasonable inquiry into the allegations would have proven otherwise. *See* TEX. CIV. PRAC. & REM.CODE § 10.001(3). White's medical records, which were in Henry's possession before he filed the lawsuit, indicated that neither physician ever prescribed or administered the drug to White. The physicians argue that Henry violated Chapter 10 by alleging that they prescribed and administered Propulsid in spite of the information to the contrary in White's medical records. We agree with the physicians.

Undeniably, the petition focuses on Propulsid, a drug used to treat gastric reflux. The first sentence of the fact section of the petition summarizes, "The Plaintiffs are victims of the Defendants' decision to manufacture, market, design, promote, and/or distribute [Propulsid]." The petition claims that Johnson & Johnson, Janssen Pharmaceutica, and Janssen Research Foundation were negligent, negligent per se, and strictly liable for the defective design, marketing, manufacture, and distribution of the drug and for the violation of specified statutes and regulations. The petition also includes fraud and misrepresentation claims against Johnson & Johnson, Janssen Pharmaceutica, and Janssen Research Foundation regarding the safety and efficacy of the drug. The petition further alleges that collectively the "defendants" breached implied and express warranties. Finally, the petition * * * alleges [in numerous places, ed.] that Drs. Low and Smith provided or prescribed the drug to White. The other paragraphs allege negligent conduct other than prescribing or providing Propulsid to White.

However, Drs. Low and Smith presented undisputed evidence at the trial court that neither doctor ever prescribed or administered Propulsid to White and that a pre-suit review of White's medical records would have confirmed that fact. Dr. Low filed an affidavit with his motion for sanctions swearing that "[a]t no time during [his] involvement with this patient did [he] ever prescribe, provide, administer or order Propulsid for Mr. White." Dr. Smith filed an affidavit making the same statement with his motion. At the July 30, 2002 hearing on the motions, the physicians again testified that they did not administer or prescribe Propulsid. The testimony established that Dr. Smith was White's doctor for less than an hour in the emergency room, and Dr. Low, an internal medicine doctor at Columbia North Bay, provided care to White for four days after he arrived at Columbia North Bay and before his transfer to a facility in Corpus Christi. Dr. Low also confirmed that "anyone familiar with reviewing a medical record could easily have confirmed [Dr. Low's] testimony and the fact that [Dr. Low] had nothing to do with Propulsid had they simply reviewed the record." Dr. Smith testified that White's medical record contains no reference to Dr. Smith's ever prescribing or administering Propulsid to White. In fact, Henry does not dispute Dr. Low's testimony that White had not been taking Propulsid approximately two weeks before his treatment by the physicians. Dr. Smith similarly testified that he was informed that White had not been taking Propulsid "for some time" before his arrival at the Columbia North Bay emergency room and his subsequent treatment by Drs. Low and Smith.

The evidence at the hearing supports the trial court's conclusion that:

> Based upon the totality of the evidence admitted during the hearing on the Motions for Sanctions, each and all of the allegations brought against Drs. Low and Smith, and therefore the lawsuit brought against these physicians, did not, on January 31, 2002, and do not now, have evidentiary support; nor were they on January 31, 2002, likely to have evidentiary support after a reasonable opportunity for further investigation . . . .

Under chapter 10 of the Texas Civil Practice and Remedies Code, the physicians were not required to specifically show bad faith or malicious intent, just that Henry certified he made a reasonable inquiry into all of the allegations when he did not and that he certified that all the allegations in the petition had evidentiary support, or were likely to have evidentiary support, when some allegations did not. We conclude that the trial court did not abuse its discretion in concluding that Henry failed to meet the standard in Chapter 10.

* * *

Finally, Henry claims that the trial court's order, including the findings of fact and conclusions of law, was not specific enough to support sanctions under chapter 10 of the Texas Civil Practice and Remedies Code. Henry first raised this complaint in his first supplemental motion to vacate, modify, correct, or reform the modified judgment, which he filed on September 23, 2002. As we held in *Moritz, M.D. v. Preiss,* "[r]ead together, Rules 5, 329b(b) and 329b(e) demonstrate that an amended motion for new trial filed more than thirty days after the trial court signs a final judgment is untimely." 121 S.W.3d 715, 720 (Tex. 2003). The trial court signed its revised order granting sanctions, including findings of fact and conclusions of law, on August 2, 2002, fifty-two days before Henry's complaint that the order was not sufficiently specific to support an award of sanctions under Chapter 10. Although we have recognized that "the trial court may, at its discretion, consider the grounds raised in an untimely motion and grant a new trial under its inherent authority before the court loses plenary power," the trial court in this case denied Henry's motion as untimely. *Id.* at 720. On appeal, Henry fails to challenge the trial court's ruling on the timeliness of his post-sanctions motions and thus has waived any complaint about the specificity of the trial court's order. *See* TEX.R.APP. P. 33.1(a). Despite Henry's waiver, as discussed below, we conclude that Henry's challenge fails on the merits: the evidence and the trial court's order support an award of sanctions under Chapter 10.

* * *

We recognize that in some cases, a party may not have evidence that proves each specific factual allegation at the time a lawsuit is filed. Certainly, the law does not require proof of a case without reasonable time for discovery. However, this does not excuse the filing of claims against parties when the attorney filing the lawsuit possesses information that a reasonable inquiry would have determined negated some of the claims made. We affirm the trial court's determination that chapter 10 was violated but hold that the trial court abused its discretion in not more specifically identifying the basis for imposing a $50,000 penalty under chapter 10 of the Texas Civil Practice and Remedies Code. We reverse the judgment of the court of appeals and remand the case to the trial court for proceedings consistent with this opinion.

Note

Unifund CCR Partners v. Villa, ---- S.W.3d-----, 53 Tex. Sup. Ct. J. 57, 2009 W.L. 3403326 (Tex. 2009): Unifund CCR Partners (Unifund) purchased a credit card debt Villa owed to Bank One. Villa later filed for bankruptcy, and his debts were discharged. In his bankruptcy filing, Villa listed Bank One, not Unifund, as creditor on the credit card debt. After Villa's bankruptcy, Unifund sued Villa on the debt. Villa answered, asserted his discharge in bankruptcy, and filed a motion for sanctions. Unifund responded by filing a notice of dismissal, and the trial court dismissed the suit with prejudice. Several months later the court assessed sanctions against Unifund pursuant to chapter 10 of the Texas Civil Practice and Remedies Code. The court of appeals affirmed. 273 S.W.3d 385. ***Held:*** We hold that the trial court abused its discretion in assessing sanctions against Unifund because there was no evidence to support the findings underlying the sanctions. ***Held:*** Reversed and judgment rendered that Villa take nothing on his claim for costs for inconvenience and harassment. The court's findings that Unifund CCR Partners subjectively knew of Villa's bankruptcy, and that it became aware of the bankruptcy before suit was filed, rely entirely on the truth of the statements in the TransUnion document. But the document was hearsay, was timely objected to, and should have been excluded from evidence. Absent the inadmissible document, there is no evidence to support Villa's motion and the trial court's findings and conclusions that Unifund violated the provisions of Chapter 10. Without evidence to support Villa's motion and the trial court's findings, the trial court abused its discretion by assessing sanctions against Unifund.

2. *Defendant's Pleadings*

Notes

1. *Nath v. Texas Children's Hospital*, ___ S.W.3d ___, 2014 WL 4352269 (Tex. 2014): Sanctions for pleading abuse (more than $1.3 million for attorney fees) were proper. Nath's pleadings were properly subject to sanctions for asserting time-barred claims and addressing matters wholly irrelevant to the lawsuit in an attempt to leverage a more favorable settlement, but in assessing the amount the trial court failed to consider whether the defendants bore at least partial responsibility for the attorney fees they incurred by litigating for more than four years before seeking sanctions. Nath may be properly deemed the true offender, yet his attorneys possess ethical obligations and may share in the blame for sanctioned conduct. But Baylor and the hospital only moved to sanction Nath—not his lawyers—and the trial court declined to sanction the lawyers on its own. Under the true-offender inquiry, the Court concludes, it must uphold the trial court's decision to sanction Nath personally because evidence supports the sanction.

2. Under the Rules of Texas Civil Procedure a special appearance needs to be filed before a motion to transfer venue or any other pleading or motion or it is waived; likewise, a motion to transfer venue needs to be filed before all pleadings other than a special appearance or it is waived. Read Rules 86 and 120a. The defendant is not required to observe any other due order of pleading rules.

a. *Plea in Abatement*

Read Rule 85 Texas Rules of Civil Procedure

WYATT
v.
SHAW PLUMBING CO.
760 S.W.2d 245
(Tex. 1988)

Ken Dahlbert, Wood & Burney, Corpus Christi, Tracy DuBose, DuBose & Short, Montgomery, Joe R. Greenhill and Larry F. York, Baker & Botts, Austin, for petitioner.

Richard J. Hatch, Prichard, Peeler, Hatch, Cartwright, Hall & Kratzig, Corpus Christi, for respondent.

RAY, JUSTICE.

This case arises out of a dispute over the services provided by a plumbing contractor in the construction of a house in Duval County. The issue presented by this appeal involves a plea in abatement filed in a second suit in Nueces County when a prior suit was pending in Duval County. The court of appeals affirmed the Nueces County district court, holding that the decision to grant a plea in abatement was within the discretion of the Nueces County court and there was no abuse of that discretion. 736 S.W.2d 763. We hold that the Nueces County district court was required to grant the plea in abatement because a previously filed suit between the parties was pending. We, therefore, reverse the judgment of the court of appeals and remand the cause to the Nueces County district court with instructions to vacate its judgment and abate all proceedings pending final disposition of the Duval County lawsuit, which was previously filed.

This controversy involves a suit between the parties in the district court of Duval County and another suit subsequently filed in the district court of Nueces County. Oscar Wyatt was building a house in Duval County. On Wyatt's behalf, Morgan Spear entered into an oral agreement with Shaw Plumbing Company for Shaw to perform work on the house. When Wyatt did not pay Shaw Plumbing for its services, Shaw made a written demand for payment. Following Shaw Plumbing's demand letter, Wyatt filed suit against Shaw in Duval County on February 7, 1983, alleging fraud and violation of the Deceptive Trade Practices Act.

On April 4, 1983, Shaw Plumbing filed a breach of contract suit against Wyatt and Spear in Nueces County to recover for its services. Wyatt filed a plea in abatement in the Nueces County suit based upon the pendency of the previously filed Duval County suit. The Nueces County district court signed an order denying Wyatt's plea in abatement on June 15, 1984. On February 13, 1986, Wyatt filed a second plea in abatement in Nueces County after he agreed to indemnify Spear for any claims against Spear by Shaw Plumbing. The Nueces County district court again denied the plea. Prior to the trial in Nueces County, the trial judge struck Wyatt's pleadings as a sanction for alleged discovery abuse. Judgment was rendered against Wyatt following a jury trial in Nueces County.

It has long been the policy of the courts and the legislature of this state to avoid a multiplicity of lawsuits. The need for judicial economy has recently become more acute because the dockets of our trial courts are overburdened, and litigants must wait far too long for their cases to be heard. In keeping with the policy to avoid multiple lawsuits, Texas Rule of Civil Procedure 97(a) was promulgated. This rule regarding compulsory counterclaims dictates that a pleading shall assert a counterclaim if it meets six elements. A counterclaim is compulsory if: (1) it is within the jurisdiction of the court; (2) it is not at the time of filing the answer the subject of a pending action; (3) the action is mature and owned by the pleader at the time of filing the answer; (4) it arises out of the transaction or occurrence that is the subject matter of the opposing party's claim; (5) it is against an opposing party in the same capacity; and (6) it does not require for its adjudication the presence of third parties over whom the court cannot acquire jurisdiction. *See* TEX. R. CIV. P. 97(a), (d); *see also* 2 R. MCDONALD, TEXAS CIVIL PRACTICE IN DISTRICT AND COUNTY COURTS § 7.49, at 253-54 (rev. 1982). If a claim meets these elements, it must be asserted in the initial action. A defendant's failure to assert a compulsory counterclaim precludes its assertion in later actions. *Gray v. Kirkland*, 550 S.W.2d 410, 411 (Tex. Civ. App.—Corpus Christi

1977, writ ref'd n.r.e.); *see* 2 R. MCDONALD, *supra*, § 7.49, at 254. Shaw Plumbing's suit against Wyatt was a compulsory counterclaim under the requirements of Rule 97(a).

In the case in which Wyatt as plaintiff sued Shaw Plumbing as defendant on tort and DTPA theories, the counties in which venue was proper were: (1) Nueces County, where the defendant had its principal office situated; (2) Duval County, where the construction and plumbing was done, and thus the cause of action arose; or (3) Harris County, where the plaintiff resided at the time the cause of action arose. Wyatt's agent, Morgan Spear, was not a party to the suit brought by Wyatt. Spear was a party, however, to Shaw Plumbing's suit in Nueces County, which was based solely on breach of contract. Because there was a difference in both issues and parties, Shaw argues that the Nueces County district court was not obliged to grant the plea in abatement. We disagree.

When an inherent interrelation of the subject matter exists in two pending lawsuits, a plea in abatement in the second action must be granted. It is not required that the exact issues and all the parties be included in the first action before the second is filed, provided that the claim in the first suit may be amended to bring in all necessary and proper parties and issues. *See* 2 R. MCDONALD, *supra*, § 7.10, at 165. In determining whether an inherent interrelationship exists, courts should be guided by the rule governing persons to be joined if feasible and the compulsory counterclaim rule. *See* TEX. R. CIV. P. 39, 97(a).

Shaw Plumbing should have brought its compulsory counterclaim on the contract in Wyatt's tort and DTPA suit in Duval County. If Shaw Plumbing had joined Morgan Spear, venue would have been proper in the Duval County suit filed by Wyatt, where the cause of action arose. If Wyatt had sued Shaw Plumbing in Nueces County, venue would have also been proper because Shaw's principal office was situated in Nueces County. However, since Wyatt filed suit first, he chose Duval County.

It is well settled that when suit would be proper in more than one county, the court in which suit is first filed acquires dominant jurisdiction to the exclusion of other courts. *Curtis v. Gibbs*, 511 S.W.2d 263, 267 (Tex. 1974); *V.D. Anderson Co. v. Young*, 128 Tex. 631, 636, 101 S.W.2d 798, 800 (1937); *Cleveland v. Ward*, 116 Tex. 1, 19, 285 S.W. 1063, 1070 (1926). As long as the forum is a proper one, it is the plaintiff's privilege to choose the forum. *Mutual Sav. & Loan Ass'n v. Earnest*, 582 S.W.2d 534, 535 (Tex. Civ. App.—Texarkana 1979, no writ). Defendants are simply not at liberty to decline to do battle in the forum chosen by the plaintiff. 2 R. MCDONALD, *supra*, § 7.49, at 254.

Abatement of a lawsuit due to the pendency of a prior suit is based on the principles of comity, convenience, and the necessity for an orderly procedure in the trial of contested issues. *See McCurdy v. Gage*, 123 Tex. 558, 565-66, 69 S.W.2d 56, 59, reh'g overruled per curiam and opinion adopted, 75 S.W.2d 1107 (Tex. Comm'n App. 1934). The plea in abatement must be raised in a timely manner, however, or it is waived. Cleveland, 116 Tex. at 21, 285 S.W.2d at 1071-72. There has been no waiver in the present case.

There are three exceptions to the rule of *Cleveland v. Ward* that the court where suit is first filed acquires dominant jurisdiction: (1) Conduct by a party that estops him from asserting prior active jurisdiction; (2) lack of persons to be joined if feasible, or the power to bring them before the court; and (3) lack of intent to prosecute the first lawsuit. *Young*, 128 Tex. at 636-37, 101 S.W.2d at 800-01; *see also Curtis*, 511 S.W.2d at 267. None of these exceptions applies in this case.

Shaw Plumbing relies on our opinion in *Dolenz v. Continental National Bank* to support its argument that the trial court's decision to grant the plea in abatement was discretionary. *Dolenz*, 620 S.W.2d 572 (Tex. 1981). In that case we held that the trial court did not abuse its discretion in denying a plea in abatement. *Dolenz* must be distinguished, however, for two reasons. First, the second lawsuit in *Dolenz* came into being as a result of Continental Bank's plea of privilege. The court in the second suit properly denied the bank's plea in abatement because a party may not request that a suit against it be severed and transferred to another court, and subsequently seek to abate the second suit. Second, we held that a judgment in the first suit would not foreclose all issues between Continental Bank and *Dolenz*. *Dolenz*, 620 S.W.2d at 575.

We reaffirm that the rule of *Cleveland v. Ward* is the law regarding conflicts of jurisdiction between Texas courts of coordinate jurisdiction. In the case at bar, both lawsuits involve the same issues. Moreover, the parties in the second suit were either present in the first suit, or parties who should have been joined in the first suit. Since venue was proper in either Duval, Harris, or Nueces County, the court where suit was first filed, Duval County, acquired dominant jurisdiction. The Nueces County district court, therefore, had no discretion to deny Wyatt's plea in abatement.

Accordingly, we reverse the judgment of the court of appeals and remand the cause to the Nueces County district court with instructions to vacate its judgment and abate all proceedings pending final disposition of the Duval County lawsuit.

KILGARLIN, J., files a concurring opinion [opinion omitted].

GONZALEZ, JUSTICE, dissenting.

I agree wholeheartedly with the court's articulation of the rule of dominant jurisdiction. We do not disagree on the law; we disagree on its application to this cause.

Unquestionably, the general rule is that the court in which suit is first filed acquires dominant jurisdiction and that any subsequent suit involving the same parties and the same controversy must be dismissed if, by a plea in abatement, a party calls the court's attention to the pendency of the prior suit. *Curtis v. Gibbs*, 511 S.W.2d 263 (Tex. 1974), *Cleveland v. Ward*, 116 Tex. 1, 285 S.W. 1063 (1926). I would not in any way abandon this general rule.

* * *

Curtis v. Gibbs, 511 S.W.2d at 267, stated the following exception to the general rule of dominant jurisdiction: [T]he plaintiff in the first suit may be guilty of such inequitable conduct as will estop him from relying on that suit to abate a subsequent proceeding brought by his adversary. In this case, Wyatt filed his DTPA suit against Shaw Plumbing after having already received Shaw Plumbing's thirty day demand letter, and he did so without giving the thirty day notice required of him under the Deceptive Trade Practices—Consumer Protection Act. TEX. BUS. & COM. CODE ANN. § 17.505 (Vernon 1987).

Wyatt's failure to give the required statutory notice enabled him to beat Shaw Plumbing to the courthouse and fix venue in Duval County. The proper remedy for a party's failure to give the required DTPA notice is ordinarily abatement rather than dismissal. *The Moving Company v. Whitten*, 717 S.W.2d 117 (Tex. App.—Houston [14th Dist.] 1986, writ ref'd n.r.e.); *see also Schepps v. Presbyterian Hospital*, 652 S.W.2d 934 (Tex. 1983). Under the circumstances of this case, I would hold that although a party's failure to comply with the statutory notice requirement will not result in dismissal, it is nevertheless a type of "inequitable conduct" that cannot be used as a vehicle for fixing venue. Thus, I would further hold that Wyatt's failure to give the required DTPA notice estops him from relying on his first-filed suit to abate the subsequent suit.

Although the court's opinion acknowledges the exceptions to the general rule of dominant jurisdiction, it summarily states that none apply. Upon analysis, I am unable to reach the same conclusion. Therefore, I dissent from the court's opinion and would affirm the judgment of the court of appeals.

PHILLIPS, C.J., and MAUZY, J., join.

Notes

1. Pleas in abatement and pleas to the jurisdiction have different objectives and different results. Sustaining a plea to the jurisdiction requires dismissal; sustaining a plea in abatement requires that the claim be abated until removal of some impediment. *See, e.g., Texas Highway Department v. Jarrell*, 418 S.W.2d 486, 488 (1967) (holding a plea in abatement, if sustained, would require an abatement of the claim or cause of action until some obstacle to its further prosecution was removed). Furthermore, an order sustaining a plea in abatement is an interlocutory order and not subject to appeal; while an order sustaining a plea to the jurisdiction is final and appealable. *See, e.g., Speer v. Stover*, 685 S.W.2d 22 (Tex. 1985).

2. *Reddy Partnership/5900 North Freeway, L.P. v. Harris Cty. Appraisal Dist.*, 370 S.W.3d 373 (Tex. 2012): Harris County Appraisal District's Appraisal Review Board's rejection of a protest to its 2008 tax assessment was challenged in timely filed a petition for judicial review filed by "Reddy Partnership ETAL." After the statute of limitations to appeal the Board's ruling had expired—and despite the fact that HCAD had mailed the notice of appraised value to "Reddy Partnership ETAL"; "Reddy Partnership ETAL" had filed a protest to the tax assessment; and HCAD's Board had mailed the order rejecting that protest to "Reddy Partnership ETAL"—HCAD filed a plea to the jurisdiction contending that the trial court lacked subject matter jurisdiction over the suit because "Reddy Partnership ETAL" was not the owner of the property on the relevant date and therefore lacked standing. To support its assertion, HCAD attached a copy of the deed by which "Reddy Partnership," a

Texas general partnership, sold the property to "Reddy Partnership/5900 North Freeway, L.P.," a Texas limited partnership. In response to HCAD's plea, "Reddy Partnership, ETAL" amended the petition to name "Reddy Partnership/5900 North Freeway, L.P." as a plaintiff in the suit and moved to substitute "Reddy Partnership/5900 North Freeway, L.P." as the true name of "Reddy Partnership, ETAL." "Reddy Partnership, ETAL" also responded to HCAD's plea, arguing that jurisdiction was not lacking because "Reddy Partnership, ETAL" is the common name for "Reddy Partnership/5900 North Freeway, L.P., as reflected in HCAD's own records." The trial court granted the plea and dismissed the suit; and the court of appeals affirmed. ***Held*:** This is plainly a case of a trivial "misnomer," that is "when a party misnames itself or another party, but the correct parties are involved." "When the correct party sues or is sued under the incorrect name, 'the court acquires jurisdiction after service with the misnomer if it is clear that no one was misled or placed at a disadvantage by the error.' " This not a case of "misidentification," which "arises when two separate legal entities actually exist and a plaintiff mistakenly sues the entity with a name similar to that of the correct entity."

3. A plea in abatement presents a legally recognized reason not to proceed with a case. The recognized pleas in abatement include:

a. Capacity to sue or be sued;
b. Nonjoinder of parties;
c. Misjoinder of parties;
d. Misnomer of parties;
e. Prematurity of suit (may also be a plea in bar in some cases); and
f. Pendency of another action

4. *Southern County Mut. Ins. Co. v. Ochoa*, 19 S.W.3d 452 (Tex. App. –Corpus Christi 2000, no pet.): A plea in abatement must be verified, but, here, it was adequately presented in concurrently filed answer and motion to transfer.

A plea in abatement is properly overruled where the party asserting dominant jurisdiction shows its' lack of intent to prosecute the first lawsuit by an unreasonable delay in procuring a citation. The required standard of diligence in procuring citation and service is that diligence to procure service which an ordinarily prudent person would have used under the same or similar circumstances. An unexplained delay of five or six months in procuring issuance and service of citation constitute a lack of due diligence, as a matter of law.

5. *In re Red Dot Building System, Inc.*, 504 S.W.3d 320 (Tex. 2016)**: Prior Suit Pending in Multiple Counties. Abate Second Filed Action. Mandamus Proper If Abatement Denied**. When two inherently interrelated suits are brought in different counties, the first-filed suit ordinarily acquires dominant jurisdiction and the second-filed suit should be abated. In the pending dispute, the second court (Hidalgo County Court at Law) should have abated the suit pending in that court, and that mandamus relief is available to secure this result. In instances where inherently interrelated suits are pending in two counties, and venue is proper in either county, the court in which suit was first filed acquires dominant jurisdiction.

b. *Special Exceptions*

Read Rules 71 & 91 Texas Rules of Civil Procedure

TEXAS DEP'T OF CORRECTIONS
v.
HERRING

513 S.W.2d 6
(Tex. 1974)

John L. Hill, Atty. Gen., Jack Sparks, Asst. Atty. Gen., Austin, for petitioner.
Moore, Morris & Payne, Louis M. Moore, Houston, for respondent.

SAM D. JOHNSON, JUSTICE.

Suit for damages brought under the Texas Tort Claims Act. James W. Herring brought this action for personal injuries against the Texas Department of Corrections. The trial court held that, as a matter of law, Herring did not have a cause of action under the Texas Tort Claims Act and rendered a take-nothing summary judgment with prejudice. The court of civil appeals reversed and remanded. 500 S.W.2d 718. We affirm the judgment of the court of civil appeals.

Plaintiff Herring, a prisoner of the Texas Department of Corrections at Huntsville, received an accidental injury to the right side of his face in a basketball game. He received medical treatment at the prison hospital and later at The University of Texas Medical Branch Hospital in Galveston. Despite such treatment Herring lost all vision in his right eye. Herring's petition did not allege specific acts of negligence; rather, his petition contained only a general allegation of negligence which was 'negligence in failing to provide adequate medical care and treatment.'

Herring served written interrogatories on '(t)he Department of Corrections, Defendant herein, by and through its Attorney of Record, John L. Hill, Attorney General of Texas, . . .' These interrogatories, among other things, sought the basic information needed to assert specific allegations of negligence: the names of doctors, nurses and paraprofessionals who treated the plaintiff, details of his injury and the medical treatment administered to him. The Department of Corrections moved to strike the interrogatories on the ground that Rule 168, Texas Rules of Civil Procedure, is not applicable to the State. The record contains no ruling on this motion. The trial court nevertheless proceeded to grant the Department of Correction's motion for summary judgment. As a result, the plaintiff's written interrogatories were not answered. In remanding the case, the court of civil appeals said it perceived no reason why the State should be exempt from Rule 168. This court agrees with the court of civil appeals.

As a general rule, the State litigates as any other party in Texas courts 'When the state becomes a litigant in the courts it must observe and is bound by the same rules of procedure that bind all other litigants, except where special provision is made to the contrary.' *Texas Company v. State*, 154 Tex. 494, 281 S.W.2d 83, 90 (1955). *See also State v. Jasco Aluminum Products Corporation*, 421 S.W.2d 409 (Tex. Civ. App.—Austin 1967, no writ). Laws and rules governing evidence, burden of proof, cross complaints, pleadings, instructed verdicts and summary judgments bind the State and other litigants uniformly. *See State v. Humble Oil & Refining Co.*, 141 Tex. 40, 169 S.W.2d 707 (1943); *Bednarz v. State*, 142 Tex. 138, 176 S.W.2d 562 (1943); and Note, 43 TEX. L. REV. 979, 982 (1965).

* * *

Aside from the preliminary question relative to interrogatories, the only issue to be resolved is whether the Department of Corrections was entitled to a summary judgment. The Texas Tort Claims Act, Article 6252-19, Section 3, reads:

> 'Sec. 3. Each unit of government in the state shall be liable for money damages for personal injuries or death when proximately caused by the negligence or wrongful act or omission of any officer or employee acting within the scope of his employment or office arising from the operation or use of a motor-driven vehicle and motor-driven equipment, other than motor-driven equipment used in connec-

tion with the operation of floodgates or water release equipment by river authorities created under the laws of this state, under circumstances where such officer or employee would be personally liable to the claimant in accordance with the law of this state, or death or personal injuries so caused from some condition or some use of tangible property, real or personal, under circumstances where such unit of government, if a private person, would be liable to the claimant in accordance with the law of this state . . . .'

Herring relies on the State's liability for 'use of tangible property.' In the plaintiff's petition, containing the very general allegation of negligence, he asserted that the Texas Department of Corrections and its agents and/or employees were negligent in 'failing to provide adequate medical care and treatment.' The Department of Corrections, without anything more than its motion to strike interrogatories, moved for summary judgment, asserting that 'Plaintiff's allegations fail to bring him within the requirements of the Texas Tort Claims Act and there is no legal authority for an action such as alleged by Plaintiff against this Defendant.' Although not pointed out specifically in the motion, the Department of Corrections argues here that a failure to give medical care cannot involve the use of tangible property, *citing Beggs v. Texas Dep't of Mental Health & Mental Ret.*, 496 S.W.2d 252 (Tex. Civ. App.—San Antonio 1973, writ ref'd). This court agrees that Herring's pleadings failed to state a cause of action since no 'use of tangible property' was alleged as required by the Texas Tort Claims Act.

However, the question to be resolved is whether Herring, under the instant circumstances, may be denied the opportunity to amend his pleadings because they were attacked via a summary judgment motion instead of a special exception. It is recognized that a party may plead himself out of court; E.g., the plaintiff may plead facts which affirmatively negate his cause of action. *See* for example *Morris v. Hargrove*, 351 S.W.2d 666 (Tex .Civ. App.—Austin 1961, writ ref'd n.r.e.), and *Schroeder v. Texas & Pacific Ry. Co.*, 243 S.W.2d 261 (Tex. Civ. App.—Dallas 1951, no writ). In such instance it is proper to grant the defendant's motion for summary judgment. The instant case is clearly distinguishable however. Here, as we have held, Herring's pleadings were insufficient; that is, they failed to state a cause of action. The Department of Corrections leveled no special exceptions to Herring's pleadings and thus no opportunity to amend his pleadings to state a cause of action was afforded.

Had the Department of Corrections filed special exceptions which were sustained by the court, Herring would have had an opportunity to amend as a matter of right. *McCamey v. Kinnear*, 484 S.W.2d 150 (Tex. Civ. App.—Beaumont 1972, writ ref'd n.r.e.). But only after a party has been given an opportunity to amend after special exceptions have been sustained may the case be dismissed for failure to state a cause of action.

In the instant case Herring was precluded opportunity to amend his pleadings once the trial court had granted the motion for summary judgment. This court believes that the protective features of special exception procedure should not be circumvented by a motion for summary judgment on the pleadings where plaintiff's pleadings, as here, fail to state a cause of action. To do so would revive the general demurrer discarded by Rule 90, Texas Rules of Civil Procedure. McDonald, *Summary Judgments*, 30 TEX. L. REV. 285, 297 (1951); Suggs and Stumberg, *Summary Judgment Procedure*, 22 TEX. L. REV. 433, 439-40 (1944); 2 McDonald, TEXAS CIVIL PRACTICE s 7.18 at 205.

We agree with the court of civil appeals that the instant motion for summary judgment alleging that the plaintiff's pleadings fail to state a cause of action cannot take the place of a special exception. Accordingly, this case must be returned to the trial court. If the Department of Corrections files a special exception which is sustained and Herring still fails to state a cause of action, then the case may properly be dismissed.

The judgment of the court of civil appeals is affirmed.

Dissenting opinion by WALKER, J., in which GREENHILL, C.J., joins (omitted).

Notes

1. A special exception is an objection to the opponent's pleading. It may question the sufficiency the pleadings to state a cause of action, or point out defects in the cause of action stated. It may also be used object to a lack of specificity or to raise matters that do not go to the merits of the case (dilatory matters). It is rare for a case to be determined by special exceptions, and they are frequently a waste of time. *See* Fitzwater, *Reexamining the Special Exception*, 37 SW.L. J. 789, 789-790 (1983).

2. Speaking demurrers are not to be used. A speaking demurrer is a special exception that relies upon matters not shown on the face of the opponent's pleading.

McCAMEY
v.
KINNEAR

484 S.W.2d 150
(Tex. Civ. App.—Beaumont 1972 writ ref'd n.r.e.)

B. J. McGinnis, Beaumont, for appellant.
Adams & Browne, Beaumont, for appellee.

KEITH, JUSTICE.

Plaintiff appeals from a judgment of dismissal of his suit wherein he sought to recover of the defendant attorney's fees paid to defendant in connection with a patent application. Plaintiff also sought recovery of certain expenses incurred by reason of the alleged inaction of defendant. At the outset we note affirmatively that while plaintiff has prosecuted the appeal with diligence, such comment does not apply to his trial court actions.

On the day the case was specially set for trial upon the 'try or dismiss' docket, defendant filed a motion to dismiss plaintiff's cause of action, the allegations being set out in the margin.[1]

The court's order, entered on January 31, 1972, recited that the defendant's motion to dismiss having been heard, and 'it appearing to the Court that said motion should be in all things granted; it is therefore ordered, adjudged and decreed that defendant's motion to dismiss be in all things granted.'

This order of dismissal was preceded by some unusual maneuvers which require mention at this point. Defendant leveled many exceptions to plaintiff's original petition, some of which were sustained by an order entered May 4, 1970, defendant's exceptions to such action being duly noted. Although plaintiff did not file amended pleadings until the very day of the dismissal (a matter which will be mentioned later), the docket sheet in our record shows that defendant procured three continuances, the last being on October 7, 1971. Upon this latter date, the trial court entered a specific and detailed order setting the case for trial on January 31, 1972, and advised counsel that it would be tried or dismissed upon said date 'depending upon any announcements which may or may not be made by counsel at such time.'

On January 31, 1972, the date set for trial, plaintiff filed what he denominated a 'Trial Amendment' but which was in fact an amended original petition. *See* Rule 71, Texas Rules of Civil Procedure. Our record does not reveal that leave was granted to file the instrument, whatever it might have been, under either Rule 63 or Rule 66, nor does the record show that such instrument ever came to the attention of the trial court before the order of dismissal was entered. On the other hand, the record is equally silent as to any motion to strike the pleading filed in violation of the rules just mentioned. See in this connection 2 MCDONALD, TEXAS CIVIL PRACTICE (1970 Rev. Vol.), s 8.06, pp. 323, et seq.

Plaintiff timely gave notice of appeal from the order of dismissal, duly perfected his appeal, and now assigns many points of error. We do not find it necessary to discuss all of such points of error under our view of the record.

---

1 'Defendant would show the Court that it is useless to pick a jury in this cause or to take up the Court's time because said Plaintiff does not state a cause of action in this suit, and it would be a waste of the Court's time and a waste of the Jury's time to pick a jury in this cause, and said suit should be in all things dismissed.'

Plaintiff devotes much of his brief to the proposition that the trial court erred in granting the defendant's motion to dismiss, contending that such motion was a general demurrer in legal disguise which is forbidden by Rule 90. Under our view of the record, we do not reach the point. Instead, we turn to the controlling issue in the appeal, the action of the trial court upon the exceptions.

When special exceptions addressed to a pleading are sustained, the party has two options available to him: (a) he may amend to meet the exceptions and this he may do as a matter of right; or, (b) he may stand upon his pleadings, refuse to amend, and test the validity of the ruling upon appeal. *Harold v. Houston Yacht Club*, 380 S.W.2d 184, 186 (Tex. Civ. App., Houston, 1964, no writ); *M. C. Winters, Inc. v. Lawless*, 407 S.W.2d 275, 277 (Tex. Civ. App., Dallas, 1966, error dism.); *and Farris v. Nortex Oil & Gas Corporation*, 393 S.W.2d 684, 690 (Tex. Civ. App., Texarkana, 1965, error ref. n.r.e.).

A reasonable time should be allowed a party desiring to amend to conform to the ruling upon the special exceptions; but this is a matter within the sound discretion of the court not to be overthrown except for an abuse of discretion. *Farias v. Besteiro*, 453 S.W.2d 314, 317 (Tex. Civ. App., Corpus Christi, 1970, error ref. n.r.e.), and cases therein cited. The plaintiff, being ever under the duty of prosecuting his suit with diligence under the penalty of having it dismissed for want of prosecution, must also use diligence in amending his pleadings after an order sustaining exceptions. 4 MCDONALD, TEXAS CIVIL PRACTICE (1971 Rev. Vol.), s 17.18, pp. 101-102 . In our case, the plaintiff waited nearly twenty months—and through three trial settings—before filing his amended pleading upon the very day the case was set upon the 'try or dismiss' docket.

Under the circumstances of this case, we hold that the long unexplained delay in filing the amended pleadings amounted in law to a refusal to amend. When a party stands firm on his pleadings, as we have held the plaintiff did in this case, the trial court may dismiss the cause if the remaining allegations fail to state a cause of action. *Rutledge v. Valley Evening Monitor*, 289 S.W.2d 952, 953 (Tex. Civ. App., San Antonio, 1956, no writ) *and City of Roma v. Starr County*, 428 S.W.2d 851, 853 (Tex. Civ. App., San Antonio, 1968, error ref. n.r.e.).

Having reviewed the remnants of the original petition, after the exceptions had been sustained, we are of the opinion that the remaining allegations of the petition failed to state a cause of action. The trial court was authorized, under these circumstances, to dismiss the case. *Rutledge v. Valley Evening Monitor, supra*; *Wiseman v. Zorn*, 309 S.W.2d 253, 259 (Tex. Civ. App., Houston, 1958, no writ).

The order sustaining the special exceptions was interlocutory in nature and plaintiff had no right of appeal therefrom. *Mueller v. Banks*, 317 S.W.2d 254, 255 (Tex. Civ. App., San Antonio, 1958, no writ). However, when the court entered the order of dismissal on January 31, 1972, following plaintiff's failure to amend within a reasonable time, plaintiff's right to appeal was then exercised. We now turn to the validity of the special exceptions and review the action of the trial court in entering the order sustaining such exceptions.

Special Exceptions 5, 8, 9 and 10 were worded identically and challenged different parts of plaintiff's pleading. We quote the exception:

> 'Plaintiff (sic, Defendant) excepts . . . (naming the particular paragraph of the petition) because said allegations are too general; because said allegations are a mere conclusion of the pleader; because no facts are alleged on which said conclusions are based; because said allegations do not inform this defendant of the facts on which the plaintiff intends to rely; because said allegations do not inform this defendant of the proof that he will be required to meet on the trial of this cause and because said allegations are calculated to surprise and prejudice the defendant on the trial of this cause; because said allegations are calculated to cause a mistrial; said allegations should be in all things stricken and of this exception the defendant prays judgment of the Court.'

It is obvious that this 'special exception' did not comply with the provisions of Rule 91 and even a cursory examination of the allegations attacked shows that in each instance the exception was without merit. The exception quoted was simply a broadside attack and did not 'point out intelligibly and with particularity the defect, omission, obscurity, duplicity, generality, or other insufficiency in the allegations in the pleading excepted to' as required by Rule 91. There were other exceptions sustained which are subject to the same criticism and the result of the court's action was to eliminate from plaintiff's pleading the necessary allegations upon which his cause of action was predicated. In effect, such exceptions were 'nothing more than the old general demurrer' which was abolished in 1941 when Rule 90 was adopted. *Huff v. Fidelity Union Life Insurance Company*, 158 Tex. 433, 312 S.W .2d 493, 499 (1958).

These particular exceptions also lacked merit for the reasons pointed out in *Helly v. Wright*, 144 Tex. 114, 188 S.W.2d 983, 985 (1945):

> 'Rule 91 provides that a special exception shall not only point out the particular pleading excepted to, but shall also point out intelligibly and with particularity the defect, omission, obscurity, duplicity, generality, or other insufficiency in the allegation in the pleading excepted to.
>
> 'The exceptions in question merely assert that the petition failed to show any grounds for equitable relief or state a cause of action. They do not point out intelligibly and with particularity the reasons for such conclusions. Therefore, the trial court erred in sustaining them.'

See also, Pargas of Canton, Inc. v. Clower, 434 S.W.2d 192, 196 (Tex. Civ. App., Tyler, 1968, no writ); *Chakur v. Zena*, 233 S.W.2d 200, 201 (Tex. Civ. App., San Antonio, 1950, no writ).

The object and purpose of pleading is to give fair and adequate notice to the party being sued of the nature of the cause of action asserted against him so that he may adequately prepare his defense thereto. Plaintiff's original petition in this case fairly and adequately advised defendant of the nature of the cause of action being asserted against him. The plaintiff was not required to plead his evidence in detail and if the defendant desired more factual detail as to the basis of the claim, he had but to invoke the discovery processes authorized by the rules.

It follows, therefore, that the trial court having erred in sustaining the special exceptions, likewise erred in dismissing the case. The judgment below must be reversed and the cause remanded. We note, however, that plaintiff, by his inaction below, has delayed a disposition of his case and has contributed to the clogging of the dockets of both the trial and appellate courts. Such action is not to be commended and it is suggested that a repetition of this spectacle could be avoided by utilizing the provisions of Rule 166.

Reversed and remanded.

Note

It is well settled that when special exceptions are sustained the pleader has two options: (1) he may, as a matter of right, amend his petition, or (2) he may refuse to amend and thereby test the validity of the ruling on appeal. *Davis v. Quality Pest Control*, 641 S.W.2d 324, 328 (Tex. App.—Houston [14th Dist.] 1982, writ ref'd n.r.e); *McCamey v. Kinnear*, 484 S.W.2d 150 (Tex. Civ. App.—Beaumont 1972, writ ref'd n.r.e). If the pleader refuses to amend his pleadings, the trial court may, by further order, strike the objectionable portion of the pleadings, *see Ship Ahoy, Inc. v. Whalen*, 347 S.W.2d 662, 663 (Tex. Civ. App.—Houston 1961, no writ), and dismiss the suit if the remaining allegations in the petition fail to state a cause of action. *Geochem Lab., Inc. v. Brown & Ruth Lab., Inc.*, 689 S.W.2d 288 (Tex. App.—Houston [1st Dist.] 1985, writ ref'd n.r.e); *Farias v. Besteiro*, 453 S.W.2d 314, 317 (Tex. Civ. App.—Corpus Christi 1970, writ ref'd n.r.e).

c. *General Denial*

Read Rule 92 Texas Rules of Civil Procedure

MOULTON
v.
ALAMO AMBULANCE SERV.

414 S.W.2d 444
(Tex. 1967)

Lieck & Lieck, Jack Leon and Eugene H. Lieck, Arch B. Haston, San Antonio, for petitioner.
Lang, Byrd, Cross, Ladon & Oppenheimer, Paul M. Green, San Antonio, for respondent.

CALVERT, CHIEF JUSTICE.

This case grew out of a three-vehicle collision at the intersection of East Commerce and Cherry Streets in the City of San Antonio, an intersection controlled by a traffic signal. Philip J. Moulton sued Alamo Ambulance Service, Inc. and Louie Cardenas and by his suit sought a joint and several judgment against the defendants for damages for personal injuries sustained in the collision. A jury trial resulted in findings that both defendants committed acts of negligence proximately causing the injuries sustained by Moulton and fixing his damages at $10,000. Cardenas filed a motion for judgment notwithstanding the verdict, and the motion was granted. The judgment rendered by the trial court awarded Moulton a recovery of his damages from Alamo but decreed that he take nothing from Cardenas. Only Alamo appealed.

In its appeal, Alamo complained of both facets of the trial court's judgment. The court of civil appeals held that the trial court erred in granting Cardenas' motion for judgment notwithstanding the verdict and in rendering judgment absolving Cardenas of liability. It then held that the trial court also erred to the prejudice of Alamo in refusing it permission to file a trial amendment. On the basis of these holdings, the court of civil appeals reversed the judgment of the trial court and remanded the cause for a new trial. 402 S.W.2d 200. Separate applications for writ of error were filed by Cardenas and Moulton and both applications were granted. We affirm the judgment of the court of civil appeals.

At the time of the collision, Alamo's station wagon, operated by its employee, Dickie Wolfe, was proceeding west on Commerce Street; Cardenas' Buick was proceeding north on Cherry Street, and the van occupied by Moulton was headed south on Cherry Street but was stopped just north of the intersection while Moulton was waiting for clearance to make a left-hand turn easterly into Commerce Street. Alamo's station wagon and Cardenas' Buick collided near the center of the intersection. Following this collision, Cardenas' Buick continued northerly for thirty-two feet and collided with Moulton's van.

Neither of the defendants pleaded that Moulton was guilty of negligence in any respect. Therefore, the crucial questions with which the jury was concerned related to the conduct of the two defendants preceding the collision with Moulton's van and the damages to be awarded. Each of the defendants sought to establish, primarily, that negligent conduct of the other was the sole proximate cause of the plaintiff's injuries, and, secondarily, was a contributing proximate cause. The jury found that no negligent act or omission of either defendant was the sole proximate cause. They found that Alamo's driver was operating its station wagon at an excessive rate of speed, failed to keep a proper lookout, failed to apply his brakes and entered the intersection when the traffic light facing him was red, and further found each of the negligent acts or omissions was a proximate cause of the collision. The jury also found that Cardenas accelerated his automobile immediately prior to his collision with the plaintiff's van, and that this act was negligence and a proximate cause of the collision. The trial court disregarded the jury findings against Cardenas on the ground that they were not supported by the evidence.

We consider first the application of Cardenas. The only questions presented by the application are whether there is evidence supporting the jury finding of acceleration of his automobile by Cardenas and whether the act of acceleration was negligence. We agree with the holding of the court of civil appeals on these questions. The evidence hearing on the questions and the applicable law are set out in the opinion of the court of civil appeals and need not be restated here. *See* 402 S.W.2d 200, 202-203. The "loss of control" cases cited by Cardenas are not controlling because loss of control of his automobile by Cardenas after the collision with Alamo's vehicle is not established either as a matter of law or by a jury finding.

Moulton's application insists that the court of civil appeals erred in reversing the trial court's judgment in so far as it awarded him a recovery of damages from Alamo.

As heretofore noted, the court of civil appeals reversed the judgment against Alamo because of the refusal of the trial court to permit Alamo to file a trial amendment. Tender of the trial amendment and refusal of the trial court to permit its filing were made in the following circumstances. Moulton was employed at the time of the accident by a vending machine company and a necessary part of his duties was to get down on his knees and service and clean the vending machines. The most serious injury suffered by Moulton was to one of his knees. His doctor, Lloyd E. Berry, testified at the trial that to relieve ill effects of the knee injury he prescribed "heat, rest and elevation of the leg," and advised Moulton "to stay off the knee and take care of it." The evidence would support a conclusion by the jury that Moulton continued to perform his duties, using his leg and working on his knee, and thus aggravated his knee injury to such an extent that he lost his job because he could no longer perform his duties acceptably and was still suffering pain at the time of trial, more than eighteen months after the injury. The doctor's testimony would also support a reasonable conclusion that Moulton's knee injury would probably have healed within a brief period of time if he had followed his doctor's advice. After the close of all the evidence, Alamo tendered its trial amendment in which it pleaded that Moulton had failed to mitigate his damages, and had in fact contributed to cause an injury of greater severity to himself than that which he received in the accident by failing to exercise the care of an ordinary prudent person in following competent medical advice to prevent the further aggravation of, or in the alternative, the complete healing of such injury. The answer on which Alamo went to trial contained no such plea but did contain a general denial.

The reasoning of the court of civil appeals in holding that the trial court abused its discretion in refusing to permit the filing of the trial amendment was as follows: An injured person is not entitled to recover damages from a wrongdoer for consequences of an injury which can be avoided by the exercise of ordinary care; mitigation of damages is an affirmative defense as to which a defendant is not entitled to submission to a jury of special issues under Rules 277 and 279, Texas Rules of Civil Procedure, in the absence of a written pleading of failure to mitigate; the testimony which would support a finding that Moulton failed to minimize his damages was admitted without objection, and the issue was therefore tried by consent; and in the absence of a showing that Moulton was surprised by the testimony, Rule 67, Texas Rules of Civil Procedure, required that the trial amendment to Alamo's answer be allowed so that justice might be done. We recognize the universality of the rule that an injured person cannot recover damages which can be avoided by that care and treatment of his injury which an ordinary prudent person would exercise in the same or similar circumstances; but we hold that mitigation of damages in this situation is not an affirmative defense, and thus that the trial court did not err in refusing to permit Alamo to file its trial amendment.

* * * The question has never been directly decided by this court and thus is an open one in this state. We hold that failure to mitigate damages by care and treatment of personal injuries is not an affirmative defense which must be specially pleaded to let in evidence of such failure and to entitle the wrongdoer to proper court instructions.

Rule 94, Texas Rules of Civil Procedure, requires that a pleading to a preceding pleading shall set forth affirmatively nineteen listed pleas "and any other matter constituting an avoidance or affirmative defense." Mitigation of damages is not one of the listed pleas. Each of the nineteen listed pleas would defeat, in whole or in specific part, the underlying cause of action or defense asserted in the preceding pleading. Unlike the listed pleas, failure to mitigate damages would not defeat the underlying cause of action in whole or in specific part, in personal injury cases. A wrongdoer is liable to an injured person for all damages proximately caused by his wrongful or negligent acts, and failure of the injured person to care for and treat his injuries as a reasonable prudent person would under the same or similar circumstances will not defeat in whole or in part the cause of action for damages thus proximately caused. Testimony that Moulton failed to heed and follow the advice of his doctor was admissible under Alamo's and Cardenas' general denials which put in issue the amount of the damages alleged by Moulton to have been suffered by him as a proximate result of the negligence of the two defendants. The rule by which we have been guided in reaching our conclusion was announced by this court in *W. L. Moody & Co. v. Rowland*, 100 Tex. 363, 99 S.W. 1112, 1115 (1907), as follows: "The defendant may, by a general denial, put the plaintiff upon proof of the facts alleged in the petition, and, Under such general denial, the defendant would be entitled to introduce evidence which tended to disprove the facts alleged in the plaintiff's petition, and to rebut evidence offered by the plaintiff. If a defendant desires to introduce evidence of a fact which does not tend to rebut the facts of the plaintiff's case, but which show(s) an independent reason why the plaintiff should not recover upon the case stated and proved, Then such defendant must plead the facts which will avoid the legal consequence of plaintiff's case, else the testimony will not be admissible * * *."

There is a strong policy reason for holding that a failure to mitigate damages in a personal injury case is not an affirmative defense. Affirmative defenses, when supported by evidence, entitle the pleader to special issues embodying the defense, and a holding that in personal injury cases failure to mitigate is an affirmative defense would result in a proliferation of special issues in an area already mired in a prolixity of complicated issues. * * *

Having held that the court of civil appeals erred in reversing the trial court's judgment because of the refusal of the trial court to permit the filing of the trial amendment, we must look . . . to see if the judgment of that court can be affirmed on any other ground. * * *

The judgment of the court of civil appeals is affirmed.

Note

A defendant is not entitled to the submission of any jury questions on defensive matters as the result of pleading only a general denial. *See* Rule 278 of the Texas Rules of Civil Procedure.

d. *Verified Denials*

Read Rule 93 Texas Rules of Civil Procedure.

Note

A general denial imposes upon the plaintiff the need to offer proof of all matters which he has pled, except those which the defendant is required to deny under oath under Rule 93. As a general rule, the purpose of a verified specific denial is to point out a specific allegation within the plaintiff's petition which is not true and require the plaintiff to offer proof on these matters. The failure of a defendant to file a verified specific denial of the matters listed in Rule 93 eliminates the need of the plaintiff to offer proof of these matters.

THE RAY MALOOLY TRUST
v.
JUHL
186 S.W.3d 568
(Tex. 2006)

Paul Frederick Grajeda, Joe Rosales, El Paso, for Petitioner.
John P. Mobbs, El Paso, for Respondent.

PER CURIAM.

The trial court entered and the court of appeals affirmed a judgment for $351,352 against "The Ray Malooly Trust." The latter appeals, pointing out that a trust is not a legal entity. While the point is well-taken, we deny the petition for review as it was waived.

The Juhls sued the Trust in May 1999, alleging a breach of lease. More than three years later, on the day trial began, the Trust filed a verified answer stating for the first time that "Defendant, The Ray Malooly Trust does not have capacity to be sued." The trial court denied leave to file the amended pleading on grounds of surprise. *See* TEX. R. CIV. P. 63.

The court of appeals stated that "a number of Texas cases indicate a trust may be named as a party without inclusion of a trustee." But a number of cases from this Court indicate the opposite. As we said in *Huie v. DeS-*

hazo, "[t]he term 'trust' refers not to a separate legal entity but rather to the fiduciary relationship governing the trustee with respect to the trust property." 922 S.W.2d 920, 926 (Tex. 1996) (holding that treating trust rather than trustee as attorney's client "is inconsistent with the law of trusts"). The general rule in Texas (and elsewhere) has long been that suits against a trust must be brought against its legal representative, the trustee. *See Werner v. Colwell*, 909 S.W.2d 866, 870 (Tex. 1995); *Smith v. Wayman*, 148 Tex. 318, 224 S.W.2d 211, 218 (1949); *Slay v. Burnett Trust*, 143 Tex. 621, 187 S.W.2d 377, 382 (1945).

The court of appeals noted that the Code Construction Act specifies that "person" includes a ". . . business trust, estate, trust, partnership, association, and any other legal entity." TEX. GOV'T CODE § 311.005(2). But the Code Construction Act addresses the construction of state codes, not the capacity to sue or be sued. *Id.* at § 311.002. For example, the Act includes estates as statutory "persons," but an estate is nonetheless "not a legal entity and may not properly sue or be sued as such." *Austin Nursing Center, Inc. v. Lovato*, 171 S.W.3d 845, 849 (Tex. 2005).

Moreover, the definitions in the Code Construction Act apply unless other statutes or contexts require a different definition. TEX. GOV'T CODE § 311.005(2). The most relevant code—the Texas Trust Code—explicitly defines a trust as a relationship rather than a legal entity. *See* TEX. PROP. CODE § 111.004(4). It states that trustees "may compromise, contest, arbitrate, or settle claims" against a trust. *Id.* § 113.019. It validates payments to and conveyances from a trustee, even if the trustee absconds with the proceeds. *Id.* §§ 114.081, 114.082. And since the trustee is "the person holding the property in trust," *id.* § 111.004(18), a judgment against that property must be brought against the person who holds it.

The court of appeals pointed to a Trust Code provision stating that in contract cases, "the plaintiff may sue the trustee in his representative capacity, and a judgment rendered in favor of the plaintiff is collectible by execution against the trust property." *Id.* § 114.084(a). From the use of "may," the court implied that plaintiffs could sue trusts in other ways too. But the word "may" (unless context or other statutes indicate otherwise) "creates discretionary authority or grants permission or a power." TEX. GOV'T CODE § 311.016(1) (emphasis added). In the context of the Trust Code as a whole, this provision grants contract claimants permission or power to sue the trustee, not to sue someone else. This is not to say that the Legislature could not allow suit by or against a trust in its own name. *See, e.g.*, TEX. REV. CIV. STAT. art 6138A, § 6.10(A)(2) (authorizing real estate investment trusts to "sue and be sued, complain and defend, in its trust name"). But there is no pleading, evidence, or argument that the Legislature has done so by specific provisions here.

Nevertheless, while the court of appeals incorrectly reasoned that a trust can sue or be sued directly, it reached the right result here because the Trust waived any objection to capacity by filing its verified pleading too late. *See* TEX. R. CIV. P. 93(1). "[P]arties who do not follow rule 93's mandate waive any right to complain about the matter on appeal." *Nootsie, Ltd. v. Williamson County Appraisal Dist.*, 925 S.W.2d 659, 662 (Tex. 1996).

"Civil suits may be maintained only by or against parties having an actual or legal existence." *Bailey v. Vanscot Concrete Co.*, 894 S.W.2d 757, 759 (Tex. 1995). If a legal representative makes a general appearance in that capacity, the judgment is treated as if it were against the legal entity, even if the latter is never named. *See Werner*, 909 S.W.2d at 870; *Henson v. Estate of Crow*, 734 S.W.2d 648, 649 (Tex. 1987).

Here, the Trust answered discovery "by and through its trustee, Raymond Malooly." Malooly was deposed, and he testified at trial. By failing to raise a timely objection to capacity, he waived any objection that judgment had to be rendered against the Trust, rather than himself as trustee.

The remaining points in the Trust's petition do not demonstrate that the court of appeals committed any other error of law. TEX. GOV'T CODE § 22.001. Accordingly, the petition for review is denied.

e. ***Affirmative Defenses***

Read Rule 94 Texas Rules of Civil Procedure

HASSELL CONSTR. CO., INC.
v.
STATURE COMMERCIAL CO. INC.
162 S.W.3d 664
(Tex. App.—Houston [14th Dist.] 2005, no pet.)

Ron Ramey, Houston, for appellant.
William S. Chesney, Houston, for appellee.

HEDGES, CHIEF JUSTICE.

Appellant Hassell Construction Company appeals a take-nothing judgment following a bench trial against Stature Commercial Company. We reverse.

Background

In mid- to late 2000, Hassell Construction Company subcontracted with Stature Commercial Company, Inc. (SCCI) to perform certain construction work on the building of the Memorial Villages Police Facility. In 2003, the owner of the project, Memorial Villages Police Department, became dissatisfied with SCCI's performance and discontinued its relationship with SCCI. SCCI's bonding company took over completion of the project. Hassell sued SCCI, claiming SCCI owed it $40,300.11 for work performed and $22,121.00 in withheld retainage. At trial, over Hassell's objections, SCCI introduced evidence that it had not been paid by the owner for work done by Hassell. According to SCCI, the contract required that Hassell would not be due funds until SCCI had been paid by the owner. After a one-day bench trial, the trial court issued findings of fact and conclusions of law, including the following:

Findings of Fact

* * *

9. Hassell testified, and the subcontract provides, that Hassell had agreed with [SCCI] that "payments shall be due Hassell for work that had been approved by the Owner". [SIC]

10. Hassell testified, and the subcontract provides, that Hassell had agreed with [SCCI] that payments shall be due subcontractor for work "for which payment has been made to [SCCI] by Owner". [SIC]

11. Hassell testified, and the subcontract provides, that Hassell had agreed with [SCCI] that payments shall be due within ten (10) working days following receipt of payment from Owner by [SCCI]." [SIC]

* * *

Conclusions of Law

* * *

4. [SCCI] has not received any monies from the Owner for the work Hassell performed and seeks payment by its suit.

5. Pursuant to the terms of the subcontract, Hassell is not entitled to any recovery from [SCCI] on its claims.

6. Hassell shall take-nothing on its claims from [SCCI].

Appellant raises seven issues: whether the trial court properly applied Rule 54 of Texas Rules of Civil Procedure; whether the trial court improperly based its findings on evidence disallowed by Texas Rule of Civil Procedure 94; whether the trial court properly applied Texas law regarding contracts, covenants, and conditions precedent; whether sufficient evidence existed for the court's findings of fact numbers nine, ten, and eleven; whether the court improperly failed to award appellant the retainage owed to it by appellee; and whether the court erred in failing to make a finding of reasonable and necessary attorneys' fees. Finding insufficient evidence for the trial court's findings, we reverse.

Rule 94 and Evidence Supporting an Affirmative Defense

We first address appellant's second issue challenging the trial court's application of the procedural requirement for specific pleading of certain defensive matters. Under Rule 94 of the Texas Rules of Civil Procedure, parties must plead affirmative defenses such as "payment, release, . . . and any other matter constituting an avoidance or affirmative defense." TEX.R. CIV. P. 94. In a contract dispute, Texas law makes certain requirements of each party, including the specific pleading of excuses for nonperformance.

The burden of proving the happening of a contingency which, by the terms of the contract, would discharge the party from liability, or any default or refusal to perform on the part of the plaintiff that would excuse the performance by the defendant, is on the party who seeks to avoid the contract or excuse a failure to perform it on that ground. As a general rule there must be specific pleading of excuses for nonperformance. *Howell v. Kelly,* 534 S.W.2d 737, 740 (Tex. Civ. App.—Houston [1st Dist.] 1976, no writ) (citations omitted).

An affirmative defense is defined as "a denial of the plaintiff's right to judgment even if the plaintiff establishes every allegation in its pleadings." *Bracton Corp. v. Evans Constr. Co.,* 784 S.W.2d 708, 710 (Tex. App.—Houston [14th Dist.] 1990, no writ). An affirmative defense allows the defendant to introduce evidence to establish an independent reason why the plaintiff should not prevail; it does not rebut the factual proposition of the plaintiff's pleading. *Heggy v. Am. Trading Employee Ret. Account Plan,* 123 S.W.3d 770, 778 (Tex. App.—Houston [14th Dist.] 2003, pet. denied). All affirmative defenses are waived when the defendant files only a general denial, and, absent trial by consent, failure to plead a matter of affirmative defense will preclude a defendant from asserting it. *Bracton Corp.,* 784 S.W.2d at 710.

In this case, SCCI's reliance on nonpayment from the owner as a basis for non-liability under the contract is an affirmative defense under Texas Rule of Civil Procedure 94. SCCI's original answer contained only a general denial and did not enumerate any specific affirmative defenses. At trial, SCCI did not contest the fact that it owed appellant for its completed work and for retainage; however, SCCI argued that it was not legally required to pay appellant. SCCI's trial counsel's opening remarks included the following:

It is not a fact of [SCCI] not wanting to pay [appellant], but indeed the subcontracted money was never paid to [SCCI] by the Owner. And therefore, pursuant to the terms of the contract on their face we have no legal obligation to pay this subcontractor unless we are paid by the Owner of the property, and that's specific in the contract terms which we will go over. That's why we're not disputing how much the gentleman is owed, anything like that.

During the trial, appellant's counsel properly objected when SCCI's counsel attempted to introduce evidence of: 1) the contract language delaying payment of the subcontractor until the contractor had been paid; and 2) the fact that the contractor had not been paid by the owner. The trial judge overruled both objections. SCCI's counsel did not request a trial amendment of its original answer. We therefore hold that the trial court erred in admitting the evidence. Appellant's second issue is sustained.

* * *

Having sustained appellant's issues two, four, five, and six, we reverse the judgment of the court below. Because of our disposition, we need not discuss appellant's first and third issues. We reverse the judgment of the trial court, render judgment in favor of appellant in the amount of $62,421.11, and remand the case to the trial court for entry of a new judgment consistent with this opinion, including a finding of the total amount of attorney's fees to be awarded to appellant and all such pre-and post-judgment interest as may be required by law.

PHILLIPS
v.
PHILLIPS
820 S.W.2d 785
(Tex. 1992)

Facts: This case arises out of a divorce settlement in which the H & W placed their assets into a limited partnership, with the H as general partner and W as limited partner. It was agreed that if the general partner (H) breached his trust he was to pay as liquidated damages, the limited partner (W) ten times the amount she losses as a result of the breach of trust. Disputes arose over accounting and operating practices. Suit ensued. The jury found that H breached the agreement and his fiduciary duty. They awarded damages.

Issue: Was W entitled to have the damages multiplied by ten as a penalty? Not in this case. Liquidated damage provisions are enforceable; penalty provisions are not enforceable. To be enforceable as liquidated damages, the damages must be uncertain and the stipulation must be reasonable. Parties are usually limited to actual damages in order to enforce a liquidated damage clause, the court must find: (1) that the harm caused by the breach is incapable or difficult of estimation, and 2) that the amount of liquidated damages called for is a reasonable forecast of just compensation. Whether it is a damage or penalty provision is a question of law.

Here, the clause was an unenforceable penalty provision because the harm caused by the breach of the contract is not incapable or difficult to estimate.

Issue: What is the effect of H's failure to plead that the clause was a penalty provision? While not listed as an affirmative defense in Rule 94, penalty is a matter constituting an avoidance or affirmative defense. Generally, an affirmative defense must be pleaded or it is waived. An exception exists for the defense of illegality (which is listed in Rule 94), which, if the illegality appears from the face of the plaintiff's pleadings, does not have to be specifically plead.

Issue: Are there exceptions to the requirement that affirmative defenses be specially pleaded? Yes. (1) When a plaintiff in his or her pleadings anticipates defensive matters and pleads them, a defendant may rely upon the defenses though his only pleading is a general denial. Pleading an agreement illegal on its face, in effect, anticipates the defense. (2) The courts will not enforce a plainly illegal contract even if the parties do not object. Enforcement of an illegal agreement violates public policy.

Held: The defense of penalty is not waived by the failure to plead it if it is apparent on the face of the petition and established as a matter of law. However, whenever the defense is not clearly established on the face of the pleadings, it does have to be plead.

Notes

1. The "constitutionality of a statute will be considered only when the question is properly raised and a decision becomes necessary and appropriate to the disposal of the case and no statute should be overruled without careful and mature consideration." *Wood v. Wood*, 320 S.W.2d 807, 813 (Tex. 1959), *cited in In re Jane Doe 2*, 19 S.W.3d 346 (2000).

2. *Federal Deposit Ins. Corp. v. Lenk*, 361 S.W.3d 602 (Tex. 2012): The statute of repose, under TEX. BUS. & COM. CODE § 4.406(f) requires a person to report unauthorized transactions to a bank within one year of account statements being made available. If a person fails to report the unauthorized transaction, the person is barred from bringing a claim for payment. Here, however, the Bank failed to raise the statue of repose as an affirmative defense in the trial court. A court cannot grant summary judgment on grounds that were not presented.

3. *Manbeck v. Austin Independent School District,* -----S.W.3d-----, ----Tex. Sup. Ct. R.---, 2012 WL 3800876 (Tex. 2012): The defense of sovereign immunity from suit sufficiently implicates subject matter jurisdiction to conclude that the defense may be raised for the first time on appeal, regardless of whether sovereign immunity equates to subject matter jurisdiction for all purposes.

4. *Moayedi v. Interstate 35/Chisam Rd., L.P.*, 438 S.W.3d 1 (Tex. 2014): A party waives the statutory right of offset under section 51.003(c) of the Property Code by agreeing to a general waiver of defenses in a

guaranty agreement. Section 51.003 creates an affirmative defense that Moayedi abandoned by the guaranty agreement.

5. JUSTICE GUZMAN in *Kingsaire, Inc. v. Meledez,* 477 S.W.3d 309, 320 (Tex. 2015) (concurring) stated:

> "An inferential rebuttal defense operates to rebut an essential element of the plaintiff's case by proof of other facts." *See Dillard v. Tex. Elec. Coop.,* 157 S.W.3d 429, 430 (Tex. 2005). In contrast, an affirmative defense enables a defendant to avoid liability even if the plaintiff successfully proves all the elements of a cause of action. *Tex. Beef Cattle Co. v. Green,* 921 S.W.2d 203, 210 (Tex. 1996). Evidence that an employee was terminated based on uniform enforcement of a reasonable leave policy rebuts the conclusion that the employee was terminated in retaliation for engaging in protected conduct. It presents a contrary theory of causation. Accordingly, the leave-policy defense illustrates the "basic characteristic" of an inferential rebuttal defense; "it presents a contrary or inconsistent theory from the claim relied upon for recovery." *Select Ins. Co. v. Boucher,* 561 S.W.2d 474, 477 (Tex. 1978). A leave-policy defense cannot be treated as an affirmative defense because doing so would impermissibly shift the burden of causation to the defendant in contravention of the retaliatory-discharge statute. *See Zorrilla v. Aypco Constr. II, LLC,* 469 S.W.3d 143, 156 (Tex. 2015) ("[T]he hallmark characteristic of [an affirmative defense] is that the burden of proof is on the defendant to present sufficient evidence to establish the defense and obtain the requisite jury findings.")"

f. *Special Pleas*

Read Rule 54 Texas Rules of Civil Procedure

GREATHOUSE
v.
CHARTER NAT'L BANK

851 S.W.2d 173
(Tex. 1992)

Gary L. McConnell, Angleton, for petitioner.
Larry Huelbig, Audrey Seldon, Houston, for respondent.

HECHT, JUSTICE.

Section 9.504 of the Uniform Commercial Code, TEX. BUS. & COM. CODE § 9.504, requires that collateral must be disposed of in a commercially reasonable manner. The Code, however, does not allocate the burden of pleading and proving whether this requirement has been met in an action by a creditor against a debtor for the deficiency due after disposition of the collateral. We granted writ of error to resolve a split among Texas courts of appeals over this procedural issue.

Forrest Allen & Associates, Inc. defaulted on a note payable to Charter National Bank-Southwest, guaranteed by Clyde R. Greathouse, and secured by an assignment of insurance expirations, commissions, accounts receivable, furniture and fixtures. Charter took the pledged collateral and sold it for $100,000, leaving a principal balance due on the note of $151,014.95. Charter then sued Forrest Allen and Greathouse for the deficiency, interest and attorney fees. Greathouse died during the pendency of the suit, and the independent executrix of his estate was substituted as a defendant.

Charter did not plead that it had disposed of the collateral in a commercially reasonable manner, but it did plead generally that: "All conditions precedent have been performed or have occurred. All just and lawful credits, payments and offsets have been allowed." Defendants answered with a general denial. At trial before the court without a jury, Charter's sole witness established the amount due on the note after foreclosure, and Charter rested its case. Greathouse then moved for judgment on the grounds that Charter had failed to plead or prove an element of its cause of action, namely, a commercially reasonable disposition of the pledged collateral. Charter responded that it had satisfied its pleading obligation by alleging generally the performance of all conditions precedent, and that it was not required to prove the commercial reasonableness of the foreclosure absent a specific denial by Greathouse. Charter relied upon Rule 54, TEX. R. CIV. P., which states: In pleading the performance or occurrence of conditions precedent, it shall be sufficient to aver generally that all conditions precedent have been performed or have occurred. When such performances or occurrences have been so plead, the party so pleading same shall be required to prove only such of them as are specifically denied by the opposite party. Charter also requested a continuance to procure evidence of the commercial reasonableness of the foreclosure sale. The trial court denied both Charter's request for a continuance and Greathouse's motion for judgment, and Greathouse rested its case without offering any evidence. After taking the case under submission, the trial court rendered judgment for Charter in the amount of $252,858.28.

Only Greathouse appealed. The court of appeals affirmed, holding "that the burden of specifically pleading a lack of commercial reasonableness or notice in a deficiency action under section 9.504 . . . rests with the debtor." 795 S.W.2d 1, 3. Once the debtor has specifically raised the issue, the court held, the burden of proof is upon the creditor. The court reasoned: "Such an approach informs a creditor which areas (if any) are disputed and which items of proof must be produced; it does not allow a creditor to avoid proving its case . . . . Without indication of a debtor's objections, a creditor is prejudiced in the preparation of its case." *Id.* at 2.

On the procedural issue before us, the Uniform Commercial Code has not achieved its purposes of simplification and uniformity of commercial law. Texas courts are severely split on the subject. Many of them indicate that the creditor must plead and prove a commercially reasonable disposition of the collateral, while others have treated commercial unreasonableness as a defense which the debtor must raise in order to shift the burden of proof to the creditor. Our sister states are equally divided. Some states place the burden on the creditor in a deficiency suit to both plead and prove compliance with the notice and commercial reasonableness requirements of section 9.504. In other states, the debtor raises the issue in pleadings as a counterclaim or a defense in order to put the creditor to proof on the matters so challenged, and the secured creditor then bears the burden of proving compliance. A few states treat the issue as an affirmative defense.

This division of authority illustrates the difficulty which attends an allocation of the burdens of pleading and proof. In discussing whether a matter should be considered an affirmative defense, Professor McDonald has observed: the allocation of an element to the plaintiff's case or to the defendant's affirmative pleading is not determined by abstract logic. There is no reason in logic, for instance, why a plaintiff should not be compelled as an element of his case to establish that he was free of contributory negligence or did not induce a particular contract by fraud; or that an assertedly subsisting claim has not been paid or released. Considerations of fairness and convenience, of the ease or difficulty of making proof, of the comparative likelihood that a particular defensive situation may exist in a reasonable proportion of the cases presented in court, and even of handicapping disfavored contentions, have contributed to the shaping of the concept of an "affirmative" defense. 2 ROY W. MCDONALD, TEXAS CIVIL PRACTICE IN DISTRICT AND COUNTY COURTS § 7.34.1.-C, at 221 (Frank W. Elliott ed., 1982 rev.). We employed one of these considerations in *Eckman v. Centennial Sav. Bank*, 784 S.W.2d 672, 675 (Tex. 1990), to assign the burden of pleading and proving whether a plaintiff has assets of $25 million or more and thus is excepted from the definition of business consumer under the Deceptive Trade Practices—Consumer Protection Act, TEX. BUS. & COM. CODE § 17.45(4). In assigning that burden to the defendant, we reasoned: The comparative likelihood that a certain situation may occur in a reasonable percentage of cases should be considered when determining whether a fact should be allocated as an element of the plaintiff's case or to the defendant as an affirmative defense. . . . Obviously, most litigants do not have assets of $25,000,000 or more. Requiring every DTPA plaintiff to prove that he is not a multimillionaire would be an inefficient and uneconomical use of judicial resources.

As Professor McDonald observed, logic alone does not dictate the assignment of the burden of pleading and proof. The division of authority throughout the country on the issue now before us demonstrates this. There is simply no clear answer to whether a creditor should be required to plead and prove that collateral has been disposed of in a commercially reasonable manner as an element of a claim for the amount due on the debt, or whether a debtor should be required to allege and show that collateral has not been so disposed of as a defense to the creditor's demand for payment. To resolve the issue, we consider factors like those Professor McDonald mentions.

A commercially reasonable disposition of collateral is in the nature of a condition to a creditor's recovery in a deficiency suit. We suggested this in *Tanenbaum v. Economics Laboratory, Inc.*, 628 S.W.2d 769, 771 (Tex. 1982), where we said: "The only limits on the creditor's disposition of the collateral is that it must be commercially reasonable, and must be made only after notification to the debtor if required by section 9.504. Then and only then is he entitled to sue for a deficiency." (Emphasis added.) Evidence on the issue will ordinarily be more readily available to the creditor, who takes the collateral and arranges for its disposition, than to the debtor, who ordinarily plays no role in the disposition and is absent when it occurs. In general, it is easier for a creditor to prove that a disposition of collateral was commercially reasonable than for a debtor to prove it was not. Furthermore, the creditor controls the disposition of the collateral, and the debtor often has little or no say in how it is done. Accordingly, the creditor bears greater responsibility to demonstrate that the disposition met the requirements of law. However, the commercial reasonableness of a disposition of collateral is not in dispute in most deficiency suits. To require proof of this issue in every case, even if it is not disputed, would be an unreasonable burden on the judicial process.

Based upon these considerations, we conclude that a creditor in a deficiency suit must plead that disposition of the collateral was commercially reasonable. This may be pleaded specifically or by averring generally that all conditions precedent have been performed or have occurred. If pleaded generally, the creditor is required to prove that the disposition of collateral was commercially reasonable only if the debtor specifically denies it in his answer. Should the creditor plead specifically, then it must, of course, prove the allegation in order to obtain a favorable judgment.

In this case, Charter met its burden of pleading by its general allegation that all conditions precedent had been performed. In answer, Greathouse did not specifically deny that Charter's disposition of the collateral was commercially unreasonable. Consequently, Charter was not required to prove commercial reasonableness at trial. The trial court did not err in rendering judgment for Charter. Therefore, the judgment of the court of appeals is

Affirmed.

DOGGETT, J., concurring in separate opinion in which MAUZY, J., joins [opinion omitted].

g. *Amendment of Pleadings*

Read Rules 63, 66, and 67 Texas Rules of Civil Procedure

GREENHALGH
v.
SERVICE LLOYDS INSURANCE COMPANY
787 S.W.2d 938
(Tex. 1990)

Ray Chester, Austin, for petitioner.
Robert D. Stokes, Austin, Janet Townsley, Ben Taylor, Michael Phillips, Houston, for respondent.

MAUZY, JUSTICE.

The issue in this case is whether a trial court abuses its discretion by allowing a post-verdict amendment increasing the amount of damages in Plaintiff's pleadings to conform to the amount awarded by the jury when Defendant presents no evidence of surprise or prejudice. We hold that under Texas Rules of Civil Procedure 63 and 66, a trial court must allow a trial amendment that increases the amount of damages sought in the pleadings to that found by the jury unless the opposing party presents evidence of prejudice or surprise.

Plaintiff Greenhalgh and Service Lloyds Insurance Company (Service Lloyds), his workers' compensation carrier, agreed to a settlement of Greenhalgh's workers' compensation claim. However, Service Lloyds refused to pay Greenhalgh's medical expenses as required by the settlement. Greenhalgh subsequently filed this bad-faith insurance claim against Service Lloyds. The jury found in favor of Greenhalgh on each of his theories of recovery: breach of the duty of good faith and fair dealing, bad-faith insurance practices, gross negligence, negligence, and intentional infliction of emotional distress. Greenhalgh pleaded for $10,000 in actual damages and $100,000 in punitive damages; the jury awarded $8,000 in actual damages and $128,000 in punitive damages.

Because Greenhalgh had pleaded for only $100,000 in punitive damages, he requested leave to amend his pleadings to conform the amount of damages to that found by the jury and supported by the evidence. In its responsive motion, Service Lloyds alleged that the amendment was prejudicial because Service Lloyds had relied on the $100,000 amount in Plaintiff's pleadings in preparing for trial and in deciding whether to settle the case. The trial court allowed the post-verdict amendment. The court of appeals held that the trial court abused its discretion in allowing the amendment and reduced the punitive damages to $100,000.

The court of appeals reasoned that "because a defendant receives notice of the upper limit of punitive damages only by way of pleadings, it is an abuse of discretion to allow a post-verdict trial amendment increasing punitive damages when proper objections are made." 771 S.W.2d 688, 697. We disagree. The holding of the court of appeals ignores the mandates of the procedural rules regarding amendment of pleadings during trial. *See* TEX. R. CIV. P. 63 and 66.

Not only did the trial court not abuse its discretion in granting the amendment, it would have been an abuse of discretion if the trial court had refused the amendment. Under Rules 63 and 66 a trial court has no discretion to refuse an amendment unless: 1) the opposing party presents evidence of surprise or prejudice, TEX. R. CIV. P. 63 and 66; *Hardin v. Hardin*, 597 S.W.2d 347, 350-51 (Tex. 1980) (Campbell, J., concurring); *see Food Source, Inc. v. Zurich Ins. Co.*, 751 S.W.2d 596, 599 (Tex. App.—Dallas 1988, writ denied); or 2) the amendment asserts a new cause of action or defense, and thus is prejudicial on its face, and the opposing party objects to the amendment. *Hardin v. Hardin*, 597 S.W.2d 347 (Tex. 1980). The burden of showing prejudice or surprise rests on the party resisting the amendment. *Patino v. Texas Employers Insurance Association*, 491 S.W.2d 754, 756 (Tex. Civ. App.—Austin 1973, writ ref'd n.r.e.). Because Greenhalgh's amendment raised no new substantive matters and because there was no showing of surprise or prejudice by Service Lloyds, the trial court properly granted leave to file the amendment.[2]

Service Lloyds relies on appellate court holdings that a trial court abuses its discretion in allowing a post-verdict amendment increasing damages to conform to the verdict. *Burk Royalty Co. v. Walls*, 596 S.W.2d 932, 938 (Tex. Civ. App.—Fort Worth 1980), aff'd on other grounds, 616 S.W.2d 911 (Tex. 1981); *Winn-Dixie Texas, Inc. v. Buck*, 719 S.W.2d 251, 255 (Tex. App.—Fort Worth 1986, no writ). We disapprove these holdings because they directly conflict with Rules 63 and 66.

TEXAS RULES OF CIVIL PROCEDURE 63 and 66

It is well established that a party may amend its pleading after verdict but before judgment. *American Produce & Vegetable Co. v. J.D. Campisi's Italian Restaurant*, 533 S.W.2d 380, 386 (Tex. Civ. App.—Tyler 1975, writ ref'd n.r.e.). Rule 63 states:

> Parties may amend their pleadings, . . . as they may desire by filing such pleas with the clerk at such time as not to operate as a surprise to the opposite party; provided, that any amendment offered for filing within seven days of the date of trial or thereafter, . . . shall be filed only after leave of the judge is obtained, which leave shall be granted by the judge unless there is a showing that such amendment will operate as a surprise of the opposite party.

(Emphasis added).

The language of Rule 63 makes it clear that without a showing of surprise the trial court must grant leave for a party to file the amendment when requested within seven days of trial or thereafter. Thus, a party's right to amend under Rule 63 is subject only to the opposing party's right to show surprise. *Hardin v. Hardin*, 597 S.W.2d 347, 349 (Tex. 1980). However, the trial court may conclude that the amendment is on its face calculated to surprise or that the amendment would reshape the cause of action, prejudicing the opposing party and unnecessarily delaying the trial. *Id.*

An amended pleading that changes only the amount of damages sought does not automatically operate as surprise within the contemplation of Rule 63. *See Drury v. Reeves*, 539 S.W.2d 390, 394 (Tex. Civ. App.—Austin 1976, no writ). A party opposing an amendment increasing damages must present evidence to show that

[2] Service Lloyds offered no evidence of how it was prejudiced or surprised by the trial amendment. In closing arguments Service Lloyds argued that no punitive damages should have been awarded. Service Lloyds has never argued that it would have changed its position at trial—that Plaintiff deserved zero punitive damages—if the pleadings requested $128,000 rather than $100,000. In its opposition to the amendment Service Lloyds failed to make any showing to the trial court that an increase in punitive damages pleaded would have forced it to change its trial posture.

the increase resulted in surprise. Because Service Lloyds presented no evidence of surprise, the trial court properly allowed the amendment as required under Rule 63.

Rule 66 further confirms the propriety of the trial court's granting leave for Greenhalgh to file his amendment. Rule 66 provides in part:

> if during the trial any defect, fault or omission in a pleading, either of form or substance, is called to the attention of the court, the court may allow the pleadings to be amended and shall do so freely when the presentation of the merits of the action will be subserved thereby and the objecting party fails to satisfy the court that the allowance of such amendment would prejudice him in maintaining his action or defense upon the merits.

(Emphasis added). In *Vermillion v. Haynes*, 147 Tex. 359, 215 S.W.2d 605, 609 (Tex. 1948), this Court held that the trial court abused its discretion in denying a trial amendment filed after the close of evidence in a nonjury trial. Rule 66 "directs that the court shall 'freely' allow an amendment" when it subserves the merits of the case and the opposing party fails to show prejudice. *Id.*

The "defect" that Greenhalgh sought to cure in his amendment was to conform his pleadings to the evidence and jury findings on punitive damages. Service Lloyds failed to complain in the trial court that the evidence did not support the jury's finding on punitive damages—nor has it made this argument on appeal. We have held that when objections carry neither suggestion nor hint that the opposing party was in any manner surprised or prejudiced, both the spirit and the intent of Rule 66 require that the amendment be permitted. *Id.* Thus the trial court properly allowed the amendment under Rules 63 and 66.

We hold that in the absence of a showing of surprise or prejudice by an opposing party, a trial court must grant leave to a party to amend his or her pleadings to conform the amount of damages requested to that awarded by the jury. We reverse the judgment of the court of appeals and affirm the judgment of the trial court.

HECHT, J., files a concurring opinion in which PHILLIPS, C.J., and COOK, J., join [opinion omitted].

Notes

1. Under *Sosa v. Central Power & Light,* 909 S.W.2d 893, 895 (Tex. 1995) *infra*, applying Rule 4 to Rule 63, the day of the filing of an amended pleading is not counted for purposes of the seven day period prior to trial or hearing during which an amended pleading may be filed without leave of court. The last day of the seven-day period, which may be the date of the hearing, is counted.

2. Do you count backwards in applying the time period under TEX. R. CIV. P. 4 or do you count forward? Compare: *Hammonds v. Thomas*, 770 S.W.2d 1, 3 (Tex. App.—Texarkana 1989, no writ) with *Old Republic Ins. Co. v. Wuensche,* 782 S.W.2d 346, 348-49 (Tex. App.—Fort Worth 1989, writ denied) and *Reichhold Chemicals, Inc. v. Puremco Mfg. Co.*, 854 S.W.2d 240 (Tex. App.—Waco 1992, writ denied).

3. The following law review article is instructing concerning trial by consent. *Trial Amendments and Trial by Consent: Properly Applying Texas Rules of Civil Procedure 66 and 67*, 45 BAYLOR L. REV. 475 (1993).

CHAPIN & CHAPIN
v.
TEXAS SAND & GRAVEL CO.
844 S.W.2d 664
(Tex. 1992)

William V. Dorsaneo, III, Dallas, Richard N. Countiss, Houston, Kenneth E. Shollenbarger, Robert O. Fleming, Jr., Amarillo, for petitioners.

Tad Fowler, Amarillo, for respondent.

PER CURIAM.

Texas Sand & Gravel Co., a subcontractor, sued its general contractor, Chapin & Chapin, Inc. on a sworn account, alleging that Chapin had failed to pay Texas Sand for sand and gravel delivered to a construction project. Chapin denied Texas Sand's allegations, contending that it paid for all such materials it received. The trial court refused to allow Chapin to verify its denial less than seven days before trial, thereby restricting the evidence Chapin was permitted to offer at trial. A directed verdict for Texas Sand was affirmed on appeal. 844 S.W.2d 754. We hold that the trial court's refusal to allow Chapin to amend its answer was an abuse of discretion.

Texas Sand originally filed suit for breach of contract, not on open account. Several months after suit was filed, Texas Sand requested a trial setting, representing to the district court that all of its pleadings were "now in order". The trial court scheduled trial for a date about a month later. Before that date arrived, however, Texas Sand moved for a continuance and amended its pleadings to allege a sworn account. Chapin joined in the motion for continuance, and the trial was postponed. Texas Sand again moved for a continuance, and trial was postponed a second time. Six days before the third trial setting, Texas Sand and Chapin appeared at docket call and announced ready for trial. The next day, however, Chapin moved for leave to amend its answer to include a verified denial of Texas Sand's open account allegations. The trial court considered the motion the morning of trial. Texas Sand objected, arguing that it was ready to proceed only on the assumption that its verified petition, without a verified denial, would establish a prima facie case, that it was surprised by Chapin's attempt to file a verified denial, and that it would be unprepared to proceed if the verified denial were allowed. The trial court denied Chapin's motion and proceeded to trial, prohibiting Chapin from adducing evidence of payment.

Rule 63, TEX. R. CIV. P. states that pleadings may be amended within seven days of trial "only after leave of the judge is obtained, which leave shall be granted by the judge unless there is a showing that such filing will operate as a surprise to the opposite party." *In re Laughlin*, 153 Tex. 183, 265 S.W.2d 805, 807 (1954), we acknowledged that under rule 66 "it has been held that amendment should be allowed to supply a necessary verification of a pleading."

Chapin argues that our recent opinion in *Greenhalgh v. Service Lloyds Ins. Co.*, 787 S.W.2d 938 (Tex. 1990), is controlling. There we held that the trial court properly allowed plaintiff to amend the amount of damages claimed after the verdict was returned in the absence of surprise or prejudice to defendant. We stated: Not only did the trial court not abuse its discretion in granting the amendment, it would have been an abuse of discretion if the trial court had refused the amendment. Under Rules 63 and 66 a trial court has no discretion to refuse an amendment unless: 1) the opposing party presents evidence of surprise or prejudice, TEX. R. CIV. P. 63 and 66; *Hardin v. Hardin*, 597 S.W.2d 347, 350-351 (Tex. 1980) (CAMPBELL, J., concurring); *see Food Source, Inc. v. Zurich Ins. Co.*, 751 S.W.2d 596, 599 (Tex. App.—Dallas 1988, writ denied); or 2) the amendment asserts a new cause of action or defense, and thus is prejudicial on its face, and the opposing party objects to the amendment. *Hardin v. Hardin*, 597 S.W.2d 347 (Tex. 1980). Texas Sand argues that *Hardin*, on which we relied in *Greenhalgh*, is controlling. *Hardin* held that the trial court did not abuse its discretion in refusing to allow a defendant to amend his pleadings the day of trial in a suit on a promissory note to assert, for the first time, duress, failure of consideration, fraud, illegality and unjust enrichment. This Court concluded: "These amendments could not have been anticipated by the plaintiff, and had they been permitted, they would have prejudiced the plaintiff's presentation of the case and resulted in unnecessary delay." 597 S.W.2d at 350.

The difference between *Greenhalgh*, in which we held that the amendment was not only proper but mandatory, and *Hardin*, in which we held that denial of the amendment was not an abuse of discretion, is that the amendment in the former case was of a formal, procedural nature—increasing the ad damnum—which simply conformed the pleadings to the evidence at trial and did not result in surprise or prejudice, while the amendment in the latter case was substantive—changing the bases of the defense—which rather clearly changed the nature of the trial itself. The present case—adding a verified denial—is more in the nature of a procedural change, like *Greenhalgh*, than a substantive change, like *Hardin*. By adding a verified denial in this case, Chapin did not change a single substantive issue for trial. Chapin's position throughout had been that it had already paid for all it got. The only change was procedural: Texas Sand would have been obliged to rebut Chapin's substantive defense and could not simply insist judgment on the pleadings. If Texas Sand had relied upon the absence of a verified denial to the extent that it was unprepared to proceed to trial and would thus have been prejudiced by Chapin's amendment, it would have been entitled to a continuance. However, Texas Sand's counsel stated that he was prepared to prove that all deliveries had been made or accounted for and that the amount claimed was owed. In these circumstances, following *Laughlin*, we conclude that the trial court's refusal to allow Chapin to verify its denial was an abuse of discretion.

Accordingly, a majority of this Court grants Chapin's motion for rehearing of its application for writ of error, grants that application, reverses the judgment of the court of appeals, and remands the case to the district court for further proceedings. TEX. R. APP. P. 170.

STATE BAR OF TEXAS
v.
KILPATRICK

874 S.W.2d 656 (Tex. 1994), *cert. denied*, 114 S.Ct. 2740 (1994)

James McCormack, Linda A. Acevedo, Austin, for petitioner.
David W. Holman, Houston, for respondent.

PER CURIAM.

In this disciplinary proceeding, the court of appeals reversed and remanded the trial court's order disbarring Donald Kilpatrick for soliciting employment in violation of State Bar disciplinary rules. We reverse the judgment of the court of appeals, and render judgment disbarring Kilpatrick.

Bill Camp, a Houston attorney, suffered brain damage during a routine medical procedure on June 13, 1989. A week later, on June 20, his wife was appointed as his temporary guardian. On September 1, 1989, she became his permanent guardian.

Kilpatrick visited Camp at the Texas Institute for Research and Rehabilitation on July 19, 1989. During this meeting, Kilpatrick obtained Camp's signature on a power of attorney, which purported to authorize Kilpatrick to represent Camp in a medical malpractice claim. Only Kilpatrick and Camp were present, and neither Camp, his family, nor any legal representative requested or authorized Kilpatrick's visit. Kilpatrick later testified he knew Camp only as a "brother in the bar," that they had not been close friends or socialized together, and that their only previous acquaintance had been as opposing counsel on some criminal cases. He said that he had heard of Camp's misfortune through a law firm that, in turn, had learned the news from the emergency room physician on duty at the time of Camp's injury. Kilpatrick learned of Camp's location by calling Camp's office.

On July 21, 1989, two days after Kilpatrick obtained Camp's signature, Hornbuckle & Montgomery, the firm that had contacted Kilpatrick, filed a malpractice lawsuit against the doctors who treated Camp. When Ms. Camp learned of Kilpatrick's actions, she told Kilpatrick that the power of attorney was invalid, that she was Camp's guardian, and that Bill Camp was in no condition to retain a lawyer. Ms. Camp also hired a probate lawyer, Robert McIntyre, to assist her with the guardianship.

At Ms. Camp's behest, McIntyre went to Kilpatrick's office and demanded that Kilpatrick relinquish any claim to represent Camp under the power of attorney. Kilpatrick refused, and insisted on a referral fee. When McIntyre repeated his demand to Kilpatrick in a letter dated October 6, 1989, Kilpatrick demanded $277,000.00 in exchange for his release.

As guardian, Ms. Camp filed a TEX. R. CIV. P. 12 Motion for Attorney to Show Authority with the probate court concerning Kilpatrick's power of attorney. On November 17, 1989, the probate court determined that

Camp was mentally incompetent on the date he signed the power of attorney, and that Kilpatrick had no authority to represent him. The probate court also directed Kilpatrick to reimburse Ms. Camp for the attorneys' fees she had incurred as a result of his actions. On December 8, 1989, the same day the court issued its order, Kilpatrick appeared at McIntyre's office with an unfiled Motion to Recuse the probate judge. Kilpatrick threatened to file the motion unless Ms. Camp paid him the requested referral fee.

In April 1991, the State Bar filed a disciplinary action against Kilpatrick, charging him with violations of five disciplinary rules. At trial, the jury found that Kilpatrick (1) initiated contact with a prospective client for the purpose of obtaining employment, (2) engaged in conduct involving dishonesty, deceit, or misrepresentation, and (3) with intent to obtain an economic benefit to himself, solicited employment for himself to prosecute or collect a claim. On March 13, the trial court rendered judgment on the verdict, disbarring Kilpatrick.

The court of appeals reversed the trial court's judgment and remanded for new trial on two grounds. 869 S.W.2d 361. First, the court of appeals held that the trial court had erroneously permitted the State Bar to amend its pleadings at trial to include an allegation of barratry. *Id.* at 364. Second, the court held that the trial court abused its discretion in ordering disbarment based on a single act of solicitation. *Id.* at 366. We disagree with the court of appeals on both counts.

The State Bar's expert witness, Fred Hagans, testified on the issue of barratry, first during cross-examination by Kilpatrick's attorney, and then on redirect examination. At the subsequent charge conference, the State Bar requested a trial amendment alleging barratry as defined in TEX. PENAL CODE ANN. § 38.12(a) (Vernon Supp. 1993), reprinted in TEX. PENAL CODE ANN. § 38.12 note (Vernon Supp. 1994) (Historical and Statutory Notes), amended by TEX. PENAL CODE ANN. § 38.12(a) (Vernon Supp. 1994). Over Kilpatrick's objection, the trial court permitted the trial amendment, and included the issue in the charge.

If evidence is objected to at trial on the ground that it is not within the issues made by the pleadings, the court may allow the pleadings to be amended and shall do so freely when the presentation of the merits will be subserved thereby and the objecting party fails to satisfy the court that the amendment would prejudice that party in maintaining the action or defense on the merits. TEX. R. CIV. P. 66 (emphasis supplied). A court may not refuse a trial amendment unless (1) the opposing party presents evidence of surprise or prejudice, or (2) the amendment asserts a new cause of action or defense, and thus is prejudicial on its face. *Greenhalgh v. Service Lloyds Ins. Co.*, 787 S.W.2d 938, 939 (Tex. 1990). The burden of showing surprise or prejudice rests on the party resisting the amendment. *Id.* If the trial amendment is not mandatory, then the decision to permit or deny the amendment rests within the sound discretion of the trial court. TEX. R. CIV. P. 66; *Greenhalgh*, 787 S.W.2d at 939. In such a case, the court's decision to allow or deny a trial amendment may be reversed only if it is a clear abuse of discretion. *Hardin v. Hardin*, 597 S.W.2d 347, 349-50 (Tex. 1980).

The court of appeals held that the trial amendment alleging barratry was "prejudicial on its face" because it added a new cause of action. 869 S.W.2d at 365. In so doing the court of appeals effectively held that all non-mandatory trial amendments under Rule 66 must be rejected. To the contrary, we hold that the decision to grant or deny the trial amendment was discretionary, and under the circumstances the trial court did not abuse that discretion.

The trial amendment added an additional cause of action to the extent it alleged another ground of attorney misconduct under former Article X, section 7 of the STATE BAR RULES. *See also* TEX. R. DISCIPLINARY P. 1.06(Q) (1992), reprinted in TEX. GOV'T. CODE ANN., tit. 2, subtit. G, app. A-1 (Vernon Supp. 1994) (current version of same rule). The initial pleadings alleged multiple forms of attorney misconduct in violation of STATE BAR RULES art. X, § 7(1), which is a general prohibition concerning acts or omissions that violate the Texas Code of Professional Responsibility. The trial amendment added an allegation under a different subdivision of the same article and section of the disciplinary rules. STATE BAR RULES art. X, § 7(5) ("engaging in conduct that constitutes barratry as defined by [TEX. PENAL CODE ANN. § 38.12(a) (Vernon Supp. 1993)]"). *See also* TEX. R. DISCIPLINARY P. 1.06(Q)(5) (1992) (current version).

The central allegation in the State Bar's initial complaint was that Kilpatrick violated former TEX. CODE PROFESSIONAL RESPONSIBILITY DR 2-103(D)(1), which prohibited attorneys from initiating contact with prospective clients for the purpose of obtaining employment if the lawyer knew or reasonably should have known the person could not have exercised reasonable judgment in employing a lawyer. *See also*, TEX. DISCIPLINARY R. PROF. CONDUCT 7.02 (1989), reprinted in TEX. GOV'T. CODE ANN., tit. 2, subtit. G, app. A (Vernon Supp. 1994) (STATE BAR RULES art. X § 9). Former DR 2-103(D)(1) shares common elements with the criminal offense of barratry, and the evidence presented at trial supported discipline under either theory. Thus, the trial court, in its discretion, could reasonably have concluded that the trial amendment did not impair Kilpatrick's ability to present his defense. We therefore hold that the trial amendment did not involve the kind of calculated surprise or unfair prejudice that would render it an abuse of discretion.

The court of appeals further based its reversal on the fact that Kilpatrick had not been convicted of barratry in criminal proceedings: "[T]here was no criminal prosecution, yet, the State Bar obtained a finding of criminal wrongdoing without the hardship of the higher burden of proof which is necessary for a conviction." 869 S.W.2d at 365. The court of appeals erred, however, in its assumption that an attorney may not be disciplined for barratry in civil proceedings without first being convicted in criminal proceedings. While barratry is a crime for which an attorney may be prosecuted, a criminal prosecution is not a prerequisite to disciplinary proceedings based on that offense. TEX. GOV'T. CODE ANN. § 82.062 (Vernon 1988) ("Any attorney who is guilty of barratry . . . may be [disciplined] . . . regardless of whether the attorney is being prosecuted for, or has been convicted of the offense."). Thus, we hold that the trial amendment resulted in no unfair prejudice, and was clearly within the trial court's discretion.

* * *

We therefore grant the application of the State Bar and, without hearing argument, a majority of the court reverses the judgment of the court of appeals, and renders judgment disbarring Donald Kilpatrick. TEX. R. APP. P. 170.

SOSA
v.
CENTRAL POWER & LIGHT

909 S.W.2d 893
(Tex. 1995)

Eugene Z. DuBose, Dallas, Hugo Xavier De Los Santon, San Antonio, for Petitioners.

F. Walter Conrad, Jr., Houston, John H. McLeod, Austin, Kevin M. Sadler, Austin, Richard T. McCarroll, Austin, Kay Andrews, Austin, J. Clifford Gunter, III, Houston, Larry F. York, Austin, Vernon B. Hill, Jr., McAllen, Allen B. Odum, Edinburg, Marc F. Wiegand, Houston, Michelle A. Blaine, Houston, John T. Dailey, San Antonio, for Respondents.

PER CURIAM.

This case involves the construction of Rule 63 of the Texas Rules of Civil Procedure. The question is whether Rule 4 governs the computation of the time period in Rule 63. Rule 63 provides that an amended pleading requires leave of court if it is filed within seven days of trial. Because we conclude Rule 4 does govern, we reverse the judgment of the court of appeals and remand the case to the trial court for further proceedings. TEX. R. APP. P. 170.

Lydia Sosa and her children sued Central Power & Light, Houston Lighting & Power Company, and General Electric for the wrongful death of Lydia's husband, Clemente M. Sosa, Jr. Sosa died from liver disease allegedly caused by exposure to toxic chemicals during the 1970s while he was employed by the defendants. The plaintiffs' first amended original petition alleged that Sosa was in good physical health before Central Power's wrongful conduct, but had been incapacitated from the date of his injuries until the date of his death approximately twenty years later. The defendants filed a motion for summary judgment asserting that the Sosas' claims were barred by the statute of limitations, and relying on the factual admissions in the Sosas' pleadings.

The summary judgment hearing was scheduled for November 17, 1993. Without first obtaining leave of court, the Sosas filed their second amended original petition on November 10, 1993. This amended petition deleted the factual allegations forming the basis of the defendants' motion for summary judgment and added the allegation that Sosa neither discovered nor should have discovered the nature of his injury until less than six months before his death. The defendants filed a motion to strike the amended petition. They asserted that Rule 63 required a party to obtain leave to amend if the amendment is filed seven days or less before the date of trial, excluding the date of filing.

At the summary judgment hearing, the Sosas made their first motion for leave to amend even though they argued that the amended petition was timely filed. The trial court granted the defendants' motion to strike the amendment, thus leaving the Sosas' first amended original petition as their only live pleading. Accordingly, the trial court granted the defendants' motion for summary judgment based on the factual admissions in the first amended petition. The court of appeals affirmed. 901 S.W.2d 562. We reverse.

Rule 63 of the Texas Rules of Civil Procedure states that "any pleadings, responses or pleas offered for filing within seven days of the date of trial or thereafter . . . shall be filed only after leave of the judge is obtained." TEX. R. CIV. P. 63 (emphasis added). This Court's comment to the rule more clearly states our intent to authorize amendment without leave of court if it is filed "seven days or more before the date of trial." *Id.*

We have never specifically dealt with how the time period prescribed in Rule 63 should be computed. However, in an opinion not cited by the court of appeals, we emphasized that Rule 4 "applies to any period of time prescribed by the rules of procedure." *Lewis v. Blake*, 876 S.W.2d 314, 316 (Tex. 1994) (emphasis in original).

Rule 4 provides:

> In computing any period of time prescribed or allowed by [the Texas Rules of Civil Procedure], . . . the day of the act, event, or default after which the designated period of time begins to run is not to be included. The last day of the period so computed is to be included.

TEX. R. CIV. P. 4. Under our facts, the Sosas filed their second amended original petition exactly one week before a scheduled summary judgment hearing. When Rule 4 is applied, the day on which the Sosas filed their amendment is not counted but the seventh day after it was filed is counted. This latter day is November 17, 1993. As we held in *Lewis*, the last day counted from the date of the filing may be the date of the hearing. *Lewis*, 876 S.W.2d at 316. Therefore, the Sosas timely filed their second amended original petition.

A number of courts of appeals have held that Rule 63 requires seven days to elapse between the date of filing and the date of hearing. *Volvo Petroleum, Inc. v. Getty Oil Co.*, 717 S.W.2d 134, 137 (Tex. App.—Houston [14th Dist.] 1986, no writ); *Sweeny Bank v. Ritchie, Hopson & Assocs., Inc.*, 628 S.W.2d 175, 176 (Tex. App.—Houston [14th Dist.] 1982, writ ref'd n.r.e.); *Dillingham v. Lynch*, 516 S.W.2d 694, 704 (Tex. Civ. App.—Austin 1974, writ ref'd n.r.e.); *Oehler v. Oehler*, 422 S.W.2d 240, 244 (Tex. Civ. App.—Austin 1967, writ ref'd n.r.e.). To the extent these cases hold contrary to our decision today, they are disapproved.

Because the Sosas timely filed their second amended original petition, it superseded their first amended original petition containing the statements on which the defendants based their motion for summary judgment. Contrary to statements in live pleadings, those contained in superseded pleadings are not conclusive and indisputable judicial admissions. *Drake Ins. Co. v. King*, 606 S.W.2d 812, 817 (Tex. 1980). Therefore, the basis for the defendants' motion no longer existed and summary judgment was improper.

Pursuant to Rule 170 of the Texas Rules of Appellate Procedure, a majority of this Court, without hearing oral argument, reverses the judgment of the court of appeals and remands the case to the trial court for further proceedings. TEX. R. APP. P. 170.

Notes

1. Rule 301 of the Texas Rules of Civil Procedure requires that the judgment conform to the pleadings, evidence and verdict. A judgment must be supported by the pleadings and, if not so supported, it is erroneous. *Fort Worth v. Gause*, 129 Tex. 25, 101 S.W.2d 221, 223 (1937). Thus, a party may not be granted relief in the absence of pleadings to support that relief. *Stoner v. Thompson*, 578 S.W.2d 679, 682 (Tex. 1979). The importance of amending pleadings should therefore be put in its proper perspective.

2. *City of Tyler v. Beck*, 196 S.W.3d 784 (Tex. 2006): The City filed two post-judgment motions, a Motion for New Trial and a Verified Motion to Reinstate, shortly after the trial court's order dismissing the case. The City filed its appeal more than thirty days after the judgment, the default period allowed to perfect an appeal, but within ninety days of the judgment, the extended period allowed when a post-judgment motion is filed. *See* TEX. R. APP. P. 26.1. The Becks argue that the City's post-judgment motions did not extend the time to perfect appeal because the motions were filed by new counsel who had not been designated as the City's attorney in charge. We disagree. Rule 8 of the Texas Rules of Civil Procedure provides that "[a]ll communications . . . with

respect to a suit shall be sent to the attorney in charge," and that any change of that designation must be made by written notice to the court and the other parties. TEX. R. CIV. P. 8. However, nothing in the rule indicates that a motion filed by an attorney other than the designated attorney in charge is void or that other attorneys are not authorized to act on behalf of the party. The City's post-judgment motions properly extended the plenary power of the court and the time for appeal.

h. *Supplemental Pleadings*

Note

Sixth RMA Partners, L.P. v. Sibley, 111 S.W.3d 46 (Tex. 2003): The original and the supplemental pleadings constitute separate and distinct parts of the pleading of each party, the former being for the purpose of stating or defending against the cause of action, and the latter for the purpose of replying to the allegations of the opposing party immediately preceding them; whereas an amendment to either, as contradistinguished from a supplemental petition or answer, is designed to "add something to, or withdraw something from" the amending party's own pleading, so as to cure its deficiencies.

The purpose of the second supplemental pleadings was to change the party name from "RMA Partners, L.P." to "Sixth RMA Partners, L.P." Although Sixth RMA Partners, L.P.'s should have used an amended pleading to state the partnership's correct name, the second supplemental pleadings filed by Sixth RMA Partners, L.P., showing the correct name, in place of the previously used incorrect assumed name, were effective to substitute its correct legal name. These allegations would properly have appeared in an amended petition, but, having been pleaded, they cannot be disregarded. The fact that the necessary factual allegations were contained in supplemental pleadings rather than amended original pleadings was a defect in form, which was waived, since it was not properly objected to.

3. *Special Pleading Forms*

a. *Suit on a Sworn Account*

Read Rules 185 and 93(10) Texas Rules of Civil Procedure.

RIZK
v.
FINANCIAL GUARDIAN INS. AGENCY
584 S.W.2d 860
(Tex. 1979)

Day & Elliott, Richard Elliott, Dallas, for petitioner.
Ronald G. Wiesenthal, Houston, for respondent.

BARROW, JUSTICE.

This is an appeal from a summary judgment granted respondent on the pleadings in its suit on a sworn account to recover insurance premiums allegedly owed by petitioner and three other individuals d/b/a Sheraton-Safari Inn. The court of civil appeals affirmed. 576 S.W.2d 110. The principal question presented here is the sufficiency of the verified answer filed by Rizk. We reverse the judgments of the lower courts and remand the cause to the trial court.

The petition filed herein by respondent contains an affidavit that meets the requirements of Rule 185, TEX. R. CIV. P. Rule 93(k), TEX. R. CIV. P. makes a similar requirement. In response to this petition, Rizk filed an amended answer which stated:

"1.

Defendant denies each and every, all and singular the material allegations contained in Plaintiff's Original Petition and demands strict proof thereof by a preponderance of the evidence as required by law.

"2.

Each and every item in Plaintiff's account attached to the Original Petition as Exhibit "A" is not just or true in whole or in part. Defendant did not request Plaintiff to furnish the items listed therein or agree or promise to pay plaintiff for the charges shown therein.

"3.

Defendant asserts his affirmative defense of failure of consideration.

"4.

Plaintiff's cause of action on its account, or a part thereof, is barred by the applicable two year statute of limitations, and accordingly should be dismissed.

"5.

Defendant denies Plaintiff is entitled to recover any attorney's fees in this cause, and furthermore denies that $4,000.00 is a reasonable attorney's fee." This answer was supported by the affidavit of Rizk that "the facts and statements contained therein are true and correct of his own personal knowledge."

The court of civil appeals concluded that the verified denial contained in Paragraph 2 of Rizk's amended answer meets the requirements of Rule 185 as a denial of the whole of the account. It held, however, that this denial was destroyed by subsequent allegations of the answer wherein inconsistent or alternative defenses were alleged. Since a verification must be positive and unequivocal to be effective, the court of civil appeals concluded that Rizk's answer was inconsistent and, therefore, did not destroy the evidentiary effect of respondent's verified petition.

Rule 185 is not a rule of substantive law but is a rule of procedure with regard to evidence necessary to establish a prima facie right of recovery. *Meaders v. Biskamp*, 159 Tex. 79, 316 S.W.2d 75 (1958). In the absence of a sworn denial meeting the requirements of the rule, the account is received as prima facie evidence as against a defendant sued thereon, and the defendant may not dispute the receipt of the items or services, or the correctness of the stated charges although he may defend on other grounds. 2 R. MCDONALD, TEXAS CIVIL PRACTICE § 7.31 (rev. 1970). Most courts have been very exacting in the nature of the language used in sworn denials of a verified account. *See Aztec Pipe & Supply Co. v. Sundance Oil Co.*, 568 S.W.2d 401 (Tex. Civ. App. Houston (1st Dist.), *writ ref'd n. r. e. per curiam*, 576 S.W.2d 780 (Tex. 1978); *P. T. Poultry Growers v. Darr Equipment Co.*, 537 S.W.2d 773 (Tex. Civ. App. Tyler 1976, writ ref'd n. r. e.); *Oliver Bass Lbr. Co. v. Kay & Herring Butane G. Co.*, 524 S.W.2d 600 (Tex. Civ. App. Tyler 1975, no writ); *Youngblood v. Central Soya Company, Inc.*, 522 S.W.2d 277 (Tex. Civ. App. Fort Worth 1975, writ ref'd n. r. e.); *cf. American Home Fence Co. v. Himes*, 374 S.W.2d 777 (Tex. Civ. App. Tyler, *writ ref'd n. r. e. per curiam*, 379 S.W.2d 290 (Tex. 1964); *Jones v. Houston Materials Company*, 477 S.W.2d 694 (Tex. Civ. App. Houston (14th Dist.) 1972, no writ).

It is settled, however, that a defendant's verified denial of the correctness of a plaintiff's sworn account In the form required by Rule 185 destroys the evidentiary effect of the itemized account attached to the petition and forces the plaintiff to put on proof of his claim. *J. E. Earnest & Co. v. Word*, 137 Tex. 16, 152 S.W.2d 325 (1941); *Cal-Tex Beef Processors, Inc. v. Frozen Food Exp.*, 530 S.W.2d 143 (Tex. Civ. App. Waco 1975, writ ref'd n. r. e.); *Charlie Thomas Courtesy Ford, Inc. v. Sid Murray Agency*, 517 S.W.2d 869 (Tex. Civ. App. Corpus Christi 1974, writ ref'd n. r. e.); *Davis Bumper To Bumper, Inc. v. American Petrofina Co.*, 420 S.W.2d 145 (Tex. Civ. App. Amarillo 1967, writ ref'd n. r. e.); *Burrus Mills, Inc. v. Hein*, 399 S.W.2d 950 (Tex. Civ. App. Houston 1966, writ ref'd n. r. e.); *Jones v. Eames*, 369 S.W.2d 524 (Tex. Civ. App. Eastland 1963, no writ).

We agree with the holding of the court of civil appeals that Rizk's verified answer that each and every item in respondent's account "is not just or true in whole or in part" was a denial of the whole account within the purview of Rule 185. However, we do not agree that this verified denial was nullified or destroyed by the other parts of Rizk's answer.

We do not see any inconsistency in the denial of the whole account in the form required by Rule 185 and the remainder of Rizk's answer which would nullify the statements in his affidavit. It is apparent that the account would not be true and correct as to Rizk if he had not ordered or agreed to pay for the items listed in the account attached to respondent's petition. In this connection it is interesting to note that In respondent's motion to sever the case as to Rizk from that of the other defendants, it was alleged that issues remained as to the existence of a partnership. Rizk's affirmative defenses of failure of consideration and statute of limitations are clearly not inconsistent with his verified denial in the form required by Rule 185. These affirmative defenses could be raised even in the absence of a verified denial under Rule 185. *King Title Co., Inc. v. Croft*, 562 S.W.2d 536 (Tex. Civ. App. El Paso 1978, no writ); *P. T. Poultry Growers v. Darr Equipment Co., supra*; *First National Bank of San Angelo v. Sheffield*, 475 S.W.2d 820 (Tex. Civ. App. Austin 1972, no writ); *Jorrie Furniture Company v. Rohm*, 442 S.W.2d 476 (Tex. Civ. App. San Antonio 1969, no writ). There is no valid reason why alternative pleadings may not be had in a suit on a sworn account within the restraints necessarily imposed by the required affidavit.

We conclude that the lower courts erred in holding that respondent was entitled to a summary judgment on its verified pleading. The verified denial by Rizk in the form required by Rule 185 destroyed the evidentiary effect of the itemized account attached to respondent's petition. There was no summary judgment evidence offered by respondent In proof of this account. Since the judgment must be set aside and the cause remanded for a new trial, it is unnecessary to consider Rizk's point complaining of the award of attorney's fees.

The judgments of the lower courts are reversed and the cause is remanded to the trial court.

Note

Airborne Freight Corp v. CRB Marketing, Inc., 566 S.W.2d 573, 574 (Tex. 1978): "It is settled that if the defendant fails to file a written denial under oath and in the form provided, he will not be permitted to dispute receipt of the items, or services or the correctness of the stated charges. * * * The defendant may, however, assert defenses in the nature of confession and avoidance without filing a sworn denial if they are properly pleaded."

b. *Trespass to Try Title*

Glance at Rules 783-809 Texas Rules of Civil Procedure.

MARTIN
v.
AMERMAN

133 S.W.3d 262
(Tex. 2004)

To prevail in a trespass-to-try-title action, a plaintiff must usually

(1) prove a regular chain of conveyances from the sovereign,
(2) establish superior title out of a common source,
(3) prove title by limitations, or
(4) prove title by prior possession coupled with proof that possession was not abandoned.

The pleading rules for a trespass to try title action are detailed and formal, and require a plaintiff to prevail on the superiority of his title, not on the weakness of a defendant's title.

The strict pleading and proof requirements applicable to trespass-to-try-title actions have been relaxed, when the sole dispute between the parties involves a boundary's location. Thus a boundary dispute may be tried by a statutory action of trespass-to-try title. In such a case, a recorded deed is sufficient to show an interest in the disputed property without having to prove a formal chain of superior title. In determining whether a case is one of boundary, the test is whether there would have been no case but for the question of boundary. However, by lessening the trespass-to-try-title action's more formal proof requirements, boundary disputes were not made a distinct cause of action.

Notes

1. *Northwest Indep. Sch. Dist. v. Carroll Indep. Sch. Dist.*, 441 S.W.3d 684 (Tex. App.—Ft. Worth 2014, pet. denied): Carroll Independent School District (CISD) sued Northwest Independent School District (NWISD) alleging a boundary dispute with NWISD. The parties disagreed over the location of the boundary line between the two districts when other litigation between their relative counties was resolved.

"After we issued our opinion in *Tarrant County v. Denton County,* our state's supreme court issued its opinion in *Martin v. Amerman,* which held a portion of our opinion invalid, stating that the use of the Declaratory Judgments Act to decide a boundary determination was incorrect and that a boundary dispute could be resolved by one method only: a trespass to try title action. *Martin,* 133 S.W.3d at 267-68 (holding trespass to try title statute governs method for determining title to real property and boundaries as well), *superseded by* TEX. CIV. PRAC. & REM.CODE Ann. § 37.004(c) (reversing *Martin's* holding that relief under the Act is unavailable for boundary disputes). Quickly, however, the state legislature overruled *Martin* by adding subsection (c) to section 37.004 of the Declaratory Judgments Act. TEX. CIV. PRAC. & REM. CODE Ann. § 37.004(c). This provision authorizes a party to seek a determination on the construction of "a *statute, municipal ordinance, contract, or franchise* " even when the only determination concerning title to real property involves the "proper boundary line between adjoining properties." *Id.* § 37.004(a), (c) (emphasis added); *see* Act of May 17, 2007, 80th Leg., R.S., ch. 305, § 1, 2007 Tex. Gen. Laws 581, 581 (adding subsection (c) effective June 15, 2007).

NWISD misconstrues the impact of the legislature's revision to section 37.004. Subsection (c) does not say that one may now *only* seek a determination of a boundary line under the Declaratory Judgments Act *if* one is seeking a determination of title. It says simply and only that *if* one is seeking a determination of title, then *notwithstanding that fact,* one may seek a determination or declaration of a boundary under the Declaratory Judgments Act. TEX. CIV. PRAC. & REM.CODE Ann. § 37.004(c). In other words, if determining a boundary line may also result in declaring title to real property, a party is no longer prohibited from seeking a declaration of rights under the Declaratory Judgments Act instead of solely under the property code's trespass to try title scheme as the supreme court had previously declared. *See Martin,* 133 S.W.3d at 267-68. The legislation simply removed the prohibition, based on the supreme court's construction of the Act in *Martin,* against using the Act to determine boundaries. Therefore, we conclude that the determination of a boundary is no longer a disqualifier under the Act, even when title may be affected."

2. *Yoast v. Yoast*, 649 S.W.2d 289 (Tex. 1983): In Texas, a trespass to try title action is a procedure by which rival claims to title or right of possession may be adjudicated. Partition issues may be resolved in a trespass to try title suit once the controversy as to title or right to possession is settled. A partition suit, as opposed to a trespass to try title action, is based on the theory of common title, rather than disputed ownership. Here ownership was disputed. The fact that there were issues of partition after the title dispute was settled, did not convert this into a partition suit.

3. *Hejl v. Wirth,* 161 Tex. 609, 343 S.W.2d 226 (Tex. 1961): "It has long been the rule in this State that in a trespass to try title suit, the plaintiff must recover upon the strength of his own title. *Kauffman v. Shellworth,* 64 Tex. 179; *Hovel v. Kaufman,* Tex.Com.App., 1926, 280 S.W. 185; *Davis v. Gale*, 1960, Tex., 330 S.W.2d 610. If the plaintiff under the circumstances fails to establish his title, the effect of a judgment of take nothing against him is to vest title in the defendant. The rule is a harsh one, but it also has been well established as a rule of land law in this State. *French v. Olive*, 1887, 67 Tex. 400, 3 S.W. 568; *Permian Oil* Co. *v. Smith*, 1934, 129 Tex. 413, 73 S.W.2d 490, 111 A.L.R. 1152."

4. The answer in a trespass to try title suit is "not guilty." Rule 788. Under the not guilty plea, the defendant "may give in evidence any lawful defense to the action except the defense of limitations, which shall be specifically pleaded." Rule 789.

5. The failure to timely comply with requests for abstracts of title, or to provide a reasonable explanation for the failure to comply, can result in the trial court precluding proof of the title that would have been shown by the abstract. Rules 791-794.

Notes

1. The legislature amended the Texas Declaratory Judgments Act to allow a party to obtain declaratory relief "when the sole issue concerning title to real property is the determination of the proper boundary line between adjoining properties." *See* TEX. CIV. PRAC. & REM. CODE ANN. § 37.004(c) (West 2008).

2. *Lance v. Robinson,* 543 S.W.3d 723 (Tex. 2018): The trespass-to-try-title statute does not apply to a claimant who seeks to establish an easement, because such a claimant "does not have such a possessory right." An easement "is a nonpossessory interest that authorizes its holder to use the property for only particular purposes." A claimant who prevails on a claim to establish an easement cannot prevail on a trespass-to-try-title claim without also establishing title or a possessory right.

3. *Permian Oil Co. v. Smith*, 129 Tex. 413, 427, 73 S.W.2d 490, 496 (1934): The doctrine has been thoroughly settled by repeated decisions of the courts of this state, that a judgment in an action of trespass to try title that plaintiff take nothing by his suit is an adjudication that the title to the land involved is in the defendant, and such a judgment is equally as effective for that purpose as one expressly vesting title in the defendant. . . . The principle announced in these cases is but an application of the provision of the statute to the effect that any final judgment in an action to recover real estate shall be conclusive as to the title or right of possession established in such action upon the party against whom it is recovered, and upon all persons claiming through or under him, by title arising after the commencement of the action. Article 7391, R. S. 1925.

c. *Other Special Pleading Forms*

The Texas Rules of Civil Procedure provide for many other types of special pleading forms. The most frequently used are those relating to various creditors' remedies. Glance at Rules of Civil Procedure 783 through 813. Furthermore, the Tort Reform Act of 2003 sets up notice and pleading requirements for health care liability claims. *See* § 74.051, TEX. CIV. PRAC. & REM. CODE. In addition, in health care liability claims the pleadings are not to state the amount of damages sought. *See* § 74.053, TEX. CIV. PRAC. & REM. CODE.

Chapter 9.
Parties and Actions

1. *Capacity of Parties*

COASTAL LIQUIDS TRANSPORTATION, L.P.
v.
HARRIS COUNTY APPRAISAL DISTRICT

46 S.W.3d 880
(Tex. 2001)

Coastal Liquids Transportation, L.P., a Delaware limited partnership, formed on 12/21/1993, sought to challenge the Appraisal District's 1994 and 1995 appraisals of six salt dome storage caverns for ad valorem tax purposes. Coastal has been transacting business in Texas since 12/21/1993. Coastal was required to register as a foreign limited partnership to appeal the Appraisal Review Board's order regarding the 1994 and 1995 appraisals. Coastal did not register until 6/1995, and did not prove that it had paid the fees and penalties for prior years. Held: Coastal lacks the capacity to maintain this lawsuit for 1994 or 1995. There is no evidence that Coastal ever properly registered by paying all necessary fees. The Court does not decide how much time a party has to cure a registration defect during a pending lawsuit, only that by the time the case reaches the Supreme Court by appeal from a final judgment is too late.

A plaintiff has standing when it is personally aggrieved, regardless of whether it is acting with legal authority; a party has capacity when it has the legal authority to act, regardless of whether it has a justiciable interest in the controversy." A party must have both standing and capacity to bring a lawsuit. And while standing as an issue cannot be waived, capacity can be.

Coastal's capacity was in issue before the trial court and the court of appeals. If it is not evident from the petition that a plaintiff foreign limited partnership lacks the capacity to sue, the burden is on the defendant to raise the issue. The burden is then on the defendant to prove that it had properly registered and paid the applicable fees, and, therefore, had capacity to sue.

Coastal waived its due process and "defending an action" arguments by not raising them until its motion for rehearing in the court of appeals. Claims not made to the trial court generally cannot be raised for the first time on appeal.

Notes

1. In *City of Galveston v. State*, 217 S.W.3d 466 (Tex. 2007) the Court dealt with litigation arising from a 1982 agreement with the Texas Department of Transportation for construction of State Highway 275, in which the City of Galveston agreed to move and maintain nearby utilities. One of those utilities, a City water line, ruptured in 2001 and allegedly caused $180,872.53 in damages to the highway. The Attorney General filed suit in the name of the State of Texas to recover damages for the City's "negligent installation, maintenance, and upkeep" of its water line and the resulting damage to state property. The City filed a plea to the jurisdiction, special exceptions, and a motion for summary judgment asserting governmental immunity; the trial court granted the jurisdictional plea. A divided court of appeals reversed, holding that cities have no immunity from suit by the State. ***Held:*** Reversed and the State's claim against the City is dismissed. The City is immune from suit by the State. Generally, a governmental unit is immune from tort liability, unless the Legislature has waived immunity. Given the novelty of this suit, the political nature of all the parties, and the sensitivity of these intergovernmental issues, the decision as to who should bear responsibility for governmental employees' misconduct should be made by the peoples' representatives. The Court does not defer to the Legislature to decide whether immunity exists; it is a common-law, court-created doctrine. Rather, the Court decides to defer to the Legislature, to decide whether and to what extent that immunity should be waived. Home-rule cities, like Galveston, derive their powers from the Texas Constitution, not the Legislature. They have all the powers of the state not inconsistent with the Constitution, the general laws, or the city's charter. Among those powers is immunity from suit for governmental functions. The State has the power to waive immunity from suit for cities, but no authority to do so without the Legislature's clear and unambiguous consent. There is no such authority here.

2. *Christi Bay Temple v. GuideOne Specialty Mut. Ins. Co.*, 330 S.W.3d 251 (Tex. 2010): Corpus Bay Temple of Corpus Christi, Texas, is a member church of the Pentecostal Church of God. Operating as an unincorporated religious association, the trustees of the church acquired title to property for its ministry in 1976. This property sustained water damages in 2001. Guide One insured the property at the time of the loss. Although GuideOne accepted coverage, the church was ultimately dissatisfied with the adjustment of its claims and sued for additional damages. GuideOne denied that it owned any more money, and filed a plea in abatement, challenging the church's capacity to sue. In this plea, GuideOne averred that the church was, in fact, a non-profit corporation that had forfeited its charter years earlier and thus, lack capacity to sue or, for that matter, even contract for insurance. The trial court granted the plea in abatement, and dismissed for want of prosecution, after the church failed to cure the problem. The court of appeals affirmed finding not abuse of discretion. Reversed and remanded. An unincorporated association organized for nonbusiness purposes generally has the legal capacity to sue and be sued in its assumed name. One challenging capacity has the burden of proof and as there was no evidence that the church lacked capacity, the courts below erred.

2. *Joinder of Parties*

Read Rules 38-41 Texas Rules of Civil Procedure.

Note

Under prior laws, parties were divided into proper, necessary, indispensable, conditionally necessary, or insistible. The failure to join an indispensable party was considered jurisdictional and a matter of fundamental error, that could be raised for the first time on appeal. *Shields v. Barrow,* 7 How. 130, 15 L.Ed. 158 (1854); *Petroleum Anchor Equipment, Inc. v. Tyra,* 406 S.W.2d 891 (Tex. 1966). A strong procedural reform movement lead to the amendment of, first, the Federal Rules, *Provident Tradesmens Bank & Trust Co. v. Patterson,* 390 U. S. 102 (1968), and then, in 1971, of the Texas Rules. *Cooper v. Texas Gulf Industries*, 513 S.W.2d 200 (Tex. 1974), shows that there are few, if any, indispensable parties, under the new rules. The absence of parties is no longer fundamental error, except in the most rare of cases. Defendants are powerless to make additional parties plaintiff. The defendant may, however, by plea in abatement urge the omission of an indispensable party or a party to be joined if feasible.

PROVIDENT TRADESMENS BANK & TRUST CO.
v.
PATTERSON
390 U.S.118-119
(1968)

The case involved a multiple party accident. Dutcher is a potential defendant, who was not joined. Dutcher owed the car, which was driven by Cionci, to whom Dutcher had given the keys. The Ps (estate of Lynch) got a judgment against Cionci. Dutcher's insurance company (Lumberman's Mutual) had refused to defend Cionci. Cionci had settled with Lynch's estate (Provident Tradesmen's Bank is the administrator of the estate of Lynch, a passenger in the car driven by Cionci). Ps brought this declaratory judgment action against Lumberman's and the Estate Cionci (Patterson is the administrator). Dutcher was not joined as a party, because to do so would destroy diversity. No objection was made to the failure to join Dutcher. In the district court, Dutcher couldn't testify about whether he had given permission or not, because his testimony was barred by the dead man's Rule, so it was presumed that he had given Cionci permission to drive the car. On appeal, the Third Circuit held that Dutcher was an indispensable party.

The Supreme Court held that Dutcher was not an indispensable party. The category of indispensable party is rejected, as a matter of substantive law, and treated as a fact specific question, requiring that the court determine factually that the situation is such that it cannot proceed without the party. Failure to join a party under Fed, R. P. 19 is not really a jurisdictional matter, in as much as the court does have subject matter jurisdiction over the action before it. What is involved is a question of whether the court should decline to adjudicate the dispute because certain persons are absent. In making the decision of whether to proceed without the missing party, the appellate court should Party. consider:

(1) the fact that the case has been tried without objection concerning the non-joinder of a party [At the appellate stage there is reason not to throw away a judgment, just because it did not theoretically settle the whole controversy];
(2) the extent to which an absent party may be prejudiced;
(3) the extent to which protective provisions may be made in the judgment; and
(4) whether in equity and good conscience the action should proceed, or be dismissed.

COOPER
v.
TEXAS GULF INDUS.

513 S.W.2d 200
(Tex. 1974)

J. Leonard Gotsdiner and Ranseler O. Wyatt, Houston, for petitioners.
Baer, Cryan, Keen & Kelly, Melvin R. Wilcox, III and Ralph A. Keen, Houston, for respondents.

JOHNSON, JUSTICE.

Petitioners Dr. Griffin Cooper and his wife, Dolores, appeal from summary judgment that they take nothing in a suit for cancellation and rescission of a sale of real estate to them by Texas Gulf Industries, Inc. (T.G.I.). Cooper and his wife sued T.G.I. on September 28, 1971 alleging fraud as ground for rescission and cancellation of the sale. T.G.I. moved for summary judgment asserting Dr. Cooper previously filed a suit on December 29, 1970, which suit was dismissed with prejudice on January 29, 1971, and that such dismissal with prejudice was res judicata of the instant action. The trial court granted T.G.I.'s motion for summary judgment that plaintiffs take nothing and the court of civil appeals affirmed. 495 S.W.2d 273. We reverse and remand.

In the prior suit filed December 29, 1970 Dr. Cooper was the sole plaintiff. He sought to terminate a management contract on the property at issue and alternatively sought to rescind the sale of the property. The trial court dismissed the first suit "with prejudice."

The Coopers argue that dismissal of the prior suit with prejudice is not res judicata of the instant suit because Dolores Cooper, being a grantee along with her husband in the deed to the real estate at issue, was a necessary party to a suit to cancel and rescind the sale. Accordingly, the Coopers assert, the trial court had no jurisdiction in the prior case and the judgment of dismissal with prejudice is invalid.

A decision on whether a wife is an indispensable party in an action which concerns her joint community property necessitates (1) a study of the Texas Family Code, Section 5.22 (1971), to determine the nature of the community property, (2) a reexamination of the rule that a husband can act for and represent his wife in an action concerning their joint community property under the doctrine of virtual representation, and (3) a discussion of the application of Rule 39, as amended, Texas Rules of Civil Procedure (1971), concerning the joinder of parties.

THE NATURE OF THE COMMUNITY PROPERTY

T.G.I. says in its brief that the property in question is community property and the record bears this out. Both Coopers were named in the deed to the property in question and both signed a deed of trust executed in favor of T.G.I. Insofar as can be ascertained, both Coopers were obligated also on the notes given as consideration. Part of the consideration was payment of $45,000 in cash; the record does not reveal the source of these funds. Under Section 5.02, Texas Family Code (Supp. 1971), property possessed by either spouse during marriage is presumed to be community property. In light of this presumption, and the absence of contrary evidence in the record, the court adopts T.G.I.'s statement that the property involved is community.

Under Section 5.22 community property falls into two categories with respect to management: Sole management community property and Joint management community property. On the basis of the record before us, the court must assume that the property is subject to joint management. Section 5.24 says, "(d)uring marriage, property is presumed to be subject to the sole management, control, and disposition of a spouse If it is held in his or her name. . . ." (Emphasis added.) All of the evidence, as noted above, indicates joint ownership of and joint liability for the property in question.

THE DOCTRINE OF VIRTUAL REPRESENTATION

One of the basic questions in this case is whether Dr. Cooper, in bringing the first suit without the joinder of his wife, acted as a representative of the community; whether he 'virtually represented' his wife in that action. If the doctrine has vitality, the dismissal with prejudice of that first suit would be binding upon the wife, Mrs. Dolores Cooper, and res judicata as to the second and instant suit. * * *

Dolores Cooper was not a party to the first suit; the doctrine of virtual representation was abolished by the new Family Code; there was no writing authorizing her husband to represent her. Accordingly, her interest in the Coopers' joint management community property is untouched by the judgment of dismissal with prejudice of the first suit.

THE JOINDER OF PARTIES

Having determined that the wife was not virtually represented by her husband, a second question is urged for consideration: was Dolores Cooper an indispensable party in the first suit? Under the traditional view, if she was an indispensable party, the judgment in the first suit would be invalid and not res judicata as to either of the Coopers; if she was not an indispensable party, then the judgment would be binding on Dr. Cooper since he was a party, although still not binding on Mrs. Cooper. *Petroleum Anchor Equipment, Inc. v. Tyra*, 406 S.W.2d 891 (Tex. 1966).

Amended Rule 39, however, initiated an entirely new method for resolving the question of joinder of parties. Amended Rule 39, effective January 1, 1971, is almost an exact copy by Texas of Federal Rule 19, Federal Rules of Civil Procedure, which is also of recent origin, having been adopted in 1966.

Prior to the amendment to Rule 39, Texas resolved questions of joinder of parties by efforts to catalogue parties as "proper," "necessary," "indispensable," "conditionally necessary," or "insistible." Typical of that approach is this court's preamendment opinion in *Petroleum Anchor Equipment, Inc. v. Tyra, supra*, where it is stated: "It is at once apparent that the 'necessary' parties of which the rule speaks fall into two categories: (1) those who under the paragraph (a) 'shall be made parties,' and (2) those who under paragraph (b) 'ought to be parties if complete relief is to be accorded between those already parties.' It is also at once apparent that 'persons having a joint interest' within the meaning of paragraph (a), properly interpreted, are indispensable parties, but that those who simply ought to be joined if complete relief is to be accorded between those already parties are not indispensable. The rule expressly confers discretion upon trial courts to proceed without joinder of persons in the second category if jurisdiction over them can be acquired only by their consent or voluntary appearance. If joinder of such persons is discretionary, their joinder cannot be essential to jurisdiction of a court to proceed to judgment." 406 S.W.2d 891 at 893.

That historical and classical approach to the joinder of parties has now been wholly replaced. The reasons and legal literature which impelled the adoption of the new approach are well summarized in 7 C. WRIGHT & A. MILLER, FEDERAL PRACTICE AND PROCEDURE § 1601 (1972). One of the aims of the revised rule was to avoid questions of jurisdiction. The text states:

> "in addition to the failure of many courts to articulate satisfactory bases of decision prior to 1966, the Advisory Committee referred to other defects in the original version of Rule 19. Paramount among these was a problem of 'jurisdiction' that arose in connection with the concept of indispensable parties. The Committee felt that the rule's (original) wording suggested that the absence of an indispensable party 'itself deprived the court of the power to adjudicate as between the parties already joined.' As is discussed in another section, failure to join a party under Rule 19 is not really a jurisdictional matter inasmuch as the court does have subject matter jurisdiction over the action before it; what is involved is a question of whether the court should decline to adjudicate the dispute because certain persons are absent. The present language of Rule 19(a) and Rule 19(b) should help eliminate this confusion." *And see* C. WRIGHT, LAW OF FEDERAL COURTS § 70 at 298-99 (2d ed. 1970).

Contrary to our emphasis under Rule 39 before it was amended, today's concern is less that of the jurisdiction of a court to proceed and is more a question of whether the court ought to proceed with those who are present. *Rippey v. Denver United States National Bank*, 42 F.R.D. 316 (D. Colo. 1967). The United States Supreme Court provides a helpful discussion of the objectives sought by its amended Rule 19 in *Provident Tradesmens Bank & Trust v. Patterson*, 390 U.S. 102, 88 S.Ct. 733, 19 L.Ed.2d 936 (1968). One of the practical factors the court took into consideration in holding that an absent party was not jurisdictionally indispensable was the fact that the case had actually been tried as to those parties who were present and there was no objection at the trial level concerning the nonjoinder of a party. As expressed in *Continental Insurance Co. of New York v. Cotten*, 427 F.2d 48, 51 (9th Cir. 1970), "at the appellate stage there is reason not to throw away a judgment just because it did not theoretically settle the whole controversy."

The amended rule includes practical considerations within the rule itself, including the extent to which an absent party may be prejudiced, the extent to which protective provisions may be made in the judgment, and whether in equity and good conscience the action should proceed or be dismissed. The factors mentioned in the rule which a judge may consider are not exclusive. *Provident Tradesmens Bank & Trust Company v. Patterson, supra; Bixby v. Bixby*, 50 F.R.D. 277 (S.D.Ill.1970); 7 C. WRIGHT & A. MILLER, FEDERAL PRACTICE AND PROCEDURE, *supra*, at 14. As expressed in *Schutten v. Shell Oil Co.*, 421 F.2d 869, 874 (5th Cir. 1970); "(t)he watchwords of Rule 19 are 'pragmatism' and 'practicality.' The court must, however, always consider the possibility of shaping a decree in order to adjudicate between the parties who have been joined."

Under the provisions of our present Rule 39 it would be rare indeed if there were a person whose presence was so indispensable in the sense that his absence deprives the court of jurisdiction to adjudicate between the parties already joined. Although not of controlling importance, the very title of the rule has been changed from "Necessary Joinder of Parties" to "Joinder of Persons Needed for Just Adjudication." Subdivision (a) provides that certain persons "shall be joined," but there is no arbitrary standard or precise formula for determining whether a particular person falls within its provisions. It is clear, moreover, that the persons described in the subdivision are to be joined only if subject to service of process. When such a person cannot be made a party, the court is required to determine "whether in equity and good conscience the action should proceed among the parties before it, or should be dismissed."

Under the foregoing analysis of Rule 39 we determine that the named parties in the first suit, Dr. Cooper and T.G.I., were properly before the court for the resolution of the issues between them; that the judgment of dismissal with prejudice resolved those issues and is necessarily res judicata as to the claims of Dr. Cooper in the second and instant suit; that the judgment of dismissal is not res judicata, however, with respect to the rights and claims of Mrs. Dolores Cooper; and finally, that the judgment of dismissal is conclusive as to Dr. Cooper except to the extent that it might have to be disregarded in giving Mrs. Cooper all the relief to which she may show herself entitled.

The judgments of the courts below are reversed and the cause remanded to the trial court for further proceedings consistent with this opinion.

WALKER, J., concurring, in which GREENHILL, C.J., joins [opinion omitted].

Notes

1. Apparently a "rare circumstance" exists in partition litigation. A party's absence from a partition proceeding has been held to deprive the court of jurisdiction. Thus, an attempted partition of a tract of land, where all the owners are not joined as parties, is not binding, even on those who are parties. *See Ward v. Hinkle*, 117 Tex. 566, 8 S.W.2d 641 (1928); *Mustang Drilling, Inc. v. Cobb*, 815 S.W.2d 774 (Tex. App.—Texarkana 1991, writ denied).

2. Failure to join a party under FED. R. P. 19 & TEX. R CIV. P. 39 is not really a jurisdictional matter, in as much as the court does have subject matter jurisdiction over the action before it. What is involved is a question of whether the court should decline to adjudicate the dispute because certain persons are absent. In making the decision of whether to proceed without the missing party, the appellate court should, as outlined in *Provident Tradesmens Bank & Trust Co. v. Patterson,* 390 U. S. 102 (1968) consider:

a. the fact that the case has been tried without objection concerning the non-joinder of a party [at the appellate stage there is reason not to throw away a judgment, just because it did not theoretically settle the whole controversy];

b. the extent to which an absent party may be prejudiced;

c. the extent to which protective provisions may be made in the judgment; and

d. whether in equity and good conscience the action should proceed, or be dismissed.

3. Section 1.105 of the Family Code provides that:

a. A spouse may sue and be sued without the joinder of the other spouse.

b. When claims or liabilities are joint and several, the spouses may be joined under the rule relating to joinder of parties generally.

4. *Geneva Brooks v. Northglen Association*, 141 S.W.3d 158 (Tex. 2004): The trial court did not lack subject matter jurisdiction, because Brooks did not join all Northglen property owners as parties in a suit to challenge additional assessments by the Homeowners Association. Northglen did not raise the issue either in the trial court or the court of appeals. *Held*: The absence of parties, within the represented sections of the subdivision, did not deprive the court of jurisdiction over those parties who were joined. TEX. R. CIV. P. 39(a)(1) requires the presence of all persons who have an interest in the litigation, so that any relief awarded will effectively and completely adjudicate the dispute. In this case, nothing in the rule precluded the trial court from rendering complete relief among Northglen and the eight homeowners who had sued for a declaration of rights. Although the parties continue to litigate its correctness, the trial court's judgment represents a final and complete adjudication of the dispute for the parties who were before the court. There is a risk that, unless each homeowner is joined in one suit, Northglen may be subject to inconsistent judgments. Northglen's dilemma, however, is the product of its own inaction in failing to urge the court to abate the case, join absent homeowners, or grant special exceptions. The trial court properly entered judgment even though a subset of the homeowners was not joined in the lawsuit. TEX. R. CIV. P. 39, like the Declaratory Judgment Act, mandates joinder of persons whose interests would be affected by the judgment. There was no objection to the failure to join the missing subset of homeowners, and the omission was not fundamental error. It will be rare indeed when an appellate court properly determines that the trial court lacked jurisdiction to adjudicate a dispute when the nonjoining person's absence is raised for the first time on appeal by one of the parties in the trial court, at least insofar as the judgment affects parties who participated in the trial, directly or indirectly, or who purposely bypassed the proceedings. The doctrine of fundamental error should no longer protect persons from the binding force of judgments when they have had an opportunity to raise the absence of the nonjoined person and waived it.

Notes

Perryman v. Spartan Texas Six Capital Partners Ltd., 546 S.W.3d 110 (Tex. 2018): TEX. CIV. PROC. 38(a) makes clear that if a plaintiff wishes to bring a claim against a third-party defendant, that claim must arise out of the transaction or occurrence forming the basis of the plaintiff's claim against the original defendant. This limitation prevents plaintiffs from gaming the system to avoid strictures such as venue by waiting until a defendant joins a third-party before the plaintiff asserts a claim against him.

RUTHART
v.
FIRST STATE BANK

431 S.W.2d 366
(Tex. Civ. App—Amarillo 1968, writ ref'd)

Sanders, Scott, Saunders, Brian & Humphrey, C. J. Humphrey, Amarillo, of counsel, for appellant.
Morehead, Sharp, Boyd & Tisdel, Joe Sharp, Plainview, of counsel, for appellee.

DENTON, CHIEF JUSTICE.

This is a suit to recover on a promissory note executed by Garland E. Ruthart payable to the First State Bank, Tulia, Texas. Both parties filed motions for summary judgment. The trial court granted the bank's motion for summary judgment against the defendant below who has timely perfected this appeal.

From the pleadings, affidavits and stipulations it is uncontradicted the defendant below, Garland E. Ruthart, an employee of R.A.R., Inc., executed a promissory note in the amount of $3,766.68 payable in 36 monthly installments to First State Bank, Tulia, Texas on April 14, 1966. The face amount of the note included principal, interest and the premium on a credit life insurance policy on the life of Ruthart with the bank being the beneficiary. The bank upon the execution of the note delivered a $3,000.00 cashier's check to Ruthart payable to R.A.R., Inc. Ruthart then delivered the cashier's check to an officer of the corporation who simultaneously issued Ruthart 150 shares of the corporation's common stock. Ruthart then assigned this stock to the bank as collateral for the loan. R.A.R., Inc. cashed the check and received the proceeds thereof. All these transactions took place in the office of the appellee bank at one meeting between appellant, R.A.R., Inc. officers and officers of the bank. Some 14 other employees of R.A.R., Inc. entered into similar transactions at the same meeting, and acquired various amounts of stock of the corporation. Demand was made upon appellant's note after he became delinquent after paying three monthly installments.

Appellant first complains the trial court erred in overruling his motion to consolidate eleven other cases filed by appellee against other employees of R.A.R., Inc.; and its refusal to make the officers and directors of R.A.R., Inc. third party defendants. It is well settled that the Rules of Civil Procedure grant the trial court broad discretion in the matter of consolidation of causes. Rule 174, Texas Rules of Civil Procedure and *Hamilton v. Hamilton*, 154 Tex. 511, 280 S.W.2d 588 and *Wilson v. Ammann & Jordan* (Tex. Civ. App.) 163 S.W.2d 660 (error dism'd) and *McKinney v. Gaiser* (Tex. Civ. App.) 366 S.W.2d 268 (ref'd n.r.e.). The trial court's action in such procedural matters will not be disturbed on appeal except for abuse of discretion, *Womack v. Berry*, 156 Tex. 44, 291 S.W.2d 677 and *Rose v. Baker*, 143 Tex. 202, 183 S.W.2d 438. Each suit sought to be consolidated with the instant case was a separate and distinct cause of action against different defendants. The fact that all the causes relate to promissory notes is not persuasive. Although the pleadings of the other cases are not a part of this record, it is apparent different questions of fact and law are quite likely to be presented. A denial of the motion to consolidate was clearly not an abuse of discretion.

Appellant sought under Rule 38, T.R.C.P. to make the officers and directors of R.A.R., Inc. third party defendants. As in other such procedural matters the trial court is clothed with considerable discretionary authority. *Hamilton v. Hamilton, supra; Nutter v. Dearing* (Tex. Civ. App.) 400 S.W.2d 346 (error ref'd n.r.e., 402 S.W.2d 889). Appellant argues the R.A.R., Inc. officers who made the financial arrangements for the several note makers with the bank, would be liable to each note maker in the event of recovery by the bank against them; and that the proposed third party defendants should be impleaded for their participation in the alleged fraudulent transaction. This is simply a suit on a promissory note, admittedly executed by appellant who concedes he received the $3,000.00 for which he executed the note. The fact such consideration was paid directly over to R.A.R., Inc. whose stock was simultaneously transferred to appellant and was given as collateral, is no defense. *Kliesing v. Neuhaus* (Tex. Civ. App.) 265 S.W.2d 215. The alleged cause of action of appellee against appellant is separate and distinct from that alleged by appellant against the proposed third party defendants. Nor can it be said appellant's alleged cause of action against the proposed third party defendants would constitute a defense to appellee's suit on the promissory note executed by appellant. Appellant's contention is without merit.

* * *

The judgment of the trial court is affirmed.

TRUEHEART
v.
BRASELTON
875 S.W.2d 412
(Tex. App.—Corpus Christi 1994, no writ)

Summary: While leave of court is required for a third party action not filed within thirty days after the service of the original answer, the plaintiff may waive the right to object, or may lose it by laches.

Facts: Plaintiff-Trueheart sued the Defendants-Braseltons in 1988 to collect on a note. The defendants filed a third party action against Sanghavi in 1990, without first having obtained leave of court. After Sanghavi failed to answer, an interlocutory default judgment was entered. Plaintiff moves to strike the third-party action, even though he did not object to the filing of the action.

Issue: Is leave of court required for the filing of a third party action? Not if done within thirty days, but it is required thereafter.

Issue: When leave of court is required (after thirty days), is it fatal if leave is not obtained? No. The opponent waives objection to the requirement of obtaining leave of court by failing to timely object. Trial courts have broad discretion in matters such as party joinder.

FORD MOTOR CO.
v.
GARCIA
363 S.W.3d 573
(Tex. 2012)

Craig A. Morgan, Austin, Michael W. Eady, Jaime A. Saenz, Joseph A. "Tony" Rodriguez, Rodriguez, Colvin, Chaney & Saenz, L.L.P., Brownsville, Barry Clark Toone, for Ford Motor Company.

Isaac Joel Tawil, Garcia Quintanilla & Palacios, McAllen, for Richard H. Garcia.

Robert E. Ammons, for other interested party Adelita Gonzales.

JUSTICE JOHNSON delivered the opinion of the Court.

This is a dispute over fees awarded to an ad litem appointed in connection with the proposed division of a personal injury settlement between an incapacitated plaintiff and his guardian. The court-appointed attorney requested fees based on an unsworn invoice that specified numerous tasks performed, but did not specify when they were performed, who performed them or the amount of time spent on them. The ad litem testified about who performed some of the tasks, but he did not testify about how much time was spent on the tasks, other than specifying that a minimum of one-quarter hour was invoiced for each one, nor did he testify about any unusual circumstances that made it necessary for persons other than him to perform tasks for which compensation was sought. The trial court awarded the full amount requested and assessed the fees as court costs. The court of appeals affirmed. We reverse the judgment of the court of appeals and remand the case to the trial court for further proceedings.

I. Background

Jesus Gonzalez was a passenger in a Ford pickup when a tire tread separated and the truck rolled over. The driver was killed and Gonzalez suffered an incapacitating brain injury. Several plaintiffs sued multiple defendants as a result of the accident. Relevant to the issues before us, Gonzalez's wife, Ramona, sued Ford Motor Company individually and as guardian of her husband. After the Gonzalezes and Ford reached a confidential settlement agreement, their attorney filed an "Unopposed Motion for Appointment of Guardian Ad Litem" for Gonzalez because of the conflict of interest between the Gonzalezes regarding division of the settlement. Pursuant to that motion, the trial court appointed attorney Richard Garcia. Garcia concluded that the agreed-upon division of the settlement between Ramona and Gonzalez should be approved by the court, and the court did so.

Ford and Garcia were unable to agree on a fee for his services, so the trial court held a hearing. At the hearing Garcia produced an unverified invoice for $28,260.00 and requested that amount as compensation. The invoice listed sixty-five separate tasks that were completed from December 9, 2008, when Garcia was appointed, to December 19, 2008, when the settlement with Ford was approved. The invoice did not set out who performed the tasks, the dates on which the tasks were performed, the time expended on any task, or a total amount of time spent on all of the tasks. Garcia testified, in relevant part, that (1) his billing rate for this matter was $300.00 per hour, (2) he performed most of the invoiced tasks but not all of them, (3) he did not know how much time it took to perform each invoiced task, and (4) he billed in quarter-hour increments. The trial court awarded the full $28,260.00 and charged the fee to Ford as court costs. The court of appeals affirmed. 363 S.W.3d 618. We granted Ford's petition for review. 54 Tex.Sup.Ct.J. 1578 (Aug. 26, 2011).

Ford argues that Garcia was appointed as a guardian ad litem subject to Rule 173 of the Texas Rules of Civil Procedure; the fee award compensates him for tasks not within the scope of his limited role as guardian ad litem; and even as to tasks within the scope of his limited role, there is neither evidence of how much time was spent on them nor who performed them. Garcia counters that he was appointed as attorney ad litem, not guardian ad litem; as attorney ad litem he was entitled to be compensated for services he performed individually as well as services he was assisted with by "his staff including other lawyers;" and his invoice and testimony were sufficient evidence of reasonableness and necessity to support the compensation award whether he was functioning as an attorney ad litem or guardian ad litem.

We first address the nature of Garcia's role.

II. Garcia's Role

Relying on *City of Houston v. Woods,* 138 S.W.3d 574, 582 (Tex. App.—Houston [14th Dist.] 2004, no pet.), Garcia contends the fee award is proper because the trial court's appointment order states he was appointed "to serve as Attorney Ad Litem in this litigation as independent counsel for the benefit of Plaintiff Jesus Gonzalez in connection with effectuating Plaintiffs' settlement with Defendant Ford Motor Company." Working from that premise, he maintains that he was properly compensated both for "his services in fulfilling his role as independent counsel to the ward, and his role as an officer and advisor to the trial court." He cites *Woods* for the proposition that an attorney ad litem is to "perform the same services as any attorney, giving legal advice, doing research and conducting litigation for an incapacitated party," and that all the activities on his invoice were proper because they were directed toward determining both whether (1) the proposed settlement was generally appropriate for Gonzalez and (2) the division and structure of the settlement was appropriate given the conflict of interest between Gonzalez and Ramona. We disagree that Garcia was entitled to be compensated for tasks that were not compensable as a guardian ad litem under Rule 173, even though some of those tasks might have been compensable had he truly been appointed as attorney ad litem.

First, *Woods,* a case involving fees for representation of minors, does not support his position. Garcia references only part of a passage in *Woods* in which the court of appeals distinguished the role of a guardian ad litem from that of an attorney ad litem. The full passage gives context to the statement on which he relies:

> Guardian ad litems and attorney ad litems serve different roles in the representation of minors. A guardian ad litem is not an attorney for the child, but an officer appointed by the court to assist in properly protecting the child's interests. An attorney ad litem, on the other hand, performs the same services as any other attorney—giving advice, doing research, and conducting litigation.

Id. at 582 (citations omitted). The court also noted that the source of fees for attorneys ad litem is different from that for guardians ad litem:

> A guardian ad litem is entitled to a reasonable fee for his services to be taxed as costs . . . . However, there is no provision to tax attorney fees as costs to the opposing party. Indeed, attorney fees may not be recovered unless provided for by statute or by contract between the parties. More specifically, no statute provides for the recovery of attorney fees in a negligence action. Instead, attorneys in personal injury cases are compensated out of the funds recovered by the plaintiff on a contingency basis.

Id. at 582-83 (citations omitted). Although attorneys representing personal injury plaintiffs in negligence suits are not always compensated on a contingency fee basis as the *Woods* court suggested, the court was correct that while a guardian ad litem's fee may be taxed as court costs pursuant to the rules of procedure, *see, e.g.*, TEX.R. CIV. P. 173.6(c), there is no provision for shifting a plaintiff's attorney's fee to the defendant absent a statute or contract allowing for shifting them. *See 1/2 Price Checks Cashed v. United Auto. Ins. Co.,* 344 S.W.3d 378, 382 (Tex. 2011) ("Texas adheres to the American Rule for the award of attorney's fees, under which attorney's fees are recoverable in a suit only if permitted by statute or by contract."). Here, Garcia does not base his claim for attorney's fees on either a statute or contract. And in *Woods,* the court of appeals held that the trial court abused its discretion by assessing attorney ad litem fees as costs to be paid by the defendant where the attorney represented minor plaintiffs in a negligence suit for personal injuries—the opposite of what Garcia contends for here. 138 S.W.3d at 583.

Second, a guardian ad litem's duties under the circumstances covered by Rule 173 are those of an officer of the court assisting in properly protecting the incapacitated person's interests when a conflict of interest has arisen between the incapacitated person and the guardian or next friend. The duty of such a guardian ad litem is not the duty of a plaintiff's attorney generally representing the incapacitated person in regard to the cause of action. *See Land Rover U.K., Ltd. v. Hinojosa,* 210 S.W.3d 604, 607 (Tex. 2006) (per curiam) ("[A] guardian ad litem . . . should not duplicate the work performed by the plaintiff's attorney."); *see also Am. Gen. Fire & Cas. Co. v. Vandewater,* 907 S.W.2d 491, 493 n. 2 (Tex. 1995) (per curiam). The context of the appointment and duties assigned to the ad litem determine the nature of the appointment and the duties of the ad litem. The burden to ensure that a guardian ad litem's services do not exceed the scope of the role assigned by the trial court is on the ad litem. *See Goodyear Dunlop Tires N. Am., Ltd. v. Gamez,* 151 S.W.3d 574, 582 (Tex. App.—San Antonio 2004, no pet.). An improper designation of the ad litem by the trial court is not controlling as to the nature of the appointment. *See Brownsville-Valley Reg. Med. Ctr., Inc. v. Gamez,* 894 S.W.2d 753, 755 n. 4 (Tex. 1995) ("The trial court's improper designation of the ad litem 'is not of controlling import.' ") (citation omitted).

Garcia does not claim that he was appointed because Ramona, acting as Gonzalez's guardian, and the attorney she hired, failed to properly represent Gonzalez's interests and Gonzalez needed a separate attorney to prosecute his personal injury claim. *See Vandewater,* 907 S.W.2d at 493 n. 2 ("In the event that the next friend takes actions sufficiently adverse to a [ward's] interests, the next friend and her attorney may be replaced."). To the contrary, Garcia's appointment was requested only after Ramona and her attorney reached a settlement with Ford that was to be divided between the Gonzalezes, and the necessity of the division created a conflict. A division was tentatively agreed upon before Ramona's lawyer filed the unopposed motion for appointment of an ad litem to "assist [Jesus Gonzalez] with the issues relating to effectuating the settlement of his claims against Ford Motor Company." The motion used the term attorney ad litem in one sentence, but as the caption and body of the motion made clear, the trial court was being asked to appoint an ad litem only to protect Jesus's interest in relation to division of the settlement. The trial court order stated that Garcia was appointed "to serve as Attorney Ad Litem in this litigation as independent counsel for the benefit of Plaintiff Jesus Gonzalez *in connection with effectuating Plaintiffs' settlement with Defendant Ford Motor Company.*" (emphasis added). The judgment awarding fees to Garcia stated that he was appointed as guardian ad litem. And Garcia's testimony at the evidentiary hearing on his compensation request confirmed his understanding that the appointment was as a guardian ad litem, not attorney ad litem:

> Q. Mr. Garcia, you are the same Judge Richard Garcia that was appointed by this Honorable Court as guardian ad litem for an incapacitated person in the proceeding that we're here on today? That would be Jesus Gonzalez?
>
> A. That's correct.

The evidence is conclusive that Garcia was not appointed to act as an attorney ad litem to generally represent Gonzalez in prosecuting his personal injury claim. Rather, he was appointed as a guardian ad litem with the limited role of assisting the trial court in protecting Gonzalez's interest because of the conflict of interest that arose between the Gonzalezes. The appointment substantively falls within the provisions of Rule 173 of the Texas Rules of Civil Procedure. Garcia's contention that his compensation request should be reviewed differently from the manner provided for by Rule 173 lacks merit.

III. The Fees

The trial court awarded Garcia $28,260.00. Ford challenges the amount for three related reasons. First, some of the activities on the invoice were admittedly performed by persons other than Garcia and the court order appointed only Garcia as ad litem. Second, there is no evidence of how much time was spent performing each invoiced task, so there is no evidence of either how much time is compensable for individual tasks or how much total time is compensable. Third, even if there had been evidence to show which of the invoiced activities Garcia individually performed and how long they took, compensation cannot be awarded for many of those tasks because they were not necessary given the purpose of his appointment.

A. Standard of Review

The amount a guardian ad litem is awarded as compensation is within the trial court's discretion and an award will not be set aside except for abuse of that discretion. *See Land Rover U.K.*, 210 S.W.3d at 607. A trial court abuses its discretion by ruling (1) arbitrarily, unreasonably, or without regard to guiding legal principles; or (2) without supporting evidence. *See Bocquet v. Herring,* 972 S.W.2d 19, 21 (Tex. 1998).

B. Rule 173 Guardian Appointments

When construing rules of procedure, we apply the same rules of construction that govern the interpretation of statutes. *In re Christus Spohn Hosp. Kleberg,* 222 S.W.3d 434, 437 (Tex. 2007). We first look to the plain language of the rule and construe it according to its plain or literal meaning. *See, e.g., In re E.A.*, 287 S.W.3d 1, 5 (Tex. 2009). In doing so we keep in mind that the rules of civil procedure are given a liberal construction so as "to obtain a just, fair, equitable and impartial adjudication of the rights of litigants under established principles of substantive law." TEX.R. CIV. P. 1.

When a guardian ad litem is appointed under circumstances covered by Rule 173, as opposed to other rules or statutes, the guardian has a limited role in the litigation and may be compensated only for limited types of activities. *See* TEX.R. CIV. P. 173.4(b), (c), (d); *Vandewater,* 907 S.W.2d at 493 n. 2. Garcia's role falls under Rule 173.4(c) which provides:

> (c) *When Settlement Proposed.* When an offer has been made to settle the claim of a party represented by a next friend or guardian, a guardian ad litem has the limited duty to determine and advise the court whether the settlement is in the party's best interest.

TEX.R. CIV. P. 173.4(c). The rule contemplates appointment of a guardian ad litem "when a party's next friend or guardian appears to have an interest adverse to the party because of the division of settlement proceeds." TEX.R. CIV. P. 173 cmt. 3. The comments to Rule 173 elaborate on the guardian's role and compensation under those circumstances:

> [T]he responsibility of the guardian ad litem as prescribed by the rule is very limited, and no reason exists for the guardian ad litem to participate in the conduct of the litigation in any other way or to review the discovery or the litigation file except to the limited extent that it may bear on the division of settlement proceeds. A guardian ad litem may, of course, choose to review the file or attend proceedings when it is unnecessary, but the guardian ad litem may not be compensated for unnecessary expenses or services.

Id. (citation omitted). Not all Rule 173 guardians ad litem seek compensation, but for those who do, Rule 173.6 prescribes how compensation is to be determined:

> 173.6. Compensation
>
> (a) *Amount.* If a guardian ad litem requests compensation, he or she may be reimbursed for reasonable and necessary expenses incurred and may be paid a reasonable hourly fee for necessary services performed.
>
> (b) *Procedure.* At the conclusion of the appointment, a guardian ad litem may file an application for compensation. The application must be verified and must detail the basis for the compensation requested. Unless all parties agree to the application, the court must conduct an evidentiary hearing to determine the total amount of fees and expenses that are reasonable and necessary. In making this determination, the court must not consider compensation as a percentage of any judgment or settlement.
>
> (c) *Taxation as Costs.* The court may tax a guardian ad litem's compensation as costs of court.

TEX.R. CIV. P. 173.6(a)-(c).

We stated in *Land Rover U.K.* that "[a] reasonable hourly rate multiplied by the number of hours spent performing necessary services within the guardian ad litem's role yields a reasonable fee." 210 S.W.3d at 608. While necessary services within the proper, limited scope of the Rule 173 guardian ad litem's role are compensable, including those legal services necessarily performed by a lawyer appointed as guardian ad litem, compensation cannot be awarded for legal or other services outside that role, even if they are performed. *See* TEX.R. CIV. P. 173.4 (defining the role of a guardian ad litem); *Land Rover U.K.,* 210 S.W.3d at 607 ("If a guardian ad litem performs work beyond the scope of this role, such work is non-compensable."). Ordinarily only the person appointed as guardian ad litem should be compensated for services under Rule 173. *See* TEX.R. CIV. P. 173.6 & 173 cmt. 7; *Gamez,* 151 S.W.3d at 588. However, Rule 173.6 does not preclude awarding compensation for persons other than the person designated in the trial court's order as guardian ad litem if the evidence shows particular, unusual circumstances making services of other persons necessary for the ad litem's duties to be fulfilled. Such circumstances might exist, for example, if paralegals or other staff under the supervision of the appointed guardian ad litem could perform tasks necessary for the ad litem to properly fulfill his or her appointed role, but at a lesser hourly rate than the ad litem, or an unexpected emergency requires the guardian ad litem to miss a mandatory hearing and an associated attorney familiar with the matter appears instead. *See, e.g.,* TEX.R. CIV. P. 173.4(d)(2). But if a guardian ad litem such as Garcia seeks compensation for activities of persons not authorized in advance by the trial court to act on behalf of the incapacitated person, he or she should identify the persons with particularity and prove the particular, unusual circumstances making the services of the persons necessary for the ad litem's duties to be fulfilled, the specific services they performed, when the services were performed, the amount of time spent performing the services, the necessity of the services in light of the ad litem's appointment, and a reasonable hourly rate for each person. *See Jocson v. Crabb,* 133 S.W.3d 268, 270 (Tex. 2004) (per curiam) (recognizing that parties would be wise to seek direction from the trial court if they disagree about an ad litem's role, but also recognizing that it could be expensive and disruptive if they had to pursue every disagreement to a hearing). Once that is done the trial court will have evidence on which to determine whether to award compensation for the activities of those persons, and if so, how much.

C. Application

Garcia's invoice and testimony are not legally sufficient evidence to support the amount of compensation he was awarded. First, Garcia was the only person the trial court's order designated to act as Gonzalez's guardian ad litem. His appointment was for a particular, narrow role: protecting Gonzalez's interest in dividing the settlement. *See* TEX.R. CIV. P. 173.4(c). As a guardian ad litem under Rule 173, he was to exercise his independent judgment about the division. That warranted his personal attention to the matter, and ordinarily it would have required only his personal involvement. Garcia does not claim there is evidence of particular, unusual circumstances showing services of other persons were necessary for his ad litem duties to be fulfilled. Even if he did, there is no evidence of who the persons were that performed services, what services they performed, why it was necessary for them to perform the services for Garcia's limited role to be fulfilled, the necessity of the services, the time it took to perform the services, and the reasonable hourly rate for each person.

Garcia admittedly did not perform all of the tasks listed on his invoice, so even if all the tasks were compensable under Rule 173 and the time for each task was proved, matters we address below, there is no evidence to support the amount of compensation awarded to Garcia for having done them. Thus, the evidence is legally insufficient to support the amount he was awarded. The trial court abused its discretion by awarding it, and the court of appeals erred by affirming the award. *See Bocquet,* 972 S.W.2d at 21.

Second, the invoice did not set out the amount of time each task took. Nor did Garcia supply the necessary evidence. . .

* * *

The only evidence of the time spent is Garcia's testimony that he invoiced a minimum of a quarter-hour for each activity, but manifestly, more than a quarter-hour was spent performing some of the activities such as traveling to where the Gonzalezes lived and conferring with them. Although there is evidence that Garcia necessarily spent time in performing his duties as ad litem, the evidence is such that the total number of hours he spent in the representation cannot be calculated on the record before us. Under Rule 173 compensation is to be based on the hours necessarily spent on the representation multiplied by a reasonable hourly fee. TEX.R. CIV. P. 173.6(a)

("If a guardian ad litem requests compensation, he or she may be . . . paid a reasonable hourly fee for necessary services performed."); *Land Rover U.K.,* 210 S.W.3d at 608. The evidence is legally insufficient to support the fees awarded, and the trial court abused its discretion by awarding them. *See Bocquet,* 972 S.W.2d at 21.

* * *

Third, many of the tasks shown on the invoice were not compensable under Rule 173 because they were not necessary to fulfill the limited role to which Garcia was appointed. *See* TEX.R. CIV. P. 173.4 (defining the role of a guardian ad litem); *Land Rover U.K.,* 210 S.W.3d at 607 ("If a guardian ad litem performs work beyond the scope of this role, such work is non-compensable."). Only those tasks directly and materially bearing on the conflict of interest between Ramona and Gonzalez regarding division of the settlement were necessary. Some of the non-compensable tasks demonstrated by this record were "Receiv[ing] and Review[ing]" (1) multiple motions to transfer venue, responses to those, orders setting hearings on the motions and correspondence relating to the motions and responses; (2) superseded petitions; (3) sundry discovery requests and responses; (4) a motion relating to admission of an attorney to practice *pro hac vice;* (5) correspondence about postponed hearings; (6) pleadings relating to already-settled claims; (7) notices of settlement of minor plaintiffs' claims; and (8) copies of citations issued for defendants. Garcia testified, in part, that the activities he performed were for the purpose of becoming familiar with the lawsuit, representing Gonzalez's interests, and advising the court. But tasks such as those enumerated above were not necessary to fulfilling the limited role for which he was appointed. The trial court did not conform to guiding rules and principles when it awarded compensation for non-necessary activities, thus it abused its discretion. *See, e.g.,* TEX.R. CIV. P. 173 & cmts. 3-4, 7; *Land Rover U.K.,* 210 S.W.3d at 607-08. The court of appeals erred by holding otherwise.

IV. Conclusion

The evidence is legally insufficient to support the full amount awarded to Garcia as compensation, although it is sufficient to show he necessarily spent some amount of time fulfilling his role as guardian ad litem. We reverse the judgment of the court of appeals and remand the case to the trial court for further proceedings consistent with this opinion. *See Guevara v. Ferrer,* 247 S.W.3d 662, 669-70 (Tex. 2007) (holding that when there is evidence to support damages other than the full amount awarded in the trial court and an appropriate remittitur could not be determined by the court of appeals, the case will be remanded to the trial court); *accord Wagner & Brown, Ltd. v. Sheppard,* 282 S.W.3d 419, 425, 430 (Tex. 2008) (reversing and remanding to the trial court for a reassessment of damages where there was at least some evidence to support an award of damages).

Notes

1. *Ford Motor Co. v. Stewart, Cox and Hatcher, P.C.*, 390 S.W.3d 294 (Tex. 2013): When there is no apparent conflict between an injured minor and next friend a court may not *sua sponte* appoint a guardian ad litem.

2. *Roberts v. Williamson*, 111 S.W.3d 113 (Tex. 2004): The trial court apportioned the ad litem costs between the plaintiffs and the D-Dr. Roberts, who had been found to be 15% at fault. TEX. R. CIV. P. 131 provides that "[t]he successful party to a suit shall recover of his adversary all costs incurred therein, except where otherwise provided." Rule 141 permits a trial court, for good cause stated on the record, to "adjudge the costs otherwise than as provided by law or [the Rules of Civil Procedure]." The trial court explained that it split the costs because an ad litem is there for the benefit of all parties, and thus, it is "fair" to split costs between the losing and prevailing parties. *Held*: Grounds of perceived fairness, without more, are insufficient to constitute good cause to apportion costs against the winning party. A guardian ad litem does not serve for the benefit of all parties. The guardian is appointed to protect the child's interests. Fairness can be good cause, but the record must substantiate the connection. Here, the trial court's finding of good cause is premised on the perception that the prevailing party incidentally benefited from the guardian ad litem's services. Assuming that such an incidental benefit might, in a particular case, provide good cause, Rule 141 still requires that the trial court state its reasons "on the record" and with more specificity than the court's general notion of fairness here.

3. *Jocson v. Crabb*, 133 S.W.3d 268 (Tex. 2004): Defendants did not waive their objections to the ad litem fees, awarded in this medical malpractice case, by (1) failing to obtain a ruling on objections they lodged to the ad litem's attendance at several depositions, and (2) failing to introduce the ad litem's files. Objections to

ad litem fees are timely if raised at the post-trial fee hearing. Introduction of the ad litem's entire file was unnecessary to preserve the fee objection raised here. Likewise, the defendants did not waive their objections to the ad litem's attendance at depositions by failing to obtain a ruling during the course of discovery. TEX. R. CIV. P. 199.6, the general rule for deposition objections provides "the failure of a party to obtain a ruling prior to trial does not waive any objection or privilege." The Supreme Court concludes that under the facts here the defendants, Hospital and Dr. Jocson, properly preserved their objections for appellate review. The Court also noted that a guardian ad litem is not an attorney for the child, but an officer appointed by the court to assist in properly protecting the child's interests. The guardian ad litem is required to participate in the case to the extent necessary to protect the minor.

4. Rule 173. Guardian Ad Litem.

When a minor, lunatic, idiot or a non-compos mentis may be a defendant to a suit and has no guardian within this State, or where such person is a party to a suit either as plaintiff, defendant or intervenor and is represented by a next friend or a guardian who appears to the court to have an interest adverse to such minor, lunatic, idiot or non-compos mentis, the court shall appoint a guardian ad litem for such person and shall allow him a reasonable fee for his services to be taxed as a part of the costs.

Rule 173.1. Appointment Governed by Statute or Other Rules.

This rule does not apply to an appointment of a guardian ad litem governed by statute or other rules.

Rule 173.2. Appointment of Guardian ad Litem.

(a) When Appointment Required or Prohibited. The court must appoint a guardian ad litem for a party represented by a next friend or guardian only if:

(1) the next friend or guardian appears to the court to have an interest adverse to the party, or

(2) the parties agree.

(b) Appointment of the Same Person for Different Parties. The court must appoint the same guardian ad litem for similarly situated parties unless the court finds that the appointment of different guardians ad litem is necessary.

Rule 173.3. Procedure.

(a) Motion Permitted But Not Required. The court may appoint a guardian ad litem on the motion of any party or on its own initiative.

(b) Written Order Required. An appointment must be made by written order.

(c) Objection. Any party may object to the appointment of a guardian ad litem.

Rule 173.4. Role of Guardian Ad Litem.

(a) Court Officer and Advisor. A guardian ad litem acts as an officer and advisor to the court.

(b) Determination of Adverse Interest. A guardian ad litem must determine and advise the court whether a party's next friend or guardian has an interest adverse to the party.

(c) When Settlement Proposed. When an offer has been made to settle the claim of a party represented by a next friend or guardian, a guardian ad litem has the limited duty to determine and advise the court whether the settlement is in the party's best interest.

(d) Participation in Litigation Limited. A guardian ad litem:

(1) may participate in mediation or a similar proceeding to attempt to reach a settlement;

(2) must participate in any proceeding before the court whose purpose is to determine whether a party's next friend or guardian has an interest adverse to the party, or whether a settlement of the party's claim is in the party's best interest;

(3) must not participate in discovery, trial, or any other part of the litigation unless:

(A) further participation is necessary to protect the party's interest that is adverse to the next friend's or guardian's, and

(B) the participation is directed by the court in a written order stating sufficient reasons.

Rule 173.5. Communications Privileged.

Communications between the guardian ad litem and the party, the next friend or guardian, or their attorney are privileged as if the guardian ad litem were the attorney for the party.

Rule 173.6. Compensation.

(a) Amount. If a guardian ad litem requests compensation, he or she may be reimbursed for reasonable and necessary expenses incurred and may be paid a reasonable hourly fee for necessary services performed.

(b) Procedure. At the conclusion of the appointment, a guardian ad litem may file an application for compensation. The application must be verified and must detail the basis for the compensation requested. Unless all parties agree to the application, the court must conduct an evidentiary hearing to determine the total amount of fees and expenses that are reasonable and necessary. In making this determination, the court must not consider compensation as a percentage of any judgment or settlement.

(c) Taxation as Costs. The court may tax a guardian ad litem's compensation as costs of court.

(d) Other Benefit Prohibited. A guardian ad litem may not receive, directly or indirectly, anything of value in consideration of the appointment other than as provided by this rule.

Rule 173.7. Review.

(a) Right of Appeal. Any party may seek mandamus review of an order appointing a guardian ad litem or directing a guardian ad litem's participation in the litigation. Any party and a guardian ad litem may appeal an order awarding the guardian ad litem compensation.

(b) Severance. On motion of the guardian ad litem or any party, the court must sever any order awarding a guardian ad litem compensation to create a final, appealable order.

(c) No Affect on Finality of Settlement or Judgment. Appellate proceedings to review an order pertaining to a guardian ad litem do not affect the finality of a settlement or judgment.

Comment—2004

1. The rule is completely revised.
2. This rule does not apply when the procedures and purposes for appointment of guardians ad litem (as well as attorneys ad litem) are prescribed by statutes, such as the Family Code and the Probate Code, or by other rules, such as the Parental Notification Rules.
3. The rule contemplates that a guardian ad litem will be appointed when a party's next friend or guardian appears to have an interest adverse to the party because of the division of settlement proceeds. In those situations, the responsibility of the guardian ad litem as prescribed by the rule is very limited, and no reason exists for the guardian ad litem to participate in the conduct of the litigation in any other way or to review the discovery or the litigation file except to the limited extent that it may bear on the division of settlement proceeds. *See Jocson v. Crabb*, 133 S.W.3d 268 (Tex. 2004) (per curiam). A guardian ad litem may, of course, choose to review the file or attend proceedings when it is unnecessary, but the guardian ad litem may not be compensated for unnecessary expenses or services.
4. Only in extraordinary circumstances does the rule contemplate that a guardian ad litem will have a broader role. Even then, the role is limited to determining whether a party's next friend or guardian has an interest adverse to the party that should be considered by the court under Rule 44. In no event may a guardian ad litem supervise or supplant the next friend or undertake to represent the party while serving as guardian ad litem.
5. As an officer and advisor to the court, a guardian ad litem should have qualified judicial immunity.
6. Though an officer and adviser to the court, a guardian ad litem must not have ex parte communications with the court. *See* TEX. CODE JUD. CONDUCT, Canon 3. 7. Because the role of guardian ad litem is limited in all but extraordinary situations, and any risk that might result from services performed is also limited, compensation, if any is sought, should ordinarily be limited.
7. Because the role of guardian ad litem is limited in all but extraordinary situations, and any risk that might result from services performed is also limited, compensation, if any is sought, should ordinarily be limited.
8. A violation of this rule is subject to appropriate sanction.

3. *Misjoinder of Claims*

FLOUR BLUFF INDEPENDENT SCHOOL DISTRICT
v.
BASS
133 S.W.3d 272
(Tex. 2004)

PER CURIAM.

Margaret Bass filed a workers' compensation claim after slipping and injuring her back while employed with Flour Bluff Independent School District (Flour Bluff). The Texas Association of School Boards (TASB) denied Bass's claim for compensation. Bass appealed the denial, and the Texas Workers' Compensation Commission Appeals Panel (Panel) denied the benefits in a decision filed October 6, 1997.

On November 14, 1997, with one day remaining on the statute of limitations, Bass filed a judicial petition for review of the Panel's decision and named TASB as the only defendant. *See* TEX. LAB. CODE § 410.252(a) (requiring that an appeal from a decision by the Panel be made within 40 days of filing the decision). TASB, however, was a third party administrator of workers' compensation benefits and therefore not the proper defendant. Flour Bluff itself carried Bass's workers' compensation benefits, and therefore Bass should have sued Flour Bluff instead.

Accordingly, in its answer to Bass's petition, TASB expressly stated that it was not Bass's workers' compensation carrier and that Bass had failed to name and join the necessary party—Flour Bluff. Two weeks after TASB's answer was filed and over a year after the statute of limitations had expired, Bass amended her original pleading and named Flour Bluff as a defendant. Bass then waited more than a year to serve Flour Bluff with process.

TASB moved for summary judgment on the grounds that it was not a proper party to the lawsuit. Flour Bluff moved for summary judgment on two alternative grounds: 1) that the statute of limitations had expired because Bass failed to timely file suit against Flour Bluff; or 2) that Bass failed to use due diligence in serving Flour Bluff with process. The trial court granted both TASB's and Flour Bluff's summary judgment motions. The court found it did not have jurisdiction over TASB and that the statute of limitations had run on the claims against Flour Bluff.

The court of appeals affirmed the summary judgment in TASB's favor, but reversed the summary judgment as to Flour Bluff, holding that a fact issue existed as to whether the statute of limitations tolled the claims against Flour Bluff when Bass mistakenly named TASB as defendant. 55 S.W.3d 735, 740. Therefore, the court of appeals reversed the trial court's summary judgment ruling for Flour Bluff without reaching the due diligence issue.

According to the court of appeals, misidentification tolls the statute of limitations in a workers' compensation appeal under Texas Labor Code section 410.252 if the appealing party establishes that the proper defendant was cognizant of the facts of the lawsuit and was not misled or placed at a disadvantage by the appealing party's pleading error. 55 S.W.3d at 737. We disagree.

The statute of limitations will be tolled in misidentification cases if there are two separate, but related, entities that use a similar trade name and the correct entity had notice of the suit and was not misled or disadvantaged by the mistake. *Chilkewitz v. Hyson*, 22 S.W.3d 825, 830 (Tex.1999). Here, TASB and Flour Bluff were two distinct parties that did not operate under a similar trade name. Bass therefore was required to sue Flour Bluff within the limitations period and serve Flour Bluff with process within a reasonable time thereafter. Accordingly, pursuant to Rule 59.1 of the Texas Rules of Appellate Procedure, without hearing oral argument, the Court grants Flour Bluff's petition for review, reverses the court of appeals' judgment, and renders judgment that Bass take nothing.

4. *Joinder of Claims*

Read Rules 51 and 97 Texas Rules of Civil Procedure.

ALLISON
v.
ARKANSAS LOUISIANA GAS CO.
624 S.W.2d 566
(Tex. 1981)

J. E. Jackson, Carthage, for petitioners.
Bankhead & Davis, Tom Bankhead, Carthage, for respondent.

PER CURIAM.

Arkansas Louisiana Gas Company ("Arkansas") filed a condemnation petition to acquire a 40-foot gas pipeline right-of-way across the Allisons' timber land. Arkansas objected to and appealed the award of the commissioners to the trial court. The Allisons, in response to the appeal, asserted a claim for trespass seeking recovery of additional damages for Arkansas' acts of clearing an additional ten-foot strip of timber and pasture grass and pushing timber, tree roots and debris off the right-of-way onto the Allisons' land. The trial court overruled Arkansas' various objections to the trespass claim, admitted evidence of the trespass acts, and submitted special issues as to trespass damage occurring during construction of the Arkansas Louisiana gas pipeline. The jury found in favor of the Allisons on the trespass claim and the trial court awarded damages of $1,000. The court of civil appeals reversed the judgment of the trial court as to the trespass damages, holding that the trial court erred in admitting testimony and submitting to the jury the issue of damages occurring from construction activities. The cause was remanded for a new trial on the trespass claim. 620 S.W.2d 207.

Both parties have filed application for writ of error. Arkansas complains generally of evidentiary rulings by the trial court regarding land owner and expert witness qualification to testify as to land value in a condemnation proceeding. Arkansas additionally asserts reversible error of the entire cause is presented because of the trial court's allowance of the trespass claim and evidence thereunder in a condemnation action. The Allisons urge the sole question of whether a trespass claim may be joined in a condemnation suit. We find no reversible error in the court of civil appeals disposition of the points presented by Arkansas, but grant the application of the Allisons to reach the issue of joinder.

Under Rule 51(a), a plaintiff or defendant is permitted to join in the same proceeding "as many claims either legal or equitable or both as he may have against an opposing party." *See also* Rule 174, TEX. R. CIV. PROC. (consolidation of actions). Such procedural matters as joinder and consolidation of parties and claims are within the discretion of the trial court. The court's rulings on these matters will not be disturbed on appeal except for abuse of discretion. *Hamilton v. Hamilton*, 154 Tex. 511, 280 S.W.2d 588, 591 (1955); *Lambert v. H. Molsen & Co., Inc.*, 551 S.W.2d 151, 155 (Tex. Civ. App.—Waco 1977, writ ref'd n. r. e.). The court of civil appeals held the trial court erred in allowing joinder of a trespass claim. The cases relied on by the appeals court, however, pre-date the adoption of the Rules of Civil Procedure. We hold that the present rule allowing joinder of claims is dispositive of the matter and that an action in tort for damages after the taking may be maintained in a condemnation suit. We find this situation analogous to that presented in *Alexander v. City of San Antonio*, 468 S.W.2d 797 (Tex. 1971), in which we stated: "(T)he landowner is not to be forced into two trials, one for damages for trespass and another in condemnation in order to obtain full redress . . . ." A trespass claim may properly be joined and tried as a separate matter in a condemnation suit, subject to the discretion of the trial court, without necessarily influencing the jury's answers to the issues of condemnation damages.

Since the severance and reversal of the trial court's judgment on the trespass claim is contrary to Rule 51(a), we grant the application for writ of error and, under Rule 483, without hearing oral argument, reform the judgment of the court of civil appeals so as to affirm the judgment of the trial court.

Note

Jameson v Zuehlke, 218 S.W.2d 326 (Tex. Civ. App.—Waco 1948, no writ): **Facts**: This case proves that Robert Frost was right in saying that good fences make good neighbors. P & D owned adjoining farms. D's cows kept getting out and eating P's crops. On the advice of the County Attorney, P kept one of the D's cows the next time it happened. D had P arrested for cattle theft. P sued D for malicious prosecution. Shortly after this, the two met at the cattle auction. D struck P & "called him out." A fight ensued, D struck P twice before P responded, but D's nose was broken, & P needed a doctor and six stitches. P amended his petition to add a claim for assault and battery. The trial court entered judgment for P for both actual & exemplary damages.

Issue: Could the P properly join the malicious prosecution action and the assault action? Yes.

Held: Yes. Where the parties are the same, Rule 51 places no restrictions on joinder outside of Rules 39, 40 & 43.

Rule 39 relates to joinder of parties, and really places no restrictions on joinder of claims.

Rule 40 relates to the permissive joinder of parties, and does require that the multiple claims arise out of "the same transaction, occurrence, or series of transactions or occurrences . . . [involving] any question of law or fact common to all of them . . . ."

Rule 43 relates to interpleader where parties have rival claims to a stake.

AKERS
v.
SIMPSON

445 S.W.2d 957
(Tex. 1969)

Jesse Shivers, John Holloway, Houston, for petitioner.
Vinson, Elkins, Searls & Connally, Gerald P. Coley and James R. Bertrand, Houston, for respondent.

STEAKLEY, JUSTICE.

James Akers, Petitioner, an employee of Fred Hayden, d/b/a Houston International Airport Limousine Service, and Jay Simpson were involved in a traffic accident on August 30, 1967. Akers was driving an airport limousine owned by Hayden. On October 23, Simpson filed a personal injury suit in the District Court of Harris County, Texas, against Hayden and Akers, and on November 20 an answer in the form of a general denial was filed in their names. On December 8, Akers filed a personal injury suit against Simpson in the District Court of Harris County, and on January 23, 1968, Simpson filed an answer to the merits.

On May 28, an agreed judgment was entered in the suit of Simpson against Hayden and Akers, the terms of which were: "ON THIS 28 day of May, 1968, came on in its regular order to be heard the above styled and numbered cause, and came plaintiffs, Jay W. Simpson, and wife, Mrs. Jay W. Simpson, by and through their attorney of record, and announced ready for trial, and came defendants, James Akers, and Fred Hayden, dba Houston International Airport Limousine Service, by and through their attorney of record, and announced ready for trial; thereupon all parties announced in open court that an agreement for settlement had been consummated herein by and under the terms of which the plaintiffs have released all their causes of action growing out of the accident made the basis of this suit and have further agreed that judgment may be entered in this cause in favor of the defendants: "IT IS, THEREFORE, ORDERED, ADJUDGED, AND DECREED BY THE COURT that the plaintiffs, Jay W. Simpson and wife, Mrs. Jay W. Simpson, take nothing by reason of this suit and that judgment be, and the same is hereby rendered in favor of the defendants. "All costs herein are adjudged against the defendants, for which let execution issue if same are not seasonably paid."

On July 5, Simpson filed a motion for summary judgment in Akers' suit in which he invoked Rule 97(a), Texas Rules of Civil Procedure, the compulsory counterclaim rule. Akers countered Simpson's motion for summary judgment by filing his affidavit and that of the Deputy Constable who handled the citations issued in Simpson's suit and made the returns thereon. These affidavits established that Hayden, the employer of Akers, was personally served with citation and that the Constable was instructed to leave the Akers citation with his employer; the return, however, recited that service was had on Akers. It was further established that the answer filed in the Simpson suit on behalf of Hayden and in the name of Akers was filed by an attorney who represented either Hayden or his insurer and that Akers did not know of and did not authorize the filing of the answer in his name. The trial court granted Simpson's motion for summary judgment and this was affirmed by the Court of Civil Appeals, 437 S.W.2d 429.

Rule 97(a) provides: "(a) Compulsory Counterclaims. A pleading shall state as a counterclaim any claim within the jurisdiction of the court, not the subject of a pending action, which at the time of filing the pleading the pleader has against any opposing party, if it arises out of the transaction or occurrence that is the subject matter of the opposing party's claim and does not require for its adjudication the presence of third parties of whom the court cannot acquire jurisdiction."

Our principal reason for granting the application of Akers for writ of error was to review the basic question of whether the lower courts correctly considered Akers an "opposing party" in the earlier Simpson suit and judgment. All other requirements for application of Rule 97(a) in Akers' suit against Simpson were clearly present. The judgment in the Simpson suit, above quoted, recited that Akers was a party defendant and appeared through an attorney of record. It is the firmly established rule in Texas that a defendant who is not served and who does not appear may not, as a matter of public policy, attack the verity of a judgment in a collateral proceeding; the jurisdictional recitals import absolute verity. *Crawford v. McDonald*, 88 Tex. 626, 33 S.W. 325 (1895), *Levy v. Roper*, 113 Tex. 356, 256 S.W. 251 (1923), and *State Mortgage Corporation v. Traylor*, 120 Tex. 148, 36 S.W.2d 440 (1931); *see* Hodges, *Collateral Attacks on Judgments*, 41 TEX. L. REV. 162-198, 499-544 (1962). A collateral attack on a judgment is an attempt to avoid its binding force in a proceeding not instituted for such purpose, *Crawford v. McDonald*, *supra*, and such is the case here. Akers chose not to institute a direct attack on the Simpson judgment by means of which he could have avoided the compulsory counterclaim effect of the judgment in the suit of Akers against Simpson. Not having done so, the jurisdictional recitals of the judgment in the Simpson suit bring Akers under the decisions which hold that Rule 97(a) bars a subsequent suit growing out of the same accident when a prior suit between the same parties is concluded by a judgment pursuant to a compromise settlement agreement. *Harris v. Jones*, 404 S.W.2d 349 (Tex. Civ. App. 1966, writ ref.); *Stringer v. Munnell*, 390 S.W.2d 484 (Tex. Civ. App. 1956, writ ref.); and *Beach v. Runnels*, 379 S.W.2d 684 (Tex. Civ. App. 1964, writ ref.).

This opinion will not be further extended since we also agree with the holdings of the Court of Civil Appeals upon the other questions there decided and brought forward in the application for writ of error.

The judgments below are affirmed.

Notes

1. The result in this case could not occur today. The proviso to Rule 97(a) was written to prevent this fact situation from ever being repeated. The proviso to Rule 97(a) reads:

> ". . . provided, however, that a judgment based upon a settlement or compromise of a claim of one party to the transaction or occurrence prior to a disposition on the merits shall not operate as a bar to the continuation or assertion of the claims of any other party to the transaction or occurrence unless the latter has consented in writing that said judgment shall operate as a bar."

2. The compulsory counterclaim rule [Rule 97(a) of the Texas Rules of Civil Procedure] is a rule of procedure designed to avoid piecemeal or duplicative litigation. It requires that a potential counterclaimant with a justiciable interest arising out of the same transaction or occurrence at issue in the opposing party's claim bring the counterclaim in the same proceeding, or it will be deemed waived. The "compelling interest" underlying the compulsory counterclaim rule is solidly in judicial economy; its purpose is to prevent multiple suits arising out of the same transaction or occurrence. *See Bard v. Charles R. Myers Ins. Agency*, 839 S.W.2d 791 (Tex. 1992).

3. If the plaintiff contesting a counterclaim does not desire to urge any defensive theories which must be verified or any affirmative defenses under Rule 94, he is not required to answer the defendant's counterclaim. *See Greater Fort Worth and Tarrant County Community Agency v. Mims*, 627 S.W.2d 149 (Tex. 1982). Furthermore, under Rule 123 of the Texas Rules of Civil Procedure it is not necessary to serve counterclaims or

cross-actions by citation—they can be served in compliance with Rule 21a of the Texas Rules of Civil Procedure.

4. Section 16.069 of the Texas Civil Practice and Remedies Code provides for an extension of the statute of limitations in the case of counterclaims and cross claims. It provides:

> (a) If a counterclaim or cross claim arises out of the same transaction or occurrence that is the basis of an action, a party to the action may file the counterclaim or cross claim even though as a separate action it would be barred by limitations on the date the party's answer is required.
>
> (b) The counterclaim or cross claim must be filed not later than the 30th day after the date on which the party's answer is required.

5. *Interpleader*

Read Rule 43 Texas Rules of Civil Procedure.

CLAYTON
v.
MONY LIFE INSURANCE CO. OF AMERICA

284 S.W.3d 398
(Tex. App.—Beaumont 2009, no pet.)

Daniel D. Clayton, Daniel D. Clayton, P.C., Beaumont, pro se.

Carl C. Scherz, W. Scott Hastings, Jeffrey A. Logan, Erik A. Marshall, Locke Lord Bissell & Liddell, LLP, Dallas, for appellee.

GAULTNEY, JUSTICE.

This is an appeal from the trial court's discharge order granting an interpleader filed by MONY Life Insurance Company of America. We conclude the court did not abuse its discretion by permitting interpleader and granting a discharge related to annuity payments tendered and made in compliance with the court order. However, the trial court erred by dismissing with prejudice certain pre-interpleader claims, and considering MONY's more than two year delay in interpleading the funds, the court erred by awarding MONY attorney's fees from the annuity. We therefore affirm the discharge order in part, reverse the order in part, and remand the case for further proceedings consistent with this opinion.

The Dispute

In exchange for $400,000, MONY issued an annuity contract to appellant in February 2003, shortly before his divorce from Nancy Clayton. MONY made regular monthly payments to appellant under the annuity contract from March 15, 2003, to July 15, 2003.

The trial court signed the decree of divorce on June 27, 2003, and the judgment was affirmed on appeal. *See In re Marriage of Clayton,* No. 07-03-0445-CV, 2004 WL 1840453, at **1-2 (Tex. App.—Amarillo Aug. 16, 2004, no pet.) (mem.op.). The judgment provides in part that Nancy is awarded "fifty percent of MONY Annuity i/n/o husband as set out in the qualified domestic relations order to be signed by the court." The parties do not direct us to a qualified domestic relations order relating to the MONY annuity. The judgment also includes a handwritten order providing that "[a]ll retirement payments awarded to a party received by other party are held in trust [and] shall be delivered to party awarded payment within 5 days."

MONY apparently learned of the divorce decree in July 2003 and stopped making payments to appellant. MONY began depositing the annuity payments into a non-interest bearing account pursuant to its own procedures.

In February 2005, appellant sued MONY, Nancy Clayton, and Jeffery Shelton (Nancy's attorney in the divorce proceeding) on contract and tort claims, all related to the annuity. MONY filed its answer and subsequently filed an amended answer asserting a plea in interpleader. MONY also filed an affidavit of its compliance director. The affidavit explained that the parties had not completed the appropriate paperwork to allow MONY to disburse the annuity after the divorce decree. Appellant filed a responsive pleading contesting MONY's entitlement to interpleader relief.

The trial court held a hearing to consider the interpleader and heard arguments by counsel. The compliance director's affidavit was not alluded to or admitted into evidence at the hearing. We find nothing in the record indicating any party filed a motion for summary judgment regarding any matter related to MONY's interpleader or appellant's liability claims against MONY. The only evidence offered at the hearing related to MONY's attorney's fees.

Appellant argued MONY was required to pay him the annuity on a monthly basis, and upon receiving the payment, he would pay Nancy Clayton her share. Counsel for Nancy explained that she had to seek and obtain a court order requiring the payment to her by appellant of her share of some of the annuity payments that had been paid directly to him.

MONY argued that the divorce judgment named Nancy as a fifty percent owner of the annuity, and that although appellant had signed some paperwork to effectuate that division, the paperwork had not been completed despite MONY's repeated requests. Counsel for MONY stated, "We've never gotten paperwork that allows us to do anything." MONY maintained that it was "in the middle" of the controversy.

The trial court ordered the annuity payments placed into the registry of the court, awarded MONY attorney's fees from appellant's share of those funds, and dismissed all claims against MONY with prejudice. The trial court severed the interpleader action, making the discharge order final and appealable. Appellant asks this Court to set aside the order.

Interpleader

Texas has long recognized the equitable remedy of interpleader. *See Williams v. Wright,* 20 Tex. 499, 500 (1857); *Nixon v. Malone,* 100 Tex. 250, 98 S.W. 380, 384-385 (1906), *amended by* 100 Tex. 250, 99 S.W. 403 (1907). Presented with conflicting claims to the stake it holds, a stakeholder who does not know which claimant to pay and fears exposure to double or multiple liability for the single stake, may apply to a court for protection. *See generally Nixon,* 98 S.W. at 384-385. By placing the fund in the control of the court pursuant to court order for the court to decide ownership, the stakeholder is relieved from the potential liability to pay the single fund more than once, and also from the litigation costs attending the rival claims. *See generally State Farm Life Ins. Co. v. Martinez,* 216 S.W.3d 799, 806-07 (Tex. 2007). If a reasonable doubt exists as to the proper party to pay, the interpleader procedure allows the court to make that decision and discharge the stakeholder from that responsibility. *See id.* at 806 ("[A]n insurer should interplead [the rival claims] and let the courts decide.").

Today, the interpleader procedure is provided in Texas as a remedial joinder-of-parties rule. *See* TEX. R. CIV. P. 43; *see also generally* 7 Charles Alan Wright, Arthur R. Miller and Mary Kay Kane, Federal Practice and Procedure § 1702 (3d ed. 2001) (In considering similar federal rule, "[i]nterpleader should be viewed as a remedial joinder device . . . ."). Rule 43 of the Texas Rules of Civil Procedure authorizes a party to join as defendants persons having conflicting claims against the party. *See* TEX. R. CIV. P. 43. The rival claimants may be "required to interplead when their claims are such that the plaintiff is or may be exposed to double or multiple liability." *Id.* As set out in Rule 43, "A defendant exposed to similar liability may obtain such interpleader by way of cross-claim or counterclaim." *Id.* A party presented with multiple claims to property in its possession may join all claimants in a lawsuit, tender the disputed property into the registry of the court, and request a discharge. *Heggy v. Am. Trading Employee Ret. Account Plan,* 123 S.W.3d 770, 775 (Tex. App.—Houston [14th Dist.] 2003, pet. denied). The trial court decides whether interpleader is appropriate. As is true of all the rules of civil procedure, the objective of Rule 43 is to obtain a just adjudication of the litigants' rights, and toward that end, we construe the rule liberally. *See* TEX. R. CIV. P. 1.

Rule 43 expressly disclaims certain pre-rule restrictions imposed on interpleader practice. *See* TEX. R. CIV. P. 43. The Rule "extended and liberalized the equitable remedy of interpleader." *Downing v. Laws,* 419 S.W.2d 217, 220 (Tex. Civ. App.—Austin 1967, writ ref'd n.r.e.). Interpleader under Rule 43 requires only conflicting claims. *See* TEX. R. CIV. P. 43; *see Martinez,* 216 S.W.3d at 807. In *Martinez,* a case involving rival claims to life insurance proceeds, the Supreme Court explained as follows:

> When insurers receive notice of adverse bona fide claims, Texas law does not require them 'to act as judge and jury,' or to pay one claim and risk liability on the other. Instead, if a reasonable doubt ex-

> ists in law or fact as to whom the proceeds belong, an insurer should interplead them and let the courts decide.

Martinez, 216 S.W.3d at 806 (footnotes omitted). Interpleader requires the rival claimants to litigate the ownership issue among themselves, rather than with a stakeholder who has no claim to the fund and simply seeks to pay the proper claimant.

In practice, interpleader generally involves two stages. *See generally Nixon,* 98 S.W. at 382; *Sparkman v. Reliastar Life Ins. Co.,* No. 13-03-500-CV, 2008 WL 2058216, at *2 (Tex. App.—Corpus Christi May 15, 2008, pet. denied) (mem.op.) (interpleader, then trial between rival claimants). In the first stage, the court determines whether interpleader is appropriate. Generally, the stakeholder is discharged from liability to the rival claimants in the first stage of the process, and so can avoid the cost of additional litigation over the stake it once held, but to which it asserts no claim. In the second stage, after interpleader has been determined to be appropriate, the rival claimants litigate their differences. *Sparkman,* 2008 WL 2058216, at *2.

Rival Claims

To be entitled to interpleader relief, MONY had to establish that it was facing rival claims to the fund, and that a reasonable doubt existed in law or fact as to which claim was valid. *See Broesche v. Jacobson,* 218 S.W.3d 267, 277 (Tex. App.—Houston [14th Dist.] 2007, pet. denied); *see also Savs. & Profit Sharing Fund of Sears Employees v. Stubbs,* 734 S.W.2d 76, 79 (Tex. App.—Austin 1987, no writ) (Party requesting interpleader remedy has burden of proof.). Appellant argued that he is the owner of the annuity contract and that MONY refused to transfer the account. He explained he had signed a "Title Change Form," and although MONY had a copy of that document, MONY made no change in the ownership of the annuity. On appeal, he argues there are no rival claims to the annuity, and the risk that payment of the annuity to him alone may leave MONY without a right of reimbursement is "not the kind of exposure to multiple liabilities that would justify [i]nterpleader relief."

It is undisputed that the divorce decree awarded fifty percent of the annuity to Nancy Clayton. Nevertheless, appellant asserted that the contract required MONY to make the annuity payments solely to him, with appellant then disbursing Nancy's share to her. Confronted with a divorce decree awarding Nancy a fifty percent interest in the annuity and two claimants disputing how and to whom the payments should be made, MONY was presented with rival claimants. Pursuant to Rule 43, under the circumstances MONY could "interplead them and let the courts decide." *See Martinez,* 216 S.W.3d at 806; *see also* TEX. R. CIV. P. 43.

"Rewriting" the Contract

Appellant generally argues that the trial court erred in rewriting the annuity contract by changing the payee and ordering the funds paid into the registry of the court. The divorce decree divided the funds, and that judgment is final. *See Clayton,* 2004 WL 1840453, at **1-2. Payment of the tendered funds into the registry of the court followed that division of the marital estate. The trial court did not rewrite the contract in the interpleader action.

Timeliness of Interpleader

Appellant argues MONY filed its interpleader late. He filed suit against MONY, Nancy Clayton, and Shelton on February 14, 2005, along with a request for disclosure and request for production of documents. MONY filed its answer on April 21, 2005, and its discovery responses and objections on May 23, 2005. On August 25, 2005, approximately six months after appellant filed suit and over two years after MONY received notice of the divorce judgment and stopped the payment of the annuity funds to appellant, MONY filed a plea in interpleader.

Delay in filing an interpleader does not bar a party from depositing disputed funds into the registry of the court. *Martinez,* 216 S.W.3d at 807 (citations omitted). The Supreme Court explained in *Martinez* as follows:

> [I]nterpleader is not improper merely because it is delayed; while some courts have listed prompt filing as an interpleader requirement, the rules of procedure require only conflicting claims. When rival claims exist, courts must decide who gets the proceeds no matter how tardy the deposit; we cannot imply "toss the money back out the clerk's window," or return it to a stakeholder who makes no claim to it.

Id. (citations omitted); *see also Sparkman,* 2008 WL 2058216, at *4. MONY was presented with conflicting claims and its interpleader is not improper merely because it was delayed. *See Martinez,* 216 S.W.3d at 807.

Unconditional Tender

Appellant argues MONY did not make an unconditional tender of the entire annuity, because MONY deposited only $61,492.23, less attorney's fees, into the court's registry, rather than $400,000. In its plea in interpleader, MONY unequivocally disclaimed any interest in the annuity proceeds that had become due. The trial court found that "at the time of the filing of the Plea in Interpleader, MONY unconditionally offered and tendered to the Court the Annuity payments which had become due at that time, $56,937.25." The trial court also found MONY "unconditionally offered and tendered to [the] Court each additional future monthly Annuity payment of $2,277.49 as they became due until further notice from the Court."

In *Heggy,* American Trading stated in its interpleader petition that it " 'unconditionally offers and is ready to deposit with the court the remaining benefits of Robert Heggy totaling $144,251.61.' " *Heggy,* 123 S.W.3d at 776. The court held that "[a]lthough American did not physically deposit the funds into the registry of the court, it tendered the funds into the court . . . [O]nly an unconditional tender, not a deposit, is required." *Id.* (citation omitted).

MONY made an unconditional tender of the annuity payments into the registry of the court for the trial court to determine who should receive the money. That unconditional tender fulfilled the purpose of interpleader. *See id.*

Independent Claims

Appellant argues he has claims against MONY which should not have been discharged. MONY's tender did not include interest on the money it retained in its possession for over two years. Appellant's claim for interest remained in dispute. He asserted causes of action against MONY for breach of contract, fraud, and breach of fiduciary duty. Appellant argues MONY placed his share as well as Nancy's share of the annuity payments in a non-interest bearing account for two years and did not tender the annuity funds by interpleader until months after he sued MONY. According to the pleadings, the conduct giving rise to these causes of action all occurred prior to MONY's August 2005 filing of the interpleader.

Courts have sometimes held that independent liability to one of the claimants precludes interpleader; essentially, the stakeholder was required to be "innocent." *See, e.g., Nixon,* 98 S.W. at 385; *Farmers State Bank of Meridian v. Nat'l Fire Ins. Co. of Hartford, Conn.,* 169 S.W.2d 545, 549 (Tex. Civ. App.—Waco 1943, no writ); *Travelers Ins. Co. v. Nelle,* 115 S.W.2d 988, 991 (Tex. App.—Austin 1938, writ dism'd); *see also Union Gas Corp. v. Gisler,* 129 S.W.3d 145, 153 (Tex. App.—Corpus Christi 2003, no pet.). That restriction did not survive the adoption of Rule 43, however. *See, e.g., Sparkman,* 2008 WL 2058216, at **4-5. We reach this conclusion from a reading of Rule 43 itself, and from the application of the rule in *Martinez. See Martinez,* 216 S.W.3d at 805-08.

Rule 43 requires only conflicting claims. *See* TEX. R. CIV. P. 43. Rule 43 provides that it is not grounds for objection that the rival claims "do not have a common origin or are not identical but are adverse to and independent of one another[.]" *Id.* It is also not grounds for objection that the stakeholder claims it is "not liable in whole or in part to any or all of the claimants." *Id.* This language indicates that interpleader is not precluded merely because one of the rival claimants alleges the stakeholder is also independently liable to that claimant, and the stakeholder denies that independent liability, but makes no claim to the stake. *See id.* Rule 43 expressly permits a defendant, exposed to "similar" double or multiple liability, to "obtain such interpleader by way of cross-claim or counterclaim [,]" and the Rule supplements and does not "in any way limit the joinder of parties permitted in any other rules." *Id.; see also* TEX. R. CIV. P. 40. (permissive joinder of parties). As the interpleader remedy was applied in *Martinez,* the insurer's pre-interpleader liability for statutory penalties—those penalties that were incurred before the interpleader was filed—did not preclude the filing of the interpleader, or the effect of the tender in halting any subsequent penalties. *See Martinez,* 216 S.W.3d at 805-08.

As one author has explained in discussing the similar federal interpleader rule, "The reasons underlying the interpleader remedy continue to have force even when there is a possibility that the stakeholder also may be liable to one of the claimants on some special basis." 7 Charles Alan Wright, Arthur R. Miller and Mary Kay Kane, Federal Practice and Procedure § 1706 (3d ed. 2001); *see also Olivier v. Humble Oil & Ref. Co.,* 225 F.Supp. 536, 539 (E.D. La. 1963) (discussing independent liability claims and federal interpleader rule). The possibility of independent liability may affect the final scope of the discharge order, but independent liability does not necessarily preclude the placement of the fund into the registry of the court, or the obtaining of a discharge from further liability for the payment in compliance with the court order. *See, e.g., Martinez,* 216 S.W.3d at 804-08; *Sparkman,* 2008 WL 2058216, at **4-5. By unconditionally tendering the annuity payment to the court for an ownership decision, MONY gained entitlement to a discharge from the trial court of MONY's possible double liability to the rival claimants for the single fund. The court determined the amount each rival claimant should receive.

The trial court erred, however, in dismissing with prejudice appellant's pre-interpleader liability claims against MONY, because there has been no adjudication of the merits of those claims by summary judgment motion or trial. Courts have applied interpleader to discharge parties from liability on related tort and contract claims. *See Petro Source Partners, Ltd. v. 3-B Rattlesnake Ref.,* 905 S.W.2d 371, 378 (Tex. App.—El Paso 1995, writ denied); *Cable Commc'ns Network, Inc.,* 838 S.W.2d 947, 949-51 (Tex. App.—Houston [14th Dist.] 1992, no writ); *Salazar v. San Benito Bank & Trust Co.,* 730 S.W.2d 21 (Tex. App.—Corpus Christi 1987, no writ). However, those cases involved a summary judgment or a judgment after a trial. While independent liability does not necessarily and automatically preclude interpleader under Rule 43, liability for the independent pre-interpleader claims is not necessarily and automatically discharged by the tender.

The hearing record does not include the annuity contract, a motion for summary judgment, or evidence concerning the claims; therefore, we do not address the merits of the pre-interpleader liability claims asserted here. The error we address is in the dismissal procedure followed. We therefore do not decide at this time whether recovery of interest on the withheld money, for the time it was withheld, is authorized in this case by contract, statute, or under principles of equity. *See, e.g., Phillips Petroleum Co. v. Stahl Petroleum Co.,* 569 S.W.2d 480, 485-89 (Tex. 1978); *see also generally Phillips Petroleum Co. v. Adams,* 513 F.2d 355, 364-67 (5th Cir.1975) (discussing Texas law).

The discharge order properly discharged MONY from the potential double liability to the rival claimants for the single fund. The interpleader tender did not serve to discharge all liability claims which arose prior to the interpleader, however. Those disputed independent claims must be adjudicated by summary judgment motion or trial.

Attorney's Fees

"Under the common law, a stakeholder is entitled to recover its attorney's fees from the deposited funds unless there were no rival claimants or the interpleader was unreasonably delayed." *Martinez,* 216 S.W.3d at 803 (citations omitted). An award of attorney's fees to the stakeholder from the fund is within the trial court's sound discretion. *Olmos v. Pecan Grove Mun. Util. Dist.,* 857 S.W.2d 734, 741 (Tex. App.—Houston [14th Dist.] 1993, no writ). Appellant argues an award of attorney's fees to MONY under the circumstances was improper, because MONY, having breached the contract with appellant and having violated its fiduciary duty, was not an innocent stakeholder but rather unreasonably delayed payment or tender of the funds. He asserts the deprivation of his funds caused him harm.

MONY says it learned "in or about July 2003" that the divorce decree awarded fifty percent of the annuity to Nancy Clayton. More than two years elapsed, during which time MONY retained all of the annuity payments due appellant and Nancy in a non-interest bearing account. Appellant sued MONY in February 2005. MONY did not file an interpleader action until August 2005. Nothing in the record suggests MONY offered to place the funds into the registry of the court at an earlier time.

Delay in interpleading may be justified or reasonable under some circumstances. *See Martinez,* 216 S.W.3d at 805 ("Some delay before filing an interpleader may benefit all concerned, if settlement can be reached before lawyers must be hired and pleadings filed.") (citations omitted). However, the mere existence of an ongoing dispute involving rival claims does not, without more, justify a lengthy delay like that here; rival claims to a single fund are the reason for the existence of the interpleader procedure and not an excuse for its non-use. The record of the hearing in this case does not support an award of attorney's fees to MONY from the annuity funds in light of the delay of more than two years before MONY filed its interpleader. *See id.* at 807 ("[D]elay may bar recovery of attorney's fees[.]").

Conclusion

We affirm the trial court's order instructing MONY to deposit the monthly annuity payments into the registry of the court until further order of the court, and discharging MONY of further liability for payments made in compliance with the court order. We reverse the trial court's award of attorney's fees to MONY. We reverse the dismissal of the pre-interpleader independent liability claims and remand the case for further proceedings consistent with this opinion.

Notes

1. Interpleader practice in Texas has changed over the years, and the reading of earlier cases should not confuse one. The distinction between past and present practice is set out in *Savings & Profit Sharing Fund of Sears Employees v. Stubbs,* 735 S.W. 76 (Tex. App.—Austin 1987, no writ):

> "1. Early Interpleader Practice. Originally, an interpleader action allowed a stakeholder to bring the disputed sum or property into court and have his own liability discharged, leaving the rival claimants to litigate whatever controversy existed. 24 MCELROY, CIVIL PRE-TRIAL PROCEDURE § 543 (Tex. Practice 1980). The remedy was for the protection of the disinterested and innocent stakeholder who claimed no interest in the property and who, because of conflicting claims and uncertain position ". . . knows not what to do . . . and asks instruction of and protection of a court of equity." *Nixon v. Malone*, 100 Tex. 250, 98 S.W. 380 (1908).
>
> "Such an 'innocent stakeholder' had to plead and prove four essential elements: (1) that he was subject to conflicting claims to the same property; (2) that the adverse claims were dependent or derived from a common source; (3) that he claimed no interest in the property; and (4) that he was not independently liable to any claimant but rather stood perfectly indifferent between them. 1 MCDONALD, TEXAS CIVIL PRACTICE § 3.38 at 289 (Rev. ed. 1981). These rather strict requirements were somewhat tempered by the adoption of the rule that every reasonable doubt would be resolved in favor of allowing the interpleader. *Nixon v. Malone, supra* 98 S.W. at 385.
>
> "2. Adoption of Rule 43. In an attempt to liberalize the remedy of interpleader and to encourage litigants to seek the protections offered thereby, the Supreme Court promulgated Rule 43 as part of the initial adoption of the Rules of Civil Procedure in 1941. Under Rule 43, a stakeholder need only show that he is or may be exposed to double or multiple liability as a result of conflicting claims justifying a reasonable doubt as to which claimant is entitled to the fund. *See e.g., Davis v. East Texas Savings & Loan Association*, 163 Tex. 361, 354 S.W.2d 926 (1962); *Downing v. Laws*, 419 S.W.2d 217 (Tex. Civ. App. 1967, writ ref'd n.r.e.)."
>
> "3. Modern Practice. Since Rule 43 was adopted, a successful petitioner at interpleader must now plead and prove three basic elements: (1) that he is either subject to, or has reasonable grounds to anticipate, rival claims to the same fund or property; (2) that he has not unreasonably delayed filing his action for interpleader; and (3) that he has unconditionally tendered the fund into the court. . . . Failure to meet any one of these three elements will defeat a petitioner's standing as an innocent stakeholder and preclude relief at interpleader."

2. The Texas rule is that the innocent stakeholder in an interpleader is entitled to attorney's fees, to be paid out of the impleaded fund. *U. S. v. Ray Thomas Gravel Co.,* 380 S.W.2d 576, 581 (Tex. 1964), so long as the interpleading party meets each one of the elements required for interpleader. Failure to meet any one of the elements defeats a petitioner's standing as an innocent, disinterested stakeholder and precludes recovery of attorney's fees in the interpleader action. *Daniels v. Pecan Valley Ranch, Inc.,* 831 S.W.2d 372 (Tex. App.—San Antonio 992, writ denied), *cert. denied* 508 U.S. 965.

3. Funds deposited into the registry of the court are to be invested by the clerk, and the interest on the fund is to be paid to the one determined to be the owner of the principal. *Sellers v. Harris County,* 483 S.W.2d 242 (Tex. 1972).

4. *State Farm Life Ins. Co. v. Martinez*, 216 S.W.3d 799 (Tex. 2007) involved a dispute over life insurance proceeds. The insurer interplead the proceeds of the policy, but did so 12 days after the time required by the "prompt payment statute" (current version at TEX. INS. CODE §§ 542.051-.061). ***Held:*** Once State Farm interpleaded the entire policy proceeds, it owed nothing more on the policy. Thus, the courts below erred in awarding penalty interest and attorney's fees for more than those 12 days. When insurers receive notice of adverse bona fide claims, Texas law does not require them to act as judge and jury, or to pay one claim and risk liability on the other. Instead, if a reasonable doubt exists in law or fact as to whom the proceeds belong, an

insurer should interplead them and let the courts decide. Every reasonable doubt should be resolved in favor of the stakeholder's right to interplead. If an insurer promptly interpleads policy proceeds, it cannot be subjected to statutory penalties for delayed payment, even if it missed the statutory deadlines. But in 1991, the Legislature changed the prompt payment statute, raising the penalty interest to 18 percent and the deadline for payment (in most cases) to 60 days. The Legislature's 1991 changes to the Insurance Code suggest the courts should not continue imposing a different deadline. But nothing in those changes suggests that statutory penalties should apply after interpleader occurs. Assessing penalty interest and attorney's fees after an interpleader is filed would punish insurers for doing what Texas law encourages. Indeed, the more difficult and protracted the dispute between rival claimants (and thus the more justified the interpleader), the larger those penalties would grow.

5. *Fort Worth Transportation Authority v. Rodriguez*, 547 S.W.3d 830 (Tex. 2018). Interpleader Is Not Available To A Potential Tortfeasor. They Are Not Disinterested Stakeholders.

Anticipating that it would be drawn into the litigation by New Hampshire Insurance, seeking what it paid Rodriguez for workers-compensation death benefits, MTI intervened as a party-defendant, counter-claimant and cross-claimant in that suit. It also filed an interpleader. In an amended petition the transit defendants asserted that Rodriguez's claims were defensible, but if the trial court accepted the interpleader and dismissed all claims against them, they would not choose to put up a defense—thereby conditioning their tender on the trial court's acceptance of their argument that their cumulative liability was capped at a single, $100,000 cap. Held: This was not a valid interpleader—it was not an unconditional tender. Interpleader jurisdiction is determined at the time the interpleader complaint is filed, MTI's potential for double liability met the requirement of Rule 43. However, the Transit Defendants—as the parties who are alleged to have negligently caused the damage—are not innocent, disinterested stakeholders. Under the unambiguous meaning of term 'disinterested stakeholder,' a party who asserts a claim to the interpleaded funds is not a disinterested stakeholder The Transit Defendants' assertion that the claims against them were defensible and that they would put up a defense if their interpleader terms were not accepted necessarily defeats their proposed status as a disinterested stakeholder. Even absent the defensibility assertion, the Transit Defendants' position as the alleged tortfeasors prevents them from being a "disinterested stakeholder." Interpleader is proper to protect an insurance company facing competing claims over benefits. But the protection of interpleader—and the accompanying attorney's fees—should not be extended to an alleged tortfeasor/defendant. Moreover, the allowance of attorney's fees for an alleged tortfeasor/defendant attempting to interplead the extent of his liability is adverse to public policy.

6. *Intervention, Severance and Separate Trials*

Read Rules 41, 60, and 174a Texas Rules of Civil Procedure.

In re UNION CARBIDE CORPORATION
273 S.W.3d 152
(Tex. 2008)

PER CURIAM.

In this case, family members who survived John Hall intervened in a pending personal injury suit filed by Kenneth Moffett. Union Carbide, a defendant in both the pending suit and the intervention, filed a motion to strike the intervention. Instead of ruling on that motion, the trial court severed the Halls' claims into a new suit that then remained pending in the same court. We conclude that (1) the trial court abused its discretion by failing to rule on Union Carbide's motion to strike before considering whether to sever the intervention; (2) the trial court only had discretion to grant the motion to strike; and (3) Union Carbide does not have an adequate remedy by appeal. We conditionally grant mandamus relief.

On January 27, 2006, Kenneth Moffett filed a personal injury action in the 212th District Court of Galveston County. Moffett alleged that he was exposed to toxic chemicals distributed, marketed, or manufactured by fourteen defendants and that the exposure caused him to develop acute myelogenous leukemia. He claims to have been exposed to the chemicals from 1974 to 2000, including short periods of time in the mid-1970s and in the 1980s when he worked at the Union Carbide facility in Texas City.

On March 5, 2007, family members who survived John Hall intervened in Moffett's lawsuit. They alleged that Hall died from myelodysplastic syndrome caused by his exposure between 1963 and 1998 to toxic chemicals at Union Carbide's Texas City facility. Some, but not all of the defendants sued by the Hall survivors were also defendants in Moffett's suit. Union Carbide was a defendant in both the Moffett and Hall suits. Union Carbide filed a motion to strike the Halls' intervention because the Halls failed to show that they possessed a justiciable interest in the Moffett suit. The trial court conducted a hearing on the motion to strike but did not rule on it. Instead, the trial court severed the Halls' claims into a separate suit and directed the suit to be docketed and maintained on the regular docket of the court. Union Carbide petitioned the court of appeals for a writ of mandamus directing the trial court to rule on and grant its motion to strike. The court of appeals denied the petition. --- S.W.3d ----.

In this Court, Union Carbide argues that the trial court abused its discretion by both refusing to rule on its motion to strike the intervention and refusing to grant the motion because the Halls did not show a justiciable interest in the Moffett suit. Union Carbide also urges it does not have an adequate appellate remedy and that the benefits of mandamus review outweigh the detriments.

Texas Rule of Civil Procedure 60 provides that "[a]ny party may intervene by filing a pleading subject to being stricken out by the court for sufficient cause on the motion of any party." The rule authorizes a party with a justiciable interest in a pending suit to intervene in the suit as a matter of right. *Guar. Fed. Sav. Bank v. Horseshoe Operating Co.*, 793 S.W.2d 652, 657 (Tex. 1990). Because intervention is allowed as a matter of right, the "justiciable interest" requirement is of paramount importance: it defines the category of non-parties who may, without consultation with or permission from the original parties or the court, interject their interests into a pending suit to which the intervenors have not been invited. Thus, the "justiciable interest" requirement protects pending cases from having interlopers disrupt the proceedings. The parties to the pending case may protect themselves from the intervention by filing a motion to strike. *Id.* If any party to the pending suit moves to strike the intervention, the intervenors have the burden to show a justiciable interest in the pending suit. *Mendez v. Brewer*, 626 S.W.2d 498, 499 (Tex. 1982).

To constitute a justiciable interest, "[t]he intervenor's interest must be such that if the original action had never been commenced, and he had first brought it as the sole plaintiff, he would have been entitled to recover in his own name to the extent at least of a part of the relief sought" in the original suit. *King v. Olds*, 71 Tex. 729, 12 S.W. 65, 65 (Tex. 1888). In other words, a party may intervene if the intervenor could have "brought the [pending] action, or any part thereof, in his own name." *Guar. Fed. Sav. Bank*, 793 S.W.2d at 657.

In this case, the Halls' petition in intervention only briefly addressed their interest in the Moffett suit:

> In the original action, Moffett claims exposure to benzene and benzene-containing products at premises including Union Carbide in Texas City and against some, if not all, of the Defendants that Intervenors are making claims. Intervenors are entitled to a recovery against the defendants and Intervenors' claims [that] arise out of the same transaction and/or series of transactions and have common questions of law and/or fact with the claims in the original action.

Neither party introduced evidence at the hearing on Union Carbide's motion to strike. In their brief the Halls claim to have met their burden of showing that they had a justiciable interest in the Moffett suit. They primarily base their argument on allegations that Hall and Moffett suffered from similar blood disorders resulting from exposure to benzene at Union Carbide's facilities. Yet the Halls do not assert that they could have brought any part of Moffett's claim. While there is a real controversy between the Halls and Union Carbide—whether John Hall's exposure to toxic chemicals while working at Union Carbide caused his disease—the Halls make no claim that their controversy will be affected or resolved by resolution of the Moffett case. Accordingly, the Halls fail to demonstrate a justiciable interest in Moffett's suit and are not entitled to intervene in the Moffett suit.

The Halls assert that even if they did not properly intervene in Moffett's suit, the trial court had discretion to sever their claims rather than striking them. First, the Halls claim that their petition met the standard for permissive joinder found in Texas Rule of Civil Procedure 40, and therefore, the trial court could properly sever their claims under Rule 41. *See* TEX.R. CIV. P. 41 (providing that "actions which have been improperly joined may be severed"). But the joinder standard does not control here because this was an intervention, and the two are distinct. *Compare* TEX.R. CIV. P. 40(a) (providing the requirements to join in an action as a plaintiff), with

Guar. Fed. Sav. Bank, 793 S.W.2d at 657 (providing the requirements to intervene in an action). Permissive joinder relates to "proper parties to an action who may be joined or omitted at the pleader's election." 1 Roy W. McDonald & Elaine A. Grafton Carlson, TEXAS CIVIL PRACTICE § 5:29 (2d ed.2004)(emphasis added). Permissive joinder and intervention are authorized and permitted by separate rules, and the rules provide different processes for addressing the different situations. TEX.R. CIV. P. 41, 60. Because interventions by uninvited participants have potential for disrupting pending suits, trial courts should rule on motions to strike interventions before considering other matters such as severance.

The Halls reference *Boswell, O'Toole, Davis & Pickering v. Stewart*, 531 S.W.2d 380, 382 (Tex. Civ. App.—Houston [14th Dist.] 1975, no writ), in which the court stated that a trial judge may "proceed to trial of the intervention claim; he may sever the intervention; he may order a separate trial; he may strike the intervention for good cause." *See also Saldana v. Saldana*, 791 S.W.2d 316, 320-21 (Tex. App.—Corpus Christi 1990, no writ). However, Rule 60 does not provide for such options as equal alternatives; it provides only that an intervention is "subject to being stricken out by the court for sufficient cause on the motion of any party." TEX. R. CIV. P. 60.

The Halls further argue that mandamus relief is not proper because the Court cannot prescribe the manner in which the trial court exercises its discretion. *See Walker v. Packer*, 827 S.W.2d 833, 839-40 (Tex. 1992) (noting that mandamus relief is available to correct a trial court's clear abuse of discretion). The Halls' argument assumes that Rule 60 afforded the trial court discretion to refuse to rule on Union Carbide's motion to strike before it considered severing the Hall case from the Moffett case. It did not. The trial court abused its discretion in failing to first rule on the motion to strike. Furthermore, the Halls did not show that they possessed any justiciable interest in the Moffett lawsuit. They did not show that they had standing to have brought and recovered for any part of Moffett's claim. Accordingly, the trial court had no discretion to deny Union Carbide's motion to strike the petition in intervention.

For mandamus to issue, a relator must show that it has no adequate remedy by appeal. *In re Prudential Ins. Co. of Am.*, 148 S.W.3d 124, 135-36 (Tex. 2004). "An appellate remedy is 'adequate' when any benefits to mandamus review are outweighed by the detriments." *Id.* at 136. Union Carbide claims that the benefits of mandamus review outweigh the detriments because (1) the issue presented is one of law that is likely to recur, yet eludes an answer by appeal; (2) the trial court's action effectively establishes a template for circumventing procedures for random assignment of cases in multi-court counties; (3) it will be difficult or impossible to show on appeal that the deprivation of a randomly assigned judge entitles Union Carbide to appellate relief; (4) the effective initiation of suit by intervention and severance deprived Union Carbide of procedural rights afforded to defendants in original actions; and (5) granting mandamus will not result in any, or at most, negligible detriment. We agree with Union Carbide.

Regardless of the other benefits claimed by Union Carbide, there is significant benefit from mandamus relief in regard to the random-assignment-of-cases question. Random assignment of cases is designed to prevent forum-shopping. Practices that subvert random assignment procedures breed "disrespect for and [threaten] the integrity of our judicial system." *See In re Bennett*, 960 S.W.2d 35, 40 (Tex. 1997). We need not consider whether the intervention was intended to circumvent Galveston County's local rule requiring random assignment of cases because regardless of the Halls' intent, the intervention and the trial court's abuse of discretion in failing to rule on and grant the motion to strike resulted in circumvention of the random assignment rule. In regard to any detriment to the parties, the Halls' claims have now been filed as a separate lawsuit that is pending in Galveston County. There will be insignificant detriment to either party or the judicial system if mandamus relief is granted. On balance, mandamus review is warranted because the benefits of establishing the priority that trial courts must give to ruling on motions to strike interventions and re-emphasizing the importance of both appearance and practice in maintaining integrity of random assignment rules outweigh any detriment to mandamus review in this instance. Thus, Union Carbide does not have an adequate remedy by appeal.

Without hearing oral argument, we conditionally grant the writ of mandamus and direct the trial court to vacate its severance order and enter an order granting Union Carbide's motion to strike. *See* TEX.R.APP. P. 52.8(c). The writ will issue only if the trial court does not do so.

Note

Texas Commerce Bank, N.A. v. Grizzle, 96 S.W.3d 240 (Tex. 2002): Plaintiff-Grizzle filed several amended petitions that attempted to add new putative class representatives. Summary judgment was entered against Grizzle, and the amended petitions were stricken. The Supreme Court held that because Grizzle has no live individual claim, the trial court properly struck the amended petitions, which sought to add new class representatives, who could not possibly have a claim or defense in common with Grizzle, who never had a claim. For the same reason, the putative class claims Grizzle brought failed, as a matter of law, and the trial court properly rendered final judgment for the TCB and Frost defendants. Regardless of when the amended petitions and purported interventions were filed, the trial court still had to consider Grizzle's standing to bring suit, before granting the interventions through the amended petitions. A plaintiff without a claim cannot be allowed to bring suit by making a class action allegation. By the same token: A third party cannot intervene in a class action suit to save a claim, as to which the original plaintiff never had a claim, for the intervenors cannot possibly have a claim or defense in common with a plaintiff who never had a claim.

Notes

1. Under the authority of Rule 174(b) of the Texas Rules of Civil Procedure the Supreme Court has held that as a general rule liability and damages may not be bifurcated into separate trials in personal injury cases. *See Iley v. Hughes*, 158 Tex. 362, 311 S.W.2d 648 (1958). However, in *Transportation Ins. Co. v. Moriel*, 879 S.W.2d 10 (Tex. 1994) the Supreme Court held that there is an exception to this general rule in punitive damages cases. In such cases there is a "requirement of bifurcated trials."

2. In the cases of *In Re: Ethyl Corporation, USX Corporation, Todd Shipyards,* 975 S.W.2d 601 (Tex. 1998) and in *In Re: Bristol-Myers Squibb Co.*, 975 S.W.2d 606 (Tex. 1998) the Court struggled with the problems of consolidation and separate trials in the context of mass tort litigation (arising out exposure to asbestos in *Ethyl,* and breast implants in *Bristol-Myers Squibb).* In *Ethyl,* the court, in passing, discussed consolidation in ordinary cases as follows:

> Under TEX. R. CIV. P. 174(b) a trial court has discretion to decline to order separate trials, but that discretion is not unlimited. A trial court is required to exercise a sound and legal discretion within limits created by the circumstances of the particular case. The express purpose of Rule 174(b) was to further convenience, to avoid prejudice, and to promote the ends of justice. The trial court has no discretion to deny separate trials, when an injustice will result: *When all of the facts and circumstances of the case unquestionably require a separate trial to prevent manifest injustice, and there is no fact or circumstance supporting, or tending to support, a contrary conclusion, and the legal rights of the parties will not be prejudiced thereby, there is no room for the exercise of discretion.* The rule then is peremptory in operation, and imposes upon the court a duty to order a separate trial. Many considerations under Rule 174(b) are shared under Rule 174(a), and the paramount objective of preventing injustice obtains whether the question is one of separate trials, or of consolidation. The rights of the parties to a fair trial cannot be compromised in the name of judicial economy.

3. *Tarrant Regional Water District v. Gragg*, 47 Tex.Sup.Ct.J. 207, ___ S.W.3d ___ (2004 WL 1439646) (Tex. 2004): The trial court, in this inverse condemnation action, did not abuse its discretion by refusing to order a separate trial on the taking issue and on the issue of reasonable compensation, if a taking was found to have occurred. TEX. R. CIV. PROC. 174(b) allows a trial court to order a separate trial on any issue, in the interest of convenience, or to avoid prejudice. Defendants typically proceed generally without knowing whether they will be found liable, or on what, if any, theory. Although it is often preferable, or even necessary, to bifurcate the trial of an inverse condemnation case, so that takings issues are tried to the bench before damage issues are submitted to the jury, the Court's statements in neither *State v. Wood Oil Distributing, Inc.*, 751 S.W.2d 863, 865 (Tex. 1988), and *State v. Heal*, 917 S.W.2d 6, 9 (Tex. 1996) support the District's argument that separate trials must be conducted on taking and compensation issues, in every case.

7. *Class Actions*

Read Rule 42 of the Texas Rules of Civil Procedure

FORD MOTOR COMPANY
v.
SHELDON
22 S.W.3d 444
(Tex. 2000)

Jessie A. Amos, John H. Coates, Craig A. Morgan, Austin, Jonathan L. Griffith, Washington, DC, for Petitioners.

Stephen E. McConnico, Ray N. Donley, Tommy Jacks, Sam Johnson, James L. Wright, Austin, Mark G. Einfalt, Houston, for Respondents.

CHIEF JUSTICE PHILLIPS delivered the opinion of the Court, in which JUSTICE HECHT, JUSTICE ENOCH, JUSTICE OWEN, JUSTICE ABBOTT, JUSTICE HANKINSON, JUSTICE O'NEILL, and JUSTICE GONZALES joined.

Seven owners of certain types of Ford vehicles, individually and on behalf of all others who bought similar vehicles in Texas, brought this class action against Ford Motor Co., a Ford dealer, and a Ford district manager. The suit prayed for damages for peeling paint, allegedly caused by the lack of spray primer in the paint process, on certain 1984-1993 vehicle models. The trial court certified the class under Texas Rule of Civil Procedure 42(b)(4). The court of appeals affirmed after modifying the class definition. *Ford Motor Company, Inc. v. Sheldon*, 965 S.W.2d 65 (Tex. App.—Austin 1998). Ford filed this interlocutory appeal in this Court under Texas Motor Vehicle Commission Code Section 6.06(g). We hold that this Court does have jurisdiction, and that the trial court's definition and the court of appeals' modified definition are both defective. Because these defects cannot be cured on appeal, we reverse the court of appeals' judgment affirming the class certification and remand for the trial court to decertify the class.

I

Barry Sheldon, Matthew Rueter, Margaret Dunayer, John Porter, William Dobbs, James Beasley, and B.J. Sanders (collectively "Purchasers") filed this consumer class action against Ford Motor Co., Leif Johnson Ford, Inc.(a Ford dealership in Austin), and Fred Capdevielle (Ford's district manager in Houston from 1984-1994) ("Ford"), alleging that Ford knowingly used a defective paint process resulting in premature paint peeling on their Ford vehicles. They contend that the cause of this defect was Ford's removal of spray primer from the paint process as a cost-saving measure in the early 1980s. Before that time, Ford applied low-build electrocoat to sheet metal and then sprayed a primer before adding the enamel topcoat. Under the new process, which was adopted for F-Series Trucks, Broncos, Bronco IIs, Rangers, and Mustangs, Ford replaced low-build electrocoat with medium- or high-build electrocoat and then applied the topcoat directly to the electrocoat. Purchasers argue that, because electrocoat is not weather-resistant, removing the primer from the paint process caused the paint on many vehicles to delaminate. When exposed to ultraviolet sunlight, the enamel paint coat could separate from the vehicle's metal surface within 18 to 36 months. Purchasers assert that Ford learned of the alleged defect within a few years after adopting the new paint process, but continued to use it until the early 1990s, selling the affected cars to Texas consumers while consciously concealing the problem.

Based on these allegations, Purchasers brought claims against Ford for violating the Texas Deceptive Trade Practices Act ("DTPA") and breaching the implied warranty of merchantability. Purchasers alleged that Ford violated section 17.46(b)(5) of the DTPA by representing that the vehicles have characteristics that they do not have, section 17.46(b)(7) by representing that the vehicles are of a particular quality when they are, in fact, of another, section 17.46(b)(23) by failing to disclose information about the vehicles that was known at the time of the transactions when such failure to disclose was intended to induce consumers into transactions that they would not have entered had the information been disclosed, and section 17.45(5) by acting unconscionably. *See* TEX. BUS. & COMM. CODE §§ 17.45(5), 17.46(b)(5), (7), (23).

Purchasers also brought breach of contract, common-law fraud and conspiracy to defraud claims. After certification, the trial court granted Ford's motion for summary judgment with respect to Purchasers' breach of contract and common-law fraud claims. The conspiracy claim, which alleges that "Defendant Ford conspired with other dealers to hide this problem from consumers and to prevent consumers from getting their vehicles promptly and properly repaired," apparently remains pending in the trial court.

Purchasers sought certification of the following class:

> All persons who purchased a new 1987-1993 Ford F-Series Truck, 1987-1993 Ford Bronco, 1987-1989 Ford Bronco II, 1987-1992 Ford Ranger or 1987-1989 Ford Mustang in Texas on or after March 8, 1988 which was painted with high build electrocoat or medium build electrocoat and no spray primer and who suffered past and/or future damage as a result of peeling or flaking paint on these vehicles caused by a defective paint process (i.e., high build electrocoat or medium build electrocoat and no spray primer) excluding persons who purchased vehicles pursuant to a fleet account or fleet identification number; and all persons who purchased a new 1984-1988 Ford F-Series Truck, 1984-1988 Ford Bronco, 1984-1988 Ford Bronco II, 1984-1988 Ford Ranger or 1984-1988 Ford Mustang in Texas prior to March 8, 1988 which was painted with high build electrocoat or medium build electrocoat and no spray primer and who paid Ford or a Ford dealership for a paint repair to their vehicle to repair peeling or flaking paint caused by a defective paint process (i.e., high build electrocoat or medium build electrocoat and no spray primer), excluding persons who purchased vehicles pursuant to a fleet account or fleet identification number.

The trial court certified the class under Texas Rule of Civil Procedure 42(b)(4), determining that these questions were common to the class: (1) whether there was a defective paint process by reason of lack of primer, (2) whether Ford had knowledge of the defect, (3) whether Ford withheld information of the defect when it had a duty to disclose, and (4) how the discovery rule applied to delay the running of limitations. The court contemplated a two-phase trial in which the common liability questions would be determined first, with the court proceeding to individualized damage inquiries only if Ford were found liable.

The court of appeals modified the certification order. Although the court approved having "a phase of individual trials following the class-wide resolution of the common issues," 965 S.W.2d at 67-68, it determined that the class definitions in the certification order "violate Rule 42 by allowing the named plaintiffs to proceed in a class action before showing that a class exists." *Id.* at 73. The court modified the definitions by inserting the phrase "who allege the peeling or flaking was" before the clause "caused by a defective paint process" in both subclasses. *Id.* at 74. As modified, the class includes those purchasers of certain specified Ford vehicles who suffered past or future diminution in value damages or out of pocket expenses from peeling paint and who allege that the cause of the peeling is the lack of spray primer in the paint process. Ford filed an interlocutory appeal in this Court under Texas Motor Vehicle Commission Code Section 6.06(g), requesting that we reverse the judgment of the court of appeals and decertify the class. *See* TEX. REV. CIV. STAT. art. 4413(36), § 6.06(g). Ford argues that the court of appeals erred in (1) redefining the class sua sponte to include those who allege that the lack of primer caused the peeling of their vehicles, thereby certifying a "failsafe" class; (2) determining that common issues exist when "a jury may reach different conclusions with respect to different class members"; (3) concluding that the common issues predominate over individual issues given the court of appeals' conclusion that "thousands of individual trials might be necessary on liability and damage issues," 965 S.W.2d at 72; (4) determining that the class action is superior to alternative means of adjudication when the DTPA provides incentives for individual adjudication; and (5) affirming a trial plan providing for adjudication of liability issues before one jury and damage issues before a second group of juries when Texas prohibits multi-stage, piecemeal trials.

II

* * *

III

The class action device originated in the equity courts of England as a means to overcome the requirement that "all persons materially interested, either legally or beneficially, in the subject matter of a suit, are to be made parties to it." DICKERSON, CLASS ACTIONS: THE LAW OF 50 STATES § 1.02[1], at 1-6 (1999) (citation omitted); *see also Phillips Petroleum Co. v. Shutts*, 472 U.S. 797, 808, 105 S.Ct. 2965, 86 L.Ed.2d 628 (1985); *Hansberry v. Lee*, 311 U.S. 32, 41, 61 S.Ct. 115, 85 L.Ed. 22 (1940). It was designed as " 'an exception to the usual rule that litigation is conducted by and on behalf of the individual named parties only.' " *General Tel. Co. v. Falcon*, 457 U.S. 147, 155, 102 S.Ct. 2364, 72 L.Ed.2d 740 (1982) (*quoting Califano v. Yamasaki*, 442 U.S. 682, 700-01, 99 S.Ct. 2545, 61 L.Ed.2d 176 (1979)). "In a class action, the complained-of wrong is allegedly committed against a class of individuals, and the judgment in the case binds the entire class, not merely named parties." *Vinson v. Texas Commerce Bank-Houston*, 880 S.W.2d 820, 823 (Tex. App.—Dallas 1994, no writ).

Although Federal Rule 23 codified the class action procedure in 1938, it "gained its current shape in an innovative 1966 revision." *Amchem Prods., Inc. v. Windsor*, 521 U.S. 591, 613, 117 S.Ct. 2231, 138 L.Ed.2d 689 (1997); *see generally* Kaplan, *Continuing Work of the Civil Committee: 1966 Amendments of the Federal Rules of Civil Procedure* (I), 81 HARV L. REV. 356 (1967). Texas Rule 42, adopted in 1941 and patterned after the federal rule, was also fully revised in 1977 to conform to the 1966 federal amendments. Thus, federal decisions and authorities interpreting current federal class action requirements are persuasive in Texas actions. *See RSR Corp. v. Hayes*, 673 S.W.2d 928, 931-32 (Tex. App.—Dallas 1984, writ dism'd).

Rule 42, like its federal counterpart, is intended to "eliminate or reduce the threat of repetitive litigation," "prevent inconsistent resolution of similar cases," and "provide an effective means of redress for individuals whose claims are too small to make it economically viable to pursue them in independent actions." *See* THE AMERICAN LAW INSTITUTE, REPORT: PRELIMINARY STUDY OF COMPLEX LITIGATION 35 (1987). When properly used, the class action device " 'saves the resources of both the courts and the parties by permitting an issue potentially affecting every class member to be litigated in an economical fashion.' " *Falcon*, 457 U.S. at 155, 102 S.Ct. 2364 (*quoting Yamasaki*, 442 U.S. at 701, 99 S.Ct. 2545) (alterations omitted).

Even though it is an efficient device, there is no right to litigate a claim as a class action. "Rather, rule 42 provides only that the court may certify a class action if the plaintiff satisfies the requirements of the rule." *Weatherly*, 905 S.W.2d at 647 (emphasis in original). Rule 42(a) establishes four initial prerequisites to class certification: numerosity, commonality, typicality, and adequacy of representation. Moreover, a proposed class action must satisfy at least one of the subdivisions of Rule 42(b), which are:

> (1) the prosecution of separate actions by or against individual members would create a risk of
>
> > (A) inconsistent or varying adjudications with respect to individual members of the class which would establish incompatible standards of conduct for the party opposing the class, or
> >
> > (B) adjudications with respect to individual members of the class which would as a practical matter be dispositive of the interests of the other members not parties to the adjudications or substantially impair or impede their ability to protect their interests; or
>
> (2) the party opposing the class has acted or refused to act on grounds generally applicable to the class, thereby making appropriate final injunctive relief or corresponding declaratory relief with respect to the class as a whole; or
>
> (3) where the object of the action is the adjudication of claims which do or may affect specific property involved in the action; or
>
> (4) the court finds that the questions of law or fact common to the members of the class predominate over any questions affecting only individual members, and that a class action is superior to other available methods for the fair and efficient adjudication of the controversy . . . . TEX. R. CIV. P. 42(b).

In this case, Purchasers sought certification of a class under the fourth class action category.

A

Although not an express requirement, "it is axiomatic that for a class action to be certified a 'class' must exist." *Simer v. Rios*, 661 F.2d 655, 669 (7th Cir.1981); *accord DeBremaecker v. Short*, 433 F.2d 733, 734 (5th Cir.1970); *Intratex Gas Co. v. Beeson*, 22 S.W.3d 398, 403 (Tex. 2000); *Reserve Life Ins. Co. v. Kirkland*, 917 S.W.2d 836, 839 (Tex. App.—Houston [14th Dist.] 1996, no writ). A properly defined class is essential to the maintenance of a class action. *See Intratex*, 22 S.W.3d at 403. A proper class definition determines who is entitled to notice, who is entitled to relief and what relief can be awarded. *Id.* In addition, the class definition specifies who will be bound by the judgment. *Id.*; *see also* FEDERAL JUDICIAL CENTER, MANUAL FOR COMPLEX LITIGATION 217 (3d ed. 1995) (concluding that the notice requirement for (b)(4) class actions mandates greater precision for class definitions brought under (b)(4) than for those brought under other class action categories). Thus, the failure to adequately define a proposed class implicates due process rights. As a distinguished judge has observed:

> [W]ithout reasonable specificity the court cannot define the class, cannot determine whether the representation is adequate, and the [defendant] does not know how to defend. And, what may be most significant, an over-broad framing of the class may be so unfair to the absent members as to approach, if not amount to, deprivation of due process.

Johnson v. Georgia Highway Express, Inc., 417 F.2d 1122, 1126 (5th Cir.1969) (GODBOLD, J., concurring).

For a class to be properly defined, the class members must be clearly ascertainable by reference to objective criteria. *See Intratex*, 22 S.W.3d at 403. While a class definition need not be so specific "that every potential member can be identified at the commencement of the action," 7A CHARLES ALAN WRIGHT, ARTHUR R. MILLER & MARY KAY KANE, FEDERAL PRACTICE & PROCEDURE, § 1760, at 117 (1986); *accord Intratex*, 22 S.W.3d at 404, a "class should not be defined by criteria that are subjective or that require an analysis of the merits of the case" because class membership would not be presently ascertainable. *Intratex*, 22 S.W.3d at 404.

The court of appeals determined that the proposed class certified by the trial court "allow[s] the named plaintiffs to proceed in a class action before showing that a class exists." 965 S.W.2d at 73. Because a "full trial . . . of some issues [would be necessary] before class membership could be ascertained," the court modified the class definitions from those "who suffered past and/or future damage as a result of peeling or flaking paint on these vehicles caused by a defective paint process" or "who paid Ford or a Ford dealership for a paint repair to their vehicle to repair peeling or flaking paint caused by a defective paint process" to those "who suffered past and/or future damage as a result of peeling or flaking paint on these vehicles who allege the peeling or flaking was caused by a defective paint process" and those "who paid Ford or a Ford dealership for a paint repair to their vehicle to repair peeling or flaking paint who allege the peeling or flaking was caused by a defective paint process" *Id.* at 73-74.

We agree with the court of appeals that the class defined by the trial court fails to meet *Intratex's* clearly-ascertainable requirement. Including the defect theory as an element of the class definition impermissibly requires a determination of the merits before the court can ensure the existence of a class. *See Intratex*, 22 S.W.3d at 404 ("[W]hen the class definition is framed as a legal conclusion, the trial court has no way of ascertaining whether a given person is a member of the class until a determination of ultimate liability as to that person is made."). Moreover, basing the class definition on a determination of the merits creates a fail-safe class because if the defendants prevail at trial and Purchasers are unable to prove their theory, then there was never a class to begin with and certification was inappropriate. *Id.* Therefore, the proposed members of the unsuccessful class would not be bound by the judgment. Clearly, the trial court abused its discretion in defining the class in this manner. *Id.*

But Ford contends that the court of appeals' class definition is also erroneous. That definition limits the class to those persons "who allege" that the peeling was caused by the lack of spray primer.

The use of state of mind in a class definition "serves as a shorthand method of alerting the court and the parties that there might be difficulty in identifying class members." *Simer*, 661 F.2d at 670 n. 25. When a class is "so highly diverse and so difficult to identify that it is not adequately defined or nearly ascertainable," *Adashunas v. Negley*, 626 F.2d 600, 604 (7th Cir. 1980), the class definition will not be sustained. *See DeBremaecker*, 433 F.2d at 734; *see also* CHARLES ALAN WRIGHT, ARTHUR R. MILLER & MARY KAY KANE, 7A FEDERAL PRACTICE & PROCEDURE, § 1760, at 123-26 (1986) ("a class defined with reference to the state of mind of its members" renders the class "too amorphous" and will not be allowed to proceed).

We need not go so far as to hold that a class definition may never require the trial court to make a subjective inquiry into the claimants' thought processes. *See Developments in the Law—Class Actions*, 89 HARV. L. REV. 1318, 1478 n.128 (1976) (concluding that the use of state of mind in class definitions does not render a class unascertainable when identification is possible otherwise). But here, there are no realistic means for the trial court to determine which class members "allege that the peeling or flaking was caused by a defective paint process." The trial court would have to inquire individually into each proposed class member's state of mind to ascertain class membership under the court of appeals' class definition. *See Forman v. Data Transfer, Inc.*, 164 F.R.D. 400, 403 (E.D.Pa.1995) (class definition was untenable because determining class membership would require mini-hearings); *Metcalf v. Edelman*, 64 F.R.D. 407, 409-10 (N.D. Ill. 1974) (class definition cannot stand when it requires individual adjudications to determine membership). Such a monumental task at the outset defeats the benefits of the class action. *See Reyes v. San Diego County Bd. of Supervisors*, 196 Cal.App.3d 1263, 242 Cal.Rptr. 339, 345 (1987) ("[W]here the administrative cost in identification [of class members] . . . is so substantial to render the likely appreciable benefits to the class de minimis in comparison, the class action should not be certified."). Therefore, the court of appeals' definition also fails to satisfy the clearly-ascertainable requirement.

B

Having found that neither the trial court's definition nor the court of appeals' modified definition satisfies the clearly ascertainable requirement, we must now determine whether we should attempt to redefine the class, if that can be done, or remand the case for the trial court to decertify the class. In *Intratex*, we refused to redefine a class, concluding that "the better course [was] to remand the action to the trial court for it to determine if the definitional problems can be eliminated." *See Intratex*, 22 S.W.3d at 405. Like the definition in *Intratex*, the trial court and the court of appeals' definitions do not lend themselves to appellate redefinition. Therefore, instead of attempting to determine whether the class can or should be redefined, we remand the case to the trial court to decertify the class. We express no opinion about whether, if the Purchasers proposed a different definition, the trial court could certify a class that would meet the requisites of Rule 42.

* * *

Because both the trial court and the court of appeals' definitions fail to meet the clearly-ascertainable requirement, we reverse the judgment of the court below and remand to the trial court to decertify the class. Our action is without prejudice to a further attempt by Purchasers to seek certification of a class consistent with this opinion.

JUSTICE BAKER filed a dissenting opinion.

Notes

1. *Henry Schein, Inc. v. Stromboe*, ___Tex. Sup. Ct. J. ___, 2002 WL 31426407 (October 31, 2002): Under Rule 42(b)(4) of the Texas Rules of Civil Procedure, the district court certified a nationwide class of some 20,000 purchasers of three dental practice management software products. There are members of this class in all fifty states. The five named plaintiffs and their counsel allege that the software was defective, and was sold under false pretenses on which buyers relied. Some of the causes of action they assert are breach of contract, breach of express and implied warranties, fraudulent and negligent misrepresentations, and violations of the Texas Deceptive Trade Practices—Consumer Protection Act. They claim actual, special, consequential, exemplary, and statutory damages, as well as restitution of all amounts paid, up to $74,000 per purchaser, or $1.48 billion overall. The district court determined to adjudicate all of these claims, including those of out-of-state purchasers, under Texas law. On interlocutory appeal, the court of appeals affirmed. Held: The class is decertified, and the case remanded to the trial court. The representative plaintiffs have failed to demonstrate, as Rule 42(b)(4) requires they must, "that the questions of law or fact common to the members of the class predominate over any questions affecting only individual members, and that a class action is superior to other available methods for the fair and efficient adjudication of the controversy."

In class actions, *Southwestern Refining Co. v. Bernal*, 22 S.W.3d 425 (Tex. 2000), does not require a "trial plan," by that name, set out in a separate document. Rather, TEX. R. CIV. P. 42 requires a rigorous analysis and a specific explanation of how class claims are to proceed to trial. Compliance with Rule 42 must be demonstrated; it cannot merely be presumed.

Class certification should be rejected when multiple states' laws must be applied.

Under the facts of this case (detailed in the opinion), the plaintiffs have failed to satisfy the superiority requirement of TEX. R. CIV. P. 42(b)(4), in that they have failed to show that a class action is either more fair or more efficient in these circumstances. Efficiency is a vital goal in any legal system—but the vision of "efficiency" underlying this class certification is the model of the central planner. The central planning model—one case, one court, one set of rules, one settlement price for all involved—suppresses information that is vital to accurate resolution. Markets instead use diversified decision making to supply and evaluate information. Thousands of traders affect prices by their purchases and sales over the course of a crop year. This method looks "inefficient" from the planner's perspective, but it produces more information, more accurate prices, and a vibrant, growing economy. When courts think of efficiency, they should think of market models rather than central-planning models.

2. The class in a class-action lawsuit may not be defined by the ultimate liability issue. Such a class is referred to as a "fail safe class." In *Intratex Gas Company v. Beeson*, 96 S.W.3d 240 (Tex. 2002) the trial court's class definition—those producers "whose natural gas was taken by the defendant in quantities less than their ratable proportions"—turns on the issue certified by the trial court—whether Intratex took nonratably from the class members. Class membership is not presently ascertainable, because the certified issue of whether Intratex took ratably has yet to be decided. Under the trial court's definition, the parties will have to await the outcome of the litigation to determine who, if anyone, is in the class, because whether Intratex took nonratably is the central issue to be determined at trial. If judgment is rendered for Plaintiffs, the various producers' ability to exercise their right to opt out of the class action will have been compromised, because the judgment will bind those producers who were taken from nonratably. But if Intratex wins at trial, there is no class because its existence is dependent on a finding that Plaintiffs were taken from nonratably. Plaintiffs cannot be bound by such a judgment because without a class, there is no way to ascertain class membership. Certification of the class under these circumstances is clearly impermissible. Furthermore, while the trial court possesses significant discretion to modify the class definition or even decertify the class as the case develops, the trial court must still certify only those classes which are sufficiently defined and meet the rule 42 requirements. Because the class definition in this case is not precise, and its members cannot be ascertained until the alleged ultimate liability issue is decided, the trial court abused its discretion when it certified the class.

3. *Union Pacific Resources Group, Inc. v. Hankins*, 69 S.W.3d 69 (Tex. 2003): The trial court certified a class consisting of gas royalty owners in Crockett County who claim that lessees breached an implied duty to "obtain the best current price reasonably obtainable." The court of appeals affirmed. As certified, the class includes some royalty owners whose leases calculate royalty payments on an amount-realized (or proceeds) basis and other royalty owners whose leases calculate royalty payments based on current market value. The Supreme Court reversed and remanded the case holding that because a covenant to obtain the best price reasonably attainable is implied under Texas law only to proceeds leases, not to market-value leases, the royalty owners have not established, as required by TEX. R. CIV. P. 42 that there are "questions of law or fact common to the class" sufficient to support certification. The threshold for commonality is not high. Yet it does require at least one issue of law or fact that inheres in the complaints of all class members. A common issue must also be applicable to the class as a whole and be subject to generalized proof. Here, unity of value cannot be established through common proof.

4. H.B. 4, the Tort Reform Act of 2003 ordered the Texas Supreme Court to adopted new rules for the "fair and efficient resolution of class actions". *See* TEX. R. CIV. PROC. 42.

5. *Compaq Computer Corporation v. Lapray*, 135 S.W.3d 657 (Tex. 2004): Plaintiffs, on behalf of themselves and all others similarly situated, sued Compaq Computer Corporation alleging that Compaq sold them computers containing defective floppy disk controllers (AFDCs"). Plaintiffs allege that the affected computers, some thirty-seven models of Compaq Presario computers, contain defective FDCs. The plaintiffs seek a declaration that (1) Compaq breached its express warranty, (2) Compaq breached its obligation to repair, replace, or refund, (3i) the FDC defect is covered by Compaq's express warranty, and (4) class members have a right to seek relief under the warranty. In the alternative, they seek damages, either in the form of a refund, the difference in value between a computer without the FDC defect and the computer as purchased, or damages for breach of the duty to repair or replace. Plaintiffs explicitly disclaim consequential damages from loss or corruption of data. The trial court certified a nationwide class under TEX. R. CIV. P. 42(b)(2) and (b)(3). The trial court also certified both the declaratory relief and the damage claims under (b)(3). The court of appeals affirmed. Held: Reversed and remanded. Rule 42(b)(3)'s predominance requirement is not satisfied. While the (b)(3) class would be automatically entitled to notice and opt-out, the trial court failed to even examine the possibility of notice and opt-out for the (b)(2) class. The Supreme Court is reluctant to affirm a (b)(2) class that includes claims for damages without the concomitant protections afforded by notice and opt-out, and cannot do so without knowing whether class members will be provided these protections. This is particularly true when, as here, the class has disclaimed consequential damages. If, in fact, some purchasers suffered such damages, their inclusion in a mandatory class may be improper; that is, due process may require that they be given notice of the

class action and an opportunity to opt out and preserve their claims. Parties may not evade *Southwestern Refining Co. v. Bernal*, 22 S.W.3d 425 (Tex. 2000) by seeking TEX. R. CIV. P. 42(b)(2) certification. Although (b)(2) does not explicitly require predominance and superiority as (b)(3) does, (b)(2) does require a rigorous analysis of "cohesiveness." Generally, (b)(2) classes are premised on an assumption of homogeneity. The members of a (b)(2) class are generally bound together through preexisting or continuing legal relationships or by some significant common trait such as race or gender.

6. In *Best Buy v. Barrera*, --- S.W.3d ----, --- Tex. Sup. Ct. J. ----, 2007 WL 4216615 (Tex.), consumers brought this class-action suit for "money had and received", to recover a restocking fee that was deducted from refunds made on certain returned merchandise. The trial court certified a statewide class, and the court of appeals affirmed. 214 S.W.3d 66, 71. ***Held:*** The class is decertified, and the case is remanded for the trial court. This case involves a claim for money had and received, and equitable defenses will be available, under the particular circumstances of each case. Equitable defenses like these demonstrate that the vast majority of the litigation could be spent trying to determine which individuals should recover their restocking fees under the equities presented and which should not. Therefore, individualized inquiry will predominate over common issues of proof, making the claim inappropriate for class certification.

CHAPTER 10.
DISCOVERY

1. *Discovery Control Plans*

Under TEX. R. CIV. P. 190.1, "[e]very case must be governed by a discovery control plan as provided in this rule. A plaintiff must allege in the first numbered paragraph of the original petition whether discovery is intended to be conduced under Level 1, 2, or 3 of this Rule."

Level 1
(Rule 190.2)

When: Level 1 applies to suits governed by the expedited action process of Rule 169 to suits for divorce where there are no children and the marital estate does not exceed $50,000 unless the parties agree that that Level 2 should apply or the court orders a discovery control plan under Rule 190.4.

Limits: Under Level 1 discovery, each party is limited to six hours of oral depositions, 15 written interrogatories, 15 requests for production, 15 requests for admission, and requests for disclosure under rule 194 including "all documents, electronic information, and tangible items that the disclosing party has in its possession, custody, or control and may use to support its claims or defenses.

Discovery Period: The discovery period "begins when the suit is filed and continues until 180 days after the date the first request for discovery of any kind is served on a party."

Level 2
(Rule 190.3)

When: Level 2 (Rule 190.3) applies to all suits not controlled by Level 1 or Level 3 discovery.

Limits: Under Level 2 discovery, each party is limited to "50 hours in oral depositions to examine and cross-examine parties on the opposing side, experts designated by those parties, and persons who are subject to those parties control. 'Side' refers to all the litigants with generally common interest in the litigation. If one side designates more than two experts, the opposing side may have an additional six hours of total deposition time for each additional expert designated. The court may modify the deposition hours and must do so when a side or party would be given unfair advantage." Each party is limited to 25 interrogatories.

Discovery Period: The discovery period "begins when suit is filed and continues until:

(A) 30 days before the date set for trial, in cases under the Family Code, or

(B) in other cases, the earlier of

(i) 30 days before the date set for trial, or

(ii) nine months after the earlier of the date of the first oral deposition or the due date of the first response to written discovery.

Level 3
(Rule 190.4)

When: "The court must, on a party's motion, and may, on its own initiative, order that discovery be conducted in accordance with a discovery control plan tailored to the circumstances of the specific suit. The parties may submit an agreed order to the court for its consideration. The court should act on a party's motion or agreed order under this subdivision as promptly as reasonably possible.

Limits: "The plan must include:

(1) a date for trial or for a conference to determine a trial setting;

(2) a discovery period during which either all discovery must be conducted or all discovery requests must be sent, for the entire case or an appropriate phase of it;

(3) appropriate limits on the amount of discovery; and

(4) for joining additional parties, amending or supplementing pleadings, and designating expert witnesses."

Modification of Discovery Plans
(Rule 190.5)

"The court may modify a discovery control plan at any time and must do so when the interest of justice requires." In stated circumstances the court must allow additional discovery (read the rule).

Note

In re BP Products North America, Inc., 244 S.W.3d 840 (Tex: 2008): Discovery Agreements Between Parties Are Permissible. TEX. R. CIV. P. 191.1 provides that "except where specifically prohibited" the parties may modify the "rules pertaining to discovery" by agreement. An agreement is enforceable when it complies with the terms of TEX. R. CIV. P. 11, or as it affects an oral deposition, if made a part of the record of the deposition. The agreement in this case complied with the requirements of Rule 11. The parties entered into a valid discovery agreement. The parties agreed to define the scope of permissible discovery, under Rule 192.3(a), limiting the expense and burden of litigating a disputed issue. Finding that subsequent events justified modifying the agreement, the trial court set it aside. Held: Writ of mandamus will issue. The trial court abused its discretion, in setting aside a valid discovery agreement, without good cause. In this case, one party had already acted in reliance on the agreed procedure, partially performing its obligations. Consistent with its powers over discovery, under TEX. R. CIV. P. 191.1, a trial court may modify discovery procedures and limitations for "good cause." This power, however, is not "unbounded." The trial court apparently set aside the agreement here based on the court's application of equitable and contract principles. The trial court found that BP's Chief Executive Officer's, Browne's, public statements justified setting aside the discovery agreement on grounds of misrepresentation, estoppel, and changed circumstances. On this record [detailed in the opinion], none of these grounds provides a valid basis for ignoring the parties' agreement. The plaintiffs identify no specific misrepresentations on which they may have relied. Nor does the record contain evidentiary support for the assertion that BP Products made a material, false representation that could have reasonably induced the plaintiffs to enter the discovery agreement.

2. *Scope of Discovery*

Notes

1. TEX. R. CIV. P. 192.3. "*a. In General.* Parties may obtain discovery regarding any matter which is relevant to the subject matter in the pending action whether it relates to the claim or defense of the party seeking discovery or the claim or defense of any other party. It is not ground for objection that the information sought will be inadmissible at the trial if the information sought appears reasonably calculated to lead to the discovery of admissible evidence."

2. The "Scope of Discovery" in Texas (at least up to 1/1/1999) is as broad as you can make it. At one time, including the time of the decision in *Carroll Cable, infra,* the rule spoke of "good cause" rather than "relevance." The move to a "relevance" standard was intended to broaden the scope of discovery.

3. *Carroll Cable Company v Miller,* 501 S.W.2d 299 (Tex. 1973). Liability insurance policies, including the limits of such policies, are discoverable. It is sufficient showing of "good cause" that an insurance agreement is not available to the moving party and that the information is needed to determine settlement and litigation strategy. [Now codified in TEX. R. CIV. P. 192.3, formerly Rule 166b (2)(f)(1)]

4. Rule 190.1 requires that every case be governed by a discovery control plan as provided by rule 190. The rule promulgates three different Levels of discovery for cases and provides discovery limitations on all cases depending on which Level the particular case falls under. The student should review that rule.

5. In *Allen v. Humphreys*, 559 S.W.2d 798 (Tex. 1977) the Court addressed the question of the scope of discovery. The case involved a workmen's compensation appeal by Allen an employee of Safeway Stores. Allen alleged that she suffered from lung cancer and that the cause of her condition had been her exposure during the course and scope of her employment in the meat department of a Safeway Store to polyvinyl chloride particles released into the air when meat wrapping film was cut with a hot wire. She sought the discovery of a wide range of documents, including information relating to tests results and reports concerning the Safeway work environment and information relating to similar claims made by other employees. In addressing the discoverability of these matters the Court stated:

> In support of the trial court order denying discovery it is argued that the information sought to be discovered is relevant only on the issue of Safeway's fault, and since fault is not an issue in a workmen's compensation suit, it is asserted the items sought do not "constitute or contain" and are not "reasonably calculated to lead to the discovery of" evidence "material to any matter involved in the action." Though undoubtedly relevant to the issue of Safeway's fault, the items sought by Relator are also relevant to the issue of whether the conditions under which Mrs. Allen worked contributed to the cause of her affliction. Any test results, reports, surveys, and complaints by similarly affected individuals might reveal a causal relationship between the working conditions experienced by the Relator and the disease suffered by her, and if not themselves admissible, such documents reasonably might be expected to lead to the discovery of relevant and admissible evidence.

6. The Supreme Court shed additional light on the scope of discovery in *Jampole v. Touchy*, 673 S.W.2d 569 (Tex. 1984). *Jampole* was a products liability lawsuit in which the plaintiff sought to recover damages as the result of the death of his wife following a post-collision, fuel feed fire. The 1976 Vega in which Mrs. Jampole was driving caught fire after being struck from the rear by another car. The plaintiff sought discovery of a vast amount of material from General Motors Corporation. General Motors resisted the discovery. In a mandamus proceeding before the Court JUSTICE SPEARS stated:

> In making this determination [whether the trial court abused its discretion in denying certain requested discovery], we note that the ultimate purpose of discovery is to seek the truth, so that disputes may be decided by what the facts reveal, not by what facts are concealed. For this reason, discovery is not limited to information that will be admissible at trial. * * *
>
> Jampole filed interrogatories to determine GMC's pre-accident knowledge of alternative designs that would have reduced the risk of fuel escaping from the Vega fuel tank on impact, entering the passenger compartment, and igniting. * * * Several interrogatories also asked about the design and performance of the 1973-75 Opel Kadetts, small cars manufactured by a foreign subsidiary of GMC and designed with an above-axle fuel tank.
>
> The trial court limited discovery to knowledge and information based on records pertaining to 1971-77 Vegas and Astres. The trial court was persuaded that other vehicles were not substantially similar to the Jampoles' 1976 Vega Hatchback; therefore, he concluded that tests on those vehicles were not relevant.
>
> Jampole contends that it was a clear abuse of discretion for the trial court to deny discovery of alternate design documents. Jampole argues that the requested documents are relevant to his strict liability claim because they could show the availability and feasibility of safer alternatives. * * * The basic issue in this lawsuit is whether the 1976 Vega hatchback fuel tank design was defective because it allowed fuel to escape. Other designs that may have prevented fuel escaping are relevant to show that the Vega tank was unreasonably dangerous. Furthermore, the documents showing GMC's knowledge of alternative designs are relevant to show conscious indifference in support of Jampole's claim of gross negligence.
>
> The trial court, in balancing the rights of the parties, took an unduly restrictive view of the degree of similarity necessary for tests on other vehicles to be relevant. The automobiles need not be identical in order for tests on one to be relevant in determining whether the design of another is defective. Design differences between vehicles that might prevent certain alternatives from being adapted to the hatchback design do not necessarily undermine the relevance or discoverability of documents relating to those alternatives. Whether a safer fuel system design suitable for one vehicle is adaptable to anoth-

er is a question of feasibility to be decided by the trier of fact, not a question to be resolved in ruling on discovery requests. Moreover, if it were impossible to incorporate a safer design in the fuel system of a 1976 Vega Hatchback, the existence of that design would be relevant to establish liability for failure to warn.

The Court concluded that the trial courts denial of certain discovery was an abuse of discretion.

7. Rule 401 of the Texas Rules of Evidence defines "relevant evidence" to mean that evidence having any tendency to make the existence of any fact that is of consequence to the determination of the action more probable or less probable than it would be without the evidence.

8. *In re North Cypress Medical Center Operating Co. Ltd.*, --- S.W.3d ----, 2018 WL 197437661, 61 Tex. Sup. Ct. J. 1038 (Tex. 2018): The crux of the plaintiff suit is whether the amount secured by North Cypress's hospital lien exceeds a reasonable and regular rate for the services provided. The trial court's order at issue in this mandamus proceeding requires the defendant hospital to produce information regarding its reimbursement rates from private insurers and public payers for the services it provided to the uninsured plaintiff. The hospital's petition for writ of mandamus is denied. The reimbursement rates sought reflect the amounts the hospital is willing to accept from the vast majority of its patients as payment in full for such services. The amount North Cypress accepts as payment for those services from other patients, including those covered by private insurance and government benefits are relevant to whether the charges to the plaintiff were reasonable and are thus discoverable.

LUNSFORD
v.
MORRIS

746 S.W.2d 471
(Tex. 1988)

Ronald D. Hinds, Dallas, for relators.

Robert R. Roby, Gwinn & Roby, Bruce W. Bowman, Jr., Vial, Hamilton, Koch & Knox, Dallas, Robert R. Estes, Fort Worth, Wayne E. Lee, Dallas, for respondent.

KILGARLIN, JUSTICE.

At issue in this mandamus proceeding is whether a defendant's net worth is subject to pre-trial discovery. We hold that such information is relevant to the issue of punitive or, as they are sometimes called, exemplary damages and therefore discoverable under TEX. R. CIV. P. 166b(2). Consequently, we conditionally grant relators' petition for writ of mandamus.

In the underlying case, relators Lunsford and Dail sued their former employer and others alleging conspiracy and malicious defamation. Their suit sought both actual and punitive damages. In connection with the latter claim, Lunsford and Dail requested production of financial statements and other documents bearing on the defendants' net worth. The trial court denied the requested discovery, and we granted leave to file a petition for writ of mandamus after denial by the court of appeals.

We first consider whether evidence of net worth is discoverable. In Texas, a party "may obtain discovery regarding any matter which is relevant to the subject matter" of a pending action. TEX. R. CIV. P. 166b(2)(a). Further, the same rule provides "it is not ground for objection that the information sought will be inadmissible at the trial if the information sought appears reasonably calculated to lead to the discovery of admissible evidence."

Since the earliest Texas decisions, punitive damages have been allowed, among other things, to punish a wrongdoer. "[P]unitive damages are justified by [a] blending of the interests of society with those of the aggrieved individual, thus giving damages not only to recompense the sufferer, but to punish the offender." *Graham v. Roder*, 5 Tex. 141, 149 (1849). In addition to punishment, punitive damages are allowed to deter the same or similar future conduct. *Cole v. Tucker*, 6 Tex. 266, 268 (1851). Our recent decisions have continued to recognize punishment and deterrence as co-purposes of punitive damages awards. *See, e.g., Hofer v. Lavender*, 679 S.W.2d 470, 474-75 (Tex. 1984); *Pace v. State*, 650 S.W.2d 64, 65 (Tex. 1983).

At least forty-three states now allow evidence of net worth to be discovered and admitted for the limited purpose of assessing punitive damages. Substantial federal court authority also supports the proposition that net worth is admissible on punitive damages. The United States Supreme Court recognizes and adheres to the majority view. *City of Newport v. Fact Concerts, Inc.*, 453 U.S. 247, 270, 101 S.Ct. 2748, 2761, 69 L.Ed.2d 616 (1981). Also, the RESTATEMENT view is in accord: "The wealth of the defendant is also relevant . . . ; the degree of punishment or deterrence resulting from a judgment is to some extent in proportion to the means of the guilty person." RESTATEMENT (SECOND) OF TORTS § 908 (comment e) (1977). *See also*, PROSSER & KEETON, PROSSER AND KEETON ON TORTS § 2 at 15 (5th ed. 1984).

Texas has allowed neither discovery nor admission of evidence concerning a defendant's net worth. One hundred years ago, this court determined that the injury inflicted, rather than the ability of a defendant to pay, was the more important consideration. *Young v. Kuhn*, 71 Tex. 645, 652, 9 S.W. 860, 862 (1888). This view has persisted to the present day despite overwhelming authority to the contrary. *See Murphy v. Waldrip*, 692 S.W.2d 584, 588 (Tex. App.—Fort Worth 1985, no writ). A defendant's "ability to pay" bears directly on the question of adequate punishment and deterrence. That which could be an enormous penalty to one may be but a mere annoyance to another. For example, one hundred dollars as a punitive award against a single mother of three small children may be a greater deterrent than one hundred thousand dollars awarded against a major corporation whose directors are shielded from the stark reality of harm done by the paneled walls and plush carpet of the corporate boardroom. We hold that in cases in which punitive or exemplary damages may be awarded, parties may discover and offer evidence of a defendant's net worth.

Although the issue in this case is one of discovery of net worth, cases involving admissibility of net worth into evidence are instructive. We therefore review briefly the positions taken in this and in other jurisdictions on discoverability and admissibility of net worth evidence. Just recently this court, in *Birchfield v. Texarkana Memorial Hospital d/b/a Wadley Hospital*, 747 S.W.2d 361 (1987), held admissible evidence of the financial condition of the hospital to demonstrate the hospital's ability to provide proper facilities. While it is true that this holding went to a gross negligence inquiry, it nevertheless demonstrates that we have previously permitted admission of evidence of the financial condition of a defendant.

Some states allowing discovery of net worth require a prima facie showing of entitlement to punitive damages before information about a defendant's net worth may be sought. *See, e.g., Curtis v. Partain*, 272 Ark. 400, 614 S.W.2d 671 (1981). Other courts would make a plaintiff wait until trial, after the jury has heard evidence warranting punitive damages, before evidence of net worth is introduced. *Ruiz v. Southern Pacific Transportation Co.*, 97 N.M. 194, 638 P.2d 406, 414 (N.M. Ct. App.1981). One state subjects a plaintiff to a show-cause hearing in which a prima facie right to punitive damages must be proved. *Leidholt v. District Court*, 619 P.2d 768, 771 (Colo. 1980). In Wyoming, a plaintiff must overcome two hurdles. First, the plaintiff must make a prima facie showing of entitlement to punitive damages before the trial court permits discovery of net worth. Then, a trial involving punitive damages is bifurcated: a jury must again find a plaintiff is entitled to punitive damages; and then the jury may consider evidence of net worth to determine damages. *Campen v. Stone*, 635 P.2d 1121, 1132 (Wyo. 1981); *see also* Annot., 32 A.L.R.4TH 432 (1984).

Our rules of civil procedure and evidence do not require similar practices before net worth may be discovered. Absent a privilege or specifically enumerated exemption, our rules permit discovery of any "relevant" matter; thus, there is no evidentiary threshold a litigant must cross before seeking discovery. TEX. R. CIV. P. 166b(2)(a). Neither do the rules of evidence contemplate exclusion of otherwise relevant proof unless the evidence proffered is unfairly prejudicial, privileged, incompetent, or otherwise legally inadmissible. TEX. R. CIV. EVID. 401, 403, 501-10, 601. *Accord, Coy v. Superior Court*, 58 Cal.2d 210, 373 P.2d 457, 23 Cal.Rptr. 393 (1962). We do not circumscribe, however, a trial judge's authority to consider on motion whether a party's discovery request involves unnecessary harassment or invasion of personal or property rights. *See* TEX. R. CIV. P. 166b(5) *and compare* TEX. R. CIV. P. 13.

Young v. Kuhn, 71 Tex. 645, 9 S.W. 860 (1888), predates both our rules of civil procedure and evidence and is no longer controlling. In a suit in which exemplary damages may be recovered, we hold the defendant's net worth is "relevant" and therefore discoverable under TEX. R. CIV. P. 166b(2)(a). Because no privilege or other specific exemption has been shown, the trial court abused its discretion by refusing to permit the requested discovery. We are confident the trial judge will withdraw his order disallowing discovery of the defendants' net worth; the writ of mandamus will issue only if he fails to do so. Relators' request for a writ of prohibition is conditionally dismissed as moot.

CULVER, J., not sitting.

Notes

1. While still the law, the holding in *Lunsford* is clearly subject to the limitations now found in TEX. R. CIV. P. 192.4.

2. *Sears, Roebuck & Co. v. Ramirez,* 824 S.W.2d 558 (Tex. 1992). Plaintiff sued Sears for wrongful termination. Plaintiff sought net worth information, requesting that Sears produce annual reports and tax returns for the 5 years preceding her suit. Sears produced the annual reports, but objected to the request for production of tax returns on the grounds of undue burden and unnecessary expense. Sears proffered evidence that its net worth was contained in the annual reports and that it would take one employee 2-3 weeks to duplicate the requested tax returns. The trial court ordered the tax returns produced. The Supreme Court held that the writ of mandamus would issue. Under the facts of this case, discovery of federal income tax statements in addition to the annual reports is unnecessarily duplicative. There is no justification for requiring Sears to produce the same information in different form. The Supreme Court is reluctant to allow uncontrolled and unnecessary discovery of federal income tax returns.

K MART CORPORATION
v.
SANDERSON
937 S.W.2d 429
(Tex. 1996)

Brock C. Akers, Evelyn T. Ailts, Phillips & Akers, Martin John de la Torre, Houston, for relators.
Chris E. Quinn, Richard J. Clarkson, Reaud Morgan & Quinn, Beaumont, for respondent.

PER CURIAM.

Much like *Dillard Department Stores, Inc. v. Hall*, 909 S.W.2d 491 (Tex. 1995) (per curiam), and *Texaco, Inc. v. Sanderson*, 898 S.W.2d 813 (Tex. 1995) (per curiam), this original mandamus proceeding involves discovery that is clearly excessively broad.

Stacey Thompson sued K Mart, a Michigan corporation, to recover actual and punitive damages not exceeding $30 million for injuries she received when she was abducted from a K Mart store parking lot in Lufkin and raped. Thompson also sued Weingarten Realty Management Company, a Texas corporation. Thompson alleged that these defendants (to whom we refer collectively as K Mart) and others were negligent and grossly negligent in failing to make adequate provisions for her safety. Although the incident occurred in Angelina County, where Thompson resides, Thompson filed suit in Jefferson County.

Thompson requested K Mart to produce all documents "which relate to, touch or concern the allegations of this lawsuit", all documents "reflecting the incident made the basis of this lawsuit", and any document "which is not work product which relates in any way to this incident". K Mart objected to these requests on the grounds that they would require production of work product and are "overly broad, unduly burdensome and would require [K Mart] to turn over its entire file and gather evidence from every known source so as to try the entire case in this discovery response." The district court overruled K Mart's objections and ordered production of the documents.

One of Thompson's three requests excludes work product; the other two do not. The order compelling production does not mention work product. Since the record does not reflect any basis for compelling K Mart to produce work product, the district court erred in doing so.

K Mart argues that Thompson's requests were improper under our decision in *Loftin v. Martin*, 776 S.W.2d 145, 148 (Tex. 1989), which held:

> Loftin has requested all evidence that supports Lumbermens' allegations. The request does not identify any particular class or type of documents but it is merely a request that Loftin be allowed to generally peruse all evidence Lumbermens might have. We hold that such request was vague, ambiguous, and overbroad and that the trial court was within its sound discretion in sustaining Lumbermens' objection. No one seeks to deny Loftin's right to see evidence against him, but he must formulate his request for production with a certain degree of specificity to allow Lumbermens to comply.

We think the request in the present case is distinguishable from the one in *Loftin*. Thompson requested all documents relating to the incident in which she was injured, not all documents which support K Mart's position or which relate to the claims and defenses in the cause of action. Because the incident was an isolated occurrence, we think a reasonable person would understand from the request what documents fit the description. It would be better, of course, to be more specific. We do not hold that a request as broad as Thompson's is proper in every circumstance. Here, however, the district court did not abuse its discretion in enforcing Thompson's requests, except for requiring production of work product.

Thompson also served the three following interrogatories on K Mart:

> 10. Please describe by date and offense type any criminal conduct that occurred in the K Mart store or parking lot in the shopping center in question during the last seven (7) years.
>
> 15. Please list all criminal activities at all property owned, leased or managed by both K Mart Corporation or Weingarten Realty Management Company in the State of Texas during the last seven years that relate in any way to the alleged failure to provide adequate security allegedly resulting in any sort of physical injury to any person.
>
> 16. Have there been other incidents at K Mart Stores owned by Weingarten Realty Management Company nationwide in which a person was abducted from the premises and raped? If so, please state the date and location of each such incident that occurred within the last ten years.

Thompson also requested production (request 19) of all documents related to interrogatory 15. K Mart objected to the interrogatories and request as being overly broad and burdensome. The district court overruled K Mart's objections.

In *Texaco, Inc. v. Sanderson*, plaintiffs claimed damages for exposure to toxic chemicals. At plaintiffs' request, the district court ordered production of all documents written by Texaco's safety director concerning "safety, toxicology, and industrial hygiene, epidemiology, fire protection and training." 898 S.W.2d at 814. We granted mandamus relief, holding the request to be so excessively broad as to be "well outside the bounds of proper discovery." *Id.* at 815. The same may be said of Thompson's interrogatory 10. It would require K Mart to give the date of every shoplifting offense for the past seven years, though shoplifting on K Mart's premises has no apparent connection to Thompson's injury or cause of action.

In *Dillard Department Stores, Inc. v. Hall*, plaintiff sued Dillard for false arrest. At plaintiff's request, the trial court ordered Dillard to produce "every claims file and incident report prepared from 1985 through 1990 in every lawsuit or claim that involved allegations of false arrest, civil rights violations, and excessive use of force" for each of its 227 stores located in twenty states. 909 S.W.2d at 491-492. We granted mandamus relief, holding that the requested discovery was "overly broad as a matter of law." *Id.* at 492. Thompson's interrogatories 15 and 16 are likewise overly broad. The likelihood that criminal conduct on the parking lot of a K Mart store or other property owned by Weingarten in El Paso or Amarillo as long ago as 1989, or outside Texas as long ago as 1986, will have even a minuscule bearing on this case is far too small to justify discovery.

A reference in *Loftin* suggests that interrogatories and depositions may properly be used for a fishing expedition when a request for production of documents cannot. *Loftin*, 776 S.W.2d at 148 ("Unlike interrogatories and depositions, Rule 167 is not a fishing rule."). We reject the notion that any discovery device can be used to "fish". The burden of answering interrogatories like those in this case is hardly less to K Mart than producing documents containing the same information. The district court's order requiring K Mart to answer interrogatories 10, 15 and 16, and to produce documents related to interrogatory 15 called for in request 19, exceeded the bounds of discovery permitted by the rules of procedure and was a clear abuse of discretion. K Mart has no adequate remedy by appeal and is therefore entitled to relief by mandamus. *Dillard*, 909 S.W.2d at 492 ("A discovery order that compels overly broad discovery 'well outside the bounds of proper discovery' is an abuse of discretion for which mandamus is the proper remedy"); *Texaco*, 898 S.W.2d at 815 ("The trial court's ruling requiring production beyond that permitted by the rules of procedure was a clear abuse of discretion. Defendants have no adequate remedy by appeal."). *See General Motors Corp. v. Lawrence*, 651 S.W.2d 732, 734 (Tex. 1983); *Walker v. Packer*, 827 S.W.2d 833, 843 (Tex. 1992).

Accordingly, the Court grants K Mart's motion for leave to file petition for writ of mandamus and, without hearing argument, grants K Mart's petition and directs the district court to vacate its order dated September 13, 1995. The writ will not issue unless the district court fails to comply promptly. Further proceedings should be consistent with this opinion.

ABBOTT, J., did not participate in the decision.

In re FORD MOTOR COMPANY
427 S.W.3d 396
(Tex. 2014)

Discovery seeking, from testifying experts, detailed financial and business information for all cases the expert's employers have handled for auto manufactures from 2000-2011, was an overbroad fishing expedition the discovery rules are intended to prevent.

Notes

1. TEX. R. 192.7, citing *Sanderson* states: "While the scope of discovery is quite broad, it is nevertheless confined by the subject matter of the case and reasonable expectations of obtaining information that will aid resolution of the dispute. The rule must be read and applied in that context."

2. *Ford Motor Co. v. Leggat*, 904 S.W.2d 643 (Tex. 1995). The amount of money paid in settlement in another matter was not discoverable absent a showing of relevance to the issues in the present case. *Accord: In Re Union Pacific Resources Co., infra.*

3. *In re Allstate County Mutual Ins. Co.*, 227 S.W.3d 667 (Tex. 2007): Discovery. Purpose. Discovery Is Not To Make A Trial More Expensive.

Discovery orders, requiring document production from an unreasonably long time period, or from distant and unrelated locales, are impermissibly overbroad.

Discovery. Overbroad Requests Are Improper, Whether Burdensome Or Not.

Discovery Must Be Reasonably Tailored. This Requires A Sense Of Proportion.

Notes

1. *In re Dana Corp.*, 138 S.W.3d 298 (Tex. 2004): This is an original mandamus proceeding, brought to challenge the trial court's discovery ruling in the underlying asbestos litigation. The real parties in this proceeding sought production of Dana's insurance policies since 1930, and also sought to learn the amount of insurance remaining under those policies. *Held*: A trial court's ruling that requires production beyond that permitted by the procedural rules is an abuse of discretion. A discovery order requiring document production from an unreasonably long time period or from distant and unrelated locales, is impermissibly overbroad and may be subject to mandamus relief.

TEX. R. CIV. P. 192.3(f) mandates disclosure of any insurance agreement that may satisfy part or all of a judgment rendered in the action. There is no special rule concerning the production of insurance policies in toxic-tort cases. But, even in an ordinary case, the rules require that a threshold showing of applicability must be made before a party can be ordered to produce multiple decades of insurance policies. Thus, while the plaintiffs' request for production should not be delayed until each plaintiff has necessarily identified a particular product and a particular period of exposure, the insurance policies need not be produced until they are shown to be applicable to a potential judgment.

2. *In re Graco Children's Products, Inc.*, --- S.W.3d ----, 2006 WL 3040580 (Tex.): This is an original mandamus proceeding. Galnares's five-week-old son was killed in a roll over accident. Galnares sued Graco, alleging that defects in the harness clip of the baby's car seat failed to restrain him in the rollover. Before trial, the Consumer Products Safety Commission announced a provisional settlement with Graco imposing a $4 million civil penalty for failing to report defects in more than a dozen products, including high chairs, swings, strollers, toddler beds, and infant carriers. None of the products had five-point harnesses, such as the one involved in this case. None mentioned defective harness buckles. Nevertheless, Galnares's attorneys sought to discover 20 categories of documents, including anything that mentioned or referred to any of the defects, products, complaints, or people who might have been involved with those products or the investigation. The trial court ordered Graco to produce two representatives for deposition as well as all the documents Galnares requested. ***Held:*** Writ of mandamus will issue. In this case, there is no apparent connection between the alleged defect and the discovery ordered. Generally, the scope of discovery is within the trial court's discretion," but "the trial court must make an effort to impose reasonable discovery limits. An order that compels overly broad discovery well outside the bounds of proper discovery is an abuse of discretion for which mandamus is the proper remedy.

3. *In re National Lloyds Ins. Co.*, ___ S.W.3d ___, 2014 WL 5785871 (Tex. 2014): Discovery order, requiring production of all claims files from two adjusters assessing storm damage in the policyholder's city, is impermissibly broad.

3. *Types of Discovery*

a. *Interrogatories*

Notes

1. *What are Interrogatories?* Under Rule 197.1 (formerly Rule 168) interrogatories to parties are questions relating to any matter within the scope of discovery, "except matters covered by Rule 195." (Rule 195 concerns "Discovery Regarding Testifying Expert Witnesses.")

2. *Who can use them?* Any party can submit them to any other party, but the answers can only be used against the party answering the interrogatories. Rule 197.3 (formerly R 168 (2)).

3. *When can they be used?* No later than 30 days before the end of the discovery period.

4. *How much time to answer?* A written response must be served on the requesting party within 30 days after service of the interrogatories, unless they are served before the defendant's answer is due, in which event, the response must be served within 50 days after service of the interrogatories.

5. *The number.* Under the old rules, each set of interrogatories could require no more than 30 *answers*, and, no more than 2 sets could be used, except by agreement or by permission of the trial court upon the showing of good cause. Under the new rules the number of interrogatories in cases falling under Level 1 and Level 2 Discovery Control Plans is 25, but a substantial limitation has been imposed by making each "discrete subpart," a separate interrogatory. Rules 190.2(c)(3) and 190.39(b)(3) state:

> "Any party may serve on any other party no more than 25 written interrogatories, excluding interrogatories asking a party only to identify or authenticate specific documents. Each discrete subpart of an interrogatory is considered a separate interrogatory."

6. *Ethical considerations.* Rule 191.3(c) provides:

> "The signature of an attorney or party on a discovery request, notice, response, or objection constitutes a certification that to the best of the signer's knowledge, information, and belief, formed after a reasonable inquiry, the request, notice, response, or objection is:
>
> > "(1) consistent with the rules of civil procedure and these discovery rules and warranted by existing law or a good faith argument for the extension, modification, or reversal of existing law'

"(2) not interposed for any improper purpose, such as to harass or to cause unnecessary delay or needless increase in the cost of litigation; and

"(3) not unreasonable or unduly burdensome or expensive, given the needs of the case, the discovery already had in the case, the amount in controversy, and the importance of the issues at stake in the litigation."

7. *Oath.* Under Rule 197.2(d), R 14 does not apply, so the attorney cannot sign for the answering person. The interrogatories must be answered under oath by the party, with two exceptions:

"(1) when answers are based on information obtained from other persons, the party may so state, and

"(2) a party need not sign answers to interrogatories about persons with knowledge of relevant facts, trial witnesses, and legal contentions."

8. *Objections.* Rule 197.2(b) provides that "A response must include the party's answers to the interrogatories and may include objections and assertions of privilege as required under these rules. Read Rule 193.2 for a complete explanation of the procedures involved in objecting to written discovery.

9. *Examples of Interrogatories*:

IN RE:	§	IN THE COUNTY COURT
	§	
ESTATE OF DIANE E. WALTERS,	§	AT LAW NO. ONE OF
	§	
DECEASED	§	NUECES COUNTY, TEXAS

APPLICANT DONALD CARRICO'S FIRST SET OF INTERROGATORIES TO DEFENDANTS SANDRA K. BOERNER and JOYCE AHLERS SHAW

TO: Defendant, SANDRA K. BOERNER and JOYCE AHLERS SHAW, by and through their attorney of record, Mr. Bradley Bunting, Bunting & Bunting, 307 NationsBank Tower, 500 N. Shoreline Blvd., Corpus Christi, Texas 78471.

Pursuant to Rule 197.1 of the Texas Rules of Civil Procedure, Plaintiff, Donald Carrico serves the following set of Interrogatories to be answered under oath and writing, separately, as required by Rule 197. The answers must be signed by the person making them, and shall be served no later than thirty (30) days of service of these interrogatories. Plaintiff is under a duty to seasonably supplement these answers in accordance with rule 193.5 of the Texas Rules of Civil Procedure request that documents be produced at the offices of Pearson & Price, PLLC, 800 N. Shoreline, Suite 1700, South Tower, Corpus Christi, Texas 78401, within thirty (30) days after the service of this request.

DEFINITIONS

1. The Estate of Diane E. Walters shall mean the Estate of Diane E. Walters, Deceased and includes representatives, agents, employees, attorneys and accountants.

2. "Defendants" shall mean Sandra K. Boerner and Joyce Ahlers Shaw and includes their representative, agents, employees, accountants, and attorneys.

3. "You" or "your" or "yours" means Defendant as defined above.

4. "Document" means any printed, typewritten, handwritten, or otherwise recorded matter of whatever character, including but without limitation, letters, work orders, takeoffs, purchase orders, invoices, memoranda, telegrams, photographs, tape recordings, motion pictures, video tapes, and any carbon or photostatic copies of any such material, as well as all non-identical copies of all of the above including copies upon which notations, interlineations, or changes have been made, if Plaintiff does not have custody or control of the original. If any doc-

ument requested to be produces was, but is no longer in Plaintiff's possession or control, or is no longer in existence, state whether it is:

a. missing or lost;
b. destroyed;
c. transferred voluntarily or involuntarily to others, and if so, to whom; or
d. otherwise disposed of; and in each instance explain the circumstances surrounding and authorization for such disposition thereof and state the approximate cause thereof.

5. "Identify" when referring:

(1) to a person, means to state his or her full name and present or last known business and residential addresses and phone numbers.
(2) to a public or private corporation, partnership, association, or other organization, or to a governmental agency, means to state its full name and present or last known pertinent business address and phone number.
(3) to a statement, means to identify who made it, who took of recorded it, and all others, if any, present during the making thereof; to state when, where and how it was taken or recorded, and to identify who has present or last know possession, custody, or control thereof.
(4) to a document, means to give a reasonably detailed description thereof, including if applicable when, where and how it was made; to identify who made it; and to identify who has present or last known possession, custody or control thereof.
(5) to any other tangible thing, means to give a reasonably detailed description thereof, including, if applicable, when, where, and how it was made, to identify who made it; and to identify who has present or last known possession, custody or control thereof.

INTERROGATORIES

INTERROGATORY NO. 1:

Please state the identity and location of the person answering these interrogatories.

ANSWER:

INTERROGATORY NO. 2:

Identify and state the location of the each and every person, business agency and/or government agency that might have knowledge relative to the issues of this case.

ANSWER:

* * *

Respectfully submitted,

PEARSON & PRICE, PLLC
Suite 1700 South Tower
800 North Shoreline Boulevard
Corpus Christi, Texas 78401
(512) 885-0077
(512) 885-0288(FAX)

By______________________________
Richard E. Flint
State Bar No. 07151500
Attorneys for Donald Carrico

CERTIFICATE OF SERVICE

I, Richard E. Flint certify on this the ____ day of _____________, 2000, a true and correct copy of the forgoing pleading was mailed by certified mail, return receipt addressed as follows:

Mr. Bradley Bunting
Bunting & Bunting
Attorneys At Law
307 NationsBank Tower
500 N. Shoreline Blvd.
Corpus Christi, Texas 78471

____
Richard E. Flint

BRADEN
v.
DOWNEY
811 S.W.2d 922
(Tex. 1991)

Facts: This is an action for a deficiency after a foreclosure sale. The Bank sent Braden requests for admissions, accompanied by interrogatories, asking Braden to "state all facts relied upon in denying the request or objecting to it" if the request was not admitted. Braden answered the interrogatory relating to his denial, that the Bank was the owner & holder of the partnership note, by stating that he was not in a position to know one way or the other. He then objected to the interrogatory because it was vague, ambiguous, overly broad, non-specific & unduly burdensome. The Bank moved the district court to compel Braden to answer all the discovery requests to which he objected & to award the bank $500 attorney's fee as sanctions. At the conclusion of the hearing on the bank's motion to compel, the district court found that both parties were abusing the discovery process. Braden was ordered to pay the Bank $10,000 within 30 days & his attorney was ordered to perform 10 hours of community service within 6 weeks.

Issue: Were the questions too vague, numerous or contentious? No. At least no abuse of discretion was shown.

Held: The district court did not abuse its discretion in overruling the objections to the discovery requests & ordering them to answer them. The thirty-answer limit in R 168, like vagueness, burdensomeness & many other standards, while not susceptible a precise definition, establishes some boundary to the range of discovery. The Bank's interrogatories in this case do not so trespass upon this boundary that it was an abuse of discretion to order that they be answered.

Issue: Can a party be required to repeat in answer to interrogatories the same information that has been given in a deposition? Not reached, but indicated that this is not a ground for objection. Here, however, Braden had not been forthcoming with his answers during the deposition, so there was clearly no abuse of discretion by the trial court.

Discovery Sanction. Court Must Defer Or Find That Sanction Will Not Preclude Access To Court.

Issue: Are there limits to the sanctions that can be imposed? Yes. They cannot limit access to the courts.

Held: Yes. The imposition of sanctions must not result in total, or even significant, preclusion of access to the courts. However, if a district court imposes monetary sanctions that are made payable prior to the entry of a final appealable order, a litigant may suffer a substantial restriction on his access to the courts. To avoid this harsh, inequitable scenario, if a litigant contends that a monetary sanction award precludes access to the court, the district judge must either (1) provide that the sanction is payable only at a date that coincides with or follows entry of a final order terminating the litigation; or (2) makes express written findings, after a prompt hearing, as to why the award does not have such a preclusive effect. This procedure allows the trial court to levy some monetary sanctions during pretrial proceedings but requires that payment of more severe sanctions be deferred until an appealable judgment is rendered.

Notes

1. *Braden* is no longer the law on the number of interrogatories, but sheds light on the Court's interpretation of the scope of an interrogatory.

2. *State Farm Fire & Casualty Company v. Morua,* 979 S.W.2d 616 (Tex. 1998). The Court noted that the purpose of interrogatories was to flesh out the facts of the case and to prevent trial by ambush. As interrogatory answers may be used at trial against the party providing them and given the fact-intensive nature of interrogatories, requiring verification to answers to interrogatories and supplemental answers promotes the purpose of discovery and avoids the inevitable disputes over who said what when. Verification is intended to promote, among other things, meaningful cross-examination at trial. However, the requirement for verification is not intended to promote "gotcha" gamesmanship, and thus the verification requirement is subject to waiver. When a party fails to verify the answers to interrogatories, the requesting party must object, or waive the right to verification. Here, because Morua waited thirteen months and failed to object to the lack of verification before trial, the trial court properly concluded that Morua waived the objection.

3. *Use of Answers. Yates v. Fisher, 998* S.W.2d 730 (Tex. 1998). As stated above, interrogatory answers may be used only *against* the party answering the interrogatories.

4. *Contention Interrogatories.* TEX. R. CIV. P. 197.1 specifically authorizes interrogatories concerning a party's contentions—such as, whether a party claims a breach of implied warranty, or when a party contends that limitations began to run—, but these interrogatories may not go so far as to require a party to marshal its proof. In other words, interrogatories that ask a party to state all legal and factual assertions are improper.

b. *Requests for Disclosure*

1. *What are they?* A request for disclosure is a non-adversarial means of obtaining information generally sought in ordinary cases. It is not automatic, but is available upon request.

2. *Who Can Use Them?* Any party may obtain disclosure from another party of the information listed in Rule 194.2 (which students should read and be familiar with).

3. *When Can They Be Used?* The request for disclosure can be made no later than 30 days before the end of any applicable discovery period.

4. *When Are Responses Due?* Written response are to be served within 30 days after service of the request, unless the request is made before the answer is due, in which event the response is due within 50 days after service of the request, or unless it is a request under Rule 194.2(f) (concerning experts), in which event the schedule in Rule 195 controls. [In general a longer period is authorized for a party to designate experts and to furnish expert information.]

5. *Objections Are Not Permitted.* Rule 194.5 provides that "No objection is permitted to a request under this rule."

6. *Limits On Admissibility.* A response to requests under Rule 194.2 (c) (legal theories and factual bases of claims or defenses) and 194.2 (d) (the amount and method of calculating economic damages) that has been changed or amended or supplemented is not admissible and may not be used for impeachment. Evidence of other changes in position is not barred.

7. *Oath.* Disclosure responses need not be verified, but are subject to the general certification requirement contained in Rule 191.3 concerning the propriety, completeness, and accuracy of the response.

8. *Example of Request for Disclosure*:

NO. 38747-1

IN RE:	§	IN THE COUNTY COURT
	§	
ESTATE OF DIANE E. WALTERS,	§	AT LAW NO. ONE OF
	§	
DECEASED	§	NUECES COUNTY, TEXAS

**APPLICANT DONALD CARRICO'S RULE 194
REQUEST FOR DISCLOSURE**

TO: Contestants, SANDRA K. BOERNER and JOYCE AHLERS SHAW, by and through their attorney of record, Mr. Bradley Bunting, Bunting & Bunting, 307 NationsBank Tower, 500 N. Shoreline Blvd., Corpus Christi, Texas 78471.

Donald Carrico, Applicant in the above styled and numbered cause pursuant to Rules 192 and 194 of the Texas Rules of Civil Procedure, requests that you disclose, within thirty (30) days of service of this request, the information or materials described in Rule 194.2(a)-(l), as applicable.

Respectfully submitted,

PEARSON & PRICE, PLLC
Suite 1700 South Tower
800 North Shoreline Boulevard
Corpus Christi, Texas 78401
(512) 885-0077
(512) 885-0288(FAX)

By________________________________
Richard E. Flint
State Bar No. 07151500
Attorneys for Donald Carrico

CERTIFICATE OF SERVICE

I, Richard E. Flint certify on this the ____ day of _____________, 2000, a true and correct copy of the forgoing pleading was mailed by certified mail, return receipt addressed as follows:

Mr. Bradley Bunting
Bunting & Bunting
Attorneys At Law
307 NationsBank Tower
500 N. Shoreline Blvd.
Corpus Christi, Texas 78471

____
Richard E. Flint

In re C.D. MORSE
153 S.W.3d 578
(Tex. App.—Amarillo 2004, no pet.)

Facts: This is a mandamus proceeding. The trial court refused to compel the defendants to disclose the identities of their present and past shareholders. These names were sought to identify potential parties.

Issue: May a party be compelled to disclose the identity of potential parties? Yes.

Held: Yes.

Rule 194.2 expressly provides that a party may request disclosure of at least 16 specific categories of information. Relying on Rule 194, and the limited case law interpreting it, the Amarillo Court of Appeals held that the relators "were entitled to disclosure of the names and addresses of the shareholders" as potential parties, and the trial court therefore abused its discretion in denying their motion to compel.

c. *Request for Admissions*

Notes

1. *What are they?* Request for Admissions from one party to another party ask the other party to admit the truth of any matter (opinions of fact or of the application of law to fact, including the genuineness of any documents described in the request) within the scope of discovery. The primary purpose of requests is to simplify trials by eliminating matters about which there is no real controversy. Each matter for which an admission is requested must be stated separately.

2. *Who can use them?* Any party can submit them to any other party. The admission binds the admitting party, and only for the pending action. Rule 198.3

3. *When can they be used?* Requests for admission can be served at anytime before the period of discovery ends.

4. *How much time to answer?* They are deemed admitted unless answered within 30 days after service of the request, except that a defendant served with a request before the defendant's answer is due need not respond until 50 days after service of the request.

5. *The number.* No limit on the number of requests for admissions is stated in the Rules.

6. *Responses:* Responses to requests for admissions must be in writing. Unless an objection is stated, or a privilege asserted, the answer must deny or set forth in detail the reasons the party cannot answer. Additionally:

   a. A response must fairly meet the substance of the request.
   b. The answer may be qualified only when good faith requires,
   c. Lack of information or knowledge is not a proper response, unless the responding party states that a reasonable inquiry was made, but that the information known or easily obtainable is insufficient to allow a response.
   d. An assertion that the request presents an issue for trial is not a proper response.

7. *Oath.* An oath is not required.

8. *Failure to Respond.* If a response is not timely served, the request is considered admitted without the necessity of a court order, i.e., the requested admissions will be deemed admitted.

9. *Objections.* Objections must set forth in detail the reasons that the answering party cannot truthfully admit or deny the matter. Lack of information is not a sufficient response, unless a reasonable inquiry fails to produce the knowledge or information necessary to respond.

10. *Effect of Admission.* Any matter admitted is conclusively established unless the court permits withdrawal or amendment of the admission.

11. *Withdrawal or Amendment of Responses.* Withdrawal or amendment can be allowed upon showing of good cause and a finding that the parties relying upon the responses and deemed admissions will not be unduly prejudiced "and that the presentation of the merits of the action will be subserved by permitting the party to amend or withdraw the admission."

STELLY
v.
PAPANIA

927 S.W.2d 620
(Tex. 1996)

Michael J. Truncale, Martha R. Campbell, Beaumont, for petitioner.
Thomas P. Roebuck, Jr., L.K. Greer, Brett S. Thomas, Beaumont, for respondent.

PER CURIAM.

We consider whether a trial court abuses its discretion by allowing a party to withdraw and amend its original answers to a request for admissions. We hold that a trial court does not abuse its discretion when the moving party shows: (1) good cause; (2) that the party relying on the responses will not be unduly prejudiced; and (3) that the withdrawal will serve the purpose of legitimate discovery and the merits of the case. Accordingly, we reverse the judgment of the court of appeals and remand the case to that court to determine the merits of the appeal.

After delivering a pizza to Ermon Stelly's house, Michael Papania slipped on a patch of mud in what he believed to be Stelly's front yard. As a result, he suffered a broken leg. Papania sued Stelly and the City of Port Neches. He alleged that the City created the mud patch when it worked on the sewer line in front of Stelly's home.

Papania sent Requests for Admissions to both Stelly and the City. Stelly mistakenly admitted that he owned the premises on which Papania fell. Papania non-suited the City and the trial court later dismissed all of Papania's claims against the City with prejudice. Later, Stelly discovered that the City owned the land where Papania fell. A surveyor's report revealed that Stelly's boundary line ended seven feet before the street curb.

Stelly moved to withdraw and amend his previous admissions. He also moved for summary judgment on grounds that he did not: (1) own the property by the street; (2) actively cause the alleged defective condition on the City's property; and (3) have a duty to keep the City's land safe.

The trial court granted both motions. The court of appeals reversed and remanded. That court held that the trial court abused its discretion because Stelly did not show that his new responses would not prejudice Papania. Because the new responses formed the basis for Stelly's motion for summary judgment, the court of appeals reversed the judgment and remanded the case for trial.

Stelly argues that the trial court did not abuse its discretion because the surveyor's report about who actually owned the land provided good cause for Stelly to amend his responses to Papania's request for admissions. Stelly also contends that his amended admissions did not prejudice Papania because: (1) Papania's claim against the City was barred because he did not give timely notice under the Texas Tort Claims Act; and (2) even if Papania had relied on Stelly's original admission, Stelly's ownership could not absolve the City of responsibility for creating a hazard. We agree.

This case presents a unique situation. We have never considered whether a party can withdraw its original response to a request for admission and substitute it with a new response. Moreover, decisions from the courts of appeals are limited to cases where parties seek to withdraw deemed admissions. *See, e.g., Burden v. John Watson Landscape Illumination, Inc.*, 896 S.W.2d 253, 256 (Tex. App.—Eastland 1995, writ denied); *North River Ins. Co. of New Jersey v. Greene*, 824 S.W.2d 697, 700 (Tex. App.—El Paso 1992, writ denied); *Employers Ins. of Wausau v. Halton*, 792 S.W.2d 462, 465 (Tex. App.—Dallas 1990, writ denied). Although this case does not involve deemed admissions, we find these cases instructive.

A party may withdraw a deemed admission "upon a showing of good cause for such withdrawal . . . if the court finds that the parties relying upon the responses . . . will not be unduly prejudiced and that the presentation of the merits of the action will be subserved thereby." TEX. R. CIV. P. 169(2). After the rule was amended in 1988, "good cause" became the threshold standard for withdrawal of deemed admissions. *Halton*, 792 S.W.2d at 465. A party can establish good cause by showing that its failure to answer was accidental or the result of a mistake, rather than intentional or the result of conscious indifference. *Greene*, 824 S.W.2d at 700; *see Halton*, 792 S.W.2d at 465.

A trial court has broad discretion to permit or deny the withdrawal of deemed admissions. *Halton*, 792 S.W.2d at 464. An appellate court should set aside the trial court's ruling only if, after reviewing the entire record, it is clear that the trial court abused its discretion. *See Simon v. York Crane & Rigging Company, Inc.* 739 S.W.2d 793, 795 (Tex. 1987); *Burden*, 896 S.W.2d at 256. An abuse of discretion occurs when a court acts without reference to guiding rules or principles, or acts arbitrarily or unreasonably. *See Downer v. Aquamarine Operators, Inc.*, 701 S.W.2d 238, 241 (Tex. 1985), *cert. denied*, 476 U.S. 1159, 106 S.Ct. 2279, 90 L.Ed.2d 721 (1986).

The purpose of the rules of civil procedure is to obtain a just, fair, equitable and impartial adjudication of the litigants' rights under established principles of substantive law. *See* TEX. R. CIV. P. 1. The "ultimate purpose of discovery is to seek the truth . . . ." *Jampole v. Touchy*, 673 S.W.2d 569, 573 (Tex. 1984). The discovery rules were not designed as traps for the unwary, nor should we construe them to prevent a litigant from presenting the truth. *See Burden*, 896 S.W.2d at 256. As we stated:

> The primary purpose of [Rule 169] is to simplify trials by eliminating matters about which there is no real controversy, but which may be difficult or expensive to prove. It was never intended to be used as a demand upon a plaintiff or defendant to admit that he had no cause of action or ground of defense. *Sanders v. Harder*, 148 Tex. 593, 227 S.W.2d 206, 208 (1950); *see also Birdo v. Parker*, 842 S.W.2d 699 (Tex. App.—Tyler 1992, writ denied).

There is evidence in the record to support the trial court's order allowing Stelly to withdraw his admissions. Stelly presented affidavit testimony that, upon discovering the faulty admissions, he immediately filed his motion to withdraw them and amend his responses. He offered the surveyor's affidavit and report to show "good cause." The report and affidavit showed that he did not own the property where Papania fell. Papania offered no controverting evidence.

Papania was not prejudiced by the withdrawal for two reasons. First, his failure to comply with the notice provision under the Texas Tort Claims Act precluded his suit against the City regardless of who owned the land. Secondly, even if Stelly's original admission were true and he did own the land, it would not affect Papania's ability to sue the City for creating the alleged hazard.

Because the trial court properly conducted a hearing on both motions and based its decision on evidence in the record, we cannot say that it abused its discretion. The court of appeals incorrectly concluded that the trial court abused its discretion on a procedural point. It, therefore, declined to consider the merits of Stelly's duty, if any, to Papania. We disagree. Without hearing oral argument the Court remands this case to the court of appeals to determine whether the trial court properly granted Stelly summary judgment. *See* TEX. R. APP. P. 170 and 184(c).

Notes

1. The procedure described by *Stelly* is incorporated into Rule 198.3.

2. *Employers Insurance of Wausau v. Halton,* 792 S.W.2d 462 (Tex. App.—Dallas 1990, writ denied) contains an excellent discussion of the issues involved with deemed admissions. The trial court possesses broad discretion to permit or deny withdrawal of deemed admissions. The court of appeals analogizes this to Rule 320 on motion for new trial and indicates that the trial court will not abuse its discretion in setting aside an admission if it was made by accident or mistake, that there is a true contested fact, and that there will be no harm or delay to the opponent.

3. *Marshall v. Vise,* 767 S.W.2d 699 (Tex. 1989). A party's failure to object at trial to testimony contrary to an opponent's deemed admissions waives the effect of those admissions. Vise waived his right to rely upon the deemed admissions by failing to object to (and by eliciting) testimony to the contrary.

d. *Request for Production*

Notes

1. *Who can use Requests for Production?* Any party may serve these on any other party.

2. *When can Requests for Production be made?* Requests must be made no later than 30 days before the end of the discovery period.

3. *Specificity Required.* The request for production from a party, however, must be specific in terms of the information or data sought. It must recite precisely what is wanted.

a. The request must specify a reasonable time and place for production.
b. If the requesting party is to test the requested item, the means, manner, and procedure for testing or sampling must be described with specificity.
c. Under Rule 196.4, if data or information that exists in electronic or magnetic form is requested, the requesting party must specifically request specify the form in which the requesting party wants it produced.

i. The responding party must produce the electronic or magnetic data that is responsive to the request and is reasonable available to the responding party in the ordinary course of business.
ii. If the responding party cannot, through reasonable efforts, retrieve the data, or cannot, through reasonable efforts, produce it in the form requested the responding party must state an objection complying with the Rules.
iii. If the court ordered the production of data that requires extraordinary costs to comply, the trial court is to order the requesting party to pay the reasonable expenses of retrieving and producing the information.

4. *Who bears the cost of production?* Unless otherwise ordered by the court, the expense of producing items will be borne by the responding party, and the expense of inspecting, sampling, testing, photographing, and copying items produced will be borne by the requesting party.

5. *Testing.* Testing, sampling, and examination of an item may not destroy or materially alter an item unless previously authorized by the court.

6. *Entry Upon Property.* Under Rule 196.7 a party may gain entry on land or other property for good cause shown, and only if the land, property, or object thereon is relevant to the subject matter of the action.

7. *Response Time.* A written response is required within 30 days after service, unless a defendant is served with the request before the defendant's answer is due, in which event, the response is due 50 days after service of the response.

8. *Content of Response.* The responding party must state objections and assert privileges, and state, as appropriate, that:

a. production, inspection, or other requested action will be permitted as requested;
b. the requested items are being served on the requesting party with the response;
c. production, inspection, or other requested action will take place at a specified time and place.

If the responding party is objecting to the time and place of production; or

d. no items have been identified—after a diligent search—that are responsive to the request.

9. *Form of production:* The party producing documents must kept them as kept in usual course of business, or organize and label them to correspond with the categories in the request. There shall be no hiding by shuffling.

10. *Production of documents within the control of a party.* Under Rule 192.3(c), "A person is required to produce a document or tangible thing that is within the person's possession, custody, or control."

11. *Production from nonparties.* Under Rule 205, nonparties may be compelled to produce documents or other tangible things pursuant to a court order or subpoena, with, or without, a deposition.

a. *Notice.* The requesting party must give notice of the request to produce to both the non-party and the party. This notice must be served before or at the same time that the subpoena is served.

b. *Motion.* Unlike the prior practice, a motion is not required when seeking production by a non-party.

c. *Response.* The nonparty must respond to the notice and subpoena in accordance with Rule 176.6.

d. *Cost.* A party requiring production of documents by a nonparty must reimburse the nonparty's reasonable costs of production.

12. *Medical Authorization.* Under TEX. R. CIV. P. 194.2(j), a party must produce, upon request, in a suit alleging physical or mental injury and damages from the occurrence that is the subject of the case, all medical records and bills that are reasonably related to the injuries or damages asserted or, in lieu thereof, an authorization permitting the disclosure of such medical records and bills. Under TEX. R. CIV. P. 194.2(k) in a suit alleging physical or mental injury, and damages from the occurrence that is the subject of the case, all medical records and bills obtained by the responding party by virtue of an authorization furnished by the requesting party.

13. *Example of Request for Production*:

NO. 38747-1

IN RE :	§	IN THE COUNTY COURT
	§	
ESTATE OF DIANE E. WALTERS,	§	AT LAW NO. ONE OF
	§	
DECEASED	§	NUECES COUNTY, TEXAS

APPLICANT DONALD CARRICO'S REQUEST FOR PRODUCTION TO SANDRA K. BOERNER and JOYCE AHLERS SHAW

TO: Contestants, SANDRA K. BOERNER and JOYCE AHLERS SHAW, by and through their attorney of record, Mr. Bradley Bunting, Bunting & Bunting, 307 NationsBank Tower, 500 N. Shoreline Blvd., Corpus Christi, Texas 78471.

Applicant Donald Carrico, pursuant to Rule 196 of the Texas Rules of Civil Procedure, files this his First Request for Production to Contestants Sandra K. Boerner and Joyce Ahlers Shaw.

Respectfully submitted,
PEARSON & PRICE, PLLC
Suite 1700 South Tower
800 North Shoreline Boulevard
Corpus Christi, Texas 78401
(512) 885-0077
(512) 885-0288(FAX)

By______________________________
Richard E. Flint
State Bar No. 07151500
Attorneys for Donald Carrico

CERTIFICATE OF SERVICE

I, Richard E. Flint certify on this the ____ day of _____________, 2000, a true and correct copy of the forgoing pleading was mailed by certified mail, return receipt addressed as follows:

Mr. Bradley Bunting
Bunting & Bunting
Attorneys At Law
307 NationsBank Tower
500 N. Shoreline Blvd.
Corpus Christi, Texas 78471

____
Richard E. Flint

INSTRUCTIONS

Pursuant to the provisions of Rule 196, Texas Rules of Civil Procedures, you are hereby requested to produce the below designated documents (including papers, books, accounts, writings, drawings, graphs, charts, photographs, or any insurance agreements under which any person or entity carrying on an insurance business may be liable to satisfy part or all of the judgment which may be rendered in this action or to indemnify or reimburse for payments made to satisfy the judgment), recordings and other data compilations from which information can be obtained, translated, if necessary by you, your agents or attorneys, through appropriate devices into reasonably usable form, and to produce the below designated tangible things which constitute or contain matters which are in the possession, custody or control of you, your agents, servants or attorneys, for inspection, sampling, testing, photographing and/or copying at 800 N. Shoreline, Suite 1700 South Tower, Corpus Christi, Texas 7840l. You are advised that, pursuant to Rule 191, you must make a written response that shall state with respect to each item or category of items that inspection will be permitted as requested and that you will comply with this request, except to the extent that objections are made, stating specific reasons why such discovery will not be allowed. You are advised that, pursuant to Rule 191, responses to these requests shall be served within thirty (30) days after receipt of the requests. You are hereby requested to produce each document, recording, tangible thing, or other datum by attaching copies of the documents requested, bound together, marked *Produced pursuant to Request for Production No.* _______ (indicate the appropriate request number), and accompanied by a bill for the reasonable cost of making copies. If a document produced in such a response is produced pursuant to another response, please include copies with both responses. A response by reference is not acceptable.

In answering the following questions and responding to the following requests, furnish all information and items available to you, including information or items in the possession of your attorneys, their investigators, and all persons acting in your behalf, and not merely such information known for your own personal knowledge. If you cannot answer a question or respond to a request in full after exercising due diligence to secure the information or item requested, so state in your response and to the extent possible, answer or respond stating whatever information or knowledge you have.

The questions which follow are continuing, and you are requested to provide by way of supplemental answers hereto, additional information as you or any other person acting on your behalf may hereafter obtain which will augment or otherwise modify your answers given to the questions below. Such supplemental responses are to be filed and served upon this party as required by Rule 197, TEX. R. CIV. P.

As used herein, the following terms shall have the meaning indicated below:

(a) ***Persons*** means natural persons, corporations, partnerships, sole proprietorships, unions, associations, federations or any other kind of entity.

(b) ***Document*** means any printed, typewritten, handwritten, mechanically or otherwise recorded matter of whatever character, including, but without limitation, letters, purchase orders, memoranda, telegrams, notes, catalogs, brochures, diaries, calendars, inter- or intra-office communications, depositions, answers to interrogatories, pleadings, judgments, newspaper articles, photographs, tape recordings, motion pictures, and any carbon or photographic copies of any such material if you do not have custody or control of the original. If any document requested to be identified was but is no longer in your possession or control or is no longer in existence, please state that such is the case.

(c) ***You*** and ***your*** shall mean the party to whom these questions are directed, as well as agents, employees, attorneys, investigators and all other "persons" acting for said party.

(d) In each question wherein you are asked to identify a person, state with respect to such person as follows: (a) his or her full name, and (b) his or her last known address and telephone number. If the person to be identified is not a natural person (e.g., a corporation), give its name and address and principal business activity. If you object to identifying any person as hereinabove defined, or producing any item requested, or you feel that a court order should be obtained by this party, please so state in your answer to the interrogatory or response to a request for production.

(e) ***Contestants*** means Sandra K. Boerner and Joyce Ahlers Shaw.

(f) ***Applicant*** means Donald Carrico.

APPLICANT DONALD CARRICO'S FIRST SET OF REQUESTS FOR PRODUCTION TO SANDRA K. BOERNER and JOYCE AHLERS SHAW

REQUEST FOR PRODUCTION NO. 1:

Any and all documents by and/or between Contestants, or either of them, and the Deceased, Diane E. Walters.

RESPONSE:

REQUEST FOR PRODUCTION NO. 2:

Any and all affidavits or statements of any persons taken, given, or in the possession of Contestants, and/or their attorney.

RESPONSE:

REQUEST FOR PRODUCTION NO. 3:

Any and all documents to support your allegation that "the Last Will and Testament of Diane E. Walters, Deceased" sought to be admitted into probate "is not a lawful and valid Will".

RESPONSE:

* * *

Notes

1. *In re Continental General Tire, Inc.*, 979 S.W.2d 609 (Tex. 1998). TEX. R. CIV. EVID. 507 provides special protection to trade secrets. Under our TEX. R. CIV. EVID. 507, a party has a privilege to refuse to disclose its trade secrets "if the allowance of the privilege will not tend to conceal fraud or otherwise work injustice." When a party resisting discovery establishes that the requested information is a trade secret under Rule 507, the burden shifts to the requesting party to establish that the information is necessary for a fair adjudication of its claim or defense.

2. *In re Union Pacific Railroad Co.*, 294 S.W.3d 589 (Tex. 2009): This is an original mandamus proceeding. ***Held:*** Writ of mandamus will issue. The trial court abused its discretion when it compelled a rail transportation company to produce confidential "rate structures," which include formulas to determine shipping rates charged to customers. When trade secret privilege is asserted, as the basis for resisting production, the trial

court must determine (1) whether the requested production constitutes a trade secret; (2) if so, the court must require the party seeking production to show reasonable necessity for the requested materials, weighing the requesting party's need for the information against the potential of harm to the resisting party from disclosure. Here, the defendant met its burden of establishing that the information sought is protected by the trade secret privilege, and the plaintiff failed to demonstrate how the information is necessary or essential to the fair adjudication of the case. If the information is a trade secret, and the requesting parties do not need it, an order that requires disclosure is a clear abuse of discretion.

Once trade secret status has been established, the burden shifts to the party seeking to discover the information protected by the trade secret, to establish that the information is necessary or essential to the fair adjudication of the case, weighing the requesting party's need for the information against the potential of harm to the resisting party from disclosure. The degree to which information is necessary in a case depends on the nature of the information and the context of the case. But, the test cannot be satisfied merely by general assertions of unfairness; instead, a party must demonstrate with specificity exactly how the lack of the information will impair the presentation of the case on the merits to the point that an unjust result is a real, rather than a merely possible, threat.

IN RE MARION SHIPMAN
540 S.W.3d 562
(Tex. 2018)

B. Russell Horton, George Brothers Kincaid & Horton LLP, Christopher L. Elliott, Graves Dougherty Hearon & Moody, P.C., Kathryn E. Allen, The Law Office of Kathryn E. Allen, PLLC, Austin TX, R. Mark Dietz, Dietz & Jarrad, P.C., Round Rock, TX, for Real Party in Interest Jamie Lynn Shelton.

D. Todd Smith, Smith Law Group LLLP, Maitreya Tomlinson, Smith Law Group LLLP, Robert C. Alden, Byrd Davis Alden & Henrichson, Austin TX, for Relator Marion Shipman.

PER CURIAM

This mandamus petition arises out of a discovery dispute. Specifically, the real party in interest suspects that the relator is unable or unwilling to diligently search his computer for responsive documents. On the real party's motion, the trial court ordered the relator to turn over his computer and other electronic devices for forensic examination. We conditionally grant mandamus relief and order the trial court to vacate its order.

Relator Marion Shipman partnered with Mark and Jamie Shelton in various real-estate ventures and auto dealerships in the 1990s and 2000s. According to Shipman, their business dealings ceased in 2010. In 2011, a bank sued Shipman and the Sheltons, seeking recovery of $1.3 million in loans made to an auto dealership owned by the Sheltons. As guarantor of the loans, Shipman settled with the bank in 2012, but the bank's case against the Sheltons moved forward. More than two years later, in October 2014, Jamie, the real party in interest here, brought a third-party action against Shipman, alleging fraud as well as breaches of contract and fiduciary duty.

Jamie sought to discover a variety of records concerning Shipman's business dealings with the Sheltons over the years. Shipman responded to two sets of discovery requests, producing responsive documents both times. But Jamie was dissatisfied with Shipman's production and filed a motion to compel.

In July 2015, the trial court ordered Shipman to produce more documents—primarily financial statements and "floor-planning" spreadsheets related to auto dealerships. In a deposition later that month, Shipman testified that he had produced all such documents in his possession. He added, however, that some relevant data was on a computer that "crashed" in 2012, more than two years before Jamie sued him. Shipman testified he was unable to retrieve records from that computer.

But a few days later, Shipman reported that his son had helped him discover files from his old computer in a "backup" folder on his replacement computer. Shipman's attorney reviewed those documents and, on August 3, produced a thumb drive containing responsive documents. In an affidavit, Shipman further attested that other documents the trial court ordered produced had been destroyed years earlier. According to Shipman, "[m]ost of the partnerships and transactions that the judge ruled I had to produce documents for dated from the late 1990s and early 2000s. In 2011, my CPA told me that I only had to keep files for 7 years, and so I cleaned my files of documents that were more than 7 years old, and I burned those files." Both Shipman and his attorney submitted affidavits insisting they had diligently searched Shipman's files, both physical and electronic, and produced all responsive documents—according to them, more than 6,000 pages.

Jamie filed a second motion to compel—the one at issue in this case—arguing that in light of Shipman's deposition testimony and belated "late-night production," it had become "crystal clear" that Shipman had "misled" the trial court at the previous motion-to-compel hearing and "had failed to produce (or even to search for) entire categories of responsive, discoverable information, and that Shipman may have destroyed material evidence in the case." Jamie asked the trial court to compel Shipman to turn over his computer for forensic inspection. Jamie offered testimony from a forensic examiner who said he could determine if more backup files existed and whether files had been deleted. He further testified he could likely recover data from the "crashed" computer, though Shipman maintains that device is no longer in his possession.

The trial court ordered Shipman to produce not only his computer but also all "media" for forensic examination, including "all internal hard drives and external media (including, without limitation, thumb drives, hard drives, CDs, DVDs, zip drives and any other storage medium) in Shipman's possession, custody or control and used by Shipman or his agents at any time during the period January 1, 2000 through the present." The order contains a detailed forensic-examination protocol to protect Shipman's privacy and legal privileges. In short, the forensic examiner would "blindly" generate a list of all file names on the media and provide the list only to Shipman's counsel, who could then make objections before turning anything over to Jamie's counsel. The Austin court of appeals denied mandamus relief in a non-substantive opinion. No. 03-16-00345-CV, 2016 WL 3677883 (Tex. App.—Austin July 8, 2016, orig. proceeding) (mem. op.).

Shipman now seeks mandamus relief from this Court, arguing the trial court abused its discretion in three ways. First, the underlying discovery request does not seek specific documents in electronic form, as Rule 196.4 requires. Thus, the trial court lacked discretion to order Shipman to turn over his computer and other media for examination. *See* TEX. R. CIV. P. 196.4. Second, the bare allegations supporting the motion are insufficient to justify such an invasive search. Shipman argues Jamie presented no evidence that he defaulted on his obligation to search his records, that his production was inadequate, or that a forensic search of his storage devices could recover responsive materials that had not already been produced. And third, the trial court's order is overly broad, covering all of Shipman's computers and electronic media for the past seventeen years, and grants more relief than Jamie requested.

"A discovery order that compels production beyond the rules of procedure is an abuse of discretion for which mandamus is the proper remedy." *In re Nat'l Lloyds Ins. Co.*, 449 S.W.3d 486, 488 (Tex. 2014) (orig. proceeding) (per curiam). "A writ of mandamus will issue only if the trial court reaches a decision so arbitrary and unreasonable as to amount to a clear and prejudicial error of law and the relator has no adequate remedy by appeal." *In re State Farm Lloyds*, 520 S.W.3d 595, 604 (Tex. 2017) (orig. proceeding) (internal quotation omitted). Appellate courts may not substitute their judgment for the trial court's determination of factual matters committed to the trial court's discretion. *See id.* "But with regard to questions of law and mixed questions of law and fact, a trial court has no discretion in determining what the law is or applying the law to the facts, even when the law is unsettled." *Id.* (internal quotations omitted).

"Intrusive discovery measures—such as ordering direct access to an opponent's electronic storage device—require, at a minimum, that the benefits of the discovery measure outweigh the burden imposed upon the discovered party." *In re Weekley Homes, L.P.*, 295 S.W.3d 309, 322 (Tex. 2009) (orig. proceeding) (citing TEX. R. CIV. P. 196.4, 192.4). "Providing access to information by ordering examination of a party's electronic storage device is particularly intrusive and should be generally discouraged, just as permitting open access to a party's file cabinets for general perusal would be." *Id.* at 317.

Shipman initially argues that Jamie failed to satisfy the Rule 196.4 requirement to "specifically request production of electronic or magnetic data and specify the form in which the requesting party wants it produced." He points out that she never sought access to his computer hard drive or other media and "did not request documents that could be obtained from only those sources." The only reference to electronic data in Jamie's discovery requests, Shipman argues, is "generic language" in her second request for production that modified the definition of "document" to include "data and information that exists in electronic or magnetic form." If a "global" definition were satisfactory, he argues, the rule would require no specificity at all.

Jamie acknowledges that her first request for production did not include a request for electronically stored information, but she argues the "generic" reference in her second request is sufficient. And, even if it isn't, she relies on *Weekley* in arguing that her second motion to compel clarified the scope of her request to include electronic data on Shipman's computer.

In *Weekley*, we concluded the request at issue was not specific enough to cover the deleted emails the requesting party sought. *See* 295 S.W.3d at 314. But we also held the requesting party's "failure to follow the rule" did not prejudice the producing party. *Id.* at 314-15. In that case, the requesting party was skeptical that the emails it received reflected the volume in the producing party's possession. *See id.* at 312. The requesting party elicited testimony at a motion-to-compel hearing that the producing party's computer system "forces employees to clear out their inboxes on a regular basis, so that deleted emails will only be saved if an employee backs them up on the employee's own personal hard drive somehow." *Id.* at 312 (cleaned up). So the requesting party sought direct access to that computer system in hopes of recovering deleted emails. *Id.* at 313.

We concluded the underlying discovery requests were not specific enough to include deleted emails but that it "became abundantly clear in the course of discovery and before the hearing on the motion to compel" that deleted emails were sought. *Id.* at 314. "The purpose of Rule 196.4's specificity requirement," we noted in *Weekley*, "is to ensure that requests for electronic information are clearly understood and disputes avoided." *Id.* Because the scope of discovery sought "was understood before trial court intervention, [the producing party] was not prejudiced by [the requesting party's] failure to follow the rule." *Id.* at 314-15.

Jamie's discovery requests do not explicitly seek direct access to Shipman's computer. Rather, Jamie seeks access to Shipman's computer through a motion to compel as a *remedy* for perceived inadequate production, not as a discovery request in itself. The function of Rule 196.4's specificity requirement is to ensure electronic-information requests are "clearly understood and disputes avoided." *Id.* at 314. Jamie's request to directly access Shipman's computer is, in her view, a response to Shipman's failure to comply with her "clearly understood" requests for electronically stored information. She properly sought that remedy through her second motion to compel; she did not need to separately lodge a Rule 196.4–specific discovery request for direct access to Shipman's computer.

Furthermore, we are not persuaded that Shipman can claim prejudice by any failure on Jamie's part to specifically request electronically stored information. Like the deleted emails sought in *Weekley*, it became "abundantly clear" throughout the course of litigation and before trial-court intervention that Jamie sought financial records she believed were relevant to this case, whether they exist in a physical file cabinet or on an electronic device. *See id.* at 315. Regardless of the specificity of Jamie's initial requests, she argued in her second motion to compel that "Shipman should be required to produce all paper and electronic records he can locate using diligent efforts, and to make his computer[s] available for forensic examination." If Jamie's discovery requests did not technically meet Rule 196.4's specificity requirement, Shipman cannot argue Jamie's intent was not "clearly understood."

Insisting her request was sufficiently specific, Jamie argues we should decline to consider Shipman's arguments because he failed to object to her request as required under Rule 196.4. *See* TEX. R. CIV. P. 194.6 ("If the responding party cannot—through reasonable efforts—retrieve the data or information requested or produce it in the form requested, the responding party must state an objection complying with these rules."). She points us to Shipman's response to her second requests for production, in which Shipman objects to some requests and agrees to others, but never takes the position that the information requested is reasonably unavailable to him under Rule 196.4. Shipman responds simply that because no specific Rule 196.4 request was made, no Rule 196.4 objection was required.

Neither Jamie's argument nor Shipman's response correctly contemplates the relationship of Rule 196.4 to this case. Rule 196.4 requires the producing party to produce "data that is responsive to the request and is reasonably available to the responding party in its ordinary course of business." Shipman's position is that all responsive documents in his possession *have* been produced. He does not claim to hold back anything on the basis that it is not reasonably available to him in the course of his business. *Cf. State Farm*, 520 S.W.3d at 600-01 (considering a producing party's argument that documents admittedly in its possession in the requested "native" format were not reasonably available in the ordinary course of business). In this case, Shipman could not lodge a Rule 196.4 objection without contradicting his position that he had produced all responsive documents in his possession.

We therefore proceed to Shipman's argument that the trial court abused its discretion in ordering Shipman to surrender his computer and all other electronic media from the past seventeen years for forensic examination. As a threshold to granting access to electronic devices, "the requesting party must show that the responding party has somehow defaulted in its obligation to search its records and produce the requested data." *Weekley*, 295 S.W.3d at 317. But we do not rely on "mere skepticism or bare allegations that the responding party has failed to comply with its discovery duties." *Id.* at 318.

The crux of Jamie's argument is that Shipman's post-deposition production, along with his equivocal deposition testimony concerning the existence of particular documents, indicates he is incapable of or unwilling to search his computer for responsive documents. She insists the evidence shows Shipman kept detailed business records on his computer—both the one that "crashed" in 2012 and his current computer—but that Shipman has proved himself "lacking the expertise" to "thoroughly and diligently search his electronic storage media." So although Shipman testified in his affidavit that he has produced all responsive documents, Jamie argues that her only assurance is that Shipman testified at his deposition that "[I] looked at my computer to see, and I don't have them on there."

This assurance, Jamie maintains, rings hollow against additional deposition testimony in which Shipman was unsure about the existence of particular documents Jamie seeks. For example, when asked about particular records concerning floor-planning payments, loans made to Mark Shelton, and a 2008 financial statement potentially provided to the bank that earlier sued Shipman and the Sheltons, Shipman provided equivocal answers such as "I'll have to look and see," "I don't know if our records go back that far," and "I don't know if I've still got it." Based on these responses, Jamie argues Shipman's position that he thoroughly searched his computer and produced all responsive documents is not credible. Jamie also insists Shipman admitted in his deposition that he deleted some computer files, though Shipman maintains those statements referred to documents stored on his old, "crashed" computer, and not his current computer. In his affidavit, Shipman swears he has not deleted any files from his new computer.

Shipman acknowledges that the backup files discovered after his deposition were produced late, but he argues that late production is not tantamount to default under *Weekley*. Otherwise, an opposing party would be entitled to search all of the producing party's computers and other electronic storage media every time the producing party supplements an initial production. The evidence shows that after his July 29 deposition, Shipman enlisted his son's assistance in searching his computer files and discovered the "backup" folder. Shipman promptly turned these files over to his attorney, who in turn quickly reviewed them and produced responsive documents to Jamie on August 3.

Of course, late production of the backup files is inconsistent with Shipman's deposition testimony that no such files existed. But Shipman's later determination that they *did* exist, paired with his prompt production of responsive files from that backup, indicates an effort to comply with discovery rather than a default. And the discovery process is best served by rules that encourage parties to produce documents belatedly discovered in good faith. They should not face the perverse incentive to conceal such information lest they be forced to hand over the underlying electronic devices for forensic examination.

Shipman's belated discovery of the "backup" folder is evidence bearing on his ability to operate a computer and to search for and retrieve responsive documents. But it gives rise only to "mere skepticism" that responsive documents remain on Shipman's computer, *see Weekley*, 295 S.W.3d at 318, and it is insufficient evidence to support a finding that he defaulted on his discovery obligation. Indeed, Jamie's insistence that Shipman kept detailed records on his computer, including "electronic check registers" and "financial statements," suggests that Shipman is competent at some level to operate a computer and create and negotiate computer files. Though he admittedly failed to discover the "backup" folder in his initial search, he *did* eventually discover and produce it. Jamie offers no evidence that he is incapable of searching the computer files he actively maintained on the device or that an exhaustive search for backup files has not now been conducted, either by Shipman or his son.

Nor does Shipman's equivocation about the existence of discrete documents at his deposition transform general skepticism into discovery default. Shipman was asked about discrete, individual documents linked to 2008 and 2009—more than five years before the deposition—and stated he was unsure if they existed. This is no evidence that he cannot reliably produce responsive documents from his computer. Shipman's affidavit testimony that he *has* produced all responsive documents is his ultimate answer on what documents are in his possession. His inability to remember off the cuff what documents he possesses, even when combined with any skepticism surrounding late production of the "backup" folder, creates only more skepticism, not evidence of default under *Weekley*.

We do not suggest that a requesting party can never establish a discovery-obligation default under *Weekley* by offering evidence of a producing party's technical ineptitude. Nor do we discount trial-court discretion in determining when that line is crossed. But the burden imposed by *Weekley* is high—forensic examination of electronic devices is "particularly intrusive and should be generally discouraged." 295 S.W.3d at 317. And notably absent from the record here is any examination of what exactly Shipman's or his son's technical capabilities actually are. Neither testified at the motion-to-compel hearing. Instead, Jamie's counsel merely recounted Shipman's equivocal deposition answers, explained the belated production from the backup folder, and then stated: "Our question is: What else is there?"

Counsel's question suggests exactly the "mere skepticism" *Weekley* prohibits as a basis for forensic examination. *Id.* at 318. Jamie's burden is to show that Shipman "somehow defaulted" in his discovery obligation and that his production "has been inadequate and that a search [of his computer] could recover . . . relevant materials." *Id.* But Jamie has only established that some of Shipman's production was late and some of his deposition answers were equivocal. There is no evidence—just suspicion—that more unrecovered data exists on Shipman's computer outside the "backup" folder. Shipman was neither pressed at his deposition nor examined at the motion-to-compel hearing concerning his computer skills or the specific steps he took to search his computer. There is no evidence that, having discovered one "backup" folder, Shipman is incapable of searching for others either by himself or through his son. And there is no evidence at all concerning the abilities of Shipman's son, who discovered the "backup" folder. If Jamie's complaint is that Shipman lacks the ability to thoroughly search his computer such that someone else should do it for him, the evidence shows he did just that. Yet Jamie made no attempt to ascertain Shipman's son's abilities, what processes he undertook, and whether *his* search was adequate.

On the evidence presented, however, the trial court ordered Shipman to surrender not just the computer at issue, but also all electronic "media," whether business or personal, and regardless of whether they are related to the issues in the lawsuit, for the past seventeen years. Shipman argues the order's breadth far exceeds the relief Jamie sought. Indeed, the parties argue only about access to Shipman's current personal computer. We agree that even if *some* relief were warranted, the trial court's order was overly broad. The trial court appeared to grant greater relief than was sought in Jamie's motion to compel, and there is no apparent connection between the vast majority of the devices and media the order covers and the documents Jamie seeks, or justification for its nearly twenty-year reach. *See State Farm*, 520 S.W.3d at 595 ("[A]ll discovery is subject to the proportionality overlay embedded in our discovery rules and inherent in the reasonableness standard to which our electronic-discovery rule is tethered.").

* * *

Jamie may ultimately be entitled to some relief, but, on the evidence presented, the trial court abused its discretion when it ordered forensic examination of all of Shipman's electronic devices. The trial court ordered Shipman to produce for forensic examination all his electronically stored files of every kind, whether business or personal, and regardless of whether they are related to the issues in the lawsuit, for seventeen years. Jamie's skepticism about Shipman's production of the relevant records does not amount to a default in Shipman's discovery obligation, nor is it enough to justify such an extraordinarily intrusive order. As such, the trial court abused its discretion and Shipman is without an adequate remedy on appeal. *See Weekley*, 295 S.W.3d at 322. We conditionally grant the writ of mandamus and order the trial court to vacate its order. We are confident the trial court will comply, and our writ will issue only if it does not.

In re STATE FARM LLOYDS
520 S.W.3d 595
(Tex. 2017)

Discovery of Electronic Data. Principles Elucidated.

Facts: Plaintiffs residential homeowners sued their insurer and other others alleging underpayment of insured hail-damage claims. The requesting party sought Electronically Stored Information (ESI) in native from while the responding party offered to produce in searchable static form. The trial court ordered production in native form.

Held: The Supreme Court elucidates the guiding principles informing the exercise of discretion over electronic-discovery disputes. Because the parties below were unaware of these principles, the request for mandamus relief is denied without prejudice to allow the relator to seek reconsideration of the trial court in light of this opinion. In clarifying the guiding principles informing the exercise of discretion over electronic-discover disputes. The Court emphasized that proportionality is the polestar. In doing so the Court furthers a guiding tenet of the Texas Rules of Civil Procedure: that litigants achieve a "just, fair, equitable and impartial adjudication . . . with as great expedition and dispatch and at the least expense . . . as may be practicable."

Discovery of Electronic Data. Principles Detailed.

Discovery of ESI must be guided by factors considered case by case, including:

Likely benefit of the requested discovery.

The needs of the case.

The amount in controversy.

The parties' resources.

Importance of the issues at stake in the litigation.

The importance of the proposed discovery in resolving the litigation.

Any other articulable factors bearing on proportionality.

e. *Oral Depositions*

Notes

1. *What are they*? An oral depositions is a pre-trial procedure allowing counsel for the parties (or the parties without counsel) to question, in person, any person, including another party, who has information within the scope of discovery. *See* TEX. R. CIV. P. 199. The testimony, objections, and any other statements during the deposition must be recorded at the time they are give or made.

2. *How is the record made?*

a. Court Reporter

b. Non-stenographic recording, including video taping. Notice must be given at least five days prior to the deposition that the deposition will recorded by other than stenographic means. Rule 199.1(c). The party requesting the non-stenographic recording will be responsible for obtaining a person authorized by law to administer the oath and for assuring that the recording will be intelligible, accurate, and trustworthy.

3. *Telephone or other remote electronic means:* There are procedures for taking depositions by telephone or other remote electronic means (e.g., closed circuit television or the Internet), and permitting lawyers to attend the deposition through those means. Rules 199.1(b), 199.5(a)(2). If a deposition is taken by telephone or other remote electronic means, the party noticing the deposition must make arrangements for all persons to attend by the same means. If the party noticing the deposition appears in person, any other party may appear by telephone

or other remote electronic means if that party makes the necessary arrangements with the deposition officer, and the party noticing the deposition. Rule 199.5 (a)(2) and Rule 195.5 (d).

4. *Who can use them?* Any party can take an oral deposition of any person (party or non-party) having information within the scope of discovery. Either party may use the deposition at trial.

5. *When can they be taken?* A notice of intent to take an oral deposition must be served on the witness and all parties a reasonable time before the deposition is taken. An oral deposition may be taken outside the discovery period only by agreement of the parties or with leave of court. Oral depositions may be taken before suit is filed, to preserve testimony. *See* TEX. R. CIV. P. 202 details the procedure for such depositions.

6. *What limits are imposed on deposition conduct?* Oral depositions are to be conducted the same manner as if the testimony were being obtained in court at trial. Rule 195.5 (d). Private conferences between the witnesses and their lawyers are prohibited except for the purpose of determining whether a privilege should be asserted. Rule 195.5 (d). If the lawyers and the witnesses do not comply with these rules, the court may admit into evidence at trial statements, discussions *and other occurrences* that reflect upon the credibility of the witness or the testimony. "Coaching" objections and colloquy are strictly prohibited. Objections to questions during the depositions are limited to "objection: form" or "objection: leading," and objections to testimony are limited to "objection: non-responsive." These objections are waived if not stated as phrased during the deposition. The witness's attorney may also instruct the witness not to answer a question if it calls for privileged information, is abusive or if any answer to the questions would be misleading. Rule 195.5(f) and comment 4. The deposing party, however, may require the objecting party to give a short and concise explanation of the basis for the objection or instruction to enable them to rephrase the question. Rules 199.5(e) and (f). Argumentative or suggestive objections or explanations are prohibited, waive the objection and may be ground for terminating the deposition. Rules 199.5(e) and (f). Objection or instructions not to answer a question in an oral deposition must be made only if there is a good faith factual and legal basis for doing so at the time. Rule 199.5(h).

7. *What time limits are imposed upon depositions.* In addition to the aggregate time limits of Rule 190, Rule 199.5(c) limits each side to six hours to examine and cross-examine an individual witness in an oral deposition. Breaks do not count against this limitation. The deposition officer (usually the court reporter) must certify the amount of time used by each party at the deposition.

8. *Duty to identify representative of organization before deposition:* If an organization is named as the witness in a deposition notice, the organization must, a reasonable time before the deposition, designate the persons who will testify on the organization's behalf and identify the matters on which each person will testify. Rule 199.2(b)(1).

9. *Reconciling of deposition document request with other rules.* If a party serves a request for production of documents with a deposition notice to a party, the request, response, objections and privilege claims are governed by the requests for production rule, Rule 197, including the deadline of thirty days for responding, as well as the general standards governing written discovery set forth in Rule 193. Rule 199.2(b)(5) & comment 1. If the witness is a nonparty, these matters are governed by the nonparty discovery rule, Rule 205.

10. *Suspending the deposition.* If the time limitations for the deposition have expired or the deposition is being conducted or defended in violation of these rules, a party or witness may suspend the oral deposition for the time necessary to obtain a ruling. Rule 195.5(g)

11. *Good faith required.* An attorney must not object to a question at an oral deposition, instruct the witness not to answer a question, or suspend the deposition unless there is a good faith factual and legal basis for doing so at the time. Rule 195.5(g).

12. *When can they be used?* Texas allows the admission of deposition testimony without regard to the availability of the witness. This is contrasted with the Texas position on the use of former testimony at a previous trial. Such former testimony is excluded, unless the witness is unavailable to testify at the trial. The witness is unavailable at the subsequent trial, when dead, insane, when physically unable to testify, when beyond the jurisdiction of the court (if their deposition could have been taken, they are not unavailable), or when whereabouts unknown and a diligent search has been made to find the witness, or when the witness has been kept from trial by the adverse party. *Hall v White,* 525 S.W.2d 860 (Tex. 1975).

13. *Subpoena Range:* TEX. R. CIV. P. 176.3 and TEX. CIV. PRAC. & REM. CODE section 22.001 provides that "A person my not be required by subpoena to appear or produce documents or other things in a court that is more than 150 miles from where the person resides or is served." (Language of Rule 176.3). Rule 176.5 provides that "A subpoena may be served at any place within the State of Texas by any sheriff or constable of the state of Texas, or any person who is not a party and is 18 years of age or older."

14. *In Re Jack Jorden,* 249 S.W.3d 416 (Tex. 2008): TEX. CIV. PRAC. & REM. CODE § 74.351(s), limits discovery in health-care lawsuits until the plaintiff serves an expert report, summarizing how each defendant violated standards of care and caused the plaintiff injury. This requirement for an expert report applies to presuit depositions authorized by Rule 202 of the Texas Rules of Civil Procedure. Because the § 74.351(s) prohibits "all discovery" other than three exceptions—and Rule 202 depositions are not listed among them—the statute prohibits such depositions until after an expert report is served.

TEX. R. CIV. P. 202 depositions are not now, and never have been, intended for routine use. There are practical as well as due process problems, with demanding discovery from someone before telling them what the issues are. Accordingly, presuit depositions are available under Rule 202, only if a trial court makes one of two findings: (1) allowing the petitioner to take the requested deposition may prevent a failure, or delay of justice, in an anticipated suit; or (2) the likely benefit of allowing the petitioner to take the requested deposition, to investigate a potential claim outweighs the burden or expense of the procedure.

15. *Crown Central Petroleum Corporation v. Garcia*, 904 S.W.2d 125 (Tex. 1995): Plaintiffs sued Defendants for the death of Otto Carl, who died in 1992 of lung cancer, allegedly as the result of asbestos exposure. In July 1994, Plaintiffs filed a motion to require Defendant-Crown Central to produce its chairman of the board and chief executive officer, Rosenberg, for a video deposition. Crown Central responded with a motion to quash deposition accompanied by Rosenberg's affidavit, to the effect that he knew nothing of the case, was not involved in the day-to-day maintenance decisions made at the Refinery where Carl worked, and had no expertise that could be brought to bear on the case. The trial court granted Plaintiffs' motion to produce Rosenberg and denied Crown Royal's motion to quash. ***Held:*** Writ of mandamus is denied because the guidelines adopted here were not before the trial court. This action is without prejudice so that the trial court may reconsider its order denying Crown Central's motion to quash Rosenberg's deposition. When a party seeks to depose a corporate president or other high level corporate official at the apex of the corporate hierarchy and that official (or the corporation) files a motion for protective order to prohibit the deposition accompanied by the official's affidavit denying any knowledge of relevant facts, the trial court should first determine whether the party seeking the deposition has arguably shown that the official has any unique or superior personal knowledge of discoverable information. If the party seeking the deposition cannot show that the official has any unique or superior personal knowledge of discoverable information, the trial court should grant the motion for protective order and first require the party seeking the deposition to attempt to obtain the discovery through less intrusive methods. Depending upon the circumstances of the particular case, these methods could include the depositions of lower level employees, the deposition of the corporation itself, and interrogatories and requests for production of documents directed to the corporation. After making a good faith effort to obtain the discovery though less intrusive methods, the party seeking the deposition may attempt to show (1) that there is a reasonable indication that the official's deposition is calculated to lead to the discovery of admissible evidence, or (2) that the less intrusive methods of discovery are unsatisfactory, insufficient or inadequate. If the party seeking the deposition makes this showing, the trial court should modify or vacate the protective order as appropriate. As with any deponent, the trial court retains discretion to restrict the duration, scope and location of the deposition. If the party seeking the deposition fails to make this showing, the trial court should leave the protective order in place.

CROWN CENTRAL PETROLEUM CORPORATION v. GARCIA

904 S.W.2d 125
(Tex. 1995)

When a party seeks to depose a corporate president or other high level corporate official at the apex of the corporate hierarchy and that official (or the corporation) files a motion for protective order to prohibit the deposition accompanied by the official's affidavit denying any knowledge of relevant facts, the trial court should first determine whether the party seeking the deposition has arguably shown that the official has any unique or superior personal knowledge of discoverable information. If the party seeking the deposition cannot show that the official has any unique or superior personal knowledge of discoverable information, the trial court should grant the motion for protective order and first require the party seeking the deposition to attempt to obtain the discovery through less intrusive methods. Depending upon the circumstances of the particular case, these methods could include the depositions of lower level employees, the deposition of the corporation itself, and interrogatories and requests for production of documents directed to the corporation.

After making a good faith effort to obtain the discovery though less intrusive methods, the party seeking the deposition may attempt to show (1) that there is a reasonable indication that the official's deposition is calculated to lead to the discovery of admissible evidence, or (2) that the less intrusive methods of discovery are unsatisfactory, insufficient or inadequate. If the party seeking the deposition makes this showing, the trial court should modify or vacate the protective order as appropriate. As with any deponent, the trial court retains discretion to restrict the duration, scope and location of the deposition. If the party seeking the deposition fails to make this showing, the trial court should leave the protective order in place.

In re ALCATEL USA, INC. f/k/a DSC COMMUNICATIONS INC.

11 S.W.3d 173
(Tex. 2000)

Timothy S. Durst, Dallas, Bob E. Shannon, Austin, Joseph D. Cheavens, Houston, Joseph R. Knight, Joe R. Greenhill, Austin, Samara L. Kline, Dallas, Scott Partridge, Houston, Michael P. Lynn, Eric W. Pinker, John Jesse Kendrick, Robert E. Goodfriend, Dallas, for relator.

R. Laurance Macon, San Antonio, Jack Hightower, Austin, David J. Healey, Houston, Nina Cortell, Dallas, Lynne Liberato, Houston, Mike A. Hatchell, Tyler, Stephan B. Rodgers, Karen Kroesche Gulde, Melanie Goins Cowart, San Antonio, Ana E. Kadala, Stephen L. Lundwall, Houston, Sharon N. Freytag, Debra Janece McComas, Dallas, for respondent.

JUSTICE ABBOTT delivered the opinion of the Court, in which CHIEF JUSTICE PHILLIPS, JUSTICE HECHT, JUSTICE OWEN and JUSTICE GONZALES join.

The issue in this mandamus proceeding is whether the trial court abused its discretion by allowing DSC Communications[1] to take the apex depositions of two high-level Samsung executives. The court of appeals conditionally granted mandamus relief, concluding that DSC failed to prove that the executives had "unique or superior knowledge that is unavailable through less intrusive means." ___ S.W.3d ___, 1998 WL 851123. We hold that DSC failed to present any evidence that arguably shows that the executives have unique or superior personal knowledge of discoverable information. Thus, the court of appeals did not err in conditionally granting the writ of mandamus because the trial court abused its discretion by overruling Samsung's motion to quash the depositions. We therefore deny Alcatel's request for mandamus relief.

---

[1] In September 1998, DSC Communications Corporation merged with and changed its name to Alcatel USA, Inc. We refer to Relator throughout this opinion as DSC, as it was referenced in the trial court and the court of appeals.

I

DSC filed this suit alleging that Samsung engaged in a plan to steal a new DSC telecommunication technology known as "intelligent network" and "next generation switching" systems. DSC asserts that Samsung identified and lured a team of engineers away from DSC and then specifically assigned them to develop the same type of product they had developed at DSC. DSC claims that Samsung's actions were the direct result of a plan engineered at the highest level of Samsung's executive structure, and that highest-level Samsung executives were involved in the plan's execution at all stages. DSC noticed the depositions of two high-level Samsung executives, Jin-Ku Kang and Kun-Hee Lee. Kang served as Chairman of defendant Samsung Electronics Co., Ltd. (SEC) during the earliest events giving rise to this case and is currently Chairman Emeritus of that corporation. Lee is currently Chairman and CEO of SEC and formerly served as the Chairman of the Samsung Chaebol during the earliest events at issue in this case. DSC and Samsung agree, and therefore we assume, that the Kang and Lee depositions qualify as apex depositions.

Samsung moved to quash both depositions. At the first evidentiary hearing on the issue, the special discovery master assigned to the case deferred ruling until after the deposition of Mr. K.H. Kim, the former President and CEO of SEC at all times relevant to this matter. After Kim's deposition, DSC renewed its request for the Kang and Lee depositions and moved to compel both. After holding another evidentiary hearing, the special discovery master denied Samsung's motion to quash and ordered that both depositions proceed. Samsung appealed the special discovery master's order to the trial court. The trial court reviewed the transcripts of these hearings and conducted a third hearing. The trial judge denied Samsung's appeal and affirmed the special discovery master's order. Samsung moved for reconsideration. After a fourth hearing on Samsung's motion to reconsider, the trial judge denied the motion.

Samsung filed a petition for writ of mandamus with the court of appeals. Basing its decision on *Crown Central Petroleum Corp. v. Garcia*, 904 S.W.2d 125 (Tex. 1995), the court of appeals held that DSC had failed to prove that it was entitled to take the apex depositions and conditionally granted mandamus relief. DSC filed a petition for writ of mandamus in this Court, arguing that the court of appeals abused its discretion by granting the writ because the trial court did not abuse its discretion.

II

Mandamus relief is available only to correct a "clear abuse of discretion" when there is no other adequate remedy at law. *See Walker v. Packer*, 827 S.W.2d 833, 839-44 (Tex. 1992). When a party alleges that the court of appeals abused its discretion by granting mandamus relief, this Court focuses on whether the trial court's ruling was an abuse of discretion. *See In re Meador*, 968 S.W.2d 346, 350 (Tex. 1998) (*citing Johnson v. Fourth Court of Appeals*, 700 S.W.2d 916, 918 (Tex.1985)). We agree with the court of appeals that the trial court's ruling was an abuse of discretion and therefore we deny DSC's request for mandamus relief.

III

This Court first adopted the apex deposition guidelines in *Crown Central Petroleum Corp. v. Garcia*, 904 S.W.2d 125 (Tex. 1995). We held that the apex deposition guidelines apply "[w]hen a party seeks to depose a corporate president or other high level corporate official." *Id.* at 128. A party initiates the *Crown Central* guideline proceedings by moving for protection and filing the corporate official's affidavit denying any knowledge of relevant facts. The trial court evaluates the motion first by deciding if the party seeking the deposition has "arguably shown that the official has any unique or superior personal knowledge of discoverable information." *Id.* "If the party seeking the deposition cannot show that the official has any unique or superior personal knowledge of discoverable information, the trial court should" not allow the deposition to go forward without a showing, after a good faith effort to obtain the discovery through less intrusive means, "(1) that there is a reasonable indication that the official's deposition is calculated to lead to the discovery of admissible evidence, and (2) that the less intrusive methods of discovery are unsatisfactory, insufficient or inadequate." *Id.*

While we agree with the court of appeals' conclusion that mandamus relief was appropriate, we disagree with that court's phrasing of the *Crown Central* guidelines. The court of appeals stated: "A party requesting an apex deposition must show that the corporate official to be deposed has an [sic] unique or superior personal knowledge that is unavailable through less intrusive means." ___ S.W.3d ___, 1998 WL 851123. That phrasing of the guidelines improperly collapses the two discrete inquiries into a single test. Under *Crown Central*, if the party seeking the deposition has "arguably shown that the official has any unique or superior personal knowledge of discoverable information," the trial court should deny the motion for protection and the party seeking discovery should be entitled to take the apex depositions. *Crown Cent.*, 904 S.W.2d at 128. The party seeking the apex deposition is required to pursue less intrusive means of discovering the information only when that party cannot make the requisite showing concerning unique or superior knowledge. *See id.* We recognize that these guidelines could be read as requiring trial courts to undertake two hearings and issue two orders: First, a hearing on whether to grant a protective order and, if one is granted, then a second hearing, after less intrusive methods of discovery have been explored, to determine whether the protective order should be dissolved. We believe that such a mechanical application of the *Crown Central* guidelines is unnecessary when, as here, the parties have already undertaken extensive discovery and the court has sufficient information to consider both prongs of the guidelines.

In this case, when Samsung moved for the protective orders the parties had already engaged in significant discovery, including more than 300 hours of depositions. At this stage of discovery, nothing in *Crown Central* precluded the trial court from considering whether DSC had attempted to gain the information by less intrusive means and otherwise satisfied the second *Crown Central* test. The parties argued both *Crown Central* tests in the trial court, and both the discovery master and trial judge denied the requested protective orders without specifying the reasons. Accordingly, mandamus is not appropriate if the trial court's order can be sustained under either *Crown Central* test. We consider first whether DSC arguably showed that Lee or Kang have unique or superior personal knowledge of discoverable information.

LEE

The most comprehensive discussion of Kun-Hee Lee's knowledge as it relates to this lawsuit is found in a document submitted by DSC titled: "Kun- Hee Lee's Significance and Connection to This Lawsuit." In that document, DSC urges several reasons why Lee's deposition is necessary. First, under the heading "Kun-Hee Lee Sets Samsung's Course," DSC claims that (1) Lee is the leader of the Samsung Chaebol, (2) Lee sets the overall vision for the Samsung companies, and (3) Samsung's goal is to be one of the world's top five telecommunications companies by 2005. Second, under the heading "Kun-Hee Lee's Ties To The Lead Defendant, Samsung Electronics Co., Ltd.," DSC states that Lee (1) was the chief executive officer and president of SEC, (2) was a long-standing director of SEC, and (3) is the largest single owner of Samsung and its subsidiaries.

Evidence tending to support these allegations does not satisfy the first *Crown Central* test; it merely demonstrates that Lee is a long-time company leader who sets the company vision with lofty goals. Virtually every company's CEO has similar characteristics. Allowing apex depositions merely because a high-level corporate official possesses apex-level knowledge would eviscerate the very guidelines established in *Crown Central*. Such evidence is too general to arguably show the official's knowledge is unique or superior.

In *AMR Corp. v. Enlow*, 926 S.W.2d 640 (Tex. App.—Fort Worth 1996, no writ), the Second Court of Appeals addressed a somewhat similar argument. In *AMR Corp.*, an American Airlines passenger became intoxicated on his flight and later had a traffic accident with the plaintiff. The plaintiff sued AMR Corp. and American Airlines under the Dramshop Act. The plaintiff sought the apex deposition of Robert Crandall, AMR's president, CEO, and chairman of the board, and American Airlines, Inc.'s CEO and chairman of the board, arguing that he "wish[ed] to depose Robert Crandall in order to determine where the authority lies within the organization for making those [alcohol service and flight attendant training] policy decisions so that Plaintiffs can understand how and why those policy decisions were made and what precisely the policies in place were." *Id.* at 643. The court of appeals held that "[t]his testimony amounts to nothing more than the simple, obvious recognition that the highest-ranking corporate officer of any corporation has the ultimate responsibility for all corporate decisions and falls far short of the [*Crown Central*] standard." *Id.* at 644. We agree with the *AMR Corp.* court of appeals. Testimony that a corporate executive possesses knowledge of company policies does not, by itself, satisfy the first *Crown Central* test because it does not show that the executive has unique or superior knowledge of discoverable information. *See In re El Paso Healthcare Sys.*, 969 S.W.2d 68, 74 (Tex. App.—El Paso 1998, no writ) ("A generalized claim that a corporate president has ultimate responsibility for all corporate decisions or has knowledge of corporate policy is insufficient to establish that the corporate president has unique or superior personal knowledge of discoverable information."); *see also AMR Corp.*, 926 S.W.2d at 644.

Under the heading "The Samsung Project At Issue In This Case Smacks Of Chairman-Level Importance," DSC claims that (1) the "[t]echnology at issue in this case involved huge investments and expected revenue," (2) "SEC's commitment to technology in this case is significant to execution" of its plan to be in the top five companies in its industry, (3) "[t]he significance of the project is illustrated by the claims made in this case," and (4) "Kun-Hee Lee has been involved with Samsung's telecommunications business." Proof of the importance of the project to Samsung, combined with the allegation that the issue in this case "smacks of chairman-level importance," at most tends to show that the chairman-level official whose deposition is sought may possess discoverable information. It does not, however, arguably show that the official's knowledge is unique or superior. Consequently, the first prong of the Crown Central guidelines has not been satisfied with regard to Lee.

KANG

* * *

IV

DSC seeks to distinguish business-related cases like this from tort-related cases like *Crown Central* and *AMR Corp*. DSC contends that the trial court, in allowing the depositions to proceed, considered that "this litigation involves two giant international multinational corporations suing each other over trade secrets and corporate direction, policy and defamation." DSC argues that, "[i]n contrast to cases like . . . *Crown Central*, this is the very kind of lawsuit in which high-level executives would be expected to participate." (Emphasis in original). The special discovery master apparently agreed with this reasoning by stating: [T]his is not the same situation as in *Crown Central* or the *Wal-Mart* case, the original apex deposition case. Mr. Lee appears to be the one person at the very top of the chain at Samsung, and it may very well be that he does not know anything that's relevant to this case, and that can be determined very quickly. But I think that DSC ought to have an opportunity to test that. (Emphasis added).

Even if a lawsuit concerns a business dispute rather than a tort claim, and regardless of whether high-level executives would be expected to participate in a decision relevant to the dispute, the *Crown Central* prerequisites must still be met. Business disputes provide no greater license than any other kind of suit to explore by apex deposition whether a high-level executive knows anything relevant to the case. It may well be true that many tort claims arise without the knowledge or involvement of a high-level officer. Conversely, it may also be true that many business disputes directly involve the decisions or actions of a high-level officer. Regardless of the truth, vel non, of these suppositions, the fact remains that the *Crown Central* guidelines must be applied.

V

Because DSC failed to arguably show that either Kang or Lee possesses unique or superior knowledge of discoverable information, the trial court's order cannot be supported under the first *Crown Central* test. Nevertheless, DSC argues that it has pursued less intrusive means and therefore is entitled to the depositions under *Crown Central*'s second guideline: If the party seeking the deposition cannot show that the official has any unique or superior personal knowledge of discoverable information, the trial court should grant the motion for protective order and first require the party seeking the deposition to attempt to obtain the discovery through less intrusive methods . . . . After making a good faith effort to obtain the discovery through less intrusive methods, the party seeking the deposition may attempt to show (1) that there is a reasonable indication that the official's deposition is calculated to lead to the discovery of admissible evidence, and (2) that the less intrusive methods of discovery are unsatisfactory, insufficient or inadequate. If the party seeking the deposition makes this showing, the trial court should modify or vacate the protective order as appropriate . . . . If the party seeking the deposition fails to make this showing, the trial court should leave the protective order in place. *Crown Cent.*, 904 S.W.2d at 128. From the record before us, DSC has not shown that it attempted to obtain the information it sought from Kang through less intrusive methods. DSC based its contention that Kang has unique or superior knowledge largely on his presence at a written and oral presentation concerning the next generation switching system. But, DSC was allowed to depose Joo-Hyung Lee, who presented the report to Kang and Song. Also, DSC deposed Song, the Samsung executive in charge of telecommunications, who also attended the presentation. Yet, DSC has failed to identify any relevant information that it seeks from Kang that it attempted and failed to obtain from either Joo-Hyung Lee or Song.

In addition, DSC failed to establish that it attempted to obtain the information that it sought from Lee through less intrusive methods. DSC argued that Lee has unique and superior knowledge regarding Samsung's policies. But the special master allowed DSC to depose Kim, the president and CEO of SEC during the relevant time. Yet, DSC failed to ask Kim any questions about Samsung's "vision" for telecommunications or any of the other issues DSC now contends justify an apex deposition of Lee. DSC also did not issue interrogatories, requests for admissions, or any other forms of discovery to Samsung regarding its corporate policies. The record simply does not show that the information sought from Lee was sought by less intrusive means or that the information sought was unobtainable from other sources.

Absent a showing that an executive arguably has unique or superior personal knowledge, a court has no discretion to allow an apex deposition unless the party seeking the deposition establishes that it has attempted to obtain the information through less intrusive methods. The special master provided DSC with the opportunity to depose other Samsung executives who at least arguably possessed the information DSC seeks. Yet, DSC either failed to take advantage of that opportunity or failed to preserve its attempts in the record. Thus, the trial court abused its discretion in overruling Samsung's motion to quash the depositions of Kang and Lee.

* * *

We agree with the court of appeals' conclusion that the trial court abused its discretion when it refused to quash the depositions of Kang and Lee because it failed to properly apply the guidelines set forth in *Crown Central v. Garcia*. Accordingly, we deny the mandamus relief requested by DSC.

JUSTICE ENOCH filed a dissenting opinion, in which JUSTICE BAKER and JUSTICE O'NEILL join.

JUSTICE HANKINSON did not participate in the decision.

JUSTICE ENOCH, joined by JUSTICE BAKER and JUSTICE O'NEILL.

This Court has held that the proper place to amend or promulgate a rule is through rulemaking, not judicial fiat. Yet today, from mere guidelines intended to aid a trial court's decision to allow or prevent apex depositions in the context of discovery harassment, the Court effectively forges an apex deposition rule—one, significantly, not found in our recently promulgated discovery rules. This new rule erects an improperly high barrier, imposing a special protection for corporate officials.

The apex guidelines arose from an evaluation of the existing Rules of Civil Procedure, which have long articulated a deponent's right to protection "from undue burden, unnecessary expense, harassment, [or] annoyance . . . ." TEX. R. CIV. P. 192.6(b). The progenitor of Texas cases analyzing the propriety of apex depositions is *Wal-Mart Stores, Inc. v. Street*. 754 S.W.2d 153 (Tex. 1988). In that case, this Court examined a business invitee's assertion in a slip-and-fall case that he should be allowed to depose the chair of Wal-Mart's Board of Directors, Sam Walton. We held that the trial judge abused his discretion by ordering the deposition to be taken at a location other than Walton's residence or place of business. Our decision in *Street* recognized the potential for harassment that high-level corporate officials face when a corporation is routinely subjected to litigation, and when the official's connection to the case is as tenuous as Walton's connection to a slip-and-fall case in one of hundreds of Wal-Mart stores.

Despite the Court's concerns signaled in *Street*, litigants continued to seek the depositions of highest ranking executives of large corporations in what appeared to be nothing more than an effort to harass or pressure settlement by needlessly increasing the costs of litigation. Deciding that it was appropriate to alert courts to such undue discovery burden and harassment, we established parameters to guide a trial court's discretion. While I strongly support the protection from harassment that our apex deposition guidelines provide, I do not countenance a de facto rule, unavailable to any other potential deponent, that extends a privilege to corporate officials to avoid depositions by virtue of their position.

* * *

Notes

1. One seeking protection from an apex deposition would move for a protective order under Rule 192.6(a).

2. Some of the problems associated with video-taped depositions are those associated with the lights and camera(s). In *Masinga v. Whittington*, 792 S.W.2d 940 (Tex. 1990), the Court held that a trial court abused its discretion in entering a protective order to prevent the video-taping of an oral deposition of a doctor who alleged that the lights and other matters would distract and cause him undue stress. The Court noted that there was no evidence that the video-taping would cause a particular, articulated and demonstrable injury sufficient to justify

the protective order. It should be noted that the trial court refused to conduct a hearing and based it decision on mere conclusions contained in the motion itself.

f. *Pre-Suit Discovery*

Notes

1. Rule 202.1 of the Texas Rules of Civil Procedure states:

A person may petition the court for an order authorizing the taking of a deposition on oral examination or written questions either:

(a) to perpetuate or obtain the person's own testimony or that of any other person for use in an anticipated suit; or

(b) to investigate a potential claim or suit.

2. *In re City of Dallas*, 501 S.W.3d 71 (Tex. 2016): **Discovery; Pre-Trial. Court Must Determine That It Has Jurisdiction Over Pre-suit Discovery.**

Facts: Navarro County and Navarro College filed a Rule 202 petition in the County Court at Law of Navarro to investigate a potential tortious interference claim against the City of Dallas. The county court denied Dallas's immunity-based plea to the jurisdiction, granted Navarro's Rule 202 petition, and authorized depositions.

Held: Mandamus will issue. The county court must first determine whether the claim would exceed $200,000 jurisdictional cap. For a party to properly obtain Rule 202 pre-suit discovery, the court must have subject-matter jurisdiction over the anticipated action. Navarro did not specify the damages it would seek in the anticipated suit.

In re John DOE a/k/a "TROOPER"
444 S.W.3d 603
(Tex. 2014)

Facts: Calling himself "the Trooper", an anonymous blogger launched an on-line attack on Reynolds & Reynolds Co. and Brockman, its chairman and CEO. To discover the Trooper's identity, Brockman and Reynolds filed a Rule 202 petition in the district court in Harris County, seeking to depose Google, Inc., which hosts the blog. The petition requests that Google disclose the name, address, and telephone number of the owner of the blog website and the email address shown on the site.

Issue: When is pre-suit discovery allowed?
Held: Mandamus will issue directing the trial court to vacate its order authorizing discovery. A "proper court" may authorize pre-suit discovery to investigate a potential claim before suit is filed

Issue: What is a "proper" court, for pre-suit discovery purposes?
Held: One that has jurisdiction, including jurisdiction over the person.
Rule 202 of the Texas Rules of Civil Procedure allows "a proper court" to authorize a deposition to investigate a potential claim before suit is filed, but a proper court must have personal jurisdiction over the potential defendant. The Court does not reach a due process issue.

Notes

1. *In re Wolfe*, 341 S.W.3d 932 (Tex. 2011): "Rule 202 is not a license for forced interrogations. Courts must strictly limit and carefully supervise pre-suit discovery to prevent abuse of the rule."

2. *In re Does,* 337 S.W.3d 862(2011): A court may not order pre-suit discovery by agreement of the witness over the objections of other interested parties without making the findings required by Rule 202.4(a) of the Texas Rules of Civil Procedure.

The court must order a deposition to be taken if, but only if, it finds that:

(1) allowing the petitioner to take the requested deposition may prevent a failure or delay of justice in an anticipated suit; or
(2) the likely benefit of allowing the petitioner to take the requested deposition to investigate a potential claim outweighs the burden or expense of the procedure.

TEX. R. CIV. P. 202.4(a). The trial court did not make either of these findings.

"[T]he required findings [may not] be implied in support of the trial court's order compelling discovery. For one thing, PRK made no effort to present the trial court with a basis for the findings. . . . The rule does not permit the findings to be implied from support in the record. The intrusion into otherwise private matters authorized by Rule 202 outside a lawsuit is not to be taken lightly. One noted commentator, Professor Lonny Hoffman, has observed that there is "cause for concern about insufficient judicial attention to petitions to take presuit discovery" and that "judges should maintain an active oversight role to ensure that [such discovery is] not misused". *Access to Information, Access to Justice: The Rule of Presuit Investigatory Discovery*, 40 U. MICH. J.L. REFORM 217, 273-74 (2007). We agree."

4. *Limitations on Discovery*

a. *Privileges and Exemptions*

SCOTT
v.
McILHANY
798 S.W.2d 556
(Tex. 1990)

Jack O'Neill, Houston, for relators.
Jess H. Hall, Jr., Houston, Bill W. Waters, Pampa, Oscar Fields, Charles R. Watson, Amarillo, Layton Z. Woodul, Lubbock, Robert L. Templeton, Amarillo, M. Kent Sims, Wheeler, and Charles L. Tighe, Midland, for respondent.

GONZALEZ, JUSTICE.

This is an original mandamus proceeding involving pretrial discovery of expert witnesses. The relators, Tom L. Scott, Inc. and others, seek relief from orders signed by the respondent, the Honorable Grainger W. McIlhany, denying discovery of six experts retained by various parties to the case. By this mandamus, relators seek to obtain the depositions of these experts. The defendants changed the designation of these experts from "testifying" experts to "consulting-only" experts after they settled with some of the plaintiffs and third-party defendants in the underlying suit. The court of appeals denied the petition for writ of mandamus. 753 S.W.2d 214. We hold that the redesignation under the facts before us violates the purpose of discovery enunciated in *Gutierrez v. Dallas Independent School District*, 729 S.W.2d 691, 693 (Tex.1987), and in *Jampole v. Touchy*, 673 S.W.2d 569, 573 (Tex.1984, orig. proceeding), and is, therefore, ineffective. Thus we conditionally grant the writ.

This case arose from the October 1981 blowout of Key Well 1-11 in Wheeler County. In terms of the gas loss, this is believed to be the largest gas well blowout in United States history. It was not brought under control for over a year. Apache Corporation operated the well and, along with El Paso Exploration Company (now known as Meridian Oil Production Company), owned the working interest. Over one hundred parties, including mineral interest owners from adjacent properties, royalty interest holders, and claimants through such properties, particularly Arkla Exploration Company, Stephens Production Company, Hobart Key, and other owners of interests in the same field, filed suits against Apache and El Paso seeking damages alleging that Apache and El Paso's wrongful acts caused the blowout. All of these cases have been consolidated by the trial court. Only the parties and actions pertinent to this mandamus proceeding will be discussed.

Apache and El Paso eventually brought third-party claims against their suppliers and contractors alleging product liability and negligence theories as causes or partial causes of the blowout. As supplier of a relief valve for the well, Axelson, Inc. and its parent corporation, U.S. Industries, Inc., were sued as third-party defendants. Apache and El Paso also added Sooner Pipe & Supply Corporation, Hydril Company and Babcock & Wilcox Company alleging that these third-party defendants supplied equipment that caused the well to blow out. The Scott group, owners of various mineral interests in the same field and relators herein, intervened as plaintiffs and alleged causes of action against Apache and El Paso.

The initial plaintiffs, Arkla, Stephens and Key (Arkla/Key), and third-party defendants, Sooner, Hydril and Babcock & Wilcox, designated the six experts in question as testifying experts. Allegedly, these experts were prepared to deliver damaging testimony against Apache and El Paso. On the morning the Arkla/Key witnesses' depositions were scheduled, Apache and El Paso settled with these parties on the condition that Apache and El Paso gain control of the experts. Following execution of the settlement, Apache and El Paso, along with the settling parties, redesignated all six as consulting-only experts.

The trial court denied requests by the Scott group to depose the experts. Specifically, the Scott group filed a motion to take depositions of the experts, and Judge McIlhany denied it. This order, along with others denying depositions of the experts, form the basis of this mandamus proceeding. We must determine whether the trial court abused its discretion. Relators assert and we agree that mandamus is the only remedy because the protective order shields the witnesses from deposition and thereby prevents the evidence from being part of the record. Therefore, it would be impossible to determine on appeal if the denial were harmful error. *Jampole*, 673 S.W.2d at 576. We next address the critical question presented in this case—whether a party may obtain an adversary's testifying experts and redesignate them as consulting-only experts to avoid discovery.

Designating these experts as testifying experts subjected their work product to discovery. Texas Rule of Civil Procedure 166b(2)(e)(1) provides in part:

> A party may obtain discovery of the identity and location (name, address and telephone number) of an expert who may be called as an expert witness, the subject matter on which the witness is expected to testify, the mental impressions and opinions held by the expert and the facts known to the expert (regardless of when the factual information was acquired) which relate to or form the basis of the mental impressions and opinions held by the expert.

Depositions were scheduled but never took place because Apache and El Paso settled with all of the parties who had made these designations. As part of the settlement agreement, all rights to the six experts were assigned to Apache and El Paso. Specifically, all of the settling parties except Key assigned their experts to Apache and El Paso. Key agreed to keep its experts confidential except as to Apache and El Paso. Additionally, the settlement agreements provided that all of the settling parties were obligated, unless ordered by a court, "to refrain from disclosing to any persons or entities," other than Apache and El Paso, "information, reports, or opinions generated by any expert."

Upon gaining control of the experts, Apache and El Paso redesignated them as consulting-only experts. The settling parties also redesignated the experts as consulting-only experts. Identities and opinions of experts are nevertheless discoverable if they are not engaged in anticipation of litigation and solely for consultation or if their work product has been reviewed or relied upon by testifying experts. *See* Tex. R. Civ. P. 166b(3)(b). The trial court allowed the redesignation and refused requests by the Scott group to depose these experts. The Scott group asks us to hold this redesignation invalid.

The primary policy behind discovery is to seek truth so that disputes may be decided by facts that are revealed rather than concealed. *Jampole*, 673 S.W.2d at 573. Privileges from discovery run contrary to this policy but serve other legitimate interests. The policy behind the consulting expert privilege is to encourage parties to seek expert advice in evaluating their case and to prevent a party from receiving undue benefit from an adversary's efforts and diligence. *Werner v. Miller*, 579 S.W.2d 455, 456 (Tex. 1979, orig. proceeding); *see also* D. KELTNER, TEXAS DISCOVERY § 3.110 (1989). But the protection afforded by the consulting expert privilege is intended to be only "a shield to prevent a litigant from taking undue advantage of his adversary's industry and effort, not a sword to be used to thwart justice or to defeat the salutary objects" of discovery. *Williamson v. Superior Court*, 21 Cal.2d 829, 148 Cal.Rptr. 39, 582 P.2d 126, 132 (1978); *see also Chuidian v. Philippine Nat'l Bank*, 734 F.Supp. 415, 423 (C.D.Cal.1990) (interpreting *Williamson* as holding agreements to suppress evidence or conceal discreditable facts are illegal); *Raytheon Co. v. Superior Court*, 208 Cal.App.3d 683, 256 Cal.Rptr. 425, 427 1989) (interpreting *Williamson* as holding agreements between adversarial codefendants to suppress expert testimony are against public policy).

The redesignation of the experts in this case was an offensive and unacceptable use of discovery mechanisms intended to defeat the salutary objectives of discovery. Attorneys for Apache and El Paso even admitted to the trial judge that the settlements were "expressly contingent" on these experts not being required to give their testimony, and that there might not be a settlement agreement if the depositions were ordered. One of the settling parties expressly told the trial court that he understood the settlement offer would expire upon the depositions being taken. The legitimate purposes and policies behind the consulting expert privilege do not countenance this conduct. We hold that, as a matter of law, the redesignation of experts under the facts of this case violates the policy underlying the rules of discovery and is therefore ineffective. *See Gutierrez*, 729 S.W.2d at 693; *Jampole*, 673 S.W.2d at 573. "If we were to hold otherwise, nothing would preclude a party in a multiparty case from in effect auctioning off a witness' testimony to the highest bidder." *Williamson*, 148 Cal.Rptr. at 45, 582 P.2d at 132. Because the redesignation of experts under the facts of this case violates the clear purpose and policy underlying the rules of discovery, the trial court abused its discretion in granting the protective order as to these six experts. We are confident Judge McIlhany will vacate his orders denying discovery and will render orders consistent with this opinion. Should he fail to do so, the clerk of the supreme court is directed to issue the writ of mandamus.

AXELSON
v.
McILHANY

798 S.W.2d 550
(Tex. 1990)

Robert L. Templeton, John Smithee, Joe L. Lovell, Amarillo, for Axelson.
Jess H. Hall, Jr., Jack O'Neill, Houston, H. Carter Burdette, Fort Worth, S. Tom Morris, Amarillo, R. Scott Hogarty, Bonnie J. White, James R. Snell, Houston, for respondent.

GONZALEZ, JUSTICE.

In this mandamus proceeding, we are asked to direct Judge McIlhany to vacate orders denying pretrial discovery. The court of appeals conditionally granted the petition for writ of mandamus on certain points but denied the petition on other points. 755 S.W.2d 170. Among other things, we are requested to grant relief regarding discovery of a kickback investigation and "dual capacity" witnesses. We conditionally grant the writ.

The underlying suit from which this action arises involves what is believed to be the largest gas well blowout in United States history. Key Well 1-11, located in Wheeler County, blew out in October 1981 and was not brought under control for over a year. Apache Corporation operates the well and, together with El Paso Exploration Company (a/k/a Meridian Oil Production, Inc.), owns the working interest. Numerous lawsuits involving over 100 parties have been filed against Apache and El Paso, alleging that their wrongful acts caused the blowout. All suits against Apache and El Paso have been consolidated.

Plaintiffs include Arkla Exploration, Stephens Production Company and Hobart Key, all of whom own mineral interests in the same field. Tom L. Scott, Inc. and other mineral interest holders ("Scott group") intervened as plaintiffs, alleging a cause of action against Apache and El Paso only. Apache and El Paso responded by adding numerous third-party defendants. Sooner Pipe & Supply Corporation, Hydril Corporation and Babcock & Wilcox Company ("Sooner") were added because they supplied well equipment that allegedly caused the blowout. Axelson, Inc. and its parent corporation, U.S. Industries, Inc. (USI), were added because Axelson manufactured a relief valve that allegedly should have prevented the blowout. Axelson and USI are the relators herein and ask that we set aside the trial court's order denying:

(1) discovery of documents reflecting Apache's internal investigation of kickback schemes at the well site;

(2) depositions from dual capacity witnesses (those witnesses who were active participants in the Key Well 1-11 operations or support and were later designated consulting-only experts);

(3) depositions of six experts originally designated as testifying experts by parties who have settled with Apache and El Paso and who were later redesignated as consulting-only experts;[1] and

(4) depositions of persons who performed gas analyses at Apache's request. We will now separately address each of the discovery requests made by Axelson and USI.

KICKBACK INVESTIGATION

For purposes unrelated to this lawsuit, Apache conducted an internal investigation concerning bribes and kickbacks from suppliers and contractors on a number of wells in western Oklahoma and Texas Panhandle fields. Illegal drug use and prostitution on the job site were also investigated. According to testimony by Apache's general counsel, wells in Oklahoma were the primary focus of the investigation, but Key Well 1-11 and the subsequent Key wells were included. Axelson and USI have tried unsuccessfully to obtain discovery of this investigation. Apache and El Paso resist discovery on the grounds of relevance, attorney-client privilege, attorney work product exemption, and the party communications exemption. The trial court did not conduct an in camera inspection of the investigation results. Instead, the court heard testimony from Apache's general counsel regarding Apache's grounds for resisting discovery of any part of the investigation results. Ultimately, the trial court denied discovery on the basis of relevance, and the court of appeals upheld the denial on this ground. 755 S.W.2d at 178.

Generally, discovery is permitted into any matter, not privileged, that is relevant to the subject matter and is "reasonably calculated to lead to the discovery of admissible evidence." TEX. R. CIV. P. 166b(2)(a); *see also Lindsey v. O'Neill*, 689 S.W.2d 400, 402 (Tex. 1985, orig. proceeding) (per curiam); *Jampole v. Touchy*, 673 S.W.2d 569, 573 (Tex. 1984, orig. proceeding). This broad grant, however, is limited by the legitimate interests of the opposing party to avoid overly broad requests, harassment, or disclosure of privileged information. *Jampole*, 673 S.W.2d at 573. Thus the trial court has discretion to narrow the scope of discovery on a case by case basis with a protective order. TEX. R. CIV. P. 166b(5).

The "relevant to the subject matter" and "reasonably calculated to lead to admissible evidence" tests are liberally construed to allow the litigants to obtain the fullest knowledge of the facts and issues prior to trial. *Gutierrez v. Dallas Indep. School Dist.*, 729 S.W.2d 691, 693 (Tex. 1987). It does not matter that the information sought may be inadmissible at trial if it appears reasonably calculated to lead to the discovery of admissible evidence. TEX. R. CIV. P. 166b(2)(a). Among other reasons, Apache conducted the investigation to determine whether the kickbacks and bribes affected the quality of equipment used. This information might reasonably lead to evidence that Apache's conduct, or that of its suppliers, was a contributing cause of the blowout. Apache also investigated whether this conduct had an inflationary effect on the drilling costs. Since Apache is seeking drilling costs in its suit against Axelson, to be able to defend against these costs, Axelson must be permitted to determine whether they were reasonable. Therefore, portions of the kickback investigation may well be relevant to Axelson's case. Furthermore, Apache's attorney testified that the scope of the investigation included Key Well 1-11, the subsequent Key wells and all suppliers to Apache wells during the time covered by the investigation. The trial court abused its discretion in denying discovery of the investigation results sight unseen. The trial court should have conducted an in camera inspection to determine if any of the kickback in-

[1] This issue is dealt with in the companion case of Scott v. McIlhany, 798 S.W.2d 556 (Tex.1990, orig. proceeding). In that case we held that agreements to silence testifying experts by redesignation as consulting-only experts pursuant to a settlement violate the purpose and policy underlying the rules of discovery. Jampole v. Touchy, 673 S.W.2d 569 (Tex.1984, orig. proceeding).

vestigation was relevant to the subject matter of the litigation and, if it was, whether any part of the investigation is reasonably calculated to lead to the discovery of admissible evidence.[2]

Apache also resists discovery based on the attorney-client privilege under Texas Rule of Civil Evidence 503(b) and the work product privilege under Texas Rule of Civil Procedure 166b(3). Since there was evidence that the investigation was disclosed to the FBI, IRS, and the Wall Street Journal, the court of appeals properly held that these privileges had been waived. TEX. R. CIV. EVID. 511. Nor does the party communications privilege apply, because the record shows that these documents were not prepared in anticipation of the litigation in which discovery of the communication was sought.

"DUAL CAPACITY" WITNESSES

Several potential witnesses in this case maintain a dual capacity—possessing firsthand knowledge of relevant facts and serving as consulting-only experts for Apache and El Paso. One of these persons, Paul Douglas Storts, is the petroleum engineer who has been in charge of the well from its inception. He also spearheaded the effort to bring the well under control after the blowout. The others include Richard Biel, Joe Fowler and Tom Hill, who were hired by Apache and El Paso to examine the wellhead equipment and have specific knowledge concerning the chain of custody of the wellhead equipment.

Axelson and USI seek to discover all facts known by Storts and his mental impressions and opinions gained while working on the well and consulting. They seek to discover only chain of custody facts from Biel, Fowler and Hill.

The trial court entered several orders from December 1984 through July 1987 limiting discovery. With regard to Storts, the trial court initially quashed his deposition, but later determined that information gained by him while working on the well was discoverable, but that information he gained while doing a combination of working on the well and consulting was not discoverable. With regard to Biel, Fowler, and Hill, the trial court allowed discovery of facts relating only to the Axelson valve. The court of appeals held that the trial court had not abused its discretion and disallowed all other discovery from these experts. 755 S.W.2d at 176-77. We disagree.

The factual knowledge and opinions acquired by an individual who is an expert and an active participant in the events material to the lawsuit are discoverable. This information is not shielded from discovery by merely changing the designation of a person with knowledge of relevant facts to a "consulting-only expert."

The scope of discovery regarding experts who serve in the dual capacity of fact witness and consulting-only expert has not been addressed thoroughly by Texas courts. Barrow and Henderson, 1984 *Amendments to the Texas Rules of Civil Procedure Affecting Discovery*, 15 ST. MARY'S L.J. 713, 729 (1984). The literal text of the exemption, however, resolves the issue presented in this mandamus. The consulting expert exemption protects the identity, mental impressions and opinions of consulting-only experts; but not the facts.[3] The rule we announce today, however, "should not extend to consulting [only] experts . . . whose only source of factual information was the consultation." *Id.* In other words, persons who gain factual information by virtue of their involvement relating to the incident or transaction giving rise to the litigation do not qualify as consulting-only experts because the consultation is not their only source of information. We now separately address Axelson's discovery requests regarding Storts, an employee designated as a consulting-only expert, and Biel, Fowler and Hill, experts designated as consulting-only who have factual knowledge of the well equipment.

---

[2] Because Apache and El Paso object to discovery requests, they have the burden of proving that the documents are privileged or otherwise not subject to discovery. They also have the burden to segregate the items or documents which they allege are exempt from discovery and produce the discovery to the court In a sealed wrapper for In camera inspection, so that the trial court can make a ruling on discovery after examining the documents. *See* TEX.R.CIV.P. 166b(4); McKinney v. National Union Fire Ins. Co., 772 S.W.2d 72 (Tex.1989).

[3] The consulting expert exemption has its genesis in the attorney work product privilege, which protects only the mental impressions, opinions, and conclusions of the lawyer and not the facts. D. KELTNER, TEXAS DISCOVERY § 3:93 (1989).

Storts

An employee may be specially employed as a consulting-only expert. *See Barker v. Dunham*, 551 S.W.2d 41, 43-44 (Tex. 1977, orig. proceeding). Nevertheless, all employees do not necessarily qualify as "consulting-only" experts. The rules provide requirements that a consulting-only expert must meet. *See* TEX. R. CIV. P. 166b(3)(b). Rule of Civil Procedure 166b(3)(b) provides: 3. Exemptions. The following matters are protected from disclosure by privilege: b. Experts. The identity, mental impressions, and opinions of an expert who has been informally consulted or of an expert who has been retained or specially employed by another party in anticipation of litigation or preparation for trial . . . *Id.* (emphasis added). Under this rule, a consulting-only expert must be informally consulted or retained or specially employed in anticipation of litigation. An employee who was employed in an area that becomes the subject of litigation can never qualify as a consulting-only expert because the employment was not in anticipation of litigation. On the other hand, an employee who was not employed in an area that becomes the subject of litigation and is reassigned specifically to assist the employer in anticipation of litigation arising out of the incident or in preparation for trial may qualify as a "consulting-only" expert. In any event, a party may discover facts known by an employee acting as a "consulting-only" expert.

In this case, evidence presented to the trial court suggested that Storts was doing a combination of both working on the well and consulting. Storts was hired to work as a petroleum engineer and he worked on Key Well 1-11 before, during and after the blowout. After litigation began Apache asserted that Storts was a consulting-only expert and resisted all discovery of Storts' mental impressions, opinions and facts. On the record before him, the trial judge abused his discretion in denying discovery of Storts' mental impressions, opinions and facts because Storts did not qualify as a consulting-only expert.

Policies previously enunciated by this court support the decision we reach today. This rule aims to effectuate the ultimate purpose of discovery, which is to seek truth, so that disputes may be decided by those facts that are revealed, rather than concealed. *Jampole*, 673 S.W.2d at 573. Additionally, although Apache and El Paso are defendants in this case, they are pursuing a cross claim and "cannot use one hand to seek affirmative relief in court and with the other lower an iron curtain of silence around the facts of the case." *Ginsberg v. Fifth Court of Appeals*, 686 S.W.2d 105, 108 (Tex. 1985, orig. proceeding).

Biel, Fowler, & Hill

Axelson sought only factual discovery from Biel, Fowler and Hill regarding the condition of wellhead equipment in addition to the condition of Axelson's relief valve. The trial judge limited the scope of discovery from these consulting-only experts to the Axelson valve. The trial judge abused his discretion in refusing discovery of these facts because the exemption for consulting-only experts does not extend to facts known to them.

* * *

CONCLUSION

We hold that the trial judge abused his discretion by refusing discovery of the kickback investigation without conducting an in camera inspection; denying the request to depose the six experts redesignated as consulting-only experts; denying discovery of a witness who does not qualify as a consulting-only expert; and denying discovery of facts known by consulting experts. We are confident Judge McIlhany will vacate his orders denying this discovery and will enter orders consistent with this opinion. Should he fail to do so, the clerk of the supreme court is directed to issue the writ of mandamus.

Notes

1. TEX.R.CIV.P. 192.3 Scope of Discovery. "(e) Testifying and consulting experts. The identity, mental impressions, and opinions of a consulting expert whose mental impressions and opinion shave not been reviewed by a testifying expert are not discoverable. A party may discover the following information regarding a testifying expert or regarding a consulting expert whose mental impressions or opinions have been reviewed by a testifying expert:

    a. the expert's name, address, and telephone number;
    b. the subject matter on which a testifying expert will testify;

c. the facts known by the expert that relate to or form the basis of the expert's mental impressions and opinions formed or made in connection with the case in which the discovery is sought, regardless of when and how the factual information was acquired;

d. the expert's mental impressions and opinions formed or made in connection with the case in which discovery is sought;

e. evidence of bias;

f. all documents, tangible things, reports, models, or data compilations that have been provided to, reviewed by, or prepared by or for the expert in anticipation of a testifying expert's testimony;

g. the experts current resume and bibliography."

2. Rule 195 governs the methods of obtaining discovery regarding testifying expert witnesses.

3. The Tort Reform Act of 2003 established qualifications of expert witnesses in suits against a physician or health care provider. *See* § 74.401, TEX. CIV. PRAC. & REM. CODE (the qualifications of a medical expert witness); § 74.402, TEX. CIV. PRAC. & REM. CODE (the qualifications of an expert witnesses in suits against health care providers); § 74.403, TEX. CIV. PRAC. & REM. CODE, (the qualification of an expert witness on causation in cases involving health care liability claims).

4. The Tort Reform Act of 2003 also established certain requirements for expert reports in health care liability cases. *See* § 74.351 TEX. CIV. PRAC. & REM. CODE. Subdivision s of § 74.351 provides "[u]ntil a claimant has served the expert report and curriculum vitae as required by subsection (a), all discovery in a health care liability claim is stayed, except for the acquisition by the claimant of information, including medical or hospital records or other documents or tangible things, related to the patient's health care through: (1) written discovery as defined in Rule 192.7, Texas Rules of Civil Procedure; (2) depositions on written questions under Rule 200, Texas Rules of Civil Procedure; and (3) discovery from nonparties under Rule 205, Texas Rules of Civil Procedure."

NATIONAL UNION FIRE INS. CO.
v.
VALDEZ

863 S.W.2d 458
(Tex. 1993)

John L. Ross, Lisa A. Stegall, for relator.
Rollins M. Koppel, Greg M. Powers, Harlingen, for respondent.

PHILLIPS, CHIEF JUSTICE.

This original mandamus action arises from a bad faith insurance case. Relator seeks relief from the trial court's order compelling production of its attorney's files from the related, previously resolved workers' compensation case. Although we conclude that a document is not automatically privileged because it reposes in an attorney's file, we hold that a request for an "attorney's files," as opposed to a request for specific documents relevant to the pending lawsuit, is objectionable under the attorney work-product exemption from discovery. Because relator timely asserted this objection, we conditionally grant the writ of mandamus.

I

Jimmy Ray Haynes was injured on July 3, 1987, in the course and scope of his employment at Wal-Mart Stores, Inc. Relator National Union Fire Insurance Co., Wal-Mart's workers' compensation carrier, disputed the extent of Haynes' on-the-job injury, and the parties submitted the claim to the Texas Industrial Accident Board. The record does not disclose the terms of the Board award, but Haynes was apparently dissatisfied, as he appealed to district court in Cameron County. While his compensation case was pending, Haynes filed a separate action against National Union and its adjustor, Corporate Services, Inc., for bad faith failure to pay benefits. In addition to a common-law bad faith claim, Haynes alleged negligence and gross negligence, negligent and intentional infliction of emotional distress, and claims under the Texas Workers' Compensation Act, the Texas Industrial Accident Board rules, Texas Insurance Code art. 21.21, and the Texas Deceptive Trade Practices Act.

Haynes ultimately prevailed in the compensation case, obtaining a judgment against National Union for $46,762. On March 20, 1991, with the bad faith case still pending, National Union paid the compensation judgment in full and obtained a judgment release signed by Haynes.

National Union moved for summary judgment in the bad faith case on July 1, 1992, arguing that the judgment release executed by Haynes in the compensation case also released National Union from liability in the bad faith case. National Union alternatively argued that the summary judgment evidence conclusively established a reasonable basis for disputing Haynes' compensation claim. As to the latter ground, National Union relied in part on the deposition testimony of Scott Schwartzberg, its lawyer in the compensation case. Schwartzberg had been associated with the law firm of Hirsch, Glover, Robinson & Sheiness (hereinafter "the law firm") while representing National Union, but he had left that firm when he was deposed in April 1992. Schwartzberg, who never represented National Union in the bad faith case, testified at his deposition that Haynes' compensation claim had been questionable due to conflicting evidence as to the extent of his compensable injury. Therefore, from the insurer's standpoint, it "deserved to be tried." He also testified, however, that he did not specifically intend for the judgment release, which he drafted, to accomplish anything beyond releasing the compensation judgment.

Shortly before National Union moved for summary judgment, Haynes caused a subpoena duces tecum to be served on the custodian of records for the law firm, requesting all records from the compensation case, "including but not limited to the investigation file, the correspondence file and the pleadings file." It is this discovery request that gives rise to the present mandamus action. National Union objected, asserting the attorney-client, work product, and party communication privileges. On July 2, 1992, after hearing argument of counsel but no evidence, the trial court directed National Union to submit the law firm files for in camera review.

National Union submitted the files to the court on September 25, 1992, along with written objections reasserting its earlier claims of privilege. In addition to general objections as to each particular file, and specific objections as to certain documents, National Union claimed that the files in their entirety were privileged as attorney work product because "the organization and labeling of the files, in addition to selection of documents to include in the files, reflect the attorneys' mental impressions, conclusions, opinions, and legal theories formed in preparation for trial."

The trial court held a second hearing on November 24, 1992, after attempting an in camera review. Complaining of their lack of organization, the court ordered all the documents produced. Apparently the court not only rejected National Union's argument that a request for an attorneys' entire file from a particular case violates the work-product exemption, but further concluded that National Union waived its objections by failing to sufficiently index the files.[4]

National Union sought mandamus relief from the court of appeals, but it denied relief on January 7, 1993, without opinion. National Union requested leave to file this action on January 19, 1993, and we stayed production of the law firm files that same day.

II

We must first determine whether it is proper for a party in an insurance bad faith action to specifically request an opponent's attorney's entire litigation file from a related, previously concluded contract case.

We start with the proposition, which National Union does not dispute, that a document is not privileged simply because it is contained in an attorney's files. There is no specific privilege under our rules or caselaw for "documents in an attorney's files." Thus, a party may not cloak a document with the attorney-client privilege simply by forwarding it to his or her attorney. *See Methodist Home v. Marshall*, 830 S.W.2d 220, 224 (Tex. App.—Dallas 1992, orig. proceeding). Similarly, a file memorandum is not necessarily attorney work product, even though prepared by a lawyer. *See Leede Oil & Gas, Inc. v. McCorkle*, 789 S.W.2d 686, 687 (Tex. App.—Houston [1st Dist.] 1990, orig. proceeding) (holding that attorney memoranda containing only neutral recitals of

4 The trial court had directed National Union at the September 25 hearing to "index" the files submitted for in camera inspection. Because we conclude that National Union asserted a valid work-product objection to Haynes' request for the entire law firm files, we need not today reach the issue of whether, or to what extent, a party must index documents submitted for in camera review, or to what extent a trial court may heighten any such duty on a producing party.

fact were not protected by the work-product privilege). In seeking to withhold specific documents from production, a party has the burden of demonstrating the applicability of a particular privilege, notwithstanding the location of these documents in its attorney's files.

National Union contends, however, that even if some of the documents in the law firm files would not otherwise be privileged, production of an attorney's entire file necessarily reveals the attorney's mental processes, thus invoking work-product protection. We agree.

Texas Rule of Civil Procedure 166b(3)(a) protects from disclosure the "work product of an attorney." This exemption shelters the "mental processes, conclusions, and legal theories of the attorney, providing a privileged area within which the lawyer can analyze and prepare his or her case." *Owens-Corning Fiberglas Corp. v. Caldwell*, 818 S.W.2d 749, 750 (Tex. 1991) (citations omitted). The exemption continues even after the litigation for which the work product was prepared concludes. *Id.* at 751-52.

An attorney's litigation file goes to the heart of the privileged work area guaranteed by the work product exemption. The organization of the file, as well as the decision as to what to include in it, necessarily reveals the attorney's thought processes concerning the prosecution or defense of the case. For example, one of the law firm files which National Union produced for in camera inspection was Schwartzberg's "trial notebook," which directly reflects his trial strategy. While a party should not be allowed to shield discoverable documents simply by placing them in an attorney's file, neither should its attorney be restricted in the organization and maintenance of his or her files by the prospect that they might have to be revealed in their entirety in either current or future litigation. As the Supreme Court recognized in *Hickman v. Taylor*, 329 U.S. 495, 511, 67 S.Ct. 385, 393, 91 L.Ed. 451 (1947): Proper presentation of a client's case demands that (the attorney) assemble information, sift what he considers to be the relevant from the irrelevant facts, prepare his legal theories and plan his strategy without undue and needless interference. Based on this doctrine, federal courts have recognized that an attorney's selection and ordering of documents in anticipation of litigation is protected work product, even where the individual documents are not privileged. *See Sporck v. Peil*, 759 F.2d 312, 315 (3d Cir. 1985); *James Julian, Inc. v. Raytheon Co.*, 93 F.R.D. 138, 144 (D.Del. 1982). The court in *Sporck* held that counsel's selection of specific documents for pre-deposition review by his client fell within the zone of work-product protection. 759 F.2d at 316. This reasoning applies with even greater force where a party seeks to discover an attorney's entire litigation file.

Moreover, no legitimate purpose is served by allowing a party to discover an opponent's litigation file. Our decision today does not prevent a party from requesting specific documents or categories of documents relevant to issues in a pending case, even though some or all of the documents may be contained in an attorney's files. It does, however, prevent a party from requesting the entire file, which is almost certain to encompass numerous irrelevant and immaterial documents, such as transmittal letters and pleadings already on file with the court, as well as privileged information.

We thus conclude that National Union raised a valid work-product objection to producing the law firm files in their entirety in response to the subpoena duces tecum. The trial court abused its discretion in ordering production of these files.

III

Haynes further argues that National Union waived its privileges by attempting to use them offensively. National Union's motion for summary judgment, filed July 1, 1992, expressly relied on Schwartzberg's opinion, given at his deposition, that National Union's denial of the compensation claim was reasonable. Haynes argues that National Union may not rely on Schwartzberg's testimony in this manner and at the same time shield his files from discovery.

We recognized in *Ginsberg v. Fifth Court of Appeals*, 686 S.W.2d 105 (Tex. 1985), that a privilege may be waived by offensive use. "A plaintiff cannot use one hand to seek affirmative relief in court and with the other lower an iron curtain of silence against otherwise pertinent and proper questions which may have a bearing upon his right to maintain his action." *Id.* at 108 (*quoting Pavlinko v. Yale-New Haven Hosp.*, 192 Conn. 138, 470 A.2d 246, 251 (1984)). Although *Ginsberg* concerned the psychotherapist-patient privilege, we have recently applied the offensive waiver principle to the attorney-client privilege, *Republic Ins. Co. v. Davis*, 856 S.W.2d 158, 164 (Tex. 1993), as well as indicating that it applies to the work-product privilege. *Owens-Corning Fiberglas Corp. v. Caldwell*, 818 S.W.2d 749, 752 (Tex. 1991).

In *Davis*, we stated that privileges "represent society's desire to protect certain relationships, and an offensive use waiver of a privilege should not lightly be found." 856 S.W.2d at 163. Accordingly, we held that such waiver requires each of the following elements: 1) the party asserting the privilege must seek affirmative relief; 2) the privileged information must be such that, if believed by the fact finder, would probably be outcome determinative; and 3) disclosure of the confidential information must be the only means by which the aggrieved party may obtain the evidence. *Id.*

In this case, National Union does not seek affirmative relief. Rather, it relies on information in the law firm files only to avoid Haynes' claims. National Union's assertion that it had a reasonable basis to deny the compensation claim is not even an affirmative defense, but is merely a rebuttal to the insurance bad-faith cause of action. *See Aranda v. Ins. Co. of North America*, 748 S.W.2d 210, 213 (Tex. 1988). Moreover, National Union subsequently amended its July 1, 1992, motion for summary judgment to delete all references to Schwartzberg's testimony, and it has represented to the trial court as well as this Court that it does not intend to rely on this testimony. Haynes thus may not show waiver by offensive use.

National Union also based its summary judgment motion on the judgment release signed by Haynes in the compensation case. Haynes argues that this constitutes another attempt by National Union to use its privileges offensively, as he believes there may be a memo in the law firm files bearing on National Union's understanding as to the scope of the release. Again, however, Haynes is unable to establish waiver by offensive use, as National Union is not seeking affirmative relief.

IV

To be entitled to mandamus relief, National Union must also demonstrate that it has no adequate remedy by appeal. *See Walker v. Packer*, 827 S.W.2d 833, 840 (Tex. 1992). We held in *Walker* that an appellate remedy is not adequate "when the trial court erroneously orders the disclosure of privileged information which will materially affect the rights of the aggrieved party . . . ." *Id.* at 843. Based on our review of the law firm files, we believe that their disclosure would materially affect National Union's rights, a conclusion Haynes does not dispute.

Accordingly, the writ of mandamus is conditionally granted. The trial court should vacate its order compelling production of the law firm files. The writ will issue only if the trial court does not comply.

Notes

1. Rule 192.5 (b)(1) states that "core work product—the work product of an attorney or an attorney's representative that contains the attorney's or the attorney's representative's mental impressions, opinions, conclusions, or legal theories—is not discoverable."

2. *In re Bexar County Criminal District Attorney's Office*, 224, S.W.3d 182 (Tex. 2007) discussed the nature of work product. In this malicious prosecution case, all of the DA's Office's work, in connection with the criminal proceeding against Crudup, and relevant to the decision to bring criminal charges against him, constitutes work product, under TEX. R. EVID. 192.5(a). The primary purpose of the work product rule is to shelter the mental processes, conclusions, and legal theories of the attorney, providing a privileged area within which the lawyer can analyze and prepare his or her case. The privilege continues indefinitely, beyond the litigation for which the materials were originally prepared. Moreover, the privilege covers more than just documents: it extends to an attorney's mental impressions, opinions, conclusions, and legal theories, as well as the selection and ordering of documents. The work product privilege is broader than the attorney-client privilege, because it includes all communications made in preparation for trial, including an attorney's interviews with parties and non-party witnesses. Rule 192.5(b)(1) distinguishes everyday work product from "core work product" and makes clear that the latter—defined as "the attorney's or the attorney's representative's mental impressions, opinions, conclusions, or legal theories"—is inviolate and flatly "not discoverable," subject to narrow exceptions that are inapplicable here. Core work product is sacrosanct, and its protection impermeable. Assuming *arguendo* that the testimony Crudup seeks is non-core work product, Crudup still bears a heavy burden: he must show that he "has substantial need" for the testimony in the preparation of his case and that he is unable, without undue hardship, to obtain the substantial equivalent of the material by other means. Even assuming the testimony sought is non-core work product, Crudup's burden of showing causation, in his malicious prosecution suit, is insufficient to constitute "substantial need." Nor has Crudup shown an inability to obtain the substantial equiva-

lent of the testimony sought, without "undue hardship." If anything, when it comes to affecting Crudup's burdens at trial, the DA's disclosure of its prosecution file did more to alleviate than to aggravate.

3. Rule 192.5(b)(2) provides that "any other work product is discoverable only upon a showing that the party seeking discovery has substantial need of the materials in the preparation of the party's case and that the party is unable without undue hardship to obtain the substantial equivalent of the material by other means."

4. Rule 192.5(b)(3) provides that "It is not a violation of subparagraph (1) if disclosure ordered pursuant to subparagraph (2) incidentally discloses by inference attorney mental processes otherwise protected under subparagraph (1)."

5. Rule 192.5(b)(4) provides that "If a court orders discovery of work product pursuant to subparagraph (2), the court must-insofar as possible—protect against disclosure of the mental impressions, opinions, conclusions, or legal theories not otherwise discoverable."

6. Rule 192.5(c) states exceptions to the work product protected from discovery.

7. *Flores v Fourth Court of Appeals,* 777 S.W.2d 38 (Tex. 1989), interpreting former TEX. R. CIV. P. 166b(3) established a controversial test for determining whether investigative documents were prepared in "anticipation of litigation," which has now been modified by *Brotherton, infra.* Under *Flores* investigative documents are prepared in "anticipation of litigation" for purposes of TEX. R. CIV. P 166b(3) if:

a. a reasonable person would have concluded from the totality of the circumstances surrounding the investigation that there was a substantial chance that litigation would ensue; and

b. the party resisting discovery believes in good faith that there was a substantial chance that litigation would ensue and conducts the investigation for the purpose of preparing for such litigation.

To determine whether there is good cause to believe a suit will be filed, so that an investigation is done in anticipation of litigation requires *a two-prong analysis. The first prong* requires an *objective examination* of the facts surrounding the investigation. Consideration should be given to the outward manifestations which indicate litigation is imminent. *The second prong* utilizes a *subjective* approach. Did the party opposing discovery have a good faith belief that litigation would ensue?

NATIONAL TANK CO.
v.
BROTHERTON
851 S.W.2d 193
(Tex. 1993)

Facts: On 8/28/90, there was an explosion at a NATCO manufacturing facility. Pease, NATCO's General Counsel and secretary sent Townsend, NATCO's safety and risk control coordinator, to investigate. Pease also notified Sneed, a representative of NATCO's liability insurer's. They initiated their own investigation at the recommendation of Pease. Wilson was an employee who was injured in the explosion and who later died. Wilson's wife sued, and requested that NATCO produce any reports prepared in connection with the accident investigation. NATCO learned that it had been sued by Wilson on 10/25/90. NATCO asserted that its investigation reports were protected by the attorney-client, work-product, witness-statement, and party-communication privileges. The trial court overruled NATCO's objections and ordered production of documents prepared before 10/25/90.

Issue: What is the work product of an attorney?

Held: "Work product" is defined as the "specific documents, reports, communications, memoranda, mental impressions, conclusions, opinions, or legal theories, prepared and assembled in actual anticipation of litigation or for trial.

Issue: Does the attorney work product privilege apply to documents prepared before the institution of litigation? The term "work product", as used in Rule 166b(3)(a)a, applies only to material prepared in anticipation of litigation. It is not necessary to further consider the scope of the work product exemption in Texas, because if the disputed documents were prepared in anticipation of litigation, they are privileged under the witness statement and party communication privileges.

History: The U.S. Supreme Court in *Hickman* recognized a common law privilege for the work product of the lawyer, consisting of interviews, memoranda, briefs and other material prepared with an eye toward litigation. It allows the attorney assemble facts and prepare a case without undue and needless interference. This was codified into FED.R.CIV.P. 26(b)(3) in 1970.

Under the federal rule, ordinary work product, is discoverable upon a showing of "substantial need" and "undue hardship,' but "opinion" or "core" work product is discoverable, if at all, upon a much higher showing.

The Texas Rule is different from the federal rule, as it simply protects the "work product of an attorney" without defining "work product." But this hasn't been important since 1941. Texas has protected communications between a party's representatives. TEX.R.CIV.P. 166(3)(d). This rule has been broad enough to protect to protect "ordinary work product." Texas, in 1973, adopted a specific work product exemption, but it did not become important until 1986 when the scope of the party communication privilege was narrowed (to require, with very limited exception, that the suit be filed before the party communication privilege could come into existence).

Issue: Were the witness statements protected under TEX.R.CIV.P. 166(b)(3)(d), which protects statements taken in anticipation of the prosecution or defense of the claims made a part of the pending litigation?

When is an investigation conducted in anticipation of litigation?

(1) Objective: When a reasonable person would have concluded from the totality of the circumstances surrounding the investigation that there was a substantial chance that litigation would ensue, and

(2) Subjective: The party conducting the investigation believes in good faith that there was a substantial chance that litigation would ensue and conducts the investigation for the purpose of preparing for such litigation.

Issue: What was the holding in the *Flores* case, and how is it changed by this decision?

Held: The decision in *Flores v 4th Court of Appeals*, 777 S.W.2d 38 (Tex. 1989) is modified to hold that investigative documents are prepared in "anticipation of litigation" for purposes of TEX.R.CIV. P 166b(3)[see 192.5] if (a) a reasonable person would have concluded from the totality of the circumstances surrounding the investigation that there was a substantial chance that litigation would ensue; & (b) the party resisting discovery believes in good faith that there was a substantial chance that litigation would ensue & conducts the investigation for the purpose of preparing for such litigation. The objective prong of *Flores* is satisfied whenever the circumstances surrounding the investigation would have indicated to a reasonable person that there was a substantial chance of litigation. The confidentiality necessary for the adversary process is not defeated because a party, reasonably anticipating future litigation, conducts an investigation prior to the time that litigation is "imminent." *Flores* is modified to the extent that it accords protection only to investigations conducted when litigation is imminent. The underlying inquiry is whether it was reasonable for the investigating party to anticipate litigation & prepare accordingly.

Requiring that the P manifest an intent to sue would also be at odds with the policy goals of the witness statement & party communication privileges. Common sense dictates that a party may reasonably anticipate suit being filed, & conduct an investigation to prepare for the expected litigation, before the P manifests an intent to sue. The second prong of the *Flores* test is subjective & plainly requires that the investigation actually be conducted for the purpose of preparing for an investigation.

Issue: Is it possible to overcome the investigation work product privilege? Yes.

Held: These privileges may be overcome where the requesting party demonstrates a substantial need for the materials & undue hardship in obtaining the substantial equivalent of the materials by other means. Because the court alters the controlling law, it denies mandamus relief without prejudice to allow the trial court to reconsider its ruling in light of this opinion.

Issue: If the investigation is conducted in the ordinary scope of business is the privilege lost?

Held: in some jurisdictions, but not in Texas. There is no "bright-line ordinary course of business exception. It may very well be that a party routinely investigates serious accidents because such accidents routinely give rise to litigation.

Discovery. R 166b(3)(a). Work Product in Anticipation Of Litigation.

Issue: What does the term "in anticipation of litigation" mean?

The term "work product" as used in R Civ P 166b(3)(a) applies only to materials prepared in anticipation of litigation.

Mandamus. Trial Court Does Not Abuse Discretion When Law Change Could Not Be Anticipated.

Having modified a controlling legal standard, the trial court should have an opportunity to reconsider its conclusion in light of this opinion. The Supreme Court therefore denies the writ of mandamus without prejudice to allow the trial court to reconsider D's objections based on the witness statement & party communication privileges.

Notes

1. Rule 192.5 (a) defines "work product" as comprising: "(1) material prepared or mental impressions developed in anticipation of litigation or for trial by or for a party or party's representative, including the party's attorneys, consultants, sureties, indemnitors, insurers, or agents, or (2) a communication made in anticipation of litigation or for trial between a party and the party's representatives or among a party's representatives." This new definition of work product encompasses the "attorney work product" and "party communication" exemptions under former Rule 166b.

2. Under Rule 192.5(b)(1) core work product (a product that contains the attorney's or the attorney's representative's mental impressions, opinions, conclusions, or legal theories) is not discoverable. Under Rule 192.5(b)(2) "Any other work product is discoverable only upon a showing that the party seeking discovery has substantial need of the materials in the preparation of the party's case and that the party is unable without undue hardship to obtain the substantial equivalent of the material by other means."

3. Rule 192.5(c) lists items that, even though prepared in anticipation of litigation, are excepted from the work product protection from discovery. Know them.

Notes

1. *Owens-Corning Fiberglass Corp. v. Caldwell*, 818 S.W.2d 749 (Tex. 1991). The investigatory privilege is not of continuing duration. However, the work product privilege continues to apply to material prepared in anticipation of terminated litigation.

2. There are four principle sources of privileges and exemption to the discovery process:

   a. TEX.R.CIV.P. 192.3, and 192.5;
   b. TEX.R.EVID;
   c. state and federal constitutions, and
   d. the Revised Statutes.

3. *Privileges and Exemptions.*

   a. *Work product.* See previous discussion *supra.*

   b. *Consulting experts.* TEX. R. CIV. P. 192.3(3) provides an exemption from discovery of the identity, mental impressions, and opinions of consulting experts (those experts informally consulted or retained or specially employed by another party in anticipation of litigation or in preparation of trial). Consulting experts are subject to discovery if the consulting expert's opinion or impressions have been reviewed by a testifying expert. Remember that facts known by a consulting expert are not protected.

   c. *Witness statements.* Written statements of potential witnesses and parties were expressly exempted from discovery under the old rules. However, under new Rule 192.3(f), "A party may obtain discovery of the statement of any person with knowledge of relevant facts—a 'witness statement'—regardless of when the statement was made." The commentary to that rule, however, indicates that a dramatic change is not intended. "Elimination of the 'witness statement' exemption does not render all witness statements automatically discoverable but subjects them to the same rules concerning the scope of discovery, work product, and privileges applicable to other documents or tangible thing." Thus, if it is obtained as "work product," it should be discoverable only upon a showing of substantial need, and an inability to obtain the substantial equivalent by other means. Rule 192.5(b)(2).

d. *Party communications.* See previous discussion of work product *supra.* Note that the present work product exemption does not include communications prepared by or for experts that are otherwise discoverable. Also note that a photograph is not a communication.

4. *Attorney-Client Privileges.* TEX. R. EVID. 503(b) provides that a client has a privilege to refuse to disclose and to prevent any other person from disclosing confidential communications made for the purpose of facilitating the rendition of professional legal services to the client:

a. between client and attorney
b. between lawyer and the lawyers' representative;
c. by the client or lawyer to a lawyer representing another party in a pending action and concerning a matter of common interest therein;
d. between representatives of the client or between the client and a representative of the client; or
e. among lawyers and their representatives representing the same client.

The rules of evidence make it clear that there is no attorney-client privilege:

a. in furtherance of a crime or fraud;
b. as to claimants through the same deceased client;
c. as to breach of duty by an attorney or client;
d. as to a document attested by an attorney;
e. as to joint clients.

5. *In re The City of Georgetown*, 53 S.W.3d 328, (Tex. 2001): Section 552.022(b) of the Government Code (the Texas Public Information Act, formerly known as the Texas Open Records Act) does not require the City to disclose to the *Austin American-Statesman* a report prepared by a consulting expert in connection with pending and anticipated litigation. Section 552.022 provides that a governmental body must disclose completed reports or evaluations "unless the category of information is expressly made confidential under other law." The Texas Rules of Civil Procedure are "other law," and consulting-expert reports are within a category of information that is expressly confidential under those rules. If documents are privileged or confidential under the Texas Rules of Civil Procedure or Texas Rules of Evidence, they are within a category of information that is expressly made confidential under other law within the meaning of section 552.022 of the Public Information Act.

b. *Asserting Exemptions and Privileges*

Notes

In re Carolina Garza, 544 S.W.3d 836 (2018): Both a party and any other person affected by the discovery request are entitled to seek protection by filing motions for protection.

In re UNION PACIFIC RESOURCES COMPANY

22 S.W.3d 338
(Tex. 1999)

Ralph H. Duggins, Fort Worth, Roy L. Barrett, Waco, Curtis E. Pritchard, John R. McLean, Cleburne, Shayne D. Moses, Fort Worth, Keith C. Cameron, Waco, Dan M. Boulware, Cleburne, for Relator.

James W. Walker, Dallas, Alfred Mackenzie, Waco, Katherine Anne Grossman, Marcus Jarrett Coleman, Kevin Lamar Sewell, Dallas, for Respondent.

PER CURIAM.

The issue in this original mandamus proceeding is whether the district court abused its discretion by partially sustaining relator's objections to discovery based on relevance when relator did not adduce evidence in support of its objections. Contrary to the court of appeals, we hold that the district court did not abuse its discretion.

Union Pacific Resources Company sued its excess insurer, Continental Insurance Company, for defense costs and payments made on liability claims covered, Union Pacific asserts, by Continental's policy. The claims related to a Corpus Christi petroleum refinery formerly owned by Union Pacific. Continental sought discovery of information pertaining to Union Pacific's settlement of entirely separate litigation with other insurers over coverage of claims relating to a waste disposal site in California that Union Pacific operated. Although Continental was not a party to the California litigation, it argues that releases in the settlement agreements might extend to the Corpus Christi litigation. Continental also argues that it needs the requested information to determine if Union Pacific has already been compensated for its claims against Continental by the California settlements.

Union Pacific objected to the requested discovery on the ground that it was not relevant to the Corpus Christi coverage dispute, and Continental moved to compel. The district court held a lengthy hearing on Continental's motion, at which each side argued its position extensively. Neither side produced evidence. Union Pacific offered to submit the settlement agreements to the court for an in camera inspection, but Continental objected, and the court did not conduct an in camera review. The court ordered Union Pacific to produce the California settlement agreements with the dollar amounts of the settlements redacted, explaining: "I think there would need to be some showing that these other settlements are relevant to this lawsuit before the amounts of the settlement could be properly discoverable in this case." After obtaining the redacted agreements, Continental again moved to compel production of the settlement amounts, arguing that how Union Pacific allocated them for purposes of its internal bookkeeping was relevant to show what the amounts were for. The district court denied Continental's motion, and Continental sought mandamus relief in the court of appeals.

The court of appeals conditionally granted relief, holding that the district court abused its discretion by refusing to order discovery when Union Pacific had not offered evidence that the requested information was irrelevant. The court of appeals relied on our decisions in *Peeples v. Honorable Fourth Supreme Judicial District*, 990 S.W.2d 941, 944, 994 S.W.2d 423, 428-429 (op. on reh'g). 701 S.W.2d 635 (Tex. 1985) and *Weisel Enterprises, Inc. v. Curry*, 718 S.W.2d 56 (Tex. 1986) (per curiam). Neither decision supports the court of appeals' holding.

In *Peeples*, the plaintiff sued to cancel a transfer of stock, and the defendant requested production of all of the plaintiff's financial information for a stated period of time, as well as other information. The plaintiff moved for protection on the ground that the requested information was irrelevant, but did not request an in camera inspection. The district court denied the plaintiff's motion without reviewing the requested documents in camera. The court of appeals held that this was an abuse of discretion and granted mandamus relief. This Court held that the district court had not abused its discretion. We stated:

> Any party who seeks to deny the production of evidence must claim a specific privilege against such production. The burden is on the party asserting a privilege from discovery to produce evidence concerning the applicability of a particular privilege.

We hold that any party who seeks to exclude documents, records or other matters from the discovery process has the affirmative duty to specifically plead the particular privilege or immunity claimed and to request a hearing on his motion. The trial court should then determine whether an in camera inspection is necessary. If such inspection is ordered by the trial court, those materials for which the inspection is sought must be segregated and produced to the court. Failure to follow the above procedure constitutes a waiver of any complaint of the trial court's action.

The requirement that evidence be produced related to a claim of privilege, not to an objection based on relevance. We concluded that the district court had discretion to require the plaintiff to follow these procedures.

In *Weisel*, the defendant moved for protection from discovery on the ground that documents requested by the plaintiff were work product and subject to the attorney-client privilege. The defendant supplied the district court with a list of documents but did not submit them to the court for an in camera inspection and offered no evidence of privilege. The district court granted the defendant's motion and a divided court of appeals denied mandamus relief. This court granted mandamus relief, holding that the defendant had failed to establish the applicability of any privilege.

Neither *Peeples* nor *Weisel* requires evidence in support of an assertion relating to discovery when evidence is unnecessary to decide the matter. We made this clear in former Rule 166b(4) of the Texas Rules of Civil Procedure, which required that "a party seeking to exclude any matter from discovery on the basis of an exemption or immunity from discovery . . . shall produce any evidence necessary to support such claim". The same provision has been carried over into current Rule 193.4(a), which states: "The party making the objection or asserting the privilege must present any evidence necessary to support the objection or privilege." As the rule recognizes, evidence may not always be necessary to support a claim of protection from discovery.

Evidence was not necessary to determine the discoverability of Union Pacific's settlement agreements related to the California litigation. Indeed, it is not clear what evidence could have been produced on the issue. The question was simply whether the settlement dollar amounts are pertinent to the issues in the current litigation. Continental's sole argument was that information concerning Union Pacific's internal allocation and budgeting of settlement proceeds from the California litigation might show that it considered some of the funds attributable to the Corpus Christi litigation. The district court could determine without hearing evidence that the purpose for payment of the settlement proceeds was determined by the terms of the agreements, which had already been produced for Continental, and not by Union Pacific's internal bookkeeping.

The district court acted well within its discretion, and consequently it was an abuse of discretion for the court of appeals to direct that the discovery order be vacated. We have previously held that if settlement information like Continental seeks is erroneously ordered produced, the producing party has no adequate remedy on appeal. Having shown an abuse of discretion and the lack of an adequate appellate remedy, Union Pacific is entitled to mandamus relief. The court of appeals is directed to withdraw its judgment and deny Continental's petition for mandamus. We are confident the court of appeals will promptly comply, and our writ will issue only if that confidence proves misplaced.

Note

To assert a claim of privilege, Rule 193.3, the party withholds the requested document or information, and notifies the requesting party that a privilege is being asserted. The requesting party is then required to request more specific information. The responding party then has 15 days to provide sufficient information which identifies the material being withheld with sufficient detail to allow the requesting party to evaluate the claim of privilege. 'Assertions of privilege are not to be made prophylactically against the threat of waiver, but only when information is actually withheld' [Court's Explanatory statement; TEX. R. CIV. P. 193, Comment 3].

HUMPHREYS
v.
CALDWELL
888 S.W.2d 469
(Tex. 1994)

Facts: There was a car wreck between Mulinax (insured by State farm) and Farley. While that suit was pending, Farley filed this suit against State Farm and its adjusters alleging bad faith and unfair settlement practices. During discovery, Farley sought production of 1) State Farms's claims file, which contains documents relating to the accident and lawsuit between Mullinax and Farley. 2) Farely sent an interrogatory asking State farm to identify all lawsuits in Texas which involved similar claims in the last five years. 3) Farley sought production of the personnel files of Humphreys and Holiner, State Farm's Adjuster. The only thing State Farm relied upon to establish the privilege for items 2 & 3 were affidavits based on "personal knowledge and/or knowledge which he has been able to acquire upon inquiry." The trial court ordered production.

Issue: How does a party exclude a matter from discovery, when claiming a privilege? A party who seeks to exclude any matter from discovery on the basis of an exemption or immunity from discovery, must specifically plead the particular exemption or immunity relied on and produce evidence supporting such claim in the form of affidavits or live testimony at a hearing. The burden is on the party asserting a privilege from discovery to produce evidence concerning it applicability.

Issue: What is required for an affidavit, supporting a privilege, to be sufficient? An affidavit must positively and unqualifiedly represent the facts as disclosed in the affidavit to be true and within the affiant's personal knowledge. Here, it was not on personal knowledge and do not state that the facts recited are true.

Issue: Was the claim file discoverable? No, because it contained documents protected by the attorney-client work product privilege. It is immaterial that these were prepared for the other suit, since the work-product privilege is of continuing duration.

Notes

1. The burden of requesting a hearing has been a vexing one. Until the new rules were promulgated, the following case settled the matter. *McKinney v. National Union Fire Ins. Co.*, 772 S.W.2d 72 (Tex. 1989): The party filing an objection of discovery no longer waives his/her objection by failing to request a hearing. *Because the party requesting discovery is in the best position to evaluate its need for information and sometimes recognizes the validity of an objection to a discovery request, the orderly administration of justice will be better served by placing responsibility for obtaining a hearing on discovery matters on the party requesting discovery. If a hearing is held, the objecting party must assume the burden of establishing its privilege, immunity or other objection to the discovery requests.*

2. *McKinney* is slightly modified by the new rules. Under TEX. R. CIV. P. 193.4(a) any party may, at any reasonable time, request a hearing on a objection or claim of privilege. Under TEX. R. CIV. P. 193.4(c) "a party need not request a ruling on that party's own objection or assertion of privilege to preserve the objection or privilege, but a party may not use—at any hearing or trial—material or information withheld from discovery without timely amending or supplementing the party's response to that discovery." In other words, to be able to use the material, once a privilege has been asserted, the objecting party must provide it to the other party.

3. Under the new rules, if a hearing is held, "The evidence [to establish the privilege] may be testimony presented at the hearing or affidavits served at least seven days before the hearing or at such other reasonable time as the court permits." TEX. R. CIV. P. 193.4(a).

4. If the court rules that the material is not privileged, the responding party must produce the requested material or information within 30 days after the court's ruling or at such time as the court orders.

5. The inadvertent production of privileged material no longer waives the privilege, if, within 10 days after the producing party discovers that such production was made, the producing party amends the response, identifying the material or information produced and stating the privilege asserted.

6. *In re E.I. DuPont de Nemours and Company,* 136, S.W.3d 218 (Tex. 2004): The party who seeks to limit discovery, by asserting a privilege, has the burden of proof. However, if a party, asserting privilege claims, makes a prima facie showing of privilege, and tenders documents to the trial court, the trial court must conduct an in camera inspection of those documents, before deciding to compel production. Generally, a trial court conducts an in camera inspection, to determine if a document is, in fact, privileged. If it is not privileged, then it may become evidence that the factfinder may consider. If the document is privileged, it is not subject to discovery, and may not be considered by the factfinder, even when the factfinder is the trial court. The trial court abuses its discretion in refusing to conduct an in camera inspection, when such review is critical to the evaluation of a privilege claim. The prima facie standard requires only the "minimum quantum of evidence necessary to support a rational inference that the allegation of fact is true." The documents themselves may constitute sufficient evidence, to make a prima facie showing of attorney-client, or work product privilege. An affidavit, even if it addresses groups of documents, rather than each document individually, is sufficient to make a prima facie showing of attorney-client, and/or work product privilege. However, an affidavit is of no probative value, if it merely presents global allegations that documents come within the asserted privilege.

Note

Under new Rule 193.6, Texas Rules of Civil Procedure, a party who fails to timely respond to a discovery request will be precluded from, using the material withheld during trial unless he can show good cause, and that the failure to timely make, amend, or supplement the discover response will not unfairly surprise or unfairly prejudice the other parties.

In re CHRISTUS SPOHN HOSPITAL KLEBERG
222 S.W.3d 434
(Tex. 2007)

Discovery. Inadvertent Disclosure To Testifying Expert. Documents Snap's Back, Unless Expert Testifies.

This is an original mandamus proceeding. In this medical malpractice proceeding, the defendant hospital seeks to recover privileged documents that were mistakenly provided to its designated testifying expert witness.

Issue: Is the privileged nature of a document lost if it is inadvertently produced? No.

Held: Writ of mandamus is denied. Texas Rule of Civil Procedure 193.3(d), known as the "snap-back" provision, preserves the privilege over Rule 192.3(e)(6)'s mandate that all documents provided to a testifying expert are discoverable.

The inadvertent nature of the production in this case preserved the privilege under Rule 193.3(d) and entitled the hospital to recover the documents, upon realizing its mistake, *provided the hospital's designated expert does not testify at trial.* The hospital has not attempted to name another testifying expert, instead indicating an intent to rely upon the expert to whom the documents were disclosed. So long as the hospital stands upon its testifying expert designation, Rule 192 compels the conclusion that the documents may not be snapped back.

The focus is on the intent to waive the privilege, not the intent to produce the material or information. A party who fails to diligently screen documents before producing them does not waive a claim of privilege.

Issue: What is discoverable from a testifying expert?

Held: Permissible discovery from a testifying expert in includes:

Facts know by the expert, no matter how acquired.

Mental impressions and opinions formed or made in connection with the case.

Any bias of the witness.

All documents, tangible things, etc. provided to, received by, or prepared by or for the expert in anticipation of a testifying expert's testimony.

5. *Relief from Improper Discovery Orders*

WALKER
v.
PACKER
827 S.W.2d 833
(Tex. 1992)

Summary: Mandamus issues only(1) (a) to correct a clear abuse of discretion or (b) the violation of a duty imposed by law and when there is no other adequate remedy by law. A party seeking review of a discovery order by mandamus must demonstrate that the remedy offered by an ordinary appeal is inadequate. Now supplanted by Prudential test.

A remedy by appeal is not inadequate merely because it might involve more delay or cost than mandamus. 1) A party will not have an adequate remedy by appeal when (1) the appellate court would not be able to cure the trial court's discovery error, (2) where the party's ability to present a viable claim or defense at trial is vitiated or severely compromised by the trial court's discovery error. Here, there was an adequate remedy by appeal since the information sought is not privileged, burdensome, or harassing, nor does it vitiate or severely compromise the Walker's ability to present a viable claim.

Facts: This is a medical malpractice lawsuit. The trial court denied Ps' requests for discovery from one of the defendants and denied discovery of documents sought by Ps from a nonparty for impeachment purposes. While the denial of the 1st request was proper, the 2nd was improper.

Issue: What record is required for writ of mandamus review. A sufficient record to establish the right to mandamus. Since an evidentiary hearing was held on the motion to compel, it was the movant's burden to provide the supreme court with the petition and affidavit, and also the statement of facts of the hearing. So, they have waived their right to mandamus relief against St. Paul. This disposes of the first request.

Issue: Were the Obstetrics Faculty Records discoverable? Yes, this was discoverable evidence, and the trial court erred in not allowing the Ps to obtain the evidence.

Ps sought documentary evidence to impeach one of the Ds' expert witnesses, Dr. Gilstrap. (They wanted to show that the department had a policy restricting faculty members from testifying for plaintiffs in medical malpractice cases. Gilstrap denied it, but Dr. Brekken, in another case, admitted there was such a policy.) Thus, *Russell v. Young* (holding that records of third party sought for impeachment were not subject to discovery), is distinguished. There was a wholesale effort to discover financial records of a potential medical witness, and the records did not relate directly to the suit. Here, there is specific evidence sought to show bias on the part of Dr. Gilstrap. The request here is narrow and specific; not wholesale. Evidence of bias is discoverable.

Issue: Granted that the trial court erred in denying the discovery, is mandamus available to correct that error?

Issue: When is mandamus available?

Held: Mandamus issues only (1) to correct a clear abuse of discretion or (2) the violation of a duty imposed by law (3) when there is no other adequate remedy by law. Traditionally, the writ of mandamus issued only to compel the performance of a ministerial act or duty. That has been expanded to allow correction of a clear abuse of discretion. A trial court clearly abuses its discretion if it reaches a decision so arbitrary and unreasonable as to amount to a clear and prejudicial error of law.

Mandamus. Clear Abuse Of Discretion. Fact v. Law Question.

Traditionally, the writ of mandamus issued only to compel the performance of a ministerial act or duty. Since the 1950's, however, the Supreme Court has used the writ to correct a "clear abuse of discretion" committed by the trial court.

Issue: When is a trial court's decision arbitrary and unreasonable?

If it relates to factual issues, the reviewing court may not substitute its judgment for that of the trial court, unless the trial court could have reached only one decision. I.e., unless the issue was established as a matter of law. However, if the issue relates to legal issues a trial court has no discretion in determining what the law is or applying the law to the facts. Thus, a clear failure by the trial court to analyze or apply the law correctly will constitute an abuse of discretion, and may result I appellate reversal by extraordinary writ.

Held: A trial court clearly abuses its discretion if it reaches a decision so arbitrary and unreasonable as to amount to a clear and prejudicial error of law. With respect to resolution of factual issues or matters committed to the trial court's discretion, for example, the reviewing court may not substitute its judgment for that of the trial court. The relator must establish that the trial court could reasonably have reached only one decision. On the other hand, review of a trial court's determination of the legal principles controlling its ruling is much less deferential. A trial court has no "discretion" in determining what the law is or applying the law to the facts. Thus, a clear failure by the trial court to analyze or apply the law correctly will constitute an abuse of discretion, and may result in appellate reversal by extraordinary writ.

Issue: Did the trial court abuse its discretion in this case? Clearly. The trial court's erroneous interpretation of the law constitutes a clear abuse of discretion. That, however, does not settle the right to a writ of mandamus.

Issue: Did the movant have an adequate remedy by appeal? Yes!

Issue: In passing on a writ of mandamus concerning discovery, when is there an adequate remedy on appeal?

Held: Writ of mandamus is denied. Mandamus issues only to correct a clear abuse of discretion or the violation of a duty imposed by law when there is no other adequate remedy by law. A normal appeal is an adequate remedy at law which will preclude issuance of mandamus. Thus, a party seeking review of a discovery order by mandamus must demonstrate that the remedy offered by an ordinary appeal is inadequate.

Further, an appellate remedy is not inadequate merely because it may involve more expense or delay than obtaining an extraordinary writ. The Supreme Court disapproves of *Cleveland v. Ward*, 116 Tex. 1, 285 S.W. 1063 (1926), *Crane v. Tunks*, 160 Tex. 182, 328 S.W.2d 434 (1959), *Jampole v. Touchy*, 673 S.W.2d 569 (Tex. 1984) and any other authorities to the extent that they imply that a remedy by appeal is inadequate merely because it might involve more delay or cost than mandamus.

Issue: When will appeal not be an adequate remedy for a discovery error?

1) A party will not have an adequate remedy by appeal when the appellate court would not be able to cure the trial court's discovery error, as where it orders the disclosure of privileged information which will materially affect the rights of the aggrieved party, or whether trade secrets are ordered disclosed without adequate protections to maintain confidentiality.

2) An appeal will not be an adequate remedy where the party's ability to present a viable claim or defense at trial is vitiated or severely compromised by the trial court's discovery error, as where discovery sanctions have been imposed which will preclude presentation of the movant's case. Cost and delay are not enough.

3) The remedy by appeal may be inadequate where the trial court disallows discovery and the missing discovery cannot be made part of the appellate record, or the trial court after proper request refuses to make it part of the record, and the reviewing court is unable to evaluate the effect of the trial court's error on the record before it.

Issue: Did the movants have an adequate remedy by appeal? Yes. The information sought is not privileged, burdensome, or harassing, nor does it vitiate or severely compromise the Walker's ability to present a viable claim.

Note

Remember that the holding in *Walker v. Packer,* concerning whether an adequate remedy by appeal exist, has been modified in *In re The Prudential Insurance Co. of America*, 148 S.W.3d 124 (Tex. 2004) [found on page 2 of this book).

Mandamus relief is available only when there is no adequate remedy on appeal. The operative word, "adequate", has no comprehensive definition; it is simply a proxy for the careful balance of jurisprudential considerations that determine when appellate courts will use original mandamus proceedings to review the actions of lower courts.

An appellate remedy is "adequate" when any benefits to mandamus review are outweighed by the detriments. When the benefits outweigh the detriments, appellate courts must consider whether the appellate remedy is adequate.

PARADIGM OIL, INC.
v.
RETAMCO OPERATING, INC.

372 S.W.3d 177
(Tex. 2012)

Susan S. Vance, Douglas W. Alexander, Alexander Dubose & Townsend, LLP, Thomas R. Phillips, Dustin Mark Howell, Baker Botts, LLP, Austin, TX, Juan M. Castillo, Roger G. Bresnahan, Farrimond Castillo & Bresnahan PC, Jeffrey D. Small, Law Office of Jeff Small, San Antonio, TX, Leslee N. Haas, Hays McComm Rice & Pickering, Houston, TX, Craig Price, Nathan C. Rogers, Griffith & Thornburgh, LLP, Santa Barbara, CA, Charles Rudolph Grebing, Wingert Grebing Brubaker & Juskie LLP, San Diego, CA, for Paradigm Oil, Inc.

James L. Drought, Calhoun Bobbitt, Drought Drought & Bobbitt LLP, Timothy Patton, Timothy Patton, PC, San Antonio, TX, for Retamco Operating, Inc.

JUSTICE MEDINA delivered the opinion of the Court.

Texas Rule of Civil Procedure 215.2(b)(5) authorizes a trial court to render a default judgment against a defendant for discovery abuse, justice and due process permitting. Commonly known as the death-penalty sanction, it is the remedy of last resort.

Discovery abuse in this case caused the trial court to strike the defendants' answer and render a default judgment. In addition to striking the defendants' answer, the discovery sanction also barred the defendants from contesting the plaintiff's damages. Because these damages were unliquidated, however, the plaintiff was required to prove them at an uncontested hearing.

The defendants do not deny their discovery abuse, nor do they question the trial court's decision to strike their pleadings and render judgment by default. Rather, they complain that the trial court abused its discretion by barring them from the damages trial. The defendants maintain that this extension of the death-penalty sanction was excessive, unjust, and therefore an abuse of discretion.

The court of appeals did not agree, holding that the discovery sanction was neither excessive nor an abuse of the trial court's discretion. The court of appeals, however, remanded the case twice on legal insufficiency grounds before affirming the uncontested damages award in this, the third appeal. *See Paradigm Oil, Inc. v. Retamco Operating, Inc.,* 161 S.W.3d 531 (Tex. App.—San Antonio 2004, pet. denied) (*Paradigm I*), *on remand,* 242 S.W.3d 67 (Tex. App.—San Antonio 2007, pet. denied) (*Paradigm II*), *on remand,* 330 S.W.3d 342 (Tex. App.—San Antonio 2010) (*Paradigm III*). Because we conclude that the defaulted defendants should have been permitted to participate in the hearing on unliquidated damages, we reverse the court of appeals' judgment and remand the case to the trial court for further proceedings.

I

The case arises out of the conveyance of oil and gas properties by Retamco Operating, Inc. almost thirty years ago. Following an economic downturn in 1984, Retamco conveyed 572 oil and gas leases to PNB Securities Corporation under a debt workout agreement (the 1984 Agreement). The agreement was complex. Under it, Retamco retained certain rights, including overriding royalty interests and after-payout working interests in certain wells PNB financed. The 1984 Agreement further allowed Retamco to continue operating certain leases in production, entitled Retamco to notice of lease terminations, sales, or assignments, and granted Retamco the option to retain certain leases that might otherwise terminate. Retamco was also to be notified when certain wells reached payout so it could elect to share in the working interest. The agreement obligated PNB to prepare a document describing Retamco's rights and record it in all applicable counties. PNB was further to notify those acquiring an interest in any of the leases of Retamco's rights and interests under the 1984 Agreement.

In 1999, Retamco sued multiple parties for damages under the 1984 Agreement. By the time of the suit, PNB had divested itself of all the leases covered under the agreement, with the last sixty-two leases having been sold to Paradigm Oil, Inc. in 1993. Before this sale, Paradigm operated one of the leases for PNB for a number of years.

Retamco's suit named both PNB and Paradigm as defendants. Retamco also joined other defendants, including PNB's successor, Bank of America, and three Paradigm affiliates, Pacific Operators, Inc., Pacific Operators of Texas, Inc., and Finley Oilwell Service, Inc. Alleging breach of contract and fraud, Retamco complained that it had not been notified of well proposals as required under the 1984 Agreement and had thereby lost the opportunity to participate in several wells. Retamco also accused Paradigm of overcharging for operating expenses and otherwise diverting proceeds, which allegedly caused Retamco to lose royalty and working-interest revenues. Retamco further alleged that Paradigm had succeeded to PNB's obligations under the 1984 Agreement by its purchase of the sixty-two leases in 1993 and was therefore jointly and severally liable for its damages.

Paradigm denied Retamco's allegations but after answering the lawsuit generally refused to participate in discovery. Retamco sought sanctions. The trial court conducted hearings on the matter, and Paradigm was ordered to pay discovery-related expenses and to provide discovery. When Paradigm failed to meet the trial court's discovery deadline, Retamco again moved for sanctions. Another hearing was conducted after which the court granted Retamco's motion, striking Paradigm's answer and rendering a $1.6 million default judgment. In sanctioning Paradigm for discovery abuse, the trial court's order not only precluded Paradigm from contesting its liability but also Retamco's damages, stating:

> Paradigm Oil, Inc., Pacific Operators, Inc. and Pacific Operators of Texas, Inc., may not, and are disallowed to, oppose Plaintiff's . . . claims to overriding royalty interests, damages, exemplary damages, pre-judgment interest, or attorney's fees, whether by cross examination, objection to evidence offered, or offer of evidence[.]
>
> Paradigm moved for a new trial, produced everything it believed Retamco requested, and offered to reimburse Retamco's legal expenses. The trial court denied the motion and thereafter severed the default judgment into a separate cause, making it a final judgment. Paradigm appealed.

The court of appeals affirmed the discovery sanction in the first appeal but did not affirm the default judgment itself. *See Paradigm I,* 161 S.W.3d at 534. Concluding that the record contained no evidence to support the $1.6 million award, the court reversed the judgment and remanded the case for a new damages hearing. *Id.* at 540. Meanwhile in the trial court, Retamco obtained a similar death-penalty sanction against Finley, the Paradigm affiliate that had not been included in the previous default judgment.

After the remand in *Paradigm I,* Retamco endeavored to prove its damages in two separate trials—one against Paradigm and affiliates Pacific Operators and Pacific Operators of Texas and the other against Finley. The two trials together resulted in approximately $5.6 million in actual damages and $40 million in punitive damages ($10 million for each of the four defendants). Paradigm and Finley separately appealed their respective judgments, and the court of appeals again reversed, holding the evidence to be legally insufficient to support the damages awarded in either trial. *See Paradigm II,* 242 S.W.3d at 69; *Finley Oilwell Serv., Inc. v. Retamco Operating, Inc.,* 248 S.W.3d 314 (Tex. App.—San Antonio 2007, pet. denied).

After these reversals, the severed actions against Paradigm and Finley were consolidated for a fourth damages trial. Once again the defendants were not permitted to participate. At the conclusion of this uncontested trial, Retamco was awarded more than $35 million, which included $20 million in exemplary damages. On the third appeal, the court of appeals reduced the judgment by $1.25 million but otherwise affirmed the trial court's judgment. *See Paradigm III,* 330 S.W.3d at 347. As it had done in the previous two appeals, Paradigm petitioned this Court for review.

II

Paradigm's petition does not contest the trial court's decision to strike its answer as a discovery sanction or the default judgment rendered against it on liability. Paradigm's appeal focuses instead on its exclusion from the trial on damages. As a general rule, a defaulted defendant has the right to participate in such a trial when, as here, the plaintiff's damages are unliquidated. *Rainwater v. Haddox,* 544 S.W.2d 729, 733 (Tex. Civ. App.—Amarillo 1976, no writ) (citing, *inter alia, Maywald Trailer Co. v. Perry,* 238 S.W.2d 826, 827-28 (Tex. Civ. App.—Galveston 1951, writ ref'd n.r.e.)). Paradigm contends that the trial court therefore abused its discretion by extending the discovery sanction to bar its participation at this trial.

Retamco responds that Paradigm waived this complaint by not raising the issue in the court of appeals. It points out that Paradigm's most recent brief in the court of appeals complained about several things but not about the discovery sanction itself. Even though the court of appeals previously upheld the sanction in the first appeal, Retamco maintains that Paradigm needed to brief and argue the issue in the court of appeals once again to preserve it for our review.

Retamco's argument, however, ignores the law-of-the-case doctrine. Under this doctrine, a decision rendered in a former appeal of a case is generally binding in a later appeal of the same case. *Briscoe v. Goodmark Corp.,* 102 S.W.3d 714, 716 (Tex. 2003). Having decided the issue in *Paradigm I,* the court of appeals was not obligated to reconsider the matter in subsequent appeals. *Id.* Neither was Paradigm required to reargue the issue in a court that already decided the matter.

Such a requirement would undermine the doctrine's purpose, which is to bring an end to litigation by winnowing the issues in each successive appeal. *Hudson v. Wakefield,* 711 S.W.2d 628, 630 (Tex. 1986). By narrowing the issues in successive appeals, the law-of-the-case doctrine further seeks to promote efficiency and uniformity in the decision-making process. *Id.* Requiring a party to reargue issues previously lost in the court of appeals as a predicate to this Court's review would obviously work at cross-purposes to the doctrine.

The court of appeals determined in the first appeal that the trial court did not abuse its discretion in denying Paradigm the right to participate in the post-default damages hearing. *See Paradigm I,* 161 S.W.3d at 537-38. That decision on Paradigm's participation became the law of the case for future proceedings in those courts. It did not, however, become the law of the case in this Court. Although we declined to review the matter in *Paradigm I,* our decision to deny Paradigm's petition for review in that appeal did not invoke the doctrine. *See Loram Maint. of Way, Inc. v. Ianni,* 210 S.W.3d 593, 596 (Tex. 2006) (holding that law-of-the-case doctrine is inapplicable when this Court simply denies a petition because the denial is not a decision on the merits). It was appropriate then for Paradigm to raise the issue again in this Court, even though it did not reargue it in the court of appeals. Paradigm's previous complaint about the death-penalty sanction in *Paradigm I* preserved the issue for our review, and we turn now to the merits of that complaint.

III

As to the merits, the parties disagree about the underlying nature of the default judgment in this case. Paradigm argues that the discovery sanction should be treated like a no-answer default judgment. It submits that, by striking its answer, the discovery sanction put it in the same position as though it had never answered the suit. Because a defendant who defaults by failing to answer a lawsuit ordinarily retains the right to participate in any subsequent trial to determine unliquidated damages, Paradigm contends that it should similarly have that right in this case. It concludes that the trial court therefore abused its discretion in denying it the right to participate.

Retamco, on the other hand, maintains that a default judgment from a discovery sanction is different from a no-answer default judgment. A defendant who simply fails to answer a lawsuit, according to Retamco, is less culpable than a defendant that answers and abuses the discovery process. Retamco contends that different rules apply because of the discovery abuse and that such rules include trial court discretion to bar the defendant's participation at the damages hearing, as was done here.

The parties' arguments recognize that default judgments are not all alike and that different rules apply in different circumstances. For example, a default judgment caused by a defendant's failure to answer after service is treated differently from a default judgment caused by a defendant's failure to appear for trial after answering a suit. *Jatoi v. Decker, Jones, McMackin, Hall & Bates,* 955 S.W.2d 430, 432 (Tex. App.—Fort Worth 1997, pet. denied); TEX.R. CIV. P. 239. In the latter instance, a post-answer default "constitutes neither an abandonment of the defendant's answer nor an implied confession of any issues thus joined by the defendant's answer." *Stoner v. Thompson,* 578 S.W.2d 679, 682 (Tex. 1979). Because the merits of the plaintiff's claim remain at issue, judgment cannot be rendered on the pleadings, and the plaintiff must prove its claim. *Id.* By contrast, the non-answering party in a no-answer default judgment is said to have admitted both the truth of facts set out in the petition and the defendant's liability on any cause of action properly alleged by those facts. *Morgan v. Compugraphic Corp.,* 675 S.W.2d 729, 731 (Tex. 1984). The defendant's default thus establishes liability, but a trial may still be necessary if the plaintiff's damages are unliquidated. *Holt Atherton Indus., Inc. v. Heine,* 835 S.W.2d 80, 83 (Tex. 1992); TEX.R. CIV. P. 243. And as a general rule, a defendant who has not answered but nevertheless appears at the post-default hearing on damages is entitled to participate.

Although default judgments may generally be categorized as pre-or post-answer, other variations exist. A default judgment as a discovery sanction is one variation that does not fit neatly into either general category. When a trial court strikes a defendant's answer as a discovery sanction, the resulting default is technically post-answer, but it is also, as Paradigm contends, similar to a no-answer default judgment. Indeed, some courts have analogized the death-penalty discovery sanction to a no-answer default judgment, finding "no distinction in the treatment of cases between those where the defendant failed to answer in a lawsuit and where the defendant's answer has been stricken from the record as a result of the imposition of sanctions." *Fiduciary Mortg. Co. v. City Nat'l Bank of Irving,* 762 S.W.2d 196, 200 (Tex. App.—Dallas 1988, writ denied); *see also In the Matter of Gober,* 100 F.3d 1195, 1205 (5th Cir. 1996); *Assicurazioni Generali, S.p.A. v. Milsap,* 760 S.W.2d 314, 317 (Tex. App.—Texarkana 1988, writ denied); *City of Dallas v. Cox,* 793 S.W.2d 701, 728 (Tex. App.—Dallas 1990, no writ).

Even though a death-penalty discovery sanction may be similar to a no-answer default judgment, it is not the same for all purposes. This type of default judgment implicates not only the broader principles that apply to default judgments generally but also the rules that apply to discovery abuse, specifically those principles that control the use of a case-ending discovery sanction. *See TransAmerican Natural Gas Corp. v. Powell,* 811 S.W.2d 913 (Tex. 1991) (explaining the limitations on death-penalty sanctions). Our review must thus take into consideration both general default judgment principles and our discovery rules.

Our discovery rules provide a variety of sanctions for discovery abuse. *See generally* TEX.R. CIV. P. 215. The law requires, however, that any sanction imposed by the trial court must be "just," *id.* 215.2(b), and we have said that two factors mark the bounds of a "just" sanction. First, a direct relationship between the offensive conduct and the sanction imposed must exist. *TransAmerican,* 811 S.W.2d at 917. Second, the sanction imposed must not be excessive. *Id.* The most extreme sanctions are also limited by due process considerations. Thus, a death-penalty sanction cannot be used to adjudicate the merits of claims or defenses unless the offending party's conduct during discovery justifies a presumption that its claims or defenses lack merit. *Id.* at 918.

* * *

We agree with Paradigm that the general rule in this state and elsewhere is that a defaulted party may participate in the post-default damages hearing. *See, e.g., Payne v. Dewitt,* 995 P.2d 1088, 1095 (Okla. 1999) (stripping the defaulted defendant "of basic due process truth-testing devices is contrary to the orderly process of assessing damages"); *Bashforth v. Zampini,* 576 A.2d 1197, 1200-01 (R.I. 1990) (holding that in a hearing on the question of damages, the defendant, even though in default, is entitled to full participation); *see also Bonilla v. Trebol Motors Corp.,* 150 F.3d 77, 82 (1st Cir. 1998) (noting general rule that a defaulting party "is entitled to contest damages and to participate in a hearing on damages, should one be held") (citing 10A CHARLES ALAN WRIGHT, ARTHUR R. MILLER & MARY KAY KANE, FEDERAL PRACTICE AND PROCEDURE § 2688 (3d. ed.1998)); B. Finberg, Annotation: *Defaulting Defendant's Right to Notice and Hearing as to Determination of Amount of Damages,* 15 A.L.R.3d 586 (1967) (collecting cases).

Retamco points out, however, that much of this authority concerns no-answer default judgments rather than defaults caused by discovery abuse. It emphasizes again that discovery abuse can include conduct that goes far beyond a mere failure to answer and submits that a trial court must have discretion in an appropriate case to prohibit the sanctioned party's further participation.

We agree that a trial court should have discretion to bar a defendant's participation, such as at the damages hearing in this case, if such a sanction is necessary to remedy the abuse. Even so, such an extreme sanction must be carefully tailored to comport with the requirements of *TransAmerican* and due process. Sanctions that preclude the admission of evidence intrude upon the fact-finding process of a trial just as much as a default judgment on liability. In the latter instance, sanctions that adjudicate the merits of a party's claim or defense cannot be imposed as mere punishment but rather are appropriate only when the sanctioned party's conduct justifies a presumption that an asserted claim or defense lacks merit. *TransAmerican,* 811 S.W.2d at 918. The justification for also barring the defaulted party from the ensuing evidentiary trial on damages must go beyond that presumption because the damages issue is materially different.

The existence, or not, of facts establishing liability lends itself to the first presumption. For instance: Did the defendant's negligence proximately cause the occurrence? *Morgan,* 675 S.W.2d at 732-33. Was the defendant indebted to the plaintiff? *Paramount Pipe & Supply Co. v. Muhr,* 749 S.W.2d 491, 496 (Tex. 1988). Striking the defendant's answer establishes the answer to these questions. The either/or character of liability facts, however, does not translate to a claim for unliquidated damages, which cannot be determined by answering "yes" or "no." By their very nature, unliquidated damages are not susceptible to exact calculation and involve a range of possible answers. For this reason, a defaulting defendant admits facts establishing liability but not any claimed amount of unliquidated damages. *See Holt Atherton,* 835 S.W.2d at 83; *see also Thomson v. Wooster,* 114 U.S. 104, 111, 5 S.Ct. 788, 29 L.Ed. 105 (1885) (allegations that are distinct and positive are confessed by default; matters not alleged with certainty or, which by their nature require examination of details, require the complainant to present proof). So what kind of abuse would justify barring a defaulted defendant's participation at the hearing on unliquidated damages? *Dynamic Health,* the case cited by the court of appeals in this case, suggests spoliation as one example. *Dynamic Health,* 32 S.W.3d at 884.

The destruction of evidence that directly and significantly impairs a party's ability to prove damages might reasonably justify a sanction like the one in this case. But the destruction of this type of evidence is not at issue in this case. The evidence needed to prove Retamco's damages is available. According to Retamco, the information on the various wells has been collected, but at great expense. Retamco asserts that Paradigm's discovery abuse forced it to spend hundreds of thousands of dollars to assemble the data needed to determine its damages—information that Retamco asserts Paradigm possessed and owed it under the 1984 Agreement.

Although punishment may be a legitimate consequence of a discovery sanction, it cannot be excessive. *See Chrysler Corp. v. Blackmon,* 841 S.W.2d 844, 849 (Tex. 1992) (listing securing compliance, deterrence, and punishment as legitimate purposes of discovery sanctions). Sanctions for discovery abuse should not be dispensed as arbitrary monetary penalties unrelated to any harm. *Ford Motor Co. v. Tyson,* 943 S.W.2d 527, 534-35 (Tex. App.—Dallas 1997, orig. proceeding). When discussing excessiveness, we have said that "the punishment should fit the crime" and that the sanction "should be no more severe than necessary to satisfy its legitimate purposes." *TransAmerican,* 811 S.W.2d at 917; *see also PR Invs. and Specialty Retailers, Inc. v. State,* 251 S.W.3d 472, 480 (Tex. 2008); *In re SCI Tex. Funeral Servs., Inc.,* 236 S.W.3d 759, 761 (Tex. 2007) (per curiam). Moreover, discovery sanctions are primarily intended to remedy discovery abuse and should be tailored to serve their remedial purpose. It is not apparent that barring Paradigm's participation in the post-default damages phase of the case served any purpose other than punishment.

Compensatory damages awarded post-default should compensate the injured party for its loss, not penalize the wrongdoer or allow the plaintiff a windfall. *See Torrington Co. v. Stutzman,* 46 S.W.3d 829, 848-49 (Tex. 2000) (noting that the role of compensatory damages is to fairly compensate the plaintiff, not punish the defendant). And although punitive damages are intended to punish the wrongdoer, they nevertheless must bear some relationship to the liability-producing conduct. *See* TEX. CIV. PRAC. & REM.CODE § 41.011(a) (requiring factfinder to consider nature of the wrong, character of conduct involved, degree of culpability, and extent to which conduct offends public sense of justice in determining exemplary damages); *see also In the Matter of Gober,* 100 F.3d at 1205 (noting that conduct sufficient to warrant punitive damages is not regarded as admitted by default). Given this authority and the death-penalty sanction that ended the liability litigation, the additional sanction of precluding Paradigm from the damages trial was excessive. Retamco might have been entitled to a lesser sanction, such as the additional costs and expenses caused by Paradigm's discovery abuse, but barring its participation in the damages trial was "more severe than necessary to satisfy its legitimate purposes." *TransAmerican,* 811 S.W.2d at 917.

* * *

The judgment of the court of appeals is reversed and the case is remanded to the trial court for further proceedings consistent with our opinion.

JUSTICE GREEN did not participate in the decision.

6. *Failure to Comply with Discovery and Related Problems of Discovery Abuse and Sanctions*

Read Rule 215 Texas Rules of Civil Procedure.

ALVARADO
v.
FARAH MFG CO.
830 S.W.2d 911
(Tex. 1992)

Evelina Ortega, Raymond C. Caballero, El Paso, Prof. J. Patrick Hazel, Austin, for petitioner.
Tom Thomas, Marc Culp, Dallas, Crawford S. Kerr, El Paso, for respondent.

HECHT, JUSTICE.

Petitioner's motion for rehearing is denied. This opinion is substituted for our prior opinion.

This is yet another case in which a witness who was not identified in response to a discovery request was nevertheless allowed to testify. The trial court apparently found good cause to allow the testimony because the witness was called as a rebuttal witness. The court of appeals held that admission of this testimony was reversible error, and remanded the cause for a new trial. 763 S.W.2d 529. Consistent with many prior opinions of this Court, we agree with the court of appeals and therefore affirm.

I

While employed by Farah Manufacturing Company, Jose Luis Lerma Alvarado experienced chest pains and was diagnosed as having a pulmonary embolism. Alvarado consulted with an attorney and filed a worker's compensation claim. After receiving medical treatment, Alvarado was released by his physicians to return to work but was restricted from sitting or standing still for long periods of time. This restriction prevented Alvarado from resuming the work he had done before his illness, which required long periods of standing. Farah had other jobs which Alvarado could perform, and he requested reassignment to one of them; but Farah advised him that there were no openings in any of those jobs. In accordance with the collective bargaining agreement which governed Alvarado's employment, Farah placed him on "sustained layoff" status, listing him with other employees in the same status. Whenever a job opening occurred in a particular department, the collective bargaining agreement required that Farah fill the position from the employees on the list, first from those who had worked in that department, by seniority, then from the others on the list, also by seniority. After one year on the list, an employee's seniority and recall rights automatically terminated.

Farah never recalled Alvarado to work, and all his rights under the collective bargaining agreement were eventually terminated. The union did not complain of Alvarado's termination. Nevertheless, Alvarado filed this action for damages against Farah, claiming that Farah had job openings which it should have offered him but did not do so in retaliation for his filing a worker's compensation claim. Thus, Alvarado claims that Farah violated TEX. REV. CIV. STAT. ANN. article 8307c, (Vernon Supp. 1992). Farah denies that it violated article 8307c and asserts that it never recalled Alvarado to work because it never had an opening for a job that Alvarado was both physically able to do and eligible to take under the seniority system which Farah had to follow.

Shortly after filing suit, Alvarado directed interrogatories to Farah, the first two of which asked: 1. Please state the name, address, telephone number, and employer of all persons having knowledge of the occurrences made the basis of this suit. 2. Please state the name, address, telephone number, and employer of each potential witness that you may use in the trial of this case. Farah responded with interrogatories to Alvarado, the first two of which were identical to those quoted above. Neither Alvarado nor Farah objected to these interrogatories; both answered them by identifying several persons.

Six days before trial was set to begin, Alvarado subpoenaed two witnesses to testify who had never been identified in answer to Farah's interrogatories. One of these witnesses, Jacqueline Arrambide, had formerly been employed by Farah in a non-union position. Like Alvarado, Arrambide had sued Farah claiming that she had been terminated in retaliation for asserting a claim for worker's compensation benefits. On the first day of trial, before voir dire commenced, Farah moved to exclude the testimony of Arrambide for the reason that she had not been identified in answer to its interrogatories. The trial court denied Farah's motion. After Farah rested its case, Alvarado called Arrambide as a witness on rebuttal. Again Farah objected, and again the trial court overruled the objection. Arrambide testified that Farah had fired her one week after Farah found out that she had hired an attorney to make a worker's compensation claim for injury to her back. She testified that the reason she was given for her termination was poor attendance at work, even though she had missed only a few days work for medical treatment.

The jury found that Farah violated article 8307c with respect to Alvarado, and that he should be awarded $139,080 actual damages and $1,000,000 exemplary damages. The trial court rendered judgment on the verdict.

II

A

Rule 215(5) of the Texas Rules of Civil Procedure states: A party who fails to respond to or supplement his response to a request for discovery shall not be entitled to present evidence which the party was under a duty to provide in a response or supplemental response or to offer the testimony of an expert witness or of any other person having knowledge of discoverable matter, unless the trial court finds that good cause sufficient to require admission exists. The burden of establishing good cause is upon the party offering the evidence and good cause must be shown in the record. To say that this rule has proven to be problematic is perhaps an understatement. On ten occasions in the eight years since the rule was first promulgated in 1984, this Court has written on whether a witness not identified in response to a discovery request should have been allowed to testify. *Sharp v. Broadway Nat'l Bank*, 784 S.W.2d 669 (Tex. 1990) (per curiam); *Rainbo Baking Co. v. Stafford*, 787 S.W.2d 41 (Tex. 1990) (per curiam); *McKinney v. National Union Fire Ins. Co.*, 772 S.W.2d 72 (Tex. 1989); *Clark v. Trailways, Inc.*, 774 S.W.2d 644 (Tex. 1989); *Boothe v. Hausler*, 766 S.W.2d 788 (Tex. 1989) (per curiam); *Gee v. Liberty Mut. Fire Ins. Co.*, 765 S.W.2d 394 (Tex. 1989); *E.F. Hutton & Co. v. Youngblood*, 741 S.W.2d 363 (Tex. 1987) (per curiam); *Gutierrez v. Dallas Indep. Sch. Dist.*, 729 S.W.2d 691 (Tex. 1987); *Morrow v. H.E.B., Inc.*, 714 S.W.2d 297 (Tex. 1986) (per curiam); *Yeldell v. Holiday Hills Retirement and Nursing Center, Inc.*, 701 S.W.2d 243 (Tex. 1985). In eight of these cases the trial courts admitted testimony which had not been timely identified in response to discovery requests; in none of them did the Court hold that "good cause sufficient to require admission" was shown.

The trial courts in these cases have given various reasons for allowing testimony despite the failure to comply with discovery rules. These reasons seem to share a basic rationale, sometimes expressed and other times implicit, that admitting the testimony allowed a full presentation of the merits of the case. In the present case, for example, the trial court permitted a previously undisclosed witness to testify "In the interest of justice in getting everything on the table, which this court tries to do when possible . . . ." While it is certainly important for the parties in a case to be afforded a full and fair opportunity to present the merits of their contentions, it is not in the interest of justice to apply the rules of procedure unevenly or inconsistently. It is both reasonable and just that a party expect that the rules he has attempted to comply with will be enforced equally against his adversary. To excuse noncompliance without a showing of good cause frustrates that expectation.

The salutary purpose of Rule 215(5) is to require complete responses to discovery so as to promote responsible assessment of settlement and prevent trial by ambush. *See Clark*, 774 S.W.2d at 646; *Gee*, 765 S.W.2d at 396; *Gutierrez*, 729 S.W.2d at 693. The rule is mandatory, and its sole sanction—exclusion of evidence—is automatic, unless there is good cause to excuse its imposition. The good cause exception permits a trial court to excuse a failure to comply with discovery in difficult or impossible circumstances. *See Clark*, 774 S.W.2d at 647 (inability to locate witness despite good faith efforts or inability to anticipate use of witness' testimony at trial might support a finding of good cause). The trial court has discretion to determine whether the offering party has met his burden of showing good cause to admit the testimony; but the trial court has no discretion to admit testimony excluded by the rule without a showing of good cause.

We have repeatedly addressed what factors, standing alone, are not in themselves good cause. Included among these are inadvertence of counsel, *Sharp*, 784 S.W.2d at 672; *E.F. Hutton*, 741 S.W.2d at 364; lack of surprise, *Sharp*, 784 S.W.2d at 671; *Gee*, 765 S.W.2d at 395 n. 2 (lack of surprise is not the standard, but may be a factor); *Morrow*, 714 S.W.2d at 298; and uniqueness of the excluded evidence, *Clark*, 774 S.W.2d at 646. The reasons in each instance are intuitive. If inadvertence of counsel, by itself, were good cause, the exception would swallow up the rule, for there would be few cases in which counsel would admit to making a deliberate decision not to comply with the discovery rules. Determining whether a party is really surprised by an offer of testimony not formally identified in discovery is difficult. The better prepared counsel is for trial, the more likely he is to have anticipated what evidence may be offered against his client, and the less likely he is to be surprised. It would hardly be right to reward competent counsel's diligent preparation by excusing his opponent from complying with the requirements of the rules. As we explained in *Sharp*: A party is entitled to prepare for trial assured that a witness will not be called because opposing counsel has not identified him or her in response to a proper interrogatory. Thus, even the fact that a witness has been fully deposed, and only his or her deposition testimony will be offered at trial, is not enough to show good cause for admitting the evidence when the witness was not identified in response to discovery. 784 S.W.2d at 671. Finally, if good cause could be shown simply by establishing the unique importance of the evidence to the presentation of the case, only unimportant evidence would ever be excluded, and the rule would be pointless.

To relax the good cause standard in Rule 215(5) would impair its purpose. Counsel should not be excused from the requirements of the rule without a strict showing of good cause. The difficulty with the rule lies not so much in the requirement of strict adherence, but in the severity of the sanction it imposes for every breach. The consequences of the rule should not be harsher in any case than the vice the rule seeks to correct. The sole sanction should not be the exclusion of all evidence not properly identified in discovery; rather, as with other failures to comply with discovery, the trial court should have a range of sanctions available to it to enforce the rules without injustice. "The punishment should fit the crime." *TransAmerican Natural Gas Corp. v. Powell*, 811 S.W.2d 913, 917 (Tex. 1991).

As written, however, Rule 215(5) prescribes a single sanction for failing to supplement discovery, and we are not free to disregard its plain language. Nor should we revise the rule by opinion. The Legislature has provided that notice be given before rules amendments become effective. TEX. GOV'T CODE § 22.004. In addition, this Court has structured the rules revision process to encourage advice and comment from the bench and bar, and from the public generally. Any revision in Rule 215(5) should be left to those processes, which are underway. Last year the Court appointed task forces to study the conduct of discovery and the imposition of sanctions, and to make recommendations for revisions in the rules. The Court's Rules Advisory Committee, the State Bar's Committee on the Administration of Justice, and other groups have undertaken similar studies. While those processes are at work, we adhere to the language of the rule and our consistent precedent.

We note, however, that the trial courts are not without power to prevent the enforcement of Rule 215(5) from operating as an injustice in a particular case. When a party has failed to timely identify evidence in response to discovery requests, the trial court has the discretion to postpone the trial and, under Rule 215(3), to impose an appropriate sanction upon the offending party for abuse of the discovery process. Such sanction may be used to compensate the non-offending party for any wasted expense in preparing for trial. Although the trial court should not allow delay to prejudice the non-offending party, the trial court should ordinarily be able to cure any prejudice by a just imposition of sanctions.

B

In the instant case each party inquired of the other the identity of all potential witnesses. Although they might both have successfully objected to the interrogatory, having undertaken to answer it, they were required to do so fully, and to supplement their answers in accordance with the rules. *See Gutierrez*, 729 S.W.2d at 693. Alvarado never supplemented his answers to identify Arrambide as a witness, even though he knew at least six days before trial when he subpoenaed her that she would be a witness. Alvarado does not contend that he did not know of Arrambide until he subpoenaed her. Rather, as good cause to admit Arrambide's testimony over Farah's objection, Alvarado argued at a pretrial hearing that Farah had long known of Arrambide because she had sued Farah herself on a similar claim, that Farah had deposed Arrambide in her own case although not in

Alvarado's, and that Arrambide would be called as a rebuttal witness. The trial court did not make a specific finding of good cause but simply overruled Farah's objection. The fact that Farah was aware of Arrambide and had deposed her in another case, is not, either in itself or in the circumstances of this case, good cause for allowing Arrambide to testify. Neither is Alvarado's use of Arrambide as a rebuttal witness. Alvarado was asked to identify "each potential witness that you may use in the trial of this case." Arrambide was clearly a potential witness, at least when Alvarado subpoenaed her, and Alvarado clearly indicated to the trial court prior to trial that he intended to call her to testify. She could just as well have testified during Alvarado's case in chief as in rebuttal. We hold that Alvarado's tactical decision prior to trial to call Arrambide on rebuttal was not good cause for failing to comply with discovery. *See Walsh v. Mullane*, 725 S.W.2d 263, 264-65 (Tex. App.—Houston [1st Dist.] 1986, writ ref'd n.r.e.). To hold otherwise would be to encourage the very kind of gamesmanship that Rule 215(5) is intended to prevent.

Later during the trial, when Alvarado called Arrambide to the witness stand and Farah renewed its objection, Alvarado asserted a further reason as good cause for allowing Arrambide to testify. Alvarado argued that Arrambide's testimony was necessary to rebut unexpected testimony by Farah's personnel director during its case in chief that Farah would rehire employees with physical limitations. Even if Alvarado's argument had merit, it could hardly support his pretrial decision to call Arrambide as a rebuttal witness. Moreover, the testimony Alvarado claims was unexpected was essentially immaterial. Regardless of whether Farah would or would not rehire employees with physical limitations, Alvarado asserted, and Farah's personnel director admitted, that Alvarado did not have any such limitations precluding his return to work. Alvarado argues, somewhat inconsistently, that he did not call Arrambide to rebut specific testimony by Farah's personnel director, but to impeach him generally. Farah's personnel director was deposed prior to trial, and his credibility was known to be in issue before trial commenced. To the extent Arrambide's testimony was used generally to impeach him, Alvarado certainly knew before trial that she was a potential witness.

We therefore hold that the trial court erred in admitting Arrambide's testimony. The question remains whether that error was harmful. *See Gee*, 765 S.W.2d at 396 (erroneous admission of surprise witness' testimony is not harmful if that testimony is "merely cumulative of properly admitted testimony"), *citing McInnes v. Yamaha Motor Corp.*, 673 S.W.2d 185, 188 (Tex. 1984), *cert. denied*, 469 U.S. 1107, 105 S.Ct. 782, 83 L.Ed.2d 777 (1985); *accord, McKinney*, 772 S.W.2d at 76. Arrambide testified that she had been fired by Farah one week after the company became aware that she had hired an attorney to file a compensation claim. She was the only witness to testify to these facts; her testimony was not cumulative. It was intended to show that Farah had a pattern of firing employees for filing compensation claims. Alvarado's insistence on using her testimony indicates how important he thought it was to his case. Under the circumstances, we hold that the error in admitting Arrambide's testimony was reversible.

* * *

Whether Rule 215(5) should be revised is an issue which we leave to the processes which exist to study such matters. In this case, consistent with the plain language of the rule and our prior precedent, we affirm the judgment of the court of appeals.

DOGGETT, J., not sitting.

MAUZY, J., dissenting [opinion omitted].

Notes

1. Since the decision in *Alvarado* the timetable for designating experts has changed. Under Rule 195.2 "Unless otherwise ordered by the court, a party must designate experts—that is, furnish information requested under Rule 194.2(f)—by the later of the following two dates: 30 days after the request is served, or

(a) with regard to all experts testifying for a party seeking affirmative relief, 90 days before the end of the discovery period;

(b) with regard to all other experts, 60 days before the end of the discovery period.

2. The 1999 Amendments to the Discovery Rules do not cover the subject of discovery sanctions. A separate Task Force is at work on revising those rules.

3. New TEX. R. CIV. P. 195 governs the methods for obtaining discovery regarding testifying expert witnesses, but does not address discovery of consulting experts whose opinions have been reviewed by testifying experts.

ALUMINUM CO. OF AMERICA
v.
BULLOCK

870 S.W.2d 2
(Tex. 1994)

Summary: A party must designate an expert as soon as practical, but not less than thirty days before trial. The penalty for the failure to designate an expert is exclusion of the expert's testimony, unless good cause has been found. The fact that it is impossible to anticipate the need for the experts, as here, may be good cause for the failure to designate the expert where the need for the testimony could not reasonably have been anticipated.

Facts: John Bullock was killed when a forklift overturned and pinned him to the ground. His survivors sued Alcoa and Eaton alleging that his death resulted from gross negligence, etc. in discovery responses, the Bullocks designed Laux, a human factors expert, as a witness. At trial, Laux changed her testimony from the deposition. Alcoa then requested that it be allowed to use two of Bullocks designated and deposed experts. Alcoa had not designed these two (Kirby and Entwisle) as their experts, but the Bullocks had had an opportunity to cross examine them at deposition, and the Bullocks had six days to prepare before the experts were allowed to testify.

Issue: When must a party designate an expert? As soon as practical, but not less than thirty days before trial.

Issue: What is the penalty for the failure to designate an expert. Exclusion of the expert's testimony, unless good cause has been found.

Issue: Did the trial court err in allowing the testimony of an undesignated experts to testify? Yes. The fact that it was impossible to anticipate the need for the experts, as here, may be good cause for the failure to designate the expert where the need for the testimony could not reasonably have been anticipated.

Note

Under Rule 192.3(d), a party is not required to disclose in discovery the identity of "rebuttal or impeaching witnesses the necessity of whose testimony cannot reasonably be anticipated before trial.

Notes

1. In *Henry S. Miller Co. v. Bynum*, 836 S.W.2d 160 (Tex. 1992) the Court held that the trial court had not abused its discretion in letting the plaintiff testify even though the plaintiff had not identified himself in response to an interrogatory that sought the names of all persons with knowledge of relevant facts. The court held that the fact that the witness permitted to testify was both a party to the litigation and had been deposed "may combine to satisfy the good cause requirement." The dissent lamented the fact that the court permitted two individually inadequate reasons of good cause to combine together to equal a positive showing of good cause. The dissent noted that in *Smith v. Southwest Feed Yards, Ltd.*, 835 S.W.2d 89 (Tex. 1992) the Court had held that there was no *per se* party exception to the automatic exclusion sanction of the rule; and noted that in *Sharp v. Broadway National Bank*, 784 S.W.2d 669 (Tex. 1990) the court had held that the fact that a witness had been deposed did not in itself constitute good cause.

2. In *Service Lloyds Insurance Co. v. Harbison*, 826 S.W.2d 930 (Tex. 1991) the Court considered the question of whether supplemental answers to interrogatories are timely filed when the trial court overrules an objection to an "expert witness" interrogatory and directs the party to answer within 30 days of trial without a showing a good cause. The Court stated:

Service Lloyds argues that when the trial court overrules the designating party's objection to an "expert witness" interrogatory and directs the designating party to supplement its answer within 30 days of trial pursuant to Rule 168.6, the answer is timely. We agree.

This court has not addressed the effect of objections under Rule 168.6 upon the admissibility of an undisclosed witness' testimony under Rule 215.5. Rule 168.6 states:

> Answers only to those interrogatories or portions thereof, to which objection is made, shall be deferred until the objections are ruled upon and for such additional time thereafter as the court may direct. Either party may request a hearing as to such objections at the earliest possible time.

TEX. R. CIV. P. 168.6. Rule 168.6 protects litigants from complying with objectionable discovery requests by staying all requirements for answering interrogatories until the date the trial court rules on the objections or directs the parties to answer. A plain reading of Rule 168.6 indicates that the trial court may admit an undisclosed witness' testimony which would otherwise be excluded under Rule 215.5, when that testimony is the product of a deferred answer to an interrogatory. Therefore, we hold that when the trial court overruled Service Lloyds' objection to the "expert witness" interrogatory and directed it to supplement its answer on or before March 2, which was within 30 days of trial, Service Lloyds' supplemental answers to interrogatories filed on February 28 were timely.

3. In *Mentis v. Barnard*, 870 S.W.2d 14 (1994) the Court addressed a party's duty to supplement a discovery request regarding the identity or subject matter of an expert witness. The Rule states that supplementation must occur "as soon as is practical, but in no event less than thirty days prior to the beginning of trial except on leave of court." Rule 215(5) states that a witness not timely designated is automatically excluded unless good cause is shown. The Court held that a party seeking to deny an opponent the right to call a witness has the burden of producing evidence to show that the designation was not "as soon as practical" if the designation is outside the thirty day period. It is only after the opponent establishes this, that a court must then address the issue of good cause.

4. In *Global Services, Inc. v. Bianchi*, 901 S.W.2d 934 (Tex. 1995) the court addressed the use of affidavits in the hearing on sanctions. The Court stated:

> "[W]hen a motion for sanctions asserts that a respondent to a discovery request has failed to produce a document within its possession, custody or control, the movant has the burden to prove the assertion." *GTE Communications Sys. Corp. v. Tanner*, 856 S.W.2d 725, 729 (Tex. 1993). [The plaintiff] has not met this burden. The only evidence he offered was his own affidavit and two exhibits submitted to the court in camera. His affidavit says only that he saw documents at GSI before leaving his employment there that he did not see at the document production seven months later. Even if it is assumed that [the plaintiff] looked through the 300,000 pages of documents GSI produced, carefully enough in less than two days to determine that documents he had seen before were not among them, [the plaintiff's] affidavit is not evidence that GSI had possession of the documents at that time and failed to produce them. [The plaintiff] has not even denied the charge by GSI's officers that if there are documents that were not produced it is because [the plaintiff] took the only copies. * * * [The plaintiff] has averred that he once saw documents in GSI's files that have not been produced. Nevertheless, his affidavit falls short of providing the necessary proof that GSI has failed to produce requested documents. We recognize that it is often difficult to prove that a party has withheld documents from discovery. Direct evidence of such conduct is seldom available, and it may be necessary to rely entirely upon circumstantial evidence. But an imposition of sanctions cannot be based merely on a party's bald assertions. There must be some evidence to show an abuse of discovery before sanctions can be imposed. *Chrysler Corp. v. Blackmon*, 841 S.W.2d 844, 850 (Tex. 1992).

TRANSAMERICAN NATURAL GAS CORP.
v.
POWELL
811 S.W.2d 913
(Tex. 1991)

James Kronzer, Don Henderson, Robert V. Holland, Jr., John C. Nabors, Karen Zuckerman, Bill Jones, Kenneth E. McKay and Joe H. Reynolds, Houston, for relator.

Michael C. Feehan, Beverly Arleen Sandifer, G. Byron Sims, Daniel J. Kasprzak, Jonathan C.S. Cox, Ann Ryan Robertson and Donald F. Hawbaker, Houston, for respondent.

HECHT, JUSTICE.

In this original mandamus proceeding, TransAmerican Natural Gas Corporation seeks to compel the Hon. William R. Powell, Judge of the 80th District Court, to set aside his orders imposing sanctions for discovery abuse. The district court struck TransAmerican's pleadings, dismissed its action against Toma Steel Supply, Inc., and granted Toma an interlocutory default judgment on its counterclaim against TransAmerican, reserving for trial only the amount of damages due Toma. We conditionally grant the writ of mandamus.

I

The underlying case is a complex, multi-party action arising out of Toma's sale of allegedly defective pipe casing to TransAmerican. TransAmerican withheld payment for the casing, apparently some $2.3 million, and sued Toma in April 1987 for damages allegedly caused by its use. Toma counterclaimed for $52 million damages resulting from TransAmerican's refusal to pay for the casing. Numerous other parties also joined in the litigation.

On July 3, 1988, the district court issued a docket control order pursuant to Rule 166 of the Texas Rules of Civil Procedure, which set a discovery cutoff date of April 3, 1989. The order allowed discovery to be conducted beyond that date only upon agreement of the parties.

On March 7, 1989, Toma noticed the deposition of TransAmerican's president, K. Craig Shephard, to take place March 16. Two days later TransAmerican's counsel, who at that time was one of the attorneys in its legal department, telephoned Toma's counsel to inform him that Shephard could not be available on March 16 because of a previously scheduled deposition in another case. When counsel could not agree on another date for Shephard's deposition, TransAmerican filed a motion for protection to quash the deposition notice and postpone the deposition. The motion stated that it would be submitted to the trial court for ruling on March 17. However, the trial court did not rule on the motion on that date.

Beginning April 3, the deadline set by the district court for completion of discovery, the parties' smoldering discovery problem started to flare. On that date, counsel for TransAmerican and Toma agreed that Shephard would be deposed after April 10 on a date to be agreed upon. Despite this understanding, counsel again failed to agree upon a date, and on April 19 Toma noticed Shephard's deposition for May 2 without TransAmerican's consent. On April 20, upon receipt of this second deposition notice, TransAmerican's counsel wrote a letter to Toma's counsel informing him that Shephard would not be available May 2 because, as before, he already had a deposition in another matter scheduled for that day. Toma's counsel replied by letter that he would not agree to reschedule the deposition. On April 27, TransAmerican reset the date for submission of its motion for protection to the trial court for ruling to May 12. By this time, of course, the motion was moot, and it is not apparent why TransAmerican continued to seek a ruling. TransAmerican did not move the trial court to postpone the May 2 deposition.

Also on April 27, Shephard's other deposition scheduled for May 2 was canceled, leaving him available to be deposed by Toma. However, TransAmerican's counsel did not advise Toma's counsel that Shephard's schedule had changed so that he could be deposed on May 2 after all, nor did Shephard appear on May 2 as noticed. TransAmerican ascribes its failure to produce Shephard for deposition to miscommunication concerning his schedule changes between attorneys in its legal department. Toma alleges that Shephard's failure to appear was purposeful and part of TransAmerican's intentional obstruction of the discovery process.

On May 8, Toma filed a response to TransAmerican's March 14 motion for protective order, even though it acknowledged that that motion was moot. Toma included in its response, however, a motion for sanctions against TransAmerican based on Shephard's failure to appear at the May 2 deposition. In return, TransAmerican filed its own sanctions motion on May 11, urging that Toma's motion for sanctions was itself an abuse of the discovery process. Toma's and TransAmerican's motions for sanctions both stated that they would be submitted to the court for ruling on May 12, the date set for submission of TransAmerican's original motion for protection.

On May 12, without hearing oral argument, the district court signed an order granting Toma's motion for sanctions and striking TransAmerican's pleadings in their entirety. TransAmerican moved for reconsideration, which the district court denied after hearing argument of counsel but refusing to hear any evidence. Based upon his May 12 order striking TransAmerican's pleadings, the district court issued an order on October 6 dismissing TransAmerican's action with prejudice, rendering an interlocutory default judgment against TransAmerican and in favor of Toma on its counterclaim, and setting the case for trial solely on the issue of the damages to be awarded Toma.

TransAmerican sought mandamus relief from the court of appeals to compel the district court to set aside his May 12 and October 6 orders. A divided court of appeals denied TransAmerican leave to file its petition for writ of mandamus in an unpublished per curiam opinion. TransAmerican then moved for leave to file its petition in this Court. We granted the motion in order to review the propriety of the discovery sanctions imposed by the district court.

II

The sanctions imposed by the district court are among those authorized for various discovery abuses under Rule 215 of the Texas Rules of Civil Procedure. The district court did not specify what provision of Rule 215 it relied upon. The portions of the rule applicable to the circumstances here are paragraphs 2(b)(5) and 3. Paragraph 2(b)(5) provides in part: If a party or an officer . . . of a party . . . fails to comply with proper discovery requests or to obey an order to provide or permit discovery, . . . the court in which the action is pending may, after notice and hearing, make such orders in regard to the failure as are just, and among others the following:

* * *

(5) An order striking out pleadings or parts thereof, . . . or dismissing with or without prejudice the action or proceedings or any part thereof, or rendering a judgment by default against the disobedient party . . . . At the time of the district court's rulings, paragraph 3 of Rule 215 stated in part: if the court finds a party is abusing the discovery process in seeking, making or resisting discovery . . . , then the court in which the action is pending may impose any sanction authorized by paragraphs (1), (2), (3), (4), (5), and (8) of paragraph 2b of this rule. Such order of sanction shall be subject to review on appeal from the final judgment.

Both paragraphs leave the choice of sanctions to the sound discretion of the trial court. *Bodnow Corp. v. City of Hondo*, 721 S.W.2d 839, 840 (Tex. 1986). However, paragraph 2(b) explicitly requires that any sanctions imposed be "just". By referring to paragraph 2(b), paragraph 3 incorporates the same requirement. Thus, whether the district court imposed sanctions under paragraph 2(b) or paragraph 3, we consider whether those sanctions were just. *See Bodnow*, 721 S.W.2d at 840.

In our view, whether an imposition of sanctions is just is measured by two standards. First, a direct relationship must exist between the offensive conduct and the sanction imposed. This means that a just sanction must be directed against the abuse and toward remedying the prejudice caused the innocent party. It also means that the sanction should be visited upon the offender. The trial court must at least attempt to determine whether the offensive conduct is attributable to counsel only, or to the party only, or to both. This we recognize will not be an easy matter in many instances. On the one hand, a lawyer cannot shield his client from sanctions; a party must bear some responsibility for its counsel's discovery abuses when it is or should be aware of counsel's conduct and the violation of discovery rules. On the other hand, a party should not be punished for counsel's conduct in which it is not implicated apart from having entrusted to counsel its legal representation. The point is, the sanctions the trial court imposes must relate directly to the abuse found.

Second, just sanctions must not be excessive. The punishment should fit the crime. A sanction imposed for discovery abuse should be no more severe than necessary to satisfy its legitimate purposes. It follows that courts must consider the availability of less stringent sanctions and whether such lesser sanctions would fully promote compliance.

These standards set the bounds of permissible sanctions under Rule 215 within which the trial court is to exercise sound discretion. The imposition of very severe sanctions is limited, not only by these standards, but by constitutional due process. The sanctions the district court imposed against TransAmerican are the most devastating a trial court can assess against a party. When a trial court strikes a party's pleadings and dismisses its action or renders a default judgment against it for abuse of the discovery process, the court adjudicates the party's claims without regard to their merits but based instead upon the parties' conduct of discovery. "[T]here are constitutional limitations upon the power of courts, even in aid of their own valid processes, to dismiss an action without affording a party the opportunity for a hearing on the merits of his cause." *Societe Internationale v. Rogers*, 357 U.S. 197, 209-10, 78 S.Ct. 1087, 1094, 2 L.Ed.2d 1255 (1958), *citing Hammond Packing Co. v. Arkansas*, 212 U.S. 322, 350-51, 29 S.Ct. 370, 379-80, 53 L.Ed. 530 (1909), *and Hovey v. Elliott*, 167 U.S. 409, 17 S.Ct. 841, 42 L.Ed. 215 (1897); *accord Insurance Corp. of Ireland, Ltd. v. Compagnie des Bauxites de Guinee*, 456 U.S. 694, 705-06, 102 S.Ct. 2099, 2105-06, 72 L.Ed.2d 492 (1982). Discovery sanctions cannot be used to adjudicate the merits of a party's claims or defenses unless a party's hindrance of the discovery process justifies a presumption that its claims or defenses lack merit. *Insurance Corp. of Ireland*, 456 U.S. 694, 705-06, 102 S.Ct. 2099, 2105-06; *Rogers*, 357 U.S. at 209-10, 78 S.Ct. at 1094; *Hammond Packing*, 212 U.S. at 350-51, 29 S.Ct. at 379-80. However, if a party refuses to produce material evidence, despite the imposition of lesser sanctions, the court may presume that an asserted claim or defense lacks merit and dispose of it. *Insurance Corp. of Ireland*, 456 U.S. at 705-06, 102 S.Ct. at 2105-06. Although punishment and deterrence are legitimate purposes for sanctions, *National Hockey League v. Metropolitan Hockey Club, Inc.*, 427 U.S. 639, 96 S.Ct. 2778, 49 L.Ed.2d 747 (1976) (per curiam); *Bodnow Corp. v. City of Hondo*, 721 S.W.2d at 840 they do not justify trial by sanctions, *Hammond Packing*, 212 U.S. at 350-51, 29 S.Ct. at 379-80; *Hovey*, 167 U.S. at 413-14, 17 S.Ct. at 843. Sanctions which are so severe as to preclude presentation of the merits of the case should not be assessed absent a party's flagrant bad faith or counsel's callous disregard for the responsibilities of discovery under the rules. *See National Hockey League*, 427 U.S. at 642-643, 96 S.Ct. at 2780-81.

In the present case, it is not clear whether TransAmerican or its counsel or both should be faulted for Shephard's failure to attend his deposition. Moreover, there is nothing in the record to indicate that the district court considered imposition of lesser sanctions or that such sanctions would not have been effective. If anything, the record strongly suggests that lesser sanctions should have been utilized and perhaps would have been effective. The district court could have ordered Shephard's deposition for a specific date and punished any failure to comply with that order by contempt or another sanction. He also could have taxed the costs of the deposition against TransAmerican and awarded Toma attorney fees. The range of sanctions available to the district court under Rule 215 is quite broad. The district court dismissed TransAmerican's claims against Toma and rendered default judgment for Toma on its counterclaim solely because, as the record before us establishes, TransAmerican's president failed to present himself for his deposition. Nothing in the record before us even approaches justification for so severe a sanction.

We recognize that we affirmed a similar sanction in *Downer v. Aquamarine Operators, Inc.*, 701 S.W.2d 238, 241-42 (Tex. 1985), *cert. denied*, 476 U.S. 1159, 106 S.Ct. 2279, 90 L.Ed.2d 721 (1986). In that case the trial court struck defendant's answer and rendered a default judgment against it based upon the failure of defendant and his employees to appear for their depositions on three separate occasions without explanation. Even assuming that *Downer* was correctly decided, the instant case does not show the same pattern of abuse present in *Downer*. Furthermore, *Downer's* approval of the sanction of default judgment was specifically based upon the facts of that case, and the holding in that case is limited to those facts. Rendition of default judgment as a discovery sanction ought to be the exception rather than the rule.

There are cases, of course, when striking pleadings, dismissal, rendition of default and other such extreme sanctions are not only just but necessary. *See National Hockey League*, 427 U.S. at 642, 96 S.Ct. at 2780. In this case, however, the record before us establishes that the severe sanctions the district court imposed against TransAmerican were manifestly unjust in violation of Rule 215.

III

We next consider whether TransAmerican has an adequate remedy by appeal. If it does, then the writ of mandamus must be denied. *State v. Walker*, 679 S.W.2d 484, 485 (Tex. 1984). Rule 215, paragraph 3 states that orders imposing discovery sanctions "shall be subject to review on appeal from the final judgment." Today we have held in *Braden v. Downey*, 811 S.W.2d 922 (1991), that sanctions should not be imposed in such a way that effective appellate review is thwarted. Whenever a trial court imposes sanctions which have the effect of adjudicating a dispute, whether by striking pleadings, dismissing an action or rendering a default judgment, but which do not result in rendition of an appealable judgment, then the eventual remedy by appeal is inadequate. Specifically, in this case TransAmerican does not have an adequate remedy by appeal because it must suffer a trial limited to the damages claimed by Toma. The entire conduct of the litigation is skewed by the removal of the merits of TransAmerican's position from consideration and the risk that the trial court's sanctions will not be set aside on appeal. Resolution of matters in dispute between the parties will be influenced, if not dictated, by the trial court's determination of the conduct of the parties during discovery. Some award of damages on Toma's counterclaim is likely, leaving TransAmerican with an appeal, not on whether it should have been liable for those damages, but on whether it should have been sanctioned for discovery abuse. This is not an effective appeal.

We therefore hold that when a trial court imposes discovery sanctions which have the effect of precluding a decision on the merits of a party's claims—such as by striking pleadings, dismissing an action, or rendering default judgment—a party's remedy by eventual appeal is inadequate, unless the sanctions are imposed simultaneously with the rendition of a final, appealable judgment. If such an order of sanctions is not immediately appealable, the party may seek review of the order by petition for writ of mandamus. Although not every such case will warrant issuance of the extraordinary writ, this case does. TransAmerican's remedy by appeal from a final judgment eventually to be rendered in Toma's favor is inadequate.

* * *

Accordingly, we hold that TransAmerican is entitled to the mandamus relief it seeks. We are confident that Judge Powell will vacate his orders of May 12 and October 6, after which he may conduct further proceedings consistent with this opinion. Our writ of mandamus will issue only in the event he fails promptly to comply.

GONZALEZ and MAUZY, JJ., concurring [opinion omitted]

Notes

1. In *Low v. Henry*, 221 S.W.3d 609, the court expounded upon the criterion to be used in determining the amount of sanctions in the following language:

> Henry claims that the $50,000 sanction, a $25,000 sanction for the petition filed against each doctor, is excessive. The amount of the sanction is limited by the trial court's duty to exercise sound discretion. *Powell,* 811 S.W.2d at 917. A trial court abuses its discretion when it acts without reference to any guiding rules or principles, not when it simply exercises that discretion in a different manner than reviewing appellate courts might. *Downer v. Aquamarine Operators, Inc.,* 701 S.W.2d 238, 241-42 (Tex. 1985). In *Powell* we held that a sanction under rule 215 of the Texas Rules of Civil Procedure, now rule 215.2, must relate directly to the abuse found and "be no more severe than necessary to satisfy its legitimate purpose." *Powell,* 811 S.W.2d at 917. Texas Rule of Civil Procedure 215.2 allows a trial court to disallow any further discovery; charge certain expenses, costs, or attorney's fees of one party against the offending party; order certain facts to be established as true; limit a party's ability to defend against or bring certain claims; strike pleadings or parts of pleadings; or find a party in contempt of court. In contrast, Chapter 10 authorizes a sanction ordering the offending party to, among other things, pay a penalty into the court, as ordered in this case. TEX. CIV. PRAC. & REM.CODE § 10.004. The only restriction on the amount of the penalty in the language of the statute is that the "sanction must be limited to what is sufficient to deter repetition of the conduct or comparable conduct by others similarly situated." *Id.* § 10.004(b); *see, e.g., Skepnek v. Mynatt,* 8 S.W.3d 377, 380 (Tex. App.—El Paso 1999, pet. denied) (upholding $25,000 sanction to be paid into registry of court under Chapter 10). The legislative history does not shed light on the question.
>
> Generally, a sanction cannot be excessive nor should it be assessed without appropriate guidelines. *See Powell,* 811 S.W.2d at 917. Although this Court has not specifically identified factors for a trial court to consider when assessing penalties under Chapter 10, *see Altus Commc'ns., Inc. v. Meltzer &*

Martin, Inc., 829 S.W.2d 878, 883 (Tex. App.—Dallas 1992, no writ), the absence of an explanation of how a trial court determined that amount of sanctions when those sanctions are especially severe is inadequate. For example, in *Cire v. Cummings,* we held the trial court was required to explain that it considered lesser sanctions before imposing severe, "death penalty" sanctions. 134 S.W.3d at 842. In *Powell,* we held that the dismissal of plaintiff's case with prejudice for failing to appear for a deposition was an excessive sanction under Texas Rule of Civil Procedure 215. 811 S.W.2d at 918-19. Because we held that the death penalty sanction at issue was "manifestly unjust," we did not identify specific factors for determining appropriate sanctions. *Id.* at 917 n. 6, 919. In his concurrence, Justice Gonzalez recognized that the American Bar Association cumulated relevant factors useful to this type of analysis. *Id.* at 920-21 (GONZALEZ, J., concurring). Although we do not require a trial court to address all of the factors listed in the report to explain the basis of a monetary sanction under Chapter 10, it should consider relevant factors in assessing the amount of the sanction. In addition, the determination of the amount of a penalty to be assessed under Chapter 10, which is not limited to attorney's fees and costs, should nevertheless begin with an acknowledgment of the costs and fees incurred because of the sanctionable conduct. This provides a monetary guidepost of the impact of the conduct on the party seeking sanctions and the burdens on the court system.

2. The suggested criterion for application of sanctions proposed by the American Bar Association alluded to by Justice Gonzalez in the *Transamerican v. Powell* case include:

a. the good faith or bad faith of the offender;
b. the degree of willfulness, vindictiveness, negligence, or frivolousness involved in the offense;
c. the knowledge, experience, and expertise of the offender;
d. any prior history of sanctionable conduct on the part of the offender;
e. the reasonableness and necessity of the out-of-pocket expenses incurred by the offended person as a result of the misconduct;
f. the nature and extent of prejudice, apart from out-of-pocket expenses, suffered by the offended person as a result of the misconduct;
g. the relative culpability of client and counsel, and the impact on their privileged relationship of an inquiry into that area;
h. the risk of chilling the specific type of litigation involved;
i. the impact of the sanction on the offender, including the offender's ability to pay a monetary sanction;
j. the impact of the sanction on the offended party, including the offended person's need for compensation;
k. the relative magnitude of sanction necessary to achieve the goal or goals of the sanction;
l. burdens on the court system attributable to the misconduct, including consumption of judicial time and incurrence of juror fees and other court costs;

* * *

n. the degree to which the offended person's own behavior caused the expenses for which recovery is sought . . . .

AMERICAN BAR ASSOCIATION, STANDARDS AND GUIDELINES FOR PRACTICE UNDER RULE 11 OF THE FEDERAL RULES OF CIVIL PROCEDURE, *reprinted in* 121 F.R.D. 101, 104 (1988).

CIRE
v.
CUMMINGS
134 S.W.3d 835
(Tex. 2004)

Byron G. Lee, Carol Patricia Keough, Coats Rose Yale Ryman & Lee, P.C., Houston, Charles R. Watson Jr., Mullin Hoard & Brown, L.L.P., Amarillo, for petitioners.

L.T." Butch" Bradt, Telschik Law Firm, Houston, for respondent.

JUSTICE SCHNEIDER delivered the opinion of the Court.

The issue in this case is when, if ever, a trial court may strike a plaintiff's pleadings as a sanction without first testing the effectiveness of lesser sanctions. We conclude that in this case, the trial court did not abuse its discretion by striking the plaintiff's pleadings and imposing death penalty sanctions when the plaintiff violated the trial court's orders by deliberately destroying dispositive evidence sought by the defendant in discovery. Thus, we reverse the court of appeals' judgment and accordingly, render a take-nothing judgment against Cummings.

Attorneys George Cire and Martha Adams and the law firm of Taylor & Cire (collectively "Cire") represented Carla Cummings ("Cummings") in a suit against Texas Utilities Fuel Company ("TUFCO"). After the TUFCO litigation settled, Cummings filed a legal malpractice fee forfeiture suit against Cire, claiming that Cire told her the settlement would be "tax free" and that Cire did not explain how the settlement or the resulting attorney's fees would be structured and paid.

During pretrial discovery of the malpractice suit, Cummings testified that she had tape-recorded several conversations with Cire during the TUFCO litigation, including discussions of the settlement negotiations. Specifically, the record reflects that Cummings made between 70 to 100 secret audiotape recordings during the eight months preceding the settlement agreement, and she kept the audiotapes in her home office.

Cire requested production of the audiotapes in discovery and Cummings objected to the request. Cire then moved to compel production. Cummings did not file a response. Without an oral hearing, the trial court entered an order compelling production. The trial court found that Cummings filed evasive, incomplete answers and frivolous objections to discovery requests. The trial court also ordered that Cummings's counsel pay $250 in attorney's fees to Cire's counsel. Cummings did not comply with the trial court's order. Instead, Cummings sought a writ of mandamus, which was denied by the court of appeals and this Court. The trial court again ordered Cummings to comply with the discovery requests, and after Cummings again refused to comply, the trial court granted Cire's second motion to compel. Again, Cummings refused to comply, so Cire filed a motion to strike Cummings's pleadings. It is not contested that Cummings had possession of the audiotapes. Nor is it an issue that Cummings had a duty to preserve the audiotapes once they were sought by Cire in discovery. *See Wal-Mart Stores, Inc. v. Johnson*, 106 S.W.3d 718, 722 (Tex.2003).

At the sanctions hearing, Cummings admitted that she had possession of the audiotapes she made recording conversations with her attorneys. There was testimony that the audiotapes contained recorded conversations regarding the TUFCO settlement and that Cummings planned to "use the audiotapes against" Cire to "help her case." Elizabeth Martinez, Cummings's friend and neighbor, testified that she had seen 70 to 100 audiotapes in Cummings's home office (approximately "two shoe boxes full") that Cummings had made of her conversations with Cire. Martinez also testified that she and several others heard portions of the audiotapes. The audiotapes were the only evidence that would support or disprove Cummings's claims of misrepresentation. The record does not reflect that there was any other evidence that would support either side's position.

Cummings testified at the hearing that she did not destroy the audiotapes and that she did not tell anyone to destroy the audiotapes. However, Cire presented evidence at the sanctions hearing that Cummings burned the audiotapes in the presence of Elizabeth Martinez, and that Cummings laughed with her friends about being a habitual liar. After listening to the evidence presented, the trial court determined that Cummings deliberately destroyed the audiotapes to avoid production, and, based on this determination, properly presumed that her actions prevented Cire from obtaining objective proof that they were not liable. * * * The trial court granted the motion to strike the pleadings as a sanction for Cumming's failure to comply with the discovery order.

In its order, the trial court's primary focus was on Cummings's failure to produce the audiotapes. The trial court found that Cummings "flagrantly violated" four discovery orders by her failure to comply with them, tried to hide her relationship with other attorneys by refusing to answer deposition questions, used forged documents "to gain an advantage with the court," gave conflicting testimony under oath, and "deliberately destroyed and/or concealed material evidence" [the audiotapes] that would "show [Cummings's] claims had no merit." The trial court found that less stringent sanctions would be "ineffective," reasoning that because Cummings's counsel never paid the $250 sanction for filing frivolous objections to discovery, monetary sanctions would not deter Cummings. In addition, the court found that less stringent sanctions could not cure Cummings's wrongdoing based on its presumption that Cummings's destruction of the audiotapes, after they had been repeatedly ordered produced, deprived Cire of objective factual evidence that went to the heart of the proof required to show that Cummings's claims lacked merit. The court of appeals reversed, holding that the trial court abused its discretion when it failed to consider alternative, lesser sanctions and when it did not explain why lesser sanctions would not suffice. 74 S.W.3d at 929. The court of appeals noted that the trial court had only issued sanctions once before striking Cummings's pleadings. Emphasizing that the fine imposed was against Cummings's attorney, the court of appeals concluded that the failure to pay the fine should not be used as evidence that a lesser sanction against Cummings would have been ineffective. The court of appeals also said that the trial court could have and should have considered other, lesser sanctions before it imposed death penalty sanctions. It suggested a less stringent sanction: a spoliation instruction to the jury directing it to assume the missing audiotapes would have been unfavorable to Cummings. Ultimately, the court of appeals concluded that the trial court violated GTE Communications *Sys. Corp. v. Tanner*, 856 S.W.2d 725, 729-30 (Tex.1993), when it refused to consider lesser sanctions.

We granted the petition to consider the issue of death penalty sanctions and to examine whether a trial court's sanctions order must recite why every conceivable sanction would be ineffective in securing compliance and curing prejudice before striking pleadings.

A trial court's ruling on a motion for sanctions is reviewed under an abuse of discretion standard. *Bodnow Corp. v. City of Hondo*, 721 S.W.2d 839, 840 (Tex.1986); *Downer v. Aquamarine Operators, Inc.*, 701 S.W.2d 238, 241 (Tex.1985). The test for an abuse of discretion is not whether, in the opinion of the reviewing court, the facts present an appropriate case for the trial court's action, but "whether the court acted without reference to any guiding rules and principles." *Downer*, 701 S.W.2d at 241; *see also Bodnow Corp.*, 721 S.W.2d at 840. The trial court's ruling should be reversed only if it was arbitrary or unreasonable. *Downer*, 701 S.W.2d at 242.

* * *

Sanctions are used to assure compliance with discovery and deter those who might be tempted to abuse discovery in the absence of a deterrent. *Downer*, 701 S.W.2d at 242. However, a trial court may not impose a sanction that is more severe than necessary to satisfy its legitimate purpose. *Hamill v. Level*, 917 S.W.2d 15, 16 (Tex.1996). Here, the court of appeals relied on our previous holdings in *TransAmerican Natural Gas Corp. v. Powell*, 811 S.W.2d 913 (Tex.1991), and *Chrysler Corp. v. Blackmon*, 841 S.W.2d 844 (Tex.1992), in concluding that the trial court's sanctions were too severe.

In *TransAmerican*, the trial court struck TransAmerican's pleadings because TransAmerican's president failed to appear for a deposition. We held that Rule 215 requires that any sanctions imposed be "just," and explained that there are two components to measuring whether an imposition of sanctions is just. First, a direct relationship must exist between the offensive conduct and the sanction imposed. *TransAmerican*, 811 S.W.2d at 917. We noted that "[t]his means that a just sanction must be directed against the abuse and toward remedying the prejudice caused the innocent party." *Id.* Second, the sanctions must not be excessive. *Id.* In other words, "[t]he punishment should fit the crime . . . courts must consider the availability of less stringent sanctions and whether such lesser sanctions would fully promote compliance." *Id.* (emphasis added). * * * Ultimately, we concluded that the trial court's sanctions in *TransAmerican* were too severe because there was nothing in the record to indicate that the trial court considered the imposition of lesser sanctions. We also noted that the record strongly suggested that lesser sanctions should have been utilized and that they might have been effective. *Id.* We gave several specific examples of lesser sanctions that the trial court could have considered or used before imposing the "death penalty" sanction:

> The district court could have ordered Shephard's deposition for a specific date and punished any failure to comply with that order by contempt or another sanction. He also could have taxed the costs of the deposition against TransAmerican and awarded Toma attorney fees.

Id.

In *Chrysler*, the second case the court of appeals relied on, the trial court struck Chrysler's pleadings when Chrysler refused to produce crash-test reports that were repeatedly requested by the plaintiffs. We noted that "lesser sanctions must first be tested to determine whether they are adequate" before a sanction that prevented a decision on the merits of a case could be justified. *Chrysler*, 841 S.W.2d at 849 (emphasis added). We conditionally granted mandamus relief and ordered the trial court to set aside the order, holding that the trial court had failed to meet the standards set out in *TransAmerican* in four ways. First, there was no direct relationship between the offensive conduct and the sanction imposed, as the plaintiffs did not show that they were unable to prepare for trial without the test reports, and the record did not demonstrate Chrysler's ability to produce the test reports. Second, striking Chrysler's pleadings and rendering a default judgment was more severe than necessary to satisfy the legitimate purposes of sanctions for discovery abuse. Third, no lesser sanction was first imposed. Finally, death penalty sanctions should not be used to deny a trial on the merits unless the court finds that the sanctioned party's conduct "justifies a presumption that its claims or defenses lack merit" and that "it would be unjust to permit the party to present the substance of that position [which is the subject of the withheld discovery] before the court." *Id.* at 850.

Our decision in *Chrysler* was soon followed by *GTE Communications Sys. Corp. v. Tanner*, 856 S.W.2d 725 (Tex.1993). In *GTE*, we conditionally granted mandamus relief when a telephone cord manufacturer was improperly sanctioned for failing to produce a memorandum when there was no evidence that it had actual or constructive possession of the document. *GTE*, 856 S.W.2d at 727. We reaffirmed our *TransAmerican* holding in *GTE*, specifically noting that a trial court was required to consider the availability of lesser sanctions before imposing death penalty sanctions. Under this standard, the trial court need not test the effectiveness of each available lesser sanction by actually imposing the lesser sanction on the party before issuing the death penalty; rather, the trial court must analyze the available sanctions and offer a reasoned explanation as to the appropriateness of the sanction imposed. *GTE*, 856 S.W.2d at 729 ("[T]he record must reflect the trial court considered the availability of lesser sanctions."); *see also Spohn Hosp. v. Mayer*, 104 S.W.3d 878, 883 (Tex.2003) (noting that the record should "contain some explanation of the appropriateness of the sanctions imposed"); *TransAmerican*, 811 S.W.2d at 917. However, we did not overrule the language in *Chrysler* requiring that lesser sanctions first be tested to determine whether they are adequate before a death penalty sanction could be justified in our *GTE* opinion. Instead, we reemphasized that case-determinative sanctions may only be imposed in "exceptional cases" where they are "clearly justified" and it is "fully apparent that no lesser sanctions would promote compliance with the rules." *GTE*, 856 S.W.2d at 729-30. This holding was reaffirmed in *Spohn Hosp. v. Mayer*, 104 S.W.3d 878, 882 (Tex.2003) (requiring a trial court to "consider less stringent measures before settling on severe sanctions," but reiterating that death penalty sanctions may only be imposed in the first instance when the facts of the case are exceptional and such a sanction is "clearly justified").

In light of the *GTE* holding, we must first decide whether the facts of this case make it one of the "exceptional" cases warranting death penalty sanctions. Second, we must determine whether the trial court's discussion of lesser sanctions in its order complies with our earlier holdings in *TransAmerican*, *Chrysler*, and *GTE* that the trial court consider the availability of less stringent sanctions, and in all but the most exceptional cases, actually test the lesser sanctions before striking the pleadings.

* * *

In *GTE*, we required the record to "reflect that the court considered the availability of lesser sanctions." *GTE*, 856 S.W.2d at 730. Nothing in the standard articulated in *GTE* requires that a trial court test the effectiveness of lesser sanctions by actually implementing and ordering each and every sanction that could possibly be imposed before striking the pleadings of a disobedient party. Nor does *GTE* require a trial court to list each possible lesser sanction in its order and then explain why each would be ineffective. *GTE* requires that the record reflect that the court "consider" the availability of appropriate lesser sanctions, and cautions that in all but the most exceptional cases, the trial court must actually test the lesser sanctions before striking the pleadings. *GTE*, 856 S.W.2d at 730. Again, we reemphasize that striking pleadings is a harsh sanction that must be used as a last resort after the trial court has considered lesser sanctions, and that in all but the most egregious and exceptional cases, the trial court must test lesser sanctions before resorting to death penalty sanctions. However, in cases of exceptional misconduct such as this one, the trial court is not required to test lesser sanctions before striking pleadings under our previous holdings in *TransAmerican*, *Chrysler*, and *GTE*, so long as the record reflects that the trial court considered lesser sanctions before striking pleadings and the party's conduct justifies the presumption that its claims lack merit. This means that a trial court must analyze the available sanctions and offer a reasoned explanation as to the appropriateness of the sanction imposed. The trial court's order in this case meets this test.

The imposition of death penalty sanctions in this case was just and not excessive. * * * The sanction was directed against Cummings, the offender, and remedied the prejudice caused to Cire when the trial court presumed evidence going to "the heart of the proof needed" to defend Cummings's claims was destroyed. In a case of such egregious conduct, death penalty sanctions will secure compliance with discovery rules, deter other litigants from destruction of dispositive evidence, and punish Cummings.

The court of appeals stresses that the trial court did not discuss one of the most obvious "lesser sanctions" used in spoliation cases: the trial court's ability to instruct the jury that they should presume that the missing audiotapes would have been unfavorable to Cummings. TEX. R. CIV. P. 215(b)(3); *see Trevino v. Ortega*, 969 S.W.2d 950, 952 (Tex.1998) (defining spoliation as an evidentiary concept that allows "the factfinder to deduce [ ] guilt from the destruction of presumably incriminating evidence"). However, the sanctions hearing record reflects that the trial court considered using a spoliation instruction as a sanction even though it ultimately chose not to do so. The attorneys discussed the *Trevino* case and the potential use of a spoliation instruction at length with the trial court.

A spoliation instruction may be given when a party has deliberately destroyed relevant evidence. *See Wal-Mart Stores, Inc.*, 106 S.W.3d at 721. In this case, although the trial court could have instructed a jury that Cummings deliberately destroyed the audiotapes after they were ordered to be produced in discovery because they would have been unfavorable to her claims, Cire would still have to prepare for and attend a trial, despite a justified presumption that Cummings's claims were meritless. Thus, the trial court did not abuse its discretion by choosing instead to strike Cummings's pleadings. Sanctions are used to punish those who violate the discovery rules, and this is an exceptional case where the only objective evidence that would have supported or disproved Cummings's claims was deliberately destroyed after the trial court thrice ordered it produced. Such intentionally egregious behavior warrants a harsher sanction. Given the extent and severity of the discovery abuses committed by Cummings, this is an "exceptional" case as contemplated in *GTE* where death penalty sanctions are justified. * * * In this case, the trial court did not abuse its discretion by striking the pleadings to promote compliance with its orders.

* * *

We reverse the court of appeals' decision to set aside the death penalty sanctions imposed by the trial court, and we render judgment that Cummings take nothing against Cire.

Notes

1. *Brookshire Bros., Ltd. v. Aldridge*, 438 S.W.3d 9 (Tex. 2014): In considering whether an act of spoliation has occurred, (1) the trial court must determine, as a question of law, whether a party spoliated evidence, and (2) if spoliation occurred, the court must assess an appropriate remedy. To conclude that a party spoliated evidence, the court must find that (1) the spoliating party had a duty to reasonably preserve evidence, and (2) the party intentionally or negligently breached that duty by failing to do so. Spoliation findings—and their related sanctions—are to be determined by the trial judge, outside the presence of the jury, in order to avoid unfairly prejudicing the jury by the presentation of evidence that is unrelated to the facts underlying the lawsuit.

Upon a finding of spoliation, the trial court has broad discretion to impose a remedy that, as with any discovery sanction, must be proportionate; that is, it must relate directly to the conduct giving rise to the sanction and may not be excessive. Key considerations in imposing a remedy are the level of culpability of the spoliating party and the degree of prejudice, if any, suffered by the nonspoliating party. Here, the trial court abused its discretion in submitting a spoliation instruction, because there is no evidence that Brookshire Brothers intentionally concealed or destroyed the video in question, or that Aldridge was deprived of any meaningful ability to present his claim to the jury at trial.

While the spectrum of remedies that may be imposed for spoliation of evidence range from an award of attorney's fees to the dismissal of the lawsuit, the harsh remedy of a spoliation instruction is warranted only when the trial court finds that the spoliating party acted with the specific intent of concealing discoverable evidence, and that a less severe remedy would be insufficient to reduce the prejudice caused by the spoliation. This intent requirement is congruent with the presumption underlying a spoliation instruction—that the evidence would have hurt the wrongdoer.

2. *Petroleum Solutions, Inc. v. Head*, ___ S.W.3d ___, 2014 WL 3511509 (Tex. 2014): Even if finished-product manufacturer spoliated evidence, the sanctions imposed were improper. In this case the trial court struck the defendant's statute of limitations defense. The Texas Supreme Court held that the trial court's sanctions were an abuse of discretion because no proof exists that Petroleum Solutions intentionally concealed evidence or that Petroleum Solutions' spoliation irreparably deprived Head of any meaningful ability to present its claims.

3. *Altesse Healthcare Solutions, Inc. v. Wilson*, 540 S.W.3d 570 (2018): Discovery Sanctions More Severe Than Death-Penalty Sanction Not Justified. The trial court's imposition of sanctions even more severe than death-penalty sanctions for the defendants' failure to comply fully with a temporary restraining order were not justified Under the *TransAmerican* standards, the beyond-death-penalty sanctions imposed by the trial court must be reconsidered. No direct relationship between the sanctions and the conduct of the party sanctioned can be discerned, beyond punishment for its own sake. The effect of the judgment and restraining order was to award the Wilsons the full value of their company at the time it was sold to Altesse, as measured by the agreed contract price. But the judgment and order also awarded the Wilsons all remaining company assets, which were returned to the Wilsons and which they admitted had some value, plus the value of the cash transfers made during the restraining order's pendency, plus attorney's fees, interest and costs. The judgment, if paid, makes the Wilsons better off than if they had never sold their company.

OCCIDENTAL CHEMICAL CORPORATION
v.
BANALES

907 S.W.2d 488
(Tex. 1995)

Joe R. Greenhill, Bob E. Shannon, Joseph R. Knight, Austin, M.W. Meredith, Jr., Clay E. Coalson, Carlos A. Mattioli, J.A. Canales, Corpus Christi, John R. Crews, Dallas, Douglas E. Chaves, Paul W. Nye, Corpus Christi, for relators.

Jeanette Cantu-Bazar, Angelina Beltran, Michael G. Terry, Douglas A. Allison, Rene Rodriguez, Guy H. Allison, Steve T. Hastings, Rose Vela, Corpus Christi, for respondent.

PER CURIAM.

This original mandamus proceeding involves an order that an attorney produce her notes to adverse counsel as a sanction for discovery abuse. We conditionally grant the writ of mandamus.

The underlying suit is a class action toxic tort proceeding. Occidental Chemical (OxyChem) conducted a flaring operation in Corpus Christi. While burning off gases emitted from chemicals that had been delivered by barge, the flame went out and a chemical cloud formed which wafted into the Robstown area. Numerous Robstown residents became ill after the incident, and these representative plaintiffs assert the chemical cloud accident caused the illness and injury.

One of the crucial issues in the case is whether only "ordinary byproducts" of butadiene production were released, or whether some harmful concentrations of toxic chemicals were released. On this issue and several weeks into a lengthy jury trial, the plaintiffs called Billy Riggs, a witness they located only shortly before trial. Riggs was an employee of an independent contractor working for the barge company the day of the accident. He testified that he smelled "pi gas" which would have consisted of a mixture of highly toxic chemicals such as benzene, toluene, and xylene. During his testimony, he revealed that defense attorney Kim McGovern had interviewed him over a year before the trial, that he told her what he observed and that he had concluded that toxic chemicals were involved.

The next day, the plaintiffs filed a motion for sanctions for OxyChem's counsel's failure to disclose Riggs' name in answer to interrogatories. At the hearing, the plaintiffs offered the testimony of Riggs. John Crews, lead defense counsel for OxyChem, offered the explanation that they had to make decisions on how to separate irrelevant names from relevant ones, and that because they had concluded that "pi gas" was natural to the ordinary production of butadiene, they omitted several names. He named seven other similarly situated potential, but omitted, witnesses. Later, when McGovern testified, she added more omitted names bringing to ten the additional potential witnesses similarly situated to Riggs. She suggested that it was more of an oversight or lack of communication by one half of the defense team with the other half that produced the omission.

Concluding that OxyChem's counsel had intentionally hidden the names of fact witnesses known to be potentially adverse to defense positions, the trial court imposed a monetary sanction against the law firm, Crews, and McGovern of $860,000.00. He further ordered that all of McGovern's notes of interviews with or activities of all such undisclosed potential witnesses be produced to plaintiffs. Only these McGovern notes are in issue here; the monetary sanction is not before us.

After an in camera inspection, we agree with relators' assertion that the McGovern notes are attorney work product. OxyChem claims that the work product privilege is "absolute," so that the judge could not order them produced, at least not as a discovery sanction. Alternatively, it argues that the fault lies with their attorneys and that the privilege belonging to the client, OxyChem, cannot be broached to sanction the attorneys' misconduct. Additionally, OxyChem argues that even if the privilege is not absolute, the plaintiffs could not claim the fraud and offensive use exceptions to the attorney work product privilege because they failed to expressly assert them and the production order is not justified as a sanction under the circumstances.

The attorney work product privilege protects two related but different concepts. First, the privilege protects the attorney's thought process, which includes strategy decisions and issue formulation, and notes or writings evincing those mental processes. Second, the privilege protects the mechanical compilation of information to the extent such compilation reveals the attorney's thought processes. *See Nat'l Union Fire Ins. Co. v. Valdez*, 863 S.W.2d 458, 461 (Tex. 1993) (noting that an attorney's litigation file goes to the heart of the work product exemption and citing federal authority holding that "an attorney's selection and ordering of documents in anticipation of litigation is protected work product even where the individual documents are not privileged"). The work product exemption is of continuing duration. *Owens-Corning Fiberglas Co. v. Caldwell*, 818 S.W.2d 749, 751-52 (Tex. 1991).

With respect to an attorney's thought processes, we agree with OxyChem that the work product privilege is absolute, subject only to the narrow exceptions found in the Texas Rules of Civil Procedure. *See* TEX. R. CIV. P. 166b(3)(a) (an attorney's work product privilege is subject to exceptions listed in TEX. R. CIV. EVID. 503(d)). To the extent the trial judge's order does not fit within these exceptions and would cause the breach of the work product privilege by requiring attorneys for OxyChem to reveal their thought processes, we agree that the order to produce the notes was an abuse of discretion.

With respect to compiled information that reveals an attorney's thought processes, the privilege is not absolute. For example, the work product privilege may be waived under the offensive use doctrine. *See Nat'l Union*, 863 S.W.2d at 461. Even though rule 215 of the Texas Rules of Civil Procedure does not expressly mention production of work product or other privileged documents as a sanction for discovery abuse, we cannot agree with OxyChem that the latter type of work product production can never be imposed as a sanction. Orders that privileged documents be produced must be an option for discovery abuse, if the court correctly finds the abuse has waived or otherwise invalidated the privilege.

Concluding that production of information compiled by an attorney is a possible sanction even though the information is the attorney's work product does not end the inquiry. The sanction imposed for discovery abuse should be no more severe than necessary to satisfy the legitimate purposes of the discovery process offended. *TransAmerican Natural Gas Corp. v. Powell*, 811 S.W.2d 913, 917 (Tex. 1991). The work product privilege is essential to the attorney-client relationship. *Owens-Corning*, 818 S.W.2d at 751. Requiring the production of the attorney's notes from interviews of witnesses is a severe sanction and should receive an appropriately strict review. Piercing the work product privilege, like the "death penalty" sanction, should apply only when lesser sanctions are inadequate to correct the discovery abuse that has occurred, i.e., when it is the only appropriate sanction. *Cf. TransAmerican Natural Gas Corp.*, 811 S.W.2d at 917. Here the record does not reflect why lesser traditional sanctions might not cure the discovery abuse. *See, e.g.*, TEX. R. CIV. P 215(2)(b) (requiring sanction to be just); *see also TransAmerican Natural Gas Corp.*, 811 S.W.2d at 918 (interpreting TEX. R. CIV. P. 215). For example, the record does not indicate that any of the ten undisclosed potential witnesses are unavailable and not subject to examination by plaintiffs. We should not be understood as holding that production of attorney work product notes concerning witness interviews can never be appropriate; rather, we conclude that it is not appropriate in this case.

The trial court's erroneous order to produce the privileged notes leaves OxyChem without an adequate remedy by appeal. *Walker v. Packer*, 827 S.W.2d 833, 843 (Tex. 1992). Accordingly, without hearing oral argument, a majority of the Court conditionally grants Relators' petition for a writ of mandamus directing the trial court to vacate its order compelling production of McGovern's notes. TEX. R. APP. P. 122. A writ of mandamus will issue only if the trial court fails to comply.

Note

The Court held in *Remington Arms Co. v. Caldwell*, 850 S.W.2d 167 (Tex. 1993) that a failure to obtain a pretrial ruling on a discovery abuse dispute constituted a waiver of any claim for sanctions based on the alleged abusive conduct. The court noted in *dicta*, however, that post-trial sanctions could be imposed for discovery abuse revealed for the first time after trial.

7. *Privacy of Discovery*

Former rule 166b(5)(c) allowed discovery to be sealed by protective order in accordance with rule 76a's provisions. TEX. R. CIV. P. 166b(5)(c) (repealed 1999); *see General Tire, Inc. v. Kepple*, 970 S.W.2d 520, 524 (Tex. 1988). Rule 192.6 has replaced rule 166b(5) without changing this requirement. TEX. R. CIV. P. 192.6(b)(5).

APPENDIX

Texas Rules of Civil Procedure

Adopted effective Sept. 1, 1941 including amendments received through January 1, 2019.

**PART I.
GENERAL RULES**

RULE 1. OBJECTIVE OF RULES.

The proper objective of rules of civil procedure is to obtain a just, fair, equitable and impartial adjudication of the rights of litigants under established principles of substantive law. To the end that this objective may be attained with as great expedition and dispatch and at the least expense both to the litigants and to the state as may be practicable, these rules shall be given a liberal construction.

RULE 2. SCOPE OF RULES.

These rules shall govern the procedure in the justice, county, and district courts of the State of Texas in all actions of a civil nature, with such exceptions as may be hereinafter stated. Where any statute in effect immediately prior to September 1, 1941, prescribed a rule of procedure in lunacy, guardianship, or estates of decedents, or any other probate proceedings in the county court differing from these Rules, and not included in the "List of Repealed Statutes," such statute shall apply; and where any statute in effect immediately prior to September 1, 1941, and not included in the "List of Repealed Statutes," prescribed a rule of procedure in any special statutory proceeding differing from these rules, such statute shall apply. All statutes in effect immediately prior to September 1, 1941, prescribing rules of procedure in bond or recognizance forfeitures in criminal cases are hereby continued in effect as rules of procedure governing such cases, but where such statutes prescribed no rules of procedure in such cases, these rules shall apply. All statutes in effect immediately prior to September 1, 1941, prescribing rules of procedure in tax suits are hereby continued in effect as rules of procedure governing such cases, but where such statutes prescribed no rules of procedure in such cases, these rules shall apply; provided, however, that Rule 117a shall control with respect to citation in tax suits.

(Amended by Order Sept. 20, 1941, eff. Dec. 31, 1941; June 16, 1943, eff. Dec. 31, 1943; Aug. 18, 1947, eff. Dec. 31, 1947; April 10, 1986, eff. Sept. 1, 1986.)

RULE 3. CONSTRUCTION OF RULES.

Unless otherwise expressly provided, the past, present or future tense shall each include the other; the masculine, feminine, or neuter gender shall each include the other; and the singular and plural number shall each include the other.

RULE 3a. LOCAL RULES.

Each administrative judicial region, district court, county court, county court at law, and probate court may make and amend local rules governing practice before such courts, provided:

(1) that any proposed rule or amendment shall not be inconsistent with these rules or with any rule of the administrative judicial region in which the court is located;

(2) no time period provided by these rules may be altered by local rules;

(3) any proposed local rule or amendment shall not become effective until it is submitted and approved by the Supreme Court of Texas;

(4) any proposed local rule or amendment shall not become effective until at least thirty days after its publication in a manner reasonably calculated to bring it to the attention of attorneys practicing before the court or courts for which it is made;

(5) all local rules or amendments adopted and approved in accordance herewith are made available upon request to members of the bar;

(6) no local rule, order, or practice of any court, other than local rules and amendments which fully comply with all requirements of this Rule 3a, shall ever be applied to determine the merits of any matter.

(Renumbered from former rule 817 and amended Dec. 5, 1983, eff. April 1, 1984. Amended April 10, 1986, eff. Sept. 1 1986; July 15, 1987, eff. Jan. 1, 1988; April 24, 1990, eff. Sept. 1, 1990.)

Notes and Comments

Comment to 1990 change: To make Texas Rules of Civil Procedure timetables mandatory and to preclude use of unpublished local rules or other "standing" orders to local practices to determine issues of substantive merit.

RULE 4. COMPUTATION OF TIME.

In computing any period of time prescribed or allowed by these rules, by order of court, or by any applicable statute, the day of the act, event, or default after which the designated period of time begins to run is not to be included. The last day of the period so computed is to be included, unless it is a Saturday, Sunday, or legal holiday, in which event the period runs until the end of the next day which is not a Saturday, Sunday, or legal holiday. Saturdays, Sundays, and legal holidays shall not be counted for any purpose in any time period of five days or less in these rules, except that Saturdays, Sundays, and legal holidays shall be counted for purpose of the three-day periods in Rules 21 and 21a, extending other periods by three days when service is made by mail.

(Amended by Order July 26, 1960, eff. Jan. 1, 1961; April 24, 1990, eff. Sept. 1, 1990; Aug. 16, 2013, eff. Jan. 1, 2014; Dec. 13, 2013, eff. Jan. 1, 2014.)

Notes and Comments

Comment to 1990 change: Amended to omit counting Saturdays, Sundays and legal holidays in all periods of less than five days with certain exceptions.

RULE 5. ENLARGEMENT OF TIME.

When by these rules or by a notice given thereunder or by order of court an act is required or allowed to be done at or within a specified time, the court for cause shown may, at any time in its discretion (a) with or without motion or notice, order the period enlarged if application therefor is made before the expiration of the period originally prescribed or as extended by a previous order; or (b) upon motion permit the act to be done after the expiration of the specified period where good cause is shown for the failure to act. The court may not enlarge the period for taking any action under the rules relating to new trials except as stated in these rules. If any document is sent to the proper clerk by first-class United States mail in an envelope or wrapper properly addressed and stamped and is deposited in the mail on or before the last day for filing same, the same, if received by the clerk not more than ten days tardily, shall be filed by the clerk and be deemed filed in time. A legible postmark affixed by the United States Postal Service shall be prima facie evidence of the date of mailing.

(Amended by Order Oct. 12, 1949, eff. March 1, 1950; July 21, 1970, eff. Jan. 1, 1971; Oct. 3, 1972, eff. Feb. 1, 1973; July 22, 1975, eff. Jan. 1, 1976; April 10, 1986, eff. Sept. 1, 1986; April 24, 1990, eff. Sept. 1, 1990.)

Notes and Comments

Comment to 1990 change: To make the last date for mailing under Rule 5 coincide with the last date for filing.

RULE 6. SUITS COMMENCED ON SUNDAY.

No civil suit shall be commenced nor process issued or served on Sunday, except in cases of injunction, attachment, garnishment, sequestration, or distress proceedings, provided that citation by publication published on Sunday shall be valid.

(Amended by Order Oct. 3, 1972, eff. Feb. 1, 1973.)

RULE 7. MAY APPEAR BY ATTORNEY.

Any party to a suit may appear and prosecute or defend his rights therein, either in person or by an attorney of the court.

RULE 8. ATTORNEY IN CHARGE.

On the occasion of a party's first appearance through counsel, the attorney whose signature first appears on the initial pleadings for any party shall be the attorney in charge, unless another attorney is specifically designated therein. Thereafter, until such designation is changed by written notice to the court and all other parties in accordance with Rule 21a, said attorney in charge shall be responsible for the suit as to such party. All communications from the court or other counsel with respect to a suit shall be sent to the attorney in charge.

(Amended by Order July 16, 1987, eff. Jan. 1, 1988.)

RULE 8a. [Suspended, *see* Misc. Docket No. 03-9207, Dec. 23, 2003, eff. Dec. 30, 2003.]

(Adopted by Order Oct. 9, 2003, eff. Jan. 1, 2004, only in cases filed on or after effective date. Order Dec. 23, 2003 suspends effective date pending further order of the Court.)

RULE 9. NUMBER OF COUNSEL HEARD.

Not more than two counsel on each side shall be heard on any question or on the trial, except in important cases, and upon special leave of the court.

RULE 10. WITHDRAWAL OF ATTORNEY.

An attorney may withdraw from representing a party only upon written motion for good cause shown. If another attorney is to be substituted as attorney for the party, the motion shall state: the name, address, telephone number, telecopier number, if any, and State Bar of Texas identification number of the substitute attorney; that the party approves the substitution; and that the withdrawal is not sought for delay only. If another attorney is not to be substituted as attorney for the party, the motion shall state: that a copy of the motion has been delivered to the party; that the party has been notified in writing of his right to object to the motion; whether the party consents to the motion, the party's last known address and all pending settings and deadlines. If the motion is granted, the withdrawing attorney shall immediately notify the party in writing of any additional settings or deadlines of which the attorney has knowledge at the time of the withdrawal and has not already notified the party. The Court may impose further conditions upon granting leave to withdraw. Notice or delivery to a party shall be either made to the party in person or mailed to the party's last known address by both certified and regular first class mail. If the attorney in charge withdraws and another attorney remains or becomes substituted, another attorney in charge must be designated of record with notice to all other parties in accordance with Rule 21a.

(Amended by Order July 15, 1987, eff. Jan. 1, 1988; April 24, 1990, eff. Sept. 1, 1990.)

Notes and Comments

Comment to 1990 change: The amendment repeals the present rule and clarifies the requirements for withdrawal.

RULE 11. AGREEMENTS TO BE IN WRITING.

Unless otherwise provided in these rules, no agreement between attorneys or parties touching any suit pending will be enforced unless it be in writing, signed and filed with the papers as part of the record, or unless it be made in open court and entered of record.

(Amended by Order July 15, 1987, eff. Jan. 1, 1988.)

Notes and Comments

Comment to 1988 change: The amendment makes it clear that Rule 11 is subject to modification by any other Rule of Civil Procedure.

RULE 12. ATTORNEY TO SHOW AUTHORITY.

A party in a suit or proceeding pending in a court of this state may, by sworn written motion stating that he believes the suit or proceeding is being prosecuted or defended without authority, cause the attorney to be cited to appear before the court and show his authority to act. The notice of the motion shall be served upon the challenged attorney at least ten days before the hearing on the motion. At the hearing on the motion, the burden of proof shall be upon the challenged attorney to show sufficient authority to prosecute or defend the suit on behalf of the other party. Upon his failure to show such authority, the court shall refuse to permit the attorney to appear in the cause, and shall strike the pleadings if no person who is authorized to prosecute or defend appears. The motion may be heard and determined at anytime before the parties have announced ready for trial, but the trial shall not be unnecessarily continued or delayed for the hearing.

(Amended by Order June 10, 1980, eff. Jan. 1, 1981.)

RULE 13. EFFECT OF SIGNING OF PLEADINGS, MOTIONS AND OTHER PAPERS; SANCTIONS.

The signatures of attorneys or parties constitute a certificate by them that they have read the pleading, motion, or other paper; that to the best of their knowledge, information, and belief formed after reasonable inquiry the instrument is not groundless and brought in bad faith or groundless and brought for the purpose of harassment. Attorneys or parties who shall bring a fictitious suit as an experiment to get an opinion of the court, or who shall file any fictitious pleading in a cause for such a purpose, or shall make statements in pleading which they know to be groundless and false, for the purpose of securing a delay of the trial of the cause, shall be held guilty of a contempt. If a pleading, motion or other paper is signed in violation of this rule, the court, upon motion or upon its own initiative, after notice and hearing, shall impose an appropriate sanction available under Rule 215-2b, upon the person who signed it, a represented party, or both.

Courts shall presume that pleadings, motions, and other papers are filed in good faith. No sanctions under this rule may be imposed except for good cause, the particulars of which must be stated in the sanction order. "Groundless" for purposes of this rule means no basis in law or fact and not warranted by good faith argument for the extension, modification, or reversal of existing law. A general denial does not constitute a violation of this rule. The amount requested for damages does not constitute a violation of this rule.

(Amended by Order July 15, 1987, eff. Jan. 1, 1988; April 24, 1990, eff. Sept. 1, 1990.)

Notes and Comments

Comment to 1990 change: To require notice and hearing before a court determines to impose sanctions, to specify that any sanction imposed be appropriate, and to eliminate the 90-day "grace" period provided in the former version of the rule.

RULE 14. AFFIDAVIT BY AGENT.

Whenever it may be necessary or proper for any party to a civil suit or proceeding to make an affidavit, it may be made by either the party or his agent or his attorney.

RULE 14a. [Repealed effective Sept. 1, 1986]

(Repealed by Order April 10, 1986, eff. Sept. 1, 1986.)

RULE 14b. RETURN OR OTHER DISPOSITION OF EXHIBITS.

The clerk of the court in which the exhibits are filed shall retain and dispose of the same as directed by the Supreme Court.

(Adopted by Order July 20, 1966, eff. Jan. 1, 1967. Amended by Order July 15, 1987, eff. Jan. 1, 1988.)

Supreme Court Order Relating to Retention and Disposition of Exhibits

In compliance with the provisions of Rule 14b, the Supreme Court hereby directs that exhibits offered or admitted into evidence shall be retained and disposed of by the clerk of the court in which the exhibits are filed upon the following basis.

This order shall apply only to: (1) those cases in which judgment has been rendered on service of process by publication and in which no motion for new trial was filed within two years after judgment was signed; and, (2) all other cases in which judgment has been signed for one year and in which no appeal was perfected or in which a perfected appeal was dismissed or concluded by a final judgement as to all parties and the issuance of the appellate court's mandate such that the case is no longer pending on appeal or in the trial court.

The party who offered an exhibit may withdraw it from the clerk's office within thirty days of the later of (1) a case becoming subject to this order, or (2) the effective date of this order. The clerk, unless otherwise directed by the court, may dispose of any exhibits remaining after such time period.

Misc. Docket No. 05-9026, Order Relating to Retention and Disposition of Deposition of Exhibits in Civil Case, Jan. 27, 2005, eff. June 1, 2005.

RULE 14c. DEPOSIT IN LIEU OF SURETY BOND.

Wherever these rules provide for the filing of a surety bond, the party may in lieu of filing the bond deposit cash or other negotiable obligation of the government of the United States of America or any agency thereof, or with leave of court, deposit a negotiable obligation of any bank or savings and loan association chartered by the government of the United States of America or any state thereof that is insured by the government of the United States of America or any agency thereof, in the amount fixed for the surety bond, conditioned in the same manner as would be a surety bond for the protection of other parties. Any interest thereon shall constitute a part of the deposit.

(Adopted by Order June 10, 1980, eff. Jan. 1, 1981.)

PART II.
RULES OF PRACTICE IN DISTRICT AND COUNTY COURTS

SECTION 1.
GENERAL RULES

RULE 15. WRITS AND PROCESS.

The style of all writs and process shall be "The State of Texas;" and unless otherwise specially provided by law or these rules every such writ and process shall be directed to any sheriff or any constable within the State of Texas, shall be made returnable on the Monday next after expiration of twenty days from the date of service thereof, and shall be dated and attested by the clerk with the seal of the court impressed thereon; and the date of issuance shall be noted thereon.

RULE 16. SHALL ENDORSE ALL PROCESS.

Every officer or authorized person shall endorse on all process and precepts coming to his hand the day and hour on which he received them, the manner in which he executed them, and the time and place the process was served and shall sign the returns officially.

(Amended by Order July 15, 1987, eff. Jan. 1, 1988.)

RULE 17. OFFICER TO EXECUTE PROCESS.

Except where otherwise expressly provided by law or these rules, the officer receiving any process to be executed shall not be entitled in any case to demand his fee for executing the same in advance of such execution, but his fee shall be taxed and collected as other costs in the case.

RULE 18. WHEN JUDGE DIES DURING TERM, RESIGNS OR IS DISABLED.

If the judge dies, resigns, or becomes unable to hold court during the session of court duly convened for the term, and the time provided by law for the holding of said court has not expired, such death, resignation, or inability on the part of the judge shall not operate to adjourn said court for the term, but such court shall be deemed to continue in session. If a successor to such judge shall qualify and assume office during the term, or if a judge be transferred to said district from some other judicial district, he may continue to hold said court for the term provided, and all motions undisposed of shall be heard and determined by him, and statements of facts and bills of exception shall be approved by him. If the time for holding such court expires before a successor shall qualify, and before a judge can be transferred to said district from some other judicial district, then all motions pending, including those for new trial, shall stand as continued in force until such successor has qualified and assumed office, or a judge has been transferred to said district who can hold said court, and thereupon such judge shall have power to act thereon at the succeeding term, or on an earlier day in vacation, on notice to all parties to the motion, and such orders shall have the same effect as if rendered in term time. The time for allowing statement of facts and bills of exception from such orders shall date from the time the motion was decided.

(Amended by Order June 16, 1943, eff. Dec. 31, 1943.)

RULE 18a. RECUSAL AND DISQUALIFICATION OF JUDGES.

(a) *Motion; Form and Contents.* A party in a case in any trial court other than a statutory probate court or justice court may seek to recuse or disqualify a judge who is sitting in the case by filing a motion with the clerk of the court in which the case is pending. The motion:

(1) must be verified;

(2) must assert one or more of the grounds listed in Rule 18.2;

(3) must not be based solely on the judge's rulings in the case; and

(4) must state with detail and particularity facts that:

(A) are within the affiant's personal knowledge, except that facts may be stated on information and belief if the basis for that belief is specifically stated;

(B) would be admissible in evidence; and

(C) if proven, would be sufficient to justify recusal or disqualification.

(b) *Time for Filing Motion.*

(1) Motion to Recuse. A motion to recuse:

(A) must be filed as soon as practicable after the movant knows of the ground stated in the motion; and

(B) must not be filed after the tenth day before the date set for trial or other hearing unless, before that day, the movant neither knew nor reasonably should have known:

(i) that the judge whose recusal is sought would preside at the trial or hearing; or

(ii) that the ground stated in the motion existed.

(2) Motion to Disqualify. A motion to disqualify should be filed as soon as practicable after the movant knows of the ground stated in the motion.

(c) *Response to Motion.*

(1) By Another Party. Any other party in the case may, but need not, file a response to the motion. Any response must be filed before the motion is heard.

(2) By the Respondent Judge. The judge whose recusal or disqualification is sought should not file a response to the motion.

(d) *Service of Motion or Response.* A party who files a motion or response must serve a copy on every other party. The method of service must be the same as the method of filing, if possible.

(e) *Duties of Clerk.*

(1) Delivery of Motion or Response. When a motion or response is filed, the clerk of the court must immediately deliver a copy to the respondent judge and to the presiding judge of the administrative judicial region in which the court is located ("the regional presiding judge").

(2) Delivery of Order of Recusal or Referral. When a respondent judge signs and files an order of recusal or referral, the clerk of the court must immediately deliver a copy to the regional presiding judge.

(f) *Duties of Respondent Judge; Failure to Comply.*

(1) Responding to Motion. Regardless of whether the motion complies with this rule, the respondent judge, within three business days after the motion is filed, must either:

(A) sign and file with the clerk an order of recusal or disqualification; or

(B) sign and file with the clerk an order referring the motion to the regional presiding judge.

(2) Restrictions on Further Action.

(A) Motion Filed Before Evidence Offered at Trial. If a motion is filed before evidence has been offered at trial, the respondent judge must take no further action in the case until the motion has been decided, except for good cause stated in writing or on the record.

(B) Motion Filed After Evidence Offered at Trial. If a motion is filed after evidence has been offered at trial, the respondent judge may proceed, subject to stay by the regional presiding judge.

(3) Failure to Comply. If the respondent judge fails to comply with a duty imposed by this rule, the movant may notify the regional presiding judge.

(g) Duties of Regional Presiding Judge.

(1) Motion. The regional presiding judge must rule on a referred motion or assign a judge to rule. If a party files a motion to recuse or disqualify the regional presiding judge, the regional presiding judge may still assign a judge to rule on the original, referred motion. Alternatively, the regional presiding judge may sign and file with the clerk an order referring the second motion to the Chief Justice of the Supreme Court of Texas for consideration.

(2) Order. The ruling must be by written order.

(3) Summary Denial for Noncompliance.

(A) Motion to Recuse. A motion to recuse that does not comply with this rule may be denied without an oral hearing. The order must state the nature of the noncompliance. Even if the motion is amended to correct the stated noncompliance, the motion will count for purposes of determining whether a tertiary recusal motion has been filed under the Civil Practice and Remedies Code.

(B) Motion to Disqualify. A motion to disqualify may not be denied on the ground that it was not filed or served in compliance with this rule.

(4) Interim Orders. The regional presiding judge or judge assigned to decide the motion may issue interim or ancillary orders in the pending case as justice may require.

(5) Discovery. Except by order of the regional presiding judge or the judge assigned to decide the motion, a subpoena or discovery request may not issue to the respondent judge and may be disregarded unless accompanied by the order.

(6) Hearing.

(A) Time. The motion must be heard as soon as practicable and may be heard immediately after it is referred to the regional presiding judge or an assigned judge.

(B) Notice. Notice of the hearing must be given to all parties in the case.

(C) By Telephone. The hearing may be conducted by telephone on the record. Documents submitted by facsimile or email, otherwise admissible under the rules of evidence, may be considered.

(7) Reassignment of Case if Motion Granted. If the motion is granted, the regional presiding judge must transfer the case to another court or assign another judge to the case.

(h) *Sanctions.* After notice and hearing, the judge who hears the motion may order the party or attorney who filed the motion, or both, to pay the reasonable attorney fees and expenses incurred by other parties if the judge determines that the motion was:

(1) groundless and filed in bad faith or for the purpose of harassment; or

(2) clearly brought for unnecessary delay and without sufficient cause.

(i) *Chief Justice.* The Chief Justice of the Supreme Court of Texas may assign judges and issue any orders permitted by this rule or pursuant to statute.

(j) *Appellate Review.*

(1) Order on Motion to Recuse.

(A) Denying Motion. An order denying a motion to recuse may be reviewed only for abuse of discretion on appeal from the final judgment.

(B) Granting Motion. An order granting a motion to recuse is final and cannot be reviewed by appeal, mandamus, or otherwise.

(2) Order on Motion to Disqualify. An order granting or denying a motion to disqualify may be reviewed by mandamus and may be appealed in accordance with other law.

(Added by Order June 10, 1980, eff. Jan. 1, 1981. Amended by Order Dec. 5 1983, eff. April 1, 1984; April 10, 1986, eff. Sept. 1, 1986; July 15, 1987, eff. Jan. 1, 1988; April 24, 1990, eff. Sept. 1, 1990; July 5, 2011, eff. Aug. 1, 2011; July 22, 2011, eff. Aug. 1, 2011.)

RULE 18b. GROUNDS FOR DISQUALIFICATION AND RECUSAL OF JUDGES.

(a) *Grounds for Disqualification.* A judge must disqualify in any proceeding in which:

(1) the judge has served as a lawyer in the matter in controversy, or a lawyer with whom the judge previously practiced law served during such association as a lawyer concerning the matter;

(2) the judge knows that, individually or as a fiduciary, the judge has an interest in the subject matter in controversy; or

(3) either of the parties may be related to the judge by affinity or consanguinity within the third degree.

(b) *Grounds for Recusal.* A judge must recuse in any proceeding in which:

(1) the judge's impartiality might reasonably be questioned;

(2) the judge has a personal bias or prejudice concerning the subject matter or a party;

(3) the judge has personal knowledge of disputed evidentiary facts concerning the proceeding;

(4) the judge or a lawyer with whom the judge previously practiced law has been a material witness concerning the proceeding;

(5) the judge participated as counsel, adviser, or material witness in the matter in controversy, or expressed an opinion concerning the merits of it, while acting as an attorney in government service;

(6) the judge knows that the judge, individually or as a fiduciary, or the judge's spouse or minor child residing in the judge's household, has a financial interest in the subject matter in controversy or in a party to the proceeding, or any other interest that could be substantially affected by the outcome of the proceeding;

(7) the judge or the judge's spouse, or a person within the third degree of relationship to either of them, or the spouse of such a person:

(A) is a party to the proceeding or an officer, director, or trustee of a party;

(B) is known by the judge to have an interest that could be substantially affected by the outcome of the proceeding; or

(C) is to the judge's knowledge likely to be a material witness in the proceeding; or

(8) the judge or the judge's spouse, or a person within the first degree of relationship to either of them, or the spouse of such a person, is acting as a lawyer in the proceeding.

(c) *Financial Interests.* A judge should inform himself or herself about personal and fiduciary financial interests, and make a reasonable effort to inform himself or herself about the personal financial interests of his or her spouse and minor children residing in the household.

(d) *Terminology and Standards.* In this rule:

(1) "proceeding" includes pretrial, trial, or other stages of litigation;

(2) the degree of relationship is calculated according to the civil law system;

(3) "fiduciary" includes such relationships as executor, administrator, trustee, and guardian;

(4) "financial interest" means ownership of a legal or equitable interest, however small, or a relationship as director, adviser, or other active participant in the affairs of a party, except that:

(A) ownership in a mutual or common investment fund that holds securities is not a "financial interest" in such securities unless the judge participates in the management of the fund;

(B) an office in an educational, religious, charitable, fraternal, or civic organization is not a "financial interest" in securities held by the organization;

(C) the proprietary interest of a policyholder in a mutual insurance company, of a depositor in a mutual savings association, or a similar proprietary interest, is a "financial interest" in the organization only if the outcome of the proceeding could substantially affect the value of the interest;

(D) ownership of government securities is a "financial interest" in the issuer only if the outcome of the proceeding could substantially affect the value of the securities; and

(E) an interest as a taxpayer or utility ratepayer, or any similar interest, is not a "financial interest" unless the outcome of the proceeding could substantially affect the liability of the judge or a person related to the judge within the third degree more than other judges.

(e) *Waiving Ground for Recusal.* The parties to a proceeding may waive any ground for recusal after it is fully disclosed on the record.

(f) *Discovery and Divestiture.* If a judge does not discover that the judge is recused under subparagraph (b)(6) or (b)(7)(C) until after the judge has devoted substantial time to the matter, the judge is not required to recuse himself or herself if the judge or the person related to the judge divests himself or herself of the interest that would otherwise require recusal.

(Adopted by Order July 15, 1987, eff. Jan. 1, 1988. Amended by Order April 24, 1990, eff. Sept. 1, 1990; July 5, 2011, eff. Aug. 1, 2011.)

Comment to 2011 Change: Rule 18a governs the procedure for recusing or disqualifying a judge sitting in any trial court other than a statutory probate court or justice court. Chapter 25 of the Government Code governs statutory probate courts, Rule 528 governs justice courts, and Chapter 29 of the Government Code governs municipal courts. Under Rule 18.a, a judge's rulings may not be the sole basis for a motion to recuse or disqualify the judge. But when one or more sufficient other bases are raised, the judge hearing the motion may consider evidence of rulings when considering whether to grant the motion. For purposes of this rule, the term "rulings" is not meant to encompass a judge's statements or remarks about a case.

The amendments to Rule 18b are not intended to be substantive.

RULE 18c. RECORDING AND BROADCASTING OF COURT PROCEEDINGS.

A trial court may permit broadcasting televising, recording, or photographing of proceedings in the courtroom only in the following circumstances:

(a) in accordance with guidelines promulgated by the Supreme Court for civil cases, or

(b) when broadcasting, televising, recording, or photographing will not unduly distract participants or impair the dignity of the proceedings and the parties have consented, and consent to being depicted or recorded is obtained from each witness whose testimony will be broadcast, televised, or photographed, or

(c) the broadcasting, televising, recording, or photographing of investiture, or ceremonial proceedings.

(Added by Order April 24, 1990, eff. Sept. 1, 1990.)

RULE 19. NON-ADJOURNMENT OF TERM.

Every term of court shall commence and convene by operation of law at the time fixed by statute without any act, order, or formal opening by a judge or other official thereof, and shall continue to be open at all times until and including the last day of the term unless sooner adjourned by the judge thereof.

(Amended by Order June 16, 1943, eff. Dec. 31, 1943.)

RULE 20. MINUTES READ AND SIGNED.

On the last day of the session, the minutes shall be read, corrected and signed in open court by the judge. Each special judge shall sign the minutes of such proceedings as were had by him.

RULE 21. FILING AND SERVING PLEADINGS AND MOTIONS.

(a) *Filing and Service Required.* Every pleading, plea, motion or application to the court for an order, whether in the form of a motion, plea or other form of request, unless presented during a hearing or trial, must be filed with the clerk of the court in writing, must state the grounds therefore, must set forth the relief or order sought, and at the same time a true copy must be served on all other parties, and must be noted on the docket.

(b) *Service of Notice of Hearing.* An application to the court for an order and notice of any hearing thereon, not presented during a hearing or trial, must be served upon all other parties not less than three days before the time specified for the hearing unless otherwise provided by these rules or shortened by the court.

(c) *Multiple Parties.* If there is more than one other party represented by different attorneys, one copy of each pleading must be served on each attorney in charge.

(d) *Certificate of Service.* The party or attorney of record, must certify to the court compliance with this rule in writing over signature on the filed pleading, plea, motion or application.

(e) *Additional Copies.* After one copy is served on a party that party may obtain another copy of the same pleading upon tendering reasonable payment for copying and delivering.

(f) *Electronic Filing.*

(1) Requirement. Except in juvenile cases under Title 3 of the Family Code and truancy cases under Title 3A of the Family Code, attorneys must electronically file documents in courts where electronic filing has been mandated. Attorneys practicing in courts where electronic filing is available but not mandated and unrepresented parties may electronically file documents, but it is not required.

(2) Email Address. The email address of an attorney or unrepresented party who electronically files a document must be included on the document.

(3) Mechanism. Electronic filing must be done through the electronic filing manager established by the Office of Court Administration and an electronic filing service provider certified by the Office of Court Administration.

(4) Exceptions.

(A) Wills are not required to be filed electronically.

(B) The following documents must not be filed electronically:

(i) documents filed under seal or presented to the court in camera; and

(ii) documents to which access is otherwise restricted by law or court order.

(C) For good cause, a court may permit a party to file other documents in paper form in a particular case.

(5) Timely Filing. Unless a document must be filed by a certain time of day, a document is considered timely filed if it is electronically filed at any time before midnight (in the court's time zone) on the filing deadline. An electronically filed document is deemed filed when transmitted to the filing party's electronic filing service provider, except:

(A) if a document is transmitted on a Saturday, Sunday, or legal holiday, it is deemed filed on the next day that is not a Saturday, Sunday, or legal holiday; and

(B) if a document requires a motion and an order allowing its filing, the document is deemed filed on the date that the motion is granted.

(6) Technical Failure. If a document is untimely due to a technical failure or a system outage, the filing party may seek appropriate relief from the court. If the missed deadline is one imposed by these rules, the filing party must be given a reasonable extension of time to complete the filing.

(7) Electronic Signatures. A document that is electronically served, filed, or issued by a court or clerk is considered signed if the document includes:

(A) a "/s/" and name typed in the space where the signature would otherwise appear, unless the document is notarized or sworn; or

(B) an electronic image or scanned image of the signature.

(8) Format. An electronically filed document must:

(A) be in text-searchable portable document format (PDF);

(B) be directly converted to PDF rather than scanned, if possible;

(C) not be locked; and

(D) otherwise comply with the Technology Standards set by the Judicial Committee on Information Technology and approved by the Supreme Court.

(9) Paper Copies. Unless required by local rule, a party need not file a paper copy of an electronically filed document.

(10) Electronic Notices From the Court. The clerk may send notices, orders, or other communications about the case to the party electronically. A court seal may be electronic.

(11) Non-Conforming Documents. The clerk may not refuse to file a document that fails to conform with this rule. But the clerk may identify the error to be corrected and state a deadline for the party to resubmit the document in a conforming format.

(12) Original Wills. When a party electronically files an application to probate a document as an original will, the original will must be filed with the clerk within three business days after the application is filed.

(13) Official Record. The clerk may designate an electronically filed document or a scanned paper document as the official court record. The clerk is not required to keep both paper and electronic versions of the same document unless otherwise required by local rule. But the clerk must retain an original will filed for probate in a numbered file folder.

(Amended by Order Sept. 20, 1941, eff. Dec. 31, 1941; Aug. 18, 1947, eff. Dec. 31, 1947; July 11, 1977, eff. Jan. 1, 1978; June 10, 1980, eff. Jan. 1, 1981; April 24, 1990, eff. Sept. 1, 1990; Aug. 16, 2013, eff. Jan. 1, 2014; Dec. 13, 2013, eff. Jan. 1, 2014; Tex. Sup. Ct. Misc. Docket No. 15-9155 Aug. 28, 2015, eff. Sept. 1, 2015.)

Comment to 2013 Change: Rule 21 is revised to incorporate rules for electronic filing, in accordance with the Supreme Court's order—Misc. Docket No. 12-9206, amended by Misc. Docket Nos. 13-9092 and 13-9164—mandating electronic filing in civil cases beginning on January 1, 2014. The mandate will be implemented according to the schedule in the order and will be completed by July 1, 2016. The revisions reflect the fact that the mandate will only apply to a subset of Texas courts until that date.

Technology Standards (These standards apply to documents filed electronically under Texas Rule of Civil Procedure 21 and Texas Rule of Appellate Procedure 9.)

RULE 21a. METHODS OF SERVICE.

(a) Methods of Service. Every notice required by these rules, and every pleading, plea, motion, or other form of request required to be served under Rule 21, other than the citation to be served upon the filing of a cause of action and except as otherwise expressly provided in these rules, may be served by delivering a copy to the party to be served, or the party's duly authorized agent or attorney of record in the manner specified below:

(1) Documents Filed Electronically. A document filed electronically under Rule 21 must be served electronically through the electronic filing manager if the email address of the party or attorney to be served is on file with the electronic filing manager. If the email address of the party or attorney to be served is not on file with the electronic filing manager, the document may be served on that party or attorney under subparagraph (2).

(2) Documents Not Filed Electronically. A document not filed electronically may be served in person, by mail, by commercial delivery service, by fax, by email, or by such other manner as the court in its discretion may direct.

(b) When Complete.

(1) Service by mail or commercial delivery service shall be complete upon deposit of the document, postpaid and properly addressed, in the mail or with a commercial delivery service.

(2) Service by fax is complete on receipt. Service completed after 5:00 p.m. local time of the recipient shall be deemed served on the following day.

(3) Electronic service is complete on transmission of the document to the serving party's electronic filing service provider. The electronic filing manager will send confirmation of service to the serving party.

(c) Time for Action After Service. Whenever a party has the right or is required to do some act within a prescribed period after the service of a notice or other paper upon him and the notice or paper is served upon him by mail, three days shall be added to the prescribed period.

(d) Who May Serve. Notice may be served by a party to the suit, an attorney of record, a sheriff or constable, or by any other person competent to testify.

(e) Proof of Service. The party or attorney of record shall certify to the court compliance with this rule in writing over signature and on the filed instrument. A certificate by a party or an attorney of record, or the return of the officer, or the affidavit of any other person showing service of a notice shall be prima facie evidence of the fact of service. Nothing herein shall preclude any party from offering proof that the document was not received, or, if service was by mail, that the document was not received within three days from the date that it was deposited in the mail, and upon so finding, the court may extend the time for taking the action required of such party or grant such other relief as it deems just.

(f) Procedures Cumulative. These provisions are cumulative of all other methods of service prescribed by these rules.

(Adopted by Order Aug. 18, 1947, eff. Dec. 31, 1947. Amended by Order July 21, 1970, eff. Jan. 1, 1971; Oct. 3, 1972, eff. Feb. 1, 1973, July 11 1977, eff. Jan. 1, 1978; June 10, 1980, eff. Jan. 1, 1981; Dec. 5, 1983, eff. April 1, 1984; April 24, 1990, eff. Sept. 1, 1990; Aug. 16, 2013, eff. Jan. 1, 2014; Dec. 13, 2013, eff. Jan. 1, 2014.)

Comment to 2013 Change: Rule 21a is revised to incorporate rules for electronic service in accordance with the Supreme Court's order—Misc. Docket No. 12-9206, amended by Misc. Docket Nos. 13-9092 and 13-9164—mandating electronic filing in civil cases beginning on January 1, 2014.

Technology Standards (These standards apply to documents filed electronically under Texas Rule of Civil Procedure 21 and Texas Rule of Appellate Procedure 9.)

RULE 21b. SANCTIONS FOR FAILURE TO SERVE OR DELIVER COPY OF PLEADINGS AND MOTIONS.

If any party fails to serve on or deliver to the other parties a copy of any pleading, plea, motion, or other application to the court for an order in accordance with Rules 21 and 21a, the court may in its discretion, after notice and hearing, impose an appropriate sanction available under Rule 215-2b.

(Adopted by Order April 24, 1990, eff. Sept. 1, 1990.)

[RULE 21c. Repealed effective September 1, 1986.]

RULE 21c. PRIVACY PROTECTION FOR FILED DOCUMENTS.

(a) Sensitive Data Defined. Sensitive data consists of:
   (1) a driver's license number, passport number, social security number, tax identification number, or similar government-issued personal identification number;
   (2) a bank account number, credit card number, or other financial account number; and
   (3) a birth date, home address, and the name of any person who was a minor when the underlying suit was filed.

(b) Filing of Documents Containing Sensitive Data Prohibited. Unless the inclusion of sensitive data is specifically required by a statute, court rule, or administrative regulation, an electronic or paper document, except for wills and documents filed under seal, containing sensitive data may not be filed with a court unless the sensitive data is redacted.

(c) Redaction of Sensitive Data; Retention Requirement. Sensitive data must be redacted by using the letter "X" in place of each omitted digit or character or by removing the sensitive data in a manner indicating that the data has been redacted. The filing party must retain an unredacted version of the filed document during the pendency of the case and any related appellate proceedings filed within six months of the date the judgment is signed.

(d) Notice to Clerk. If a document must contain sensitive data, the filing party must notify the clerk by:
   (1) designating the document as containing sensitive data when the document is electronically filed; or
   (2) if the document is not electronically filed, by including, on the upper lefthand side of the first page, the phrase: "NOTICE: THIS DOCUMENT CONTAINS SENSITIVE DATA."

(e) Non-Conforming Documents. The clerk may not refuse to file a document that contains sensitive data in violation of this rule. But the clerk may identify the error to be corrected and state a deadline for the party to resubmit a redacted, substitute document.

(f) Restriction on Remote Access. Documents that contain sensitive data in violation of this rule must not be posted on the Internet.

(Adopted by Order Aug. 16, 2013, eff. Jan. 1, 2014; Dec. 13, 2013, eff. Jan. 1, 2014.)

Comment to 2013 Change: Rule 21c is added to provide privacy protection for documents filed in civil cases.

SECTION 2.
INSTITUTION OF SUIT

RULE 22. COMMENCED BY PETITION.

A civil suit in the district or county court shall be commenced by a petition filed in the office of the clerk.

RULE 23. SUITS TO BE NUMBERED CONSECUTIVELY.

It shall be the duty of the clerk to designate the suits by regular consecutive numbers, called file numbers, and he shall mark on each paper in every case the file number of the cause.

RULE 24. DUTY OF CLERK.

When a petition is filed with the clerk he shall indorse thereon the file number, the day on which it was filed and the time of filing, and sign his name officially thereto.

RULE 25. CLERK'S FILE DOCKET.

Each clerk shall keep a file docket which shall show in convenient form the number of the suit, the names of the attorneys, the names of the parties to the suit, and the nature thereof, and, in brief form, the officer's return on the process, and all subsequent proceedings had in the case with the dates thereof.

RULE 26. CLERK'S COURT DOCKET.

Each clerk shall also keep a court docket in a permanent record that shall include the number of the case and the names of the parties, the names of the attorneys, the nature of the action, the pleas, the motions, and the ruling of the court as made.

(Amended by Order April 24, 1990, eff. Sept. 1, 1990.)

RULE 27. ORDER OF CASES.

The cases shall be placed on the docket as they are filed.

SECTION 3.
PARTIES TO SUITS

RULE 28. SUITS IN ASSUMED NAME.

Any partnership, unincorporated association, private corporation, or individual doing business under an assumed name may sue or be sued in its partnership, assumed or common name for the purpose of enforcing for or against it a substantive right, but on a motion by any party or on the court's own motion the true name may be substituted.

(Amended by Order July 21, 1970, eff. Jan. 1, 1971.)

RULE 29. SUIT ON CLAIM AGAINST DISSOLVED CORPORATION.

When no receiver has been appointed for a corporation which has dissolved, suit may be instituted on any claim against said corporation as though the same had not been dissolved, and service of process may be obtained on the president, directors, general manager, trustee, assignee, or other person in charge of the affairs of the corporation at the time it was dissolved, and judgment may be rendered as though the corporation had not been dissolved.

RULE 30. PARTIES TO SUITS.

Assignors, endorsers and other parties not primarily liable upon any instruments named in the chapter of the Business and Commerce Code, dealing with commercial paper, may be jointly sued with their principal obligors, or may be sued alone in the cases provided for by statute.

(Amended by Order July 15, 1987, eff. Jan. 1, 1988.)

RULE 31. SURETY NOT TO BE SUED ALONE.

No surety shall be sued unless his principal is joined with him, or unless a judgment has previously been rendered against his principal, except in cases otherwise provided for in the law and these rules.

RULE 32. MAY HAVE QUESTION OF SURETYSHIP TRIED.

When any suit is brought against two or more defendants upon any contract, any one or more of the defendants being surety for the other, the surety may cause the question of suretyship to be tried and determined upon the issue made for the parties defendant at the trial of the cause, or at any time before or after the trial or at a subsequent term. Such proceedings shall not delay the suit of the plaintiff.

RULE 33. SUITS OR AGAINST COUNTIES.

Suits by or against a county or incorporated city, town or village shall be in its corporate name.

RULE 34. AGAINST SHERIFF, ETC.

Whenever a sheriff, constable, or a deputy or either has been sued for damages for any act done in his official character, and has taken an indemnifying bond for the acts upon which the suit is based, he may make the principal and surety on such bond parties defendant in such suit, and the cause may be continued to obtain service on such parties.

RULE 35. ON OFFICIAL BONDS.

In suits brought by the State or any county, city, independent school district, irrigation district, or other political subdivision of the State, against any officer who has held an office for more than one term, or against any depository which has been such depository for more than one term, or has given more than one official bond the sureties on each and all such bonds may be joined as defendants in the same suit whenever it is difficult to determine when the default sued for occurred and which set of sureties on such bonds is liable therefor.

(Amended by Order June 16, 1943, eff. Dec. 13, 1943.)

RULE 36. DIFFERENT OFFICIALS AND BONDSMEN.

In suits by the State upon the official bond of a State officer, any subordinate officer who has given bond, payable either to the State or such superior officer, to cover all or part of the default sued for together with the sureties on his official bond, may be joined as defendants with such superior officer and his bondsmen whenever it is alleged in the petition that both of such officers are liable for the money sued for.

RULE 37. ADDITIONAL PARTIES.

Before a case is called for trial, additional parties, necessary or proper parties to the suit, may be brought in, either by the plaintiff or the defendant, upon such terms as the court may prescribe; but not at a time nor in a manner to unreasonably delay the trial of the case.

RULE 38. THIRD-PARTY PRACTICE.

(a) **When Defendant May Bring in Third Party.** At any time after commencement of the action a defending party, as a third-party plaintiff, may cause a citation and petition to be served upon a person not a party to the action who is or may be liable to him or to the plaintiff for all or part of the plaintiff's claim against him. The third-party plaintiff need not obtain leave to make the service if he files the third-party petition not later than thirty (30) days after he serves his original answer. Otherwise, he must obtain leave on motion upon notice to all parties to the action. The person served, hereinafter called the third-party defendant, shall make his defenses to the third-party plaintiff's claim under the rules applicable to the defendant, and his counterclaims against the third-party plaintiff and cross-claims against other third-party defendants as provided in Rule 97. The third-party defendant may assert against the plaintiff any defenses which the third-party plaintiff has to the plaintiff's claim. The third-party defendant may also assert any claim against the plaintiff arising out of the transaction or occurrence that is the subject matter of the plaintiff's claim against the third-party plaintiff The plaintiff may assert any claim against the third-party defendant arising out of the transaction or occurrence that is the subject matter of the plaintiff's claim against the third-party plaintiff, and the third-party defendant thereupon shall assert his defenses and his counterclaims and cross-claims. Any party may move to strike the third-party claim, or for its severance or separate trial. A third-party defendant may proceed under this rule against any person not a party to the action who is or who may be liable to him or to the third-party plaintiff for all or part of the claim made in the action against the third-party defendant.

(b) **When Plaintiff May Bring in Third Party.** When a counterclaim is asserted against a plaintiff, he may cause a third party to be brought in under circumstances which under this rule would entitle a defendant to do so.

(c) This rule shall not be applied, in tort cases, so as to permit the joinder of a liability or indemnity insurance company, unless such company is by statute or contract liable to the person injured or damaged.

(d) This rule shall not be applied so as to violate any venue statute, as venue would exist absent this rule.

(Amended by Order March 31, 1941, eff. Sept. 1, 1941; Dec. 5, 1983, eff. April 1, 1984.)

RULE 39. JOINDER OF PERSONS NEEDED FOR JUST ADJUDICATION.

(a) Persons to Be Joined if Feasible. A person who is subject to service of process shall be joined as a party in the action if

- (1) in his absence complete relief cannot be accorded among those already parties or
- (2) he claims an interest relating to the subject of the action and is so situated that the disposition of the action in his absence may
  - (i) as a practical matter impair or impede his ability to protect that interest or
  - (ii) leave any of the persons already parties subject to a substantial risk of incurring double, multiple, or otherwise inconsistent obligations by reason of his claimed interest. If he has not been so joined, the court shall order that he be made a party. If he should join as a plaintiff but refuses to do so, he may be made a defendant, or, in a proper case, an involuntary plaintiff.

(b) **Determination by Court Whenever Joinder Not Feasible.** If a person as described in subdivision (a)(1)-(2) hereof cannot be made a party, the court shall determine whether in equity and good conscience the action should proceed among the parties before it or should be dismissed, the absent person being thus regarded as indispensable. The factors to be considered by the court include: first, to what extent a judgment rendered in the person's absence might be prejudicial to him or those already parties; second, the extent to which, by protective provisions in the judgment, by the shaping of relief, or other measures the prejudice can be lessened or avoided, third whether a judgment rendered in the person's absence will be adequate; fourth, whether the plaintiff will have an adequate remedy if the action is dismissed for non-joinder.

(c) **Pleading Reasons for Nonjoinder.** A pleading asserting a claim for relief shall state the names, if known to the pleader, of any persons as described in subdivision (a)(1)-(2) hereof who are not joined, and the reasons why they are not joined.

(d) **Exception of Class Actions.** This rule is subject to the provisions of Rule 42.

(Amended by Order July 21, 1970, eff. Jan. 1, 1971.)

RULE 40. PERMISSIVE JOINDER OF PARTIES.

(a) **Permissive Joinder.** All persons may join in one action as plaintiffs if they assert any right to relief jointly, severally, or in the alternative in respect of or arising out of the same transaction, occurrence, or series of transactions or occurrences and if any question of law or fact common to all of them will arise in the action. All persons may be joined in one action as defendants if there is asserted against them jointly, severally, or in the alternative any right to relief in respect of or arising out of the same transaction, occurrence, or series of transactions or occurrences and if any question of law or fact common to all of them will arise in the action. A plaintiff or defendant need not be interested in obtaining or defending against all the relief demanded. Judgment may be given for one or more of the plaintiffs according to their respective rights to relief, and against one or more defendants according to their respective liabilities.

(b) **Separate Trials.** The court may make such orders as will prevent a party from being embarrassed, delayed, or put to expense by the inclusion of a party against whom he asserts no claim and who asserts no claim against him, and may order separate trials or make other orders to prevent delay or prejudice.

RULE 41. MISJOINDER AND NONJOINDER OF PARTIES.

Misjoinder of parties is not ground for dismissal of an action. Parties may be dropped or added, or suits filed separately may be consolidated, or actions which have been improperly joined may be severed and each ground of recovery improperly joined may be docketed as a separate suit between the same parties, by order of the court on motion of any party or on its own initiative at any stage of the action, before the time of submission to the jury or to the court if trial is without a jury, on such terms as are just. Any claim against a party may be severed and proceeded with separately.

(Amended by Order March 31, 1941, eff. Sept. 1, 1941.)

RULE 42. CLASS ACTIONS.

(a) Prerequisites to a Class Action. One or more members of a class may sue or be sued as representative parties on behalf of all only if (1) the class is so numerous that joinder of all members is impracticable, (2) there are questions of law or fact common to the class, (3) the claims or defenses of the representative parties are typical of the claims or defenses of the class, and (4) the representative parties will fairly and adequately protect the interests of the class.

(b) Class Actions Maintainable. An action may be maintained as a class action if the prerequisites of subdivision (a) are satisfied, and in addition:

- (1) the prosecution of separate actions by or against individual members of the class would create a risk of
  - (A) inconsistent or varying adjudications with respect to individual members of the class which would establish incompatible standards of conduct for the party opposing the class, or
  - (B) adjudications with respect to individual members of the class which would as a practical matter be dispositive of the interests of the other members not parties to the adjudications or substantially impair or impede their ability to protect their interests; or
- (2) the party opposing the class has acted or refused to act on grounds generally applicable to the class, thereby making appropriate final injunctive relief or corresponding declaratory relief with respect to the class as a whole; or
- (3) the questions of law or fact common to the members of the class predominate over any questions affecting only individual members, and a class action is superior to other available methods for the fair and efficient adjudication of the controversy. The matters pertinent to these issues include:
  - (A) the interest of members of the class in individually controlling the prosecution or defense of separate actions;
  - (B) the extent and nature of any litigation concerning the controversy already commenced by or against members of the class;
  - (C) the desirability or undesirability of concentrating the litigation of the claims in the particular forum; and
  - (D) the difficulties likely to be encountered in the management of a class action.

(c) **Determination by Order Whether to Certify a Class Action; Notice and Membership in Class.**

- (1) (A) When a person sues or is sued as a representative of a class, the court must—at an early practicable time—determine by order whether to certify the action as a class action.

(B) An order certifying a class action must define the class and the class claims, issues, or defenses, and must appoint class counsel under Rule 42(g).

(C) An order under Rule 42(c)(1) may be altered or amended before final judgment. The court may order the naming of additional parties in order to insure the adequacy of representation.

(D) An order granting or denying certification under Rule 42(b)(3) must state:

(i) he elements of each claim or defense asserted in the pleadings;

(ii) any issues of law or fact common to the class members;

(iii) any issues of law or fact affecting only individual class members;

(iv) the issues that will be the object of most of the efforts of the litigants and the court;

(v) other available methods of adjudication that exist for the controversy;

(vi) why the issues common to the members of the class do or do not predominate over individual issues;

(vii) why a class action is or is not superior to other available methods for the fair and efficient adjudication of the controversy; and

(viii)if a class is certified, how the class claims and any issues affecting only individual members, raised by the claims or defenses asserted in the pleadings, will be tried in a manageable, time efficient manner.

(2) (A) For any class certified under Rule 42(b)(1) or (2), the court may direct appropriate notice to the class.

(B) For any class certified under Rule 42(b)(3), the court must direct to class members the best notice practicable under the circumstances, including individual notice to all members who can be identified through reasonable effort. The notice must concisely and clearly state in plain, easily understood language:

(i) the nature of the action;

(ii) the definition of the class certified;

(iii) the class claims, issues, or defenses;

(iv) that a class member may enter an appearance through counsel if the member so desires;

(v) that the court will exclude from the class any member who requests exclusion, stating when and how members may elect to be excluded; and

(vi) the binding effect of a class judgment on class members under Rule 42(c)(3).

(3) The judgment in an action maintained as a class action under subdivision (b)(1) or (b)(2) whether or not favorable to the class, shall include and describe those whom the court finds to be members of the class. The judgment in an action maintained as a class action under subdivision (b)(3), whether or not favorable to the class, shall include and specify or describe those to whom the notice provided in subdivision (c)(2) was directed, and who have not requested exclusion, and whom the court finds to be members of the class.

(d) **Actions Conducted Partially as Class Actions; Multiple Classes and Subclasses.** When appropriate (1) an action may be brought or maintained as a class action with respect to particular issues, or (2) a class may be divided into subclasses and each subclass treated as a class, and the provisions of this rule shall then be construed and applied accordingly.

(e) **Settlement, Dismissal or, Compromise.**

(1) (A) The court must approve any settlement, dismissal, or compromise of the claims, issues, or defenses of a certified class.

(B) Notice of the material terms of the proposed settlement, dismissal or compromise, together with an explanation of when and how the members may elect to be excluded from the class, shall be given to all members in such manner as the court directs.

(C) The court may approve a settlement, dismissal, or compromise that would bind class members only after a hearing and on finding that the settlement, dismissal, or compromise is fair, reasonable, and adequate.

(2) The parties seeking approval of a settlement, dismissal, or compromise under Rule 42(e)(1) must file a statement identifying any agreement made in connection with the proposed settlement, dismissal, or compromise.

(3) In an action previously certified as a class action under Rule 42(b)(3), the court may not approve a settlement unless it affords a new opportunity to request exclusion to individual class members who had an earlier opportunity to request exclusion but did not do so.

(4)(A) Any class member may object to a proposed settlement, dismissal, or compromise that requires court approval under Rule 42(e)(1)(A).

(B) An objection made under Rule 42(e)(4)(A) may be withdrawn only with the court's approval.

(f) **Discovery.** Unnamed members of a class action are not to be considered as parties for purposes of discovery.

(g) **Class Counsel.**

(1) Appointing Class Counsel.

(A) Unless a statute provides otherwise, a court that certifies a class must appoint class counsel.

(B) An attorney appointed to serve as class counsel must fairly and adequately represent the interests of the class.

(C) In appointing class counsel, the court

(i) must consider:

- the work counsel has done in identifying or investigating potential claims in the action;
- counsel's experience in handling class actions, other complex litigation, and claims of the type asserted in the action;
- counsel's knowledge of the applicable law; and
- the resources counsel will commit to representing the class;

(ii) may consider any other matter pertinent to counsel's ability to fairly and adequately represent the interests of the class;

(iii) may direct potential class counsel to provide information on any subject pertinent to the appointment and to propose terms for attorney fees and nontaxable costs; and

(iv) may make further orders in connection with the appointment.

(2) Appointment Procedure.

(A) The court may designate interim counsel to act on behalf of the putative class before determining whether to certify the action as a class action.

(B) When there is one applicant for appointment as class counsel, the court may appoint that applicant only if the applicant is adequate under Rule 42(g)(1)(B) and (C). If more than one adequate applicant seeks appointment as class counsel, the court must appoint the applicant or applicants best able to represent the interests of the class.

(C) The order appointing class counsel may include provisions about the award of attorney fees or nontaxable costs under Rule 42(h) and (i).

(h) **Procedure for determining Attorney Fees Award.** In an action certified as a class action, the court may award attorney fees in accordance with subdivision (i) and nontaxable costs authorized by law or by agreement of the parties as follows:

(1) Motion for Award of Attorney Fees. A claim for an award of attorney fees and nontaxable costs must be made by motion, subject to the provisions of this subdivision, at a time set by the court. Notice of the motion must be served on all parties and, for motions by class counsel, directed to class members in a reasonable manner.

(2) Objections to Motion. A class member, or a party from whom payment is sought, may object to the motion.

(3) Hearing and Findings. The court must hold a hearing in open court and must find the facts and state its conclusions of law on the motion. The court must state its findings and conclusions in writing or orally on the record.

(i) **Attorney's Fees Award.**

(1) In awarding attorney fees, the court must first determine a lodestar figure by multiplying the number of hours reasonably worked times a reasonable hourly rate. The attorney fees award must be in the range of 25% to 400% of the lodestar figure. In making these determinations, the court must consider the factors specified in Rule 1.04(b), Tex. Disciplinary R. Prof. Conduct.

(2) If any portion of the benefits recovered for the class are in the form of coupons or other noncash common benefits, the attorney fees awarded in the action must be in cash and noncash amounts in the same proportion as the recovery for the class.

(j) **Effective Date.** Rule 42(i) applies only in actions filed after September 1, 2003.

(Amended by Order Sept. 20, 1941, eff. Dec. 31, 1941; May 9, 1977, eff. Sept. 1, 1977; Dec. 5, 1983, eff. April 1, 1984; Oct. 9, 2003, eff. Jan. 1, 2004, except that Rule 42(i) applies only in cases filed on or after Sept. 1, 2003.)

RULE 43. INTERPLEADER.

Persons having claims against the plaintiff may be joined as defendants and required to interplead when their claims are such that the plaintiff is or may be exposed to double or multiple liability. It is not ground for objection to the joinder that the claims of the several claimants or the titles on which their claims depend do not have a common origin or are not identical but are adverse to and independent of one another, or that the plaintiff avers that he is not liable in whole or in part to any or all of the claimants. A defendant exposed to similar liability may obtain such interpleader by way of cross-claim or counterclaim. The provisions of this rule supplement and do not in any way limit the joinder of parties permitted in any other rules.

RULE 44. MAY APPEAR BY NEXT FRIEND.

Minors, lunatics, idiots, or persons non compos mentis who have no legal guardian may sue and be represented by "next friend" under the following rules:

(1) Such next friend shall have the same rights concerning such suits as guardians have, but shall give security for costs, or affidavits in lieu thereof, when required.

(2) Such next friend or his attorney of record may with the approval of the court compromise suits and agree to judgments, and such judgments, agreements and compromises, when approved by the court, shall be forever binding and conclusive upon the party plaintiff in such suit.

SECTION 4. PLEADING

A. GENERAL

RULE 45. DEFINITION AND SYSTEM.

Pleadings in the district and county court shall

(a) be by petition and answer;

(b) consist of a statement in plain and concise language of the plaintiff's cause of action or the defendant's grounds of defense. That an allegation be evidentiary or be of legal conclusion shall not be grounds for an objection when fair notice to the opponent is given by the allegations as a whole; and

(c) contain any other matter which may be required by any law or rule authorizing or regulating any particular action or defense.

Pleadings that are not filed electronically must be in writing, on paper measuring approximately 8 ½ inches by 11 inches, and signed by the party or his attorney. The use of recycled paper is strongly encouraged.

All pleadings shall be construed so as to do substantial justice.

(Amended by Order July 15, 1987. eff. Jan. 1, 1988; April 24, 1990, eff. Sept. 1, 1990; Sept. 4, 1990; Dec. 13, 2013, eff. Jan. 1, 2014.)

RULE 46. PETITION AND ANSWER; EACH ONE INSTRUMENT OF WRITING.

The original petition, first supplemental petition, second supplemental petition, and every other, shall each be contained in one instrument of writing, and so with the original answer and each of the supplemental answers.

RULE 47. CLAIMS FOR RELIEF.

An original pleading which sets forth a claim for relief, whether an original petition, counterclaim, cross-claim, or third party claim, shall contain:

(a) a short statement of the cause of action sufficient to give fair notice of the claim involved;

(b) a statement that the damages sought are within the jurisdictional limits of the court;

(c) except in suits governed by the Family Code, a statement that the party seeks:

  (1) only monetary relief of $ 100,000 or less, including damages of any kind, penalties, costs, expenses, prejudgment interest, and attorney fees; or

  (2) monetary relief of $ 100.000 or less and non-monetary relief; or

  (3) monetary relief over $ 100.000 but not more than $200.000; or

  (4) monetary relief over $200.000 but not more than $ 1.000.000; or

  (5) monetary relief over $ 1.000.000: and

(d) a demand for judgment for all the other relief to which the party deems himself entitled.

Relief in the alternative or of several different types may be demanded; provided, further, that upon special exception the court shall require the pleader to amend so as to specify the maximum amount claimed. A party that fails to comply with (c) may not conduct discovery until the party's pleading is amended to comply.

(Amended by Order July 11, 1977, eff. Jan. 1, 1978; April 24, 1990, eff. Sept. 1. 1990; Nov. 13, 2012, eff. March 1, 2013; Feb 12, 2013, eff. March 1, 2013. (Applies to cases filed on or after March 1, 2013, except those filed in justice court.))

Comment to 2013 change: Rule 47 is amended to require a more specific statement of the relief sought by a party. The amendment requires parties to plead into or out of the expedited actions process governed by Rule 169, added to implement section 22.004(h) of the Texas Government Code. Except in a in a suit governed by the Family Code, the Property Code, the Tax Code, or Chapter 74 of the Civil Practice & Remedies Code, a suit in which the original petition contains the statement in paragraph (c)(l) is governed by the expedited actions process. The further specificity in paragraphs (c)(2)-(5) is to provide information regarding the nature of cases filed and does not affect a party's substantive rights.

RULE 48. ALTERNATIVE CLAIMS FOR RELIEF.

A party may set forth two or more statements of a claim or defense alternatively or hypothetically, either in one count or defense or in separate counts or defenses. When two or more statements are made in the alternative and one of them if made independently would be sufficient, the pleading is not made insufficient by the insufficiency of one or more of the alternative statements. A party may also state as many separate claims or defenses as he has regardless of consistency and whether based upon legal or equitable grounds or both.

RULE 49. WHERE SEVERAL COUNTS.

Where there are several counts in the petition, and entire damages are given, the verdict or judgment, as the case may be, shall be good, notwithstanding one or more of such counts may be defective.

RULE 50. PARAGRAPHS, SEPARATE STATEMENTS.

All averments of claim or defense shall be made in numbered paragraphs, the contents of each of which shall be limited as far as practicable to a statement of a single set of circumstances; and a paragraph may be referred to by number in all succeeding pleadings, so long as the pleading containing such paragraph has not been superseded by an amendment as provided by Rule 65. Each claim founded upon a separate transaction or occurrence and each defense other than denials shall be stated in a separate count or defense whenever a separation facilitates the clear presentation of the matters set forth.

RULE 51. JOINDER OF CLAIMS AND REMEDIES

(a) **Joinder of Claims.** The plaintiff in his petition or in a reply setting forth a counterclaim and the defendant in an answer setting forth a counterclaim may join either as independent or as alternate claims as many claims either legal or equitable or both as he may have against an opposing party. There may be a like joinder of claims when there are multiple parties if the requirements of Rules 39, 40, and 43 are satisfied. There may be a like joinder of cross claims or third-party claims if the requirements of Rules 38 and 97, respectively, are satisfied.

(b) **Joinder of Remedies.** Whenever a claim is one heretofore cognizable only after another claim has been prosecuted to a conclusion, the two claims may be joined in a single action; but the court shall grant relief in that action only in accordance with the relative substantive rights of the parties. This rule shall not be applied in tort cases so as to permit the joinder of a liability or indemnity insurance company, unless such company is by statute or contract directly liable to the person injured or damaged.

(Amended by Order Sept. 20, 1941, eff. Dec. 31, 1941; July 26, 1960, eff. Jan. 1, 1961.)

RULE 52. ALLEGING A CORPORATION.

An allegation that a corporation is incorporated shall be taken as true, unless denied by the affidavit of the adverse party, his agent or attorney, whether such corporation is a public or private corporation and however created.

RULE 53. SPECIAL ACT OR LAW.

A pleading founded wholly or in part on any private or special act or law of this State or of the Republic of Texas need only recite the title thereof, the date of its approval, and set out in substance so much of such act or laws as may be pertinent to the cause of action or defense.

RULE 54. CONDITIONS PRECEDENT.

In pleading the performance or occurrence of conditions precedent, it shall be sufficient to aver generally that all conditions precedent have been performed or have occurred. When such performances or occurrences have been so plead, the party so pleading same shall be required to prove only such of them as are specifically denied by the opposite party.

(Amended by Order March 31, 1941, eff. Sept. 1, 1941.)

RULE 55. JUDGMENT.

In pleading a judgment or decision of a domestic or foreign court, judicial or quasi-judicial tribunal, or of a board or officer, it shall be sufficient to aver the judgment or decision without setting forth matter showing jurisdiction to render it.

RULE 56. SPECIAL DAMAGE.

When items of special damage are claimed, they shall be specifically stated.

RULE 57. SIGNING OF PLEADINGS.

Every pleading of a party represented by an attorney shall be signed by at least one attorney of record in his individual name, with his State Bar of Texas identification number, address, telephone number, email address, and if available, fax number. A party not represented by an attorney shall sign his pleadings, state his address, telephone number, email address, and, if available, fax number.

(Amended by Order June 10, 1980, eff. Jan. 1, 1981; April 24, 1990, eff. Sept. 1, 1990; Dec. 13, 2013, eff. Jan. 1, 2014.)

RULE 58. ADOPTION BY REFERENCE.

Statements in a pleading may be adopted by reference in a different part of the same pleading or in another pleading or in any motion, so long as the pleading containing such statements has not been superseded by an amendment as provided by Rule 65.

RULE 59. EXHIBITS AND PLEADING.

Notes, accounts, bonds, mortgages, records, and all other written instruments, constituting, in whole or in part, the claim sued on, or the matter set up in defense, may be made a part of the pleadings by copies thereof, or the originals, being attached or filed and referred to as such, or by copying the same in the body of the pleading in aid and explanation of the allegations in the petition or answer made in reference to said instruments and shall be deemed a part thereof for all purposes. Such pleadings shall not be deemed defective because of the lack of any allegations which can be supplied from said exhibit. No other instrument of writing shall be made an exhibit in the pleading.

RULE 60. INTERVENOR'S PLEADINGS.

Any party may intervene by filing a pleading, subject to being stricken out by the court for sufficient cause on the motion of any party.

(Amended by Order April 24, 1990, eff. Sept. 1, 1990.)

RULE 61. TRIAL: INTERVENORS: RULES APPLY TO ALL PARTIES.

These rules of pleading shall apply equally, so far as it may be practicable to intervenors and to parties, when more than one, who may plead separately.

RULE 62. AMENDMENT DEFINED.

The object of an amendment, as contra-distinguished from a supplemental petition or answer, is to add something to, or withdraw something from, that which has been previously pleaded so as to perfect that which is or may be deficient, or to correct that which has been incorrectly stated by the party making the amendment, or to plead new matter, additional to that formerly pleaded by the amending party, which constitutes an additional claim or defense permissible to the suit.

RULE 63. AMENDMENTS AND RESPONSIVE PLEADINGS.

Parties may amend their pleadings, respond to pleadings on file of other parties, file suggestions of death and make representative parties and file such other pleas as they may desire by filing such pleas with the clerk at such time as not to operate as a surprise to the opposite party; provided that any pleadings, responses or pleas offered for filing within seven days of the date of trial or thereafter, or after such time as may be ordered by the judge under Rule 166, shall be filed only after leave of the judge is obtained, which leave shall be granted by the judge unless there is a showing that such filing will operate as a surprise to the opposite party.

(Amended by Order July 26, 1960, eff. Jan. 1, 1961; April 24, 1990, eff. Sept. 1, 1990.)

RULE 64. AMENDED INSTRUMENT.

The party amending shall point out the instrument amended, as "original petition," or "plaintiff's first supplemental petition," or as "original answer," or "defendant's first supplemental answer" or other instrument filed by the party and shall amend by filing a substitute therefor, entire and complete in itself, indorsed "amended original petition," or "amended first supplemental petition," or "amended original answer," or "amended first supplemental answer," accordingly as said instruments of pleading are designated.

RULE 65. SUBSTITUTED INSTRUMENT TAKES PLACE OF ORIGINAL.

Unless the substituted instrument shall be set aside on exceptions, the instrument for which it is substituted shall no longer be regarded as a part of the pleading in the record of the cause, unless some error of the court in deciding upon the necessity of the amendment, or otherwise in superseding it, be complained of, and exception be taken to the action of the court, or unless it be necessary to look to the superseded pleading upon a question of limitation.

RULE 66. TRIAL AMENDMENT.

If evidence is objected to at the trial on the ground that it is not within the issues made by the pleading, or if during the trial any defect, fault or omission in a pleading, either of form or substance, is called to the attention of the court, the court may allow the pleadings to be amended and shall do so freely when the presentation of the merits of the action will be subserved thereby and the objecting party fails to satisfy the court that the allowance of such amendment would prejudice him in maintaining his action or defense upon the merits. The court may grant a postponement to enable the objecting party to meet such evidence.

(Amended by Order March 31, 1941, eff. Sept. 1, 1941.)

RULE 67. AMENDMENTS TO CONFORM TO ISSUES TRIED WITHOUT OBJECTION.

When issues not raised by the pleadings are tried by express or implied consent of the parties, they shall be treated in all respects as if they had been raised in the pleadings. In such case such amendment of the pleadings as may be necessary to cause them to conform to the evidence and to raise these issues may be made by leave of court upon motion of any party at any time up to the submission of the case to the Court or jury, but failure so to amend shall not affect the result of the trial of these issues; provided that written pleadings, before the time of submission, shall be necessary to the submission of questions, as is provided in Rules 277 and 279.

(Amended by Order March 31, 1941, eff. Sept. 1, 1941; April 24, 1990, eff. Sept. 1, 1990.)

RULE 68. COURT MAY ORDER REPLEADER.

The court, when deemed necessary in any case, may order a repleader on the part of one or both of the parties, in order to make their pleadings substantially conform to the rules.

RULE 69. SUPPLEMENTAL PETITION OR ANSWER.

Each supplemental petition or answer, made by either party, shall be a response to the last preceding pleading by the other party, and shall not repeat allegations formerly pleaded further than is necessary as an introduction to that which is stated in the pleading then being drawn up. These instruments, to wit, the original petition and its several supplements, and the original answer and its several supplements, shall respectively, constitute separate and distinct parts of the pleadings of each party; and the position and identity, by number and name, with the indorsement of each instrument, shall be preserved throughout the pleadings of either party.

RULE 70. PLEADING: SURPRISE: COST.

When either a supplemental or amended pleading is of such character and is presented at such time as to take the opposite party by surprise, the court may charge the continuance of the cause, if granted, to the party causing the surprise if the other party satisfactorily shows that he is not ready for trial because of the allowance of the filing of such supplemental or amended pleading, and the court may, in such event, in its discretion require the party filing such pleading to pay to the surprised party the amount of reasonable costs and expenses incurred by the other party as a result of the continuance, including attorney fees, or make such other order with respect thereto as may be just.

(Amended by Order June 10, 1980, eff. Jan. 1, 1981.)

RULE 71. MISNOMER OF PLEADING.

When a party has mistakenly designated any plea or pleading, the court, if justice so requires, shall treat the plea or pleading as if it had been properly designated. Pleadings shall be docketed as originally designated and shall remain identified as designated, unless the court orders redesignation. Upon court order filed with the clerk, the clerk shall modify the docket and all other clerk records to reflect redesignation.

(Amended by Order July 15, 1987, eff. Jan. 1, 1988.)

RULE 72. [REPEALED]

(Repealed by Order April 24, 1990, eff. Sept. 1, 1990.)

RULE 73. [REPEALED]

(Repealed by Order April 24, 1990, eff. Sept. 1, 1990.)

RULE 74. FILING WITH THE COURT DEFINED.

The filing of pleadings, other papers and exhibits as required by these rules shall be made by filing them with the clerk of the court, except that the judge may permit the papers to be filed with him, in which event he shall note thereon the filing date and time and forthwith transmit them to the office of the clerk.

(Amended by Order July 20, 1966, eff. Jan. 1, 1967.)

RULE 75. FILED PLEADINGS; WITHDRAWAL.

All filed pleadings shall remain at all times in the clerk's office or in the court or in custody of the clerk, except that the court may by order entered on the minutes allow a filed pleading to be withdrawn for a limited time whenever necessary, on leaving a certified copy on file. The party withdrawing such pleading shall pay the costs of such order and certified copy.

RULE 75a. FILING EXHIBITS: COURT REPORTER TO FILE WITH CLERK.

The court reporter or stenographer shall file with the clerk of the court all exhibits which were admitted in evidence or tendered on bill of exception during the course of any hearing, proceeding, or trial.

(Added July 20, 1966, eff. Jan. 1, 1967.)

RULE 75b. FILED EXHIBITS: WITHDRAWAL.

All filed exhibits admitted in evidence or tendered on bill of exception shall, until returned or otherwise disposed of as authorized by Rule 14b, remain at all times in the clerk's office or in the court or in the custody of the clerk except as follows:

(a) The court may by order entered on the minutes allow a filed exhibit to be withdrawn by any party only upon such party's leaving on file a certified, photo, or other reproduced copy of such exhibit. The party withdrawing such exhibit shall pay the costs of such order and copy.

(b) The court reporter or stenographer of the court conducting the hearing, proceedings, or trial in which exhibits are admitted or offered in evidence, shall have the right to withdraw filed exhibits, upon giving the clerk proper receipt therefor, whenever necessary for the court reporter or stenographer to transmit such original exhibits to an appellate court under the provisions of Rule 379 or to otherwise discharge the duties imposed by law upon said court reporter or stenographer.

(Adopted by Order July 20, 1966, eff. Jan. 1, 1967.)

RULE 76. MAY INSPECT PAPERS.

Each attorney at law practicing in any court shall be allowed at all reasonable times to inspect the papers and records relating to any suit or other matter in which he may be interested.

RULE 76a. SEALING COURT RECORDS.

1. **Standard for Sealing Court Records.** Court records may not be removed from court files except as permitted by statute or rule. No court order or opinion issued in the adjudication of a case may be sealed. Other court records, as defined in this rule, are presumed to be open to the general public and may be sealed only upon a showing of all of the following:
   - (a) a specific, serious and substantial interest which clearly outweighs:
     - (1) this presumption of openness;
     - (2) any probable adverse effect that sealing will have upon the general public health or safety;
   - (b) no less restrictive means than sealing records will adequately and effectively protect the specific interest asserted.
2. **Court Records.** For purposes of this rule, court records means:
   - (a) all documents of any nature filed in connection with any matter before any civil court, except:
     - (1) documents filed with a court in camera, solely for the purpose of obtaining a ruling on the discoverability of such documents;
     - (2) documents in court files to which access is otherwise restricted by law;
     - (3) documents filed in an action originally arising under the Family Code.
   - (b) settlement agreements not filed of record, excluding all reference to any monetary consideration, that seek to restrict disclosure of information concerning matters that have a probable adverse effect upon the general public health or safety, or the administration of public office, or the operation of government.
   - (c) discovery, not filed of record, concerning matters that have a probable adverse effect upon the general public health or safety, or the administration of public office, or the operation of government, except discovery in cases originally initiated to preserve bona fide trade secrets or other intangible property rights.
3. **Notice.** Court records may be sealed only upon a party's written motion, which shall be open to public inspection. The movant shall post a public notice at the place where notices for meetings of county governmental bodies are required to be posted, stating: that a hearing will be held in open court on a motion to seal court records in the specific case, that any person may intervene and be heard concerning the sealing of court records; the specific time and place of the hearing; the style and number of the case, a brief but specific description of both the nature of the case and the records which are sought to be sealed; and the identity of the movant. Immediately after posting such notice, the movant shall file a verified copy of the posted notice with the clerk of the court in which the case is pending and with the Clerk of the Supreme Court of Texas.

4. **Hearing.** A hearing, open to the public, on a motion to seal court records shall be held in open court as soon as practicable, but not less than fourteen days after the motion is filed and notice is posted. Any party may participate in the hearing. Nonparties may intervene as a matter of right for the limited purpose of participating in the proceedings, upon payment of the fee required for filing a plea in intervention. The court may inspect records in camera when necessary. The court may determine a motion relating to sealing or unsealing court records in accordance with the procedures prescribed by Rule 120a.
5. **Temporary Sealing Order.** A temporary sealing order may issue upon motion and notice to any parties who have answered in the case pursuant to Rules 21 and 21a upon a showing of compelling need for specific facts shown by affidavit or by verified petition that immediate and irreparable injury will result to a specific interest of the applicant before notice can be posted and a hearing held as otherwise provided herein. The temporary order shall set the time for the hearing required by paragraph 4 and shall direct that the movant immediately give the public notice required by paragraph 3. The court may modify or withdraw any temporary order upon motion by any party or intervenor, notice to the parties, and hearing conducted as soon as practicable. Issuance of a temporary order shall not reduce in any way the burden of proof of a party requesting sealing at the hearing required by paragraph 4.
6. **Order on Motion to Seal Court Records.** A motion relating to sealing or unsealing court records shall be decided by written order, open to the public, which shall state: the style and number of the case; the specific reasons for finding and concluding whether the showing required by paragraph 1 has been made; the specific portions of court records which are to be sealed; and the time period for which the sealed portions of the court records are to be sealed. The order shall not be included in any judgment or other order but shall be a separate document in the case; however, the failure to comply with this requirement shall not affect its appealability.
7. **Continuing Jurisdiction.** Any person may intervene as a matter of right at any time before or after judgment to seal or unseal court records. A court that issues a sealing order retains continuing jurisdiction to enforce, alter, or vacate that order. An order sealing or unsealing court records shall not be reconsidered on motion of any party or intervenor who had actual notice of the hearing preceding issuance of the order, without first showing changed circumstances materially affecting the order. Such circumstances need not be related to the case in which the order was issued. However, the burden of making the showing required by paragraph 1 shall always be on the party seeking to seal records.
8. **Appeal.** Any order (or portion of an order or judgment) relating to sealing or unsealing court records shall be deemed to be severed from the case and a final judgment which may be appealed by any party or intervenor who participated in the hearing preceding issuance of such order. The appellate court may abate the appeal and order the trial court to direct that further public notice be given, or to hold further hearings, or to make additional findings.
9. **Application.** Access to documents in court files not defined as court records by this rule remains governed by existing law. This rule does not apply to any court records sealed in an action in which a final judgment has been entered before its effective date. This rule applies to cases already pending on its effective date only with regard to:
   (a) all court records filed or exchanged after the effective date;
   (b) any motion to alter or vacate an order restricting access to court records, issued before the effective date.

(Adopted by Order April 24, 1990, eff. Sept. 1, 1990.)

RULE 77. LOST RECORDS AND PAPERS.

When any papers or records are lost or destroyed during the pendency of a suit, the parties may, with the approval of the judge, agree in writing on a brief statement of the matters contained therein; or either party may supply such lost records or papers as follows:

a. After three days' notice to the adverse party or his attorney, make written sworn motion before the court stating the loss or destruction of such record or papers, accompanied by certified copies of the originals if obtainable, or by substantial copies thereof.
b. If, upon hearing, the court be satisfied that they are substantial copies of the original, an order shall be made substituting such copies or brief statement for the originals.
c. Such substituted copies or brief statement shall be filed with the clerk, constitute a part of the cause, and have the force and effect of the originals.

(Amended by Order June 16, 1943, eff. Dec. 31, 1943.)

B.
PLEADINGS OF PLAINTIFF

RULE 78. PETITION; ORIGINAL AND SUPPLEMENTAL; INDORSEMENT.

The pleading of plaintiff shall consist of an original petition, and such supplemental petitions as may be necessary in the course of pleading by the parties to the suit. The original petition and the supplemental petitions shall be indorsed, so as to show their respective positions in the process of pleading, as "original petition," "plaintiff's first supplemental petition," "plaintiff's second supplemental petition," and so on, to be successively numbered, named, and indorsed.

RULE 78a. CASE INFORMATION SHEET.

(a) *Requirement*. A civil case information sheet, in the form promulgated by the Supreme Court of Texas, must accompany the filing of:

(1) an original petition or application; and

(2) a post-judgment petition for modification or motion for enforcement in a case arising under the Family Code.

(b) *Signature*. The civil case information sheet must be signed by the attorney for the party filing the pleading or by the party.

(c) *Enforcement*. The court and clerk must take appropriate measures to enforce this rule. But the clerk may not reject a pleading because the pleading is not accompanied by a civil case information sheet.

(d) *Limitation on Use*. The civil case information sheet is for data collection for statistical and administrative purposes and does not affect any substantive right.

(e) *Applicability*. The civil case information sheet is not required in cases filed injustice courts or small-claims courts, or in cases arising under Title 3 of the Family Code.

(Adopted by Order August 16, 2010, eff. Sept. 1, 2010.)

Comment: Rule 78a is added to require the submission of a civil case information sheet to collect data for statistical and administrative purposes, *see*, *e.g.*, TEX. GOV'T CODE § 71.035. A civil case information sheet is not a pleading. Rule 78a is placed with other rules regarding pleadings because civil case information sheets must accompany pleadings.

[Civil Case Information Sheet as provided in Misc. Docket No. 13-9022, Feb. 12, 2013, eff March 1, 2013 and applies to all cases filed on or after March 1, 2013.]

RULE 79. THE PETITION.

The petition shall state the names of the parties and their residences, if known, together with the contents prescribed in Rule 47 above.

RULE 80. PLAINTIFF'S SUPPLEMENTAL PETITION.

The plaintiff's supplemental petitions may contain special exceptions, general denials, and the allegations of new matter not before alleged by him, in reply to those which have been alleged by the defendant.

RULE 81. DEFENSIVE MATTERS.

When the defendant sets up a counter claim, the plaintiff may plead thereto under rules prescribed for pleadings of defensive matter by the defendant, so far as applicable. Whenever the defendant is required to plead any matter of defense under oath, the plaintiff shall be required to plead such matters under oath when relied on by him.

RULE 82. SPECIAL DEFENSES.

The plaintiff need not deny any special matter of defense pleaded by the defendant, but the same shall be regarded as denied unless expressly admitted.

C.
PLEADINGS OF DEFENDANT

RULE 83. ANSWER; ORIGINAL AND SUPPLEMENTAL; INDORSEMENT.

The answer of defendant shall consist of an original answer, and such supplemental answers as may be necessary, in the course of pleading by the parties to the suit. The original answer and the supplemental answers shall be indorsed, so as to show their respective positions in the process of pleading, as "original answer," "defendant's first supplemental answer," "defendant's second supplemental answer," and so on, to be successively numbered, named and indorsed.

RULE 84. ANSWER MAY INCLUDE SEVERAL MATTERS.

The defendant in his answer may plead as many several matters, whether of law or fact, as he may think necessary for his defense, and which may be pertinent to the cause, and such matters shall be heard in such order as may be directed by the court, special appearance and motion to transfer venue, and the practice thereunder being excepted herefrom.

(Amended by Order Oct. 12, 1949, eff. March 1, 1950; April 12, 1962, eff. Sept. 1, 1962; June 15, 1983, eff. Sept. 1, 1983.)

RULE 85. ORIGINAL ANSWER; CONTENTS.

The original answer may consist of motions to transfer venue, pleas to the jurisdiction, in abatement, or any other dilatory pleas; of special exceptions, of general denial, and any defense by way of avoidance or estoppel, and it may present a cross-action, which to that extent will place defendant in the attitude of a plaintiff. Matters in avoidance and estoppel may be stated together, or in several special pleas, each presenting a distinct defense, and numbered so as to admit of separate issues to be formed on them.

(Amended by Order June 16, 1983, eff. Sept. 1, 1983.)

RULE 86. MOTION TO TRANSFER VENUE.

1. **Time to File.** An objection to improper venue is waived if not made by written motion filed prior to or concurrently with any other plea, pleading or motion except a special appearance motion provided for in Rule 120a. A written consent of the parties to transfer the case to another county may be filed with the clerk of the court at any time. A motion to transfer venue because an impartial trial cannot be had in the county where the action is pending is governed by the provisions of Rule 257.
2. **How to File.** The motion objecting to improper venue may be contained in a separate instrument filed concurrently with or prior to the filing of the movant's first responsive pleading or the motion may be combined with other objections and defenses and included in the movant's first responsive pleading.
3. **Requisites of Motion.** The motion, and any amendments to it, shall state that the action should be transferred to another specified county of proper venue because:
   (a) The county where the action is pending is not a proper county; or
   (b) Mandatory venue of the action in another county is prescribed by one or more specific statutory provisions which shall be clearly designated or indicated.

The motion shall state the legal and factual basis for the transfer of the action and request transfer of the action to a specific county of mandatory or proper venue. Verification of the motion is not required. The motion may be accompanied by supporting affidavits as provided in Rule 87.

4. **Response and Reply.** Except as provided in paragraph 3(a) of Rule 87, a response to the motion to transfer is not required. Verification of a response is not required.
5. **Service.** A copy of any instrument filed pursuant to Rule 86 shall be served in accordance with Rule 21a.

(Amended by Order March 31, 1941, eff. Sept. 1, 1941; June 16, 1943 eff. Dec. 31, 1943; July 20, 1954, eff. Jan. 1, 1955; April 12, 1962, eff. Sept. 1, 1962; June 15, 1983, eff. Sept. 1, 1983.)

RULE 87. DETERMINATION OF MOTION TO TRANSFER.

1. **Consideration of Motion.** The determination of a motion to transfer venue shall be made promptly by the court and such determination must be made in a reasonable time prior to commencement of the trial on the merits. The movant has the duty to request a setting on the motion to transfer. Except on leave of court each party is entitled to at least 45 days notice of a hearing on the motion to transfer.

Except on leave of court, any response or opposing affidavits shall be filed at least 30 days prior to the hearing of the motion to transfer. The movant is not required to file a reply to the response but any reply and additional affidavits supporting the motion to transfer must, except on leave of court, be filed not later than 7 days prior to the hearing date.

2. **Burden of Establishing Venue.**
   (a) **In General.** A party who seeks to maintain venue of the action in a particular county in reliance upon Section 15.001 (General Rule), Sections 15.011-15.017 (Mandatory Venue), Sections 15.031-15.040 (Permissive Venue), or Sections 15.061 and 15.062 (Multiple Claims), Civil Practice and Remedies Code, has the burden to make proof, as provided in paragraph 3 of this rule, that venue is maintainable in the county of suit. A party who seeks to transfer venue of the action to another specified county under Section 15.001 (General Rule), Sections 15.011 & REM.-15.017 (Mandatory Venue), Sections 15.031-15.040 (Permissive Venue), or Sections 15.061 and 15.062 (Multiple Claims), Civil Practice and Remedies Code, has the burden to make proof, as provided in paragraph 3 of this rule, that venue is maintainable in the county to which transfer is sought. A party who seeks to transfer venue of the action to another specified county under Sections 15.011-15.017, Civil Practice and Remedies Code on the basis that a mandatory venue provision is applicable and controlling has the burden to make proof, as provided in paragraph 3 of this rule, that venue is maintainable in the county to which transfer is sought by virtue of one or more mandatory venue exceptions.
   (b) **Cause of Action.** It shall not be necessary for a claimant to prove the merits of a cause of action, but the existence of a cause of action, when pleaded properly, shall be taken as established as alleged by the pleadings. When the defendant specifically denies the venue allegations, the claimant is required, by prima facie proof as provided in paragraph 3 of this rule, to support such pleading that the cause of action taken as established by the pleadings, or a part of such cause of action, accrued in the county of suit. If a defendant seeks transfer to a county where the cause of

action or a part thereof accrued, it shall be sufficient for the defendant to plead that if a cause of action exists, then the cause of action or part thereof accrued in the specific county to which transfer is sought, and such allegation shall not constitute an admission that a cause of action in fact exists. But the defendant shall be required to support his pleading by prima facie proof as provided in paragraph 3 of this rule, that, if a cause of action exists, it or a part thereof accrued in the county to which transfer is sought.

(c) **Other Rules.** A motion to transfer venue based on the written consent of the parties shall be determined in accordance with Rule 255. A motion to transfer venue on the basis that an impartial trial cannot be had in the courts where the action is pending shall be determined in accordance with Rules 258 and 259.

3. **Proof.**

(a) **Affidavit and Attachments.** All venue facts, when properly pleaded, shall be taken as true unless specifically denied by the adverse party. When a venue fact is specifically denied, the party pleading the venue fact must make prima facie proof of that venue fact; provided, however, that no party shall ever be required for venue purposes to support by prima facie proof the existence of a cause of action or part thereof, and at the hearing the pleadings of the parties shall be taken as conclusive on the issues of existence of a cause of action. Prima facie proof is made when the venue facts are properly pleaded and an affidavit, and any duly proved attachments to the affidavit, are filed fully and specifically setting forth the facts supporting such pleading. Affidavits shall be made on personal knowledge, shall set forth specific facts as would be admissible in evidence, and shall show affirmatively that the affiant is competent to testify.

(b) **The Hearing.** The court shall determine the motion to transfer venue on the basis of the pleadings, any stipulations made by and between the parties and such affidavits and attachments as may be filed by the parties in accordance with the preceding subdivision of this paragraph 3 or of Rule 88.

(c) If a claimant has adequately pleaded and made prima facie proof that venue is proper in the county of suit as provided in subdivision (a) of paragraph 3, then the cause shall not be transferred but shall be retained in the county of suit, unless the motion to transfer is based on the grounds that an impartial trial cannot be had in the county where the action is pending as provided in Rules 257-259 or on an established ground of mandatory venue. A ground of mandatory venue is established when the party relying upon a mandatory exception to the general rule makes prima facie proof as provided in subdivision (a) of paragraph 3 of this rule.

(d) In the event that the parties shall fail to make prima facie proof that the county of suit or the specific county to which transfer is sought is a county of proper venue, then the court may direct the parties to make further proof.

4. **No Jury.** All venue challenges shall be determined by the court without the aid of a jury.

5. **Motion for Rehearing.** If venue has been sustained as against a motion to transfer, or if an action has been transferred to a proper county in response to a motion to transfer, then no further motions to transfer shall be considered regardless of whether the movant was a party to the prior proceedings or was added as a party subsequent to the venue proceedings, unless the motion to transfer is based on the grounds that an impartial trial cannot be had under Rules 257-259 or on the ground of mandatory venue, provided that such claim was not available to the other movant or movants.

Parties who are added subsequently to an action and are precluded by this rule from having a motion to transfer considered may raise the propriety of venue on appeal, provided that the party has timely filed a motion to transfer.

6. There shall be no interlocutory appeals from such determination.

(Amended by Order Sept. 20, 1941, eff. Dec. 31, 1941; June 16, 1943, eff. Dec. 31, 1943; Aug. 18, 1947, eff. Dec. 13, 1947; June 15, 1983, eff. Sept. 1, 1983, July 15, 1987, eff. Jan. 1, 1988; April 24, 1990, eff. Sept. 1, 1990.)

RULE 88. DISCOVERY AND VENUE.

Discovery shall not be abated or otherwise affected by pendency of a motion to transfer venue. Issuing process for witnesses and taking depositions shall not constitute a waiver of a motion to transfer venue, but depositions taken in such case may be read in evidence in any subsequent suit between the same parties concerning the same subject matter in like manner as if taken in such subsequent suit. Deposition transcripts, responses to requests for admission, answers to interrogatories and other discovery products containing information relevant to a determination of proper venue may be considered by the court in making the venue determination when they are attached to, or incorporated by reference in, an affidavit of a party, a witness or an attorney who has knowledge of such discovery.

(Amended by Order June 15, 1983, eff. Sept. 1, 1983; July 15, 1987, eff. Jan. 1, 1988.)

RULE 89. TRANSFERRED IF MOTION IS SUSTAINED.

If a motion to transfer venue is sustained, the cause shall not be dismissed, but the court shall transfer said cause to the proper court; and the costs incurred prior to the time such suit is filed in the court to which said cause is transferred shall be taxed against the plaintiff. The clerk shall make up a transcript of all the orders made in said cause, certifying thereto officially under the seal of the court, and send it with the original papers in the cause to the clerk of the court to which the venue has been changed. Provided, however, if the cause be severable as to parties defendant and shall be ordered transferred as to one or more defendants but not as to all, the clerk, instead of sending the original papers, shall make certified copies of such filed papers as directed by the court and forward the same to the clerk of the court to which the venue has been changed. After the cause has been transferred, as above provided for the clerk of the court to which the cause has been transferred shall mail notification to the plaintiff or his attorney that transfer of the cause has been completed, that the filing fee in the proper court is due and payable within thirty days from the mailing of such notification, and that the case may be dismissed if the filing fee is not timely paid; and if such filing fee is timely paid, the cause will be subject to trial at the expiration of thirty days after the mailing of notification to the parties or their attorneys by the clerk that the papers have been filed in the court to which the cause has been transferred; and if the filing fee is not timely paid, any court of the transferee county to which the case might have been assigned, upon its own motion or the motion of a party, may dismiss the cause without prejudice to the refiling of same.

(Amended by Order June 16, 1943 eff. Dec. 31, 1943; June 15, 1983 eff. Sept. 1, 1983.)

RULE 90. WAIVER OF DEFECTS IN PLEADING.

General demurrers shall not be used. Every defect omission or fault in a pleading either of form or of substance, which is not specifically pointed out by exception in writing and brought to the attention of the judge in the trial court before the instruction or charge to the jury or, in a non-jury case, before the judgment is signed, shall be deemed to have been waived by the party seeking reversal on such account; provided that this rule shall not apply as to any party against whom default judgment is rendered.

(Amended by Order June 10, 1980, eff. Jan. 1, 1981.)

RULE 91. SPECIAL EXCEPTIONS.

A special exception shall not only point out the particular pleading excepted to, but it shall also point out intelligibly and with particularity the defect, omission, obscurity, duplicity, generality, or other insufficiency in the allegations in the pleading excepted to.

(Amended by Order March 31, 1941, eff. Sept. 1, 1941.)

Rule 91a. Dismissal of Baseless Causes of Action.

91a.1. Motion and Grounds.

Except in a case brought under the Family Code or a case governed by Chapter 14 of the Texas Civil Practice and Remedies Code, a party may move to dismiss a cause of action on the grounds that it has no basis in law or fact. A cause of action has no basis in law if the allegations, taken as true, together with inferences reasonably drawn from them, do not entitle the claimant to the relief sought. A cause of action has no basis in fact if no reasonable person could believe the facts pleaded.

91a.2. Contents of Motion.

A motion to dismiss must state that it is made pursuant to this rule, must identify each cause of action to which it is addressed, and must state specifically the reasons the cause of action has no basis in law, no basis in fact, or both.

91a.3. Time for Motion and Ruling.

A motion to dismiss must be:

(a) filed within 60 days after the first pleading containing the challenged cause of action is served on the movant;

(b) filed at least 21 days before the motion is heard; and

(c) granted or denied within 45 days after the motion is filed.

91a.4. Time for Response.

Any response to the motion must be filed no later than 7 days before the date of the hearing.

91a.5. Effect of Nonsuit or Amendment; Withdrawal of Motion.

(a) The court may not rule on a motion to dismiss if, at least 3 days before the date of the hearing, the respondent files a nonsuit of the challenged cause of action, or the movant files a withdrawal of the motion.

(b) If the respondent amends the challenged cause of action at least 3 days before the date of the hearing, the movant may, before the date of the hearing, file a withdrawal of the motion or an amended motion directed to the amended cause of action.

(c) Except by agreement of the parties, the court must rule on a motion unless it has been withdrawn or the cause of action has been nonsuited in accordance with (a) or (b). In ruling on the motion, the court must not consider a nonsuit or amendment not filed as permitted by paragraphs (a) or (b).

(d) An amended motion filed in accordance with (b) restarts the time periods in this rule.

91a.6. Hearing; No Evidence Considered.

Each party is entitled to at least 14 days' notice of the hearing on the motion to dismiss. The court may, but is not required to, conduct an oral hearing on the motion. Except as required by 91 a. 7, the court may not consider evidence in ruling on the motion and must decide the motion based solely on the pleading of the cause of action, together with any pleading exhibits permitted by Rule 59.

91a.7. Award of Costs and Attorney Fees Required.

Except in an action by or against a governmental entity or a public official acting in his or her official capacity or under color of law, the court must award the prevailing party on the motion all costs and reasonable and necessary attorney fees incurred with respect to the challenged cause of action in the trial court. The court must consider evidence regarding costs and fees in determining the award.

91a.8. Effect on Venue and Personal Jurisdiction.

This rule is not an exception to the pleading requirements of Rules 86 and 120a, but a party does not, by filing a motion to dismiss pursuant to this rule or obtaining a ruling on it, waive a special appearance or a motion to transfer venue. By filing a motion to dismiss, a party submits to the court's jurisdiction only in proceedings on the motion and is bound by the court's ruling, including an award of attorney fees and costs against the party.

91a.9. Dismissal Procedure Cumulative.

This rule is in addition to, and does not supersede or affect, other procedures that authorize dismissal.

(Adopted by Order Nov. 13, 2012, eff. March 1, 2013; Order Feb. 12, 2013, eff. March 1, 2013. (Applies to all cases, including those pending on March 1, 2013.))

Comment to 2013 change: Rule 91a is a new rule implementing section 22.004(g) of the Texas Government Code, which was added in 2011 and calls for rules to provide for the dismissal of causes of action that have no basis in law or fact on motion and without evidence. A motion to dismiss filed under this rule must be ruled on by the court within 45 days unless the motion, pleading, or cause of action is withdrawn, amended, or nonsuited as specified in 9 1a. 5. If an amended motion is filed in response to an amended cause of action in accordance with 91a.5(b), the court must rule on the motion within 45 days of the filing of the amended motion and the respondent must be given an opportunity to respond to the amended motion. The term "hearing" in the rule includes both submission and an oral hearing. Attorney fees awarded under 91a.7 are limited to those associated with challenged cause of action, including fees for preparing or responding to the motion to dismiss.

RULE 92. GENERAL DENIAL.

A general denial of matters pleaded by the adverse party which are not required to be denied under oath, shall be sufficient to put the same in issue. When the defendant has pleaded a general denial, and the plaintiff shall afterward amend his pleading, such original denial shall be presumed to extend to all matters subsequently set up by the plaintiff.

When a counterclaim or cross-claim is served upon a party who has made an appearance in the action, the party so served, in the absence of a responsive pleading, shall be deemed to have pleaded a general denial of the counterclaim or cross-claim, but the party shall not be deemed to have waived any special appearance or motion to transfer venue. In all other respects the rules prescribed for pleadings of defensive matter are applicable to answers to counterclaims and cross-claims.

(Amended by Order Dec. 5, 1983, eff. April 1, 1984; Dec. 19, 1984, eff. April 1, 1985.)

RULE 93. CERTAIN PLEAS TO BE VERIFIED.

A pleading setting up any of the following matters, unless the truth of such matters appear of record, shall be verified by affidavit.

1. That the plaintiff has not legal capacity to sue or that the defendant has not legal capacity to be sued.
2. That the plaintiff is not entitled to recover in the capacity in which he sues, or that the defendant is not liable in the capacity in which he is sued.
3. That there is another suit pending in this State between the same parties involving the same claim.
4. That there is a defect of parties, plaintiff or defendant.
5. A denial of partnership as alleged in any pleading as to any party to the suit.
6. That any party alleged in any pleading to be a corporation is not incorporated as alleged.
7. Denial of the execution by himself or by his authority of any instrument in writing, upon which any pleading is founded, in whole or in part and charged to have been executed by him or by his authority, and not alleged to be lost or destroyed. Where such instrument in writing is charged to have been executed by a person then deceased, the affidavit shall be sufficient if it states that the affiant has reason to believe and does believe that such instrument

was not executed by the decedent or by his authority. In the absence of such a sworn plea, the instrument shall be received in evidence as fully proved.

8. A denial of the genuineness of the indorsement or assignment of a written instrument upon which suit is brought by an indorsee or assignee and in the absence of such a sworn plea, the indorsement or assignment thereof shall be held as fully proved. The denial required by this subdivision of the rule may be made upon information and belief.
9. That a written instrument upon which a pleading is founded is without consideration, or that the consideration of the same has failed in whole or in part.
10. A denial of an account which is the foundation of the plaintiff's action, and supported by affidavit.
11. That a contract sued upon is usurious. Unless such plea is filed, no evidence of usurious interest as a defense shall be received.
12. That notice and proof of loss or claim for damage has not been given as alleged. Unless such plea is filed such notice and proof shall be presumed and no evidence to the contrary shall be admitted. A denial of such notice or such proof shall be made specifically and with particularity.
13. In the trial of any case appealed to the court from the Industrial Accident Board the following, if pleaded, shall be presumed to be true as pleaded and have been done and filed in legal time and manner unless denied by verified pleadings:
    (a) Notice of injury.
    (b) Claim for compensation.
    (c) Award of the Board.
    (d) Notice of intention not to abide by the award of the Board.
    (e) Filing of suit to set aside the award.
    (f) That the insurance company alleged to have been the carrier of the workers' compensation insurance at the time of the alleged injury was in fact the carrier thereof.
    (g) That there was good cause for not filing claim with the Industrial Accident Board within the one year period provided by statute.
    (h) Wage rate. A denial of any of the matters set forth in subdivisions (a) or (g) of paragraph 13 may be made on information and belief. Any such denial may be made in original or amended pleadings; but if in amended pleadings the same must be filed not less than seven days before the case proceeds to trial. In case of such denial the things so denied shall not be presumed to be true, and if essential to the case of the party alleging them, must be proved.
14. That a party plaintiff or defendant is not doing business under an assumed name or trade name as alleged.
15. In the trial of any case brought against an automobile insurance company by an insured under the provisions of an insurance policy in force providing protection against uninsured motorists, an allegation that the insured has complied with all the terms of the policy as a condition precedent to bringing the suit shall be presumed to be true unless denied by verified pleadings which may be upon information and belief.
16. Any other matter required by statute to be pleaded under oath.

(Amended by Order March 31, 1941, eff. Sept. 1, 1941; Sept. 20, 1941 eff. Dec. 31, 1941; June 16, 1943, eff. Dec. 31, 1943; Oct. 12, 1949, eff. March 1, 1950; July 21, 1970, eff. Jan. 1, 1971; July 22, 1975, eff. Jan. 1, 1976; June 15, 1983, eff. Sept. 1, 1983; Dec. 5, 1983, eff. April 1, 1984.)

RULE 94. AFFIRMATIVE DEFENSES.

In pleading to a preceding pleading, a party shall set forth affirmatively accord and satisfaction, arbitration and award, assumption of risk, contributory negligence, discharge in bankruptcy, duress, estoppel, failure of consideration, fraud, illegality, injury by fellow servant, laches, license, payment, release, res judicata, statute of frauds, statute of limitations, waiver, and any other matter constituting an avoidance or affirmative defense. Where the suit is on an insurance contract which insures against certain general hazards, but contains other provisions limiting such general liability, the party suing on such contract shall never be required to allege that the loss was not due to a risk or cause coming within any of the exceptions specified in the contract, nor shall the insurer be allowed to raise such issue unless it shall specifically allege that the loss was due to a risk or cause coming within a particular exception to the general liability; provided that nothing herein shall be construed to change the burden of proof on such issue as it now exists.

(Amended by Order March 31, 1941, eff. Sept. 1, 1941.)

RULE 95. PLEAS OF PAYMENT.

When a defendant shall desire to prove payment, he shall file with his plea an account stating distinctly the nature of such payment, and the several items thereof; failing to do so, he shall not be allowed to prove the same, unless it be so plainly and particularly described in the plea as to give the plaintiff full notice of the character thereof.

RULE 96. NO DISCONTINUANCE.

Where the defendant has filed a counterclaim seeking affirmative relief, the plaintiff shall not be permitted by a discontinuance of his suit, to prejudice the right of the defendant to be heard on such counter-claim.

RULE 97. COUNTERCLAIM AND CROSS-CLAIM.

(a) **Compulsory Counterclaims.** A pleading shall state as a counterclaim any claim within the jurisdiction of the court, not the subject of a pending action, which at the time of filing the pleading the pleader has against any opposing party, if it arises out of the transaction or occurrence that is the subject matter of the opposing party's claim and does not require for its adjudication the presence of third parties of whom the court cannot acquire jurisdiction; provided, however, that a judgment based upon a settlement or compromise of a claim of one party to the transaction or occurrence prior to a disposition on the merits shall not operate as a bar to the continuation or assertion of the claims of any other party to the transaction or occurrence unless the latter has consented in writing that said judgment shall operate as a bar.

(b) **Permissive Counterclaims.** A pleading may state as a counterclaim any claim against an opposing party whether or not arising out of the transaction or occurrence that is the subject matter of the opposing party's claim.

(c) **Counterclaim Exceeding Opposing Claim.** A counterclaim may or may not diminish or defeat the recovery sought by the opposing party. It may claim relief exceeding in amount or different in kind from that sought in the pleading of the opposing party, so long as the subject matter is within the jurisdiction of the court.

(d) **Counterclaim Maturing or Acquired After Pleading.** A claim which either matured or was acquired by the pleader after filing his pleading may be presented as a counterclaim by amended pleading.

(e) **Cross-Claim Against Co-party.** A pleading may state as a cross-claim any claim by one party against a co-party arising out of the transaction or occurrence that is the subject matter either of the original action or of a counterclaim therein. Such cross-claim may include a claim that the party against whom it is asserted is or may be liable to the cross-claimant for all or part of a claim asserted in the action against the cross-claimant.

(f) **Additional Parties.** Persons other than those made parties to the original action may be made parties to a third party action, counterclaim or crossclaim in accordance with the provisions of Rules 38, 39 and 40.

(g) Tort shall not be the subject of set-off or counterclaim against a contractual demand nor a contractual demand against tort unless it arises out of or is incident to or is connected with same.

(h) **Separate Trials; Separate Judgments.** If the court orders separate trials as provided in Rule 174, judgment on a counterclaim or cross-claim may be rendered when the court has jurisdiction so to do, even if the claims of the opposing party have been dismissed or otherwise disposed of.

(Amended by Order March 31, 1941, eff. Sept. 1, 1941; July 21, 1970, eff. Jan. 1, 1971; Dec. 5, 1983, eff. April 1, 1984.)

RULE 98. SUPPLEMENTAL ANSWERS.

The defendant's supplemental answers may contain special exceptions, general denial, and the allegations of new matter not before alleged by him, in reply to that which has been alleged by the plaintiff.

(Amended by Order March 31, 1941, eff. Sept. 1, 1941.)

SECTION 5.
CITATION

RULE 99. ISSUANCE AND FORM OF CITATION.

a. **Issuance.** Upon the filing of the petition, the clerk, when requested, shall forthwith issue a citation and deliver the citation as directed by the requesting party. The party requesting citation shall be responsible for obtaining service of the citation and a copy of the petition. Upon request, separate or additional citations shall be issued by the clerk. The clerk must retain a copy of the citation in the court's file.

b. **Form.** The citation shall (1) be styled "The State of Texas," (2) be signed by the clerk under seal of court, (3) contain name and location of the court, (4) show date of filing of the petition, (5) show date of issuance of citation, (6) show file number, (7) show names of parties, (8) be directed to the defendant, (9) show the name and address of attorney for plaintiff, otherwise the address of plaintiff, (10) contain the time within which these rules require the defendant to file a written answer with the clerk who issued citation, (11) contain address of the clerk, and (12) shall notify the defendant that in case of failure of defendant to file an answer, judgment by default may be rendered for the relief demanded in the petition. The citation shall direct the defendant to file a written answer to the plaintiff's petition on or before 10:00 a.m. on the Monday next after the expiration of twenty days after the date of service thereof. The requirement of subsections 10 and 12 of this section shall be in the form set forth in section c of this rule.

c. **Notice.** The citation shall include the following notice to the defendant: "You have been sued. You may employ an attorney. If you or your attorney do not file a written answer with the clerk who issued this citation by 10:00 a.m. on the

Monday next following the expiration of twenty days after you were served this citation and petition, a default judgment may be taken against you."

d. **Copies.** The party filing any pleading upon which citation is to be issued and served shall furnish the clerk with a sufficient number of copies thereof for use in serving the parties to be served, and when copies are so furnished the clerk shall make no charge for the copies.

(Amended by Order Oct. 10, 1945, eff. Feb. 1, 1946; July 16, 1987, eff. Jan. 1, 1988; Oct. 17, 2011, eff. Jan. 1, 2012; Order Dec. 12, 2011, eff. Jan. 1, 2012.)

RULE 100 TO 102. [REPEALED]

(Repealed by Order July 15, 1987, eff. Jan. 1, 1988.)

RULE 103. WHO MAY SERVE.

Process—including citation and other notices, writs, orders, and other papers issued by the court—may be served anywhere by (1) any sheriff or constable or other person authorized by law or, (2) any person authorized by law or by written order of the court who is not less than eighteen years of age, or (3) any person certified under order of the Supreme Court. Service by registered or certified mail and citation by publication shall, if requested, be made by the clerk of the court in which the case is pending. But no person who is a party to or interested in the outcome of a suit may serve any process. The order authorizing a person to serve process may be made without written motion and no fee may be imposed for issuance of such order.

(Amended by Order June 10, 1980, eff. Jan. 1, 1981; July 15, 1987, eff. Jan. 1, 1988; Oct. 7, 2004, eff. Feb. 1, 2005, extended by Order Jan. 27, 2005 to July. 1, 2005, in all pending cases; June 29, 2005, eff. July 1, 2005, in all pending cases.)

Comment – 2005: Subsection (a) is amended to include among the persons authorized to effect service those who meet certification requirements promulgated by the Supreme Court and to prohibit private individuals from serving certain types of process unless, in rare circumstances, a court authorizes an individual to do so.

Certification of Persons
Authorized to Serve Process Under
Rules 103 and 536(a), Texas Rules of Civil Procedure

Rules 103 and 536(a), Texas Rules of Civil Procedure, allow process to be served by any person who is not a party to or interested in the outcome of a suit and who is certified under order of the Supreme Court of Texas. To improve the standards for persons authorized to serve process and to reduce the disparity among Texas civil courts for approving persons to serve process,

IT IS ORDERED:

1. To be certified to serve process under Rules 103 and 536(a), Texas Rules of Civil Procedure, a person must file with the Clerk of the Supreme Court a sworn application in the form prescribed by the Court. The application must contain a statement that the applicant has not been convicted of a felony or of a misdemeanor involving moral turpitude. Form applications may be obtained in the Clerk's office or on the Supreme Court website. The application must include a criminal history record obtained within the preceding 90 days from the Texas Department of Public Safety in Austin, Texas, and a certificate from the director of a civil process service course approved as provided by this Order that the applicant has completed the approved course within the prior year.

2. Applications will be reviewed and approved or rejected for good cause by the Texas Process Service Review Board, appointed by the Court. The Board will notify each applicant of its action, and for each person certified, will post on a list maintained on the Supreme Court website the person's name and an assigned identification number. The Office of Court Administration will provide clerical assistance to the Board.

3. Certification is effective for three years from the last day of the month it issues.

4. Certification may be revoked for good cause, including a conviction of a felony or of a misdemeanor involving moral turpitude. A person suffering such a conviction must immediately notify the Clerk of the Supreme Court and cease to serve process.

5. A person must not represent that he or she is certified under this Order if certification has not been approved, has expired, or has been revoked.

6. The following civil process service courses are approved:

   a. the course now offered by the Houston Young Lawyer's Association, for certification for every state court;

   b. the course now offered by the Texas Process Server's Association, for certification except for courts in Harris County;

   c. a course offered by an academy or other provider licensed or approved by the Texas Commission on Law Enforcement, for certification for every state court.

7. A civil process service course that meets the following requirements, similar to the courses approved in paragraph 6, may apply to the Board for approval by the Court:

   a. a minimum of 7 hours of monitored instruction;

b. instruction on applicable laws, including the historical development of the law, with emphasis on practical training of proper service and return of service (for example, using sample returns depicting both correct and incorrect returns of service);

c. instruction on a process server's exposure to criminal liability;

d. instruction on unique issues involving family law cases; and

e. basic competence testing upon completion of the course.

8. No organization that offers an approved civil process service course may make membership in the organization a prerequisite to taking the course.

9. The effective date of this Order is July 1, 2005. A person who on that date is shown to have met the requirements for an approved private process server already in place in Dallas County, Denton County, or Harris County, having provided a criminal history record there and having completed a course listed in paragraph 6, is considered to have been certified under this Order, to the extent permitted by paragraph 6, as if the person had complied with this Order on that date.

(Adopted by Order Oct. 7, 2004, eff. Feb. 1, 2005, extended by Order Jan. 27, 2005 to July. 1, 2005; June 29, 2005, eff. July 1, 2005.)

RULE 104. [REPEALED]

(Repealed by Order July 15, 1987, eff. Jan. 1, 1988.)

RULE 105. DUTY OF OFFICER OR PERSON RECEIVING.

The officer or authorized person to whom process is delivered shall endorse thereon the day and hour on which he received it, and shall execute and return the same without delay.

(Amended by Order July 11, 1977, eff. Jan. 1, 1978; July 15, 1987, eff. Jan. 1, 1988.)

RULE 106. METHOD OF SERVICE

(a) Unless the citation or an order of the court otherwise directs, the citation shall be served by any person authorized by Rule 103 by

(1) delivering to the defendant, in person, a true copy of the citation with the date of delivery endorsed thereon with a copy of the petition attached thereto, or

(2) mailing to the defendant by registered or certified mail, return receipt requested, a true copy of the citation with a copy of the petition attached thereto.

(b) Upon motion supported by affidavit stating the location of the defendant's usual place of business or usual place of abode or other place where the defendant can probably be found and stating specifically the facts showing that service has been attempted under either (a)(1) or (a)(2) at the location named in such affidavit but has not been successful, the court may authorize service

(1) by leaving a true copy of the citation, with a copy of the petition attached, with anyone over sixteen years of age at the location specified in such affidavit, or

(2) in any other manner that the affidavit or other evidence before the court shows will be reasonably effective to give the defendant notice of the suit.

(Amended by Order Aug. 18, 1947, eff. Dec. 31, 1947; July 22, 1975, eff. Jan. 1, 1976; July 11, 1977, eff. Jan. 1, 1978; June 10, 1980, eff. Jan. 1, 1981; July 15, 1987, eff. Jan. 1, 1988; April 24, 1990, eff. Sept. 1, 1990.)

RULE 107. RETURN OF SERVICE

(a) The officer or authorized person executing the citation must complete a return of service. The return may, but need not, be endorsed on or attached to the citation.

(b) The return, together with any document to which it is attached, must include the following information:

(1) the cause number and case name;

(2) the court in which the case is filed;

(3) a description of what was served;

(4) the date and time the process was received for service;

(5) the person or entity served;

(6) the address served;

(7) the date of service or attempted service;

(8) the manner of delivery of service or attempted service;

(9) the name of the person who served or attempted to serve the process;

(10) if the person named in (9) is a process server certified under order of the Supreme Court, his or her identification number and the expiration date of his or her certification; and

(11) any other information required by rule or law.

(c) When the citation was served by registered or certified mail as authorized by Rule 106, the return by the officer or authorized person must also contain the return receipt with the addressee's signature.

(d) When the officer or authorized person has not served the citation, the return shall show the diligence used by the officer or authorized person to execute the same and the cause of failure to execute it, and where the defendant is to be found, if ascertainable.

(e) The officer or authorized person who serves or attempts to serve a citation must sign the return. If the return is signed by a person other than a sheriff, constable, or the clerk of the court, the return must either be verified or be signed under penalty of perjury. A return signed under penalty of perjury must contain the statement below in substantially the following form:

"My name is ___________________________, my date of birth is
(First) (Middle) (Last)
_________, and my address is _______, ___, ____, ______, and
(Street) (City)(State)(Zip Code)
__________, I declare under penalty of perjury that the foregoing is
(Country)
true and correct.
Executed in _______ County, State of ____, on the day of _____, _____
(Month) (Year)

____
Declarant"

(f) Where citation is executed by an alternative method as authorized by Rule 106, proof of service shall be made in the manner ordered by the court.

(g) The return and any document to which it is attached must be filed with the court and may be filed electronically or by facsimile, if those methods of filing are available.

(h) No default judgment shall be granted in any cause until proof of service as provided by this rule or by Rules 108 or 108a, or as ordered by the court in the event citation is executed by alternative method under Rule 106, shall have been on file with the clerk of the court ten days, exclusive of the day of filing and the day of judgment.

(Amended by Order July 11, 1977, eff. Jan. 1, 1978; June 10, 1980, eff. Jan. 1, 1981; July 15, 1987, eff. Jan. 1, 1988; April 24, 1990, eff. Sept. 1, 1990; Oct. 17, 2011, eff. Jan. 1, 2012; Order Dec. 12, 2011, eff. Jan. 1, 2012.)

RULE 108. SERVICE IN ANOTHER STATE

Where the defendant is absent from the State, or is a nonresident of the State, the form of notice to such defendant of the institution of the suit shall be the same as prescribed for citation to a resident defendant; and such notice may be served by any disinterested person who is not less than eighteen years of age, in the same manner as provided in Rule 106 hereof The return of service in such cases shall be in accordance with Rule 107. A defendant served with such notice shall be required to appear and answer in the same manner and time and under the same penalties as if he had been personally served with a citation within this State to the full extent that he may be required to appear and answer under the Constitution of the United States in an action either in rem or in personam.

(Amended by Order July 22, 1975, eff. Jan. 1, 1976; Oct. 17, 2011, eff. Jan. 1, 2012; Order Dec. 12, 2011, eff. Jan. 1, 2012.)

RULE 108a. SERVICE OF PROCESS IN FOREIGN COUNTRIES.

(1) **Manner.** Service of process may be effected upon a party in a foreign country if service of the citation and petition is made: (a) in the manner prescribed by the law of the foreign country for service in that country in an action in any of its courts of general jurisdiction; or (b) as directed by the foreign authority in response to a letter rogatory or a letter of request; or (c) in the manner provided by Rule 106; or (d) pursuant to the terms and provisions of any applicable treaty or convention; or (e) by diplomatic or consular officials when authorized by the United States Department of State; or (f) by any other means directed by the court that is not prohibited by the law of the country where service is to be made. The method for service of process in a foreign country must be reasonably calculated, under all of the circumstances, to give actual notice of the proceedings to the defendant in time to answer and defend. A defendant served with process under this rule shall be required to appear and answer in the same manner and time and under the same penalties as if he had been personally served with citation within this state to the full extent that he may be required to appear and answer under the Constitution of the United States or under any applicable convention or treaty in an action either in rem or in personam.

(2) **Return.** Proof of service may be made as prescribed by the law of the foreign country, by order of the court, by Rule 107, or by a method provided in any applicable treaty or convention.

(Added Dec. 5, 1983, eff. April 1, 1984.)

RULE 109. CITATION BY PUBLICATION.

When a party to a suit, his agent or attorney, shall make oath that the residence of any party defendant is unknown to affiant, and to such party when the affidavit is made by his agent or attorney, or that such defendant is a transient person, and that after due diligence such party and the affiant have been unable to locate the whereabouts of such defendant, or that such defendant is absent from or is a nonresident of the State, and that the party applying for the citation has attempted to obtain personal service of nonresident notice as provided for in Rule 108, but has been unable to do so, the clerk shall issue citation for such defendant for service by publication. In such cases it shall be the duty of the court trying the case to inquire into the sufficiency of the 1 exercised in attempting to ascertain the residence or whereabouts of the defendant or to obtain service of nonresident notice, as the case may be, before granting any judgment on such service.

(Amended by Order Oct. 10, 1945, eff. Feb. 1, 1946; July 22, 1975, eff. Jan. 1, 1976; Dec. 5, 1983, eff. April 1, 1984.)

RULE 109a. OTHER SUBSTITUTED SERVICE.

Whenever citation by publication is authorized, the court may, on motion, prescribe a different method of substituted service, if the court finds, and so recites in its order, that the method so prescribed would be as likely as publication to give defendant actual notice. When such method of substituted service is authorized, the return of the officer executing the citation shall state particularly the manner in which service is accomplished, and shall attach any return receipt, returned mail, or other evidence showing the result of such service. Failure of defendant to respond to such citation shall not render the service invalid. When such substituted service has been obtained and the defendant has not appeared, the provisions of Rules 244 and 329 shall apply as if citation had been served by publication.

(Added July 22, 1975, eff. Jan. 1, 1976.)

RULE 110. EFFECT OF RULES ON OTHER STATUTES.

Where by statute or these rules citation by publication is authorized and the statute or rules do not specify the requisites of such citation or the method of service thereof, or where they direct that such citation be issued or served as in other civil actions, the provisions of these rules shall govern. Where, however, the statute authorizing citation by publication provides expressly for requisites of such citation or service thereof, or both, differing from the provisions of Rules 114, 115, and 116, these rules shall not govern, but the special statutory procedure shall continue in force; provided, however, that Rule 117a shall control with respect to citation in tax suits.

(Amended by Order Aug. 18, 1947, eff. Dec. 31, 1947.)

RULE 111. CITATION BY PUBLICATION IN ACTION AGAINST UNKNOWN HEIRS OR STOCKHOLDERS OF DEFUNCT CORPORATIONS.

If the plaintiff, his agent, or attorney, shall make oath that the names of the heirs or stockholders against whom an action is authorized by Section 17.004, Civil Practice and Remedies Code, are unknown to the affiant, the clerk shall issue a citation for service by publication. Such citation shall be addressed to the defendants by a concise description of their classification, as "the Unknown Heirs of A.B. deceased," or "Unknown Stockholders of ___________ Corporation," as the case may be, and shall contain the other requisites prescribed in Rules 114 and 115 and shall be served as provided by Rule 116.

(Amended by Order July 15, 1987, eff. Jan. 1, 1988.)

RULE 112. PARTIES TO ACTIONS AGAINST UNKNOWN OWNERS OR CLAIMANTS OF INTEREST IN LAND.

In suits authorized by Section 17.005, Civil Practice and Remedies Code, all persons claiming under such conveyance whose names are known to plaintiff shall be made parties by name and cited to appear, in the manner now provided by law as in other suits; all other persons claiming any interest in such land under such conveyance may be made parties to the suit and cited by publication under the designation "all persons claiming any title or interest in land under deed heretofore given to _______________ of ______________ as grantee" (inserting in the blanks the name and residence of grantee as given in such conveyance). It shall be permissible to join in one suit all persons claiming under two or more conveyances affecting title to the same tract of land.

(Amended by Order July 15, 1987, eff. Jan. 1, 1988.)

RULE 113. CITATION BY PUBLICATION IN ACTIONS AGAINST UNKNOWN OWNERS OR CLAIMANTS OF INTEREST IN LAND.

In suits authorized by Section 17.005, Civil Practice and Remedies Code, plaintiff, his agent or attorney shall make and file with the clerk of the court an affidavit, stating

(a) the name of the grantee as set out in the conveyance constituting source of title of defendants, and

(b) stating that affiant does not know the names of any persons claiming title or interest under such conveyance other than as stated in plaintiff's petition and

(c) if the conveyance is to a company or association name as grantee, further stating whether grantee is incorporated or unincorporated, if such fact is known and if such fact is unknown, so stating.

Said clerk shall thereupon issue a citation for service upon all persons claiming any title or interest in such land under such conveyance. The citation in such cases shall contain the requisites and be served in the manner provided by Rules 114, 115 and 116.

(Amended by Order July 20, 1954, eff. Jan. 1, 1955; July 15, 1987, eff. Jan. 1, 1988; April 24, 1990 eff. Sept. 1, 1990.)

RULE 114. CITATION BY PUBLICATION; REQUISITES.

Where citation by publication is authorized by these rules, the citation shall contain the requisites prescribed by Rules 1., and 99, in so far as they are not inconsistent herewith, provided that no copy of the plaintiff's petition shall accompany this citation, and the citation shall be styled "The State of Texas" and shall be directed to the defendant or defendants by name, if their names are known, or to the defendant or defendants as designated in the petition, if unknown or such other classification as may be fixed by any statute or by these rules. Where there are two or more defendants or classes of defendants to be served by publication, the citation may be directed to all of them by name and classification, so that service may be completed by publication of the one citation for the required number of times. The citation shall contain the names of the parties, a brief statement of the nature of the suit (which need not contain the details and particulars of the claim) a description of any property involved and of the interest of the named or unknown defendant or defendants, and, where the suit involves land, the requisites of Rule 115. If issued from the district or county court, the citation shall command such parties to appear and answer at or before 10 o'clock a.m. of the first Monday after the expiration of 42 days from the date of issuance thereof, specifying the day of the week, the day of the month, and the time of day the defendant is required to answer. If issued from the justice of the peace court, such citation shall command such parties to appear and answer on or before the first day of the first term of court which convenes after the expiration of 42 days from the date of issue thereof, specifying the day of the week, and the day of the month, that such term will meet.

(Amended by Order Sept. 20, 1941, eff. Dec. 31, 1941.)

RULE 115. FORM OF PUBLISHED CITATION IN ACTIONS INVOLVING LAND.

In citations by publication involving land, it shall be sufficient in making the brief statement of the claim in such citation to state the kind of suit, the number of acres of land involved in the suit, or the number of the lot and block, or any other plat description that may be of record if the land is situated in a city or town the survey on which and the county in which the land is situated, and any special pleas which are relied upon in such suit.

RULE 116. SERVICE OF CITATION BY PUBLICATION.

The citation, when issued, shall be served by the sheriff or any constable of any county of the State of Texas or by the clerk of the court in which the case is pending, by having the same published once each week for four (4) consecutive weeks, the first publication to be at least twenty-eight (28) days before the return day of the citation. In all suits which do not involve the title to land or the partition of real estate, such publication shall be made in the county where the suit is pending, if there be a newspaper published in said county, but if not, then in an adjoining county where a newspaper is published. In all suits which involve the title to land or partition of real estate, such publication shall be made in the county where the land, or a portion thereof, is situated, if there be a newspaper in such county, but if not, then in an adjoining county to the county where the land or a part thereof is situated, where a newspaper is published.

(Amended by Order Dec. 5, 1983, eff. April 1, 1984.)

RULE 117. RETURN OF CITATION BY PUBLICATION.

The return of the officer executing such citation shall show how and when the citation was executed, specifying the dates of such publication be signed by him officially and shall be accompanied by a printed copy of such publication.

(Amended by Order Oct. 17, 2011, eff. Jan. 1, 2012; Order Dec. 12, 2011, eff. Jan. 1, 2012.)

RULE 117a. CITATION IN SUITS FOR DELINQUENT AD VALOREM TAXES.

In all suits for collection of delinquent ad valorem taxes, the rules of civil procedure governing issuance and service of citation shall control the issuance and service of citation therein, except as herein otherwise specially provided.

1. **Personal Service: Owner and Residence Known, Within State.** Where any defendant in a tax suit is a resident of the State of Texas and is not subject to citation by publication under subdivision 3 below, the process shall conform substantially to the form hereinafter set out for personal service and shall contain the essential elements and be served and returned and otherwise regulated by the provisions of Rules 99 to 107, inclusive.
2. **Personal Service: Owner and Residence Known, Out of State.** Where any such defendant is absent from the State or is a nonresident of the State and is not subject to citation by publication under subdivision 3 below, the process shall conform substantially to the form hereinafter set out for personal service and shall contain the essential elements and be served and returned and otherwise regulated by the provisions of Rule 108.
3. **Service by Publication: Nonresident, Absent from State, Transient, Name Unknown, Residence Unknown, Owner Unknown, Heirs Unknown, Corporate Officers, Trustees, Receivers or Stockholders Unknown, Any Other Unknown Persons Owing or Claiming or Having an Interest.** Where any defendant in a tax suit is a nonresident of the State, or is absent from the State, or is a transient person, or the name or the residence of any owner of any interest in any property upon which a tax lien is sought to be foreclosed, is unknown to the attorney requesting the issuance of process or filing the suit for the taxing unit, and such attorney shall make affidavit that such defendant is a nonresident of the State, or is absent from the State, or is a transient person, or that the name or residence of such owner is unknown and cannot be ascertained after diligent inquiry, each such person in every such class above mentioned, together with any and all other persons, including adverse claimants, owning or claiming or having any legal or equitable interest in or lien upon such property, may be cited by publication. All unknown owners of any interest in any property upon which any taxing unit seeks to foreclose a lien for taxes, including stockholders of corporations—defunct or otherwise—their successors, heirs, and assigns, may be joined in such suit under the designation of "unknown owners" and citation be had upon them as such; provided, however, that record owners of such property or of any apparent interest therein, including, without limitation, record lien holders, shall not be included in the designation of "unknown owners"; and provided further that where any record owner has rendered the property involved within five years before the tax suit is filed, citation on such record owner may not be had by publication or posting unless citation for personal service has been issued as to such record owner, with a notation thereon setting forth the same address as is contained on the rendition sheet made within such five years, and the sheriff or other person to whom citation has been delivered makes his return thereon that he is unable to locate the defendant. Where any attorney filing a tax suit for a taxing unit, or requesting the issuance of process in such suit, shall make affidavit that a corporation is the record owner of any interest in any property upon which a tax lien is sought to be foreclosed, and that he does not know, and after diligent inquiry has been unable to ascertain, the location of the place of business, if any, of such corporation, or the name or place of residence of any officer of such corporation upon whom personal service may be had, such corporation may be cited by publication as herein provided. All defendants of the classes enumerated above may be joined in the same citation by publication.

   An affidavit which complies with the foregoing requirements therefor shall be sufficient basis for the citation above mentioned in connection with it but shall be held to be made upon the criminal responsibility of affiant.

   Such citation by publication shall be directed to the defendants by names or by designation as hereinabove provided, and shall be issued and signed by the clerk of the court in which such tax suit is pending. It shall be sufficient if it states the file number and style of the case, the date of the filing of the petition, the names of all parties by name or by designation as hereinabove provided, and the court in which the suit is pending; shall command such parties to appear and defend such suit at or before 10 o'clock a.m. of the first Monday after the expiration of forty-two days from the date of the issuance thereof, specifying such date when such parties are required to answer; shall state the place of holding the court, the nature of the suit, and the date of the issuance of the citation; and shall be signed and sealed by the clerk.

   The citation shall be published in the English language one time a week for two weeks in some newspaper published in the county in which the property is located, which newspaper must have been in general circulation for at least one year immediately prior to the first publication and shall in every respect answer the requirements of the law applicable to newspapers which are employed for such a purpose, the first publication to be not less than twenty-eight days prior to the return day fixed in the citation; and the affidavit of the editor or publisher of the newspaper giving the date of publication, together with a printed copy of the citation as published, shall constitute sufficient proof of due publication when returned and filed in court. If there is no newspaper published in the county, then the publication may be made in a newspaper in an adjoining county, which newspaper shall in every respect answer the requirements of the law applicable to newspapers which are employed for such a purpose. The maximum fee for publishing the citation shall be the lowest published word or line rate of that newspaper for classified advertising. If the publication of the citation cannot be had for this fee, chargeable as costs and payable upon sale of the property, as provided by law, and this fact is supported by the affidavit of the attorney for the plaintiff or the attorney requesting the issuance of the process, then service of the citation may be made by posting a copy at the courthouse door of the county in which the suit is pending, the citation to be posted at least twenty-eight days prior to the return day fixed in the citation. Proof of the posting of the citation shall be made by affidavit of the attorney for the plaintiff, or of the person posting it. When citation is served as here provided it shall be sufficient, and no other form of citation or notice to the named defendants therein shall be necessary.

4. **Citation in Tax Suits: General Provisions.**. Any process authorized by this rule may issue jointly in behalf of all taxing units who are plaintiffs or intervenors in any tax suit. The statement of the nature of the suit, to be set out in the citation, shall be sufficient if it contains a brief general description of the property upon which the taxes are due and the amount of such taxes, exclusive of interest, penalties, and costs, and shall state, in substance, that in such suit the plaintiff and all other taxing units who may set up their claims therein seek recovery of the delinquent ad valorem taxes due on said property, and the (establishment and foreclosure) of liens, if any, securing the payment of same, as provided by law; that in addition to the taxes all interest, penalties, and costs allowed by law up to and including the day of judgment are included in the suit; and that all parties to the suit, including plaintiff, defendants, and intervenors, shall take notice that claims for any taxes on said property becoming delinquent subsequent to the filing of the suit and up to the day of judgment, together with all interest, penalties, and costs allowed by law thereon, may, upon request therefor, be recovered therein without further citation or notice to any parties thereto. Such citation need not be accompanied by a copy of plaintiff's petition and no such copy need be served. Such citation shall also show the names of all taxing units which assess and collect taxes on said property not made parties to such suit, and shall contain, in substance, a recitation that each party to such suit shall take notice of, and plead and answer to, all claims and pleadings then on file or thereafter filed in said cause by all other parties therein, or who may intervene therein and set up their respective tax claims against said property. After citation or notice has been given on behalf of any plaintiff or intervenor taxing unit, the court shall have jurisdiction to hear and determine the tax claims of all taxing units who are parties plaintiff, intervenor or defendant at the time such process is issued and of all taxing units intervening after such process is issued, not only for the taxes, interest, penalties, and costs which may be due on said property at the time the suit is filed, but those becoming delinquent thereon at any time thereafter up to and including the day of judgment, without the necessity of further citation or notice to any party to said suit; and any taxing unit having a tax claim against said property may, by answer or intervention, set up and have determined its tax claim without the necessity of further citation or notice to any parties to such suit.

5. **Form of Citation by Publication or Posting.** The form of citation by publication or posting shall be sufficient if it is in substantially the following form with proper changes to make the same applicable to personal property, where necessary, and if the suit includes or is for the recovery of taxes assessed on personal property, a general description of such personal property shall be sufficient:

THE STATE OF TEXAS)
COUNTY OF ________________)
In the name and by the authority of the State of Texas
Notice is hereby given as follows:
To

____

and any and all other persons, including adverse claimants, owning or having or claiming any legal or equitable interest in or lien upon the following described property delinquent to Plaintiff herein, for taxes, to-wit:

____

____

____

Which said property is delinquent to Plaintiff for taxes in the following amounts:

$ ______, exclusive of interest, penalties, and costs, and there is included in this suit in addition to the taxes all said interest, penalties, and costs thereon allowed by law up to and including the day of judgment herein.

You are hereby notified that suit has been brought by ___________ as Plaintiffs, against __________ as Defendants, by petition filed on the ______ day of ________________, 19__, in a certain suit styled ____________ v. ___________ for collection of the taxes on said property and that said suit is now pending in the District Court of ________________ County, Texas, ________________ Judicial District, and the file number of said suit is ________________, that the names of all taxing units which assess and collect taxes on the property hereinabove described not made parties to this suit, are ________________.

Plaintiff and all other taxing units who may set up their tax claims herein seek recovery of delinquent ad valorem taxes on the property hereinabove described, and in addition to the taxes all interest, penalties, and costs allowed by law thereon up to and including the day of judgment herein, and the establishment and foreclosure of liens, if any, securing the payment of same, as provided by law.

All parties to this suit, including plaintiff, defendants, and intervenors, shall take notice that claims not only for any taxes which were delinquent on said property at the time this suit was filed but all taxes becoming delinquent thereon at any time thereafter up to the day of judgment, including all interest, penalties, and costs allowed by law thereon, may, upon request therefor, be recovered herein without further citation or notice to any parties herein, and all said parties shall take notice of and plead and answer to all claims and pleadings now on file and which may hereafter be filed in said cause by all other parties herein, and all of those taxing units above named who may intervene herein and set up their respective tax claims against said property.

You are hereby commanded to appear and defend such suit on the first Monday after the expiration of forty-two (42) days from and after the date of issuance hereof, the same being the _____ day of __________ A.D., 19__ (which is the return day of such citation), before the honorable District Court of ______________ County, Texas, to be held at the courthouse thereof, then and there to show cause why judgment shall not be rendered for such taxes, penalties, interest, and costs, and condemning said property and ordering foreclosure of the constitutional and statutory tax liens thereon for taxes due the plaintiff and the taxing units parties hereto, and those who may intervene herein, together with all interest, penalties, and costs allowed by law up to and including the day of judgment herein, and all costs of this suit.

Issued and given under my hand and seal of said court in the City of __________,____________County, Texas, this ____ day of _________, A.D., 19__.

____
Clerk of the District Court.
____________ County, Texas,
____________ Judicial District.

6. **Form of Citation by Personal Service In or Out of State.** The form of citation for personal service shall be sufficient if it is in substantially the following form, with proper changes to make the same applicable to personal property, where necessary, and if the suit includes or is for the recovery of taxes assessed on personal property, a general description of such personal property shall be sufficient:

THE STATE OF TEXAS
To ________________, Defendant,
GREETING:

YOU ARE HEREBY COMMANDED to appear and answer before the Honorable District Court, _________________ Judicial District, _______________ County, Texas, at the Courthouse of said county in __________, Texas, at or before 10 o'clock a.m. of the Monday next after the expiration of 20 days from the date of service of this citation, then and there to answer the petition of ____________ Plaintiff, filed in said Court on the __________ day of ___________, A.D., 19__, against ____________, Defendant, said suit being number _______ on the docket of said Court, the nature of which demand is a suit to collect delinquent ad valorem taxes on the property hereinafter described.

The amount of taxes due Plaintiff, exclusive of interest, penalties, and costs, is the sum of $ __________, said property being described as follows, to-wit: ____.

The names of all taxing units which assess and collect taxes on said property, not made parties to this suit, are: ____

Plaintiff and all other taxing units who may set up their tax claims herein seek recovery of delinquent ad valorem taxes on the property hereinabove described, and in addition to the taxes all interest, penalties, and costs allowed by law thereon up to and including the day of judgment herein, and the establishment and foreclosure of liens securing the payment of same, as provided by law.

All parties to this suit, including plaintiff, defendants, and intervenors, shall take notice that claims not only for any taxes which were delinquent on said property at the time this suit was filed but all taxes becoming delinquent thereon at any time thereafter up to the day of judgment, including all interest, penalties, and costs allowed by law thereon, may, upon request therefor, be recovered herein without further citation or notice to any parties herein, and all said parties shall take notice of and plead and answer to all claims and pleadings now on file and which may hereafter be filed in this cause by all other parties hereto, and by all of those taxing units above named, who may intervene herein and set up their respective tax claims against said property.

If this citation is not served within 90 days after the date of its issuance, it shall be returned unserved.

The officer executing this return shall promptly serve the same according to the requirements of law and the mandates hereof and make due return as the law directs.

Issued and given under my hand and seal of said Court at _________________, Texas, this the ___________ day of _____________, A.D., 19__.

____
Clerk of the District Court of
______________ County, Texas.
By ______________________, Deputy.

(Added Aug. 18, 1947, eff. Dec. 31, 1947. Amended by Order May 4, 1948, eff. Oct. 1, 1948; July 17, 1950, eff. Dec. 1, 1950; July 15, 1987, eff. Jan. 1, 1988.)

RULE 118. AMENDMENT.

At any time in its discretion and upon such notice and on such terms as it deems just, the court may allow any process or proof of service thereof to be amended, unless it clearly appears that material prejudice would result to the substantial rights of the party against whom the process issued.

RULE 119. ACCEPTANCE OF SERVICE.

The defendant may accept service of process, or waive the issuance or service thereof by a written memorandum signed by him, or by his duly authorized agent or attorney, after suit is brought, sworn to before a proper officer other than an attorney in the case, and filed among the papers of the cause, and such waiver or acceptance shall have the same force and effect as if the citation had been issued and served as provided by law. The party signing such memorandum shall be delivered a copy of plaintiff's petition, and the receipt of the same shall be acknowledged in such memorandum. In every divorce action such memorandum shall also include the defendant's mailing address.

(Amended by Order Sept. 20, 1941, eff. Dec. 31, 1941; July 20, 1954, eff. Jan. 1, 1955; July 26, 1960, eff. Jan. 1, 1961.)

RULE 119a. COPY OF DECREE.

The district clerk shall forthwith mail a certified copy of the final divorce decree or order of dismissal to the party signing a memorandum waiving issuance or service of process. Such divorce decree or order of dismissal shall be mailed to the signer of the memorandum at the address stated in such memorandum or to the office of his attorney of record.

(Added July 20, 1954, eff. Jan. 1, 1955.)

RULE 120. ENTERING APPEARANCE.

The defendant may, in person, or by attorney, or by his duly authorized agent, enter an appearance in open court. Such appearance shall be noted by the judge upon his docket and entered in the minutes, and shall have the same force and effect as if the citation had been duly issued and served as provided by law.

RULE 120a. SPECIAL APPEARANCE.

1. Notwithstanding the provisions of Rules 121, 122 and 123, a special appearance may be made by any party either in person or by attorney for the purpose of objecting to the jurisdiction of the court over the person or property of the defendant on the ground that such party or property is not amenable to process issued by the courts of this State. A special appearance may be made as to an entire proceeding or as to any severable claim involved therein. Such special appearance shall be made by sworn motion filed prior to motion to transfer venue or any other plea, pleading or motion; provided however, that a motion to transfer venue and any other plea, pleading, or motion may be contained in the same instrument or filed subsequent thereto without waiver of such special appearance; and may be amended to cure defects. The issuance of process for witnesses, the taking of depositions, the serving of requests for admissions, and the use of discovery processes, shall not constitute a waiver of such special appearance. Every appearance, prior to judgment, not in compliance with this rule is a general appearance.
2. Any motion to challenge the jurisdiction provided for herein shall be heard and determined before a motion to transfer venue or any other plea or pleading may be heard. No determination of any issue of fact in connection with the objection to jurisdiction is a determination of the merits of the case or any aspect thereof.
3. The court shall determine the special appearance on the basis of the pleadings, any stipulations made by and between the parties, such affidavits and attachments as may be filed by the parties, the results of discovery processes, and any oral testimony. The affidavits, if any, shall be served at least seven days before the hearing, shall be made on personal knowledge, shall set forth specific facts as would be admissible in evidence, and shall show affirmatively that the affiant is competent to testify.

   Should it appear from the affidavits of a party opposing the motion that he cannot for reasons stated present by affidavit facts essential to justify his opposition, the court may order a continuance to permit affidavits to be obtained or depositions to be taken or discovery to be had or may make such other order as is just.

   Should it appear to the satisfaction of the court at any time that any of such affidavits are presented in violation of Rule 13, the court shall impose sanctions in accordance with that rule.
4. If the court sustains the objection to jurisdiction, an appropriate order shall be entered. If the objection to jurisdiction is overruled, the objecting party may thereafter appear generally for any purpose. Any such special appearance or such general appearance shall not be deemed a waiver of the objection to jurisdiction when the objecting party or subject matter is not amenable to process issued by the courts of this State.

(Added April 12, 1962, eff. Sept. 1, 1962. Amended by Order July 22, 1975, eff. Jan. 1, 1976; June 15, 1983, eff. Sept. 1, 1983; April 24, 1990, eff. Sept. 1, 1990.)

RULE 121. ANSWER IS APPEARANCE.

An answer shall constitute an appearance of the defendant so as to dispense with the necessity for the issuance or service of citation upon him.

RULE 122. CONSTRUCTIVE APPEARANCE.

If the citation or service thereof is quashed on motion of the defendant, such defendant shall be deemed to have entered his appearance at ten o'clock a.m. on the Monday next after the expiration of twenty (20) days after the day on which the citation or service is quashed, and such defendant shall be deemed to have been duly served so as to require him to appear and answer at that time, and if he fails to do so, judgment by default may be rendered against him.

RULE 123. REVERSAL OF JUDGMENT.

Where the judgment is reversed on appeal or writ of error for the want of service, or because of defective service of process, no new citation shall be issued or served, but the defendant shall be presumed to have entered his appearance to the term of the court at which the mandate shall be filed.

RULE 124. NO JUDGMENT WITHOUT SERVICE.

In no case shall judgment be rendered against any defendant unless upon service, or acceptance or waiver of process, or upon an appearance by the defendant, as prescribed in these rules, except where otherwise expressly provided by law or these rules.

When a party asserts a counterclaim or a cross-claim against another party who has entered an appearance, the claim may be served in any manner prescribed for service of citation or as provided in Rule 21(a).

(Amended by Order Dec. 5, 1983, eff. April 1, 1984.)

SECTION 6.
COSTS AND SECURITY THEREFOR

RULE 125. PARTIES RESPONSIBLE.

Each party to a suit shall be liable to the officers of the court for all costs incurred by himself.

RULE 126. FEE FOR SERVICE OF PROCESS IN A COUNTY OTHER THAN IN THE COUNTY OF SUIT.

(a) *General Rule: Fee Due Before Service.* A sheriff or constable may require payment before serving process in a case pending in a county other than the county in which the sheriff or constable is an officer.

(b) *Exception: Statement of Inability to Afford Payment of Court Costs Filed.* If a Statement of Inability to Afford Payment of Court Costs has been filed in a case in which the declarant requests service of process in a county other than in the county of suit, the clerk must indicate on the document to be served that a Statement of Inability to Afford Payment of Court Costs has been filed. The sheriff or constable must execute the service without demanding payment.

(Amended by Tex. Sup. Ct. Misc. Docket No. 16-9056, eff. Sept. 1, 2016; Tex. Sup. Ct. Misc. Docket No. 16-9122, eff. Sept. 1, 2016.)

[Statement of Inability to Afford Payment of Court Costs as provided in Tex. Sup. Ct. Misc. Docket No. 16-9122, eff. Sept. 1, 2016 and applies to any contest of, or challenge to, a claim of inability to afford payment of court costs that is pending on September 1, 2016.]

RULE 127. PARTIES LIABLE FOR OTHER COSTS.

Each party to a suit shall be liable for all costs incurred by him. If the costs cannot be collected from the party against whom they have been adjudged, execution may issue against any party in such suit for the amount of costs incurred by such party, but no more.

RULE 128. [REPEALED]

(Repealed by Order Dec. 5, 1983, eff. April 1, 1984.)

RULE 129. HOW COSTS COLLECTED.

If any party responsible for costs fails or refuses to pay the same within ten days after demand for payment, the clerk or justice of the peace may make certified copy of the bill of costs then due, and place the same in the hands of the sheriff or constable for collection. All taxes imposed on law proceedings shall be included in the bill of costs. Such certified bill of costs shall have the force and effect of an execution. The removal of a case by appeal shall not prevent the issuance of an execution for costs.

(Amended by Order Dec. 5, 1983, eff. April 1, 1984.)

RULE 130. OFFICER TO LEVY.

The sheriff or constable upon demand and failure to pay said bill of costs, may levy upon a sufficient amount of property of the person from whom said costs are due to satisfy the same, and sell such property as under execution. Where such party is not a resident of the county where such suit is pending, the payment of such costs may be demanded of his attorney of record; and neither the clerk nor justice of the peace shall be allowed to charge any fee for making out such certified bill of costs, unless he is compelled to make a levy.

RULE 131. SUCCESSFUL PARTY TO RECOVER.

The successful party to a suit shall recover of his adversary all costs incurred therein, except where otherwise provided.

RULE 132. [REPEALED]

(Repealed by Order Dec. 5, 1983, eff. April 1, 1984.)

RULE 133. COSTS OF MOTION.

The court may give or refuse costs on motions at its discretion, except where otherwise provided by law or these rules.

RULES 134 AND 135. [REPEALED]

(Repealed by Order Dec. 5, 1983, eff. April 1, 1984.)

RULE 136. DEMAND REDUCED BY PAYMENTS.

Where the plaintiff's demand is reduced by payment to an amount which would not have been within the jurisdiction of the court, the defendant shall recover his costs.

RULE 137. IN ASSAULT AND BATTERY, ETC.

In civil actions for assault and battery, slander and defamation of character, if the verdict or judgment shall be for the plaintiff, but for less than twenty dollars, the plaintiff shall not recover his costs, but each party shall be taxed with the costs incurred by him in such suit.

RULE 138. COST OF NEW TRIALS.

The costs of new trials may either abide the result of the suit or may be taxed against the party to whom the new trial is granted, as the court may adjudge when he grants such new trial.

RULE 139. ON APPEAL AND CERTIORARI.

When a case is appealed, if the judgment of the higher court be against the appellant, but for less amount than the original judgment, such party shall recover the costs of the higher court but shall be adjudged to pay the costs of the court below; if the judgment be against him for the same or a greater amount than in the court below, the adverse party shall recover the costs of both courts. If the judgment of the court above be in favor of the party appealing and for more than the original judgment, such party shall recover the costs of both courts; if the judgment be in his favor, but for the same or a less amount than in the court below, he shall recover the costs of the court below, and pay the costs of the court above.

RULE 140. NO FEE FOR COPY.

No fee for a copy of a paper not required by law or these rules to be copied shall be taxed in the bill of costs.

RULE 141. COURT MAY OTHERWISE ADJUDGE COSTS.

The court may, for good cause, to be stated on the record, adjudge the costs otherwise than as provided by law or these rules.

RULE 142. SECURITY FOR COSTS.

The clerk shall require from the plaintiff fees for services rendered before issuing any process unless filing is requested pursuant to Rule 145 of these rules.

(Amended by Order March 31, 1941, eff. Sept. 1, 1941; July 15, 1987, eff. Jan. 1, 1988.)

RULE 143. RULE FOR COSTS.

A party seeking affirmative relief may be ruled to give security for costs at any time before final judgment, upon motion of any party, or any officer of the court interested in the costs accruing in such suit, or by the court upon its own motion. If such rule be entered against any party and he failed to comply therewith on or before twenty (20) days after notice that such rule has been entered, the claim for affirmative relief of such party shall be dismissed.

(Amended by Order July 21, 1970, eff. Jan. 1, 1971.)

RULE 143a. COSTS ON APPEAL TO COUNTY COURT.

If the appellant fails to pay the costs on appeal from a judgment of a justice of the peace or small claims court within twenty (20) days after being notified to do so by the county clerk, the appeal shall be deemed not perfected and the county clerk shall return all papers in said cause to the justice of the peace having original jurisdiction and the justice of the peace shall proceed as though no appeal had been attempted.

(Added July 22, 1975, eff. Jan. 1, 1976.)

RULE 144. JUDGMENT ON COST BOND.

All bonds given as security for costs shall authorize judgment against all the obligors in such bond for the said costs, to be entered in the final judgment of the cause.

RULE 145. PAYMENT OF COSTS NOT REQUIRED.

(a) *General Rule.* A party who files a Statement of Inability to Afford Payment of Court Costs cannot be required to pay costs except by order of the court as provided by this rule. After the Statement is filed, the clerk must docket the case, issue citation, and provide any other service that is ordinarily provided to a party. The Statement must either be sworn to before a notary or made under penalty of perjury. In this rule, "declarant" means the party filing the Statement.

(b) *Supreme Court Form; Clerk to Provide.* The declarant must use the form Statement approved by the Supreme Court, or the Statement must include the information required by the Court-approved form. The clerk must make the form available to all persons without charge or request.

(c) *Costs Defined.* "Costs" mean any fee charged by the court or an officer of the court that could be taxed in a bill of costs, including, but not limited to, filing fees, fees for issuance and service of process, fees for a court-appointed professional, and fees charged by the clerk or court reporter for preparation of the appellate record.

(d) *Defects.* The clerk may refuse to file a Statement that is not sworn to before a notary or made under penalty of perjury. No other defect is a ground for refusing to file a Statement or requiring the party to pay costs. If a defect or omission in a Statement is material, the court—on its own motion or on motion of the clerk or any party—may direct the declarant to correct or clarify the Statement.

(e) *Evidence of Inability to Afford Costs Required.* The Statement must say that the declarant cannot afford to pay costs. The declarant must provide in the Statement, and, if available, in attachments to the Statement, evidence of the declarant's inability to afford costs, such as evidence that the declarant:

(1) receives benefits from a government entitlement program, eligibility for which is dependent on the recipient's means;

(2) is being represented in the case by an attorney who is providing free legal services to the declarant, without contingency, through:

(A) a provider funded by the Texas Access to Justice Foundation;

(B) a provider funded by the Legal Services Corporation; or

(C) a nonprofit that provides civil legal services to persons living at or below 200% of the federal poverty guidelines published annually by the United States Department of Health and Human Services;

(3) has applied for free legal services for the case through a provider listed in(e)(2) and was determined to be financially eligible but was declined representation; or

(4) does not have funds to afford payment of costs.

(f) *Requirement to Pay Costs Notwithstanding Statement.* The court may order the declarant to pay costs only as follows:

(1) *On Motion by the Clerk or a Party.* The clerk or any party may move to require the declarant to pay costs only if the motion contains sworn evidence, not merely on information or belief:

(A) that the Statement was materially false when it was made; or

(B) that because of changed circumstances, the Statement is no longer true in material respects.

(2) *On Motion by the Attorney Ad Litem for a Parent in Certain Cases.* An attorney ad litem appointed to represent a parent under Section 107.013,Family Code, may move to require the parent to pay costs only if the motion complies with (f)(1).

(3) *On Motion by the Court Reporter.* When the declarant requests the preparation of a reporter's record but cannot make arrangements to pay for it, the court reporter may move to require the declarant to prove the inability to afford costs.

(4) *On the Court's Own Motion.* Whenever evidence comes before the court that the declarant may be able to afford costs, or when an officer or professional must be appointed in the case, the court may require the declarant to prove the inability to afford costs.

(5) *Notice and Hearing.* The declarant may not be required to pay costs without an oral evidentiary hearing. The declarant must be given 10 days' notice of the hearing. Notice must either be in writing and served in accordance with Rule 21a or given in open court. At the hearing, the burden is on the declarant to prove the inability to afford costs.

(6) *Findings Required.* An order requiring the declarant to pay costs must be supported by detailed findings that the declarant can afford to pay costs.

(7) *Partial and Delayed Payment.* The court may order that the declarant pay the part of the costs the declarant can afford or that payment be made in installments. But the court must not delay the case if payment is made in installments.

(g) *Review of Trial Court Order.*

(1) *Only Declarant May Challenge; Motion.* Only the declarant may challenge an order issued by the trial court under this rule. The declarant may challenge the order by motion filed in the court of appeals with jurisdiction over an appeal from the judgment in the case. The declarant is not required to pay any filing fees related to the motion in the court of appeals.

(2) *Time for Filing; Extension.* The motion must be filed within 10 days after the trial court's order is signed. The court of appeals may extend the deadline by 15 days if the declarant demonstrates good cause for the extension in writing.

(3) *Record.* After a motion is filed, the court of appeals must promptly send notice to the trial court clerk and the court reporter requesting preparation of the record of all trial court proceedings on the declarant's claim of indigence. The court may set a deadline for filing the record. The record must be provided without charge.

(4) *Court of Appeals to Rule Promptly.* The court of appeals must rule on the motion at the earliest practicable time.

(h) *Judgment.* The judgment must not require the declarant to pay costs, and a provision in the judgment purporting to do so is void, unless the court has issued an order under (f), or the declarant has obtained a monetary recovery, and the court orders the recovery to be applied toward payment of costs.

Comment to 2016 Change: The rule has been rewritten. Access to the civil justice system cannot be denied because a person cannot afford to pay court costs. Whether a particular fee is a court cost is governed by this rule, Civil Practice and Remedies Code Section 31.007, and case law.

The issue is not merely whether a person can pay costs, but whether the person can afford to pay costs. A person may have sufficient cash on hand to pay filing fees, but the person cannot afford the fees if paying them would preclude the person from paying for basic essentials, like housing or food. Experience indicates that almost all filers described in (e)(1)-(3), and most filers described in (e)(4), cannot in fact afford to pay costs.

Because costs to access the system—filing fees, fees for issuance of process and notices, and fees for service and return—are kept relatively small, the expense involved in challenging a claim of inability to afford costs often exceeds the costs themselves. Thus, the rule does not allow the clerk or a party to challenge a litigant's claim of inability to afford costs without sworn evidence that the claim is false. The filing of a Statement of Inability to Afford Payment of Court Costs—which may either be sworn to before a notary or made under penalty of perjury, as permitted by Civil Practice and Remedies Code Section 132.001—is all that is needed to require the clerk to provide ordinary services without payment of fees and costs. But evidence may come to light that the claim was false when made. And the declarant's circumstances may change, so that the claim is no longer true. Importantly, costs may increase with the appointment of officers or professionals in the case, or when a reporter's record must be prepared. The reporter is always allowed to challenge a claim of inability to afford costs before incurring the substantial expense of record preparation. The trial court always retains discretion to require evidence of an inability to afford costs.

(Amended by Order Dec. 5, 1983, eff. April 1, 1984; July 15, 1987, eff. Jan. 1, 1988; Tex. Sup. Ct. Misc. Docket No. 16-9056, eff. Sept. 1, 2016; Tex. Sup. Ct. Misc. Docket No. 16-9122, eff. Sept. 1, 2016.)

[Statement of Inability to Afford Payment of Court Costs as provided in Tex. Sup. Ct. Misc. Docket No. 16-9122, eff. Sept. 1, 2016 and applies to any contest of, or challenge to, a claim of inability to afford payment of court costs that is pending on September 1, 2016.]

RULE 146. DEPOSIT FOR COSTS.

In lieu of a bond for costs, the party required to give the same may deposit with the clerk of court or the justice of the peace such sum as the court or justice from time to time may designate as sufficient to pay the accrued costs.

RULE 147. APPLIES TO ANY PARTY.

The foregoing rules as to security and rule for costs shall apply to any party who seeks a judgment against any other party.

(Amended by Order Dec. 5, 1983, eff. April 1, 1984.)

RULE 148. SECURED BY OTHER BOND.

No further security shall be required if the costs are secured by the provisions of an attachment or other bond filed by the party required to give security for costs.

RULE 149. EXECUTION FOR COSTS.

When costs have been adjudged against a party and are not paid, the clerk or justice of the court in which the suit was determined may issue execution, accompanied by an itemized bill of costs, against such party to be levied and collected as in other cases; and said officer, on demand of any party to whom any such costs are due, shall issue execution for costs at once. This rule shall not apply to executors, administrators or guardians in cases where costs are adjudged against the estate of a deceased person or of a ward. No execution shall issue in any case for costs until after judgment rendered therefor by the court.

SECTION 7.
ABATEMENT AND DISCONTINUANCE OF SUIT

RULE 150. DEATH OF PARTY.

Where the cause of action is one which survives, no suit shall abate because of the death of any party thereto before the verdict or decision of the court is rendered, but such suit may proceed to judgment as hereinafter provided.

RULE 151. DEATH OF PLAINTIFF.

If the plaintiff dies, the heirs, or the administrator or executor of such decedent may appear and upon suggestion of such death being entered of record in open court, may be made plaintiff, and the suit shall proceed in his or their name. If no such appearance and suggestion be made within a reasonable time after the death of the plaintiff, the clerk upon the application of defendant, his agent or attorney, shall issue a scire facias for the heirs or the administrator or executor of such decedent, requiring him to appear and prosecute such suit. After service of such scire facias, should such heir or administrator or executor fail to enter appearance within the time provided, the defendant may have the suit dismissed.

(Amended by Order Dec. 5, 1983, eff. April 1, 1984.)

RULE 152. DEATH OF DEFENDANT.

Where the defendant shall die, upon the suggestion of death being entered of record in open court, or upon petition of the plaintiff, the clerk shall issue a scire facias for the administrator or executor or heir requiring him to appear and defend the suit and upon the return of such service, the suit shall proceed against such administrator or executor or heir.

RULE 153. WHEN EXECUTOR, ETC., DIES.

When an executor or administrator shall be a party to any suit, whether as plaintiff or as defendant, and shall die or cease to be such executor or administrator, the suit may be continued by or against the person succeeding him in the administration, or by or against the heirs, upon like proceedings being had as provided in the two preceding rules, or the suit may be dismissed, as provided in Rule 151.

(Amended by Order Dec. 5, 1983, eff. April 1, 1984.)

RULE 154. REQUISITES OF SCIRE FACIAS.

The scire facias and returns thereon, provided for in this section, shall conform to the requisites of citations and the returns thereon, under the provisions of these rules.

RULE 155. SURVIVING PARTIES.

Where there are two or more plaintiffs or defendants, and one or more of them die, upon suggestion of such death being entered upon the record, the suit shall at the instance of either party proceed in the name of the surviving plaintiffs or against the surviving defendants, as the case may be.

RULE 156. DEATH AFTER VERDICT OR CLOSE OF EVIDENCE.

When a party in a jury case dies between verdict and judgment, or a party in a non-jury case dies after the evidence is closed and before judgment is pronounced, judgment shall be rendered and entered as if all parties were living.

(Amended by Order July 11, 1977, eff. Jan. 1, 1978.)

RULE 157. [REPEALED]

(Repealed by Order July 15, 1987, eff. Jan. 1, 1988.)

RULE 158. SUIT FOR THE USE OF ANOTHER.

When a plaintiff suing for the use of another shall die before verdict, the person for whose use such suit was brought, upon such death being suggested on the record in open court, may prosecute the suit in his own name, and shall be as responsible for costs as if he brought the suit.

RULE 159. SUIT FOR INJURIES RESULTING IN DEATH.

In cases arising under the provisions of the title relating to injuries resulting in death, the suit shall not abate by the death of either party pending the suit, but in such case, if the plaintiff dies, where there is only one plaintiff, some one or more of the parties entitled to the money recovered may be substituted and the suit prosecuted to judgment in the name of such party or parties, for the benefit of the person entitled, if the defendant dies, his executor, administrator or heir may be made a party, and the suit prosecuted to judgment.

RULE 160. DISSOLUTION OF CORPORATION.

The dissolution of a corporation shall not operate to abate any pending suit in which such corporation is a defendant, but such suit shall continue against such corporation and judgment shall be rendered as though the same were not dissolved.

RULE 161. WHERE SOME DEFENDANTS NOT SERVED.

When some of the several defendants in a suit are served with process in due time and others are not so served, the plaintiff may either dismiss as to those not so served and proceed against those who are, or he may take new process against those not served, or may obtain severance of the case as between those served and those not served, but no dismissal shall be allowed as to a principal obligor without also dismissing the parties secondarily liable except in cases provided by statute. No defendant against whom any suit may be so dismissed shall be thereby exonerated from any liability, but may at any time be proceeded against as if no such suit had been brought and no such dismissal ordered.

(Amended by Order Dec. 5, 1983, eff. April 1, 1984; April 24, 1984, eff. Oct. 1, 1984; July 15, 1987, eff. Jan. 1, 1988.)

RULE 162. DISMISSAL OR NON-SUIT.

At any time before the plaintiff has introduced all of his evidence other than rebuttal evidence, the plaintiff may dismiss a case, or take a non-suit, which shall be entered in the minutes. Notice of the dismissal or non-suit shall be served in accordance with Rule 21a on any party who has answered or has been served with process without necessity of court order.

Any dismissal pursuant to this rule shall not prejudice the right of an adverse party to be heard on a pending claim for affirmative relief or excuse the payment of all costs taxed by the clerk. A dismissal under this rule shall have no effect on any motion for sanctions, attorney's fees or other costs, pending at the time of dismissal, as determined by the court. Any dismissal pursuant to this rule which terminates the case shall authorize the clerk to tax court costs against dismissing party unless otherwise ordered by the court.

(Amended by Order Dec. 5, 1983, eff. April 1, 1984; July 15, 1987, eff. Jan. 1, 1988.)

RULE 163. DISMISSAL AS TO PARTIES SERVED, ETC.

When it will not prejudice another party, the plaintiff may dismiss his suit as to one or more of several parties who were served with process, or who have answered, but no such dismissal shall in any case, be allowed as to a principal obligor, except in the cases provided for by statute.

(Amended by Order Dec. 5, 1983, eff. April 1, 1984; July 15, 1987, eff. Jan. 1, 1988.)

RULE 164. [REPEALED]

(Repealed by Order July 15, 1987, eff. Jan. 1, 1988.)

RULE 165. ABANDONMENT.

A party who abandons any part of his claim or defense, as contained in the pleadings, may have that fact entered of record, so as to show that the matters therein were not tried.

RULE 165a. DISMISSAL FOR WANT OF PROSECUTION.

1. **Failure to Appear.** A case may be dismissed for want of prosecution on failure of any party seeking affirmative relief to appear for any hearing or trial of which the party had notice. Notice of the court's intention to dismiss and the date and place of the dismissal hearing shall be sent by the clerk to each attorney of record, and to each party not represented by an attorney and whose address is shown on the docket or in the papers on file, by posting same in the United States Postal Service. At the dismissal hearing, the court shall dismiss for want of prosecution unless there is good cause for the case to be maintained on the docket. If the court determines to maintain the case on the docket, it shall render a pretrial order assigning a trial date for the case and setting deadlines for the joining of new parties, all discovery, filing of all pleadings, the making of a response or supplemental responses to discovery and other pretrial matters. The case may be continued thereafter only for valid and compelling reasons specifically determined by court order. Notice of the signing of the order of dismissal shall be given as provided in Rule 306a. Failure to mail notices as required by this rule shall not affect any of the periods mentioned in Rule 306a except as provided in that rule.
2. **Non-compliance With Time Standards.** Any case not disposed of within time standards promulgated by the Supreme Court under its Administrative Rules may be placed on a dismissal docket.
3. **Reinstatement.** A motion to reinstate shall set forth the grounds therefor and be verified by the movant or his attorney. It shall be filed with the clerk within 30 days after the order of dismissal is signed or within the period provided by Rule

306a. A copy of the motion to reinstate shall be served on each attorney of record and each party not represented by an attorney whose address is shown on the docket or in the papers on file. The clerk shall deliver a copy of the motion to the judge, who shall set a hearing on the motion as soon as practicable. The court shall notify all parties or their attorneys of record of the date, time and place of the hearing.

The court shall reinstate the case upon finding after a hearing that the failure of the party or his attorney was not intentional or the result of conscious indifference but was due to an accident or mistake or that the failure has been otherwise reasonably explained.

In the event for any reason a motion for reinstatement is not decided by signed written order within seventy-five days after the judgment is signed, or, within such other time as may be allowed by Rule 306a, the motion shall be deemed overruled by operation of law. If a motion to reinstate is timely filed by any party, the trial court, regardless of whether an appeal has been perfected, has plenary power to reinstate the case until 30 days after all such timely filed motions are overruled, either by a written and signed order or by operation of law, whichever occurs first.

4. **Cumulative Remedies.** This dismissal and reinstatement procedure shall be cumulative of the rules and laws governing any other procedures available to the parties in such cases. The same reinstatement procedures and timetable are applicable to all dismissals for want of prosecution including cases which are dismissed pursuant to the court's inherent power, whether or not a motion to dismiss has been filed.

(Added Oct. 3, 1972, eff. Feb. 1, 1973. Amended July 22, 1975, eff. Jan. 1, 1976; Dec. 5, 1983; July 15, 1987, eff. Jan. 1, 1988.)

SECTION 8.
PRE-TRIAL PROCEDURE

RULE 166. PRETRIAL CONFERENCE.

In an appropriate action, to assist in the disposition of the case without undue expense or burden to the parties, the court may in its discretion direct the attorneys for the parties and the parties or their duly authorized agents to appear before it for a conference to consider:

(a) All pending dilatory pleas, motions and exceptions;
(b) The necessity or desirability of amendments to the pleadings;
(c) A discovery schedule;
(d) Requiring written statements of the parties' contentions;
(e) Contested issues of fact and simplification of the issues;
(f) The possibility of obtaining stipulations of fact;
(g) The identification of legal matters to be ruled on or decided by the court;
(h) The exchange of a list of direct fact witnesses, other than rebuttal or impeaching witnesses the necessity of whose testimony cannot reasonably be anticipated before the time of trial, who will be called to testify at trial, stating their address and telephone number, and the subject of the testimony of each such witness;
(i) The exchange of a list of expert witnesses who will be called to testify at trial, stating their address and telephone number, and the subject of the testimony and opinions that will be proffered by each expert witness;
(j) Agreed applicable propositions of law and contested issues of law;
(k) Proposed jury charge questions, instructions, and definitions for a jury case or proposed findings of fact and conclusions of law for a nonjury case;
(l) The marking and exchanging of all exhibits that any party may use at trial and stipulation to the authenticity and admissibility of exhibits to be used at trial;
(m) Written trial objections to the opposite party's exhibits, stating the basis for each objection;
(n) The advisability of a preliminary reference of issues to a master or auditor for findings to be used as evidence when the trial is to be by jury;
(o) The settlement of the case, and to aid such consideration, the court may encourage settlement;
(p) Such other matters as may aid in the disposition of the action.

The court shall make an order that recites the action taken at the pretrial conference, the amendments allowed to the pleadings, the time within which same may be filed, and the agreements made by the parties as to any of the matters considered, and which limits the issues for trial to those not disposed of by admissions, agreements of counsel, or rulings of the court; and such order when issued shall control the subsequent course of the action, unless modified at the trial to prevent manifest injustice. The court in its discretion may establish by rule a pretrial calendar on which actions may be placed for consideration as above provided and may either confine the calendar to jury actions or extend it to all actions.

Pretrial proceedings in multidistrict litigation may also be governed by Rules 11 and 13 of the Rules of Judicial Administration.

(Amended by Order July 26, 1960, eff. Jan. 1, 1961; April 24, 1990, eff. Sept. 1, 1990; Aug. 29, 2003, eff. Sept. 1, 2003.)

RULE 166a. SUMMARY JUDGMENT.

(a) **For Claimant.** A party seeking to recover upon a claim, counterclaim, or cross-claim or to obtain a declaratory judgment may, at any time after the adverse party has appeared or answered, move with or without supporting affidavits for a summary judgment in his favor upon all or any part thereof A summary judgment, interlocutory in character, may be rendered on the issue of liability alone although there is a genuine issue as to amount of damages.

(b) **For Defending Party.** A party against whom a claim, counterclaim, or cross-claim is asserted or a declaratory judgment is sought may, at any time, move with or without supporting affidavits for a summary judgment in his favor as to all or any part thereof.

(c) **Motion and Proceedings Thereon.** The motion for summary judgment shall state the specific grounds therefor. Except on leave of court, with notice to opposing counsel, the motion and any supporting affidavits shall be filed and served at least twenty-one days before the time specified for hearing. Except on leave of court, the adverse party, not later than seven days prior to the day of hearing may file and serve opposing affidavits or other written response. No oral testimony shall be received at the hearing. The judgment sought shall be rendered forthwith if (i) the deposition transcripts, interrogatory answers, and other discovery responses referenced or set forth in the motion or response, and (ii) the pleadings, admissions, affidavits, stipulations of the parties, and authenticated or certified public records, if any, on file at the time of the hearing, or filed thereafter and before judgment with permission of the court, show that, except as to the amount of damages, there is no genuine issue as to any material fact and the moving party is entitled to judgment as a matter of law on the issues expressly set out in the motion or in an answer or any other response. Issues not expressly presented to the trial court by written motion, answer or other response shall not be considered on appeal as grounds for reversal. A summary judgment may be based on uncontroverted testimonial evidence of an interested witness, or of an expert witness as to subject matter concerning which the trier of fact must be guided solely by the opinion testimony of experts, if the evidence is clear, positive and direct, otherwise credible and free from contradictions and inconsistencies, and could have been readily controverted.

(d) **Appendices, References and Other Use of Discovery Not Otherwise on File.** Discovery products not on file with the clerk may be used as summary judgment evidence if copies of the material, appendices containing the evidence, or a notice containing specific references to the discovery or specific references to other instruments, are filed and served on all parties together with a statement of intent to use the specified discovery as summary judgment proofs: (i) at least twenty-one days before the hearing if such proofs are to be used to support the summary judgment; or (ii) at least seven days before the hearing if such proofs are to be used to oppose the summary judgment.

(e) **Case Not Fully Adjudicated on Motion.** If summary judgment is not rendered upon the whole case or for all the relief asked and a trial is necessary, the judge may at the healing examine the pleadings and the evidence on file, interrogate counsel, ascertain what material fact issues exist and make an order specifying the facts that are established as a matter of law, and directing such further proceedings in the action as are just.

(f) **Form of Affidavits; Further Testimony.** Supporting and opposing affidavits shall be made on personal knowledge, shall set forth such facts as would be admissible in evidence, and shall show affirmatively that the affiant is competent to testify to the matters stated therein. Sworn or certified copies of all papers or parts thereof referred to in an affidavit shall be attached thereto or served therewith. The court may permit affidavits to be supplemented or opposed by depositions or by further affidavits. Defects in the form of affidavits or attachments will not be grounds for reversal unless specifically pointed out by objection by an opposing party with opportunity, but refusal, to amend.

(g) **When Affidavits Are Unavailable.** Should it appear from the affidavits of a party opposing the motion that he cannot for reasons stated present by affidavit facts essential to justify his opposition, the court may refuse the application for judgment or may order a continuance to permit affidavits to be obtained or depositions to be taken or discovery to be had or may make such other order as is just.

(h) **Affidavits Made in Bad Faith.** Should it appear to the satisfaction of the court at any time that any of the affidavits presented pursuant to this rule are presented in bad faith or solely for the purpose of delay, the court shall forthwith order the party employing them to pay to the other party the amount of the reasonable expenses which the filing of the affidavits caused him to incur, including reasonable attorney's fees, and any offending party or attorney may be adjudged guilty of contempt.

(i) **No-Evidence Motion.** After adequate time for discovery, a party without presenting summary judgment evidence may move for summary judgment on the ground that there is no evidence of one or more essential elements of a claim or defense on which an adverse party would have the burden of proof at trial. The motion must state the elements as to which there is no evidence. The court must grant the motion unless the respondent produces summary judgment evidence raising a genuine issue of material fact.

(Added Oct. 12, 1949. eff. March 1, 1950. Amended by Order Oct. 1, 1951, eff. March 1, 1952; July 20, 1966, eff. Jan. 1, 1967; July 21, 1970, eff. Jan. 1, 1971; July 11, 1977, eff. Jan. 1, 1978; June 10, 1980, eff. Jan. 1, 1981; Dec. 5, 1983, eff. April 1, 1984; July 15, 1987, eff. Jan. 1, 1988; April 24, 1990, eff. Sept. 1, 1990; April 16, 1997 and August 15, 1997, effective September 1, 1997.)

RULE 167. OFFER OF SETTLEMENT; AWARD OF LITIGATION COSTS.

167.1. Generally.

Certain litigation costs may be awarded against a party who rejects an offer made substantially in accordance with this rule to settle a claim for monetary damages—including a counterclaim, crossclaim, or third-party claim — except in:

(a) a class action;

(b) a shareholder's derivative action;

(c) an action by or against the State, a unit of state government, or a political subdivision of the State;

(d) an action brought under the Family Code;

(e) an action to collect workers' compensation benefits under title 5, subtitle A of the Labor Code; or

(f) an action filed in a justice of the peace court or small claims court.

167.2. Settlement Offer.

(a) *Defendant's declaration a prerequisite; deadline.* A settlement offer under this rule may not be made until a defendant — a party against whom a claim for monetary damages is made — files a declaration invoking this rule. When a defendant files such a declaration, an offer or offers may be made under this rule to settle only those claims by and against that defendant. The declaration must be filed no later than 45 days before the case is set for conventional trial on the merits.

(b) *Requirements of an offer.* A settlement offer must:

(1) be in writing;

(2) state that it is made under Rule 167 and Chapter 42 of the Texas Civil Practice and Remedies Code;

(3) identify the party or parties making the offer and the party or parties to whom the offer is made;

(4) state the terms by which all monetary claims — including any attorney fees, interest, and costs that would be recoverable up to the time of the offer — between the offeror or offerors on the one hand and the offeree or offerees on the other may be settled;

(5) state a deadline — no sooner than 14 days after the offer is served — by which the offer must be accepted;

(6) be served on all parties to whom the offer is made.

(c) *Conditions of offer.* An offer may be made subject to reasonable conditions, including the execution of appropriate releases, indemnities, and other documents. An offeree may object to a condition by written notice served on the offeror before the deadline stated in the offer. A condition to which no such objection is made is presumed to have been reasonable. Rejection of an offer made subject to a condition determined by the trial court to have been unreasonable cannot be the basis for an award of litigation costs under this rule.

(d) *Non-monetary and excepted claims not included.* An offer must not include non-monetary claims and other claims to which this rule does not apply.

(e) *Time limitations.* An offer may not be made:

(1) before a defendant's declaration is filed;

(2) within 60 days after the appearance in the case of the offeror or offeree, whichever is later;

(3) within 14 days before the date the case is set for a conventional trial on the merits, except that an offer may be made within that period if it is in response to, and within seven days of, a prior offer.

(f) *Successive offers.* A party may make an offer after having made or rejected a prior offer. A rejection of an offer is subject to imposition of litigation costs under this rule only if the offer is more favorable to the offeree than any prior offer.

167.3. Withdrawal, Acceptance, and Rejection of Offer.

(a) *Withdrawal of offer.* An offer can be withdrawn before it is accepted. Withdrawal is effective when written notice of the withdrawal is served on the offeree. Once an unaccepted offer has been withdrawn, it cannot be accepted or be the basis for awarding litigation costs under this rule.

(b) *Acceptance of offer.* An offer that has not been withdrawn can be accepted only by written notice served on the offeror by the deadline stated in the offer. When an offer is accepted, the offeror or offeree may file the offer and acceptance and may move the court to enforce the settlement.

(c) *Rejection of offer.* An offer that is not withdrawn or accepted is rejected. An offer may also be rejected by written notice served on the offeror by the deadline stated in the offer.

(d) *Objection to offer made before an offeror's joinder or designation of responsible third party.* An offer made before an offeror joins another party or designates a responsible third party may not be the basis for awarding litigation costs under this rule against an offeree who files an objection to the offer within 15 days after service of the offeror's pleading or designation.

167.4. Awarding Litigation Costs.

(a) *Generally.* If a settlement offer made under this rule is rejected, and the judgment to be awarded on the monetary claims covered by the offer is significantly less favorable to the offeree than was the offer, the court must award the offeror litigation costs against the offeree from the time the offer was rejected to the time of judgment.

(b) *"Significantly less favorable" defined.* A judgment award on monetary claims is significantly less favorable than an offer to settle those claims if:

(1) the offeree is a claimant and the judgment would be less than 80 percent of the offer; or

(2) the offeree is a defendant and the judgment would be more than 120 percent of the offer.

(c) *Litigation costs.* Litigation costs are the expenditures actually made and the obligations actually incurred — directly in relation to the claims covered by a settlement offer under this rule — for the following:

(1) court costs;

(2) reasonable deposition costs, in cases filed on or after September1, 2011;

(3) reasonable fees for not more than two testifying expert witnesses; and

(3) reasonable fees for not more than two testifying witnesses; and

(4) reasonable attorney fees.

(d) *Limits on litigation costs.*

(1) In cases filed before September 1, 2011, the litigation costs that may be awarded under this rule must not exceed the following amount:

(A) the sum of the noneconomic damages, the exemplary or additional damages, and one-half of the economic damages to be awarded to the claimant in the judgment; minus

(B) the amount of any statutory or contractual liens in connection with the occurrences or incidents giving rise to the claim.

(2) In cases filed on or after September I, 2011, the litigation costs that may be awarded to any party under this rule must not exceed the total amount that the claimant recovers or would recover before adding an award of litigation costs under this rule in favor of the claimant or subtracting as an offset an award of litigation costs under this rule in favor of the defendant.

(e) *No double recovery permitted.* A party who is entitled to recover attorney fees and costs under another law may not recover those same attorney fees and costs as litigation costs under this rule.

(f) *Limitation on attorney fees and costs recovered by a party against whom litigation costs are awarded.* A party against whom litigation costs are awarded may not recover attorney fees and costs under another law incurred after the date the party rejected the settlement offer made the basis of the award.

(g) *Litigation costs to be awarded to defendant as a setoff.* Litigation costs awarded to a defendant must be made a setoff to the claimant's judgment against the defendant.

167.5. Procedures.

(a) *Modification of time limits.* On motion, and for good cause shown, the court may — by written order made before commencement of trial on the merits — modify the time limits for filing a declaration under Rule 167.2(a) or for making an offer.

(b) *Discovery permitted.* On motion, and for good cause shown, a party against whom litigation costs are to be awarded may conduct discovery to ascertain the reasonableness of the costs requested. If the court determines the costs to be reasonable, it must order the party requesting discovery to pay all attorney fees and expenses incurred by other parties in responding to such discovery.

(c) *Hearing required.* The court must, upon request, conduct a hearing on a request for an award of litigation costs, at which the affected parties may present evidence.

167.6. Evidence Not Admissible.

Evidence relating to an offer made under this rule is not admissible except for purposes of enforcing a settlement agreement or obtaining litigation costs. The provisions of this rule may not be made known to the jury by any means.

167.7. Other Settlement Offers Not Affected.

This rule does not apply to any offer made in a mediation or arbitration proceeding. A settlement offer not made in compliance with this rule, or a settlement offer not made under this rule, or made in an action to which this rule does not apply, cannot be the basis for awarding litigation costs under this rule as to any party. This rule does not limit or affect a party's right to make a settlement offer that does not comply with this rule, or in an action to which this rule does not apply.

(Adopted Oct. 9, 2003, eff. Jan. 1, 2004, only in cases filed on or after effective date. Amended by Order Aug. 31, 2011, eff. Sept. 1, 2011; Sept. 9, 2011, eff. Sept. 9, 2011.)

Rule 168. Permission to Appeal.

On a party's motion or on its own initiative, a trial court may permit an appeal from an interlocutory order that is not otherwise appealable, as provided by statute. Permission must be stated in the order to be appealed. An order previously issued may be amended to include such permission. The permission must identify the controlling question of law as to which there is a substantial ground for difference of opinion, and must state why an immediate appeal may materially advance the ultimate termination of the litigation.

(Adopted by Order Aug. 31, 2011, eff. Sept. 1, 2011. Amended by Order Sept. 9, 2011, eff. Sept. 9, 2011.)

Comment to 2011 change: Rule 168 is a new rule, added to implement amendments to section 51.0 14(d)-(f) of the Texas Civil Practice and Remedies Code. Rule 168 applies only to cases filed on or after September 1, 2011. Rule 168 clarifies that the trial court's permission to appeal should be included in the order to be appealed rather than in a separate order. Rule of Appellate Procedure 28.3 sets out the corollary requirements for permissive appeals in the courts of appeals.

RULE 166B to 169. [REPEALED]

(Repealed by Order Aug. 5, 1998, and Nov. 9, 1998, eff. Jan. 1, 1999.)

Rule 169. Expedited Actions.

(a) *Application.*
  (1) The expedited actions process in this rule applies to a suit in which all claimants, other than counter-claimants, affirmatively plead that they seek only monetary relief aggregating $100,000 or less, including damages of any kind, penalties, costs, expenses, pre-judgment interest, and attorney fees.
  (2) The expedited actions process does not apply to a suit in which a party has filed a claim governed by the Family Code, the Property Code, the Tax Code, or Chapter 74 of the Civil Practice & Remedies Code.

(b) *Recovery.* In no event may a party who prosecutes a suit under this rule recover a judgment in excess of $ 100,000, excluding post-judgment interest.

(c) *Removal from Process.*
  (1) A court must remove a suit from the expedited actions process:
    (A) on motion and a showing of good cause by any party; or
    (B) if any claimant, other than a counter-claimant, files a pleading or an amended or supplemental pleading that seeks any relief other than the monetary relief allowed by (a)(l).
  (2) A pleading, amended pleading, or supplemental pleading that removes a suit from the expedited actions process may not be filed without leave of court unless it is filed before the earlier of 30 days after the discovery period is closed or 30 days before the date set for trial. Leave to amend may be granted only if good cause for filing the pleading outweighs any prejudice to an opposing party.
  (3) If a suit is removed from the expedited actions process, the court must reopen discovery under Rule 190.2(c).

(d) *Expedited Actions Process.*
  (1) Discovery. Discovery is governed by Rule 190.2.
  (2) Trial Setting; Continuances. On any party's request, the court must set the case for a trial date that is within 90 days after the discovery period in Rule 190.2(b)(l) ends. The court may continue the case twice, not to exceed a total of 60 days.
  (3) Time Limits for Trial. Each side is allowed no more than eight hours to complete jury selection, opening statements, presentation of evidence, examination and cross-examination of witnesses, and closing arguments. On motion and a showing of good cause by any party, the court may extend the time limit to no more than twelve hours per side.
    (A) The term "side" has the same definition set out in Rule 233.
    (B) Time spent on objections, bench conferences, bills of exception, and challenges for cause to a juror under Rule 228 are not included in the time limit.
  (4) Alternative Dispute Resolution.
    (A) Unless the parties have agreed not to engage in alternative dispute resolution, the court may refer the case to an alternative dispute resolution procedure once, and the procedure must:
      (i) not exceed a half-day in duration, excluding scheduling time;
      (ii) not exceed a total cost of twice the amount of applicable civil filing fees; and
      (iii) be completed no later than 60 days before the initial trial setting.
    (B) The court must consider objections to the referral unless prohibited by statute.
    (C) The parties may agree to engage in alternative dispute resolution other than that provided for in (A).

(5) Expert Testimony. Unless requested by the party sponsoring the expert, a party may only challenge the admissibility of expert testimony as an objection to summary judgment evidence under Rule 166a or during the trial on the merits. This paragraph does not apply to a motion to strike for late designation.

(Adopted by Order Nov. 13, 2012, eff. March 1, 2013. Amended by Order Feb 12, 2013, eff. March 1, 2013. (Applies to cases filed on or after March 1, 2013, except those filed in justice court.))

Comments to 2013 change:

1. Rule 169 is a new rule implementing section 22.004(h) of the Texas Government Code, which was added in 2011 and calls for rules to promote the prompt, efficient, and cost-effective resolution of civil actions when the amount in controversy does not exceed $100,000.

2. The expedited actions process created by Rule 169 is mandatory; any suit that falls within the definition of 169(a)(l) is subject to the provisions of the rule.

3. In determining whether there is good cause to remove the case from the process or extend the time limit for trial, the court should consider factors such as whether the damages sought by multiple claimants against the same defendant exceed in the aggregate the relief allowed under 169(a)(l), whether a defendant has filed a compulsory counterclaim in good faith that seeks relief other than that allowed under 169(a)(l), the number of parties and witnesses, the complexity of the legal and factual issues, and whether an interpreter is necessary.

4. Rule 169(b) specifies that a party who prosecutes a suit under this rule cannot recover a judgment in excess of $100,000. Thus, the rule in *Greenhalgh v. Service Lloyds Ins. Co.*, 787 S.W.2d 938 (Tex. 1990), does not apply if a jury awards damages in excess of $100,000 to the party. The limitation in 169(b) does not apply to a counter-claimant that seeks relief other than that allowed under 5. The discovery limitations for expedited actions are set out in Rule 190.2, which is also amended to implement section 22.004(h) of the Texas Government Code.

RULE 170. [REPEALED]

(Repealed by Order Dec. 5, 1983, eff. April 1, 1984.)

RULE 171. MASTER IN CHANCERY.

The court may, in exceptional cases, for good cause appoint a master in chancery, who shall be a citizen of this State, and not an attorney for either party to the action, nor related to either party, who shall perform all of the duties required of him by the court, and shall be under orders of the court, and have such power as the master of chancery has in a court of equity.

The order of reference to the master may specify or limit his powers, and may direct him to report only upon particular issues, or to do or perform particular acts, or to receive and report evidence only and may fix the time and place for beginning and closing the hearings, and for the filing of the master's report. Subject to the limitations and specifications stated in the order, the master has and shall exercise the power to regulate all proceedings in every hearing before him and to do all acts and take all measures necessary or proper for the efficient performance of his duties under the order. He may require the production before him of evidence upon all matters embraced in the reference, including the production of books, papers, vouchers, documents and other writings applicable thereto. He may rule upon the admissibility of evidence, unless otherwise directed by the order of reference and has the authority to put witnesses on oath, and may, himself, examine them, and may call the parties to the action and examine them upon oath. When a party so requests, the master shall make a record of the evidence offered and excluded in the same manner as provided for a court sitting in the trial of a case.

The clerk of the court shall forthwith furnish the master with a copy of the order of reference.

The parties may procure the attendance of witnesses before the master by the issuance and service of process as provided by law and these rules.

The court may confirm, modify, correct, reject, reverse or recommit the report, after it is filed, as the court may deem proper and necessary in the particular circumstances of the case. The court shall award reasonable compensation to such master to be taxed as costs of suit.

(Amended by Order Sept. 20, 1941, eff. Dec. 31, 1941.)

RULE 172. AUDIT.

When an investigation of accounts or examination of vouchers appears necessary for the purpose of justice between the parties to any suit, the court shall appoint an auditor or auditors to state the accounts between the parties and to make report thereof to the court as soon as possible. The auditor shall verify his report by his affidavit stating that he has carefully examined the state of the account between the parties, and that his report contains a true statement thereof, so far as the same has come within his knowledge. Exceptions to such report or of any item thereof must be filed within 30 days of the filing of such report. The court shall award reasonable compensation to such auditor to be taxed as costs of suit.

(Amended by Order July 15, 1987, eff. Jan. 1, 1988.)

RULE 173. GUARDIAN AD LITEM.

173.1. Appointment Governed by Statute or Other Rules.

This rule does not apply to an appointment of a guardian ad litem governed by statute or other rules.

173.2. Appointment of Guardian Ad Litem.

(a) ***When Appointment Required or Prohibited.*** The court must appoint a guardian ad litem for a party represented by a next friend or guardian only if:

- **(1)** the next friend or guardian appears to the court to have an interest adverse to the party, or
- **(2)** the parties agree.

(b) ***Appointment of the Same Person for Different Parties.*** The court must appoint the same guardian ad litem for similarly situated parties unless the court finds that the appointment of different guardians ad litem is necessary.

173.3. Procedure.

(a) ***Motion Permitted But Not Required.*** The court may appoint a guardian ad litem on the motion of any party or on its own initiative.

(b) ***Written Order Required.*** An appointment must be made by written order.

(c) ***Objection.*** Any party may object to the appointment of a guardian ad litem.

173.4. Role of Guardian Ad Litem.

(a) ***Court Officer and Advisor.*** A guardian ad litem acts as an officer and advisor to the court.

(b) ***Determination of Adverse Interest.*** A guardian ad litem must determine and advise the court whether a party's next friend or guardian has an interest adverse to the party.

(c) ***When Settlement Proposed.*** When an offer has been made to settle the claim of a party represented by a next friend or guardian, a guardian ad litem has the limited duty to determine and advise the court whether the settlement is in the party's best interest.

(d) ***Participation in Litigation Limited.*** A guardian ad litem:

- **(1)** may participate in mediation or a similar proceeding to attempt to reach a settlement;
- **(2)** must participate in any proceeding before the court whose purpose is to determine whether a party's next friend or guardian has an interest adverse to the party, or whether a settlement of the party's claim is in the party's best interest;
- **(3)** must not participate in discovery, trial, or any other part of the litigation unless:
  - **(A)** further participation is necessary to protect the party's interest that is adverse to the next friend's or guardian's, and
  - **(B)** the participation is directed by the court in a written order stating sufficient reasons.

173.5. Communications Privileged.

Communications between the guardian ad litem and the party, the next friend or guardian, or their attorney are privileged as if the guardian ad litem were the attorney for the party.

173.6. Compensation.

(a) ***Amount.*** If a guardian ad litem requests compensation, he or she may be reimbursed for reasonable and necessary expenses incurred and may be paid a reasonable hourly fee for necessary services performed.

(b) ***Procedure.*** At the conclusion of the appointment, a guardian ad litem may file an application for compensation. The application must be verified and must detail the basis for the compensation requested. Unless all parties agree to the application, the court must conduct an evidentiary hearing to determine the total amount of fees and expenses that are reasonable and necessary. In making this determination, the court must not consider compensation as a percentage of any judgment or settlement.

(c) ***Taxation as Costs.*** The court may tax a guardian ad litem's compensation as costs of court.

(d) ***Other Benefit Prohibited.*** A guardian ad litem may not receive, directly or indirectly, anything of value in consideration of the appointment other than as provided by this rule.

173.7. Review.

(a) ***Right of Appeal.*** Any party may seek mandamus review of an order appointing a guardian ad litem or directing a guardian ad litem's participation in the litigation. Any party and a guardian ad litem may appeal an order awarding the guardian ad litem compensation.

(b) ***Severance.*** On motion of the guardian ad litem or any party, the court must sever any order awarding a guardian ad litem compensation to create a final, appealable order.

(c) ***No Effect on Finality of Settlement or Judgment.*** Appellate proceedings to review an order pertaining to a guardian ad litem do not affect the finality of a settlement or judgment.

(Amended by Order June 16, 1943, eff. Dec. 31, 1943; Jan. 27, 2005, eff. Feb. 1, 2005 in all pending cases.)

Comment - 2005

1. The rule is completely revised.
2. This rule does not apply when the procedures and purposes for appointment of guardians ad litem (as well as attorneys ad litem) are prescribed by statutes, such as the Family Code and the Probate Code, or by other rules, such as the Parental Notification Rules.
3. The rule contemplates that a guardian ad litem will be appointed when a party's next friend or guardian appears to have an interest adverse to the party because of the division of settlement proceeds. In those situations, the responsibility of the guardian ad litem as prescribed by the rule is very limited, and no reason exists for the guardian ad litem to participate in the conduct of the litigation in any other way or to review the discovery or the litigation file except to the limited extent that it may bear on the division of settlement proceeds. *See Jocson v. Crabb*, 133 S.W.3d 268 (Tex. 2004)(per curiam). A guardian ad litem may, of course, choose to review the file or attend proceedings when it is unnecessary, but the guardian ad litem may not be compensated for unnecessary expenses or services.
4. Only in extraordinary circumstances does the rule contemplate that a guardian ad litem will have a broader role. Even then, the role is limited to determining whether a party's next friend or guardian has an interest adverse to the party that should be considered by the court under Rule 44. In no event may a guardian ad litem supervise or supplant the next friend or undertake to represent the party while serving as guardian ad litem.
5. As an officer and advisor to the court, a guardian ad litem should have qualified judicial immunity.
6. Though an officer and adviser to the court, a guardian ad litem must not have *ex parte* communications with the court. *See* TEX. CODE JUD. CONDUCT, Canon 3.
7. Because the role of guardian ad litem is limited in all but extraordinary situations, and any risk that might result from services performed is also limited, compensation, if any is sought, should ordinarily be limited.
8. A violation of this rule is subject to appropriate sanction.

RULE 174. CONSOLIDATION; SEPARATE TRIALS.

(a) *Consolidation.* When actions involving a common question of law or fact are pending before the court, it may order a joint hearing or trial of any or all the matters in issue in the actions; it may order all the actions consolidated; and it may make such orders concerning proceedings therein as may tend to avoid unnecessary costs or delay.

(b) *Separate Trials.* The court in furtherance of convenience or to avoid prejudice may order a separate trial of any claim, cross-claim, counterclaim, or third-party claim, or of any separate issue or of any number of claims, cross-claims, counterclaims, third-party claims, or issues.

RULE 175. ISSUE OF LAW AND DILATORY PLEAS.

When a case is called for trial in which there has been no pretrial hearing as provided by Rule 166, the issues of law arising on the pleadings, all pleas in abatement and other dilatory pleas remaining undisposed of shall be determined; and it shall be no cause for postponement of a trial of the issues of law that a party is not prepared to try the issues of fact.

SECTION 9.
EVIDENCE AND DISCOVERY

EXPLANATORY STATEMENT ACCOMPANYING THE 1999 AMENDMENTS TO THE RULES OF CIVIL PROCEDURE GOVERNING DISCOVERY.

The rules pertaining to discovery have been substantively revised and reorganized to clarify and streamline discovery procedures and to reduce costs and delays associated with discovery practice. The notes and comments appended to the rules, unlike most other notes and comments in the Rules of Civil Procedure, are intended to inform their construction and application by both courts and practitioners.

Discovery in civil cases is founded on the principle that justice is best served when litigants may obtain information not in their possession to prosecute and defend claims. Discovery provides access to that information, but at a price. Recent years' experience has shown that discovery may be misused to deny justice to parties by driving up the costs of litigation until it is unaffordable and stalling resolution of cases. As any litigant on a budget knows, the benefits to be gained by discovery in a particular case must be weighed against its costs. The rules of procedure must provide both adequate access to information and effective means of curbing discovery when appropriate to preserve litigation as a viable, affordable, and expeditious dispute resolution mechanism.

These revisions recognize the importance of discovery as well as the necessity for reasonable limits. The scope of discovery, always broad, is unchanged. All the forms of discovery under the prior rules are retained, and a new one—disclosure—is added. Disclosure is not required unless requested and thus does not burden cases in which it is not sought. When requested, it provides ready access to basic information without objection. At the same time, the necessity of a discovery control plan in each case, whether by rule or by order, is intended to focus courts and parties on both the need for discovery and its costs in each case. The Level 1 plan allows a party seeking recovery of no more than $60,000 to insist that discovery be minimal. The Level 2 plan will provide adequate discovery in most cases, and Level 3 is available for cases needing special attention. No single set of rules can address so diverse and changing a practice as discovery, and thus the rules maintain the ability of parties by agreement and courts by order to tailor discovery to individual cases.

Presentation of objections and assertions of privilege are streamlined under these rules. A party who objects to only part of a discovery request must usually comply with the rest of the request. Assertions of privilege are not to be made prophylactically against the threat of waiver, but only when information is actually withheld. Documents produced in discovery are now presumed to be authentic for use against the party producing them, thus avoiding the cost of proving authentication when there is no dispute. Procedures for oral depositions are revised to encourage focused examination by imposing time limits and to discourage colloquy between counsel.

An important aspect of these revisions has been the regrouping of provisions in a more logical sequence and the elimination of archaic and confusing language.

A.
EVIDENCE

RULE 176. SUBPOENAS

176.1. Form.

Every subpoena must be issued in the name of "The State of Texas" and must:

(a) state the style of the suit and its cause number;

(b) state the court in which the suit is pending;

(c) state the date on which the subpoena is issued;

(d) identify the person to whom the subpoena is directed;

(e) state the time, place, and nature of the action required by the person to whom the subpoena is directed, as provided in Rule 176.2;

(f) identify the party at whose instance the subpoena is issued, and the party's attorney of record, if any;

(g) state the text of Rule 176.8(a); and

(h) be signed by the person issuing the subpoena.

176.2. Required Actions.

A subpoena must command the person to whom it is directed to do either or both of the following:

(a) attend and give testimony at a deposition, hearing, or trial;

(b) produce and permit inspection and copying of designated documents or tangible things in the possession, custody, or control of that person.

176.3. Limitations.

(a) **Range**. A person may not be required by subpoena to appear or produce documents or other things in a county that is more than 150 miles from where the person resides or is served. However, a person whose appearance or production at a deposition may be compelled by notice alone under Rules 199.3 or 200.2 may be required to appear and produce documents or other things at any location permitted under Rules 199.2(b)(2).

(b) **Use for discovery.** A subpoena may not be used for discovery to an extent, in a manner, or at a time other than as provided by the rules governing discovery.

176.4. Who May Issue.

A subpoena may be issued by:

(a) the clerk of the appropriate district, county, or justice court, who must provide the party requesting the subpoena with an original and a copy for each witness to be completed by the party;

(b) an attorney authorized to practice in the State of Texas, as an officer of the court; or

(c) an officer authorized to take depositions in this State, who must issue the subpoena immediately on a request accompanied by a notice to take a deposition under Rules 199 or 200, or a notice under Rule 205.3, and who may also serve the notice with the subpoena.

176.5. Service.

(a) **Manner of service.** A subpoena may be served at any place within the State of Texas by any sheriff or constable of the State of Texas, or any person who is not a party and is 18 years of age or older. A subpoena must be served by delivering a copy to the witness and tendering to that person any fees required by law. If the witness is a party and is represented by an attorney of record in the proceeding, the subpoena may be served on the witness's attorney of record.

(b) **Proof of service.** Proof of service must be made by filing either:

(1) the witness's signed written memorandum attached to the subpoena showing that the witness accepted the subpoena; or

(2) a statement by the person who made the service stating the date, time, and manner of service, and the name of the person served.

176.6. Response.

(a) **Compliance required**. Except as provided in this subdivision, a person served with a subpoena must comply with the command stated therein unless discharged by the court or by the party summoning such witness. A person commanded to appear and give testimony must remain at the place of deposition hearing, or trial from day to day until discharged by the court or by the party summoning the witness.

(b) **Organizations**. If a subpoena commanding testimony is directed to a corporation, partnership, association, governmental agency, or other organization, and the matters on which examination is requested are described with reasonable particularity, the organization must designate one or more persons to testify on its behalf as to matters known or reasonably available to the organization.

(c) **Production of documents or tangible things**. A person commanded to produce documents or tangible things need not appear in person at the time and place of production unless the person is also commanded to attend and give testimony, either in the same subpoena or a separate one. A person must produce documents as they are kept in the usual course of business or must organize and label them to correspond with the categories in the demand. A person may withhold material or information claimed to be privileged but must comply with Rule 193.3. A nonparty's production of a document authenticates the document for use against the nonparty to the same extent as a party's production of a document is authenticated for use against the party under Rule 193.7.

(d) **Objections**. A person commanded to produce and permit inspection or copying of designated documents and things may serve on the party requesting issuance of the subpoena—before the time specified for compliance—written objections to producing any or all of the designated materials. A person need not comply with the part of a subpoena to which objection is made as provided in this paragraph unless ordered to do so by the court. The party requesting the subpoena may move for such an order at any time after an objection is made.

(e) **Protective orders**. A person commanded to appear at a deposition, hearing, or trial, or to produce and permit inspection and copying of designated documents and things, and any other person affected by the subpoena, may move for a protective order under Rule 192.6(b)—before the time specified for compliance—either in the court in which the action is pending or in a district court in the county where the subpoena was served. The person must serve the motion on all parties in accordance with Rule 21a. A person need not comply with the part of a subpoena from which protection is sought under this paragraph unless ordered to do so by the court. The party requesting the subpoena may seek such an order at any time after the motion for protection is filed.

(f) **Trial subpoenas**. A person commanded to attend and give testimony, or to produce documents or things, at a hearing or trial, may object or move for protective order before the court at the time and place specified for compliance, rather than under paragraphs (d) and (e).

176.7. Protection of Person from Undue Burden and Expense.

A party causing a subpoena to issue must take reasonable steps to avoid imposing undue burden or expense on the person served. In ruling on objections or motions for protection, the court must provide a person served with a subpoena an adequate time for compliance, protection from disclosure of privileged material or information, and protection from undue burden or expense. The court may impose reasonable conditions on compliance with a subpoena, including compensating the witness for undue hardship.

176.8. Enforcement of Subpoena.

(a) **Contempt**. Failure by any person without adequate excuse to obey a subpoena served upon that person may be deemed a contempt of the court from which the subpoena is issued or a district court in the county in which the subpoena is served, and may be punished by fine or confinement, or both.

(b) **Proof of payment of fees required for fine or attachment**. A fine may not be imposed, nor a person served with a subpoena attached, for failure to comply with a subpoena without proof by affidavit of the party requesting the subpoena or the party's attorney of record that all fees due the witness by law were paid or tendered.

(Added Aug. 5, 1998. Amended Nov. 9, 1998, eff. Jan. 1, 1999.)

Comments to 1999 change:

1. This rule combines the former rules governing subpoenas for trial and discovery. When a subpoena is used for discovery, the protections from undue burden and expense apply, just as with any discovery.

2. Rule 176.3(b) prohibits the use of a subpoena to circumvent the discovery rules. Thus, for example, a deposition subpoena to a party is subject to the procedures of Rules 196, 199, and 200, and a deposition subpoena to a nonparty is subject to the procedures of Rule 205.

[No change in Rules 180-185.]

RULES 177, 178, and 179. [REPEALED]

(Repealed by Order Aug. 5, 1998, and Nov. 9, 1998, eff. Jan. 1, 1999.)

RULE 180. REFUSAL TO TESTIFY.

Any witness refusing to give evidence may be committed to jail, there to remain without bail until such witness shall consent to give evidence.

RULE 181. PARTY AS WITNESS.

Either party to a suit may examine the opposing party as a witness, and shall have the same process to compel his attendance as in the case of any other witness.

RULE 182 and 182a. [REPEALED]

(Repealed by Order July 15, 1987, eff. Jan. 1, 1988.)

RULE 183. INTERPRETERS.

The court may appoint an interpreter of its own selection and may fix the interpreter's reasonable compensation. The compensation shall be paid out of funds provided by law or by one or more of the parties as the court may direct, and may be taxed ultimately as costs, in the discretion of the court.

(Amended by Order April 24, 1990, eff. Sept. 1, 1990.)

RULE 184 and 184a. [REPEALED]

(Repealed by Order April 24, 1990, eff. Sept. 1, 1990.)

RULE 185. SUIT ON ACCOUNT.

When any action or defense is founded upon an open account or other claim for goods, wares and merchandise, including any claim for a liquidated money demand based upon written contract or founded on business dealings between the parties, or is for personal service rendered, or labor done or labor or materials furnished, on which a systematic record has been kept, and is supported by the affidavit of the party, his agent or attorney taken before some officer authorized to administer oaths, to the effect that such claim is, within the knowledge of affiant, just and true, that it is due, and that all just and lawful offsets, payments and credits have been allowed, the same shall be taken as prima facie evidence thereof, unless the party resisting such claim shall file a written denial, under oath. A party resisting such a sworn claim shall comply with the rules of pleading as are required in any other kind of suit, provided, however, that if he does not timely file a written denial, under oath, he shall not be permitted to deny the claim, or any item therein, as the case may be. No particularization or description of the nature of the component parts of the account or claim is necessary unless the trial court sustains special exceptions to the pleadings.

(Amended by Order Oct. 12, 1949, eff. March 1, 1950; July 21, 1970, eff. Jan. 1, 1971; Dec. 5, 1983, eff. April 1, 1984.)

B.
DISCOVERY

RULES 186, 187, 188, and 189. [REPEALED]

(Rules 186 and 189 repealed Dec. 5, 1983, eff. April 1, 1984; Rules 187 and 188 repealed Aug. 5, 1998, and Nov. 9, 1998, eff. Jan. 1, 1999.)

RULE 190. DISCOVERY LIMITATIONS

190.1. Discovery Control Plan Required.

Every case must be governed by a discovery control plan as provided in this Rule. A plaintiff must allege in the first numbered paragraph of the original petition whether discovery is intended to be conducted under Level 1, 2, or 3 of this Rule.

190.2. Discovery Control Plan—Expedited Actions and Divorces Involving $50,000 or Less (Level 1).

(a) **Application**. This subdivision applies to:

(1) any suit that is governed by the expedited actions process in Rule 169; and

(2) unless the parties agree that Rule 190.3 should apply or the court orders a discovery control plan under Rule 190.4, any suit for divorce not involving children in which a party pleads that the value of the marital estate is more than zero but not more than $50,000.

(b) **Limitations**. Discovery is subject to the limitations provided elsewhere in these rules and to the following additional limitations:

(1) **Discovery Period**. All discovery must be conducted during the discovery period, which begins when the suit is filed and continues until 180 days after the date the first request for discovery of any kind is served on a party.

(2) **Total Time for Oral Depositions**. Each party may have no more than six hours in total to examine and cross-examine all witnesses in oral depositions. The parties may agree to expand this limit up to ten hours in total, but not more except by court order. The court may modify the deposition hours so that no party is given unfair advantage.

(3) **Interrogatories**. Any party may serve on any other party no more than 15 written interrogatories, excluding interrogatories asking a party only to identify or authenticate specific documents. Each discrete subpart of an interrogatory is considered a separate interrogatory.

(4) **Requests for Production**. Any party may serve on any other party no more than 15 written requests for production. Each discrete subpart of a request for production is considered a separate request for production.

(5) **Requests for Admissions**. Any party may serve on any other party no more than 15 written requests for admissions. Each discrete subpart of a request for admission is considered a separate request for admission.

(6) **Requests for Disclosure**. In addition to the content subject to disclosure under Rule 194.2. a party may request disclosure of all documents, electronic information, and tangible items that the disclosing party has in its possession, custody, or control and may use to support its claims or defenses. A request for disclosure made pursuant to this paragraph is not considered a request for production.

(c) **Reopening Discovery**. If a suit is removed from the expedited actions process in Rule 169 or. in a divorce, the filing of a pleading renders this subdivision no longer applicable, the discovery period reopens, and discovery must be completed within the limitations provided in Rules 190.3 or 190.4, whichever is applicable. Any person previously deposed may be redeposed. On motion of any party, the court should continue the trial date if necessary to permit completion of discovery.

(Amended by Order Nov. 13, 2012, eff. March 1, 2013; Feb 12, 2013, eff. March 1, 2013 (Applies to cases filed on or after March 1, 2013, except those filed in justice court).)

190.3. Discovery Control Plan—By Rule (Level 2).

(a) **Application**. Unless a suit is governed by a discovery control plan under Rules 190.2 or 190.4 discovery must be conducted in accordance with this subdivision.

(b) **Limitations**. Discovery is subject to the limitations provided elsewhere in these rules and to the following additional limitations:

(1) **Discovery period**. All discovery must be conducted during the discovery period, which begins when suit is filed and continues until:

(A) 30 days before the date set for trial, in cases under the Family Code; or

(B) in other cases, the earlier of

(i) 30 days before the date set for trial, or

(ii) nine months after the earlier of the date of the first oral deposition or the due date of the first response to written discovery.

(2) **Total time for oral depositions**. Each side may have no more than 50 hours in oral depositions to examine and cross-examine parties on the opposing side, experts designated by those parties, and persons who are subject to those parties' control. "Side" refers to all the litigants with generally common interests in the litigation. If one side designates more than two experts, the opposing side may have an additional six hours of total deposition time for each additional expert designated. The court may modify the deposition hours and must do so when a side or party would be given unfair advantage.

(3) **Interrogatories**. Any party may serve on any other party no more than 25 written interrogatories, excluding interrogatories asking a party only to identify or authenticate specific documents. Each discrete subpart of an interrogatory is considered a separate interrogatory.

190.4. Discovery Control Plan—By Order (Level 3).

(a) **Application**. The court must, on a party's motion, and may, on its own initiative, order that discovery be conducted in accordance with a discovery control plan tailored to the circumstances of the specific suit. The parties may submit an agreed order to the court for its consideration. The court should act on a party's motion or agreed order under this subdivision as promptly as reasonably possible.

(b) **Limitations**. The discovery control plan ordered by the court may address any issue concerning discovery or the matters listed in Rule 166, and may change any limitation on the time for or amount of discovery set forth in these rules. The discovery limitations of Rule 190.2, if applicable, or otherwise of Rule 190.3 apply unless specifically changed in the discovery control plan ordered by the court. The plan must include:

(1) a date for trial or for a conference to determine a trial setting;

(2) a discovery period during which either all discovery must be conducted or all discovery requests must be sent, for the entire case or an appropriate phase of it;

(3) appropriate limits on the amount of discovery; and

(4) deadlines for joining additional parties, amending or supplementing pleadings, and designating expert witnesses.

190.5. Modification of Discovery Control Plan.

The court may modify a discovery control plan at any time and must do so when the interest of justice requires. Unless a suit is governed by the expedited actions process in Rule 169, the court must allow additional discovery:

(a) related to new, amended or supplemental pleadings, or new information disclosed in a discovery response or in an amended or supplemental response, if:

(1) the pleadings or responses were made after the deadline for completion of discovery or so nearly before that deadline that an adverse party does not have an adequate opportunity to conduct discovery related to the new matters, and

(2) the adverse party would be unfairly prejudiced without such additional discovery;

(b) regarding matters that have changed materially after the discovery cutoff if trial is set or postponed so that the trial date is more than three months after the discovery period ends.

(Amended by Order Nov. 13, 2012, eff. March 1, 2013; Feb 12, 2013, eff. March 1, 2013.)

Comment to 2013 change: Rule 190 is amended to implement section 22.004(h) of the Texas Government Code, which calls for rules to promote the prompt, efficient, and cost-effective resolution of civil actions when the amount in controversy does not exceed $100,000. Rule 190.2 now applies to expedited actions, as defined by Rule 169. Rule 190.2 continues to apply to divorces not involving children in which the value of the marital estate is not more than $50,000, which are otherwise exempt from the expedited actions process. Amended Rule 190.2(b) ends the discovery period 180 days after the date the first discovery request is served; imposes a fifteen limit maximum on interrogatories, requests for production, and requests for admission; and allows for additional disclosures. Although expedited actions are not subject to mandatory additional discovery under amended Rule 190.5, the court may still allow additional discovery if the conditions of Rule 190(a) are met.

190.6. Certain Types of Discovery Excepted.

This rule's limitations on discovery do not apply to or include discovery conducted under Rule 202 ("Depositions Before Suit or to Investigate Claims"), or Rule 621a ("Discovery and Enforcement of Judgment"). But Rule 202 cannot be used to circumvent the limitations of this rule.

(Added Aug. 5, 1998, and amended Nov. 9, 1998 and Dec. 31, 1998, to apply to all cases filed on or after Jan. 1, 1999, but a court may adopt an appropriate discovery control plan in previously filed cases.)

Comments to 1999 change:

1. This rule establishes three tiers of discovery plans and requires that every case be in one at all times. A case is in Level 1 if it is pleaded by the plaintiff so as to invoke application of Level 1, as provided by Rule 190.2(a). If a plaintiff does not or cannot plead the case in compliance with Rule 190.2(a) so as to invoke the application of Level 1, the case is automatically in Level 2. A

case remains in Level 1 or Level 2, as determined by the pleadings, unless and until it is moved to Level 3. To be in Level 3, the court must order a specific plan for the case, either on a party's motion or on the court's own initiative. The plan may be one agreed to by the parties and submitted as an agreed order. A Level 3 plan may simply adopt Level 1 or Level 2 restrictions. Separate Level 3 plans for phases of the case may be appropriate. The initial pleading required by Rule 190.1 is merely to notify the court and other parties of the plaintiff's intention; it does not determine the applicable discovery level or bind the court or other parties. Thus, a plaintiff's failure to state in the initial pleading that the case should be in Level 1, as provided in Rule 190.1, does not alone make the case subject to Level 2 because the discovery level is determined by Rule 190.2. Likewise, a plaintiff's statement in the initial paragraph of the petition that the case is to be governed by Level 3 does not make Level 3 applicable, as a case can be in Level 3 only by court order. A plaintiff's failure to plead as required by Rule 190.1 is subject to special exception.

2. Rule 190.2 does not apply to suits for injunctive relief or divorces involving children. The requirement of an affirmative pleading of limited relief (*e.g.*: "Plaintiff affirmatively pleads that he seeks only monetary relief aggregating $50,000 or less, excluding costs, pre-judgment interest and attorneys' fees") does not conflict with other pleading requirements, such as Rule 47 and TEX. REV. CIV. STAT. ANN. art. 4590i, § 5.01. In a suit to which Rule 190.2 applies, the relief awarded cannot exceed the limitations of Level 1 because the purpose of the rule, unlike Rule 47, is to bind the pleader to a maximum claim. To this extent, the rule in *Greenhalgh v. Service Lloyds Ins. Co.*, 787 S.W.2d 938 (Tex. 1990), does not apply.

3. "Discrete subparts" of interrogatories are counted as single interrogatories, but not every separate factual inquiry is a discrete subpart. *See* FED. R. CIV. P. 33(a). While not susceptible of precise definition, *see Braden v. Downey*, 811 S.W.2d 922, 927-928 (Tex. 1991), a "discrete subpart" is, in general, one that calls for information that is not logically or factually related to the primary interrogatory. The number of sets of interrogatories is no longer limited to two.

4. As other rules make clear, unless otherwise ordered or agreed, parties seeking discovery must serve requests sufficiently far in advance of the end of the discovery period that the deadline for responding will be within the discovery period. The court may order a deadline for sending discovery requests in lieu of or in addition to a deadline for completing discovery.

5. Use of forms of discovery other than depositions and interrogatories, such as requests for disclosure, admissions, or production of documents, are not restricted in Levels 1 and 2. But depositions on written questions cannot be used to circumvent the limits on interrogatories.

6. The concept of "side" in Rule 190.3(b)(2) borrows from Rule 233, which governs the allocation of peremptory strikes, and from FED. R. CIV. P. 30(a)(2). In most cases there are only two sides—plaintiffs and defendants. In complex cases, however, there may be more than two sides, such as when defendants have sued third parties not named by plaintiffs, or when defendants have sued each other. As an example, if P1 and P2 sue D1, D2, and D3, and D1 sues D2 and D3, Ps would together be entitled to depose Ds and others permitted by the rule (*i.e.*, Ds' experts and persons subject to Ds' control) for 50 hours, and Ds would together be entitled to depose Ps and others for 50 hours. D1 would also be entitled to depose D2 and D3 and others for 50 hours on matters in controversy among them, and D2 and D3 would together be entitled to depose D1 and others for 50 hours.

7. Any matter listed in Rule 166 may be addressed in an order issued under Rule 190.4. A pretrial order under Rule 166 may be used in individual cases regardless of the discovery level.

8. For purposes of defining discovery periods, "trial" does not include summary judgment.

RULE 191. MODIFYING DISCOVERY PROCEDURES AND LIMITATIONS; CONFERENCE REQUIREMENT; SIGNING DISCLOSURES, DISCOVERY REQUESTS, RESPONSES, AND OBJECTIONS; FILING REQUIREMENTS.

191.1. Modification of Procedures.

Except where specifically prohibited, the procedures and limitations set forth in the rules pertaining to discovery may be modified in any suit by the agreement of the parties or by court order for good cause. An agreement of the parties is enforceable if it complies with Rule 11 or, as it affects an oral deposition, if it is made a part of the record of the deposition.

191.2. Conference.

Parties and their attorneys are expected to cooperate in discovery and to make any agreements reasonably necessary for the efficient disposition of the case. All discovery motions or requests for hearings relating to discovery must contain a certificate by the party filing the motion or request that a reasonable effort has been made to resolve the dispute without the necessity of court intervention and the effort failed.

191.3. Signing of Disclosures, Discovery Requests, Notices, Responses, and Objections.

(a) **Signature required**. Every disclosure, discovery request, notice, response, and objection must be signed:

 (1) by an attorney, if the party is represented by an attorney, and must show the attorney's State Bar of Texas identification number, address, telephone number, and fax number, if any; or

 (2) by the party, if the party is not represented by an attorney, and must show the party's address, telephone number, and fax number, if any.

(b) **Effect of signature on disclosure**. The signature of an attorney or party on a disclosure constitutes a certification that to the best of the signer's knowledge, information, and belief, formed after a reasonable inquiry, the disclosure is complete and correct as of the time it is made.

(c) **Effect of signature of discovery request, notice, response, or objection**. The signature of an attorney or party on a discovery request, notice, response, or objection constitutes a certification that to the best of the signer's knowledge, information, and belief, formed after a reasonable inquiry, the request, notice, response, or objection:

(1) is consistent with the rules of civil procedure and these discovery rules and warranted by existing law or a good faith argument for the extension, modification, or reversal of existing law;

(2) has a good faith factual basis;

(3) is not interposed for any improper purpose, such as to harass or to cause unnecessary delay or needless increase in the cost of litigation; and

(4) is not unreasonable or unduly burdensome or expensive, given the needs of the case, the discovery already had in the case, the amount in controversy, and the importance of the issues at stake in the litigation.

(d) **Effect of failure to sign**. If a request, notice, response, or objection is not signed, it must be stricken unless it is signed promptly after the omission is called to the attention of the party making the request, notice, response, or objection. A party is not required to take any action with respect to a request or notice that is not signed.

(e) **Sanctions**. If the certification is false without substantial justification, the court may, upon motion or its own initiative, impose on the person who made the certification, or the party on whose behalf the request, notice, response, or objection was made, or both, an appropriate sanction as for a frivolous pleading or motion under Chapter 10 of the Civil Practice and Remedies Code.

191.4. Filing of Discovery Materials.

(a) **Discovery materials not to be filed**. The following discovery materials must not be filed:

(1) discovery requests, deposition notices, and subpoenas required to be served only on parties;

(2) responses and objections to discovery requests and deposition notices, regardless on whom the requests or notices were served;

(3) documents and tangible things produced in discovery; and

(4) statements prepared in compliance with Rule 193.3 (b) or (d).

(b) **Discovery materials to be filed**. The following discovery materials must be filed:

(1) discovery requests, deposition notices, and subpoenas required to be served on nonparties;

(2) motions and responses to motions pertaining to discovery matters; and

(3) agreements concerning discovery matters, to the extent necessary to comply with Rule 11.

(c) **Exceptions**. Notwithstanding paragraph (a)—

(1) the court may order discovery materials to be filed;

(2) a person may file discovery materials in support of or in opposition to a motion or for other use in a court proceeding; and

(3) a person may file discovery materials necessary for a proceeding in an appellate court.

(d) **Retention requirement for persons**. Any person required to serve discovery materials not required to be filed must retain the original or exact copy of the materials during the pendency of the case and any related appellate proceedings begun within six months after judgment is signed, unless otherwise provided by the trial court.

(e) **Retention requirement for courts**. The clerk of the court shall retain and dispose of deposition transcripts and depositions upon written questions as directed by the Supreme Court. [See Misc. Docket No. 05-9025, Order Relating to Retention and Disposition of Deposition Transcripts in Civil Cases, Jan. 27, 2005, eff. June 1, 2005.]

191.5. Service of Discovery Materials.

Every disclosure, discovery request, notice, response, and objection required to be served on a party or person must be served on all parties of record.

(Added Aug. 5, 1998, and amended Nov. 9, 1998, eff. Jan. 1, 1999, except that Rules 191.3 and 191.4 apply only to discovery conducted on or after that date.)

Comments to 1999 change:

1. Rule 191.1 preserves the ability of parties by agreement and trial courts by order to adapt discovery to different circumstances. That ability is broad but not unbounded. Parties cannot merely by agreement modify a court order without the court's concurrence. Trial courts cannot simply "opt out" of these rules by form orders or approve or order a discovery control plan that does not contain the matters specified in Rule 190.4, but trial courts may use standard or form orders for providing discovery plans, scheduling, and other pretrial matters. In individual instances, courts may order, or parties may agree, to use discovery methods other than those prescribed in these rules if appropriate. Because the general rule is stated here, it is not repeated in each context in which it applies. Thus, for example, parties can agree to enlarge or shorten the time permitted for a deposition and to change the manner in which a deposition is conducted, notwithstanding Rule 199.5, although parties could not agree to be abusive toward a witness.

2. Rule 191.2 expressly states the obligation of parties and their attorneys to cooperate in conducting discovery.

3. The requirement that discovery requests, notices, responses, and objections be signed also applies to documents used to satisfy the purposes of such instruments. An example is a statement that privileged material or information has been withheld, which may be separate from a response to the discovery request but is nevertheless part of the response.

RULE 192. PERMISSIBLE DISCOVERY: FORMS AND SCOPE; WORK PRODUCT; PROTECTIVE ORDERS; DEFINITIONS.

192.1. Forms of Discovery.

Permissible forms of discovery are:

(a) requests for disclosure;

(b) requests for production and inspection of documents and tangible things;

(c) requests and motions for entry upon and examination of real property;

(d) interrogatories to a party;

(e) requests for admission;

(f) oral or written depositions; and

(g) motions for mental or physical examinations.

192.2. Sequence of Discovery.

The permissible forms of discovery may be combined in the same document and may be taken in any order or sequence.

192.3. Scope of Discovery.

(a) **Generally**. In general, a party may obtain discovery regarding any matter that is not privileged and is relevant to the subject matter of the pending action, whether it relates to the claim or defense of the party seeking discovery or the claim or defense of any other party. It is not a ground for objection that the information sought will be inadmissible at trial if the information sought appears reasonably calculated to lead to the discovery of admissible evidence.

(b) **Documents and tangible things**. A party may obtain discovery of the existence, description, nature, custody, condition, location, and contents of documents and tangible things (including papers, books, accounts, drawings, graphs, charts, photographs, electronic or videotape recordings, data, and data compilations) that constitute or contain matters relevant to the subject matter of the action. A person is required to produce a document or tangible thing that is within the person's possession, custody, or control.

(c) **Persons with knowledge of relevant facts**. A party may obtain discovery of the name, address, and telephone number of persons having knowledge of relevant facts, and a brief statement of each identified person's connection with the case. A person has knowledge of relevant facts when that person has or may have knowledge of any discoverable matter. The person need not have admissible information or personal knowledge of the facts. An expert is "a person with knowledge of relevant facts" only if that knowledge was obtained first-hand or if it was not obtained in preparation for trial or in anticipation of litigation.

(d) **Trial witnesses**. A party may obtain discovery of the name, address, and telephone number of any person who is expected to be called to testify at trial. This paragraph does not apply to rebuttal or impeaching witnesses the necessity of whose testimony cannot reasonably be anticipated before trial.

(e) **Testifying and consulting experts**. The identity, mental impressions, and opinions of a consulting expert whose mental impressions and opinions have not been reviewed by a testifying expert are not discoverable. A party may discover the following information regarding a testifying expert or regarding a consulting expert whose mental impressions or opinions have been reviewed by a testifying expert:

(1) the expert's name, address, and telephone number;

(2) the subject matter on which a testifying expert will testify;

(3) the facts known by the expert that relate to or form the basis of the expert's mental impressions and opinions formed or made in connection with the case in which the discovery is sought, regardless of when and how the factual information was acquired;

(4) the expert's mental impressions and opinions formed or made in connection with the case in which discovery is sought, and any methods used to derive them;

(5) any bias of the witness;

(6) all documents, tangible things, reports, models, or data compilations that have been provided to, reviewed by, or prepared by or for the expert in anticipation of a testifying expert's testimony;

(7) the expert's current resume and bibliography.

(f) **Indemnity and insuring agreements**. Except as otherwise provided by law, a party may obtain discovery of the existence and contents of any indemnity or insurance agreement under which any person may be liable to satisfy part or all of a judgment rendered in the action or to indemnify or reimburse for payments made to satisfy the judgment. Information concerning the indemnity or insurance agreement is not by reason of disclosure admissible in evidence at trial.

(g) **Settlement agreements**. A party may obtain discovery of the existence and contents of any relevant portions of a settlement agreement. Information concerning a settlement agreement is not by reason of disclosure admissible in evidence at trial.

(h) **Statements of persons with knowledge of relevant facts**. A party may obtain discovery of the statement of any person with knowledge of relevant facts—a "witness statement"—regardless of when the statement was made. A witness statement is

(1) a written statement signed or otherwise adopted or approved in writing by the person making it, or

(2) a stenographic, mechanical, electrical, or other type of recording of a witness's oral statement, or any substantially verbatim transcription of such a recording. Notes taken during a conversation or interview with a witness are not a witness statement. Any person may obtain, upon written request, his or her own statement concerning the lawsuit, which is in the possession custody or control of any party.

(i) **Potential parties**. A party may obtain discovery of the name, address, and telephone number of any potential party.

(j) **Contentions**. A party may obtain discovery of any other party's legal contentions and the factual bases for those contentions.

192.4. Limitations on Scope of Discovery.

The discovery methods permitted by these rules should be limited by the court if it determines, on motion or on its own initiative and on reasonable notice, that:

(a) the discovery sought is unreasonably cumulative or duplicative, or is obtainable from some other source that is more convenient, less burdensome, or less expensive; or

(b) the burden or expense of the proposed discovery outweighs its likely benefit, taking into account the needs of the case, the amount in controversy, the parties' resources, the importance of the issues at stake in the litigation, and the importance of the proposed discovery in resolving the issues.

192.5. Work Product.

(a) **Work product defined**. Work product comprises:

(1) material prepared or mental impressions developed in anticipation of litigation or for trial by or for a party or a party's representatives, including the party's attorneys, consultants, sureties, indemnitors, insurers, employees, or agents; or

(2) a communication made in anticipation of litigation or for trial between a party and the party's representatives or among a party's representatives, including the party's attorneys, consultants, sureties, indemnitors, insurers, employees, or agents.

(b) **Protection of work product**.

(1) **Protection of core work product-attorney mental processes**. Core work product—the work product of an attorney or an attorney's representative that contains the attorney's or the attorney's representative's mental impressions, opinions, conclusions, or legal theories—is not discoverable.

(2) **Protection of other work product**. Any other work product is discoverable only upon a showing that the party seeking discovery has substantial need of the materials in the preparation of the party's case and that the party is unable without undue hardship to obtain the substantial equivalent of the material by other means.

(3) **Incidental disclosure of attorney mental processes**. It is not a violation of subparagraph (1) if disclosure ordered pursuant to subparagraph (2) incidentally discloses by inference attorney mental processes otherwise protected under subparagraph (1).

(4) **Limiting disclosure of mental processes**. If a court orders discovery of work product pursuant to subparagraph (2), the court must—insofar as possible—protect against disclosure of the mental impressions, opinions, conclusions, or legal theories not otherwise discoverable.

(c) **Exceptions**. Even if made or prepared in anticipation of litigation or for trial, the following is not work product protected from discovery:

(1) information discoverable under Rule 192.3 concerning experts, trial witnesses, witness statements, and contentions;

(2) trial exhibits ordered disclosed under Rule 166 or Rule 190.4;

(3) the name, address, and telephone number of any potential party or any person with knowledge of relevant facts;

(4) any photograph or electronic image of underlying facts (e.g., a photograph of the accident scene) or a photograph or electronic image of any sort that a party intends to offer into evidence; and

(5) any work product created under circumstances within an exception to the attorney-client privilege in Rule 503 (d) of the Rules of Evidence.

(d) **Privilege**. For purposes of these rules, an assertion that material or information is work product is an assertion of privilege.

192.6. Protective Orders.

(a) **Motion**. A person from whom discovery is sought, and any other person affected by the discovery request, may move within the time permitted for response to the discovery request for an order protecting that person from the discovery sought. A person should not move for protection when an objection to written discovery or an assertion of privilege is appropriate, but a motion does not waive the objection or assertion of privilege. If a person seeks protection regarding the time or place of discovery, the person must state a reasonable time and place for discovery with which the person will comply. A person must comply with a request to the extent protection is not sought unless it is unreasonable under the circumstances to do so before obtaining a ruling on the motion.

(b) **Order**. To protect the movant from undue burden, unnecessary expense, harassment, annoyance, or invasion of personal, constitutional, or property rights, the court may make any order in the interest of justice and may—among other things—order that:

(1) the requested discovery not be sought in whole or in part;

(2) the extent or subject matter of discovery be limited;

(3) the discovery not be undertaken at the time or place specified;

(4) the discovery be undertaken only by such method or upon such terms and conditions or at the time and place directed by the court;

(5) the results of discovery be sealed or otherwise protected, subject to the provisions of Rule 76a.

192.7. Definitions.

As used in these rules—

(a) Written discovery means requests for disclosure, requests for production and inspection of documents and tangible things, requests for entry onto property, interrogatories, and requests for admission.

(b) Possession, custody, or control of an item means that the person either has physical possession of the item or has a right to possession of the item that is equal or superior to the person who has physical possession of the item.

(c) A testifying expert is an expert who may be called to testify as an expert witness at trial.

(d) A consulting expert is an expert who has been consulted, retained, or specially employed by a party in anticipation of litigation or in-preparation for trial, but who is not a testifying expert.

(Added Aug. 5, 1998, and amended Nov. 9, 1998, eff. Jan. 1, 1999.)

Comments to 1999 change:

1. While the scope of discovery is quite broad, it is nevertheless confined by the subject matter of the case and reasonable expectations of obtaining information that will aid resolution of the dispute. The rule must be read and applied in that context. *See In re American Optical Corp.*, ___ S.W.2d ___ (Tex. 1998) (per curiam); *K-Mart v. Sanderson*, 937 S.W.2d 429 (Tex. 1996) (per curiam); *Dillard Dept. Stores v. Hall*, 909 S.W.2d 491 (Tex. 1995) (per curiam); *Texaco, Inc. v. Sanderson*, 898 S.W.2d 813 (Tex. 1995) (per curiam); *Loftin v. Martin*, 776 S.W.2d 145, 148 (Tex. 1989).

2. The definition of documents and tangible things has been revised to clarify that things relevant to the subject matter of the action are within the scope of discovery regardless of their form.

3. Rule 192.3(c) makes discoverable a "brief statement of each identified person's connection with the case." This provision does not contemplate a narrative statement of the facts the person knows, but at most a few words describing the person's identity as relevant to the lawsuit. For instance: "treating physician," "eyewitness," "chief financial officer," "director," "plaintiff's mother and eyewitness to accident." The rule is intended to be consistent with *Axelson v. McIlhany*, 798 S.W.2d 550 (Tex. 1990).

4. Rule 192.3(g) does not suggest that settlement agreements in other cases are relevant or irrelevant.

5. Rule 192.3(j) makes a party's legal and factual contentions discoverable but does not require more than a basic statement of those contentions and does not require a marshaling of evidence.

6. The sections in former Rule 166b concerning land and medical records are not included in this rule. They remain within the scope of discovery and are discussed in other rules.

7. The court's power to limit discovery based on the needs and circumstances of the case is expressly stated in Rule 192.4. The provision is taken from Rule 26(b)(2) of the Federal Rules of Civil Procedure. Courts should limit discovery under this rule only to prevent unwarranted delay and expense as stated more fully in the rule. A court abuses its discretion in unreasonably restricting a party's access to information through discovery.

8. Work product is defined for the first time, and its exceptions stated. Work product replaces the "attorney work product" and "party communication" discovery exemptions from former Rule 166b.

9. Elimination of the "witness statement" exemption does not render all witness statements automatically discoverable but subjects them to the same rules concerning the scope of discovery and privileges applicable to other documents or tangible things.

RULE 193. WRITTEN DISCOVERY: RESPONSE; OBJECTION; ASSERTION OF PRIVILEGE; SUPPLEMENTATION AND AMENDMENT; FAILURE TO TIMELY RESPOND; PRESUMPTION OF AUTHENTICITY.

193.1. Responding to Written Discovery; Duty to Make Complete Response.

A party must respond to written discovery in writing within the time provided by court order or these rules. When responding to written discovery, a party must make a complete response, based on all information reasonably available to the responding party or its attorney at the time the response is made. The responding party's answers, objections, and other responses must be preceded by the request to which they apply.

193.2. Objecting to Written Discovery.

(a) **Form and time for objections**. A party must make any objection to written discovery in writing—either in the response or in a separate document—within the time for response. The party must state specifically the legal or factual basis for the objection and the extent to which the party is refusing to comply with the request.

(b) **Duty to respond when partially objecting objection to time or place of production**. A party must comply with as much of the request to which the party has made no objection unless it is unreasonable under the circumstances to do so before obtaining a ruling on the objection. If the responding party objects to the requested time or place of production, the responding party must state a reasonable time and place for complying with the request and must comply at that time and place without further request or order.

(c) **Good faith basis for objection**. A party may object to written discovery only if a good faith factual and legal basis for the objection exists at the time the objection is made.

(d) **Amendment**. An objection or response to written discovery may be amended or supplemented to state an objection or basis that, at the time the objection or response initially was made, either was inapplicable or was unknown after reasonable inquiry.

(e) **Waiver of objection**. An objection that is not made within the time required, or that is obscured by numerous unfounded objections, is waived unless the court excuses the waiver for good cause shown.

(f) **No objection to preserve privilege**. A party should not object to a request for written discovery on the grounds that it calls for production of material or information that is privileged but should instead comply with Rule 193.3. A party who objects to production of privileged material or information does not waive the privilege but must comply with Rule 193.3 when the error is pointed out.

193.3. Asserting a Privilege.

A party may preserve a privilege from written discovery in accordance with this subdivision.

(a) **Withholding privileged material or information**. A party who claims that material or information responsive to written discovery is privileged may withhold the privileged material or information from the response. The party must state—in the response (or an amended or supplemental response) or in a separate document—that:

  (1) information or material responsive to the request has been withheld,

  (2) the request to which the information or material relates, and

  (3) the privilege or privileges asserted.

(b) **Description of withheld material or information**. After receiving a response indicating that material or information has been withheld from production, the party seeking discovery may serve a written request that the withholding party identify the information and material withheld. Within 15 days of service of that request, the withholding party must serve a response that:

  (1) describes the information or materials withheld that, without revealing the privileged information itself or otherwise waiving the privilege, enables other parties to assess the applicability of the privilege, and

  (2) asserts a specific privilege for each item or group of items withheld.

(c) **Exemption**. Without complying with paragraphs (a) and (b), a party may withhold a privileged communication to or from a lawyer or lawyer's representative or a privileged document of a lawyer or lawyer's representative—

  (1) created or made from the point at which a party consults a lawyer with a view to obtaining professional legal services from the lawyer in the prosecution or defense of a specific claim in the litigation in which discovery is requested, and

  (2) concerning the litigation in which the discovery is requested.

(d) **Privilege not waived by production**. A party who produces material or information without intending to waive a claim of privilege does not waive that claim under these rules or the Rules of Evidence if—within ten days or a shorter time ordered by the court, after the producing party actually discovers that such production was made—the producing party amends the response, identifying the material or information produced and stating the privilege asserted. If the producing party thus amends the response to assert a privilege, the requesting party must promptly return the specified material or information and any copies pending any ruling by the court denying the privilege.

193.4. Hearing and Ruling on Objections and Assertions of Privilege.

(a) **Hearing**. Any party may at any reasonable time request a hearing on an objection or claim of privilege asserted under this rule. The party making the objection or asserting the privilege must present any evidence necessary to support the objection or privilege. The evidence may be testimony presented at the hearing or affidavits served at least seven days before the hearing or at such other reasonable time as the court permits. If the court determines that an in camera review of some or all of the requested discovery is necessary, that material or information must be segregated and produced to the court in a sealed wrapper within a reasonable time following the hearing.

(b) **Ruling**. To the extent the court sustains the objection or claim of privilege, the responding party has no further duty to respond to that request. To the extent the court overrules the objection or claim of privilege, the responding party must produce the requested material or information within 30 days after the court's ruling or at such time as the court orders. A party need not request a ruling on that party's own objection or assertion of privilege to preserve the objection or privilege.

(c) **Use of material or information withheld under claim of privilege**. A party may not use—at any hearing or trial—material or information withheld from discovery under a claim of privilege, including a claim sustained by the court, without timely amending or supplementing the party's response to that discovery.

193.5. Amending or Supplementing Responses to Written Discovery.

(a) **Duty to amend or supplement**. If a party learns that the party's response to written discovery was incomplete or incorrect when made, or, although complete and correct when made, is no longer complete and correct, the party must amend or supplement the response:

    (1) to the extent that the written discovery sought the identification of persons with knowledge of relevant facts, trial witnesses, or expert witnesses, and

    (2) to the extent that the written discovery sought other information, unless the additional or corrective information has been made known to the other parties in writing, on the record at a deposition, or through other discovery responses.

(b) **Time and form of amended or supplemental response**. An amended or supplemental response must be made reasonably promptly after the party discovers the necessity for such a response. Except as otherwise provided by these rules, it is presumed that an amended or supplemental response made less than 30 days before trial was not made reasonably promptly. An amended or supplemental response must be in the same form as the initial response and must be verified by the party if the original response was required to be verified by the party, but the failure to comply with this requirement does not make the amended or supplemental response untimely unless the party making the response refuses to correct the defect within a reasonable time after it is pointed out.

193.6. Failing to Timely Respond—Effect on Trial.

(a) **Exclusion of evidence and exceptions**. A party who fails to make, amend, or supplement a discovery response in a timely manner may not introduce in evidence the material or information that was not timely disclosed, or offer the testimony of a witness (other than a named party) who was not timely identified, unless the court finds that:

    (1) there was good cause for the failure to timely make, amend, or supplement the discovery response; or

    (2) the failure to timely make, amend, or supplement the discovery response will not unfairly surprise or unfairly prejudice the other parties.

(b) **Burden of establishing exception**. The burden of establishing good cause or the lack of unfair surprise or unfair prejudice is on the party seeking to introduce the evidence or call the witness. A finding of good cause or of the lack of unfair surprise or unfair prejudice must be supported by the record.

(c) **Continuance.** Even if the party seeking to introduce the evidence or call the witness fails to carry the burden under paragraph (b), the court may grant a continuance or temporarily postpone the trial to allow a response to be made, amended, or supplemented, and to allow opposing parties to conduct discovery regarding any new information presented by that response.

193.7. Production of Documents Self-Authenticating.

A party's production of a document in response to written discovery authenticates the document for use against that party in any pretrial proceeding or at trial unless—within ten days or a longer or shorter time ordered by the court, after the producing party has actual notice that the document will be used—the party objects to the authenticity of the document, or any part of it, stating the specific basis for objection. An objection must be either on the record or in writing and must have a good faith factual and legal basis. An objection made to the authenticity of only part of a document does not affect the authenticity of the remainder. If objection is made, the party attempting to use the document should be given a reasonable opportunity to establish its authenticity.

(Added Aug. 5, 1998, and amended Nov. 9, 1998 and Dec. 31, 1998, eff. Jan. 1, 1999, except that a response to a discovery request, an objection to a discovery request, an assertion of privilege, or an amendment or supplementation to a discovery response made before that date need not comply with the new rule.)

Comments to 1999 change:

1. This rule imposes a duty upon parties to make a complete response to written discovery based upon all information reasonably available, subject to objections and privileges.

2. An objection to written discovery does not excuse the responding party from complying with the request to the extent no objection is made. But a party may object to a request for "all documents relevant to the lawsuit" as overly broad and not in compliance with the rule requiring specific requests for documents and refuse to comply with it entirely. *See Loftin v. Martin*, 776 S.W.2d 145 (Tex. 1989). A party may also object to a request for a litigation file on the ground that it is overly broad and may assert that on its face the request seeks only materials protected by privilege. *See National Union Fire Ins. Co. v. Valdez*, 863 S.W.2d 458 (Tex. 1993). A party who objects to production of documents from a remote time period should produce documents from a more recent period unless that production would be burdensome and duplicative should the objection be overruled.

3. This rule governs the presentation of all privileges including work product. It dispenses with objections to written discovery requests on the basis that responsive information or materials are protected by a specific privilege from discovery. Instead, the rule requires parties to state that information or materials have been withheld and to identify the privilege upon which the party relies. The statement should not be made prophylactically, but only when specific information and materials have been withheld. The party must amend or supplement the statement if additional privileged information or material is found subsequent to the initial response. Thus, when large numbers of documents are being produced, a party may amend the initial response when documents are found as to which the party claims privilege. A party need not state that material created by or for lawyers for the litigation has been withheld as it can be assumed that such material will be withheld from virtually any request on the grounds of attorney-client privilege or work product. However, the rule does not prohibit a party from specifically requesting the material or information if the party has a good faith basis for asserting that it is discoverable. An example would be material or information described by Rule 503(d)(1) of the Rules of Evidence.

4. Rule 193.3(d) is a new provision that allows a party to assert a claim of privilege to material or information produced inadvertently without intending to waive the privilege. The provision is commonly used in complex cases to reduce costs and risks in large document productions. The focus is on the intent to waive the privilege, not the intent to produce the material or information. A party who fails to diligently screen documents before producing them does not waive a claim of privilege. This rule is thus broader than TEX. R. EVID. 511 and overturns *Granada Corp. v. First Court of Appeals*, 844 S.W.2d 223 (Tex. 1992), to the extent the two conflict. The ten-day period (which may be shortened by the court) allowed for an amended response does not run from the production of the material or information but from the party's first awareness of the mistake. To avoid complications at trial, a party may identify prior to trial the documents intended to be offered, thereby triggering the obligation to assert any overlooked privilege under this rule. A trial court may also order this procedure.

5. This rule imposes no duty to supplement or amend deposition testimony. The only duty to supplement deposition testimony is provided in Rule 195.6.

6. Any party can request a hearing in which the court will resolve issues brought up in objections or withholding statements. The party seeking to avoid discovery has the burden of proving the objection or privilege.

7. The self-authenticating provision is new. Authentication is, of course, but a condition precedent to admissibility and does not establish admissibility. *See* TEX. R. EVID. 901(a). The ten-day period allowed for objection to authenticity (which period may be altered by the court in appropriate circumstances) does not run from the production of the material or information but from the party's actual awareness that the document will be used. To avoid complications at trial, a party may identify prior to trial the documents intended to be offered, thereby triggering the obligation to object to authenticity. A trial court may also order this procedure. An objection to authenticity must be made in good faith.

RULE 194. REQUESTS FOR DISCLOSURE.

194.1. Request.

A party may obtain disclosure from another party of the information or material listed in Rule 194.2 by serving the other party—no later than 30 days before the end of any applicable discovery period—the following request: "Pursuant to Rule 194, you are requested to disclose, within 30 days of service of this request, the information or material described in Rule [state rule, e.g., 194.2, or 194.2 (a), (c), and (f), or 194.2 (d)-(g)]."

194.2. Content.

A party may request disclosure of any or all of the following:

(a) the correct names of the parties to the lawsuit;

(b) the name, address, and telephone number of any potential parties;

(c) the legal theories and, in general, the factual bases of the responding party's claims or defenses (the responding party need not marshal all evidence that may be offered at trial);

(d) the amount and any method of calculating economic damages;

(e) the name, address, and telephone number of persons having knowledge of relevant facts, and a brief statement of each identified person's connection with the case;

(f) for any testifying expert:
  (1) the expert's name, address, and telephone number;
  (2) the subject matter on which the expert will testify;
  (3) the general substance of the expert's mental impressions and opinions and a brief summary of the basis for them, or if the expert is not retained by, employed by, or otherwise subject to the control of the responding party, documents reflecting such information;
  (4) if the expert is retained by, employed by, or otherwise subject to the control of the responding party:
    (A) all documents, tangible things, reports, models, or data compilations that have been provided to, reviewed by, or prepared by or for the expert in anticipation of the expert's testimony; and
    (B) the expert's current resume and biography;

(g) any indemnity and insuring agreements described in Rule 192.3 (f);

(h) any settlement agreements described in Rule 192.3 (g);

(i) any witness statements described in Rule 192.3 (h);

(j) in a suit alleging physical or mental injury and damages from the occurrence that is the subject of the case, all medical records and bills that are reasonably related to the injuries or damages asserted or, in lieu thereof, an authorization permitting the disclosure of such medical records and bills;

(k) in a suit alleging physical or mental injury and damages from the occurrence that is the subject of the case, all medical records and bills obtained by the responding party by virtue of an authorization furnished by the requesting party;

(l) the name, address, and telephone number of any person who may be designated as a responsible party.

(Amended by Order Mar. 3, 2004, effective in cases filed on or after July 1, 2003, in which a request for disclosure under Rule 194.1 is made on or after May 1, 2004.)

2004 Amendment: Rule 194.2(l) is added as required by changes in chapter 33 of the Texas Civil Practice and Remedies Code. The amendment applies in all cases filed on or after July 1, 2003, in which a request under Rule 194.1 is made after May 1, 2004.

194.3. Response.

The responding party must serve a written response on the requesting party within 30 days after service of the request, except that:

(a) a defendant served with a request before the defendant's answer is due need not respond until 50 days after service of the request, and

(b) a response to a request under Rule 194.2(f) is governed by Rule 195.

194.4. Production.

Copies of documents and other tangible items ordinarily must be served with the response. But if the responsive documents are voluminous, the response must state a reasonable time and place for the production of documents. The responding party must produce the documents at the time and place stated, unless otherwise agreed by the parties or ordered by the court, and must provide the requesting party a reasonable opportunity to inspect them.

194.5. No Objection or Assertion of Work Product.

No objection or assertion of work product is permitted to a request under this rule.

194.6. Certain Responses Not Admissible.

A response to requests under Rule 194.2 (c) and (d) that has been changed by an amended or supplemental response is not admissible and may not be used for impeachment.

(Added Aug. 5, 1998 and Nov. 9, 1998, and amended Dec. 31, 1998, eff. Jan. 1, 1999. Rule 194.2 amended Mar. 3, 2004.)

Comments to 1999 change:

1. Disclosure is designed to afford parties basic discovery of specific categories of information, not automatically in every case, but upon request, without preparation of a lengthy inquiry, and without objection or assertion of work product. In those extremely rare cases when information ordinarily discoverable should be protected, such as when revealing a person's residence might result in harm to the person, a party may move for protection. A party may assert any applicable privileges other than work product using the procedures of Rule 193.3 applicable to other written discovery. Otherwise, to fail to respond fully to a request for disclosure would be an abuse of the discovery process.

2. Rule 194.2(c) and (d) permit a party further inquiry into another's legal theories and factual claims than is often provided in notice pleadings. So-called "contention interrogatories" are used for the same purpose. Such interrogatories are not properly used to require a party to marshal evidence or brief legal issues. Paragraphs (c) and (d) are intended to require disclosure of a party's basic assertions, whether in prosecution of claims or in defense. Thus, for example, a plaintiff would be required to disclose

that he or she claimed damages suffered in a car wreck caused by defendant's negligence in speeding, and would be required to state how loss of past earnings and future earning capacity was calculated, but would not be required to state the speed at which defendant was allegedly driving. Paragraph (d) does not require a party, either a plaintiff or a defendant, to state a method of calculating non-economic damages, such as for mental anguish. In the same example, defendant would be required to disclose his or her denial of the speeding allegation and any basis for contesting the damage calculations.

3. Responses under Rule 194.2(c) and (d) that have been amended or supplemented are inadmissible and cannot be used for impeachment, but other evidence of changes in position is not likewise barred.

RULE 195. DISCOVERY REGARDING TESTIFYING EXPERT WITNESSES.

195.1. Permissible Discovery Tools.

A party may request another party to designate and disclose information concerning testifying expert witnesses only through a request for disclosure under Rule 194 and through depositions and reports as permitted by this rule.

195.2. Schedule for Designating Experts.

Unless otherwise ordered by the court, a party must designate experts—that is, furnish information requested under Rule 194.2 (f)—by the later of the following two dates: 30 days after the request is served, or—

(a) with regard to all experts testifying for a party seeking affirmative relief, 90 days before the end of the discovery period;

(b) with regard to all other experts, 60 days before the end of the discovery period.

195.3. Scheduling Depositions.

(a) **Experts for party seeking affirmative relief**. A party seeking affirmative relief must make an expert retained by, employed by, or otherwise in the control of the party available for deposition as follows:

 (1) **If no report furnished**. If a report of the expert's factual observations, tests, supporting data, calculations, photographs, and opinions is not produced when the expert is designated, then the party must make the expert available for deposition reasonably promptly after the expert is designated. If the deposition cannot—due to the actions of the tendering party—reasonably be concluded more than 15 days before the deadline for designating other experts, that deadline must be extended for other experts testifying on the same subject.

 (2) **If report furnished**. If a report of the expert's factual observations, tests, supporting data, calculations, photographs, and opinions is produced when the expert is designated, then the party need not make the expert available for deposition until reasonably promptly after all other experts have been designated.

(b) **Other experts**. A party not seeking affirmative relief must make an expert retained by, employed by, or otherwise in the control of the party available for deposition reasonably promptly after the expert is designated and the experts testifying on the same subject for the party seeking affirmative relief have been deposed.

195.4. Oral Deposition.

In addition to disclosure under Rule 194, a party may obtain discovery concerning the subject matter on which the expert is expected to testify, the expert's mental impressions and opinions, the facts known to the expert (regardless of when the factual information was acquired) that relate to or form the basis of the testifying expert's mental impressions and opinions, and other discoverable matters, including documents not produced in disclosure, only by oral deposition of the expert and by a report prepared by the expert under this rule.

195.5. Court-Ordered Reports.

If the discoverable factual observations, tests, supporting data, calculations, photographs, or opinions of an expert have not been recorded and reduced to tangible form, the court may order these matters reduced to tangible form and produced in addition to the deposition.

195.6. Amendment and Supplementation.

A party's duty to amend and supplement written discovery regarding a testifying expert is governed by Rule 193.5. If an expert witness is retained by, employed by, or otherwise under the control of a party, that party must also amend or supplement any deposition testimony or written report by the expert, but only with regard to the expert's mental impressions or opinions and the basis for them.

195.7. Cost of Expert Witnesses.

When a party takes the oral deposition of an expert witness retained by the opposing party, all reasonable fees charged by the expert for time spent in preparing for, giving, reviewing, and correcting the deposition must be paid by the party that retained the expert.

(Added Aug. 5, 1998, and amended Nov. 9, 1998 and Dec. 31, 1998, eff. Jan. 1, 1999, except that interrogatories that have been served but not answered as of that date and request information pertaining to experts should be answered; and the rule should not be applied to disrupt expert discovery that is in progress or impending, or that has been scheduled by order or by agreement of the parties.)

Comments to 1999 change:

1. This rule does not limit the permissible methods of discovery concerning consulting experts whose mental impressions or opinions have been reviewed by a testifying expert. *See* Rule 192.3(e). Information concerning purely consulting experts, of course, is not discoverable.

2. This rule and Rule 194 do not address depositions of testifying experts who are not retained by, employed by, or otherwise subject to the control of the responding party, nor the production of the materials identified in Rule 192.3(e)(5) and (6) relating to such experts. Parties may obtain this discovery, however, through Rules 176 and 205.

3. In scheduling the designations and depositions of expert witnesses, the rule attempts to minimize unfair surprise and undue expense. A party seeking affirmative relief must either produce an expert's report or tender the expert for deposition before an opposing party is required to designate experts. A party who does not wish to incur the expense of a report may simply tender the expert for deposition, but a party who wishes an expert to have the benefit of an opposing party's expert's opinions before being deposed may trigger designation by providing a report. Rule 191.1 permits a trial court, for good cause, to modify the order or deadlines for designating and deposing experts and the allocation of fees and expenses.

RULE 196. REQUESTS FOR PRODUCTION AND INSPECTION TO PARTIES; REQUESTS AND MOTIONS FOR ENTRY UPON PROPERTY.

196.1. Request for Production and Inspection to Parties.

(a) **Request**. A party may serve on another party—no later than 30 days before the end of the discovery period—a request for production or for inspection, to inspect, sample, test, photograph and copy documents or tangible things within the scope of discovery.

(b) **Contests of request**. The request must specify the items to be produced or inspected, either by individual item or by category, and describe with reasonable particularity each item and category. The request must specify a reasonable time (on or after the date on which the response is due) and place for production. If the requesting party will sample or test the requested items, the means, manner and procedure for testing or sampling must be described with sufficient specificity to inform the producing party of the means, manner, and procedure for testing or sampling.

(c) **Requests for production of medical or mental health records regarding nonparties**.

(1) **Service of request on nonparty**. If a party requests another party to produce medical or mental health records regarding a nonparty, the requesting party must serve the nonparty with the request for production under Rule 21a.

(2) **Exceptions**. A party is not required to serve the request for production on a nonparty whose medical records are sought if:

(A) the nonparty signs a release of the records that is effective as to the requesting party;

(B) the identity of the nonparty whose records are sought will not directly or indirectly be disclosed by production of the records; or

(C) the court, upon a showing of good cause by the party seeking the records, orders that service is not required.

(3) **Confidentiality**. Nothing in this rule excuses compliance with laws concerning the confidentiality of medical or mental health records.

196.2. Response to Request for Production and Inspection.

(a) **Time for response**. The responding party must serve a written response on the requesting party within 30 days after service of the request, except that a defendant served with a request before the defendant's answer is due need not respond until 50 days after service of the request.

(b) **Content of response**. With respect to each item or category of items, the responding party must state objections and assert privileges as required by these rules, and state, as appropriate, that:

(1) production, inspection, or other requested action will be permitted as requested,

(2) the requested items are being served on the requesting party with the response;

(3) production, inspection, or other requested action will take place at a specified time and place, if the responding party is objecting to the time and place of production; or

(4) no items have been identified—after a diligent search—that are responsive to the request.

196.3. Production.

(a) **Time and place of production**. Subject to any objections stated in the response, the responding party must produce the requested documents or tangible things within the person's possession, custody or control at either the time and place requested or the time and place stated in the response, unless otherwise agreed by the parties or ordered by the court, and must provide the requesting party a reasonable opportunity to inspect them.

(b) **Copies**. The responding party may produce copies in lieu of originals unless a question is raised as to the authenticity of the original or in the circumstances it would be unfair to produce copies in lieu of originals. If originals are produced, the responding party is entitled to retain the originals while the requesting party inspects and copies them.

(c) **Organization**. The responding party must either produce documents and tangible things as they are kept in the usual course of business or organize and label them to correspond with the categories in the request.

196.4. Electronic or Magnetic Data.

To obtain discovery of data or information that exists in electronic or magnetic form, the requesting party must specifically request production of electronic or magnetic data and specify the form in which the requesting party wants it produced. The responding party must produce the electronic or magnetic data that is responsive to the request and is reasonably available to the responding party in its ordinary course of business. If the responding party cannot—through reasonable efforts—retrieve the data or information requested or produce it in the form requested, the responding party must state an objection complying with these rules. If the court orders the responding party to comply with the request, the court must also order that the requesting party pay the reasonable expenses of any extraordinary steps required to retrieve and produce the information.

196.5. Destruction or Alteration.

Testing, sampling or examination of an item may not destroy or materially alter an item unless previously authorized by the court.

196.6. Expenses of Production.

Unless otherwise ordered by the court for good cause, the expense of producing items will be borne by the responding party and the expense of inspecting, sampling, testing, photographing, and copying items produced will be borne by the requesting party.

196.7. Request or Motion for Entry Upon Property.

(a) **Request or motion**. A party may gain entry on designated land or other property to inspect, measure, survey, photograph, test, or sample the property or any designated object or operation thereon by serving—no later than 30 days before the end of any applicable discovery period -

  (1) a request on all parties if the land or property belongs to a party, or

  (2) a motion and notice of hearing on all parties and the nonparty if the land or property belongs to a nonparty. If the identity or address of the nonparty is unknown and cannot be obtained through reasonable diligence, the court must permit service by means other than those specified in Rule 21a that are reasonably calculated to give the nonparty notice of the motion and hearing.

(b) **Time, place, and other conditions**. The request for entry upon a party's property, or the order for entry upon a nonparty's property, must state the time, place, manner, conditions, and scope of the inspection, and must specifically describe any desired means, manner, and procedure for testing or sampling, and the person or persons by whom the inspection, testing, or sampling is to be made.

(c) **Response to request for entry**.

  (1) **Time to Respond**. The responding party must serve a written response on the requesting party within 30 days after service of the request, except that a defendant served with a request before the defendant's answer is due need not respond until 50 days after service of the request.

  (2) **Content of response**. The responding party must state objections and assert privileges as required by these rules, and state, as appropriate, that:

    (A) entry or other requested action will be permitted as requested;

    (B) entry or other requested action will take place at a specified time and place, if the responding party is objecting to the time and place of production; or

    (C) entry or other requested action cannot be permitted for reasons stated in the response.

(d) **Requirements for order for entry on nonparty's property**. An order for entry on a nonparty's property may issue only for good cause shown and only if the land, property, or object thereon as to which discovery is sought is relevant to the subject matter of the action.

(Added Aug. 5, 1998, and amended Nov. 9, 1998 and Dec. 31, 1998, eff. Jan. 1, 1999.)

Comments to 1999 change:

1. "Document and tangible things" are defined in Rule 192.3(b).
2. A party requesting sampling or testing must describe the procedure with sufficient specificity to enable the responding party to make any appropriate objections.
3. A party requesting production of magnetic or electronic data must specifically request the data, specify the form in which it wants the data produced, and specify any extraordinary steps for retrieval and translation. Unless ordered otherwise, the responding party need only produce the data reasonably available in the ordinary course of business in reasonably usable form.
4. The rule clarifies how the expenses of production are to be allocated absent a court order to the contrary.
5. The obligation of parties to produce documents within their possession, custody or control is explained in Rule 192.3(b).
6. Parties may request production and inspection of documents and tangible things from nonparties under Rule 205.3.
7. Rule 196.3(b) is based on TEX. R. EVID. 1003.
8. Rule 196.1(c) is merely a notice requirement and does not expand the scope of discovery of a nonparty's medical records.

RULE 197. INTERROGATORIER TO PARTIES.

197.1. Interrogatories.

A party may serve on another party—no later than 30 days before the end of the discovery period—written interrogatories to inquire about any matter within the scope of discovery except matters covered by Rule 195. An interrogatory may inquire whether a party makes a specific legal or factual contention and may ask the responding party to state the legal theories and to describe in general the factual bases for the party's claims or defenses, but interrogatories may not be used to require the responding party to marshal all of its available proof or the proof the party intends to offer at trial.

197.2. Response to Interrogatories.

(a) **Time for response**. The responding party must serve a written response on the requesting party within 30 days after service of the interrogatories, except that a defendant served with interrogatories before the defendant's answer is due need not respond until 50 days after service of the interrogatories.

(b) **Content of response**. A response must include the party's answers to the interrogatories and may include objections and assertions of privilege as required under these rules.

(c) **Option to produce records**. If the answer to an interrogatory may be derived or ascertained from public records, from the responding party's business records, or from a compilation, abstract or summary of the responding party's business records, and the burden of deriving or ascertaining the answer is substantially the same for the requesting party as for the responding party, the responding party may answer the interrogatory by specifying and, if applicable, producing the records or compilation, abstract or summary of the records. The records from which the answer may be derived or ascertained must be specified in sufficient detail to permit the requesting party to locate and identify them as readily as can the responding party. If the responding party has specified business records, the responding party must state a reasonable time and place for examination of the documents. The responding party must produce the documents at the time and place stated, unless otherwise agreed by the parties or ordered by the court, and must provide the requesting party a reasonable opportunity to inspect them.

(d) **Verification required, exceptions**. A responding party—not an agent or attorney as otherwise permitted by Rule 14—must sign the answers under oath except that:

(1) when answers are based on information obtained from other persons, the party may so state, and

(2) a party need not sign answers to interrogatories about persons with knowledge of relevant facts, trial witnesses, and legal contentions.

197.3. Use.

Answers to interrogatories may be used only against the responding party. An answer to an interrogatory inquiring about matters described in Rule 194.2 (c) and (d) that has been amended or supplemented is not admissible and may not be used for impeachment.

(Added Aug. 5, 1998, and amended Nov. 9, 1998 and Dec. 31, 1998, eff. Jan. 1, 1999.)

Comments to 1999 change:

1. Interrogatories about specific legal or factual assertions—such as, whether a party claims a breach of implied warranty, or when a party contends that limitations began to run—are proper, but interrogatories that ask a party to state all legal and factual assertions are improper. As with requests for disclosure, interrogatories may be used to ascertain basic legal and factual claims and defenses but may not be used to force a party to marshal evidence. Use of the answers to such interrogatories is limited, just as the use of similar disclosures under Rule 194.6 is.
2. Rule 191's requirement that a party's attorney sign all discovery responses and objections applies to interrogatory responses and objections. In addition, the responding party must sign some interrogatory answers under oath, as specified by the rule. Answers in amended and supplemental responses must be signed by the party under oath only if the original answers were required to be signed under oath. The failure to sign or verify answers is only a formal defect that does not otherwise impair the answers unless the party refuses to sign or verify the answers after the defect is pointed out.

RULE 198. REQUESTS FOR ADMISSIONS.

198.1. Request for Admissions.

A party may serve on another party—no later than 30 days before the end of the discovery period—written requests that the other party admit the truth of any matter within the scope of discovery, including statements of opinion or of fact or of the application of law to fact, or the genuineness of any documents served with the request or otherwise made available for inspection and copying. Each matter for which an admission is requested must be stated separately.

198.2. Response to Requests for Admissions.

(a) **Time for response**. The responding party must serve a written response on the requesting party within 30 days after service of the request, except that a defendant served with a request before the defendant's answer is due need not respond until 50 days after service of the request.

(b) **Content of response**. Unless the responding party states an objection or asserts a privilege, the responding party must specifically admit or deny the request or explain in detail the reasons that the responding party cannot admit or deny the request. A response must fairly meet the substance of the request. The responding party may qualify an answer, or deny a request in part, only when good faith requires. Lack of information or knowledge is not a proper response unless the responding party states that a reasonable inquiry was made but that the information known or easily obtainable is insufficient to enable the responding party to admit or deny. An assertion that the request presents an issue for trial is not; a proper response.

(c) **Effect of failure to respond**. If a response is not timely served, the request is considered admitted without the necessity of a court order.

198.3. Effect of Admissions; Withdrawal or Amendment.

Any admission made by a party under this rule may be used solely in the pending action and not in any other proceeding. A matter admitted under this rule is conclusively established as to the party making the admission unless the court permits the party to withdraw or amend the admission. The court may permit the party to withdraw or amend the admission if:

(a) the party shows good cause for the withdrawal or amendment; and

(b) the court finds that the parties relying upon the responses and deemed admissions will not be unduly prejudiced and that the presentation of the merits of the action will be subserved by permitting the party to amend or withdraw the admission.

(Added Aug. 5, 1998, and Nov. 9, 1998, eff. Jan. 1, 1999.)

RULE 199. DEPOSITIONS UPON ORAL EXAMINATION.

199.1. Oral Examination; Alternative Methods of Conducting or Recording.

(a) **Generally**. A party may take the testimony of any person or entity by deposition on oral examination before any officer authorized by law to take depositions. The testimony, objections, and any other statements during the deposition must be recorded at the time they are given or made.

(b) **Depositions by telephone or other remote electronic means**. A party may take an oral deposition by telephone or other remote electronic means if the party gives reasonable prior written notice of intent to do so. For the purposes of these rules, an oral deposition taken by telephone or other remote electronic means is considered as having been taken in the district and at the place where the witness is located when answering the questions. The officer taking the deposition may be located with the party noticing the deposition instead of with the witness if the witness is placed under oath by a person who is present with the witness and authorized to administer oaths in that jurisdiction.

(c) **Nonstenographic recording**. Any party may cause a deposition upon oral examination to be recorded by other than stenographic means, including videotape recording. The party requesting the nonstenographic recording will be responsible for obtaining a person authorized by law to administer the oath and for assuring that the recording will be intelligible, accurate, and trustworthy. At least five days prior to the deposition, the party must serve on the witness and all parties a notice, either in the notice of deposition or separately, that the deposition will be recorded by other than stenographic means. This notice must state the method of nonstenographic recording to be used and whether the deposition will also be recorded stenographically. Any other party may then serve written notice designating another method of recording in addition to the method specified, at the expense of such other party unless the court orders otherwise.

199.2. Procedure for Noticing Oral Deposition.

(a) **Time to notice deposition**. A notice of intent to take an oral deposition must be served on the witness and all parties a reasonable time before the deposition is taken. An oral deposition may be taken outside the discovery period only by agreement of the parties or with leave of court.

(b) **Content of notice**.

(1) **Identity of witness; organizations**. The notice must state the name of the witness, which may be either an individual or a public or private corporation, partnership, association, governmental agency, or other organization. If an organization is named as the witness, the notice must describe with reasonable particularity the matters on which examination is requested. In response, the organization named in the notice must—a reasonable time before the deposition—designate one or more individuals to testify on its behalf and set forth, for each individual designated, the matters on which the individual will testify. Each individual designated must testify as to matters that are known or reasonably available to the organization. This subdivision does not preclude taking a deposition by any other procedure authorized by these rules.

(2) **Time and Place**. The notice must state a reasonable time and place for the oral deposition. The place may be in:

(A) the county of the witness's residence;

(B) the county where the witness is employed or regularly transacts business in person;

(C) the county of suit, if the witness is a party or a person designated by a party under Rule 199.2 (b)(1);

(D) the county where the witness was served with the subpoena, or within 150 miles of the place of service, if the witness is not a resident of Texas or is a transient person; or

(E) subject to the foregoing, at any other convenient place directed by the court in which the cause is pending.

(3) **Alternative means of conducting and recording**. The notice must state whether the deposition is to be taken by telephone or other remote electronic means and identify the means. If the deposition is to be recorded by nonstenographic means, the notice may include the notice required by Rule 199.1 (c).

(4) **Additional attendees**. The notice may include the notice concerning additional attendees required by Rule 199.5 (a)(3).

(5) **Request for production of documents**. A notice may include a request that the witness produce at the deposition documents or tangible things within the scope of discovery and within the witness's possession, custody, or control. If the witness is a nonparty, the request must comply with Rule 205 and the designation of materials required to be identified in the subpoena must be attached to, or included in, the notice. The nonparty's response to the request is governed by Rules 176 and 205. When the witness is a party or subject to the control of a party, document requests under this subdivision are governed by Rules 193 and 196.

199.3. Compelling Witness to Attend.

A party may compel the witness to attend the oral deposition by serving the witness with a subpoena under Rule 176. If the witness is a party or is retained by, employed by, or otherwise subject to the control of a party, however, service of the notice of oral deposition upon the party's attorney has the same effect as a subpoena served on the witness.

199.4. Objections to Time and Place of Oral Deposition.

A party or witness may object to the time and place designated for an oral deposition by motion for protective order or by motion to quash the notice of deposition. If the motion is filed by the third business day after service of the notice of deposition an objection to the time and place of a deposition stays the oral deposition until the motion can be determined.

199.5. Examination, Objection, and Conduct During Oral Depositions.

(a) Attendance.

(1) **Witness**. The witness must remain in attendance from day to day until the deposition is begun and completed.

(2) **Attendance by party**. A party may attend an oral deposition in person, even if the deposition is taken by telephone or other remote electronic means. If a deposition is taken by telephone or other remote electronic means, the party noticing the deposition must make arrangements for all persons to attend by the same means. If the party noticing the deposition appears in person, any other party may appear by telephone or other remote electronic means if that party makes the necessary arrangements with the deposition officer and the party noticing the deposition.

(3) **Other attendees**. If any party intends to have in attendance any persons other than the witness, parties, spouses of parties, counsel, employees of counsel, and the officer taking the oral deposition, that party must give reasonable notice to all parties, either in the notice of deposition or separately, of the identity of the other persons.

(b) **Oath; examination**. Every person whose deposition is taken by oral examination must first be placed under oath. The parties may examine and cross-examine the witness. Any party, in lieu of participating in the examination, may serve written questions in a sealed envelope on the party noticing the oral deposition, who must deliver them to the deposition officer, who must open the envelope and propound them to the witness.

(c) **Time limitation**. No side may examine or cross-examine an individual witness for more than six hours. Breaks during depositions do not count against this limitation.

(d) **Conduct during the oral deposition, conferences**. The oral deposition must be conducted in the same manner as if the testimony were being obtained in court during trial. Counsel should cooperate with and be courteous to each other and to the witness. The witness should not be evasive and should not unduly delay the examination. Private conferences between the witness and the witness's attorney during the actual taking of the deposition are improper except for the purpose of determining whether a privilege should be asserted. Private conferences may be held, however, during agreed recesses and adjournments. If the lawyers and witnesses do not comply with this rule, the court may allow in evidence at trial statements, objections, discussions, and other occurrences during the oral deposition that reflect upon the credibility of the witness or the testimony.

(e) **Objections**. Objections to questions during the oral deposition are limited to "Objection, leading" and "Objection, form." Objections to testimony during the oral deposition are limited to "Objection, nonresponsive." These objections are waived if not stated as phrased during the oral deposition. All other objections need not be made or recorded during the oral deposition to be later raised with the court. The objecting party must give a clear and concise explanation of an objection if requested by the party taking the oral deposition, or the objection is waived. Argumentative or suggestive objections or explanations waive objection and may be grounds for terminating the oral deposition or assessing costs or other sanctions. The officer taking the oral deposition will not rule on objections but must record them for ruling by the court. The officer taking the oral deposition must not fail to record testimony because an objection has been made.

(f) **Instructions not to answer**. An attorney may instruct a witness not to answer a question during an oral deposition only if necessary to preserve a privilege, comply with a court order or these rules, protect a witness from an abusive question or one for which any answer would be misleading, or secure a ruling pursuant to paragraph (g). The attorney instructing the witness not to answer must give a concise, nonargumentative, nonsuggestive explanation of the grounds for the instruction if requested by the party who asked the question.

(g) **Suspending the deposition**. If the time limitations for the deposition have expired or the deposition is being conducted or defended in violation of these rules, a party or witness may suspend the oral deposition for the time necessary to obtain a ruling.

(h) **Good faith required**. An attorney must not ask a question at an oral deposition solely to harass or mislead the witness, for any other improper purpose, or without a good faith legal basis at the time. An attorney must not object to a question at an oral deposition, instruct the witness not to answer a question, or suspend the deposition unless there is a good faith factual and legal basis for doing so at the time.

199.6. Hearing on Objections.

Any party may, at any reasonable time, request a hearing on an objection or privilege asserted by an instruction not to answer or suspension of the deposition; provided the failure of a party to obtain a ruling prior to trial does not waive any objection or privilege. The party seeking to avoid discovery must present any evidence necessary to support the objection or privilege either by testimony at the hearing or by affidavits served on opposing parties at least seven days before the hearing If the court determines that an in camera review of some or all of the requested discovery is necessary to rule, answers to the deposition questions may be made *in camera*, to be transcribed and sealed in the event the privilege is sustained, or made in an affidavit produced to the court in a sealed wrapper.

(Added Aug. 5, 1998, and amended Nov. 9, 1998, eff. Jan. 1, 1999.)

Comments to 1999 change:

1. Rule 199.2(b)(5) incorporates the procedures and limitations applicable to requests for production or inspection under Rule 196, including the 30-day deadline for responses, as well as the procedures and duties imposed by Rule 193.

2. For purposes of Rule 199.5(c), each person designated by an organization under Rule 199.2(b)(1) is a separate witness.

3. The requirement of Rule 199.5(d) that depositions be conducted in the same manner as if the testimony were being obtained in court is a limit on the conduct of the lawyers and witnesses in the deposition, not on the scope of the interrogation permitted by Rule 192.

4. An objection to the form of a question includes objections that the question calls for speculation, calls for a narrative answer, is vague, is confusing, or is ambiguous. Ordinarily, a witness must answer a question at a deposition subject to the objection. An objection may therefore be inadequate if a question incorporates such unfair assumptions or is worded so that any answer would necessarily be misleading. A witness should not be required to answer whether he has yet ceased conduct he denies ever doing, subject to an objection to form (*i.e.*, that the question is confusing or assumes facts not in evidence) because any answer would necessarily be misleading on account of the way in which the question is put. The witness may be instructed not to answer. Abusive questions include questions that inquire into matters clearly beyond the scope of discovery or that are argumentative, repetitious, or harassing.

RULE 200. DEPOSITIONS UPON WRITTEN QUESTIONS.

200.1. Procedure for Noticing Deposition Upon Written Questions.

(a) **Who may be noticed, when**. A party may take the testimony of any person or entity by deposition on written questions before any person authorized by law to take depositions on written questions. A notice of intent to take the deposition must be served on the witness and all parties at least 20 days before the deposition is taken. A deposition on written questions may be taken outside the discovery period only by agreement of the parties or with leave of court. The party noticing the deposition must also deliver to the deposition officer a copy of the notice and of all written questions to be asked during the deposition.

(b) **Content of notice**. The notice must comply with Rules 199.1 (b), 199.2 (b), and 199.5 (a)(3). If the witness is an organization, the organization must comply with the requirements of that provision. The notice also may include a request for production of documents as permitted by Rule 199.2 (b)(5), the provisions of which will govern the request, service, and response.

200.2. Compelling Witness to Attend.

A party may compel the witness to attend the deposition on written questions by serving the witness with a subpoena under Rule 176. If the witness is a party or is retained by, employed by, or otherwise subject to the control of a party, however, service of the deposition notice upon the party's attorney has the same effect as a subpoena served on the witness.

200.3. Questions and Objections.

(a) **Direct questions**. The direct questions to be propounded to the witness must be attached to the notice.

(b) **Objections and additional questions**. Within ten days after the notice and direct questions are served, any party may object to the direct questions and serve cross-questions on all other parties. Within five days after cross-questions are served, any party may object to the cross-questions and serve redirect questions on all other parties. Within three days after redirect questions are served, any party may object to the redirect questions and serve recross questions on all other parties. Objections to recross questions must be served within five days after the earlier of when recross questions are served or the time of the deposition on written questions.

(c) **Objections to form of questions**. Objections to the form of a question are waived unless asserted in accordance with this subdivision.

200.4. Conducting the Deposition Upon Written Questions.

The deposition officer must: take the deposition on written questions at the time and place designated; record the testimony of the witness under oath in response to the questions; and prepare, certify, and deliver the deposition transcript in accordance with Rule 203. The deposition officer has authority when necessary to summon and swear an interpreter to facilitate the taking of the deposition.

(Added Aug. 5 1998 and Nov. 9, 1998, and amended Dec. 31, 1998, eff. Jan. 1, 1999.)

Comments to 1999 change:

1. The procedures for asserting objections during oral depositions under Rule 199.5(e) do not apply to depositions on written questions.

2. Section 20.001 of the Civil Practice and Remedies Code provides that a deposition on written questions of a witness who is alleged to reside or to be in this state may be taken by a clerk of a district court, a judge or clerk of a county court, or a notary public of this state.

RULE 201. DEPOSITIONS IN FOREIGN JURISDICTIONS FOR USE IN TEXAS PROCEEDINGS; DEPOSITIONS IN TEXAS FOR USE IN FOREIGN PROCEEDINGS.

201.1. Depositions in Foreign Jurisdictions for Use in Texas Proceedings.

(a) **Generally**. A party may take a deposition on oral examination or written questions of any person or entity located in another state or a foreign country for use in proceedings in this State. The deposition may be taken by:

(1) notice;

(2) letter rogatory, letter of request, or other such device;

(3) agreement of the parties; or

(4) court order.

(b) **By notice**. A party may take the deposition by notice in accordance with these rules as if the deposition were taken in this State, except that the deposition officer may be a person authorized to administer oaths in the place where the deposition is taken.

(c) **By letter rogatory**. On motion by a party, the court in which an action is pending must issue a letter rogatory on terms that are just and appropriate, regardless of whether any other manner of obtaining the deposition is impractical or inconvenient. The letter must:

  (1) be addressed to the appropriate authority in the jurisdiction in which the deposition is to be taken;

  (2) request and authorize that authority to summon the witness before the authority at a time and place stated in the letter for examination on oral or written questions; and

  (3) request and authorize that authority to cause the witness's testimony to be reduced to writing and returned, together with any items marked as exhibits, to the party requesting the letter rogatory.

(d) **By letter of request or other such device**. On motion by a party, the court in which an action is pending, or the clerk of that court, must issue a letter of request or other such device in accordance with an applicable treaty or international convention on terms that are just and appropriate. The letter or other device must be issued regardless of whether any other manner of obtaining the deposition is impractical or inconvenient. The letter or other device must:

  (1) be in the form prescribed by the treaty or convention under which it is issued, as presented by the movant to the court or clerk; and

  (2) must state the time, place, and manner of the examination of the witness.

(e) **Objections to form of letter rogatory, letter of request, or other such device**. In issuing a letter rogatory, letter of request, or other such device, the court must set a time for objecting to the form of the device. A party must make any objection to the form of the device in writing and serve it on all other parties by the time set by the court, or the objection is waived.

(f) **Admissibility of evidence**. Evidence obtained in response to a letter rogatory, letter of request, or other such device is not inadmissible merely because it is not a verbatim transcript, or the testimony was not taken under oath, or for any similar departure from the requirements for depositions taken within this State under these rules.

(g) **Deposition by electronic means**. A deposition in another jurisdiction may be taken by telephone, videoconference, teleconference, or other electronic means under the provisions of Rule 199.

201.2. Depositions in Texas for Use in Proceedings in Foreign Jurisdictions.

If a court of record of any other state or foreign jurisdiction issues a mandate, writ, or commission that requires a witness's oral or written deposition testimony in this State, the witness may be compelled to appear and testify in the same manner and by the same process used for taking testimony in a proceeding pending in this State.

(Added Aug. 5, 1998 and Nov. 9, 1998, eff. Jan. 1, 1999.)

Comments to 1999 change:

1. Rule 201.1 sets forth procedures for obtaining deposition testimony of a witness in another state or foreign jurisdiction for use in Texas court proceedings. It does not, however, address whether any of the procedures listed are, in fact, permitted or recognized by the law of the state or foreign jurisdiction where the witness is located. A party must first determine what procedures are permitted by the jurisdiction where the witness is located before using this rule.

2. Section 20.001 of the Civil Practice and Remedies Code provides a nonexclusive list of persons who are qualified to take a written deposition in Texas and who may take depositions (oral or written) in another state or outside the United States.

3. Rule 201.2 is based on Section 20.002 of the Civil Practice and Remedies Code.

RULE 202. DEPOSITIONS BEFORE SUIT OR TO INVESTIGATE CLAIMS.

202.1. Generally.

A person may petition the court for an order authorizing the taking of a deposition on oral examination or written questions either:

  (a) to perpetuate or obtain the person's own testimony or that of any other person for use in an anticipated suit; or

  (b) to investigate a potential claim or suit.

202.2. Petition.

The petition must:

  (a) be verified;

  (b) be filed in a proper court of any county:

    (1) where venue of the anticipated suit may lie, if suit is anticipated; or

    (2) where the witness resides, if no suit is yet anticipated;

  (c) be in the name of the petitioner;

  (d) state either:

    (1) that the petitioner anticipates the institution of a suit in which the petitioner may be a party; or

(2) that the petitioner seeks to investigate a potential claim by or against petitioner;

(e) state the subject matter of the anticipated action, if any, and the petitioner's interest therein;

(f) if suit is anticipated, either:

(1) state the names of the persons petitioner expects to have interests adverse to petitioner's in the anticipated suit, and the addresses and telephone numbers for such persons; or

(2) state that the names, addresses, and telephone numbers of persons petitioner expects to have interests adverse to petitioner's in the anticipated suit cannot be ascertained through diligent inquiry, and describe those persons;

(g) state the names, addresses and telephone numbers of the persons to be deposed, the substance of the testimony that the petitioner expects to elicit from each, and the petitioner's reasons for desiring to obtain the testimony of each; and

(h) request an order authorizing the petitioner to take the depositions of the persons named in the petition.

202.3. Notice and Service.

(a) **Personal service on witnesses and persons named**. At least 15 days before the date of the hearing on the petition, the petitioner must serve the petition and a notice of the hearing—in accordance with Rule 21a—on all persons petitioner seeks to depose and, if suit is anticipated, on all persons petitioner expects to have interests adverse to petitioner's in the anticipated suit.

(b) **Service by publication on persons not named**.

(1) **Manner**. Unnamed persons described in the petition whom the petitioner expects to have interests adverse to petitioner's in the anticipated suit if any, may be served by publication with the petition and notice of the hearing. The notice must state the place for the hearing and the time it will be held, which must be more than 14 days after the first publication of the notice. The petition and notice must be published once each week for two consecutive weeks in the newspaper of broadest circulation in the county in which the petition is filed, or if no such newspaper exists, in the newspaper of broadest circulation in the nearest county where a newspaper is published.

(2) **Objection to depositions taken on notice by publication**. Any interested party may move, in the proceeding or by bill of review, to suppress any deposition, in whole or in part, taken on notice by publication, and may also attack or oppose the deposition by any other means available.

(c) **Service in probate cases**. A petition to take a deposition in anticipation of an application for probate of a will, and notice of the hearing on the petition, may be served by posting as prescribed by Section 33(f)(2) of the Probate Code. The notice and petition must be directed to all parties interested in the testator's estate and must comply with the requirements of Section 33(c) of the Probate Code insofar as they may be applicable.

(d) **Modification by order**. As justice or necessity may require, the court may shorten or lengthen the notice periods under this rule and may extend the notice period to permit service on any expected adverse party.

202.4. Order.

(a) **Required findings**. The court must order a deposition to be taken if, but only if, it finds that:

(1) allowing the petitioner to take the requested deposition may prevent a failure or delay of justice in an anticipated suit: or

(2) the likely benefit of allowing the petitioner to take the requested deposition to investigate a potential claim outweighs the burden or expense of the procedure.

(b) **Contents**. The order must state whether a deposition will be taken an oral examination or written questions. The order may also state the time and place at which a deposition will be taken. If the order does not state the time and place at which a deposition will be taken, the petitioner must notice the deposition as required by Rules 199 or 200. The order must contain any protections the court finds necessary or appropriate to protect the witness or any person who may be affected by the procedure.

202.5. Manner of Taking and Use.

Except as otherwise provided in this rule, depositions authorized by this rule are governed by the rules applicable to depositions of nonparties in a pending suit. The scope of discovery in depositions authorized by this rule is the same as if the anticipated suit or potential claim had been filed. A court may restrict or prohibit the use of a deposition taken under this rule in a subsequent suit to protect a person who was not served with notice of the deposition from any unfair prejudice or to prevent abuse of this rule.

(Added Aug. 5. 1998 and Nov. 8, 1998, to apply to proceedings filed on or after Jan. 1, 1999, but a court may use the rule for guidance in previously filed proceedings.)

Comments to 1999 change:

1. This rule applies to all discovery before suit covered by former rules governing depositions to perpetuate testimony and bills of discovery.

2. A deposition taken under this rule may be used in a subsequent suit as permitted by the rules of evidence, except that a court may restrict or prohibit its use to prevent taking unfair advantage of a witness or others. The bill of discovery procedure, which Rule 202 incorporates, is equitable in nature, and a court must not permit it to be used inequitably.

RULE 203. SIGNING, CERTIFICATION AND USE OF ORAL AND WRITTEN DEPOSITIONS.

203.1. Signature and Changes.

(a) **Deposition transcript to be provided to witness**. The deposition officer must provide the original deposition transcript to the witness for examination and signature. If the witness is represented by an attorney at the deposition, the deposition officer must provide the transcript to the attorney instead of the witness.

(b) **Changes by witness; signature**. The witness may change responses as reflected in the deposition transcript by indicating the desired changes, in writing, on a separate sheet of paper, together with a statement of the reasons for making the changes. No erasures or obliterations of any kind may be made to the original deposition transcript. The witness must then sign the transcript under oath and return it to the deposition officer. If the witness does not return the transcript to the deposition officer within 20 days of the date the transcript was provided to the witness or the witness's attorney, the witness may be deemed to have waived the right to make the changes.

(c) **Exceptions**. The requirements of presentation and signature under this subdivision do not apply:

(1) if the witness and all parties waive the signature requirement;

(2) to depositions on written questions; or

(3) to nonstenographic recordings of oral depositions.

203.2. Certification.

The deposition officer must file with the court, serve on all parties, and attach as part of the deposition transcript or nonstenographic recording of an oral deposition a certificate duly sworn by the officer stating:

(a) that the witness was duly sworn by the officer and that the transcript or nonstenographic recording of the oral deposition is a true record of the testimony given by the witness;

(b) that the deposition transcript, if any, was submitted to the witness or to the attorney for the witness for examination and signature, the date on which the transcript was submitted, whether the witness returned the transcript, and if so, the date on which it was returned.

(c) that changes, if any, made by the witness are attached to the deposition transcript;

(d) that the deposition officer delivered the deposition transcript or nonstenographic recording of an oral deposition in accordance with Rule 203.3;

(e) the amount of time used by each party at the deposition;

(f) the amount of the deposition officer's charges for preparing the original deposition transcript, which the clerk of the court must tax as costs; and

(g) that a copy of the certificate was served on all parties and the date of service.

203.3. Delivery.

(a) **Endorsement, to whom delivered**. The deposition officer must endorse the title of the action and "Deposition of (name of witness)" on the original deposition transcript (or a copy, if the original was not returned) or the original nonstenographic recording of an oral deposition, and must return:

(1) the transcript to the party who asked the first question appearing in the transcript, or

(2) the recording to the party who requested it.

(b) **Notice**. The deposition officer must serve notice of delivery on all other parties.

(c) **Inspection and copying; copies**. The party receiving the original deposition transcript or nonstenographic recording must make it available upon reasonable request for inspection and copying by any other party. Any party or the witness is entitled to obtain a copy of the deposition transcript or nonstenographic recording from the deposition officer upon payment of a reasonable fee.

203.4. Exhibits.

At the request of a party, the original documents and things produced for inspection during the examination of the witness must be marked for identification by the deposition officer and annexed to the deposition transcript or nonstenographic recording. The person producing the materials may produce copies instead of originals if the party gives all other parties fair opportunity at the deposition to compare the copies with the originals. If the person offers originals rather than copies, the deposition officer must, after the conclusion of the deposition, make copies to be attached to the original deposition transcript or nonstenographic recording, and then return the originals to the person who produced them. The person who produced the originals must preserve them for hearing or trial and make them available for inspection or copying by any other party upon seven days' notice. Copies annexed to the original deposition transcript or nonstenographic recording may be used for all purposes.

203.5. Motion to Suppress.

A party may object to any errors and irregularities in the manner in which the testimony is transcribed, signed, delivered, or otherwise dealt with by the deposition officer by filing a motion to suppress all or part of the deposition. If the deposition officer complies with Rule 203.3 at least one day before the case is called to trial, with regard to a deposition transcript, or 30 days before the case is called to trial, with regard to a nonstenographic recording, the party must file and serve a motion to suppress before trial commences to preserve the objections.

203.6. Use.

(a) **Nonstenographic recording; transcription**. A nonstenographic recording of an oral deposition, or a written transcription of all or part of such a recording, may be used to the same extent as a deposition taken by stenographic means. However, the court, for good cause shown, may require that the party seeking to use a nonstenographic recording or written transcription first obtain a complete transcript of the deposition recording from a certified court reporter. The court reporter's transcription must be made from the original or a certified copy of the deposition recording. The court reporter must, to the extent applicable, comply with the provisions of this rule, except that the court reporter must deliver the original transcript to the attorney requesting the transcript, and the court reporter's certificate must include a statement that the transcript is a true record of the nonstenographic recording. The party to whom the court reporter delivers the original transcript must make the transcript available, upon reasonable request, for inspection and copying by the witness or any party.

(b) **Same proceeding**. All or part of a deposition may be used for any purpose in the same proceeding in which it was taken. If the original is not filed, a certified copy may be used. "Same proceeding" includes a proceeding in a different court but involving the same subject matter and the same parties or their representatives or successors in interest. A deposition is admissible against a party joined after the deposition was taken if:

(1) the deposition is admissible pursuant to Rule 804 (b)(1) of the Rules of Evidence, or

(2) that party has had a reasonable opportunity to redepose the witness and has failed to do so.

(c) **Different proceeding**. Depositions taken in different proceedings may be used as permitted by the Rules of Evidence.

(Added Aug. 5, 1998 and Nov. 9, 1998, eff. Jan. 1, 1999.)

RULE 204. PHYSICAL AND MENTAL EXAMINATIONS.

204.1. Motion and Order Required.

(a) **Motion**. A party may—no later than 30 days before the end of any applicable discovery period—move for an order compelling another party to:

(1) submit to a physical or mental examination by a qualified physician or a mental examination by a qualified psychologist; or

(2) produce for such examination a person in the other party's custody, conservatorship or legal control.

(b) **Service**. The motion and notice of hearing must be served on the person to be examined and all parties.

(c) **Requirements for obtaining order**. The court may issue an order for examination only for good cause shown and only in the following circumstances:

(1) when the mental or physical condition (including the blood group) of a party, or of a person in the custody, conservatorship or under the legal control of a party, is in controversy; or

(2) except as provided in Rule 204.4, an examination by a psychologist may be ordered when the party responding to the motion has designated a psychologist as a testifying expert or has disclosed a psychologist's records for possible use at trial.

(d) **Requirements of order**. The order must be in writing and must specify the time, place, manner, conditions, and scope of the examination and the person or persons by whom it is to be made.

204.2. Report of Examining Physician or Psychologist.

(a) **Right to report**. Upon request of the person ordered to be examined, the party causing the examination to be made must deliver to the person a copy of a detailed written report of the examining physician or psychologist setting out the findings, including results of all tests made, diagnoses and conclusions, together with like reports of all earlier examinations of the same condition. After delivery of the report, upon request of the party causing the examination, the party against whom the order is made must produce a like report of any examination made before or after the ordered examination of the same condition, unless the person examined is not a party and the party shows that the party is unable to obtain it. The court on motion may limit delivery of a report on such terms as are just. If a physician or psychologist fails or refuses to make a report the court may exclude the testimony if offered at the trial.

(b) **Agreements; relationship to other rules**. This subdivision applies to examinations made by agreement of the parties, unless the agreement expressly provides otherwise. This subdivision does not preclude discovery of a report of an examining physician or psychologist or the taking of a deposition of the physician or psychologist in accordance with the provisions of any other rule.

204.3. Effect of No Examination.

If no examination is sought either by agreement or under this subdivision, the party whose physical or mental condition is in controversy must not comment to the court or jury concerning the party's willingness to submit to an examination, or on the right or failure of any other party to seek an examination.

204.4. Cases Arising Under Titles II or V, Family Code.

In cases arising under Family Code Titles II or V, the court may—on its own initiative or on motion of a party—appoint:

(a) one or more psychologists or psychiatrists to make any and all appropriate mental examinations of the children who are the subject of the suit or of any other parties, and may make such appointment irrespective of whether a psychologist or psychiatrist has been designated by any party as a testifying expert;

(b) one or more experts who are qualified in paternity testing to take blood, body fluid, or tissue samples to conduct paternity tests as ordered by the court.

204.5. Definition.

For the purpose of this rule, a psychologist is a person licensed or certified by a state or the District of Columbia as a psychologist.

(Added Aug. 5, 1998 and Nov. 9, 1998, eff. Jan. 1, 1999.)

RULE 205. DISCOVERY FROM NONPARTIES.

205.1. Forms of Discovery; Subpoena Requirement.

A party may compel discovery from a nonparty—that is, a person who is not a party or subject to a party's control—only by obtaining a court order under Rules 196.7, 202, or 204, or by serving a subpoena compelling:

(a) an oral deposition;

(b) a deposition on written questions;

(c) a request for production of documents or tangible things, pursuant to Rule 199.2(b)(5) or Rule 200.1(b), served with a notice of deposition on oral examination or written questions; and

(d) a request for production of documents and tangible things under this rule.

205.2. Notice.

A party seeking discovery by subpoena from a nonparty must serve, on the nonparty and all parties, a copy of the form of notice required under the rules governing the applicable form of discovery. A notice of oral or written deposition must be served before or at the same time that a subpoena compelling attendance or production under the notice is served. A notice to produce documents or tangible things under Rule 205.3 must be served at least 10 days before the subpoena compelling production is served.

205.3. Production of Documents and Tangible Things Without Deposition.

(a) **Notice; subpoena**. A party may compel production of documents and tangible things from a nonparty by serving—a reasonable time before the response is due but no later than 30 days before the end of any applicable discovery period—the notice required in Rule 205.2 and a subpoena compelling production or inspection of documents or tangible things.

(b) **Contents of notice**. The notice must state:

(1) the name of the person from whom production or inspection is sought to be compelled;

(2) a reasonable time and place for the production or inspection; and

(3) the items to be produced or inspected, either by individual item or by category, describing each item and category with reasonable particularity, and, if applicable, describing the desired testing and sampling with sufficient specificity to inform the nonparty of the means, manner, and procedure for testing or sampling.

(c) **Requests for production of medical or mental health records of other nonparties**. If a party requests a nonparty to produce medical or mental health records of another nonparty, the requesting party must serve the nonparty whose records are sought with the notice required under this rule. This requirement does not apply under the circumstances set forth in Rule 196.1 (c)(2).

(d) **Response**. The nonparty must respond to the notice and subpoena in accordance with Rule 176.6.

(e) **Custody, inspection and copying**. The party obtaining the production must make all materials produced available for inspection by any other party on reasonable notice, and must furnish copies to any party who requests at that party's expense.

(f) **Cost of production**. A party requiring production of documents by a nonparty must reimburse the nonparty's reasonable costs of production.

(Added Aug. 5, 1998 and Nov. 9, 1998, and amended Dec. 31, 1998, eff. Jan. 1, 1999.)

Comments to 1999 change: Under this rule, a party may subpoena production of documents and tangible things from nonparties without need for a motion or oral or written deposition.

RULES 206, 207, 208, 208a, 209, 210, 211, 212, 213, and 214. [REPEALED]

(Rules 206 to 209 repealed Aug. 5, 1998 and Nov. 9, 1998, eff. Jan. 1, 1999; Rules 210 to 214 repealed Dec. 5, 1983, eff. April 1, 1984.)

RULE 215. ABUSE OF DISCOVERY; SANCTIONS.

215.1. Motion for Sanctions or Order Compelling Discovery.

A party, upon reasonable notice to other parties and all other persons affected thereby, may apply for sanctions or an order compelling discovery as follows:

(a) **Appropriate court**. On matters relating to a deposition, an application for an order to a party may be made to the court in which the action is pending, or to any district court in the district where the deposition is being taken. An application for an order to a deponent who is not a party shall be made to the court in the district where the deposition is being taken. As to all other discovery matters, an application for an order will be made to the court in which the action is pending.

(b) **Motion**.

(1) If a party or other deponent which is a corporation or other entity fails to make a designation under Rules 199.2 (b)(1) or 200.1 (b); or

(2) If a party, or other deponent, or a person designated to testify on behalf of a party or other deponent fails:

(A) to appear before the officer who is to take his deposition, after being served with a proper notice; or

(B) to answer a question propounded or submitted upon oral examination or upon written questions; or

(3) if a party fails:

(A) to serve answers or objections to interrogatories submitted under Rule 197, after proper service of the interrogatories; or

(B) to answer an interrogatory submitted under Rule 197; or

(C) to serve a written response to a request for inspection submitted under Rule 196, after proper service of the request; or

(D) to respond that discovery will be permitted as requested or fails to permit discovery as requested in response to a request for inspection submitted under Rule 196; the discovering party may move for an order compelling a designation, an appearance, an answer or answers, or inspection or production in accordance with the request, or apply to the court in which the action is pending for the imposition of any sanction authorized by Rule 215.2 (b) without the necessity of first having obtained a court order compelling such discovery. When taking a deposition on oral examination, the proponent of the question may complete or adjourn the examination before he applies for an order. If the court denies the motion in whole or in part, it may make such protective order as it would have been empowered to make on a motion pursuant to Rule 192.6.

(c) **Evasive or incomplete answer**. For purposes of this subdivision an evasive or incomplete answer is to be treated as a failure to answer.

(d) **Disposition of motion to compel: award of expenses**. If the motion is granted, the court shall, after opportunity for hearing, require a party or deponent whose conduct necessitated the motion or the party or attorney advising such conduct or both of them to pay, at such time as ordered by the court, the moving party the reasonable expenses incurred in obtaining the order, including attorney fees, unless the court finds that the opposition to the motion was substantially justified or that other circumstances make an award of expenses unjust. Such an order shall be subject to review on appeal from the final judgment. If the motion is denied, the court may, after opportunity for hearing, require the moving party or attorney advising such motion to pay to the party or deponent who opposed the motion the reasonable expenses incurred in opposing the motion, including attorney fees, unless the court finds that the making of the motion was substantially justified or that other circumstances make an award of expenses unjust. If the motion is granted in part and denied in part, the court may apportion the reasonable expenses incurred in relation to the motion among the parties and persons in a just manner. In determining the amount of reasonable expenses, including attorney fees, to be awarded in connection with a motion, the trial court shall award expenses which are reasonable in relation to the amount of work reasonably expended in obtaining an order compelling compliance or in opposing a motion which is denied.

(e) **Providing person's own statement**. If a party fails to comply with any person's written request for the person's own statement as provided in Rule 192.3(h), the person who made the request may move for an order compelling compliance. If the motion is granted, the movant may recover the expenses incurred in obtaining the order, including attorney fees, which are reasonable in relation to the amount of work reasonably expended in obtaining the order.

215.2. Failure to Comply with Order or with Discovery Request.

(a) **Sanctions by court in district where deposition is taken**. If a deponent fails to appear or to be sworn or to answer a question after being directed to do so by a district court in the district in which the deposition is being taken, the failure may be considered a contempt of that court.

(b) **Sanctions by court in which action is pending**. If a party or an officer, director, or managing agent of a party or a person designated under Rules 199.2 (b)(1) or 200.1 (b) to testify on behalf of a party fails to comply with proper discovery requests or to obey an order to provide or permit discovery, including an order made under Rules 204 or 215.1, the court in which the action is pending may, after notice and hearing, make such orders in regard to the failure as are just, and among others the following:

(1) an order disallowing any further discovery or any kind or of a particular kind by the disobedient party;

(2) an order charging all or any portion of the expenses of discovery or taxable court costs or both against the disobedient party or the attorney advising him;

(3) an order that the matters regarding which the order was made or any other designated facts shall be taken to be established for the purposes of the action in accordance with the claim of the party obtaining the order;

(4) an order refusing to allow the disobedient party to support or oppose designated claims or defenses, or prohibiting him from introducing designated matters in evidence;

(5) an order striking out pleadings or parts thereof, or staying further proceedings until the order is obeyed, or dismissing with or without prejudice the action or proceedings or any part thereof, or rendering a judgment by default against the disobedient party;

(6) in lieu of any of the foregoing orders or in addition thereto, an order treating as a contempt of court the failure to obey any orders except an order to submit to a physical or mental examination;

(7) when a party has failed to comply with an order under Rule 204 requiring him to appear or produce another for examination, such orders as are listed in paragraphs (1), (2), (3), (4) or (5) of this subdivision, unless the person failing to comply shows that he is unable to appear or to produce such person for examination.

(8) In lieu of any of the foregoing orders or in addition thereto, the court shall require the party failing to obey the order or the attorney advising him, or both, to pay, at such time as ordered by the court, the reasonable expenses, including attorney fees, caused by the failure, unless the court finds that the failure was substantially justified or that other circumstances make an award of expenses unjust. Such an order shall be subject to review on appeal from the final judgment.

(c) **Sanction against nonparty for violation of Rules 196.7 or 205.3**. If a nonparty fails to comply with an order under Rules 196.7 or 205.3, the court which made the order may treat the failure to obey as contempt of court.

215.3. Abuse of Discovery Process in Seeking, Making, or Resisting Discovery.

If the court finds a party is abusing the discovery process in seeking, making or resisting discovery or if the court finds that any interrogatory or request for inspection or production is unreasonably frivolous, oppressive, or harassing, or that a response or answer is unreasonably frivolous or made for purposes of delay, then the court in which the action is pending may, after notice and hearing, impose any appropriate sanction authorized by paragraphs (1), (2), (3), (4), (5), and (8) of Rule 215.2(b). Such order of sanction shall be subject to review on appeal from the final judgment.

215.4. Failure to Comply with Rule 198.

(a) **Motion**. A party who has requested an admission under Rule 198 may move to determine the sufficiency of the answer or objection. For purposes of this subdivision an evasive or incomplete answer may be treated as a failure to answer.

Unless the court determines that an objection is justified, it shall order that an answer be served. If the court determines that an answer does not comply with the requirements of Rule 198, it may order either that the matter is admitted or that an amended answer be served. The provisions of Rule 215.1 (d) apply to the award of expenses incurred in relation to the motion.

(b) **Expenses on failure to admit**. If a party fails to admit the genuineness of any document or the truth of any matter as requested under Rule 198 and if the party requesting the admissions thereafter proves the genuineness of the document or the truth of the matter, he may apply to the court for an order requiring the other party to pay him the reasonable expenses incurred in making that proof, including reasonable attorney fees. The court shall make the order unless it finds that

(1) the request was held objectionable pursuant to Rule 193, or

(2) the admission sought was of no substantial importance, or

(3) the party failing to admit had a reasonable ground to believe that he might prevail on the matter, or

(4) there was other good reason for the failure to admit.

215.5. Failure of Party or Witness to Attend or to Serve Subpoena; Expenses.

(a) **Failure of party giving notice to attend**. If the party giving the notice of the taking of an oral deposition fails to attend and proceed therewith and another party attends in person or by attorney pursuant to the notice, the court may order the party giving the notice to pay such other party the reasonable expenses incurred by him and his attorney in attending, including reasonable attorney fees.

(b) **Failure of witness to attend**. If a party gives notice of the taking of an oral deposition of a witness and the witness does not attend because of the fault of the party giving the notice, if another party attends in person or by attorney because he expects the deposition of that witness to be taken, the court may order the party giving the notice to pay such other party the reasonable expenses incurred by him and his attorney in attending, including reasonable attorney fees.

215.6. Exhibits to Motions and Responses.

Motions or responses made under this rule may have exhibits attached including affidavits, discovery pleadings, or any other documents.

(Amended by Order Aug. 5, 1998, and Nov. 9, 1998, eff. Jan. 1, 1999.)

Comments to 1999 change: The references in this rule to other discovery rules are changed to reflect the revisions in those rules, and former Rule 203 is added as Rule 215.5 in place of the former provision, which is superseded by Rule 193.6.

SECTION 10.
THE JURY IN COURT

RULE 216. REQUEST AND FEE FOR JURY TRIAL.

a. **Request**. No jury trial shall be had in any civil suit, unless a written request for a jury trial is filed with the clerk of the court a reasonable time before the date set for trial of the cause on the non-jury docket, but not less than thirty days in advance.

b. **Jury Fee**. Unless otherwise provided by law, a fee of ten dollars if in the district court and five dollars if in the county court must be deposited with the clerk of the court within the time for making a written request for a jury trial. The clerk shall promptly enter a notation of the payment of such fee upon the court's docket sheet.

(Amended by Order March 31, 1941, eff. Sept. 1, 1941; Sept. 20, 1941, eff. Dec. 31, 1941; Oct. 12, 1949, eff. March 1, 1950; July 15, 1987, eff. Jan. 1, 1988; April 24, 1990, eff. Sept. 1, 1990.)

RULE 217. OATH OF INABILITY.

The deposit for a jury fee shall not be required when the party shall within the time for making such deposit, file with the clerk his affidavit to the effect that he is unable to make such deposit, and that he can not, by the pledge of property or otherwise, obtain the money necessary for that purpose; and the court shall then order the clerk to enter the suit on the jury docket.

RULE 218. JURY DOCKET.

The clerks of the district and county courts shall each keep a docket, styled, "The Jury Docket," in which shall be entered in their order the cases in which jury fees have been paid or affidavit in lieu thereof has been filed as provided in the two preceding rules.

RULE 219. JURY TRIAL DAY.

The court shall designate the days for taking up the jury docket and the trial of jury cases. Such order may be revoked or changed in the court's discretion.

(Amended by Order Dec. 5, 1983, eff. April 1, 1984.)

RULE 220. WITHDRAWING CAUSE FROM JURY DOCKET.

When any party has paid the fee for a jury trial, he shall not be permitted to withdraw the cause from the jury docket over the objection of the parties adversely interested. If so permitted, the court in its discretion may by an order permit him to withdraw also his jury fee deposit. Failure of a party to appear for trial shall be deemed a waiver by him of the right to trial by jury.

(Amended by Order Aug. 18, 1947, eff. Dec. 31, 1947; July 21, 1970, eff. Jan. 1, 1971.)

RULE 221. CHALLENGE TO THE ARRAY.

When the jurors summoned have not been selected by jury commissioners or by drawing the names from a jury wheel, any party to a suit which is to be tried by a jury may, before the jury is drawn challenge the array upon the ground that the officer summoning the jury has acted corruptly, and has wilfully summoned jurors known to be prejudiced against the party challenging or biased in favor of the adverse party. All such challenges must be in writing setting forth distinctly the grounds of such challenge and supported by the affidavit of the party or some other credible person. When such challenge is made, the court shall hear evidence and decide without delay whether or not the challenge shall be sustained.

RULE 222. WHEN CHALLENGE IS SUSTAINED.

If the challenge be sustained, the array of jurors summoned shall be discharged, and the court shall order other jurors summoned in their stead, and shall direct that the officer who summoned the persons so discharged, and on account of whose misconduct the challenge has been sustained, shall not summon any other jurors in the case.

RULE 223. JURY LIST IN CERTAIN COUNTIES.

In counties governed as to juries by the laws providing for interchangeable juries, the names of the jurors shall be placed upon the general panel in the order in which they are randomly selected, and jurors shall be assigned for service from the top thereof, in the order in which they shall be needed, and jurors returned to the general panel after service in any of such courts shall be enrolled at the bottom of the list in the order of their respective return; provided, however, after such assignment to a particular court, the trial judge of such court, upon the demand prior to voir dire examination by any party or attorney in the case reached for trial in such court, shall cause the names of all members of such assigned jury panel in such case to be placed in a receptacle, shuffled, and drawn, and such names shall be transcribed in the order drawn on the jury list from which the jury is to be selected to try such case. There shall be only one shuffle and drawing by the trial judge in each case.

(Amended by Order April 24, 1990, eff. Sept. 1, 1990.)

RULE 224. PREPARING JURY LIST.

In counties not governed as to juries by the laws providing for interchangeable juries, when the parties have announced ready for trial the clerk shall write the name of each regular juror entered of record for that week on separate slips of paper, as near the same size and appearance as may be, and shall place the slips in a box and mix them well. The clerk shall draw from the box, in the presence of the court, the names of twenty-four jurors, if in the district court, or so many as there may be, if there be a less number in the box; and the names of twelve jurors if in the county court, or so many as there may be, and write the names as drawn upon two slips of paper and deliver one slip to each party to the suit or his attorney.

RULE 225. SUMMONING TALESMAN.

When there are not as many as twenty-four names drawn from the box, if in the district court, or as many as twelve, if in the county court, the court shall direct the sheriff to summon such number of qualified persons as the court deems necessary to complete the panel. The names of those thus summoned shall be placed in the box and drawn and entered upon the slips as provided in the preceding rules.

RULE 226. OATH TO JURY PANEL.

Before the parties or their attorneys begin the examination of the jurors whose names have thus been listed, the jurors shall be sworn by the court or under its direction, as follows: "You, and each of you, do solemnly swear that you will true answers give to all questions propounded to you concerning your qualifications as a juror, so help you God."

RULE 226a. INSTRUCTIONS TO JURY PANEL AND JURY.

The court must give instructions to the jury panel and the jury as prescribed by order of the Supreme Court under this rule.

(Added July 20, 1966, eff. Jan. 1, 1967. Amended by Order July 15, 1987, eff. Jan. 1, 1988; Jan. 27, 2005, eff. Feb. 1, 2005 in all pending cases.)

Comment – 2005:
The rule is clarified. With these amendments, the Supreme Court has ordered changes in the prescribed jury instructions consistent with Act of June 2, 2003, 78th Leg., R.S., c. 204, § 13.04, 2003 Tex. Gen. Laws 847, 888, codified as TEX. CIV. PRAC. & REM. CODE § 41.003.

AMENDMENTS TO JURY INSTRUCTIONS UNDER RULE 226a, TEXAS RULES OF CIVIL PROCEDURE

To implement Act of June 2, 2003, 78th Leg., R.S., c. 204, § 13.04, 2003 Tex. Gen. Laws 847, 888, codified as TEX. CIV. PRAC. & REM. CODE § 41.003, Part III of the jury instructions prescribed under Rule 226a, Texas Rules of Civil Procedure, by orders dated July 20, 1966 (effective January 1, 1967), July 21, 1970 (effective January 1, 1971), October 3, 1972 (effective February 1, 1973), December 5, 1983 (effective April 1, 1984), March 10, 1987 (effective January 1, 1988), December 16, 1987 (effective January 1, 1988), and January 28, 1988 (effective January 1, 1988), and March 15, 2011 (effective April 1, 2011), and April 13, 2011 (effective April 13, 2011) is amended as follows.

Jury Instructions Prescribed by Order Under Rule 226a

I.

That the following oral instructions, with such modifications as the circumstances of the particular case may require, shall be given by the court to the members of the jury panel after they have been sworn in as provided in Rule 226 and before the voir dire examination:

Members of the Jury Panel [or Ladies and Gentlemen of the Jury Panel]:

Thank you for being here. We are here to select a jury. Twelve [six] of you will be chosen for the jury. Even if you are not chosen for the jury, you are performing a valuable service that is your right and duty as a citizen of a free country.

Before we begin: Turn off all phones and other electronic devices. While you are in the courtroom, do not communicate with anyone through any electronic device. [For example, do not communicate by phone, text message, email message, chat room, blog, or social networking websites such as Facebook, Twitter, or Myspace.] [I will give you a number where others may contact you in case of an emergency.] Do not record or photograph any part of these court proceedings, because it is prohibited by law.

If you are chosen for the jury, your role as jurors will be to decide the disputed facts in this case. My role will be to ensure that this case is tried in accordance with the rules of law.

Here is some background about this case. This is a civil case. It is a lawsuit that is not a criminal case. The parties are as follows: The plaintiff is __________, and the defendant is __________. Representing the plaintiff is __________, and representing the defendant is __________. They will ask you some questions during jury selection. But before their questions begin, I must give you some instructions for jury selection.

Every juror must obey these instructions. You may be called into court to testify about any violations of these instructions. If you do not follow these instructions, you will be guilty of juror misconduct, and I might have to order a new trial and start this process over again. This would waste your time and the parties' money, and would require the taxpayers of this county to pay for another trial.

These are the instructions.

1. To avoid looking like you are friendly with one side of the case, do not mingle or talk with the lawyers, witnesses, parties, or anyone else involved in the case. You may exchange casual greetings like "hello" and "good morning." Other than that, do not talk with them at all. They have to follow these instructions too, so you should not be offended when they follow the instructions.
2. Do not accept any favors from the lawyers, witnesses, parties, or anyone else involved in the case, and do not do any favors for them. This includes favors such as giving rides and food.
3. Do not discuss this case with anyone, even your spouse or a friend, either in person or by any other means [including by phone, text message, email message, chat room, blog, or social networking websites such as Facebook, Twitter, or Myspace]. Do not allow anyone to discuss the case with you or in your hearing. If anyone tries to discuss the case with you or in your hearing, tell me immediately. We do not want you to be influenced by something other than the evidence admitted in court.
4. The parties, through their attorneys, have the right to ask you questions about your background, experiences, and attitudes. They are not trying to meddle in your affairs. They are just being thorough and trying to choose fair jurors who do not have any bias or prejudice in this particular case.
5. Remember that you took an oath that you will tell the truth, so be truthful when the lawyers ask you questions, and always give complete answers. If you do not answer a question that applies to you, that violates your oath. Sometimes a lawyer will ask a question of the whole panel instead of just one person. If the question applies to you, raise your hand and keep it raised until you are called on.

Do you understand these instructions? If you do not, please tell me now.

The lawyers will now begin to ask their questions.

II.

That the following oral and written instructions, with such modifications as the circumstances of the particular case may require, shall be given by the court to the jury immediately after the jurors are selected for the case:

Members of the Jury [or Ladies and Gentlemen]:

You have been chosen to serve on this jury. Because of the oath you have taken and your selection for the jury, you become officials of this court and active participants in our justice system.

[Hand out the written instructions.]

You have each received a set of written instructions. I am going to read them with you now. Some of them you have heard before and some are new.

1. Turn off all phones and other electronic devices. While you are in the courtroom and while you are deliberating, do not communicate with anyone through any electronic device. [For example, do not communicate by phone, text message, email message, chat room, blog, or social networking websites such as Facebook, Twitter, or Myspace.] [I will give you a number where others may contact you in case of an emergency.] Do not post information about the case on the Internet before these court proceedings end and you are released from jury duty. Do not record or photograph any part of these court proceedings, because it is prohibited by law.

2. To avoid looking like you are friendly with one side of the case, do not mingle or talk with the lawyers, witnesses, parties, or anyone else involved in the case. You may exchange casual greetings like "hello" and "good morning." Other than that, do not talk with them at all. They have to follow these instructions too, so you should not be offended when they follow the
instructions.

3. Do not accept any favors from the lawyers, witnesses, parties, or anyone else involved in the case, and do not do any favors for them. This includes favors such as giving rides and food.

4. Do not discuss this case with anyone, even your spouse or a friend, either in person or by any other means [including by phone, text message, email message, chat room, blog, or social networking websites such as Facebook, Twitter, or Myspace]. Do not allow anyone to discuss the case with you or in your hearing. If anyone tries to discuss the case with you or in your hearing, tell me immediately. We do not want you to be influenced by something other than the evidence admitted in court.

5. Do not discuss this case with anyone during the trial, not even with the other jurors, until the end of the trial. You should not discuss the case with your fellow jurors until the end of the trial so that you do not form opinions about the case before you have heard everything. After you have heard all the evidence, received all of my instructions, and heard all of the lawyers' arguments, you will then go to the jury room to discuss the case with the other jurors and reach a verdict.

6. Do not investigate this case on your own. For example, do not:

   a. try to get information about the case, lawyers, witnesses, or issues from outside this courtroom;
   b. go to places mentioned in the case to inspect the places;
   c. inspect items mentioned in this case unless they are presented as evidence in court;
   d. look anything up in a law book, dictionary, or public record to try to learn more about the case;
   e. look anything up on the Internet to try to learn more about the case; or
   f. let anyone else do any of these things for you.

This rule is very important because we want a trial based only on evidence admitted in open court. Your conclusions about this case must be based only on what you see and hear in this courtroom because the law does not permit you to base your conclusions on information that has not been presented to you in open court. All the information must be presented in open court so the parties and their lawyers can test it and object to it. Information from other sources, like the Internet, will not go through this important process in the courtroom. In addition, information from other sources could be completely unreliable. As a result, if you investigate this case on your own, you could compromise the fairness to all parties in this case and jeopardize the results of this trial.

7. Do not tell other jurors about your own experiences or other people's experiences. For example, you may have special knowledge of something in the case, such as business, technical, or professional information. You may even have expert knowledge or opinions, or you may know what happened in this case or another similar case. Do not tell the other jurors about it. Telling other jurors about it is wrong because it means the jury will be considering things that were not admitted in court.

8. Do not consider attorneys' fees unless I tell you to. Do not guess about attorneys' fees.

9. Do not consider or guess whether any party is covered by insurance unless I tell you to.

10. During the trial, if taking notes will help focus your attention on the evidence, you may take notes using the materials the court has provided. Do not use any personal electronic devices to take notes. If taking notes will distract your attention from the evidence, you should not take notes. Your notes are for your own personal use. They are not evidence. Do not show or read your notes to anyone, including other jurors.

You must leave your notes in the jury room or with the bailiff. The bailiff is instructed not to read your notes and to give your notes to me promptly after collecting them from you. I will make sure your notes are kept in a safe, secure location and not disclosed to anyone.

[You may take your notes back into the jury room and consult them during deliberations. But keep in mind that your notes are not evidence. When you deliberate, each of you should rely on your independent recollection of the evidence and not be influenced by the fact that another juror has or has not taken notes. After you complete your deliberations, the bailiff will collect your notes.]

When you are released from jury duty, the bailiff will promptly destroy your notes so that nobody can read what you wrote.

11. I will decide matters of law in this case. It is your duty to listen to and consider the evidence and to determine fact issues that I may submit to you at the end of the trial. After you have heard all the evidence, I will give you instructions to follow as you make your decision. The instructions also will have questions for you to answer. You will not be asked and you should not consider which side will win. Instead, you will need to answer the specific questions I give you.

Every juror must obey my instructions. If you do not follow these instructions, you will be guilty of juror misconduct, and I may have to order a new trial and start this process over again. This would waste your time and the parties' money, and would require the taxpayers of this county to pay for another trial.

Do you understand these instructions? If you do not, please tell me now.

Please keep these instructions and review them as we go through this case. If anyone does not follow these instructions, tell me.

III.
Court's Charge

Before closing arguments begin, the court must give to each member of the jury a copy of the charge, which must include the following written instructions, with such modifications as the circumstances of the particular case may require:

Members of the Jury [or Ladies & Gentlemen of the Jury]:

After the closing arguments, you will go to the jury room to decide the case, answer the questions that are attached, and reach a verdict. You may discuss the case with other jurors only when you are all together in the jury room.

Remember my previous instructions: Do not discuss the case with anyone else, either in person or by any other means. Do not do any independent investigation about the case or conduct any research. Do not look up any words in dictionaries or on the Internet. Do not post information about the case on the Internet. Do not share any special knowledge or experiences with the other jurors. Do not use your phone or any other electronic device during your deliberations for any reason. [I will give you a number where others may contact you in case of an emergency.]

[Any notes you have taken are for your own personal use. You may take your notes back into the jury room and consult them during deliberations, but do not show or read your notes to your fellow jurors during your deliberations. Your notes are not evidence. Each of you should rely on your independent recollection of the evidence and not be influenced by the fact that another juror has or has not taken notes.]

[You must leave your notes with the bailiff when you are not deliberating. The bailiff will give your notes to me promptly after collecting them from you. I will make sure your notes are kept in a safe, secure location and not disclosed to anyone. After you complete your deliberations, the bailiff will collect your notes. When you are released from jury duty, the bailiff will promptly destroy your notes so that nobody can read what you wrote.]

Here are the instructions for answering the questions.

1. Do not let bias, prejudice, or sympathy play any part in your decision.
2. Base your answers only on the evidence admitted in court and on the law that is in these instructions and questions. Do not consider or discuss any evidence that was not admitted in the courtroom.
3. You are to make up your own minds about the facts. You are the sole judges of the credibility of the witnesses and the weight to give their testimony. But on matters of law, you must follow all of my instructions.
4. If my instructions use a word in a way that is different from its ordinary meaning, use the meaning I give you, which will be a proper legal definition.
5. All the questions and answers are important. No one should say that any question or answer is not important.
6. Answer "yes" or "no" to all questions unless you are told otherwise. A "yes" answer must be based on a preponderance of the evidence [unless you are told otherwise]. Whenever a question requires an answer other than "yes" or "no," your answer must be based on a preponderance of the evidence [unless you are told otherwise].

   The term "preponderance of the evidence" means the greater weight of credible evidence presented in this case. If you do not find that a preponderance of the evidence supports a "yes" answer, then answer "no." A preponderance of the evidence is not measured by the number of witnesses or by the number of documents admitted in evidence. For a fact to be proved by a preponderance of the evidence, you must find that the fact is more likely true than not true.
7. Do not decide who you think should win before you answer the questions and then just answer the questions to match your decision. Answer each question carefully without considering who will win. Do not discuss or consider the effect your answers will have.

8. Do not answer questions by drawing straws or by any method of chance.

9. Some questions might ask you for a dollar amount. Do not agree in advance to decide on a dollar amount by adding up each juror's amount and then figuring the average.

10. Do not trade your answers. For example, do not say, "I will answer this question your way if you answer another question my way."

11. [Unless otherwise instructed] The answers to the questions must be based on the decision of at least 10 of the 12 [5 of the 6] jurors. The same 10 [5] jurors must agree on every answer. Do not agree to be bound by a vote of anything less than 10 [5] jurors, even if it would be a majority.

As I have said before, if you do not follow these instructions, you will be guilty of juror misconduct, and I might have to order a new trial and start this process over again. This would waste your time and the parties' money, and would require the taxpayers of this county to pay for another trial. If a juror breaks any of these rules, tell that person to stop and report it to me immediately.

[Definitions, questions, and special instructions given to the jury will be transcribed here. If exemplary damages are sought against a defendant, the jury must unanimously find, with respect to that defendant, (i) liability on at least one claim for actual damages that will support an award of exemplary damages, (ii) any additional conduct, such as malice or gross negligence, required for an award of exemplary damages, and (iii) the amount of exemplary damages to be awarded. The jury's answers to questions regarding (ii) and (iii) must be conditioned on a unanimous finding regarding (i), except in an extraordinary circumstance when the conditioning instruction would be erroneous. The jury need not be unanimous in finding the amount of actual damages. Thus, if questions regarding (ii) and (iii) are submitted to the jury for defendants D1 and D2, instructions in substantially the following form must immediately precede such questions:

Preceding question (ii):

Answer Question (ii) for D1 only if you unanimously answered "Yes" to Question[s] (i) regarding D1. Otherwise, do not answer Question (ii) for D1. [Repeat for D2.]

You are instructed that in order to answer "Yes" to [any part of] Question (ii), your answer must be unanimous. You may answer "No" to [any part of] Question (ii) only upon a vote of 10 [5] or more jurors. Otherwise, you must not answer [that part of] Question (ii).

Preceding question (iii):

Answer Question (iii) for D1 only if you answered "Yes" to Question (ii) for D1. Otherwise, do not answer Question (iii) for D1. [Repeat for D2.]

You are instructed that you must unanimously agree on the amount of any award of exemplary damages.

These examples are given by way of illustration.]

Presiding Juror:

1. When you go into the jury room to answer the questions, the first thing you will need to do is choose a presiding juror.

2. The presiding juror has these duties:

   a. have the complete charge read aloud if it will be helpful to your deliberations;

   b. preside over your deliberations, meaning manage the discussions, and see that you follow these instructions;

   c. give written questions or comments to the bailiff who will give them to the judge;

   d. write down the answers you agree on;

   e. get the signatures for the verdict certificate; and

   f. notify the bailiff that you have reached a verdict.

Do you understand the duties of the presiding juror? If you do not, please tell me now.

Instructions for Signing the Verdict Certificate:

1. [Unless otherwise instructed] You may answer the questions on a vote of 10 [5] jurors. The same 10 [5] jurors must agree on every answer in the charge. This means you may not have one group of 10 [5] jurors agree on one answer and a different group of 10 [5] jurors agree on another answer.

2. If 10 [5] jurors agree on every answer, those 10 [5] jurors sign the verdict.

   If 11 jurors agree on every answer, those 11 jurors sign the verdict.

   If all 12 [6] of you agree on every answer, you are unanimous and only the presiding juror signs the verdict.

3. All jurors should deliberate on every question. You may end up with all 12 [6] of you

agreeing on some answers, while only 10 [5] or 11 of you agree on other answers. But when you sign the verdict, only those 10 [5] who agree on every answer will sign the verdict.

4. [Added if the charge requires some unanimity] There are some special instructions before Questions _______ explaining how to answer those questions. Please follow the instructions. If all 12 [6] of you answer those questions, you will need to complete a second verdict certificate for those questions.

Do you understand these instructions? If you do not, please tell me now.

____
Judge Presiding

Verdict Certificate

Check one:

_____ Our verdict is unanimous. All 12 [6] of us have agreed to each and every answer. The presiding juror has signed the certificate for all 12 [6] of us.

______________________ ______________________
Signature of Presiding Juror Printed Name of Presiding Juror

_____ Our verdict is not unanimous. Eleven of us have agreed to each and every answer and have signed the certificate below.

_____ Our verdict is not unanimous. Ten [Five] of us have agreed to each and every answer and have signed the certificate below.

SIGNATURE	NAME PRINTED
1. ______________________	______________________
2. ______________________	______________________
3. ______________________	______________________
4. ______________________	______________________
5. ______________________	______________________
6. ______________________	______________________
7. ______________________	______________________
8. ______________________	______________________
9. ______________________	______________________
10. ______________________	______________________
11. ______________________	______________________

If you have answered Question No. ________ [the exemplary damages amount], then you must sign this certificate also.

Additional Certificate

[Used when some questions require unanimous answers]

I certify that the jury was unanimous in answering the following questions. All 12 [6] of us agreed to each of the answers. The presiding juror has signed the certificate for all 12 [6] of us.

[Judge to list questions that require a unanimous answer, including the predicate liability question.]

______________________ ______________________
Signature of Presiding Juror Printed Name of Presiding Juror

IV.

That the following oral instructions shall be given by the court to the jury after the verdict has been accepted by the court and before the jurors are released from jury duty:

Thank you for your verdict.

I have told you that the only time you may discuss the case is with the other jurors in the jury room. I now release you from jury duty. Now you may discuss the case with anyone. But you may also choose not to discuss the case; that is your right.

After you are released from jury duty, the lawyers and others may ask you questions to see if the jury followed the instructions, and they may ask you to give a sworn statement. You are free to discuss the case with them and to give a sworn statement. But you may choose not to discuss the case and not to give a sworn statement; that is your right.

Instructions adopted by orders dated July 20, 1966 (eff. Jan. 1, 1967). Amended by Orders July 21, 1970 (eff. Jan. 1, 1971); Oct. 3, 1972 (eff. Feb. 1, 1973); Dec. 5, 1983 (eff. April 1, 1984); March 10, 1987 (eff. Jan. 1, 1988); Dec. 16, 1987 (eff. Jan. 1, 1988); Jan. 28, 1988 (eff. Jan. 1, 1988); Jan. 27, 2005 (eff. Feb. 1, 2005, in all cases filed on or after Sept. 1, 2003); March 15, 2011 (effective April 1, 2011); April 13, 2011 (effective April 13, 2011).

RULE 227. CHALLENGE TO JUROR.

A challenge to a particular juror is either a challenge for cause or a peremptory challenge. The court shall decide without delay any such challenge, and if sustained, the juror shall be discharged from the particular case. Either such challenge may be made orally on the formation of a jury to try the case.

RULE 228. "CHALLENGE FOR CAUSE" DEFINED.

A challenge for cause is an objection made to a juror, alleging some fact which by law disqualifies him to serve as a juror in the case or in any case, or which in the opinion of the court, renders him an unfit person to sit on the jury. Upon such challenge the examination is not confined to the answers of the juror, but other evidence may be heard for or against the challenge.

RULE 229. CHALLENGE FOR CAUSE.

When twenty-four or more jurors, if in the district court, or twelve or more, if in the county court, are drawn, and the lists of their names delivered to the parties, if either party desires to challenge any juror for cause, the challenge shall then be made. The name of a juror challenged and set aside for cause shall be erased from such lists.

RULE 230. CERTAIN QUESTIONS NOT TO BE ASKED.

In examining a juror, he shall not be asked a question the answer to which may show that he has been convicted of an offense which disqualifies him, or that he stands charged by some legal accusation with theft or any felony.

RULE 231. NUMBER REDUCED BY CHALLENGES.

If the challenges reduce the number of jurors to less than twenty-four, if in the district court, or to less than twelve, if in the county court, the court shall order other jurors to be drawn from the wheel or from the central jury panel or summoned, as the practice may be in the particular county, and their names written upon the list instead of those set aside for cause. Such jurors so summoned may likewise be challenged for cause.

RULE 232. MAKING PEREMPTORY CHALLENGES.

If there remain on such lists not subject to challenge for cause, twenty-four names, if in the district court, or twelve names, if in the county court, the parties shall proceed to make their peremptory challenges. A peremptory challenge is made to a juror without assigning any reason therefor.

RULE 233. NUMBER OF PEREMPTORY CHALLENGES.

Except as provided below, each party to a civil action is entitled to six peremptory challenges in a case tried in the district court, and to three in the county court.

Alignment of the Parties. In multiple party cases, it shall be the duty of the trial judge to decide whether any of the litigants aligned on the same side of the docket are antagonistic with respect to any issued to be submitted to the jury, before the exercise of peremptory challenges.

Definition of Side. The term "side" as used in this rule is not synonymous with "party," "litigant," or "person." Rather, "side" means one or more litigants who have common interests on the matters with which the jury is concerned.

Motion to Equalize. In multiple party cases, upon motion of any litigant made prior to the exercise of peremptory challenges, it shall be the duty of the trial judge to equalize the number of peremptory challenges so that no litigant or side is given unfair advantage as a result of the alignment of the litigants and the award of peremptory challenges to each litigant or side. In determining how the challenges should be allocated the court shall consider any matter brought to the attention of the trial judge concerning the ends of justice and the elimination of an unfair advantage.

(Amended by Order Dec. 5, 1983, eff. April 1, 1984.)

RULE 234. LISTS RETURNED TO THE CLERK.

When the parties have made or declined to make their peremptory challenges, they shall deliver their lists to the clerk. The clerk shall, if the case be in the district court, call off the first twelve names on the lists that have not been erased; and if the case be in the county court, he shall call off the first six names on the lists that have not been erased; those whose names are called shall be the jury.

RULE 235. IF JURY IS INCOMPLETE.

When by peremptory challenges the jury is left incomplete, the court shall direct other jurors to be drawn or summoned to complete the jury; and such other jurors shall be impaneled as in the first instance.

RULE 236. OATH TO JURY.

The jury shall be sworn by the court or under its direction, in substance as follows: "You, and each of you, do solemnly swear that in all cases between parties which shall be to you submitted, you will a true verdict render, according to the law, as it may be given you in charge by the court, and to the evidence submitted to you under the rulings of the court. So help you God."

SECTION 11.
TRIAL OF CAUSES

A.
APPEARANCE AND PROCEDURE

RULE 237. APPEARANCE DAY.

If a defendant, who has been duly cited, is by the citation required to answer on a day which is in term time, such day is appearance day as to him. If he is so required to answer on a day in vacation, he shall plead or answer accordingly, and the first day of the next term is appearance day as to him.

(Amended by Order March 31, 1941, eff. Sept. 1, 1941; July 20, 1954, eff. Jan. 1, 1955.)

RULE 237a. CASES REMANDED FROM FEDERAL COURT.

When any cause is removed to the Federal Court and is afterwards remanded to the state court, the plaintiff shall file a certified copy of the order of remand with the clerk of the state court and shall forthwith give written notice of such filing to the attorneys of record for all adverse parties. All such adverse parties shall have fifteen days from the receipt of such notice within which to file an answer. No default judgment shall be rendered against a party in a removed action remanded from federal court if that party filed an answer in federal court during removal.

(Added July 20, 1954, eff. Jan. 1, 1955. Amended by Order Dec. 5, 1983, eff. April 1, 1984; caption amended by order of July 15, 1987, eff. Jan. 1, 1988; April 24, 1990, eff. Sept. 1, 1990.)

RULE 238. CALL OF APPEARANCE DOCKET.

On the appearance day of a particular defendant and at the hour named in the citation, or as soon thereafter as may be practicable, the court or clerk in open court shall call, in their order, all the cases on the docket in which such day is appearance day as to any defendant, or, the court or clerk failing therein, any such case shall be so called on request of the plaintiff's attorney.

RULE 239. JUDGMENT BY DEFAULT.

Upon such call of the docket, or at any time after a defendant is required to answer, the plaintiff may in term time take judgment by default against such defendant if he has not previously filed an answer, and provided that return of service shall have been on file with the clerk for the length of time required by Rule 107.

(Amended by Order April 12, 1962, eff. Sept. 1, 1962; Oct. 17, 2011, eff. Jan. 1, 2012.)

RULE 239a. NOTICE OF DEFAULT JUDGMENT.

At or immediately prior to the time in interlocutory or final default judgment is rendered, the party taking the same or his attorney shall certify to the clerk in writing the last known mailing address of the party against whom the judgment is taken, which certificate shall be filed among the papers in the cause. Immediately upon the signing of the judgment, the clerk shall mail written notice thereof to the party against whom the judgment was rendered at the address shown in the certificate, and note the fact of such mailing on the docket. The notice shall state the number and style of the case, the court in which the case is pending, the names of the parties in whose favor and against whom the judgment was rendered, and the date of the signing of the judgment. Failure to comply with the provisions of this rule shall not affect the finality of the judgment.

(Added July 20, 1966, eff. Jan. 1, 1967. Amended by Order July 15, 1987, eff. Jan. 1, 1988.)

RULE 240. WHERE ONLY SOME ANSWER.

Where there are several defendants, some of whom have answered or have not been duly served and some of whom have been duly served and have made default, an interlocutory judgment by default may be entered against those who have made default, and the cause may proceed or be postponed as to the others.

RULE 241. ASSESSING DAMAGES ON LIQUIDATED DEMANDS.

When a judgment by default is rendered against the defendant, or all of several defendants, if the claim is liquidated and proved by an instrument in writing, the damages shall be assessed by the court, or under its direction, and final judgment shall be rendered therefor, unless the defendant shall demand and be entitled to a trial by jury.

(Amended by Order Dec. 5, 1983, eff. April 1, 1984.)

RULE 242. [REPEALED]

(Repealed by Order Sept. 20, 1941, eff. Dec. 31, 1941.)

RULE 243. UNLIQUIDATED DEMANDS.

If the cause of action is unliquidated or be not proved by an instrument in writing, the court shall hear evidence as to damages and shall render judgment therefor, unless the defendant shall demand and be entitled to a trial by jury in which case the judgment by default shall be noted, a writ of inquiry awarded, and the cause entered on the jury docket.

(Amended by Order March 31, 1941, eff. Sept. 1, 1941.)

RULE 244. ON SERVICE BY PUBLICATION.

Where service has been made by publication, and no answer has been filed nor appearance entered within the prescribed time, the court shall appoint an attorney to defend the suit in behalf of the defendant, and judgment shall be rendered as in other cases; but, in every such case a statement of the evidence, approved and signed by the judge, shall be filed with the papers of the cause as a part of the record thereof The court shall allow such attorney a reasonable fee for his services, to be taxed as part of the costs.

RULE 245. ASSIGNMENT OF CASES FOR TRIAL.

The court may set contested cases on written request of any party, or on the court's own motion, with reasonable notice of not less than forty-five days to the parties of a first setting for trial, or by agreement of the parties; provided, however, that when a case previously has been set for trial, the Court may reset said contested case to a later date on any reasonable notice to the parties or by agreement of the parties. Noncontested cases may be tried or disposed of at any time whether set or not, and may be set at any time for any other time.

A request for trial setting constitutes a representation that the requesting party reasonably and in good faith expects to be ready for trial by the date requested, but no additional representation concerning the completion of pretrial proceedings or of current readiness for trial shall be required in order to obtain a trial setting in a contested case.

(Amended by Order July 22, 1975, eff. Jan. 1, 1976; Dec. 5, 1983, eff. April 1, 1984; April 24, 1990, eff. Sept. 1, 1990.)

RULE 246. CLERK TO GIVE NOTICE OF SETTINGS.

The clerk shall keep a record in his office of all cases set for trial, and it shall be his duty to inform any non-resident attorney of the date of setting of any case upon request by mail from such attorney, accompanied by a return envelope properly addressed and stamped. Failure of the clerk to furnish such information on proper request shall be sufficient ground for continuance or for a new trial when it appears to the court that such failure has prevented the attorney from preparing or presenting his claim or defense.

RULE 247. TRIED WHEN SET.

Every suit shall be tried when it is called, unless continued or postponed to a future day or placed at the end of the docket to be called again for trial in its regular order. No cause which has been set upon the trial docket of the court shall be taken from the trial docket for the date set except by agreement of the parties or for good cause upon motion and notice to the opposing party.

(Amended by Order Dec. 5, 1983, eff. April 1, 1984.)

RULE 248. JURY CASES.

When a jury has been demanded, questions of law, motions, exceptions to pleadings, and other unresolved pending matters shall, as far as practicable, be heard and determined by the court before the trial commences, and jurors shall be summoned to appear on the day so designated.

(Amended by Order Dec. 5, 1983, eff. April 1, 1984; April 24, 1990, eff. Sept. 1, 1990.)

RULE 249. CALL OF NONJURY DOCKET.

The nonjury docket shall be taken up at such times as not unnecessarily to interfere with the dispatch of business on the jury docket.

RULE 250. [REPEALED]

(Repealed by Order Sept. 20, 1941, eff. Dec. 31, 1941.)

B.
CONTINUANCE AND CHANGE OF VENUE

RULE 251. CONTINUANCE.

No application for a continuance shall be heard before the defendant files his defense, nor shall any continuance be granted except for sufficient cause supported by affidavit, or by consent of the parties, or by operation of law.

RULE 252. APPLICATION FOR CONTINUANCE.

If the ground of such application be the want of testimony, the party applying therefor shall make affidavit that such testimony is material, showing the materiality thereof, and that he has used due diligence to procure such testimony, stating such diligence, and the cause of failure, if known; that such testimony cannot be procured from any other source; and, if it be for the absence of a witness, he shall state the name and residence of the witness, and what he expects to prove by him; and also state that the continuance is not sought for delay only, but that justice may be done; provided that, on a first application for a continuance, it shall not be necessary to show that the absent testimony cannot be procured from any other source.

The failure to obtain the deposition of any witness residing within 100 miles of the courthouse of the county in which the suit is pending shall not be regarded as want of diligence when diligence has been used to secure the personal attendance of such witness under the rules of law, unless by reason of age, infirmity or sickness, or official duty, the witness will be unable to attend the court, or unless such witness is about to leave, or has left, the State or county in which the suit is pending and will not probably be present at the trial.

(Amended by Order Dec. 5, 1983, eff. April 1, 1984.)

RULE 253. ABSENCE OF COUNSEL AS GROUND FOR CONTINUANCE.

Except as provided elsewhere in these rules, absence of counsel will not be good cause for a continuance or postponement of the cause when called for trial, except it be allowed in the discretion of the court, upon cause shown or upon matters within the knowledge or information of the judge to be stated on the record.

RULE 254. ATTENDANCE ON LEGISLATURE.

In all civil actions, including matters of probate, and in all matters ancillary to such suits which require action by or the attendance of an attorney, including appeals but excluding temporary restraining orders, at any time within thirty days of a date when the legislature is to be in session, or at any time the legislature is in session, or when the legislature sits as a Constitutional Convention, it shall be mandatory that the court continue the cause if it shall appear to the court, by affidavit, that any party applying for continuance, or any attorney for any party to the cause, is a member of either branch of the legislature, and will be or is in actual attendance on a session of the same. If the member of the legislature is an attorney for a party to the cause, his affidavit shall contain a declaration that it is his intention to participate actively in the preparation and/or presentation of the case. Where a party to any cause, or an attorney for any party to a cause, is a member of the legislature, his affidavit need not be corroborated. On the filing of such affidavit, the court shall continue the cause until thirty days after adjournment of the legislature and the affidavit shall be proof of the necessity for the continuance, and the continuance shall be deemed one of right and shall not be charged against the movant upon any subsequent application for continuance.

The right to a continuance shall be mandatory, except only where the attorney was employed within ten days of the date the suit is set for trial, the right to continuance shall be discretionary.

(Amended by Order June 10, 1980, eff. Jan. 1, 1981.)

RULE 255. CHANGE OF VENUE BY CONSENT.

Upon the written consent of the parties filed with the papers of the cause, the court, by an order entered on the minutes, may transfer the same for trial to the court of any other county having jurisdiction of the subject matter of such suit.

RULE 256. [REPEALED]

(Repealed by Order March 31, 1941, eff. Sept. 1, 1941.)

RULE 257. GRANTED ON MOTION.

A change of venue may be granted in civil causes upon motion of either party, supported by his own affidavit and the affidavit of at least three credible persons, residents of the county in which the suit is pending, for any following cause:

(a) That there exists in the county where the suit is pending so great a prejudice against him that he cannot obtain a fair and impartial trial.

(b) That there is a combination against him instigated by influential persons, by reason of which he cannot expect a fair and impartial trial.

(c) That an impartial trial cannot be had in the county where the action is pending.

(d) For other sufficient cause to be determined by the court.

(Amended by Order June 15, 1983, eff. Sept. 1, 1983.)

RULE 258. SHALL BE GRANTED.

Where such motion to transfer venue is duly made, it shall be granted, unless the credibility of those making such application, or their means of knowledge or the truth of the facts set out in the said application are attacked by the affidavit of a credible person; when thus attacked, the issue thus formed shall be tried by the judge; and the application either granted or refused. Reasonable discovery in support of, or in opposition to, the application shall be permitted, and such discovery as is relevant, including deposition testimony on file, may be attached to, or incorporated by reference in, the affidavit of a party, a witness, or an attorney who has knowledge of such discovery.

(Amended by Order June 15, 1983, eff. Sept. 1, 1983.)

RULE 259. TO WHAT COUNTY.

If the motion under Rule 257 is granted, the cause shall be removed:

(a) If from a district court, to any county of proper venue in the same or an adjoining district;

(b) If from a county court, to any adjoining county of proper venue;

(c) If (a) or (b) are not applicable, to any county of proper venue;

(d) If a county of proper venue (other than the county of suit) cannot be found, then if from

  (1) A district court, to any county in the same or an adjoining district or to any district where an impartial trial can be had;

  (2) A county court, to any adjoining county or to any district where an impartial trial can be had; but the parties may agree that venue shall be changed to some other county, and the order of the court shall conform to such agreement.

(Amended by Order June 15, 1983, eff. Sept. 1, 1983.)

RULE 260. [REPEALED]

(Repealed by Order April 24, 1990, eff. Sept. 1, 1990.)

RULE 261. TRANSCRIPT ON CHANGE.

When a change of venue has been granted, the clerk shall immediately make out a correct transcript of all the orders made in said cause, certifying thereto officially under the seal of the court, and send the same, with the original papers in the cause, to the clerk of the court to which the venue has been changed.

C.
THE TRIAL

RULE 262. TRIAL BY THE COURT.

The rules governing the trial of causes before a jury shall govern in trials by the court in so far as applicable.

RULE 263. AGREED CASE.

Parties may submit matters in controversy to the court upon an agreed statement of facts filed with the clerk, upon which judgment shall be rendered as in other cases; and such agreed statement signed and certified by the court to be correct and the judgment rendered thereon shall constitute the record of the cause.

RULE 264. VIDEOTAPE TRIAL.

By agreement of the parties, the trial court may allow that all testimony and such other evidence as may be appropriate be presented at trial by videotape. The expenses of such videotape recordings shall be taxed as costs. If any party withdraws agreement to a videotape trial, the videotape costs that have accrued will be taxed against the party withdrawing from the agreement.

(Added July 15, 1987, eff. Jan. 1, 1988.)

RULE 265. ORDER OF PROCEEDINGS ON TRIAL BY JURY.

The trial of cases before a jury shall proceed in the following order unless the court should, for good cause stated in the record, otherwise direct:

(a) The party upon whom rests the burden of proof on the whole case shall state to the jury briefly the nature of his claim or defense and what said party expects to prove and the relief sought. Immediately thereafter, the adverse party may make a similar statement, and intervenors and other parties will be accorded similar rights in the order determined by the court.

(b) The party upon whom rests the burden of proof on the whole case shall then introduce his evidence.

(c) The adverse party shall briefly state the nature of his claim or defense and what said party expects to prove and the relief sought unless he has already done so.

(d) He shall then introduce his evidence.

(e) The intervenor and other parties shall make their statement, unless they have already done so, and shall introduce their evidence.

(f) The parties shall then be confined to rebutting testimony on each side.

(g) But one counsel on each side shall examine and cross-examine the same witness, except on leave granted.

(Amended by Order March 31, 1941, eff. Sept. 1, 1941; July 20, 1966, eff. Jan. 1, 1967; July 11, 1977, eff. Jan. 1, 1978.)

RULE 266. OPEN AND CLOSE—ADMISSION.

Except as provided in Rule 269 the plaintiff shall have the right to open and conclude both in adducing his evidence and in the argument, unless the burden of proof on the whole case under the pleadings rests upon the defendant, or unless the defendant or all of the defendants, if there should be more than one, shall, after the issues of fact are settled and before the trial commences, admit that the plaintiff is entitled to recover as set forth in the petition, except so far as he may be defeated, in whole or in part, by the allegations of the answer constituting a good defense, which may be established on the trial; which admission shall be entered of record, whereupon the defendant, or the defendants, if more than one, shall have the right to open and conclude in adducing the evidence and in the argument of the cause. The admission shall not serve to admit any allegation which is inconsistent with such defense, which defense shall be one that defendant has the burden of establishing, as for example, and without excluding other defenses: accord and satisfaction, adverse possession, arbitration and award, contributory negligence, discharge in bankruptcy, duress, estoppel, failure of consideration, fraud, release, res judicata, statute of frauds, statute of limitations, waiver, and the like.

RULE 267. WITNESSES PLACED UNDER RULE.

(a) At the request of either party, in a civil case, the witnesses on both sides shall be sworn and removed out of the courtroom to some place where they cannot hear the testimony as delivered by any other witness in the cause. This is termed placing witnesses under the rule.

(b) This rule does not authorize exclusion of (1) a party who is a natural person or the spouse of such natural person, or (2) an officer or employee of a party that is not a natural person and who is designated as its representative by its attorney, or (3) a person whose presence is shown by a party to be essential to the presentation of the cause.

(c) If any party be absent, the court in its discretion may exempt from the rule a representative of such party.

(d) Witnesses, when placed under Rule 614 of the Texas Rules of Civil Evidence, shall be instructed by the court that they are not to converse with each other or with any other person about the case other than the attorneys in the case, except by permission of the court, and that they are not to read any report of or comment upon the testimony in the case while under the rule.

(e) Any witness or other person violating such instructions may be punished for contempt of court.

(Amended by Order July 15, 1987, eff. Jan. 1, 1988.)

RULE 268. MOTION FOR INSTRUCTED VERDICT.

A motion for directed verdict shall state the specific grounds therefor.

RULE 269. ARGUMENT.

(a) After the evidence is concluded and the charge is read, the parties may argue the case to the jury. The party having the burden of proof on the whole case, or on all matters which are submitted by the charge, shall be entitled to open and conclude the argument; where there are several parties having separate claims or defenses, the court shall prescribe the order of argument between them.

(b) In all arguments, and especially in arguments on the trial of the case, the counsel opening shall present his whole case as he relies on it, both of law and facts, and shall be heard in the concluding argument only in reply to the counsel on the other side.

(c) Counsel for an intervenor shall occupy the position in the argument assigned by the court according to the nature of the claim.

(d) Arguments on questions of law shall be addressed to the court, and counsel should state the substance of the authorities referred to without reading more from books than may be necessary to verify the statement. On a question on motions, exceptions to the evidence, and other incidental matters, the counsel will be allowed only such argument as may be necessary to present clearly the question raised and refer to authorities on it, unless further discussion is invited by the court.

(e) Arguments on the facts should be addressed to the jury, when one is impaneled in a case that is being tried, under the supervision of the court. Counsel shall be required to confine the argument strictly to the evidence and to the arguments of opposing counsel. Mere personal criticism by counsel upon each other shall be avoided, and when indulged in shall be promptly corrected as a contempt of court.

(f) Side-bar remarks, and remarks by counsel of one side, not addressed to the court, while the counsel on the other side is examining a witness or arguing any question to the court, or addressing the jury, will be rigidly repressed by the court.

(g) The court will not be required to wait for objections to be made when the rules as to arguments are violated; but should they not be noticed and corrected by the court, opposing counsel may ask leave of the court to rise and present his point of objection. But the court shall protect counsel from any unnecessary interruption made on frivolous and unimportant grounds.

(h) It shall be the duty of every counsel to address the court from his place at the bar, and in addressing the court to rise to his feet; and while engaged in the trial of a case he shall remain at his place in the bar.

(Amended by Order March 31, 1941, eff. Sept. 1, 1941; April 24, 1990, eff. Sept. 1, 1990.)

RULE 270. ADDITIONAL TESTIMONY.

When it clearly appears to be necessary to the due administration of justice, the court may permit additional evidence to be offered at any time; provided that in a jury case no evidence on a controversial matter shall be received after the verdict of the jury.

(Amended by Order Dec. 5, 1983, eff. April 1, 1984.)

D.
CHARGE TO THE JURY

RULE 271. CHARGE TO THE JURY.

Unless expressly waived by the parties, the trial court shall prepare and in open court deliver a written charge to the jury.

(Amended by Order May 25, 1973, eff. Sept. 1, 1973; July 15, 1987, eff. Jan. 1, 1988.)

RULE 272. REQUISITES.

The charge shall be in writing, signed by the court, and filed with the clerk, and shall be a part of the record of the cause. It shall be submitted to the respective parties or their attorneys for their inspection, and a reasonable time given them in which to examine and present objections thereto outside the presence of the jury, which objections shall in every instance be presented to the court in writing, or be dictated to the court reporter in the presence of the court and opposing counsel, before the charge is read to the jury. All objections not so presented shall be considered as waived. The court shall announce its rulings thereon before reading the charge to the jury and shall endorse the rulings on the objections if written or dictate same to the court reporter in the presence of counsel. Objections to the charge and the court's rulings thereon may be included as a part of any transcript or statement of facts on appeal and, when so included in either, shall constitute a sufficient bill of exception to the rulings of the court thereon. It shall be presumed, unless otherwise noted in the record, that the party making such objections presented the same at the proper time and excepted to the ruling thereon.

(Amended by Order Sept. 20, 1941, eff. Dec. 31, 1941; May 25, 1973, eff. Sept. 1, 1973; July 22, 1975, eff. Jan. 1, 1976; July 15, 1987, eff. Jan. 1, 1988.)

RULE 273. JURY SUBMISSIONS.

Either party may present to the court and request written questions, definitions, and instructions to be given to the jury; and the court may give them or a part thereof, or may refuse to give them, as may be proper. Such requests shall be prepared and presented to the court and submitted to opposing counsel for examination and objection within a reasonable time after the charge is given to the parties or their attorneys for examination. A request by either party for any questions, definitions, or instructions shall be made separate and apart from such party's objections to the court's charge.

(Amended by Order Oct. 12, 1949, eff. March 1, 1950; July 15, 1987, eff. Jan. 1, 1988.)

RULE 274. OBJECTIONS AND REQUESTS.

A party objecting to a charge must point out distinctly the objectionable matter and the grounds of the objection. Any complaint as to a question, definition, or instruction, on account of any defect, omission, or fault in pleading, is waived unless specifically included in the objections. When the complaining party's objection, or requested question, definition, or instruction is, in the opinion of the appellate court, obscured or concealed by voluminous unfounded objections, minute differentiations or numerous unnecessary requests, such objection or request shall be untenable. No objection to one part of the charge may be adopted and applied to any other part of the charge by reference only.

(Amended by Order Sept. 20, 1941, eff. Dec. 31, 1941; July 15, 1987, eff. Jan. 1, 1988.)

RULE 275. CHARGE READ BEFORE ARGUMENT.

Before the argument is begun, the trial court shall read the charge to the jury in the precise words in which it was written, including all questions, definitions, and instructions which the court may give.

(Amended by Order July 15, 1987, eff. Jan. 1, 1988.)

RULE 276. REFUSAL OR MODIFICATION.

When an instruction, question, or definition is requested and the provisions of the law have been complied with and the trial judge refuses the same, the judge shall endorse thereon "Refused," and sign the same officially. If the trial judge modifies the same the judge shall endorse thereon "Modified as follows: (stating in what particular the judge has modified the same) and given, and exception allowed" and sign the same officially. Such refused or modified instruction, question, or definition, when so endorsed shall constitute a bill of exceptions, and it shall be conclusively presumed that the party asking the same presented it at the proper time, excepted to its refusal or modification, and that all the requirements of law have been observed, and such procedure shall entitle the party requesting the same to have the action of the trial judge thereon reviewed without preparing a formal bill of exceptions.

(Amended by Order July 15, 1987, eff. Jan. 1, 1988.)

RULE 277. SUBMISSION TO THE JURY.

In all jury cases the court shall, whenever feasible, submit the cause upon broad-form questions. The court shall submit such instructions and definitions as shall be proper to enable the jury to render a verdict.

Inferential rebuttal questions shall not be submitted in the charge. The placing of the burden of proof may be accomplished by instructions rather than by inclusion in the question.

In any cause in which the jury is required to apportion the loss among the parties the court shall submit a question or questions inquiring what percentage, if any, of the negligence or causation, as the case may be, that caused the occurrence or injury in question is attributable to each of the persons found to have been culpable. The court shall also instruct the jury to answer the damage question or questions without any reduction because of the percentage of negligence or causation, if any, of the person injured. The court may predicate the damage question or questions upon affirmative findings of liability.

The court may submit a question disjunctively when it is apparent from the evidence that one or the other of the conditions or facts inquired about necessarily exists.

The court shall not in its charge comment directly on the weight of the evidence or advise the jury of the effect of their answers, but the court's charge shall not be objectionable on the ground that it incidentally constitutes a comment on the weight of the evidence or advises the jury of the effect of their answers when it is properly a part of an instruction or definition.

(Amended by Order March 31, 1941, eff. Sept. 1, 1941; May 25, 1973, eff. Sept. 1, 1973; Dec. 5, 1983, eff. April 1, 1984; July 15, 1987, eff. Jan. 1, 1988.)

RULE 278. SUBMISSION OF QUESTIONS, DEFINITIONS, AND INSTRUCTIONS.

The court shall submit the questions, instructions and definitions in the form provided by Rule 277, which are raised by the written pleadings and the evidence. Except in trespass to try title, statutory partition proceedings, and other special proceedings in which the pleadings are specially defined by statutes or procedural rules, a party shall not be entitled to any submission of any question raised only by a general denial and not raised by affirmative written pleading by that party. Nothing herein shall change the burden of proof from what it would have been under a general denial. A judgment shall not be reversed because of the failure to submit other and various phases or different shades of the same question. Failure to submit a question shall not be deemed a ground for reversal of the judgment, unless its submission, in substantially correct wording, has been requested in writing and tendered by the party complaining of the judgment; provided, however, that objection to such failure shall suffice in such respect if the question is one relied upon by the opposing party. Failure to submit a definition or instruction shall not be deemed a ground for reversal of the judgment unless a substantially correct definition or instruction has been requested in writing and tendered by the party complaining of the judgment.

(Added July 15, 1987, eff. Jan. 1, 1988.)

RULE 279. OMISSIONS FROM THE CHARGE.

Upon appeal all independent grounds of recovery or of defense not conclusively established under the evidence and no element of which is submitted or requested are waived. When a ground of recovery or defense consists of more than one element, if one or more of such elements necessary to sustain such ground of recovery or defense, and necessarily referable thereto, are submitted to and found by the jury, and one or more of such elements are omitted from the charge, without request or objection, and there is factually sufficient evidence to support a finding thereon, the trial court, at the request of either party, may after notice and hearing and at any time before the judgment is rendered, make and file written findings on such omitted element or elements in support of the judgment. If no such written findings are made, such omitted element or elements shall be deemed found by the court in such manner as to support the judgment. A claim that the evidence was legally or factually insufficient to warrant the submission of any question may be made for the first time after verdict, regardless of whether the submission of such question was requested by the complainant.

(Amended by Order March 31, 1941, eff. Sept. 1, 1941; July 15, 1987, eff. Jan. 1, 1988.)

E.
CASE TO THE JURY

RULE 280. PRESIDING JUROR OF JURY.

Each jury shall appoint one of their body presiding juror.

(Amended by Order Dec. 5, 1983, eff. April 1, 1984.)

RULE 281. PAPERS TAKEN TO JURY ROOM.

With the court's permission, the jury may take with them to the jury room any notes they took during the trial. In addition, the jury may, and on request shall, take with them in their retirement the charges and instructions, general or special, which were given and read to them, and any written evidence, except the depositions of witnesses, but shall not take with them any special charges which have been refused. Where only part of a paper has been read in evidence, the jury shall not take the same with them, unless the part so read to them is detached from that which was excluded.

(Amended by Order Dec. 5, 1983, eff. April 1, 1984; March 15, 2011, eff. April 1, 2011.)

RULE 282. JURY KEPT TOGETHER.

The jury may either decide a case in court or retire for deliberation. If they retire, they shall be kept together in some convenient place, under the charge of an officer, until they agree upon a verdict or are discharged by the court; but the court in its discretion may permit them to separate temporarily for the night and at their meals, and for other proper purposes.

RULE 283. DUTY OF OFFICER ATTENDING JURY.

The officer in charge of the jury shall not make nor permit any communication to be made to them, except to inquire if they have agreed upon a verdict, unless by order of the court; and he shall not before their verdict is rendered communicate to any person the state of their deliberations or the verdict agreed upon.

RULE 284. JUDGE TO CAUTION JURY.

Immediately after jurors are selected for a case, the court must instruct them to turn off their phones and other electronic devices and not to communicate with anyone through any electronic device while they are in the courtroom or while they are deliberating. The court must also instruct them that, while they are serving as jurors, they must not post any information about the case on the Internet or search for any information outside of the courtroom, including on the Internet, to try to learn more about the case.

If jurors are permitted to separate before they are released from jury duty, either during the trial or after the case is submitted to them, the court must instruct them that it is their duty not to communicate with, or permit themselves to be addressed by, any other person about any subject relating to the case.

(Amended by Order March 15, 2011, eff. April 1, 2011.)

RULE 285. JURY MAY COMMUNICATE WITH COURT.

The jury may communicate with the court by making their wish known to the officer in charge, who shall inform the court, and they may then in open court, and through their presiding juror, communicate with the court, either verbally or in writing. If the communication is to request further instructions, Rule 286 shall be followed.

(Amended by Order Dec. 5, 1983, eff. April 1, 1984.)

RULE 286. JURY MAY RECEIVE FURTHER INSTRUCTIONS.

After having retired, the jury may receive further instructions from the court touching any matter of law, either at their request or upon the court's own motion. For this purpose they shall appear before the judge in open court in a body, and if the instruction is being given at their request, they shall through their presiding juror state to the court, in writing, the particular question of law upon which they desire further instruction. The court shall give such instruction in writing, but no instruction shall be given except in conformity with the rules relating to the charge. Additional argument may be allowed in the discretion of the court.

(Amended by Order Dec. 5, 1983, eff. April 1, 1984; July 15, 1987, eff. Jan. 1, 1988.)

RULE 287. DISAGREEMENT AS TO EVIDENCE.

If the jury disagree as to the statement of any witness, they may, upon applying to the court, have read to them from the court reporter's notes that part of such witness' testimony on the point in dispute; but, if there be no such reporter, or if his notes cannot be read to the jury, the court may cause such witness to be again brought upon the stand and the judge shall direct him to repeat his testimony as to the point in dispute, and no other, as nearly as he can in the language used on the trial; and on their notifying the court that they disagree as to any portion of a deposition or other paper not permitted to be carried with them in their retirement, the court may, in like manner, permit such portion of said deposition or paper to be again read to the jury.

RULE 288. COURT OPEN FOR JURY.

The court, during the deliberations of the jury, may proceed with other business or recess from time to time, but shall be deemed open for all purposes connected with the case before the jury.

RULE 289. DISCHARGE OF JURY.

The jury to whom a case has been submitted may be discharged by the court when they cannot agree and the parties consent to their discharge, or when they have been kept together for such time as to render it altogether improbable that they can agree, or when any calamity or accident may, in the opinion of the court, require it, or when by sickness or other cause their number is reduced below the number constituting the jury in such court.

The cause shall again be placed on the jury docket and shall again be set for trial as the court directs.

(Amended by Order Dec. 5, 1983, eff. April 1, 1984.)

F.
VERDICT

RULE 290. DEFINITION AND SUBSTANCE.

A verdict is a written declaration by a jury of its decision, comprehending the whole or all the issues submitted to the jury, and shall be either a general or special verdict, as directed, which shall be signed by the presiding juror of the jury.

A general verdict is one whereby the jury pronounces generally in favor of one or more parties to the suit upon all or any of the issues submitted to it. A special verdict is one wherein the jury finds the facts only on issues made up and submitted to them under the direction of the court.

A special verdict shall, as between the parties, be conclusive as to the facts found.

(Amended by Order Dec. 5, 1983, eff. April 1, 1984.)

RULE 291. FORM OF VERDICT.

No special form of verdict is required, and the judgment shall not be arrested or reversed for mere want of form therein if there has been substantial compliance with the requirements of the law in rendering a verdict.

(Amended by Order Oct. 3, 1972, eff. Feb. 1, 1973.)

RULE 292. VERDICT BY PORTION OF ORIGINAL JURY.

(a) Except as provided in subsection (b), a verdict may be rendered in any cause by the concurrence, as to each and all answers made, of the same ten or more members of an original jury of twelve or of the same five or more members of an original jury of six. However, where as many as three jurors die or be disabled from sitting and there are only nine of the jurors remaining of an original jury of twelve, those remaining may render and return a verdict. If less than the original twelve or six jurors render a verdict, the verdict must be signed by each juror concurring therein.

(b) A verdict may be rendered awarding exemplary damages only if the jury was unanimous in finding liability for and the amount of exemplary damages.

(Amended by Order Oct. 3, 1972, eff. Feb. 1, 1973; Jan. 27, 2005, eff. Feb. 1, 2005 in all cases filed on or after Sept. 1, 2003.)

Comment - 2005

The rule is divided into two subsections. Subsection (a) is clarified. Subsection (b) is added to make the rule consistent with Act of June 2, 2003, 78th Leg., R.S., c. 204, § 13.04, 2003 Tex. Gen. Laws 847, 888, codified as TEX. CIV. PRAC. & REM. CODE § 41.003.

RULE 293. WHEN THE JURY AGREE.

When the jury agree upon a verdict, they shall be brought into court by the proper officer, and they shall deliver their verdict to the clerk; and if they state that they have agreed, the verdict shall be read aloud by the clerk. If the verdict is in proper form, no juror objects to its accuracy, no juror represented as agreeing thereto dissents therefrom, and neither party requests a poll of the jury, the verdict shall be entered upon the minutes of the court.

(Amended by Order Oct. 3, 1972, eff. Feb. 1, 1973.)

RULE 294. POLLING THE JURY.

Any party shall have the right to have the jury polled. A jury is polled by reading once to the jury collectively the general verdict, or the questions and answers thereto consecutively, and then calling the name of each juror separately and asking the juror if it is the juror's verdict. If any juror answers in the negative when the verdict is returned signed only by the presiding juror as a unanimous verdict, or if any juror shown by the juror's signature to agree to the verdict should answer in the negative, the jury shall be retired for further deliberation.

(Amended by Order Oct. 3, 1972, eff. Feb. 1, 1973; Dec. 5, 1983, eff. April 1, 1984; April 24, 1990, eff. Sept. 1, 1990.)

RULE 295. CORRECTION OF VERDICT.

If the purported verdict is defective, the court may direct it to be reformed. If it is incomplete, or not responsive to the questions contained in the court's charge, or the answers to the questions are in conflict, the court shall in writing instruct the jury in open court of the nature of the incompleteness, unresponsiveness, or conflict, provide the jury such additional instructions as may be proper, and retire the jury for further deliberations.

(Amended by Order July 15, 1987, eff. Jan. 1, 1988.)

G.
FINDINGS BY COURT

RULE 296. REQUESTS FOR FINDINGS OF FACTS AND CONCLUSIONS OF LAW.

In any case tried in the district or county court without a jury, any party may request the court to state in writing its findings of fact and conclusions of law. Such request shall be entitled "Request for Findings of Fact and Conclusions of Law" and shall be filed within twenty days after judgment is signed with the clerk of the court, who shall immediately call such request to the attention of the judge who tried the case. The party making the request shall serve it on all other parties in accordance with Rule 21a.

(Amended by Order March 19, 1957, eff. Sept. 1, 1957; June 10, 1980, eff. Jan. 1, 1981; Dec. 5, 1983, eff. April 1, 1984; April 24, 1990, eff. Sept. 1, 1990.)

RULE 297. TIME TO FILE FINDINGS OF FACT AND CONCLUSIONS OF LAW.

The court shall file its findings of fact and conclusions of law within twenty days after a timely request is filed. The court shall cause a copy of its findings and conclusions to be mailed to each party in the suit.

If the court fails to file timely findings of fact and conclusions of law, the party making the request shall, within thirty days after filing the original request, file with the clerk and serve on all other parties in accordance with Rule 21a a "Notice of Past Due Findings of Fact and Conclusions of Law" which shall be immediately called to the attention of the court by the clerk. Such notice shall state the date the original request was filed and the date the findings and conclusions were due. Upon filing this notice, the time for the court to file findings of fact and conclusions of law is extended to forty days from the date the original request was filed.

(Amended by Order June 10, 1980, eff. Jan. 1, 1981; Dec. 5, 1983, eff. April 1, 1984; April 24, 1990, eff. Sept. 1, 1990.)

RULE 298. ADDITIONAL OR AMENDED FINDINGS OF FACT AND CONCLUSIONS OF LAW.

After the court files original findings of fact and conclusions of law, any party may file with the clerk of the court a request for specified additional or amended findings or conclusions. The request for these findings shall be made within ten days after the filing of the original findings and conclusions by the court. Each request made pursuant to this rule shall be served on each party to the suit in accordance with Rule 21a.

The court shall file any additional or amended findings and conclusions that are appropriate within ten days after such request is filed, and cause a copy to be mailed to each party to the suit. No findings or conclusions shall be deemed or presumed by any failure of the court to make any additional findings or conclusions.

(Amended by Order March 19, 1957, eff. Sept. 1. 1957; April 24, 1990, eff. Sept. 1, 1990.)

RULE 299. OMITTED FINDINGS.

When findings of fact are filed by the trial court they shall form the basis of the judgment upon all grounds of recovery and of defense embraced therein. The judgment may not be supported upon appeal by a presumed finding upon any ground of recovery or defense, no element of which has been included in the findings of fact; but when one or more elements thereof have been found by the trial court, omitted unrequested elements, when supported by evidence, will be supplied by presumption in support of the judgment. Refusal of the court to make a finding requested shall be reviewable on appeal.

(Amended by Order Sept. 20, 1941, eff. Dec. 31, 1941; April 24, 1990, eff. Sept. 1, 1990.)

RULE 299a. FINDINGS OF FACT TO BE SEPARATELY FILED AND NOT RECITED IN A JUDGMENT.

Findings of fact shall not be recited in a judgment. If there is a conflict between findings of fact recited in a judgment in violation of this rule and findings of fact made pursuant to Rules 297 and 298, the latter findings will control for appellate purposes. Findings of fact shall be filed with the clerk of the court as a document or documents separate and apart from the judgment.

(Added by Order April 24, 1990, eff. Sept. 1, 1990.)

H.
JUDGMENTS

RULE 300. COURT TO RENDER JUDGMENT.

Where a special verdict is rendered, or the conclusions of fact found by the judge are separately stated the court shall render judgment thereon unless set aside or a new trial is granted, or judgment is rendered notwithstanding verdict or jury finding under these rules.

RULE 301. JUDGMENTS.

The judgment of the court shall conform to the pleadings, the nature of the case proved and the verdict, if any, and shall be so framed as to give the party all the relief to which he may be entitled either in law or equity. Provided, that upon motion and reasonable notice the court may render judgment non obstante veredicto if a directed verdict would have been proper, and provided further that the court may upon like motion and notice, disregard any jury finding on a question that has no support in the evidence. Only one final judgment shall be rendered in any cause except where it is otherwise specially provided by law. Judgment may, in a proper case, be given for or against one or more of several plaintiffs, and for or against one or more of several defendants or intervenors.

(Amended by Order July 15, 1987, eff. Jan. 1, 1988; April 24, 1990, eff. Sept. 1, 1990; amendment withdrawn Sept. 4, 1990, eff. retroactively to Sept. 1, 1990.)

RULE 302. ON COUNTERCLAIM.

If the defendant establishes a demand against the plaintiff upon a counterclaim exceeding that established against him by the plaintiff, the court shall render judgment for defendant for such excess.

(Amended by Order Dec. 5, 1983, eff. April 1, 1984.)

RULE 303. ON COUNTERCLAIM FOR COSTS.

When a counterclaim is pleaded, the party in whose favor final judgment is rendered shall also recover the costs, unless it be made to appear on the trial that the counterclaim of the defendant was acquired after the commencement of the suit, in which case, if the plaintiff establishes a claim existing at the commencement of the suit, he shall recover his costs.

(Amended by Order Dec. 5, 1983, eff. April 1, 1984.)

RULE 304. JUDGMENT UPON RECORD.

Judgments rendered upon questions raised upon citations, pleadings, and all other proceedings, constituting the record proper as known at common law, must be entered at the date of each term when pronounced.

RULE 305. PROPOSED JUDGMENT.

Any party may prepare and submit a proposed judgment to the court for signature.

Each party who submits a proposed judgment for signature shall serve the proposed judgment on all other parties to the suit who have appeared and remain in the case, in accordance with Rule 21a.

Failure to comply with this rule shall not affect the time for perfecting an appeal.

(Amended by Order April 24, 1990, eff. Sept. 1, 1990.)

RULE 306. RECITATION OF JUDGMENT.

The entry of the judgment shall contain the full names of the parties, as stated in the pleadings, for and against whom the judgment is rendered. In a suit for termination of the parent-child relationship or a suit affecting the parent-child relationship filed by a governmental entity for managing conservatorship. the judgment must state the specific grounds for termination or for appointment of the managing conservator.

(Amended by Order July 21, 1970, eff. Jan. 1, 1971; Order Dec. 12, 2011, eff. March 1, 2012; Order Feb. 13, 2012, eff. March 1, 2012.)

RULE 306a. PERIODS TO RUN FROM SIGNING OF JUDGMENT.

1. **Beginning of Periods**. The date of judgment or order is signed as shown of record shall determine the beginning of the periods prescribed by these rules for the court's plenary power to grant a new trial or to vacate, modify, correct or reform a judgment or order and for filing in the trial court the various documents that these rules authorize a party to file within such periods including, but not limited to, motions for new trial, motions to modify judgment, motions to reinstate a case dismissed for want of prosecution, motions to vacate judgment and requests for findings of fact and conclusions of law; but this rule shall not determine what constitutes rendition of a judgment or order for any other purpose.
2. **Date to Be Shown**. Judges, attorneys and clerks are directed to use their best efforts to cause all judgments, decisions and orders of any kind to be reduced to writing and signed by the trial judge with the date of signing stated therein. If the date of signing is not recited in the judgment or order, it may be shown in the record by a certificate of the judge or otherwise; provided, however, that the absence of a showing of the date in the record shall not invalidate any judgment or order.
3. **Notice of Judgment**. When the final judgment or other appealable order is signed, the clerk of the court shall immediately give notice to the parties or their attorneys of record by first-class mail advising that the judgment or order was signed. Failure to comply with the provisions of this rule shall not affect the periods mentioned in paragraph (1) of this rule, except as provided in paragraph (4).
4. **No Notice of Judgment**. If within twenty days after the judgment or other appealable order is signed, a party adversely affected by it or his attorney has neither received the notice required by paragraph (3) of this rule nor acquired actual knowledge of the order, then with respect to that party all the periods mentioned in paragraph (1) shall begin on the date that such party or his attorney received such notice or acquired actual knowledge of the signing, whichever occurred first, but in no event shall such periods begin more than ninety days after the original judgment or other appealable order was signed.
5. **Motion, Notice and Hearing**. In order to establish the application of paragraph (4) of this rule, the party adversely affected is required to prove in the trial court, on sworn motion and notice, the date on which the party or his attorney first either received a notice of the judgment or acquired actual knowledge of the signing and that this date was more than twenty days after the judgment was signed.
6. **Nunc Pro Tunc Order**. When a collected judgment has been signed after expiration of the court's plenary power pursuant to Rule 316, the periods mentioned in paragraph (1) of this rule shall run from the date of signing the corrected judgment with respect to any complaint that would not be applicable to the original document.
7. **When Process Served by Publication**. With respect to a motion for new trial filed more than thirty days after the judgment was signed pursuant to Rule 329 when process has been served by publication, the periods provided by paragraph (1) shall be computed as if the judgment were signed on the date of filing the motion.

(Added by Order June 16, 1943, eff. Dec. 31, 1943. Amended by Order Oct. 10, 1945, eff. Feb. 1, 1946; June 10, 1980, eff. Jan. 1, 1981; Dec. 5, 1983, eff. April 1, 1984; April 10, 1986, eff. Sept. 1, 1986; July 15, 1987, eff. Jan. 1, 1988.)

RULE 306b. [REPEALED]

(Repealed by Order Dec. 5, 1983, eff. April 1, 1984.)

RULE 306c. PREMATURELY FILED DOCUMENTS.

No motion for new trial or request for findings of fact and conclusions of law shall be held ineffective because prematurely filed; but every such motion shall be deemed to have been filed on the date of but subsequent to the time of signing of the judgment the motion assails, and every such request for findings of fact and conclusions of law shall be deemed to have been filed on the date of but subsequent to the time of signing of the judgment.

(Added by Order Oct. 10, 1945, eff. Feb. 1, 1946. Amended by Order April 12, 1962, eff. Sept. 1, 1962; July 22, 1975, eff. Jan. 1, 1976; Dec. 5, 1983, eff. April 1, 1984; April 10, 1986, eff. Sept. 1, 1986; April 24, 1990, eff. Sept. 1, 1990.)

RULE 306d. [REPEALED]

(Repealed by Order Dec. 5, 1983, eff. April 1, 1984.)

RULE 307. EXCEPTIONS, ETC., TRANSCRIPT.

In non-jury cases, where findings of fact and conclusions of law are requested and filed, and in jury cases, where a special verdict is returned, any party claiming that the findings of the court or the jury, as the case may be, do not support the judgment, may have noted in the record an exception to said judgment and thereupon take an appeal or writ of error, where such writ is allowed, without a statement of facts or further exceptions in the transcript, but the transcript in such cases shall contain the conclusions of law and fact or the special verdict and the judgment rendered thereon.

RULE 308. COURT SHALL ENFORCE ITS DECREES.

The court shall cause its judgments and decrees to be carried into execution; and where the judgment is for personal property, and it is shown by the pleadings and evidence and the verdict, if any, that such property has an especial value to the plaintiff, the court may award a special writ for the seizure and delivery of such property to the plaintiff; and in such case may enforce its judgment by attachment, fine and imprisonment.

RULE 308a. IN SUITS AFFECTING THE PARENT-CHILD RELATIONSHIP.

When the court has ordered child support or possession of or access to a child and it is claimed that the order has been violated, the person claiming that a violation has occurred shall make this known to the court. The court may appoint a member of the bar to investigate the claim to determine whether there is reason to believe that the court order has been violated. If the attorney in good faith believes that the order has been violated, the attorney shall take the necessary action as provided under Chapter 14, Family Code. On a finding of a violation, the court may enforce its order as provided in Chapter 14, Family Code.

Except by order of the court, no fee shall be charged by or paid to the attorney representing the claimant. If the court determines that an attorney's fee should be paid, the fee shall be adjudged against the party who violated the court's order. The fee may be assessed as costs of court, or awarded by judgment, or both.

(Added by Order Oct. 12, 1949, eff. March 1, 1950. Amended by Order Oct. 10, 1951, eff. March 1, 1952; July 15, 1987, eff. Jan. 1, 1988; April 24, 1990, eff. Sept. 1, 1990.)

Rule 308B. determining the enforceability of a judgement or arbitration award based on foreign law in certain Suits under the family code.

(a) *Definitions*. In this rule:

  (1) *Comity* means the recognition by a court of one jurisdiction of the laws and judicial decisions of another jurisdiction.

  (2) *Foreign law* means a law, rule, or code of a jurisdiction outside of the states and territories of the United States.

(b) *Applicability of This Rule.*

  (1) Except as provided in (2) and (3), this rule applies to the recognition or enforcement of a judgment or arbitration award based on foreign law in a suit involving a marriage relationship or a parent-child relationship under the Family Code.

  (2) This rule does not apply to an action brought under the International Child Abduction Remedies Act (22 U.S.C. § 9001 *et seq.*) concerning rights under the Hague Convention on the Civil Aspects of International Child Abduction.

  (3) In the event of a conflict between this rule and any federal or state law, the federal or state law will prevail.

(c) *Applicability of Texas Rule of Evidence 203.*

  (1) Paragraphs (c) and (d) of Rule 203, Texas Rules of Evidence, apply to an action under this rule.

  (2) Paragraphs (a) and (b) of Rule 203, Texas Rules of Evidence, do not apply to an action under this rule.

(d) *Notice.*

(1) *Party Seeking Enforcement of a Judgment or Arbitration Award Based on Foreign Law.* Within 60 days of filing an original pleading, the party seeking enforcement must give written notice to the court and all parties that describes the court's authority to enforce or decide to enforce the judgment or award.

(2) *Party Opposing Enforcement of a Judgment or Arbitration Award Based on Foreign Law.* Within 30 days of the date that a notice under (1) is served, a party opposing enforcement must give written notice to the court and all parties that explains the basis for the party's opposition and states whether the party asserts that the judgment or award violates constitutional rights or public policy.

(e) *Pretrial Conference.* Within 75 days of the date that a notice under (d)(1) is served, the court must conduct a pretrial conference to set deadlines and make other appropriate orders regarding:

(1) the submission of materials for the court to consider in determining foreign law;

(2) the translation of foreign-language documents; and

(3) the designation of expert witnesses.

(f) *Determination Hearing and Order.*

(1) At least 30 days before trial, the court must conduct a hearing on the record to determine whether to enforce the judgment or award. The parties must have timely notice of the hearing.

(2) Within 15 days of the hearing, the Court must issue a written order on the determination that includes findings of fact and conclusions of law. This deadline must not be altered absent extraordinary circumstances.

(3) The court may issue any order necessary to preserve the principles of comity or the freedom to contract for arbitration while protecting against violations of constitutional rights and public policy.

(4) The court must comply with all requirements of this paragraph and make an independent determination whether to enforce the judgment or award even if no party opposes enforcement of the judgment or award.

(g) *Temporary Orders.* Notwithstanding any other provision of this rule, the court may set filing deadlines and conduct the determination hearing to accommodate the circumstances of the case in connection with issuing temporary orders.

(Adopted by Tex. Sup. Ct. Misc. Docket No. 16-9018 Dec. 28, 2017, eff. Jan. 1, 2018.)

RULE 309. IN FORECLOSURE PROCEEDINGS.

Judgments for the foreclosure of mortgages and other liens shall be that the plaintiff recover his debt, damages and costs, with a foreclosure of the plaintiff's lien on the property subject thereto, and, except in judgments against executors, administrators and guardians, that an order of sale shall issue to any sheriff or any constable within the State of Texas, directing him to seize and sell the same as under execution, in satisfaction of the judgment; and, if the property cannot be found, or if the proceeds of such sale be insufficient to satisfy the judgment, then to take the money or any balance thereof remaining unpaid, out of any other property of the defendant, as in case of ordinary executions.

(Amended by Order July 20, 1966, eff. Jan. 1, 1967.)

RULE 310. WRIT OF POSSESSION.

When an order foreclosing a lien upon real estate is made in a suit having for its object the foreclosure of such lien, such order shall have all the force and effect of a writ of possession as between the parties to the foreclosure suit and any person claiming under the defendant to such suit by any right acquired pending such suit; and the court shall so direct in the judgment providing for the issuance of such order. The sheriff or other officer executing such order of sale shall proceed by virtue of such order of sale to place the purchaser of the property sold thereunder in possession thereof within thirty days after the day of sale.

RULE 311. ON APPEAL FROM PROBATE COURT.

Judgment on appeal or certiorari from any county court sitting in probate shall be certified to such county court for observance.

RULE 312. ON APPEAL FROM JUSTICE COURT.

Judgment on appeal or certiorari from a justice court shall be enforced by the county or district court rendering the judgment.

RULE 313. AGAINST EXECUTORS, ETC.

A judgment for the recovery of money against an executor, administrator or guardian, as such, shall state that it is to be paid in the due course of administration. No execution shall issue thereon, but it shall be certified to the county court, sitting in matters of probate, to be there enforced in accordance with law, but judgment against an executor appointed and acting under a will dispensing with the action of the county court in reference to such estate shall be enforced against the property of the testator in the hands of such executor, by execution, as in other cases.

RULE 314. CONFESSION OF JUDGMENT.

Any person against whom a cause of action exists may, without process, appear in person or by attorney, and confess judgment therefor in open court as follows:

(a) A petition shall be filed and the justness of the debt or cause of action be sworn to by the person in whose favor the judgment is confessed.

(b) If the judgment is confessed by attorney, the power of attorney shall be filed and its contents be recited in the judgment.

(c) Every such judgment duly made shall operate as a release of all errors in the record thereof, but such judgment may be impeached for fraud or other equitable cause.

I.
REMITTITUR AND CORRECTION

RULE 315. REMITTITUR.

Any party in whose favor a judgment has been rendered may remit any part thereof in open court, or by executing and filing with the clerk a written remittitur signed by the party or the party's attorney of record, and duly acknowledged by the party or the party's attorney. Such remittitur shall be a part of the record of the cause. Execution shall issue for the balance only of such judgment.

(Amended by Order July 15, 1987, eff. Jan. 1, 1988.)

RULE 316. CORRECTION OF CLERICAL MISTAKES IN JUDGMENT RECORD.

Clerical mistakes in the record of any judgment may be corrected by the judge in open court according to the truth or justice of the case after notice of the motion therefor has been given to the parties interested in such judgment, as provided in Rule 21a, and thereafter the execution shall conform to the judgment as amended.

(Amended by Order June 16, 1943, eff. Dec. 31, 1943; July 15, 1987, eff. Jan. 1, 1988.)

RULES 317 TO 319. [REPEALED]

(Repealed by Order July 15, 1987, eff. Jan. 1, 1988.)

J.
NEW TRIALS

RULE 320. MOTION AND ACTION OF COURT THEREON.

New trials may be granted and judgment set aside for good cause, on motion or on the court's own motion on such terms as the court shall direct. New trials may be granted when the damages are manifestly too small or too large. When it appears to the court that a new trial should be granted on a point or points that affect only a part of the matters in controversy and that such part is clearly separable without unfairness to the parties, the court may grant a new trial as to that part only, provided that a separate trial on unliquidated damages alone shall not be ordered if liability issues are contested. Each motion for new trial shall be in writing and signed by the party of his attorney.

(Amended by Order July 20, 1964, eff. Jan. 1, 1955; July 22, 1975, eff. Jan. 1, 1976; July 11, 1977, eff. Jan. 1, 1978, June 10, 1980, eff. Jan. 1, 1981; Dec. 5, 1983, eff. April 1, 1984; July 15, 1987, eff. Jan. 1, 1988.)

RULE 321. FORM.

Each point relied upon in a motion for new trial or in arrest of judgment shall briefly refer to that part of the ruling of the court, charge given to the jury, or charge refused, admission or rejection of evidence, or other proceedings which are designated to be complained of, in such a way that the objection can be clearly identified and understood by the court.

(Amended by Order June 10, 1980, eff. Jan. 1, 1981.)

RULE 322. GENERALITY TO BE AVOIDED.

Grounds of objections couched in general terms—as that the court erred in its charge, in sustaining or overruling exceptions to the pleadings, and in excluding or admitting evidence, the verdict of the jury is contrary to law, and the like—shall not be considered by the court.

RULE 323. [REPEALED]

(Repealed by Order July 11, 1977, eff. Jan. 1, 1978.)

RULE 324. PREREQUISITES OF APPEAL.

(a) **Motion for New Trial Not Required**. A point in a motion for new trial is not a prerequisite to a complaint on appeal in either a jury or a nonjury case, except as provided in subdivision (b).

(b) **Motion for New Trial Required**. A point in a motion for new trial is a prerequisite to the following complaints on appeal:

(1) A complaint on which evidence must be heard such as one of jury misconduct or newly discovered evidence or failure to set aside a judgment by default;

(2) A complaint of factual insufficiency of the evidence to support a jury finding;

(3) A complaint that a jury finding is against the overwhelming weight of the evidence;

(4) A complaint of inadequacy or excessiveness of the damages found by the jury; or

(5) Incurable jury argument if not otherwise ruled on by the trial court.

(c) **Judgment Notwithstanding Findings; Cross-Points**. When judgment is rendered non obstante veredicto or notwithstanding the findings of a jury on one or more questions, the appellee may bring forward by cross-point contained in his brief filed in the Court of Appeals any ground which would have vitiated the verdict or would have prevented an affirmance of the judgment had one been rendered by the trial court in harmony with the verdict, including although not limited to the ground that one or more of the jury's findings have insufficient support in the evidence or are against the overwhelming preponderance of the evidence as a matter of fact, and the ground that the verdict and judgment based thereon should be set aside because of improper argument of counsel. The failure to bring forward by cross-points such grounds as would vitiate the verdict shall be deemed a waiver thereof; provided, however, that if a cross-point is upon a ground which requires the taking of evidence in addition to that adduced upon the trial of the cause, it is not necessary that the evidentiary hearing be held until after the appellate court determines that the cause be remanded to consider such a cross-point.

(Amended by Order March 31, 1941, eff. Sept. 1, 1941; Sept. 20, 1941, eff. Dec. 31, 1941; July 20, 1954, eff. Jan. 1, 1955; March 19, 1957, eff. Sept. 1, 1957; April 12, 1962, eff. Sept. 1, 1962; July 11, 1977, eff. Jan. 1, 1978; June 10, 1980, eff. Jan. 1, 1981; Dec. 5, 1983, eff. April 1, 1984; July 15, 1987, eff. Jan. 1, 1988.)

RULE 325. [REPEALED]

(Repealed by Order July 11, 1977, eff. Jan. 1, 1978.)

RULE 326. NOT MORE THAN TWO.

Not more than two new trials shall be granted either party in the same cause because of insufficiency or weight of the evidence.

RULE 327. FOR JURY MISCONDUCT.

a. When the ground of a motion for new trial, supported by affidavit, is misconduct of the jury or of the officer in charge of them, or because of any communication made to the jury, or that a juror gave an erroneous or incorrect answer on voir dire examination, the court shall hear evidence thereof from the jury or others in open court, and may grant a new trial if such misconduct proved, or the communication made, or the erroneous or incorrect answer on voir dire examination, be material, and if it reasonably appears from the evidence both on the hearing of the motion and the trial of the case and from the record as a whole that injury probably resulted to the complaining party.

b. A juror may not testify as to any matter or statement occurring during the course of the jury's deliberations or to the effect of anything upon his or any other juror's mind or emotions as influencing him to assent to or dissent from the verdict concerning his mental processes in connection therewith, except that a juror may testify whether any outside influence was improperly brought to bear upon any juror. Nor may his affidavit or evidence of any statement by him concerning a matter about which he would be precluded from testifying be received for these purposes.

(Amended by Order July 20, 1954, eff. Jan. 1, 1955; Dec. 5, 1983, eff. April 1, 1984.)

RULE 328. [REPEALED]

(Repealed by Order July 15, 1987, eff. Jan. 1, 1988.)

RULE 329. MOTION FOR NEW TRIAL ON JUDGMENT FOLLOWING CITATION BY PUBLICATION

In cases in which judgment has been rendered on service of process by publication, when the defendant has not appeared in person or by attorney of his own selection:

(a) The court may grant a new trial upon petition of the defendant showing good cause, supported by affidavit, filed within two years after such judgment was signed. The parties adversely interested in such judgment shall be cited as in other cases.

(b) Execution of such judgment shall not be suspended unless the party applying therefor shall give a good and sufficient bond payable to the plaintiff in the judgment, in an amount fixed in accordance with Appellate Rule 47 relating to supersedeas bonds, to be approved by the clerk, and conditioned that the party will prosecute his petition for new trial to effect and will perform such judgment as may be rendered by the court should its decision be against him.

(c) If property has been sold under the judgment and execution before the process was suspended, the defendant shall not recover the property so sold, but shall have judgment against the plaintiff in the judgment for the proceeds of such sale.

(d) If the motion is filed more than thirty days after the judgment was signed, the time period shall be computed pursuant to Rule 306a(7).

(Amended by Order June 10, 1980, eff. Jan. 1, 1981; Dec. 5, 1983, eff. April 1, 1984; July 15, 1987, eff. Jan. 1, 1988.)

RULE 329a. COUNTY COURT CASES.

If a case or other matter is on trial or in the process of hearing when the term of the county court expires, such trial, hearing or other matter may be proceeded with at the next or any subsequent term of court and no motion or plea shall be considered as waived or overruled, because not acted upon at the term of court at which it was filed, but may be acted upon at any time the judge may fix or at which it may have been postponed or continued by agreement of the parties with leave of the court. This subdivision is not applicable to original or amended motions for new trial which are governed by Rule 329b.

(Added by Order July 20, 1954 eff. Jan. 1, 1955. Amended by Order March 19, 1957, eff. Sept. 1, 1957; July 26, 1960, eff. Jan. 1, 1961.)

RULE 329b. TIME FOR FILING MOTIONS.

The following rules shall be applicable to motions for new trial and motions to modify, correct, or reform judgments (other than motions to correct the record under Rule 316) in all district and county courts:

(a) A motion for new trial, if filed, shall be filed prior to or within thirty days after the judgment or other order complained of is signed.

(b) One or more amended motions for new trial may be filed without leave of court before any preceding motion for new trial filed by the movant is overruled and within thirty days after the judgment or other order complained of is signed.

(c) In the event an original or amended motion for new trial or a motion to modify, correct or reform a judgment is not determined by written order signed within seventy-five days after the judgment was signed, it shall be considered overruled by operation of law on expiration of that period.

(d) The trial court, regardless of whether an appeal has been perfected, has plenary power to grant a new trial or to vacate, modify, correct, or reform the judgment within thirty days after the judgment is signed.

(e) If a motion for new trial is timely filed by any party, the trial court, regardless of whether an appeal has been perfected, has plenary power to grant a new trial or to vacate, modify, correct, or reform the judgment until thirty days after all such timely-filed motions are overruled, either by a written and signed order or by operation of law, whichever occurs first.

(f) On expiration of the time within which the trial court has plenary power, a judgment cannot be set aside by the trial court except by bill of review for sufficient cause, filed within the time allowed by law; provided that the court may at any time correct a clerical error in the record of a judgment and render judgment nunc pro tunc under Rule 316, and may also sign an order declaring a previous judgment or order to be void because signed after the court's plenary power had expired.

(g) A motion to modify, correct, or reform a judgment (as distinguished from motion to correct the record of a judgment under Rule 316), if filed, shall be filed and determined within the time prescribed by this rule for a motion for new trial and shall extend the trial court's plenary power and the time for perfecting an appeal in the same manner as a motion for new trial. Each such motion shall be in writing and signed by the party or his attorney and shall specify the respects in which the judgment should be modified, corrected, or reformed. The overruling of such a motion shall not preclude the filing of a motion for new trial, nor shall the overruling of a motion for new trial preclude the filing of a motion to modify, correct, or reform.

(h) If a judgment is modified, corrected or reformed in any respect, the time for appeal shall run from the time the modified, corrected, or reformed judgment is signed, but if a correction is made pursuant to Rule 316 after expiration of the period of plenary power provided by this rule, no complaint shall be heard on appeal that could have been presented in an appeal from the original judgment.

(Added by Order July 20, 1954, eff. Jan. 1, 1955. Amended by Order July 26, 1960), eff. Jan. 1, 1961; July 20, 1966, eff. Jan. 1, 1967; Oct. 3, 1972, eff. Feb. 1, 1973; July 11, 1977, eff. Jan. 1, 1978; June 10, 1980, eff. Jan. 1, 1981; Dec. 5, 1983, eff. April 1, 1984; July 15, 1987, eff. Jan. 1, 1988.)

K.
CERTAIN DISTRICT COURTS

RULE 330. RULES OF PRACTICE AND PROCEDURE IN CERTAIN DISTRICT COURTS.

The following rules of practice and procedure shall govern and be followed in all civil actions in district courts in counties where the only district court of said county vested with civil jurisdiction, or all the district courts thereof having civil jurisdiction, have successive terms in said county throughout the year, without more than two days intervening between any of such terms, whether or not any one or more of such district courts include one or more other counties within its jurisdiction.

(a) **Appealed Cases**. In cases appealed to said district courts from inferior courts, the appeal, including transcript, shall be filed in the district court within thirty (30) days after the rendition of the judgment or order appealed from, and the appellee shall enter his appearance on the docket or answer to said appeal on or before ten o'clock a.m. of the Monday next after the expiration of twenty (20) days from the date the appeal is filed in the district court.

(b) Repealed by order of July 22, 1975, eff. Jan. 1, 1976.

(c) **Postponement or Continuance**. Cases may be postponed or continued by agreement with the approval of the court, or upon the court's own motion or for cause. When a case is called for trial and only one party is ready, the court may for good cause either continue the case for the term or postpone and reset it for a later day in the same or succeeding term.

(d) **Cases May Be Reset**. A case that is set and reached for trial may be postponed for a later day in the term or continued and reset for a day certain in the succeeding term on the same grounds as an application for continuance would be granted in other district courts. After any case has been set and reached in its due order and called for trial two (2) or more times and not tried, the court may dismiss the same unless the parties agree to a postponement or continuance but the court shall respect written agreements of counsel for postponement and continuance if filed in the case when or before it is called for trial unless to do so will unreasonably delay or interfere with other business of the court.

(e) **Exchange and Transfer**. Where in such county there are two or more district courts having civil jurisdiction, the judges of such courts may, in their discretion, exchange benches or districts from time to time, and may transfer cases and other proceedings from one court to another, and any of them may in his own courtroom try and determine any case or proceeding pending in another court without having the case transferred, or may sit in any other of said courts and there hear and determine any case there pending, and every judgment and order shall be entered in the minutes of the court in which the case is pending and at the time the judgment or order is rendered, and two (2) or more judges may try different cases in the same court at the same time, and each may occupy his own courtroom or the room of any other court. The judge of any such court may issue restraining orders and injunctions returnable to any other judge or court, and any judge may transfer any case or proceeding pending in his court to any other of said courts, and the judge of any court to which a case or proceeding is transferred shall receive and try the same, and in turn shall have power in his discretion to transfer any such case to any other of said courts and any other judge may in his courtroom try any case pending in any other of such courts.

(f) **Cases Transferred to Judges Not Occupied**. Where in such counties there are two or more district courts having civil jurisdiction, when the judge of any such court shall become disengaged, he shall notify the presiding judge, and the presiding judge shall transfer to the court of the disengaged judge the next case which is ready for trial in any of said courts. Any judge not engaged in his own court may try any case in any other court.

(g) **Judge May Hear Only Part of Case**. Where in such counties there are two or more district courts having civil jurisdiction, any judge may hear any part of any case or proceeding pending in any of said courts and determine the same, or may hear and determine any question in any case, and any other judge may complete the hearing and render judgment in the case.

(h) **Any Judge May Hear Dilatory Pleas**. Where in such county there are two or more district courts having civil jurisdiction, any judge may hear and determine motions, petitions for injunction, applications for appointment of receivers, interventions, pleas of privilege, pleas in abatement, all dilatory pleas and special exceptions, motions for a new trial and all preliminary matters, questions and proceedings and may enter judgment or order thereon in the court in which the case is pending without having the case transferred to the court of the judge acting, and the judge in whose court the case is pending may thereafter proceed to hear, complete and determine the case or other matter, or any part thereof, and render final judgment therein. Any judgment rendered or action taken by any judge in any of said courts in the county shall be valid and binding.

(i) **Acts in Succeeding Terms**. If a case or other matter is on trial, or in the process of hearing when the term of court expires, such trial, hearing or other matter may be proceeded with at the next or any subsequent term of court and no motion or plea shall be considered as waived or overruled, because not acted upon at the term of court at which it was filed, but may be acted upon at any time the judge may fix or at which it may have been postponed or continued by agreement of the parties with leave of the court. This subdivision is not applicable to original or amended motions for new trial which are governed by Rule 329b.

(Amended by Order July 20, 1954, eff. Jan. 1, 1955; July 26, 1960, eff. Jan. 1, 1961; Oct. 3, 1972, eff. Feb. 1, 1973; July 22, 1975, eff. Jan. 1, 1976.)

RULE 331. [REPEALED]

(Repealed by Order July 15, 1987, eff. Jan. 1, 1988.)

SECTION 12.
REVIEW BY DISTRICT COURTS OF COUNTY COURT RULINGS

RULES 332 TO 351. [REPEALED]

(Repealed by Order July 22, 1975, eff. Jan. 1, 1976.)

PART III.
RULES OF PROCEDURE FOR THE COURTS OF APPEALS

RULES 352 TO 358. [REPEALED]

(Repealed by Order April 10, 1986, eff. Sept. 1, 1986.)

RULE 359. [REPEALED]

(Repealed by Order Dec. 5, 1983, eff. April 1, 1984.)

RULE 360. [REPEALED]

(Repealed by Order April 10, 1986, eff. Sept. 1, 1986.)

RULES 361 AND 362. [REPEALED]

(Repealed by Order Dec. 5, 1983, eff. April 1, 1984.)

RULES 363 TO 369a. [REPEALED]

(Repealed by Order April 10, 1986, eff. Sept. 1, 1986.)

RULE 370. [REPEALED]

(Repealed by Order June 10, 1980, eff. Jan. 1, 1981.)

RULES 371 TO 373. [REPEALED]

(Repealed by Order April 10, 1986, eff. Sept. 1, 1986.)

RULE 374. [REPEALED]

(Repealed by Order July 11, 1977, eff. Jan. 1, 1978.)

RULES 375 AND 376. [REPEALED]

(Repealed by Order April 10, 1986, eff. Sept. 1, 1986.)

RULE 376a TO 389a. [REPEALED]

(Repealed by Order April 10, 1986, eff. Sept. 1, 1986.)

RULE 390. [REPEALED]

(Repealed by Order Dec. 5, 1983, eff. April 1, 1984.)

RULE 391. [REPEALED]

(Repealed by Order Oct. 12, 1949, eff. March 1, 1950.)

RULE 392. [REPEALED]

(Repealed by Order Dec. 5, 1983, eff. April 1, 1984.)

RULES 393 TO 414. [REPEALED]

(Repealed by Order April 10, 1986, eff. Sept. 1, 1986.)

RULES 415 TO 417. [REPEALED]

(Repealed by Order Dec. 5, 1983, eff. April 4, 1984.)

RULES 418 TO 420. [REPEALED]

(Repealed by Order April 10, 1986, eff. Sept. 1, 1986.)

RULE 421. [REPEALED]

(Repealed by Order June 10, 1980, eff. Jan. 1, 1981.)

RULE 422. [REPEALED]

(Repealed by Order April 10, 1986, eff. Sept. 1, 1986.)

RULE 423. [REPEALED]

(Repealed by Order April 10, 1986, eff. Sept. 1, 1986.)

RULES 424 TO 427. [REPEALED]

(Repealed by Order Dec. 5, 1983, eff. April 1, 1984.)

RULES 428 AND 429. [REPEALED]

(Repealed by Order April 10, 1986, eff. Sept. 1, 1986.)

RULES 430 TO 432. [REPEALED]

(Repealed by Order Dec. 5, 1983, eff. April 1, 1984.)

RULES 433 TO 442. [REPEALED]

(Repealed by Order April 10, 1986, eff. Sept. 1, 1986.)

RULES 443 AND 444. [REPEALED]

(Repealed by Order Dec. 5, 1983, eff. April 1, 1984.)

RULE 445. [REPEALED]

(Repealed by Order July 11, 1977, eff. Jan. 1, 1978.)

RULES 446 TO 448. [REPEALED]

(Repealed by Order April 10, 1986, eff. Sept. 1, 1986.)

RULES 449 AND 450. [REPEALED]

(Repealed by Order Dec. 5, 1983, eff. April 1, 1984.)

RULES 451 AND 452. [REPEALED]

(Repealed by Order April 10, 1986, eff. Sept. 1, 1986.)

RULES 453 TO 455. [REPEALED]

(Repealed by Order Dec. 5, 1983, eff. April 1, 1984.)

RULES 456 TO 458. [REPEALED]

(Repealed by Order April 10, 1986, eff. Sept. 1, 1986.)

RULE 459. [REPEALED]

(Repealed by Order Sept. 20, 1941, eff. Dec. 31, 1941.)

RULES 460 TO 462. [REPEALED]

(Repealed by Order April 10, 1986, eff. Sept. 1, 1986.)

RULES 463 AND 464. [REPEALED]

(Repealed by Order Dec. 5, 1983, eff. April 1, 1984.)

RULES 465 AND 466. [REPEALED]

(Repealed by Order April 10, 1986, eff. Sept. 1, 1986.)

RULE 467. [REPEALED]

(Repealed by Order Dec. 5, 1983, eff. April 1, 1984.)

RULES 468 TO 470. [REPEALED]

(Repealed by Order April 10, 1986, eff. Sept. 1, 1986.)

RULE 471. [REPEALED]

(Repealed by Order Dec. 5, 1983, eff. April 1, 1984.)

RULE 472. [REPEALED]

(Repealed by Order April 10, 1986, eff. Sept. 1, 1986.)

RULE 473. [REPEALED]

(Repealed by Order Dec. 5, 1983, eff. April 1, 1984.)

PART IV.
RULES OF PRACTICE FOR THE SUPREME COURT

RULES 474 TO 481. [REPEALED]

(Repealed by Order April 10, 1986, eff. Sept. 1, 1986)

RULE 482. [REPEALED]

(Repealed by Order Dec. 5, 1983, eff. April 1, 1984.)

RULES 483 TO 486. [REPEALED]

(Repealed by Order April 10, 1986, eff. Sept. 1, 1986.)

RULE 487. [REPEALED]

(Repealed by Order Oct. 10, 1945, eff. Feb. 1, 1946.)

RULES 488 TO 491. [REPEALED]

(Repealed by Order April 10, 1986, eff. Sept. 1, 1986.)

RULE 492. [REPEALED]

(Repealed by Order April 10, 1986, eff. Sept. 1, 1986.)

RULE 493. [REPEALED]

(Repealed by Order April 10, 1986, eff. Sept. 1, 1986.)

RULE 494. [REPEALED]

(Repealed by Order Oct. 10, 1945, eff. Feb. 1, 1946.)

RULE 495. [REPEALED]

(Repealed by Order April 10, 1986, eff. Sept. 1, 1986.)

RULE 496. [REPEALED]

(Repealed by Order April 10, 1986, eff. Sept. 1, 1986.)

RULES 497 TO 505. [REPEALED]

(Repealed by Order April 10, 1986, eff. Sept., 1, 1986.)

RULE 506. [REPEALED]

(Repealed by Order Dec. 5, 1983, eff. April 1, 1984.)

RULE 507. [REPEALED]

(Repealed by Order April 10, 1986, eff. Sept. 1, 1986.)

RULE 508. [REPEALED]

(Repealed by Order Dec. 5, 1983, eff. April 1, 1984.)

RULE 509. [REPEALED]

(Repealed by Order July 11, 1977, eff. Jan. 1, 1978.)

RULE 510. [REPEALED]

(Repealed by Order April 10, 1986, eff. Sept. 1, 1986.)

RULES 511 TO 513. [REPEALED]

(Repealed by Order Dec. 5, 1983, eff. April 1, 1984.)

RULES 514 AND 515. [REPEALED]

(Repealed by Order April 10, 1986, eff. Sept. 1, 1986.)

RULES 516 AND 517. [REPEALED]

(Repealed by Order Dec. 5, 1983, eff. April 1, 1984.)

RULES 518 TO 522. [REPEALED]

(Repealed by Order Oct. 10, 1945, eff. Feb. 1, 1946.)

PART V.
IN RULES OF PRACTICE IN JUSTICE COURTS

[Rules of Civil Procedure 500-510 govern cases filed on or after August 31 , 2013, and cases pending on August 31 , 2013, except to the extent that in the opinion of the court their application in a case pending on August 31 , 2013, would not be feasible or would work injustice, in which event the formerly applicable procedure applies. An action taken before August 31 , 2013, in a case pending on August 31, 2013, that was done pursuant to any previously applicable procedure must be treated as valid. Where citation or other process was issued or served prior to August 31, 2013 , in compliance with any previously applicable procedure, the party served has the time provided for under the previously applicable procedure to answer or otherwise respond.]

RULE 500. GENERAL RULES.

RULE 500.1. CONSTRUCTION OF RULES.

Unless otherwise expressly provided, in Part V of these Rules of Civil Procedure:

(a) the past, present, and future tense each includes the other;

(b) the term "it" includes a person of either gender or an entity; and

(c) the singular and plural each includes the other.

RULE 500.2. DEFINITIONS.

In Part V of these Rules of Civil Procedure:

(a) "Answer" is the written response that a party who is sued must file with the court after being served with a citation.

(b) "Citation" is the court-issued document required to be served upon a party to inform the party that it has been sued.

(c) "Claim" is the legal theory and alleged facts that, if proven, entitle a party to relief against another party in court.

(d) "Clerk" is a person designated by the judge as a justice court clerk, or the judge if there is no clerk available.

(e) "Counterclaim" is a claim brought by a party who has been sued against the party who filed the lawsuit, for example, a defendant suing a plaintiff.

(f) "County court" is the county court, statutory county court, or district court in a particular county with jurisdiction over appeals of civil cases from justice court.

(g) "Cross-claim" is a claim brought by one party against another party on the same side of a lawsuit. For example, if a plaintiff sues two defendants, the defendants can seek relief against each other by means of a cross-claim.

(h) "Default judgment" is a judgment awarded to a plaintiff when the defendant fails to answer and dispute the plaintiff s claims in the lawsuit.

(i) "Defendant" is a party who is sued, including a plaintiff against whom a counterclaim is filed.

(j) "Defense" is an assertion by a defendant that the plaintiff is not entitled to relief from the court.

(k) "Discovery" is the process through which parties obtain information from each other in order to prepare for trial or enforce a judgment. The term does not refer to any information that a party is entitled to under applicable law.

(l) "Dismissed without prejudice" means a case has been dismissed but has not been finally decided and may be refiled.

(m) "Dismissed with prejudice" means a case has been dismissed and finally decided and may not be refiled.

(n) "Judge" is a justice of the peace.

(o) "Judgment" is a final order by the court that states the relief, if any, a party is entitled to or must provide.

(p) "Jurisdiction" is the authority of the court to hear and decide a case.

(q) "Motion" is a request that the court make a specified ruling or order.

(r) "Notice" is a document prepared and delivered by the court or a party stating that something is required of the party receiving the notice.

(s) "Party" is a person or entity involved in the case that is either suing or being sued, including all plaintiffs, defendants, and third parties that have been joined in the case.

(t) "Petition" is a formal written application stating a party's claims and requesting relief from the court. It is the first document filed with the court to begin a lawsuit.

(u) "Plaintiff' is a party who sues, including a defendant who files a counterclaim.

(v) "Pleading" is a written document filed by a party, including a petition and an answer, that states a claim or defense and outlines the relief sought.

(w) "Relief' is the remedy a party requests from the court, such as the recovery of money or the return of property.

(x) "Serve" and "service" are delivery of citation as required by Rule 50 1 .2, or of a document as required by Rule 501 .4.

(y) "Sworn" means signed in front of someone authorized to take oaths, such as a notary, or signed under penalty of perjury. Filing a false sworn document can result in criminal prosecution.

(z) "Third party claim" is a claim brought by a party being sued against someone who is not yet a party to the case.

RULE 500.3. APPLICATION OF RULES IN JUSTICE COURT CASES.

(a) *Small Claims Case.* A small claims case is a lawsuit brought for the recovery of money damages, civil penalties, personal property, or other relief allowed by law. The claim can be for no more than $ 1 0,000, excluding statutory interest and court costs but including attorney fees, if any. Small claims cases are governed by Rules 500-507 of Part V of the Rules of Civil Procedure.

(b) *Debt Claim Case.* A debt claim case is a lawsuit brought to recover a debt by an assignee of a claim, a debt collector or collection agency, a financial institution, or a person or entity primarily engaged in the business of lending money at interest. The claim can be for no more than $ 1 0,000, excluding statutory interest and court costs but including attorney fees, if any. Debt claim cases injustice court are governed by Rules 500-507 and 508 of Part V of the Rules of Civil Procedure. To the extent of any conflict between Rule 508 and the rest of Part V, Rule 508 applies.

(c) *Repair and Remedy Case.* A repair and remedy case is a lawsuit filed by a residential tenant under Chapter 92, Subchapter B of the Texas Property Code to enforce the landlord's duty to repair or remedy a condition materially affecting the physical health or safety of an ordinary tenant. The relief sought can be for no more than $ 1 0,000, excluding statutory interest and court costs but including attorney fees, if any. Repair and remedy cases are governed by Rules 500-507 and 509 of Part V of the Rules of Civil Procedure. To the extent of any conflict between Rule 509 and the rest of Part V, Rule 509 applies.

(d) *Eviction Case.* An eviction case is a lawsuit brought to recover possession of real property under Chapter 24 of the Texas Property Code, often by a landlord against a tenant. A claim for rent may be joined with an eviction case if the amount of rent due and unpaid is not more than $10,000, excluding statutory interest and court costs but including attorney fees, if any. Eviction cases are governed by Rules 500-507 and 5 1 0 of Part V of the Rules of Civil Procedure. To the extent of any conflict between Rule 5 1 0 and the rest of Part V, Rule 510 applies.

(e) *Application of Other Rules.* The other Rules of Civil Procedure and the Rules of Evidence do not apply except:
   (1) when the judge hearing the case determines that a particular rule must be followed to ensure that the proceedings are fair to all parties; or
   (2) when otherwise specifically provided by law or these rules.

(f) *Examination of Rules.* The court must make the Rules of Civil Procedure and the Rules of Evidence available for examination, either in paper form or electronically, during the court's business hours.

RULE 500.4. REPRESENTATION IN JUSTICE COURT CASES.

(a) *Representation of an Individual.* An individual may:
   (1) represent himself or herself;
   (2) be represented by an authorized agent in an eviction case; or
   (3) be represented by an attorney.

(b) *Representation of a Corporation or Other Entity.* A corporation or other entity may:
   (1) be represented by an employee, owner, officer, or partner of the entity who is not an attorney;
   (2) be represented by a property manager or other authorized agent in an eviction case; or
   (3) be represented by an attorney.

(c) *Assisted Representation.* The court may, for good cause, allow an individual representing himself or herself to be assisted in court by a family member or other individual who is not being compensated.

RULE 500.5. COMPUTATION OF TIME; TIMELY FILING.

(a) *Computation of Time.* To compute a time period in these rules:

(1) exclude the day of the event that triggers the period;

(2) count every day, including Saturdays, Sundays, and legal holidays; and

(3) include the last day of the period, but

(A) if the last day is a Saturday, Sunday, or legal holiday, the time period is extended to the next day that is not a Saturday, Sunday, or legal holiday; and

(B) if the last day for filing falls on a day during which the court is closed before 5:00p.m., the time period is extended to the court's next business day.

(b) *Timely Filing by Mail.* Any document required to be filed by a given date is considered timely filed if deposited in the U.S. mail on or before that date, and received within 10 days of the due date. A legible postmark affixed by the United States Postal Service is evidence of the date of mailing.

(c) *Extensions.* The judge may, for good cause shown, extend any time period under these rules except those relating to new trial and appeal.

RULE 500.6. JUDGE TO DEVELOP THE CASE.

In order to develop the facts of the case, a judge may question a witness or party and may summon any person or party to appear as a witness when the judge considers it necessary to ensure a correct judgment and a speedy disposition.

RULE 500.7. EXCLUSION OF WITNESSES.

The court must, on a party's request, or may, on its own initiative, order witnesses excluded so that they cannot hear the testimony of other witnesses. This rule does not authorize the exclusion of:

(a) a party who is a natural person or the spouse of such natural person;

(b) an officer or employee designated as a representative of a party who is not a natural person; or

(c) a person whose presence is shown by a party to be essential to the presentation of the party's case.

RULE 500.8. SUBPOENAS.

(a) *Use.* A subpoena may be used by a party or the judge to command a person or entity to attend and give testimony at a hearing or trial. A person may not be required by subpoena to appear in a county that is more than ISO miles from where the person resides or is served.

(b) *Who Can Issue.* A subpoena may be issued by the clerk of the justice court or an attorney authorized to practice in the State of Texas, as an officer of the court.

(c) *Form.* Every subpoena must be issued in the name of the "State of Texas" and must:

(1) state the style of the suit and its case number;

(2) state the court in which the suit is pending;

(3) state the date on which the subpoena is issued;

(4) identify the person to whom the subpoena is directed;

(5) state the date, time, place, and nature of the action required by the person to whom the subpoena is directed;

(6) identify the party at whose instance the subpoena is issued, and the party's attorney of record, if any;

(7) state that "Failure by any person without adequate excuse to obey a subpoena served upon that person may be deemed a contempt of court from which the subpoena is issued and may be punished by fine or confinement, or both"; and

(8) be signed by the person issuing the subpoena.

(d) *Service: Where, By Whom, How.* A subpoena may be served at any place within the State of Texas by any sheriff or constable of the State of Texas, or by any person who is not a party and is 18 years of age or older. A subpoena must be served by delivering a copy to the witness and tendering to that person any fees required by law. If the witness is a party and is represented by an attorney of record in the proceeding, the subpoena may be served on the witness's attorney of record. Proof of service must be made by filing either:

(1) the witness's signed written memorandum attached to the subpoena showing that the witness accepted the subpoena; or

(2) a statement by the person who made the service stating the date, time, and manner of service, and the name of the person served.

(e) *Compliance Required.* A person commanded by subpoena to appear and give testimony must remain at the hearing or trial from day to day until discharged by the court or by the party summoning the witness. If a subpoena commanding testimony is directed to a corporation, partnership, association, governmental agency, or other organization, and the matters on which examination is requested are described with reasonable particularity, the organization must designate one or more persons to testify on its behalf as to matters known or reasonably available to the organization.

(f) *Objection.* A person commanded to attend and give testimony at a hearing or trial may object or move for a protective order before the court at or before the time and place specified for compliance. A party causing a subpoena to issue must take reasonable steps to avoid imposing undue burden or expense on the person served. In ruling on objections or motions for protection, the court must provide a person served with a subpoena an adequate time for compliance and protection from undue burden or expense. The court may impose reasonable conditions on compliance with a subpoena, including compensating the witness for undue hardship.

(g) *Enforcement.* Failure by any person without adequate excuse to obey a subpoena served upon that person may be deemed a contempt of the court from which the subpoena is issued or of a district court in the county in which the subpoena is served, and may be punished by fine or confinement, or both. A fine may not be imposed, nor a person served with a subpoena attached, for failure to comply with a subpoena without proof of service and proof by affidavit of the party requesting the subpoena or the party's attorney of record that all fees due the witness by law were paid or tendered.

RULE 500.9. DISCOVERY.

(a) *Pretrial Discovery.* Pretrial discovery is limited to that which the judge considers reasonable and necessary. Any requests for pretrial discovery must be presented to the court for approval by written motion. The motion must be served on the responding party. Unless a hearing is requested, the judge may rule on the motion without a hearing. The discovery request must not be served on the responding party unless the judge issues a signed order approving the request. Failure to comply with a discovery order can result in sanctions, including dismissal of the case or an order to pay the other party's discovery expenses.

(b) *Post-judgment Discovery.* Post-judgment discovery is not required to be filed with the court. The party requesting discovery must give the responding party at least 3 0 days to respond to a post-judgment discovery request. The responding party may file a written objection with the court within 30 days of receiving the request. If an objection is filed, the judge must hold a hearing to determine if the request is valid. If the objection is denied, the judge must order the party to respond to the request. If the objection is upheld, the judge may reform the request or dismiss it entirely.

(Adopted by Order Feb 12, 2013 and Order April 15, 2013, eff. Aug. 31, 2013.)

Rules of Civil Procedure 500-510 govern cases filed on or after August 31 , 2013, and cases pending on August 31 , 2013, except to the extent that in the opinion of the court their application in a case pending on August 31 , 2013, would not be feasible or would work injustice, in which event the formerly applicable procedure applies. An action taken before August 31 , 2013, in a case pending on August 31, 2013, that was done pursuant to any previously applicable procedure must be treated as valid. Where citation or other process was issued or served prior to August 31, 2013 , in compliance with any previously applicable procedure, the party served has the time provided for under the previously applicable procedure to answer or otherwise respond.

RULE 501. CITATION AND SERVICE.

RULE 501.1. CITATION.

(a) *Issuance.* When a petition is filed with a justice court to initiate a suit, the clerk must promptly issue a citation and deliver the citation as directed by the plaintiff. The plaintiff is responsible for obtaining service on the defendant of the citation and a copy of the petition with any documents filed with the petition. Upon request, separate or additional citations must be issued by the clerk. The clerk must retain a copy of the citation in the court's file.

(b) *Form.* The citation must:

(1) be styled "The State of Texas";

(2) be signed by the clerk under seal of court or by the judge;

(3) contain the name, location, and address of the court;

(4) show the date of filing of the petition;

(5) show the date of issuance of the citation;

(6) show the file number and names of parties;

(7) be directed to the defendant;

(8) show the name and address of attorney for plaintiff, or if the plaintiff does not have an attorney, the address of plaintiff; and

(9) notify defendant that if the defendant fails to file an answer, judgment by default may be rendered for the relief demanded in the petition.

(c) *Notice.* The citation must include the following notice to the defendant in boldface type:

"You have been sued. You may employ an attorney to help you in defending against this lawsuit. But you are not required to employ an attorney. You or your attorney must file an answer with the court. Your answer is due by the end of the 14th day after the day you were served with these papers. If the 14th day is a Saturday, Sunday, or legal holiday, your answer is due by the end of the first day following the 14th day that is not a Saturday, Sunday, or legal holiday. Do not ignore these papers. If you do not file an answer by the due date, a default judgment may be taken against you. For further information, consult Part V of the Texas Rules of Civil Procedure, which is available online and also at the court listed on this citation."

(d) *Copies.* The plaintiff must provide enough copies to be served on each defendant. If the plaintiff fails to do so, the clerk may make copies and charge the plaintiff the allowable copying cost.

RULE 501.2. SERVICE OF CITATION.

(a) *Who May Serve.* No person who is a party to or interested in the outcome of the suit may serve citation in that suit, and, unless otherwise authorized by written court order, only a sheriff or constable may serve a citation in an eviction case, a writ that requires the actual taking of possession of a person, property or thing, or process requiring that an enforcement action be physically enforced by the person delivering the process. Other citations may be served by:
   (1) a sheriff or constable;
   (2) a process server certified under order of the Supreme Court;
   (3) the clerk of the court, if the citation is served by registered or certified mail; or
   (4) a person authorized by court order who is 18 years of age or older.

(b) *Method of Service.* Citation must be served by:
   (1) delivering a copy of the citation with a copy of the petition attached to the defendant in person, after endorsing the date of delivery on the citation; or
   (2) mailing a copy of the citation with a copy of the petition attached to the defendant by registered or certified mail, restricted delivery, with return receipt or electronic return receipt requested.

(c) *Service Fees.* A plaintiff must pay all fees for service unless the plaintiff has filed a Statement of Inability to Afford Payment of Court Costs with the court. If the plaintiff has filed a Statement, the plaintiff must arrange for the citation to be served by a sheriff, constable, or court clerk.

(d) *Service on Sunday.* A citation cannot be served on a Sunday except in attachment, garnishment, sequestration, or distress proceedings.

(e) *Alternative Service of Citation.* If the methods under (b) are insufficient to serve the defendant, the plaintiff, or the constable, sheriff, process server certified under order of the Supreme Court, or other person authorized to serve process, may make a request for alternative service. This request must include a sworn statement describing the methods attempted under (b) and stating the defendant's usual place of business or residence, or other place where the defendant can probably be found. The court may authorize the following types of alternative service:
   (1) mailing a copy of the citation with a copy of the petition attached by first class mail to the defendant at a specified address, and also leaving a copy of the citation with petition attached at the defendant's residence or other place where the defendant can probably be found with any person found there who is at least 16 years of age; or
   (2) mailing a copy of the citation with a copy of the petition attached by first class mail to the defendant at a specified address, and also serving by any other method that the court finds is reasonably likely to provide the defendant with notice of the suit.

(f) *Service by Publication.* In the event that service of citation by publication is necessary, the process is governed by the rules in county and district court.

(Amended by Tex. Sup. Ct. Misc. Docket No. 16-9122, eff. Sept. 1, 2016.)

[Statement of Inability to Afford Payment of Court Costs as provided in Tex. Sup. Ct. Misc. Docket No. 16-9122, eff. Sept. 1, 2016 and applies to any contest of, or challenge to, a claim of inability to afford payment of court costs that is pending on September 1, 2016.]

RULE 501.3. DUTIES OF OFFICER OR PERSON RECEIVING CITATION; RETURN OF SERVICE.

(a) *Endorsement; Execution; Return.* The officer or authorized person to whom process is delivered must:
   (1) endorse on the process the date and hour on which he or she received it;
   (2) execute and return the same without delay; and
   (3) complete a return of service, which may, but need not, be endorsed on or attached to the citation.

(b) *Contents of Return.* The return, together with any document to which it is attached, must include the following information:
   (1) the case number and case name;
   (2) the court in which the case is filed;
   (3) a description of what was served;
   (4) the date and time the process was received for service;
   (5) the person or entity served;

(6) the address served;
(7) the date of service or attempted service;
(8) the manner of delivery of service or attempted service;
(9) the name of the person who served or attempted service;
(10) if the person named in (9) is a process server certified under Supreme Court Order, his or her identification number and the expiration date of his or her certification; and
(11) any other information required by rule or law.

(c) *Citation by Mail.* When the citation is served by registered or certified mail as authorized by Rule 501.2(b)(2), the return by the officer or authorized person must also contain the receipt with the addressee's signature.

(d) *Failure to Serve.* When the officer or authorized person has not served the citation, the return must show the diligence used by the officer or authorized person to execute the same and the cause of failure to execute it, and where the defendant is to be found, if ascertainable.

(e) *Signature.* The officer or authorized person who serves or attempts to serve a citation must sign the return. If the return is signed by a person other than a sheriff; constable, or clerk of the court, the return must either be verified or be signed under penalty of perjury. A return signed under penalty of perjury must contain the statement below in substantially the following form:

"My name is (First) (Middle) (Last), my date of birth is (Month) (Day), (Year), and my address is (Street), (City), (State) (Zip Code), (Country). I declare under penalty of perjury that the foregoing is true and correct.
Executed in ________________ County, State of ____________, on the _______ day of (Month), (Year).

____
Declarant"

(f) *Alternative Service.* Where citation is executed by an alternative method as authorized by 501.2(e), proof of service must be made in the manner ordered by the court.

(g) *Filing Return.* The return and any document to which it is attached must be filed with the court and may be filed electronically or by fax, if those methods of filing are available.

(h) *Prerequisite for Default Judgment.* No default judgment may be granted in any case until proof of service as provided by this rule, or as ordered by the court in the event citation is executed by an alternative method under 501.2(e), has been on tile with the clerk of the court 3 days, exclusive of the day of filing and the day of judgment.

RULE 501.4. SERVICE OF PAPERS OTHER THAN CITATION.

(a) *Method of Service.* Other than a citation or oral motions made during trial or when all parties are present, every notice required by these rules, and every pleading, plea, motion, application to the court for an order, or other form of request, must be served on all other parties in one of the following ways:
   (1) In person. A copy may be delivered to the party to be served, or the party's duly authorized agent or attorney of record, in person or by agent.
   (2) Mail or courier. A copy may be sent by courier-receipted delivery or by certified or registered mail, to the party's last known address. Service by certified or registered mail is complete when the document is properly addressed and deposited in the United States mail, postage prepaid.
   (3) Fax. A copy may be faxed to the recipient's current fax number. Service by fax after 5:00 p.m. local time of the recipient will be deemed to have been served on the following day.
   (4) Email. A copy may be sent to an email address expressly provided by the receiving party, if the party has consented to email service in writing. Service by email after 5:00 p.m. local time of the recipient will be deemed to have been served on the following day.
   (5) Other. A copy may be delivered in any other manner directed by the court.

(b) *Timing.* If a document is served by mail, 3 days will be added to the length of time a party has to respond to the document. Notice of any hearing requested by a party must be served on all other parties not less than 3 days before the time specified for the hearing.

(c) *Who May Serve.* Documents other than a citation may be served by a party to the suit, an attorney of record, a sheriff or constable, or by any other person competent to testify.

(d) *Certificate of Service.* The party or the party's attorney of record must include in writing on all documents filed a signed statement describing the manner in which the document was served on the other party or parties and the date of service. A certificate by a party or the party's attorney of record, or the return of the officer, or the sworn statement of any other person showing service of a notice is proof of service.

(e) *Failure to Serve*. A party may offer evidence or testimony that a notice or document was not received, or, if service was by mail, that it was not received within 3 days from the date of mailing, and upon so finding, the court may extend the time for taking the action required of the party or grant other relief as it deems just.

(Adopted by Order Feb 12, 2013 and Order April 15, 2013, eff. Aug. 31, 2013.)

Rules of Civil Procedure 500-510 govern cases filed on or after August 31 , 2013, and cases pending on August 31 , 2013, except to the extent that in the opinion of the court their application in a case pending on August 31 , 2013, would not be feasible or would work injustice, in which event the formerly applicable procedure applies. An action taken before August 31 , 2013, in a case pending on August 31, 2013, that was done pursuant to any previously applicable procedure must be treated as valid. Where citation or other process was issued or served prior to August 31, 2013 , in compliance with any previously applicable procedure, the party served has the time provided for under the previously applicable procedure to answer or otherwise respond.

RULE 502. INSTITUTION OF SUIT.

RULE 502.1. PLEADINGS AND MOTIONS MUST BE WRITTEN, SIGNED, AND FILED.

Except for oral motions made during trial or when all parties are present, every pleading, plea, motion, application to the court for an order, or other form of request must be written and signed by the party or its attorney and must be filed with the court. A document may be filed with the court by personal or commercial delivery, by mail, or electronically, if the court allows electronic filing. Electronic filing is governed by Rule 21.

(Amended by Order Aug. 16, 2013, eff. Jan. 1, 2014; Dec. 13, 2013, eff. Jan. 1, 2013.)

RULE 502.2. PETITION.

(a) *Contents*. To initiate a lawsuit, a petition must be filed with the court. A petition must contain:

(1) the name of the plaintiff;

(2) the name, address, telephone number, and fax number, if any, of the plaintiff's attorney, if applicable, or the address, telephone number, and fax number, if any, of the plaintiff;

(3) the name, address, and telephone number, if known, of the defendant;

(4) the amount of money, if any, the plaintiff seeks;

(5) a description and claimed value of any personal property the plaintiff seeks;

(6) a description of any other relief requested;

(7) the basis for the plaintiff's claim against the defendant; and

(8) if the plaintiff consents to email service of the answer and any other motions or pleadings, a statement consenting to email service and email contact information.

(b) *Justice Court Civil Case Information Sheet*. A justice court civil case information sheet, in the form promulgated by the Supreme Court of Texas, must accompany the filing of a petition and must be signed by the plaintiff or the plaintiff's attorney. The justice court civil case information sheet is for data collection for statistical and administrative purposes and does not affect any substantive right. The court may not reject a pleading because the pleading is not accompanied by a justice court civil case information sheet.

[Justice Court Civil Case Information Sheet as provided in Misc. Docket No. 13-9049, Feb. 12, 2013, eff Aug. 31, 2013; April 15, 2013, eff. Aug. 31, 2013 and applies to all cases filed on or after Aug. 31, 2013.]

RULE 502.3. FEES; INABILITY TO AFFORD FEES.

(a) *Fees and Statement of Inability to Afford Payment of Court Costs*. On filing the petition, the plaintiff must pay the appropriate filing fee and service fees, if any, with the court. A plaintiff who is unable to afford to pay the fees must file a Statement of Inability to Afford Payment of Court Costs. The Statement must either be sworn to before a notary or made under penalty of perjury. Upon filing the Statement, the clerk must docket the action, issue citation, and provide any other customary serv1ces.

(b) *Supreme Court Form; Contents of Statement*. The plaintiff must use the form Statement approved by the Supreme Court, or the Statement must include the information required by the Court-approved form. The clerk must make the form available to all persons without charge or request.

(c) *Certificate of Legal-Aid Provider*. If the party is represented by an attorney who is providing free legal services because of the party's indigence, without contingency, and the attorney is providing services either directly or by referral from legal-aid provider described in Rule 145(e)(2), the attorney may file a certificate confirming that the provider screened the party for eligibility under the income and asset guidelines established by the provider. A Statement that is accompanied by the certificate of a legal-aid provider may not be contested under (d).

(d) *Contest*. Unless a certificate is filed under (c), the defendant may file a contest of the Statement at any time within 7 days after the day the defendant's answer is due. If the Statement attests to receipt of government entitlement based on indigence, the Statement may only be contested with regard to the veracity of the attestation. If contested, the judge must hold a hearing to determine the plaintiffs ability to afford the fees. At the hearing, the burden is on the plaintiff to prove the inability to afford fees. The judge may, regardless of whether the defendant contests the Statement, examine the Statement and conduct a hearing to determine the plaintiffs ability to afford fees. If the judge determines that the plaintiff is able to afford the fees, the judge must enter a written order listing the reasons for the determination, and the plaintiff must pay the fees in the time specified in the order or the case will be dismissed without prejudice.

(Amended by Tex. Sup. Ct. Misc. Docket No. 16-9056 and Tex. Sup. Ct. Misc. Docket No. 16-9122, eff. Sept. 1, 2016.)

[Statement of Inability to Afford Payment of Court Costs as provided in Tex. Sup. Ct. Misc. Docket No. 16-9122, eff. Sept. 1, 2016 and applies to any contest of, or challenge to, a claim of inability to afford payment of court costs that is pending on September 1, 2016.]

RULE 502.4. VENUE—WHERE A LAWSUIT MAY BE BROUGHT.

(a) *Applicable Law*. Laws specifying the venue—the county and precinct where a lawsuit may be brought—are found in Chapter 15, Subchapter E of the Texas Civil Practice and Remedies Code, which is available online and for examination during the court's business hours.

(b) *General Rule*. Generally, a defendant in a small claims case as described in Rule 500.3(a) or a debt claim case as described in Rule 500.3(b) is entitled to be sued in one of the following venues:

(1) the county and precinct where the defendant resides;

(2) the county and precinct where the incident, or the majority of incidents, that gave rise to the claim occurred;

(3) the county and precinct where the contract or agreement, if any, that gave rise to the claim was to be performed; or

(4) the county and precinct where the property is located, in a suit to recover personal property.

(c) *Non-Resident Defendant; Defendant's Residence Unknown*. If the defendant is a non-resident of Texas, or if defendant's residence is unknown, the plaintiff may file the suit in the county and precinct where the plaintiff resides.

(d) *Motion to Transfer Venue*. If a plaintiff files suit in an improper venue, a defendant may challenge the venue selected by filing a motion to transfer venue. The motion must be filed before trial, no later than 21 days after the day the defendant's answer is filed, and must contain a sworn statement that the venue chosen by the plaintiff is improper and a specific county and precinct of proper venue to which transfer is sought. If the defendant fails to name a county and precinct, the court must instruct the defendant to do so and allow the defendant 7 days to cure the defect. If the defendant fails to correct the defect, the motion will be denied, and the case will proceed in the county and precinct where it was originally filed.

(1) *Procedure*.

(A) Judge to Set Hearing. If a defendant files a motion to transfer venue, the judge must set a hearing on the motion.

(B) Response. A plaintiff may file a response to a defendant's motion to transfer venue.

(C) Hearing. The parties may present evidence at the hearing. A witness may testify at a hearing, either in person or, with permission of the court, by means of telephone or an electronic communication system.

(D) Judge's Decision. If the motion is granted, the judge must sign an order designating the court to which the case will be transferred. If the motion is denied, the case will be heard in the court in which the plaintiff initially filed suit.

(E) Review. Motions for rehearing and interlocutory appeals of the judge's ruling on venue are not permitted.

(F) Time for Trial of the Case. No trial may be held until at least the 14th day after the judge's ruling on the motion to transfer venue.

(G) Order. An order granting a motion to transfer venue must state the reason for the transfer and the name of the court to which the transfer is made. When such an order of transfer is made, the judge who issued the order must immediately make out a true and correct transcript of all the entries made on the docket in the case, certify the transcript, and send the transcript, with a certified copy of the bill of costs and the original papers in the case, to the court in the precinct to which the case has been transferred. The court receiving the case must then notify the plaintiff that the case has been received and, if the case is transferred to a different county, that the plaintiff has 14 days after receiving the notice to pay the filing fee in the new court, or file a Statement of Inability to Afford Payment of Court Costs. The plaintiff is not entitled to a refund of any fees already paid. Failure to pay the fee or file a Statement will result in dismissal of the case without prejudice.

(e) *Fair Trial Venue Change*. If a party believes it cannot get a fair trial in a specific precinct or before a specific judge, the party may file a sworn motion stating such, supported by the sworn statements of two other credible persons, and specifying if the party is requesting a change of location or a change of judge. Except for good cause shown, this motion must be filed no less than 7 days before trial. If the party seeks a change of judge, the judge must exchange benches with another qualified justice of the peace, or if no judge is available to exchange benches, the county judge must appoint a visiting judge to hear the case. If the party seeks a change in location, the case must be transferred to the nearest justice court in the county that is not subject to the same or some other disqualification. If there is only one justice of the peace precinct in the county, then the judge must exchange benches with another qualified justice of the peace, or if no judge is available to exchange benches, the county judge must appoint a visiting judge to hear the case. In cases where exclusive jurisdiction is within a specific precinct, as in eviction cases, the only remedy available is a change of judge. A party may apply for relief under this rule only one time in any given lawsuit.

(f) *Transfer of Venue by Consent.* On the written consent of all parties or their attorneys, filed with the court, venue must be transferred to the court of any other justice of the peace of the county, or any other county.

(Amended by Tex. Sup. Ct. Misc. Docket No. 16-9122, eff. Sept. 1, 2016.)

[Statement of Inability to Afford Payment of Court Costs as provided in Tex. Sup. Ct. Misc. Docket No. 16-9122, eff. Sept. 1, 2016 and applies to any contest of, or challenge to, a claim of inability to afford payment of court costs that is pending on September 1, 2016.]

RULE 502.5. ANSWER.

(a) *Requirements.* A defendant must file with the court a written answer to a lawsuit as directed by the citation and must also serve a copy of the answer on the plaintiff. The answer must contain:
   (1) the name of the defendant;
   (2) the name, address, telephone number, and fax number, if any, of the defendant's attorney, if applicable, or the address, telephone number, and fax number, if any, of the defendant; and
   (3) if the defendant consents to email service, a statement consenting to email service and email contact information.

(b) *General Denial.* An answer that denies all of the plaintiffs allegations without specifying the reasons is sufficient to constitute an answer or appearance and does not bar the defendant from raising any defense at trial.

(c) *Answer Docketed.* The defendant' s appearance must be noted on the court's docket.

(d) *Due Date.* Unless the defendant is served by publication, the defendant's answer is due by the end of the 1 4th day after the day the defendant was served with the citation and petition, but
   (1) if the 14th day is a Saturday, Sunday, or legal holiday, the answer is due on the next day that is not a Saturday, Sunday, or legal holiday; and
   (2) if the 14th day falls on a day during which the court is closed before 5:00 p.m., the answer is due on the court' s next business day.

(e) *Due Date When Defendant Served by Publication.* If a defendant is served by publication, the defendant' s answer is due by the end of the 42nd day after the day the citation was issued, but
   (1) if the 42nd day is a Saturday, Sunday, or legal holiday, the answer is due on the next day that is not a Saturday, Sunday, or legal holiday; and
   (2) if the 42nd day falls on a day during which the court is closed before 5:00 p.m., the answer is due on the court's next business day.

RULE 502.6. COUNTERCLAIM; CROSS-CLAIM; THIRD PARTY CLAIM.

(a) *Counterclaim.* A defendant may file a petition stating as a counterclaim any claim against a plaintiff that is within the jurisdiction of the justice court, whether or not related to the claims in the plaintiff s petition. The defendant must file a counterclaim petition as provided in Rule 502.2, and must pay a filing fee or provide a Statement of Inability to Afford Payment of Court Costs. The court need not generate a citation for a counterclaim and no answer to the counterclaim need be filed. The defendant must serve a copy of the counterclaim as provided by Rule 501.4.

(b) *Cross-Claim.* A plaintiff seeking relief against another plaintiff, or a defendant seeking relief against another defendant may file a cross-claim. The filing party must file a cross-claim petition as provided in Rule 502.2, and must pay a filing fee or provide a Statement of Inability to Afford Payment of Court Costs. A citation must be issued and served as provided by Rule 501.2 on any party that has not yet filed a petition or an answer, as appropriate. If the party filed against has filed a petition or an answer, the filing party must serve the cross-claim as provided by Rule 501.4.

(c) *Third Party Claim.* A defendant seeking to bring another party into a lawsuit who may be liable for all or part of the plaintiffs claim against the defendant may file a petition as provided in Rule 502.2, and must pay a filing fee or provide a Statement of Inability to Afford Payment of Court Costs. A citation must be issued and served as provided by Rule 501.2.

(Amended by Tex. Sup. Ct. Misc. Docket No. 16-9122, eff. Sept. 1, 2016.)

[Statement of Inability to Afford Payment of Court Costs as provided in Tex. Sup. Ct. Misc. Docket No. 16-9122, eff. Sept. 1, 2016 and applies to any contest of, or challenge to, a claim of inability to afford payment of court costs that is pending on September 1, 2016.]

RULE 502.7. AMENDING AND CLARIFYING PLEADINGS.

(a) *Amending Pleadings.* A party may withdraw something from or add something to a pleading, as long as the amended pleading is filed and served as provided by Rule 501.4 not less than 7 days before trial. The court may allow a pleading to be amended less than 7 days before trial if the amendment will not operate as a surprise to the opposing party.

(b) *Insufficient Pleadings.* A party may file a motion with the court asking that another party be required to clarify a pleading. The court must determine if the pleading is sufficient to place all parties on notice of the issues in the lawsuit, and may hold a hearing to make that determination. If the court determines a pleading is insufficient, the court must order the party to amend the pleading and set a date by which the party must amend. If a party fails to comply with the court's order, the pleading may be stricken.

(Adopted by Order Feb 12, 2013 and Order April 15, 2013, eff. Aug. 31, 2013.)

Rules of Civil Procedure 500-510 govern cases filed on or after August 31 , 2013, and cases pending on August 31 , 2013, except to the extent that in the opinion of the court their application in a case pending on August 31 , 2013, would not be feasible or would work injustice, in which event the formerly applicable procedure applies. An action taken before August 31 , 2013, in a case pending on August 31, 2013, that was done pursuant to any previously applicable procedure must be treated as valid. Where citation or other process was issued or served prior to August 31, 2013 , in compliance with any previously applicable procedure, the party served has the time provided for under the previously applicable procedure to answer or otherwise respond.

RULE 503. DEFAULT JUDGMENT; PRE-TRIAL MATTERS; TRIAL.

RULE 503.1. IF DEFENDANT FAILS TO ANSWER.

(a) *Default Judgment.* If the defendant fails to file an answer by the date stated in Rule 502.5, the judge must ensure that service was proper, and may hold a hearing for this purpose. If it is determined that service was proper, the judge must render a default judgment in the following manner:
   (1) *Claim Based on Written Document.* If the claim is based on a written document signed by the defendant, and a copy of the document has been filed with the court and served on the defendant, along with a sworn statement from the plaintiff that this is a true and accurate copy of the document and the relief sought is owed, and all payments, offsets or credits due to the defendant have been accounted for, the judge must render judgment for the plaintiff in the requested amount, without any necessity for a hearing. The plaintiff's attorney may also submit affidavits supporting an award of attorney fees to which the plaintiff is entitled, if any.
   (2) *Other Cases.* Except as provided in (1), a plaintiff who seeks a default judgment against a defendant must request a hearing, orally or in writing. The plaintiff must appear at the hearing and provide evidence of its damages. If the plaintiff proves its damages, the judge must render judgment for the plaintiff in the amount proven. If the plaintiff is unable to prove its damages, the judge must render judgment in favor of the defendant. With the permission of the court, a party may appear at a hearing by means of telephone or an electronic communication system.

(b) *Appearance.* If a defendant files an answer or otherwise appears in a case before a default judgment is signed by the judge, the judge must not enter a default judgment and the case must be set for trial as described in Rule 503.3.

(c) *Post-Answer Default.* If a defendant who has answered fails to appear for trial, the court may proceed to hear evidence on liability and damages and render judgment accordingly.

(d) *Notice.* The plaintiff requesting a default judgment must provide to the clerk in writing the last known mailing address of the defendant at or before the time the judgment is signed. When a default judgment is signed, the clerk must immediately mail written notice of the judgment to the defendant at the address provided by the plaintiff, and note the fact of such mailing on the docket. The notice must state the number and style of the case, the court in which the case is pending, the names of the parties in whose favor and against whom the judgment was rendered, and the date the judgment was signed. Failure to comply with the provisions of this rule does not affect the finality of the judgment.

RULE 503.2. SUMMARY DISPOSITION.

(a) *Motion.* A party may file a sworn motion for summary disposition of all or part of a claim or defense without a trial. The motion must set out all supporting facts. All documents on which the motion relies must be attached. The motion must be granted if it shows that:
   (1) there are no genuinely disputed facts that would prevent a judgment in favor of the party;
   (2) there is no evidence of one or more essential elements of a defense which the defendant must prove to defeat the plaintiff s claim; or
   (3) there is no evidence of one or more essential elements of the plaintiffs claim.

(b) *Response.* The party opposing the motion may tile a sworn written response to the motion.

(c) *Hearing.* The court must not consider a motion for summary disposition until it has been on file for at least 14 days. The judge may consider evidence offered by the parties at the hearing. By agreement of the parties, the judge may decide the motion and response without a hearing.

(d) *Order.* The judge may enter judgment as to the entire case or may specify the facts that are established and direct such further proceedings in the case as are just.

RULE 503.3. SETTINGS AND NOTICE; POSTPONING TRIAL.

(a) *Settings and Notice.* After the defendant answers, the case will be set on a trial docket at the discretion of the judge. The court must send a notice of the date, time, and place of this setting to all parties at their address of record no less than 45 days before the setting date, unless the judge determines that an earlier setting is required in the interest of justice. Reasonable notice of all subsequent settings must be sent to all parties at their addresses of record.

(b) *Postponing Trial.* A party may file a motion requesting that the trial be postponed. The motion must state why a postponement is necessary. The judge, for good cause, may postpone any trial for a reasonable time.

RULE 503.4. PRETRIAL CONFERENCE.

(a) *Conference Set; Issues.* If all parties have appeared in a lawsuit, the court, at any party's request or on its own, may set a case for a pretrial conference. Reasonable notice must be sent to all parties at their addresses of record. Appropriate issues for the pretrial conference include:

(1) discovery;
(2) the amendment or clarification of pleadings;
(3) the admission of facts and documents to streamline the trial process;
(4) a limitation on the number of witnesses at trial;
(5) the identification of facts, if any, which are not in dispute between the parties;
(6) mediation or other alternative dispute resolution services;
(7) the possibility of settlement;
(8) trial setting dates that are amenable to the court and all parties;
(9) the appointment of interpreters, if needed;
(10) the application of a Rule of Civil Procedure not in Part V or a Rule of Evidence; and
(11) any other issue that the court deems appropriate.

(b) *Eviction Cases.* The court must not schedule a pretrial conference in an eviction case if it would delay trial.

RULE 503.5. ALTERNATIVE DISPUTE RESOLUTION.

(a) *State Policy.* The policy of this state is to encourage the peaceable resolution of disputes through alternative dispute resolution, including mediation, and the early settlement of pending litigation through voluntary settlement procedures. For that purpose, the judge may order any case to mediation or another appropriate and generally accepted alternative dispute resolution process.

(b) *Eviction Cases.* The court must not order mediation or any other alternative dispute resolution process in an eviction case if it would delay trial.

RULE 503.6. TRIAL.

(a) *Docket Called.* On the day of the trial setting, the judge must call all of the cases set for trial that day.

(b) *If Plaintiff Fails to Appear.* If the plaintiff fails to appear when the case is called for trial, the judge may postpone or dismiss the suit.

(c) *If Defendant Fails to Appear.* If the defendant fails to appear when the case is called for trial, the judge may postpone the case, or may proceed to take evidence. If the plaintiff proves its case, judgment must be awarded for the relief proven. If the plaintiff fails to prove its case, judgment must be rendered against the plaintiff.

(Adopted by Order Feb 12, 2013 and Order April 15, 2013, eff. Aug. 31, 2013.)

Rules of Civil Procedure 500-510 govern cases filed on or after August 31 , 2013, and cases pending on August 31 , 2013, except to the extent that in the opinion of the court their application in a case pending on August 31 , 2013, would not be feasible or would work injustice, in which event the formerly applicable procedure applies. An action taken before August 31 , 2013, in a case pending on August 31, 2013, that was done pursuant to any previously applicable procedure must be treated as valid. Where citation or other process was issued or served prior to August 31, 2013 , in compliance with any previously applicable procedure, the party served has the time provided for under the previously applicable procedure to answer or otherwise respond.

RULE 504. JURY.

RULE 504.1. JURY TRIAL DEMANDED.

(a) *Demand.* Any party is entitled to a trial by jury. A written demand for a jury must be filed no later than 1 4 days before the date a case is set for trial. If the demand is not timely, the right to a jury is waived unless the late filing is excused by the judge for good cause.

(b) *Jury Fee.* Unless otherwise provided by law, a party demanding a jury must pay a fee of $22.00 or must file a Statement of Inability to Afford Payment of Court Costs at or before the time the party files a written request for a jury.

(c) *Withdrawal of Demand.* If a party who demands a jury and pays the fee withdraws the demand, the case will remain on the jury docket unless all other parties present agree to try the case without a jury. A party that withdraws its jury demand is not entitled to a refund of the jury fee.

(d) *No Demand.* If no party timely demands a jury and pays the fee, the judge will try the case without a jury.

(Amended by Tex. Sup. Ct. Misc. Docket No. 16-9122, eff. Sept. 1, 2016.)

[Statement of Inability to Afford Payment of Court Costs as provided in Tex. Sup. Ct. Misc. Docket No. 16-9122, eff. Sept. 1, 2016 and applies to any contest of, or challenge to, a claim of inability to afford payment of court costs that is pending on September 1, 2016.]

RULE 504.2. EMPANELING THE JURY.

(a) *Drawing Jury and Oath.* If no method of electronic draw has been implemented, the judge must write the names of all prospective jurors present on separate slips of paper as nearly alike as may be, place them in a box, mix them well, and then draw the names one by one from the box. The judge must list the names drawn and deliver a copy to each of the parties or their attorneys.

(b) *Oath.* After the draw, the judge must swear the panel as follows: "You solemnly swear or affirm that you will give true and correct answers to all questions asked of you concerning your qualifications as a juror."

(c) *Questioning the Jury.* The judge, the parties, or their attorneys will be allowed to question jurors as to their ability to serve impartially in the trial but may not ask the jurors how they will rule in the case. The judge will have discretion to allow or disallow specific questions and determine the amount of time each side will have for this process.

(d) *Challenge for Cause.* A party may challenge any juror for cause. A challenge for cause is an objection made to a juror alleging some fact, such as a bias or prejudice, that disqualifies the juror from serving in the case or that renders the juror unfit to sit on the jury. The challenge must be made during jury questioning. The party must explain to the judge why the juror should be excluded from the jury. The judge must evaluate the questions and answers given and either grant or deny the challenge. When a challenge for cause has been sustained, the juror must be excused.

(e) *Challenges Not for Cause.* After the judge determines any challenges for cause, each party may select up to 3 jurors to excuse for any reason or no reason at all. But no prospective juror may be excused for membership in a constitutionally protected class.

(f) *The Jury.* After all challenges, the first 6 prospective jurors remaining on the list constitute the jury to try the case.

(g) *If Jury Is Incomplete.* If challenges reduce the number of prospective jurors below 6, the judge may direct the sheriff or constable to summon others and allow them to be questioned and challenged by the parties as before, until at least 6 remain.

(h) *Jury Sworn.* When the jury has been selected, the judge must require them to take substantially the following oath: "You solemnly swear or affirm that you will render a true verdict according to the law and the evidence presented."

RULE 504.3. JURY NOT CHARGED.

The judge must not charge the jury.

RULE 504.4. JURY VERDICT FOR SPECIFIC ARTICLES.

When the suit is for the recovery of specific articles and the jury finds for the plaintiff, the jury must assess the value of each article separately, according to the evidence presented at trial.

RULE 505. JUDGMENT; NEW TRIAL.

RULE 505.1. JUDGMENT.

(a) *Judgment Upon Jury Verdict.* Where a jury has returned a verdict, the judge must announce the verdict in open court, note it in the court's docket, and render judgment accordingly. The judge may render judgment on the verdict or, if the verdict is contrary to the law or the evidence, judgment notwithstanding the verdict.

(b) *Case Tried by Judge.* When a case has been tried before the judge without a jury, the judge must announce the decision in open court, note the decision in the court's docket, and render judgment accordingly.

(c) *Form.* A judgment must:

(1) clearly state the determination of the rights of the parties in the case;

(2) state who must pay the costs;

(3) be signed by the judge; and

(4) be dated the date of the judge's signature.

(d) *Costs.* The judge must award costs allowed by law to the successful party.

(e) *Judgment for Specific Articles.* Where the judgment is for the recovery of specific articles, the judgment must order that the plaintiff recover such specific articles, if they can be found, and if not, then their value as assessed by the judge or jury with interest at the prevailing post-judgment interest rate.

RULE 505.2. ENFORCEMENT OF JUDGMENT.

Justice court judgments are enforceable in the same method as in county and district court, except as provided by law. When the judgment is for personal property, the court may award a special writ for the seizure and delivery of such property to the plaintiff, and may, in addition to the other relief granted in such cases, enforce its judgment by attachment or fine.

RULE 505.3. MOTION TO SET ASIDE; MOTION TO REINSTATE; MOTION FOR NEW TRIAL.

(a) *Motion to Reinstate after Dismissal.* A plaintiff whose case is dismissed may file a motion to reinstate the case no later than 1 4 days after the dismissal order is signed. The plaintiff must serve the defendant with a copy of the motion no later than the next business day using a method approved under Rule 50 1 .4. The court may reinstate the case for good cause shown.

(b) *Motion to Set Aside Default.* A defendant against whom a default judgment is granted may file a motion to set aside the judgment no later than 1 4 days after the judgment is signed. The defendant must serve the plaintiff with a copy of the motion no later than the next business day using a method approved under Rule 501.4. The court may set aside the judgment and set the case for trial for good cause shown.

(c) *Motion for New Trial.* A party may file a motion for a new trial no later than 1 4 days after the judgment is signed. The party must serve all other parties with a copy of the motion no later than the next business day using a method approved under Rule 50 1 .4. The judge may grant a new trial upon a showing that justice was not done in the trial of the case. Only one new trial may be granted to either party.

(d) *Motion Not Required.* Failure to file a motion under this rule does not affect a party's right to appeal the underlying judgment.

(e) *Motion Denied as a Matter of Law.* If the judge has not ruled on a motion to set aside, motion to reinstate, or motion for new trial, the motion is automatically denied at 5:00 p.m. on the 21st day after the day the judgment was signed.

(Adopted by Order Feb 12, 2013 and Order April 15, 2013, eff. Aug. 31, 2013.)

Rules of Civil Procedure 500-510 govern cases filed on or after August 31 , 2013, and cases pending on August 31 , 2013, except to the extent that in the opinion of the court their application in a case pending on August 31 , 2013, would not be feasible or would work injustice, in which event the formerly applicable procedure applies. An action taken before August 31 , 2013, in a case pending on August 31, 2013, that was done pursuant to any previously applicable procedure must be treated as valid. Where citation or other process was issued or served prior to August 31, 2013 , in compliance with any previously applicable procedure, the party served has the time provided for under the previously applicable procedure to answer or otherwise respond.

RULE 506. APPEAL.

RULE 506.1. APPEAL.

(a) *How Taken; Time.* A party may appeal a judgment by filing a bond, making a cash deposit, or filing a Statement of Inability to Afford Payment of Court Costs with the justice court within 2 1 days after the judgment is signed or the motion to reinstate, motion to set aside, or motion for new trial, if any, is denied.

(b) *Amount of Bond; Sureties; Terms.* A plaintiff must file a $500 bond. A defendant must file a bond in an amount equal to twice the amount of the judgment. The bond must be supported by a surety or sureties approved by the judge. The bond must be payable to the appellee and must be conditioned on the appellant's prosecution of its appeal to effect and payment of any judgment and all costs rendered against it on appeal.

(c) *Cash Deposit in Lieu of Bond.* In lieu of filing a bond, an appellant may deposit with the clerk of the court cash in the amount required of the bond. The deposit must be payable to the appellee and must be conditioned on the appellant's prosecution of its appeal to effect and payment of any judgment and all costs rendered against it on appeal.

(d) *Statement of Inability to Afford Payment of Court Costs.*

(1) Filing. An appellant who cannot furnish a bond or pay a cash deposit in the amount required may instead file a Statement of Inability to Afford Payment of Court Costs. The Statement must be on the form approved by the Supreme Court or include the information required by the Court-approved for and may be the same one that was filed with the petition.

(2) Contest. The Statement may be contested as provided in Rule 502.3(d) within 7 days after the opposing party receives notice that the Statement was filed.

(3) Appeal If Contest Sustained. If the contest is sustained, the appellant may appeal that decision by filing notice with the justice court within 7 days of that court's written order. The justice court must then forward all related documents to the county court for resolution. The county court must set the matter for hearing within 1 4 days and hear

the contest de novo, as if there had been no previous hearing, and if the appeal is granted, must direct the justice court to transmit to the clerk of the county court the transcript, records, and papers of the case, as provided in these rules.

(4) If No Appeal or If Appeal Overruled. If the appellant does not appeal the ruling sustaining the contest, or if the county court denies the appeal, the appellant may, within five days, post an appeal bond or make a cash deposit in compliance with this rule.

(e) *Notice to Other Parties Required.* If a Statement of Inability to Afford Payment of Court Costs is filed, the court must provide notice to all other parties that the statement was filed no later than the next business day. Within 7 days of filing a bond or making a cash deposit, an appellant must serve written notice of the appeal on all other parties using a method approved under Rule 501.4.

(f) *No Default on Appeal Without Compliance With Rule.* The county court to which an appeal is taken must not render default judgment against any party without first determining that the appellant has fully complied with this rule.

(g) *No Dismissal of Appeal Without Opportunity for Correction.* An appeal must not be dismissed for defects or irregularities in procedure, either of form or substance, without allowing the appellant, after 7 days' notice from the court, the opportunity to correct such defect.

(h) *Appeal Perfected.* An appeal is perfected when a bond, cash deposit, or Statement of Inability to Afford Payment of Court Costs is filed in accordance with this rule.

(i) *Costs.* The appellant must pay the costs on appeal to a county court in accordance with Rule 1 43a.

(Amended by Tex. Sup. Ct. Misc. Docket No. 16-9122, eff. Sept. 1, 2016.)

[Statement of Inability to Afford Payment of Court Costs as provided in Tex. Sup. Ct. Misc. Docket No. 16-9122, eff. Sept. 1, 2016 and applies to any contest of, or challenge to, a claim of inability to afford payment of court costs that is pending on September 1, 2016.]

RULE 506.2. RECORD ON APPEAL.

When an appeal has been perfected from the justice court, the judge must immediately send to the clerk of the county court a certified copy of all docket entries, a certified copy of the bill of costs, and the original papers in the case.

RULE 506.3. TRIAL DE NOVO.

The case must be tried de novo in the county court. A trial de novo is a new trial in which the entire case is presented as if there had been no previous trial.

RULE 506.4. WRIT OF CERTIORARI.

(a) *Application.* Except in eviction cases, after final judgment in a case tried in justice court, a party may apply to the county court for a writ of certiorari.

(b) *Grounds.* An application must be granted only if it contains a sworn statement setting forth facts showing that either:

(1) the justice court did not have jurisdiction; or

(2) the final determination of the suit worked an injustice to the applicant that was not caused by the applicant's own inexcusable neglect.

(c) *Bond, Cash Deposit, or Sworn Statement of Indigency to Pay Required.* If the application is granted, a writ of certiorari must not issue until the applicant has filed a bond, made a cash deposit, or filed a Statement of Inability to Afford Payment of Court Costs that complies with Rule 145.

(d) *Time for Filing.* An application for writ of certiorari must be filed within 90 days after the date the final judgment is signed.

(e) *Contents of Writ.* The writ of certiorari must command the justice court to immediately make and certify a copy of the entries in the case on the docket, and immediately transmit the transcript of the proceedings in the justice court, together with the original papers and a bill of costs, to the proper court.

(f) *Clerk to Issue Writ and Citation.* When the application is granted and the bond, cash deposit, or sworn Statement of Inability to Afford Payment of Court Costs has been filed, the clerk must issue a writ of certiorari to the justice court and citation to the adverse party.

(g) *Stay of Proceedings.* When the writ of certiorari is served on the justice court, the court must stay further proceedings on the judgment and comply with the writ.

(h) *Cause Docketed.* The action must be docketed in the name of the original plaintiff, as plaintiff, and of the original defendant, as defendant.

(i) *Motion to Dismiss.* Within 30 days after the service of citation on the writ of certiorari, the adverse party may move to dismiss the certiorari for want of sufficient cause appearing in the affidavit, or for want of sufficient bond. If the certiorari is dismissed, the judgment must direct the justice court to proceed with the execution of the judgment below.

(j) *Amendment of Bond or Oath.* The affidavit or bond may be amended at the discretion of the court in which it is filed.

(k) *Trial De Novo.* The case must be tried de novo in the county court and judgment must be rendered as in cases appealed from justice courts. A trial de novo is a new trial in which the entire case is presented as if there had been no previous trial.

(Adopted by Order Feb 12, 2013 and Order April 15, 2013, eff. Aug. 31, 2013. Amended by Tex. Sup. Ct. Misc. Docket No. 16-9122, eff. Sept. 1, 2016.)

Rules of Civil Procedure 500-510 govern cases filed on or after August 31 , 2013, and cases pending on August 31 , 2013, except to the extent that in the opinion of the court their application in a case pending on August 31 , 2013, would not be feasible or would work injustice, in which event the formerly applicable procedure applies. An action taken before August 31 , 2013, in a case pending on August 31, 2013, that was done pursuant to any previously applicable procedure must be treated as valid. Where citation or other process was issued or served prior to August 31, 2013 , in compliance with any previously applicable procedure, the party served has the time provided for under the previously applicable procedure to answer or otherwise respond.

[Statement of Inability to Afford Payment of Court Costs as provided in Tex. Sup. Ct. Misc. Docket No. 16-9122, eff. Sept. 1, 2016 and applies to any contest of, or challenge to, a claim of inability to afford payment of court costs that is pending on September 1, 2016.]

RULE 507. ADMINISTRATIVE RULES FOR JUDGES AND COURT PERSONNEL.

RULE 507.1. PLENARY POWER.

A justice court loses plenary power over a case when an appeal is perfected or if no appeal is perfected, 2 1 days after the later of the date judgment is signed or the date a motion to set aside, motion to reinstate, or motion for new trial, if any, is denied.

RULE 507.2. FORMS.

The court may provide forms to enable a party to file documents that comply with these rules. No party may be forced to use the court's forms.

RULE 507.3. DOCKET AND OTHER RECORDS.

(a) *Docket.* Each judge must keep a civil docket in a permanent record containing the following information:
  (1) the title of all suits commenced before the court;
  (2) the date when the first process was issued against the defendant, when returnable, and the nature of that process;
  (3) the date when the parties, or either of them, appeared before the court, either with or without a citation;
  (4) a description of the petition and any documents filed with the petition;
  (5) every adjournment, stating at whose request and to what time;
  (6) the date of the trial, stating whether the same was by a jury or by the judge;
  (7) the verdict of the jury, if any;
  (8) the judgment signed by the judge and the date the judgment was signed;
  (9) all applications for setting aside judgments or granting new trials and the orders of the judge thereon, with the date;
  (10) the date of issuing execution, to whom directed and delivered, and the amount of debt, damages and costs and, when any execution is returned, the date of the return and the manner in which it was executed; and
  (11) all stays and appeals that may be taken, and the date when taken, the amount of the bond and the names of the sureties.

(b) *Other Records.* The judge must also keep copies of all documents filed; other dockets, books, and records as may be required by law or these rules; and a fee book in which all costs accruing in every suit commenced before the court are taxed.

(c) *Form of Records.* All records required to be kept under this rule may be maintained electronically.

RULE 507.4. ISSUANCE OF WRITS.

Every writ from the justice courts must be in writing and be issued and signed by the judge officially. The style thereof must be "The State of Texas." It must, except where otherwise specially provided by law or these rules, be directed to the person or party upon whom it is to be served, be made returnable to the court, and note the date of its issuance.

(Adopted by Order Feb 12, 2013 and Order April 15, 2013, eff. Aug. 31, 2013.)

Rules of Civil Procedure 500-510 govern cases filed on or after August 31 , 2013, and cases pending on August 31 , 2013, except to the extent that in the opinion of the court their application in a case pending on August 31 , 2013, would not be feasible or would work injustice, in which event the formerly applicable procedure applies. An action taken before August 31 , 2013, in a case pending on August 31, 2013, that was done pursuant to any previously applicable procedure must be treated as valid. Where citation or other process was issued or served prior to August 31, 2013 , in compliance with any previously applicable procedure, the party served has the time provided for under the previously applicable procedure to answer or otherwise respond.

RULE 508. DEBT CLAIM CASES.

RULE 508.1. APPLICATION.

Rule 508 applies to a claim for the recovery of a debt brought by an assignee of a claim, a financial institution, a debt collector or collection agency, or a person or entity primarily engaged in the business of lending money at interest.

RULE 508.2. PETITION.

(a) *Contents.* In addition to the information required by Rule 502.2, a petition filed in a lawsuit governed by this rule must contain the following information:

(1) Credit Accounts. In a claim based upon a credit card, revolving credit, or open account, the petition must state:

(A) the account name or credit card name;

(B) the account number (which may be masked);

(C) the date of issue or origination of the account, if known;

(D) the date of charge-off or breach of the account, if known;

(E) the amount owed as of a date certain; and

(F) whether the plaintiff seeks ongoing interest.

(2) Personal and Business Loans. In a claim based upon a promissory note or other promise to pay a specific amount as of a date certain, the petition must state:

(A) the date and amount of the original loan;

(B) whether the repayment of the debt was accelerated, if known;

(C) the date final payment was due;

(D) the amount due as of the final payment date;

(E) the amount owed as of a date certain; and

(F) whether plaintiff seeks ongoing interest.

(3) Ongoing Interest. If a plaintiff seeks ongoing interest, the petition must state:

(A) the effective interest rate claimed;

(B) whether the interest rate is based upon contract or statute; and

(C) the dollar amount of interest claimed as of a date certain.

(4) Assigned Debt. If the debt that is the subject of the claim has been assigned or transferred, the petition must state:

(A) that the debt claim has been transferred or assigned;

(B) the date of the transfer or assignment;

(C) the name of any prior holders of the debt; and

(D) the name or a description of the original creditor.

RULE 508.3. DEFAULT JUDGMENT.

(a) *Generally.* If the defendant does not file an answer to a claim by the answer date or otherwise appear in the case, the judge must promptly render a default judgment upon the plaintiffs proof of the amount of damages.

(b) *Proof of the Amount of Damages.*

(1) Evidence Must Be Served or Submitted. Evidence of plaintiff's damages must either be attached to the petition and served on the defendant or submitted to the court after defendant's failure to answer by the answer date.

(2) Form of Evidence. Evidence of plaintiff's damages may be offered in a sworn statement or in live testimony. The evidence offered may include documentary evidence.

(3) Establishment of the Amount of Damages. The amount of damages is established by evidence:

(A) that the account or loan was issued to the defendant and the defendant is obligated to pay it;

(B) that the account was closed or the defendant breached the terms of the account or loan agreement;

(C) of the amount due on the account or loan as of a date certain after all payment credits and offsets have been applied; and

(D) that the plaintiff owns the account or loan and, if applicable, how the plaintiff acquired the account or loan.

(4) Documentary Evidence Offered By Sworn Statement. Documentary evidence may be considered if it is attached to a sworn statement made by the plaintiff or its representative, a prior holder of the debt or its representative, or the original creditor or its representative, that attests to the following:

(A) the documents were kept in the regular course of business;

(B) it was the regular course of business for an employee or representative with knowledge of the act recorded to make the record or to transmit information to be included in such record;

(C) the documents were created at or near the time or reasonably soon thereafter; and

(D) the documents attached are the original or exact duplicates of the original.

(5) Consideration of Sworn Statement. A judge is not required to accept a sworn statement if the source of information or the method or circumstances of preparation indicate lack of trustworthiness. But a judge may not reject a sworn statement only because it is not made by the original creditor or because the documents attested to were created by a third party and subsequently incorporated into and relied upon by the business of the plaintiff.

(c) *Hearing.* The judge may enter a default judgment without a hearing if the plaintiff submits sufficient written evidence of its damages and should do so to avoid undue expense and delay. Otherwise, the plaintiff may request a default judgment hearing at which the plaintiff must appear, in person or by telephonic or electronic means, and prove its damages. If the plaintiff proves its damages, the judge must render judgment for the plaintiff in the amount proven. If the plaintiff is unable to prove its damages, the judge must render judgment in favor of the defendant.

(d) *Appearance.* If the defendant files an answer or otherwise appears in a case before a default judgment is signed by the judge, the judge must not render a default judgment and must set the case for trial.

(e) *Post-Answer Default.* If a defendant who has answered fails to appear for trial, the court may proceed to hear evidence on liability and damages and render judgment accordingly.

(Adopted by Order Feb 12, 2013 and Order April 15, 2013, eff. Aug. 31, 2013.)

Rules of Civil Procedure 500-510 govern cases filed on or after August 31 , 2013, and cases pending on August 31 , 2013, except to the extent that in the opinion of the court their application in a case pending on August 31 , 2013, would not be feasible or would work injustice, in which event the formerly applicable procedure applies. An action taken before August 31 , 2013, in a case pending on August 31, 2013, that was done pursuant to any previously applicable procedure must be treated as valid. Where citation or other process was issued or served prior to August 31, 2013 , in compliance with any previously applicable procedure, the party served has the time provided for under the previously applicable procedure to answer or otherwise respond.

RULE 509. REPAIR AND REMEDY CASES.

RULE 509.1. APPLICABILITY OF RULE.

Rule 509 applies to a lawsuit filed in a justice court by a residential tenant under Chapter 92, Subchapter B of the Texas Property Code to enforce the landlord' s duty to repair or remedy a condition materially affecting the physical health or safety of an ordinary tenant.

RULE 509.2. CONTENTS OF PETITION; COPIES; FORMS AND AMENDMENTS.

(a) *Contents of Petition.* The petition must be in writing and must include the following:

(1) the street address of the residential rental property;

(2) a statement indicating whether the tenant has received in writing the name and business street address of the landlord and landlord's management company;

(3) to the extent known and applicable, the name, business street address, and telephone number of the landlord and the landlord's management company, on-premises manager, and rent collector serving the residential rental property;

(4) for all notices the tenant gave to the landlord requesting that the condition be repaired or remedied:

(A) the date of the notice;

(B) the name of the person to whom the notice was given or the place where the notice was given;

(C) whether the tenant' s lease is in writing and requires written notice;

(D) whether the notice was in writing or oral;

(E) whether any written notice was given by certified mail, return receipt requested, or by registered mail; and

(F) whether the rent was current or had been timely tendered at the time notice was given;

(5) a description of the property condition materially affecting the physical health or safety of an ordinary tenant that the tenant seeks to have repaired or remedied;

(6) a statement of the relief requested by the tenant, including an order to repair or remedy a condition, a reduction in rent, actual damages, civil penalties, attorney's fees, and court costs;

(7) if the petition includes a request to reduce the rent:

(A) the amount of rent paid by the tenant, the amount of rent paid by the government, if known, the rental period, and when the rent is due; and

(B) the amount of the requested rent reduction and the date it should begin;

(8) a statement that the total relief requested does not exceed $ 1 0,000, excluding interest and court costs but including attorney's fees; and

(9) the tenant's name, address, and telephone number.

(b) *Copies.* The tenant must provide the court with copies of the petition and any attachments to the petition for service on the landlord.

(c) *Forms and Amendments.* A petition substantially in the form promulgated by the Supreme Court is sufficient. A suit may not be dismissed for a defect in the petition unless the tenant is given an opportunity to correct the defect and does not promptly correct it.

RULE 509.3. CITATION: ISSUANCE; APPEARANCE DATE; ANSWER.

(a) *Issuance.* When the tenant files a written petition with a justice court, the judge must immediately issue citation directed to the landlord, commanding the landlord to appear before such judge at the time and place named in the citation.

(b) *Appearance Date; Answer.* The appearance date on the citation must not be less than 10 days nor more than 21 days after the petition is filed. For purposes of this rule, the appearance date on the citation is the trial date. The landlord may, but is not required to, file a written answer on or before the appearance date.

RULE 509.4. SERVICE AND RETURN OF CITATION; ALTERNATIVE SERVICE OF CITATION.

(a) *Service and Return of Citation.* The sheriff, constable, or other person authorized by Rule 50 1 .2 who receives the citation must serve the citation by delivering a copy of it, along with a copy of the petition and any attachments, to the landlord at least 6 days before the appearance date. At least one day before the appearance date, the person serving the citation must file a return of service with the court that issued the citation. The citation must be issued, served, and returned in like manner as ordinary citations issued from a justice court.

(b) *Alternative Service of Citation.*

(1) If the petition does not include the landlord's name and business street address, or if, after making diligent efforts on at least two occasions, the officer or authorized person is unsuccessful in serving the citation on the landlord under (a), the officer or authorized person must serve the citation by delivering a copy of the citation, petition, and any attachments to:

(A) the landlord's management company if the tenant has received written notice of the name and business street address of the landlord's management company; or

(B) if (b)(I)(A) does not apply and the tenant has not received the landlord's name and business street address in writing, the landlord's authorized agent for service of process, which may be the landlord's management company, on-premise manager, or rent collector serving the residential rental property.

(2) If the officer or authorized person is unsuccessful in serving citation under (b)(1) after making diligent efforts on at least two occasions at either the business street address of the landlord's management company, if (b)(1)(A) applies, or at each available business street address of the landlord's authorized agent for service of process, if (b)(I)(B) applies, the officer or authorized person must execute and file in the justice court a sworn statement that the officer or authorized person made diligent efforts to serve the citation on at least two occasions at all available business street addresses of the landlord and, to the extent applicable, the landlord's management company, on-premises manager, and rent collector serving the residential rental property, providing the times, dates, and places of each attempted service. The judge may then authorize the officer or authorized person to serve citation by:

(A) delivering a copy of the citation, petition, and any attachments to someone over the age of 1 6 years, at any business street address listed in the petition, or, if nobody answers the door at a business street address, either placing the citation, petition, and any attachments through a door mail chute or slipping them under the front door, and if neither of these latter methods is practical, affixing the citation, petition, and any attachments to the front door or main entry to the business street address;

(B) within 24 hours of complying with (b)(2)(A), sending by first class mail a true copy of the citation, petition, and any attachments addressed to the landlord at the landlord's business street address provided in the petition; and

(C) noting on the return of the citation the date of delivery under (b)(2)(A) and the date of mailing under (b)(2)(B).

The delivery and mailing to the business street address under (b)(2)(A)-(B) must occur at least 6 days before the appearance date. At least one day before the appearance date, a return of service must be completed and filed in accordance with Rule 50 1 .3 with the court that issued the citation. It is not necessary for the tenant to request the alternative service authorized by this rule.

RULE 509.5. DOCKETING AND TRIAL; FAILURE TO APPEAR.

(a) *Docketing and Trial.* The case must be docketed and tried as other cases. The judge may develop the facts of the case in order to ensure justice.

(b) *Failure to Appear.*

(1) If the tenant appears at trial and the landlord has been duly served and fails to appear at trial, the judge may proceed to hear evidence. If the tenant establishes that the tenant is entitled to recover, the judge must render judgment against the landlord in accordance with the evidence.

(2) If the tenant fails to appear for trial, the judge may dismiss the lawsuit.

RULE 509.6. JUDGMENT: AMOUNT; FORM AND CONTENT; ISSUANCE AND SERVICE; FAILURE TO COMPLY.

(a) *Amount.* Judgment may be rendered against the landlord for failure to repair or remedy a condition at the residential rental property if the total judgment does not exceed $ 10,000, excluding interest and court costs but including attorney's fees. Any party who prevails in a lawsuit brought under these rules may recover the party's court costs and reasonable attorney's fees as allowed by law.

(b) *Form and Content.*

(1) The judgment must be in writing, signed, and dated and must include the names of the parties to the proceeding and the street address of the residential rental property where the condition is to be repaired or remedied.

(2) In the judgment, the judge may:

(A) order the landlord to take reasonable action to repair or remedy the condition;

(B) order a reduction in the tenant's rent, from the date of the first repair notice, in proportion to the reduced rental value resulting from the condition until the condition is repaired or remedied;

(C) award a civil penalty of one month's rent plus $500;

(D) award the tenant's actual damages; and

(E) award court costs and attorney's fees, excluding any attorney's fees for a claim for damages relating to a personal injury.

(3) If the judge orders the landlord to repair or remedy a condition, the judgment must include in reasonable detail the actions the landlord must take to repair or remedy the condition and the date when the repair or remedy must be completed.

(4) If the judge orders a reduction in the tenant's rent, the judgment must state:

(A) the amount of the rent the tenant must pay, if any;

(B) the frequency with which the tenant must pay the rent;

(C) the condition justifying the reduction of rent;

(D) the effective date of the order reducing rent;

(E) that the order reducing rent will terminate on the date the condition is repaired or remedied; and

(F) that on the day the condition is repaired or remedied, the landlord must give the tenant written notice, served in accordance with Rule 501.4, that the condition justifying the reduction of rent has been repaired or remedied and the rent will revert to the rent amount specified in the lease.

(c) *Issuance and Service.* The judge must issue the judgment. The judgment may be served on the landlord in open court or by any means provided in Rule 501 .4 at an address listed in the citation, the address listed on any answer, or such other address the landlord furnishes to the court in writing. Unless the judge serves the landlord in open court or by other means provided in Rule 50 1 .4, the sheriff, constable, or other authorized person who serves the landlord must promptly file a return of service in the justice court.

(d) *Failure to Comply.* If the landlord fails to comply with an order to repair or remedy a condition or reduce the tenant's rent, the failure is grounds for citing the landlord for contempt of court under Section 2 1 .002 of the Texas Government Code.

RULE 509.7. COUNTERCLAIMS.

Counterclaims and the joinder of suits against third parties are not permitted in suits under these rules. Compulsory counterclaims may be brought in a separate suit. Any potential causes of action, including a compulsory counterclaim, that are not asserted because of this rule are not precluded.

RULE 509.8. APPEAL: TIME AND MANNER; PERFECTION; EFFECT; COSTS; TRIAL ON APPEAL.

(a) *Time and Manner.* Either party may appeal the decision of the justice court to a statutory county court or, if there is no statutory county court with jurisdiction, a county court or district court with jurisdiction by filing a written notice of appeal with the justice court within 2 1 days after the date the judge signs the judgment. If the judgment is amended in any respect, any party has the right to appeal within 2 1 days after the date the judge signs the new judgment, in the same manner set out in this rule.

(b) *Perfection.* The posting of an appeal bond is not required for an appeal under this rule, and the appeal is considered perfected with the filing of a notice of appeal. Otherwise, the appeal is in the manner provided by law for appeal from a justice court.

(c) *Effect.* The timely filing of a notice of appeal stays the enforcement of any order to repair or remedy a condition or reduce the tenant's rent, as well as any other actions.

(d) *Costs.* The appellant must pay the costs on appeal to a county court in accordance with Rule 143a.

(e) *Trial on Appeal.* On appeal, the parties are entitled to a trial de novo. A trial de novo is a new trial in which the entire case is presented as if there had been no previous trial. Either party is entitled to trial by jury on timely request and payment of a fee, if required. An appeal of a judgment of a justice court under these rules takes precedence in the county court and may be held at any time after the eighth day after the date the transcript is filed in the county court.

RULE 509.9. EFFECT OF WRIT OF POSSESSION.

If a judgment for the landlord for possession of the residential rental property becomes final, any order to repair or remedy a condition is vacated and unenforceable.

(Adopted by Order Feb 12, 2013 and Order April 15, 2013, eff. Aug. 31, 2013.)

Rules of Civil Procedure 500-510 govern cases filed on or after August 31 , 2013, and cases pending on August 31 , 2013, except to the extent that in the opinion of the court their application in a case pending on August 31 , 2013, would not be feasible or would work injustice, in which event the formerly applicable procedure applies. An action taken before August 31 , 2013, in a case pending on August 31, 2013, that was done pursuant to any previously applicable procedure must be treated as valid. Where citation or other process was issued or served prior to August 31, 2013 , in compliance with any previously applicable procedure, the party served has the time provided for under the previously applicable procedure to answer or otherwise respond.

RULE 510. EVICTION CASES.

RULE 510.1. APPLICATION.

Rule 510 applies to a lawsuit to recover possession of real property under Chapter 24 of the Texas Property Code.

RULE 510.2. COMPUTATION OF TIME FOR EVICTION CASES.

Rule 500.5 applies to the computation of time in an eviction case. But if a document is filed by mail and not received by the court by the due date, the court may take any action authorized by these rules, including issuing a writ of possession requiring a tenant to leave the property.

RULE 510.3. PETITION.

(a) *Contents.* In addition to the requirements of Rule 502.2, a petition in an eviction case must be sworn to by the plaintiff and must contain:

(1) a description, including the address, if any, of the premises that the plaintiff seeks possession of;

(2) a description of the facts and the grounds for eviction;

(3) a description of when and how notice to vacate was delivered;

(4) the total amount of rent due and unpaid at the time of filing, if any; and

(5) a statement that attorney fees are being sought, if applicable.

(b) *Where Filed.* The petition must be filed in the precinct where the premises is located. If it is filed elsewhere, the judge must dismiss the case. The plaintiff will not be entitled to a refund of the filing fee, but will be refunded any service fees paid if the case is dismissed before service is attempted.

(c) *Defendants Named.* If the eviction is based on a written residential lease, the plaintiff must name as defendants all tenants obligated under the lease residing at the premises whom plaintiff seeks to evict. No judgment or writ of possession may issue or be executed against a tenant obligated under a lease and residing at the premises who is not named in the petition and served with citation.

(d) *Claim for Rent.* A claim for rent within the justice court's jurisdiction may be asserted in
an eviction case.

(e) *Only Issue.* The court must adjudicate the right to actual possession and not title.

Counterclaims and the joinder of suits against third parties are not permitted in eviction cases. A claim that is not asserted because of this rule can be brought in a separate suit in a court of proper jurisdiction.

RULE 510.4. ISSUANCE, SERVICE, AND RETURN OF CITATION.

(a) *Issuance of Citation; Contents.* When a petition is filed, the court must immediately issue citation directed to each defendant. The citation must:

(1) be styled "The State of Texas";
(2) be signed by the clerk under seal of court or by the judge;
(3) contain the name, location, and address of the court;
(4) state the date of filing of the petition;
(5) state the date of issuance of the citation;
(6) state the file number and names of parties;
(7) state the plaintiffs cause of action and relief sought;
(8) be directed to the defendant;
(9) state the name and address of attorney for plaintiff, or if the plaintiff does not have an attorney, the address of plaintiff;
(10) state the day the defendant must appear in person for trial at the court issuing citation, which must not be less than I 0 days nor more than 21 days after the petition is filed;
(11) notify the defendant that if the defendant fails to appear in person for trial, judgment by default may be rendered for the relief demanded in the petition;
(12) inform the defendant that, upon timely request and payment of a jury fee no later than 3 days before the day set for trial, the case will be heard by a jury;
(13) contain all warnings required by Chapter 24 of the Texas Property Code; and
(14) include the following statement: "For further information, consult Part V of the Texas Rules of Civil Procedure, which is available online and also at the court listed on this citation."

(b) *Service and Return of Citation.*
  (1) Who May Serve. Unless otherwise authorized by written court order, citation must be served by a sheriff or constable.
  (2) Method of Service. The constable, sheriff, or other person authorized by written court order receiving the citation must execute it by delivering a copy with a copy of the petition attached to the defendant, or by leaving a copy with a copy of the petition attached with some person, other than the plaintiff, over the age of 1 6 years, at the defendant's usual place of residence, at least 6 days before the day set for trial.
  (3) Return of Service. At least one day before the day set for trial, the constable, sheriff, or other person authorized by written court order must complete and file a return of service in accordance with Rule 501.3 with the court that issued the citation.

(c) *Alternative Service by Delivery to the Premises.*
  (1) When Allowed. The citation may be served by delivery to the premises if:
    (A) the constable, sheriff, or other person authorized by written court order is unsuccessful in serving the citation under (b);
    (B) the petition lists all home and work addresses of the defendant that are known to the plaintiff and states that the plaintiff knows of no other home or work addresses of the defendant in the county where the premises are located; and
    (C) the constable, sheriff, or other person authorized files a sworn statement that it has made diligent efforts to serve such citation on at least two occasions at all addresses of the defendant in the county where the premises are located, stating the times and places of attempted service.
  (2) Authorization. The judge must promptly consider a sworn statement filed under (1)(C) and determine whether citation may be served by delivery to the premises. The plaintiff is not required to make a request or motion for alternative service.
  (3) Method. If the judge authorizes service by delivery to the premises, the constable, sheriff, or other person authorized by written court order must, at least 6 days before the day set for trial:
    (A) deliver a copy of the citation with a copy of the petition attached to the premises by placing it through a door mail chute or slipping it under the front door; if neither method is possible, the officer may securely affix the citation to the front door or main entry to the premises; and
    (B) deposit in the mail a copy of the citation with a copy of the petition attached, addressed to defendant at the premises and sent by first class mail.
  (4) Notation on Return. The constable, sheriff, or other person authorized by written court order must note on the return of service the date the citation was delivered and the date it was deposited in the mail.

RULE 510.5. REQUEST FOR IMMEDIATE POSSESSION.

(a) *Immediate Possession Bond.* The plaintiff may, at the time of filing the petition or at any time prior to final judgment, file a possession bond to be approved by the judge in the probable amount of costs of suit and damages that may result to defendant in the event that the suit has been improperly instituted, and conditioned that the plaintiff will pay defendant all such costs and damages that are adjudged against plaintiff.

(b) *Notice to Defendant.* The court must notify a defendant that the plaintiff has filed a possession bond. The notice must be served in the same manner as service of citation and must inform the defendant that if the defendant does not file an answer or appear for trial, and judgment for possession is granted by default, an officer will place the plaintiff in possession of the property on or after the 7th day after the date defendant is served with the notice.

(c) *Time for Issuance and Execution of Writ.* If judgment for possession is rendered by default and a possession bond has been filed, approved, and served under this rule, a writ of possession must issue immediately upon demand and payment of any required fees. The writ must not be executed before the 7th day after the date defendant is served with notice under (b).

(d) *Effect of Appearance.* If the defendant files an answer or appears at trial, no writ of possession may issue before the 6th day after the date a judgment for possession is signed or the day following the deadline for the defendant to appeal the judgment, whichever is later.

RULE 510.6. TRIAL DATE; ANSWER; DEFAULT JUDGMENT.

(a) *Trial Date and Answer.* The defendant must appear for trial on the day set for trial in the citation. The defendant may, but is not required to, file a written answer with the court on or before the day set for trial in the citation.

(b) *Default Judgment.* If the defendant fails to appear at trial and fails to file an answer before the case is called for trial, and proof of service has been filed in accordance with Rule 510.4, the allegations of the complaint must be taken as admitted and judgment by default rendered accordingly. If a defendant who has answered fails to appear for trial, the court may proceed to hear evidence and render judgment accordingly.

(c) *Notice of Default.* When a default judgment is signed, the clerk must immediately mail written notice of the judgment by first class mail to the defendant at the address of the premises.

RULE 510.7. TRIAL.

(a) *Trial.* An eviction case will be docketed and tried as other cases. No eviction trial may be held less than 6 days after service under Rule 5 1 0.4 has been obtained.

(b) *Jury Trial Demanded.* Any party may file a written demand for trial by jury by making a request to the court at least 3 days before the trial date. The demand must be accompanied by payment of a jury fee or by filing a Statement of Inability to Afford Payment of Court Costs. If a jury is demanded by either party, the jury will be impaneled and sworn as in other cases; and after hearing the evidence it will return its verdict in favor of the plaintiff or the defendant. If no jury is timely demanded by either party, the judge will try the case.

(c) *Limit on Postponement.* Trial in an eviction case must not be postponed for more than 7 days total unless both parties agree in writing.

(Amended by Tex. Sup. Ct. Misc. Docket No. 16-9122, eff. Sept. 1, 2016.)

[Statement of Inability to Afford Payment of Court Costs as provided in Tex. Sup. Ct. Misc. Docket No. 16-9122, eff. Sept. 1, 2016 and applies to any contest of, or challenge to, a claim of inability to afford payment of court costs that is pending on September 1, 2016.]

RULE 510.8. JUDGMENT; WRIT; NO NEW TRIAL.

(a) *Judgment Upon Jury Verdict.* Where a jury has returned a verdict, the judge may render judgment on the verdict or, if the verdict is contrary to the law or the evidence, judgment notwithstanding the verdict.

(b) *Judgment for Plaintiff.* If the judgment is in favor of the plaintiff, the judge must render judgment for plaintiff or possession of the premises, costs, delinquent rent as of the date of entry of judgment, if any, and attorney fees if recoverable by law.

(c) *Judgment for Defendant.* If the judgment is in favor of the defendant, the judge must render judgment for defendant against the plaintiff for costs and attorney fees if recoverable by law.

(d) *Writ.* If the judgment or verdict is in favor of the plaintiff, the judge must award a writ of possession upon demand of the plaintiff and payment of any required fees.

   (1) Time to Issue. Except as provided by Rule 510.5, no writ of possession may issue before the 6th day after the date a judgment for possession is signed or the day following the deadline for the defendant to appeal the judgment, whichever is later. A writ of possession may not issue more than 60 days after a judgment for possession is signed. For good cause, the court may extend the deadline for issuance to 90 days after a judgment for possession is signed.

   (2) Time to Execute. A writ of possession may not be executed after the 90th day after a judgment for possession is signed.

   (3) Effect of Appeal. A writ of possession must not issue if an appeal is perfected and, if applicable, rent is paid into the registry, as required by these rules.

(e) *No Motion For New Trial.* No motion for new trial may be filed.

RULE 510.9. APPEAL.

(a) *How Taken; Time.* A party may appeal a judgment in an eviction case by filing a bond, making a cash deposit, or Statement of Inability to Afford Payment of Court Costs with the justice court within 5 days after the judgment is signed.

(b) *Amount of Security; Terms.* The justice court judge will set the amount of the bond or cash deposit to include the items enumerated in Rule 510.11. The bond or cash deposit must be payable to the appellee and must be conditioned on the appellant's prosecution of its appeal to effect and payment of any judgment and all costs rendered against it on appeal.

(c) *Statement of Inability to Afford Payment of Court Costs.*

(1) Filing. An appellant who cannot furnish a bond or pay a cash deposit in the amount required may instead Statement of Inability to Afford Payment of Court Costs. The Statement must be on a form approved by the Supreme Court or include the information required by the Court-approved form.

(2) Contest. The Statement may be contested as provided in Rule 502.3(d) within 5 days after the opposing party receives notice that the Statement was filed.

(3) Appeal If Contest Sustained. If the contest is sustained, the appellant may appeal that decision by filing notice with the justice court within 5 days of that court's written order. The justice court must then forward all related documents to the county court for resolution. The county court must set the matter for hearing within 5 days and hear the contest de novo, as if there had been no previous hearing, and, if the appeal is granted, must direct the justice court to transmit to the clerk of the county court the transcript, records, and papers of the case, as provided in these rules.

(4) If No Appeal or If Appeal Overruled. If the appellant does not appeal the ruling sustaining the contest, or if the county court denies the appeal, the appellant may, within one business day, post an appeal bond or make a cash deposit in compliance with this rule.

(5) Payment of Rent in Nonpayment of Rent Appeals.

(A) Notice. If a defendant appeals an eviction for nonpayment of rent by filing a Statement of Inability to Afford Payment of Court Costs, the justice court must provide to the defendant a written notice at the time the Statement is filed that contains the following information in bold or conspicuous type:

(i) the amount of the initial deposit of rent, equal to one rental period's rent under the terms of the rental agreement, that the defendant must pay into the justice court registry;

(ii) whether the initial deposit must be paid in cash, cashier's check, or money order, and to whom the cashier's check or money order, if applicable, must be made payable;

(iii) the calendar date by which the initial deposit must be paid into the justice court registry, which must be within 5 days of the date the Statement of Inability to Afford Payment of Court Costs is filed; and

(iv) a statement that failure to pay the required amount into the justice court registry by the required date may result in the court issuing a writ of possession without hearing.

(B) Defendant May Remain in Possession. A defendant who appeals an eviction for nonpayment of rent by filing a Statement of Inability to Afford Payment of Court Costs is entitled to stay in possession of the premises during the pendency of the appeal by complying with the following procedure:

(i) Within 5 days of the date that the defendant files a Statement of Inability to Afford Payment of Court Costs, it must pay into the justice court registry the amount set forth in the notice provided at the time the defendant filed the Statement. If the defendant was provided with notice and fails to pay the designated amount into the justice court registry within 5 days, and the transcript has not been transmitted to the county clerk, the plaintiff is entitled, upon request and payment of the applicable fee, to a writ of possession, which the justice court must issue immediately and without hearing.

(ii) During the appeal process as rent becomes due under the rental agreement, the defendant must pay the designated amount into the county court registry within 5 days of the rental due date under the terms of the rental agreement.

(iii) If a government agency is responsible for all or a portion of the rent, the defendant must pay only that portion of the rent determined by the justice court to be paid during appeal. Either party may contest the portion of the rent that the justice court determines must be paid into the county court registry by filing a contest within 5 days after the judgment is signed. If a contest is filed, the justice court must notify the parties and hold a hearing on the contest within 5 days. If the defendant objects to the justice court's ruling at the hearing, the defendant is required to pay only the portion claimed to be owed by the defendant until the issue is tried in county court.

(iv) If the defendant fails to pay the designated amount into the court registry within the time limits prescribed by these rules, the plaintiff may file a sworn motion that the defendant is in default in county court. The plaintiff must notify the defendant of the motion and the hearing date. Upon a showing that the defendant is in default, the court must issue a writ of possession.

(v) The plaintiff may withdraw any or all rent in the county court registry upon sworn motion and hearing, prior to final determination of the case, showing just cause; dismissal of the appeal; or order of the court after final hearing.

(vi) All hearings and motions under this subparagraph are entitled to precedence in the county court.

(d) *Notice to Other Parties Required.* If a Statement of Inability to Afford Payment of Court Costs is filed, the court must provide notice to all other parties that the Statement was filed no later than the next business day. Within 5 days of filing a bond or making a cash deposit, an appellant must serve written notice of the appeal on all other parties using a method approved under Rule 501.4.

(e) *No Default on Appeal Without Compliance With Rule.* No judgment may be taken by default against the adverse party in the court to which the case has been appealed without first showing substantial compliance with this rule.

(f) *Appeal Perfected.* An appeal is perfected when a bond, cash deposit, or Statement of Inability to Afford Payment of Court Costs is filed in accordance with this rule.

(Amended by Tex. Sup. Ct. Misc. Docket No. 16-9122, eff. Sept. 1, 2016.)

[Statement of Inability to Afford Payment of Court Costs as provided in Tex. Sup. Ct. Misc. Docket No. 16-9122, eff. Sept. 1, 2016 and applies to any contest of, or challenge to, a claim of inability to afford payment of court costs that is pending on September 1, 2016.]

RULE 510.10. RECORD ON APPEAL; DOCKETING; TRIAL DE NOVO.

(a) *Preparation and Transmission of Record.* Unless otherwise provided by law or these rules, when an appeal has been perfected, the judge must stay all further proceedings on the judgment and must immediately send to the clerk of the county court a certified copy of all docket entries, a certified copy of the bill of costs, and the original papers in the case together with any money in the court registry, including sums tendered pursuant to Rule 510.9(c)(5)(B).

(b) *Docketing; Notice.* The county clerk must docket the case and must immediately notify the parties of the date of receipt of the transcript and the docket number of the case. The notice must advise the defendant that it must file a written answer in the county court within 8 days if one was not filed in the justice court.

(c) *Trial De Novo.* The case must be tried de novo in the county court. A trial de novo is a new trial in which the entire case is presented as if there had been no previous trial. The trial, as well as any hearings and motions, is entitled to precedence in the county court.

RULE 510.11. DAMAGES ON APPEAL.

On the trial of the case in the county court the appellant or appellee will be permitted to plead, prove and recover his damages, if any, suffered for withholding or defending possession of the premises during the pendency of the appeal. Damages may include but are not limited to loss of rentals during the pendency of the appeal and attorney fees in the justice and county courts provided, as to attorney fees, that the requirements of Section 24.006 of the Texas Property Code have been met. Only the party prevailing in the county court will be entitled to recover damages against the adverse party. The prevailing party will also be entitled to recover court costs and to recover against the sureties on the appeal bond in cases where the adverse party has executed an appeal bond.

RULE 510.12. JUDGMENT BY DEFAULT ON APPEAL.

An eviction case appealed to county court will be subject to trial at any time after the expiration of 8 days after the date the transcript is filed in the county court. If the defendant has filed a written answer in the justice court, it must be taken to constitute his appearance and answer in the county court and may be amended as in other cases. If the defendant made no answer in writing in the justice court and fails to file a written answer within 8 days after the transcript is filed in the county court, the allegations of the complaint may be taken as admitted and judgment by default may be entered accordingly.

RULE 510.13. WRIT OF POSSESSION ON APPEAL.

The writ of possession, or execution, or both, will be issued by the clerk of the county court according to the judgment rendered, and the same will be executed by the sheriff or constable, as in other cases. The judgment of the county court may not be stayed unless within 10 days from the judgment the appellant files a supersedeas bond in an amount set by the county court pursuant to Section 24.007 of the Texas Property Code.

(Adopted by Order Feb 12, 2013 and Order April 15, 2013, eff. Aug. 31, 2013.)

Rules of Civil Procedure 500-510 govern cases filed on or after August 31 , 2013, and cases pending on August 31 , 2013, except to the extent that in the opinion of the court their application in a case pending on August 31 , 2013, would not be feasible or would work injustice, in which event the formerly applicable procedure applies. An action taken before August 31 , 2013, in a case pending on August 31, 2013, that was done pursuant to any previously applicable procedure must be treated as valid. Where citation or other process was issued or served prior to August 31, 2013 , in compliance with any previously applicable procedure, the party served has the time provided for under the previously applicable procedure to answer or otherwise respond.

PART V.
IN RULES OF PRACTICE JUSTICE COURTS

RULES 523-591. [Repealed.]

(Repealed by Order Feb 12, 2013 and Order April 15, 2013, eff. Aug. 31, 2013.)

PART VI.
RULES RELATING TO ANCILLARY PROCEEDINGS

SECTION 1.
ATTACHMENT

RULE 592. APPLICATION FOR WRIT OF ATTACHMENT AND ORDER.

Either at the commencement of a suit or at any time during its progress the plaintiff may file an application for the issuance of a writ of attachment. Such application shall be supported by affidavits of the plaintiff, his agent, his attorney, or other persons having knowledge of relevant facts. The application shall comply with all statutory requirements and shall state the grounds for issuing the writ and the specific facts relied upon by the plaintiff to warrant the required findings by the court. The writ shall not be quashed because two or more grounds are stated conjunctively or disjunctively. The application and any affidavits shall be made on personal knowledge and shall set forth such facts as would be admissible in evidence; provided that facts may be stated based upon information and belief if the grounds of such belief are specifically stated.

No writ shall issue except upon written order of the court after a hearing, which may be ex parte. The court, in its order granting the application, shall make specific findings of facts to support the statutory grounds found to exist, and shall specify the maximum value of property that may be attached, and the amount of bond required of plaintiff, and, further shall command that the attached property be kept safe and preserved subject to further orders of the court. Such bond shall be in an amount which, in the opinion of the court, will adequately compensate the defendant in the event plaintiff fails to prosecute his suit to effect, and to pay all damages and costs which may be adjudged against him for wrongfully suing out the writ of attachment. The court shall further find in its order the amount of bond required of defendant to replevy, which, unless the defendant chooses to exercise his option as provided in Rule 599, shall be the amount of plaintiff's claim, one year's accrual of interest if allowed by law on the claim, and the estimated costs of court. The order may direct the issuance of several writs at the same time, or in succession, to be sent to different counties.

(Amended by Order July 11, 1977, eff. Jan. 1, 1978.)

RULE 592a. BOND FOR ATTACHMENT.

No writ of attachment shall issue until the party applying therefor has filed with the officer authorized to issue such writ a bond payable to the defendant in the amount fixed by the court's order, with sufficient surety or sureties as provided by statute to be approved by such officer, conditioned that the plaintiff will prosecute his suit to effect and pay to the extent of the penal amount of the bond all damages and costs as may be adjudged against him for wrongfully suing out such writ of attachment.

After notice to the opposite party, either before or after the issuance of the writ, the defendant or plaintiff may file a motion to increase or reduce the amount of such bond, or to question the sufficiency of the sureties thereon, in the court in which such suit is pending. Upon hearing, the court shall enter its order with respect to such bond and sufficiency of the sureties.

(Added July 11, 1977, eff. Jan. 1, 1978.)

RULE 592b. FORM OF ATTACHMENT BOND.

The following form of bond may be used:

"The State of Texas,
"County of ________________,

"We, the undersigned, ____________________________ as principal, and ____________________________ and ______________________ as sureties, acknowledge ourselves bound to pay to C.D. the sum of ______________________ dollars, conditioned that the above bound plaintiff in attachment against the said C.D., defendant, will prosecute his said suit to effect, and that he will pay all such damages and costs to the extent of the penal amount of this bond as shall be adjudged against him for wrongfully suing out such attachment. Witness our hands this _______ day of ________, 19__."

(Renumbered from Rule 592 and amended by Order July 11, 1977, eff. Jan. 1, 1978.)

RULE 593. REQUISITES FOR WRIT.

A writ of attachment shall be directed to the sheriff or any constable within the State of Texas. It shall command him to attach and hold, unless replevied, subject to the further order of the court, so much of the property of the defendant, of a reasonable value in approximately the amount fixed by the court, as shall be found within his county.

(Amended by Order July 11, 1977, eff. Jan. 1, 1978.)

RULE 594. FORM OF WRIT.

The following form of writ may be issued:

"The State of Texas. "To the Sheriff or any Constable of any County of the State of Texas, greeting:
"We command you that you attach forthwith so much of the property of C.D., if it be found in your county, repleviable on security, as shall be of value sufficient to make the sum of ________ dollars, and the probable costs of suit, to satisfy the demand of A.B., and that you keep and secure in your hands the property so attached, unless replevied, that the same may be liable to further proceedings thereon to be had before our court in ____________, County of _________________. You will true return make of this writ on or before 10 a.m. of Monday, the _______ day of _______, 19__, showing how you have executed the same."

RULE 595. SEVERAL WRITS.

Several writs of attachment may, at the option of the plaintiff, be issued at the same time, or in succession and sent to different counties, until sufficient property shall be attached to satisfy the writ.

RULE 596. DELIVERY OF WRIT.

The writ of attachment shall be dated and tested as other writs, and may be delivered to the sheriff or constable by the officer issuing it, or he may deliver it to the plaintiff, his agent or attorney, for that purpose.

RULE 597. DUTY OF OFFICER.

The sheriff or constable receiving the writ shall immediately proceed to execute the same by levying upon so much of the property of the defendant subject to the writ, and found within his county, as may be sufficient to satisfy the command of the writ.

RULE 598. LEVY, HOW MADE.

The writ of attachment shall be levied in the same manner as is, or may be, the writ of execution upon similar property.

RULE 598a. SERVICE OF WRIT ON DEFENDANT.

The defendant shall be served in any manner prescribed for service of citation, or as provided in Rule 21a, with a copy of the writ of attachment, the application, accompanying affidavits, and orders of the court as soon as practicable following the levy of the writ. There shall be prominently displayed on the face of the copy of the writ served on the defendant, in ten-point type and in a manner calculated to advise a reasonably attentive person of its contents, the following:

"To ________________________, Defendant:
"You are hereby notified that certain properties alleged to be owned by you have been attached. If you claim any rights in such property, you are advised:
"YOU HAVE A RIGHT TO REGAIN POSSESSION OF THE PROPERTY BY FILING A REPLEVY BOND. YOU HAVE A RIGHT TO SEEK TO REGAIN POSSESSION OF THE PROPERTY BY FILING WITH THE COURT A MOTION TO DISSOLVE THIS WRIT."

(Added by Order July 11, 1977, eff. Jan. 1, 1978.)

RULE 599. DEFENDANT MAY REPLEVY.

At any time before judgment, should the attached property not have been previously claimed or sold, the defendant may replevy the same, or any part thereof, or the proceeds from the sale of the property if it has been sold under order of the court, by giving bond with sufficient surety or sureties as provided by statute, to be approved by the officer who levied the writ, payable to plaintiff, in the amount fixed by the court's order, or, at the defendant's option, for the value of the property sought to be replevied (to be estimated by the officer), plus one year's interest thereon at the legal rate from the date of the bond, conditioned that the defendant shall satisfy, to the extent of the penal amount of the bond, any judgment which may be rendered against him in such action.

On reasonable notice to the opposing party (which may be less than three days) either party shall have the right to prompt judicial review of the amount of bond required, denial of bond, sufficiency of sureties, and estimated value of the property, by the court which authorized issuance of the writ. The court's determination may be made upon the basis of affidavits, if uncontroverted, setting forth such facts as would be admissible in evidence; otherwise, the parties shall submit evidence. The court shall forthwith enter its order either approving or modifying the requirements of the officer or of the court's prior order, and such order of the court shall supersede and control with respect to such matters.

On reasonable notice to the opposing party (which may be less than three days) the defendant shall have the right to move the court for a substitution of property, of equal value as that attached, for the property attached. Provided that there has been located sufficient property of the defendants to satisfy the order of attachment, the court may authorize substitution of one or more items of defendant's property for all or for part of the property attached. The court shall first make findings as to the value of the property to be substituted. If property is substituted, the property released from attachment shall be delivered to defendant, if such property is personal property, and all liens upon such property from the original order of attachment or modification thereof shall be terminated. Attachment of substituted property shall be deemed to have existed from the date of levy on the original property attached, and no property on which liens have become affixed since the date of levy on the original property may be substituted.

(Amended by Order July 11, 1977, eff. Jan. 1, 1978.)

RULE 600. SALE OF PERISHABLE PROPERTY.

Whenever personal property which has been attached shall not have been claimed or replevied, the judge, or justice of the peace, out of whose court the writ was issued, may, either in term time or in vacation, order the same to be sold, when it shall be made to appear that such property is in danger of serious and immediate waste or decay, or that the keeping of the same until the trial will necessarily be attended with such expense or deterioration in value as greatly to lessen the amount likely to be realized therefrom.

RULE 601. TO PROTECT INTERESTS.

In determining whether the property attached is perishable, and the necessity or advantage of ordering a sale thereof, the judge or justice of the peace may act upon affidavits in writing or oral testimony, and may by a preliminary order entered of record, with or without notice to the parties as the urgency of the case in his opinion requires, direct the sheriff or constable to sell such property at public auction for cash, and thereupon the officer shall sell it accordingly.

RULE 602. BOND OF APPLICANT FOR SALE.

If the application for an order of sale be filed by any person or party other than the defendant from whose possession the property was taken by levy, the court shall not grant such order unless the applicant shall file with such court a bond payable to such defendant with two or more good and sufficient sureties, to be approved by said court, conditioned that they will be responsible to the defendant for such damages as he may sustain in case such sale be illegally and unjustly applied for, or be illegally and unjustly made.

RULE 603. PROCEDURE FOR SALE.

Such sale of attached perishable personal property shall be conducted in the same manner as sales of personal property under execution; provided, however, that the time of the sale, and at the time of advertisement thereof, may be fixed by the judge or justice of the peace at a time earlier than ten days according to the exigency of the case, and in such event notice thereof shall be given in such manner as directed by the order.

RULE 604. RETURN OF SALE.

The officer making such sale of perishable property shall promptly pay the proceeds of such sale to the clerk of such court or justice of the peace, as the case may be, and shall make written return of the order of sale signed by him officially, stating the time and place of the sale, the name of the purchaser, and the amount of money received, with an itemized account of the expenses attending the sale. Such return shall be filed with the papers of the case.

RULE 605. JUDGE MAY MAKE NECESSARY ORDERS.

When the perishable personal property levied on under the attachment writ has not been claimed or replevied, the judge or justice of the peace may make such orders, either in term time or vacation, as may be necessary for its preservation or use.

RULE 606. RETURN OF WRIT.

The officer executing the writ of attachment shall return the writ, with his action endorsed thereon, or attached thereto, signed by him officially, to the court from which it issued, at or before 10 o'clock a.m. of the Monday next after the expiration of fifteen days from the date of issuance of the writ. Such return shall describe the property attached with sufficient certainty to identify it, and state when the same was attached, and whether any personal property attached remains still in his hands, and, if not, the disposition made of the same. When property has been replevied he shall deliver the replevy bond to the clerk or justice of the peace to be filed with the papers of the cause.

RULE 607. REPORT OF DISPOSITION OF PROPERTY.

When the property levied on is claimed, replevied or sold, or otherwise disposed of after the writ has been returned, the officer having the custody of the same shall immediately make a report in writing, signed by him officially, to the clerk, or justice of the peace, as the case may be, showing such disposition of the property. Such report shall be filed among the papers of the cause.

RULE 608. DISSOLUTION OR MODIFICATION OF WRIT OF ATTACHMENT.

A defendant whose property has been attached or any intervening party who claims an interest in such property, may by sworn written motion, seek to vacate, dissolve, or modify the writ, and the order directing its issuance, for any grounds or cause, extrinsic or intrinsic. Such motion shall admit or deny each finding of the order directing the issuance of the writ except where the movant is unable to admit or deny the finding, in which case movant shall set forth the reasons why he cannot admit or deny. Unless the parties agree to an extension of time, the motion shall be heard promptly, after reasonable notice to the plaintiff (which may be less than three days), and the issue shall be determined not later than ten days after the motion is filed. The filing of the motion shall stay any further proceedings under the writ, except for any orders concerning the care, preservation, or sale of perishable property, until a hearing is had and the issue is determined. The writ shall be dissolved unless at such hearing, the plaintiff shall prove the grounds relied upon for its issuance, but the court may modify its previous order granting the writ and the writ issued pursuant thereto. The movant shall, however, have the burden to prove that the reasonable value of the property attached exceeds the amount necessary to secure the debt, interest for one year, and probable costs. He shall also have the burden to prove the facts to justify substitution of property.

The court's determination may be made upon the basis of affidavits, if uncontroverted, setting forth such facts as would be admissible in evidence; otherwise, the parties shall submit evidence. The court may make all such orders, including orders concerning the care, preservation, or disposition of the property (or the proceeds therefrom if the same has been sold), as justice may require. If the movant has given a replevy bond, an order to vacate or dissolve the writ shall vacate the replevy bond and discharge the sureties thereon, and if the court modifies its order or the writ issued pursuant thereto, it shall make such further orders with respect to the bond as may be consistent with its modification.

(Amended by Order July 11, 1977, eff. Jan. 1, 1978.)

RULE 609. AMENDMENT.

Clerical errors in the affidavit, bond, or writ of attachment, or the officer's return thereof, may upon application in writing to the judge or justice of the court in which the suit is filed, and after notice to the opponent, be amended in such manner and on such terms as the judge or justice shall authorize by an order entered in the minutes of the court or noted on the docket of the justice of the peace, provided the amendment does not change or add to the grounds of such attachment as stated in the affidavit, and provided such amendment appears to the judge or justice to be in furtherance of justice.

SECTION 2.
DISTRESS WARRANT

RULE 610. APPLICATION FOR DISTRESS WARRANT AND ORDER.

Either at the commencement of a suit or at any time during its progress the plaintiff may file an application for the issuance of a distress warrant with the justice of the peace. Such application may be supported by affidavits of the plaintiff, his agent, his attorney, or other persons having knowledge of relevant facts, but shall include a statement that the amount sued for is rent, or advances described by statute, or shall produce a writing signed by the tenant to that effect, and shall further swear that such warrant is not sued out for the purpose of vexing and harassing the defendant. The application shall comply with all statutory requirements and shall state the grounds for issuing the warrant and the specific facts relied upon by the plaintiff to warrant the required findings by the justice of the peace. The warrant shall not be quashed because two or more grounds are stated conjunctively or disjunctively. The application and any affidavits shall be made on personal knowledge and shall set forth such facts as would be admissible in evidence provided that facts may be stated based upon information and belief if the grounds of such belief are specifically stated.

No warrant shall issue before final judgment except on written order of the justice of the peace after a hearing, which may be ex parte. Such warrant shall be made returnable to a court having jurisdiction of the amount in controversy. The justice of the peace in his order granting the application shall make specific findings of fact to support the statutory grounds found to exist, and shall specify the maximum value of property that may be seized, and the amount of bond required of plaintiff, and, further shall command that property be kept safe and preserved subject to further orders of the court having jurisdiction. Such bond shall be in an amount which, in the opinion of the court, shall adequately compensate defendant in the event plaintiff fails to prosecute his suit to effect, and pay all damages and costs as shall be adjudged against him for wrongfully suing out the warrant. The justice of the peace shall further find in his order the amount of bond required to replevy, which, unless the defendant chooses to exercise his option as provided in Rule 614, shall be the amount of plaintiff's claim, one year's accrual of interest if allowed by law on the claim, and the estimated costs of court. The order may direct the issuance of several warrants at the same time, or in succession, to be sent to different counties.

(Added by Order June 10, 1980, eff. Jan. 1, 1981.)

RULE 611. BOND FOR DISTRESS WARRANT.

No distress warrant shall issue before final judgment until the party applying therefor has filed with the justice of the peace authorized to issue such warrant a bond payable to the defendant in an amount approved by the justice of the peace, with sufficient surety or sureties as provided by statute, conditioned that the plaintiff will prosecute his suit to effect and pay all damages and costs as may be adjudged against him for wrongfully suing out such warrant.

After notice to the opposite party, either before or after the issuance of the warrant, the defendant or plaintiff may file a motion to increase or reduce the amount of such bond, or to question the sufficiency of the sureties thereon, in a court having jurisdiction of the subject matter. Upon hearing, the court shall enter its order with respect to such bond and sufficiency of the sureties.

(Added by Order June 10, 1980, eff. Jan. 1, 1981.)

RULE 612. REQUISITES FOR WARRANT.

A distress warrant shall be directed to the sheriff or any constable within the State of Texas. It shall command him to attach and hold, unless replevied, subject to the further orders of the court having jurisdiction, so much of the property of the defendant, not exempt by statute, of reasonable value in approximately the amount fixed by the justice of the peace, as shall be found within his county.

(Added by Order June 10, 1980, eff. Jan. 1, 1981.)

RULE 613. SERVICE OF WARRANT ON DEFENDANT.

The defendant shall be served in any manner prescribed for service of citation, or as provided in Rule 21a, with a copy of the distress warrant, the application, accompanying affidavits, and orders of the justice of the peace as soon as practicable following the levy of the warrant. There shall be prominently displayed on the face of the copy of the warrant served on the defendant, in 10-point type and in a manner calculated to advise a reasonably attentive person of its contents, the following:

To _________________, Defendant:

You are hereby notified that certain properties alleged to be owned by you have been seized. If you claim any rights in such property, you are advised: "YOU HAVE A RIGHT TO REGAIN POSSESSION OF THE PROPERTY BY FILING A REPLEVY BOND. YOU HAVE A RIGHT TO SEEK TO REGAIN POSSESSION OF THE PROPERTY BY FILING WITH THE COURT A MOTION TO DISSOLVE THIS WARRANT."

(Added by Order June 10, 1980, eff. Jan. 1, 1981.)

RULE 614. DEFENDANT MAY REPLEVY.

At any time before judgment, should the seized property not have been previously claimed or sold, the defendant may replevy the same, or any part thereof, or the proceeds from the sale of the property if it has been sold under order of the court, by giving bond with sufficient surety or sureties as provided by statute, to be approved by a court having jurisdiction of the amount in controversy payable to plaintiff in double the amount of the plaintiff's debt, or, at the defendant's option for not less than the value of the property sought to be replevied, plus one year's interest thereon at the legal rate from the date of the bond conditioned that the defendant shall satisfy to the extent of the penal amount of the bond any judgment which may be rendered against him in such action.

On reasonable notice to the opposing party (which may be less than three days) either party shall have the right to prompt judicial review of the amount of bond required, denial of bond, sufficiency of sureties and estimated value of the property, by a court having jurisdiction of the amount in controversy. The court's determination may be made upon the basis of affidavits if uncontroverted setting forth such facts as would be admissible in evidence, otherwise the parties shall submit evidence. The court shall forthwith enter its order either approving or modifying the requirements of the order of the justice of the peace, and such order of the court shall supersede and control with respect to such matters.

On reasonable notice to the opposing party (which may be less than three days) the defendant shall have the right to move the court for a substitution of property, of equal value as that attached, for the property seized. Provided that there has been located sufficient property of the defendant's to satisfy the order of seizure, the court may authorize substitution of one or more items of defendant's property for all or part of the property seized. The court shall first make findings as to the value of the property to be substituted. If property is substituted, the property released from seizure shall be delivered to defendant, if such property is personal property, and all liens upon such property from the original order of seizure or modification thereof shall be terminated. Seizure of substituted property shall be deemed to have existed from the date of levy on the original property seized, and no property on which liens have become affixed since the date of levy on the original property may be substituted.

(Added by Order June 10, 1980, eff. Jan. 1, 1981.)

RULE 614a. DISSOLUTION OR MODIFICATION OF DISTRESS WARRANT.

A defendant whose property has been seized or any intervening claimant who claims an interest in such property, may by sworn written motion, seek to vacate, dissolve, or modify the seizure, and the order directing its issuance, for any grounds or cause, extrinsic or intrinsic. Such motion shall admit or deny each finding of the order directing the issuance of the warrant except where the movant is unable to admit or deny the finding, in which case movant shall set forth the reasons why he cannot admit or deny. Unless the parties agree to an extension of time, the motion shall be heard promptly, after reasonable notice to the plaintiff (which may be less than three days), and the issue shall be determined not later than 10 days after the motion is filed. The filing of the motion shall stay any further proceedings under the warrant, except for any orders concerning the care, preservation, or sale of any perishable property, until a hearing is had, and the issue is determined. The warrant shall be dissolved unless, at such hearing, the plaintiff shall prove the specific facts alleged and the grounds relied upon for its issuance, but the court may modify the order of the justice of the peace granting the warrant and the warrant issued pursuant thereto. The movant shall however have the burden to prove that the reasonable value of the property seized exceeds the amount necessary to secure the debt, interest for one year, and probable costs. He shall also have the burden to prove the facts to justify substitution of property.

The court's determination may be made upon the basis of affidavits setting forth such facts as would be admissible in evidence, but additional evidence, if tendered by either party shall be received and considered. The court may make all such orders, including orders concerning the care, preservation, or disposition of the property (or the proceeds therefrom if the same has been sold), as justice may require. If the movant has given a replevy bond, an order to vacate or dissolve the warrant shall vacate the replevy bond and discharge the sureties thereon, and if the court modifies the order of the justice of the peace of the warrant issued pursuant thereto, it shall make such further orders with respect to the bond as may be consistent with its modification.

(Added by Order June 10, 1980, eff. Jan. 1, 1981.)

RULE 615. SALE OF PERISHABLE PROPERTY.

Whenever personal property which has been levied on under a distress warrant shall not have been claimed or replevied, the judge, or justice of the peace, to whose court such writ is made returnable may, either in term time or in vacation, order the same to be sold, when it shall be made to appear that such property is in danger of serious and immediate waste or decay, or that the keeping of the same until the trial will necessarily be attended with such expense or deterioration in value as greatly to lessen the amount likely to be realized therefrom.

RULE 616. TO PROTECT INTERESTS.

In determining whether the property levied upon is perishable, and the necessity or advantage of ordering a sale thereof, the judge or justice of the peace may act upon affidavits in writing or oral testimony, and may by a preliminary order entered of record with or without notice to the parties as the urgency of the case in his opinion requires, direct the sheriff or constable to sell such property at public auction for cash, and thereupon the sheriff or constable shall sell it accordingly. If the application for an order of sale be filed by any person or party other than the defendant from whose possession the property was taken by levy, the court shall not grant such order, unless the applicant shall file with such court a bond payable to such defendant, with two or more good and sufficient sureties, to be approved by said court, conditioned that they will be responsible to the defendant for such damages as he may sustain in case such sale be illegally and unjustly applied for, or be illegally and unjustly made.

RULE 617. PROCEDURE FOR SALE.

Such sale of perishable personal property shall be conducted in the same manner as sales of personal property under execution; provided, however, that the time of the sale, and the time of advertisement thereof, may be fixed by the judge or justice of the peace at a time earlier than ten days, according to the exigency of the case, and in such event notice thereof shall be given in such manner as directed by the order.

RULE 618. RETURN OF SALE.

The officer making such sale of perishable property shall promptly pay the proceeds of such sale to the clerk of such court or to the justice of the peace, as the case may be, and shall make written return of the order of sale, signed by him officially, stating the time and place of the sale, the name of the purchaser, and the amount of money received, with an itemized account of the expenses attending the sale. Such return shall be filed with the papers of the case.

RULE 619. CITATION FOR DEFENDANT.

The justice at the time he issues the warrant shall issue a citation to the defendant requiring him to answer before such justice at the first day of the next succeeding term of court, stating the time and place of holding the same, if he has jurisdiction to finally try the cause, and upon its being returned served, to proceed to judgment as in ordinary cases; and, if he has not such jurisdiction, the citation shall require the defendant to answer before the court to which the warrant was made returnable at or before ten o'clock a.m. of the Monday next after the expiration of twenty days from the date of service thereof, stating the place of holding the court, and shall be returned with the other papers to such court. If the defendant has removed from the county without service, the proper officer shall state this fact in his return on the citation; and the court shall proceed to try the case ex parte, and may enter judgment.

RULE 620. PETITION.

When the warrant is made returnable to the district or county court, the plaintiff shall file his petition within ten days from the date of the issuance of the writ.

SECTION 3.
EXECUTIONS

RULE 621. ENFORCEMENT OF JUDGMENT.

The judgments of the district, county, and justice courts shall be enforced by execution or other appropriate process. Such execution or other process shall be returnable in thirty, sixty, or ninety days as requested by the plaintiff, his agent or attorney.

RULE 621a. DISCOVERY AND ENFORCEMENT OF JUDGMENT.

At any time after rendition of judgment, and so long as said judgment has not been suspended by a supersedeas bond or by order of a proper court and has not become dormant as provided by Article 3773, V.A.T.S., the successful party may, for the purpose of obtaining information to aid in the enforcement of such judgment, initiate and maintain in the trial court in the same suit in which said judgment was rendered any discovery proceeding authorized by these rules for pre-trial matters. Also, at any time after rendition of judgment, either party may, for the purpose of obtaining information relevant to motions allowed by Texas Rules of Appellate Procedure 47 and 49 initiate and maintain in the trial court in the same suit in which said judgment was rendered any discovery proceeding authorized by these rules for pre-trial matters. The rules governing and related to such pre-trial discovery proceedings shall apply in like manner to discovery proceedings after judgment. The rights herein granted to the parties shall inure to their successors or assignees, in whole or in part. Judicial supervision of such discovery proceedings after judgment shall be the same as that provided by law or these rules for pre-trial discovery and proceedings insofar as applicable.

(Added by Order July 21, 1970, eff. Jan. 1, 1971. Amended by Order July 15, 1987, eff. Jan. 1, 1988.)

RULE 622. EXECUTION.

An execution is a process of the court from which it is issued. The clerk of the district or county court or the justice of the peace, as the case may be, shall tax the costs in every case in which a final judgment has been rendered and shall issue execution to enforce such judgment and collect such costs. The execution and subsequent executions shall not be addressed to a particular county, but shall be addressed to any sheriff or any constable within the State of Texas.

(Amended by Order Sept. 20, 1941, eff. Dec. 31, 1941.)

RULE 623. ON DEATH OF EXECUTOR.

When an executor, administrator, guardian or trustee of an express trust dies, or ceases to be such executor, administrator, guardian or trustee after judgment, execution shall issue on such judgment in the name of his successor, upon an affidavit of such death or termination being filed with the clerk of the court or the justice of the peace, as the case may be, together with the certificate of the appointment of such successor under the hand and seal of the clerk of the court wherein the appointment was made.

RULE 624. ON DEATH OF NOMINAL PLAINTIFF.

When a person in whose favor a judgment is rendered for the use of another dies after judgment, execution shall issue in the name of the party for whose use the suit was brought upon an affidavit of such death being filed with the clerk of the court or the justice of the peace.

RULE 625. ON MONEY OF DECEASED.

If a sole defendant dies after judgment for money against him, execution shall not issue thereon, but the judgment may be proved up and paid in due course of administration.

RULE 626. ON PROPERTY OF DECEASED.

In any case of judgment other than a money judgment, where the sole defendant, or one or more of several joint defendants, shall die after judgment, upon an affidavit of such death being filed with the clerk, together with the certificate of the appointment of a representative of such decedent under the hand and seal of the clerk of the court wherein such appointment was made, the proper process on such judgment shall issue against such representative.

RULE 627. TIME FOR ISSUANCE.

If no supersedeas bond or notice of appeal, as required of agencies exempt from filing bonds, has been filed and approved, the clerk of the court or justice of the peace shall issue the execution upon such judgment upon application of the successful party or his attorney after the expiration of thirty days from the time a final judgment is signed. If a timely motion for new trial or in arrest of judgment is filed, the clerk shall issue the execution upon the judgment on application of the party or his attorney after the expiration of thirty days from the time the order overruling the motion is signed or from the time the motion is overruled by operation of law.

(Amended by Order July 22, 1975, eff. Jan. 1, 1976; June 10, 1980, eff. Jan. 1, 1981; Dec. 5, 1983, eff. April 1, 1984.)

RULE 628. EXECUTION WITHIN THIRTY DAYS.

Such execution may be issued at any time before the thirtieth day upon the filing of an affidavit by the plaintiff in the judgment or his agent or attorney that the defendant is about to remove his personal property subject to execution by law out of the county, or is about to transfer or secrete such personal property for the purpose of defrauding his creditors.

(Amended by Order July 22, 1976, eff. Jan. 1, 1976.)

RULE 629. REQUISITES OF EXECUTION.

The style of the execution shall be "The State of Texas." It shall be directed to any sheriff or any constable within the State of Texas. It shall be signed by the clerk or justice officially, and bear the seal of the court, if issued out of the district or county court, and shall require the officer to execute it according to its terms, and to make the costs which have been adjudged against the defendant in execution and the further costs of executing the writ. It shall describe the judgment, stating the court in which, and the time when, rendered, and the names of the parties in whose favor and against whom the judgment was rendered. A correct copy of the bill of costs taxed against the defendant in execution shall be attached to the writ. It shall require the officer to return it within thirty, sixty, or ninety days, as directed by the plaintiff or his attorney.

(Amended by Order Sept. 20, 1941, eff. Dec. 2, 1941.)

RULE 630. EXECUTION ON JUDGMENT FOR MONEY.

When an execution is issued upon a judgment for a sum of money, or directing the payment simply of a sum of money, it must specify in the body thereof the sum recovered or directed to be paid and the sum actually due when it is issued and the rate of interest upon the sum due. It must require the officer to satisfy the judgment and costs out of the property of the judgment debtor subject to execution by law.

RULE 631. EXECUTION FOR SALE OF PARTICULAR PROPERTY.

An execution issued upon a judgment for the sale of particular estates or personal property or real estate, must particularly describe the property, and shall direct the officer to make the sale by previously giving the public notice of the time and place of sale required by law and these rules.

RULE 632. EXECUTION FOR DELIVERY OF CERTAIN PROPERTY.

An execution issued upon a judgment for the delivery of the possession of a chattel or personal property, or for the delivery of the possession of real property, shall particularly describe the property, and designate the party to whom the judgment awards the possession. The writ shall require the officer to deliver the possession of the property to the party entitled thereto.

RULE 633. EXECUTION FOR POSSESSION OR VALUE OF PERSONAL PROPERTY.

If the judgment be for the recovery of personal property or its value, the writ shall command the officer, in case a delivery thereof cannot be had, to levy and collect the value thereof for which the judgment was recovered, to be specified therein, out of any property of the party against whom judgment was rendered, liable to execution.

RULE 634. EXECUTION SUPERSEDED.

The clerk or justice of the peace shall immediately issue a writ of supersedeas suspending all further proceedings under any execution previously issued when a supersedeas bond is afterward filed and approved within the time prescribed by law or these rules.

RULE 635. STAY OF EXECUTION IN JUSTICE COURT.

At any time within ten days after the rendition of any judgment in a justice court, the justice may grant a stay of execution thereof for three months from the date of such judgment, if the person against whom such judgment was rendered shall, with one or more good and sufficient sureties, to be approved by the justice, appear before him and acknowledge themselves and each of them bound to the successful party in such judgment for the full amount thereof, with interest and costs, which acknowledgment shall be entered in writing on the docket, and signed by the persons binding themselves as sureties; provided, no such stay of execution shall be granted unless the party applying therefor shall first file an affidavit with the justice that he has not the money with which to pay such judgment, and that the enforcement of same by execution prior to three months would be a hardship upon him and would cause a sacrifice of his property which would not likely be caused should said execution be stayed. Such acknowledgment shall be entered by the justice on his docket and shall constitute a judgment against the defendant and such sureties, upon which execution shall issue in case the same is not paid on or before the expiration of such day.

RULE 636. INDORSEMENTS BY OFFICER.

The officer receiving the execution shall indorse thereon the exact hour and day when he received it. If he receives more than one on the same day against the same person he shall number them as received.

RULE 637. LEVY OF EXECUTION.

When an execution is delivered to an officer he shall proceed without delay to levy the same upon the property of the defendant found within his county not exempt from execution, unless otherwise directed by the plaintiff, his agent or attorney. The officer shall first call upon the defendant, if he can be found, or, if absent, upon his agent within the county, if known, to point out property to be levied upon, and the levy shall first be made upon the property designated by the defendant, or his agent. If in the opinion of the officer the property so designated will not sell for enough to satisfy the execution and costs of sale, he shall require an additional designation by the defendant. If no property be thus designated by the defendant, the officer shall levy the execution upon any property of the defendant subject to execution.

RULE 638. PROPERTY NOT TO BE DESIGNATED.

A defendant in execution shall not point out property which he has sold, mortgaged or conveyed in trust, or property exempt from forced sale.

RULE 639. LEVY.

In order to make a levy on real estate, it shall not be necessary for the officer to go upon the ground but it shall be sufficient for him to indorse such levy on the writ. Levy upon personal property is made by taking possession thereof, when the defendant in execution is entitled to the possession. Where the defendant in execution has an interest in personal property, but is not entitled to the possession thereof, a levy is made thereon by giving notice thereof to the person who is entitled to the possession, or one of them where there are several.

RULE 640. LEVY ON STOCK RUNNING AT LARGE.

A levy upon livestock running at large in a range, and which cannot be herded and penned without great inconvenience and expense, may be made by designating by reasonable estimate the number of animals and describing them by their marks and brands, or either; such levy shall be made in the presence of two or more credible persons, and notice thereof shall be given in writing to the owner or his herder or agent, if residing within the county and known to the officer.

RULE 641. LEVY ON SHARES OF STOCK.

A levy upon shares of stock of any corporation or joint stock company for which a certificate is outstanding is made by the officer seizing and taking possession of such certificate. Provided, however, that nothing herein shall be construed as restricting any rights granted under Section 8.317 of the Texas Uniform Commercial Code.

(Amended by Order Aug. 18, 1947, eff. Dec. 31, 1947; July 21, 1970, eff. Jan. 1, 1971.)

RULE 642. [REPEALED]

(Repealed by Order July 22, 1975, eff. Jan. 1, 1976.)

RULE 643. LEVY ON GOODS PLEDGED OR MORTGAGED.

Goods and chattels pledged, assigned or mortgaged as security for any debt or contract, may be levied upon and sold on execution against the person making the pledge, assignment or mortgage subject thereto; and the purchaser shall be entitled to the possession when it is held by the pledgee, assignee or mortgagee, on complying with the conditions of the pledge, assignment or mortgage.

RULE 644. MAY GIVE DELIVERY BOND.

Any personal property taken in execution may be returned to the defendant by the officer upon the delivery by the defendant to him of a bond, payable to the plaintiff, with two or more good and sufficient sureties, to be approved by the officer, conditioned that the property shall be delivered to the officer at the time and place named in the bond, to be sold according to law, or for the payment to the officer of a fair value thereof, which shall be stated in the bond.

RULE 645. PROPERTY MAY BE SOLD BY DEFENDANT.

Where property has been replevied, as provided in the preceding rule, the defendant may sell or dispose of the same, paying the officer the stipulated value thereof.

RULE 646. FORFEITED DELIVERY BOND.

In case of the non-delivery of the property according to the terms of the delivery bond, and nonpayment of the value thereof, the officer shall forthwith indorse the bond "Forfeited" and return the same to the clerk of the court or the justice of the peace from which the execution issued; whereupon, if the judgment remain unsatisfied in whole or in part, the clerk or justice shall issue execution against the principal debtor and the sureties on the bond for the amount due, not exceeding the stipulated value of the property, upon which execution no delivery bond shall be taken, which instruction shall be indorsed by the clerk or justice on the execution.

RULE 646a. SALE OF REAL PROPERTY.

Real property taken by virtue of any execution shall be sold at public auction, at the courthouse door of the county, unless the court orders that such sale be at the place where the real property is situated, on the first Tuesday of the month, between the hours of ten o'clock, a.m. and four o'clock, p.m.

(Added by Order July 26, 1960, eff. Jan. 1, 1961.)

RULE 647. NOTICE OF SALE OF REAL ESTATE.

The time and place of sale of real estate under execution, order of sale, or venditioni exponas, shall be advertised by the officer by having the notice thereof published in the English language once a week for three consecutive weeks preceding such sale, in some newspaper published in said county. The first of said publications shall appear not less than twenty days immediately preceding the day of sale. Said notice shall contain a statement of the authority by virtue of which the sale is to be made, the time of levy, and the time and place of sale, it shall also contain a brief description of the property to be sold, and shall give the number of acres, original survey, locality in the county, and the name by which the land is most generally known, but it shall not be necessary for it to contain field notes. Publishers of newspapers shall charge the legal rate of Two (2) Cents per word for the first insertion of such publication and One (1) Cent per word for such subsequent insertions, or such newspapers shall be entitled to charge for such publication at a rate equal to but not in excess of the published word or line rate of that newspaper for such class of advertising. If there be no newspaper published in the county, or none which will publish the notice of sale for the compensation herein fixed, the officer shall then post such notice in writing in three public places in the county, one of which shall be at the courthouse door of such county, for at least twenty days successively next before the day of sale. The officer making the levy shall give the defendant, or his attorney, written notice of such sale, either in person or by mail, which notice shall substantially conform to the foregoing requirements.

(Amended by Order Sept. 20, 1941, eff. Dec. 31, 1941.)

RULE 648. "COURTHOUSE DOOR" DEFINED.

By the term "courthouse door" of a county is meant either of the principal entrances to the house provided by the proper authority for the holding of the district court. If from any cause there is no such house, the door of the house where the district court was last held in that county shall be deemed to be the courthouse door. Where the courthouse, or house used by the court, has been destroyed by fire or other cause, and another has not been designated by the proper authority, the place where such house stood shall be deemed to be the courthouse door.

RULE 649. SALE OF PERSONAL PROPERTY.

Personal property levied on under execution shall be offered for sale on the premises where it is taken in execution, or at the courthouse door of the county, or at some other place if, owing to the nature of the property, it is more convenient to exhibit it to purchasers at such place. Personal property susceptible of being exhibited shall not be sold unless the same be present and subject to the view of those attending the sale, except shares of stock in joint stock or incorporated companies, and in cases where the defendant in execution has merely an interest without right to the exclusive possession in which case the interest of defendant may be sold and conveyed without the presence or delivery of the property. When a levy is made upon livestock running at large on the range, it is not necessary that such stock, or any part thereof, be present at the place of sale, and the purchaser at such sale is authorized to gather and pen such stock and select therefrom the number purchased by him.

RULE 650. NOTICE OF SALE OF PERSONAL PROPERTY.

Previous notice of the time and place of the sale of any personal property levied on under execution shall be given by posting notice thereof for ten days successively immediately prior to the day of sale at the courthouse door of any county and at the place where the sale is to be made.

RULE 651. WHEN EXECUTION NOT SATISFIED.

When the property levied upon does not sell for enough to satisfy the execution, the officer shall proceed anew, as in the first instance, to make the residue.

RULE 652. PURCHASER FAILING TO COMPLY.

If any person shall bid off property at any sale made by virtue of an execution, and shall fail to comply with the terms of the sale, he shall be liable to pay the plaintiff in execution twenty per cent on the value of the property thus bid off, besides costs, to be recovered on motion, five days notice of such motion being given to such purchaser; and should the property on a second sale bring less than on the former, he shall be liable to pay to the defendant in execution all loss which he sustains thereby, to be recovered on motion as above provided.

RULE 653. RESALE OF PROPERTY.

When the terms of the sale shall not be complied with by the bidder the levying officer shall proceed to sell the same property again on the same day, if there be sufficient time, but if not, he shall readvertise and sell the same as in the first instance.

RULE 654. RETURN OF EXECUTION.

The levying officer shall make due return of the execution, in writing and signed by him officially, stating concisely what such officer has done in pursuance of the requirements of the writ and of the law. The return shall be filed with the clerk of the court or the justice of the peace as the case may be. The execution shall be returned forthwith if satisfied by the collection of the money or if ordered by the plaintiff or his attorney indorsed thereon.

RULE 655. RETURN OF EXECUTION BY MAIL.

When an execution is placed in the hands of an officer of a county other than the one in which the judgment is rendered, return may be made by mail; but money cannot be thus sent except by direction of the party entitled to receive the same or his attorney of record.

RULE 656. EXECUTION DOCKET.

The clerk of each court shall keep an execution docket in which he shall enter a statement of all executions as they are issued by him, specifying the names of the parties, the amount of the judgment, the amount due thereon, the rate of interest when it exceeds six per cent, the costs, the date of issuing the execution, to whom delivered, and the return of the officer thereon, with the date of such return. Such docket entries shall be taken and deemed to be a record. The clerk shall keep an index and cross-index to the execution docket. When execution is in favor or against several persons, it shall be indexed in the name of each person. Any clerk who shall fail to keep said execution docket and index thereto, or shall neglect to make the entries therein, shall be liable upon his official bond to any person injured for the amount of damages sustained by such neglect.

SECTION 4.
GARNISHMENT

RULE 657. JUDGMENT FINAL FOR GARNISHMENT.

In the case mentioned in subsection 3, section 63.001, Civil Practice and Remedies Code, the judgment whether based upon a liquidated demand or an unliquidated demand, shall be deemed final and subsisting for the purpose of garnishment from and after the date it is signed, unless a supersedeas bond shall have been approved and filed in accordance with Texas Rule of Appellate Procedure 47.

(Amended by Order June 10, 1980, eff. Jan. 1, 1981; July 15, 1987, eff. Jan. 1, 1988.)

RULE 658. APPLICATION FOR WRIT OF GARNISHMENT AND ORDER.

Either at the commencement of a suit or at any time during its progress the plaintiff may file an application for a writ of garnishment. Such application shall be supported by affidavits of the plaintiff, his agent, his attorney, or other person having knowledge of relevant facts. The application shall comply with all statutory requirements and shall state the grounds for issuing the writ and the specific facts relied upon by the plaintiff to warrant the required findings by the court. The writ shall not be quashed because two or more grounds are stated conjunctively or disjunctively. The application and any affidavits shall be made on personal knowledge and shall set forth such facts as would be admissible in evidence; provided that facts may be stated based upon information and belief if the grounds of such belief are specifically stated.

No writ shall issue before final judgment except upon written order of the court after a hearing, which may be ex parte. The court in its order granting the application shall make specific findings of facts to support the statutory grounds found to exist, and shall specify the maximum value of property or indebtedness that may be garnished and the amount of bond required of plaintiff. Such bond shall be in an amount which, in the opinion of the court, shall adequately compensate defendant in the event plaintiff fails to prosecute his suit to effect, and pay all damages and costs as shall be adjudged against him for wrongfully suing out the writ of garnishment. The court shall further find in its order the amount of bond required of defendant to replevy, which, unless defendant exercises his option as provided under Rule 664, shall be the amount of plaintiff's claim, one year's accrual of interest if allowed by law on the claim, and the estimated costs of court. The order may direct the issuance of several writs at the same time, or in succession, to be sent to different counties.

(Amended by Order Aug. 18, 1947, eff. Dec. 31, 1947; July 11, 1977, eff. Jan. 1, 1978.)

RULE 658a. BOND FOR GARNISHMENT.

No writ of garnishment shall issue before final judgment until the party applying therefor has filed with the officer authorized to issue such writ a bond payable to the defendant in the amount fixed by the court's order, with sufficient surety or sureties as provided by statute, conditioned that the plaintiff will prosecute his suit to effect and pay to the extent of the penal amount of the bond all damages and costs as may be adjudged against him for wrongfully suing out such writ of garnishment.

After notice to the opposite party, either before or after the issuance of the writ, the defendant or plaintiff may file a motion to increase or reduce the amount of such bond, or to question the sufficiency of the sureties. Upon hearing, the court shall enter its order with respect to such bond and the sufficiency of the sureties.

Should it be determined from the garnishee's answer if such is not controverted that the garnishee is indebted to the defendant, or has in his hands effects belonging to the defendant, in an amount or value less than the amount of the debt claimed by the plaintiff, then after notice to the defendant the court in which such garnishment is pending upon hearing may reduce the required amount of such bond to double the sum of the garnishee's indebtedness to the defendant plus the value of the effects in his hands belonging to the defendant.

(Added by Order July 26, 1960, eff. Jan. 1, 1961. Amended by Order July 11, 1977, eff. Jan. 1, 1978.)

RULE 659. CASE DOCKETED.

When the foregoing requirements of these rules have been complied with, the judge, or clerk, or justice of the peace, as the case may be, shall docket the case in the name of the plaintiff as plaintiff and of the garnishee as defendant; and shall immediately issue a writ of garnishment directed to the garnishee commanding him to appear before the court out of which the same is issued at or before 10 o'clock a.m. of the Monday next following the expiration of twenty days from the date the writ was served, if the writ is issued out of the district or county court, or the Monday next after the expiration of ten days from the date the writ was served, if the writ is issued out of the justice court. The writ shall command the garnishee to answer under oath upon such return date what, if anything, he is indebted to the defendant, and was when the writ was served, and what effects, if any, of the defendant he has in his possession, and had when such writ was served, and what other persons, if any, within his knowledge, are indebted to the defendant or have effects belonging to him in their possession.

(Amended by Order Sept. 20, 1941, eff. Dec. 31, 1941; Aug. 18, 1947, eff. Dec. 31, 1947; July 11, 1977, eff. Jan. 1, 1978.)

RULE 660. [REPEALED]

(Repealed by Order Aug. 18, 1947, eff. Dec. 31, 1947.)

RULE 661. FORM OF WRIT.

The following form of writ may be used:

"The State of Texas.

"To E.F., Garnishee, greeting:

"Whereas, in the ________________ Court of ______________ County (if a justice court, state also the number of the precinct), in a certain cause wherein A.B. is plaintiff and C.D. is defendant, the plaintiff, claiming an indebtedness against the said C.D. of _________ dollars, besides interest and costs of suit, has applied for a writ of garnishment against you, E.F.; therefore you are hereby commanded to be and appear before said court at ________________ in said county (if the writ is issued from the county or district court, here proceed: 'at 10 o'clock a.m. on the Monday next following the expiration of twenty days from the date of service hereof.' If the writ is issued from a justice of the peace court, here proceed: 'at or before 10 o'clock a.m. on the Monday next after the expiration of ten days from the date of service hereof.' In either event, proceed as follows:) then and there to answer upon oath what, if anything, you are indebted to the said C.D., and were when this writ was served upon you, and what effects, if any, of the said C.D. you have in your possession, and had when this writ was served, and what other persons, if any, within your knowledge, are indebted to the said C.D. or have effects belonging to him in their possession. You are further commanded NOT to pay to defendant any debt or to deliver to him any effects, pending further order of this court. Herein fail not, but make due answer as the law directs."

(Amended by Order Sept. 20, 1941, eff. Dec. 31, 1941; Aug. 18, 1947 eff. Dec. 31, 1947: July 11, 1977. eff. Jan. 1, 1978.)

RULE 662. DELIVERY OF WRIT.

The writ of garnishment shall be dated and tested as other writs, and may be delivered to the sheriff or constable by the officer who issued it, or he may deliver it to the plaintiff, his agent or attorney, for that purpose.

RULE 663. EXECUTION AND RETURN OF WRIT.

The sheriff or constable receiving the writ of garnishment shall immediately proceed to execute the same by delivering a copy thereof to the garnishee, and shall make return thereof as of other citations.

RULE 663a. SERVICE OF WRIT ON DEFENDANT.

The defendant shall be served in any manner prescribed for service of citation or as provided in Rule 21a with a copy of the writ of garnishment, the application, accompanying affidavits and orders of the court as soon as practicable following the service of the writ. There shall be prominently displayed on the face of the copy of the writ served on the defendant, in ten-point type and in a manner calculated to advise a reasonably attentive person of its contents, the following:

"To ______________________, Defendant:

"You are hereby notified that certain properties alleged to be owned by you have been garnished. If you claim any rights in such property, you are advised:

"YOU HAVE A RIGHT TO REGAIN POSSESSION OF THE PROPERTY BY FILING A REPLEVY BOND. YOU HAVE A RIGHT TO SEEK TO REGAIN POSSESSION OF THE PROPERTY BY FILING WITH THE COURT A MOTION TO DISSOLVE THIS WRIT."

(Added by Order July 11, 1977, eff. Jan. 1, 1978.)

RULE 664. DEFENDANT MAY REPLEVY.

At any time before judgment, should the garnished property not have been previously claimed or sold, the defendant may replevy the same, or any part thereof, or the proceeds from the sale of the property if it has been sold under order of the court, by giving bond with sufficient surety or sureties as provided by statute, to be approved by the officer who levied the writ, payable to plaintiff, in the amount fixed by the court's order, or, at the defendant's option, for the value of the property or indebtedness sought to be replevied (to be estimated by the officer), plus one year's interest thereon at the legal rate from the date of the bond, conditioned that the defendant, garnishee, shall satisfy, to the extent of the penal amount of the bond, any judgment which may be rendered against him in such action.

On reasonable notice to the opposing party (which may be less than three days) either party shall have the right to prompt judicial review of the amount of bond required, denial of bond, sufficiency of sureties, and estimated value of the property, by the court which authorized issuance of the writ. The court's determination may be made upon the basis of affidavits, if uncontroverted, setting forth such facts as would be admissible in evidence; otherwise, the parties shall submit evidence. The court shall forthwith enter its order either approving or modifying the requirements of the officer or of the court's prior order, and such order of the court shall supersede and control with respect to such matters.

On reasonable notice to the opposing party (which may be less than three days) the defendant shall have the right to move the court for a substitution of property, of equal value as that garnished, for the property garnished. Provided that there has been located sufficient property of the defendant's to satisfy the order of garnishment, the court may authorize substitution of one or more items of defendant's property for all or for part of the property garnished. The court shall first make findings as to the value of the property to be substituted. If property is substituted, the property released from garnishment shall be delivered to defendant, if such property is personal property, and all liens upon such property from the original order of garnishment or modification thereof shall be terminated. Garnishment of substituted property shall be deemed to have existed from date of garnishment on the original property garnished, and no property on which liens have become affixed since the date of garnishment of the original property may be substituted.

(Amended by Order July 11, 1977, eff. Jan. 1, 1978.)

RULE 664a. DISSOLUTION OR MODIFICATION OF WRIT OF GARNISHMENT.

A defendant whose property or account has been garnished or any intervening party who claims an interest in such property or account, may by sworn written motion, seek to vacate, dissolve or modify the writ of garnishment, and the order directing its issuance, for any grounds or cause, extrinsic or intrinsic. Such motion shall admit or deny each finding of the order directing the issuance of the writ except where the movant is unable to admit or deny the finding, in which case movant shall set forth the reasons why he cannot admit or deny. Unless the parties agree to an extension of time, the motion shall be heard promptly, after reasonable notice to the plaintiff (which may be less than three days), and the issue shall be determined not later than ten days after the motion is filed. The filing of the motion shall stay any further proceedings under the writ, except for any orders concerning the care, preservation or sale of any perishable property, until a hearing is had, and the issue is determined. The writ shall be dissolved unless, at such hearing, the plaintiff shall prove the grounds relied upon for its issuance, but the court may modify its previous order granting the writ and the writ issued pursuant thereto. The movant shall, however, have the burden to prove that the reasonable value of the property garnished exceeds the amount necessary to secure the debt, interest for one year, and probable costs. He shall also have the burden to prove facts to justify substitution of property.

The court's determination may be made upon the basis of affidavits, if uncontroverted, setting forth such facts as would be admissible in evidence; otherwise, the parties shall submit evidence. The court may make all such orders including orders concerning the care, preservation or disposition of the property (or the proceeds therefrom if the same has been sold), as justice may require. If the movant has given a replevy bond, an order to vacate or dissolve the writ shall vacate the replevy bond and discharge the sureties thereon, and if the court modifies its order or the writ issued pursuant thereto, it shall make such further orders with respect to the bond as may be consistent with its modification.

(Added by Order July 11, 1977, eff. Jan. 1, 1978.)

RULE 665. ANSWER TO WRIT.

The answer of the garnishee shall be under oath, in writing and signed by him, and shall make true answers to the several matters inquired of in the writ of garnishment.

RULE 666. GARNISHEE DISCHARGED.

If it appears from the answer of the garnishee that he is not indebted to the defendant, and was not so indebted when the writ of garnishment was served upon him, and that he has not in his possession any effects of the defendant and had not when the writ was served, and if he has either denied that any other persons within his knowledge are indebted to the defendant or have in their possession effects belonging to the defendant, or else has named such persons, should the answer of the garnishee not be controverted as hereinafter provided, the court shall enter judgment discharging the garnishee.

(Amended by Order Aug. 18, 1947, eff. Dec. 31, 1947.)

RULE 667. JUDGMENT BY DEFAULT.

If the garnishee fails to file an answer to the writ of garnishment at or before the time directed in the writ, it shall be lawful for the court, at any time after judgment shall have been rendered against the defendant, and on or after appearance day, to render judgment by default, as in other civil cases, against such garnishee for the full amount of such judgment against the defendant together with all interest and costs that may have accrued in the main case and also in the garnishment proceedings. The answer of the garnishee may be filed as in any other civil case at any time before such default judgment is rendered.

RULE 668. JUDGMENT WHEN GARNISHEE IS INDEBTED.

Should it appear from the answer of the garnishee or should it be otherwise made to appear and be found by the court that the garnishee is indebted to the defendant in any amount, or was so indebted when the writ of garnishment was served, the court shall render judgment for the plaintiff against the garnishee for the amount so admitted or found to be due to the defendant from the garnishee, unless such amount is in excess of the amount of the plaintiff's judgment against the defendant with interest and costs, in which case, judgment shall be rendered against the garnishee for the full amount of the judgment already rendered against the defendant, together with interest and costs of the suit in the original case and also in the garnishment proceedings. If the garnishee fail or refuse to pay such judgment rendered against him, execution shall issue thereon in the same manner and under the same conditions as is or may be provided for the issuance of execution in other cases.

RULE 669. JUDGMENT FOR EFFECTS.

Should it appear from the garnishee's answer, or otherwise, that the garnishee has in his possession, or had when the writ was served, any effects of the defendant liable to execution, including any certificates of stock in any corporation or joint stock company, the court shall render a decree ordering sale of such effects under execution in satisfaction of plaintiff's judgment and directing the garnishee to deliver them, or so much thereof as shall be necessary to satisfy plaintiff's judgment, to the proper officer for that purpose.

(Amended by Order Aug. 18, 1947, eff. Dec. 31, 1947.)

RULE 670. REFUSAL TO DELIVER EFFECTS.

Should the garnishee adjudged to have effects of the defendant in his possession, as provided in the preceding rule, fail or refuse to deliver them to the sheriff or constable on such demand, the officer shall immediately make return of such failure or refusal, whereupon on motion of the plaintiff, the garnishee shall be cited to show cause upon a date to be fixed by the court why he should not be attached for contempt of court for such failure or refusal. If the garnishee fails to show some good and sufficient excuse for such failure or refusal, he shall be fined for such contempt and imprisoned until he shall deliver such effects.

RULE 671. [REPEALED]

(Repealed by Order Aug. 18, 1947, eff. Dec. 31, 1947.)

RULE 672. SALE OF EFFECTS.

The sale so ordered shall be conducted in all respects as other sales of personal property under execution; and the officer making such sale shall execute a transfer of such effects or interest to the purchaser, with a brief recital of the judgment of the court under which the same was sold.

(Amended by Order Aug. 18, 1947, eff. Dec. 31, 1947.)

RULE 673. MAY TRAVERSE ANSWER.

If the plaintiff should not be satisfied with the answer of any garnishee, he may controvert the same by his affidavit stating that he has good reason to believe, and does believe, that the answer of the garnishee is incorrect, stating in what particular he believes the same to be incorrect. The defendant may also, in like manner, controvert the answer of the garnishee.

RULE 674. TRIAL OF ISSUE.

If the garnishee whose answer is controverted, is a resident of the county in which the proceeding is pending, an issue shall be formed under the direction of the court and tried as in other cases.

RULE 675. DOCKET AND NOTICE.

The clerk of the court or the justice of the peace, on receiving certified copies filed in the county of the garnishee's residence under the provisions of the statutes, shall docket the case in the name of the plaintiff as plaintiff, and of the garnishee as defendant, and issue a notice to the garnishee, stating that his answer has been so controverted, and that such issue will stand for trial on the docket of such court. Such notice shall be directed to the garnishee, be dated and tested as other process from such court, and served by delivering a copy thereof to the garnishee. It shall be returnable, if issued from the district or county court, at ten o'clock a.m. of the Monday next after the expiration of twenty days from the date of its service; and if issued from the justice court, to the next term of such court convening after the expiration of twenty days after the service of such notice.

(Amended by Order Sept. 20, 1941, eff. Dec. 31, 1941.)

RULE 676. ISSUE TRIED AS IN OTHER CASES.

Upon the return of such notice served, an issue shall be formed under the direction of the court and tried as in other cases.

RULE 677. COSTS.

Where the garnishee is discharged upon his answer, the costs of the proceeding, including a reasonable compensation to the garnishee, shall be taxed against the plaintiff; where the answer of the garnishee has not been controverted and the garnishee is held thereon, such costs shall be taxed against the defendant and included in the execution provided for in this section; where the answer is contested, the costs shall abide the issue of such contest.

RULE 678. GARNISHEE DISCHARGED ON PROOF.

It shall be a sufficient answer to any claim of the defendant against the garnishee founded on an indebtedness of such garnishee, or on the possession by him of any effects, for the garnishee to show that such indebtedness has been paid, or such effects, including any certificates of stock in any incorporated or joint stock company, have been delivered to any sheriff or constable as provided for in Rule 669.

(Amended by Order Aug. 18, 1947, eff. Dec. 31, 1947.)

RULE 679. AMENDMENT.

Clerical errors in the affidavit, bond, or writ of garnishment or the officer's return thereof, may upon application in writing to the judge or justice of the court in which the suit is filed, and after notice to the opponent, be amended in such manner and on such terms as the judge or justice shall authorize by an order entered in the minutes of the court (or noted on the docket of the justice of the peace), provided such amendment appears to the judge or justice to be in furtherance of justice.

SECTION 5.
INJUNCTIONS

RULE 680. TEMPORARY RESTRAINING ORDER.

No temporary restraining order shall be granted without notice to the adverse party unless it clearly appears from specific facts shown by affidavit or by the verified complaint that immediate and irreparable injury, loss, or damage will result to the applicant before notice can be served and a hearing had thereon. Every temporary restraining order granted without notice shall be endorsed with the date and hour of issuance; shall be filed forthwith in the clerk's office and entered of record; shall define the injury and state why it is irreparable and why the order was granted without notice, and shall expire by its terms within such time after signing, not to exceed fourteen days, as the court fixes, unless within the time so fixed the order, for good cause shown, is extended for a like period or unless the party against whom the order is directed consents that it may be extended for a longer period. The reasons for the extension shall be entered of record. No more than one extension may be granted unless subsequent extensions are unopposed. In case a temporary restraining order is granted without notice, the application for a temporary injunction shall be set down for hearing at the earliest possible date and takes precedence of all matters except older matters of the same character; and when the application comes on for hearing the party who obtained the temporary restraining order shall proceed with the application for a temporary injunction and, if he does not do so, the court shall dissolve the temporary restraining order. On two days' notice to the party who obtained the temporary restraining order without notice or on such shorter notice to that party as the court may prescribe, the adverse party may appear and move its dissolution or modification and in that event the court shall proceed to hear and determine such motion as expeditiously as the ends of justice require.

Every restraining order shall include an order setting a certain date for hearing on the temporary or permanent injunction sought.

(Amended by Order Dec. 5, 1983, eff. April 1, 1984; July 15, 1987, eff. Jan. 1, 1988.)

RULE 681. TEMPORARY INJUNCTIONS: NOTICE.

No temporary injunction shall be issued without notice to the adverse party.

RULE 682. SWORN PETITION.

No writ of injunction shall be granted unless the applicant therefor shall present his petition to the judge verified by his affidavit and containing a plain and intelligible statement of the grounds for such relief.

(Amended by Order March 31, 1941, eff. Sept. 1, 1941.)

RULE 683. FORM AND SCOPE OF INJUNCTION OR RESTRAINING ORDER.

Every order granting an injunction and every restraining order shall set forth the reasons for its issuance, shall be specific in terms shall describe in reasonable detail and not by reference to the complaint or other document, the act or acts sought to be restrained; and is binding only upon the parties to the action, their officers, agents, servants, employees, and attorneys, and upon those persons in active concert or participation with them who receive actual notice of the order by personal service or otherwise.

Every order granting a temporary injunction shall include an order setting the cause for trial on the merits with respect to the ultimate relief sought. The appeal of a temporary injunction shall constitute no cause for delay of the trial.

(Amended by Order Dec. 5, 1983, eff. April 1, 1984.)

RULE 684. APPLICANT'S BOND.

In the order granting any temporary restraining order or temporary injunction, the court shall fix the amount of security to be given by the applicant. Before the issuance of the temporary restraining order or temporary injunction the applicant shall execute and file with the clerk a bond to the adverse party, with two or more good and sufficient sureties, to be approved by the clerk, in the sum fixed by the judge, conditioned that the applicant will abide the decision which may be made in the cause, and that he will pay all sums of money and costs that may be adjudged against him if the restraining order or temporary injunction shall be dissolved in whole or in part.

Where the temporary restraining order or temporary injunction is against the State, a municipality, a State agency, or a subdivision of the State in its governmental capacity, and is such that the State, municipality, State agency, or subdivision of the State in its governmental capacity, has no pecuniary interest in the suit and no monetary damages can be shown, the bond shall be allowed in the sum fixed by the judge, and the liability of the applicant shall be for its face amount if the restraining order or temporary injunction shall be dissolved in whole or in part. The discretion of the trial court in fixing the amount of the bond shall be subject to review. Provided that under equitable circumstances and for good cause shown by affidavit or otherwise the court rendering judgment on the bond may allow recovery for less than its full face amount, the action of the court to be subject to review.

(Amended by Order June 16, 1943, eff. Dec. 31, 1943; Oct. 12, 1949, eff. March 1, 1950; June 10, 1980, eff. Jan. 1, 1981.)

RULE 685. FILING AND DOCKETING.

Upon the grant of a temporary restraining order or an order fixing a time for hearing upon an application for a temporary injunction, the party to whom the same is granted shall file his petition therefor, together with the order of the judge, with the clerk of the proper court; and, if such orders do not pertain to a pending suit in said court, the cause shall be entered on the docket of the court in its regular order in the name of the party applying for the writ as plaintiff and of the opposite party as defendant.

RULE 686. CITATION.

Upon the filing of such petition and order not pertaining to a suit pending in the court, the clerk of such court shall issue a citation to the defendant as in other civil cases, which shall be served and returned in like manner as ordinary citations issued from said court; provided, however, that when a temporary restraining order is issued and is accompanied with a true copy of plaintiff's petition, it shall not be necessary for the citation in the original suit to be accompanied with a copy of plaintiffs petition, nor contain a statement of the nature of plaintiffs demand, but it shall be sufficient for said citation to refer to plaintiff's claim as set forth in a true copy of plaintiffs petition which accompanies the temporary restraining order; and provided further that the court may have a hearing upon an application for a temporary restraining order or temporary injunction at such time and upon such reasonable notice given in such manner as the court may direct.

(Amended by Order June 16, 1943, eff. Dec. 31, 1943; Aug. 18, 1947, eff. Dec. 31, 1947.)

RULE 687. REQUISITES OF WRIT.

The writ of injunction shall be sufficient if it contains substantially the following requisites:

(a) Its style shall be, "The State of Texas."

(b) It shall be directed to the person or persons enjoined.

(c) It must state the names of the parties to the proceedings, plaintiff and defendant, and the nature of the plaintiff's application, with the action of the judge thereon.

(d) It must command the person or persons to whom it is directed to desist and refrain from the commission or continuance of the act enjoined, or to obey and execute such order as the judge has seen proper to make.

(e) If it is a temporary restraining order, it shall state the day and time set for hearing, which shall not exceed fourteen days from the date of the court's order granting such temporary restraining order; but if it is a temporary injunction, issued after notice, it shall be made returnable at or before ten o'clock a.m. of the Monday next after the expiration of twenty days from the date of service thereof, as in the case of ordinary citations.

(f) It shall be dated and signed by the clerk officially and attested with the seal of his office and the date of its issuance must be indorsed thereon.

(Amended by Order April 24, 1990, eff. Sept. 1, 1990.)

RULE 688. CLERK TO ISSUE WRIT.

When the petition, order of the judge and bond have been filed, the clerk shall issue the temporary restraining order or temporary injunction, as the case may be, in conformity with the terms of the order, and deliver the same to the sheriff or any constable of the county of the residence of the person enjoined, or to the applicant, as the latter shall direct. If several persons are enjoined, residing in different counties, the clerk shall issue such additional copies of the writ as shall be requested by the applicant. The clerk must retain a copy of the temporary restraining order or temporary injunction in the court's file.

(Amended by Order Oct. 17, 2011, eff. Jan. 1, 2012; Order Dec. 12, 2011, eff. Jan. 1, 2012.)

RULE 689. SERVICE AND RETURN.

The officer receiving a writ of injunction shall indorse thereon the date of its receipt by him, and shall forthwith execute the same by delivering to the party enjoined a true copy thereof. The officer must complete and file a return in accordance with Rule 107.

(Amended by Order Oct. 17, 2011, eff. Jan. 1, 2012; Order Dec. 12, 2011, eff. Jan. 1, 2012.)

RULE 690. THE ANSWER.

The defendant to an injunction proceeding may answer as in other civil actions; but no injunction shall be dissolved before final hearing because of the denial of the material allegations of the plaintiff's petition, unless the answer denying the same is verified by the oath of the defendant.

RULE 691. BOND ON DISSOLUTION.

Upon the dissolution of an injunction restraining the collection of money, by an interlocutory order of the court or judge, made in term time or vacation, if the petition be continued over for trial, the court or judge shall require of the defendant in such injunction proceedings a bond, with two or more good and sufficient sureties, to be approved by the clerk of the court, payable to the complainant in double the amount of the sum enjoined, and conditioned to refund to the complainant the amount of money, interest and costs which may be collected of him in the suit or proceeding enjoined if such injunction is made perpetual on final hearing. If such injunction is so perpetuated, the court, on motion of the complainant, may enter judgment against the principal and sureties in such bond for such amount as may be shown to have been collected from such defendant.

RULE 692. DISOBEDIENCE.

Disobedience of an injunction may be punished by the court or judge, in term time or in vacation, as a contempt. In case of such disobedience, the complainant, his agent or attorney, may file in the court in which such injunction is pending or with the judge in vacation, his affidavit stating what person is guilty of such disobedience and describing the acts constituting the same; and thereupon the court or judge shall cause to be issued an attachment for such person, directed to the sheriff or any constable of any county, and requiring such officer to arrest the person therein named if found within his county and have him before the court or judge at the time and place named in such writ; or said court or judge may issue a show cause order, directing and requiring such person to appear on such date as may be designated and show cause why he should not be adjudged in contempt of court. On return of such attachment or show cause order, the judge shall proceed to hear proof; and if satisfied that such person has disobeyed the injunction, either directly or indirectly, may commit such person to jail without bail until he purges himself of such contempt, in such manner and form as the court or judge may direct.

(Amended by Order June 16, 1943, eff. Dec. 31, 1943.)

RULE 693. PRINCIPLES OF EQUITY APPLICABLE.

The principles, practice and procedure governing courts of equity shall govern proceedings in injunctions when the same are not in conflict with these rules or the provisions of the statutes.

RULE 693a. BOND IN DIVORCE CASE.

In a divorce case the court in its discretion may dispense with the necessity of a bond in connection with an ancillary injunction in behalf of one spouse against the other.

(Added by Order June 16, 1943, eff. Dec. 31, 1943.)

SECTION 6.
MANDAMUS

RULE 694. NO MANDAMUS WITHOUT NOTICE.

No mandamus shall be granted by the district or county court on ex parte hearing, and any peremptory mandamus granted without notice shall be abated on motion.

SECTION 7.
RECEIVERS

RULE 695. NO RECEIVER OF IMMOVABLE PROPERTY APPOINTED WITHOUT NOTICE.

Except where otherwise provided by statute, no receiver shall be appointed without notice to take charge of property which is fixed and immovable. When an application for appointment of a receiver to take possession of property of this type is filed, the judge or court shall set the same down for hearing and notice of such hearing shall be given to the adverse party by serving notice thereof not less than three days prior to such hearing. If the order finds that the defendant is a nonresident or that his whereabouts is unknown, the notice may be served by affixing the same in a conspicuous manner and place upon the property or if that is impracticable it may be served in such other manner as the court or judge may require.

(Amended by Order June 16, 1943, eff. Dec. 31, 1943.)

RULE 695a. BOND, AND BOND IN DIVORCE CASE.

No receiver shall be appointed with authority to take charge of property until the party applying therefor has filed with the clerk of the court a good and sufficient bond, to be approved by such clerk, payable to the defendant in the amount fixed by the court, conditioned for the payment of all damages and cost in such suit, in case it should be decided that such receiver was wrongfully appointed to take charge of such property. The amount of such bond shall be fixed at a sum sufficient to cover all such probable damages and costs. In a divorce case the court or judge, as a matter of discretion, may dispense with the necessity of a bond.

(Added by Order June 16, 1940, eff. Dec. 31, 1943.)

SECTION 8.
SEQUESTRATION

RULE 696. APPLICATION FOR WRIT OF SEQUESTRATION AND ORDER.

Either at the commencement of a suit or at any time during its progress the plaintiff may file an application for a writ of sequestration. The application shall be supported by affidavits of the plaintiff, his agent, his attorney, or other persons having knowledge of relevant facts. The application shall comply with all statutory requirements and shall state the grounds for issuing the writ, including the description of the property to be sequestered with such certainty that it may be identified and distinguished from property of a like kind, giving the value of each article of the property and the county in which it is located, and the specific facts relied upon by the plaintiff to warrant the required findings by the court. The writ shall not be quashed because two or more grounds are stated conjunctively or disjunctively. The application and any affidavits shall be made on personal knowledge and shall set forth such facts as would be admissible in evidence, provided that facts may be stated based upon information and belief if the grounds of such belief are specifically stated.

No writ shall issue except upon written order of the court after a hearing, which may be ex parte. The court, in its order granting the application, shall make specific findings of facts to support the statutory grounds found to exist, and shall describe the property to be sequestered with such certainty that it may be identified and distinguished from property of a like kind, giving the value of each article of the property and the county in which it is located. Such order shall further specify the amount of bond required of plaintiff which shall be in an amount which, in the opinion of the court, shall adequately compensate defendant in the event plaintiff fails to prosecute his suit to effect and pay all damages and costs as shall be adjudged against him for wrongfully suing out the writ of sequestration including the elements of damages stated in Sections 62.044 and 62.045, Civil Practice and Remedies Code. The court shall further find in its order the amount of bond required of defendant to replevy, which shall be in an amount equivalent to the value of the property sequestered or to the amount of plaintiff's claim and one year's accrual of interest if allowed by law on the claim, whichever is the lesser amount, and the estimated costs of court. The order may direct the issuance of several writs at the same time, or in succession, to be sent to different counties.

(Amended by Order July 11, 1977, eff. Jan. 1, 1978; July 15, 1987, eff. Jan. 1, 1988.)

RULE 697. PETITION.

If the suit be in the district or county court, no writ of sequestration shall issue, unless a petition shall have been first filed therein, as in other suits in said courts.

RULE 698. BOND FOR SEQUESTRATION.

No writ of sequestration shall issue until the party applying therefor has filed with the officer authorized to issue such writ a bond payable to the defendant in the amount fixed by the court's order, with sufficient surety or sureties as provided by statute to be approved by such officer, conditioned that the plaintiff will prosecute his suit to effect and pay to the extent of the penal amount of the bond all damages and costs as may be adjudged against him for wrongfully suing out such writ of sequestration, and plaintiff may further condition the bond pursuant to the provisions of Rule 708, in which case he shall not be required to give additional bond to replevy unless so ordered by the court.

After notice to the opposite party, either before or after the issuance of the writ, the defendant or plaintiff may file a motion to increase or reduce the amount of such bond, or to question the sufficiency of the sureties thereon, in the court in which such suit is pending. Upon hearing, the court shall enter its order with respect to such bond and sufficiency of the sureties as justice may require.

(Amended by Order July 11, 1977, eff. Jan. 1, 1978.)

RULE 699. REQUISITES OF WRIT.

The writ of sequestration shall be directed "To the Sheriff or any Constable within the State of Texas" (not naming a specific county) and shall command him to take into his possession the property, describing the same as it is described in the application or affidavits, if to be found in his county, and to keep the same subject to further orders of the court, unless the same is replevied. There shall be prominently displayed on the face of the writ, in ten-point type and in a manner calculated to advise a reasonably attentive person of its contents, the following:

"YOU HAVE A RIGHT TO REGAIN POSSESSION OF THE PROPERTY BY FILING A REPLEVY BOND. YOU HAVE A RIGHT TO SEEK TO REGAIN POSSESSION OF THE PROPERTY BY FILING WITH THE COURT A MOTION TO DISSOLVE THIS WRIT."

(Amended by Order July 11, 1977, eff. Jan. 1, 1978.)

RULE 700. AMENDMENT.

Clerical errors in the affidavit, bond, or writ of sequestration or the officer's return thereof may upon application in writing to the judge of the court in which the suit is filed and after notice to the opponent, be amended in such manner and on such terms as the judge shall authorize by an order entered in the minutes of the court, provided the amendment does not change or add to the grounds of such sequestration as stated in the affidavit, and provided such amendment appears to the judge to be in furtherance of justice.

RULE 700a. SERVICE OF WRIT ON DEFENDANT.

The defendant shall be served in any manner provided for service of citation or as provided in Rule 21a, with a copy of the writ of sequestration, the application, accompanying affidavits, and orders of the court as soon as practicable following the levy of the writ. There shall also be prominently displayed on the face of the copy of the writ served on defendant, in ten-point type and in a manner calculated to advise a reasonably attentive person of its contents, the following:

"To ____________________, Defendant:

"You are hereby notified that certain properties alleged to be claimed by you have been sequestered. If you claim any rights in such property, you are advised:

"YOU HAVE A RIGHT TO REGAIN POSSESSION OF THE PROPERTY BY FILING A REPLEVY BOND. YOU HAVE A RIGHT TO SEEK TO REGAIN POSSESSION OF THE PROPERTY BY FILING WITH THE COURT A MOTION TO DISSOLVE THIS WRIT."

(Added by Order July 11, 1977, eff. Jan. 1, 1978.)

RULE 701. DEFENDANT MAY REPLEVY.

At any time before judgment, should the sequestered property not have been previously claimed, replevied, or sold, the defendant may replevy the same, or any part thereof, or the proceeds from the sale of the property if it has been sold under order of the court, by giving bond, with sufficient surety or sureties as provided by statute, to be approved by the officer who levied the writ, payable to plaintiff in the amount fixed by the court's order, conditioned as provided in Rule 702 or Rule 703.

On reasonable notice to the opposing party (which may be less than three days) either party shall have the right to prompt judicial review of the amount of bond required, denial of bond, sufficiency of sureties, and estimated value of the property, by the court which authorized issuance of the writ. The court's determination may be made upon the basis of affidavits, if uncontroverted, setting forth such facts as would be admissible in evidence; otherwise, the parties shall submit evidence. The court shall forthwith enter its order either approving or modifying the requirements of the officer or of the court's prior order, and such order of the court shall supersede and control with respect to such matters.

(Amended by Order July 11, 1977, eff. Jan. 1, 1978.)

RULE 702. BOND FOR PERSONAL PROPERTY.

If the property to be replevied be personal property, the condition of the bond shall be that the defendant will not remove the same out of the county, or that he will not waste, ill-treat, injure, destroy, or dispose of the same, according to the plaintiff's affidavit, and that he will have such property, in the same condition as when it is replevied, together with the value of the fruits, hire or revenue thereof, forthcoming to abide the decision of the court, or that he will pay the value thereof, or the difference between its value at the time of replevy and the time of judgment and of the fruits, hire or revenue of the same in case he shall be condemned to do so.

RULE 703. BOND FOR REAL ESTATE.

If the property be real estate, the condition of such bond shall be that the defendant will not injure the property, and that he will pay the value of the rents of the same in case he shall be condemned so to do.

RULE 704. RETURN OF BOND AND ENTRY OF JUDGMENT.

The bond provided for in the three preceding rules shall be returned with the writ to the court from whence the writ issued. In case the suit is decided against the defendant, final judgment shall be rendered against all the obligors in such bond, jointly and severally, for the value of the property replevied as of the date of the execution of the replevy bond, and the value of the fruits, hire, revenue, or rent thereof, as the case may be.

(Amended by Order June 10, 1980, eff. Jan. 1, 1981.)

RULE 705. DEFENDANT MAY RETURN SEQUESTERED PROPERTY.

Within ten days after final judgment for personal property the defendant may deliver to the plaintiff, or to the officer who levied the sequestration or to his successor in office the personal property in question, and such officer shall deliver same to plaintiff upon his demand therefor; or such defendant shall deliver such property to the officer demanding same under execution issued therefor upon a judgment for the title or possession of the same; and such officer shall receipt the defendant for such property; provided, however, that such delivery to the plaintiff or to such officer shall be without prejudice to any rights of the plaintiff under the replevy bond given by the defendant. Where a mortgage or other lien of any kind is foreclosed upon personal property sequestered and replevied, the defendant shall deliver such property to the officer calling for same under order of sale issued upon a judgment foreclosing such mortgage or other lien, either in the county of defendant's residence or in the county where sequestered, as demanded by such officer; provided, however, that such delivery by the defendant shall be without prejudice to any rights of the plaintiff under the replevy bond given by the defendant.

(Amended by Order Sept. 20, 1941, eff. Dec. 31, 1941.)

RULE 706. DISPOSITION OF THE PROPERTY BY OFFICER.

When the property is tendered back by the defendant to the officer who sequestered the same or to the officer calling for same under an order of sale, such officer shall receive said property and hold or dispose of the same as ordered by the court; provided, however, that such return to and receipt of same by the officer and any sale or disposition of said property by the officer under order or judgment of the court shall not affect or limit any rights of the plaintiff under the bond provided for in Rule 702.

(Amended by Order Sept. 20, 1941, eff. Dec. 31, 1941.)

RULE 707. EXECUTION.

If the property be not returned and received, as provided in the two preceding rules, execution shall issue upon said judgment for the amount due thereon, as in other cases.

RULE 708. PLAINTIFF MAY REPLEVY.

When the defendant fails to replevy the property within ten days after the levy of the writ and service of notice on defendant, the officer having the property in possession shall at any time thereafter and before final judgment, deliver the same to the plaintiff upon his giving bond payable to defendant in a sum of money not less than the amount fixed by the court's order, with sufficient surety or sureties as provided by statute to be approved by such officer. If the property to be replevied be personal property, the condition of the bond shall be that he will have such property, in the same condition as when it is replevied, together with the value of the fruits, hire or revenue thereof, forthcoming to abide the decision of the court, or that he will pay the value thereof, or the difference between its value at the time of replevy and the time of judgment (regardless of the cause of such difference in value, and of the fruits, hire or revenue of the same in case he shall be condemned to do so). If the property be real estate, the condition of such bond shall be that the plaintiff will not injure the property, and that he will pay the value of the rents of the same in case he shall be condemned to do so.

On reasonable notice to the opposing party (which may be less than three days) either party shall have the right to prompt judicial review of the amount of bond required, denial of bond, sufficiency of sureties, and estimated value of the property, by the court which authorized issuance of the writ. The court's determination may be made upon the basis of affidavits, if uncontroverted, setting forth such facts as would be admissible in evidence, otherwise, the parties shall submit evidence. The court shall forthwith enter its order either approving or modifying the requirements of the officer or of the court's prior order, and such order of the court shall supersede and control with respect to such matters.

(Amended by Order July 11, 1977, eff. Jan. 1, 1978; Dec. 5, 1983, eff. April 1, 1984.)

RULE 709. WHEN BOND FORFEITED.

The bond provided for in the preceding rule shall be returned by the officer to the court issuing the writ immediately after he has approved same, and in case the suit is decided against the plaintiff, final judgment shall be entered against all the obligors in such bond, jointly and severally for the value of the property replevied as of the date of the execution of the replevy bond, and the value of the fruits, hire, revenue or rent thereof as the case may be. The same rules which govern the discharge or enforcement of a judgment against the obligors in the defendant's replevy bond shall be applicable to and govern in case of a judgment against the obligors in the plaintiff's replevy bond.

RULE 710. SALE OF PERISHABLE GOODS.

If after the expiration of ten days from the levy of a writ of sequestration the defendant has failed to replevy the same, if the plaintiff or defendant shall make affidavit in writing that the property levied upon, or any portion thereof, is likely to be wasted or destroyed or greatly depreciated in value by keeping, and if the officer having possession of such property shall certify to the truth of such affidavit, it shall be the duty of the judge or justice of the peace to whose court the writ is returnable, upon the presentation of such affidavit and certificate, either in term time or vacation, to order the sale of said property or so much thereof as is likely to be so wasted, destroyed or depreciated in value by keeping, but either party may replevy the property at any time before such sale.

RULE 711. ORDER OF SALE FOR.

The judge or justice granting the order provided for in the preceding rule shall issue an order directed to the officer having such property in possession, commending such officer to sell such property in the same manner as under execution.

RULE 712. RETURN OF ORDER.

The officer making such sale shall, within five days thereafter, return the order of sale to the court from whence the same issued, with his proceedings thereon, and shall, at the time of making such return, pay over to the clerk or justice of the peace the proceeds of such sale.

RULE 712a. DISSOLUTION OR MODIFICATION OF WRIT OF SEQUESTRATION.

A defendant whose property has been sequestered or any intervening party who claims an interest in such property, may by sworn written motion, seek to vacate, dissolve, or modify the writ and the order directing its issuance, for any grounds or cause, extrinsic or intrinsic, including a motion to reduce the amount of property sequestered when the total amount described and authorized by such order exceeds the amount necessary to secure the plaintiffs claim, one year's interest if allowed by law on the claim, and costs. Such motion shall admit or deny each finding of the order directing the issuance of the writ except where the movant is unable to admit or deny the finding, in which case movant shall set forth the reasons why he cannot admit or deny. Unless the parties agree to an extension of time, the motion shall be heard promptly, after reasonable notice to the plaintiff (which may be less than three days), and the issue shall be determined not later than ten days after the motion is filed. The filing of the motion shall stay any further proceedings under the writ, except for any orders concerning the care, preservation, or sale of any perishable property, until a hearing is had, and the issue is determined. The writ shall be dissolved unless, at such hearing, the plaintiff shall prove the grounds relied upon for its issuance, but the court may modify its previous order granting the writ and the writ issued pursuant thereto. The movant shall, however, have the burden to prove that the reasonable value of the property sequestered exceeds the amount necessary to secure the debt, interest for one year, and probable costs.

The court's determination may be made upon the basis of affidavits, if uncontroverted, setting forth such facts as would be admissible in evidence; otherwise, the parties shall submit evidence. The court may make all such orders, including orders concerning the care, preservation, or disposition of the property (or the proceeds therefrom if the same has been sold) as justice may require. If the movant has given a replevy bond, an order to vacate or dissolve the writ shall vacate the replevy bond and discharge the sureties thereon, and if the court modifies its order or the writ issued pursuant thereto, it shall make such further orders with respect to the bond as may be consistent with its modification.

(Added by Order July 11, 1977, eff. Jan. 1, 1978.)

RULE 713. SALE ON DEBT NOT DUE.

If the suit in which the sequestration issued be for a debt or demand not yet due, and the property sequestered be likely to be wasted, destroyed or greatly depreciated in value by keeping, the judge or justice of the peace shall, under the regulations hereinbefore provided, order the same to be sold, giving credit on such sale until such debt or demand shall become due.

RULE 714. PURCHASER'S BOND.

In the case of a sale as provided for in the preceding rule, the purchaser of the property shall execute his bond, with two or more good and sufficient sureties, to be approved by the officer making the sale, and payable to such officer, in a sum not less than double the amount of the purchase money, conditioned that such purchaser shall pay such purchase money at the expiration of the time given.

RULE 715. RETURN OF BOND.

The bond provided for in the preceding rule shall be returned by the officer taking the same to the clerk or justice of the peace from whose court the order of sale issued, with such order, and shall be filed among the papers in the cause.

RULE 716. RECOVERY ON BOND.

In case the purchaser does not pay the purchase money at the expiration of the time given, judgment shall be rendered against all the obligors in such bond for the amount of such purchase money, interest thereon and all costs incurred in the enforcement and collection of the same; and execution shall issue thereon in the name of the plaintiff in the suit, as in other cases, and the money when collected shall be paid to the clerk or justice of the peace to abide the final decision of the cause.

SECTION 9.
TRIAL OF THE RIGHT OF PROPERTY

RULE 717. CLAIMANT MUST MAKE AFFIDAVIT.

Whenever a distress warrant, writ of execution, sequestration, attachment, or other like writ is levied upon personal property, and such property, or any part thereof, shall be claimed by any claimant who is not a party to such writ, such claimant may make application that such claim is made in good faith, and file such application with the court in which such suit is pending. Such application may be supported by affidavits of the claimant, his agent, his attorney, or other persons having knowledge of relevant facts. The application shall comply with all statutory requirements and shall state the grounds for such claim and the specific facts relied upon by the claimant to warrant the required findings by the court.

The claim shall not be quashed because two or more grounds are stated conjunctively or disjunctively. The application and any affidavits shall be made on personal knowledge and shall set forth such facts as would be admissible in evidence provided that facts may be stated based upon information and belief if the grounds of such belief are specifically stated.

No property shall be delivered to the claimant except on written order of the court after a hearing pursuant to Rule 718. The court in its order granting the application shall make specific findings of facts to support the statutory grounds found to exist and shall specify the amount of the bond required of the claimant.

(Added by Order June 10, 1980, eff. Jan. 1, 1981.)

RULE 718. PROPERTY DELIVERED TO CLAIMANT.

Any claimant who claims an interest in property on which a writ has been levied may, by sworn written motion, seek to obtain possession of such property. Such motion shall admit or deny each finding of the order directing the issuance of the writ except where the claimant is unable to admit or deny the finding, in which case claimant shall set forth the reasons why he cannot admit or deny. Such motion shall also contain the reasons why the claimant has superior right or title to the property claimed as against the plaintiff in the writ. Unless the parties agree to an extension of time, the motion shall be heard promptly, after reasonable notice to the plaintiff (which may be less than three days), and the issue shall be determined not later than 10 days after the motion is filed. The filing of the motion shall stay any further proceedings under the writ, except for any orders concerning the care, preservation, or sale of any perishable property, until a hearing is had, and the issue is determined. The claimant shall have the burden to show superior right or title to the property claimed as against the plaintiff and defendant in the writ.

The court's determination may be made upon the basis of affidavits, if uncontroverted, setting forth such facts as would be admissible in evidence, but additional evidence, if tendered by either party shall be received and considered. The court may make all such orders, including orders concerning the care, preservation, or disposition of the property, or the proceeds therefrom if the same has been sold, as justice may require, and if the court modifies its order or the writ issued pursuant thereto, it shall make such further orders with respect to the bond as may be consistent with its modification.

(Added by Order June 10, 1980, eff. Jan. 1, 1981.)

RULE 719. BOND.

No property shall be put in the custody of the claimant until the claimant has filed with the officer who made the levy, a bond in an amount fixed by the court's order equal to double the value of the property so claimed, payable to the plaintiff in the writ, with sufficient surety or sureties as provided by statute to be approved by such officer, conditioned that the claimant will return the same to the officer making the levy, or his successor, in as good condition as he received it, and shall also pay the reasonable value of the use, hire, increase and fruits thereof from the date of said bond, or, in case he fails so to return said property and pay for the use of the same, that he shall pay the plaintiff the value of said property, with legal interest thereon from the date of the bond, and shall also pay all damages and costs that may be awarded against him for wrongfully suing out such claim.

The plaintiff or claimant may file a motion to increase or reduce the amount of such bond, or to question the sufficiency of the sureties thereon, in the court in which such suit is pending. Upon hearing, the court shall enter its order with respect to such bond and sufficiency of the sureties.

(Added by Order June 10, 1980, eff. Jan. 1, 1981.)

RULE 720. RETURN OF BOND.

Whenever any person shall claim property and shall duly make the application and give the bond, if the writ under which the levy was made was issued by a justice of the peace or a court of the county where such levy was made, the officer receiving such application and bond shall endorse on the writ that such claim has been made and application and bond given, and by whom; and shall also endorse on such bond the value of the property as assessed by himself, and shall forthwith return such bond with a copy of the writ to the proper court having jurisdiction to try such claim.

(Added by Order June 10, 1980, eff. Jan. 1, 1981.)

RULE 721. OUT-COUNTY LEVY.

Whenever any person shall claim property and shall make the application and give the bond as provided for herein, if the writ under which such levy was made was issued by a justice of the peace or a court of another county than that in which such levy was made, then the officer receiving such bond shall endorse on such bond the value of the property as assessed by himself. and shall forthwith return such bond with a copy of the writ, to the proper court having jurisdiction to try such claim.

(Added by Order June 10, 1980, eff. Jan. 1, 1981.)

RULE 722. RETURN OF ORIGINAL WRIT.

The officer taking such bond shall also endorse on the original writ, if in his possession, that such claim has been made and application and bond given, stating by whom, the names of the surety or sureties, and to what justice or court the bond has been returned; and he shall forthwith return such original writ to the tribunal from which it issued.

(Added by Order June 10, 1980, eff. Jan 1, 1981.)

RULE 723. DOCKETING CAUSE.

Whenever any bond for the trial of the right of property shall be returned, the clerk of the court, or such justice of the peace, shall docket the same in the original writ proceeding in the name of the plaintiff in the writ as the plaintiff, and the claimant of the property as intervening claimant.

(Added by Order June 10, 1980, eff. Jan. 1, 1981.)

RULE 724. ISSUE MADE UP.

After the claim proceedings have been docketed, and on the hearing day set by the court, then the court, or the justice of the peace, as the case may be shall enter an order directing the making and joinder of issues by the parties. Such issues shall be in writing and signed by each party or his attorney. The plaintiff shall make a brief statement of the authority and right by which he seeks to subject the property levied on to the process, and it shall be sufficient for the claimant and other parties to make brief statements of the nature of their claims thereto.

(Added by Order June 10, 1980, eff. Jan. 1, 1981.)

RULE 725. JUDGMENT BY DEFAULT.

If the plaintiff appears and the claimant fails to appear or neglects or refuses to join issue under the direction of the court or justice within the time prescribed for pleading, the plaintiff shall have judgment by default.

(Added by Order June 10, 1980, eff. Jan. 1, 1981.)

RULE 726. JUDGMENT OF NON-SUIT.

If the plaintiff does not appear, he shall be nonsuited.

(Amended by Order June 10, 1980, eff. Jan. 1, 1981.)

RULE 727. PROCEEDINGS.

The proceedings and practice on the trial shall be as nearly as may be the same as in other cases before such court or justice.

(Amended by Order June 10, 1980, eff. Jan. 1, 1981.)

RULE 728. BURDEN OF PROOF.

If the property was taken from the possession of the claimant pursuant to the original writ, the burden of proof shall be on the plaintiff in the writ. If it was taken from the possession of the defendant in such writ, or any other person than the claimant, the burden of proof shall be on the claimant.

(Added by Order June 10, 1980, eff. Jan. 1, 1981.)

RULE 729. COPY OF WRIT EVIDENCE.

In all trials of the right of property, under the provisions of this section in any county other than that in which the writ issued under which the levy was made, the copy of the writ herein required to be returned by the officer making the levy shall be received in evidence in like manner as the original could be.

(Amended by Order June 10, 1980, eff. Jan. 1, 1981.)

RULE 730. FAILURE TO ESTABLISH TITLE.

Where any claimant has obtained possession of property, and shall ultimately fail to establish his right thereto, judgment may be rendered against him and his sureties for the value of the property, with legal interest thereon from the date of such bond. Such judgment shall be rendered in favor of the plaintiff or defendant in the writ, or of the several plaintiffs or defendants, if more than one, and shall fix the amount of the claim of each.

(Added by Order June 10, 1980, eff. Jan. 1, 1981.)

RULE 731. EXECUTION SHALL ISSUE.

If such judgment should not be satisfied by a return of the property, then after the expiration of ten days from the date of the judgment, execution shall issue thereon in the name of the plaintiff or defendant for the amount of the claim, or of all the plaintiffs or defendants for the sum of their several claims, provided the amount of such judgment shall inure to the benefit of any person who shall show superior right or title to the property claimed as against the claimant; but if such judgment be for a less amount than the sum of the several plaintiffs' or defendants' claims, then the respective rights and priorities of the several plaintiffs or defendants shall be fixed and adjusted in the judgment.

(Amended by Order June 10, 1980, eff. Jan. 1, 1981.)

RULE 732. RETURN OF PROPERTY BY CLAIMANT.

If, within ten days from the rendition of said judgment, the claimant shall return such property in as good condition as he received it, and pay for the use of the same together with the damages and costs, such delivery and payment shall operate as a satisfaction of such judgment.

(Added by Order June 10, 1980, eff. Jan. 1, 1981.)

RULE 733. CLAIM IS A RELEASE OF DAMAGES.

A claim made to the property, under the provisions of this section, shall operate as a release of all damages by the claimant against the officer who levied upon said property.

(Added by Order June 10, 1980, eff. Jan. 1, 1981.)

RULE 734. LEVY ON OTHER PROPERTY.

Proceedings for the trial of right of property under these rules shall in no case prevent the plaintiff in the writ from having a levy made upon any other property of the defendant.

(Amended by Order June 10, 1980, eff. Jan. 1, 1981.)

PART VII.
RULES RELATING SPECIAL PROCEEDINGS

SECTION 1.
PROCEDURES RELATED TO FORECLOSURES OF CERTAIN LIENS

RULE 735. FORECLOSURES REQUIRING A COURT ORDER.

735.1. Liens Affected.

Rule 736 provides the procedure for obtaining a court order, when required, to allow foreclosure of a lien containing a power of sale in the security instrument, dedicatory instrument, or declaration creating the lien, including a lien securing any of the following:

(a) a home equity loan, reverse mortgage, or home equity line of credit under article XVI, sections 50(a)(6), 50(k), and 50(t) of the Texas Constitution;

(b) a tax lien transfer or property tax loan under sections 32.06 and 32.065 of the Tax Code; or

(c) a property owners' association assessment under section 209.0092 of the Property Code.

735.2. Other Statutory and Contractual Foreclosure Provisions Unaltered.

A Rule 736 order does not alter any foreclosure requirement or duty imposed under applicable law or the terms of the loan agreement, contract, or lien sought to be foreclosed. The only issue to be determined in a Rule 736 proceeding is whether a party may obtain an order under Rule 736 to proceed with foreclosure under applicable law and the terms of the loan agreement, contract, or lien sought to be foreclosed.

735.3. Judicial Foreclosure Unaffected.

A Rule 736 order is not a substitute for a judgment for judicial foreclosure, but any loan agreement, contract, or lien that may be foreclosed using Rule 736 procedures may also be foreclosed by judgment in an action for judicial foreclosure.

(Adopted by Order Oct. 17, 2011, eff. Jan. 1, 2012; Order Dec. 30, 2011, eff. Jan 1, 2012.)

RULE 736. EXPEDITED ORDER PROCEEDING.

736.1. Application.

(a) *Where Filed.* An application for an expedited order allowing the foreclosure of a lien listed in Rule 735 to proceed must be filed in a county where all or part of the real property encumbered by the loan agreement, contract, or lien sought to be foreclosed is located or in a probate court with jurisdiction over proceedings involving the property.

(b) *Style.* An application must be styled "In re: Order for Foreclosure Concerning [state: property's mailing address] under Tex. R. Civ. P. 736."

(c) *When Filed.* An application may not be filed until the opportunity to cure has expired under applicable law and the loan agreement, contract, or lien sought to be foreclosed.

(d) *Contents.* The application must:

(1) Identify by name and last known address each of the following parties:

(A) "Petitioner" - any person legally authorized to prosecute the foreclosure;

(B) "Respondent" - according to the records of the holder or servicer of the loan agreement, contract, or lien sought to be foreclosed;

(i) for a home equity loan, reverse mortgage, or home equity line of credit, each person obligated to pay the loan agreement, contract, or lien sought to be foreclosed and each mortgagor, if any, of the loan agreement, contract, or lien sought to be foreclosed;

(ii) for a tax lien transfer or property tax loan, each person obligated to pay the loan agreement, contract, or lien sought to be foreclosed, each mortgagor, if any, of the loan agreement, contract, or lien sought to be foreclosed, each owner of the property, and the holder of any recorded preexisting first lien secured by the property;

(iii) for a property owners' association assessment, each person obligated to pay the loan agreement, contract, or lien sought to be foreclosed who has a current ownership interest in the property.

(2) Identify the property encumbered by the loan agreement, contract, or lien sought to be foreclosed by its commonly known street address and legal description.

(3) Describe or state:

(A) the type of lien listed in Rule 735 sought to be foreclosed and its constitutional or statutory reference;

(B) the authority of the party seeking foreclosure, whether as the servicer, beneficiary, lender, investor, property owners' association, or other person with authority to prosecute the foreclosure;

(C) each person obligated to pay the loan agreement, contract, or lien sought to be foreclosed;

(D) each mortgagor, if any, of the loan agreement, contract, or lien sought to be foreclosed who is not a maker or assumer of the underlying debt;

(E) as of a date that is not more than sixty days prior to the date the application is filed:

(i) if the default is monetary, the number of unpaid scheduled payments,

(ii) if the default is monetary, the amount required to cure the default,

(iii) if the default is non-monetary, the facts creating the default, and

(iv) if applicable, the total amount required to pay off the loan agreement, contract or lien;

(F) that the requisite notice or notices to cure the default has or have been mailed to each person as required under applicable law and the loan agreement, contract, or lien sought to be foreclosed and that the opportunity to cure has expired; and

(G) that before the application was filed, any other action required under applicable law and the loan agreement, contract, or lien sought to be foreclosed was performed.

(4) For a tax lien transfer or property tax loan, state all allegations required to be contained in the application in accordance with section 32.06(c-1)(1) of the Tax Code.

(5) Conspicuously state:

(A) that legal action is not being sought against the occupant of the property unless the occupant is also names as a respondent in the application; and

(B) that if the petitioner obtains a court order, the petitioner will proceed with a foreclosure of the property in accordance with applicable law and the terms of the loan agreement, contract, or lien sought to be foreclosed.

(6) Include an affidavit of material facts in accordance with Rule 166a(f) signed by the petitioner or the servicer describing the basis for foreclosure and, depending on the type of lien sought to be foreclosed, attach a legible copy of:

(A) the note, original recorded lien, or pertinent part of a property owners' association declaration or dedicatory instrument establishing the lien, and current assignment of the lien, if assigned;

(B) each notice required to be mailed to any person under applicable law and the loan agreement, contract, or lien sought to be foreclosed before the application was filed and proof of mailing of each notice; and

(C) for a tax lien transfer or property tax loan:

(i) the property owner's sworn document required under section 32.06(-1) of the Tax Code; and

(ii) the taxing authority's certified statement attesting to the transfer of the lien, required under section 32.06(b) of the Tax Code.

736.2. Costs.

All filing, citation, mailing, service, and other court costs and fees are costs of court and must be paid by petitioner at the time of filing an application with the clerk of the court.

736.3. Citation.

(a) *Issuance.*

(1) When the application is filed, the clerk must issue a separate citation for each respondent named in the application and one additional citation for the occupant of the property sought to be foreclosed.

(2) Each citation that is directed to a respondent must state that any response to the application is due the first Monday after the expiration of 38 days from the date the citation was placed in the custody of the U.S. Postal Service in accordance with the clerk's standard mailing procedures and state the date that the citation was placed in the custody of the U.S. Postal Service by the clerk.

(b) *Service and Return.*

(1) The clerk of the court must serve each citation, with a copy of the application attached, by both first class mail and certified mail. A citation directed to a respondent must be mailed to the respondent's last known address that is stated in the application. A citation directed to the occupant of the property sought to be foreclosed must be mailed to Occupant of [state: property's mailing address] at the address of the property sought to be foreclosed that is stated in the application.

(2) Concurrently with service, the clerk must complete a return of service in accordance with Rule 107, except that the return of service need not contain a return receipt. For a citation mailed by the clerk in accordance with (b)(1), the date of service is the date and time the citation was placed in the custody of the U.S. Postal Service in a properly addressed, postage prepaid envelope in accordance with the clerk's standard mailing procedures.

(3) The clerk must only charge one fee per respondent or occupant served under this rule.

736.4. Discovery.

No discovery is permitted in a Rule 736 proceeding.

736.5. Response.

(a) *Generally.* A respondent may file a response contesting the application.

(b) *Due Date.* Any response to the application is due the first Monday after the expiration of 38 days from the date the citation was placed in the custody of the U.S. Postal Service in accordance with the clerk's standard mailing procedures, as stated on the citation.

(c) *Form.* A response must be signed in accordance with Rule 57 and may be in the form of a general denial under Rule 92, except that a respondent must affirmatively plead:

(1) why the respondent believes a respondent did not sign a loan agreement document, if applicable, that is specifically identified by the respondent;

(2) why the respondent is not obligated for payment of the lien;

(3) why the number of months of alleged default or the reinstatement or pay off amounts are materially incorrect;

(4) why any document attached to the application is not a true and correct copy of the original; or

(5) proof of payment in accordance with Rule 95.

(d) *Other Claims.* A response may not state an independent claim for relief. The court must, without a hearing, strike and dismiss any counterclaim, cross claim, third party claim, intervention, or cause of action filed by any person in a Rule 736 proceeding.

736.6. Hearing Required When Response Filed.

The court must not conduct a hearing under this rule unless a response is filed. If a response is filed, the court must hold a hearing after reasonable notice to the parties. The hearing on the application must not be held earlier than 20 days or later than 30 days after a request for a hearing is made by any party. At the hearing, the petitioner has the burden to prove by affidavits on file or evidence presented the grounds for granting the order sought in the application.

736.7. Default When No Response Filed.

(a) If no response to the application is filed by the due date, the petitioner may file a motion and proposed order to obtain a default order. For the purposes of obtaining a default order, all facts alleged in the application and supported by the affidavit of material facts constitute prima facie evidence of the truth of the matters alleged.

(b) The court must grant the application by default order no later than 30 days after a motion is filed under (a) if the application complies with the requirements of Rule 736.1 and was properly served in accordance with Rule 736.3. The petitioner need not appear in court to obtain a default order.

(c) The return of service must be on file with the clerk of the court for at least 10 days before the court may grant the application by default.

736.8. Order.

(a) The court must issue an order granting the application if the petitioner establishes the basis for the foreclosure. Otherwise, the court must deny the application.

(b) An order granting the application must describe:
   (1) the material facts establishing the basis for foreclosure;
   (2) the property to be foreclosed by commonly known mailing address and legal description;
   (3) the name and last known address of each respondent subject to the order; and
   (4) the recording or indexing information of each lien to be foreclosed.

(c) An order granting or denying the application is not subject to a motion for rehearing, new trial, bill of review, or appeal. Any challenge to a Rule 736 order must be made in a suit filed in a separate, independent, original proceeding in a court of competent jurisdiction.

736.9. Effect of the Order.

An order is without prejudice and has no res judicata, collateral estoppel, estoppel by judgment, or other effect in any other judicial proceeding. After an order is obtained, a person may proceed with the foreclosure process under applicable law and the terms of the lien sought to be foreclosed.

736.10. Bankruptcy.

If a respondent provides proof to the clerk of the court that respondent filed bankruptcy before an order is signed, the proceeding under this rule must be abated so long as the automatic stay is effective.

736.11. Automatic Stay and Dismissal if Independent Suit Filed.

(a) A proceeding or order under this rule is automatically stayed if a respondent files a separate, original proceeding in a court of competent jurisdiction that puts in issue any matter related to the origination, servicing, or enforcement of the loan agreement, contract, or lien sought to be foreclosed prior to 5:00 p.m. on the Monday before the scheduled foreclosure sale.

(b) Respondent must give prompt notice of the filing of the suit to petitioner or petitioner's attorney and the foreclosure trustee or substitute trustee by any reasonable means necessary to stop the scheduled foreclosure sale.

(c) Within ten days of filing suit, the respondent must file a motion and proposed order to dismiss or vacate with the clerk of the court in which the application was filed giving notice that respondent has filed an original proceeding contesting the right to foreclose in a court of competent jurisdiction. If no order has been signed, the court must dismiss a pending proceeding. If an order has been signed, the court must vacate the Rule 736 order.

(d) If the automatic stay under this rule is in effect, any foreclosure sale of the property is void. Within 10 business days of notice that the foreclosure sale was void, the trustee or substitute trustee must return to the buyer of the foreclosed property the purchase price paid by the buyer.

(e) The court may enforce the Rule 736 process under chapters 9 and 10 of the Civil Practices and Remedies Code.

736.12. Attachment of Order to Trustee's Deed.

A conformed copy of the order must be attached to the trustee or substitute trustee's foreclosure deed.

736.13. Promulgated Forms.

The Supreme Court of Texas may promulgate forms that conform to this rule.

(Added by Order Jan. 27, 1998. Amended by Order May 15, 1998, eff. May 15, 1998; Order effective April 15, 2000; Order Oct. 17, 2011, eff. Jan. 1, 2012; Order Dec. 30, 2011, eff. Jan 1, 2012.)

Comment to 2011 change

Rules 735 and 736 have been rewritten and expanded to cover property owners' associations' assessment liens, in accordance with amendments to chapter 209 of the Property Code. Rule 735.1 makes the expedited procedures of Rule 736 available only when the lienholder has a power of sale but a court order is nevertheless required by law to foreclose the lien. Rule 735.2 makes clear that Rule 736 is procedural only and does not affect other contractual or legal rights or duties. Any lien which can be foreclosed under Rule 736 may also be foreclosed in an action for judicial foreclosure, as Rule 735.3 states, but no lienholder is required to obtain both a Rule 736 order and a judgment for judicial foreclosure. The requirement of conspicuousness in Rule 736.1(d)(5) has reference to section 1.201(b)(10) of the Business and Commerce Code.

Forms for Expedited Foreclosure Proceedings (Pursuant to the Act of May 27, 2013, 83rd Leg., R.S., c. 1044 (HB 2978) and section 22.018 of the Texas Government Code, the Supreme Court of Texas approves the following set of forms for use in expedited foreclosure proceedings under Texas Rule of Civil Procedure 736.)

RULES 737-755. [REPEALED.]

(Repealed by Order Feb 12, 2013, eff. Aug. 31, 2013; Order April 15, 2013, eff. Aug. 31, 2013.)

SECTION 4.
PARTITION REAL ESTATE

RULE 756. PETITION.

The plaintiff's petition shall state:

(a) The names and residence, if known, of each of the other joint owners, or joint claimants, of such property.

(b) The share or interest which the plaintiff and the other joint owners, or joint claimants, of same own or claim so far as known to the plaintiff.

(c) The land sought to be partitioned shall be so described as that the same may be distinguished from any other and the estimated value thereof stated.

RULE 757. CITATION AND SERVICE.

Upon the filing of a petition for partition, the clerk shall issue citation for each of the joint owners, or joint claimants, named therein, as in other cases, and such citations shall be served in the manner and for the time provided for the service of citations in other cases.

RULE 758. WHERE DEFENDANT IS UNKNOWN OR RESIDENCE IS UNKNOWN.

If the plaintiff, his agent or attorney, at the commencement of any suit, or during the progress thereof, for the partition of land, shall make affidavit that an undivided portion of the land described in plaintiff's petition in said suit is owned by some person unknown to affiant, or that the place of residence of any known party owning an interest in land sought to be partitioned is unknown to affiant, the Clerk of the Court shall issue citation for publication, conforming to the requirements of Rules 114 and 115, and served in accordance with the directions of Rule 116. In case of unknown residence or party, the affidavit shall include a statement that after due diligence plaintiff and the affiant have been unable to ascertain the name or locate the residence of such party, as the case may be, and in such case it shall be the duty of the court trying the action to inquire into the sufficiency of the diligence so stated before granting any judgment.

(Amended by Order July 20, 1954, eff. Jan. 1, 1955; Dec. 19, 1984, eff. April 1, 1985.)

RULE 759. JUDGMENT WHERE DEFENDANT CITED BY PUBLICATION.

When the defendant has been duly cited by publication in accordance with the preceding rule, and no appearance is entered within the time prescribed for pleadings, the court shall appoint an attorney to defend in behalf of such owner or owners, and proceed as in other causes where service is made by publication. It shall be the special duty of the court in all cases to see that its decree protects the rights of the unknown parties thereto. The judge of the court shall fix the fee of the attorney so appointed, which shall be entered and collected as costs against said unknown owner or owners.

RULE 760. COURT SHALL DETERMINE, WHAT.

Upon the hearing of the cause, the court shall determine the share or interest of each of the joint owners or claimants in the real estate sought to be divided, and all questions of law or equity affecting the title to such land which may arise.

RULE 761. APPOINTMENT OF COMMISSIONERS.

The court shall determine before entering the decree of partition whether the property, or any part thereof, is susceptible of partition; and, if the court determines that the whole, or any part of such property is susceptible of partition, then the court for that part of such property held to be susceptible of partition shall enter a decree directing the partition of such real estate, describing the same, to be made in accordance with the respective shares or interests of each of such parties entitled thereto, specify in such decree the share or interest of each party, and shall appoint three or more competent and disinterested persons as commissioners to make such partition in accordance with such decree and the law, a majority of which commissioners may act.

RULE 762. WRIT OF PARTITION.

The clerk shall issue a writ a partition, directed to the sheriff or any constable of the county, commanding such sheriff or constable to notify each of the commissioners of their appointment as such, and shall accompany such writ with a certified copy of the decree of the court directing the partition.

RULE 763. SERVICE OF WRIT OF PARTITION.

The writ of partition shall be served by reading the same to each of the persons named therein as commissioners, and by delivering to any one of them the accompanying certified copy of the decree of the court.

RULE 764. MAY APPOINT SURVEYOR.

The court may, should it be deemed necessary, appoint a surveyor to assist the commissioners in making the partition, in which case the writ of partition shall name such surveyor, and shall be served upon him by reading the same to him.

RULE 765. RETURN OF WRIT.

A writ of partition, unless otherwise directed by the court, shall be made returnable twenty days from date of service on the commissioner last served; and the officer serving it shall endorse thereon the time and manner of such service.

RULE 766. SHALL PROCEED TO PARTITION.

The commissioners, or a majority of them, shall proceed to partition the real estate described in the decree of the court, in accordance with the directions contained in such decree and with the provisions of law and these rules.

RULE 767. MAY CAUSE SURVEY.

If the commissioners deem it necessary, they may cause to be surveyed the real estate to be partitioned into several tracts or parcels.

RULE 768. SHALL DIVIDE REAL ESTATE.

The commissioners shall divide the real estate to be partitioned into as many shares as there are persons entitled thereto, as determined by the court, each share to contain one or more tracts or parcels, as the commissioners may think proper, having due regard in the division to the situation, quantity and advantages of each share, so that the shares may be equal in value, as nearly as may be, in proportion to the respective interests of the parties entitled. The commissioners shall then proceed by lot to set apart to each of the parties entitled one of said shares, as determined by the decrees of the court.

RULE 769. REPORT OF COMMISSIONERS.

When the commissioners have completed the partition, they shall report the same in writing and under oath to the court, which report shall show:

(a) The property divided, describing the same.

(b) The several tracts or parcels into which the same was divided by them, describing each particularly

(c) The number of shares and the land which constitutes each share, and the estimated value of each share.

(d) The allotment of each share.

(e) The report shall be accompanied by such field notes and maps as may be necessary to make the same intelligible. The clerk shall immediately mail written notice of the filing of the report to all parties.

(Amended by Order April 24, 1990, eff. Sept. 1, 1990.)

RULE 770. PROPERTY INCAPABLE OF DIVISION.

Should the court be of the opinion that a fair and equitable division of the real estate, or any part thereof, cannot be made, it shall order a sale of so much as is incapable of partition, which sale shall be for cash, or upon such other terms as the court may direct, and shall be made as under execution or by private or public sale through a receiver, if the court so order, and the proceeds thereof shall be returned into court and be partitioned among the persons entitled thereto, according to their respective interests.

(Amended by Order Oct. 12, 1949, eff. March 1, 1950.)

RULE 771. OBJECTIONS TO REPORT.

Either party to the suit may file objections to any report of the commissioners in partition within thirty days of the date the report is filed, and in such case a trial of the issues thereon shall be had as in other cases. If the report be found to be erroneous in any material respect, or unequal and unjust, the same shall be rejected, and other commissioners shall be appointed by the Court, and the same proceedings had as in the first instance.

(Amended by Order April 24, 1990, eff. Sept. 1, 1990.)

SECTION 5.
PARTITION OF PERSONAL PROPERTY

RULE 772. PROCEDURE.

An action seeking partition of personal property as authorized by Section 23.001, Texas Property Code, shall be commenced in the same manner as other civil suits, and the several owners or claimants of such property shall be cited as in other cases.

(Amended by Order July 15, 1987, eff. Jan. 1, 1988.)

RULE 773. VALUE ASCERTAINED.

The separate value of each article of such personal property, and the allotment in kind to which each owner is entitled, shall be ascertained by the court, with or without a jury.

RULE 774. DECREE OF COURT EXECUTED.

When partition in kind of personal property is ordered by the judgment of the court, a writ shall be issued in accordance with such judgment, commanding the sheriff or constable of the county where the property may be to put the parties forthwith in possession of the property allotted to each respectively.

RULE 775. PROPERTY SOLD.

When personal property will not admit of a fair and equitable partition, the court shall ascertain the proportion to which each owner thereof is entitled, and order the property to be sold, and execution shall be issued to the sheriff or any constable of the county where the property may be describing such property and commanding such officer to sell the same as in other cases of execution, and pay over the proceeds of sale to the parties entitled thereto, in the proportion ascertained by the judgment of the court.

SECTION 6. PARTITION:
MISCELLANEOUS PROVISIONS

RULE 776. CONSTRUCTION.

No provision of the statutes or rules relating to partition shall affect the mode of proceeding prescribed by law for the partition of estates of decedents among the heirs and legatees, nor preclude partition in any other manner authorized by the rules of equity, which rules shall govern in proceedings for partition in all respects not provided for by law or these rules.

RULE 777. PLEADING AND PRACTICE.

The same rules of pleading, practice and evidence which govern in other civil actions shall govern in suits for partition, when not in conflict with any provisions of the law or these rules relating to partition.

RULE 778. COSTS.

The court shall adjudge the costs in a partition suit to be paid by each party to whom a share has been allotted in proportion to the value of such share.

SECTION 7.
QUO WARRANTO

RULE 779. JOINDER OF PARTIES.

When it appears to the court or judge that the several rights of divers parties to the same office or franchise may properly be determined on one information, the court or judge may give leave to join all such persons in the same information in order to try their respective rights to such office or franchise.

RULE 780. CITATION TO ISSUE.

When such information is filed, the clerk shall issue citation as in civil actions, commanding the defendant to appear and answer the relator in an information in the nature of a quo warranto.

RULE 781. PROCEEDINGS AS IN CIVIL CASES.

Every person or corporation who shall be cited as hereinbefore provided shall be entitled to all the rights in the trial and investigation of the matters alleged against him, as in cases of trial of civil cases in this State. Either party may prosecute an appeal or writ of error from any judgment rendered, as in other civil cases, subject, however, to the provisions of Rule 42, Texas Rules of Appellate Procedure, and the appellate court shall give preference to such case, and hear and determine the same as early as practicable.

(Amended by Order Aug. 18, 1947, eff. Dec. 31, 1947; April 24, 1990, eff. Sept. 1, 1990.)

RULE 782. REMEDY CUMULATIVE.

The remedy and mode of procedure hereby prescribed shall be construed to be cumulative of any now existing.

SECTION 8.
TRESPASS TO TRY TITLE

RULE 783. REQUISITES OF PETITION.

The petition shall state:

(a) The real names of the plaintiff and defendant and their residences, if known.

(b) A description of the premises by metes and bounds, or with sufficient certainty to identify the same, so that from such description possession thereof may be delivered, and state the county or counties in which the same are situated.

(c) The interest which the plaintiff claims in the premises, whether it be a fee simple or other estate; and, if he claims an undivided interest, the petition shall state the same and the amount thereof.

(d) That the plaintiff was in possession of the premises or entitled to such possession.

(e) That the defendant afterward unlawfully entered upon and dispossessed him of such premises, stating the date, and withholds from him the possession thereof.

(f) If rents and profits or damages are claimed, such facts as show the plaintiff to be entitled thereto and the amount thereof.

(g) It shall conclude with a prayer for the relief sought.

RULE 784. THE POSSESSOR SHALL BE DEFENDANT.

The defendant in the action shall be the person in possession if the premises are occupied, or some person claiming title thereto in case they are unoccupied.

RULE 785. MAY JOIN AS DEFENDANTS, WHEN.

The plaintiff may join as a defendant with the person in possession, any other person who, as landlord, remainderman, reversioner or otherwise, may claim title to the premises, or any part thereof, adversely to the plaintiff.

RULE 786. WARRANTOR, ETC., MAY BE MADE A PARTY.

When a party is sued for lands, the real owner or warrantor may make himself, or may be made, a party defendant in the suit, and shall be entitled to make such defense as if he had been the original defendant in the action.

RULE 787. LANDLORD MAY BECOME DEFENDANT.

When such action shall be commenced against a tenant in possession, the landlord may enter himself as the defendant, or he may be made a party on motion of such tenant; and he shall be entitled to make the same defense as if the suit had been originally commenced against him.

RULE 788. MAY FILE PLEA OF "NOT GUILTY" ONLY.

The defendant in such action may file only the plea of "not guilty," which shall state in substance that he is not guilty of the injury complained of in the petition filed by the plaintiff against him, except that if he claims an allowance for improvements, he shall state the facts entitling him to the same.

RULE 789. PROOF UNDER SUCH PLEA.

Under such plea of "not guilty" the defendant may give in evidence any lawful defense to the action except the defense of limitations, which shall be specially pleaded.

RULE 790. ANSWER TAKEN AS ADMITTING POSSESSION.

Such plea or any other answer to the merits shall be an admission by the defendant, for the purpose of that action, that he was in possession of the premises sued for, or that he claimed title thereto at the time of commencing the action, unless he states distinctly in his answer the extent of his possession or claim, in which case it shall be an admission to such extent only.

RULE 791. MAY DEMAND ABSTRACT OF TITLE.

After answer filed, either party may, by notice in writing, duly served on the opposite party or his attorney of record, not less than ten days before the trial of the cause, demand an abstract in writing of the claim or title to the premises in question upon which he relies.

RULE 792. TIME TO FILE ABSTRACT.

Such abstract of title shall be filed with the papers of the cause that within thirty days after the service of the notice, or within such further time that the court on good cause shown may grant; and in default thereof, the court may, after notice and hearing prior to the beginning of trial, order that no written instruments which are evidence of the claim or title of such opposite party be given on trial.

(Amended by Order July 15, 1987, eff. Jan. 1, 1988; April 24, 1990, eff. Sept. 1, 1990.)

RULE 793. ABSTRACT SHALL STATE, WHAT.

The abstract mentioned in the two preceding rules shall state:

(a) The nature of each document or written instrument intended to be used as evidence and its date;

(b) If a contract or conveyance, its date, the parties thereto and the date of the proof of acknowledgment, and before what officer the same was made; and

(c) Where recorded, stating the book and page of the record.

(d) If not recorded in the county when the trial is had, copies of such instrument, with the names of the subscribing witnesses, shall be included. If such unrecorded instrument be lost or destroyed it shall be sufficient to state the nature of such instrument and its loss or destruction.

RULE 794. AMENDED ABSTRACT.

The court may allow either party to file an amended abstract of title, under the same rules, which authorize the amendment of pleadings so far as they are applicable; but in all cases the documentary evidence of title shall at the trial be confined to the matters contained in the abstract of title.

RULE 795. RULES IN OTHER CASES OBSERVED.

The trial shall be conducted according to the rules of pleading, practice and evidence in other cases in the district court and conformable to the principles of trial by ejectment, except as otherwise provided by these rules.

RULE 796. SURVEYOR APPOINTED, ETC.

The judge of the court may, either in term time or in vacation, at his own discretion, or on motion of either party to the action appoint a surveyor, who shall survey the premises in controversy pursuant to the order of the court, and report his action under oath to such court. If said report be not rejected for good cause shown, the same shall be admitted as evidence on the trial.

RULE 797. SURVEY UNNECESSARY, WHEN.

Where there is no dispute as to the lines or boundaries of the land in controversy, or where the defendant admits that he is in possession of the lands or tenements included in the plaintiff's claim, or title, an order of survey shall be unnecessary.

RULE 798. COMMON SOURCE OF TITLE.

It shall not be necessary for the plaintiff to deraign title beyond a common source. Proof of a common source may be made by the plaintiff by certified copies of the deeds showing a chain of title to the defendant emanating from and under such common source. Before any such certified copies shall be read in evidence, they shall be filed with the papers of the suit three days before the trial, and the adverse party served with notice of such filing as in other cases. Such certified copies shall not be evidence of title in the defendant unless offered in evidence by him. The plaintiff may make any legal objection to such certified copies, or the originals thereof, when introduced by the defendant.

RULE 799. JUDGMENT BY DEFAULT.

If the defendant, who has been personally served with citation according to law or these rules fails to appear and answer by himself or attorney within the time prescribed by law or these rules for other actions in the district court, then judgment by default may be entered against him and in favor of the plaintiff for the title to the premises, or the possession thereof, or for both, according to the petition, and for all costs, without any proof of title by the plaintiff.

RULE 800. PROOF EX PARTE.

If the defendant has been cited only by publication, and fails to appear and answer by himself, or by attorney of his own selection, or if any defendant, having answered, fails to appear by himself or attorney when the case is called for trial on its merits, the plaintiff shall make such proof as will entitle him prima facie to recover, whereupon the proper judgment shall be entered.

RULE 801. WHEN DEFENDANT CLAIMS PART ONLY.

Where the defendant claims part of the premises only, the answer shall be equivalent to a disclaimer of the balance.

RULE 802. WHEN PLAINTIFF PROVES PART.

Where the defendant claims the whole premises, and the plaintiff shows himself entitled to recover part, the plaintiff shall recover such part and costs.

RULE 803. MAY RECOVER A PART.

When there are two or more plaintiffs or defendants any one or more of the plaintiffs may recover against one or more of the defendants the premises, or any part thereof, or any interest therein, or damages, according to the rights of the parties.

RULE 804. THE JUDGMENT.

Upon the finding of the jury, or of the court where the case is tried by the court, in favor of the plaintiff for the whole or any part of the premises in controversy, the judgment shall be that the plaintiff recover of the defendant the title or possession, or both, as the case may be, of such premises, describing them, and where he recovers the possession, that he have his writ of possession.

RULE 805. DAMAGES.

Where it is alleged and proved that one of the parties is in possession of the premises, the court or jury, if they find for the adverse party, shall assess the damages for the use and occupation of the premises. If special injury to the property be alleged and proved, the damages for such injury shall also be assessed, and the proper judgment shall be entered therefor, on which execution may issue.

RULE 806. CLAIM FOR IMPROVEMENTS.

When the defendant or person in possession has claimed an allowance for improvements in accordance with Sections 22.021-22.024, Texas Property Code, the claim for use and occupation and damages mentioned in the preceding rule shall be considered and acted on in connection with such claim by the defendant or person in possession.

(Amended by Order Dec. 5, 1983, eff. April 1, 1984; July 15, 1987, eff. Jan. 1, 1988.)

RULE 807. JUDGMENT WHEN CLAIM FOR IMPROVEMENTS IS MADE.

When a claim for improvements is successfully made under Sections 22.021 PROP.-22.024, Texas Property Code, the judgment shall recite the estimated value of the premises without the improvements, and shall also include the conditions, stipulations and directions contained in Sections 22.021-22.024., Texas Property Code so far as applicable to the case before the court.

(Amended by Order Dec. 5, 1983, eff. April 1, 1984; July 15, 1987, eff. Jan. 1, 1988.)

RULE 808. THESE RULES SHALL NOT GOVERN, WHEN.

Nothing in Sections 22.001-22.045, Texas Property Code, shall be so construed as to alter, impair or take away the rights of parties, as arising under the laws in force before the introduction of the common law, but the same shall be decided by the principles of the law under which the same accrued, or by which the same were regulated or in any manner affected.

(Amended by Order Dec. 5, 1983, eff. April 1, 1984; July 15, 1987, eff. Jan. 1, 1988.)

RULE 809. THESE RULES SHALL NOT GOVERN, WHEN.

Nothing in these rules relating to trespass to try title shall be so construed as to alter, impair or take away the rights of parties, as arising under the laws in force before the introduction of the common law, but the same shall be decided by the principles of the law under which the same accrued, or by which the same were regulated or in any manner affected.

SECTION 9.
SUITS AGAINST NON-RESIDENTS

RULE 810. REQUISITES OF PLEADINGS.

The petition in actions authorized by section 17.003, Civil Practice and Remedies Code, shall state the real names of the plaintiff and defendant, and shall describe the property involved with sufficient certainty to identify the same, the interest which the plaintiff claims, and such proceedings shall be had in such action as may be necessary to fully settle and determine the question of right or title in and to said property between the parties to said suit, and to decree the title or right of the party entitled thereto; and the court may issue the appropriate order to carry such decree, judgment or order into effect; and whenever such petition has been duly filed and citation thereon has been duly served by publication as required by Rules 114-116, the plaintiff may, at any time prior to entering the decree by leave of court first had and obtained, file amended and supplemental pleadings that do not subject additional property to said suit without the necessity of reciting the defendants so cited as aforesaid.

(Amended by Order Dec. 5, 1983, eff. April 1, 1984; July 15, 1987, eff. Jan. 1, 1988.)

RULE 811. SERVICE BY PUBLICATION IN ACTIONS UNDER SECTION 17.003 CIV. PRAC. & REM, CIVIL PRACTICE AND REMEDIES CODE.

In actions authorized by Section 17.003, Civil Practice and Remedies Code, service on the defendant or defendants may be made by publication as is provided by Rules 114-116 or by service of notice of the character and in the manner provided by Rule 108.

(Amended by Order Dec. 5, 1983, eff. April 1, 1984; July 15, 1987, eff. Jan. 1, 1988.)

RULE 812. NO JUDGMENT BY DEFAULT.

No judgment by default shall be taken in such case when service has been had by publication, but in such case the facts entitling the plaintiff to judgment shall be exhibited to the court on the trial; and a statement of facts shall be filed as provided by law and these rules in suits against nonresidents of this State served by publication, where no appearance has been made by them.

(Amended by Order Oct. 12, 1949, eff. March 1, 1950.)

RULE 813. SUIT TO EXTINGUISH LIEN.

If said suit shall be for the extinguishment of a lien or claim for money on said property that may be held by the defendant, the amount thereof, with interest, shall be ascertained by the court; and the same deposited in the registry of the court, subject to the drawn by the parties entitled thereto; but in such case no decree shall be entered until said sum is deposited; which fact shall be noted in said decree.

PART VIII.
CLOSING RULES

RULE 814. EFFECTIVE DATE.

These rules shall take effect on September 1st, 1941. They shall govern all proceedings in actions brought after they take effect, and also all further proceedings in actions then pending, except to the extent that in the opinion of the court their application in a particular action pending when the rules take effect would not be feasible or would work injustice, in which event the former procedure shall apply. All things properly done under any previously existing rule or statutes prior to the taking effect of these rules shall be treated as valid. Where citation or other process is issued and served in compliance with existing rules or laws prior to the taking effect of these rules, the party upon whom such citation or other process has been served shall have the time provided for under such previously existing rules or laws in which to comply therewith.

RULE 815. SUBSTANTIVE RIGHTS UNAFFECTED.

These rules shall not be construed to enlarge or diminish any substantive rights or obligations of any parties to any civil action.

RULE 816. JURISDICTION AND VENUE UNAFFECTED.

These rules shall not be construed to extend or limit the jurisdiction of the courts of the State of Texas nor the venue of actions therein.

RULE 817. [RENUMBERED]

(Renumbered as rule 3a Dec. 5, 1983, eff. April 1, 1984.)

RULE 818. REFERENCE TO FORMER STATUTES.

Wherever any statute or rule refers to any practice or procedure in any law, laws, statute or statutes, or to a title, chapter, section, or article of the statutes, or contains any reference of any such nature, and the matter referred to has been supplanted in whole or in part by these rules, every such reference shall be deemed to be to the pertinent part or parts of these rules.

RULE 819. PROCEDURE CONTINUED.

All procedure prescribed by statutes of the State of Texas not specifically listed in the accompanying enumeration of repealed articles shall, insofar as the same is not inconsistent with the provisions of these rules, continue in accordance with the provisions of such statutes as rules of court. In case of inconsistency between the provisions of these rules and any statutory procedure not specifically listed as repealed, these rules shall apply.

RULE 820. WORKERS' COMPENSATION LAW.

All portions of the Workers' Compensation Law, Articles 8306-8309-1, Revised Civil Statutes, and amendments thereto, which relate to matters of practice and procedure are hereby adopted and retained in force and effect as rules of court.

(Amended by Order Dec. 5, 1983, eff. April 1, 1984.)

RULE 821. PRIOR COURT RULES REPEALED.

These rules shall supersede all Court Rules heretofore promulgated for any court; and all of said prior Court Rules are hereby repealed; provided, however, any rules of procedure heretofore adopted by a particular county or district court or by any Court of Appeals which were not of general application but were solely to regulate procedure in the particular court promulgating such rules are to remain in force and effect insofar as they are not inconsistent with these rules.

(Amended by Order Dec. 5, 1983, eff. April 1, 1984.)

RULE 822. TITLE.

These rules may be known and cited as the Texas Rules of Civil Procedure.

Texas Rules of Appellate Procedure

Adopted effective Sept. 1, 1997 including amendments received through August 1, 2017.

SECTION ONE.
GENERAL PROVISIONS

RULE 1. SCOPE OF RULES; LOCAL RULES OF COURTS OF APPEALS

1.1. Scope.

These rules govern procedure in appellate courts and before appellate judges and post-trial procedure in trial courts in criminal cases.

1.2. Local Rules.

(a) Promulgation. A court of appeals may promulgate rules governing its practice that are not inconsistent with these rules. Local rules governing civil cases must first be approved by the Supreme Court. Local rules governing criminal cases must first be approved by the Court of Criminal Appeals.

(b) Copies. The clerk must provide a copy of the court's local rules to anyone who requests it.

(c) Party's Noncompliance. A court must not dismiss an appeal for noncompliance with a local rule without giving the noncomplying party notice and a reasonable opportunity to cure the noncompliance.

(Adopted by Order eff. Sept. 1, 1997.)

Comment to 1997 change: Subdivision 1.1 is simplified without substantive change. Subdivision 1.2 is amended to make clear that any person is entitled to a copy of local rules. Paragraph 1.2(c), restricting dismissal of a case for noncompliance with a local rule, is added.

RULE 2. SUSPENSION OF RULES.

On a party's motion or on its own initiative an appellate court may—to expedite a decision or for other good cause—suspend a rule's operation in a particular case and order a different procedure; but a court must not construe this rule to suspend any provision in the Code of Criminal Procedure or to alter the time for perfecting an appeal in a civil case.

Comment to 1997 change: Former subdivision (a) regarding appellate court jurisdiction is deleted. The power to suspend rules is extended to civil cases. Other nonsubstantive changes are made.

RULE 3. DEFINITIONS; UNIFORM TERMINOLOGY

3.1. Definitions.

(a) Appellant means a party taking an appeal to an appellate court.

(b) Appellate court means the courts of appeals, the Court of Criminal Appeals, and the Supreme Court.

(c) Appellee means a party adverse to an appellant.

(d) Applicant means a person seeking relief by a habeas corpus in a criminal case.

(e) Petitioner means a party petitioning the Supreme Court or the Court of Criminal Appeals for review.

(f) Relator means a person seeking relief in an original proceeding in an appellate court other than by habeas corpus in a criminal case.

(g) Reporter or court reporter means the court reporter or court recorder.

(h) Respondent means:

(1) a party adverse to a petitioner in the Supreme Court or the Court of Criminal Appeals; or

(2) a party against whom relief is sought in an original proceeding in an appellate court.

3.2. Uniform Terminology in Criminal Cases.

In documents filed in criminal appeals, the parties are the State and the appellant. But if the State has appealed under **Article 44.01 of the Code of Criminal Procedure**, the defendant is the appellee. Otherwise, papers should use real names for parties, and such labels as appellee, petitioner, respondent, and movant should be avoided unless necessary for clarity. In habeas corpus proceedings, the person for whose relief the writ is requested is the applicant; **Code of Criminal Procedure article 11.13.**

(Adopted by Order eff. Sept. 1, 1997.)

Comment to 1997 change: The definition of court below and the reference to "suing out a writ of error to the court of appeals," are deleted as those terms are no longer used in these rules. Other changes are made.

RULE 4. TIME AND NOTICE PROVISIONS

4.1. Computing Time.

(a) In General. The day of an act, event, or default after which a designated period begins to run is not included when computing a period prescribed or allowed by these rules, by court order, or by statute. The last day of the period is included, but if that day is a Saturday, Sunday, or legal holiday, the period extends to the end of the next day that is not a Saturday, Sunday, or legal holiday.

(b) Clerk's Office Closed or Inaccessible. If the act to be done is filing a document, and if the clerk's office where the document is to be filed is closed or inaccessible during regular hours on the last day for filing the document, the period for filing the document extends to the end of the next day when the clerk's office is open and accessible. The closing or inaccessibility of the clerk's office may be proved by a certificate of the clerk or counsel, by a party's affidavit, or by other satisfactory proof, and may be controverted in the same manner.

4.2. No Notice of Trial Court's Judgment in Civil Case.

(a) Additional Time to File Documents.

(1) In general. If a party affected by a judgment or other appealable order has not—within 20 days after the judgment or order was signed—either received the notice required by Texas Rule of Civil Procedure 306a.3 or acquired actual knowledge of the signing, then a period that, under these rules, runs from the signing will begin for that party on the earlier of the date when the party receives notice or acquires actual knowledge of the signing. But in no event may the periods begin more than 90 days after the judgment or order was signed.

(2) Exception for restricted appeal. Subparagraph (1) does not extend the time for perfecting a restricted appeal.

(b) Procedure to Gain Additional Time. The procedure to gain additional time is governed by Texas Rule of Civil Procedure 306a.5.

(c) The Court's Order. After hearing the motion, the trial court must sign a written order that finds the date when the party or the party's attorney first either received notice or acquired actual knowledge that the judgment or order was signed.

4.3. Periods Affected by Modified Judgment in Civil Case.

(a) During Plenary-Power Period. If a judgment is modified in any respect while the trial court retains plenary power, a period that, under these rules, runs from the date when the judgment is signed will run from the date when the modified judgment is signed.

(b) After Plenary Power Expires. If the trial court corrects or reforms the judgment under > Texas Rule of Civil Procedure 316 after expiration of the trial court's plenary power, all periods provided in these rules that run from the date the judgment is signed run from the date the corrected judgment is signed for complaints that would not apply to the original judgment.

4.4. Periods Affected When Process Served by Publication.

If process was served by publication and if a motion for new trial was filed under Texas Rule of Civil Procedure 329 more than 30 days after the judgment was signed, a period that, under these rules, runs from the date when the judgment is signed will be computed as if the judgment were signed on the date when the motion for new trial was filed.

4.5. No Notice of Judgment or Order of Appellate Court; Effect on Time to File Certain Documents.

(a) Additional Time to File Documents. A party may move for additional time to file a motion for rehearing or en banc reconsideration in the court of appeals, a petition for review, or a petition for discretionary review, if the party did not—until after the time expired for filing the document—either receive notice of the judgment or order from the clerk or acquire actual knowledge of the rendition of the judgment or order.

(b) Procedure to Gain Additional Time. The motion must state the earliest date when the party or the party's attorney received notice or acquired actual knowledge that the judgment or order had been rendered. The motion must be filed within 15 days of that date but in no event more than 90 days after the date of the judgment or order.

(c) Where to File.

(1) A motion for additional time to file a motion for rehearing or en banc reconsideration in the court of appeals must be filed in and ruled on by the court of appeals in which the case is pending.

(2) A motion for additional time to file a petition for review must be filed in and ruled on by the Supreme Court.

(3) A motion for additional time to file a petition for discretionary review must be filed in and ruled on by the Court of Criminal Appeals.

(d) Order of the Court. If the court finds that the motion for additional time was timely filed and the party did not—within the time for filing the motion for rehearing or en banc reconsideration, petition for review, or petition for discretionary review, as the case may be—receive the notice or have actual knowledge of the judgment or order, the court must grant the motion. If the court grants the motion, the time for filing the document will begin to run on the date when the court grants the motion.

(Adopted by Order eff. Sept. 1, 1997. Amended by Order Dec. 23, 2002 eff. Jan. 1, 2003; Order Aug. 20, 2008, eff. Sept. 1, 2008.)

Comment to 2002 change: Subdivision 4.5 is amended to clarify that a party may obtain additional time to file documents when the party fails to receive notice not only of an appellate court judgment, but of an appellate court order—such as one denying a motion for rehearing—that triggers the appeal period.

Comment to 2008 change: Subdivision 4.5 is changed, consistent with other changes in the rules, to specifically address a motion for en banc reconsideration and treat it as a motion for rehearing.

Rule 4.6. No Notice of Trial Court's Order on Motion for Forensic DNA Testing

(a) *Additional Time to File Notice of Appeal.* Notwithstanding Rules 26.2 and 26.3, a defendant may move for additional time to file a notice of appeal under Code of Criminal Procedure chapter 64 (Motion for Forensic DNA Testing) if the defendant neither received notice nor acquired actual knowledge that the trial judge signed an appealable order before the time for filing a notice of appeal had expired.

(b) *Contents of Motion for Additional Time.* The motion must be in writing and sworn, state the earliest date when the defendant first received notice or acquired actual knowledge that the appealable order had been signed, and comply with Rule 10.5(b)(2).

(c) *When and Where to File.*

(1) The motion must be filed within 30 days of the date upon which the defendant first received notice or acquired actual knowledge of the trial court's signing of the appealable order. But in no event may the motion be filed more than 120 days after the date the appealable order was signed.

(2) The motion must be filed in the proper court of appeals.

(d) *Order of the Court.* The court of appeals must grant a motion for additional time if it finds that the defendant neither received notice nor acquired actual knowledge of the trial judge's signing of an appealable order before the time for filing a notice of appeal had expired and that the defendant timely filed the motion for additional time. The time for filing the document will begin to run on the date when the court grants the motion.

(Adopted by Tex. Sup. Ct. Misc. Docket No. 16-9061 June 13, 2017, eff. Sept. 1, 2017.)

RULE 5. FEES IN CIVIL CASES

A party who is not excused by statute or these rules from paying costs must pay—at the time an item is presented for filing—whatever fees are required by statute or Supreme Court order. The appellate court may enforce this rule by any order that is just.

(Adopted by Order eff. Sept. 1, 1997.)

Comment to 1997 change: This is former Rule 13. The rule is simplified. The fees an appellate court may charge in a civil case are now specified by Supreme Court order.

RULE 6. REPRESENTATION BY COUNSEL

6.1. Lead Counsel.

(a) For Appellant. Unless another attorney is designated, lead counsel for an appellant is the attorney whose signature first appears on the notice of appeal.

(b) For a Party Other Than Appellant. Unless another attorney is designated, lead counsel for a party other than an appellant is the attorney whose signature first appears on the first document filed in the appellate court on that party's behalf.

(c) How to Designate. The original or a new lead counsel may be designated by filing a notice stating that attorney's name, mailing address, telephone number, fax number, if any, email address, and State Bar of Texas identification number. If a new lead counsel is being designated, both the new attorney and either the party or the former lead counsel must sign the notice.

(Amended by Order Aug. 16, 2013, eff. Jan. 1, 2014; Order Dec. 13, 2013, eff. Jan. 1, 2014.)

6.2. Appearance of Other Attorneys.

An attorney other than lead counsel may file a notice stating that the attorney represents a specified party to the proceeding and giving that attorney's name, mailing address, telephone number, fax number, if any, email address, and State Bar of Texas identification number. The clerk will note on the docket the attorney's appearance. When a brief or motion is filed, the clerk will note on the docket the name of each attorney, if not already noted, who appears on the document.

(Amended by Order Aug. 16, 2013, eff. Jan. 1, 2014; Order Dec. 13, 2013, eff. Jan. 1, 2014.)

6.3. To Whom Communications Sent.

Any notice, copies of documents filed in an appellate court, or other communications must be sent to:

(a) each party's lead counsel on appeal;

(b) a party's lead counsel in the trial court if:

(1) that party was represented by counsel in the trial court;

(2) lead counsel on appeal has not yet been designated for that party; and

(3) lead counsel in the trial court has not filed a nonrepresentation notice or been allowed to withdraw;

(c) a party if the party is not represented by counsel.

6.4. Nonrepresentation Notice.

(a) In General. If, in accordance with paragraph 6.3(b), the lead counsel in the trial court is being sent notices, copies of documents, or other communications, that attorney may file a nonrepresentation notice in the appellate court. The notice must:

(1) state that the attorney is not representing the party on appeal;

(2) state that the court and other counsel should communicate directly with the party in the future;

(3) give the party's name and last known address and telephone number; and

(4) be signed by the party.

(b) Appointed Counsel. In a criminal case, an attorney appointed by the trial court to represent an indigent party cannot file a nonrepresentation notice.

6.5. Withdrawal.

An appellate court may, on appropriate terms and conditions, permit an attorney to withdraw from representing a party in the appellate court.

(a) Contents of Motion. A motion for leave to withdraw must contain the following:

(1) a list of current deadlines and settings in the case;

(2) the party's name and last known address and telephone number;

(3) a statement that a copy of the motion was delivered to the party; and

(4) a statement that the party was notified in writing of the right to object to the motion.

(b) Delivery to Party. The motion must be delivered to the party in person or mailed—both by certified and by first-class mail—to the party at the party's last known address.

(c) If Motion Granted. If the court grants the motion, the withdrawing attorney must immediately notify the party, in writing, of any deadlines or settings that the attorney knows about at the time of withdrawal but that were not previously disclosed to the party. The withdrawing attorney must file a copy of that notice with the court clerk.

(d) Exception for Substitution of Counsel. If an attorney substitutes for a withdrawing attorney, the motion to withdraw need not comply with (a) but must state only the substitute attorney's name, mailing address, telephone number, fax number, if any, and State Bar of Texas identification number. The withdrawing attorney must comply with (b) but not (c).

6.6. Agreements of Parties or Counsel.

To be enforceable, an agreement of parties or their counsel concerning an appellate court proceeding must be in writing and signed by the parties or their counsel. Such an agreement is subject to any appellate court order necessary to ensure that the case is properly presented.

(Adopted by Order eff. Sept. 1, 1997.)

Comment to 1997 change: Former Rules 7 and 57 are merged and substantially revised. Former Rule 8 regarding agreements of counsel is included here as subdivision 6.6 and the requirement that an agreement be filed and included in the record is deleted.

RULE 7. SUBSTITUTING PARTIES

7.1. Parties Who Are Not Public Officers.

(a) Death of a Party.

(1) Civil Cases. If a party to a civil case dies after the trial court renders judgment but before the case has been finally disposed of on appeal, the appeal may be perfected, and the appellate court will proceed to adjudicate the appeal as if all parties were alive. The appellate court's judgment will have the same force and effect as if rendered when all parties were living. The decedent party's name may be used on all papers.

(2) Criminal Cases. If the appellant in a criminal case dies after an appeal is perfected but before the appellate court issues the mandate, the appeal will be permanently abated.

(b) Substitution for Other Reasons. If substitution of a party in the appellate court is necessary for a reason other than death, the appellate court may order substitution on any party's motion at any time.

7.2. Public Officers.

(a) Automatic Substitution of Officer. When a public officer is a party in an official capacity to an appeal or original proceeding, and if that person ceases to hold office before the appeal or original proceeding is finally disposed of, the public officer's successor is automatically substituted as a party if appropriate. Proceedings following substitution are to be in the name of the substituted party, but any misnomer that does not affect the substantial rights of the parties may be disregarded. Substitution may be ordered at any time, but failure to order substitution of the successor does not affect the substitution.

(b) Abatement. If the case is an original proceeding under Rule 52, the court must abate the proceeding to allow the successor to reconsider the original party's decision. In all other cases, the suit will not abate, and the successor will be bound by the appellate court's judgment or order as if the successor were the original party.

(Adopted by Order eff. Sept. 1, 1997.)

Comment to 1997 change: This is former Rule 9. Former subdivision (a) regarding death of a party in a civil case is now subparagraph 7.1(a)(1). Former subdivision (b) regarding death of a party in a criminal case is now subparagraph 7.1(a)(2). Former subdivision (c) regarding separation of office by public officers is now subdivision 7.2. Former paragraph (c)(3) regarding a successor's liability for costs is omitted as unnecessary. Former subdivision (d) regarding substitution for other causes is now paragraph 7.1(b). Subdivision 7.2 is revised to make it applicable to all cases in which a public officer is a party, and to make substitution automatic if appropriate.

RULE 8. BANKRUPTCY IN CIVIL CASES

8.1. Notice of Bankruptcy.

Any party may file a notice that a party is in bankruptcy. The notice must contain:

(a) the bankrupt party's name;

(b) the court in which the bankruptcy proceeding is pending;

(c) the bankruptcy proceeding's style and case number; and

(d) the date when the bankruptcy petition was filed.

(Amended by Order March 10, 2008 eff. Sept. 1, 2008; Order Aug. 20, 2008, eff. Sept. 1, 2008.)

Comment to 2008 change: The amendment eliminates the former requirement that the bankruptcy notice contain certain pages of the bankruptcy petition, in recognition that electronic filing is now prevale28.1.nt in bankruptcy courts and access to bankruptcy petitions is widely available through the federal PACER system.

8.2. Effect of Bankruptcy.

A bankruptcy suspends the appeal and all periods in these rules from the date when the bankruptcy petition is filed until the appellate court reinstates or severs the appeal in accordance with federal law. A period that began to run and had not expired at the time the proceeding was suspended begins anew when the proceeding is reinstated or severed under 8.3. A document filed by a party while the proceeding is suspended will be deemed filed on the same day, but after, the court reinstates or severs the appeal and will not be considered ineffective because it was filed while the proceeding was suspended.

8.3. Motion to Reinstate or Sever Appeal Suspended by Bankruptcy.

(a) Motion to Reinstate. If a case has been suspended by a bankruptcy filing, a party may move that the appellate court reinstate the appeal if permitted by federal law or the bankruptcy court. If the bankruptcy court has lifted or terminated the stay, a certified copy of the order must be attached to the motion.

(b) Motion to Sever. A party may move to sever the appeal with respect to the bankrupt party and to reinstate the appeal with respect to the other parties. The motion must show that the case is severable and must comply with applicable federal law regarding severance of a bankrupt party. The court may proceed under this paragraph on its own initiative.

(Adopted by Order eff. Sept. 1, 1997.)

Comment to 1997 change: This is a new rule.

RULE 9. DOCUMENTS GENERALLY

9.1. Signing.

(a) Represented Parties. If a party is represented by counsel, a document filed on that party's behalf must be signed by at least one of the party's attorneys. For each attorney whose name appears on a document as representing that party, the document must contain that attorney's State Bar of Texas identification number, mailing address, telephone number, fax number, if any, and email address.

(b) Unrepresented Parties. A party not represented by counsel must sign any document that the party files and give the party's mailing address, telephone number, and fax number, if any, and email address.

(c) Electronic Signatures. A document that is electronically served, filed, or issued by a court or clerk is considered signed if the document includes:

(1) a "/s/" and name typed in the space where the signature would otherwise appear, unless the document is notarized or sworn; or

(2) an electronic image or scanned image of the signature.

(Amended by Order Aug. 16, 2013, eff. Jan. 1, 2014; Order Dec. 13, 2013, eff. Jan. 1, 2014.)

9.2. Filing.

(a) With Whom. A document is filed in an appellate court by delivering it to:

(1) the clerk of the court in which the document is to be filed; or

(2) a justice or judge of that court who is willing to accept delivery. A justice or judge who accepts delivery must note on the document the date and time of delivery, which will be considered the time of filing, and must promptly send it to the clerk.

(b) Filing by Mail.

(1) Timely Filing. A document received within ten days after the filing deadline is considered timely filed if:

(A) it was sent to the proper clerk by United States Postal Service first class, express, registered, or certified mail or a commercial delivery service;

(B) it was placed in an envelope or wrapper properly addressed and stamped; and

(C) it was deposited in the mail or delivered to a commercial delivery service on or before the last day for filing.

(2) Proof of Mailing. Though it may consider other proof, the appellate court will accept the following as conclusive proof of the date of mailing:

(A) a legible postmark affixed by the United States Postal Service;

(B) a receipt for registered or certified mail if the receipt is endorsed by the United States Postal Service;

(C) a certificate of mailing by the United States Postal Service;

(D) a receipt endorsed by the commercial delivery service.

(c) Electronic Filing.

(1) Requirement. Attorneys in civil cases must electronically file documents. Attorneys in criminal cases must electronically file documents except for good cause shown in a motion filed in the appellate court. Unrepresented parties in civil and criminal cases may electronically file documents, but it is not required.

(2) Mechanism. Electronic filing must be done through the electronic filing manager established by the Office of Court Administration and an electronic filing service provider certified by the Office of Court Administration.

(3) Exceptions. Documents filed under seal, subject to a pending motion to seal, or to which access is otherwise restricted by law or court order must not be electronically filed. For good cause, an appellate court may permit a party to file other documents in paper form in a particular case.

(4) Timely Filing. Unless a document must be filed by a certain time of day, a document is considered timely filed if it is electronically filed at any time before midnight (in the court's time zone) on the filing deadline. An electronically filed document is deemed filed when transmitted to the filing party's electronic filing service provider, except:

(A) if a document is transmitted on a Saturday, Sunday, or legal holiday, it is deemed filed on the next day that is not a Saturday, Sunday, or legal holiday; and

(B) if a document requires a motion and an order allowing its filing, the document is deemed filed on the date the motion is granted.

(5) Technical Failure. If a document is untimely due to a technical failure or a system outage, the filing party may seek appropriate relief from the court.

(6) Confirmation of Filing. The electronic filing manager will send a filing confirmation notice to the filing party.

(7) Electronic Notices From the Court. The clerk may send notices, orders, or other communications about the case to the party electronically. A court seal may be electronic.

(Amended by Order June 27, 2011, eff. June 30, 2011; Order Aug. 16, 2013, eff. Jan. 1, 2014; Order Dec. 13, 2013, eff. Jan. 1, 2014.)

9.3. Number of Copies.

(a) Courts of Appeals.

(1) Document Filed in Paper Form. If a document is not electronically filed, a party must file the original and one unbound copy of the document unless otherwise required by local rule. The unbound copy of an appendix must contain a separate page before each document and must not include tabs that extend beyond the edge of the page.

(2) Electronically Filed Document. Unless required by local rule, a party need not file a paper copy of an electronically filed document.

(b) Supreme Court and Court of Criminal Appeals.

(1) Document Filed in Paper Form. If a document is not electronically filed, a party must file the original and 11 copies of any document addressed to either the Supreme Court or the Court of Criminal Appeals, except that in the Supreme Court only an original and one copy must be filed of any motion, response to the motion, and reply in support of the motion, and in the Court of Criminal Appeals, only the original must be filed of a motion for extension of time or a response to the motion, or a pleading under Code of Criminal Procedure article 11.07.

(2) Electronically Filed Document. Paper copies of each document that is electronically filed with the Supreme Court or the Court of Criminal Appeals must be mailed or hand-delivered to the Supreme Court or the Court of Criminal Appeals, as appropriate, within three business days after the document is electronically filed. The number of paper copies required shall be determined, respectively, by order of the Supreme Court or the Court of Criminal Appeals.

(c) Exception for Record. Only the original record need be filed in any proceeding.

(Amended by Order March 10, 2008, eff. Sept. 1, 2008; Order Aug. 20, 2008, eff. Sept. 1, 2008; Order June 27, 2011, eff. June 30, 2011; Order Aug. 16, 2013, eff. Jan. 1, 2014; Order Dec. 13, 2013, eff. Jan. 1, 2014.)

APPENDIX A

Local Rule _____. Electronic Copies of Documents Filed in Paper Form.

(a) Electronic copies of documents required. For the convenience of the court, attorneys, parties, and the public, an attorney for a party must email to the court an electronic copy of every document filed with the court, except a document under seal or subject to a motion to seal. A party who is not represented by an attorney is encouraged to email to the court an electronic copy of every document filed with the court, except a document under seal or subject to a motion to seal. [Courts may add exceptions for attorneys and unrepresented parties.]

(b) Filing required. An electronic copy does not constitute a filing. Documents must continue to be filed as provided by the Texas Rules of Appellate Procedure[, except that only the original and [insert number] copies must be filed of any document other than a petition for discretionary review. A party must file the original and 11 copies of a petition for discretionary review].

(c) Time to email electronic copy. The electronic copy must be emailed to the court at [insert applicable email address] on the same day the original document is filed. Also on that day, the electronic copy must be emailed to each other party's lead counsel for whom the filing attorney has an email address.

(d) Identification of document. The email subject line must identify the document by case number and by name. The electronic copy must be named as follows: [insert court's desired naming conventions here].

(e) Redaction of electronic copies. An electronic copy must be substantively identical to the original document filed with the court, except it must not contain a social security number; a birth date; a home address; the name of any person who was a minor when the underlying suit was filed; a driver's license number, passport number, tax identification number, or similar government issued personal identification number; or a bank account number, credit card number, or other financial account number. The attorney emailing the electronic copy must redact all such information in accordance with the redaction guidelines posted by the Supreme Court's Clerk on the Supreme Court's website; however, the electronic copy may contain a reference to this information as long as the reference does not include any part of the actual information (e.g., "passport number"). For good cause, the court may order redaction of additional information.

(f) Certification of counsel. The submission of an electronic copy constitutes a certification by all attorneys of record for the party filing the document that the electronic copy complies with paragraph (e).

(g) Posting of electronic copies. The clerk may post electronic copies of documents in a case on the court's website. By letter to the clerk, a party to the case may request that electronic copies posted on the court's website be redacted further or removed altogether. The request must identify with particularity the document(s) to be removed or the information to be redacted and state specific reasons for the request. If the request is for further redaction, the party must email a copy of the requested version of the document.

(h) Format of electronic copies. An electronic copy must be formatted as follows:

(1) An electronic copy must be in text-searchable portable document format (PDF) compatible with the latest version of Adobe Reader.

(2) Except as otherwise provided by this rule, an electronic copy of a document created by a word processing program must not be a scan of the original but must instead be converted from the original directly into a PDF file using Adobe Acrobat, a word processing program's PDF conversion utility, or another software program.

(3) Records filed in original proceedings and appendix materials may be scanned if necessary, but scanning creates larger file sizes with images of lesser quality and should be avoided when possible. An appendix must be combined into one computer file with the document it is associated with, unless the resulting computer file would exceed the size limits in paragraph (i). If a record filed in an original proceeding or an appendix contains more than one item, it should include a table of contents and either bookmarks to assist in locating each item or separator pages with the title of the item immediately following and any number or letter associated with the item in the table of contents.

(4) A scanned document must be made searchable using optical-character-recognition software, such as Adobe Acrobat, and have a resolution of 300 dots per inch (dpi).

(5) An electronic copy may contain hyperlinks to another part of the same document, an external source cited in the document, an appendix item associated with the document, an embedded case, or a record cite. Hyperlinks within an appendix item are also permitted.

(6) An electronic copy must not contain a virus or malware. The submission of an electronic copy constitutes a certification by all attorneys of record for the party filing the document that the electronic copy has been checked for viruses and malware.

(7) An electronic copy need not be signed.

(i) Size of electronic copies. A electronic copy must not exceed 20 megabytes. Electronic copies larger than 20 megabytes must be divided into smaller files.

(j) Communications with the clerk. An attorney who emails an electronic copy of a document must supply the clerk with an email address to which the clerk may send notices or other communications about the case in lieu of mailing paper documents. If the attorney's email address changes, the attorney must provide the clerk with the new email address within one business day of the change. Lead counsel must register for Casemail and follow the instructions for receiving notices for cases in which they represent a party.

APPENDIX B

Local Rule _____. Electronic Filings of Documents.

(a) Electronic filing permitted. A party may electronically file (e-file) any document that may be filed with the court in paper form, except a document under seal or subject to a motion to seal.

(b) E-filing mechanism. E-filing must be done through Texas.gov, the portal established by the Texas Legislature. Directions for its use may be found on its website. This is a summary. A person must first register with an Electronic Filing Service Provider (EFSP). A list of approved EFSPs is on the Texas.gov website. The EFSP will provide the registrant with a confidential, secure username and password to use when e-filing a document. This username and password will also function as a signature on each e-filed document, and will authorize payment of all filing fees and service fees. A document to be e-filed must be transmitted to the EFSP, which will send the document to Texas.gov, which in turn will send the document to the clerk. The e-filer will receive by email an immediate acknowledgment of the e-filing, a confirmation of the clerk's acceptance of the filing, and a file-stamped copy of the document. Fees charged by Texas.gov for the e-filing of a document are in addition to any filing fees and are costs of court.

(c) Electronic service. A party who has registered to e-file documents through an EFSP may electronically serve (e-serve) documents through that EFSP on any other party who has consented to e-service by registering for the e-service option with an EFSP or by setting up a complimentary account with Texas.gov. Directions may be found on the Texas.gov website.

(1) Service through an EFSP is complete on transmission to the e-served person's EFSP or complimentary Texas.gov account. The e-filer's EFSP will send proof of service to the e-filer. Fees that an EFSP charges for e-service are not costs of court.

(2) If an e-filer must serve a copy of a document on a party who has not consented to eservice, the e-filer must comply with the service requirements in Texas Rule of Appellate Procedure 9.5 and, on the same day the document is e-filed, must send the document to:

(A) the party's lead counsel by email if the e-filer has an email address for the lead counsel; or

(B) if the party is not represented by counsel, to the party by email if the e-filer has the party's email address.

(d) Redaction of information in e-filed document.

(1) Unless the court orders otherwise, an e-filed document must not contain a social security number; a birth date; a home address; the name of any person who was a minor when the underlying suit was filed; a driver's license number, passport number, tax identification number, or similar government-issued personal identification number; or a bank account number, credit card number, or other financial account number. The e-filer must redact all of this information in accordance with the redaction guidelines posted by the Supreme Court's Clerk on the Supreme Court's website; however, the e-filed document may contain a reference to this information as long as the reference does not include any part of the actual information (e.g., "passport number"). For good cause, the court may order redaction of additional information.

(2) The e-filing of a document constitutes a certification by all attorneys of record for the party filing the document that the document complies with paragraph (1) of this rule.

(3) If an e-filer believes any information described in paragraph (1) of this rule is essential to an e-filed document or that the e-filed document would be confusing without the information, the e-filer may submit the information to the court in a reference list that is in paper form and under seal. The reference list must specify an appropriate identifier that corresponds uniquely to each item listed. Any reference in the e-filed document to a listed identifier will be construed to refer to the corresponding item of information. If the e-filer provides a reference list pursuant to this rule, the front page of the e-filed document must indicate that the reference list has been, or will be, provided.

(4) On its own initiative, the court may order a sealed reference list in any case. The court may also order that a document be filed under seal in paper form, without redaction. The court may later unseal the document or order the filer to provide a redacted version of the document for the public record.

(e) Format of e-filed document. An e-filed document must be formatted as follows:

(1) An e-filed document must be formatted in accordance with Texas Rule of Appellate Procedure 9.4(b)-(e). The "paper" requirements in Rule 9.4(b)-(c) apply equally to a "page" of the e-filed document.

(2) An e-filed document must be in text-searchable portable document format (PDF) compatible with the latest version of Adobe Reader. An EFSP will convert each e-filed document from its original form into a PDF file that complies with this rule.

(3) Records filed in original proceedings and appendix materials may be scanned if necessary, but scanning creates larger file sizes with images of lesser quality and should be avoided when possible. An appendix must be combined into one computer file with the document it is associated with, unless the resulting computer file would exceed Texas.gov's size limits for the document. If a record filed in an original proceeding or an appendix contains more than one item, it should include a table of contents

and either bookmarks to assist in locating each item or separator pages with the title of the item immediately following and any number or letter associated with the item in the table of contents.

(4) A scanned document must be made searchable using optical-character-recognition software, such as Adobe Acrobat, and have a resolution of 300 dots per inch (dpi).

(5) An e-filed document may contain hyperlinks to another part of the same document, an external source cited in the document, an appendix item associated with the document, an embedded case, or a record cite. Hyperlinks within an appendix item are also permitted.

(6) An e-filed document must not contain a virus or malware. The e-filing of a document constitutes a certification by the e-filer that the document has been checked for viruses and malware.

(7) The court may strike an e-filed document for nonconformance with this rule.

(f) Signatures on e-filed documents.

(1) Except as otherwise provided by this rule, the confidential, secure username and password that the e-filer must use to e-file a document constitute the e-filer's signature on the document, in compliance with signature requirements in the Texas Rules of Appellate Procedure. When a signature is provided in this manner, the e-filer must also include either an "/s/" and the e-filer's name typed in the space where the e-filer's signature would otherwise appear or an electronic image of the e-filer's signature, which may take the form of a public key-based digital signature or a scanned image of the e-filer's signature. The efiler must not allow the e-filer's username or password to be used by anyone other than an agent who is authorized by the e-filer.

(2) If a document must be notarized, sworn to, or made under oath, the e-filer must e-file the document as a scanned image containing the necessary signature(s).

(3) If a document requires the signature of an opposing party, the e-filer must e-file the document as a scanned image containing the opposing party's signature.

(4) When an e-filer e-files a scanned image of a document pursuant to paragraph (2) or (3) of this rule, the e-filer must retain the original document from which the scanned image was made until the case in which the document was filed is resolved. If the original document is in another party's possession, that party must retain the original document until the case in which the document was filed is resolved.

(5) If an e-served document was also e-filed and the person who completes a certificate of service under Texas Rule of Appellate Procedure 9.5(e) is different from the person who e-filed the document, the person who completes the certificate of service must sign the certificate by including either an'Vs/" and his or her name typed in the space where his or her signature would otherwise appear or an electronic image of his or her signature.

(g) Time of e-filing. A document will be considered filed timely if it is e-filed at any time before midnight (in the court's time zone) on the date on which the document is due.

(1) An e-filed document is deemed filed when the e-filer transmits the document to the e-filer's EFSP, unless the document is transmitted on a Saturday, Sunday, or legal holiday or requires a motion and an order allowing its filing.

(2) If a document is transmitted on a Saturday, Sunday, or legal holiday, it will be deemed filed on the next day that is not a Saturday, Sunday, or legal holiday.

(3) If a document requires a motion and an order allowing its filing, it will be deemed filed on the date the motion is granted.

(4) If an e-filed document is untimely due to a technical failure or a system outage, the e-filer may seek appropriate relief from the court.

(h) Paper copies.

OPTION 1: An e-filer is not required to file any paper copies of an e-filed document, except that paper copies of a petition for discretionary review must still be filed in accordance with Rule 9 of the Texas Rules of Appellate Procedure within one business day after the petition is e-filed.

OPTION 2: An e-filer must file 11 paper copies of an e-filed petition for discretionary review and [insert number] paper copies of any other e-filed document in accordance with Rule 9 of the Texas Rules of Appellate Procedure within one business day after the document is e-filed.

(i) Email address requirements and communications with the clerk. An e-filed document must include the e-filer's email address, in addition to any other information required by the Texas Rules of Appellate Procedure. If the e-filer's email address changes, the e-filer must provide the clerk and the e-filer's EFSP with the new email address within one business day of the change. If there is a change in the email address of a party who has consented to receive e-service, the party must provide Texas.gov or, if applicable, the party's EFSP with the new email address within one business day of the change. The clerk may send notices or other communications about a case to an attorney's email address in lieu of mailing paper documents.

(j) Casemail registration. Lead counsel must register for Casemail and follow the instructions for receiving notices for cases in which they represent a party.

(k) Construction of rules. This rule must be liberally construed so as to avoid undue prejudice to any person who makes a good-faith effort to comply with requirements in this rule.

9.4. Form.

Except for the record, a document filed with an appellate court, including a paper copy of an electronically filed document, must—unless the court accepts another form in the interest of justice—be in the following form:

(a) Printing. A document may be produced by standard typographic printing or by any duplicating process that produces a distinct black image. For a paper document, printing may be on both sides of the paper.

(b) Paper Type and Size. The paper on which a document is produced must 8½ by 11 inches, white or nearly white, and opaque.

(c) Margins. Documents must have at least one-inch margins on both sides and at the top and bottom.

(d) Spacing. Text must be double-spaced, but footnotes, block quotations, short lists, and issues or points of error may be single-spaced.

(e) Typeface. A document produced on a computer must be printed in a conventional typeface no smaller than 14-point except for footnotes, which must be no smaller than 12-point. A typewritten document must be printed in standard 10-character-per-inch (cpi) monospaced typeface.

(f) Binding and Covering. A paper document must be bound so as to ensure that it will not lose its cover or fall apart in regular use. A paper document should be stapled once in the top left-hand corner or be bound so that it will lie flat when open. A paper petition or brief should have durable front and back covers which must not be plastic or be red, black, or dark blue.

(g) Contents of Cover. A document's front cover, if any, must contain the case style, the case number, the title of the document being filed, the name of the party filing the document, and the name, mailing address, telephone number, fax number, if any, email address, and State Bar of Texas identification number of the lead counsel for the filing party. If a party requests oral argument in the court of appeals, the request must appear on the front cover of that party's first brief.

(h) Appendix and Original Proceeding Record. A paper appendix may be bound either with the document to which it is related or separately. If separately bound, the appendix must comply with paragraph (f). A paper record in an original proceeding or a paper appendix must be tabbed and indexed. An electronically filed record in an original proceeding or an electronically filed appendix that includes more than one item must contain bookmarks to assist in locating each item.

(i) Length.

(1) Contents Included and Excluded. In calculating the length of a document, every word and every part of the document, including headings, footnotes, and quotations, must be counted except the following: caption, identity of parties and counsel, statement regarding oral argument, table of contents, index of authorities, statement of the case, statement of issues presented, statement of jurisdiction, statement of procedural history, signature, proof of service, certification, certificate of compliance, and appendix.

(2) Maximum Length. The documents listed below must not exceed the following limits:

(A) A brief and response in a direct appeal to the Court of Criminal Appeals in a case in which the death penalty has been assessed: 37.500 words if computer-generated, and 125 pages if not.

(B) A brief and response in an appellate court (other than a brief under subparagraph (A)) and a petition and response in an original proceeding in the court of appeals: 15.000 words if computer generated, and 50 pages if not. In a civil case in the court of appeals, the aggregate of all briefs filed by a party must not exceed 27,000 words if computer-generated, and 90 pages if not.

(C) A reply brief in an appellate court and a reply to a response to a petition in an original proceeding in the court of appeals: 7,500 words if computer-generated, and 25 pages if not.

(D) A petition and response in an original proceeding in the Supreme Court, a petition for review and response in the Supreme Court, a petition for discretionary review and response in the Court of Criminal Appeals, and a motion for rehearing and response in an appellate court: 4,500 words if computer-generated, and 15 pages if not.

(E) A reply to a response to a petition for review in the Supreme Court, a reply to a response to a petition in an original proceeding in the Supreme Court, and a reply to a response to a petition for discretionary review in the Court of Criminal Appeals: 2.400 words if computer-generated, and 8 pages if not.

(3) Certificate of Compliance. A computer-generated document that is subject to a word limit under this rule must include a certificate by counsel or an unrepresented party stating the number of words in the document. The person certifying may rely on the word count of the computer program used to prepare the document.

(4) Extensions. A court may, on motion, permit a document that exceeds the prescribed limit.

(j) Electronically Filed Documents. An electronically filed document must:

(1) be in text-searchable portable document format (PDF);

(2) be directly converted to PDF rather than scanned, if possible;

(3) not be locked;

(4) be combined with any appendix into one computer file, unless that file would exceed the size limit prescribed by the electronic file manager; and

(5) otherwise comply with the Technology Standards promulgated by the Judicial Committee on Information Technology and approved by the Supreme Court.

(k) Nonconforming Documents. If a document fails to conform with these rules, the court may strike the document or identify the error and permit the party to resubmit the document in a conforming format by a specified deadline.

(Amended by Order Aug. 10, 2012, eff. Dec. 1, 2012; Order Nov. 13, 2012, eff. Dec. 1, 2012; Order March 4, 2013, eff. March 4, 2013; Order Aug. 16, 2013, eff. Jan. 1, 2014; Order Dec. 13, 2013, eff. Jan. 1, 2014; Order March 4, 2013, eff. March 4, 2013.)

Comment to 2012 Change: Rule 9 is revised to consolidate all length limits and establish word limits for documents produced on a computer. All documents produced on a computer must comply with the word limits. Page limits are retained for documents that are typewritten or otherwise not produced on a computer.

9.5. Service.

(a) Service of All Documents Required. At or before the time of a document's filing, the filing party must serve a copy on all parties to the proceeding. Service on a party represented by counsel must be made on that party's lead counsel. Except in original proceedings, a party need not serve a copy of the record.

(b) Manner of Service.

(1) Documents Filed Electronically. A document filed electronically under Rule 9.2 must be served electronically through the electronic filing manager if the email address of the party or attorney to be served is on file with the electronic filing manager. If the email address of the party or attorney to be served is not on file with the electronic filing manager, the document may be served on that party or attorney under subparagraph (2).

(2) Documents Not Filed Electronically. A document that is not filed electronically may be served in person, by mail, by commercial delivery service, by fax, or by email. Personal service includes delivery to any responsible person at the office of the lead counsel for the party served.

(c) When Complete.

(1) Service by mail is complete on mailing.

(2) Service by commercial delivery service is complete when the document is placed in the control of the delivery service.

(3) Service by fax is complete on receipt.

(4) Electronic service is complete on transmission of the document to the serving party's electronic filing service provider. The electronic filing manager will send confirmation of service to the serving party.

(d) Proof of Service. A document presented for filing must contain a proof of service in the form of either an acknowledgment of service by the person served or a certificate of service. Proof of service may appear on or be affixed to the filed document. The clerk may permit a document to be filed without proof of service, but will require the proof to be filed promptly.

(e) Certificate Requirements. A certificate of service must be signed by the person who made the service and must state:

(1) the date and manner of service;

(2) the name and address of each person served; and

(3) if the person served is a party's attorney, the name of the party represented by that attorney.

(Amended by Order Dec. 23, 2002, eff. Jan. 1, 2003; Order Aug. 16, 2013, eff. Jan. 1, 2014; Order Dec. 13, 2013, eff. Jan. 1, 2014.)

Comment to 2002 change: The change clarifies that the filing party must serve a copy of the document filed on all other parties, not only in an appeal or review, but in original proceedings as well. The rule applies only to filing *parties*. Thus, when the clerk or court reporter is responsible for filing the record, as in cases on appeal, a copy need not be served on the parties. The rule for original civil proceedings, in which a party is responsible for filing the record, is stated in subdivision 52.7.

9.6. Communications With the Court.

Parties and counsel may communicate with the appellate court about a case only through the clerk.

(Adopted by Order eff. Sept. 1, 1997.)

Comment to 1997 change: This is former Rule 4. Subdivision 9.4, prescribing the form of documents filed in the appellate courts, is changed and the form to be used is stated in significantly more detail. Former subdivisions (f) and (g), regarding service of documents, are merged into subdivision 9.5. Former Rule 6 is included as subdivision 9.6, but no substantive change is made. Other changes are made throughout the rule. Electronic filing is authorized by §§ 51.801-.807 of the Government Code.

9.7. Adoption by Reference.

Any party may join in or adopt by reference all or any part of a brief, petition, response, motion, or other document filed in an appellate court by another party in the same case.

(Amended by Order Dec. 23, 2002 eff. Jan. 1, 2003.)

Comment to 2002 change: Subdivision 9.7 is added to provide express authorization for the practice of adopting by reference all or part of another party's filing.

9.8. Protection of Minor's identity in parental-rights termination cases or juvenile court cases.

(a) Alias Defined. For purposes of this rule, an alias means one or more of a person's initials or fictitious name, used to refer to the person.

(b) Parental-Rights Termination Cases.

(1) except for a docketing statement, in all papers submitted to the court, including all appendix items submitted with a brief, petition, or motion:

(A) a minor must be identified only by an alias unless the court orders otherwise;

(B) the court may order that a minor's parent or other family member be identified only by an alias if necessary to protect a minor's identity; and

(C) all documents must be redacted accordingly;

(2) the court must, in its opinion, use an alias to refer to a minor, and if necessary to protect the minor's identity, to the minor's parent or other family member.

(c) Juvenile Court Cases. In an appeal or an original proceeding in an appellate court, including all appendix items submitted with a brief, petition, or motion;

(1) except for a docketing statement, in all papers submitted to the court, including all appendix items submitted with a brief, petition, or motion:

(A) a minor must be identified only by an alias;

(B) a minor's parent of other family member must be identified only by an alias; and

(C) all documents must be redacted accordingly;

(2) the court must, in its opinion, use an alias to refer to a minor and to the minor's parent or other family member.

(d) No Alteration of Appellate Record. Nothing in this rule permits alteration of the original appellate record except as specifically authorized by court order.

(Adopted by Order March 10, 2008 eff. Sept. 1, 2008; Order Aug. 20, 2008, eff. Sept. 1, 2008.)

9.9. Privacy Protection for Documents Filed in Civil Cases.

(a) Sensitive Data Defined. Sensitive data consists of:

(1) a driver's license number, passport number, social security number, tax identification number or similar government-issued personal identification number;

(2) a bank account number, credit card number, or other financial account number; and

(3) a birth date, home address, and the name of any person who was a minor when the underlying suit was filed.

(b) Filing of Documents Containing Sensitive Data Prohibited. Unless the inclusion of sensitive data is specifically required by a statute, court rule, or administrative regulation, an electronic or paper document containing sensitive data may not be filed with a court unless the sensitive data is redacted, except for the record in an appeal under Section Two.

(c) Redaction of Sensitive Data; Retention Requirement. Sensitive data must be redacted by using the letter "X" in place of each omitted digit or character or by removing the sensitive data in a manner indicating that the data has been redacted. The filing party must retain an unredacted version of the filed document during the pendency of the appeal and any related proceedings filed within six months of the date the judgment is signed.

(d) Notice to Clerk. If a document must contain sensitive data, the filing party must notify the clerk by:

(1) designating the document as containing sensitive data when the document is electronically filed; or

(2) if the document is not electronically filed, by including, on the upper lefthand side of the first page, the phrase: "NOTICE: THIS DOCUMENT CONTAINS SENSITIVE DATA."

(e) Restriction on Remote Access. Documents that contain unredacted sensitive data in violation of this rule must not be posted on the Internet.

(Adopted by Order Aug. 16, 2013, eff. Jan. 1, 2014; Order Dec. 13, 2013, eff. Jan. 1, 2014.)

Comment to 1997 change: This is former Rule 4. Subdivision 9.4, prescribing the form of documents filed in the appellate courts, is changed and the form to be used is stated in significantly more detail. Former subdivisions (f) and (g), regarding service of documents, are merged into subdivision 9.5. Former Rule 6 is included as subdivision 9.6, but no substantive change is made. Other changes are made throughout the rule. Electronic filing is authorized by §§ 51.801-.807 of the Government Code.

Comment to 2002 change: The change [to Rule 9.5(a)] clarifies that the filing party must serve a copy of the document filed on all other parties, not only in an appeal or review, but in original proceedings as well. The rule applies only to filing parties. Thus, when the clerk or court reporter is responsible for filing the record, as in cases on appeal, a copy need not be served on the parties. The rule for original civil proceedings, in which a party is responsible for filing the record, is stated in subdivision 52.7. Subdivision 9.7 is added to provide express authorization for the practice of adopting by reference all or part of another party's filing.

Comment to 2008 change: Subdivision 9.3 is amended to reduce the number of copies of a motion for extension of time or response filed in the Supreme Court. Subdivision 9.8 is new. To protect the privacy of minors in suits affecting the parent-child relationship (SAPCR), including suits to terminate parental rights, Section 109.002(d) of the Family Code authorizes appellate courts, in their opinions, to identify parties only by fictitious names or by initials. Similarly, Section 56.01(j) of the Family Code prohibits identification of a minor or a minor's family in an appellate opinion related to juvenile court proceedings. But as appellate briefing becomes more widely available through electronic media sources, appellate courts' efforts to protect minors' privacy by disguising their identities in appellate opinions may be defeated if the same children are fully identified in briefs and other court papers available to the public. The rule provides protection from such disclosures. Any fictitious name should not be pejorative or suggest the person's true identity. The rule does not limit an appellate court's authority to disguise parties' identities in appropriate circumstances in other cases. Although appellate courts are authorized to enforce the rule's provisions requiring redaction, parties and amici curiae are responsible for ensuring that briefs and other papers submitted to the court fully comply with the rule.

Comment to 2012 Change: Rule 9 is revised to consolidate all length limits and establish word limits for documents produced on a computer. All documents produced on a computer must comply with the word limits. Page limits are retained for documents that are typewritten or otherwise not produced on a computer.

Comment to 2013 Change: Rule 9 is revised to incorporate rules for electronic filing, in accordance with the Supreme Court's order—Misc. Docket No. 12-9206, amended by Misc. Docket Nos. 13-9092 and 13-9164—mandating electronic filing in civil cases in appellate courts, effective January 1, 2014. In addition, Rule 9.9 is added to provide privacy protection for all documents, both paper and electronic, filed in civil cases in appellate courts.

Technology Standards (These standards apply to documents filed electronically under Texas Rule of Civil Procedure 21 and Texas Rule of Appellate Procedure 9.)

9.10. Privacy Protection for Documents Filed in Criminal Cases

(a) Sensitive Data Defined. Sensitive data consists of:

(1) a driver's license number, passport number, social security number, tax identification number or similar government-issued personal identification number;

(2) bank account number, credit card number, and other financial account number;

(3) a birth date, a home address, and the name of any person who was a minor at the time the offense was committed.

(b) Redacted Filings. Unless a court orders otherwise, an electronic or paper filing with the court, including the contents of any appendices, must not contain sensitive data.

(c) Redaction procedures. Sensitive data must be redacted by using the letter "X" in place of each omitted digit or character or by removing the sensitive data in a manner indicating that the data has been redacted. The filer must retain an unredacted version of the filed document during the pendency of the appeal and any related proceedings filed within three years of the date the judgment is signed. If a district court clerk or appellate court clerk discovers unredacted sensitive data in the record, the clerk shall notify the parties and seek a ruling from the court.

(d) Certification. The filing of a document constitutes a certification by the filer that the document complies with paragraphs (a) and (b) of this rule.

(e) Reference List. If a filer believes any information described in paragraph (a) of this rule is essential to a document or that the document would be confusing without the information, the filer may submit the information to the court in a reference list that is in paper form and under seal. The reference list must specify an appropriate identifier that corresponds uniquely to each item listed. Any reference in the document to a listed identifier will be construed to refer to the corresponding item of information. If the filer provides a reference list pursuant to this rule, the front page of the document containing the redacted information must indicate that the reference list has been, or will be, provided. On its own initiative, the court may order a sealed reference list in any case.

(f) Sealed materials. Materials that are required by statute to be sealed, redacted, or kept confidential, such as the items set out in Articles 35.29 (Personal Information About Jurors), 38.45 (Evidence Depicting or Describing Abuse of or Sexual Conduct by Child or Minor), and 42.12, § 9(j), must be treated in accordance with the pertinent statutes and shall not be publicly available on the Internet. A court may also order that a document be filed under seal in paper form or electronic form, without redaction. The court may later unseal the document or order the filer to provide a redacted version of the document for the public record. If a court orders material sealed, whether it be sensitive data or other materials, the court's sealing order must be affixed to the outside of the sealed container if the sealed material is filed in paper form, or be the first document that appears if filed in electronic form. Sealed portions of the clerk's and reporter's records should be clearly marked and separated from unsealed portions and tendered as separate records, whether in paper form or electronic form. Sealed material shall not be available either on the Internet or in other form without court order.

(Adopted by Order Dec. 13, 2013, eff. Jan. 1, 2014.)

RULE 10. MOTIONS IN THE APPELLATE COURTS.

10.1. Contents of Motions; Response.

(a) Motion. Unless these rules prescribe another form, a party must apply by motion for an order or other relief. The motion must:

(1) contain or be accompanied by any matter specifically required by a rule governing such a motion;

(2) state with particularity the grounds on which it is based;

(3) set forth the order or relief sought;

(4) be served and filed with any brief, affidavit, or other paper filed in support of the motion; and

(5) in civil cases, except for motions for rehearing and motions for en banc reconsideration, contain or be accompanied by a certificate stating that the filing party conferred, or made a reasonable attempt to confer, with all other parties about the merits of the motion and whether those parties oppose the motion.

(b) Response. A party may file a response to a motion at any time before the court rules on the motion or by any deadline set by the court. The court may determine a motion before a response is filed.

(Amended by Order March 10, 2008 eff. Sept. 1, 2008; Order Aug. 20, 2008, eff. Sept. 1, 2008.)

Comment to 2008 change: It is presumed that non-movants will oppose the relief sought in motions for rehearing and motions for en banc reconsideration. To encourage consistent application of the certificate-of-conference requirement, Rule 10.1(a)(5) is amended—and Rule 49.11 is added—to exempt those motions from the certificate requirement.

10.2. Evidence on Motions.

A motion need not be verified unless it depends on the following types of facts, in which case the motion must be supported by affidavit or other satisfactory evidence. The types of facts requiring proof are those that are:

(a) not in the record;

(b) not within the court's knowledge in its official capacity; and

(c) not within the personal knowledge of the attorney signing the motion.

(Amended by Order March 10, 2008 eff. Sept. 1, 2008; Order Aug. 20, 2008, eff. Sept. 1, 2008.)

10.3. Determining Motions.

(a) Time for Determination. A court should not hear or determine a motion until 10 days after the motion was filed, unless:

(1) the motion is to extend time to file a brief, a petition for review, or a petition for discretionary review;

(2) the motion states that the parties have conferred and that no party opposes the motion; or

(3) the motion is an emergency.

(b) Reconsideration. If a motion is determined prematurely, any party adversely affected may request the court to reconsider its order.

10.4. Power of Panel or Single Justice or Judge to Entertain Motions.

(a) Single Justice. In addition to the authority expressly conferred by these rules or by law, a single justice or judge of an appellate court may grant or deny a request for relief that these rules allow to be sought by motion. But in a civil case, a single justice should not do the following:

(1) act on a petition for an extraordinary writ; or

(2) dismiss or otherwise determine an appeal or a motion for rehearing.

(b) Panel. An appellate court may provide, by order or rule, that a panel or the full court must act on any motion or class of motions.

10.5. Particular Motions.

(a) Motions Relating to Informalities in the Record. A motion relating to informalities in the manner of bringing a case into court must be filed within 30 days after the record is filed in the court of appeals. The objection, if waivable, will otherwise be deemed waived.

(b) Motions to Extend Time.

(1) Contents of Motion in General. All motions to extend time, except a motion to extend time for filing a notice of appeal, must state:

(A) the deadline for filing the item in question;

(B) the length of the extension sought;

(C) the facts relied on to reasonably explain the need for an extension; and

(D) the number of previous extensions granted regarding the item in question.

(2) Contents of Motion to Extend Time to File Notice of appeal. A motion to extend the time for filing a notice of appeal must:

(A) comply with (1)(A) and (C);

(B) identify the trial court;

(C) state the date of the trial court's judgment or appealable order; and

(D) state the case number and style of the case in the trial court.

(3) Contents of Motion to Extend Time to File Petition for Review or Petition for Discretionary Review. A motion to extend time to file a petition for review or petition for discretionary review must also specify:

(A) the court of appeals;

(B) the date of the court of appeals' judgment; and

(C) the case number and style of the case in the court of appeals; and

(D) the date every motion for rehearing or en banc reconsideration was filed, and either the date and nature of the court of appeals' ruling on the motion, or that if remains pending.

(c) Motions to Postpone Argument. Unless all parties agree, or unless sufficient cause is apparent to the court, a motion to postpone argument of a case must be supported by sufficient cause.

(Adopted by Order eff. Sept. 1, 1997. Amended by Order Aug. 20, 2008, eff. Sept. 1, 2008)

Comment to 1997 change: This is former Rule 19. Under subdivision 10.1, a response may be filed at any time before the court rules on the motion. The provision of former subdivision (b) regarding docketing motions is incorporated in Rule 12.2. The provision of former subdivision (b) for noting attorneys' names on the docket is incorporated in Rule 6.2. Former subdivision (c), requiring the clerk to send notices of the filing of motions is deleted as unnecessary because the parties must serve all motions under Rule 9.5. Subdivision 10.2 is amended to eliminate the requirement of an oath where the facts are within the personal knowledge of the attorney. Subdivision 10.5 is new and incorporates the provisions of other rules concerning motions, as follows: 10.5(a) from former Rule 71; 10.5(b) from former Rules 73, 130(d), and 160; and 10.5(c) from former Rule 70. Other changes are made.

Comment to 2008 change: It happens so infrequently that a non-movant does not oppose a motion for rehearing on en banc reconsideration that such motions are excepted from the certificate-of-conference requirement in Subdivision 10.1(a)(5). Subdivision 10.2 is revised to clarify that facts supporting a motion need not be verified by the filer if supporting evidence is in the record, the facts are known to the court, or the filer has personal knowledge of them. Subdivision 10.5(b)(3)(D) is added.

RULE 11. AMICUS CURIAE BRIEFS.

An appellate clerk may receive, but not file, an amicus curiae brief. But the court for good cause may refuse to consider the brief and order that it be returned. An amicus curiae brief must:

(a) comply with the briefing rules for parties;

(b) identify the person or entity on whose behalf the brief is tendered;

(c) disclose the source of any fee paid or to be paid for preparing the brief; and

(d) certify that copies have been served on all parties.

(Amended by Order Dec. 23, 2002 eff. Jan. 1, 2003.)

Comment to 2002 change: The change expressly recognizes that a court may refuse to consider an amicus curiae brief for good cause.

RULE 12. DUTIES OF APPELLATE CLERK.

12.1. Docketing the Case.

On receiving a copy of the notice of appeal, the petition for review, the petition for discretionary review, the petition in an original proceeding, or a certified question, the appellate clerk must:

(a) endorse on the document the date of receipt;

(b) collect any filing fee;

(c) docket the case;

(d) notify all parties of the receipt of the document; and

(e) if the document filed is a petition for review filed in the Supreme Court, notify the court of appeals clerk of the filing of the petition.

12.2. Docket Numbers.

The clerk must put the case's docket number on each item received in connection with the case and must put the docket number on the envelope in which the record is stored.

(a) Numbering System. Each case filed in a court of appeals must be assigned a docket number consisting of the following four parts, separated by hyphens:

(1) the number of the court of appeals district;

(2) the last two digits of the year in which the case is filed;

(3) the number assigned to the case; and

(4) the designation "CV" for a civil case or "CR" for a criminal case.

(b) Numbering Order. Each case must be docketed in the order of its filing.

(c) Multiple Notices of Appeal. All notices of appeal filed in the same case must be given the same docket number.

(d) Appeals Not Yet Filed. A motion relating to an appeal that has been perfected but not yet filed must be docketed and assigned a docket number that will also be assigned to the appeal when it is filed.

12.3. Custody of Papers.

The clerk must safeguard the record and every other item filed in a case. If the record or any part of it or any other item is missing, the court will make an order for the replacement of the record or item that is just under the circumstances.

12.4. Withdrawing Papers.

The clerk may permit the record or other filed item to be taken from the clerk's office at any time, on the following conditions:

(a) the clerk must have a receipt for the record or item;

(b) the clerk should make reasonable conditions to ensure that the withdrawn record or item is preserved and returned;

(c) the clerk may demand the return of the record or item at any time;

(d) after the case is submitted to the court and before the court's decision, the record cannot be withdrawn;

(e) after the court's decision, the losing party must be given priority in withdrawing the record;

(f) the clerk may not allow original documents filed under Rule 34.5(f) or original exhibits filed under Rule 34.6(g) to be taken from the clerk's office;

(g) if the court allows an original document or exhibit to be taken by a party and it is not returned, the court may accept the opposing party's statement concerning the document's or exhibit's nature and contents;

(h) withdrawn material must not be removed from the court's jurisdiction; and

(i) the court may, on the motion of any party or its own initiative, modify any of these conditions.

12.5. Clerk's Duty to Account.

The clerk of an appellate court who receives money due another court must promptly pay the money to the court to whom it is due. This rule is enforceable by the Supreme Court.

12.6. Notices of Court's Judgments and Orders.

In any proceeding, the clerk of an appellate court must promptly send a notice of any judgment, mandate, or other court order to all parties to the proceeding.

(Adopted by Order eff. Sept. 1, 1997. Amended by Order Dec. 23, 2002, eff. Jan. 1, 2003.)

Comment to 2002 change: Subdivision 12.6 is amended to require the clerk to notify the parties of all of the court's rulings, including the mandate.

RULE 13. COURT REPORTERS AND COURT RECORDERS.

13.1. Duties of Court Reporters and Recorders.

The official court reporter or court recorder must:

(a) unless excused by agreement of the parties, attend court sessions and make a full record of the proceedings;

(b) take all exhibits offered in evidence during a proceeding and ensure that they are marked;

(c) file all exhibits with the trial court clerk after a proceeding ends;

(d) perform the duties prescribed by Rules 34.6 and 35; and

(e) perform other acts relating to the reporter's or recorder's official duties, as the trial court directs.

(Amended by Order Dec. 23, 2002, eff. Jan. 1, 2003.)

Comment to 2002 change: Subdivision 13.1(a) is amended merely for clarification.

13.2. Additional Duties of Court Recorder.

The official court recorder must also:

(a) ensure that the recording system functions properly throughout the proceeding and that a complete, clear, and transcribable recording is made;

(b) make a detailed, legible log of all proceedings being recorded, showing:

(1) the number and style of the case before the court;

(2) the name of each person speaking;

(3) the event being recorded such as the voir dire, the opening statement, direct and cross-examinations, and bench conferences;

(4) each exhibit offered, admitted, or excluded;

(5) the time of day of each event; and

(6) the index number on the recording device showing where each event is recorded;

(c) after a proceeding ends, file with the clerk the original log;

(d) have the original recording stored to ensure that it is preserved and is accessible; and

(e) ensure that no one gains access to the original recording without the court's written order.

13.3. Priorities of Reporters.

The trial court must help ensure that the court reporter's work is timely accomplished by setting work priorities. The reporter's duties relating to proceedings before the court take preference over other work.

13.4. Report of Reporters.

To aid the trial court in setting priorities under 13.3, each court reporter must give the trial court a monthly written report showing the amount and nature of the business pending in the reporter's office. A copy of this report must be filed with the appellate clerk of each district in which the court sits.

13.5 Appointing Deputy Reporter.

When the official court reporter is unable to perform the duties in 13.1 or 13.2 because of illness, press of official work, or unavoidable absence or disability, the trial court may designate a deputy reporter. If the court appoints a deputy reporter, that person must file with the trial court clerk a document stating:

(a) the date the deputy worked;

(b) the court in which the deputy worked; and

(c) the number and style of the case on which the deputy worked.

13.6. Filing of Notes in a Criminal Case.

When a defendant is convicted and sentenced, or is granted deferred adjudication for a felony other than a state jail felony, and does not appeal, the court reporter must—within 20 days after the time to perfect the appeal has expired—file the untranscribed notes or the original recording of the proceeding with the trial court clerk. The trial court clerk need not retain the notes beyond 15 years of their filing date.

(Adopted by Order eff. Sept. 1, 1997.)

Comment to 1997 change: Former Rules 11 and 12 are merged. Former Rules 11(a), (c) and (d) now appear as subdivisions 13.1, 13.5 and 13.6. Former Rule 11(b) is omitted as unnecessary. The provisions of former Rule 12(a) are moved to Rule 35.3. Former Rules 12(b) and (c) now appear as subdivisions 13.3 and 13.4. The rule is made to apply to court recorders as well as court reporters. Paragraph 13.1(a) merges paragraphs (a)(1) and (2) of former Rule 11, and now requires the reporter to make a record of voir dire and closing argument unless excused by agreement of the parties. Paragraph 13.1(b) is new, but codifies current practice. Subdivision 13.2 is new and specifies rules for electronic recording of proceedings. A provision requiring a deputy court reporter to file with the trial court clerk a document identifying the proceedings in which the reporter worked is included in paragraph 13.5. Other changes are made.

RULE 14. RECORDING AND BROADCASTING COURT PROCEEDINGS.

14.1. Recording and Broadcasting Permitted.

An appellate court may permit courtroom proceedings to be broadcast, televised, recorded, or photographed in accordance with this rule.

14.2. Procedure.

(a) Request to Cover Court Proceeding.

(1) A person wishing to broadcast, televise, record, or photograph a court proceeding must file with the court clerk a request to cover the proceeding. The request must state:

(A) the case style and number;

(B) the date and time when the proceeding is to begin;

(C) the name of the requesting person or organization;

(D) the type of coverage requested (for example, televising or photographing); and

(E) the type and extent of equipment to be used.

(2) A request to cover argument of a case must be filed no later than five days before the date the case is set for argument and must be served on all parties to the case. A request to cover any other proceeding must be filed no later than two days before the date when the proceeding is to begin.

(b) Response. Any party may file a response to the request. If the request is to cover argument, the response must be filed no later than two days before the date set for argument. If a party objects to coverage of the argument, the response should state the injury that will allegedly result from coverage.

(c) Court May Shorten Time. The court may, in the interest of justice, shorten the time for filing a document under this rule if no party or interested person would be unduly prejudiced.

(d) Decision of Court. In deciding whether to allow coverage, the court may consider information known ex parte to the court. The court may allow, deny, limit, or terminate coverage for any reason the court considers necessary or appropriate, such as protecting the parties' rights or the dignity of the court and ensuring the orderly conduct of the proceedings.

14.3. Equipment and Personnel.

The court may, among other things:

(a) require that a person seeking to cover a proceeding demonstrate or display the equipment that will be used;
(b) prohibit equipment that produces distracting sound or light;
(c) prohibit signal lights or devices showing when equipment is operating, or require their concealment;
(d) prohibit moving lights, flash attachments, or sudden lighting changes;
(e) require the use of the courtroom's existing video, audio, and lighting systems, if any;
(f) specify the placement of personnel and equipment;
(g) determine the number of cameras to be allowed in the courtroom; and
(h) require pooling of equipment if more than one person wishes to cover a proceeding.

14.4. Enforcement.

The court may sanction a violation of this rule by measures that include barring a person or organization from access to future coverage of proceedings in that court for a defined period.

(Adopted by Order eff. Sept. 1, 1997.)

Comment to 1997 change: This is former Rule 21. The rule is rewritten and now allows recording and broadcasting of court proceedings at the discretion of the court and subject to the stated guidelines.

RULE 15. ISSUANCE OF WRIT OR PROCESS BY APPELLATE COURT.

15.1. In General.

(a) Signature Under Seal. A writ or process issuing from an appellate court must bear the court's seal and be signed by the clerk.

(b) To Whom Directed; by Whom Served. Unless a rule or statute provides otherwise, the writ or process must be directed to the person or court to be served. The writ or process may be served by the sheriff, constable, or other peace officer whose jurisdiction includes the county in which the person or court to be served may be found.

(c) Return; Lack of Execution; Simultaneous Writs. The writ or process must be returned to the issuing court according to the writ's direction. If the writ or process is not executed, the clerk may issue another writ or process if requested by the party who requested the former writ or process. At a party's request, the clerk may issue two or more writs simultaneously.

15.2. Appearance Without Service; Actual Knowledge.

A party who appears in person or by attorney in an appellate court proceeding—or who has actual knowledge of the court's opinion, judgment, or order related to a writ or process—is bound by the opinion, judgment, or order to the same extent as if personally served under 15.1.

(Adopted by Order eff. Sept. 1, 1997.)

Comment to 1997 change: This is former Rule 17. Nonsubstantive changes are made.

RULE 16. DISQUALIFICATION OR RECUSAL OF APPELLATE JUDGES.

16.1. Grounds for Disqualification.

The grounds for disqualification of an appellate court justice or judge are determined by the Constitution and laws of Texas.

16.2. Grounds for Recusal.

The grounds for recusal of an appellate court justice or judge are the same as those provided in the Rules of Civil Procedure. In addition, a justice or judge must recuse in a proceeding if it presents a material issue which the justice or judge participated in deciding while serving on another court in which the proceeding was pending.

16.3. Procedure for Recusal.

(a) Motion. A party may file a motion to recuse a justice or judge before whom the case is pending. The motion must be filed promptly after the party has reason to believe that the justice or judge should not participate in deciding the case.

(b) Decision. Before any further proceeding in the case, the challenged justice or judge must either remove himself or herself from all participation in the case or certify the matter to the entire court, which will decide the motion by a majority of the remaining judges sitting en banc. The challenged justice or judge must not sit with the remainder of the court to consider the motion as to him or her.

(c) Appeal. An order of recusal is not reviewable, but the denial of a recusal motion is reviewable.

(Adopted by Order eff. Sept. 1, 1997.)

Comment to 1997 change: Former Rules 15 and 15a are merged. Former Rule 15a appears as subdivision 16.2. For grounds for disqualification, reference is made to the Constitution and statutes rather than the Rules of Civil Procedure. The procedure for disqualification is not specified. The nature of prior participation in a proceeding that requires recusal is clarified. Former subdivision (b) of Rule 15, requiring service of the motion, is omitted as unnecessary. The remaining subdivisions of former Rule 15 are contained in subdivision 16.3. Other changes are made.

RULE 17. COURT OF APPEALS UNABLE TO TAKE IMMEDIATE ACTION.

17.1. Inability to Act.

A court of appeals is unable to take immediate action if it cannot—within the time when action must be taken—assemble a panel because members of the court are ill, absent, or unavailable. A justice who is disqualified or recused is unavailable. A court of appeals' inability to act immediately may be established by certificate of the clerk, a member of the court, or a party's counsel, or by affidavit of a party.

17.2. Nearest Available Court of Appeals.

If a court of appeals is unable to take immediate action, the nearest court of appeals that is able to take immediate action may do so with the same effect as the other court. The nearest court of appeals is the one whose courthouse is nearest—measured by a straight line—the courthouse of the trial court.

17.3. Further Proceedings.

After acting or refusing to act, the nearest court of appeals must promptly send a copy of its order, and the original or a copy of any document presented to it, to the other court, which will conduct any further proceedings in the matter.

(Adopted by Order eff. Sept. 1, 1997.)

Comment to 1997 change: This is former Rule 16. The rule is rewritten and simplified.

RULE 18. MANDATE.

18.1. Issuance.

The clerk of the appellate court that rendered the judgment must issue a mandate in accordance with the judgment and send it to the clerk of the court to which it is directed and to all parties to the proceeding when one of the following periods expires:

(a) In the Court of Appeals.

(1) Ten days after the time has expired for filing a motion to extend time to file a petition for review or a petition for discretionary review if:

(A) no timely petition for review or petition for discretionary review has been filed;

(B) no timely filed motion to extend time to file a petition for review or petition for discretionary review is pending; and

(C) in a criminal case, the Court of Criminal Appeals has not granted review on its own initiative.

(2) Ten days after the time has expired for filing a motion to extend time to file a motion for rehearing of a denial, refusal, or dismissal of a petition for review, or a refusal or dismissal of a petition for discretionary review, if no timely filed motion for rehearing or motion to extend time is pending.

(b) In the Supreme Court and the Court of Criminal Appeals. Ten days after the time has expired for filing a motion to extend time to file a motion for rehearing if no timely filed motion for rehearing or motion to extend time is pending.

(c) Agreement to Issue. The mandate may be issued earlier if the parties so agree, or for good cause on the motion of a party.

(Amended by Order Dec. 23, 2002, eff. Jan. 1, 2003.)

Comment to 2002 change: Subdivision 18.1 is amended consistent with the change in subdivision 12.6.

18.2. Stay of Mandate.

A party may move to stay issuance of the mandate pending the United States Supreme Court's disposition of a petition for writ of certiorari. The motion must state the grounds for the petition and the circumstances requiring the stay. The appellate court authorized to issue the mandate may grant a stay if it finds that the grounds are substantial and that the petitioner or others would incur serious hardship from the mandate's issuance if the United States Supreme Court were later to reverse the judgment. In a criminal case, the stay will last for no more than 90 days, to permit the timely filing of a petition for writ of certiorari. After that period and others mentioned in this rule expire, the mandate will issue.

18.3. Trial Court Case Number.

The mandate must state the trial court case number.

18.4. Filing of Mandate.

The clerk receiving the mandate will file it with the case's other papers and note it on the docket.

18.5. Costs.

The mandate will be issued without waiting for costs to be paid. If the Supreme Court declines to grant review, Supreme Court costs must be included in the court of appeals' mandate.

18.6. Mandate in Accelerated Appeals.

The appellate court's judgment on an appeal from an interlocutory order takes effect when the mandate is issued. The court may issue the mandate with its judgment or delay the mandate until the appeal is finally disposed of. If the mandate is issued, any further proceeding in the trial court must conform to the mandate.

18.7. Recall of Mandate.

If an appellate court vacates or modifies its judgment or order after issuing its mandate, the appellate clerk must promptly notify the clerk of the court to which the mandate was directed and all parties. The mandate will have no effect and a new mandate may be issued.

(Adopted by Order eff. Sept. 1, 1997.)

Comment to 1997 change: This is a new rule that combines the provisions of former Rules 43(g), 86, 186, 231, and 232.

RULE 19. PLENARY POWER OF THE COURTS OF APPEALS AND EXPIRATION OF TERM.

19.1. Plenary Power of Courts of Appeals.

A court of appeals' plenary power over its judgment expires:

(a) 60 days after judgment if no timely filed motion for rehearing or timely filed motion en banc reconsideration, or timely filed motion to extend time to file such a motion, is then pending; or

(b) 30 days after the court overrules all timely filed motions for rehearing or en banc reconsideration, and all timely filed motions to extend time to file such a motion.

(Amended by Order Dec. 23, 2002, eff. Jan. 1, 2003; Order March 10, 2008, eff. Sept. 1, 2008.)

Comment to 2002 change: Subdivision 19.1 is changed, consistent with other changes in the rules, to specifically address a motion for en banc reconsideration and treat it as a motion for rehearing.

Comment to 2008 change: The provisions of Rule 19 governing the courts of appeals' plenary power are revised in conjunction with the amendments to Rules 49 and 53.7 concerning motions for en banc reconsideration.

19.2. Plenary Power Continues After Petition Filed.

In a civil case, the court of appeals retains plenary power to vacate or modify its judgment during the periods prescribed in 19.1 even if a party has filed a petition for review in the Supreme Court.

19.3. Proceedings After Plenary Power Expires.

After its plenary power expires, the court cannot vacate or modify its judgment. But the court may:

(a) correct a clerical error in its judgment or opinion;

(b) issue and recall its mandate as these rules provide;

(c) enforce or suspend enforcement of its judgment as these rules or applicable law provide;

(d) order or modify the amount and type of security required to suspend a judgment, and decide the sufficiency of the sureties, under Rule 24; and

(e) order its opinion published in accordance with Rule 47.

19.4. Expiration of Term.

The expiration of the appellate court's term does not affect the court's plenary power or its jurisdiction over a case that is pending when the court's term expires.

(Adopted by Order eff. Sept. 1, 1997.)

Comment to 1997 change: This is a new rule except the provisions of former Rule 234 are incorporated in subdivision 19.4.

RULE 20. WHEN PARTY IS INDIGENT.

20.1. Civil Cases.

(a) *Costs Defined.* In this rule, "costs" mean filing fees charged by the appellate court. Fees charged for preparation of the appellate record are governed by Texas Rule of Civil Procedure 145.

(b) *When a Statement Was Filed in the Trial Court.*

(1) *General Rule; Status in Trial Court Carries Forward.* A party who filed a Statement of Inability to Afford Payment of Court Costs in the trial court is not required to pay costs in the appellate court unless the trial court overruled the party's claim of indigence in an order that complies with Texas Rule of Civil Procedure 145. A party is not required to pay costs in the appellate court if the trial court ordered the party to pay partial costs or to pay costs in installments.

(2) *Establishing the Right to Proceed Under the General Rule.* To establish the right to proceed without payment of costs under (1), a party must communicate to the appellate court clerk in writing that the party is presumed indigent under this rule. In an appeal under Section Two of these rules, the applicability of the presumption should be stated in the notice of appeal and in the docketing statement.

(3) *Exception; Material Change in Circumstances.* An appellate court may permit a party who is not entitled to proceed under (1) to proceed without payment of costs if the party establishes that the party's financial circumstances have materially changed since the date of the trial court's order under Texas Rule of Civil Procedure 145.

(A) *Requirements.* The party must file a motion in the appellate court alleging that the party's financial circumstances have materially changed since the date of the trial court's order and a current Statement of Inability to Afford Payment of Court Costs that complies with Texas Rule of Civil Procedure 145. The Statement that was filed in the trial court does not meet the requirements of this rule.

(B) *Action by Appellate Court.* The appellate court may decide the motion based on the record or refer the motion to the trial court with instructions to hear evidence and issue findings of fact. If a motion is referred to the trial court, the appellate court must review the trial court's findings and the record of the hearing before ruling on the motion.

(c) *When No Statement Was Filed in the Trial Court.* An appellate court may permit a party who did not file a Statement of Inability to Afford Payment of Court Costs in the trial court to proceed without payment of costs. The court may require the party to file a Statement in the appellate court. If the court denies the party's request to proceed without payment of costs, it must do so in a written order.

(Amended by Order March 10, 2008 eff. Sept. 1, 2008; Order Aug. 20, 2008, eff. Sept. 1, 2008; Order Aug. 31, 2011, eff. Sept. 1, 2011; Order Dec. 12, 2011, eff. March 1, 2012; Order Feb. 13, 2012, eff. March 1, 2012; Tex. Sup. Ct. Misc. Docket No. 16-9056, eff. Sept. 1, 2016; Tex. Sup. Ct. Misc. Docket No. 16-9122, eff. Sept. 1, 2016.)

[Statement of Inability to Afford Payment of Court Costs as provided in Tex. Sup. Ct. Misc. Docket No. 16-9122, eff. Sept. 1, 2016 and applies to any contest of, or challenge to, a claim of inability to afford payment of court costs that is pending on September 1, 2016.]

Comment to 2016 Change: The rule has been rewritten so that it only governs filing fees and any other fee charged by the appellate court. Texas Rule of Civil Procedure 145 governs a party's claim that the party is unable to afford costs for preparation of the appellate record.

Because appellate filing fees are minimal, a party that filed a Statement of Inability to Afford Payment of Court Costs in the trial court is not required to file a new Statement in the appellate court unless the trial court made affirmative findings under Texas Rule of Civil Procedure 145 that the party is able to afford all court costs and to pay those costs as they are incurred. Furthermore, because a determination of indigence by the trial court carries forward to appeal in all cases, Family Code section 107.013 is satisfied.

Experience has shown that, in most cases, a party's financial circumstances do not change substantially between the trial court proceedings and the appellate court proceedings. Nonetheless, (b)(3) permits a party whom the trial court determined is able to afford all costs to demonstrate to the appellate court that the party's circumstances have changed since the trial court's ruling and that the party is unable to afford appellate filing fees.

Comment to 2008 change: Subdivision 20.1(a) is added to provide, as in Texas Rule of Civil Procedure 145, that an affidavit of indigence accompanied by an IOLTA or other Texas Access to Justice Foundation certificate cannot be challenged. Subdivision 20.1(c)(1) is revised to clarify that an affidavit of indigence filed to proceed in the trial court without advance payment of costs is insufficient to establish indigence on appeal; a separate affidavit must be filed with or before the notice of appeal. Subdivision 20.1(c)(3) is revised to provide that an appellate court must give an appellant who fails to file a proper appellate indigence affidavit notice of the defect and an opportunity to cure it before dismissing the appeal or affirming the judgment on that basis. *See Higgins v. Randall County Sheriff's Office*, 193 S.W .3d 898 (Tex. 2006). The limiting phrase "under (c)(2)" in Subdivision 20.1(d)(2) is deleted to clarify that the appellate clerk's duty to forward copies of the affidavit to the trial court clerk and the court reporter, along with a notice setting a deadline to contest the affidavit, applies to affidavits on appeal erroneously filed in the appellate court, not only to affidavits in other appellate proceedings properly filed in the appellate court under subdivision 20.1(c)(2). Although Subdivision 3.1(g) defines "court reporter" to include court recorder, subdivision 20.1(e) is amended to make clear that a court recorder can contest an affidavit.

20.2. Criminal Cases.

Within the time for perfecting the appeal, an appellant who is unable to pay for the appellate record may, by motion and affidavit, ask the trial court to have the appellate record furnished without charge. If after hearing the motion the court finds that the appellant cannot pay or give security for the appellate record, the court must order the reporter to transcribe the proceedings. When the court certifies that the appellate record has been furnished to the appellant, the reporter must be paid from the general funds of the county in which the offense was committed, in the amount set by the trial court.

(Adopted by Order eff. Sept. 1, 1997.)

Comment to 1997 change: The rule is new and combines the provisions of former Rules 13(k), 40(a)(3), and 53(j). The procedure for proceeding in civil cases in an appellate court without advance payment of costs, in both appeals and original proceedings, is stated. The information that must be given in the affidavit is prescribed. An extension of time to file the affidavit is now available. The indigent party is no longer required to serve the court reporter, but must file the affidavit with the appropriate clerk who is to notify the court reporter. A contest need not be under oath. Provision is made for later ability to pay the costs. Nonsubstantive changes are made to the rule for criminal cases.

Reference

See also: Civil Practice and Remedies Code § 13.003.

**SECTION TWO.
APPEALS FROM TRIAL COURT JUDGMENTS AND ORDERS**

RULE 21. NEW TRIALS IN CRIMINAL CASES.

21.1. Definitions.

(a) *New trial* means the rehearing of a criminal action after the trial court has, on the defendant's motion, set aside a finding or verdict of guilt.

(b) *New trial on punishment* means a new hearing of the punishment stage of a criminal action after the trial court has, on the defendant's motion, set aside an assessment of punishment without setting aside a finding or verdict of guilt.

21.2. When Motion for New Trial Required.

A motion for new trial is a prerequisite to presenting a point of error on appeal only when necessary to adduce facts not in the record.

21.3. Grounds.

The defendant must be granted a new trial, or a new trial on punishment, for any of the following reasons:

(a) except in a misdemeanor case in which the maximum possible punishment is a fine, when the defendant has been unlawfully tried in absentia or has been denied counsel;

(b) when the court has misdirected the jury about the law or has committed some other material error likely to injure the defendant's rights;

(c) when the verdict has been decided by lot or in any manner other than a fair expression of the jurors' opinion;

(d) when a juror has been bribed to convict or has been guilty of any other corrupt conduct;

(e) when a material defense witness has been kept from court by force, threats, or fraud, or when evidence tending to establish the defendant's innocence has been intentionally destroyed or withheld, thus preventing its production at trial;

(f) when, after retiring to deliberate, the jury has received other evidence; when a juror has talked with anyone about the case; or when a juror became so intoxicated that his or her vote was probably influenced as a result;

(g) when the jury has engaged in such misconduct that the defendant did not receive a fair and impartial trial; or

(h) when the verdict is contrary to the law and the evidence.

21.4. Time to File and Amend Motion.

(a) To File. The defendant may file a motion for new trial before, but no later than 30 days after, the date when the trial court imposes or suspends sentence in open court.

(b) To Amend. Within 30 days after the date when the trial court imposes or suspends sentence in open court but before the court overrules any preceding motion for new trial, a defendant may, without leave of court, file one or more amended motions for new trial.

21.5. State May Controvert; Effect.

The State may oppose in writing any reason the defendant sets forth in the motion for new trial. The State's having opposed a motion for new trial does not affect a defendant's responsibilities under 21.6.

21.6. Time to Present.

The defendant must present the motion for new trial to the trial court within 10 days of filing it, unless the trial court in its discretion permits it to be presented and heard within 75 days from the date when the court imposes or suspends sentence in open court.

21.7. Types of Evidence Allowed at Hearing.

The court may receive evidence by affidavit or otherwise.

21.8. Court's Ruling.

(a) Time to Rule. The court must rule on a motion for new trial within 75 days after imposing or suspending sentence in open court.

(b) Ruling. In ruling on a motion for new trial, the court may make oral or written findings of fact. The granting of a motion for new trial must be accomplished by written order. A docket entry does not constitute a written order.

(c) Failure to Rule. A motion not timely ruled on by written order will be deemed denied when the period prescribed in (a) expires.

21.9. Granting a new trial.

(a) A court must grant a new trial when it has found a meritorious ground for new trial, but a court must grant only a new trial on punishment when it has found a ground that affected only the assessment of punishment.

(b) Granting a new trial restores the case to its position before the former trial, including, at any party's option, arraignment or pretrial proceedings initiated by that party.

(c) Granting a new trial on punishment restores the case to its position after the defendant was found guilty. Unless the defendant, State, and trial court all agree to a change, punishment in a new trial shall be assessed in accordance with the defendant's original election under article 37.07, § 2(b) of the Code of Criminal Procedure.

(d) A finding or verdict of guilt in the former trial must not be regarded as a presumption of guilt, nor may it be alluded to in the presence of the jury that hears the case on retrial of guilt. A finding of fact or an assessment of punishment in the former trial may not be alluded to in the presence of the jury that hears the case on retrial of punishment.

(Adopted by Order eff. Sept. 1, 1997. Amended by Order Dec. 13, 2006 eff. Jan. 1, 2007.)

Comment to 1997 change: Former Rules 30, 31, and 32 are merged. Paragraph (b)(6) of former Rule 30 is deleted because the rule-making authority of the Court of Criminal Appeals was withdrawn. *See* Code of Criminal Procedure article 40.001. Other nonsubstantive changes are made.

RULE 22. ARREST OF JUDGMENT IN CRIMINAL CASES.

22.1. Definition.

Motion in arrest of judgment means a defendant's oral or written suggestion that, for reasons stated in the motion, the judgment rendered against the defendant was contrary to law. Such a motion is made in the trial court.

22.2. Grounds.

The motion may be based on any of the following grounds:

(a) that the indictment or information is subject to an exception on substantive grounds;

(b) that in relation to the indictment or information a verdict is substantively defective; or

(c) that the judgment is invalid for some other reason.

22.3. Time to File Motion.

A defendant may file a motion in arrest of judgment before, but no later than 30 days after, the date when the trial court imposes or suspends sentence in open court.

22.4. Court's Ruling.

(a) Time to Rule; Form of Ruling. The court must rule on a motion in arrest of judgment within 75 days after imposing or suspending sentence in open court. The ruling may be oral or in writing.

(b) Failure to Rule. A motion not timely ruled on will be deemed denied when the period prescribed in (a) expires.

22.5. Effect of Denying.

For purposes of the defendant's giving notice of appeal, an order denying a motion in arrest of judgment will be considered an order denying a motion for new trial.

22.6. Effect of Granting.

(a) Defendant Restored. If judgment is arrested, the defendant is restored to the position that he or she had before the indictment or information was presented.

(b) Defendant Discharged or Remanded. If the judgment is arrested, the defendant will be discharged. But the trial court may remand the defendant to custody or fix bail if the court determines, from the evidence adduced at trial, that the defendant may be convicted on a proper indictment or information, or on a proper verdict in relation to the indictment or information.

(Adopted by Order eff. Sept. 1, 1997.)

Comment to 1997 change: Former Rules 33, 34, and 35 are merged without substantive change.

RULE 23. NUNC PRO TUNC PROCEEDINGS IN CRIMINAL CASES.

23.1. Judgment and Sentence.

Unless the trial court has granted a new trial or arrested the judgment, or unless the defendant has appealed, a failure to render judgment and pronounce sentence may be corrected at any time by the court's doing so.

23.2. Credit on Sentence.

When sentence is pronounced, the trial court must give the defendant credit on that sentence for:

(a) all time the defendant has been confined since the time when judgment and sentence should have been entered and pronounced; and

(b) all time between the defendant's arrest and confinement to the time when judgment and sentence should have been entered and pronounced.

(Adopted by Order eff. Sept. 1, 1997.)

Comment to 1997 change: This is former Rule 36. The rule is amended without substantive change.

RULE 24. SUSPENSION OF ENFORCEMENT OF JUDGMENT PENDING APPEAL IN CIVIL CASES.

24.1. Suspension of Enforcement.

(a) Methods. Unless the law or these rules provide otherwise, a judgment debtor may supersede the judgment by:

(1) filing with the trial court clerk a written agreement with the judgment creditor for suspending enforcement of the judgment;

(2) filing with the trial court clerk a good and sufficient bond;

(3) making a deposit with the trial court clerk in lieu of a bond; or

(4) providing alternate security ordered by the court.

(b) Bonds.

(1) A bond must be:

(A) in the amount required by 24.2;

(B) payable to the judgment creditor;

(C) signed by the judgment debtor or the debtor's agent;

(D) signed by a sufficient surety or sureties as obligors; and

(E) conditioned as required by (d).

(2) To be effective a bond must be approved by the trial court clerk. On motion of any party, the trial court will review the bond.

(c) Deposit in Lieu of Bond.

(1) Types of Deposits. Instead of filing a surety bond, a party may deposit with the trial court clerk:

(A) cash;

(B) a cashier's check payable to the clerk, drawn on any federally insured and federally or state-chartered bank or savings-and-loan association; or

(C) with leave of court, a negotiable obligation of the federal government or of any federally insured and federally or state-chartered bank or savings-and-loan association.

(2) Amount of Deposit. The deposit must be in the amount required by 24.2.

(3) Clerk's Duties. The clerk must promptly deposit any cash or a cashier's check in accordance with law. The clerk must hold the deposit until the conditions of liability in (d) are extinguished. The clerk must then release any remaining funds in the deposit to the judgment debtor.

(d) Conditions of Liability. The surety or sureties on a bond, any deposit in lieu of a bond, or any alternate security ordered by the court is subject to liability for all damages and costs that may be awarded against the debtor—up to the amount of the bond, deposit, or security—if:

(1) the debtor does not perfect an appeal or the debtor's appeal is dismissed, and the debtor does not perform the trial court's judgment;

(2) the debtor does not perform an adverse judgment final on appeal; or

(3) the judgment is for the recovery of an interest in real or personal property, and the debtor does not pay the creditor the value of the property interest's rent or revenue during the pendency of the appeal.

(e) Orders of Trial Court. The trial court may make any order necessary to adequately protect the judgment creditor against loss or damage that the appeal might cause.

(f) Effect of Supersedeas. Enforcement of a judgment must be suspended if the judgment is superseded. Enforcement begun before the judgment is superseded must cease when the judgment is superseded. If execution has been issued, the clerk will promptly issue a writ of supersedeas.

24.2. Amount of Bond, Deposit or Security.

(a) Type of Judgment.

(1) For Recovery of Money. When the judgment is for money, the amount of the bond, deposit, or security must equal the sum of compensatory damages awarded in the judgment, interest for the estimated duration of the appeal, and costs awarded in the judgment. But the amount must not exceed the lesser of:

(A) 50 percent of the judgment debtor's current net worth; or

(B) 25 million dollars.

(2) For Recovery of Property. When the judgment is for the recovery of an interest in real or personal property, the trial court will determine the type of security that the judgment debtor must post. The amount of that security must be at least:

(A) the value of the property interest's rent or revenue, if the property interest is real; or

(B) the value of the property interest on the date when the court rendered judgment, if the property interest is personal.

(3) Other Judgment. When the judgment is for something other than money or an interest in property, the trial court must set the amount and type of security that the judgment debtor must post. The security must adequately protect the judgment creditor against loss or damage that the appeal might cause. But the trial court may decline to permit the judgment to be superseded if the judgment creditor posts security ordered by the trial court in an amount and type that will secure the judgment debtor against any loss or damage caused by the relief granted the judgment creditor if an appellate court determines, on final disposition, that that relief was improper. When the judgment debtor is the state, a department of this state, or the head of a department of this state, the trial court must permit a judgment to be superseded except in a matter arising from a contested case in an administrative enforcement action.

(4) Conservatorship or Custody. When the judgment involves the conservatorship or custody of a minor or other person under legal disability, enforcement of the judgment will not be suspended, with or without security, unless ordered by the trial court. But upon a proper showing, the appellate court may suspend enforcement of the judgment with or without security.

(5) For a Governmental Entity. When a judgment in favor of a governmental entity in its governmental capacity is one in which the entity has no pecuniary interest, the trial court must determine whether to suspend enforcement, with or without security, taking into account the harm that is likely to result to the judgment debtor if enforcement is not suspended, and the harm that is likely to result to others if enforcement is suspended. The appellate court may review the trial court's determination and suspend enforcement of the judgment, with or without security, or refuse to suspend the judgment. If security is required, recovery is limited to the governmental entity's actual damages resulting from suspension of the judgment.

(b) Lesser Amount. The trial court must lower the amount of security required by (a) to an amount that will not cause the judgment debtor substantial economic harm if, after notice to all parties and a hearing, the court finds that posting a bond, deposit, or security in the amount required by (a) is likely to cause the judgment debtor substantial economic harm.

(c) Determination of Net Worth.

(1) Judgment Debtor's Affidavit Required; Contents; Prima Facie Evidence. A judgment debtor who provides a bond, deposit, or security under (a)(1)(2) in an amount based on the debtor's net worth must simultaneously file with the trial court clerk an affidavit that states the debtor's net worth and states complete, detailed information concerning the debtor's assets and liabilities from which net worth can be ascertained. An affidavit that meets these requirements is prima facie evidence of the debtor's net worth for the purpose of establishing the amount of the bond, deposit, or security required to suspend enforcement of the judgment. A trial court clerk must receive and file a net worth affidavit tendered for filing by a judgment debtor.

(2) Contest; Discovery. A judgment creditor may file a contest to the debtor's claimed net worth. The contest need not be sworn. The creditor may conduct reasonable discovery concerning the judgment debtor's net worth.

(3) Hearing; Burden of Proof; Findings; Additional Security. The trial court must hear a judgment creditor's contest of the judgment debtor's claimed net worth promptly after any discovery has been completed. The judgment debtor has the burden of proving net worth. The trial court must issue an order that states the debtor's net worth and states with particularity the factual basis for that determination. If the trial court orders additional or other security to supercede the judgment, the enforcement of the judgment will be suspended for twenty days after the trial court's order. If the judgment debtor does not comply with the order within that period, the judgment may be enforced against the judgment debtor.

(d) Injunction. The trial court may enjoin the judgment debtor from dissipating or transferring assets to avoid satisfaction of the judgment, but the trial court may not make any order that interferes with the judgment debtor's use, transfer, conveyance, or dissipation of assets in the normal course of business.

(Amended by Order August 29, 2003, effective in all cases in which a final judgment is signed on or after Sept. 1. 2003; Order March 10, 2008, eff. Sept. 1, 2008; Order Aug. 20, 2008, eff. Sept. 1, 2008; Misc. Docket No. 18-9061 April 2, 2018, eff May 1, 2018..)

24.3. Continuing Trial Court Jurisdiction; Duties of Judgment Debtor.

(a) Continuing Jurisdiction. Even after the trial court's plenary power expires, the trial court has continuing jurisdiction to do the following:

(1) order the amount and type of security and decide the sufficiency of sureties; and

(2) if circumstances change, modify the amount or type of security required to continue the suspension of a judgment's execution.

(b) Duties of Judgment Debtor. If, after jurisdiction attaches in an appellate court, the trial court orders or modifies the security or decides the sufficiency of sureties, the judgment debtor must notify the appellate court of the trial court's action.

24.4. Appellate Review.

(a) Motions; Review. A party may seek review of the trial court's ruling by motion filed in the court of appeals with jurisdiction or potential jurisdiction over the appeal from the judgment in the case. A party may seek review of the court of appeals' ruling on the motion by petition for writ of mandamus in the Supreme Court. The appellate court may review:

(1) the sufficiency or excessiveness of the amount of security, but when the judgment is for money, the appellate court must not modify the amount of security to exceed the limits imposed by rule 24.2(a)(1);

(2) the sureties on any bond;

(3) the type of security;

(4) the determination whether to permit suspension of enforcement; and

(5) the trial court's exercise of discretion under Rule 24.3(a).

(b) Grounds of Review. Review may be based both on conditions as they existed at the time the trial court signed an order, and on changes in those conditions afterward.

(c) Temporary Orders. The appellate court may issue any temporary orders necessary to preserve the parties' rights.

(d) Filing in Appellate Court. A motion filed under paragraph (a) should be filed in the court of appeals having potential appellate jurisdiction over the underlying judgment. The court of appeals' ruling is subject to review on petition for writ of mandamus to the Texas Supreme Court.

(e) Action by Appellate Court. The motion must be heard at the earliest practicable time. The appellate court may require that the amount of a bond, deposit, or other security be increased or decreased, and that another bond, deposit, or security be provided and approved by the trial court clerk. The appellate court may require other changes in the trial court order. The appellate court may remand to the trial court for entry of findings of fact or for the taking of evidence.

(f) Effect of Ruling. If the appellate court orders additional or other security to supersede the judgment, enforcement will be suspended for 20 days after the appellate court's order. If the judgment debtor does not comply with the order within that period, the judgment may be enforced. When any additional bond, deposit, or security has been filed, the trial court clerk must notify the appellate court. The posting of additional security will not release the previously posted security or affect any alternative security arrangements that the judgment debtor previously made unless specifically ordered by the appellate court.

(Adopted by Order eff. Sept. 1, 1997. Amended by Order Aug. 29, 2003, eff. Sept. 1, 2003; Order March 10, 2008 eff. Sept. 1, 2008; Order Aug. 20, 2008, eff. Sept. 1, 2008.)

Comment to 1997 change: Former Rules 47, 48, and 49 are merged. The rule is substantially revised. Paragraph 24.1(a) now provides for superseding the judgment by agreement. Paragraph 24.1(c) is taken from former Rule 48 and provides for a deposit in lieu of the bond, including specific provisions for the release of the deposit. Paragraph 24.1(d) provides the conditions for the surety to honor the bond and for the deposit to be paid to the judgment creditor. In subdivision 24.2, the provisions for determining the amount of the bond or deposit are simplified. All provisions regarding superseding a judgment for an interest in property are merged into subparagraph 24.2(a)(2). The procedure for allowing security in a lesser amount is moved to paragraph 24.2(b) and is made applicable to all judgments. Subdivision 24.4 is taken from former Rule 49. The procedure for appellate review is more precisely stated.

Comment to 2008 changes: Subdivision 24.2(c) is amended to clarify the procedure in determining net worth. A debtor's affidavit of net worth must be detailed, but the clerk must file what is tendered without determining whether it complies with the rule. If the trial court orders that additional or other security be given, the debtor is afforded time to comply. Subdivision 24.4(a) is revised to clarify that a party seeking relief from a supersedeas ruling should file a motion in the court of appeals that has or presumably will have jurisdiction of the appeal. After the court of appeals has ruled, a party may seek review by filing a petition for writ of mandamus in the Supreme Court. *See In re Smith/In re Main Place Custom Homes, Inc.*, 192 S.W.3d 564, 568 (Tex. 2006) (per curiam).

RULE 25. PERFECTING APPEALs.

25.1. Civil Cases.

(a) Notice of Appeal. An appeal is perfected when a written notice of appeal is filed with the trial court clerk. If a notice of appeal is mistakenly filed with the appellate court, the notice is deemed to have been filed the same day with the trial court clerk, and the appellate clerk must immediately send the trial court clerk a copy of the notice.

(b) Jurisdiction of Appellate Court. The filing of a notice of appeal by any party invokes the appellate court's jurisdiction over all parties to the trial court's judgment or order appealed from. Any party's failure to take any other step required by these rules, including the failure of another party to perfect an appeal under (c), does not deprive the appellate court of jurisdiction but is ground only for the appellate court to act appropriately, including dismissing the appeal.

(c) Who Must File Notice. A party who seeks to alter the trial court's judgment or other appealable order must file a notice of appeal. Parties whose interests are aligned may file a joint notice of appeal. The appellate court may not grant a party who does not file a notice of appeal more favorable relief than did the trial court except for just cause.

(d) Contents of Notice. The notice of appeal must:

(1) identify the trial court and state the case's trial court number and style;

(2) state the date of the judgment or order appealed from;

(3) state that the party desires to appeal;

(4) state the court to which the appeal is taken unless the appeal is to either the First or Fourteenth Court of Appeals, in which case the notice must state that the appeal is to either of those courts;

(5) state the name of each party filing the notice;

(6) n an accelerated appeal, state that the appeal is accelerated and state whether it is a parental termination or child protection case, as defined in Rule 28.4;

(7) in a restricted appeal:

(A) state that the appellant is a party affected by the trial court's judgment but did not participate—either in person or through counsel—in the hearing that resulted in the judgment complained of;

(B) state that the appellant did not timely file either a postjudgment motion, request for findings of fact and conclusions of law, or notice of appeal; and

(C) be verified by the appellant if the appellant does not have counsel.

(8) state, if applicable, that the appellant is presumed indigent and may proceed without paying costs under Rule 20.1.

(e) Service of Notice. The notice of appeal must be served on all parties to the trial court's final judgment or, in an interlocutory appeal, on all parties to the trial court proceeding.

(f) Clerk's Duties. The trial court clerk must immediately send a copy of the notice of appeal to the appellate court clerk and to the court reporter or court reporters responsible for preparing the reporter's record.

(g) Amending the Notice. An amended notice of appeal correcting a defect or omission in an earlier filed notice may be filed in the appellate court at any time before the appellant's brief is filed. The amended notice is subject to being struck for cause on the motion of any party affected by the amended notice. After the appellant's brief is filed, the notice may be amended only on leave of the appellate court and on such terms as the court may prescribe.

(h) Enforcement of Judgment Not Suspended by Appeal. The filing of a notice of appeal does not suspend enforcement of the judgment. Enforcement of the judgment may proceed unless:

(1) the judgment is superseded in accordance with Rule 24, or

(2) the appellant is entitled to supersede the judgment without security by filing a notice of appeal.

(Amended by Order Aug. 31, 2011, eff. Sept. 1, 2011; Order Dec. 12, 2011, eff. March 1, 2012; Order Feb. 13, 2012, eff. March 1, 2012; Tex. Sup. Ct. Misc. Docket No. 16-9056, eff. Sept. 1, 2016; Amended by Tex. Sup. Ct. Misc. Docket No. 16-9122, eff. Sept. 1, 2016.)

[Statement of Inability to Afford Payment of Court Costs as provided in Tex. Sup. Ct. Misc. Docket No. 16-9122, eff. Sept. 1, 2016 and applies to any contest of, or challenge to, a claim of inability to afford payment of court costs that is pending on September 1, 2016.]

25.2. Criminal Cases.

(a) Rights to Appeal.

(1) Of the State. The State is entitled to appeal a court's order in a criminal case as provided by Code of Criminal Procedure article 44.01.

(2) Of the Defendant. A defendant in a criminal case has the right of appeal under Code of Criminal Procedure article 44.02 and these rules. The trial court shall enter a certification of the defendant's right of appeal each time it enters a judgment of guilt or other appealable order. In a plea bargain case—that is, a case in which a defendant's plea was guilty or nolo contendere and the punishment did not exceed the punishment recommended by the prosecutor and agreed to by the defendant—a defendant may appeal only:

(A) those matters that were raised by written motion filed and ruled on before trial, or

(B) after getting the trial court's permission to appeal.

(b) Perfection of Appeal. In a criminal case, appeal is perfected by timely filing a sufficient notice of appeal. In a death-penalty case it is unnecessary to file a notice of appeal, but, in every death-penalty case, the clerk of the trial court shall file a notice of conviction with the Court of Criminal Appeals within thirty days after the defendant is sentenced to death.

(c) Form and Sufficiency of Notice.

(1) Notice must be given in writing and filed with the trial court clerk. If the notice of appeal is received in the court of appeals, the clerk of that court shall immediately record on the notice the date that it was received and send the notice to the trial court clerk.

(2) Notice is sufficient if it shows the party's desire to appeal from the judgment or other appealable order, and, if the State is the appellant, the notice complies with Code of Criminal Procedure article 44.01.

(d) Certification of Defendant's Right of Appeal. If the defendant is the appellant, the record must include the trial court's certification of the defendant's right of appeal under Rule 25.2(a)(2). The certification shall include a notice that the defendant has been informed of his rights concerning an appeal, as well as any right to file a *pro se* petition for discretionary review. This notification shall be signed by the defendant, with a copy given to him. The certification should be part of the record when notice is filed, but may be added by timely amendment or supplementation under this rule or Rule 34.5(c)(1) or Rule 37.1 or by order of the appellate court under Rule 34.5(c)(2). The appeal must be dismissed if a certification that shows the defendant has the right of appeal has not been made part of the record under these rules.

(e) Clerk's Duties. The trial court clerk must note on the copies of the notice of appeal and the trial court's certification of the defendant's right of appeal the case number and the date when each was filed. The clerk must then immediately send one copy to the clerk of the appropriate court of appeals and, if the defendant is the appellant, one copy of each to the State's attorney.

(f) Amending the Notice or Certification. An amended notice of appeal or trial court's certification of the defendant's right of appeal correcting a defect or omission in an earlier filed notice or certification, including a defect in the notification of the defendant's appellate rights, may be filed in the appellate court in accordance with Rule 37.1, or at any time before the appealing party's brief is filed if the court of appeals has not used Rule 37.1. The amended notice or certification is subject to being struck for cause on the motion of any party affected by the amended notice or certification. After the appealing party's brief is filed, the notice or certification may be amended only on leave of the appellate court and on such terms as the court may prescribe.

(g) Effect of Appeal. Once the record has been filed in the appellate court, all further proceedings in the trial court—except as provided otherwise by law or by these rules—will be suspended until the trial court receives the appellate-court mandate.

(h) Advice of Right of Appeal. When a court enters a judgment or other appealable order and the defendant has a right of appeal, the court (orally or in writing) shall advise the defendant of his right of appeal and of the requirements for timely filing a sufficient notice of appeal.

(Amended by Order Dec. 23, 2002 eff. Jan. 1, 2003; Order Dec. 13, 2006 eff. Jan. 1, 2007; Order May 2, 2007 eff. Sept. 1, 2007; Order Aug. 20, 2008, eff. Sept. 1, 2008.)

Comment on 2002 change: Rule 25.2, for criminal cases, is amended. Subdivision 25.2(a) states the parties' right of appeal that are established by Code of Criminal Procedure article 44.01 and by article 44.02, the proviso of which was repealed when rulemaking power was given to the Court of Criminal Appeals. Subdivision 25.2(b) is given the requirement that a notice of appeal be in "sufficient" form, which codifies the decisional law. The requirement in former subdivision 25.2(b)(3) that a plea-bargain appellant's notice of appeal specify the right of appeal is replaced by a requirement in subdivision 25.2(d) that the trial court certify the defendant's right of appeal in every case in which a judgment or other appealable order is entered. The certificate should be signed at the time of judgment or other appealable order is pronounced. The form of certification of the defendant's right of appeal is provided in an appendix [see below] to these rules. If the record does not include the trial court's certification that the defendant has the right of appeal, the appeal must be dismissed. If a sufficient notice of appeal or certification is not filed after the appellate court deals with the defect (*See* Rules 34.5(c) and 37.1), preparation of an appellate record and representation by an appointed attorney may cease.

[Form to be included in Appendix and is omitted.]

RULE 26. TIME TO PERFECT APPEAL.

26.1. Civil Cases.

The notice of appeal must be filed within 30 days after the judgment is signed, except as follows:

(a) the notice of appeal must be filed within 90 days after the judgment is signed if any party timely files:

(1) a motion for new trial;

(2) a motion to modify the judgment;

(3) a motion to reinstate under Texas Rule of Civil Procedure 165a; or

(4) a request for findings of fact and conclusions of law if findings and conclusions either are required by the Rules of Civil Procedure or, if not required, could properly be considered by the appellate court;

(b) in an accelerated appeal, the notice of appeal must be filed within 20 days after the judgment or order is signed;

(c) in a restricted appeal, the notice of appeal must be filed within six months after the judgment or order is signed; and

(d) if any party timely files a notice of appeal, another party may file a notice of appeal within the applicable period stated above or 14 days after the first filed notice of appeal, whichever is later.

26.2. Criminal Cases.

(a) By the Defendant. The notice of appeal must be filed:

(1) within 30 days after the day sentence is imposed or suspended in open court, or after the day the trial court enters an appealable order; or

(2) within 90 days after the day sentence is imposed or suspended in open court if the defendant timely files a motion for new trial.

(b) By the State. The notice of appeal must be filed within 20 days after the day the trial court enters the order, ruling, or sentence to be appealed.

(Amended by Order March 10, 2008, eff. Sept. 1, 2008; Order Aug. 20, 2008, eff. Sept. 1, 2008.)

26.3. Extension of Time.

The appellate court may extend the time to file the notice of appeal if, within 15 days after the deadline for filing the notice of appeal, the party:

(a) files in the trial court the notice of appeal; and

(b) files in the appellate court a motion complying with Rule 10.5(b).

(Adopted by Order eff. Sept. 1, 1997.)

Comment to 1997 change: This is former Rule 41. All times for perfecting appeal in civil cases—including the time for perfecting a restricted appeal—are stated. An extension of time is available for all appeals. The provisions of former Rule 41(c) regarding prematurely filed documents are moved to Rule 27. Nonsubstantive changes are made in the rule for criminal cases.

RULE 27. PREMATURE FILINGS.

27.1. Prematurely Filed Notice of Appeal.

(a) Civil Cases. In a civil case, a prematurely filed notice of appeal is effective and deemed filed on the day of, but after, the event that begins the period for perfecting the appeal.

(b) Criminal Cases. In a criminal case, a prematurely filed notice of appeal is effective and deemed filed on the same day, but after, sentence is imposed or suspended in open court, or the appealable order is signed by the trial court. But a notice of appeal is not effective if filed before the trial court makes a finding of guilt or receives a jury verdict.

27.2. Other Premature Actions.

The appellate court may treat actions taken before an appealable order is signed as relating to an appeal of that order and give them effect as if they had been taken after the order was signed. The appellate court may allow an appealed order that is not final to be modified so as to be made final and may allow the modified order and all proceedings relating to it to be included in a supplemental record.

27.3. If Appealed Order Modified or Vacated.

After an order or judgment in a civil case has been appealed, if the trial court modifies the order or judgment, or if the trial court vacates the order or judgment and replaces it with another appealable order or judgment, the appellate court must treat the appeal as from the subsequent order or judgment and may treat actions relating to the appeal of the first order or judgment as relating to the appeal of the subsequent order or judgment. The subsequent order or judgment and actions relating to it may be included in the original or supplemental record. Any party may nonetheless appeal from the subsequent order or judgment.

(Adopted by Order eff. Sept. 1, 1997.)

Comment to 1997 change: This rule is new and combines the provisions of former Rules 41(c) and 58.

RULE 28. ACCELERATED, Agreed, and Permissive APPEALS IN CIVIL CASES.

28.1. Civil cases—Appeal as of Right.

(a) Types of Accelerated Appeals. Appeals from interlocutory orders (when allowed by statute), appeals in quo warranto proceedings, appeals required by statute to be accelerated or expedited, and appeals required by law to be filed or perfected within less than 30 days after the date of the order or judgment being appealed are accelerated appeals.

(b) Perfection of Accelerated Appeal. Unless otherwise provided by statute, an accelerated appeal is perfected by filing a notice of appeal in compliance with Rule 25.1 within the time allowed by Rule 26.1(b) or as extended by Rule 26.3. Filing a motion for new trial, any other post-trial motion, or a request for findings of fact will not extend the time to perfect an accelerated appeal.

(c) Appeals of Interlocutory Orders. The trial court need not file findings of fact and conclusions of law but may do so within 30 days after the order is signed.

(d) Quo Warranto Appeals. The trial court may grant a motion for new trial timely filed under Texas Rule of Civil Procedure 329b(a)-(b) until 50 days after the trial court's final judgment is signed. If not determined by signed written order within that period, the motion will be deemed overruled by operation of law on expiration of that period.

(e) Record and Briefs. In lieu of the clerk's record, the appellate court may hear an accelerated appeal on the original papers forwarded by the trial court or on sworn and uncontroverted copies of those papers. The appellate court may allow the case to be submitted without briefs. The deadlines and procedures for filing the record and briefs in an accelerated appeal are provided in Rules 35.1 and 38.6.

(Amended by Order March 10, 2008, eff. Sept. 1, 2008; Order Aug. 20, 2008, eff. Sept. 1, 2008; Order Aug. 20, 2008, eff. Sept. 1, 2008; Order Aug. 25, 2008, eff. Sept. 1, 2008.)

28.2. Agreed Interlocutory Appeals in Civil Cases.

(a) Perfecting Appeal. An agreed appeal of an interlocutory order permitted by statute must be perfected as provided in Rule 25.1. The notice of appeal must be filed no later than the 20th day after the date the trial court signs a written order granting permission to appeal, unless the court of appeals extends the time for filing pursuant to Rule 26.3.

(b) Other Requirements. In addition to perfecting appeal, the appellant must file with the clerk of the appellate court a docketing statement as provided in Rule 32.1 and pay to the clerk of the appellate court all required fees authorized to be collected by the clerk.

(c) Contents of Notice. The notice of accelerated appeal must contain, in addition to the items required by Rule 25.1(d), the following:

(1) a list of the names of all parties to the trial court proceeding and the names, addresses, and telefax numbers of all trial and appellate counsel;

(2) a copy of the trial court's order granting permission to appeal;

(3) a copy of the trial court order appealed from;

(4) a statement that all parties to the trial court proceeding agreed to the trial court's order granting permission to appeal;

(5) a statement that all parties to the trial court proceeding agreed that the order granting permission to appeal involves a controlling question of law as to which there is a substantial ground for difference of opinion;

(6) a brief statement of the issues or points presented; and

(7) a concise explanation of how an immediate appeal may materially advance the ultimate termination of litigation.

(d) Determination of Jurisdiction. If the court of appeals determines that a notice of appeal filed under this rule does not demonstrate the court's jurisdiction, it may order the appellant to file an amended notice of appeal. On a party's motion or its own initiative, the court of appeals may also order the appellant or any other party to file briefing addressing whether the appeal meets the statutory requirements, and may direct the parties to file supporting evidence. If, after providing an opportunity to file an amended notice of appeal or briefing addressing potential jurisdictional defects, the court of appeals concludes that a jurisdictional defect exists, it may dismiss the appeal for want of jurisdiction at any stage of the appeal.

(e) Record; Briefs. The rules governing the filing of the appellate record and briefs in accelerated appeals apply. A party may address in its brief any issues related to the court of appeals' jurisdiction, including whether the appeal meets the statutory requirements.

(f) No Automatic Stay of Proceedings in Trial Court. An agreed appeal of an interlocutory order permitted by statute does not stay proceedings in the trial court except as agreed by the parties and ordered by the trial court or the court of appeals.

28.3. Permissive Appeals in Civil Cases.

(a) Petition Required. When a trial court has permitted an appeal from an interlocutory order that would not otherwise be appealable, a party seeking to appeal must petition the court of appeals for permission to appeal.

(b) Where Filed. The petition must be filed with the clerk of the court of appeals having appellate jurisdiction over the action in which the order to be appealed is issued. The First and Fourteenth Courts of Appeals must determine in which of those two courts a petition will be filed.

(c) When Filed. The petition must be filed within 15 days after the order to be appealed is signed. If the order is amended by the trial court, either on its own or in response to a party's motion, to include the court's permission to appeal, the time to petition the court of appeals runs from the date the amended order is signed.

(d) Extension of Time to File Petition. The court of appeals may extend the time to file the petition if the party;

(1) files the petition within 15 days after the deadline, and

(2) files a motion complying with Rule 10.5(b).

(e) Contents. The petition must:

(1) contain the information required by Rule 25.1 (d) to be included in a notice of appeal:

(2) attach a copy of the order from which appeal is sought;

(3) contain a table of contents, index of authorities, issues presented, and a statement of facts; and

(4) argue clearly and concisely why the order to be appealed involves a controlling question of law as to which there is a substantial ground for difference of opinion and how an immediate appeal from the order may materially advance the ultimate termination of the litigation.

(f) Response; Reply; Cross-Petition; Time for Filing. If any party timely files a petition, any other party may file a response or a cross-petition within 10 days. A party may file a response to a cross-petition within 10 days of the date the cross-petition is filed. A petitioner or cross-petitioner may reply to any matter in a response within 7 days of the date the response is filed. The court of appeals may extend the time to file a response, reply, and cross-petition.

(g) Length of Petition. Cross-Petition, Response, and Reply. A petition, cross-petition, response, and reply must comply with the page limitations in Rule 9.4(i)(2)(D)-(E).

(h) Service. A petition, cross-petition, response, and reply must be served on all parties to the trial court proceeding.

(i) Docketing Statement. Upon filing the petition, the petitioner must file the docketing statement required by Rule 32.1.

(j) Time for Determination. Unless the court of appeals orders otherwise, a petition, and any cross-petition, response, and reply, will be determined without oral argument, no earlier than 10 days after the petition is filed.

(k) When Petition Granted. If the petition is granted, a notice of appeal is deemed to have been filed under Rule 26. Kb) on that date, and the appeal is governed by the rules for accelerated appeals. A separate notice of appeal need not be filed. A copy of the order granting the petition must be filed with the trial court clerk.

(Amended by Order March 4, 2013, eff. March 4, 2013.)

28.4. Accelerated Appeals in Parental Termination and Child Protection Cases

(a) Application and Definitions.

(1) Appeals in parental termination and child protection cases are governed by the rules of appellate procedure for accelerated appeals, except as otherwise provided in Rule 28.4.

(2) In Rule 28.4:

(A) a "parental termination case" means a suit in which termination of the parent-child relationship is at issue.

(B) a "child protection case" means a suit affecting the parent-child relationship filed by a governmental entity for managing conservatorship.

(b) Appellate Record.

(1) Responsibility for Preparation of Reporter's Record. In addition to the responsibility imposed on the trial court in Rule 35.3(c), when the reporter's responsibility to prepare, certify and timely file the reporter s record arises under Rule 35.3(b), the trial court must direct the official or deputy reporter to immediately commence the preparation of the reporter's record. The trial court must arrange for a substitute reporter, if necessary.

(2) Extension of Time. The appellate court may grant an extension of time to file a record under Rule 35.3(c); however, the extension or extensions granted must not exceed 30 days cumulatively, absent extraordinary circumstances.

(3) Restriction on Preparation Inapplicable. Section 13.003 of the Civil Practice & Remedies Code does not apply to an appeal from a parental termination or child protection case.

(c) Remand for New Trial. If the judgment of the appellate court reverses and remands a parental termination or child protection case for a new trial, the judgment must instruct the trial court to commence the new trial no later than 180 days after the mandate is issued by the appellate court.

(Adopted by Order eff. Sept. 1, 1997. Amended by Order March 10, 2008 eff. Sept. 1, 2008; Order Aug. 20, 2008, eff. Sept. 1, 2008; Order Aug. 31, 2011, eff. Sept. 1, 2011; Order Sept. 9, 2011, eff. Sept. 9, 2011; Order Dec. 12, 2011, eff. March 1, 2012; Order Feb. 13, 2012, eff. March 1, 2012.)

Comment to 1997 change: This is former Rule 42. A motion for new trial is now permitted in an appeal from an interlocutory order, but it does not extend the time to perfect appeal. The deadlines for filing items in an accelerated appeal are moved to other rules. *See* Rules 26.1, 35.1 and 38.6. Former Rule 42(b), regarding discretionary acceleration, is omitted as unnecessary. *See* Rule 40.1. The provision in former Rule 42(c) allowing the court to shorten the time to file briefs is omitted as unnecessary. *See* Rule 38.6.

Comment to 2008 changes: Rule 28 is rewritten. Subdivision 28.1 more clearly defines accelerated appeals and provides a uniform appellate timetable. But many statutes that provide for accelerated or expedited appeals also set appellate timetables, and statutory deadlines govern over deadlines provided in the rule. Subdivision 28.2 provides procedures for an agreed appeal of an interlocutory order permitted by statute. Such appeals are now permitted under Section 51.014(d) of the Civil Practice and Remedies Code. The requirements for perfecting appeal are generally set out in Rule 25.1, and as provided there, only the notice of appeal is jurisdictional.

Comment to 2011 Change: Section 51.014(d)-(f) of the Texas Civil Practice and Remedies Code, as amended in 2011, provides for appeals of orders not otherwise appealable when permitted by the trial court. The 2011 amendments, which explicitly apply only to cases commenced on or after September 1, 2011, eliminated the prior requirement that the parties agree to the appeal and reinstated a requirement that the court of appeals also permit the appeal. Act of May 25, 2011, 82nd Leg., R.S., ch. 203, §§ 3.01, 6.01 [HB 274], amending Act of May 27, 2005, 79th Leg. R.S., ch. 1051 [HB 1294], §§ 1-2, 2005 Tex. Gen. Laws 3512, 3512-3513 and Act of May 17, 2001, 77th Leg., R.S., ch. 1389 [HB 978], § 1, 2001 Tex. Gen. Laws 3575. The amendments necessitated the addition of Rule 28.3 and the adoption of Rule of Civil Procedure 168, which governs the procedure for obtaining permission to appeal from the trial court.

New Rule 28.3 applies only to appeals in cases that were filed in the trial court on or after September 1, 2011. Rule 28.2 applies only to appeals in cases that were filed in the trial court before September 1, 2011.

Rule of Civil Procedure 168 clarifies that the trial court's permission to appeal should be included in the order to be appealed rather than in a separate order. As stated in Rule 28.3(c), if a prior order containing the trial court's ruling is amended to include such permission, the time for appeal runs from the amended order. Rule 28.3(k) further clarifies that if the petition is granted, appeal is thereby perfected, and the appeal proceeds as an accelerated appeal, with all deadlines-including deadlines and obligations for preparing the record-running from the date the petition was granted. A separate notice of appeal need not be filed. The petition procedure in Rule 28.3 is intended to be similar to the Rule 53 procedure governing petitions for review in the Supreme Court.

RULE 29. ORDERS PENDING INTERLOCUTORY APPEAL IN CIVIL CASES.

29.1. Effect of Appeal.

Perfecting an appeal from an order granting interlocutory relief does not suspend the order appealed from unless:

(a) the order is superseded in accordance with 29.2; or

(b) the appellant is entitled to supersede the order without security by filing a notice of appeal.

29.2. Security.

The trial court may permit an order granting interlocutory relief to be superseded pending an appeal from the order, in which event the appellant may supersede the order in accordance with Rule 24. If the trial court refuses to permit the appellant to supersede the order, the appellant may move the appellate court to review that decision for abuse of discretion.

29.3. Temporary Orders of Appellate Court.

When an appeal from an interlocutory order is perfected, the appellate court may make any temporary orders necessary to preserve the parties' rights until disposition of the appeal and may require appropriate security. But the appellate court must not suspend the trial court's order if the appellant's rights would be adequately protected by supersedeas or another order made under Rule 24.

29.4. Enforcement of Temporary Orders.

While an appeal from an interlocutory order is pending, only the appellate court in which the appeal is pending may enforce the order. But the appellate court may refer any enforcement proceeding to the trial court with instructions to:

(a) hear evidence and grant appropriate relief; or

(b) make findings and recommendations and report them to the appellate court.

29.5. Further Proceedings in Trial Court.

While an appeal from an interlocutory order is pending, the trial court retains jurisdiction of the case and unless prohibited by statute may make further orders, including one dissolving the order complained of on appeal. If permitted by law, the trial court may proceed with a trial on the merits. But the court must not make an order that:

(a) is inconsistent with any appellate court temporary order; or

(b) interferes with or impairs the jurisdiction of the appellate court or effectiveness of any relief sought or that may be granted on appeal.

(Amended by Order Dec. 23, 2002 eff. Jan. 1, 2003. Amended by Order March 10, 2008 eff. Sept. 1, 2008; Order Aug. 20, 2008, eff. Sept. 1, 2008.)

Comment to 2002 change: Rule 29.5 is amended to acknowledge that a trial court may be prohibited by law from proceeding to trial during the pendency of an interlocutory appeal, as for example by section 51.014(b) of the Texas Civil Practice and Remedies Code.

Comment to 2008 changes: Rule 29.5 is amended to be consistent with § 51.014(b) of the Civil Practice and Remedies Code, as amended in 2003, staying all proceedings in the trial court pending resolution of interlocutory appeals of class certification orders, denials of summary judgments based on assertions of immunity by governmental officers or employees, and orders granting or denying a governmental unit's plea to the jurisdiction.

29.6. Review of Further Orders.

(a) Motion to Review Further Orders. While an appeal from an interlocutory order is pending, on a party's motion or on the appellate court's own initiative, the appellate court may review the following:

(1) a further appealable interlocutory order concerning the same subject matter; and

(2) any interlocutory order that interferes with or impairs the effectiveness of the relief sought or that may be granted on appeal.

(b) Record. The party filing the motion may rely on the original record or may file a supplemental record with the motion.

(Adopted by Order eff. Sept. 1, 1997.)

Comment to 1997 change: This is former Rule 43. The provision in the former rule that an appeal from an order certifying a class suspends the order is repealed. The provision in the former rule that an order denying interlocutory relief cannot be suspended is omitted as unnecessary because the rule provides for superseding only orders granting relief. No substantive change is intended. The provision in former Rule 43(d) prohibiting the trial court from making an order granting substantially the same relief as the order appealed is repealed as being too broad. The provisions of former Rule 43(g) regarding the mandate are moved to Rule 18.6 and 18.7. The provision of former Rule 43(h) regarding rehearings is moved to Rule 49.4.

RULE 30. RESTRICTED APPEAL TO COURT OF APPEALS IN CIVIL CASES.

A party who did not participate—either in person or through counsel—in the hearing that resulted in the judgment complained of and who did not timely file a postjudgment motion or request for findings of fact and conclusions of law, or a notice of appeal within the time permitted by Rule 26.1(a), may file a notice of appeal within the time permitted by Rule 26.1(c). Restricted appeals replace writ of error appeals to the court of appeals. Statutes pertaining to writ of error appeals to the court of appeals apply equally to restricted appeals.

(Adopted by Order eff. Sept. 1, 1997.)

Comment to 1997 change: This is former Rule 45. The appeal by writ of error procedure is repealed. A procedure for an appeal filed within 6 months—called a restricted appeal—is substituted. This rule sets out who may take a restricted appeal. Rules 25.1 and 26.1 set out the method of perfection and the time for perfecting the appeal.

RULE 31. APPEALS IN HABEAS CORPUS, BAIL, AND EXTRADITION PROCEEDINGS IN CRIMINAL CASES.

31.1. Filing the Record; Submission.

When written notice of appeal from a judgment or order in a habeas corpus or bail proceeding is filed, the trial court clerk must prepare and certify the clerk's record and, if the appellant requests, the court reporter must prepare and certify a reporter's record. The clerk must send the clerk's record and the court reporter must send the reporter's record to the appellate court within 15 days after the notice of appeal is filed. On reasonable explanation, the appellate court may shorten or extend the time to file the record. When the appellate court receives the record, the court will—if it desires briefs—set the time for filing briefs, and will set the appeal for submission.

31.2. Hearing.

An appeal in a habeas corpus or bail proceeding will be heard at the earliest practicable time. The applicant need not personally appear, and the appeal will be heard and determined upon the law and the facts shown by the record. The appellate court will not review any incidental question that might have arisen on the hearing of the application before the trial court. The sole purpose of the appeal is to do substantial justice to the parties.

31.3. Orders on Appeal.

The appellate court will render whatever judgment and make whatever orders the law and the nature of the case require. The court may make an appropriate order relating to costs, whether allowing costs and fixing the amount, or allowing no costs.

31.4. Stay of Mandate.

(a) When Motion for Stay Required. Despite Rule 18 or any other of these rules, in the following circumstances a party who in good faith intends to seek discretionary review must—within 15 days after the court of appeals renders judgment—file with the court of appeals clerk a motion for stay of mandate, to which is appended the party's petition for discretionary review showing reasons why the Court of Criminal Appeals should review the appellate court judgment:

(1) when a court of appeals affirms the judgment of the trial court in an extradition matter and thereby sanctions a defendant's extradition; or

(2) when a court of appeals reverses the trial court's judgment in a bail matter—including bail pending appeal under > Code of Criminal Procedure article 44.04(g)—and thereby grants or reduces the amount of bail.

(b) Determination of the Motion. The clerk must promptly submit the motion and appendix to the court of appeals, or to one or more judges as the court deems appropriate, for immediate consideration and determination.

(1) If the motion for stay is granted, the clerk will file the petition for discretionary review and process the case in accordance with Rule 68.7.

(2) If the motion is denied, the clerk will issue a mandate in accordance with the court of appeals' judgment.

(c) Denial of Stay. If the motion for stay is denied under 31.4(b)(2), the losing party may then present the motion and appendix to the clerk of the Court of Criminal Appeals, who will promptly submit them to the Court, or to one or more judges as the Court deems appropriate, for immediate consideration and determination. The Court of Criminal Appeals may deny the motion or stay or recall the mandate. If the mandate is stayed or recalled, the court of appeals clerk will file the petition for discretionary review and process the case in accordance with Rule 68.7.

31.5. Judgment Conclusive.

The court of appeals' judgment is final and conclusive if the Court of Criminal Appeals does not grant discretionary review. If the Court of Criminal Appeals grants discretionary review, that court's judgment is final and conclusive. In either case, no further application in the same case can be made for the writ unless the law provides otherwise.

31.6. Defendant Detained by Other Than Officer.

If the defendant is held by a person other than an officer, the sheriff receiving the appellate court mandate so ordering must immediately cause the defendant to be discharged, for which discharge the mandate is sufficient authority.

31.7. Judgment to Be Certified.

The appellate court clerk will certify the court's judgment to the officer holding the defendant in custody or, if the defendant is held by a person other than an officer, to the appropriate sheriff.

(Adopted by Order eff. Sept. 1, 1997.)

Comment to 1997 change: This is former Rule 44. Since the purpose of the appeal is to do substantial justice, it is extended to both parties in recognition that both parties now have the right to appeal. Other nonsubstantive changes are made.

RULE 32. DOCKETING STATEMENT.

32.1. Civil Cases.

Promptly upon filing the notice of appeal in a civil case, the appellant must file in the appellate court a docketing statement that includes the following information:

(a)(1) if the appellant filing the statement has counsel, the name of that appellant and the name, address, telephone number, fax number, if any, and State Bar of Texas identification number of the appellant's lead counsel; or

(2) if the appellant filing the statement is not represented by an attorney, that party's name, address, telephone number, and fax number, if any;

(b) the date the notice of appeal was filed in the trial court and, if mailed to the trial court clerk, the date of mailing;

(c) the trial court's name and county, the name of the judge who tried the case, and the date the judgment or order appealed from was signed;

(d) the date of filing of any motion for new trial, motion to modify the judgment, request for findings of fact, motion to reinstate, or other filing that affects the time for perfecting the appeal;

(e) the names of all other parties to the trial court's judgment or the order appealed from, and:

(1) if represented by counsel, their lead counsel's names, addresses, telephone numbers, and fax numbers, if any; or

(2) if not represented by counsel, the name, address, and telephone number of the party, or a statement that the appellant diligently inquired but could not discover that information;

(f) the general nature of the case—for example, personal injury, breach of contract, or temporary injunction;

(g) whether the appeal's submission should be given priority, whether the appeal is an accelerated one under Rule 28 or another rule or statute and whether it is a parental termination or child protection case, as defined in Rule 28.4;

(h) whether the appellant has requested or will request a reporter's record, and whether the trial was electronically recorded;

(i) the name of the court reporter;

(j) whether the appellant intends to seek temporary or ancillary relief while the appeal is pending;

(k) if the appellant filed a Statement of Inability to Afford Payment of Court Costs in the trial court:

(1) the date the Statement was filed;

(2) the date of filing of any motion challenging the Statement;

(3) the date of any hearing on the appellant's ability to afford costs; and

(4) if the trial court signed an order under Texas Rule of Civil Procedure 145, the court's findings regarding the appellant's ability to afford costs and the date that the order was signed.

(l) whether the appellant has filed or will file a supersedeas bond; and

(m) any other information the appellate court requires.

(Amended by Order Dec. 12, 2011, eff. March 1, 2012; Order Feb. 13, 2012, eff. March 1, 2012; Tex. Sup. Ct. Misc. Docket No. 16-9056, eff. Sept. 1, 2016; Amended by Tex. Sup. Ct. Misc. Docket No. 16-9122, eff. Sept. 1, 2016.)

[Statement of Inability to Afford Payment of Court Costs as provided in Tex. Sup. Ct. Misc. Docket No. 16-9122, eff. Sept. 1, 2016 and applies to any contest of, or challenge to, a claim of inability to afford payment of court costs that is pending on September 1, 2016.]

32.2. Criminal Cases.

Upon perfecting the appeal in a criminal case, the appellant must file in the appellate court a docketing statement that includes the following information:

(a)(1) if the appellant has counsel, the name of the appellant and the name, address, telephone number, fax number, if any, and State Bar of Texas identification number of the appellant's counsel, and whether the counsel is appointed or retained; or

(2) if the appellant is not represented by an attorney, that party's name, address, telephone number, and fax number, if any;

(b) the date the notice of appeal was filed in the trial court and, if mailed to the trial court clerk, the date of mailing;

(c) the trial court's name and county, and the name of the judge who tried the case;

(d) the date the trial court imposed or suspended sentence in open court, or the date the judgment or order appealed from was signed;

(e) the date of filing any motion for new trial, motion in arrest of judgment, or any other filing that affects the time for perfecting the appeal;

(f) the offense charged and the date of the offense;

(g) the defendant's plea;

(h) whether the trial was jury or nonjury;

(i) the punishment assessed;

(j) whether the appeal is from a pretrial order;

(k) whether the appeal involves the validity of a statute, ordinance, or rule;

(l) whether a reporter's record has been or will be requested, and whether the trial was electronically recorded;

(m) the name of the court reporter;

(n)(1) the dates of filing of any motion and affidavit of indigence;

(2) the date of any hearing;

(3) the date of any order; and

(4) whether the motion was granted or denied; and

(o) any other information the appellate court requires.

32.3. Supplemental Statements.

Any party may file a statement supplementing or correcting the docketing statement.

32.4. Purpose of Statement.

The docketing statement is for administrative purposes and does not affect the appellate court's jurisdiction.

(Adopted by Order eff. Sept. 1, 1997.)

Comment to 1997 change: The rule is new.

RULE 33. PRESERVATION OF APPELLATE COMPLAINTS

33.1. Preservation; How Shown.

(a) In General. As a prerequisite to presenting a complaint for appellate review, the record must show that:

(1) the complaint was made to the trial court by a timely request, objection, or motion that:

(A) stated the grounds for the ruling that the complaining party sought from the trial court with sufficient specificity to make the trial court aware of the complaint, unless the specific grounds were apparent from the context; and

(B) complied with the requirements of the Texas Rules of Evidence or the Texas Rules of Civil or Appellate Procedure; and

(2) the trial court:

(A) ruled on the request, objection, or motion, either expressly or implicitly; or

(B) refused to rule on the request, objection, or motion, and the complaining party objected to the refusal.

(b) Ruling by Operation of Law. In a civil case, the overruling by operation of law of a motion for new trial or a motion to modify the judgment preserves for appellate review a complaint properly made in the motion, unless taking evidence was necessary to properly present the complaint in the trial court.

(c) Formal Exception and Separate Order Not Required. Neither a formal exception to a trial court ruling or order nor a signed, separate order is required to preserve a complaint for appeal.

(d) Sufficiency of Evidence Complaints in Civil Nonjury Cases. In a civil nonjury case, a complaint regarding the legal or factual insufficiency of the evidence—including a complaint that the damages found by the court are excessive or inadequate, as distinguished from a complaint that the trial court erred in refusing to amend a fact finding or to make an additional finding of fact—may be made for the first time on appeal in the complaining party's brief.

(Amended by Order Dec. 23, 2002, eff. Jan. 1, 2003; Order Tex. Sup. Ct. Misc. Docket No. 16-9018 and Final Order Misc. Docket No. 17-9067, eff. July 1, 2017.)

Comment to 2002 change: The last sentence of former Rule 52(d) of the Rules of Appellate Procedure has been reinstated in substance.

Comment to 2017 change: The 2017 amendment is intended only to clarify, and not to change existing law.

33.2. Formal Bills of Exception.

To complain on appeal about a matter that would not otherwise appear in the record, a party must file a formal bill of exception.

(a) Form. No particular form of words is required in a bill of exception. But the objection to the court's ruling or action, and the ruling complained of, must be stated with sufficient specificity to make the trial court aware of the complaint.

(b) Evidence. When the appellate record contains the evidence needed to explain a bill of exception, the bill itself need not repeat the evidence, and a party may attach and incorporate a transcription of the evidence certified by the court reporter.

(c) Procedure.

(1) The complaining party must first present a formal bill of exception to the trial court.

(2) If the parties agree on the contents of the bill of exception, the judge must sign the bill and file it with the trial court clerk. If the parties do not agree on the contents of the bill, the trial judge must—after notice and hearing—do one of the following things:

(A) sign the bill of exception and file it with the trial court clerk if the judge finds that it is correct;

(B) suggest to the complaining party those corrections to the bill that the judge believes are necessary to make it accurately reflect the proceedings in the trial court, and if the party agrees to the corrections, have the corrections made, sign the bill, and file it with the trial court clerk; or

(C) if the complaining party will not agree to the corrections suggested by the judge, return the bill to the complaining party with the judge's refusal written on it, and prepare, sign, and file with the trial court clerk such bill as will, in the judge's opinion, accurately reflect the proceedings in the trial court.

(3) If the complaining party is dissatisfied with the bill of exception filed by the judge under (2)(C), the party may file with the trial court clerk the bill that was rejected by the judge. That party must also file the affidavits of at least three people who observed the matter to which the bill of exception is addressed. The affidavits must attest to the correctness of the bill as presented by the party. The matters contained in that bill of exception may be controverted and maintained by additional affidavits filed by any party within ten days after the filing of that bill. The truth of the bill of exception will be determined by the appellate court.

(d) Conflict. If a formal bill of exception conflicts with the reporter's record, the bill controls.

(e) Time to File.

(1) Civil Cases. In a civil case, a formal bill of exception must be filed no later than 30 days after the filing party's notice of appeal is filed.

(2) Criminal Cases. In a criminal case, a formal bill of exception must be filed:

(A) no later than 60 days after the trial court pronounces or suspends sentence in open court; or

(B) if a motion for new trial has been timely filed, no later than 90 days after the trial court pronounces or suspends sentence in open court.

(3) Extension of Time. The appellate court may extend the time to file a formal bill of exception if, within 15 days after the deadline for filing the bill, the party files in the appellate court a motion complying with Rule 10.5(b).

(f) Inclusion in Clerk's Record. When filed, a formal bill of exception should be included in the appellate record.

(Adopted by Order eff. Sept. 1, 1997.)

Comment to 1997 change: This is former Rule 52. Subdivision 33.1 is rewritten. Former Rule 52(b), regarding offers of proof, is omitted as unnecessary. *See* TEX. R. CIV. EVID. 103; TEX. R. CRIM. EVID. 103. Subdivision 33.2 is also rewritten and the procedure is more definitely stated. Former Rule 52(d), regarding motions for new trial, is omitted as unnecessary. *See* TEX. R. CIV. P. 324(a) & (b).

RULE 34. APPELLATE RECORD.

34.1. Contents.

The appellate record consists of the clerk's record and, if necessary to the appeal, the reporter's record. Even if more than one notice of appeal is filed, there should be only one appellate record in a case.

34.2. Agreed Record.

By written stipulation filed with the trial court clerk, the parties may agree on the contents of the appellate record. An agreed record will be presumed to contain all evidence and filings relevant to the appeal. To request matter to be included in the agreed record, the parties must comply with the procedures in Rules 34.5 and 34.6.

34.3. Agreed Statement of the Case.

In lieu of a reporter's record, the parties may agree on a brief statement of the case. The statement must be filed with the trial court clerk and included in the appellate record.

34.4. Form.

The Supreme Court and Court of Criminal Appeals will prescribe the form of the appellate record.

APPENDIX C
IN THE SUPREME COURT OF TEXAS
ORDER DIRECTING
THE FORM OF THE APPELLATE RECORD IN CIVIL CASES

ORDERED that:

Pursuant to Texas Rule of Appellate Procedure 34.4, the Supreme Court orders that the appellate record in civil cases be in the form specified below:

RULE 1. CLERK'S RECORD

1.1. Preparation of Electronic or Paper Clerk's Record.

The trial court clerk must prepare and file the clerk's record in accordance with Rules of Appellate Procedure 34.5 and 35. Even if more than one notice of appeal or request for inclusion of items is filed, the clerk should prepare only one consolidated record in a case. To prepare the clerk's record, the trial court clerk must:

(a) gather the documents required by Rule of Appellate Procedure 34.5(a) and those requested by a party under Rule of Appellate Procedure 34.5(b);

(b) start each document on a new page;

(c) include the date of filing on each document;

(d) arrange the documents in ascending chronological order, by date of filing or occurrence;

(e) start the page numbering on the front cover of the first volume of the clerk's record and continue to number all pages consecutively—including the front and back covers, tables of contents, certification page, and separator pages, if any—until the final page of the clerk's record, without regard for the number of volumes in the clerk's record, and place each page number at the bottom of each page;

(f) prepare, label, and certify the clerk's record as required by this rule;

(g) as far as practicable, include the date of signing by the judge on each order and judgment;

(h) include on the front cover of the first volume, and any subsequent volumes, of the clerk's record, whether filed in paper or electronic form, the following information, in substantially the following form:

CLERK'S RECORD
VOLUME ____ of ____

Trial Court Cause No. ______________________
In the ______ (District or County) Court
of __________ County, Texas,
Honorable ______________, Judge Presiding

__________________, Plaintiff(s)
vs.
__________________, Defendant(s)

Appealed to the
(Supreme Court of Texas at Austin, Texas,
or Court of Criminal Appeals of Texas at Austin, Texas,
or Court of Appeals for the _____ District of Texas, at ______________, Texas).

Attorney for Appellant(s):
Name ____
Address ____
Telephone no.: ____________________
Fax no.: ________________________
E-mail address: ____________________
SBOT no.: ______________________
Attorney for: ______________________, Appellant(s)

Name of clerk preparing the clerk's record: ________________________

(i) prepare and include after the front cover of the clerk's record a detailed table of contents identifying each document in the entire record (including sealed documents), the date each document was filed, and, except for sealed documents, the page on which each document begins. The table of contents must be double-spaced and conform to the order in which documents appear in the clerk's record, rather than in alphabetical order. If the clerk's record consists of multiple volumes, the table of contents must indicate the page on which each volume begins. If the clerk's record is filed in electronic form, the clerk must use bookmarks to link each document description in the table of contents, except descriptions of sealed documents, to the page on which each document begins; and

(j) conclude the clerk's record with a certificate in substantially the following form:

The State of Texas)
County of ____________)

I, __________, Clerk of the _____ Court of ________ County, Texas do hereby certify that the documents contained in this record to which this certification is attached are all of the documents specified by Texas Rule of Appellate Procedure 34.5(a) and all other documents timely requested by a party to this proceeding under Texas Rule of Appellate Procedure 34.5(b).

GIVEN UNDER MY HAND AND SEAL at my office in ________, County, Texas this ___ day of ____________.

signature of clerk ____________________
name of clerk ____________________
title ____________________

If the clerk's record is filed in electronic form, the trial court clerk must include either a scanned image of the clerk's signature or "/s/" and the clerk's name typed in the space where the signature would otherwise appear.

1.2. Filing an Electronic Clerk's Record.

The clerk of a court subject to mandatory civil electronic filing must file the record electronically. The clerk of any other court must file the record electronically, if possible. When filing a clerk's record in electronic form, the trial court clerk must:

(a) file each computer file in text-searchable Portable Document Format (PDF);

(b) create electronic bookmarks to mark the first page of each document in the clerk's record;

(c) limit the size of each computer file to 100 MB or less, if possible;

(d) directly convert, rather than scan, the record to PDF, if possible;

(e) comply with the Technology Standards promulgated by the Judicial Committee on Information Technology;

(f) include the following elements in the computer file name, exemplified as CR (01 of 02).pdf:

(1) "CR";

(2) the volume number, using at least two digits, with leading zeroes if needed; "of"; and the total number of volumes;

(3) a period; and

(4) "pdf";

(g) file each sealed document separately from the remainder of the clerk's record and include the word "sealed" in the computer file name;

(h) if filing a supplement to the clerk's record, include the number of the supplement and "Supp";

(i) if filing a supplement to the clerk's record, include a hyphen, the number of the supplement, the term "Supp," and another hyphen after the term "CLR" in the computer file name (e.g., FortBend-DC-09-29-CLR-1Supp-Vol001.pdf, FortBend-DC-09-29-CLR-2Supp-Vol001.pdf);

(j) submit each computer file to the Texas Appeals Management and E-filing System (TAMES) web portal using the instructions provided on the appellate court's website; and

(k) not lock any document that is part of the record.

1.3. Filing a Paper Clerk's Record.

When filing a paper record with the appellate court, the trial court clerk must:

(a) bind the documents together in one or more volumes with a top bound, two-inch capacity, two-and-three-quarter-inch, center-to-center removable fastener and no other binding materials, like wax, ribbon, glue, staples, tape, etc.;

(b) include no more than 500 pages in each volume, or limit the thickness of each volume to a maximum of two inches;

(c) include only one-sided copies in the clerk's record;

(d) number the first volume "1" and each succeeding volume sequentially;

(e) if practicable, make a legible copy of the documents on opaque, white, 8½ x 11 inch paper; and

(f) place each sealed document in a securely sealed, manila envelope that is not bound with the other documents in the clerk's record.

1.4. Non-Conforming Records and Supplements.

In the event of a material violation of this rule in the preparation or filing of the clerk's record, on motion of a party or on its own initiative, the appellate court may require the trial court clerk to amend the clerk's record or to prepare a new clerk's record in proper form—and provide it to any party who has previously made a copy of the original, defective clerk's record—at the trial clerk's expense. A supplement to a clerk's record must also be prepared in conformity with this rule.

RULE 2. ELECTRONIC REPORTER'S RECORD.

(a) The court reporter or court recorder must prepare and file the reporter's record in accordance with Rules of Appellate Procedure 34.6 and 35 and the Uniform Format Manual for Texas Reporters' Records, and the court's local rules. Even if more than one notice of appeal or request for preparation of the record is filed, the court reporter or court recorder should prepare only one consolidated record in the case.

(b) If proceedings were recorded stenographically, the court reporter or recorder must file the reporter's record in an electronic format via the Texas Appeals Management and E-filing System (TAMES) web portal and in accordance with Section 8 of the Uniform Format Manual for Texas Reporters' Records, the court's local rules, and any guidelines posted on the appellate court's website.

(c) If the record is filed in electronic format, the court reporter or recorder must include either a scanned image of any required signature or "/s/" and name typed in the space where the signature would otherwise appear.

(d) A court reporter or recorder must not lock any document that is part of the record.

(e) In exhibit volumes, the court reporter or recorder must create bookmarks to mark the first page of each exhibit document.

(f) In the event of a material violation of this rule in the preparation of a reporter's record, on motion of a party or on the court's own initiative, the appellate court may require the court reporter or court recorder to amend the reporter's record or to prepare a new reporter's record in proper form - and provide it to any party who has previously made a copy of the original, defective reporter's record - at the reporter's or recorder's expense. A court reporter who fails to comply with the requirements of the Uniform Format Manual for Texas Reporters' Records is also subject to discipline by the Court Reporters Certification Board.

(Appendix C adopted by Order Aug. 16, 2013, eff. Jan. 1, 2014; Dec. 13, 2013, eff. Jan. 1, 2014.)

34.5. Clerk's Record.

(a) Contents. Unless the parties designate the filings in the appellate record by agreement under Rule 34.2, the record must include copies of the following:

(1) in civil cases, all pleadings on which the trial was held;

(2) in criminal cases, the indictment or information, any special plea or defense motion that was presented to the court and overruled, any written waiver, any written stipulation, and, in cases in which a plea of guilty or nolo contendere has been entered, any documents executed for the plea;

(3) the court's docket sheet;

(4) the court's charge and the jury's verdict, or the court's findings of fact and conclusions of law;

(5) the court's judgment or other order that is being appealed;

(6) any request for findings of fact and conclusions of law, any post-judgment motion, and the court's order on the motion;

(7) the notice of appeal;

(8) any formal bill of exception;

(9) any request for a reporter's record, including any statement of points or issues under Rule 34.6(c);

(10) any request for preparation of the clerk's record;

(11) in civil cases, a certified bill of costs including the cost of preparing the clerk's record, showing credits for payments made;

(12) in criminal cases, the trial court's certification of the defendant's right of appeal under Rule 25.2; and

(13) subject to (b), any filing that a party designates to have included in the record.

(b) Request for Additional Items.

(1) Time for Request. At any time before the clerk's record is prepared, any party may file with the trial court clerk a written designation specifying items to be included in the record.

(2) Request Must Be Specific. A party requesting that an item be included in the clerk's record must specifically describe the item so that the clerk can readily identify it. The clerk will disregard a general designation, such as one for "all papers filed in the case."

(3) Requesting Unnecessary Items. In a civil case, if a party requests that more items than necessary be included in the clerk's record or any supplement, the appellate court may—regardless of the appeal's outcome—require that party to pay the costs for the preparation of the unnecessary portion.

(4) Failure to Timely Request. An appellate court must not refuse to file the clerk's record or a supplemental clerk's record because of a failure to timely request items to be included in the clerk's record.

(c) Supplementation.

(1) If a relevant item has been omitted from the clerk's record, the trial court, the appellate court, or any party may by letter direct the trial court clerk to prepare, certify, and file in the appellate court a supplement containing the omitted item.

(2) If the appellate court in a criminal case orders the trial court to prepare and file findings of fact and conclusions of law as required by law, or certification of the defendant's right of appeal as required by these rules, the trial court clerk must prepare, certify, and file in the appellate court a supplemental clerk's record containing those findings and conclusions.

(3) Any supplemental clerk's record will be part of the appellate record.

(d) Defects or Inaccuracies. If the clerk's record is defective or inaccurate, the appellate clerk must inform the trial court clerk of the defect or inaccuracy and instruct the clerk to make the correction.

(e) Clerk's Record Lost or Destroyed. If a filing designated for inclusion in the clerk's record has been lost or destroyed, the parties may, by written stipulation, deliver a copy of that item to the trial court clerk for inclusion in the clerk's record or a supplement. If the parties cannot agree, the trial court must—on any party's motion or at the appellate court's request—determine what constitutes an accurate copy of the missing item and order it to be included in the clerk's record or a supplement.

(f) Original Documents. If the trial court determines that original documents filed with the trial court clerk should be inspected by the appellate court or sent to that court in lieu of copies, the trial court must make an order for the safekeeping, transportation, and return of those original documents. The order must list the original documents and briefly describe them. All the documents must be arranged in their listed sequence and bound firmly together. On any party's motion or its own initiative, the appellate court may direct the trial court clerk to send it any original document.

(g) Additional Copies of Clerk's Record in Criminal Cases. In a criminal case, the clerk's record must be made in duplicate, and in a case in which the death penalty was assessed, in triplicate. The trial court clerk must retain the copy or copies for the parties to use with the court's permission.

(h) Clerk May Consult With Parties. The clerk may consult with the parties concerning the contents of the clerk's record.

(Amended by Order Dec. 23, 2002 eff. Jan. 1, 2003.)

Comment to 2002 change: Rule 34.5(a) is amended to require that the record in a criminal case include the certification of defendant's right of appeal; *see* Rule 25.2(d). Rule 34.5(c) is amended to make clear that an appellate court may order the trial court to make such a certification for inclusion in a supplemental clerk's record.

34.6. Reporter's Record.

(a) Contents.

(1) Stenographic Recording. If the proceedings were stenographically recorded, the reporter's record consists of the court reporter's transcription of so much of the proceedings, and any of the exhibits, that the parties to the appeal designate.

(2) Electronic Recording. If the proceedings were electronically recorded, the reporter's record consists of certified copies of all tapes or other audio-storage devices on which the proceedings were recorded, any of the exhibits that the parties to the appeal designate, and certified copies of the logs prepared by the court recorder under Rule 13.2.

(b) Request for Preparation.

(1) Request to Court Reporter. At or before the time for perfecting the appeal, the appellant must request in writing that the official reporter prepare the reporter's record. The request must designate the exhibits to be included. A request to the court reporter—but not the court recorder—must also designate the portions of the proceedings to be included.

(2) Filing. The appellant must file a copy of the request with the trial court clerk.

(3) Failure to Timely Request. An appellate court must not refuse to file a reporter's record or a supplemental reporter's record because of a failure to timely request it.

(c) Partial Reporter's Record.

(1) Effect on Appellate Points or Issues. If the appellant requests a partial reporter's record, the appellant must include in the request a statement of the points or issues to be presented on appeal and will then be limited to those points or issues.

(2) Other Parties May Designate Additions. Any other party may designate additional exhibits and portions of the testimony to be included in the reporter's record.

(3) Costs; Requesting Unnecessary Matter. Additions requested by another party must be included in the reporter's record at the appellant's cost. But if the trial court finds that all or part of the designated additions are unnecessary to the appeal, the trial court may order the other party to pay the costs for the preparation of the unnecessary additions. This paragraph does not affect the appellate court's power to tax costs differently.

(4) Presumptions. The appellate court must presume that the partial reporter's record designated by the parties constitutes the entire record for purposes of reviewing the stated points or issues. This presumption applies even if the statement includes a point or issue complaining of the legal or factual insufficiency of the evidence to support a specific factual finding identified in that point or issue.

(5) Criminal Cases. In a criminal case, if the statement contains a point complaining that the evidence is insufficient to support a finding of guilt, the record must include all the evidence admitted at the trial on the issue of guilt or innocence and punishment.

(d) Supplementation. If anything relevant is omitted from the reporter's record, the trial court, the appellate court, or any party may by letter direct the official court reporter to prepare, certify, and file in the appellate court a supplemental reporter's record containing the omitted items. Any supplemental reporter's record is part of the appellate record.

(e) Inaccuracies in the Reporter's Record.

(1) Correction of Inaccuracies by Agreement. The parties may agree to correct an inaccuracy in the reporter's record, including an exhibit, without the court reporter's recertification.

(2) Correction of Inaccuracies by Trial Court. If the parties cannot agree on whether or not to correct the reporter's record so that the text accurately discloses what occurred in the trial court and the exhibits are accurate, the trial court must—after notice and hearing—settle the dispute. If the court finds any inaccuracy, it must order the court reporter to conform the reporter's record (including text and any exhibits) to what occurred in the trial court, and to file certified corrections in the appellate court.

(3) Correction After Filing in Appellate Court. If the dispute arises after the reporter's record has been filed in the appellate court, that court may submit the dispute to the trial court for resolution. The trial court must then proceed as under subparagraph (e)(2).

(f) Reporter's Record Lost or Destroyed. An appellant is entitled to a new trial under the following circumstances:

(1) if the appellant has timely requested a reporter's record;

(2) if, without the appellant's fault, a significant exhibit or a significant portion of the court reporter's notes and records has been lost or destroyed or—if the proceedings were electronically recorded—a significant portion of the recording has been lost or destroyed or is inaudible;

(3) if the lost, destroyed, or inaudible portion of the reporter's record, or the lost or destroyed exhibit, is necessary to the appeal's resolution; and

(4) if the lost, destroyed or inaudible portion of the reporter's record cannot be replaced by agreement of the parties, or the lost or destroyed exhibit cannot be replaced either by agreement of the parties or with a copy determined by the trial court to accurately duplicate with reasonable certainty the original exhibit.

(g) Original Exhibits.

(1) Reporter May Use in Preparing Reporter's Record. At the court reporter's request, the trial court clerk must give all original exhibits to the reporter for use in preparing the reporter's record. Unless ordered to include original exhibits in the reporter's record, the court reporter must return the original exhibits to the clerk after copying them for inclusion in the reporter's record. If someone other than the trial court clerk possesses an original exhibit, either the trial court or the appellate court may order that person to deliver the exhibit to the trial court clerk.

(2) Use of Original Exhibits by Appellate Court. If the trial court determines that original exhibits should be inspected by the appellate court or sent to that court in lieu of copies, the trial court must make an order for the safekeeping, transportation, and return of those exhibits. The order must list the exhibits and briefly describe them. To the extent practicable, all the exhibits must be arranged in their listed order and bound firmly together before being sent to the appellate clerk. On any party's motion or its own initiative, the appellate court may direct the trial court clerk to send it any original exhibit.

(h) Additional Copies of Reporter's Record in Criminal Cases. In a criminal case in which a party requests a reporter's record, the court reporter must prepare a duplicate of the reporter's record and file it with the trial court clerk. In a case where the death penalty was assessed, the court reporter must prepare two duplicates of the reporter's record.

(i) Supreme Court and Court of Criminal Appeals May Set Fee. From time to time, the Supreme Court and the Court of Criminal Appeals may set the fee that the court reporters may charge for preparing the reporter's record.

(Amended by Order Dec. 23, 2002 eff. Jan. 1, 2003.)

Comment to 2002 change: Subparagraphs 34.6(e) and (f) are amended to clarify the application to exhibits. The language in subparagraph (e)(2) referring to the text of the record is simplified without substantive change. Subparagraph (e)(3) incorporates the procedures specified in (e)(2). The language in subparagraph (f) is clarified to require agreement only as to the portion of the text at issue, and to provide that the trial court may determine that a copy of an exhibit should be used even if the parties cannot agree.

RULE 35. TIME TO FILE RECORD; RESPONSIBILITY FOR FILING RECORD.

35.1. Civil Cases.

The appellate record must be filed in the appellate court within 60 days after the judgment is signed, except as follows:

(a) if Rule 26.1(a) applies, within 120 days after the judgment is signed;

(b) if Rule 26.1(b) applies, within 10 days after the notice of appeal is filed; or

(c) if Rule 26.1(c) applies, within 30 days after the notice of appeal is filed.

35.2. Criminal Cases.

The appellate record must be filed in the appellate court:

(a) if a motion for new trial is not filed, within 60 days after the date the sentence is imposed or suspended in open court or the order appealed from is signed;

(b) if a timely motion for new trial is filed and denied, within 120 days after the date the sentence is imposed or suspended in open court; or

(c) if a motion for new trial is granted, within 60 days after the order granting the motion is signed.

35.3. Responsibility for Filing Record.

(a) Clerk's Record. The trial court clerk is responsible for preparing, certifying, and timely filing the clerk's record if:

(1) a notice of appeal has been filed, and in criminal proceedings, the trial court has certified the defendant's right of appeal, as required by Rule 25.2(d); and

(2) the party responsible for paying for the preparation of the clerk's record has paid the clerk's fee, has made satisfactory arrangements with the clerk to pay the fee, or is entitled to appeal without paying the fee.

(b) Reporter's Record. The official or deputy reporter is responsible for preparing, certifying, and timely filing the reporter's record if:

(1) a notice of appeal has been filed;

(2) the appellant has requested that the reporter's record be prepared; and

(3) the party responsible for paying for the preparation of the reporter's record has paid the reporter's fee, or has made satisfactory arrangements with the reporter to pay the fee, or is entitled to appeal without paying the fee.

(c) Courts to Ensure Record Timely Filed. The trial and appellate courts are jointly responsible for ensuring that the appellate record is timely filed. The appellate court may extend the deadline to file the record if requested by the clerk or reporter. Each extension must not exceed 30 days in an ordinary or restricted appeal, or 10 days in an accelerated appeal. The appellate court must allow the record to be filed late when the delay is not the appellant's fault, and may do so when the delay is the appellant's fault. The appellate court may enter any order necessary to ensure the timely filing of the appellate record.

(Adopted by Order eff. Sept. 1, 1997. Amended by Order Dec. 13, 2006, eff. Jan. 1, 2007; Order Dec. 12, 2011, eff. March 1, 2012; Order Feb. 13, 2012, eff. March 1, 2012.)

Comment to 1997 change: This is former Rule 54. In subdivision 35.1, the time to file the record in civil cases is based on the date the judgment is signed except in accelerated and restricted appeals, in which the time to file the record is based on the date the notice of appeal is filed. Subdivision 35.3 is new and makes it the responsibility of the trial court clerk and court reporter to file the record. Former Rule 54(c), providing for an extension of time to file the record, is repealed as unnecessary. The trial court clerk and court reporter should make arrangements with the court of appeals if additional time is required to file the record, as suggested in Rule 37.3.

RULE 36. AGENCY RECORD IN ADMINISTRATIVE APPEALS.

36.1. Scope.

This rule applies only to cases involving judicial review of state agency decisions in contested cases under the Administrative Procedure Act.

36.2. Inclusion in Appellate Record.

The record of an agency proceeding filed in the trial court may be included in either the clerk's record or the reporter's record.

36.3. Correcting the Record.

(a) Correction by Agreement. At any stage of the proceeding, the parties may agree to correct an agency record filed under Section 2001.175(b) of the Government Code to ensure that the agency record accurately reflects the contested case proceedings before the agency. The court reporter need not recertify the agency record.

(b) Correction by Trial Court. If the parties cannot agree to a correction to the agency record, the appellate court must—on any party's motion or its own incentive—send the question to the trial court. After notice and hearing, the trial court must determine what constitutes an accurate copy of the agency record and order the agency to send an accurate copy to the clerk of the court in which the case is pending.

(Adopted by Order eff. Sept. 1, 1997.)

Comment to 1997 change: The rule is new.

RULE 37. DUTIES OF THE APPELLATE CLERK ON RECEIVING THE NOTICE OF APPEAL AND RECORD.

37.1. On Receiving the Notice of Appeal.

If the appellate clerk determines that the notice of appeal or certification of defendant's rights of appeal in a criminal case is defective, the clerk must notify the parties of the defect so that it can be remedied, if possible. If a proper notice of appeal or certification of a criminal defendant's right of appeal is not filed in the trial court within 30 days of the date of the clerk's notice, the clerk must refer the matter to the appellate court, which will make an appropriate order under this rule or Rule 34.5(c)(2).

(Amended by Order Dec. 23, 2002, eff. Jan. 1, 2003.)

37.2. On Receiving the Record.

On receiving the clerk's record or the reporter's record, the appellate clerk must determine whether each complies with the Supreme Court's and Court of Criminal Appeals' order on preparation of the record. If so, the clerk must endorse on each the date of receipt, file it, and notify the parties of the filing and the date. If not, the clerk must endorse on the clerk's record or reporter's record—whichever is defective—the date of receipt and return it to the official responsible for filing it. The appellate court clerk must specify the defects and instruct the official to correct the defects and return the record to the appellate court by a specified date. In a criminal case, the record must not be posted on the Internet.

(Amended by Order Dec. 13, 2013, eff. Jan. 1, 2014.)

37.3. If No Record Filed.

(a) Notice of Late Record.

(1) Civil Cases. If the clerk's record or reporter's record has not been timely filed, the appellate clerk must send notice to the official responsible for filing it, stating that the record is late and requesting that the record be filed within 30 days if an ordinary or restricted appeal, or 10 days if an accelerated appeal. The appellate clerk must send a copy of this notice to the parties and the trial court. If the clerk does not receive the record within the stated period, the clerk must refer the matter to the appellate court. The court must make whatever order is appropriate to avoid further delay and to preserve the parties' rights.

(2) Criminal Cases. If the clerk's record or reporter's record has not been timely filed, the appellate court clerk must refer the matter to the appellate court. The court must make whatever order is appropriate to avoid further delay and to preserve the parties' rights.

(b) If No Clerk's Record Filed Due to Appellant's Fault. If the trial court clerk failed to file the clerk's record because the appellant failed to pay or make arrangements to pay the clerk's fee for preparing the clerk's record, the appellate court may—on a party's motion or its own initiative—dismiss the appeal for want of prosecution unless the appellant was entitled to proceed without payment of costs. The court must give the appellant a reasonable opportunity to cure before dismissal.

(c) If No Reporter's Record Filed Due to Appellant's Fault. Under the following circumstances, and if the clerk's record has been filed, the appellate court may—after first giving the appellant notice and a reasonable opportunity to cure—consider and decide those issues or points that do not require a reporter's record for a decision. The court may do this if no reporter's record has been filed because:

(1) the appellant failed to request a reporter's record; or

(2)(A) appellant failed to pay or make arrangements to pay the reporter's fee to prepare the reporter's record; and

(B) the appellant is not entitled to proceed without payment of costs.

(Adopted by Order eff. Sept. 1, 1997.)

Comment to 1997 change: Former Rules 56 and 57(a) are merged. Subdivisions 37.2 and 37.3 are new.

RULE 38. REQUISITES OF BRIEFS.

38.1. Appellant's Brief.

The appellant's brief must, under appropriate headings and in the order here indicated, contain the following:

(a) Identity of Parties and Counsel. The brief must give a complete list of all parties to the trial court's judgment or order appealed from, and the names and addresses of all trial and appellate counsel, except as otherwise provided in Rule 9.8.

(b) Table of Contents. The brief must have a table of contents with references to the pages of the brief. The table of contents must indicate the subject matter of each issue or point, or group of issues or points.

(c) Index of Authorities. The brief must have an index of authorities arranged alphabetically and indicating the pages of the brief where the authorities are cited.

(d) Statement of the Case. The brief must state concisely the nature of the case (e.g., whether it is a suit for damages, on a note, or involving a murder prosecution), the course of proceedings, and the trial court's disposition of the case. The statement should be supported by record references, should seldom exceed one-half page, and should not discuss the facts.

(e) Any Statement Regarding Oral Argument. The brief may include a statement explaining why oral argument should, or should not, be permitted. Any such statement must not exceed one page and should not address how the court's decisional process would, or would not, be aided by oral argument. As required by Rule 39.7, any party requesting oral argument must note that request on the front cover of its brief.

(f) Issues Presented. The brief must state concisely all issues or points presented for review. The statement of an issue or point will be treated as covering every subsidiary question that is fairly included.

(g) Statement of Facts. The brief must state concisely and without argument the facts pertinent to the issues or points presented. In a civil case, the court will accept as true the facts stated unless another party contradicts them. The statement must be supported by record references.

(h) Summary of the Argument. The brief must contain a succinct, clear, and accurate statement of the arguments made in the body of the brief. This summary must not merely repeat the issues or points presented for review.

(i) Argument. The brief must contain a clear and concise argument for the contentions made, with appropriate citations to authorities and to the record.

(j) Prayer. The brief must contain a short conclusion that clearly states the nature of the relief sought.

(k) Appendix in Civil Cases.

(1) Necessary Contents. Unless voluminous or impracticable, the appendix must contain a copy of:

(A) the trial court's judgment or other appealable order from which relief is sought;

(B) the jury charge and verdict, if any, or the trial court's findings of fact and conclusions of law, if any; and

(C) the text of any rule, regulation, ordinance, statute, constitutional provision, or other law (excluding case law) on which the argument is based, and the text of any contract or other document that is central to the argument.

(2) Optional Contents. The appendix may contain any other item pertinent to the issues or points presented for review, including copies or excerpts of relevant court opinions, laws, documents on which the suit was based, pleadings, excerpts from the reporter's record, and similar material. Items should not be included in the appendix to attempt to avoid the page limits for the brief.

(Amended by Order March 10, 2008, eff. Sept. 1, 2008; Order Aug. 20, 2008, eff. Sept. 1, 2008.)

Comment to 2008 change: A party may choose to include a statement in the brief regarding oral argument.

38.2. Appellee's Brief.

(a) Form of Brief.

(1) An appellee's brief must conform to the requirements of Rule 38.1, except that:

(A) the list of parties and counsel is not required unless necessary to supplement or correct the appellant's list;

(B) the appellee's brief need not include a statement of the case, a statement of the issues presented, or a statement of facts, unless the appellee is dissatisfied with that portion of the appellant's brief; and

(C) the appendix to the appellee's brief need not contain any item already contained in an appendix filed by the appellant.

(2) When practicable, the appellee's brief should respond to the appellant's issues or points in the order the appellant presented those issues or points.

(b) Cross-Points.

(1) Judgment Notwithstanding the Verdict. When the trial court renders judgment notwithstanding the verdict on one or more questions, the appellee must bring forward by cross-point any issue or point that would have vitiated the verdict or that would have prevented an affirmance of the judgment if the trial court had rendered judgment on the verdict. Failure to bring forward by cross-point an issue or point that would vitiate the verdict or prevent an affirmance of the judgment waives that complaint. Included in this requirement is a point that:

(A) the verdict or one or more jury findings have insufficient evidentiary support or are against the overwhelming preponderance of the evidence as a matter of fact; or

(B) the verdict should be set aside because of improper argument of counsel.

(2) When Evidentiary Hearing Needed. The appellate court must remand a case to the trial court to take evidence if:

(A) the appellate court has sustained a point raised by the appellant; and

(B) the appellee raised a cross-point that requires the taking of additional evidence.

(Amended by Order Dec. 23, 2002, eff. Jan. 1, 2003.)

38.3. Reply Brief.

The appellant may file a reply brief addressing any matter in the appellee's brief. However, the appellate court may consider and decide the case before a reply brief is filed.

38.4. Repealed by Order Nov. 13, 2012, eff. Dec. 1, 2012.

38.5. Appendix for Cases Recorded Electronically.

In cases where the proceedings were electronically recorded, the following rules apply:

(a) Appendix.

(1) In General. At or before the time a party's brief is due, the party must file one copy of an appendix containing a transcription of all portions of the recording that the party considers relevant to the appellate issues or points. Unless another party objects, the transcription will be presumed accurate.

(2) Repetition Not Required. A party's appendix need not repeat evidence included in any previously filed appendix.

(3) Form. The form of the appendix and transcription must conform to any specifications of the Supreme Court and Court of Criminal Appeals concerning the form of the reporter's record except that it need not have the reporter's certificate.

(4) Notice. At the time the appendix is filed, the party must give written notice of the filing to all parties to the trial court's judgment or order. The notice must specify, by referring to the index numbers in the court recorder's logs, those parts of the recording that are included in the appendix. The filing party need not serve a copy of the appendix but must make a copy available to all parties for inspection and copying.

(b) Presumptions. The same presumptions that apply to a partial reporter's record under Rule 34.6(c)(4) apply to the parties' appendixes. The appellate court need not review any part of the electronic recording.

(c) Supplemental Appendix. The appellate court may direct or allow a party to file a supplemental appendix containing a transcription of additional portions of the recording.

(d) Inability to Pay. A party who cannot pay the cost of an appendix must file the affidavit provided for by Rule 20. The party must also state in the affidavit or a supplemental affidavit that the party has neither the access to the equipment necessary nor the skill necessary to prepare the appendix. If a contest to the affidavit is not sustained by written order, the court recorder must transcribe or have transcribed those portions of the recording that the party designates and must file the transcription as that party's appendix, along with all exhibits.

(e) Inaccuracies.

(1) Correction by Agreement. The parties may agree to correct an inaccuracy in the transcription of the recording.

(2) Correction by Appellate or Trial Court. If the parties dispute whether an electronic recording or transcription accurately discloses what occurred in the trial court but cannot agree on corrections, the appellate court may:

(A) settle the dispute by reviewing the recording; or

(B) submit the dispute to the trial court, which must—after notice and hearing—settle the dispute and ensure that the recording or transcription is made to conform to what occurred in the trial court.

(f) Costs. The actual expense of preparing the appendixes or the amount prescribed for official reporters, whichever is less, is taxed as costs. The appellate court may disallow the cost of any portion of the appendixes that it considers surplusage or that does not conform to any specifications prescribed by the Supreme Court or Court of Criminal Appeals.

38.6. Time to File Briefs.

(a) Appellant's Filing Date. Except in a habeas corpus or bail appeal, which is governed by Rule 31, an appellant must file a brief within 30 days—20 days in an accelerated appeal—after the later of:

(1) the date the clerk's record was filed; or

(2) the date the reporter's record was filed.

(b) Appellee's Filing Date. The appellee's brief must be filed within 30 days—20 days in an accelerated appeal—after the date the appellant's brief was filed. In a civil case, if the appellant has not filed a brief as provided in this rule, an appellee may file a brief within 30 days—20 days in an accelerated appeal—after the date the appellant's brief was due.

(c) Filing Date for Reply Brief. A reply brief, if any, must be filed within 20 days after the date the appellee's brief was filed.

(d) Modifications of Filing Time. On motion complying with Rule 10.5(b), the appellate court may extend the time for filing a brief and may postpone submission of the case. A motion to extend the time to file a brief may be filed before or after the date the brief is due. The court may also, in the interests of justice, shorten the time for filing briefs and for submission of the case.

(Amended by Order Dec. 23, 2002, eff. Jan. 1, 2003.)

Comment to 2002 change: Rule 38.6(d) is amended to clarify that an appellate court may postpone the filing of any brief, not just the appellant's brief.

38.7. Amendment or Supplementation.

A brief may be amended or supplemented whenever justice requires, on whatever reasonable terms the court may prescribe.

38.8. Failure of Appellant to File Brief.

(a) Civil Cases. If an appellant fails to timely file a brief, the appellate court may:

(1) dismiss the appeal for want of prosecution, unless the appellant reasonably explains the failure and the appellee is not significantly injured by the appellant's failure to timely file a brief;

(2) decline to dismiss the appeal and give further direction to the case as it considers proper; or

(3) if an appellee's brief is filed, the court may regard that brief as correctly presenting the case and may affirm the trial court's judgment upon that brief without examining the record.

(b) Criminal Cases.

(1) Effect. An appellant's failure to timely file a brief does not authorize either dismissal of the appeal or, except as provided in (4), consideration of the appeal without briefs.

(2) Notice. If the appellant's brief is not timely filed, the appellate clerk must notify counsel for the parties and the trial court of that fact. If the appellate court does not receive a satisfactory response within ten days, the court must order the trial court to immediately conduct a hearing to determine whether the appellant desires to prosecute his appeal, whether the appellant is indigent, or, if not indigent, whether retained counsel has abandoned the appeal, and to make appropriate findings and recommendations.

(3) Hearing. In accordance with (2), the trial court must conduct any necessary hearings, make appropriate findings and recommendations, and have a record of the proceedings prepared, which record—including any order and findings—must be sent to the appellate court.

(4) Appellate Court Action. Based on the trial court's record, the appellate court may act appropriately to ensure that the appellant's rights are protected, including initiating contempt proceedings against appellant's counsel. If the trial court has found that the appellant no longer desires to prosecute the appeal, or that the appellant is not indigent but has not made the necessary arrangements for filing a brief, the appellate court may consider the appeal without briefs, as justice may require.

38.9. Briefing Rules to Be Construed Liberally.

Because briefs are meant to acquaint the court with the issues in a case and to present argument that will enable the court to decide the case, substantial compliance with this rule is sufficient, subject to the following.

(a) Formal Defects. If the court determines that this rule has been flagrantly violated, it may require a brief to be amended, supplemented, or redrawn. If another brief that does not comply with this rule is filed, the court may strike the brief, prohibit the party from filing another, and proceed as if the party had failed to file a brief.

(b) Substantive Defects. If the court determines, either before or after submission, that the case has not been properly presented in the briefs, or that the law and authorities have not been properly cited in the briefs, the court may postpone submission, require additional briefing, and make any other order necessary for a satisfactory submission of the case.

(Adopted by Order eff. Sept. 1, 1997.)

Comment to 1997 change: This is former Rule 74. The rule is substantially rewritten. Paragraph 38.1(e) now specifically allows a party to either present issues or points of error. Paragraphs 38.1(f) and (g) are new and require a brief to include a statement of facts and summary of the argument. Paragraph 38.2(b) is new and gives specific requirements for cross-points. *See also* TEX. R. CIV. P. 324(c). Subdivision 38.3 is new and provides for a reply brief. Subdivision 38.4 imposes a total brief limit of 90 pages on each party. Thus, if more than one party has filed a notice of appeal, there will be multiple appellant's, appellee's, and reply briefs, but each party is limited to a total of 90 pages. Subdivision 38.5 is new and provides for an appendix in cases recorded electronically in the trial court. Paragraph 38.6(b) now provides that the appellee has 30—rather than 25—days to file a brief. The provisions of former Rules 74(i) (Number of Copies), (j) (Briefs Typewritten or Printed), and (q) (Service of Briefs) are omitted as unnecessary. *See* Rule 9.

RULE 39. ORAL ARGUMENT; DECISION WITHOUT ARGUMENT.

39.1. Right to Oral Argument.

Any party who has filed a brief and who has timely requested oral argument may argue the case to the court unless the court, after examining the briefs, decides that oral argument is unnecessary for any of the following reasons:

(1) the appeal is frivolous;

(2) the dispostive issue or issues have been authoritatively decided;

(3) the facts and legal arguments are adequately presented in the briefs and record; or

(4) the decisional process would not be significantly aided by oral argument.

(Amended by Order March 10, 2008, eff. Sept. 1, 2008; Order Aug. 20, 2008, eff. Sept. 1, 2008.)

39.2. Purpose of Argument.

Oral argument should emphasize and clarify the written arguments in the briefs. Counsel should not merely read from prepared text. Counsel should assume that all members of the court have read the briefs before oral argument and counsel should be prepared to respond to questions. A party should not refer to or comment on matters not involved in or pertaining to what is in the record.

39.3 Time Allowed.

The court will set the time that will be allowed for argument. Counsel must complete argument in the time allotted and may continue after the expiration of the allotted time only with permission of the court. Counsel is not required to use all the allotted time. The appellant must be allowed to conclude the argument.

39.4. Number of Counsel.

Generally, only one counsel should argue for each side. Except on leave of court, no more than two counsel on each side may argue. Only one counsel may argue in rebuttal.

39.5. Argument by Amicus.

With leave of court obtained before the argument and with a party's consent, an amicus curiae may share allotted time with that party. Otherwise, counsel for amicus may not argue.

39.6. When Only One Party Files a Brief.

If counsel for only one party has filed a brief, the court may allow that party to argue.

39.7. Request and Waiver.

A party desiring oral argument must note that request on the front cover of the party's brief. A party's failure to request oral argument waives the party's right to argue. But even if a party has waived oral argument, the court may direct the party to appear and argue.

39.8 Clerk's Notice.

The clerk must send to the parties—at least 21 days before the date the case is set for argument or submission without argument—a notice telling the parties:

(a) whether the court will allow oral argument or will submit the case without argument;

(b) the date of argument or submission without argument;

(c) if argument is allowed, the time allotted for argument; and.

(d) the names of the members of the panel to which the case will be argued or submitted, subject to change by the court.

A party's failure to receive the notice does not prevent a case's argument or submission on the scheduled date.

(Adopted by Order eff. Sept. 1, 1997. Amended by Order March 10, 2008 eff. Sept. 1, 2008; Order Aug. 20, 2008, eff. Sept. 1, 2008.)

Comment to 1997 change: This is former Rule 75. Technical and nonsubstantive changes are made.

Comment to 2008 change: Subdivision 39.1 is amended to provide for oral argument unless the court determines it is unnecessary and to set out the reasons why argument may be unnecessary. The appellate court must evaluate these reasons in view of the traditional importance of oral argument. The court need not agree on, and generally should not announce, a specific reason or reasons for declining oral argument.

RULE 40. ORDER OF DECISION.

40.1. Civil Cases.

The court of appeals may determine the order in which civil cases will be decided. But the following types of cases have precedence over all others:

(a) a case given precedence by law;

(b) an accelerated appeal; and

(c) a case that the court determines should be given precedence in the interest of justice.

40.2. Criminal Cases.

In cases not otherwise given precedence by law, the court of appeals must hear and determine a criminal appeal at the earliest possible time, having due regard for the parties' rights and for the proper administration of justice.

(Adopted by Order eff. Sept. 1, 1997.)

Reference

See Code of Criminal Procedure article 44.01(f).

Comment on 1997 change: The provisions of former Rules 76, 77 and 78 are merged. Civil cases involving the Railroad Commission, the State, and "cases submitted on oral argument for all parties" are no longer given preference unless given preference by law.

RULE 41. PANEL AND EN BANC DECISION.

41.1. Decision by Panel.

(a) Constitution of Panel. Unless a court of appeals with more than three justices votes to decide a case en banc, a case must be assigned for decision to a panel of the court consisting of three justices, although not every member of the panel must be present for argument. If the case is decided without argument, three justices must participate in the decision. A majority of the panel, which constitutes a quorum, must agree on the judgment. Except as otherwise provided in these rules, a panel's opinion constitutes the court's opinion, and the court must render a judgment in accordance with the panel opinion.

(b) When Panel Cannot Agree on Judgment. After argument, if for any reason a member of the panel cannot participate in deciding a case, the case may be decided by the two remaining justices. If they cannot agree on a judgment, the chief justice of the court of appeals must:

(1) designate another justice of the court to sit on the panel to consider the case;

(2) request the Chief Justice of Supreme Court to temporarily assign an eligible justice of judge to sit on the panel to consider the case; or

(3) or convene the court en banc to consider the case.

The reconstituted panel or the en banc court may order the case reargued.

(c) When Court Cannot Agree on Judgment. After argument, if for any reason a member of a court consisting of only three justices cannot participate in deciding a case, the case may be decided by the two remaining justices. If they cannot agree on a judgment, that fact must be certified to the Chief Justice of the Supreme Court. The Chief Justice may then temporarily assign an eligible justice or judge to sit with the court of appeals to consider the case. The reconstituted court may order the case reargued.

(Amended by Order March 10, 2008, eff. Sept. 1, 2008; Order Aug. 20, 2008, eff. Sept. 1, 2008.)

41.2. Decision by En Banc Court.

(a) Constitution of En Banc Court. An en banc court consists of all members of the court who are not disqualified or recused and—if the case was originally argued before or decided by a panel—any members of the panel who are not members of the court but remain eligible for assignment to the court. A majority of the en banc court constitutes a quorum. A majority of the en banc court must agree on a judgment.

(b) When En Banc Court Cannot Agree on Judgment. If a majority of an en banc court cannot agree on a judgment, that fact must be certified to the Chief Justice of the Supreme Court. The Chief Justice may then temporarily assign an eligible justice or judge to sit with the court of appeals to consider the case. The reconstituted court may order the case reargued.

(c) En Banc Consideration Disfavored. En banc consideration of a case is not favored and should not be ordered unless necessary to secure or maintain uniformity of the court's decisions or unless extraordinary circumstances require en banc consideration. A vote to determine whether a case will be heard or reheard en banc need not be taken unless a justice of the court requests a vote. If a vote is requested and a majority of the court's members vote to hear or rehear the case en banc, the en banc court will hear or rehear the case. Otherwise, a panel of the court will consider the case.

(Adopted by Order eff. Sept. 1, 1997. Amended by Order March 10, 2008, eff. Sept. 1, 2008 ; Order Aug. 20, 2008, eff. Sept. 1, 2008.)

41.3. Precedent in Transferred Cases.

In cases transferred by the Supreme Court from on court of appeals to another, the court of appeals to which the case is transferred must decide the case in accordance with the precedent of the transferor court under principles of stare decisis if the transferee court's decision otherwise would have been inconsistent with the precedent of the transferor court. The court's opinion may state whether the outcome would have been different had the transferee court not been required to decide the case in accordance with the transferor court's precedent.

(Amended by Order March 10, 2008, eff. Sept. 1, 2008; Order Aug. 20, 2008, eff. Sept. 1, 2008.)

Comment to 1997 change: This is former Rule 79. The rule is reorganized. Paragraphs 41.1(b) and (c) are amended to make clear that a three judge panel must hear the case. Therefore, only if a member of a panel is lost after argument do the provisions for appointment of another justice to break a deadlock come into play. Paragraph 41.2(a) is amended to define an en banc court.

Comment to 2008 changes: Subdivisions 41.1 and 41.2 are amended to acknowledge the full authority of the Chief Justice of the Supreme Court to temporarily assign a justice or judge to hear a matter pending in an appellate court. The statutory provisions governing the assignment of judges to appellate courts are located in Chapters 74 and 75 of the Government Code. Other minor changes are made for consistency. Subdivision 41.3 is added to require, in appellate cases transferred by the Supreme Court under Section 73.001 of the Government Code for docket equalization or other purposes, that the transferee court must generally resolve any conflict between the precedent of the transferor court and the precedent of the transferee court—or that of any other intermediate appellate court the transferee court otherwise would have followed—by following the precedent of the transferor court, unless it appears that the transferor court itself would not be bound by that precedent. The rule requires the transferee court to "stand in the shoes" of the transferor court so that an appellate transfer will not produce a different outcome, based on application of substantive law, than would have resulted had the case not been transferred. The transferee court is not expected to follow the transferor courts local rules or otherwise supplant its own local procedures with those of the transferor court.

RULE 42. DISMISSAL; SETTLEMENT.

42.1. Voluntary Dismissal and Settlement in Civil Cases.

(a) On Motion or By Agreement. The appellate court may dispose of an appeal as follows:

(1) On Motion of Appellant. In accordance with a motion of appellant, the court may dismiss the appeal of affirm the appealed judgment or order unless such disposition would prevent a party from seeking relief to which it would otherwise be entitled.

(2) By Agreement. In accordance with an agreement signed by the parties or their attorneys and filed with the clerk, the court may:

(A) render judgment effectuating the parties' agreement;

(B) set aside the trial court's judgment without regard to the merits and remand the case to the trial court for rendition of judgment in accordance with the agreement; or

(C) abate the appeal and permit proceedings in the trial court to effectuate the agreement.

(b) Partial Disposition. A severable portion of the proceeding may be disposed of under (a) if it will not prejudice the remaining parties.

(c) Effect on Court's Opinion. In dismissing a proceeding, the appellate court will determine whether to withdraw any opinion it has already issued. An agreement or motion for dismissal cannot be conditioned on withdrawal of the opinion.

(d) Costs. Absent agreement of the parties, the court will tax costs against the appellant.

(Amended by Order Dec. 23, 2002, eff. Jan. 1, 2003.)

Comment to 2002 change: Rule 42.1 is amended to clarify the procedures for implementing settlements on appeal and to expressly give courts flexibility in effectuating settlements. The rule is also clarified to expressly permit the dismissal of an appeal without dismissal of the action itself. The rule does not permit an appellate court to order a new trial merely on the agreement of the parties absent reversible error, or to vacate a trial court's judgment absent reversible error or a settlement.

42.2. Voluntary Dismissal in Criminal Cases.

(a) At any time before the appellate court's decision, the appellate court may dismiss the appeal upon the appellant's motion. The appellant and his or her attorney must sign the written motion to dismiss and file it in duplicate with the appellate clerk, who must immediately send the duplicate copy to the trial court clerk.

(b) After the court of appeals hands down its opinion, it may not grant a appellant's motion to dismiss the appeal unless the other parties consent. It the other parties consent and the court of appeals grants the appellant's motion to dismiss the appeal, the appellate opinion must be withdrawn and the appeal dismissed. The appellate clerk must send notice of the dismissal to the trial court clerk.

(Amended by Order Oct. 16, 2000, eff. Jan. 1, 2001. Amended by Order Dec. 13, 2006, eff. Jan. 1, 2007.)

Comment to 2000 change: In the first sentence of Rule 42.2(a) "appellant" is replaced by "party that appealed," to make it clear that the rule applies to the State when it is the appealing party. *See State v. Miles*, 994 S.W.2d 410 (Tex.App.—Waco 1999). The requirement that the appellant's attorney must sign the withdrawal is deleted, and the last sentence is added, to remove any implication that the attorney may veto the appellant's decision to withdraw the notice of appeal. The word "personally" is added to emphasize that the appellant must participate in the withdrawal of his or her appeal. The provisions of Rule 9.1(a) do not restrict the appellant's ability to withdraw the notice of appeal.

42.3. Involuntary Dismissal in Civil Cases.

Under the following circumstances, on any party's motion—or on its own initiative after giving ten days' notice to all parties—the appellate court may dismiss the appeal or affirm the appealed judgment or order. Dismissal or affirmance may occur if the appeal is subject to dismissal:

(a) for want of jurisdiction;

(b) for want of prosecution; or

(c) because the appellant has failed to comply with a requirement of these rules, a court order, or a notice from the clerk requiring a response or other action within a specified time.

42.4. Involuntary Dismissal in Criminal Cases.

The appellate court must dismiss an appeal on the State's motion, supported by affidavit, showing that the appellant has escaped from custody pending the appeal and that to the affiant's knowledge, the appellant has not, within ten days after escaping, voluntarily returned to lawful custody within the state.

(a) Timely Return to Custody; Reinstatement. The appeal may not be dismissed—or, if dismissed, must be reinstated—if an affidavit of an officer or other credible person is filed showing that the appellant, within ten days after escaping, voluntarily returned to lawful custody within the state.

(b) Life Sentence. The appellate court may overrule the motion to dismiss—or, if the motion was granted, may reinstate the appeal—if:

(1) the appellant received a life sentence; and

(2) the appellant is recaptured or voluntarily surrenders within 30 days after escaping.

(Adopted by Order eff. Sept. 1, 1997.)

Comment to 1997 change: Former Rules 59 and 60 are merged. Paragraph 42.1(c), allowing a court of appeals to withdraw its opinion, is new. Provision is made in paragraph 42.3(c) for dismissal of an appeal for failure to comply with a notice from the clerk. Other changes are made.

RULE 43. JUDGMENT OF THE COURT OF APPEALS.

43.1. Time.

The court of appeals should render its judgment promptly after submission of a case.

43.2. Types of Judgment.

The court of appeals may:

(a) affirm the trial court's judgment in whole or in part;

(b) modify the trial court's judgment and affirm it as modified;

(c) reverse the trial court's judgment in whole or in part and render the judgment that the trial court should have rendered;

(d) reverse the trial court's judgment and remand the case for further proceedings;

(e) vacate the trial court's judgment and dismiss the case; or

(f) dismiss the appeal.

43.3. Rendition Appropriate Unless Remand Necessary.

When reversing a trial court's judgment, the court must render the judgment that the trial court should have rendered, except when:

(a) a remand is necessary for further proceedings; or

(b) the interests of justice require a remand for another trial.

43.4. Judgment for Costs in Civil Cases.

The court of appeals' judgment should award to the prevailing party costs incurred by that party related to the appeal, including filing fees in the court of appeals and costs for preparation of the record. The court of appeals may tax costs otherwise as required by law or for good cause. But the judgment must not require the payment of costs by a party who was entitled to proceed without payment of costs under Rule 20.1, and a provision in the judgment purporting to do so is void.

(Amended by Tex. Sup. Ct. Misc. Docket No. 16-9122, eff. Sept. 1, 2016.)

[Statement of Inability to Afford Payment of Court Costs as provided in Tex. Sup. Ct. Misc. Docket No. 16-9122, eff. Sept. 1, 2016 and applies to any contest of, or challenge to, a claim of inability to afford payment of court costs that is pending on September 1, 2016.]

43.5. Judgment Against Sureties in Civil Cases.

When a court of appeals affirms the trial court judgment, or modifies that judgment and renders judgment against the appellant, the court of appeals must render judgment against the sureties on the appellant's supersedeas bond, if any, for the performance of the judgment and for any costs taxed against the appellant.

43.6. Other Orders.

The court of appeals may make any other appropriate order that the law and the nature of the case require.

(Adopted by Order eff. Sept. 1, 1997.)

Comment to 1997 changes: Former Rules 80(a)-(c) and 82 are merged. Paragraph 43.2(e) allows the court of appeals to vacate the trial court's judgment and dismiss the case; paragraph 43.2(f) allows the court of appeals to dismiss the appeal. Both provisions are new but codify current practice. Paragraph 43.3(a) is moved here from former Rule 81(c). Paragraph 43.3(b), allowing a remand in the interest of justice, is new. Subdivisions 43.4 and 43.5 are from former Rule 82.

RULE 44. REVERSIBLE ERROR.

44.1. Reversible Error in Civil Cases.

(a) Standard for Reversible Error. No judgment may be reversed on appeal on the ground that the trial court made an error of law unless the court of appeals concludes that the error complained of:

(1) probably caused the rendition of an improper judgment; or

(2) probably prevented the appellant from properly presenting the case to the court of appeals.

(b) Error Affecting Only Part of Case. If the error affects part of, but not all, the matter in controversy and that part is separable without unfairness to the parties, the judgment must be reversed and a new trial ordered only as to the part affected by the error. The court may not order a separate trial solely on unliquidated damages if liability is contested.

44.2. Reversible Error in Criminal Cases.

(a) Constitutional Error. If the appellate record in a criminal case reveals constitutional error that is subject to harmless error review, the court of appeals must reverse a judgment of conviction or punishment unless the court determines beyond a reasonable doubt that the error did not contribute to the conviction or punishment.

(b) Other Errors. Any other error, defect, irregularity, or variance that does not affect substantial rights must be disregarded.

(c) Presumptions. Unless the following matters were disputed in the trial court, or unless the record affirmatively shows the contrary, the court of appeals must presume:

(1) that venue was proved in the trial court;

(2) that the jury was properly impaneled and sworn;

(3) that the defendant was arraigned;

(4) that the defendant pleaded to the indictment or other charging instrument; and

(5) that the court's charge was certified by the trial court and filed by the clerk before it was read to the jury.

44.3. Defects in Procedure.

A court of appeals must not affirm or reverse a judgment or dismiss an appeal for formal defects or irregularities in appellate procedure without allowing a reasonable time to correct or amend the defects or irregularities.

44.4. Remediable Error of the Trial Court.

(a) Generally. A court of appeals must not affirm or reverse a judgment or dismiss an appeal if:

(1) the trial court's erroneous action or failure or refusal to act prevents the proper presentation of a case to the court of appeals; and

(2) the trial court can correct its action or failure to act.

(b) Court of Appeals Direction if Error Remediable. If the circumstances described in (a) exist, the court of appeals must direct the trial court to correct the error. The court of appeals will then proceed as if the erroneous action or failure to act had not occurred.

(Adopted by Order eff. Sept. 1, 1997.)

Comment to 1997 change: Former Rules 80(d), 81 and 83 are merged. The reversible error standard in subdivision 44.1 is amended to omit the reference to an action "reasonably calculated to cause" an improper judgment, but no substantive change is intended. Paragraph 44.2(a) is amended to limit its standard of review to constitutional errors that are subject to harmless error review. Paragraph 44.2(b) is new and is taken from Federal Rule of Criminal Procedure 52(a) without substantive change. Paragraph 44.2(c) is former Rule 80(d) without substantive change. Subdivision 44.3 is amended to delete the reference to defects of "substance" and to delete the provisions regarding the late filing of the record.

RULE 45. DAMAGES FOR FRIVOLOUS APPEALS IN CIVIL CASES.

If the court of appeals determines that an appeal is frivolous, it may—on motion of any party or on its own initiative, after notice and a reasonable opportunity for response—award each prevailing party just damages. In determining whether to award damages, the court must not consider any matter that does not appear in the record, briefs, or other papers filed in the court of appeals.

(Adopted by Order eff. Sept. 1, 1997.)

Comment to 1997 change: This is former Rule 84. The limit on the amount of the sanction that may be imposed is repealed. A requirement of notice and opportunity to respond is added.

RULE 46. REMITTITUR IN CIVIL CASES.

46.1. Remittitur After Appeal Perfected.

If the trial court suggests a remittitur but the case is appealed before the remittitur is filed, the party who would make the remittitur may do so in the court of appeals in the same manner as in the trial court. The court of appeals must then render the judgment that the trial court should have rendered if the remittitur had been made in the trial court.

46.2. Appeal on Remittitur.

If a party makes the remittitur at the trial judge's suggestion and the party benefiting from the remittitur appeals, the remitting party is not barred from contending in the court of appeals that all or part of the remittitur should not have been required, but the remitting party must perfect an appeal to raise that point. If the court of appeals sustains the remitting party's contention that remittitur should not have been required, the court must render the judgment that the trial court should have rendered.

46.3. Suggestion of Remittitur by Court of Appeals.

The court of appeals may suggest a remittitur. If the remittitur is timely filed, the court must reform and affirm the trial court's judgment in accordance with the remittitur. If the remittitur is not timely filed, the court must reverse the trial court's judgment.

46.4. Refusal to Remit Must Not Be Mentioned in Later Trial.

If the court of appeals suggests a remittitur, but no remittitur is filed, evidence of the court's determination regarding remittitur is inadmissible in a later trial of the case.

46.5. Voluntary Remittitur.

If a court of appeals reverses the trial court's judgment because of a legal error that affects only part of the damages awarded by the judgment, the affected party may—within 15 days after the court of appeals' judgment—voluntarily remit the amount that the affected party believes will cure the reversible error. A party may include in a motion for rehearing—without waiving any complaint that the court of appeals erred—a conditional request that the court accept the remittitur and affirm the trial court's judgment as reduced. If the court of appeals determines that the voluntary remittitur is not sufficient to cure the reversible error, but that remittitur is appropriate, the court must suggest a remittitur in accordance with Rule 46.3. If the remittitur is timely filed and the court of appeals determines that the voluntary remittitur cures the reversible error, then the court must accept the remittitur and reform and affirm the trial court judgment in accordance with the remittitur.

(Amended by Order Dec. 23, 2002 eff. Jan. 1, 2003.)

Comment to 2002 change: Subdivision 46.5 is amended to clarify the procedure for offering a voluntary remittitur. The offer may be made in a motion for rehearing without waiving any complaint that the court of appeals erred, thereby extending the deadlines for further appeal.

RULE 47. OPINIONS, DISTRIBUTION, PUBLICATION, AND CITATION.

47.1. Written Opinions.

The court of appeals must hand down a written opinion that is as brief as practicable but that addresses every issue raised and necessary to final disposition of the appeal.

(Amended by Order Dec. 23, 2002 eff. Jan. 1, 2003.)

47.2. Designation and Signing of Opinions; Participating Justices.

(a) Civil and Criminal Cases. Each opinion of the court must be designated either an "Opinion" or a "Memorandum Opinion." A majority of the justices who participate in considering the case must determine whether the opinion will be signed by a justice or will be per curiam and whether it will be designated an opinion or memorandum opinion. The names of the participating justices must be noted on all written opinions or orders of the court or a panel of the court.

(b) Criminal Cases. In addition, each opinion and memorandum opinion in a criminal case must bear the notation "publish" or "do not publish" as determined—before the opinion is handed down—by a majority of the justices who participate in considering the case. Any party may move the appellate court to change the notation, but the court of appeals must not change the notation after the Court of Criminal Appeals has acted on any party's petition for discretionary review or other request for relief. The Court of Criminal Appeals may, at any time, order that a "do not publish" notation be changed to "publish."

(c) Civil Cases. Opinions and memorandum opinions in civil cases issued on or after January 1, 2003 shall not be designated "do not publish."

(Amended by Order Dec. 23, 2002, eff. Jan. 1, 2003. Amended by Order March 10, 2008, eff. Sept. 1, 2008; Order Aug. 20, 2008, eff. Sept. 1, 2008.)

47.3. Distribution of Opinions.

All opinions of the courts of appeals are open to the public and must be made available to public reporting services, print or electronic.

(Amended by Order Dec. 23, 2002, eff. Jan. 1, 2003.)

47.4. Memorandum Opinions.

If the issues are settled, the court should write a brief memorandum opinion no longer than necessary to advise the parties of the court's decision and the basic reasons for it. An opinion may not be designated a memorandum opinion if the author of a concurrence or dissent opposes that designation. An opinion must be designated a memorandum opinion unless it does any of the following:

(a) establishes a new rule of law, alters or modifies an existing rule, or applies an existing rule to a novel fact situation likely to recur in future cases;

(b) involves issues of constitutional law or other legal issues important to the jurisprudence of Texas;

(c) criticizes existing law; or

(d) resolves an apparent conflict of authority.

(Amended by Order Dec. 23, 2002, eff. Jan. 1, 2003.)

47.5. Concurring and Dissenting Opinions.

Only a justice who participated in the decision of a case may file or join in an opinion concurring in or dissenting from the judgment of the court of appeals. Any justice on the court may file an opinion in connection with a denial of a hearing or rehearing en banc.

(Amended by Order Dec. 23, 2002 eff. Jan. 1, 2003.)

47.6. Change in Designation by En Banc Court.

A court en banc may change a panel's designation of an opinion.

(Amended by Order Dec. 23, 2002, eff. Jan. 1, 2003.)

47.7. Citation of Unpublished Opinions.

(a) Criminal Cases. Opinions and memorandum opinions not designated for publication by the court of appeals under these or prior rules have no precedential value but may be cited with the notation, "(not designated for publication)."

(b) Civil Cases. Opinions and memorandum opinions designated "do not publish" under these rules by the court of appeals prior to January 1, 2003 have no precedential value but may be cited with the notation, "(not designated for publication)." If an opinion or memorandum opinion issued on or after that date is erroneously designated "do not publish," the erroneous designation will not affect the precedential value of the decision.

(Amended by Order Dec. 23, 2002, eff. Jan. 1, 2003. Amended by Order March 10, 2008, eff. Sept. 1, 2008; Order Aug. 20, 2008, eff. Sept. 1, 2008.)

Comment to 2002 change: The rule is substantively changed to discontinue the use of the "do no publish" designation in civil cases, to require that all opinions of the court of appeals be made available to public reporting services, and to remove prospectively any prohibition against the citation of opinions as authority in civil cases. The rule favors the use of "memorandum opinions" designated as such except in certain types of cases but does not change other requirements, such as those in *Pool v. Ford Motor Co.*, 715 S.W.2d 629, 635-636 (Tex. 1986). An opinion previously designated "do not publish" has no precedential value but may be cited. The citation must include the notation, "(not designated for publication)." Of course, whenever an opinion not readily available is cited, copies should be furnished to the court and opposing counsel.

Comment to 2008 changes: Effective January 1, 2003, Rule 47 was amended to discontinue in civil cases, on a prospective basis, the practice of allowing courts of appeals to designate opinions as either "published" or "unpublished." Rule 47.7 is revised to clarify that, with respect to civil cases, only opinions issued prior to the 2003 amendment and affirmatively designated "do not publish" should be considered "unpublished" cases lacking precedential value. All opinions and memorandum opinions in civil cases issued after the 2003 amendment have precedential value. The provisions governing citation of unpublished opinions in criminal cases are substantively unchanged. Rules 47.2 and 47.7 are amended to clarify that memorandum opinions are subject to those rules.

RULE 48. COPY OF OPINION AND JUDGMENT TO INTERESTED PARTIES AND OTHER COURTS.

48.1. recipients of Opinion and Judgment in All Cases.

On the date when an appellate court's opinion is handed down, the appellate clerk must send or deliver copies of the opinion and judgment to the following persons:

(a) the trial judge;
(b) the trial court clerk;
(c) the regional administrative judge; and
(d) all parties to the appeal.

(Amended by Order Dec. 13, 2013, eff. Jan. 1, 2014.)

48.2. Additional Recipients in Criminal Cases.

In criminal cases, copies of the opinion and judgment will also be mailed or delivered to the State Prosecuting Attorney.

48.3. Filing Opinion and Judgment.

The trial court clerk must file a copy of the opinion and judgment among the papers of the case in that court.

48.4. Opinion Sent to Criminal Defendant.

In criminal cases, the attorney representing the defendant on appeal shall, within five days after the opinion is handed down, send his client a copy of the opinion and judgment, along with notification of the defendant's right to file a *pro se* petition for discretionary review under Rule 68. This notification shall be sent certified mail, return receipt requested, to the defendant at his last known address. The attorney shall also send the court of appeals a letter certifying his compliance with this rule and attaching a copy of the return receipt within the time for filing a motion for rehearing. The court of appeals shall file this letter in its record of the appeal.

(Adopted by Order eff. Sept. 1, 1997. Amended by Order May 2, 2007, eff. Sept. 1, 2007.)

Comment to 1997 change: This is former Rule 91 with changes.

RULE 49. MOTION FOR REHEARING AND EN BANC RECONSIDERATION.

49.1. Motion for Rehearing.

A motion for rehearing may be filed within 15 days after the court of appeals' judgment or order is rendered. The motion must clearly state the points relied on for the rehearing. After a motion for rehearing is decided, another motion for rehearing may be filed within 15 days of the court's action only if the court:

(a) modifies its judgment;
(b) vacates its judgment and renders a new judgment; or
(c) issues an opinion in overruling a motion for rehearing.

(Amended by Order March 10, 2008, eff. Sept. 1, 2008.)

49.2. Response.

No response to a motion for rehearing need be filed unless the court so requests. A motion will not be granted unless a response has been filed or requested by the court.

49.3. Decision on Motion.

A motion for rehearing may be granted by a majority of the justices who participated in the decision of the case. Otherwise, it must be denied. If rehearing is granted, the court or panel may dispose of the case with or without rebriefing and oral argument.

49.4. Accelerated Appeals.

In an accelerated appeal, the appellate court may deny the right to file a motion for rehearing or shorten the time to file such a motion.

49.5. Further motion for rehearing.

After a motion for rehearing is decided, a further motion for rehearing may be filed within 15 days of the court's action if the court:

(a) modifies its judgment;

(b) vacates its judgment and renders a new judgment; or

(c) issues a different opinion.

(Adopted by Order Aug. 20, 2008, eff. Sept. 1, 2008.)

49.6. Amendments.

A motion for rehearing or a motion for en banc reconsideration may be amended as a matter of right anytime before the 15-day period allowed for filing the motion expires, and with leave of the court, anytime before the court of appeals decides the motion.

(Amended by Order March 10, 2008, eff. Sept. 1, 2008; Order Aug. 20, 2008, eff. Sept. 1, 2008.)

49.7. En Banc Reconsideration.

A party may file a motion for en banc reconsideration as a separate motion, with or without filing a motion for rehearing. The motion must be filed within 15 days after the court of appeals' judgment or order, or when permitted, within 15 days after the court of appeals' denial of the party's last timely filed motion for rehearing or en banc reconsideration. While the court has plenary power a majority of the en banc court may, with or without a motion, order en banc reconsideration of a panel's decision. If a majority orders reconsideration, the panel's judgment or order does not become final, and the case will be resubmitted to the court for en banc review and disposition.

(Amended by Order March 10, 2008, eff. Sept. 1, 2008; Order Aug. 20, 2008, eff. Sept. 1, 2008; Order Aug. 25, 2008, eff. Sept. 1, 2008.)

49.8. Extensions of Time.

A court of appeals may extend the time for filing a motion for rehearing or a motion for en banc reconsideration if a party files a motion complying with Rule 10.5(b) no later than 15 days after the last date for filing the motion for rehearing.

(Amended by Order March 10, 2008, eff. Sept. 1, 2008; Order Aug. 20, 2008, eff. Sept. 1, 2008.)

49.9. Not Required for Review.

A motion for rehearing is not required to preserve error and is not a prerequisite to filing:

(a) a motion for en banc reconsideration as provided by Rule 49.6;

(b) a petition for review in the Supreme Court; or

(c) a petition for discretionary review to the Court of Criminal Appeals.

(Amended by Order March 10, 2008, eff. Sept. 1, 2008; Order Aug. 20, 2008, eff. Sept. 1, 2008.)

49.10. Repealed by Order Nov. 13, 2012, Eff. Dec. 1, 2012.

49.11. Relationship to Petition for Review.

A party may not file a motion for rehearing in the court of appeals after that party has filed a petition for review in the Supreme Court unless the court of appeals modifies its opinion or judgment after the petition for review is filed. The filing of a petition for review does not preclude another party from filing a motion for rehearing or the court of appeals from ruling on the motion. If a motion for rehearing in timely filed after a petition for review is filed, the petitioner must immediately notify the Supreme Court clerk of the filing of the motion, and must notify the clerk when the last timely filed motion is overruled by the court of appeals.

(Adopted by Order March 10, 2008, eff. Sept. 1, 2008; Order Aug. 20, 2008, eff. Sept. 1, 2008.)

49.12. Certificate of Conference Not Required.

A certificate of conference is not required for a motion for rehearing or for a motion for en banc reconsideration of a panel's decision.

(Amended by Order March 10, 2008, eff. Sept. 1, 2008; Order Aug. 20, 2008, eff. Sept. 1, 2008.)

Comment to 1997 change: This is former Rule 100. Subdivision 49.4 is moved here from former Rule 43(h). Subdivisions 49.9 and 49.10 are added.

Comment to 2008 changes: Rule 49 is revised to treat a motion for en banc reconsideration as a motion for rehearing and to include procedures governing the filing of a motion for en banc reconsideration. Subdivision 49.5(c) is amended to clarify that a further motion for rehearing may be filed if the court issues a different opinion, irrespective of whether the opinion is issued in connection with the overruling of a prior motion for rehearing. Issuance of a new opinion that is not substantially different should not occasion a further motion for rehearing, but a motion's lack of merit does not affect appellate deadlines. The provisions of former Rule 53.7(b) that address motions for rehearing are moved to new subdivision 49.11 without change, leaving the provisions of Rule 53.7(b) that address petitions for review undisturbed. Subdivision 49.12 mirrors Rule 10.1(a)(5) in excepting motions for rehearing and motions for en banc reconsideration from the certificate-of-conference requirement.

RULE 50. RECONSIDERATION ON PETITION FOR DISCRETIONARY REVIEW.

Within 60 days after a petition for discretionary review is filed with the clerk of the court of appeals that delivered the decision, the justices who participated in the decision may, as provided by subsection (a), reconsider and correct or modify the court's opinion or judgment. Within the same period of time, any of the justices who participated in the decision may issue a concurring of dissenting opinion.

(a) If the court's original opinion or judgment is corrected or modified, that opinion or judgment is withdrawn and the modified or corrected opinion or judgment is substituted as the opinion or judgment of the court. No further opinions may be issued by the court of appeals. The original petition for discretionary review is not dismissed by operation of law, unless the filing party files a new petition in the court of appeals. In the alternative, the petitioning party shall submit to the court of appeals copies of the corrected or modified opinion or judgment as an amendment to the original petition.

(b) Any party may then file with the court of appeals a new petition for discretionary review seeking review of the corrected or modified opinion or judgment, including any dissents or concurrences, under Rule 68.2.

(Adopted by Order eff. Sept. 1, 1997. Amended by Order March 10, 2008, eff. Sept. 1, 2008; Order Aug. 20, 2008, eff. Sept. 1, 2008.)

Comment to 1997 change: This is former Rule 101. The rule is amended to allow 30 days for the court of appeals to review the petition for discretionary review and to require the withdrawal of the prior opinion and judgment if the court of appeals renders a new judgment or hands down a new opinion.

RULE 51. ENFORCEMENT OF JUDGMENTS AFTER MANDATE.

51.1. Civil Cases.

(a) Statement of Costs. The appellate clerk must prepare, and send to the trial court clerk with the mandate, a statement of costs showing:

(1) the preparation costs for the appellate record, and any court of appeals filing fees, with a notation of those items that have been paid and those that are owing; and

(2) the party or parties against whom costs have been adjudged.

(b) Enforcement of Judgment. When the trial court clerk receives the mandate, the appellate court's judgment must be enforced. Appellate court costs must be included with the trial court costs in any process to enforce the judgment. If all or part of the costs are collected, the trial court clerk must immediately remit to the appellate court clerk any amount due to that clerk. The trial court need not make any further order in the case, and the appellate court's judgment may be enforced as in other cases, when the appellate judgment:

(1) affirms the trial court's judgment;

(2) modifies the trial court's judgment and, as so modified, affirms that judgment; or

(3) renders the judgment the trial court should have rendered.

51.2. Criminal Cases.

When the trial court clerk receives the mandate, the appellate court's judgment must be enforced as follows:

(a) Clerk's Duties. The trial court clerk must:

(1) send an acknowledgment to the appellate clerk of the mandate's receipt; and

(2) immediately file the mandate.

(b) Judgment of Affirmance; Defendant Not in Custody.

(1) Capias to Be Issued. If the judgment contains a sentence of confinement or imprisonment that has not been suspended, the trial court must promptly issue a capias for the defendant's arrest so that the court's sentence can be executed.

(2) Contents of Capias. The capias may issue to any county of this state and must be executed and returned as in felony cases, except that no bail may be taken. The capias must:

(A) recite the fact of conviction;

(B) set forth the offense and the court's judgment and sentence;

(C) state that the judgment was appealed from and affirmed, and that the mandate has been filed; and

(D) command the sheriff to arrest and take the defendant into his custody, and to place and keep the defendant in custody until delivered to the proper authorities as directed by the sentence.

(3) Sheriff's Duties. The sheriff must promptly execute the capias as directed. The sheriff must notify the trial court clerk and the appellate clerk when the mandate has been carried out and executed.

(c) Judgment of Reversal.

(1) When New Trial Ordered. When the appellate court reverses the trial court's judgment and grants the defendant a new trial, the procedure is governed by Code of Criminal Procedure article 44.29. If the defendant is in custody and entitled to bail, the defendant must be released upon giving bail.

(2) When Case Dismissed. When the appellate court reverses the trial court's judgment and orders the case to be dismissed, the defendant—if in custody—must be discharged.

(d) Judgment of Acquittal. When the appellate court reverses a judgment and orders the defendant's acquittal, the defendant—if in custody—must be discharged, and no further order or judgment of the trial court is necessary.

(Adopted by Order eff. Sept. 1, 1997.)

Comment to 1997 change: Former Rules 87 and 88 are merged. The reference to costs in tax suits is deleted.

SECTION THREE.
ORIGINAL PROCEEDINGS IN THE SUPREME COURT AND THE COURTS OF APPEALS

RULE 52. ORIGINAL PROCEEDINGS.

52.1. Commencement.

An original appellate proceeding seeking extraordinary relief—such as a writ of habeas corpus, mandamus, prohibition, injunction, or quo warranto—is commenced by filing a petition with the clerk of the appropriate appellate court. The petition must be captioned "In re [name of relator]."

52.2. Designation of Parties.

The party seeking the relief is the relator. In original proceedings other than habeas corpus, the person against whom relief is sought—whether a judge, court, tribunal, officer, or other person—is the respondent. A person whose interest would be directly affected by the relief sought is a real party in interest and a party to the case.

52.3. Form and Contents of Petition.

The petition must, under appropriate headings and in the order here indicated, contain the following:

(a) Identity of Parties and Counsel. The petition must give a complete list of all parties, and the names, and addresses of all counsel.

(b) Table of Contents. The petition must include a table of contents with references to the pages of the petition. The table of contents must indicate the subject matter of each issue or point, or group of issues or points.

(c) Index of Authorities. The petition must include an index of authorities arranged alphabetically and indicating the pages of the petition where the authorities are cited.

(d) Statement of the Case. The petition must contain a statement of the case that should seldom exceed one page and should not discuss the facts. The statement must contain the following:

(1) a concise description of the nature of any underlying proceeding (e.g., a suit for damages, a contempt proceeding for failure to pay child support, or the certification of a candidate for inclusion on an election ballot);

(2) if the respondent is a judge, the name of the judge, the designation of the court in which the judge was sitting, and the county in which the court is located; and if the respondent is an official other than a judge, the designation and location of the office held by the respondent;

(3) a concise description of the respondent's action from which the relator seeks relief;

(4) if the relator seeks a writ of habeas corpus, a statement describing how and where the relator is being deprived of liberty;

(5) if the petition is filed in the Supreme Court after a petition requesting the same relief was filed in the court of appeals:

(A) the date the petition was filed in the court of appeals;

(B) the district of the court of appeals and the names of the justices who participated in the decision;

(C) the author of any opinion for the court of appeals and the author of any separate opinion;

(D) the citation of the court's opinion;

(E) the disposition of the case by the court of appeals, and the date of the court of appeals' order.

(e) Statement of Jurisdiction. The petition must state, without argument, the basis of the court's jurisdiction. If the Supreme Court and the court of appeals have concurrent jurisdiction, the petition must be presented first to the court of appeals unless there is a compelling reason not to do so. If the petition is filed in the Supreme Court without first being presented to the court of appeals, the petition must state the compelling reason why the petition was not first presented to the court of appeals.

(f) Issues Presented. The petition must state concisely all issues or points presented for relief. The statement of an issue or point will be treated as covering every subsidiary question that is fairly included.

(g) Statement of Facts. The petition must state concisely and without argument the facts pertinent to the issues or points presented. Every statement of fact in the petition must be supported by citation to competent evidence included in the appendix or record.

(h) Argument. The petition must contain a clear and concise argument for the contentions made, with appropriate citations to authorities and to the appendix or record.

(i) Prayer. The petition must contain a short conclusion that clearly states the nature of the relief sought.

(j) Certification. The person filing the petition must certify that he or she has reviewed the petition and concluded that every factual statement in the petition is supported by competent evidence included in the appendix or record.

(k) Appendix.

(1) Necessary Contents. The appendix must contain:

(A) a certified or sworn copy of any order complained of, or any other document showing the matter complained of;

(B) any order or opinion of the court of appeals, if the petition is filed in the Supreme Court;

(C) unless voluminous or impracticable, the text of any rule, regulation, ordinance, statute, constitutional provision, or other law (excluding case law) on which the argument is based; and

(D) if a writ of habeas corpus is sought, proof that the relator is being restrained.

(2) Optional Contents. The appendix may contain any other item pertinent to the issues or points presented for review, including copies or excerpts of relevant court opinions, statutes, constitutional provisions, documents on which the suit was based, pleadings, and similar material. Items should not be included in the appendix to attempt to avoid the page limits for the petition. The appendix should not contain any evidence or other item that is not necessary for a decision.

(Amended by Order March 10, 2008, eff. Sept. 1, 2008 ; Order Aug. 20, 2008, eff. Sept. 1, 2008.)

Comment to 2008 changes: The reference to "unpublished" opinions in Subdivision 52.3(d)(5)(D) is deleted. The filer should provide the best cite available for the court of appeals' opinion, which may be a LEXIS, Westlaw, or other citation to an electronic medium. Subdivision 52.3 is further amended to delete the requirement that all factual statements be verified by affidavit. Instead, the filer—in the usual case of a party with legal representation, the lead counsel—must include a statement certifying that all factual statements are supported by competent evidence in the appendix or record to which the petition has cited. The certification required by subdivision 52.3(j) does not count against the page limitations.

52.4. Response.

Any party may file a response to the petition, but it is not mandatory. The court must not grant relief—other than temporary relief—before a response has been filed or requested by the court. The response must conform to the requirements of 52.3, except that:

(a) the list of parties and counsel is not required unless necessary to supplement or correct the list contained in the petition;

(b) the response need not include a statement of the case, a statement of the issues presented, or a statement of the facts unless the responding party is dissatisfied with that portion of the petition;

(c) a statement of jurisdiction should be omitted unless the petition fails to assert valid grounds for jurisdiction, in which case the reasons why the court lacks jurisdiction must be concisely stated;

(d) the argument must be confined to the issues or points presented in the petition; and

(e) the appendix to the response need not contain any item already contained in an appendix filed by the relator.

52.5. Relator's Reply to Response.

The relator may file a reply addressing any matter in the response. However, the court may consider and decide the case before a reply brief is filed.

52.6. Repealed by Order Nov. 13, 2012, Eff. Dec. 1, 2012.

52.7. Record.

(a) Filing by Relator Required. Relator must file with the petition:

(1) a certified or sworn copy of every document that is material to the relator's claim for relief and that was filed in any underlying proceeding; and

(2) a properly authenticated transcript of any relevant testimony from any underlying proceeding, including any exhibits offered in evidence, or a statement that no testimony was adduced in connection with the matter complained.

(b) Supplementation Permitted. After the record is filed, relator or any other party to the proceeding may file additional materials for inclusion in the record.

(c) Service of Record on All Parties. Relator and any party who files materials for inclusion in the record must—at the same time—serve on each party:

(1) those materials not previously served on that party as part of the record in another original appellate proceeding in the same or another court; and

(2) an index listing the materials filed and describing them in sufficient detail to identify them.

(Amended by Order Dec. 23, 2002, eff. Jan. 1, 2003.)

Comment to 2002 change: Subdivision 52.7(c) is added to specify how record materials in original proceedings are to be served. Ordinarily, a party must serve record materials and an index of those materials on all other parties. But when materials have already been served in related original proceedings, they need not be served again. Examples are when original proceedings raising the same issues are brought in both the court of appeals and the Supreme Court, or when separate original proceedings are filed arising out of the same underlying lawsuit. The purpose of this procedure is to ensure that all parties have record materials readily available without requiring unnecessary duplication.

52.8. Action on Petition.

(a) Relief Denied. If the court determines from the petition and any response and reply that the relator is not entitled to the relief sought, the court must deny the petition. If the relator in a habeas corpus proceeding has been released on bond, the court must remand the relator to custody and issue an order of commitment. If the relator is not returned to custody, the court may declare the bond to be forfeited and render judgment against the surety.

(b) Interim Action. If the court is of the tentative opinion that relator is entitled to the relief sought or that a serious question concerning the relief requires further consideration:

(1) the court must request a response if one has not been filed;

(2) the Supreme Court may request full briefing under Rule 55;

(3) in a habeas corpus proceeding, the court may order that relator be discharged on execution and filing of a bond in an amount set by the court; and

(4) the court may set the case for oral argument.

(c) Relief Granted. If the court determines that relator is entitled to relief, it must make an appropriate order. The court may grant relief without hearing oral argument.

(d) Opinion. When denying relief, the court may hand down an opinion but is not required to do so. When granting relief, the court must hand down an opinion as in any other case. Rule 47 is applicable to an order or opinion by a court of appeals except that the court of appeals may not order an unpublished opinion published after the Supreme Court or Court of Criminal Appeals has acted on any party's petition for extraordinary relief addressing the same issues.

52.9. Motion for Rehearing.

Any party may file a motion for rehearing within 15 days after the final order is rendered. The motion must clearly state the points relied on for the rehearing. No response to a motion for rehearing need be filed unless the court so requests. The court will not grant a motion for rehearing unless a response has been filed or requested.

(Amended by Order March 4, 2013, eff. March 4, 2013.)

52.10. Temporary Relief.

(a) Motion for Temporary Relief; Certificate of Compliance. The relator may file a motion to stay any underlying proceedings or for any other temporary relief pending the court's action on the petition. The relator must notify or make a diligent effort to notify all parties by expedited means (such as by telephone or fax) that a motion for temporary relief has been or will be filed and must certify to the court that the relator has complied with this paragraph before temporary relief will be granted.

(b) Grant of Temporary Relief. The court—on motion of any party or on its own initiative—may without notice grant any just relief pending the court's action on the petition. As a condition of granting temporary relief, the court may require a bond to protect the parties who will be affected by the relief. Unless vacated or modified, an order granting temporary relief is effective until the case is finally decided.

(c) Motion to Reconsider. Any party may move the court at any time to reconsider a grant of temporary relief.

52.11. Groundless Petition or Misleading Statement or Record.

On motion of any party or on its own initiative, the court may—after notice and a reasonable opportunity to respond—impose just sanctions on a party or attorney who is not acting in good faith as indicated by any of the following:

(a) filing a petition that is clearly groundless;

(b) bringing the petition solely for delay of an underlying proceeding;

(c) grossly misstating or omitting an obviously important and material fact in the petition or response; or

(d) filing an appendix or record that is clearly misleading because of the omission of obviously important and material evidence or documents.

(Adopted by Order eff. Sept. 1, 1997.)

Comment to 1997 change: Former Rules 120, 121, and 122 are merged into this rule. The requirement of a motion for leave in original proceedings is repealed. The form of the petition and response, contents of the appendix and record, page limits, and relief that may be granted are specifically stated. Specific provision is now made for a motion for rehearing. A provision for sanctions is added.

**SECTION FOUR.
PROCEEDINGS IN THE SUPREME COURT**

RULE 53. PETITION FOR REVIEW.

53.1. Method of Review.

The Supreme Court may review a court of appeals' final judgment on a petition for review addressed to "The Supreme Court of Texas." A party who seeks to alter the court of appeals' judgment must file a petition for review. The petition for review procedure replaces the writ of error procedure. Statutes pertaining to the writ of error in the Supreme Court apply equally to the petition for review.

53.2. Contents of Petition.

The petition for review must, under appropriate headings and in the order here indicated, contain the following items:

(a) Identity of Parties and Counsel. The petition must give a complete list of all parties to the trial court's final judgment, and the names and addresses of all trial and appellate counsel.

(b) Table of Contents. The petition must have a table of contents with references to the pages of the petition. The table of contents must indicate the subject matter of each issue or point, or group of issues or points.

(c) Index of Authorities. The petition must have an index of authorities arranged alphabetically and indicating the pages of the petition where the authorities are cited.

(d) Statement of the Case. The petition must contain a statement of the case that should seldom exceed one page and should not discuss the facts. The statement must contain the following:

(1) a concise description of the nature of the case (e.g., whether it is a suit for damages, on a note, or in trespass to try title);

(2) the name of the judge who signed the order or judgment appealed from;

(3) the designation of the trial court and the county in which it is located;

(4) the disposition of the case by the trial court;

(5) the parties in the court of appeals;

(6) the district of the court of appeals;

(7) the names of the justices who participated in the decision in the court of appeals, the author of the opinion for the court, and the author of any separate opinion;

(8) the citation for the court of appeals' opinion; and

(9) the disposition of the case by the court of appeals, including the court's disposition of any motions for rehearing or motions for en banc reconsideration and whether any motions for rehearing or motions for en banc reconsideration are pending in the court of appeals at the time the petition for review is filed.

(e) Statement of Jurisdiction. The petition must state, without argument, the basis of the Court's jurisdiction.

(f) Issues Presented. The petition must state concisely all issues or points presented for review. The statement of an issue or point will be treated as covering every subsidiary question that is fairly included. If the matter complained of originated in the trial court, it should have been preserved for appellate review in the trial court and assigned as error in the court of appeals.

(g) Statement of Facts. The petition must affirm that the court of appeals correctly stated the nature of the case, except in any particulars pointed out. The petition must state concisely and without argument the facts and procedural background pertinent to the issues or points presented. The statement must be supported by record references.

(h) Summary of the Argument. The petition must contain a succinct, clear, and accurate statement of the arguments made in the body of the petition. This summary must not merely repeat the issues or points presented for review.

(i) Argument. The petition must contain a clear and concise argument for the contentions made, with appropriate citations to authorities and to the record. The argument need not address every issue or point included in the statement of issues or points. Any issue or point not addressed may be addressed in the brief on the merits if one is requested by the Court. The argument should state the reasons why the Supreme Court should exercise jurisdiction to hear the case with specific reference to the factors listed in Rule 56.1(a). The petition need not quote at length from a matter included in the appendix; a reference to the appendix is sufficient. The Court will consider the court of appeals' opinion along with the petition, so statements in that opinion need not be repeated.

(j) Prayer. The petition must contain a short conclusion that clearly states the nature of the relief sought.

(k) Appendix.

(1) Necessary Contents. Unless voluminous or impracticable, the appendix must contain a copy of:

(A) the judgment or other appealable order of the trial court from which relief in the court of appeals was sought;

(B) the jury charge and verdict, if any, or the trial court's findings of fact and conclusions of law, if any;

(C) the opinion and judgment of the court of appeals; and

(D) the text of any rule, regulation, ordinance, statute, constitutional provision, or other law on which the argument is based (excluding case law), and the text of any contract or other document that is central to the argument.

(2) Optional Contents. The appendix may contain any other item pertinent to the issues or points presented for review, including copies or excerpts of relevant court opinions, statutes, constitutional provisions, documents on which the suit was based, pleadings, and similar material. Items should not be included in the appendix to attempt to avoid the page limits for the petition.

(Amended by Order March 10, 2008, eff. Sept. 1, 2008; Order Aug. 20, 2008, eff. Sept. 1, 2008.)

53.3. Response to Petition for Review.

Any other party to the appeal may file a response to the petition for review, but it is not mandatory. If no response is timely filed, or if a party files a waiver of response, the Court will consider the petition without a response. A petition will not be granted before a response has been filed or requested by the Court. The response must conform to the requirements of 53.2, except that:

(a) the list of parties and counsel is not required unless necessary to supplement or correct the list contained in the petition;

(b) a statement of the case and a statement of the facts need not be made unless the respondent is dissatisfied with that portion of the petition;

(c) a statement of the issues presented need not be made unless:

(1) the respondent is dissatisfied with the statement made in the petition;

(2) the respondent is asserting independent grounds for affirmance of the court of appeals' judgment; or

(3) the respondent is asserting grounds that establish the respondent's right to a judgment that is less favorable to the respondent than the judgment rendered by the court of appeals but more favorable to the respondent than the judgment that might be awarded to the petitioner (e.g., a remand for a new trial rather than a rendition of judgment in favor of the petitioner);

(d) a statement of jurisdiction should be omitted unless the petition fails to assert valid grounds for jurisdiction, in which case the reasons why the Supreme Court lacks jurisdiction must be concisely stated;

(e) the respondent's argument must be confined to the issues or points presented in the petition or asserted by the respondent in the respondent's statement of issues; and

(f) the appendix to the response need not contain any item already contained in an appendix filed by the petitioner.

53.4. Points Not Considered in Court of Appeals.

To obtain a remand to the court of appeals for consideration of issues or points briefed in that court but not decided by that court, or to request that the Supreme Court consider such issues or points, a party may raise those issues or points in the petition, the response, the reply, any brief, or a motion for rehearing.

53.5. Petitioner's Reply to Response.

The petitioner may file a reply addressing any matter in the response. However, the Court may consider and decide the case before a reply brief is filed.

53.6. Repealed by Order Nov. 13, 2012, Eff. Dec. 1, 2012.

53.7. Time and Place of Filing.

(a) Petition. Unless the Supreme Court for good cause orders an earlier filing deadline, the petition must be filed with the Supreme Court clerk within 45 days after the following:

(1) the date the court of appeals rendered judgment, if no motion for rehearing or motion for enbanc reconsideration is timely filed; or

(2) the date of the court of appeals' last ruling on all timely filed motions for rehearing or en banc reconsideration.

(b) Premature Filing. A petition filed before the last ruling on all timely filed motions for rehearing and en banc reconsideration is treated as having been filed on the date of, but after, the last ruling on any such motion. If a party files a petition for review while a motion for rehearing or en banc reconsideration is pending in the court of appeals, the party must include that information in its petition for review.

(c) Petitions Filed by Other Parties. If a party files a petition for review within the time specified in 53.7(a)—or within the time specified by the Supreme Court in an order granting an extension of time to file a petition—any other party required to file a petition may do so within 45 days after the last timely motion for rehearing is overruled or within 30 days after any preceding petition is filed, whichever date is later.

(d) Response. Any response must be filed with the Supreme Court clerk within 30 days after the petition is filed.

(e) Reply. Any reply must be filed with the Supreme Court clerk within 15 days after the response is filed.

(f) Extension of Time. The Supreme Court may extend the time to file a petition for review if a party files a motion complying with Rule 10.5(b) no later than 15 days after the last day for filing the petition. The Supreme Court may extend the time to file a response or reply if a party files a motion complying with Rule 10.5(b) either before or after the response or reply is due.

(g) Petition Filed in Court of Appeals. If a petition is mistakenly filed in the court of appeals, the petition is deemed to have been filed the same day with the Supreme Court clerk, and the court of appeals clerk must immediately send the petition to the Supreme Court clerk.

(Amended by Order March 10, 2008, eff. Sept. 1, 2008; Order Aug. 20, 2008, eff. Sept. 1, 2008.)

53.8. Amendment.

On motion showing good cause, the Court may allow the petition, response, or reply to be amended on such reasonable terms as the Court may prescribe.

53.9. Court May Require Revision.

If a petition, response, or reply does not conform with these rules, the Supreme Court may require the document to be revised or may return the document to the party who filed it and consider the case without allowing the document to be revised.

(Adopted by Order eff. Sept. 1, 1997.)

Comment to 1997 change: Former Rules 130 and 131 are merged. The 50-page application for writ of error is replaced by a 15-page petition for review, which is filed in the Supreme Court and should concentrate on the reasons the Court should exercise jurisdiction to hear the case. The contents of the petition and response, the length of the documents, the time for filing are all specifically stated.

Comment to 2008 change: Subdivision 53.7(a)is amended to clarify that the Supreme Court may shorten the time for filing a petition for review and that the timely filing of a motion for en banc reconsideration tolls the commencement of the 45-day period for filing a petition for review until the motion is overruled. Subdivision 53.2(d)(8) is amended to delete the reference to unpublished opinions in civil cases. Subdivision 53.2(d)(9) is amended to require a party that prematurely files a petition for review to notify the Supreme Court of any panel rehearing or en banc reconsideration motions still pending in the court of appeals. Subdivision 53.7(b) is revised to reference this new requirement and to relocate to new Rule 49.11 those provisions governing motions for rehearing.

RULE 54. FILING THE RECORD.

54.1. Request for Record.

With or without granting the petition for review, the Supreme Court may request that the record from the court of appeals be filed with the clerk of the Supreme Court.

54.2. Duty of Court of Appeals Clerk.

(a) Request for Record. The court of appeals clerk must not send the record to the Supreme Court unless it is requested. Upon receiving the Supreme Court clerk's request for the record, the court of appeals clerk must promptly send to the Supreme Court clerk all of the following:

(1) the original record;

(2) any motion filed in the court of appeals;

(3) copies of all orders of the court of appeals; and

(4) copies of all opinions and the judgment of the court of appeals.

(b) Nondocumentary Exhibits. The clerk should not send any nondocumentary exhibits unless the Supreme Court specifically requests.

54.3. Expenses.

The petitioner must pay to the court of appeals clerk a sum sufficient to pay the cost of mailing or shipping the record to and from the Supreme Court clerk.

54.4. Duty of Supreme Court Clerk.

Upon receiving the record, the Supreme Court clerk must file it and enter the filing on the docket. The clerk may refuse the record if the charges for mailing or shipping have not been paid.

(Adopted by Order eff. Sept. 1, 1997.)

Comment to 1997 change: This is former Rule 132. Subdivision 54.1 is new and provides for the Supreme Court to request the filing of the record. Other changes are made.

RULE 55. BRIEFS ON THE MERITS.

55.1. Request by Court.

A brief on the merits must not be filed unless requested by the Court. With or without granting the petition for review, the Court may request the parties to file briefs on the merits. In appropriate cases, the Court may realign parties and direct that parties file consolidated briefs.

(Amended by Order Dec. 23, 2002 eff. Jan. 1, 2003.)

Comment to 2002 change: Subdivision 55.1 is clarified to provide that the Court may realign parties require consolidated briefing for a clearer and more efficient presentation of the case.

55.2. Petitioner's Brief on the Merits.

The petitioner's brief on the merits must be confined to the issues or points stated in the petition for review and must, under appropriate headings and in the order here indicated, contain the following items:

(a) Identity of Parties and Counsel. The brief must give a complete list of all parties to the trial court's final judgment, and the names and addresses of all trial and appellate counsel.

(b) Table of Contents. The brief must have a table of contents with references to the pages of the brief. The table of contents must indicate the subject matter of each issue or point, or group of issues or points.

(c) Index of Authorities. The brief must have an index of authorities arranged alphabetically and indicating the pages of the brief where the authorities are cited.

(d) Statement of the Case. The brief must contain a statement of the case that should seldom exceed one page and should not discuss the facts. The statement must contain the following:

(1) a concise description of the nature of the case (e.g., whether it is a suit for damages, on a note, or in trespass to try title);

(2) the name of the judge who signed the order or judgment appealed from;

(3) the designation of the trial court and the county in which it is located;

(4) the disposition of the case by the trial court;

(5) the parties in the court of appeals;

(6) the district of the court of appeals;

(7) the names of the justices who participated in the decision in the court of appeals, the author of the opinion for the court, and the author of any separate opinion;

(8) the citation for the court of appeals' opinion, if available, or a statement that the opinion was unpublished; and

(9) the disposition of the case by the court of appeals;

(e) Statement of Jurisdiction. The brief must state, without argument, the basis of the Court's jurisdiction.

(f) Issues Presented. The brief must state concisely all issues or points presented for review. The statement of an issue or point will be treated as covering every subsidiary question that is fairly included. The phrasing of the issues or points need not be identical to the statement of issues or points in the petition for review, but the brief may not raise additional issues or points or change the substance of the issues or points presented in the petition.

(g) Statement of Facts. The brief must affirm that the court of appeals correctly stated the nature of the case, except in any particulars pointed out. The brief must state concisely and without argument the facts and procedural background pertinent to the issues or points presented. The statement must be supported by record references.

(h) Summary of the Argument. The brief must contain a succinct, clear, and accurate statement of the arguments made in the body of the brief. This summary must not merely repeat the issues or points presented for review.

(i) Argument. The brief must contain a clear and concise argument for the contentions made, with appropriate citations to authorities and to the record.

(j) Prayer. The brief must contain a short conclusion that clearly states the nature of the relief sought.

(Amended by Order Dec. 23, 2002, eff. Jan. 1, 2003.)

55.3. Respondent's Brief.

If the petitioner files a brief on the merits, any other party to the appeal may file a brief in response, which must conform to 55.2, except that:

(a) the list of parties and counsel is not required unless necessary to supplement or correct the list contained in the petitioner's brief;

(b) a statement of the case and a statement of the facts need not be made unless the respondent is dissatisfied with that portion of the petitioner's brief; and

(c) a statement of the issues presented need not be made unless:

(1) the respondent is dissatisfied with the statement made in the petitioner's brief;

(2) the respondent is asserting independent grounds for affirmance of the court of appeals' judgment; or

(3) the respondent is asserting grounds that establish the respondent's right to a judgment that is less favorable to the respondent than the judgment rendered by the court of appeals but more favorable to the respondent than the judgment that might be awarded to the petitioner (e.g., a remand for a new trial rather than a rendition of judgment in favor of the petitioner);

(d) a statement of jurisdiction should be omitted unless the petition fails to assert valid grounds for jurisdiction; and

(e) the respondent's argument must be confined to the issues or points presented in the petitioner's brief or asserted by the respondent in the respondent's statement of issues.

55.4. Petitioner's Brief in Reply.

The petitioner may file a reply brief addressing any matter in the brief in response. However, the Court may consider and decide the case before a reply brief is filed.

55.5. Reliance on Prior Brief.

As a brief on the merits or a brief in response, a party may file the brief that the party filed in the court of appeals.

55.6. Repealed by Order Nov. 13, 2012, eff. Dec. 1, 2012.

55.7. Time and Place of Filing; Extension of Time.

Briefs must be filed with the Supreme Court clerk in accordance with the schedule stated in the clerk's notice that the Court has requested briefs on the merits. If no schedule is stated in the notice, petitioner must file a brief on the merits within 30 days after the date of the notice, respondent must file a brief in response within 20 days after receiving petitioner's brief, and petitioner must file any reply brief within 15 days after receiving respondent's brief. On motion complying with Rule 10.5(b) either before or after the brief is due, the Supreme Court may extend the time to file a brief.

55.8. Amendment.

On motion showing good cause, the Court may allow a party to amend a brief on such reasonable terms as the Court may prescribe.

55.9. Court May Require Revision.

If a brief does not conform with these rules, the Supreme Court may require the brief to be revised or may return it to the party who filed it and consider the case without further briefing by that party.

(Adopted by Order eff. Sept. 1, 1997.)

Comment to 1997 change: The rule is new and provides for a 50 page brief on the merits if requested by the Supreme Court.

RULE 56. ORDERS ON PETITION FOR REVIEW.

56.1. Orders on Petition for Review.

(a) Considerations in Granting Review. Whether to grant review is a matter of judicial discretion. Among the factors the Supreme Court considers in deciding whether to grant a petition for review are the following:

(1) whether the justices of the court of appeals disagree on an important point of law;

(2) whether there is a conflict between the courts of appeals on an important point of law;

(3) whether a case involves the construction or validity of a statute;

(4) whether a case involves constitutional issues;

(5) whether the court of appeals appears to have committed an error of law of such importance to the state's jurisprudence that it should be corrected; and

(6) whether the court of appeals has decided an important question of state law that should be, but has not been, resolved by the Supreme Court.

(b) Petition Denied or Dismissed. When the petition has been on file in the Supreme Court for 30 days, the Court may deny or dismiss the petition—whether or not a response has been filed—with one of the following notations:

(1) "Denied." If the Supreme Court is not satisfied that the opinion of the court of appeals has correctly declared the law in all respects, but determines that the petition presents no error that requires reversal or that is of such importance to the jurisprudence of the state as to require correction, the Court will deny the petition with the notation "Denied."

(2) "Dismissed w.o.j." If the Supreme Court lacks jurisdiction, the Court will dismiss the petition with the notation "Dismissed for Want of Jurisdiction."

(c) Petition Refused. If the Supreme Court determines—after a response has been filed or requested—that the court of appeals' judgment is correct and that the legal principles announced in the opinion are likewise correct, the Court will refuse the petition with the notation "Refused." The court of appeals' opinion in the case has the same precedential value as an opinion of the Supreme Court.

(d) Improvident Grant. If the Court has granted review but later decides that review should not have been granted, the Court may, without opinion, set aside the order granting review and dismiss the petition or deny or refuse review as though review had never been granted.

56.2. Moot Cases.

If a case is moot, the Supreme Court may, after notice to the parties, grant the petition and, without hearing argument, dismiss the case or the appealable portion of it without addressing the merits of the appeal.

56.3. Settled Cases.

If a case is settled by agreement of the parties and all parties so move, the Supreme Court may grant the petition if it has not already been granted and, without hearing argument or considering the merits, render a judgment to effectuate the agreement. The Supreme Court's action may include setting aside the judgment of the court of appeals or the trial court without regard to the merits and remanding the case to the trial court for rendition of a judgment in accordance with the agreement. The Supreme Court may abate the case until the lower court's proceedings to effectuate the agreement are complete. A severable portion of the proceeding may be disposed of if it will not prejudice the remaining parties. In any event, the Supreme Court's order does not vacate the court of appeals' opinion unless the order specifically provides otherwise. An agreement or motion cannot be conditioned on vacating the court of appeals' opinion.

(Amended by Order Dec. 23, 2002, eff. Jan. 1, 2003.)

Comment to 2002 change: Subdivision 56.3 is clarified to provide for partial settlements.

56.4. Notice to Parties.

When the Supreme Court grants, denies, refuses, or dismisses a petition for review, the Supreme Court clerk must send a written notice of the disposition to the court of appeals, the trial court, and all parties to the appeal.

56.5. Return of Documents to Court of Appeals.

When the Supreme Court denies, refuses, or dismisses a petition for review, the clerk will retain the petition, together with the record and accompanying papers, for 30 days after the order is rendered. If no motion for rehearing has been filed by the end of that period or when any motion for rehearing of the order has been overruled, the clerk must send a certified copy of its order to the court of appeals and return the record and all papers (except for documents filed in the Supreme Court) to the court of appeals clerk.

(Adopted by Order eff. Sept. 1, 1997.)

Comment to 1997 change: The rule is from former Rule 133. Subdivision 56.3 regarding settled cases is added.

RULE 57. DIRECT APPEALS TO THE SUPREME COURT.

57.1. Application.

This rule governs direct appeals to the Supreme Court that are authorized by the Constitution and by statute. Except when inconsistent with a statute or this rule, the rules governing appeals to courts of appeals also apply to direct appeals to the Supreme Court.

57.2. Jurisdiction.

The Supreme Court may not take jurisdiction over a direct appeal from the decision of any court other than a district court or county court, or over any question of fact. The Supreme Court may decline to exercise jurisdiction over a direct appeal of an interlocutory order if the record is not adequately developed, or if its decision would be advisory, or if the case is not of such importance to the jurisprudence of the state that a direct appeal should be allowed.

57.3. Statement of Jurisdiction.

Appellant must file with the record a statement fully but plainly setting out the basis asserted for exercise of the Supreme Court's jurisdiction. Appellee may file a response to appellant's statement of jurisdiction within ten days after the statement is filed.

57.4. Preliminary Ruling on Jurisdiction.

If the Supreme Court notes probable jurisdiction over a direct appeal, the parties must file briefs under Rule 38 as in any other case. If the Supreme Court does not note probable jurisdiction over a direct appeal, the appeal will be dismissed.

57.5. Direct Appeal Exclusive While Pending.

If a direct appeal to the Supreme Court is filed, the parties to the appeal must not, while that appeal is pending, pursue an appeal to the court of appeals. But if the direct appeal is dismissed, any party may pursue any other appeal available at the time when the direct appeal was filed. The other appeal must be perfected within ten days after dismissal of the direct appeal.

(Adopted by Order eff. Sept. 1, 1997.)

Comment to 1997 change: This is former Rule 140. The rule is amended without substantive change except subdivision 57.5 is amended to make clear that no party to the direct appeal may pursue the appeal in the court of appeals while the direct appeal is pending, but allowing 10 days to perfect a subsequent appeal.

RULE 58. CERTIFICATION OF QUESTIONS OF LAW BY UNITED STATES COURTS.

58.1. Certification.

The Supreme Court of Texas may answer questions of law certified to it by any federal appellate court if the certifying court is presented with determinative questions of Texas law having no controlling Supreme Court precedent. The Supreme Court may decline to answer the questions certified to it.

58.2. Contents of the Certification Order.

An order from the certifying court must set forth:

(a) the questions of law to be answered; and

(b) a stipulated statement of all facts relevant to the questions certified, showing fully the nature of the controversy in which the questions arose.

58.3. Transmission of Certification Order.

The clerk of the certifying court must send to the clerk of the Supreme Court of Texas the following:

(a) the certification order under the certifying court's official seal;

(b) a list of the names of all parties to the pending case, giving the address and telephone number, if known, of any party not represented by counsel; and

(c) a list of the names, addresses, and telephone numbers of counsel for each party.

58.4. Transmission of Record.

The certifying court should not send the Supreme Court of Texas the record in the pending case with the certification order. The Supreme Court may later require the original or copies of all or part of the record before the certifying court to be filed with the Supreme Court clerk.

58.5. Fees and Costs.

Unless the certifying court orders otherwise in its certification order, the parties must bear equally the fees under Rule 5.

58.6. Notice.

If the Supreme Court agrees to answer the questions certified to it, the Court will notify all parties and the certifying court. The Supreme Court clerk must also send a notice to the Attorney General of Texas if:

(a) the constitutionality of a Texas statute is the subject of a certified question that the Supreme Court has agreed to answer; and

(b) the State of Texas or an officer, agency, or employee of the state is not a party to the proceeding in the certifying court.

58.7. Briefs and Oral Argument.

(a) Briefs. The appealing party in the certifying court must file a brief with the Supreme Court clerk within 30 days after the date of the notice. Opposing parties must file an answering brief within 20 days after receiving the opening brief. Briefs must comply with Rule 55 to the extent its provisions apply. On motion complying with Rule 10.5(b), either before or after the brief is due, the Supreme Court may extend the time to file a brief.

(b) Oral Argument. Oral argument may be granted either on a party's request or on the Court's own initiative. Argument is governed by Rule 59.

58.8. Intervention by the State.

If the constitutionality of a Texas statute is the subject of a certified question that the Supreme Court has agreed to answer the State of Texas may intervene at any reasonable time for briefing and oral argument (if argument is allowed), on the question of constitutionality.

58.9. Opinion on Certified Questions.

If the Supreme Court has agreed to answer a certified question, it will hand down an opinion as in any other case.

58.10. Answering Certified Questions.

After all motions for rehearing have been overruled, the Supreme Court clerk must send to the certifying court the written opinion on the certified questions. The opinion must be under the Supreme Court's seal.

(Adopted by Order eff. Sept. 1, 1997.)

Comment to 1997 change: This is former Rule 114. The rule is substantially revised, but no substantive change in procedure is intended.

RULE 59. SUBMISSION AND ARGUMENT.

59.1. Submission Without Argument.

If at least six members of the Court so vote, a petition may be granted and an opinion handed down without oral argument.

59.2. Submission With Argument.

If the Supreme Court decides that oral argument would aid the Court, the Court will set the case for argument. The clerk will notify all parties of the submission date.

59.3. Purpose of Argument.

Oral argument should emphasize and clarify the written arguments in the briefs. Counsel should not merely read from a prepared text. Counsel should assume that all Justices have read the briefs before oral argument and should be prepared to respond to the Justices' questions.

59.4. Time for Argument.

Each side is allowed only as much time as the Court orders. Counsel is not required to use all the allotted time. On motion filed before the day of argument, the Court may extend the time for argument. The Court may also align the parties for purposes of presenting argument.

59.5. Number of Counsel.

Generally, only one counsel should argue for each side. Except on leave of court, no more than two counsel on each side may argue. Only one counsel may argue in rebuttal.

59.6. Argument by Amicus Curiae.

With leave of court obtained before the argument and with a party's consent, an amicus may share allotted time with that party. Otherwise, counsel for amicus curiae may not argue.

(Adopted by Order eff. Sept. 1, 1997.)

Comment to 1997 change: Former Rules 170, 171, and 172 are merged. Subdivisions 59.2 and 59.3 are new. Other changes are made.

RULE 60. JUDGMENTS IN THE SUPREME COURT.

60.1. Announcement of Judgments.

The Court's judgments will be announced by the clerk.

60.2. Types of Judgment.

The Supreme Court may:

(a) affirm the lower court's judgment in whole or in part;

(b) modify the lower court's judgment and affirm it as modified;

(c) reverse the lower court's judgment in whole or in part and render the judgment that the lower court should have rendered;

(d) reverse the lower court's judgment and remand the case for further proceedings;

(e) vacate the judgments of the lower courts and dismiss the case; or

(f) vacate the lower court's judgment and remand the case for further proceedings in light of changes in the law.

60.3. Remand in the Interest of Justice.

When reversing the court of appeals' judgment, the Supreme Court may, in the interest of justice, remand the case to the trial court even if a rendition of judgment is otherwise appropriate.

60.4. Judgment for Costs.

The Supreme Court's judgment will award to the prevailing party the costs incurred by that party in the Supreme Court. If appropriate, the judgment may also award the prevailing party the costs—including preparation costs for the record—incurred by that party in the court of appeals and in the trial court. But the Court may tax costs otherwise as required by law or for good cause.

60.5. Judgment Against Sureties.

When affirming, modifying, or rendering a judgment against the party who was the appellant in the court of appeals, the Supreme Court must render judgment against the sureties on that party's supersedeas bond, if any, for the performance of the judgment. If the Supreme Court taxes costs against the party who was the appellant in the court of appeals, the Court must render judgment for those costs against the sureties on that party's supersedeas bond, if any.

60.6. Other Orders.

The Supreme Court may make any other appropriate order required by the law and the nature of the case.

(Adopted by Order eff. Sept. 1, 1997.)

Comment to 1997 change: Former Rules 180 and 182(a) are merged. Subdivision 60.1 is from former Rule 181. Paragraphs 60.2(b), (c), and (f) are new but codify current practice. Subdivision 60.6 is new. Other changes are made.

RULE 61. REVERSIBLE ERROR.

61.1. Standard for Reversible Error.

No judgment may be reversed on appeal on the ground that the trial court made an error of law unless the Supreme Court concludes that the error complained of:

(a) probably caused the rendition of an improper judgment; or

(b) probably prevented the petitioner from properly presenting the case to the appellate courts.

61.2. Error Affecting Only Part of the Case.

If the error affects a part, but not all, of the matter in controversy, and that part is separable without unfairness to the parties, the judgment must be reversed and a new trial ordered only as to the part affected by the error. The Court may not order a separate trial solely on unliquidated damages if liability is contested.

61.3. Defects in Procedure.

The Supreme Court will not affirm or reverse a judgment or dismiss a petition for review for formal defects or irregularities in appellate procedure without allowing a reasonable time to correct or amend the defects or irregularities.

61.4. Remediable Error of the Trial Court or Court of Appeals.

(a) Generally. The Supreme Court will not affirm or reverse a judgment or dismiss a petition for review if:

(1) the trial court's or court of appeals' erroneous action or failure or refusal to act prevents the proper presentation of a case to the Supreme Court; and

(2) the trial court or court of appeals can correct its action or failure to act.

(b) Supreme Court Direction if Error Remediable. If the circumstances described in (a) exist, the Supreme Court will direct the trial court or court of appeals to correct the error. The Supreme Court will then proceed as if the error had not occurred.

(Adopted by Order eff. Sept. 1, 1997.)

Comment to 1997 change: Former Rules 184 and 185 are merged. The reversible error standard is amended to omit the reference to an action "reasonably calculated to cause" an improper judgment, but no substantive change is intended. Subdivision 61.3 is amended to delete the reference to defects of "substance."

RULE 62. DAMAGES FOR FRIVOLOUS APPEALS.

If the Supreme Court determines that a direct appeal or a petition for review is frivolous, it may—on motion of any party or on its own initiative, after notice and a reasonable opportunity for response—award to each prevailing party just damages. In determining whether to award damages, the Court must not consider any matter that does not appear in the record, briefs, or other papers filed in the court of appeals or the Supreme Court.

(Adopted by Order eff. Sept. 1, 1997.)

Comment to 1997 change: This is former Rule 182(b). The rule is changed from allowing a sanction when an appeal "filed for delay and without sufficient cause" to allowing a sanction when the appeal is "frivolous." A requirement for notice and an opportunity to respond is included.

RULE 63. OPINIONS; COPY OF OPINION AND JUDGMENT TO INTERESTED PARTIES AND OTHER COURTS.

The Supreme Court will hand down a written opinion in all cases in which it renders a judgment. The clerk will send a copy of the opinion and judgment to the court of appeals clerk, the trial court clerk, the regional administrative judge, and all parties to the appeal.

(Adopted by Order eff. Sept. 1, 1997.)

Comment to 1997 change: This is former Rule 181 with changes.

RULE 64. MOTION FOR REHEARING.

64.1. Time for Filing.

A motion for rehearing may be filed with the Supreme Court clerk within 15 days from the date when the Court renders judgment or makes an order disposing of a petition for review. In exceptional cases, if justice requires, the Court may shorten the time within which the motion may be filed or even deny the right to file it altogether.

64.2. Contents.

The motion must specify the points relied on for the rehearing.

64.3. Response and Decision.

No response to a motion for rehearing need be filed unless the Court so requests. A motion will not be granted unless a response has been filed or requested by the Court. But in exceptional cases, if justice so requires, the Court may deny the right to file a response and act on a motion any time after it is filed.

64.4. Second Motion.

The Court will not consider a second motion for rehearing unless the Court modifies its judgment, vacates its judgment and renders a new judgment, or issues a different opinion.

(Amended by Order Aug. 20, 2008, eff. Sept. 1, 2008.)

Comment to 2008 change: Subdivision 64.4 is amended to reflect the Court's practice of considering a second motion for rehearing after modifying its judgment or opinion in response to a prior motion for rehearing. When the Court modifies its opinion without modifying its judgment, the Court will ordinarily deny a second motion for rehearing unless the new opinion is substantially different from the original opinion.

64.5. Extensions of Time.

The Court may extend the time to file a motion for rehearing in the Supreme Court, if a motion complying with Rule 10.5(b) is filed with the Court no later than 15 days after the last date for filing a motion for rehearing.

64.6. Repealed by Order Nov. 13, 2012, eff. Dec. 1, 2012.

Comment to 1997 change: This is former Rule 190. The service and notice provisions of former subdivisions (b) and (c) are deleted. *See* Rule 9.5. Other changes are made.

RULE 65. ENFORCEMENT OF JUDGMENT AFTER MANDATE.

65.1. Statement of Costs.

The Supreme Court clerk will prepare, and send to the clerk to whom the mandate is directed, a statement of costs showing:

(a) the costs that were incurred in the Supreme Court, with a notation of those items that have been paid and those that are owing; and

(b) the party or parties against whom costs have been adjudged.

65.2. Enforcement of Judgment.

If the Supreme Court renders judgment, the trial court need not make any further order. Upon receiving the Supreme Court's mandate, the trial court clerk must proceed to enforce the judgment of the Supreme Court's as in any other case. Appellate court costs must be included with the trial court costs in any process to enforce the judgment. If all or part of the costs are collected, the trial court clerk must immediately remit to the appellate court clerk any amount due to that clerk.

(Adopted by Order eff. Sept. 1, 1997.)

Comment to 1997 change: Subdivision 65.1 is new. Subdivision 65.2 is from former Rule 183.

SECTION FIVE.
PROCEEDINGS IN THE COURT OF CRIMINAL APPEALS

RULE 66. DISCRETIONARY REVIEW IN GENERAL.

66.1. With or Without Petition.

The Court of Criminal Appeals may review a court of appeals' decision in a criminal case on its own initiative under Rule 67 or on the petition of a party under Rule 68.

66.2. Not a Matter of Right.

Discretionary review by the Court of Criminal Appeals is not a matter of right, but of the Court's discretion.

66.3. Reasons for Granting Review.

While neither controlling nor fully measuring the Court of Criminal Appeals' discretion, the following will be considered by the Court in deciding whether to grant discretionary review:

(a) whether a court of appeals' decision conflicts with another court of appeals' decision on the same issue;

(b) whether a court of appeals has decided an important question of state or federal law that has not been, but should be, settled by the Court of Criminal Appeals;

(c) whether a court of appeals has decided an important question of state or federal law in a way that conflicts with the applicable decisions of the Court of Criminal Appeals or the Supreme Court of the United States;

(d) whether a court of appeals has declared a statute, rule, regulation, or ordinance unconstitutional, or appears to have misconstrued a statute, rule, regulation, or ordinance;

(e) whether the justices of a court of appeals have disagreed on a material question of law necessary to the court's decision; and

(f) whether a court of appeals has so far departed from the accepted and usual course of judicial proceedings, or so far sanctioned such a departure by a lower court, as to call for an exercise of the Court of Criminal Appeals' power of supervision.

66.4. Documents to Aid Decision.

(a) Acquiring Documents. The Court of Criminal Appeals—or any judge of the Court—may order the court of appeals clerk to promptly send the following items to the Court in order to aid it in deciding whether to grant discretionary review:

(1) the appellate record;

(2) a copy of the opinions of the court of appeals;

(3) a copy of the motions filed in the court of appeals; and

(4) certified copies of any judgment or order of the court of appeals.

(b) Return of Documents. If discretionary review is not granted, the clerk of the Court of Criminal Appeals will return the appellate record to the court of appeals clerk.

(Adopted by Order eff. Sept. 1, 1997.)

Comment to 1997 change: This is former Rule 200. The former rule's reference to motions for rehearing now appears in Rule 49.9. The rule is otherwise amended without substantive change.

RULE 67. DISCRETIONARY REVIEW WITHOUT PETITION.

67.1. Four Judges' Vote.

By a vote of at least four judges, the Court of Criminal Appeals may grant review of a court of appeals' decision in a criminal case at any time before the mandate of the court of appeals issues. An order granting review will be filed with the clerk of the Court of Criminal Appeals, who must send a copy to the court of appeals clerk.

(Amended by Order Oct. 16, 2000 eff. Jan. 1, 2003.)

Comment to 2000 change: Language which was in the catchline of former Rule 201 has been deleted from Rule 67.1, to restore the substance of the rule, and to remove any implication that the court may not grant review on its own motion when a petition for discretionary review has been filed.

67.2. Order Staying Mandate.

To provide enough time for the Court of Criminal Appeals to decide whether to grant discretionary review under 67.1, the Court—or any judge of the Court—may file with the clerk of the court of appeals an order staying the court of appeals' mandate. The order must be signed by a judge of the Court of Criminal Appeals. The clerk of the Court of Criminal Appeals must immediately send a copy of the order to the court of appeals clerk.

67.3. Time to Issue Mandate Extended.

Unless otherwise limited in the order itself, an order staying the court of appeals' mandate under 67.2 will extend for an additional 45 days the time before issuance of the court of appeals' mandate. An order granting review prevents the issuance of the court of appeals' mandate pending the further order of the Court of Criminal Appeals. If four judges do not agree to grant review within that time the court of appeals clerk must issue the mandate.

(Adopted by Order eff. Sept. 1, 1997.)

Comment to 1997 change: This is former Rule 201. The rule is amended without substantive change.

RULE 68. DISCRETIONARY REVIEW WITH PETITION.

68.1. Generally.

On petition by any party, the Court of Criminal Appeals may review a court of appeals' decision in a criminal case.

68.2. Time to File Petition.

(a) First Petition. The petition must be filed within 30 days after either the day the court of appeals' judgment was rendered or the day the last timely motion for rehearing was overruled by the court of appeals.

(b) Subsequent Petition. Even if the time specified in (a) has expired, a party who otherwise may file a petition may do so within 10 days after the timely filing of another party's petition.

(c) Extension of Time. The Court of Criminal Appeals may extend the time to file a petition for discretionary review if a party files a motion complying with Rule 10.5(b) no later than 15 days after the last day for filing the petition. The Court of

Criminal Appeals may extend the time to file a response or reply if a party files a motion complying with Rule 10.5(b) either before or after the response or reply is due.

68.3. Where to File Petition.

The petition and all copies of the petition must be filed with the clerk of the court of appeals, but if the State's Prosecuting Attorney files a petition, the State's Prosecuting Attorney may file the copies of the petition—but not the original—with the clerk of the Court of Criminal Appeals instead of with the court of appeals clerk.

68.4. Contents of Petition.

A petition for discretionary review must be as brief as possible. It must be addressed to the "Court of Criminal Appeals of Texas" and must state the name of the party or parties applying for review. The petition must contain the following items:

(a) Identity of Judge, Parties, and Counsel. The petition must list the trial court judge, all parties to the judgment or order appealed from, and the names and addresses of all trial and appellate counsel.

(b) Table of Contents. The petition must include a table of contents with references to the pages of the petition. The table of contents must indicate the subject matter of each ground or question presented for review.

(c) Index of Authorities. The petition must include an index of authorities arranged alphabetically and indicating the pages of the petition where the authorities are cited.

(d Statement Regarding Oral Argument. The petition must include a short statement of why oral argument would be helpful, or a statement that oral argument is waived. If a reply or cross-petition is filed, it likewise must include a statement of why oral argument should or should not be heard.

(e) Statement of the Case. The petition must state briefly the nature of the case. This statement should seldom exceed half a page. The details of the case should be reserved and stated with the pertinent grounds or questions.

(f) Statement of Procedural History. The petition must state:

(1) the date any opinion of the court of appeals was handed down, or the date of any order of the court of appeals disposing of the case without an opinion;

(2) the date any motion for rehearing was filed (or a statement that none was filed); and

(3) the date the motion for rehearing was overruled or otherwise disposed of.

(g) Grounds for Review. The petition must state briefly, without argument, the grounds on which the petition is based. The grounds must be separately numbered. If the petitioner has access to the record, the petitioner must (after each ground) refer to the page of the record where the matter complained of is found. Instead of listing grounds for review, the petition may contain the questions presented for review, expressed in the terms and circumstances of the case but without unnecessary detail. The statement of questions should be short and concise, not argumentative or repetitious.

(h) Argument. The petition must contain a direct and concise argument, with supporting authorities, amplifying the reasons for granting review. *See* Rule 66.3. The court of appeals' opinions will be considered with the petition, and statements in those opinions need not be repeated if counsel accepts them as correct.

(i) Prayer for Relief. The petition must state clearly the nature of the relief sought.

(j) Appendix. The petition must contain a copy of any opinion of the court of appeals.

(Amended by Order Dec. 23, 2002, eff. Jan. 1, 2003; Dec. 13, 2013, eff. Jan. 1, 2014.)

Comment to 2002 change: The original catchline of subdivision 68.4(g) was "Reasons for Review," which caused confusion because of its similarity to the catch line in subdivision 66.3 ("Reasons for Granting Review"). It is changed to "Argument."

68.5. Repealed by Order Nov. 13, 2012, eff. Dec. 1, 2012.

68.6. Nonconforming Petition.

The Court may strike, order redrawn, or summarily refuse a petition for discretionary review that is unnecessarily lengthy or that does not conform to these rules.

68.7. Court of Appeals Clerk's Duties.

(a) On Filing of the Petition. Upon receiving the petition, the court of appeals clerk must file the original petition and note the filing on the docket.

(b) Reply. The opposing party has 30 days after the timely filing of the petition in the court of appeals to file a reply to the petition with the clerk of the court of appeals. Upon receiving a reply to the petition, the clerk for the court of appeals must file the reply and note the filing on the docket.

(c) Sending Petition and Reply to Court of Criminal Appeals. Unless a petition for discretionary review is dismissed under Rule 50, the clerk of the court of appeals must, within 60 days after the petition is filed, send to the clerk of the Court of Criminal Appeals the petition and any copies furnished by counsel, the reply, if any, and any copies furnished by counsel, together with the record, copies of the motions filed in the case, and copies of any judgments, opinions, and orders of the court of appeals. The clerk need not forward any nondocumentary exhibits unless ordered to do so by the Court of Criminal Appeals.

(Amended by Order March 10, 2008, eff. Sept. 1, 2008; Order Aug. 20, 2008, eff. Sept. 1, 2008.)

68.8. Court of Criminal Appeals Clerk's Duties on Receipt of Petition.

The clerk of the Court of Criminal Appeals will receive a petition for discretionary review, file the petition and the accompanying record from the court of appeals, note the filing of the petition and record on the docket, and notify the parties by U.S. Mail of the filing. The Court may dispense with notice and grant or refuse the petition immediately upon its filing.

68.9. Amendment.

The petition or a reply may be amended or supplemented within 30 days after the original petition was filed in the court of appeals or at any time when justice requires. The record may be amended in the Court of Criminal Appeals under the same circumstances and in the same manner as in the court of appeals.

68.10. Service on State Prosecuting Attorney.

In addition to the service required by Rule 9.5, service of the petition, the reply, and any amendment or supplementation of a petition or reply must be made on the State Prosecuting Attorney, P.O. Box 12405, Austin, Texas 78711.

(Adopted by Order eff. Sept. 1, 1997.)

Comment to 1997 change: This is former Rule 202. Subdivisions (k) and (l) of the former rule have been relocated to Rule 69. The new rule limits the length of a petition and reply. The time for amendment of a petition or reply is increased to conform with the amendment in Rule 50. The rule is otherwise amended without substantive change.

RULE 69. ACTION OF COURT ON PETITION FOR DISCRETIONARY REVIEW AND AFTER GRANTING REVIEW.

69.1. Granting or Refusal.

If four judges do not vote to grant a petition for discretionary review, the Court will enter a docket notation that the petition is refused. If four judges vote to grant a petition, the Court will enter a docket notation that discretionary review is granted.

69.2. Setting Case for Submission.

If discretionary review is granted, either on the petition of a party or by the Court on its own initiative, the case will be set for submission.

69.3. Improvident Grant of Review.

If, after granting discretionary review, five judges are of the opinion that discretionary review should not have been granted, the case will be dismissed.

69.4. Clerk's Duties.

(a) On Refusal or Dismissal. When the Court refuses or dismisses a petition, the clerk will send to the parties and the State Prosecuting Attorney a notice informing them that the petition was refused or dismissed. The clerk will retain the petition and all other items filed in the case for at least 15 days from the date of the refusal or dismissal. At the end of that time, if no motion for rehearing has been timely filed, or upon the overruling or dismissal of such a motion, the clerk will send to the court of appeals clerk a certified copy of the order refusing or dismissing the petition (as well as any order overruling a motion for rehearing). The clerk of the Court of Criminal Appeals will return the appellate record to the court of appeals clerk but will retain the petition, and other documents filed in the Court of Criminal Appeals.

(b) On Granting Review. If the Court grants discretionary review, the clerk will send to the parties and the State Prosecuting Attorney a notice informing them that discretionary review was granted.

(Adopted by Order eff. Sept. 1, 1997.)

Comment to 1997 change: This is former subdivisions (k) and (l) of Rule 202. Internal procedures of the Court are deleted. Provisions are added in 69.4(a) and (b) for the clerk to send notice of the granting, refusal, or dismissal of a petition for discretionary review. Other nonsubstantive changes are made.

RULE 70. BRIEF ON THE MERITS.

70.1. Initial Brief.

If review is granted, the petitioner—or, if there was no petition, the party who lost in the court of appeals—must file a brief within 30 days after review is granted.

70.2. Respondent's Brief.

The opposing party must file a brief within 30 days after the petitioner's brief is filed.

(Amended by Order Dec. 13, 2013, eff. Jan. 1, 2014.)

70.3. Brief Contents and Form.

Briefs must comply with the requirements of Rules 9 and 38, except that they need not contain the appendix (Rule 38.1(k)). Copies must be served as required by Rule 68.11.

(Amended by Order March 10, 2008, eff. Sept. 1, 2008; Order Aug. 20, 2008, eff. Sept. 1, 2008; Order Aug. 10, 2012, eff. Dec. 1, 2012; Order Nov. 13, 2012, eff. Dec. 1, 2012.)

70.4. Other Briefs.

The Court of Criminal Appeals may direct that a party file a brief, or an additional brief, in a particular case. Additionally, upon motion by a party the Court may permit the filing of additional briefs.

(Adopted by Order eff. Sept. 1, 1997. Amended by Order Dec. 13, 2013, eff. Jan. 1, 2014.)

Comment to 1997 change: This is former Rule 203. The rule is amended without substantive change.

RULE 71. DIRECT APPEALS.

71.1. Direct Appeal.

Cases in which the death penalty has been assessed under Code of Criminal Procedure article 37.071, and cases in which bail has been denied in non-capital cases under Article I, Section 11a of the Constitution, are appealed directly to the Court of Criminal Appeals.

(Amended by Order Dec. 23, 2002 eff. Jan. 1, 2003.)

71.2. Record.

The appellate record should be prepared and filed in accordance with Rules 31, 32, 34, 35 and 37, except that the record must be filed in the Court of Criminal Appeals. After disposition of the appeal, the Court may discard copies of juror information cards or other portions of the clerk's record that are not relevant to an issue on appeal.

(Amended by Order Dec. 23, 2002 eff. Jan. 1, 2003.)

71.3. Briefs.

Briefs in a direct appeal should be prepared and filed in accordance with Rule 38, except that the brief need not contain an appendix (Rule 38.1(k)). All briefs must be filed in the Court of Criminal Appeals. The brief must include a short statement of why oral argument would be helpful, or a statement that oral argument is waived.

(Amended by Order Dec. 23, 2002, eff. Jan. 1, 2003; Order March 10, 2008, eff. Sept. 1, 2008; Order Aug. 20, 2008, eff. Sept. 1, 2008; Order Aug. 10, 2012, eff. Dec. 1, 2012; Order Nov. 13, 2012, eff. Dec. 1, 2012.)

Comment to 2002 change: A requirement that briefs include a statement regarding oral argument is added.

71.4. Additional briefs.

Upon motion by a party the Court may permit the filing of additional briefs other than those provided for in Rule 38.

(Adopted by Order Dec. 13, 2013, eff. Jan. 1, 2014.)

RULE 72. EXTRAORDINARY MATTERS.

72.1. Leave to File.

A motion for leave to file must accompany an original petition for writ of habeas corpus, mandamus, procedendo, prohibition, certiorari, or other extraordinary writ, or any other motion not otherwise provided for in these rules.

72.2. Disposition.

If five judges tentatively believe that the case should be filed and set for submission, the motion for leave will be granted and the case will then be handled and disposed of in accordance with Rule 52.7. If the motion for leave is denied, no motions for rehearing or reconsideration will be entertained. But the Court may, on its own initiative, reconsider a denial of a motion for leave.

(Adopted by Order eff. Sept. 1, 1997.)

Comment to 1997 change: This is former Rule 211. The rule is amended to include all the Court's jurisdiction of extraordinary matters. Internal procedures of the Court are deleted. Other nonsubstantive changes are made.

RULE 73. POSTCONVICTION APPLICATIONS FOR WRITS OF HABEAS CORPUS.

73.1. Form for Application Filed Under Article 11.07 of the Code of Criminal Procedure.

(a) Prescribed Form. An application filed under Article 11.07 must be on the form prescribed by the Court of Criminal Appeals.

(b) Availability of Form. The district clerk of the county of conviction shall make the forms available to applicants on request, without charge.

(c) Contents. The applicant or petitioner must provide all information required by the form. The form must include all grounds for relief and set forth in summary fashion the facts supporting each ground. Any ground not raised on the form will not be considered. Legal citations and arguments may be made in a separate memorandum. The form must be computer-generated, typewritten, or legibly handwritten.

(d) Length. Each ground for relief and supporting facts raised on the form shall not exceed the two pages provided for each ground in the form. The applicant or petitioner may file a separate memorandum. This memorandum shall comply with these rules and shall not exceed 15,000 words if computer-generated or 50 pages if not. If the total number of pages, including those in the original and any additional memoranda, exceed the word or page limits, an application may be dismissed unless the convicting court for good cause shown grants leave to exceed the prescribed limits. The prescribed limits do not include appendices, exhibits, cover page, table of contents, table of authorities, and certificate of compliance.

(e) Typeface. A computer-generated memorandum must be printed in a conventional typeface no smaller than 14-point except for footnotes, which must be no smaller than 12-point. A typewritten document must be printed in standard 10-character-per-inch (cpi) monospaced typeface.

(f) Certificate of Compliance. A computer-generated memorandum, including any additional memoranda, must include a certificate by the applicant or petitioner stating the number of words in the document. The person certifying may rely on the word count of the computer program used to prepare the document.

(g) Verification. The application must be verified by either:

(1) oath made before a notary public or other officer authorized to administer oaths; or

(2) if the person making the application is an inmate in the Institutional Division of the Department of Criminal Justice or in a county jail, an unsworn declaration in substantially the form required in Civil Practices and Remedies Code chapter 132.

(Adopted by Order Oct. 16, 2000, eff. Jan. 1, 2001. Amended by Order Dec. 13, 2013, eff. Jan. 1, 2014.)

73.2. Noncompliant Applications.

The Court of Criminal Appeals may dismiss an application that does not comply with these rules.

(Adopted by Order Oct. 16, 2000, eff. Jan. 1, 2001. Amended by Order Dec. 13, 2013, eff. Jan. 1, 2014.)

73.3. State's Response.

Any response by the State must comply with length, typeface, and certificate of compliance requirements set out in rule 73.1 (d),(e) and (f).

(Adopted by Order Dec. 13, 2013, eff. Jan. 1, 2014.)

73.4. Filing and Transmission of Habeas Record.

(a) The district clerk of the county of conviction shall accept and file all Code of Criminal Procedure article 11.07 applications.

(b) In addition to the duties set out in Article 11.07, the clerk shall do the following:

(1) If the convicting court enters an order designating issues, the clerk shall immediately transmit to the Court of Criminal Appeals a copy of that order and proof of the date the district attorney received the habeas application.

(2) When any pleadings, objections, motions, affidavits, exhibits, proposed or entered findings of fact and conclusions of law, or other orders are filed or made a part of the record, the district clerk shall immediately send a copy to all parties in the case. A party has ten days from the date he receives the trial court's findings of facts and conclusions of law to file objections, but the trial court may, nevertheless, order the district clerk to transmit the record to the Court of Criminal Appeals before the expiration of the ten days.

(3) When a district clerk transmits the record in a postconviction application for a writ of habeas corpus under Code of Criminal Procedure articles 11.07 or 11.071, the district clerk must prepare and transmit a summary sheet that includes the following information:

(A) the convicting court's name and county, and the name of the judge who tried the case;

(B) the applicant's name, the offense, the plea, the cause number, the sentence, and the date of sentence, as shown in the judgment of conviction;

(C) the cause number of any appeal from the conviction and the citation to any published report;

(D) whether a hearing was held on the application, whether findings of fact were made, any recommendation of the convicting court, and the name of the judge who presided over the application.;

(E) the name of counsel if applicant is represented.

The Court of Criminal Appeals may by order adopt a form of summary sheet that the district clerks must use.

(4) The district clerk shall also include in the record transmitted to the Court of Criminal Appeals, among any other pertinent papers or supplements, the indictment or information, any plea papers, the court's docket sheet, the court's charge and the jury's verdict, any proposed findings of fact and conclusions of law, the court's findings of fact and conclusions of law, any objections to the court's findings of fact and conclusions of law filed by either party, and the transcript of any hearings held.

(5) On the 181st day from the date of receipt of the application by the State of a postconviction application for writ of habeas corpus under Article 11.07, the district clerk shall forward the writ record to this Court unless the district court has received an extension of time from the Court of Criminal Appeals pursuant to Rule 73.5.

(Adopted by Order eff. Sept. 1, 1997. Amended by Order Nov. 8, 2000, eff. Jan. 1, 2001; Dec. 13, 2013, eff. Jan. 1, 2014; Tex. Sup. Ct. Misc. Docket No. 15-006 Dec. 7, 2015, eff. Jan. 1, 2016; Tex. Sup. Ct. Misc. Docket No. 16-9012 Feb. 29, 2016, eff. Jan. 1, 2016.)

73.5. Time Frame for Resolution of Claims Raised in Application.

Within 180 days from the date of receipt of the application by the State, the convicting court shall resolve any issues that the court has timely designated for resolution. Any motion for extension of time must be filed in the Court of Criminal Appeals before the expiration of the 180-day period.

(Adopted by Order Dec. 13, 2013, eff. Jan. 1, 2014.)

73.6. Action on Application.

The Court may deny relief based upon its own review of the application or may issue such other instructions or orders as may be appropriate.

(Adopted by Order eff. Sept. 1, 1997. Amended by Order Nov. 8, 2000, eff. Jan. 1, 2001.)

Notes and Comments

Comment to 1997 change: This is former Rule 4 of the Appendix for Criminal Cases. The rule is amended without substantive change.

Comment to 2000 change: Rules 73.1 and 73.2 are added, and a form is added in an appendix. [Appendix is omitted.]

RULE 74. REVIEW OF CERTIFIED STATE CRIMINAL-LAW QUESTIONS.

74.1. Certification.

The Court of Criminal Appeals may answer questions of Texas criminal law certified to it by any federal appellate court if the certifying court is presented with determinative questions of Texas criminal law having no controlling Court of Criminal Appeals precedent. The Court may decline to answer the questions certified to it.

74.2. Contents of the Certification Order.

An order from the certifying court must set forth:

(a) the questions of law to be answered; and

(b) a stipulated statement of all facts relevant to the questions certified, showing fully the nature of the controversy in which the questions arose.

74.3. Transmission of Certification Order.

The clerk of the certifying court must send to the clerk of the Court of Criminal Appeals the following:

(a) the certification order under the certifying court's official seal;

(b) a list of the names of each party to the pending case, giving the address and telephone number, if known, of any party not represented by counsel; and

(c) a list of the names and addresses of counsel for each party.

74.4. Transmission of Record.

The certifying court should not send to the Court of Criminal Appeals the record in the pending case with the certification order. The Court of Criminal Appeals may later require the original or copies of all or part of the record before the certifying court to be filed with the Court of Criminal Appeals clerk.

74.5. Notice.

If the Court of Criminal Appeals agrees to answer the questions certified to it, the Court will notify all parties and the certifying court. The Court of Criminal Appeals clerk must also send a notice to the Attorney General of Texas if:

(a) the constitutionality of a Texas statute is the subject of a certified question that the Court of Criminal Appeals has agreed to answer; and

(b) the State of Texas or an officer, agency, or employee of the State is not a party to the proceeding in the certifying court.

74.6. Briefs and Oral Argument.

(a) Briefs. The appealing party in the certifying court must file a brief with the clerk of the Court of Criminal Appeals within 30 days after the date of the notice. Opposing parties must file an answering brief within 15 days of receiving the opening brief. Briefs must comply with Rule 38 to the extent that its provisions apply.

(b) Oral Argument. Oral argument may be granted either on a party's request or on the Court's own initiative. Argument is governed by Rule 39.

74.7. Intervention by the State.

If the constitutionality of a Texas statute is the subject of a certified question that the Court of Criminal Appeals has agreed to answer, the State of Texas may intervene at any reasonable time for briefing and oral argument (if argument is allowed) on the question of constitutionality.

74.8. Opinion on Certified Question.

If the Court of Criminal Appeals has agreed to answer a certified question, it will hand down an opinion as in any other case.

74.9. Motion for Rehearing.

Any party may file a motion for rehearing within 15 days after the opinion is handed down. The motion must clearly state the points relied on for the rehearing. No reply to a motion for rehearing need be filed unless the Court so requests. The Court will not grant a motion for rehearing unless a response has been filed or requested.

74.10. Answering Certified Questions.

After all motions for rehearing have been overruled, the clerk of the Court of Criminal Appeals must send to the certifying court the written opinion on the certified questions. The opinion must be under the Court of Criminal Appeals' seal.

(Adopted by Order eff. Sept. 1, 1997.)

Comment to 1997 change: This is former Rule 214. The rule is amended without substantive change.

RULE 75. NOTIFICATION; ORAL ARGUMENT.

75.1. Notification of Argument or Submission.

Oral argument will be permitted only in cases designated by the Court of Criminal Appeals. If the Court permits argument in a case, the clerk will notify the parties of the date set for argument. If a case will be submitted without argument, the clerk will notify the parties of the date of submission. The clerk must use all reasonable diligence to notify counsel of settings, but counsel's failure to receive notice will not necessarily prevent argument or submission of the case on the day it is set.

75.2. Request for Argument.

If a case is not designated for oral argument but counsel desires oral argument, counsel may—within 30 days of the date of the clerk's notice—petition the Court to allow oral argument. This petition must contain specific reasons why oral argument is desired.

75.3. Oral Argument.

Unless extended in a special case, the total maximum time for oral argument is 20 minutes per side. Counsel for the appellant or petitioner is entitled to open and conclude the argument. Counsel should not read at length from the briefs, records, or authorities. Counsel may orally correct a brief, but multiple additional citations should not be given orally; instead, these citations should be filed in writing with the clerk.

(Adopted by Order eff. Sept. 1, 1997.)

Comment to 1997 change: This is former Rule 220. The rule is amended without substantive change.

RULE 76. SUBMISSIONS EN BANC.

The Court will sit en banc to consider the following types of cases:

(a) direct appeals;
(b) cases of discretionary review;
(c) cases in which leave to file was granted under Rule 72;
(d) cases that were docketed under Code of Criminal Procedure articles 11.07 or 11.071;
(e) certified questions; and
(f) rehearings under Rule 79.

(Adopted by Order eff. Sept. 1, 1997.)

Comment to 1997 change: This is former Rule 222. The rule is expanded to include other kinds of cases. Internal procedures of the Court are deleted. Other nonsubstantive changes are made.

RULE 77. OPINIONS.

77.1. Generally.

In each case that is argued or submitted without argument to the Court of Criminal Appeals, the Court will hand down a written opinion setting forth the reasons for its decision and any germane precedent. Any judge may file an opinion dissenting from or concurring in the Court's judgment.

77.2. Signing; Publication.

A majority of the judges will determine whether an opinion will be signed by a judge or issued per curiam, and whether the opinion (or a portion of the opinion) will be published.

77.3. Unpublished Opinions.

Unpublished opinions have no precedential value and must not be cited as authority by counsel or by a court.

77.4. Copies.

On the date when an opinion is handed down or an order rendered, the clerk of the Court of Criminal Appeals must mail copies of the opinion or order to:

(a) the parties;
(b) the State Prosecuting Attorney;
(c) the trial court clerk; and
(d) if the case is of discretionary review, the court of appeals clerk.

(Adopted by Order eff. Sept. 1, 1997.)

Comment to 1997 change: This is former Rule 223. The rule is amended without substantive change.

RULE 78. JUDGMENTS IN THE COURT OF CRIMINAL APPEALS.

78.1. Types of Judgment.

The Court of Criminal Appeals may:

(a) affirm the lower court's judgment in whole or in part;

(b) modify the lower court's judgment and affirm it as modified;

(c) reverse the court's judgment in whole or in part and render the judgment that the lower court should have rendered;

(d) reverse the lower court's judgment and remand the case for further proceedings;

(e) vacate the judgments of the lower courts and dismiss the case;

(f) vacate the lower court's judgment and remand the case for further proceedings in light of changes in the law; or

(g) dismiss the appeal.

78.2. Remand in the Interests of Justice.

When reversing the court of appeals' judgment, the Court of Criminal Appeals may, in the interests of justice, remand the case to the trial court even if a rendition of judgment is otherwise appropriate.

78.3. Other Orders.

The Court of Criminal Appeals may make any other appropriate order required by the law and the nature of the case.

(Adopted by Order eff. Sept. 1, 1997.)

Comment to 1997 change: The rule is new.

RULE 79. REHEARINGS.

79.1. Motion for Rehearing.

A motion for rehearing may be filed with the Court of Criminal Appeals clerk within 15 days from the date of the judgment or order. In exceptional cases, if justice requires, the Court may shorten the time within which the motion may be filed or even deny the right to file it altogether.

79.2. Contents.

(a) The motion must briefly and distinctly state the grounds and arguments relied on for rehearing.

(b) A motion for rehearing an order that grants discretionary review may not be filed.

(c) A motion for rehearing an order that refuses a petition for discretionary review may be grounded only on substantial intervening circumstances or on other significant circumstances which are specified in the motion. Counsel must certify that the motion is so grounded and that the motion is made in good faith and not for delay.

(d) A motion for rehearing an order that denies habeas corpus relief or dismisses a habeas corpus application under Code of Criminal Procedure, articles 11.07 or 11.071, may not be filed. The Court may on its own initiative reconsider the case.

(Amended by Tex. Sup. Ct. Misc. Docket No. 15-006 Dec. 7, 2015, eff. Jan. 1, 2016; Tex. Sup. Ct. Misc. Docket No. 16-9012 Feb. 29, 2016, eff. Jan. 1, 2016.)

79.3. Amendments.

A motion for rehearing may be amended anytime before the period allowed for filing the motion expires, and with leave of the court, anytime before the Court decides the motion.

79.4. Decision.

If the Court grants rehearing, the case will be set for submission. Oral argument may, but normally will not, be permitted.

79.5. Further Motion for Rehearing.

The Court will not consider a second motion for rehearing after rehearing is denied. If rehearing is granted and the Court delivers an opinion on rehearing, a party may file a further motion for rehearing.

79.6. Extension of Time.

The Court may extend the time for filing a motion or a further motion for rehearing if a party files a motion complying with Rule 10.5(b) within the time for filing a motion or further motion for rehearing.

79.7. Service.

The requirements of Rule 68.11 apply.

(Adopted by Order eff. Sept. 1, 1997.)

Comment to 1997 change: This is former Rule 230, and the portion of former Rule 213 that prohibited motions for rehearing. The Court may now permit oral argument after granting rehearing, although it is disfavored. A further motion for rehearing may now be filed by any party, rather than only the losing party. Other nonsubstantive changes are made.

TABLE OF CASES

4M Linen & Uniform Supply Co. v. W.P. Ballard & Co., Inc. 25

-A-

Acevedo v. Commission for Lawyer Discipline 278
Acker v. Denton Publishing Company 286
Akers v. Simpson 404
Alcatel, USA, Inc. f/k/a DSC Communications, Inc. 452
Alexander v. Hagedorn 174
Alexander v. Lynda's Boutique 100
Allison v. Arkansas Louisiana Gas Co. 403
Allstate Indemnity Company v. Forth 14
Aluminum Co. of America v. Bullock 487
Alvarado v. Farah Mfg Co. 483
American Home Products Corporation v. Clark 322
Amigo Helicopters, Inc. v. Jones 58
Andel v. Eastman Kodak Company 78
Ashley v. Hawkins 258
Attorney General v. Sailer 76
Axelson v. McIlhany 460

-B-

Baker v. Goldsmith 186
Bailey v. Cherokee County Appraisal District 59
Bay Area Healthcare Group, LTD. v. McShane 18
Baylor Medical Center at Garland, In re 134
Bennett, In re 103
Braden v. Downey 434
Bridges v. Richardson 22
Brookshire Grocery Company, In re 138
Browning v. Prostok 206
Bryant, Ex parte 58
Bushell v. Dean 20

-C-

C.D. Morse, In re 437
Caldwell v. Barnes 188
Campus Investments, Inc. v. Cullever 270
Carpenter v. Cimarron Hydrocarbons Corporation 160
Carroll v. Carroll 65
Chapin & Chapin v. Texas Sand & Gravel Co. 377
Christus Spohn Hospital Kleberg, In re 475
Cire v. Cummings 494
Clayton v. Hurt 39
Clayton v. MONY Life Insurance Co. of America 406
Coastal Liquids Transportation, L.P. v. Harris County Appraisal District 387
Comet Aluminum Co. v. Dibrell 144
Conner, In re 94
Cooper v. Texas Gulf Indus. 389
Craddock v. Sunshine Bus Lines 152

Crawford v. McDonald 201
Crown Central Petroleum Corporation v. Garcia 452

-D-

De Ayala v. Mackie 121
Deen v. Kirk 132
Del Valle Indep. Sch. Dist. v. Lopez 118
Dolgencorp of Texas, Inc. v. Lerma 161
Donovan v. City of Dallas 80
Dubai Petroleum Company v. Kazi 42

-E-

E.A., et al., In the Interest of 256
E.R., In the Interest of 272
Edwards Feed Mill v. Johnson 334
Escobar v. Escobar 146

-F-

Faulkner v. Culver 136
Fidelity and Guaranty Insurance Company v. Drewery Construction Company, Inc. 154
Flour Bluff Independent School District v. Bass 402
Flynt v. Garcia 68
Ford Motor Company, In re 430
Ford Motor Company v. Garcia 394
Ford Motor Company v. Sheldon 416
Fruehauf Corp. v. Carrillo 134

-G-

Garza v. Garcia 139, 327
Gonzalez v. Reliant Energy, Inc. 302
Greathouse v. Charter Nat'l Bank 372
Greenhalgh v. Service Lloyds Insurance Company 374

-H-

Hanks v. Rosser 180
Harris County v. Sykes 80
Hassell Constr. Co., Inc. v. Stature Commercial Co., Inc. 369
Higginbotham v. General Life & Accident In. Co. 252
Holt Atherton Indus. v. Heine 86
Humphreys v. Caldwell 474
Hyundai Motor Co. v. Alvarado 102

-J-

Jamar v. Patterson 138
Jenkins v. Northwestern Pipe & Supply Co 344
John v. Marshall Health Services, Inc. 130
John DOE a/k/a "Trooper", In re 457
Jud v. City of San Antonio 51

-K-

K.M.L., a Child, In the Interest of 246
K Mart Corporation v. Sanderson 428
Kawasaki Steel Corporation v. Middleton 244

-L-

L.M. Healthcare, Inc. v. Childs 140
Lane Bank Equipment Co. v. Smith Southern Equipment, Inc. 148
Levit v. Adams 147
Lovito-Nelson, In re 137
Low v. Henry 351
Lunsford v. Morris 426

-M-

Mackie v. McKenzie 142
Mapco, Inc. v. Carter 16
Martin v. Amerman 384
Mayhew v. Caprito 214
McCamey v. Kinnear 362
McCauley v. Consolidated Underwriters 5
McCraw v. Maris 34
McEwen v. Harrison 165
McKanna v. Edgar 240
Mentis v. Barnard 36
Missouri Pacific Railroad Company, In re 291
Moki Mac River Expeditions v. Drugg 227
Morrow v. Corbin 45
Moulton v. Alamo Ambulance Serv. 365

-N-

National Tank Co. v. Brotherton 468
National Union Fire Ins. Co. v. Valdez 464
North East Independent School District v. Aldridge 125

-O-

Occidental Chemical Corporation v. Banales 498

-P-

Padilla v. LaFrance 107
Palmer v. Coble Wall Trust Co. 61
Paradigm Oil, Inc. v. Retamco Operating, Inc. 478
Paramount Pipe & Supply Co. v. Muhr 85
Peek v. Equipment Serv. Co. of San Antonio 69
Peralta v. Heights Medical Ctr. 236
Phillips v. Phillips 371
Pirtle v. Gregory 9
Pleasant Homes v. Allied Bank of Dallas 253
PNS Stores, Inc. v. Rivera 191
Primate Constr. v. Silver 254
Provident Tradesmens Bank & Trust Co. v. Patterson 388
Prudential Insurance Co. of America, In re The 2

-R-

Ramirez v. Collier, Shannon, Scott, PLLC 326
Ray Malooly Trust, The v. Juhl 367
Reliance Steel & Aluminum Co. v. Sevcik 30
Rizk v. Financial Guardian Ins. Agency 382
Ross v. National Center for the Employment of the Disabled 196
Ruthart v. First State Bank 393

-S-

Schlichting v. Lehman Brothers Bank FSB 66
Schlobohm v. Schapiro 217
Scott v. McIlhany 458
Sherrod v. Bailey 346
Shipman, In re Marion 444
Smith v. Babcock & Wilcox Construction Company, Inc. 99
Smith v. Clary Corporation 78
Smith v. Commercial Equip. Leasing Co. 252
Snyder v. Pitts 279
Sosa v. Central Power & Light 380
Spir Star AG v. Kimich 221
State Bar of Texas v. Kilpatrick 378
State Employees Workers' Compensation v. Evans 157
State Farm Fire & Casualty Co. v. Costley 261
State Farm Lloyds, In re 449
Stelly v. Papania 438
Stewart v. USA Custom Paint & Body Shop 209
Stoner v. Thompson 340

-T-

Team Rocket, L.P., In re 306
Templeton v. Ferguson 203
Texaco, Inc. v. Central Power & Light Company 170
Texaco v. McEwen 168
Texas Association of Business v. Texas Air Control Board, et al 11
Texas Association of School Boards, Inc., In re 289
Texas Dept. of Corrections v. Herring 360
Texas Dept. of Trans., In re 316
Texas Employment Commission v. International Union of Electrical, Radio and Machine Workers, Local Union No. 782 74
Trafalgar House Oil & Gas Inc. v. De Hinojosa 298
Transamerican Natural Gas Corp. v. Powell 489
Trueheart v. Braselton 394
TV Azteca v. Ruiz 228

-U-

United Services Auto. Assn. v. Brite 72
Union Carbide Corporation, In re 412
Union Pacific Resources Company, In re 472
University of Texas v. Morris 80
USAA Texas Lloyds Co. v. Menchaca 6

-V-

Villarreal v. San Antonio Truck & Equipment 91

-W-

Waldron v. Waldron 50
Walker v. Harrison 96
Walker v. Packer 476
White v. Jackson 336
Whitney v. L & L Realty Corporation 268
Wilson v. Dunn 262
Wood v. Brown 271
WTFO, Inc. v. Braithwaite 311
Wyatt v. Shaw Plumbing Co. 356

-Y-

York v. Texas 242